Geigy Scientific Tables

Geigy Scientific Tables

Volume 2

Introduction to Statistics
Statistical Tables
Mathematical Formulae

Edited by C. Lentner

Compiled by K. Diem and J. Seldrup

Eighth, revised and enlarged edition
Published by CIBA-GEIGY

ISBN 0-914168-51-7
Library of Congress Catalogue No. 81-70045

Editor: Cornelius Lentner
Associate editors: Charlotte Lentner and Anthony Wink
International Medical and Pharmaceutical Information, Ciba-Geigy Limited, Basle

American edition published by Medical Education Division, Ciba-Geigy Corporation, West Caldwell, New Jersey 07006

International edition published by Ciba-Geigy Limited, Basle, Switzerland

Printed in the USA

By way of explanation

This completely revised and expanded 8th edition of the *Geigy Scientific Tables* represents the continuation of a work that has stood the test of time. Its aim is to provide scientists and, in particular, doctors with a concise compendium of scientific data backed by literature references and thus to spare them much laborious searching.

The vast increase in the amount of subject matter to be included has meant that the *Geigy Scientific Tables* have had to be steadily extended, with the result that they are becoming too voluminous to be published in a single book. Dividing the book up into several separate volumes has made it possible to incorporate a number of additional chapters and has also helped to ensure that the data on the various branches of knowledge are more up-to-date than they could have been in a single-volume work. The other volumes are in preparation.

CIBA-GEIGY Limited, Basle

Foreword

Life is short, the art long, timing is exact, experience is treacherous, judgement difficult. — HIPPOCRATES

The mathematical-statistical part of the 7th edition of the *Geigy Scientific Tables* appears in the 8th edition as a separate volume. This edition is extended considerably and now includes two new chapters on some of the more common non-parametric (distribution-free) statistics. Several parts of the text have also been rearranged and updated. Many of the examples have been reworked and new examples added. A few tables have been omitted from this edition as they have become obsolete with the advent of calculators and computers but other tables have been extended, notably the tables of the F-distribution, the Binomial distribution, the Poisson distribution and the Wilcoxon distributions (both for the paired and unpaired test). New tables have been added on distribution-free tolerance limits.

Basle, October 1982 — *The Editors*

Content of tables

Content of text

Acknowledgments

The publishers and editors are indebted to

Dr. h. c. K. Diem
'Im Rebholz'
CH-4117 Burg im Leimental, Switzerland

and

Dr. J. Seldrup
Head of Statistics Department
Ciba-Geigy Pharmaceuticals Division
Horsham, West Sussex RH12 4AB, UK

for compiling this volume of the Geigy Scientific Tables. We also wish to thank the following scientific bodies, journals and publishers for permission to reproduce data or illustrations:

American Statistical Association, Washington, D. C.
(pages 60, 70, 71, 163)
American Telephone & Telegraph Company, New York, N. Y.
(page 166)
Associated Book Publishers Limited, London
(pages 18–20, 23)
Biometrics, Ithaca, N. Y.
(pages 57, 60, 235)
Birkhäuser Verlag, Basle
(page 167)
Cambridge University Press, Cambridge
(pages 55, 58)
Columbia University Press, New York, N. Y.
(pages 27, 29, 66, 67, 73)
Ch. Griffin & Co. Limited, London and High Wycombe
(page 163)
Imperial College of Science and Technology, London
(pages 55, 56, 58, 59, 60, 163)
Institute of Mathematical Statistics, Hayward, California
(pages 60, 72, 165, 166)
Longman Group Limited, Harlow, Essex
(pages 29, 68, 69)
McGraw-Hill Book Company Inc., New York, N. Y.
(pages 52, 53)

Notes for the guidance of users

In addition to the preceding lists of contents this volume contains at the back an alphabetically arranged list of key words which should be a useful guide to the use of the book.
Tables commence opposite. Definitions of mathematical symbols, abbreviations etc. are given from page 168 onwards. The statistical text starts on page 182.
Note the difference between the minus sign (for example: $1-2\alpha$) and the use of the somewhat shorter and lighter hyphen meaning 'to' (for example: $N = 85$–90). A point above a digit in a number indicates the period of a fraction, for example:

$1{,}\dot{6} = 1{,}666666...$
$1{,}65\dot{2}7\dot{8} = 1{,}65278278278...$

The literature references on page 235 have naturally had to be restricted and we have tended to include the original research papers, but some more general texts, review papers and books have also been included. The journal abbreviations follow the UNESCO standard (Clegg, H. A. [Ed.], *World Medical Periodicals*, 3rd ed., World Medical Association, New York, 1961, and Ware, M. [Ed.], supplement to 3rd edition, New York, 1968).

Mathematical constants

Bernoulli numbers	
n	B_n
1	1/6
2	1/30
3	1/42
4	1/30
5	5/66
6	691/2730
7	7/6
8	3617/510
9	43867/798
10	1 74611/330
11	8 54513/138
12	2363 64091/2730
13	85 53103/6

Euler numbers	
n	E_n
1	1
2	5
3	61
4	1385
5	50521
6	27 02765
7	1993 60981
8	1 93915 12145
9	240 48796 75441
10	37037 11882 37525
11	69 34887 43931 37901
12	15514 53416 35570 86905
13	40 87072 50929 31238 92361

Prime numbers < 100	
Number	$\log_{10}$ (mantissa)
2	30102 99956 63981 19521
3	47712 12547 19662 43730
5	69897 00043 36018 80479
7	84509 80400 14256 83071
11	04139 26851 58225 04075
13	11394 33523 06836 76921
17	23044 89213 78273 92854
19	27875 36009 52828 96154
23	36172 78360 17592 87887
29	46239 79978 98956 08733
31	49136 16938 34272 67967
37	56820 17240 66994 99681
41	61278 38567 19735 49451
43	63346 84555 79586 52641
47	67209 78579 35717 46441
53	72427 58696 00789 04563
59	77085 20116 42144 19026
61	78532 98350 10767 03389
67	82607 48027 00826 43415
71	85125 83487 19075 28609
73	86332 28601 20455 90107
79	89762 70912 90441 42799
83	91907 80923 76073 90383
89	94939 00066 44912 78472
97	98677 17342 66244 85178

Constants		
Constant	Value	$\log_{10}$
π	3,14159 26535 89793 23846	0,49714 98726 94133 85435
π^2	9,86960 44010 89358 61883	0,99429 97453 88267 70870
$(2\pi)^{-1/2}$	0,39894 22804 01432 67794	0,60091 00658 20942 47522–1
e	2,71828 18284 59045 23536	M
$M = \log_{10} e = \lg e$	0,43429 44819 03251 82765	
$1/M = \log_e 10 = \ln 10$	2,30258 50929 94045 68402	
γ (Euler's constant)	0,57721 56649 01532 86061	0,76133 81087 83167 61054–1

Greek alphabet

Greek character Upright	Greek character Italics	Greek name	Roman equivalent
Α α	*Α α*	alpha	A a
Β β	*Β β*	beta	B b
Γ γ	*Γ γ*	gamma	G g
Δ δ	*Δ δ*	delta	D d
Ε ε, ϵ	*Ε ε, ϵ*	epsilon	Ě ě
Ζ ζ	*Ζ ζ*	zeta	Z z
Η η	*Η η*	eta	Ē ē
Θ ϑ, θ	*Θ ϑ, θ*	theta	Th th
Ι ι	*Ι ι*	iota	I i
Κ ϰ, κ	*Κ ϰ, κ*	kappa	K k
Λ λ	*Λ λ*	lambda	L l
Μ μ	*Μ μ*	mu	M m
Ν ν	*Ν ν*	nu	N n
Ξ ξ	*Ξ ξ*	xi	X x
Ο ο	*Ο ο*	omicron	Ŏ ŏ
Π π, ϖ	*Π π, ϖ*	pi	P p
Ρ ϱ	*Ρ ϱ*	rho	R r
Σ σ, ς	*Σ σ, ς*	sigma	S s
Τ τ	*Τ τ*	tau	T t
Υ υ	*Υ υ*	upsilon	Y y
Φ φ, ϕ	*Φ φ, ϕ*	phi	Ph ph
Χ χ	*Χ χ*	chi	Ch ch
Ψ ψ	*Ψ ψ*	psi	Ps ps
Ω ω	*Ω ω*	omega	Ō ō

All values conform to the international convention (i.e. 0,1 instead of 0.1).

Prefixes and symbols for multiples and fractions of SI units

Power of ten	Prefix	Symbol
10^{18}	exa	E
10^{15}	peta	P
10^{12}	tera	T
10^{9}	giga	G
10^{6}	mega	M
10^{3}	kilo	k
10^{2}	hecto	h
10^{1}	deca	da
10^{-1}	deci	d
10^{-2}	centi	c
10^{-3}	milli	m
10^{-6}	micro	µ
10^{-9}	nano	n
10^{-12}	pico	p
10^{-15}	femto	f
10^{-18}	atto	a

Four-Place Common Logarithms ($\log_{10} x$)

	$\log_{10} x$										Proportional parts								
x	0	1	2	3	4	5	6	7	8	9	1	2	3	4	5	6	7	8	9
100	0000	0004	0009	0013	0017	0022	0026	0030	0035	0039	0	1	1	2	2	3	3	3	4
101	0043	0048	0052	0056	0060	0065	0069	0073	0077	0082	0	1	1	2	2	3	3	3	4
102	0086	0090	0095	0099	0103	0107	0111	0116	0120	0124	0	1	1	2	2	3	3	3	4
103	0128	0133	0137	0141	0145	0149	0154	0158	0162	0166	0	1	1	2	2	3	3	3	4
104	0170	0175	0179	0183	0187	0191	0195	0199	0204	0208	0	1	1	2	2	2	3	3	4
105	0212	0216	0220	0224	0228	0233	0237	0241	0245	0249	0	1	1	2	2	2	3	3	4
106	0253	0257	0261	0265	0269	0273	0278	0282	0286	0290	0	1	1	2	2	2	3	3	4
107	0294	0298	0302	0306	0310	0314	0318	0322	0326	0330	0	1	1	2	2	2	3	3	4
108	0334	0338	0342	0346	0350	0354	0358	0362	0366	0370	0	1	1	2	2	2	3	3	4
109	0374	0378	0382	0386	0390	0394	0398	0402	0406	0410	0	1	1	2	2	2	3	3	4
10	0000	0043	0086	0128	0170	0212	0253	0294	0334	0374	4	8	12	17	21	25	29	33	37
11	0414	0453	0492	0531	0569	0607	0645	0682	0719	0755	4	8	11	15	19	23	26	30	34
12	0792	0828	0864	0899	0934	0969	1004	1038	1072	1106	3	7	10	14	17	21	24	28	31
13	1139	1173	1206	1239	1271	1303	1335	1367	1399	1430	3	6	10	13	16	19	23	26	29
14	1461	1492	1523	1553	1584	1614	1644	1673	1703	1732	3	6	9	12	15	18	21	24	27
15	1761	1790	1818	1847	1875	1903	1931	1959	1987	2014	3	6	8	11	14	17	20	22	25
16	2041	2068	2095	2122	2148	2175	2201	2227	2253	2279	3	5	8	11	13	16	18	21	24
17	2304	2330	2355	2380	2405	2430	2455	2480	2504	2529	2	5	7	10	12	15	17	20	22
18	2553	2577	2601	2625	2648	2672	2695	2718	2742	2765	2	5	7	9	12	14	16	19	21
19	2788	2810	2833	2856	2878	2900	2923	2945	2967	2989	2	4	7	9	11	13	16	18	20
20	3010	3032	3054	3075	3096	3118	3139	3160	3181	3201	2	4	6	8	11	13	15	17	19
21	3222	3243	3263	3284	3304	3324	3345	3365	3385	3404	2	4	6	8	10	12	14	16	18
22	3424	3444	3464	3483	3502	3522	3541	3560	3579	3598	2	4	6	8	10	12	14	15	17
23	3617	3636	3655	3674	3692	3711	3729	3747	3766	3784	2	4	6	7	9	11	13	15	17
24	3802	3820	3838	3856	3874	3892	3909	3927	3945	3962	2	4	5	7	9	11	12	14	16
25	3979	3997	4014	4031	4048	4065	4082	4099	4116	4133	2	3	5	7	9	10	12	14	15
26	4150	4166	4183	4200	4216	4232	4249	4265	4281	4298	2	3	5	7	8	10	11	13	15
27	4314	4330	4346	4362	4378	4393	4409	4425	4440	4456	2	3	5	6	8	9	11	13	14
28	4472	4487	4502	4518	4533	4548	4564	4579	4594	4609	2	3	5	6	8	9	11	12	14
29	4624	4639	4654	4669	4683	4698	4713	4728	4742	4757	1	3	4	6	7	9	10	12	13
30	4771	4786	4800	4814	4829	4843	4857	4871	4886	4900	1	3	4	6	7	9	10	11	13
31	4914	4928	4942	4955	4969	4983	4997	5011	5024	5038	1	3	4	6	7	8	10	11	12
32	5051	5065	5079	5092	5105	5119	5132	5145	5159	5172	1	3	4	5	7	8	9	11	12
33	5185	5198	5211	5224	5237	5250	5263	5276	5289	5302	1	3	4	5	6	8	9	10	12
34	5315	5328	5340	5353	5366	5378	5391	5403	5416	5428	1	3	4	5	6	8	9	10	11
35	5441	5453	5465	5478	5490	5502	5514	5527	5539	5551	1	2	4	5	6	7	9	10	11
36	5563	5575	5587	5599	5611	5623	5635	5647	5658	5670	1	2	4	5	6	7	8	10	11
37	5682	5694	5705	5717	5729	5740	5752	5763	5775	5786	1	2	3	5	6	7	8	9	10
38	5798	5809	5821	5832	5843	5855	5866	5877	5888	5899	1	2	3	5	6	7	8	9	10
39	5911	5922	5933	5944	5955	5966	5977	5988	5999	6010	1	2	3	4	5	7	8	9	10
40	6021	6031	6042	6053	6064	6075	6085	6096	6107	6117	1	2	3	4	5	6	8	9	10
41	6128	6138	6149	6160	6170	6180	6191	6201	6212	6222	1	2	3	4	5	6	7	8	9
42	6232	6243	6253	6263	6274	6284	6294	6304	6314	6325	1	2	3	4	5	6	7	8	9
43	6335	6345	6355	6365	6375	6385	6395	6405	6415	6425	1	2	3	4	5	6	7	8	9
44	6435	6444	6454	6464	6474	6484	6493	6503	6513	6522	1	2	3	4	5	6	7	8	9
45	6532	6542	6551	6561	6571	6580	6590	6599	6609	6618	1	2	3	4	5	6	7	8	9
46	6628	6637	6646	6656	6665	6675	6684	6693	6702	6712	1	2	3	4	5	6	7	7	8
47	6721	6730	6739	6749	6758	6767	6776	6785	6794	6803	1	2	3	4	5	5	6	7	8
48	6812	6821	6830	6839	6848	6857	6866	6875	6884	6893	1	2	3	4	4	5	6	7	8
49	6902	6911	6920	6928	6937	6946	6955	6964	6972	6981	1	2	3	4	4	5	6	7	8
50	6990	6998	7007	7016	7024	7033	7042	7050	7059	7067	1	2	3	3	4	5	6	7	8
51	7076	7084	7093	7101	7110	7118	7126	7135	7143	7152	1	2	3	3	4	5	6	7	8
52	7160	7168	7177	7185	7193	7202	7210	7218	7226	7235	1	2	2	3	4	5	6	7	7
53	7243	7251	7259	7267	7275	7284	7292	7300	7308	7316	1	2	2	3	4	5	6	6	7
54	7324	7332	7340	7348	7356	7364	7372	7380	7388	7396	1	2	2	3	4	5	6	6	7
55	7404	7412	7419	7427	7435	7443	7451	7459	7466	7474	1	2	2	3	4	5	5	6	7
56	7482	7490	7497	7505	7513	7520	7528	7536	7543	7551	1	2	2	3	4	5	5	6	7
57	7559	7566	7574	7582	7589	7597	7604	7612	7619	7627	1	2	2	3	4	5	5	6	7
58	7634	7642	7649	7657	7664	7672	7679	7686	7694	7701	1	1	2	3	4	4	5	6	7
59	7709	7716	7723	7731	7738	7745	7752	7760	7767	7774	1	1	2	3	4	4	5	6	7
60	7782	7789	7796	7803	7810	7818	7825	7832	7839	7846	1	1	2	3	4	4	5	6	6
61	7853	7860	7868	7875	7882	7889	7896	7903	7910	7917	1	1	2	3	4	4	5	6	6
62	7924	7931	7938	7945	7952	7959	7966	7973	7980	7987	1	1	2	3	3	4	5	6	6
63	7993	8000	8007	8014	8021	8028	8035	8041	8048	8055	1	1	2	3	3	4	5	5	6
64	8062	8069	8075	8082	8089	8096	8102	8109	8116	8122	1	1	2	3	3	4	5	5	6
65	8129	8136	8142	8149	8156	8162	8169	8176	8182	8189	1	1	2	3	3	4	5	5	6
66	8195	8202	8209	8215	8222	8228	8235	8241	8248	8254	1	1	2	3	3	4	5	5	6
67	8261	8267	8274	8280	8287	8293	8299	8306	8312	8319	1	1	2	3	3	4	5	5	6
68	8325	8331	8338	8344	8351	8357	8363	8370	8376	8382	1	1	2	3	3	4	4	5	6
69	8388	8395	8401	8407	8414	8420	8426	8432	8439	8445	1	1	2	2	3	4	4	5	6
70	8451	8457	8463	8470	8476	8482	8488	8494	8500	8506	1	1	2	2	3	4	4	5	6
71	8513	8519	8525	8531	8537	8543	8549	8555	8561	8567	1	1	2	2	3	4	4	5	5
72	8573	8579	8585	8591	8597	8603	8609	8615	8621	8627	1	1	2	2	3	4	4	5	5
73	8633	8639	8645	8651	8657	8663	8669	8675	8681	8686	1	1	2	2	3	4	4	5	5
74	8692	8698	8704	8710	8716	8722	8727	8733	8739	8745	1	1	2	2	3	4	4	5	5
75	8751	8756	8762	8768	8774	8779	8785	8791	8797	8802	1	1	2	2	3	3	4	5	5
76	8808	8814	8820	8825	8831	8837	8842	8848	8854	8859	1	1	2	2	3	3	4	5	5
77	8865	8871	8876	8882	8887	8893	8899	8904	8910	8915	1	1	2	2	3	3	4	4	5
78	8921	8927	8932	8938	8943	8949	8954	8960	8965	8971	1	1	2	2	3	3	4	4	5
79	8976	8982	8987	8993	8998	9004	9009	9015	9020	9025	1	1	2	2	3	3	4	4	5
80	9031	9036	9042	9047	9053	9058	9063	9069	9074	9079	1	1	2	2	3	3	4	4	5
81	9085	9090	9096	9101	9106	9112	9117	9122	9128	9133	1	1	2	2	3	3	4	4	5
82	9138	9143	9149	9154	9159	9165	9170	9175	9180	9186	1	1	2	2	3	3	4	4	5
83	9191	9196	9201	9206	9212	9217	9222	9227	9232	9238	1	1	2	2	3	3	4	4	5
84	9243	9248	9253	9258	9263	9269	9274	9279	9284	9289	1	1	2	2	3	3	4	4	5
85	9294	9299	9304	9309	9315	9320	9325	9330	9335	9340	1	1	2	2	3	3	4	4	5
86	9345	9350	9355	9360	9365	9370	9375	9380	9385	9390	1	1	2	2	3	3	4	4	5
87	9395	9400	9405	9410	9415	9420	9425	9430	9435	9440	0	1	1	2	2	3	3	4	4
88	9445	9450	9455	9460	9465	9469	9474	9479	9484	9489	0	1	1	2	2	3	3	4	4
89	9494	9499	9504	9509	9513	9518	9523	9528	9533	9538	0	1	1	2	2	3	3	4	4
90	9542	9547	9552	9557	9562	9566	9571	9576	9581	9586	0	1	1	2	2	3	3	4	4
91	9590	9595	9600	9605	9609	9614	9619	9624	9628	9633	0	1	1	2	2	3	3	4	4
92	9638	9643	9647	9652	9657	9661	9666	9671	9675	9680	0	1	1	2	2	3	3	4	4
93	9685	9689	9694	9699	9703	9708	9713	9717	9722	9727	0	1	1	2	2	3	3	4	4
94	9731	9736	9741	9745	9750	9754	9759	9763	9768	9773	0	1	1	2	2	3	3	4	4
95	9777	9782	9786	9791	9795	9800	9805	9809	9814	9818	0	1	1	2	2	3	3	4	4
96	9823	9827	9832	9836	9841	9845	9850	9854	9859	9863	0	1	1	2	2	3	3	4	4
97	9868	9872	9877	9881	9886	9890	9894	9899	9903	9908	0	1	1	2	2	3	3	4	4
98	9912	9917	9921	9926	9930	9934	9939	9943	9948	9952	0	1	1	2	2	3	3	4	4
99	9956	9961	9965	9969	9974	9978	9983	9987	9991	9996	0	1	1	2	2	3	3	3	4

All values conform to the international convention (i.e. 0,1 instead of 0.1).

Four-Place Common Antilogarithms $\log_{10}^{-1} x$ (or antilog$_{10}$ x)

$\log_{10} x$	x 0	1	2	3	4	5	6	7	8	9	Proportional parts 1	2	3	4	5	6	7	8	9
,00	1000	1002	1005	1007	1009	1012	1014	1016	1019	1021	0	0	1	1	1	1	2	2	2
,01	1023	1026	1028	1030	1033	1035	1038	1040	1042	1045	0	0	1	1	1	1	2	2	2
,02	1047	1050	1052	1054	1057	1059	1062	1064	1067	1069	0	0	1	1	1	1	2	2	2
,03	1072	1074	1076	1079	1081	1084	1086	1089	1091	1094	0	0	1	1	1	1	2	2	2
,04	1096	1099	1102	1104	1107	1109	1112	1114	1117	1119	0	1	1	1	1	2	2	2	2
,05	1122	1125	1127	1130	1132	1135	1138	1140	1143	1146	0	1	1	1	1	2	2	2	2
,06	1148	1151	1153	1156	1159	1161	1164	1167	1169	1172	0	1	1	1	1	2	2	2	2
,07	1175	1178	1180	1183	1186	1189	1191	1194	1197	1199	0	1	1	1	1	2	2	2	2
,08	1202	1205	1208	1211	1213	1216	1219	1222	1225	1227	0	1	1	1	1	2	2	2	3
,09	1230	1233	1236	1239	1242	1245	1247	1250	1253	1256	0	1	1	1	1	2	2	2	3
,10	1259	1262	1265	1268	1271	1274	1276	1279	1282	1285	0	1	1	1	1	2	2	2	3
,11	1288	1291	1294	1297	1300	1303	1306	1309	1312	1315	0	1	1	1	2	2	2	2	3
,12	1318	1321	1324	1327	1330	1334	1337	1340	1343	1346	0	1	1	1	2	2	2	2	3
,13	1349	1352	1355	1358	1361	1365	1368	1371	1374	1377	0	1	1	1	2	2	2	3	3
,14	1380	1384	1387	1390	1393	1396	1400	1403	1406	1409	0	1	1	1	2	2	2	3	3
,15	1413	1416	1419	1422	1426	1429	1432	1435	1439	1442	0	1	1	1	2	2	2	3	3
,16	1445	1449	1452	1455	1459	1462	1466	1469	1472	1476	0	1	1	1	2	2	2	3	3
,17	1479	1483	1486	1489	1493	1496	1500	1503	1507	1510	0	1	1	1	2	2	2	3	3
,18	1514	1517	1521	1524	1528	1531	1535	1538	1542	1545	0	1	1	1	2	2	2	3	3
,19	1549	1552	1556	1560	1563	1567	1570	1574	1578	1581	0	1	1	1	2	2	3	3	3
,20	1585	1589	1592	1596	1600	1603	1607	1611	1614	1618	0	1	1	1	2	2	3	3	3
,21	1622	1626	1629	1633	1637	1641	1644	1648	1652	1656	0	1	1	2	2	2	3	3	3
,22	1660	1663	1667	1671	1675	1679	1683	1687	1690	1694	0	1	1	2	2	2	3	3	3
,23	1698	1702	1706	1710	1714	1718	1722	1726	1730	1734	0	1	1	2	2	2	3	3	4
,24	1738	1742	1746	1750	1754	1758	1762	1766	1770	1774	0	1	1	2	2	2	3	3	4
,25	1778	1782	1786	1791	1795	1799	1803	1807	1811	1816	0	1	1	2	2	2	3	3	4
,26	1820	1824	1828	1832	1837	1841	1845	1849	1854	1858	0	1	1	2	2	3	3	3	4
,27	1862	1866	1871	1875	1879	1884	1888	1892	1897	1901	0	1	1	2	2	3	3	3	4
,28	1905	1910	1914	1919	1923	1928	1932	1936	1941	1945	0	1	1	2	2	3	3	4	4
,29	1950	1954	1959	1963	1968	1972	1977	1982	1986	1991	0	1	1	2	2	3	3	4	4
,30	1995	2000	2004	2009	2014	2018	2023	2028	2032	2037	0	1	1	2	2	3	3	4	4
,31	2042	2046	2051	2056	2061	2065	2070	2075	2080	2084	0	1	1	2	2	3	3	4	4
,32	2089	2094	2099	2104	2109	2113	2118	2123	2128	2133	0	1	1	2	2	3	3	4	4
,33	2138	2143	2148	2153	2158	2163	2168	2173	2178	2183	0	1	1	2	2	3	3	4	4
,34	2188	2193	2198	2203	2208	2213	2218	2223	2228	2234	1	1	2	2	3	3	4	4	5
,35	2239	2244	2249	2254	2259	2265	2270	2275	2280	2286	1	1	2	2	3	3	4	4	5
,36	2291	2296	2301	2307	2312	2317	2323	2328	2333	2339	1	1	2	2	3	3	4	4	5
,37	2344	2350	2355	2360	2366	2371	2377	2382	2388	2393	1	1	2	2	3	3	4	4	5
,38	2399	2404	2410	2415	2421	2427	2432	2438	2443	2449	1	1	2	2	3	3	4	4	5
,39	2455	2460	2466	2472	2477	2483	2489	2495	2500	2506	1	1	2	2	3	3	4	5	5
,40	2512	2518	2523	2529	2535	2541	2547	2553	2559	2564	1	1	2	2	3	4	4	5	5
,41	2570	2576	2582	2588	2594	2600	2606	2612	2618	2624	1	1	2	2	3	4	4	5	5
,42	2630	2636	2642	2649	2655	2661	2667	2673	2679	2685	1	1	2	2	3	4	4	5	6
,43	2692	2698	2704	2710	2716	2723	2729	2735	2742	2748	1	1	2	3	3	4	4	5	6
,44	2754	2761	2767	2773	2780	2786	2793	2799	2805	2812	1	1	2	3	3	4	4	5	6
,45	2818	2825	2831	2838	2844	2851	2858	2864	2871	2877	1	1	2	3	3	4	5	5	6
,46	2884	2891	2897	2904	2911	2917	2924	2931	2938	2944	1	1	2	3	3	4	5	5	6
,47	2951	2958	2965	2972	2979	2985	2992	2999	3006	3013	1	1	2	3	3	4	5	5	6
,48	3020	3027	3034	3041	3048	3055	3062	3069	3076	3083	1	1	2	3	4	4	5	6	6
,49	3090	3097	3105	3112	3119	3126	3133	3141	3148	3155	1	1	2	3	4	4	5	6	6
,50	3162	3170	3177	3184	3192	3199	3206	3214	3221	3228	1	1	2	3	4	4	5	6	7
,51	3236	3243	3251	3258	3266	3273	3281	3289	3296	3304	1	2	2	3	4	5	5	6	7
,52	3311	3319	3327	3334	3342	3350	3357	3365	3373	3381	1	2	2	3	4	5	5	6	7
,53	3388	3396	3404	3412	3420	3428	3436	3443	3451	3459	1	2	2	3	4	5	6	6	7
,54	3467	3475	3483	3491	3499	3508	3516	3524	3532	3540	1	2	2	3	4	5	6	6	7
,55	3548	3556	3565	3573	3581	3589	3597	3606	3614	3622	1	2	2	3	4	5	6	7	7
,56	3631	3639	3648	3656	3664	3673	3681	3690	3698	3707	1	2	3	3	4	5	6	7	8
,57	3715	3724	3733	3741	3750	3758	3767	3776	3784	3793	1	2	3	3	4	5	6	7	8
,58	3802	3811	3819	3828	3837	3846	3855	3864	3873	3882	1	2	3	4	4	5	6	7	8
,59	3890	3899	3908	3917	3926	3936	3945	3954	3963	3972	1	2	3	4	5	5	6	7	8
,60	3981	3990	3999	4009	4018	4027	4036	4046	4055	4064	1	2	3	4	5	6	6	7	8
,61	4074	4083	4093	4102	4111	4121	4130	4140	4150	4159	1	2	3	4	5	6	7	8	9
,62	4169	4178	4188	4198	4207	4217	4227	4236	4246	4256	1	2	3	4	5	6	7	8	9
,63	4266	4276	4285	4295	4305	4315	4325	4335	4345	4355	1	2	3	4	5	6	7	8	9
,64	4365	4375	4385	4395	4406	4416	4426	4436	4446	4457	1	2	3	4	5	6	7	8	9
,65	4467	4477	4487	4498	4508	4519	4529	4539	4550	4560	1	2	3	4	5	6	7	8	9
,66	4571	4581	4592	4603	4613	4624	4634	4645	4656	4667	1	2	3	4	5	6	7	9	10
,67	4677	4688	4699	4710	4721	4732	4742	4753	4764	4775	1	2	3	4	5	7	8	9	10
,68	4786	4797	4808	4819	4831	4842	4853	4864	4875	4887	1	2	3	4	6	7	8	9	10
,69	4898	4909	4920	4932	4943	4955	4966	4977	4989	5000	1	2	3	5	6	7	8	9	10
,70	5012	5023	5035	5047	5058	5070	5082	5093	5105	5117	1	2	4	5	6	7	8	9	11
,71	5129	5140	5152	5164	5176	5188	5200	5212	5224	5236	1	2	4	5	6	7	8	10	11
,72	5248	5260	5272	5284	5297	5309	5321	5333	5346	5358	1	2	4	5	6	7	9	10	11
,73	5370	5383	5395	5408	5420	5433	5445	5458	5470	5483	1	3	4	5	6	8	9	10	11
,74	5495	5508	5521	5534	5546	5559	5572	5585	5598	5610	1	3	4	5	6	8	9	10	12
,75	5623	5636	5649	5662	5675	5689	5702	5715	5728	5741	1	3	4	5	7	8	9	10	12
,76	5754	5768	5781	5794	5808	5821	5834	5848	5861	5875	1	3	4	5	7	8	9	11	12
,77	5888	5902	5916	5929	5943	5957	5970	5984	5998	6012	1	3	4	5	7	8	10	11	12
,78	6026	6039	6053	6067	6081	6095	6109	6124	6138	6152	1	3	4	6	7	8	10	11	13
,79	6166	6180	6194	6209	6223	6237	6252	6266	6281	6295	1	3	4	6	7	9	10	11	13
,80	6310	6324	6339	6353	6368	6383	6397	6412	6427	6442	1	3	4	6	7	9	10	12	13
,81	6457	6471	6486	6501	6516	6531	6546	6561	6577	6592	2	3	5	6	8	9	11	12	14
,82	6607	6622	6637	6653	6668	6683	6699	6714	6730	6745	2	3	5	6	8	9	11	12	14
,83	6761	6776	6792	6808	6823	6839	6855	6871	6887	6902	2	3	5	6	8	9	11	13	14
,84	6918	6934	6950	6966	6982	6998	7015	7031	7047	7063	2	3	5	6	8	10	11	13	15
,85	7079	7096	7112	7129	7145	7161	7178	7194	7211	7228	2	3	5	7	8	10	12	13	15
,86	7244	7261	7278	7295	7311	7328	7345	7362	7379	7396	2	3	5	7	8	10	12	13	15
,87	7413	7430	7447	7464	7482	7499	7516	7534	7551	7568	2	3	5	7	9	10	12	14	16
,88	7586	7603	7621	7638	7656	7674	7691	7709	7727	7745	2	4	5	7	9	11	12	14	16
,89	7762	7780	7798	7816	7834	7852	7870	7889	7907	7925	2	4	5	7	9	11	13	14	16
,90	7943	7962	7980	7998	8017	8035	8054	8072	8091	8110	2	4	6	7	9	11	13	15	17
,91	8128	8147	8166	8185	8204	8222	8241	8260	8279	8299	2	4	6	8	9	11	13	15	17
,92	8318	8337	8356	8375	8395	8414	8433	8453	8472	8492	2	4	6	8	10	12	14	15	17
,93	8511	8531	8551	8570	8590	8610	8630	8650	8670	8690	2	4	6	8	10	12	14	16	18
,94	8710	8730	8750	8770	8790	8810	8831	8851	8872	8892	2	4	6	8	10	12	14	16	18
,95	8913	8933	8954	8974	8995	9016	9036	9057	9078	9099	2	4	6	8	10	12	15	17	19
,96	9120	9141	9162	9183	9204	9226	9247	9268	9290	9311	2	4	6	8	11	13	15	17	19
,97	9333	9354	9376	9397	9419	9441	9462	9484	9506	9528	2	4	7	9	11	13	15	17	20
,98	9550	9572	9594	9616	9638	9661	9683	9705	9727	9750	2	4	7	9	11	13	16	18	20
,99	9772	9795	9817	9840	9863	9886	9908	9931	9954	9977	2	5	7	9	11	14	16	18	20

All values conform to the international convention (i.e. 0,1 instead of 0.1).

Natural Logarithms* (ln x) for $x = 0{,}000–0{,}999$

x	0,000	0,001	0,002	0,003	0,004	0,005	0,006	0,007	0,008	0,009
0,000	−∞	−6,90776	−6,21461	−5,80914	−5,52146	−5,29832	−5,11600	−4,96185	−4,82831	−4,71053
010	−4,60517	−4,50986	−4,42285	−4,34281	−4,26870	−4,19971	−4,13517	−4,07454	−4,01738	−3,96332
020	−3,91202	−3,86323	−3,81671	−3,77226	−3,72970	−3,68888	−3,64966	−3,61192	−3,57555	54046
030	50656	47377	44202	41125	38139	35241	32424	29684	27017	24419
040	21888	19418	17009	14656	12357	10109	07911	05761	03655	01593
0,050	−2,99573	−2,97593	−2,95651	−2,93746	−2,91877	−2,90042	−2,88240	−2,86470	−2,84731	−2,83022
060	81341	79688	78062	76462	74887	73337	71810	70306	68825	67365
070	65926	64508	63109	61730	60369	59027	57702	56395	55105	53831
080	52573	51331	50104	48891	47694	46510	45341	44185	43042	41912
090	40795	39690	38597	37516	36446	35388	34341	33304	32279	31264
0,100	−2,30259	−2,29263	−2,28278	−2,27303	−2,26336	−2,25379	−2,24432	−2,23493	−2,22562	−2,21641
110	20727	19823	18926	18037	17156	16282	15417	14558	13707	12863
120	12026	11196	10373	09557	08747	07944	07147	06357	05573	04794
130	04022	03256	02495	01741	00992	00248	−1,99510	−1,98777	−1,98050	−1,97328
140	−1,96611	−1,95900	−1,95193	−1,94491	−1,93794	−1,93102	92415	91732	91054	90381
0,150	−1,89712	−1,89048	−1,88387	−1,87732	−1,87080	−1,86433	−1,85790	−1,85151	−1,84516	−1,83885
160	83258	82635	82016	81401	80789	80181	79577	78976	78379	77786
170	77196	76609	76026	75446	74870	74297	73727	73161	72597	72037
180	71480	70926	70375	69827	69282	68740	68201	67665	67131	66601
190	66073	65548	65026	64507	63990	63476	62964	62455	61949	61445
0,200	−1,60944	−1,60445	−1,59949	−1,59455	−1,58964	−1,58475	−1,57988	−1,57504	−1,57022	−1,56542
210	56065	55590	55117	54646	54178	53712	53248	52786	52326	51868
220	51413	50959	50508	50058	49611	49165	48722	48281	47841	47403
230	46968	46534	46102	45672	45243	44817	44392	43970	43548	43129
240	42712	42296	41882	41469	41059	40650	40242	39837	39433	39030
0,250	−1,38629	−1,38230	−1,37833	−1,37437	−1,37042	−1,36649	−1,36258	−1,35868	−1,35480	−1,35093
260	34707	34323	33941	33560	33181	32803	32426	32051	31677	31304
270	30933	30564	30195	29828	29463	29098	28735	28374	28013	27654
280	27297	26940	26585	26231	25878	25527	25176	24827	24479	24133
290	23787	23443	23100	22758	22418	22078	21740	21402	21066	20731
0,300	−1,20397	−1,20065	−1,19733	−1,19402	−1,19073	−1,18744	−1,18417	−1,18091	−1,17766	−1,17441
310	17118	16796	16475	16155	15836	15518	15201	14885	14570	14256
320	13943	13631	13320	13010	12701	12393	12086	11780	11474	11170
330	10866	10564	10262	09961	09661	09362	09064	08767	08471	08176
340	07881	07587	07294	07002	06711	06421	06132	05843	05555	05268
0,350	−1,04982	−1,04697	−1,04412	−1,04129	−1,03846	−1,03564	−1,03282	−1,03002	−1,02722	−1,02443
360	02165	01888	01611	01335	01060	00786	00512	00239	−0,99967	−0,99696
370	−0,99425	−0,99155	−0,98886	−0,98618	−0,98350	−0,98083	−0,97817	−0,97551	97286	97022
380	96758	96496	96233	95972	95711	95451	95192	94933	94675	94418
390	94161	93905	93649	93395	93140	92887	92634	92382	92130	91879
0,400	−0,91629	−0,91379	−0,91130	−0,90882	−0,90634	−0,90387	−0,90140	−0,89894	−0,89649	−0,89404
410	89160	88916	88673	88431	88189	87948	87707	87467	87227	86988
420	86750	86512	86275	86038	85802	85567	85332	85097	84863	84630
430	84397	84165	83933	83702	83471	83241	83011	82782	82554	82326
440	82098	81871	81645	81419	81193	80968	80744	80520	80296	80073
0,450	−0,79851	−0,79629	−0,79407	−0,79186	−0,78966	−0,78746	−0,78526	−0,78307	−0,78089	−0,77871
460	77653	77436	77219	77003	76787	76572	76357	76143	75929	75715
470	75502	75290	75078	74866	74655	74444	74234	74024	73814	73605
480	73397	73189	72981	72774	72567	72361	72155	71949	71744	71539
490	71335	71131	70928	70725	70522	70320	70118	69917	69716	69515
0,500	−0,69315	−0,69115	−0,68916	−0,68717	−0,68518	−0,68320	−0,68122	−0,67924	−0,67727	−0,67531
510	67334	67139	66943	66748	66553	66359	66165	65971	65778	65585
520	65393	65201	65009	64817	64626	64436	64245	64055	63866	63677
530	63488	63299	63111	62923	62736	62549	62362	62176	61990	61804
540	61619	61434	61249	61065	60881	60697	60514	60331	60148	59966
0,550	−0,59784	−0,59602	−0,59421	−0,59240	−0,59059	−0,58879	−0,58699	−0,58519	−0,58340	−0,58161
560	57982	57803	57625	57448	57270	57093	56916	56740	56563	56387
570	56212	56037	55862	55687	55513	55339	55165	54991	54818	54645
580	54473	54300	54128	53957	53785	53614	53444	53273	53103	52933
590	52763	52594	52425	52256	52088	51919	51751	51584	51416	51249
0,600	−0,51083	−0,50916	−0,50750	−0,50584	−0,50418	−0,50253	−0,50088	−0,49923	−0,49758	−0,49594
610	49430	49266	49102	48939	48776	48613	48451	48289	48127	47965
620	47804	47642	47482	47321	47160	47000	46840	46681	46522	46362
630	46204	46045	45887	45728	45571	45413	45256	45099	44942	44785
640	44629	44473	44317	44161	44006	43850	43696	43541	43386	43232
0,650	−0,43078	−0,42925	−0,42771	−0,42618	−0,42465	−0,42312	−0,42159	−0,42007	−0,41855	−0,41703
660	41552	41400	41249	41098	40947	40797	40647	40497	40347	40197
670	40048	39899	39750	39601	39453	39304	39156	39008	38861	38713
680	38566	38419	38273	38126	37980	37834	37688	37542	37397	37251
690	37106	36962	36817	36673	36528	36384	36241	36097	35954	35810
0,700	−0,35667	−0,35525	−0,35382	−0,35240	−0,35098	−0,34956	−0,34814	−0,34672	−0,34531	−0,34390
710	34249	34108	33968	33827	33687	33547	33408	33268	33129	32989
720	32850	32712	32573	32435	32296	32158	32021	31883	31745	31608
730	31471	31334	31197	31061	30925	30788	30653	30517	30381	30246
740	30111	29975	29841	29706	29571	29437	29303	29169	29035	28902
0,750	−0,28768	−0,28635	−0,28502	−0,28369	−0,28236	−0,28104	−0,27971	−0,27839	−0,27707	−0,27575
760	27444	27312	27181	27050	26919	26788	26657	26527	26397	26266
770	26136	26007	25877	25748	25618	25489	25360	25231	25103	24974
780	24846	24718	24590	24462	24335	24207	24080	23953	23826	23699
790	23572	23446	23319	23193	23067	22941	22816	22690	22565	22439
0,800	−0,22314	−0,22189	−0,22065	−0,21940	−0,21816	−0,21691	−0,21567	−0,21443	−0,21319	−0,21196
810	21072	20949	20825	20702	20579	20457	20334	20212	20089	19967
820	19845	19723	19601	19480	19358	19237	19116	18995	18874	18754
830	18633	18513	18392	18272	18152	18032	17913	17793	17674	17554
840	17435	17316	17198	17079	16960	16842	16724	16605	16487	16370
0,850	−0,16252	−0,16134	−0,16017	−0,15900	−0,15782	−0,15665	−0,15548	−0,15432	−0,15315	−0,15199
860	15032	14966	14850	14734	14618	14503	14387	14272	14156	14041
870	13926	13811	13697	13582	13467	13353	13239	13125	13011	12897
880	12783	12670	12556	12443	12330	12217	12104	11991	11878	11766
890	11653	11541	11429	11317	11205	11093	10981	10870	10759	10647
0,900	−0,10536	−0,10425	−0,10314	−0,10203	−0,10093	−0,09982	−0,09872	−0,09761	−0,09651	−0,09541
910	09431	09321	09212	09102	08992	08883	08774	08665	08556	08447
920	08338	08230	08121	08013	07904	07796	07688	07580	07472	07365
930	07257	07150	07042	06935	06828	06721	06614	06507	06401	06294
940	06188	06081	05975	05869	05763	05657	05551	05446	05340	05235
0,950	−0,05129	−0,05024	−0,04919	−0,04814	−0,04709	−0,04604	−0,04500	−0,04395	−0,04291	−0,04186
960	04082	03978	03874	03770	03666	03563	03459	03356	03252	03149
970	03046	02943	02840	02737	02634	02532	02429	02327	02225	02122
980	02020	01918	01816	01715	01613	01511	01410	01309	01207	01106
990	01005	00904	00803	00702	00602	00501	00401	00300	00200	00100

*To find the natural logarithm (ln) of a number which is a power of ten less or greater than a number given in the table: if the number concerned is *less*, e.g., 1/10 (10^{-1}), 1/100 (10^{-2}), 1/1000 (10^{-3}), etc., *subtract* from the given logarithm ln 10, 2 ln 10, 3 ln 10, etc.; if the number concerned is *greater*, e.g., 10 times (10^1), 100 times (10^2), 1000 times (10^3), etc., *add* to the given logarithm ln 10, 2 ln 10, 3 ln 10, etc. Examples: ln 0,02 = ln 0,2 − ln 10; ln 2000 = ln 200 + ln 10.

All values conform to the international convention (i.e. 0,1 instead of 0.1).

Natural Logarithms* (ln x) for x=1,00–9,99

x	0,00	0,01	0,02	0,03	0,04	0,05	0,06	0,07	0,08	0,09
1,00	0,00000	0,00995	0,01980	0,02956	0,03922	0,04879	0,05827	0,06766	0,07696	0,08618
10	09531	10436	11333	12222	13103	13976	14842	15700	16551	17395
20	18232	19062	19885	20701	21511	22314	23111	23902	24686	25464
30	26236	27003	27763	28518	29267	30010	30748	31481	32208	32930
40	33647	34359	35066	35767	36464	37156	37844	38526	39204	39878
1,50	0,40547	0,41211	0,41871	0,42527	0,43178	0,43825	0,44469	0,45108	0,45742	0,46373
60	47000	47623	48243	48858	49470	50078	50682	51282	51879	52473
70	53063	53649	54232	54812	55389	55962	56531	57098	57661	58222
80	58779	59333	59884	60432	60977	61519	62058	62594	63127	63658
90	64185	64710	65233	65752	66269	66783	67294	67803	68310	68813
2,00	0,69315	0,69813	0,70310	0,70804	0,71295	0,71784	0,72271	0,72755	0,73237	0,73716
10	74194	74669	75142	75612	76081	76547	77011	77473	77932	78390
20	78846	79299	79751	80200	80648	81093	81536	81978	82418	82855
30	83291	83725	84157	84587	85015	85442	85866	86289	86710	87129
40	87547	87963	88377	88789	89200	89609	90016	90422	90826	91228
2,50	0,91629	0,92028	0,92426	0,92822	0,93216	0,93609	0,94001	0,94391	0,94779	0,95166
60	95551	95935	96317	96698	97078	97456	97833	98208	98582	98954
70	99325	99695	1,00063	1,00430	1,00796	1,01160	1,01523	1,01885	1,02245	1,02604
80	1,02962	1,03318	03674	04028	04380	04732	05082	05431	05779	06126
90	06471	06815	07158	07500	07841	08181	08519	08856	09192	09527
3,00	1,09861	1,10194	1,10526	1,10856	1,11186	1,11514	1,11841	1,12168	1,12493	1,12817
10	13140	13462	13783	14103	14422	14740	15057	15373	15688	16002
20	16315	16627	16938	17248	17557	17865	18173	18479	18784	19089
30	19392	19695	19996	20297	20597	20896	21194	21491	21788	22083
40	22378	22671	22964	23256	23547	23837	24127	24415	24703	24990
3,50	1,25276	1,25562	1,25846	1,26130	1,26413	1,26695	1,26976	1,27257	1,27536	1,27815
60	28093	28371	28647	28923	29198	29473	29746	30019	30291	30563
70	30833	31103	31372	31641	31909	32176	32442	32708	32972	33237
80	33500	33763	34025	34286	34547	34807	35067	35325	35584	35841
90	36098	36354	36609	36864	37118	37372	37624	37877	38128	38379
4,00	1,38629	1,38879	1,39128	1,39377	1,39624	1,39872	1,40118	1,40364	1,40610	1,40854
10	41099	41342	41585	41828	42070	42311	42552	42792	43031	43270
20	43508	43746	43984	44220	44456	44692	44927	45161	45395	45629
30	45862	46094	46326	46557	46787	47018	47247	47476	47705	47933
40	48160	48387	48614	48840	49065	49290	49515	49739	49962	50185
4,50	1,50408	1,50630	1,50851	1,51072	1,51293	1,51513	1,51732	1,51951	1,52170	1,52388
60	52606	52823	53039	53256	53471	53687	53902	54116	54330	54543
70	54756	54969	55181	55393	55604	55814	56025	56235	56444	56653
80	56862	57070	57277	57485	57691	57898	58104	58309	58515	58719
90	58924	59127	59331	59534	59737	59939	60141	60342	60543	60744
5,00	1,60944	1,61144	1,61343	1,61542	1,61741	1,61939	1,62137	1,62334	1,62531	1,62728
10	62924	63120	63315	63511	63705	63900	64094	64287	64481	64673
20	64866	65058	65250	65441	65632	65823	66013	66203	66393	66582
30	66771	66959	67147	67335	67523	67710	67896	68083	68269	68455
40	68640	68825	69010	69194	69378	69562	69745	69928	70111	70293
5,50	1,70475	1,70656	1,70838	1,71019	1,71199	1,71380	1,71560	1,71740	1,71919	1,72098
60	72277	72455	72633	72811	72988	73166	73342	73519	73695	73871
70	74047	74222	74397	74572	74746	74920	75094	75267	75440	75613
80	75786	75958	76130	76302	76473	76644	76815	76985	77156	77326
90	77495	77665	77834	78002	78171	78339	78507	78675	78842	79009
6,00	1,79176	1,79342	1,79509	1,79675	1,79840	1,80006	1,80171	1,80336	1,80500	1,80665
10	80829	80993	81156	81319	81482	81645	81808	81970	82132	82294
20	82455	82616	82777	82938	83098	83258	83418	83578	83737	83896
30	84055	84214	84372	84530	84688	84845	85003	85160	85317	85473
40	85630	85786	85942	86097	86253	86408	86563	86718	86872	87026
6,50	1,87180	1,87334	1,87487	1,87641	1,87794	1,87947	1,88099	1,88251	1,88403	1,88555
60	88707	88858	89010	89160	89311	89462	89612	89762	89912	90061
70	90211	90360	90509	90658	90806	90954	91102	91250	91398	91545
80	91692	91839	91986	92132	92279	92425	92571	92716	92862	93007
90	93152	93297	93442	93586	93730	93874	94018	94162	94305	94448
7,00	1,94591	1,94734	1,94876	1,95019	1,95161	1,95303	1,95445	1,95586	1,95727	1,95869
10	96009	96150	96291	96431	96571	96711	96851	96991	97130	97269
20	97408	97547	97685	97824	97962	98100	98238	98376	98513	98650
30	98787	98924	99061	99198	99334	99470	99606	99742	99877	2,00013
40	2,00148	2,00283	2,00418	2,00553	2,00687	2,00821	2,00956	2,01089	2,01223	01357
7,50	2,01490	2,01624	2,01757	2,01890	2,02022	2,02155	2,02287	2,02419	2,02551	2,02683
60	02815	02946	03078	03209	03340	03471	03601	03732	03862	03992
70	04122	04252	04381	04511	04640	04769	04898	05027	05156	05284
80	05412	05540	05668	05796	05924	06051	06179	06306	06433	06560
90	06686	06813	06939	07065	07191	07317	07443	07568	07694	07819
8,00	2,07944	2,08069	2,08194	2,08318	2,08443	2,08567	2,08691	2,08815	2,08939	2,09063
10	09186	09310	09433	09556	09679	09802	09924	10047	10169	10291
20	10413	10535	10657	10779	10900	11021	11142	11263	11384	11505
30	11626	11746	11866	11986	12106	12226	12346	12465	12585	12704
40	12823	12942	13061	13180	13298	13417	13535	13653	13771	13889
8,50	2,14007	2,14124	2,14242	2,14359	2,14476	2,14593	2,14710	2,14827	2,14943	2,15060
60	15176	15292	15409	15524	15640	15756	15871	15987	16102	16217
70	16332	16447	16562	16677	16791	16905	17020	17134	17248	17361
80	17475	17589	17702	17816	17929	18042	18155	18267	18380	18493
90	18605	18717	18830	18942	19054	19165	19277	19389	19500	19611
9,00	2,19722	2,19834	2,19944	2,20055	2,20166	2,20276	2,20387	2,20497	2,20607	2,20717
10	20827	20937	21047	21157	21266	21375	21485	21594	21703	21812
20	21920	22029	22138	22246	22354	22462	22570	22678	22786	22894
30	23001	23109	23216	23324	23431	23538	23645	23751	23858	23965
40	24071	24177	24284	24390	24496	24601	24707	24813	24918	25024
9,50	2,25129	2,25234	2,25339	2,25444	2,25549	2,25654	2,25759	2,25863	2,25968	2,26072
60	26176	26280	26384	26488	26592	26696	26799	26903	27006	27109
70	27213	27316	27419	27521	27624	27727	27829	27932	28034	28136
80	28238	28340	28442	28544	28646	28747	28849	28950	29051	29152
90	29253	29354	29455	29556	29657	29757	29858	29958	30058	30158

*To find the natural logarithm (ln) of a number which is a power of ten less or greater than a number given in the table: if the number concerned is *less*, e.g., 1/10 (10^{-1}), 1/100 (10^{-2}), 1/1000 (10^{-3}), etc., *subtract* from the given logarithm ln 10, 2 ln 10, 3 ln 10, etc.; if the number concerned is *greater*, e.g., 10 times (10^1), 100 times (10^2), 1000 times (10^3), etc., *add* to the given logarithm ln 10, 2 ln 10, 3 ln 10, etc. Examples: ln 0,02 = ln 0,2 − ln 10; ln 2000 = ln 200 + ln 10.

All values conform to the international convention (i.e. 0,1 instead of 0.1).

Natural Logarithms* (ln x) for $x=10{,}0–99{,}9$

x	0,0	0,1	0,2	0,3	0,4	0,5	0,6	0,7	0,8	0,9
10,0	2,30259	2,31254	2,32239	2,33214	2,34181	2,35138	2,36085	2,37024	2,37955	2,38876
11,0	39790	40695	41591	42480	43361	44235	45101	45959	46810	47654
12,0	48491	49321	50144	50960	51770	52573	53370	54160	54945	55723
13,0	56495	57261	58022	58776	59525	60269	61007	61740	62467	63189
14,0	63906	64617	65324	66026	66723	67415	68102	68785	69463	70136
15,0	2,70805	2,71469	2,72130	2,72785	2,73437	2,74084	2,74727	2,75366	2,76001	2,76632
16,0	77259	77882	78501	79117	79728	80336	80940	81541	82138	82731
17,0	83321	83908	84491	85071	85647	86220	86790	87356	87920	88480
18,0	89037	89591	90142	90690	91235	91777	92316	92852	93386	93916
19,0	94444	94969	95491	96011	96527	97041	97553	98062	98568	99072
20,0	2,99573	3,00072	3,00568	3,01062	3,01553	3,02042	3,02529	3,03013	3,03495	3,03975
21,0	3,04452	04927	05400	05871	06339	06805	07269	07731	08191	08649
22,0	09104	09558	10009	10459	10906	11352	11795	12236	12676	13114
23,0	13549	13983	14415	14845	15274	15700	16125	16548	16969	17388
24,0	17805	18221	18635	19048	19458	19867	20275	20680	21084	21487
25,0	3,21888	3,22287	3,22684	3,23080	3,23475	3,23868	3,24259	3,24649	3,25037	3,25424
26,0	25810	26194	26576	26957	27336	27714	28091	28466	28840	29213
27,0	29584	29953	30322	30689	31054	31419	31782	32143	32504	32863
28,0	33220	33577	33932	34286	34639	34990	35341	35690	36038	36384
29,0	36730	37074	37417	37759	38099	38439	38777	39115	39451	39786
30,0	3,40120	3,40453	3,40784	3,41115	3,41444	3,41773	3,42100	3,42426	3,42751	3,43076
31,0	43399	43721	44042	44362	44681	44999	45316	45632	45947	46261
32,0	46574	46886	47197	47507	47816	48124	48431	48738	49043	49347
33,0	49651	49953	50255	50556	50856	51155	51453	51750	52046	52342
34,0	52636	52930	53223	53515	53806	54096	54385	54674	54962	55249
35,0	3,55535	3,55820	3,56105	3,56388	3,56671	3,56953	3,57235	3,57515	3,57795	3,58074
36,0	58352	58629	58906	59182	59457	59731	60005	60278	60550	60821
37,0	61092	61362	61631	61899	62167	62434	62700	62966	63231	63495
38,0	63759	64021	64284	64545	64806	65066	65325	65584	65842	66099
39,0	66356	66612	66868	67122	67377	67630	67883	68135	68387	68638
40,0	3,68888	3,69138	3,69387	3,69635	3,69883	3,70130	3,70377	3,70623	3,70868	3,71113
41,0	71357	71601	71844	72086	72328	72569	72810	73050	73290	73529
42,0	73767	74005	74242	74479	74715	74950	75185	75420	75654	75887
43,0	76120	76352	76584	76815	77046	77276	77506	77735	77963	78191
44,0	78419	78646	78872	79098	79324	79549	79773	79997	80221	80444
45,0	3,80666	3,80888	3,81110	3,81331	3,81551	3,81771	3,81991	3,82210	3,82428	3,82647
46,0	82864	83081	83298	83514	83730	83945	84160	84374	84588	84802
47,0	85015	85227	85439	85651	85862	86073	86283	86493	86703	86912
48,0	87120	87328	87536	87743	87950	88156	88362	88568	88773	88978
49,0	89182	89386	89589	89792	89995	90197	90399	90600	90801	91002
50,0	3,91202	3,91402	3,91602	3,91801	3,91999	3,92197	3,92395	3,92593	3,92790	3,92986
51,0	93183	93378	93574	93769	93964	94158	94352	94546	94739	94932
52,0	95124	95316	95508	95700	95891	96081	96272	96462	96651	96840
53,0	97029	97218	97406	97594	97781	97968	98155	98341	98527	98713
54,0	98898	99083	99268	99452	99636	99820	4,00003	4,00186	4,00369	4,00551
55,0	4,00733	4,00915	4,01096	4,01277	4,01458	4,01638	4,01818	4,01998	4,02177	4,02356
56,0	02535	02714	02892	03069	03247	03424	03601	03777	03954	04130
57,0	04305	04480	04655	04830	05004	05178	05352	05526	05699	05872
58,0	06044	06217	06389	06560	06732	06903	07073	07244	07414	07584
59,0	07754	07923	08092	08261	08429	08598	08766	08933	09101	09268
60,0	4,09434	4,09601	4,09767	4,09933	4,10099	4,10264	4,10429	4,10594	4,10759	4,10923
61,0	11087	11251	11415	11578	11741	11904	12066	12228	12390	12552
62,0	12713	12875	13036	13196	13357	13517	13677	13836	13996	14155
63,0	14313	14472	14630	14789	14946	15104	15261	15418	15575	15732
64,0	15888	16044	16200	16356	16511	16667	16821	16976	17131	17285
65,0	4,17439	4,17592	4,17746	4,17899	4,18052	4,18205	4,18358	4,18510	4,18662	4,18814
66,0	18965	19117	19268	19419	19570	19720	19870	20020	20170	20320
67,0	20469	20618	20767	20916	21065	21213	21361	21509	21656	21804
68,0	21951	22098	22244	22391	22537	22683	22829	22975	23120	23266
69,0	23411	23555	23700	23844	23989	24133	24276	24420	24563	24707
70,0	4,24850	4,24992	4,25135	4,25277	4,25419	4,25561	4,25703	4,25845	4,25986	4,26127
71,0	26268	26409	26549	26690	26830	26970	27110	27249	27388	27528
72,0	27667	27805	27944	28082	28221	28359	28496	28634	28772	28909
73,0	29046	29183	29320	29456	29592	29729	29865	30000	30136	30271
74,0	30407	30542	30676	30811	30946	31080	31214	31348	31482	31615
75,0	4,31749	4,31882	4,32015	4,32149	4,32281	4,32413	4,32546	4,32678	4,32810	4,32942
76,0	33073	33205	33336	33467	33598	33729	33860	33990	34120	34251
77,0	34381	34510	34640	34769	34899	35028	35157	35286	35414	35543
78,0	35671	35800	35927	36055	36182	36310	36437	36564	36691	36818
79,0	36945	37071	37198	37324	37450	37576	37701	37827	37952	38078
80,0	4,38203	4,38328	4,38452	4,38577	4,38701	4,38826	4,38950	4,39074	4,39198	4,39321
81,0	39445	39568	39692	39815	39938	40060	40183	40305	40428	40550
82,0	40672	40794	40916	41037	41159	41280	41401	41522	41643	41764
83,0	41884	42004	42125	42245	42365	42485	42604	42724	42843	42963
84,0	43082	43201	43319	43438	43557	43675	43793	43912	44030	44147
85,0	4,44265	4,44383	4,44500	4,44617	4,44735	4,44852	4,44969	4,45085	4,45202	4,45318
86,0	45435	45551	45667	45783	45899	46014	46130	46245	46361	46476
87,0	46591	46706	46820	46935	47050	47164	47278	47392	47506	47620
88,0	47734	47847	47961	48074	48187	48300	48413	48526	48639	48751
89,0	48864	48976	49088	49200	49312	49424	49536	49647	49758	49870
90,0	4,49981	4,50092	4,50203	4,50314	4,50424	4,50535	4,50645	4,50756	4,50866	4,50976
91,0	51086	51196	51305	51415	51525	51634	51743	51852	51961	52070
92,0	52179	52287	52396	52504	52613	52721	52829	52937	53045	53152
93,0	53260	53367	53475	53582	53689	53796	53903	54010	54116	54223
94,0	54329	54436	54542	54648	54754	54860	54966	55071	55177	55282
95,0	4,55388	4,55493	4,55598	4,55703	4,55808	4,55913	4,56017	4,56122	4,56226	4,56331
96,0	56435	56539	56643	56747	56851	56954	57058	57161	57265	57368
97,0	57471	57574	57677	57780	57883	57985	58088	58190	58292	58395
98,0	58497	58599	58701	58802	58904	59006	59107	59208	59310	59411
99,0	59512	59613	59714	59815	59915	60016	60116	60217	60317	60417

*To find the natural logarithm (ln) of a number which is a power of ten less or greater than a number given in the table: if the number concerned is *less*, e.g., 1/10 (10^{-1}), 1/100 (10^{-2}), 1/1000 (10^{-3}), etc., *subtract* from the given logarithm ln 10, 2 ln 10, 3 ln 10, etc.; if the number concerned is *greater*, e.g., 10 times (10^1), 100 times (10^2), 1000 times (10^3), etc., *add* to the given logarithm ln 10, 2 ln 10, 3 ln 10, etc. Examples: $\ln 0{,}02 = \ln 0{,}2 - \ln 10$; $\ln 2000 = \ln 200 + \ln 10$.

All values conform to the international convention (i.e. 0,1 instead of 0.1).

Natural Logarithms* (ln *x*) for *x* = 0–999

x	0	1	2	3	4	5	6	7	8	9
00	∞	0,00000	0,69315	1,09861	1,38629	1,60944	1,79176	1,94591	2,07944	2,19722
10	2,30259	2,39790	2,48491	2,56495	2,63906	2,70805	2,77259	2,83321	89037	94444
20	99573	3,04452	3,09104	3,13549	3,17805	3,21888	3,25810	3,29584	3,33220	3,36730
30	3,40120	43399	46574	49651	52636	55535	58352	61092	63759	66356
40	68888	71357	73767	76120	78419	80666	82864	85015	87120	89182
50	3,91202	3,93183	3,95124	3,97029	3,98898	4,00733	4,02535	4,04305	4,06044	4,07754
60	4,09434	4,11087	4,12713	4,14313	4,15888	17439	18965	20469	21951	23411
70	24850	26268	27667	29046	30407	31749	33073	34381	35671	36945
80	38203	39445	40672	41884	43082	44265	45435	46591	47734	48864
90	49981	51086	52179	53260	54329	55388	56435	57471	58497	59512
100	4,60517	4,61512	4,62497	4,63473	4,64439	4,65396	4,66344	4,67283	4,68213	4,69135
110	70048	70953	71850	72739	73620	74493	75359	76217	77068	77912
120	78749	79579	80402	81218	82028	82831	83628	84419	85203	85981
130	86753	87520	88280	89035	89784	90527	91265	91998	92725	93447
140	94164	94876	95583	96284	96981	97673	98361	99043	99721	5,00395
150	5,01064	5,01728	5,02388	5,03044	5,03695	5,04343	5,04986	5,05625	5,06260	5,06890
160	07517	08140	08760	09375	09987	10595	11199	11799	12396	12990
170	13580	14166	14749	15329	15906	16479	17048	17615	18178	18739
180	19296	19850	20401	20949	21494	22036	22575	23111	23644	24175
190	24702	25227	25750	26269	26786	27300	27811	28320	28827	29330
200	5,29832	5,30330	5,30827	5,31321	5,31812	5,32301	5,32788	5,33272	5,33754	5,34233
210	34711	35186	35659	36129	36598	37064	37528	37990	38450	38907
220	39363	39816	40268	40717	41165	41610	42053	42495	42935	43372
230	43808	44242	44674	45104	45532	45959	46383	46806	47227	47646
240	48064	48480	48894	49306	49717	50126	50533	50939	51343	51745
250	5,52146	5,52545	5,52943	5,53339	5,53733	5,54126	5,54518	5,54908	5,55296	5,55683
260	56068	56452	56834	57215	57595	57973	58350	58725	59099	59471
270	59842	60212	60580	60947	61313	61677	62040	62402	62762	63121
280	63479	63835	64191	64545	64897	65249	65599	65948	66296	66643
290	66988	67332	67675	68017	68358	68698	69036	69373	69709	70044
300	5,70378	5,70711	5,71043	5,71373	5,71703	5,72031	5,72359	5,72685	5,73010	5,73334
310	73657	73979	74300	74620	74939	75257	75574	75890	76205	76519
320	76832	77144	77455	77765	78074	78383	78690	78996	79301	79606
330	79909	80212	80513	80814	81114	81413	81711	82008	82305	82600
340	82895	83188	83481	83773	84064	84354	84644	84932	85220	85507
350	5,85793	5,86079	5,86363	5,86647	5,86930	5,87212	5,87493	5,87774	5,88053	5,88332
360	88610	88888	89164	89440	89715	89990	90263	90536	90808	91080
370	91350	91620	91889	92158	92426	92693	92959	93225	93489	93754
380	94017	94280	94542	94803	95064	95324	95584	95842	96101	96358
390	96615	96871	97126	97381	97635	97889	98141	98394	98645	98896
400	5,99146	5,99396	5,99645	5,99894	6,00141	6,00389	6,00635	6,00881	6,01127	6,01372
410	6,01616	6,01859	6,02102	6,02345	02587	02828	03069	03309	03548	03787
420	04025	04263	04501	04737	04973	05209	05444	05678	05912	06146
430	06379	06611	06843	07074	07304	07535	07764	07993	08222	08450
440	08677	08904	09131	09357	09582	09807	10032	10256	10479	10702
450	6,10925	6,11147	6,11368	6,11589	6,11810	6,12030	6,12249	6,12468	6,12687	6,12905
460	13123	13340	13556	13773	13988	14204	14419	14633	14847	15060
470	15273	15486	15698	15910	16121	16331	16542	16752	16961	17170
480	17379	17587	17794	18002	18208	18415	18621	18826	19032	19236
490	19441	19644	19848	20051	20254	20456	20658	20859	21060	21261
500	6,21461	6,21661	6,21860	6,22059	6,22258	6,22456	6,22654	6,22851	6,23048	6,23245
510	23441	23637	23832	24028	24222	24417	24611	24804	24998	25190
520	25383	25575	25767	25958	26149	26340	26530	26720	26910	27099
530	27288	27476	27664	27852	28040	28227	28413	28600	28786	28972
540	29157	29342	29527	29711	29895	30079	30262	30445	30628	30810
550	6,30992	6,31173	6,31355	6,31536	6,31716	6,31897	6,32077	6,32257	6,32436	6,32615
560	32794	32972	33150	33328	33505	33683	33859	34036	34212	34388
570	34564	34739	34914	35089	35263	35437	35611	35784	35957	36130
580	36303	36475	36647	36819	36990	37161	37332	37502	37673	37843
590	38012	38182	38351	38519	38688	38856	39024	39192	39359	39526
600	6,39693	6,39859	6,40026	6,40192	6,40357	6,40523	6,40688	6,40853	6,41017	6,41182
610	41346	41510	41673	41836	41999	42162	42325	42487	42649	42811
620	42972	43133	43294	43455	43615	43775	43935	44095	44254	44413
630	44572	44731	44889	45047	45205	45362	45520	45677	45834	45990
640	46147	46303	46459	46614	46770	46925	47080	47235	47389	47543
650	6,47697	6,47851	6,48004	6,48158	6,48311	6,48464	6,48616	6,48768	6,48920	6,49072
660	49224	49375	49527	49677	49828	49979	50129	50279	50429	50578
670	50728	50877	51026	51175	51323	51471	51619	51767	51915	52062
680	52209	52356	52503	52649	52796	52942	53088	53233	53379	53524
690	53669	53814	53959	54103	54247	54391	54535	54679	54822	54965
700	6,55108	6,55251	6,55393	6,55536	6,55678	6,55820	6,55962	6,56103	6,56244	6,56386
710	56526	56667	56808	56948	57088	57228	57368	57508	57647	57786
720	57925	58064	58203	58341	58479	58617	58755	58893	59030	59167
730	59304	59441	59578	59715	59851	59987	60123	60259	60394	60530
740	60665	60800	60935	61070	61204	61338	61473	61607	61740	61874
750	6,62007	6,62141	6,62274	6,62407	6,62539	6,62672	6,62804	6,62936	6,63068	6,63200
760	63332	63463	63595	63726	63857	63988	64118	64249	64379	64509
770	64639	64769	64898	65028	65157	65286	65415	65544	65673	65801
780	65929	66058	66185	66313	66441	66568	66696	66823	66950	67077
790	67203	67330	67456	67582	67708	67834	67960	68085	68211	68336
800	6,68461	6,68586	6,68711	6,68835	6,68960	6,69084	6,69208	6,69332	6,69456	6,69580
810	69703	69827	69950	70073	70196	70319	70441	70564	70686	70808
820	70930	71052	71174	71296	71417	71538	71659	71780	71901	72022
830	72143	72263	72383	72503	72623	72743	72863	72982	73102	73221
840	73340	73459	73578	73697	73815	73934	74052	74170	74288	74406
850	6,74524	6,74641	6,74759	6,74876	6,74993	6,75110	6,75227	6,75344	6,75460	6,75577
860	75693	75809	75926	76041	76157	76273	76388	76504	76619	76734
870	76849	76964	77079	77194	77308	77422	77537	77651	77765	77878
880	77992	78106	78219	78333	78446	78559	78672	78784	78897	79010
890	79122	79234	79347	79459	79571	79682	79794	79906	80017	80128
900	6,80239	6,80351	6,80461	6,80572	6,80683	6,80793	6,80904	6,81014	6,81124	6,81235
910	81344	81454	81564	81674	81783	81892	82002	82111	82220	82329
920	82437	82546	82655	82763	82871	82979	83087	83195	83303	83411
930	83518	83626	83733	83841	83948	84055	84162	84268	84375	84482
940	84588	84694	84801	84907	85013	85118	85224	85330	85435	85541
950	6,85646	6,85751	6,85857	6,85961	6,86066	6,86171	6,86276	6,86380	6,86485	6,86589
960	86693	86797	86901	87005	87109	87213	87316	87420	87523	87626
970	87730	87833	87936	88038	88141	88244	88346	88449	88551	88653
980	88755	88857	88959	89061	89163	89264	89366	89467	89568	89669
990	89770	89871	89972	90073	90174	90274	90375	90475	90575	90675

*To find the natural logarithm (ln) of a number which is a power of ten less or greater than a number given in the table: if the number concerned is *less*, e. g., 1/10 (10^{-1}), 1/100 (10^{-2}), 1/1000 (10^{-3}), etc., *subtract* from the given logarithm ln 10, 2 ln 10, 3 ln 10, etc.; if the number concerned is *greater*, e. g., 10 times (10^1), 100 times (10^2), 1000 times (10^3), etc., *add* to the given logarithm ln 10, 2 ln 10, 3 ln 10, etc. Examples: ln 0,02 = ln 0,2 − ln 10; ln 2000 = ln 200 + ln 10.

All values conform to the international convention (i.e. 0,1 instead of 0.1).

Exponential Functions

x	e^x	$\log_{10}(e^x)$	e^{-x}	x	e^x	$\log_{10}(e^x)$	e^{-x}	x	e^x	$\log_{10}(e^x)$	e^{-x}
0,00	1,0000	0,00000	1,000000	**1,00**	2,7183	0,43429	0,367879	**2,00**	7,3891	0,86859	0,135335
0,01	1,0101	00434	0,990050	1,01	2,7456	43864	364219	2,01	7,4633	87293	133989
0,02	1,0202	00869	980199	1,02	2,7732	44298	360595	2,02	7,5383	87727	132655
0,03	1,0305	01303	970446	1,03	2,8011	44732	357007	2,03	7,6141	88162	131336
0,04	1,0408	01737	960789	1,04	2,8292	45167	353455	2,04	7,6906	88596	130029
0,05	1,0513	0,02171	0,951229	**1,05**	2,8577	0,45601	0,349938	**2,05**	7,7679	0,89030	0,128735
0,06	1,0618	02606	941765	1,06	2,8864	46035	346456	2,06	7,8460	89465	127454
0,07	1,0725	03040	932394	1,07	2,9154	46470	343009	2,07	7,9248	89899	126186
0,08	1,0833	03474	923116	1,08	2,9447	46904	339596	2,08	8,0045	90333	124930
0,09	1,0942	03909	913931	1,09	2,9743	47338	336216	2,09	8,0849	90768	123687
0,10	1,1052	0,04343	0,904837	**1,10**	3,0042	0,47772	0,332871	**2,10**	8,1662	0,91202	0,122456
0,11	1,1163	04777	895834	1,11	3,0344	48207	329559	2,11	8,2482	91636	121238
0,12	1,1275	05212	886920	1,12	3,0649	48641	326280	2,12	8,3311	92070	120032
0,13	1,1388	05646	878095	1,13	3,0957	49075	323033	2,13	8,4149	92505	118837
0,14	1,1503	06080	869358	1,14	3,1268	49510	319819	2,14	8,4994	92939	117655
0,15	1,1618	0,06514	0,860708	**1,15**	3,1582	0,49944	0,316637	**2,15**	8,5849	0,93373	0,116484
0,16	1,1735	06949	852144	1,16	3,1899	50378	313486	2,16	8,6711	93808	115325
0,17	1,1853	07383	843665	1,17	3,2220	50812	310367	2,17	8,7583	94242	114178
0,18	1,1972	07817	835270	1,18	3,2544	51247	307279	2,18	8,8463	94676	113042
0,19	1,2092	08252	826959	1,19	3,2871	51681	304221	2,19	8,9352	95110	111917
0,20	1,2214	0,08686	0,818731	**1,20**	3,3201	0,52115	0,301194	**2,20**	9,0250	0,95545	0,110803
0,21	1,2337	09120	810584	1,21	3,3535	52550	298197	2,21	9,1157	95979	109701
0,22	1,2461	09554	802519	1,22	3,3872	52984	295230	2,22	9,2073	96413	108609
0,23	1,2586	09989	794534	1,23	3,4212	53418	292293	2,23	9,2999	96848	107528
0,24	1,2712	10423	786628	1,24	3,4556	53853	289384	2,24	9,3933	97282	106459
0,25	1,2840	0,10857	0,778801	**1,25**	3,4903	0,54287	0,286505	**2,25**	9,4877	0,97716	0,105399
0,26	1,2969	11292	771052	1,26	3,5254	54721	283654	2,26	9,5831	98151	104350
0,27	1,3100	11726	763379	1,27	3,5609	55155	280832	2,27	9,6794	98585	103312
0,28	1,3231	12160	755784	1,28	3,5966	55590	278037	2,28	9,7767	99019	102284
0,29	1,3364	12595	748264	1,29	3,6328	56024	275271	2,29	9,8749	99453	101266
0,30	1,3499	0,13029	0,740818	**1,30**	3,6693	0,56458	0,272532	**2,30**	9,9742	0,99888	0,100259
0,31	1,3634	13463	733447	1,31	3,7062	56893	269820	2,31	10,074	1,00322	099261
0,32	1,3771	13897	726149	1,32	3,7434	57327	267135	2,32	10,176	00756	098274
0,33	1,3910	14332	718924	1,33	3,7810	57761	264477	2,33	10,278	01191	097296
0,34	1,4049	14766	711770	1,34	3,8190	58195	261846	2,34	10,381	01625	096328
0,35	1,4191	0,15200	0,704688	**1,35**	3,8574	0,58630	0,259240	**2,35**	10,486	1,02059	0,095369
0,36	1,4333	15635	697676	1,36	3,8962	59064	256661	2,36	10,591	02493	094420
0,37	1,4477	16069	690734	1,37	3,9354	59498	254107	2,37	10,697	02928	093481
0,38	1,4623	16503	683861	1,38	3,9749	59933	251579	2,38	10,805	03362	092551
0,39	1,4770	16937	677057	1,39	4,0149	60367	249075	2,39	10,913	03796	091630
0,40	1,4918	0,17372	0,670320	**1,40**	4,0552	0,60801	0,246597	**2,40**	11,023	1,04231	0,090718
0,41	1,5068	17806	663650	1,41	4,0960	61236	244143	2,41	11,134	04665	089815
0,42	1,5220	18240	657047	1,42	4,1371	61670	241714	2,42	11,246	05099	088922
0,43	1,5373	18675	650509	1,43	4,1787	62104	239309	2,43	11,359	05534	088037
0,44	1,5527	19109	644036	1,44	4,2207	62538	236928	2,44	11,473	05968	087161
0,45	1,5683	0,19543	0,637628	**1,45**	4,2631	0,62973	0,234570	**2,45**	11,588	1,06402	0,086294
0,46	1,5841	19978	631284	1,46	4,3060	63407	232236	2,46	11,705	06836	085435
0,47	1,6000	20412	625002	1,47	4,3492	63841	229925	2,47	11,822	07271	084585
0,48	1,6161	20846	618783	1,48	4,3929	64276	227638	2,48	11,941	07705	083743
0,49	1,6323	21280	612626	1,49	4,4371	64710	225373	2,49	12,061	08139	082910
0,50	1,6487	0,21715	0,606531	**1,50**	4,4817	0,65144	0,223130	**2,50**	12,182	1,08574	0,082085
0,51	1,6653	22149	600496	1,51	4,5267	65578	220910	2,51	12,305	09008	081268
0,52	1,6820	22583	594521	1,52	4,5722	66013	218712	2,52	12,429	09442	080460
0,53	1,6989	23018	588605	1,53	4,6182	66447	216536	2,53	12,554	09877	079659
0,54	1,7160	23452	582748	1,54	4,6646	66881	214381	2,54	12,680	10311	078866
0,55	1,7333	0,23886	0,576950	**1,55**	4,7115	0,67316	0,212248	**2,55**	12,807	1,10745	0,078082
0,56	1,7507	24320	571209	1,56	4,7588	67750	210136	2,56	12,936	11179	077305
0,57	1,7683	24755	565525	1,57	4,8066	68184	208045	2,57	13,066	11614	076536
0,58	1,7860	25189	559898	1,58	4,8550	68619	205975	2,58	13,197	12048	075774
0,59	1,8040	25623	554327	1,59	4,9037	69053	203926	2,59	13,330	12482	075020
0,60	1,8221	0,26058	0,548812	**1,60**	4,9530	0,69487	0,201897	**2,60**	13,464	1,12917	0,074274
0,61	1,8404	26492	543351	1,61	5,0028	69921	199888	2,61	13,599	13351	073535
0,62	1,8589	26926	537944	1,62	5,0531	70356	197899	2,62	13,736	13785	072803
0,63	1,8776	27361	532592	1,63	5,1039	70790	195930	2,63	13,874	14219	072078
0,64	1,8965	27795	527292	1,64	5,1552	71224	193980	2,64	14,013	14654	071361
0,65	1,9155	0,28229	0,522046	**1,65**	5,2070	0,71659	0,192050	**2,65**	14,154	1,15088	0,070651
0,66	1,9348	28663	516851	1,66	5,2593	72093	190139	2,66	14,296	15522	069948
0,67	1,9542	29098	511709	1,67	5,3122	72527	188247	2,67	14,440	15957	069252
0,68	1,9739	29532	506617	1,68	5,3656	72961	186374	2,68	14,585	16391	068563
0,69	1,9937	29966	501576	1,69	5,4195	73396	184520	2,69	14,732	16825	067881
0,70	2,0138	0,30401	0,496585	**1,70**	5,4739	0,73830	0,182684	**2,70**	14,880	1,17260	0,067206
0,71	2,0340	30835	491644	1,71	5,5290	74264	180866	2,71	15,029	17694	066537
0,72	2,0544	31269	486752	1,72	5,5845	74699	179066	2,72	15,180	18128	065875
0,73	2,0751	31703	481909	1,73	5,6407	75133	177284	2,73	15,333	18562	065219
0,74	2,0959	32138	477114	1,74	5,6973	75567	175520	2,74	15,487	18997	064570
0,75	2,1170	0,32572	0,472367	**1,75**	5,7546	0,76002	0,173774	**2,75**	15,643	1,19431	0,063928
0,76	2,1383	33006	467666	1,76	5,8124	76436	172045	2,76	15,800	19865	063292
0,77	2,1598	33441	463013	1,77	5,8709	76870	170333	2,77	15,959	20300	062662
0,78	2,1815	33875	458406	1,78	5,9299	77304	168638	2,78	16,119	20734	062039
0,79	2,2034	34309	453845	1,79	5,9895	77739	166960	2,79	16,281	21168	061421
0,80	2,2255	0,34744	0,449329	**1,80**	6,0496	0,78173	0,165299	**2,80**	16,445	1,21602	0,060810
0,81	2,2479	35178	444858	1,81	6,1104	78607	163654	2,81	16,610	22037	060205
0,82	2,2705	35612	440432	1,82	6,1719	79042	162026	2,82	16,777	22471	059606
0,83	2,2933	36046	436049	1,83	6,2339	79476	160414	2,83	16,945	22905	059013
0,84	2,3164	36481	431711	1,84	6,2965	79910	158817	2,84	17,116	23340	058426
0,85	2,3396	0,36915	0,427415	**1,85**	6,3598	0,80344	0,157237	**2,85**	17,288	1,23774	0,057844
0,86	2,3632	37349	423162	1,86	6,4237	80779	155673	2,86	17,462	24208	057269
0,87	2,3869	37784	418952	1,87	6,4883	81213	154124	2,87	17,637	24643	056699
0,88	2,4109	38218	414783	1,88	6,5535	81647	152590	2,88	17,814	25077	056135
0,89	2,4351	38652	410656	1,89	6,6194	82082	151072	2,89	17,993	25511	055576
0,90	2,4596	0,39087	0,406570	**1,90**	6,6859	0,82516	0,149569	**2,90**	18,174	1,25945	0,055023
0,91	2,4843	39521	402524	1,91	6,7531	82950	148080	2,91	18,357	26380	054476
0,92	2,5093	39955	398519	1,92	6,8210	83385	146607	2,92	18,541	26814	053934
0,93	2,5345	40389	394554	1,93	6,8895	83819	145148	2,93	18,728	27248	053397
0,94	2,5600	40824	390628	1,94	6,9588	84253	143704	2,94	18,916	27683	052866
0,95	2,5857	0,41258	0,386741	**1,95**	7,0287	0,84687	0,142274	**2,95**	19,106	1,28117	0,052340
0,96	2,6117	41692	382893	1,96	7,0993	85122	140858	2,96	19,298	28551	051819
0,97	2,6379	42127	379083	1,97	7,1707	85556	139457	2,97	19,492	28985	051303
0,98	2,6645	42561	375311	1,98	7,2427	85990	138069	2,98	19,688	29420	050793
0,99	2,6912	42995	371577	1,99	7,3155	86425	136695	2,99	19,886	29854	050287

All values conform to the international convention (i.e. 0,1 instead of 0.1).

x	e^x	$\log_{10}(e^x)$	e^{-x}	x	e^x	$\log_{10}(e^x)$	e^{-x}	x	e^x	$\log_{10}(e^x)$	e^{-x}
3,00	20,086	1,30288	0,049787	4,00	54,598	1,73718	0,018316	5,00	148,41	2,17147	0,006738
3,01	20,287	1,30723	049292	4,01	55,147	1,74152	018133	5,01	149,90	2,17582	006671
3,02	20,491	1,31157	048801	4,02	55,701	1,74586	017953	5,02	151,41	2,18016	006605
3,03	20,697	1,31591	048316	4,03	56,261	1,75021	017774	5,03	152,93	2,18450	006539
3,04	20,905	1,32026	047835	4,04	56,826	1,75455	017597	5,04	154,47	2,18884	006474
3,05	21,115	1,32460	0,047359	4,05	57,397	1,75889	0,017422	5,05	156,02	2,19319	0,006409
3,06	21,328	1,32894	046888	4,06	57,974	1,76324	017249	5,06	157,59	2,19753	006346
3,07	21,542	1,33328	046421	4,07	58,557	1,76758	017077	5,07	159,17	2,20187	006282
3,08	21,758	1,33763	045959	4,08	59,145	1,77192	016907	5,08	160,77	2,20622	006220
3,09	21,977	1,34197	045502	4,09	59,740	1,77626	016739	5,09	162,39	2,21056	006158
3,10	22,198	1,34631	0,045049	4,10	60,340	1,78061	0,016573	5,10	164,02	2,21490	0,006097
3,11	22,421	1,35066	044601	4,11	60,947	1,78495	016408	5,11	165,67	2,21924	006036
3,12	22,646	1,35500	044157	4,12	61,559	1,78929	016245	5,12	167,34	2,22359	005976
3,13	22,874	1,35934	043718	4,13	62,178	1,79364	016083	5,13	169,02	2,22793	005917
3,14	23,104	1,36368	043283	4,14	62,803	1,79798	015923	5,14	170,72	2,23227	005858
3,15	23,336	1,36803	0,042852	4,15	63,434	1,80232	0,015764	5,15	172,43	2,23662	0,005799
3,16	23,571	1,37237	042426	4,16	64,072	1,80667	015608	5,16	174,16	2,24096	005742
3,17	23,807	1,37671	042004	4,17	64,715	1,81101	015452	5,17	175,91	2,24530	005685
3,18	24,047	1,38106	041586	4,18	65,366	1,81535	015299	5,18	177,68	2,24965	005628
3,19	24,288	1,38540	041172	4,19	66,023	1,81969	015146	5,19	179,47	2,25399	005572
3,20	24,533	1,38974	0,040762	4,20	66,686	1,82404	0,014996	5,20	181,27	2,25833	0,005517
3,21	24,779	1,39409	040357	4,21	67,357	1,82838	014846	5,21	183,09	2,26267	005462
3,22	25,028	1,39843	039955	4,22	68,033	1,83272	014699	5,22	184,93	2,26702	005407
3,23	25,280	1,40277	039557	4,23	68,717	1,83707	014552	5,23	186,79	2,27136	005354
3,24	25,534	1,40711	039164	4,24	69,408	1,84141	014408	5,24	188,67	2,27570	005300
3,25	25,790	1,41146	0,038774	4,25	70,105	1,84575	0,014264	5,25	190,57	2,28005	0,005248
3,26	26,050	1,41580	038388	4,26	70,810	1,85009	014122	5,26	192,48	2,28439	005195
3,27	26,311	1,42014	038006	4,27	71,522	1,85444	013982	5,27	194,42	2,28873	005144
3,28	26,576	1,42449	037628	4,28	72,240	1,85878	013843	5,28	196,37	2,29307	005092
3,29	26,843	1,42883	037254	4,29	72,966	1,86312	013705	5,29	198,34	2,29742	005042
3,30	27,113	1,43317	0,036883	4,30	73,700	1,86747	0,013569	5,30	200,34	2,30176	0,004992
3,31	27,385	1,43751	036516	4,31	74,440	1,87181	013434	5,31	202,35	2,30610	004942
3,32	27,660	1,44186	036153	4,32	75,189	1,87615	013300	5,32	204,38	2,31045	004893
3,33	27,938	1,44620	035793	4,33	75,944	1,88050	013168	5,33	206,44	2,31479	004844
3,34	28,219	1,45054	035437	4,34	76,708	1,88484	013037	5,34	208,51	2,31913	004796
3,35	28,503	1,45489	0,035084	4,35	77,478	1,88918	0,012907	5,35	210,61	2,32348	0,004748
3,36	28,789	1,45923	034735	4,36	78,257	1,89352	012778	5,36	212,72	2,32782	004701
3,37	29,079	1,46357	034390	4,37	79,044	1,89787	012651	5,37	214,86	2,33216	004654
3,38	29,371	1,46792	034047	4,38	79,838	1,90221	012525	5,38	217,02	2,33650	004608
3,39	29,666	1,47226	033709	4,39	80,640	1,90655	012401	5,39	219,20	2,34085	004562
3,40	29,964	1,47660	0,033373	4,40	81,451	1,91090	0,012277	5,40	221,41	2,34519	0,004517
3,41	30,265	1,48094	033041	4,41	82,269	1,91524	012155	5,41	223,63	2,34953	004472
3,42	30,569	1,48529	032712	4,42	83,096	1,91958	012034	5,42	225,88	2,35388	004427
3,43	30,877	1,48963	032387	4,43	83,931	1,92392	011914	5,43	228,15	2,35822	004383
3,44	31,187	1,49397	032065	4,44	84,775	1,92827	011796	5,44	230,44	2,36256	004339
3,45	31,500	1,49832	0,031746	4,45	85,627	1,93261	0,011679	5,45	232,76	2,36690	0,004296
3,46	31,817	1,50266	031430	4,46	86,488	1,93695	011562	5,46	235,10	2,37125	004254
3,47	32,137	1,50700	031117	4,47	87,357	1,94130	011447	5,47	237,46	2,37559	004211
3,48	32,460	1,51134	030807	4,48	88,235	1,94564	011333	5,48	239,85	2,37993	004169
3,49	32,786	1,51569	030501	4,49	89,121	1,94998	011221	5,49	242,26	2,38428	004128
3,50	33,115	1,52003	0,030197	4,50	90,017	1,95433	0,011109				
3,51	33,448	1,52437	029897	4,51	90,922	1,95867	010998				
3,52	33,784	1,52872	029599	4,52	91,836	1,96301	010889				
3,53	34,124	1,53306	029305	4,53	92,759	1,96735	010781				
3,54	34,467	1,53740	029013	4,54	93,691	1,97170	010673	5,5	244,69	2,38862	0,004087
3,55	34,813	1,54175	0,028725	4,55	94,632	1,97604	0,010567	5,6	270,43	2,43205	003698
3,56	35,163	1,54609	028439	4,56	95,583	1,98038	010462	5,7	298,87	2,47548	003346
3,57	35,517	1,55043	028156	4,57	96,544	1,98473	010358	5,8	330,30	2,51891	003028
3,58	35,874	1,55477	027876	4,58	97,514	1,98907	010255	5,9	365,04	2,56234	002739
3,59	36,234	1,55912	027598	4,59	98,494	1,99341	010153	6,0	403,43	2,60577	0,002479
3,60	36,598	1,56346	0,027324	4,60	99,484	1,99775	0,010052	6,1	445,86	2,64920	002243
3,61	36,966	1,56780	027052	4,61	100,48	2,00210	009952	6,2	492,75	2,69263	002029
3,62	37,338	1,57215	026783	4,62	101,49	2,00644	009853	6,3	544,57	2,73606	001836
3,63	37,713	1,57649	026516	4,63	102,51	2,01078	009755	6,4	601,85	2,77948	001662
3,64	38,092	1,58083	026252	4,64	103,54	2,01513	009658	6,5	665,14	2,82291	0,001503
3,65	38,475	1,58517	0,025991	4,65	104,58	2,01947	0,009562	6,6	735,10	2,86634	001360
3,66	38,861	1,58952	025733	4,66	105,64	2,02381	009466	6,7	812,41	2,90977	001231
3,67	39,252	1,59386	025476	4,67	106,70	2,02816	009372	6,8	897,85	2,95320	001114
3,68	39,646	1,59820	025223	4,68	107,77	2,03250	009279	6,9	992,27	2,99663	001008
3,69	40,045	1,60255	024972	4,69	108,85	2,03684	009187	7,0	1096,6	3,04006	0,000912
3,70	40,447	1,60689	0,024724	4,70	109,95	2,04118	0,009095	7,1	1212,0	3,08349	000825
3,71	40,854	1,61123	024478	4,71	111,05	2,04553	009005	7,2	1339,4	3,12692	000747
3,72	41,264	1,61558	024234	4,72	112,17	2,04987	008915	7,3	1480,3	3,17035	000676
3,73	41,679	1,61992	023993	4,73	113,30	2,05421	008826	7,4	1636,0	3,21378	000611
3,74	42,098	1,62426	023754	4,74	114,43	2,05856	008739	7,5	1808,0	3,25721	0,000553
3,75	42,521	1,62860	0,023518	4,75	115,58	2,06290	0,008652	7,6	1998,2	3,30064	000501
3,76	42,948	1,63295	023284	4,76	116,75	2,06724	008566	7,7	2208,3	3,33407	000453
3,77	43,380	1,63729	023052	4,77	117,92	2,07158	008480	7,8	2440,6	3,38750	000410
3,78	43,816	1,64163	022823	4,78	119,10	2,07593	008396	7,9	2697,3	3,43093	000371
3,79	44,256	1,64598	022596	4,79	120,30	2,08027	008312	8,0	2981,0	3,47436	0,000336
3,80	44,701	1,65032	0,022371	4,80	121,51	2,08461	0,008230	8,1	3294,5	3,51779	000304
3,81	45,150	1,65466	022148	4,81	122,73	2,08896	008148	8,2	3641,0	3,56121	000275
3,82	45,604	1,65900	021928	4,82	123,97	2,09330	008067	8,3	4023,9	3,60464	000249
3,83	46,063	1,66335	021710	4,83	125,21	2,09764	007987	8,4	4447,1	3,64807	000225
3,84	46,525	1,66769	021494	4,84	126,47	2,10199	007907	8,5	4914,8	3,69150	0,000204
3,85	46,993	1,67203	0,021280	4,85	127,74	2,10633	0,007828	8,6	5431,7	3,73493	000184
3,86	47,465	1,67638	021068	4,86	129,02	2,11067	007750	8,7	6002,9	3,77836	000167
3,87	47,942	1,68072	020858	4,87	130,32	2,11501	007673	8,8	6634,2	3,82179	000151
3,88	48,424	1,68506	020651	4,88	131,63	2,11936	007597	8,9	7332,0	3,86522	000136
3,89	48,911	1,68941	020445	4,89	132,95	2,12370	007521	9,0	8103,1	3,90865	0,000123
3,90	49,402	1,69375	0,020242	4,90	134,29	2,12804	0,007447	9,1	8955,3	3,95208	000112
3,91	49,899	1,69809	020041	4,91	135,64	2,13239	007372	9,2	9897,1	3,99551	000101
3,92	50,400	1,70243	019841	4,92	137,00	2,13673	007299	9,3	10938	4,03894	000091
3,93	50,907	1,70678	019644	4,93	138,38	2,14107	007227	9,4	12088	4,08237	000083
3,94	51,419	1,71112	019448	4,94	139,77	2,14541	007155	9,5	13360	4,12580	0,000075
3,95	51,935	1,71546	0,019255	4,95	141,17	2,14976	0,007083	9,6	14765	4,16923	000068
3,96	52,457	1,71981	019063	4,96	142,59	2,15410	007013	9,7	16318	4,21266	000061
3,97	52,985	1,72415	018873	4,97	144,03	2,15844	006943	9,8	18034	4,25609	000056
3,98	53,517	1,72849	018686	4,98	145,47	2,16279	006874	9,9	19930	4,29952	000050
3,99	54,055	1,73283	018500	4,99	146,94	2,16713	006806	10,0	22026	4,34294	0,000045

All values conform to the international convention (i.e. 0,1 instead of 0.1).

n	0	1	2	3	4	5	6	7	8	9
0		1	0,50000000	0,33333333	0,25000000	0,20000000	0,16666667	0,14285714	0,12500000	0,11111111
10	0,10000000	0,09090909	0,08333333	0,07692308	0,07142857	0,06666667	0,06250000	0,05882353	0,05555556	0,05263158
20	0,05000000	4761905	4545455	4347826	4166667	4000000	3846154	3703704	3571429	3448276
30	3333333	3225806	3125000	3030303	2941176	2857143	2777778	2702703	2631579	2564103
40	2500000	2439024	2380952	2325581	2272727	2222222	2173913	2127660	2083333	2040816
50	0,02000000	0,01960784	0,01923077	0,01886792	0,01851852	0,01818182	0,01785714	0,01754386	0,01724138	0,01694915
60	1666667	1639344	1612903	1587302	1562500	1538462	1515152	1492537	1470588	1449275
70	1428571	1408451	1388889	1369863	1351351	1333333	1315789	1298701	1282051	1265823
80	1250000	1234568	1219512	1204819	1190476	1176471	1162791	1149425	1136364	1123596
90	1111111	1098901	1086957	1075269	1063830	1052632	1041667	1030928	1020408	1010101
100	0,010000000	0,009900990	0,009803922	0,009708738	0,009615385	0,009523810	0,009433962	0,009345794	0,009259259	0,009174312
110	0,009090909	9009009	8928571	8849558	8771930	8695652	8620690	8547009	8474576	8403361
120	8333333	8264463	8196721	8130081	8064516	8000000	7936508	7874016	7812500	7751938
130	7692308	7633588	7575758	7518797	7462687	7407407	7352941	7299270	7246377	7194245
140	7142857	7092199	7042254	6993007	6944444	6896552	6849315	6802721	6756757	6711409
150	0,006666667	0,006622517	0,006578947	0,006535948	0,006493506	0,006451613	0,006410256	0,006369427	0,006329114	0,006289308
160	6250000	6211180	6172840	6134969	6097561	6060606	6024096	5988024	5952381	5917160
170	5882353	5847953	5813953	5780347	5747126	5714286	5681818	5649718	5617978	5586592
180	5555556	5524862	5494505	5464481	5434783	5405405	5376344	5347594	5319149	5291005
190	5263158	5235602	5208333	5181347	5154639	5128205	5102041	5076142	5050505	5025126
200	0,005000000	0,004975124	0,004950495	0,004926108	0,004901961	0,004878049	0,004854369	0,004830918	0,004807692	0,004784689
210	4761905	4739336	4716981	4694836	4672897	4651163	4629630	4608295	4587156	4566210
220	4545455	4524887	4504505	4484305	4464286	4444444	4424779	4405286	4385965	4366812
230	4347826	4329004	4310345	4291845	4273504	4255319	4237288	4219409	4201681	4184100
240	4166667	4149378	4132231	4115226	4098361	4081633	4065041	4048583	4032258	4016064
250	0,004000000	0,003984064	0,003968254	0,003952569	0,003937008	0,003921569	0,003906250	0,003891051	0,003875969	0,003861004
260	3846154	3831418	3816794	3802281	3787879	3773585	3759398	3745318	3731343	3717472
270	3703704	3690037	3676471	3663004	3649635	3636364	3623188	3610108	3597122	3584229
280	3571429	3558719	3546099	3533569	3521127	3508772	3496503	3484321	3472222	3460208
290	3448276	3436426	3424658	3412969	3401361	3389831	3378378	3367003	3355705	3344482
300	0,003333333	0,003322259	0,003311258	0,003300330	0,003289474	0,003278689	0,003267974	0,003257329	0,003246753	0,003236246
310	3225806	3215434	3205128	3194888	3184713	3174603	3164557	3154574	3144654	3134796
320	3125000	3115265	3105590	3095975	3086420	3076923	3067485	3058104	3048780	3039514
330	3030303	3021148	3012048	3003003	2994012	2985075	2976190	2967359	2958580	2949853
340	2941176	2932551	2923977	2915452	2906977	2898551	2890173	2881844	2873563	2865330
350	0,002857143	0,002849003	0,002840909	0,002832861	0,002824859	0,002816901	0,002808989	0,002801120	0,002793296	0,002785515
360	2777778	2770083	2762431	2754821	2747253	2739726	2732240	2724796	2717391	2710027
370	2702703	2695418	2688172	2680965	2673797	2666667	2659574	2652520	2645503	2638522
380	2631579	2624672	2617801	2610966	2604167	2597403	2590674	2583979	2577320	2570694
390	2564103	2557545	2551020	2544529	2538071	2531646	2525253	2518892	2512563	2506266
400	0,002500000	0,002493766	0,002487562	0,002481390	0,002475248	0,002469136	0,002463054	0,002457002	0,002450980	0,002444988
410	2439024	2433090	2427184	2421308	2415459	2409639	2403846	2398082	2392344	2386635
420	2380952	2375297	2369668	2364066	2358491	2352941	2347418	2341920	2336449	2331002
430	2325581	2320186	2314815	2309469	2304147	2298851	2293578	2288330	2283105	2277904
440	2272727	2267574	2262443	2257336	2252252	2247191	2242152	2237136	2232143	2227171
450	0,002222222	0,002217295	0,002212389	0,002207506	0,002202643	0,002197802	0,002192982	0,002188184	0,002183406	0,002178649
460	2173913	2169197	2164502	2159827	2155172	2150538	2145923	2141328	2136752	2132196
470	2127660	2123142	2118644	2114165	2109705	2105263	2100840	2096436	2092050	2087683
480	2083333	2079002	2074689	2070393	2066116	2061856	2057613	2053388	2049180	2044990
490	2040816	2036660	2032520	2028398	2024291	2020202	2016129	2012072	2008032	2004008
500	0,002000000	0,001996008	0,001992032	0,001988072	0,001984127	0,001980198	0,001976285	0,001972387	0,001968504	0,001964637
510	1960784	1956947	1953125	1949318	1945525	1941748	1937984	1934236	1930502	1926782
520	1923077	1919386	1915709	1912046	1908397	1904762	1901141	1897533	1893939	1890359
530	1886792	1883239	1879699	1876173	1872659	1869159	1865672	1862197	1858736	1855288
540	1851852	1848429	1845018	1841621	1838235	1834862	1831502	1828154	1824818	1821494
550	0,001818182	0,001814882	0,001811594	0,001808318	0,001805054	0,001801802	0,001798561	0,001795332	0,001792115	0,001788909
560	1785714	1782531	1779359	1776199	1773050	1769912	1766784	1763668	1760563	1757469
570	1754386	1751313	1748252	1745201	1742160	1739130	1736111	1733102	1730104	1727116
580	1724138	1721170	1718213	1715266	1712329	1709402	1706485	1703578	1700680	1697793
590	1694915	1692047	1689189	1686341	1683502	1680672	1677852	1675042	1672241	1669449
600	0,001666667	0,001663894	0,001661130	0,001658375	0,001655629	0,001652893	0,001650165	0,001647446	0,001644737	0,001642036
610	1639344	1636661	1633987	1631321	1628664	1626016	1623377	1620746	1618123	1615509
620	1612903	1610306	1607717	1605136	1602564	1600000	1597444	1594896	1592357	1589825
630	1587302	1584786	1582278	1579779	1577287	1574803	1572327	1569859	1567398	1564945
640	1562500	1560062	1557632	1555210	1552795	1550388	1547988	1545595	1543210	1540832
650	0,001538462	0,001536098	0,001533742	0,001531394	0,001529052	0,001526718	0,001524390	0,001522070	0,001519757	0,001517451
660	1515152	1512859	1510574	1508296	1506024	1503759	1501502	1499250	1497006	1494768
670	1492537	1490313	1488095	1485884	1483680	1481481	1479290	1477105	1474926	1472754
680	1470588	1468429	1466276	1464129	1461988	1459854	1457726	1455604	1453488	1451379
690	1449275	1447178	1445087	1443001	1440922	1438849	1436782	1434720	1432665	1430615
700	0,001428571	0,001426534	0,001424501	0,001422475	0,001420455	0,001418440	0,001416431	0,001414427	0,001412429	0,001410437
710	1408451	1406470	1404494	1402525	1400560	1398601	1396648	1394700	1392758	1390821
720	1388889	1386963	1385042	1383126	1381215	1379310	1377410	1375516	1373626	1371742
730	1369863	1367989	1366120	1364256	1362398	1360544	1358696	1356852	1355014	1353180
740	1351351	1349528	1347709	1345895	1344086	1342282	1340483	1338688	1336898	1335113
750	0,001333333	0,001331558	0,001329787	0,001328021	0,001326260	0,001324503	0,001322751	0,001321004	0,001319261	0,001317523
760	1315789	1314060	1312336	1310616	1308901	1307190	1305483	1303781	1302083	1300390
770	1298701	1297017	1295337	1293661	1291990	1290323	1288660	1287001	1285347	1283697
780	1282051	1280410	1278772	1277139	1275510	1273885	1272265	1270648	1269036	1267427
790	1265823	1264223	1262626	1261034	1259446	1257862	1256281	1254705	1253133	1251564
800	0,001250000	0,001248439	0,001246883	0,001245330	0,001243781	0,001242236	0,001240695	0,001239157	0,001237624	0,001236094
810	1234568	1233046	1231527	1230012	1228501	1226994	1225490	1223990	1222494	1221001
820	1219512	1218027	1216545	1215067	1213592	1212121	1210654	1209190	1207729	1206273
830	1204819	1203369	1201923	1200480	1199041	1197605	1196172	1194743	1193317	1191895
840	1190476	1189061	1187648	1186240	1184834	1183432	1182033	1180638	1179245	1177856
850	0,001176471	0,001175088	0,001173709	0,001172333	0,001170960	0,001169591	0,001168224	0,001166861	0,001165501	0,001164144
860	1162791	1161440	1160093	1158749	1157407	1156069	1154734	1153403	1152074	1150748
870	1149425	1148106	1146789	1145475	1144165	1142857	1141553	1140251	1138952	1137656
880	1136364	1135074	1133787	1132503	1131222	1129944	1128668	1127396	1126126	1124859
890	1123596	1122334	1121076	1119821	1118568	1117318	1116071	1114827	1113586	1112347
900	0,001111111	0,001109878	0,001108647	0,001107420	0,001106195	0,001104972	0,001103753	0,001102536	0,001101322	0,001100110
910	1098901	1097695	1096491	1095290	1094092	1092896	1091703	1090513	1099325	1088139
920	1086957	1085776	1084599	1083424	1082251	1081081	1079914	1078749	1077586	1076426
930	1075269	1074114	1072961	1071811	1070664	1069519	1068376	1067236	1066098	1064963
940	1063830	1062699	1061571	1060445	1059322	1058201	1057082	1055966	1054852	1053741
950	0,001052632	0,001051525	0,001050420	0,001049318	0,001048218	0,001047120	0,001046025	0,001044932	0,001043841	0,001042753
960	1041667	1040583	1039501	1038422	1037344	1036269	1035197	1034126	1033058	1031992
970	1030928	1029866	1028807	1027749	1026694	1025641	1024590	1023541	1022495	1021450
980	1020408	1019368	1018330	1017294	1016260	1015228	1014199	1013171	1012146	1011122
990	1010101	1009082	1008065	1007049	1006036	1005025	1004016	1003009	1002004	1001001

[7] COMRIE, L. J. (Ed.), *Barlow's Tables of Squares, Cubes, Square Roots, Cube Roots and Reciprocals of All Integers up to 12500*, 4th ed., Chapman, London, 1970. Reprinted by kind permission of the editor and publishers.

All values conform to the international convention (i.e. 0,1 instead of 0.1).

n	0	1	2	3	4	5	6	7	8	9
0	0	1	8	27	64	125	216	343	512	729
10	1000	1331	1728	2197	2744	3375	4096	4913	5832	6859
20	8000	9261	10648	12167	13824	15625	17576	19683	21952	24389
30	27000	29791	32768	35937	39304	42875	46656	50653	54872	59319
40	64000	68921	74088	79507	85184	91125	97336	103823	110592	117649
50	125000	132651	140608	148877	157464	166375	175616	185193	195112	205379
60	216000	226981	238328	250047	262144	274625	287496	300763	314432	328509
70	343000	357911	373248	389017	405224	421875	438976	456533	474552	493039
80	512000	531441	551368	571787	592704	614125	636056	658503	681472	704969
90	729000	753571	778688	804357	830584	857375	884736	912673	941192	970299
100	1000000	1030301	1061208	1092727	1124864	1157625	1191016	1225043	1259712	1295029
110	1331000	1367631	1404928	1442897	1481544	1520875	1560896	1601613	1643032	1685159
120	1728000	1771561	1815848	1860867	1906624	1953125	2000376	2048383	2097152	2146689
130	2197000	2248091	2299968	2352637	2406104	2460375	2515456	2571353	2628072	2685619
140	2744000	2803221	2863288	2924207	2985984	3048625	3112136	3176523	3241792	3307949
150	3375000	3442951	3511808	3581577	3652264	3723875	3796416	3869893	3944312	4019679
160	4096000	4173281	4251528	4330747	4410944	4492125	4574296	4657463	4741632	4826809
170	4913000	5000211	5088448	5177717	5268024	5359375	5451776	5545233	5639752	5735339
180	5832000	5929741	6028568	6128487	6229504	6331625	6434856	6539203	6644672	6751269
190	6859000	6967871	7077888	7189057	7301384	7414875	7529536	7645373	7762392	7880599
200	8000000	8120601	8242408	8365427	8489664	8615125	8741816	8869743	8998912	9129329
210	9261000	9393931	9528128	9663597	9800344	9938375	10077696	10218313	10360232	10503459
220	10648000	10793861	10941048	11089567	11239424	11390625	11543176	11697083	11852352	12008989
230	12167000	12326391	12487168	12649337	12812904	12977875	13144256	13312053	13481272	13651919
240	13824000	13997521	14172488	14348907	14526784	14706125	14886936	15069223	15252992	15438249
250	15625000	15813251	16003008	16194277	16387064	16581375	16777216	16974593	17173512	17373979
260	17576000	17779581	17984728	18191447	18399744	18609625	18821096	19034163	19248832	19465109
270	19683000	19902511	20123648	20346417	20570824	20796875	21024576	21253933	21484952	21717639
280	21952000	22188041	22425768	22665187	22906304	23149125	23393656	23639903	23887872	24137569
290	24389000	24642171	24897088	25153757	25412184	25672375	25934336	26198073	26463592	26730899
300	27000000	27270901	27543608	27818127	28094464	28372625	28652616	28934443	29218112	29503629
310	29791000	30080231	30371328	30664297	30959144	31255875	31554496	31855013	32157432	32461759
320	32768000	33076161	33386248	33698267	34012224	34328125	34645976	34965783	35287552	35611289
330	35937000	36264691	36594368	36926037	37259704	37595375	37933056	38272753	38614472	38958219
340	39304000	39651821	40001688	40353607	40707584	41063625	41421736	41781923	42144192	42508549
350	42875000	43243551	43614208	43986977	44361864	44738875	45118016	45499293	45882712	46268279
360	46656000	47045881	47437928	47832147	48228544	48627125	49027896	49430863	49836032	50243409
370	50653000	51064811	51478848	51895117	52313624	52734375	53157376	53582633	54010152	54439939
380	54872000	55306341	55742968	56181887	56623104	57066625	57512456	57960603	58411072	58863869
390	59319000	59776471	60236288	60698457	61162984	61629875	62099136	62570773	63044792	63521199
400	64000000	64481201	64964808	65450827	65939264	66430125	66923416	67419143	67917312	68417929
410	68921000	69426531	69934528	70444997	70957944	71473375	71991296	72511713	73034632	73560059
420	74088000	74618461	75151448	75686967	76225024	76765625	77308776	77854483	78402752	78953589
430	79507000	80062991	80621568	81182737	81746504	82312875	82881856	83453453	84027672	84604519
440	85184000	85766121	86350888	86938307	87528384	88121125	88716536	89314623	89915392	90518849
450	91125000	91733851	92345408	92959677	93576664	94196375	94818816	95443993	96071912	96702579
460	97336000	97972181	98611128	99252847	99897344	100544625	101194696	101847563	102503232	103161709
470	103823000	104487111	105154048	105823817	106496424	107171875	107850176	108531333	109215352	109902239
480	110592000	111284641	111980168	112678587	113379904	114084125	114791256	115501303	116214272	116930169
490	117649000	118370771	119095488	119823157	120553784	121287375	122023936	122763473	123505992	124251499
500	125000000	125751501	126506008	127263527	128024064	128787625	129554216	130323843	131096512	131872229
510	132651000	133432831	134217728	135005697	135796744	136590875	137388096	138188413	138991832	139798359
520	140608000	141420761	142236648	143055667	143877824	144703125	145531576	146363183	147197952	148035889
530	148877000	149721291	150568768	151419437	152273304	153130375	153990656	154854153	155720872	156590819
540	157464000	158340421	159220088	160103007	160989184	161878625	162771336	163667323	164566592	165469149
550	166375000	167284151	168196608	169112377	170031464	170953875	171879616	172808693	173741112	174676879
560	175616000	176558481	177504328	178453547	179406144	180362125	181321496	182284263	183250432	184220009
570	185193000	186169411	187149248	188132517	189119224	190109375	191102976	192100033	193100552	194104539
580	195112000	196122941	197137368	198155287	199176704	200201625	201230056	202262003	203297472	204336469
590	205379000	206425071	207474688	208527857	209584584	210644875	211708736	212776173	213847192	214921799
600	216000000	217081801	218167208	219256227	220348864	221445125	222545016	223648543	224755712	225866529
610	226981000	228099131	229220928	230346397	231475544	232608375	233744896	234885113	236029032	237176659
620	238328000	239483061	240641848	241804367	242970624	244140625	245314376	246491883	247673152	248858189
630	250047000	251239591	252435968	253636137	254840104	256047875	257259456	258474853	259694072	260917119
640	262144000	263374721	264609288	265847707	267089984	268336125	269586136	270840023	272097792	273359449
650	274625000	275894451	277167808	278445077	279726264	281011375	282300416	283593393	284890312	286191179
660	287496000	288804781	290117528	291434247	292754944	294079625	295408296	296740963	298077632	299418309
670	300763000	302111711	303464448	304821217	306182024	307546875	308915776	310288733	311665752	313046839
680	314432000	315821241	317214568	318611987	320013504	321419125	322828856	324242703	325660672	327082769
690	328509000	329939371	331373888	332812557	334255384	335702375	337153536	338608873	340068392	341532099
700	343000000	344472101	345948408	347428927	348913664	350402625	351895816	353393243	354894912	356400829
710	357911000	359425431	360944128	362467097	363994344	365525875	367061696	368601813	370146232	371694959
720	373248000	374805361	376367048	377933067	379503424	381078125	382657176	384240583	385828352	387420489
730	389017000	390617891	392223168	393832837	395446904	397065375	398688256	400315553	401947272	403583419
740	405224000	406869021	408518488	410172407	411830784	413493625	415160936	416832723	418508992	420189749
750	421875000	423564751	425259008	426957777	428661064	430368875	432081216	433798093	435519512	437245479
760	438976000	440711081	442450728	444194947	445943744	447697125	449455096	451217663	452984832	454756609
770	456533000	458314011	460099648	461889917	463684824	465484375	467288576	469097433	470910952	472729139
780	474552000	476379541	478211768	480048687	481890304	483736625	485587656	487443403	489303872	491169069
790	493039000	494913671	496793088	498677257	500566184	502459875	504358336	506261573	508169592	510082399
800	512000000	513922401	515849608	517781627	519718464	521660125	523606616	525557943	527514112	529475129
810	531441000	533411731	535387328	537367797	539353144	541343375	543338496	545338513	547343432	549353259
820	551368000	553387661	555412248	557441767	559476224	561515625	563559976	565609283	567663552	569722789
830	571787000	573856191	575930368	578009537	580093704	582182875	584277056	586376253	588480472	590589719
840	592704000	594823321	596947688	599077107	601211584	603351125	605495736	607645423	609800192	611960049
850	614125000	616295051	618470208	620650477	622835864	625026375	627222016	629422793	631628712	633839779
860	636056000	638277381	640503928	642735647	644972544	647214625	649461896	651714363	653972032	656234909
870	658503000	660776311	663054848	665338617	667627624	669921875	672221376	674526133	676836152	679151439
880	681472000	683797841	686128968	688465387	690807104	693154125	695506456	697864103	700227072	702595369
890	704969000	707347971	709732288	712121957	714516984	716917375	719323136	721734273	724150792	726572699
900	729000000	731432701	733870808	736314327	738763264	741217625	743677416	746142643	748613312	751089429
910	753571000	756058031	758550528	761048497	763551944	766060875	768575296	771095213	773620632	776151559
920	778688000	781229961	783777448	786330467	788889024	791453125	794022776	796597983	799178752	801765089
930	804357000	806954491	809557568	812166237	814780504	817400375	820025856	822656953	825293672	827936019
940	830584000	833237621	835896888	838561807	841232384	843908625	846590536	849278123	851971392	854670349
950	857375000	860085351	862801408	865523177	868250664	870983875	873722816	876467493	879217912	881974079
960	884736000	887503681	890277128	893056347	895841344	898632125	901428696	904231063	907039232	909853209
970	912673000	915498611	918330048	921167317	924010424	926859375	929714176	932574833	935441352	938313739
980	941192000	944076141	946966168	949862087	952763904	955671625	958585256	961504803	964430272	967361669
990	970299000	973242271	976191488	979146657	982107784	985074875	988047936	991026973	994011992	997002999

[1] COMRIE, L. J. (Ed.), *Barlow's Tables of Squares, Cubes, Square Roots, Cube Roots and Reciprocals of All Integers up to 12500*, 4th ed., Chapman, London, 1970. Reprinted by kind permission of the editor and publishers.

All values conform to the international convention (i.e. 0,1 instead of 0.1).

Squares and Square Roots[1] of $n = 1$–399

$\sqrt{100\,n} = 10\sqrt{n}$ $\sqrt{1000\,n} = 10\sqrt{10\,n}$ $\sqrt{0{,}1\,n} = 0{,}1\sqrt{10\,n}$ $\sqrt{0{,}01\,n} = 0{,}1\sqrt{n}$ $\sqrt{0{,}001\,n} = 0{,}01\sqrt{10\,n}$

n	n^2	$\sqrt{n}$	$\sqrt{10n}$	n	n^2	$\sqrt{n}$	$\sqrt{10n}$	n	n^2	$\sqrt{n}$	$\sqrt{10n}$	n	n^2	$\sqrt{n}$	$\sqrt{10n}$
				100	10000	10,0000000	31,622777	200	40000	14,1421356	44,721360	300	90000	17,3205081	54,772256
1	1	1,0000000	3,1622777	101	10201	10,0498756	31,780497	201	40401	14,1774469	44,833024	301	90601	17,3493516	54,863467
2	4	1,4142136	4,4721360	102	10404	10,0995049	31,937439	202	40804	14,2126704	44,944410	302	91204	17,3781472	54,954527
3	9	1,7320508	5,4772256	103	10609	10,1488916	32,093613	203	41209	14,2478068	45,055521	303	91809	17,4068952	55,045436
4	16	2,0000000	6,3245553	104	10816	10,1980390	32,249031	204	41616	14,2828569	45,166359	304	92416	17,4355958	55,136195
5	25	2,2360680	7,0710678	105	11025	10,2469508	32,403703	205	42025	14,3178211	45,276926	305	93025	17,4642492	55,226805
6	36	2,4494897	7,7459667	106	11236	10,2956301	32,557641	206	42436	14,3527001	45,387223	306	93636	17,4928557	55,317267
7	49	2,6457513	8,3666003	107	11449	10,3440804	32,710854	207	42849	14,3874946	45,497253	307	94249	17,5214155	55,407581
8	64	2,8284271	8,9442719	108	11664	10,3923048	32,863353	208	43264	14,4222051	45,607017	308	94864	17,5499288	55,497748
9	81	3,0000000	9,4868330	109	11881	10,4403065	33,015148	209	43681	14,4568323	45,716518	309	95481	17,5783958	55,587768
10	100	3,1622777	10,0000000	110	12100	10,4880885	33,166248	210	44100	14,4913767	45,825757	310	96100	17,6068169	55,677644
11	121	3,3166248	10,4880885	111	12321	10,5356538	33,316662	211	44521	14,5258390	45,934736	311	96721	17,6351921	55,767374
12	144	3,4641016	10,9544512	112	12544	10,5830052	33,466401	212	44944	14,5602198	46,043458	312	97344	17,6635217	55,856960
13	169	3,6055513	11,4017543	113	12769	10,6301458	33,615473	213	45369	14,5945195	46,151923	313	97969	17,6918060	55,946403
14	196	3,7416574	11,8321596	114	12996	10,6770783	33,763886	214	45796	14,6287388	46,260134	314	98596	17,7200451	56,035703
15	225	3,8729833	12,2474487	115	13225	10,7238053	33,911650	215	46225	14,6628783	46,368092	315	99225	17,7482393	56,124861
16	256	4,0000000	12,6491106	116	13456	10,7703296	34,058773	216	46656	14,6969385	46,475800	316	99856	17,7763888	56,213877
17	289	4,1231056	13,0384048	117	13689	10,8166538	34,205263	217	47089	14,7309199	46,583259	317	100489	17,8044938	56,302753
18	324	4,2426407	13,4164079	118	13924	10,8627805	34,351128	218	47524	14,7648231	46,690470	318	101124	17,8325545	56,391489
19	361	4,3588989	13,7840488	119	14161	10,9087121	34,496377	219	47961	14,7986486	46,797436	319	101761	17,8605711	56,480085
20	400	4,4721360	14,1421356	120	14400	10,9544512	34,641016	220	48400	14,8323970	46,904158	320	102400	17,8885438	56,568542
21	441	4,5825757	14,4913767	121	14641	11,0000000	34,785054	221	48841	14,8660687	47,010637	321	103041	17,9164729	56,656862
22	484	4,6904158	14,8323970	122	14884	11,0453610	34,928498	222	49284	14,8996644	47,116876	322	103684	17,9443584	56,745044
23	529	4,7958315	15,1657509	123	15129	11,0905365	35,071356	223	49729	14,9331845	47,222876	323	104329	17,9722008	56,833089
24	576	4,8989795	15,4919334	124	15376	11,1355287	35,213634	224	50176	14,9666295	47,328638	324	104976	18,0000000	56,920998
25	625	5,0000000	15,8113883	125	15625	11,1803399	35,355339	225	50625	15,0000000	47,434165	325	105625	18,0277564	57,008771
26	676	5,0990195	16,1245155	126	15876	11,2249722	35,496479	226	51076	15,0332964	47,539457	326	106276	18,0554701	57,096410
27	729	5,1961524	16,4316767	127	16129	11,2694277	35,637059	227	51529	15,0665192	47,644517	327	106929	18,0831413	57,183914
28	784	5,2915026	16,7332005	128	16384	11,3137085	35,777088	228	51984	15,0996689	47,749346	328	107584	18,1107703	57,271284
29	841	5,3851648	17,0293864	129	16641	11,3578167	35,916570	229	52441	15,1327460	47,853944	329	108241	18,1383571	57,358522
30	900	5,4772256	17,3205081	130	16900	11,4017543	36,055513	230	52900	15,1657509	47,958315	330	108900	18,1659021	57,445626
31	961	5,5677644	17,6068169	131	17161	11,4455231	36,193922	231	53361	15,1986842	48,062459	331	109561	18,1934054	57,532599
32	1024	5,6568542	17,8885438	132	17424	11,4891253	36,331804	232	53824	15,2315462	48,166378	332	110224	18,2208672	57,619441
33	1089	5,7445626	18,1659021	133	17689	11,5325626	36,469165	233	54289	15,2643375	48,270074	333	110889	18,2482876	57,706152
34	1156	5,8309519	18,4390889	134	17956	11,5758369	36,606010	234	54756	15,2970585	48,373546	334	111556	18,2756669	57,792733
35	1225	5,9160798	18,7082869	135	18225	11,6189500	36,742346	235	55225	15,3297097	48,476799	335	112225	18,3030052	57,879185
36	1296	6,0000000	18,9736660	136	18496	11,6619038	36,878178	236	55696	15,3622915	48,579831	336	112896	18,3303028	57,965507
37	1369	6,0827625	19,2353841	137	18769	11,7046999	37,013511	237	56169	15,3948043	48,682646	337	113569	18,3575598	58,051701
38	1444	6,1644140	19,4935887	138	19044	11,7473401	37,148351	238	56644	15,4272486	48,785244	338	114244	18,3847763	58,137767
39	1521	6,2449980	19,7484177	139	19321	11,7898261	37,282704	239	57121	15,4596248	48,887626	339	114921	18,4119526	58,223707
40	1600	6,3245553	20,0000000	140	19600	11,8321596	37,416574	240	57600	15,4919334	48,989795	340	115600	18,4390889	58,309519
41	1681	6,4031242	20,2484567	141	19881	11,8743421	37,549967	241	58081	15,5241747	49,091751	341	116281	18,4661853	58,395205
42	1764	6,4807407	20,4939015	142	20164	11,9163753	37,682887	242	58564	15,5563492	49,193496	342	116964	18,4932420	58,480766
43	1849	6,5574385	20,7364414	143	20449	11,9582607	37,815341	243	59049	15,5884573	49,295030	343	117649	18,5202592	58,566202
44	1936	6,6332496	20,9761770	144	20736	12,0000000	37,947332	244	59536	15,6204994	49,396356	344	118336	18,5472370	58,651513
45	2025	6,7082039	21,2132034	145	21025	12,0415946	38,078866	245	60025	15,6524758	49,497475	345	119025	18,5741756	58,736701
46	2116	6,7823300	21,4476106	146	21316	12,0830460	38,209946	246	60516	15,6843871	49,598387	346	119716	18,6010752	58,821765
47	2209	6,8556546	21,6794834	147	21609	12,1243557	38,340579	247	61009	15,7162336	49,699095	347	120409	18,6279360	58,906706
48	2304	6,9282032	21,9089023	148	21904	12,1655251	38,470768	248	61504	15,7480157	49,799598	348	121104	18,6547581	58,991525
49	2401	7,0000000	22,1359436	149	22201	12,2065556	38,600518	249	62001	15,7797338	49,899900	349	121801	18,6815417	59,076222
50	2500	7,0710678	22,3606798	150	22500	12,2474487	38,729833	250	62500	15,8113883	50,000000	350	122500	18,7082869	59,160798
51	2601	7,1414284	22,5831796	151	22801	12,2882057	38,858718	251	63001	15,8429795	50,099900	351	123201	18,7349940	59,245253
52	2704	7,2111026	22,8035085	152	23104	12,3288280	38,987177	252	63504	15,8745079	50,199602	352	123904	18,7616630	59,329588
53	2809	7,2801099	23,0217289	153	23409	12,3693169	39,115214	253	64009	15,9059737	50,299105	353	124609	18,7882942	59,413803
54	2916	7,3484692	23,2379001	154	23716	12,4096736	39,242834	254	64516	15,9373775	50,398413	354	125316	18,8148877	59,497899
55	3025	7,4161985	23,4520788	155	24025	12,4498996	39,370039	255	65025	15,9687194	50,497525	355	126025	18,8414437	59,581876
56	3136	7,4833148	23,6643191	156	24336	12,4899960	39,496835	256	65536	16,0000000	50,596443	356	126736	18,8679623	59,665736
57	3249	7,5498344	23,8746728	157	24649	12,5299641	39,623226	257	66049	16,0312195	50,695167	357	127449	18,8944436	59,749477
58	3364	7,6157731	24,0831892	158	24964	12,5698051	39,749214	258	66564	16,0623784	50,793700	358	128164	18,9208879	59,833101
59	3481	7,6811457	24,2899156	159	25281	12,6095202	39,874804	259	67081	16,0934769	50,892043	359	128881	18,9472953	59,916609
60	3600	7,7459667	24,4948974	160	25600	12,6491106	40,000000	260	67600	16,1245155	50,990195	360	129600	18,9736660	60,000000
61	3721	7,8102497	24,6981781	161	25921	12,6885775	40,124805	261	68121	16,1554944	51,088159	361	130321	19,0000000	60,083276
62	3844	7,8740079	24,8997992	162	26244	12,7279221	40,249224	262	68644	16,1864141	51,185936	362	131044	19,0262976	60,166436
63	3969	7,9372539	25,0998008	163	26569	12,7671453	40,373258	263	69169	16,2172747	51,283526	363	131769	19,0525589	60,249481
64	4096	8,0000000	25,2982213	164	26896	12,8062485	40,496913	264	69696	16,2480768	51,380930	364	132496	19,0787840	60,332413
65	4225	8,0622577	25,4950976	165	27225	12,8452326	40,620192	265	70225	16,2788206	51,478151	365	133225	19,1049732	60,415230
66	4356	8,1240384	25,6904652	166	27556	12,8840987	40,743098	266	70756	16,3095064	51,575188	366	133956	19,1311265	60,497934
67	4489	8,1853528	25,8843582	167	27889	12,9228480	40,865633	267	71289	16,3401346	51,672043	367	134689	19,1572441	60,580525
68	4624	8,2462113	26,0768096	168	28224	12,9614814	40,987803	268	71824	16,3707055	51,768716	368	135424	19,1833261	60,663004
69	4761	8,3066239	26,2678511	169	28561	13,0000000	41,109610	269	72361	16,4012195	51,865210	369	136161	19,2093727	60,745370
70	4900	8,3666003	26,4575131	170	28900	13,0384048	41,231056	270	72900	16,4316767	51,961524	370	136900	19,2353841	60,827625
71	5041	8,4261498	26,6458252	171	29241	13,0766968	41,352146	271	73441	16,4620776	52,057660	371	137641	19,2613603	60,909769
72	5184	8,4852814	26,8328157	172	29584	13,1148770	41,472883	272	73984	16,4924225	52,153619	372	138384	19,2873015	60,991803
73	5329	8,5440037	27,0185122	173	29929	13,1529464	41,593269	273	74529	16,5227116	52,249402	373	139129	19,3132079	61,073726
74	5476	8,6023253	27,2029410	174	30276	13,1909060	41,713307	274	75076	16,5529454	52,345009	374	139876	19,3390796	61,155539
75	5625	8,6602540	27,3861279	175	30625	13,2287566	41,833001	275	75625	16,5831240	52,440442	375	140625	19,3649167	61,237244
76	5776	8,7177979	27,5680975	176	30976	13,2664992	41,952354	276	76176	16,6132477	52,535702	376	141376	19,3907194	61,318839
77	5929	8,7749644	27,7488739	177	31329	13,3041347	42,071368	277	76729	16,6433170	52,630789	377	142129	19,4164878	61,400326
78	6084	8,8317609	27,9284801	178	31684	13,3416641	42,190046	278	77284	16,6733320	52,725705	378	142884	19,4422221	61,481705
79	6241	8,8881944	28,1069386	179	32041	13,3790882	42,308392	279	77841	16,7032931	52,820451	379	143641	19,4679223	61,562976
80	6400	8,9442719	28,2842712	180	32400	13,4164079	42,426407	280	78400	16,7332005	52,915026	380	144400	19,4935887	61,644140
81	6561	9,0000000	28,4604989	181	32761	13,4536240	42,544095	281	78961	16,7630546	53,009433	381	145161	19,5192213	61,725197
82	6724	9,0553851	28,6356421	182	33124	13,4907376	42,661458	282	79524	16,7928556	53,103672	382	145924	19,5448203	61,806149
83	6889	9,1104336	28,8097206	183	33489	13,5277493	42,778499	283	80089	16,8226038	53,197744	383	146689	19,5703858	61,886994
84	7056	9,1651514	28,9827535	184	33856	13,5646600	42,895221	284	80656	16,8522995	53,291650	384	147456	19,5959179	61,967734
85	7225	9,2195445	29,1547595	185	34225	13,6014705	43,011626	285	81225	16,8819430	53,385391	385	148225	19,6214169	62,048368
86	7396	9,2736185	29,3257566	186	34596	13,6381817	43,127717	286	81796	16,9115345	53,478968	386	148996	19,6468827	62,128898
87	7569	9,3273791	29,4957624	187	34969	13,6747943	43,243497	287	82369	16,9410743	53,572381	387	149769	19,6723156	62,209324
88	7744	9,3808315	29,6647939	188	35344	13,7113092	43,358967	288	82944	16,9705627	53,665631	388	150544	19,6977156	62,289646
89	7921	9,4339811	29,8328678	189	35721	13,7477271	43,474130	289	83521	17,0000000	53,758720	389	151321	19,7230829	62,369865
90	8100	9,4868330	30,0000000	190	36100	13,7840488	43,588989	290	84100	17,0293864	53,851648	390	152100	19,7484177	62,449980
91	8281	9,5393920	30,1662063	191	36481	13,8202750	43,703547	291	84681	17,0587221	53,944416	391	152881	19,7737199	62,529993
92	8464	9,5916630	30,3315018	192	36864	13,8564065	43,817805	292	85264	17,0880075	54,037024	392	153664	19,7989899	62,609903
93	8649	9,6436508	30,4959014	193	37249	13,8924440	43,931765	293	85849	17,1172428	54,129474	393	154449	19,8242276	62,689712
94	8836	9,6953597	30,6594194	194	37636	13,9283883	44,045431	294	86436	17,1464282	54,221767	394	155236	19,8494332	62,769419
95	9025	9,7467943	30,8220700	195	38025	13,9642400	44,158804	295	87025	17,1755640	54,313902	395	156025	19,8746069	62,849025
96	9216	9,7979590	30,9838668	196	38416	14,0000000	44,271887	296	87616	17,2046505	54,405882	396	156816	19,8997487	62,928531
97	9409	9,8488578	31,1448230	197	38809	14,0356688	44,384682	297	88209	17,2336879	54,497706	397	157609	19,9248588	63,007936
98	9604	9,8994949	31,3049517	198	39204	14,0712473	44,497191	298	88804	17,2626765	54,589376	398	158404	19,9499373	63,087241
99	9801	9,9498744	31,4642654	199	39601	14,1067360	44,609416	299	89401	17,2916165	54,680892	399	159201	19,9749844	63,166447

[1] COMRIE, L. J. (Ed.), *Barlow's Tables of Squares, Cubes, Square Roots, Cube Roots and Reciprocals of All Integers up to 12500*, 4th ed., Chapman, London, 1970. Reprinted by kind permission of the editor and publishers.

All values conform to the international convention (i.e. 0,1 instead of 0.1).

Squares and Square Roots of $n = 400$–799

$\sqrt{100\,n} = 10\sqrt{n}$ $\sqrt{1000\,n} = 10\sqrt{10\,n}$ $\sqrt{0{,}1\,n} = 0{,}1\sqrt{10\,n}$ $\sqrt{0{,}01\,n} = 0{,}1\sqrt{n}$ $\sqrt{0{,}001\,n} = 0{,}01\sqrt{10\,n}$

n	n^2	$\sqrt{n}$	$\sqrt{10n}$	n	n^2	$\sqrt{n}$	$\sqrt{10n}$	n	n^2	$\sqrt{n}$	$\sqrt{10n}$	n	n^2	$\sqrt{n}$	$\sqrt{10n}$
400	160000	20,0000000	63,245553	**500**	250000	22,3606798	70,710678	**600**	360000	24,4948974	77,459667	**700**	490000	26,4575131	83,666003
401	160801	20,0249844	63,324561	501	251001	22,3830293	70,781353	601	361201	24,5153013	77,524190	701	491401	26,4764046	83,725743
402	161604	20,0499377	63,403470	502	252004	22,4053565	70,851958	602	362404	24,5356883	77,588659	702	492804	26,4952826	83,785440
403	162409	20,0748599	63,482281	503	253009	22,4276615	70,922493	603	363609	24,5560583	77,653075	703	494209	26,5141472	83,845095
404	163216	20,0997512	63,560994	504	254016	22,4499443	70,992957	604	364816	24,5764115	77,717437	704	495616	26,5329983	83,904708
405	164025	20,1246118	63,639610	**505**	255025	22,4722051	71,063352	**605**	366025	24,5967478	77,781746	**705**	497025	26,5518361	83,964278
406	164836	20,1494417	63,718129	506	256036	22,4944438	71,133677	606	367236	24,6170673	77,846002	706	498436	26,5706605	84,023806
407	165649	20,1742410	63,796552	507	257049	22,5166605	71,203932	607	368449	24,6373700	77,910205	707	499849	26,5894716	84,083292
408	166464	20,1990099	63,874878	508	258064	22,5388553	71,274119	608	369664	24,6576560	77,974355	708	501264	26,6082694	84,142736
409	167281	20,2237484	63,953108	509	259081	22,5610283	71,344236	609	370881	24,6779254	78,038452	709	502681	26,6270539	84,202138
410	168100	20,2484567	64,031242	**510**	260100	22,5831796	71,414284	**610**	372100	24,6981781	78,102497	**710**	504100	26,6458252	84,261498
411	168921	20,2731349	64,109282	511	261121	22,6053091	71,484264	611	373321	24,7184142	78,166489	711	505521	26,6645833	84,320816
412	169744	20,2977831	64,187226	512	262144	22,6274170	71,554175	612	374544	24,7386338	78,230429	712	506944	26,6833281	84,380092
413	170569	20,3224014	64,265076	513	263169	22,6495033	71,624018	613	375769	24,7588368	78,294317	713	508369	26,7020598	84,439327
414	171396	20,3469899	64,342832	514	264196	22,6715681	71,693793	614	376996	24,7790234	78,358152	714	509796	26,7207784	84,498521
415	172225	20,3715488	64,420494	**515**	265225	22,6936114	71,763500	**615**	378225	24,7991935	78,421936	**715**	511225	26,7394839	84,557673
416	173056	20,3960781	64,498062	516	266256	22,7156334	71,833140	616	379456	24,8193473	78,485667	716	512656	26,7581763	84,616783
417	173889	20,4205779	64,575537	517	267289	22,7376340	71,902712	617	380689	24,8394847	78,549348	717	514089	26,7768557	84,675853
418	174724	20,4450483	64,652920	518	268324	22,7596134	71,972217	618	381924	24,8596058	78,612976	718	515524	26,7955220	84,734881
419	175561	20,4694895	64,730209	519	269361	22,7815715	72,041655	619	383161	24,8797106	78,676553	719	516961	26,8141754	84,793868
420	176400	20,4939015	64,807407	**520**	270400	22,8035085	72,111026	**620**	384400	24,8997992	78,740079	**720**	518400	26,8328157	84,852814
421	177241	20,5182845	64,884513	521	271441	22,8254244	72,180330	621	385641	24,9198716	78,803553	721	519841	26,8514432	84,911719
422	178084	20,5426386	64,961527	522	272484	22,8473193	72,249567	622	368884	24,9399278	78,866977	722	521284	26,8700577	84,970583
423	178929	20,5669638	65,038450	523	273529	22,8691933	72,318739	623	388129	24,9599679	78,930349	723	522729	26,8886593	85,029407
424	179776	20,5912603	65,115282	524	274576	22,8910463	72,387844	624	389376	24,9799920	78,993671	724	524176	26,9072481	85,088190
425	180625	20,6155281	65,192024	**525**	275625	22,9128785	72,456884	**625**	390625	25,0000000	79,056942	**725**	525625	26,9258240	85,146932
426	181476	20,6397674	65,268675	526	276676	22,9346899	72,525857	626	391876	25,0199920	79,120162	726	527076	26,9443872	85,205634
427	182329	20,6639783	65,345237	527	277729	22,9564806	72,594766	627	393129	25,0399681	79,183332	727	528529	26,9629375	85,264295
428	183184	20,6881609	65,421709	528	278784	22,9782506	72,663608	628	394384	25,0599282	79,246451	728	529984	26,9814751	85,322916
429	184041	20,7123152	65,498092	529	279841	23,0000000	72,732386	629	395641	25,0798724	79,309520	729	531441	27,0000000	85,381497
430	184900	20,7364414	65,574385	**530**	280900	23,0217289	72,801099	**630**	396900	25,0998008	79,372539	**730**	532900	27,0185122	85,440037
431	185761	20,7605395	65,650590	531	281961	23,0434372	72,869747	631	398161	25,1197134	79,435508	731	534361	27,0370117	85,498538
432	186624	20,7846097	65,726707	532	283024	23,0651252	72,938330	632	399424	25,1396102	79,498428	732	535824	27,0554985	85,556999
433	187489	20,8086520	65,802736	533	284089	23,0867928	73,006849	633	400689	25,1594913	79,561297	733	537289	27,0739727	85,615419
434	188356	20,8326667	65,878676	534	285156	23,1084400	73,075304	634	401956	25,1793566	79,624117	734	538756	27,0924344	85,673800
435	189225	20,8566536	65,954530	**535**	286225	23,1300670	73,143694	**635**	403225	25,1992063	79,686887	**735**	540225	27,1108834	85,732141
436	190096	20,8806130	66,030296	536	287296	23,1516738	73,212021	636	404496	25,2190404	79,749608	736	541696	27,1293199	85,790442
437	190969	20,9045450	66,105976	537	288369	23,1732605	73,280284	637	405769	25,2388589	79,812280	737	543169	27,1477439	85,848704
438	191844	20,9284495	66,181568	538	289444	23,1948270	73,348483	638	407044	25,2586619	79,874902	738	544644	27,1661554	85,906926
439	192721	20,9523268	66,257075	539	290521	23,2163735	73,416619	639	408321	25,2784493	79,937476	739	546121	27,1845544	85,965109
440	193600	20,9761770	66,332496	**540**	291600	23,2379001	73,484692	**640**	409600	25,2982213	80,000000	**740**	547600	27,2029410	86,023253
441	194481	21,0000000	66,407831	541	292681	23,2594067	73,552702	641	410881	25,3179778	80,062476	741	549081	27,2213152	86,081357
442	195364	21,0237960	66,483081	542	293764	23,2808935	73,620649	642	412164	25,3377189	80,124902	742	550564	27,2396769	86,139422
443	196249	21,0475652	66,558245	543	294849	23,3023604	73,688534	643	413449	25,3574447	80,187281	743	552049	27,2580263	86,197448
444	197136	21,0713075	66,633325	544	295936	23,3238076	73,756356	644	414736	25,3771551	80,249611	744	553536	27,2763634	86,255435
445	198025	21,0950231	66,708320	**545**	297025	23,3452351	73,824115	**645**	416025	25,3968502	80,311892	**745**	555025	27,2946881	86,313383
446	198916	21,1187121	66,783231	546	298116	23,3666429	73,891813	646	417316	25,4165301	80,374125	746	556516	27,3130006	86,371292
447	199809	21,1423745	66,858059	547	299209	23,3880311	73,959448	647	418609	25,4361947	80,436310	747	558009	27,3313007	86,429162
448	200704	21,1660105	66,932802	548	300304	23,4093998	74,027022	648	419904	25,4558441	80,498447	748	559504	27,3495887	86,486993
449	201601	21,1896201	67,007462	549	301401	23,4307490	74,094534	649	421201	25,4754784	80,560536	749	561001	27,3678644	86,544786
450	202500	21,2132034	67,082039	**550**	302500	23,4520788	74,161985	**650**	422500	25,4950976	80,622577	**750**	562500	27,3861279	86,602540
451	203401	21,2367606	67,156534	551	303601	23,4733892	74,229374	651	423801	25,5147016	80,684571	751	564001	27,4043792	86,660256
452	204304	21,2602916	67,230945	552	304704	23,4946802	74,296702	652	425104	25,5342907	80,746517	752	565504	27,4226184	86,717934
453	205209	21,2837967	67,305275	553	305809	23,5159520	74,363970	653	426409	25,5538647	80,808415	753	567009	27,4408455	86,775573
454	206116	21,3072758	67,379522	554	306916	23,5372046	74,431176	654	427716	25,5734237	80,870266	754	568516	27,4590604	86,833173
455	207025	21,3307290	67,453688	**555**	308025	23,5584380	74,498322	**655**	429025	25,5929678	80,932070	**755**	570025	27,4772633	86,890736
456	207936	21,3541565	67,527772	556	309136	23,5796522	74,565408	656	430336	25,6124969	80,993827	756	571536	27,4954542	86,948260
457	208849	21,3775583	67,601775	557	310249	23,6008474	74,632433	657	431649	25,6320112	81,055537	757	573049	27,5136330	87,005747
458	209764	21,4009346	67,675697	558	311364	23,6220236	74,699398	658	432964	25,6515107	81,117199	758	574564	27,5317998	87,063195
459	210681	21,4242853	67,749539	559	312481	23,6431808	74,766303	659	434281	25,6709953	81,178815	759	576081	27,5499546	87,120606
460	211600	21,4476106	67,823300	**560**	313600	23,6643191	74,833148	**660**	435600	25,6904652	81,240384	**760**	577600	27,5680975	87,177979
461	212521	21,4709106	67,896981	561	314721	23,6854386	74,899933	661	436921	25,7099203	81,301906	761	579121	27,5862284	87,235314
462	213444	21,4941853	67,970582	562	315844	23,7065392	74,966659	662	438244	25,7293607	81,363382	762	580644	27,6043475	87,292611
463	214369	21,5174348	68,044103	563	316969	23,7276210	75,033326	663	439569	25,7487864	81,424812	763	582169	27,6224546	87,349871
464	215296	21,5406592	68,117545	564	318096	23,7486842	75,099933	664	440896	25,7681975	81,486195	764	583696	27,6405499	87,407094
465	216225	21,5638587	68,190908	**565**	319225	23,7697286	75,166482	**665**	442225	25,7875939	81,547532	**765**	585225	27,6586334	87,464278
466	217156	21,5870331	68,264193	566	320356	23,7907545	75,232971	666	443556	25,8069758	81,608823	766	586756	27,6767050	87,521426
467	218089	21,6101828	68,337398	567	321489	23,8117618	75,299402	667	444889	25,8263431	81,670068	767	588289	27,6947648	87,578536
468	219024	21,6333077	68,410526	568	322624	23,8327506	75,365775	668	446224	25,8456960	81,731267	768	589824	27,7128129	87,635609
469	219961	21,6564078	68,483575	569	323761	23,8537209	75,432089	669	447561	25,8650343	81,792420	769	591361	27,7308492	87,692645
470	220900	21,6794834	68,556546	**570**	324900	23,8746728	75,498344	**670**	448900	25,8843582	81,853528	**770**	592900	27,7488739	87,749644
471	221841	21,7025344	68,629440	571	326041	23,8956063	75,564542	671	450241	25,9036677	81,914590	771	594441	27,7668868	87,806606
472	222784	21,7255610	68,702256	572	327184	23,9165215	75,630682	672	451584	25,9229628	81,975606	772	595984	27,7848880	87,863531
473	223729	21,7485632	68,774995	573	328329	23,9374184	75,696763	673	452929	25,9422435	82,036577	773	597529	27,8028775	87,920419
474	224676	21,7715411	68,847658	574	329476	23,9582971	75,762788	674	454276	25,9615100	82,097503	774	599076	27,8208555	87,977270
475	225625	21,7944947	68,920244	**575**	330625	23,9791576	75,828754	**675**	455625	25,9807621	82,158384	**775**	600625	27,8388218	88,034084
476	226576	21,8174242	68,992753	576	331776	24,0000000	75,894664	676	456976	26,0000000	82,219219	776	602176	27,8567766	88,090862
477	227529	21,8403297	69,065187	577	332929	24,0208243	75,960516	677	458329	26,0192237	82,280010	777	603729	27,8747197	88,147603
478	228484	21,8632111	69,137544	578	334084	24,0416306	76,026311	678	459684	26,0384331	82,340755	778	605284	27,8926514	88,204308
479	229441	21,8860686	69,209826	579	335241	24,0624188	76,092050	679	461041	26,0576284	82,401456	779	606841	27,9105715	88,260977
480	230400	21,9089023	69,282032	**580**	336400	24,0831892	76,157731	**680**	462400	26,0768096	82,462113	**780**	608400	27,9284801	88,317609
481	231361	21,9317122	69,354164	581	337561	24,1039416	76,223356	681	463761	26,0959767	82,522724	781	609961	27,9463772	88,374204
482	232324	21,9544984	69,426220	582	338724	24,1246762	76,288924	682	465124	26,1151297	82,583291	782	611524	27,9642629	88,430764
483	233289	21,9772610	69,498201	583	339889	24,1453929	76,354437	683	466489	26,1342687	82,643814	783	613089	27,9821372	88,487287
484	234256	22,0000000	69,570109	584	341056	24,1660919	76,419893	684	467856	26,1533937	82,704293	784	614656	28,0000000	88,543774
485	235225	22,0227155	69,641941	**585**	342225	24,1867732	76,485293	**685**	469225	26,1725047	82,764727	**785**	616225	28,0178515	88,600226
486	236196	22,0454077	69,713700	586	343396	24,2074369	76,550637	686	470596	26,1916017	82,825117	786	617796	28,0356915	88,656641
487	237169	22,0680765	69,785385	587	344569	24,2280829	76,615925	687	471969	26,2106848	82,885463	787	619369	28,0535203	88,713020
488	238144	22,0907220	69,856997	588	345744	24,2487113	76,681158	688	473344	26,2297541	82,945765	788	620944	28,0713377	88,769364
489	239121	22,1133444	69,928535	589	346921	24,2693222	76,746335	689	474721	26,2488095	83,006024	789	622521	28,0891438	88,825672
490	240100	22,1359436	70,000000	**590**	348100	24,2899156	76,811457	**690**	476100	26,2678511	83,066239	**790**	624100	28,1069386	88,881944
491	241081	22,1585198	70,071392	591	349281	24,3104916	76,876524	691	477481	26,2868789	83,126410	791	625681	28,1247222	88,938181
492	242064	22,1810730	70,142712	592	350464	24,3310501	76,941536	692	478864	26,3058929	83,186537	792	627264	28,1424946	88,994382
493	243049	22,2036033	70,213959	593	351649	24,3515913	77,006493	693	480249	26,3248932	83,246622	793	628849	28,1602557	89,050547
494	244036	22,2261108	70,285134	594	352836	24,3721152	77,071395	694	481636	26,3438797	83,306662	794	630436	28,1780056	89,106678
495	245025	22,2485955	70,356236	**595**	354025	24,3926218	77,136243	**695**	483025	26,3628527	83,366660	**795**	632025	28,1957444	89,162773
496	246016	22,2710575	70,427267	596	355216	24,4131112	77,201036	696	484416	26,3818119	83,426614	796	633616	28,2134720	89,218832
497	247009	22,2934968	70,498227	597	356409	24,4335834	77,265775	697	485809	26,4007576	83,486526	797	635209	28,2311884	89,274856
498	248004	22,3159136	70,569115	598	357604	24,4540385	77,330460	698	487204	26,4196896	83,546394	798	636804	28,2488938	89,330846
499	249001	22,3383079	70,639932	599	358801	24,4744765	77,395090	699	488601	26,4386081	83,606220	799	638401	28,2665881	89,386800

All values conform to the international convention (i.e. 0,1 instead of 0.1).

Squares and Square Roots of $n = 800–1199$

$\sqrt{100n} = 10\sqrt{n}$ $\sqrt{1000n} = 10\sqrt{10n}$ $\sqrt{0{,}1n} = 0{,}1\sqrt{10n}$ $\sqrt{0{,}01n} = 0{,}1\sqrt{n}$ $\sqrt{0{,}001n} = 0{,}01\sqrt{10n}$

n	n^2	$\sqrt{n}$	$\sqrt{10n}$	n	n^2	$\sqrt{n}$	$\sqrt{10n}$	n	n^2	. $\sqrt{n}$	$\sqrt{10n}$	n	n^2	$\sqrt{n}$	$\sqrt{10n}$
800	640000	28,2842712	89,442719	**900**	810000	30,0000000	94,868330	**1000**	1000000	31,622777	100,000000	**1100**	1210000	33,166248	104,880885
801	641601	28,3019434	89,498603	901	811801	30,0166620	94,921020	1001	1002001	31,638584	100,049988	1101	1212201	33,181320	104,928547
802	643204	28,3196045	89,554453	902	813604	30,0333148	94,973681	1002	1004004	31,654384	100,099950	1102	1214404	33,196385	104,976188
803	644809	28,3372546	89,610267	903	815409	30,0499584	95,026312	1003	1006009	31,670175	100,149888	1103	1216609	33,211444	105,023807
804	646416	28,3548938	89,666047	904	817216	30,0665928	95,078915	1004	1008016	31,685959	100,199800	1104	1218816	33,226495	105,071404
805	648025	28,3725219	89,721792	**905**	819025	30,0832179	95,131488	**1005**	1010025	31,701735	100,249688	**1105**	1221025	33,241540	105,118980
806	649636	28,3901391	89,777503	906	820836	30,0998339	95,184032	1006	1012036	31,717503	100,299551	1106	1223236	33,256578	105,166535
807	651249	28,4077454	89,833179	907	822649	30,1164407	95,236548	1007	1014049	31,733263	100,349390	1107	1225449	33,271610	105,214068
808	652864	28,4253408	89,888820	908	824464	30,1330383	95,289034	1008	1016064	31,749016	100,399203	1108	1227664	33,286634	105,261579
809	654481	28,4429253	89,944427	909	826281	30,1496269	95,341491	1009	1018081	31,764760	100,448992	1109	1229881	33,301652	105,309069
810	656100	28,4604989	90,000000	**910**	828100	30,1662063	95,393920	**1010**	1020100	31,780497	100,498756	**1110**	1232100	33,316662	105,356538
811	657721	28,4780617	90,055538	911	829921	30,1827765	95,446320	1011	1022121	31,796226	100,548496	1111	1234321	33,331667	105,403985
812	659344	28,4956137	90,111043	912	831744	30,1993377	95,498691	1012	1024144	31,811947	100,598211	1112	1236544	33,346664	105,451411
813	660969	28,5131549	90,166513	913	833569	30,2158899	95,551033	1013	1026169	31,827661	100,647901	1113	1238769	33,361655	105,498815
814	662596	28,5306852	90,221949	914	835396	30,2324329	95,603347	1014	1028196	31,843367	100,697567	1114	1240996	33,376639	105,546198
815	664225	28,5482048	90,277350	**915**	837225	30,2489669	95,655632	**1015**	1030225	31,859065	100,747208	**1115**	1243225	33,391616	105,593560
816	665856	28,5657137	90,332718	916	839056	30,2654919	95,707889	1016	1032256	31,874755	100,796825	1116	1245456	33,406586	105,640901
817	667489	28,5832119	90,388052	917	840889	30,2820079	95,760117	1017	1034289	31,890437	100,846418	1117	1247689	33,421550	105,688221
818	669124	28,6006993	90,443352	918	842724	30,2985148	95,812317	1018	1036324	31,906112	100,895986	1118	1249924	33,436507	105,735519
819	670761	28,6181760	90,498619	919	844561	30,3150128	95,864488	1019	1038361	31,921779	100,945530	1119	1252161	33,451457	105,782796
820	672400	28,6356421	90,553851	**920**	846400	30,3315018	95,916630	**1020**	1040400	31,937439	100,995049	**1120**	1254400	33,466401	105,830052
821	674041	28,6530976	90,609050	921	848241	30,3479818	95,968745	1021	1042441	31,953091	101,044545	1121	1256641	33,481338	105,877287
822	675684	28,6705424	90,664216	922	850084	30,3644529	96,020831	1022	1044484	31,968735	101,094016	1122	1258884	33,496268	105,924501
823	677329	28,6879766	90,719347	923	851929	30,3809151	96,072889	1023	1046529	31,984371	101,143462	1123	1261129	33,511192	105,971694
824	678976	28,7054002	90,774446	924	853776	30,3973683	96,124919	1024	1048576	32,000000	101,192885	1124	1263376	33,526109	106,018866
825	680625	28,7228132	90,829511	**925**	855625	30,4138127	96,176920	**1025**	1050625	32,015621	101,242284	**1125**	1265625	33,541020	106,066017
826	682276	28,7402157	90,884542	926	857476	30,4302481	96,228894	1026	1052676	32,031235	101,291658	1126	1267876	33,555923	106,113147
827	683929	28,7576077	90,939540	927	859329	30,4466747	96,280839	1027	1054729	32,046841	101,341008	1127	1270129	33,570821	106,160256
828	685584	28,7749891	90,994505	928	861184	30,4630924	96,332757	1028	1056784	32,062439	101,390335	1128	1272384	33,585711	106,207344
829	687241	28,7923601	91,049437	929	863041	30,4795013	96,384646	1029	1058841	32,078030	101,439637	1129	1274641	33,600595	106,254412
830	688900	28,8097206	91,104336	**930**	864900	30,4959014	96,436508	**1030**	1060900	32,093613	101,488916	**1130**	1276900	33,615473	106,301458
831	690561	28,8270706	91,159201	931	866761	30,5122926	96,488341	1031	1062961	32,109189	101,538170	1131	1279161	33,630343	106,348484
832	692224	28,8444102	91,214034	932	868624	30,5286750	96,540147	1032	1065024	32,124757	101,587401	1132	1281424	33,645208	106,395489
833	693889	28,8617394	91,268834	933	870489	30,5450487	96,591925	1033	1067089	32,140317	101,636608	1133	1283689	33,660065	106,442473
834	695556	28,8790582	91,323600	934	872356	30,5614136	96,643675	1034	1069156	32,155870	101,685791	1134	1285956	33,674916	106,489436
835	697225	28,8963666	91,378334	**935**	874225	30,5777697	96,695398	**1035**	1071225	32,171416	101,734950	**1135**	1288225	33,689761	106,536379
836	698896	28,9136646	91,433036	936	876096	30,5941171	96,747093	1036	1073296	32,186954	101,784085	1136	1290496	33,704599	106,583301
837	700569	28,9309523	91,487704	937	877969	30,6104557	96,798760	1037	1075369	32,202484	101,833197	1137	1292769	33,719431	106,630202
838	702244	28,9482297	91,542340	938	879844	30,6267857	96,850400	1038	1077444	32,218007	101,882285	1138	1295044	33,734256	106,677083
839	703921	28,9654967	91,596943	939	881721	30,6431069	96,902012	1039	1079521	32,233523	101,931349	1139	1297321	33,749074	106,723943
840	705600	28,9827535	91,651514	**940**	883600	30,6594194	96,953597	**1040**	1081600	32,249031	101,980390	**1140**	1299600	33,763886	106,770783
841	707281	29,0000000	91,706052	941	885481	30,6757233	97,005155	1041	1083681	32,264532	102,029408	1141	1301881	33,778692	106,817602
842	708964	29,0172363	91,760558	942	887364	30,6920185	97,056684	1042	1085764	32,280025	102,078401	1142	1304164	33,793490	106,864400
843	710649	29,0344623	91,815031	943	889249	30,7083051	97,108187	1043	1087849	32,295511	102,127371	1143	1306449	33,808283	106,911178
844	712336	29,0516781	91,869473	944	891136	30,7245830	97,159662	1044	1089936	32,310989	102,176318	1144	1308736	33,823069	106,957936
845	714025	29,0688837	91,923882	**945**	893025	30,7408523	97,211110	**1045**	1092025	32,326460	102,225242	**1145**	1311025	33,837849	107,004673
846	715716	29,0860791	91,978258	946	894916	30,7571130	97,262531	1046	1094116	32,341923	102,274141	1146	1313316	33,852622	107,051390
847	717409	29,1032644	92,032603	947	896809	30,7733651	97,313925	1047	1096209	32,357379	102,323018	1147	1315609	33,867388	107,098086
848	719104	29,1204396	92,086915	948	898704	30,7896086	97,365292	1048	1098304	32,372828	102,371871	1148	1317904	33,882149	107,144762
849	720801	29,1376046	92,141196	949	900601	30,8058436	97,416631	1049	1100401	32,388269	102,420701	1149	1320201	33,896903	107,191418
850	722500	29,1547595	92,195445	**950**	902500	30,8220700	97,467943	**1050**	1102500	32,403703	102,469508	**1150**	1322500	33,911650	107,238053
851	724201	29,1719043	92,249661	951	904401	30,8382879	97,519229	1051	1104601	32,419130	102,518291	1151	1324801	33,926391	107,284668
852	725904	29,1890390	92,303846	952	906304	30,8544972	97,570487	1052	1106704	32,434549	102,567051	1152	1327104	33,941125	107,331263
853	727609	29,2061637	92,357999	953	908209	30,8706981	97,621719	1053	1108809	32,449961	102,615788	1153	1329409	33,955854	107,377838
854	729316	29,2232784	92,412120	954	910116	30,8868904	97,672924	1054	1110916	32,465366	102,664502	1154	1331716	33,970576	107,424392
855	731025	29,2403830	92,466210	**955**	912025	30,9030743	97,724101	**1055**	1113025	32,480764	102,713193	**1155**	1334025	33,985291	107,470926
856	732736	29,2574777	92,520268	956	913936	30,9192497	97,775252	1056	1115136	32,496154	102,761861	1156	1336336	34,000000	107,517440
857	734449	29,2745623	92,574294	957	915849	30,9354166	97,826377	1057	1117249	32,511536	102,810505	1157	1338649	34,014703	107,563934
858	736164	29,2916370	92,628289	958	917764	30,9515751	97,877474	1058	1119364	32,526912	102,859127	1158	1340964	34,029399	107,610408
859	737881	29,3087018	92,682253	959	919681	30,9677251	97,928545	1059	1121481	32,542280	102,907726	1159	1343281	34,044089	107,656862
860	739600	29,3257566	92,736185	**960**	921600	30,9838668	97,979590	**1060**	1123600	32,557641	102,956301	**1160**	1345600	34,058773	107,703296
861	741321	29,3428015	92,790086	961	923521	31,0000000	98,030607	1061	1125721	32,572995	103,004854	1161	1347921	34,073450	107,749710
862	743044	29,3598365	92,843955	962	925444	31,0161248	98,081599	1062	1127844	32,588341	103,053384	1162	1350244	34,088121	107,796104
863	744769	29,3768616	92,897793	963	927369	31,0322413	98,132563	1063	1129969	32,603681	103,101891	1163	1352569	34,102786	107,842478
864	746496	29,3938769	92,951600	964	929296	31,0483494	98,183502	1064	1132096	32,619013	103,150376	1164	1354896	34,117444	107,888832
865	748225	29,4108823	93,005376	**965**	931225	31,0644491	98,234414	**1065**	1134225	32,634338	103,198837	**1165**	1357225	34,132096	107,935166
866	749956	29,4278779	93,059121	966	933156	31,0805405	98,285299	1066	1136356	32,649655	103,247276	1166	1359556	34,146742	107,981480
867	751689	29,4448637	93,112835	967	935089	31,0966236	98,336158	1067	1138489	32,664966	103,295692	1167	1361889	34,161382	108,027774
868	753424	29,4618397	93,166518	968	937024	31,1126984	98,386991	1068	1140624	32,680269	103,344085	1168	1364224	34,176015	108,074049
869	755161	29,4788059	93,220169	969	938961	31,1287648	98,437798	1069	1142761	32,695565	103,392456	1169	1366561	34,190642	108,120303
870	756900	29,4957624	93,273791	**970**	940900	31,1448230	98,488578	**1070**	1144900	32,710854	103,440804	**1170**	1368900	34,205263	108,166538
871	758641	29,5127091	93,327381	971	942841	31,1608729	98,539332	1071	1147041	32,726136	103,489130	1171	1371241	34,219877	108,212753
872	760384	29,5296461	93,380940	972	944784	31,1769145	98,590060	1072	1149184	32,741411	103,537433	1172	1373584	34,234486	108,258949
873	762129	29,5465734	93,434469	973	946729	31,1929479	98,640762	1073	1151329	32,756679	103,585713	1173	1375929	34,249088	108,305125
874	763876	29,5634910	93,487967	974	948676	31,2089731	98,691438	1074	1153476	32,771939	103,633971	1174	1378276	34,263683	108,351281
875	765625	29,5803989	93,541435	**975**	950625	31,2249900	98,742088	**1075**	1155625	32,787193	103,682207	**1175**	1380625	34,278273	108,397417
876	767376	29,5972972	93,594872	976	952576	31,2409987	98,792712	1076	1157776	32,802439	103,730420	1176	1382976	34,292856	108,443534
877	769129	29,6141858	93,648278	977	954529	31,2569992	98,843310	1077	1159929	32,817678	103,778611	1177	1385329	34,307434	108,489631
878	770884	29,6310648	93,701654	978	956484	31,2729915	98,893883	1078	1162084	32,832910	103,826779	1178	1387684	34,322005	108,535708
879	772641	29,6479342	93,755000	979	958441	31,2889757	98,944429	1079	1164241	32,848135	103,874925	1179	1390041	34,336569	108,581766
880	774400	29,6647939	93,808315	**980**	960400	31,3049517	98,994949	**1080**	1166400	32,863353	103,923048	**1180**	1392400	34,351128	108,627805
881	776161	29,6816442	93,861600	981	962361	31,3209195	99,045444	1081	1168561	32,878564	103,971150	1181	1394761	34,365681	108,673824
882	777924	29,6984848	93,914855	982	964324	31,3368792	99,095913	1082	1170724	32,893768	104,019229	1182	1397124	34,380227	108,719823
883	779689	29,7153159	93,968080	983	966289	31,3528308	99,146356	1083	1172889	32,908965	104,067286	1183	1399489	34,394767	108,765803
884	781456	29,7321375	94,021274	984	968256	31,3687743	99,196774	1084	1175056	32,924155	104,115321	1184	1401856	34,409301	108,811764
885	783225	29,7489496	94,074439	**985**	970225	31,3847097	99,247166	**1085**	1177225	32,939338	104,163333	**1185**	1404225	34,423829	108,857705
886	784996	29,7657521	94,127573	986	972196	31,4006369	99,297533	1086	1179396	32,954514	104,211324	1186	1406596	34,438351	108,903627
887	786769	29,7825452	94,180677	987	974169	31,4165561	99,347874	1087	1181569	32,969683	104,259292	1187	1408969	34,452866	108,949530
888	788544	29,7993289	94,233752	988	976144	31,4324673	99,398189	1088	1183744	32,984845	104,307238	1188	1411344	34,467376	108,995413
889	790321	29,8161030	94,286797	989	978121	31,4483704	99,448479	1089	1185921	33,000000	104,355163	1189	1413721	34,481879	109,041277
890	792100	29,8328678	94,339811	**990**	980100	31,4642654	99,498744	**1090**	1188100	33,015148	104,403065	**1190**	1416100	34,496377	109,087121
891	793881	29,8496231	94,392796	991	982081	31,4801525	99,548983	1091	1190281	33,030289	104,450945	1191	1418481	34,510868	109,132946
892	795664	29,8663690	94,445752	992	984064	31,4960315	99,599197	1092	1192464	33,045423	104,498804	1192	1420864	34,525353	109,178753
893	797449	29,8831056	94,498677	993	986049	31,5119025	99,649385	1093	1194649	33,060551	104,546640	1193	1423249	34,539832	109,224539
894	799236	29,8998328	94,551573	994	988036	31,5277655	99,699549	1094	1196836	33,075671	104,594455	1194	1425636	34,554305	109,270307
895	801025	29,9165506	94,604440	**995**	990025	31,5436206	99,749687	**1095**	1199025	33,090784	104,642248	**1195**	1428025	34,568772	109,316056
896	802816	29,9332591	94,657277	996	992016	31,5594677	99,799800	1096	1201216	33,105891	104,690019	1196	1430416	34,583233	109,361785
897	804609	29,9499583	94,710084	997	994009	31,5753068	99,849887	1097	1203409	33,120990	104,737768	1197	1432809	34,597688	109,407495
898	806404	29,9666481	94,762862	998	996004	31,5911380	99,899950	1098	1205604	33,136083	104,785495	1198	1435204	34,612137	109,453186
899	808201	29,9833287	94,815611	999	998001	31,6069613	99,949987	1099	1207801	33,151169	104,833201	1199	1437601	34,626579	109,498858

All values conform to the international convention (i.e. 0,1 instead of 0.1).

n	0	1	2	3	4	5	6	7	8	9
0		1	0,7071068	0,5773503	0,5000000	0,4472136	0,4082483	0,3779645	0,3535534	0,3333333
10	0,3162278	0,3015113	2886751	2773501	2672612	2581989	2500000	2425356	2357023	2294157
20	2236068	2182179	2132007	2085144	2041241	2000000	1961161	1924501	1889822	1856953
30	1825742	1796053	1767767	1740777	1714986	1690309	1666667	1643990	1622214	1601282
40	1581139	1561738	1543034	1524986	1507557	1490712	1474420	1458650	1443376	1428571
50	0,1414214	0,1400280	0,1386750	0,1373606	0,1360828	0,1348400	0,1336306	0,1324532	0,1313064	0,1301889
60	1290994	1280369	1270001	1259882	1250000	1240347	1230915	1221694	1212678	1203859
70	1195229	1186782	1178511	1170411	1162476	1154701	1147079	1139606	1132277	1125088
80	1118034	1111111	1104315	1097643	1091089	1084652	1078328	1072113	1066004	1059998
90	1054093	1048285	1042572	1036952	1031421	1025978	1020621	1015346	1010153	1005038
100	0,1000000	0,0995037	0,0990148	0,0985329	0,0980581	0,0975900	0,0971286	0,0966736	0,0962250	0,0957826
110	0953463	0949158	0944911	0940721	0936586	0932505	0928477	0924500	0920575	0916698
120	0912871	0909091	0905357	0901670	0898027	0894427	0890871	0887357	0883883	0880451
130	0877058	0873704	0870388	0867110	0863868	0860663	0857493	0854358	0851257	0848189
140	0845154	0842152	0839181	0836242	0833333	0830455	0827606	0824786	0821995	0819232
150	0,0816497	0,0813788	0,0811107	0,0808452	0,0805823	0,0803219	0,0800641	0,0798087	0,0795557	0,0793052
160	0790569	0788110	0785674	0783260	0780869	0778499	0776151	0773823	0771517	0769231
170	0766965	0764719	0762493	0760286	0758098	0755929	0753778	0751646	0749532	0747435
180	0745356	0743294	0741249	0739221	0737210	0735215	0733236	0731272	0729325	0727393
190	0725476	0723575	0721688	0719816	0717958	0716115	0714286	0712470	0710669	0708881
200	0,0707107	0,0705346	0,0703598	0,0701862	0,0700140	0,0698430	0,0696733	0,0695048	0,0693375	0,0691714
210	0690066	0688428	0686803	0685189	0683586	0681994	0680414	0678844	0677285	0675737
220	0674200	0672673	0671156	0669650	0668153	0666667	0665190	0663723	0662266	0660819
230	0659380	0657952	0656532	0655122	0653720	0652328	0650945	0649570	0648204	0646846
240	0645497	0644157	0642824	0641500	0640184	0638877	0637577	0636285	0635001	0633724
250	0,0632456	0,0631194	0,0629941	0,0628695	0,0627456	0,0626224	0,0625000	0,0623783	0,0622573	0,0621370
260	0620174	0618984	0617802	0616626	0615457	0614295	0613139	0611990	0610847	0609711
270	0608581	0607457	0606339	0605228	0604122	0603023	0601929	0600842	0599760	0598684
280	0597614	0596550	0595491	0594438	0593391	0592349	0591312	0590281	0589256	0588235
290	0587220	0586210	0585206	0584206	0583212	0582223	0581238	0580259	0579284	0578315
300	0,0577350	0,0576390	0,0575435	0,0574485	0,0573539	0,0572598	0,0571662	0,0570730	0,0569803	0,0568880
310	0567962	0567048	0566139	0565233	0564333	0563436	0562544	0561656	0560772	0559893
320	0559017	0558146	0557278	0556415	0555556	0554700	0553849	0553001	0552158	0551318
330	0550482	0549650	0548821	0547997	0547176	0546358	0545545	0544735	0543928	0543125
340	0542326	0541530	0540738	0539949	0539164	0538382	0537603	0536828	0536056	0535288
350	0,0534522	0,0533761	0,0533002	0,0532246	0,0531494	0,0530745	0,0529999	0,0529256	0,0528516	0,0527780
360	0527046	0526316	0525588	0524864	0524142	0523424	0522708	0521996	0521286	0520579
370	0519875	0519174	0518476	0517780	0517088	0516398	0515711	0515026	0514345	0513665
380	0512989	0512316	0511645	0510976	0510310	0509647	0508987	0508329	0507673	0507020
390	0506370	0505722	0505076	0504433	0503793	0503155	0502519	0501886	0501255	0500626
400	0,0500000	0,0499376	0,0498755	0,0498135	0,0497519	0,0496904	0,0496292	0,0495682	0,0495074	0,0494468
410	0493865	0493264	0492665	0492068	0491473	0490881	0490290	0489702	0489116	0488532
420	0487950	0487370	0486792	0486217	0485643	0485071	0484502	0483934	0483368	0482805
430	0482243	0481683	0481125	0480569	0480015	0479463	0478913	0478365	0477818	0477274
440	0476731	0476190	0475651	0475114	0474579	0474045	0473514	0472984	0472456	0471929
450	0,0471405	0,0470882	0,0470360	0,0469841	0,0469323	0,0468807	0,0468293	0,0467780	0,0467269	0,0466760
460	0466252	0465746	0465242	0464739	0464238	0463739	0463241	0462745	0462250	0461757
470	0461266	0460776	0460287	0459800	0459315	0458831	0458349	0457869	0457389	0456912
480	0456435	0455961	0455488	0455016	0454545	0454077	0453609	0453143	0452679	0452216
490	0451754	0451294	0450835	0450377	0449921	0449467	0449013	0448561	0448111	0447661
500	0,0447214	0,0446767	0,0446322	0,0445878	0,0445435	0,0444994	0,0444554	0,0444116	0,0443678	0,0443242
510	0442807	0442374	0441942	0441511	0441081	0440653	0440225	0439799	0439375	0438951
520	0438529	0438108	0437688	0437269	0436852	0436436	0436021	0435607	0435194	0434783
530	0434372	0433963	0433555	0433148	0432742	0432338	0431934	0431532	0431131	0430730
540	0430331	0429934	0429537	0429141	0428746	0428353	0427960	0427569	0427179	0426790
550	0,0426401	0,0426014	0,0425628	0,0425243	0,0424859	0,0424476	0,0424094	0,0423714	0,0423334	0,0422955
560	0422577	0422200	0421825	0421450	0421076	0420703	0420331	0419961	0419591	0419222
570	0418854	0418487	0418121	0417756	0417392	0417029	0416667	0416305	0415945	0415586
580	0415227	0414870	0414513	0414158	0413803	0413449	0413096	0412744	0412393	0412043
590	0411693	0411345	0410997	0410651	0410305	0409960	0409616	0409273	0408930	0408589
600	0,0408248	0,0407909	0,0407570	0,0407231	0,0406894	0,0406558	0,0406222	0,0405887	0,0405554	0,0405220
610	0404888	0404557	0404226	0403896	0403567	0403239	0402911	0402585	0402259	0401934
620	0401610	0401286	0400963	0400642	0400320	0400000	0399680	0399362	0399043	0398726
630	0398410	0398094	0397779	0397464	0397151	0396838	0396526	0396214	0395904	0395594
640	0395285	0394976	0394669	0394362	0394055	0393750	0393445	0393141	0392837	0392534
650	0,0392232	0,0391931	0,0391630	0,0391330	0,0391031	0,0390732	0,0390434	0,0390137	0,0389841	0,0389545
660	0389249	0388955	0388661	0388368	0388075	0387783	0387492	0387202	0386912	0386622
670	0386334	0386046	0385758	0385472	0385186	0384900	0384615	0384331	0384048	0383765
680	0383482	0383201	0382920	0382639	0382360	0382080	0381802	0381524	0381246	0380970
690	0380693	0380418	0380143	0379869	0379595	0379322	0379049	0378777	0378506	0378235
700	0,0377964	0,0377695	0,0377426	0,0377157	0,0376889	0,0376622	0,0376355	0,0376089	0,0375823	0,0375558
710	0375293	0375029	0374766	0374503	0374241	0373979	0373718	0373457	0373197	0372937
720	0372678	0372419	0372161	0371904	0371647	0371391	0371135	0370879	0370625	0370370
730	0370117	0369863	0369611	0369358	0369107	0368856	0368605	0368355	0368105	0367856
740	0367607	0367359	0367112	0366864	0366618	0366372	0366126	0365881	0365636	0365392
750	0,0365148	0,0364905	0,0364662	0,0364420	0,0364179	0,0363937	0,0363696	0,0363456	0,0363216	0,0362977
760	0362738	0362500	0362262	0362024	0361787	0361551	0361315	0361079	0360844	0360609
770	0360375	0360141	0359908	0359675	0359443	0359211	0358979	0358748	0358517	0358287
780	0358057	0357828	0357599	0357371	0357143	0356915	0356688	0356462	0356235	0356009
790	0355784	0355559	0355335	0355110	0354887	0354663	0354441	0354218	0353996	0353775
800	0,0353553	0,0353333	0,0353112	0,0352892	0,0352673	0,0352454	0,0352235	0,0352017	0,0351799	0,0351581
810	0351364	0351147	0350931	0350715	0350500	0350285	0350070	0349856	0349642	0349428
820	0349215	0349002	0348790	0348578	0348367	0348155	0347945	0347734	0347524	0347314
830	0347105	0346896	0346688	0346479	0346272	0346064	0345857	0345651	0345444	0345238
840	0345033	0344828	0344623	0344418	0344214	0344010	0343807	0343604	0343401	0343199
850	0,0342997	0,0342796	0,0342594	0,0342393	0,0342193	0,0341993	0,0341793	0,0341593	0,0341394	0,0341196
860	0340997	0340799	0340601	0340404	0340207	0340010	0339814	0339618	0339422	0339227
870	0339032	0338837	0338643	0338449	0338255	0338062	0337869	0337676	0337484	0337292
880	0337100	0336909	0336718	0336527	0336336	0336146	0335957	0335767	0335578	0335389
890	0335201	0335013	0334825	0334637	0334450	0334263	0334077	0333890	0333704	0333519
900	0,0333333	0,0333148	0,0332964	0,0332779	0,0332595	0,0332411	0,0332228	0,0332045	0,0331862	0,0331679
910	0331497	0331315	0331133	0330952	0330771	0330590	0330409	0330229	0330049	0329870
920	0329690	0329511	0329332	0329154	0328976	0328798	0328620	0328443	0328266	0328089
930	0327913	0327737	0327561	0327385	0327210	0327035	0326860	0326686	0326512	0326338
940	0326164	0325991	0325818	0325645	0325472	0325300	0325128	0324956	0324785	0324614
950	0,0324443	0,0324272	0,0324102	0,0323932	0,0323762	0,0323592	0,0323423	0,0323254	0,0323085	0,0322917
960	0322749	0322581	0322413	0322245	0322078	0321911	0321745	0321578	0321412	0321246
970	0321081	0320915	0320750	0320585	0320421	0320256	0320092	0319928	0319765	0319601
980	0319438	0319275	0319113	0318950	0318788	0318626	0318465	0318304	0318142	0317982
990	0317821	0317660	0317500	0317340	0317181	0317021	0316862	0316703	0316544	0316386

[1] COMRIE, L. J. (Ed.), *Barlow's Tables of Squares, Cubes, Square Roots, Cube Roots and Reciprocals of All Integers up to 12500*, 4th ed., Chapman, London, 1970. Reprinted by kind permission of the editor and publishers.

All values conform to the international convention (i.e. 0,1 instead of 0.1).

Common Logarithms ($\log_{10} n$) of Factorials* of $n = 0-999$

$n! = n \times (n-1) \times \cdots \times 3 \times 2 \times 1;\ 0! = 1$

n	0	1	2	3	4	5	6	7	8	9
0	0,00000	0,00000	0,30103	0,77815	1,38021	2,07918	2,85733	3,70243	4,60552	5,55976
10	6,55976	7,60116	8,68034	9,79428	10,94041	12,11650	13,32062	14,55107	15,80634	17,08509
20	18,38612	19,70834	21,05077	22,41249	23,79271	25,19065	26,60562	28,03698	29,48414	30,94654
30	32,42366	33,91502	35,42017	36,93869	38,47016	40,01423	41,57054	43,13874	44,71852	46,30959
40	47,91165	49,52443	51,14768	52,78115	54,42460	56,07781	57,74057	59,41267	61,09391	62,78410
50	64,48307	66,19064	67,90665	69,63092	71,36332	73,10368	74,85187	76,60774	78,37117	80,14202
60	81,92017	83,70550	85,49790	87,29724	89,10342	90,91633	92,73587	94,56195	96,39446	98,23331
70	100,07841	101,92966	103,78700	105,65032	107,51955	109,39461	111,27543	113,16192	115,05401	116,95164
80	118,85473	120,76321	122,67703	124,59610	126,52038	128,44980	130,38430	132,32382	134,26830	136,21769
90	138,17194	140,13098	142,09476	144,06325	146,03638	148,01410	149,99637	151,98314	153,97437	155,97000
100	157,97000	159,97433	161,98293	163,99576	166,01280	168,03398	170,05929	172,08867	174,12210	176,15952
110	178,20092	180,24624	182,29546	184,34854	186,40544	188,46614	190,53060	192,59878	194,67067	196,74621
120	198,82539	200,90818	202,99454	205,08444	207,17787	209,27478	211,37515	213,47895	215,58616	217,69675
130	219,81069	221,92797	224,04854	226,17239	228,29950	230,42983	232,56337	234,70009	236,83997	238,98298
140	241,12911	243,27833	245,43062	247,58595	249,74432	251,90568	254,07004	256,23735	258,40762	260,58080
150	262,75689	264,93587	267,11771	269,30240	271,48993	273,68026	275,87338	278,06928	280,26794	282,46933
160	284,67345	286,88028	289,08980	291,30198	293,51683	295,73431	297,95442	300,17713	302,40244	304,63033
170	306,86078	309,09378	311,32930	313,56735	315,80790	318,05094	320,29645	322,54442	324,79484	327,04770
180	329,30297	331,56065	333,82072	336,08317	338,34799	340,61516	342,88467	345,15651	347,43067	349,70713
190	351,98589	354,26692	356,55022	358,83578	361,12358	363,41362	365,70587	368,00034	370,29700	372,59586
200	374,89689	377,20008	379,50544	381,81293	384,12256	386,43432	388,74818	391,06415	393,38222	395,70236
210	398,02458	400,34887	402,67520	405,00358	407,33400	409,66643	412,00089	414,33735	416,67580	419,01625
220	421,35867	423,70306	426,04942	428,39772	430,74797	433,10015	435,45426	437,81029	440,16822	442,52806
230	444,88978	447,25340	449,61888	451,98624	454,35546	456,72652	459,09944	461,47418	463,85076	466,22916
240	468,60937	470,99139	473,37520	475,76081	478,14820	480,53737	482,92830	485,32100	487,71545	490,11165
250	492,50959	494,90926	497,31066	499,71378	502,11862	504,52516	506,93340	509,34333	511,75495	514,16825
260	516,58322	518,99986	521,41816	523,83812	526,25972	528,68297	531,10785	533,53436	535,96250	538,39225
270	540,82361	543,25658	545,69115	548,12731	550,56506	553,00439	555,44530	557,88778	560,33183	562,77743
280	565,22459	567,67330	570,12354	572,57533	575,02865	577,48349	579,93986	582,39774	584,85713	587,31803
290	589,78043	592,24432	594,70971	597,17657	599,64492	602,11474	604,58603	607,05879	609,53301	612,00868
300	614,48580	616,96436	619,44437	621,92581	624,40869	626,89299	629,37871	631,86585	634,35440	636,84436
310	639,33572	641,82848	644,32263	646,81818	649,31511	651,81342	654,31310	656,81416	659,31659	661,82038
320	664,32553	666,83204	669,33989	671,84910	674,35964	676,87152	679,38474	681,89929	684,41516	686,93236
330	689,45087	691,97070	694,49184	697,01428	699,53803	702,06307	704,58941	707,11704	709,64596	712,17616
340	714,70764	717,24039	719,77442	722,30971	724,84627	727,38409	729,92317	732,46350	735,00508	737,54790
350	740,09197	742,63728	745,18382	747,73160	750,28060	752,83083	755,38228	757,93495	760,48883	763,04392
360	765,60023	768,15773	770,71644	773,27635	775,83745	778,39974	780,96323	783,52789	786,09374	788,66077
370	791,22897	793,79834	796,36888	798,94059	801,51347	804,08750	806,66268	809,23903	811,81652	814,39516
380	816,97494	819,55587	822,13793	824,72113	827,30546	829,89092	832,47751	835,06522	837,65405	840,24400
390	842,83507	845,42724	848,02053	850,61492	853,21042	855,80701	858,40471	861,00350	863,60338	866,20436
400	868,80642	871,40956	874,01379	876,61909	879,22547	881,83293	884,44146	887,05105	889,66171	892,27343
410	894,88622	897,50006	900,11496	902,73091	905,34791	907,96595	910,58505	913,20518	915,82636	918,44857
420	921,07182	923,69611	926,32142	928,94776	931,57512	934,20351	936,83292	939,46335	942,09480	944,72725
430	947,36072	949,99520	952,63068	955,26717	957,90466	960,54315	963,18263	965,82312	968,46459	971,10705
440	973,75051	976,39495	979,04037	981,68677	984,33415	986,98251	989,63185	992,28216	994,93344	997,58568
450	1000,23889	1002,89307	1005,54821	1008,20431	1010,86136	1013,51937	1016,17834	1018,83825	1021,49912	1024,16093
460	1026,82369	1029,48739	1032,15203	1034,81761	1037,48413	1040,15158	1042,81997	1045,48929	1048,15953	1050,83071
470	1053,50280	1056,17582	1058,84977	1061,52463	1064,20041	1066,87710	1069,55471	1072,23322	1074,91265	1077,59299
480	1080,27423	1082,95637	1085,63942	1088,32337	1091,00821	1093,69395	1096,38059	1099,06812	1101,75654	1104,44585
490	1107,13604	1109,82712	1112,51909	1115,21194	1117,90566	1120,60027	1123,29575	1125,99211	1128,68934	1131,38744
500	1134,08641	1136,78624	1139,48695	1142,18851	1144,89094	1147,59424	1150,29839	1153,00339	1155,70926	1158,41598
510	1161,12355	1163,83197	1166,54124	1169,25135	1171,96232	1174,67412	1177,38677	1180,10026	1182,81459	1185,52976
520	1188,24576	1190,96260	1193,68027	1196,39877	1199,11810	1201,83826	1204,55925	1207,28106	1210,00369	1212,72715
530	1215,45142	1218,17652	1220,90243	1223,62916	1226,35670	1229,08505	1231,81422	1234,54419	1237,27497	1240,00656
540	1242,73896	1245,47215	1248,20615	1250,94095	1253,67655	1256,41295	1259,15014	1261,88813	1264,62691	1267,36648
550	1270,10684	1272,84799	1275,58993	1278,33266	1281,07617	1283,82046	1286,56554	1289,31139	1292,05803	1294,80544
560	1297,55363	1300,30259	1303,05232	1305,80283	1308,55411	1311,30616	1314,05898	1316,81256	1319,56691	1322,32202
570	1325,07790	1327,83453	1330,59193	1333,35008	1336,10899	1338,86866	1341,62908	1344,39026	1347,15219	1349,91487
580	1352,67829	1355,44247	1358,20739	1360,97306	1363,73948	1366,50663	1369,27453	1372,04317	1374,81254	1377,58266
590	1380,35351	1383,12510	1385,89742	1388,67048	1391,44426	1394,21878	1396,99403	1399,77000	1402,54670	1405,32413
600	1408,10228	1410,88115	1413,66075	1416,44107	1419,22210	1422,00386	1424,78633	1427,56952	1430,35343	1433,13804
610	1435,92337	1438,70941	1441,49617	1444,28363	1447,07179	1449,86067	1452,65025	1455,44054	1458,23152	1461,02322
620	1463,81561	1466,60870	1469,40249	1472,19698	1474,99216	1477,78804	1480,58462	1483,38188	1486,17984	1488,97849
630	1491,77784	1494,57787	1497,37858	1500,17999	1502,98208	1505,78485	1508,58831	1511,39245	1514,19727	1517,00277
640	1519,80895	1522,61581	1525,42334	1528,23155	1531,04044	1533,85000	1536,66023	1539,47114	1542,28271	1545,09496
650	1547,90787	1550,72145	1553,53570	1556,35061	1559,16619	1561,98243	1564,79933	1567,61690	1570,43513	1573,25401
660	1576,07356	1578,89376	1581,71461	1584,53613	1587,35830	1590,18112	1593,00459	1595,82872	1598,65350	1601,47892
670	1604,30500	1607,13172	1609,95909	1612,78710	1615,61576	1618,44507	1621,27501	1624,10560	1626,93683	1629,76870
680	1632,60121	1635,43436	1638,26814	1641,10256	1643,93762	1646,77331	1649,60964	1652,44659	1655,28418	1658,12240
690	1660,96125	1663,80073	1666,64083	1669,48157	1672,32293	1675,16491	1678,00752	1680,85075	1683,69461	1686,53909
700	1689,38418	1692,22990	1695,07624	1697,92320	1700,77077	1703,61896	1706,46776	1709,31718	1712,16721	1715,01786
710	1717,86912	1720,72099	1723,57347	1726,42656	1729,28026	1732,13456	1734,98948	1737,84500	1740,70112	1743,55785
720	1746,41518	1749,27312	1752,13165	1754,99079	1757,85053	1760,71087	1763,57181	1766,43334	1769,29547	1772,15820
730	1775,02152	1777,88544	1780,74995	1783,61505	1786,48075	1789,34704	1792,21391	1795,08138	1797,94944	1800,81808
740	1803,68731	1806,55713	1809,42754	1812,29853	1815,17010	1818,04225	1820,91499	1823,78831	1826,66222	1829,53670
750	1832,41176	1835,28740	1838,16362	1841,04041	1843,91778	1846,79573	1849,67425	1852,55335	1855,43302	1858,31326
760	1861,19407	1864,07546	1866,95741	1869,83994	1872,72303	1875,60669	1878,49092	1881,37571	1884,26108	1887,14700
770	1890,03349	1892,92055	1895,80816	1898,69634	1901,58508	1904,47439	1907,36425	1910,25467	1913,14565	1916,03718
780	1918,92928	1921,82193	1924,71514	1927,60890	1930,50321	1933,39808	1936,29351	1939,18948	1942,08601	1944,98308
790	1947,88071	1950,77889	1953,67761	1956,57689	1959,47671	1962,37707	1965,27799	1968,17944	1971,08145	1973,98399
800	1976,88708	1979,79072	1982,69489	1985,59961	1988,50486	1991,41066	1994,31699	1997,22387	2000,13128	2003,03922
810	2005,94771	2008,85673	2011,76629	2014,67638	2017,58700	2020,49816	2023,40985	2026,32207	2029,23482	2032,14811
820	2035,06192	2037,97626	2040,89114	2043,80654	2046,72246	2049,63892	2052,55590	2055,47340	2058,39143	2061,30999
830	2064,22906	2067,14867	2070,06879	2072,98943	2075,91060	2078,83229	2081,75449	2084,67722	2087,60046	2090,52422
840	2093,44850	2096,37330	2099,29861	2102,22444	2105,15078	2108,07764	2111,00501	2113,93289	2116,86129	2119,79019
850	2122,71961	2125,64954	2128,57998	2131,51093	2134,44239	2137,37435	2140,30683	2143,23981	2146,17330	2149,10729
860	2152,04179	2154,97679	2157,91230	2160,84831	2163,78482	2166,72184	2169,65936	2172,59737	2175,53589	2178,47491
870	2181,41443	2184,35445	2187,29497	2190,23598	2193,17749	2196,11950	2199,06200	2202,00500	2204,94850	2207,89249
880	2210,83697	2213,78195	2216,72741	2219,67338	2222,61983	2225,56677	2228,51420	2231,46213	2234,41054	2237,35944
890	2240,30883	2243,25871	2246,20908	2249,15993	2252,11126	2255,06309	2258,01540	2260,96819	2263,92146	2266,87522
900	2269,82947	2272,78419	2275,73940	2278,69509	2281,65125	2284,60790	2287,56503	2290,52264	2293,48072	2296,43929
910	2299,39833	2302,35785	2305,31784	2308,27831	2311,23926	2314,20068	2317,16258	2320,12495	2323,08779	2326,05111
920	2329,01489	2331,97915	2334,94388	2337,90909	2340,87476	2343,84090	2346,80751	2349,77459	2352,74214	2355,71015
930	2358,67864	2361,64759	2364,61700	2367,58688	2370,55723	2373,52804	2376,49932	2379,47106	2382,44326	2385,41593
940	2388,38906	2391,36265	2394,33670	2397,31121	2400,28618	2403,26161	2406,23750	2409,21385	2412,19066	2415,16793
950	2418,14565	2421,12383	2424,10247	2427,08156	2430,06111	2433,04112	2436,02157	2439,00249	2441,98385	2444,96567
960	2447,94794	2450,93066	2453,91384	2456,89747	2459,88154	2462,86607	2465,85105	2468,83647	2471,82235	2474,80867
970	2477,79545	2480,78266	2483,77033	2486,75844	2489,74700	2492,73601	2495,72546	2498,71535	2501,70569	2504,69647
980	2507,68770	2510,67937	2513,67148	2516,66403	2519,65703	2522,65047	2525,64434	2528,63866	2531,63342	2534,62861
990	2537,62425	2540,62032	2543,61683	2546,61378	2549,61117	2552,60899	2555,60725	2558,60595	2561,60508	2564,60464

All values conform to the international convention (i.e. 0,1 instead of 0.1).

Common Logarithms ($\log_{10} n$) of the Reciprocal of Factorials* of n=0–999

The **bold figures** are negative characteristics; the mantissae are positive

n	0	1	2	3	4	5	6	7	8	9
0	00000	00000	1 69897	1 22185	2 61979	3 92082	3 14267	4 29757	5 39448	6 44024
10	7 44024	8 39884	9 31966	10 20572	11 05959	13 88350	14 67938	15 44893	16 19366	18 91491
20	19 61388	20 29166	22 94923	23 58751	24 20729	26 80935	27 39438	29 96302	30 51586	31 05346
30	33 57634	34 08498	36 57983	37 06131	39 52984	41 98577	42 42946	44 86126	45 28148	47 69041
40	48 08835	50 47557	52 85232	53 21885	55 57540	57 92219	58 25943	60 58733	62 90609	63 21590
50	65 51693	67 80936	68 09335	70 36908	72 63668	74 89632	75 14813	77 39226	79 62883	81 85798
60	82 07983	84 29450	86 50210	88 70276	90 89658	91 08367	93 26413	95 43805	97 60554	99 76669
70	101 92159	102 07034	104 21300	106 34968	108 48045	110 60539	112 72457	114 83808	116 94599	117 04836
80	119 14527	121 23679	123 32297	125 40390	127 47962	129 55020	131 61570	133 67618	135 73170	137 78231
90	139 82806	141 86902	143 90524	145 93675	147 96362	149 98590	150 00363	152 01686	154 02563	156 03000
100	158 03000	160 02567	162 01707	164 00424	167 98720	169 96602	171 94071	173 91133	175 87790	177 84048
110	179 79908	181 75376	183 70454	185 65146	187 59456	189 53386	191 46940	193 40122	195 32933	197 25379
120	199 17461	201 09182	203 00546	206 91556	208 82213	210 72522	212 62485	214 52105	216 41384	218 30325
130	220 18931	222 07203	225 95146	227 82761	229 70050	231 57017	233 43663	235 29991	237 16003	239 01702
140	242 87089	244 72167	246 56938	248 41405	250 25568	252 09432	255 92996	257 76265	259 59238	261 41920
150	263 24311	265 06413	268 88229	270 69760	272 51007	274 31974	276 12662	279 93072	281 73206	283 53067
160	285 32655	287 11972	290 91020	292 69802	294 48317	296 26569	298 04558	301 82287	303 59756	305 36967
170	307 13922	310 90622	312 67070	314 43265	316 19210	319 94906	321 70355	323 45558	325 20516	328 95230
180	330 69703	332 43935	334 17928	337 91683	339 65201	341 38484	343 11533	346 84349	348 56933	350 29287
190	352 01411	355 73308	357 44978	359 16422	362 87642	364 58638	366 29413	369 99966	371 70300	373 40414
200	375 10311	378 79992	380 49456	382 18707	385 87744	387 56568	389 25182	392 93585	394 61778	396 29764
210	399 97542	401 65113	403 32480	406 99642	408 66600	410 33357	413 99911	415 66265	417 32420	420 98375
220	422 64133	424 29694	427 95058	429 60228	431 25203	434 89985	436 54574	438 18971	441 83178	443 47194
230	445 11022	448 74660	450 38112	452 01376	455 64454	457 27348	460 90056	462 52582	464 14924	467 77084
240	469 39063	471 00861	474 62480	476 23919	479 85180	481 46263	483 07170	486 67900	488 28455	491 88835
250	493 49041	495 09074	498 68934	500 28622	503 88138	505 47484	507 06660	510 65667	512 24505	515 83175
260	517 41678	519 00014	522 58184	524 16188	527 74028	529 31703	532 89215	534 46564	536 03750	539 60775
270	541 17639	544 74342	546 30885	549 87269	551 43494	554 99561	556 55470	558 11222	561 66817	563 22257
280	566 77541	568 32670	571 87646	573 42467	576 97135	578 51651	580 06014	583 60226	585 14287	588 68197
290	590 21957	593 75568	595 29029	598 82343	600 35508	603 88526	605 41397	608 94121	610 46699	613 99132
300	615 51420	617 03564	620 55563	622 07419	625 59131	627 10701	630 62129	632 13415	635 64560	637 15564
310	640 66428	642 17152	645 67737	647 18182	650 68489	652 18658	655 68690	657 18584	660 68341	662 17962
320	665 67447	667 16796	670 66011	672 15090	675 64036	677 12848	680 61526	682 10071	685 58484	687 06764
330	690 54913	692 02930	695 50816	698 98572	700 46197	703 93693	705 41059	708 88296	710 35404	713 82384
340	715 29236	718 75961	720 22558	723 69029	725 15373	728 61591	730 07683	733 53650	736 99492	738 45210
350	741 90803	743 36272	746 81618	748 26840	751 71940	753 16917	756 61772	758 06505	761 51117	764 95608
360	766 39977	769 84227	771 28356	774 72365	776 16255	779 60026	781 03677	784 47211	787 90626	789 33923
370	792 77103	794 20166	797 63112	799 05941	802 48653	805 91250	807 33732	810 76097	812 18348	815 60484
380	817 02506	820 44413	823 86207	825 27887	828 69454	830 10908	833 52249	836 93478	838 34595	841 75600
390	843 16493	846 57276	849 97947	851 38508	854 78958	856 19299	859 59529	862 99650	864 39662	867 79564
400	869 19358	872 59044	875 98621	877 38091	880 77453	882 16707	885 55854	888 94895	890 33829	893 72657
410	895 11378	898 49994	901 88504	903 26909	906 65209	908 03405	911 41495	914 79482	916 17364	919 55143
420	922 92818	924 30389	927 67858	929 05224	932 42488	935 79649	937 16708	940 53665	943 90520	945 27275
430	948 63928	950 00480	953 36932	956 73283	958 09534	961 45685	964 81737	966 17688	969 53541	972 89295
440	974 24949	977 60505	980 95963	982 31323	985 66585	987 01749	990 36815	993 71784	995 06656	998 41432
450	1001 76111	1003 10693	1006 45179	1009 79569	1011 13864	1014 48063	1017 82166	1019 16175	1022 50088	1025 83907
460	1027 17631	1030 51261	1033 84797	1035 18239	1038 51587	1041 84842	1043 18003	1046 51071	1049 84047	1051 16929
470	1054 49720	1057 82418	1059 15023	1062 47537	1065 79959	1067 12290	1070 44529	1073 76678	1075 08735	1078 40701
480	1081 72577	1083 04363	1086 36058	1089 67663	1092 99179	1094 30605	1097 61941	1100 93188	1102 24346	1105 55415
490	1108 86396	1110 17288	1113 48091	1116 78806	1118 09434	1121 39973	1124 70425	1126 00789	1129 31066	1132 61256
500	1135 91359	1137 21376	1140 51305	1143 81149	1145 10906	1148 40576	1151 70161	1154 99661	1156 29074	1159 58402
510	1162 87645	1164 16803	1167 45876	1170 74865	1172 03768	1175 32588	1178 61323	1181 89974	1183 18541	1186 47024
520	1189 75424	1191 03740	1194 31973	1197 60123	1200 88190	1202 16174	1205 44075	1208 71894	1211 99631	1213 27285
530	1216 54858	1219 82348	1221 09757	1224 37084	1227 64330	1230 91495	1232 18578	1235 45581	1238 72503	1241 99344
540	1243 26104	1246 52785	1249 79385	1251 05905	1254 32345	1257 58705	1260 84986	1262 11187	1265 37309	1268 63352
550	1271 89316	1273 15201	1276 41007	1279 66734	1282 92383	1284 17954	1287 43446	1290 68861	1293 94197	1295 19456
560	1298 44637	1301 69741	1304 94768	1306 19717	1309 44589	1312 69384	1315 94102	1317 18744	1320 43309	1323 67798
570	1326 92210	1328 16547	1331 40807	1334 64992	1337 89101	1339 13134	1342 37092	1345 60974	1348 84781	1350 08513
580	1353 32171	1356 55753	1359 79261	1361 02694	1364 26052	1367 49337	1370 72547	1373 95683	1375 18746	1378 41734
590	1381 64649	1384 87490	1386 10258	1389 32952	1392 55574	1395 78122	1397 00597	1400 23000	1403 45330	1406 67587
600	1409 89772	1411 11885	1414 33925	1417 55893	1420 77790	1423 99614	1425 21367	1428 43048	1431 64657	1434 86196
610	1436 07663	1439 29059	1442 50383	1445 71637	1448 92821	1450 13933	1453 34975	1456 55946	1459 76848	1462 97678
620	1464 18439	1467 39130	1470 59751	1473 80302	1475 00784	1478 21196	1481 41538	1484 61812	1487 82016	1489 02151
630	1492 22216	1495 42213	1498 62142	1501 82001	1503 01792	1506 21515	1509 41169	1512 60755	1515 80273	1518 99723
640	1520 19105	1523 38419	1526 57666	1529 76845	1532 95956	1534 15000	1537 33977	1540 52886	1543 71729	1546 90504
650	1548 09213	1551 27855	1554 46430	1557 64939	1560 83381	1562 01757	1565 20067	1568 38310	1571 56487	1574 74599
660	1577 92644	1579 10624	1582 28539	1585 46387	1588 64170	1591 81888	1594 99541	1596 17128	1599 34650	1602 52108
670	1605 69500	1608 86828	1610 04091	1613 21290	1616 38424	1619 55493	1622 72499	1625 89440	1627 06317	1630 23130
680	1633 39879	1636 56564	1639 73186	1642 89744	1644 06238	1647 22669	1650 39036	1653 55341	1656 71582	1659 87760
690	1661 03875	1664 19927	1667 35917	1670 51843	1673 67707	1676 83509	1679 99248	1681 14925	1684 30539	1687 46091
700	1690 61582	1693 77010	1696 92376	1698 07680	1701 22923	1704 38104	1707 53224	1710 68282	1713 83279	1716 98214
710	1718 13088	1721 27901	1724 42653	1727 57344	1730 71974	1733 86544	1735 01052	1738 15500	1741 29888	1744 44215
720	1747 58482	1750 72688	1753 86835	1755 00921	1758 14947	1761 28913	1764 42819	1767 56666	1770 70453	1773 84180
730	1776 97848	1778 11456	1781 25005	1784 38495	1787 51925	1790 65296	1793 78609	1796 91862	1798 05056	1801 18192
740	1804 31269	1807 44287	1810 57246	1813 70147	1816 82990	1819 95775	1821 08501	1824 21169	1827 33778	1830 46330
750	1833 58824	1836 71260	1839 83638	1842 95959	1844 08222	1847 20427	1850 32575	1853 44665	1856 56698	1859 68674
760	1862 80593	1865 92454	1867 04259	1870 16006	1873 27697	1876 39331	1879 50908	1882 62429	1885 73892	1888 85300
770	1891 96651	1893 07945	1896 19184	1899 30366	1902 41492	1905 52561	1908 63575	1911 74533	1914 85435	1917 96282
780	1919 07072	1922 17807	1925 28486	1928 39110	1931 49679	1934 60192	1937 70649	1940 81052	1943 91399	1945 01692
790	1948 11929	1951 22111	1954 32239	1957 42311	1960 52329	1963 62293	1966 72201	1969 82056	1972 91855	1974 01601
800	1977 11292	1980 20928	1983 30511	1986 40039	1989 49514	1992 58934	1995 68301	1998 77613	2001 86872	2004 96078
810	2006 05229	2009 14327	2012 23371	2015 32362	2018 41300	2021 50184	2024 59015	2027 67793	2030 76518	2033 85189
820	2036 93808	2038 02374	2041 10886	2044 19346	2047 27754	2050 36108	2053 44410	2056 52660	2059 60857	2062 69001
830	2065 77094	2068 85133	2071 93121	2073 01057	2076 08940	2079 16771	2082 24551	2085 32278	2088 39954	2091 47578
840	2094 55150	2097 62670	2100 70139	2103 77556	2106 84922	2109 92236	2112 99499	2114 06711	2117 13871	2120 20981
850	2123 28039	2126 35046	2129 42002	2132 48907	2135 55761	2138 62565	2141 69317	2144 76019	2147 82670	2150 89271
860	2153 95821	2155 02321	2158 08770	2161 15169	2164 21518	2167 27816	2170 34064	2173 40263	2176 46411	2179 52509
870	2182 58557	2185 64555	2188 70503	2191 76402	2194 82251	2197 88050	2200 93800	2203 99500	2205 05150	2208 10751
880	2211 16303	2214 21805	2217 27259	2220 32662	2223 38017	2226 43323	2229 48580	2232 53787	2235 58946	2238 64056
890	2241 69117	2244 74129	2247 79092	2250 84007	2253 88874	2256 93691	2259 98460	2261 03181	2264 07854	2267 12478
900	2270 17053	2273 21581	2276 26060	2279 30491	2282 34875	2285 39210	2288 43497	2291 47736	2294 51928	2297 56071
910	2300 60167	2303 64215	2306 68216	2309 72169	2312 76074	2315 79932	2318 83742	2321 87505	2324 91221	2327 94889
920	2330 98511	2332 02085	2335 05612	2338 09091	2341 12524	2344 15910	2347 19249	2350 22541	2353 25786	2356 28985
930	2359 32136	2362 35241	2365 38300	2368 41312	2371 44277	2374 47196	2377 50068	2380 52894	2383 55674	2386 58407
940	2389 61094	2392 63735	2395 66330	2398 68879	2401 71382	2404 73839	2407 76250	2410 78615	2413 80934	2416 83207
950	2419 85435	2422 87617	2425 89753	2428 91844	2431 93889	2434 95888	2437 97843	2440 99751	2442 01615	2445 03433
960	2448 05206	2451 06934	2454 08616	2457 10253	2460 11846	2463 13393	2466 14895	2469 16353	2472 17765	2475 19133
970	2478 20455	2481 21734	2484 22967	2487 24156	2490 25300	2493 26399	2496 27454	2499 28465	2502 29431	2505 30353
980	2508 31230	2511 32063	2514 32852	2517 33597	2520 34297	2523 34953	2526 35566	2529 36134	2532 36658	2535 37139
990	2538 37575	2541 37968	2544 38317	2547 38622	2550 38883	2553 39101	2556 39275	2559 39405	2562 39492	2565 39536

All values conform to the international convention (i.e. 0,1 instead of 0.1).

Integral → Deviation c

$\int_{-\infty}^{c}$	0,000	0,001	0,002	0,003	0,004	0,005	0,006	0,007	0,008	0,009
	*	*	*	*	*	*	*	*	*	*
0,00	–	*3,0902*	*2,8782*	*2,7478*	*2,6521*	*2,5758*	*2,5121*	*2,4573*	*2,4089*	*2,3656*
0,01	*2,3263*	*2,2904*	*2,2571*	*2,2262*	*2,1973*	*2,1701*	*2,1444*	*2,1201*	*2,0969*	*2,0749*
0,02	*2,0537*	*2,0335*	*2,0141*	*1,9954*	*1,9774*	*1,9600*	*1,9431*	*1,9268*	*1,9110*	*1,8957*
0,03	*1,8808*	*1,8663*	*1,8522*	*1,8384*	*1,8250*	*1,8119*	*1,7991*	*1,7866*	*1,7744*	*1,7624*
0,04	*1,7507*	*1,7392*	*1,7279*	*1,7169*	*1,7060*	*1,6954*	*1,6849*	*1,6747*	*1,6646*	*1,6546*
0,05	*1,6449*	*1,6352*	*1,6258*	*1,6164*	*1,6072*	*1,5982*	*1,5893*	*1,5805*	*1,5718*	*1,5632*
0,06	*1,5548*	*1,5464*	*1,5382*	*1,5301*	*1,5220*	*1,5141*	*1,5063*	*1,4985*	*1,4909*	*1,4833*
0,07	*1,4758*	*1,4684*	*1,4611*	*1,4538*	*1,4466*	*1,4395*	*1,4325*	*1,4255*	*1,4187*	*1,4118*
0,08	*1,4051*	*1,3984*	*1,3917*	*1,3852*	*1,3787*	*1,3722*	*1,3658*	*1,3595*	*1,3532*	*1,3469*
0,09	*1,3408*	*1,3346*	*1,3285*	*1,3225*	*1,3165*	*1,3106*	*1,3047*	*1,2988*	*1,2930*	*1,2873*
0,10	*1,2816*	*1,2759*	*1,2702*	*1,2646*	*1,2591*	*1,2536*	*1,2481*	*1,2426*	*1,2372*	*1,2319*
0,11	*1,2265*	*1,2212*	*1,2160*	*1,2107*	*1,2055*	*1,2004*	*1,1952*	*1,1901*	*1,1850*	*1,1800*
0,12	*1,1750*	*1,1700*	*1,1650*	*1,1601*	*1,1552*	*1,1503*	*1,1455*	*1,1407*	*1,1359*	*1,1311*
0,13	*1,1264*	*1,1217*	*1,1170*	*1,1123*	*1,1077*	*1,1031*	*1,0985*	*1,0939*	*1,0893*	*1,0848*
0,14	*1,0803*	*1,0758*	*1,0714*	*1,0669*	*1,0625*	*1,0581*	*1,0537*	*1,0494*	*1,0450*	*1,0407*
0,15	*1,0364*	*1,0322*	*1,0279*	*1,0237*	*1,0194*	*1,0152*	*1,0110*	*1,0069*	*1,0027*	*0,9986*
0,16	*0,9945*	*0,9904*	*0,9863*	*0,9822*	*0,9782*	*0,9741*	*0,9701*	*0,9661*	*0,9621*	*0,9581*
0,17	*0,9542*	*0,9502*	*0,9463*	*0,9424*	*0,9385*	*0,9346*	*0,9307*	*0,9269*	*0,9230*	*0,9192*
0,18	*0,9154*	*0,9116*	*0,9078*	*0,9040*	*0,9002*	*0,8965*	*0,8927*	*0,8890*	*0,8853*	*0,8816*
0,19	*0,8779*	*0,8742*	*0,8705*	*0,8669*	*0,8633*	*0,8596*	*0,8560*	*0,8524*	*0,8488*	*0,8452*
0,20	*0,8416*	*0,8381*	*0,8345*	*0,8310*	*0,8274*	*0,8239*	*0,8204*	*0,8169*	*0,8134*	*0,8099*
0,21	*0,8064*	*0,8030*	*0,7995*	*0,7961*	*0,7926*	*0,7892*	*0,7858*	*0,7824*	*0,7790*	*0,7756*
0,22	*0,7722*	*0,7688*	*0,7655*	*0,7621*	*0,7588*	*0,7554*	*0,7521*	*0,7488*	*0,7454*	*0,7421*
0,23	*0,7388*	*0,7356*	*0,7323*	*0,7290*	*0,7257*	*0,7225*	*0,7192*	*0,7160*	*0,7128*	*0,7095*
0,24	*0,7063*	*0,7031*	*0,6999*	*0,6967*	*0,6935*	*0,6903*	*0,6871*	*0,6840*	*0,6808*	*0,6776*
0,25	*0,6745*	*0,6713*	*0,6682*	*0,6651*	*0,6620*	*0,6588*	*0,6557*	*0,6526*	*0,6495*	*0,6464*
0,26	*0,6433*	*0,6403*	*0,6372*	*0,6341*	*0,6311*	*0,6280*	*0,6250*	*0,6219*	*0,6189*	*0,6158*
0,27	*0,6128*	*0,6098*	*0,6068*	*0,6038*	*0,6008*	*0,5978*	*0,5948*	*0,5918*	*0,5888*	*0,5858*
0,28	*0,5828*	*0,5799*	*0,5769*	*0,5740*	*0,5710*	*0,5681*	*0,5651*	*0,5622*	*0,5592*	*0,5563*
0,29	*0,5534*	*0,5505*	*0,5476*	*0,5446*	*0,5417*	*0,5388*	*0,5359*	*0,5330*	*0,5302*	*0,5273*
0,30	*0,5244*	*0,5215*	*0,5187*	*0,5158*	*0,5129*	*0,5101*	*0,5072*	*0,5044*	*0,5015*	*0,4987*
0,31	*0,4959*	*0,4930*	*0,4902*	*0,4874*	*0,4845*	*0,4817*	*0,4789*	*0,4761*	*0,4733*	*0,4705*
0,32	*0,4677*	*0,4649*	*0,4621*	*0,4593*	*0,4565*	*0,4538*	*0,4510*	*0,4482*	*0,4454*	*0,4427*
0,33	*0,4399*	*0,4372*	*0,4344*	*0,4316*	*0,4289*	*0,4261*	*0,4234*	*0,4207*	*0,4179*	*0,4152*
0,34	*0,4125*	*0,4097*	*0,4070*	*0,4043*	*0,4016*	*0,3989*	*0,3961*	*0,3934*	*0,3907*	*0,3880*
0,35	*0,3853*	*0,3826*	*0,3799*	*0,3772*	*0,3745*	*0,3719*	*0,3692*	*0,3665*	*0,3638*	*0,3611*
0,36	*0,3585*	*0,3558*	*0,3531*	*0,3505*	*0,3478*	*0,3451*	*0,3425*	*0,3398*	*0,3372*	*0,3345*
0,37	*0,3319*	*0,3292*	*0,3266*	*0,3239*	*0,3213*	*0,3186*	*0,3160*	*0,3134*	*0,3107*	*0,3081*
0,38	*0,3055*	*0,3029*	*0,3002*	*0,2976*	*0,2950*	*0,2924*	*0,2898*	*0,2871*	*0,2845*	*0,2819*
0,39	*0,2793*	*0,2767*	*0,2741*	*0,2715*	*0,2689*	*0,2663*	*0,2637*	*0,2611*	*0,2585*	*0,2559*
0,40	*0,2533*	*0,2508*	*0,2482*	*0,2456*	*0,2430*	*0,2404*	*0,2378*	*0,2353*	*0,2327*	*0,2301*
0,41	*0,2275*	*0,2250*	*0,2224*	*0,2198*	*0,2173*	*0,2147*	*0,2121*	*0,2096*	*0,2070*	*0,2045*
0,42	*0,2019*	*0,1993*	*0,1968*	*0,1942*	*0,1917*	*0,1891*	*0,1866*	*0,1840*	*0,1815*	*0,1789*
0,43	*0,1764*	*0,1738*	*0,1713*	*0,1687*	*0,1662*	*0,1637*	*0,1611*	*0,1586*	*0,1560*	*0,1535*
0,44	*0,1510*	*0,1484*	*0,1459*	*0,1434*	*0,1408*	*0,1383*	*0,1358*	*0,1332*	*0,1307*	*0,1282*
0,45	*0,1257*	*0,1231*	*0,1206*	*0,1181*	*0,1156*	*0,1130*	*0,1105*	*0,1080*	*0,1055*	*0,1030*
0,46	*0,1004*	*0,0979*	*0,0954*	*0,0929*	*0,0904*	*0,0878*	*0,0853*	*0,0828*	*0,0803*	*0,0778*
0,47	*0,0753*	*0,0728*	*0,0702*	*0,0677*	*0,0652*	*0,0627*	*0,0602*	*0,0577*	*0,0552*	*0,0527*
0,48	*0,0502*	*0,0476*	*0,0451*	*0,0426*	*0,0401*	*0,0376*	*0,0351*	*0,0326*	*0,0301*	*0,0276*
0,49	*0,0251*	*0,0226*	*0,0201*	*0,0175*	*0,0150*	*0,0125*	*0,0100*	*0,0075*	*0,0050*	*0,0025*
0,50	0,0000	0,0025	0,0050	0,0075	0,0100	0,0125	0,0150	0,0175	0,0201	0,0226
0,51	0,0251	0,0276	0,0301	0,0326	0,0351	0,0376	0,0401	0,0426	0,0451	0,0476
0,52	0,0502	0,0527	0,0552	0,0577	0,0602	0,0627	0,0652	0,0677	0,0702	0,0728
0,53	0,0753	0,0778	0,0803	0,0828	0,0853	0,0878	0,0904	0,0929	0,0954	0,0979
0,54	0,1004	0,1030	0,1055	0,1080	0,1105	0,1130	0,1156	0,1181	0,1206	0,1231
0,55	0,1257	0,1282	0,1307	0,1332	0,1358	0,1383	0,1408	0,1434	0,1459	0,1484
0,56	0,1510	0,1535	0,1560	0,1586	0,1611	0,1637	0,1662	0,1687	0,1713	0,1738
0,57	0,1764	0,1789	0,1815	0,1840	0,1866	0,1891	0,1917	0,1942	0,1968	0,1993
0,58	0,2019	0,2045	0,2070	0,2096	0,2121	0,2147	0,2173	0,2198	0,2224	0,2250
0,59	0,2275	0,2301	0,2327	0,2353	0,2378	0,2404	0,2430	0,2456	0,2482	0,2508
0,60	0,2533	0,2559	0,2585	0,2611	0,2637	0,2663	0,2689	0,2715	0,2741	0,2767
0,61	0,2793	0,2819	0,2845	0,2871	0,2898	0,2924	0,2950	0,2976	0,3002	0,3029
0,62	0,3055	0,3081	0,3107	0,3134	0,3160	0,3186	0,3213	0,3239	0,3266	0,3292
0,63	0,3319	0,3345	0,3372	0,3398	0,3425	0,3451	0,3478	0,3505	0,3531	0,3558
0,64	0,3585	0,3611	0,3638	0,3665	0,3692	0,3719	0,3745	0,3772	0,3799	0,3826
0,65	0,3853	0,3880	0,3907	0,3934	0,3961	0,3989	0,4016	0,4043	0,4070	0,4097
0,66	0,4125	0,4152	0,4179	0,4207	0,4234	0,4261	0,4289	0,4316	0,4344	0,4372
0,67	0,4399	0,4427	0,4454	0,4482	0,4510	0,4538	0,4565	0,4593	0,4621	0,4649
0,68	0,4677	0,4705	0,4733	0,4761	0,4789	0,4817	0,4845	0,4874	0,4902	0,4930
0,69	0,4959	0,4987	0,5015	0,5044	0,5072	0,5101	0,5129	0,5158	0,5187	0,5215
0,70	0,5244	0,5273	0,5302	0,5330	0,5359	0,5388	0,5417	0,5446	0,5476	0,5505
0,71	0,5534	0,5563	0,5592	0,5622	0,5651	0,5681	0,5710	0,5740	0,5769	0,5799
0,72	0,5828	0,5858	0,5888	0,5918	0,5948	0,5978	0,6008	0,6038	0,6068	0,6098
0,73	0,6128	0,6158	0,6189	0,6219	0,6250	0,6280	0,6311	0,6341	0,6372	0,6403
0,74	0,6433	0,6464	0,6495	0,6526	0,6557	0,6588	0,6620	0,6651	0,6682	0,6713
0,75	0,6745	0,6776	0,6808	0,6840	0,6871	0,6903	0,6935	0,6967	0,6999	0,7031
0,76	0,7063	0,7095	0,7128	0,7160	0,7192	0,7225	0,7257	0,7290	0,7323	0,7356
0,77	0,7388	0,7421	0,7454	0,7488	0,7521	0,7554	0,7588	0,7621	0,7655	0,7688
0,78	0,7722	0,7756	0,7790	0,7824	0,7858	0,7892	0,7926	0,7961	0,7995	0,8030
0,79	0,8064	0,8099	0,8134	0,8169	0,8204	0,8239	0,8274	0,8310	0,8345	0,8381
0,80	0,8416	0,8452	0,8488	0,8524	0,8560	0,8596	0,8633	0,8669	0,8705	0,8742
0,81	0,8779	0,8816	0,8853	0,8890	0,8927	0,8965	0,9002	0,9040	0,9078	0,9116
0,82	0,9154	0,9192	0,9230	0,9269	0,9307	0,9346	0,9385	0,9424	0,9463	0,9502
0,83	0,9542	0,9581	0,9621	0,9661	0,9701	0,9741	0,9782	0,9822	0,9863	0,9904
0,84	0,9945	0,9986	1,0027	1,0069	1,0110	1,0152	1,0194	1,0237	1,0279	1,0322
0,85	1,0364	1,0407	1,0450	1,0494	1,0537	1,0581	1,0625	1,0669	1,0714	1,0758
0,86	1,0803	1,0848	1,0893	1,0939	1,0985	1,1031	1,1077	1,1123	1,1170	1,1217
0,87	1,1264	1,1311	1,1359	1,1407	1,1455	1,1503	1,1552	1,1601	1,1650	1,1700
0,88	1,1750	1,1800	1,1850	1,1901	1,1952	1,2004	1,2055	1,2107	1,2160	1,2212
0,89	1,2265	1,2319	1,2372	1,2426	1,2481	1,2536	1,2591	1,2646	1,2702	1,2759
0,90	1,2816	1,2873	1,2930	1,2988	1,3047	1,3106	1,3165	1,3225	1,3285	1,3346
0,91	1,3408	1,3469	1,3532	1,3595	1,3658	1,3722	1,3787	1,3852	1,3917	1,3984
0,92	1,4051	1,4118	1,4187	1,4255	1,4325	1,4395	1,4466	1,4538	1,4611	1,4684
0,93	1,4758	1,4833	1,4909	1,4985	1,5063	1,5141	1,5220	1,5301	1,5382	1,5464
0,94	1,5548	1,5632	1,5718	1,5805	1,5893	1,5982	1,6072	1,6164	1,6258	1,6352
0,95	1,6449	1,6546	1,6646	1,6747	1,6849	1,6954	1,7060	1,7169	1,7279	1,7392
0,96	1,7507	1,7624	1,7744	1,7866	1,7991	1,8119	1,8250	1,8384	1,8522	1,8663
0,97	1,8808	1,8957	1,9110	1,9268	1,9431	1,9600	1,9774	1,9954	2,0141	2,0335
0,98	2,0537	2,0749	2,0969	2,1201	2,1444	2,1701	2,1973	2,2262	2,2571	2,2904
0,99	2,3263	2,3656	2,4089	2,4573	2,5121	2,5758	2,6521	2,7478	2,8782	3,0902

[7] Calculated from *Tables of Normal Probability Functions* (see page 27).
* *Italic figures* are negative values.

Deviation c → Integral

c	0,00	0,01	0,02	0,03	0,04	0,05	0,06	0,07	0,08	0,09
	0,	0,	0,	0,	0,	0,	0,	0,	0,	0,
−3,2	00069	00066	00064	00062	00060	00058	00056	00054	00052	00050
−3,1	00097	00094	00090	00087	00084	00082	00079	00076	00074	00071
−3,0	00135	00131	00126	00122	00118	00114	00111	00107	00104	00100
−2,9	00187	00181	00175	00169	00164	00159	00154	00149	00144	00139
−2,8	00256	00248	00240	00233	00226	00219	00212	00205	00199	00193
−2,7	00347	00336	00326	00317	00307	00298	00289	00280	00272	00264
−2,6	00466	00453	00440	00427	00415	00402	00391	00379	00368	00357
−2,5	00621	00604	00587	00570	00554	00539	00523	00508	00494	00480
−2,4	00820	00798	00776	00755	00734	00714	00695	00676	00657	00639
−2,3	01072	01044	01017	00990	00964	00939	00914	00889	00866	00842
−2,2	01390	01355	01321	01287	01255	01222	01191	01160	01130	01101
−2,1	01786	01743	01700	01659	01618	01578	01539	01500	01463	01426
−2,0	02275	02222	02169	02118	02068	02018	01970	01923	01876	01831
−1,9	02872	02807	02743	02680	02619	02559	02500	02442	02385	02330
−1,8	03593	03515	03438	03362	03288	03216	03144	03074	03005	02938
−1,7	04457	04363	04272	04182	04093	04006	03920	03836	03754	03673
−1,6	05480	05370	05262	05155	05050	04947	04846	04746	04648	04551
−1,5	06681	06552	06426	06301	06178	06057	05938	05821	05705	05592
−1,4	08076	07927	07780	07636	07493	07353	07215	07078	06944	06811
−1,3	09680	09510	09342	09176	09012	08851	08691	08534	08379	08226
−1,2	11507	11314	11123	10935	10749	10565	10383	10204	10027	09853
−1,1	13567	13350	13136	12924	12714	12507	12302	12100	11900	11702
−1,0	15866	15625	15386	15151	14917	14686	14457	14231	14007	13786
−0,9	18406	18141	17879	17619	17361	17106	16853	16602	16354	16109
−0,8	21186	20897	20611	20327	20045	19766	19489	19215	18943	18673
−0,7	24196	23885	23576	23270	22965	22663	22363	22065	21770	21476
−0,6	27425	27093	26763	26435	26109	25785	25463	25143	24825	24510
−0,5	30854	30503	30153	29806	29460	29116	28774	28434	28096	27760
−0,4	34458	34090	33724	33360	32997	32636	32276	31918	31561	31207
−0,3	38209	37828	37448	37070	36693	36317	35942	35569	35197	34827
−0,2	42074	41683	41294	40905	40517	40129	39743	39358	38974	38591
−0,19	42465	42426	42387	42348	42309	42270	42231	42191	42152	42113
−0,18	42858	42818	42779	42740	42701	42661	42622	42583	42544	42505
−0,17	43251	43211	43172	43133	43093	43054	43015	42975	42936	42897
−0,16	43644	43605	43565	43526	43487	43447	43408	43369	43329	43290
−0,15	44038	43999	43959	43920	43880	43841	43802	43762	43723	43683
−0,14	44433	44393	44354	44315	44275	44236	44196	44157	44117	44078
−0,13	44828	44789	44749	44710	44670	44631	44591	44552	44512	44473
−0,12	45224	45185	45145	45105	45066	45026	44987	44947	44907	44868
−0,11	45620	45581	45541	45502	45462	45422	45383	45343	45303	45264
−0,10	46017	45978	45938	45898	45858	45819	45779	45739	45700	45660
−0,09	46414	46375	46335	46295	46255	46216	46176	46136	46097	46057
−0,08	46812	46772	46732	46693	46653	46613	46573	46534	46494	46454
−0,07	47210	47170	47130	47090	47051	47011	46971	46931	46891	46852
−0,06	47608	47568	47528	47488	47449	47409	47369	47329	47289	47249
−0,05	48006	47966	47926	47887	47847	47807	47767	47727	47687	47648
−0,04	48405	48365	48325	48285	48245	48205	48166	48126	48086	48046
−0,03	48803	48763	48724	48684	48644	48604	48564	48524	48484	48445
−0,02	49202	49162	49122	49083	49043	49003	48963	48923	48883	48843
−0,01	49601	49561	49521	49481	49441	49402	49362	49322	49282	49242
−0,00	50000	49960	49920	49880	49840	49801	49761	49721	49681	49641
+0,00	50000	50040	50080	50120	50160	50199	50239	50279	50319	50359
+0,01	50399	50439	50479	50519	50559	50598	50638	50678	50718	50758
+0,02	50798	50838	50878	50917	50957	50997	51037	51077	51117	51157
+0,03	51197	51237	51276	51316	51356	51396	51436	51476	51516	51555
+0,04	51595	51635	51675	51715	51755	51795	51834	51874	51914	51954
+0,05	51994	52034	52074	52113	52153	52193	52233	52273	52313	52352
+0,06	52392	52432	52472	52512	52551	52591	52631	52671	52711	52751
+0,07	52790	52830	52870	52910	52949	52989	53029	53069	53109	53148
+0,08	53188	53228	53268	53307	53347	53387	53427	53466	53506	53546
+0,09	53586	53625	53665	53705	53745	53784	53824	53864	53903	53943
+0,10	53983	54022	54062	54102	54142	54181	54221	54261	54300	54340
+0,11	54380	54419	54459	54498	54538	54578	54617	54657	54697	54736
+0,12	54776	54815	54855	54895	54934	54974	55013	55053	55093	55132
+0,13	55172	55211	55251	55290	55330	55369	55409	55448	55488	55527
+0,14	55567	55607	55646	55685	55725	55764	55804	55843	55883	55922
+0,15	55962	56001	56041	56080	56120	56159	56198	56238	56277	56317
+0,16	56356	56395	56435	56474	56513	56553	56592	56631	56671	56710
+0,17	56749	56789	56828	56867	56907	56946	56985	57025	57064	57103
+0,18	57142	57182	57221	57260	57299	57339	57378	57417	57456	57495
+0,19	57535	57574	57613	57652	57691	57730	57769	57809	57848	57887
+0,2	57926	58317	58706	59095	59483	59871	60257	60642	61026	61409
+0,3	61791	62172	62552	62930	63307	63683	64058	64431	64803	65173
+0,4	65542	65910	66276	66640	67003	67364	67724	68082	68439	68793
+0,5	69146	69497	69847	70194	70540	70884	71226	71566	71904	72240
+0,6	72575	72907	73237	73565	73891	74215	74537	74857	75175	75490
+0,7	75804	76115	76424	76730	77035	77337	77637	77935	78230	78524
+0,8	78814	79103	79389	79673	79955	80234	80511	80785	81057	81327
+0,9	81594	81859	82121	82381	82639	82894	83147	83398	83646	83891
+1,0	84134	84375	84614	84849	85083	85314	85543	85769	85993	86214
+1,1	86433	86650	86864	87076	87286	87493	87698	87900	88100	88298
+1,2	88493	88686	88877	89065	89251	89435	89617	89796	89973	90147
+1,3	90320	90490	90658	90824	90988	91149	91309	91466	91621	91774
+1,4	91924	92073	92220	92364	92507	92647	92785	92922	93056	93189
+1,5	93319	93448	93574	93699	93822	93943	94062	94179	94295	94408
+1,6	94520	94630	94738	94845	94950	95053	95154	95254	95352	95449
+1,7	95543	95637	95728	95818	95907	95994	96080	96164	96246	96327
+1,8	96407	96485	96562	96638	96712	96784	96856	96926	96995	97062
+1,9	97128	97193	97257	97320	97381	97441	97500	97558	97615	97670
+2,0	97725	97778	97831	97882	97932	97982	98030	98077	98124	98169
+2,1	98214	98257	98300	98341	98382	98422	98461	98500	98537	98574
+2,2	98610	98645	98679	98713	98745	98778	98809	98840	98870	98899
+2,3	98928	98956	98983	99010	99036	99061	99086	99111	99134	99158
+2,4	99180	99202	99224	99245	99266	99286	99305	99324	99343	99361
+2,5	99379	99396	99413	99430	99446	99461	99477	99492	99506	99520
+2,6	99534	99547	99560	99573	99585	99598	99609	99621	99632	99643
+2,7	99653	99664	99674	99683	99693	99702	99711	99720	99728	99736
+2,8	99744	99752	99760	99767	99774	99781	99788	99795	99801	99807
+2,9	99813	99819	99825	99831	99836	99841	99846	99851	99856	99861
+3,0	99865	99869	99874	99878	99882	99886	99889	99893	99896	99900
+3,1	99903	99906	99910	99913	99916	99918	99921	99924	99926	99929
+3,2	99931	99934	99936	99938	99940	99942	99944	99946	99948	99950

All values conform to the international convention (i.e. 0,1 instead of 0.1).

Integral → Deviation c

$\int_{-c}^{c}$	0,000	0,001	0,002	0,003	0,004	0,005	0,006	0,007	0,008	0,009
0,00	0,0000	0,0013	0,0025	0,0038	0,0050	0,0063	0,0075	0,0088	0,0100	0,0113
0,01	0,0125	0,0138	0,0150	0,0163	0,0175	0,0188	0,0201	0,0213	0,0226	0,0238
0,02	0,0251	0,0263	0,0276	0,0288	0,0301	0,0313	0,0326	0,0338	0,0351	0,0364
0,03	0,0376	0,0389	0,0401	0,0414	0,0426	0,0439	0,0451	0,0464	0,0476	0,0489
0,04	0,0502	0,0514	0,0527	0,0539	0,0552	0,0564	0,0577	0,0589	0,0602	0,0615
0,05	0,0627	0,0640	0,0652	0,0665	0,0677	0,0690	0,0702	0,0715	0,0728	0,0740
0,06	0,0753	0,0765	0,0778	0,0790	0,0803	0,0816	0,0828	0,0841	0,0853	0,0866
0,07	0,0878	0,0891	0,0904	0,0916	0,0929	0,0941	0,0954	0,0967	0,0979	0,0992
0,08	0,1004	0,1017	0,1030	0,1042	0,1055	0,1067	0,1080	0,1093	0,1105	0,1118
0,09	0,1130	0,1143	0,1156	0,1168	0,1181	0,1193	0,1206	0,1219	0,1231	0,1244
0,10	0,1257	0,1269	0,1282	0,1295	0,1307	0,1320	0,1332	0,1345	0,1358	0,1370
0,11	0,1383	0,1396	0,1408	0,1421	0,1434	0,1446	0,1459	0,1472	0,1484	0,1497
0,12	0,1510	0,1522	0,1535	0,1548	0,1560	0,1573	0,1586	0,1598	0,1611	0,1624
0,13	0,1637	0,1649	0,1662	0,1675	0,1687	0,1700	0,1713	0,1726	0,1738	0,1751
0,14	0,1764	0,1776	0,1789	0,1802	0,1815	0,1827	0,1840	0,1853	0,1866	0,1878
0,15	0,1891	0,1904	0,1917	0,1929	0,1942	0,1955	0,1968	0,1981	0,1993	0,2006
0,16	0,2019	0,2032	0,2045	0,2057	0,2070	0,2083	0,2096	0,2109	0,2121	0,2134
0,17	0,2147	0,2160	0,2173	0,2186	0,2198	0,2211	0,2224	0,2237	0,2250	0,2263
0,18	0,2275	0,2288	0,2301	0,2314	0,2327	0,2340	0,2353	0,2366	0,2378	0,2391
0,19	0,2404	0,2417	0,2430	0,2443	0,2456	0,2469	0,2482	0,2495	0,2508	0,2521
0,20	0,2533	0,2546	0,2559	0,2572	0,2585	0,2598	0,2611	0,2624	0,2637	0,2650
0,21	0,2663	0,2676	0,2689	0,2702	0,2715	0,2728	0,2741	0,2754	0,2767	0,2780
0,22	0,2793	0,2806	0,2819	0,2832	0,2845	0,2858	0,2871	0,2885	0,2898	0,2911
0,23	0,2924	0,2937	0,2950	0,2963	0,2976	0,2989	0,3002	0,3015	0,3029	0,3042
0,24	0,3055	0,3068	0,3081	0,3094	0,3107	0,3121	0,3134	0,3147	0,3160	0,3173
0,25	0,3186	0,3200	0,3213	0,3226	0,3239	0,3252	0,3266	0,3279	0,3292	0,3305
0,26	0,3319	0,3332	0,3345	0,3358	0,3372	0,3385	0,3398	0,3411	0,3425	0,3438
0,27	0,3451	0,3465	0,3478	0,3491	0,3505	0,3518	0,3531	0,3545	0,3558	0,3571
0,28	0,3585	0,3598	0,3611	0,3625	0,3638	0,3651	0,3665	0,3678	0,3692	0,3705
0,29	0,3719	0,3732	0,3745	0,3759	0,3772	0,3786	0,3799	0,3813	0,3826	0,3840
0,30	0,3853	0,3867	0,3880	0,3894	0,3907	0,3921	0,3934	0,3948	0,3961	0,3975
0,31	0,3989	0,4002	0,4016	0,4029	0,4043	0,4056	0,4070	0,4084	0,4097	0,4111
0,32	0,4125	0,4138	0,4152	0,4166	0,4179	0,4193	0,4207	0,4220	0,4234	0,4248
0,33	0,4261	0,4275	0,4289	0,4303	0,4316	0,4330	0,4344	0,4358	0,4372	0,4385
0,34	0,4399	0,4413	0,4427	0,4441	0,4454	0,4468	0,4482	0,4496	0,4510	0,4524
0,35	0,4538	0,4552	0,4565	0,4579	0,4593	0,4607	0,4621	0,4635	0,4649	0,4663
0,36	0,4677	0,4691	0,4705	0,4719	0,4733	0,4747	0,4761	0,4775	0,4789	0,4803
0,37	0,4817	0,4831	0,4845	0,4860	0,4874	0,4888	0,4902	0,4916	0,4930	0,4944
0,38	0,4959	0,4973	0,4987	0,5001	0,5015	0,5029	0,5044	0,5058	0,5072	0,5086
0,39	0,5101	0,5115	0,5129	0,5144	0,5158	0,5172	0,5187	0,5201	0,5215	0,5230
0,40	0,5244	0,5258	0,5273	0,5287	0,5302	0,5316	0,5330	0,5345	0,5359	0,5374
0,41	0,5388	0,5403	0,5417	0,5432	0,5446	0,5461	0,5476	0,5490	0,5505	0,5519
0,42	0,5534	0,5548	0,5563	0,5578	0,5592	0,5607	0,5622	0,5636	0,5651	0,5666
0,43	0,5681	0,5695	0,5710	0,5725	0,5740	0,5754	0,5769	0,5784	0,5799	0,5814
0,44	0,5828	0,5843	0,5858	0,5873	0,5888	0,5903	0,5918	0,5933	0,5948	0,5963
0,45	0,5978	0,5993	0,6008	0,6023	0,6038	0,6053	0,6068	0,6083	0,6098	0,6113
0,46	0,6128	0,6143	0,6158	0,6174	0,6189	0,6204	0,6219	0,6234	0,6250	0,6265
0,47	0,6280	0,6295	0,6311	0,6326	0,6341	0,6357	0,6372	0,6387	0,6403	0,6418
0,48	0,6433	0,6449	0,6464	0,6480	0,6495	0,6511	0,6526	0,6542	0,6557	0,6573
0,49	0,6588	0,6604	0,6620	0,6635	0,6651	0,6666	0,6682	0,6698	0,6713	0,6729
0,50	0,6745	0,6761	0,6776	0,6792	0,6808	0,6824	0,6840	0,6855	0,6871	0,6887
0,51	0,6903	0,6919	0,6935	0,6951	0,6967	0,6983	0,6999	0,7015	0,7031	0,7047
0,52	0,7063	0,7079	0,7095	0,7111	0,7128	0,7144	0,7160	0,7176	0,7192	0,7209
0,53	0,7225	0,7241	0,7257	0,7274	0,7290	0,7306	0,7323	0,7339	0,7356	0,7372
0,54	0,7388	0,7405	0,7421	0,7438	0,7454	0,7471	0,7488	0,7504	0,7521	0,7537
0,55	0,7554	0,7571	0,7588	0,7604	0,7621	0,7638	0,7655	0,7671	0,7688	0,7705
0,56	0,7722	0,7739	0,7756	0,7773	0,7790	0,7807	0,7824	0,7841	0,7858	0,7875
0,57	0,7892	0,7909	0,7926	0,7943	0,7961	0,7978	0,7995	0,8012	0,8030	0,8047
0,58	0,8064	0,8082	0,8099	0,8116	0,8134	0,8151	0,8169	0,8186	0,8204	0,8221
0,59	0,8239	0,8257	0,8274	0,8292	0,8310	0,8327	0,8345	0,8363	0,8381	0,8398
0,60	0,8416	0,8434	0,8452	0,8470	0,8488	0,8506	0,8524	0,8542	0,8560	0,8578
0,61	0,8596	0,8614	0,8633	0,8651	0,8669	0,8687	0,8705	0,8724	0,8742	0,8761
0,62	0,8779	0,8797	0,8816	0,8834	0,8853	0,8871	0,8890	0,8909	0,8927	0,8946
0,63	0,8965	0,8983	0,9002	0,9021	0,9040	0,9059	0,9078	0,9097	0,9116	0,9135
0,64	0,9154	0,9173	0,9192	0,9211	0,9230	0,9249	0,9269	0,9288	0,9307	0,9327
0,65	0,9346	0,9365	0,9385	0,9404	0,9424	0,9443	0,9463	0,9483	0,9502	0,9522
0,66	0,9542	0,9561	0,9581	0,9601	0,9621	0,9641	0,9661	0,9681	0,9701	0,9721
0,67	0,9741	0,9761	0,9782	0,9802	0,9822	0,9842	0,9863	0,9883	0,9904	0,9924
0,68	0,9945	0,9965	0,9986	1,001	1,003	1,005	1,007	1,009	1,011	1,013
0,69	1,015	1,017	1,019	1,022	1,024	1,026	1,028	1,030	1,032	1,034
0,70	1,036	1,039	1,041	1,043	1,045	1,047	1,049	1,052	1,054	1,056
0,71	1,058	1,060	1,063	1,065	1,067	1,069	1,071	1,074	1,076	1,078
0,72	1,080	1,083	1,085	1,087	1,089	1,092	1,094	1,096	1,098	1,101
0,73	1,103	1,105	1,108	1,110	1,112	1,115	1,117	1,119	1,122	1,124
0,74	1,126	1,129	1,131	1,134	1,136	1,138	1,141	1,143	1,146	1,148
0,75	1,150	1,153	1,155	1,158	1,160	1,163	1,165	1,168	1,170	1,172
0,76	1,175	1,177	1,180	1,183	1,185	1,188	1,190	1,193	1,195	1,198
0,77	1,200	1,203	1,206	1,208	1,211	1,213	1,216	1,219	1,221	1,224
0,78	1,227	1,229	1,232	1,235	1,237	1,240	1,243	1,245	1,248	1,251
0,79	1,254	1,256	1,259	1,262	1,265	1,267	1,270	1,273	1,276	1,279
0,80	1,282	1,284	1,287	1,290	1,293	1,296	1,299	1,302	1,305	1,308
0,81	1,311	1,314	1,317	1,320	1,323	1,326	1,329	1,332	1,335	1,338
0,82	1,341	1,344	1,347	1,350	1,353	1,356	1,359	1,363	1,366	1,369
0,83	1,372	1,375	1,379	1,382	1,385	1,388	1,392	1,395	1,398	1,402
0,84	1,405	1,408	1,412	1,415	1,419	1,422	1,426	1,429	1,433	1,436
0,85	1,440	1,443	1,447	1,450	1,454	1,457	1,461	1,465	1,468	1,472
0,86	1,476	1,480	1,483	1,487	1,491	1,495	1,499	1,502	1,506	1,510
0,87	1,514	1,518	1,522	1,526	1,530	1,534	1,538	1,542	1,546	1,551
0,88	1,555	1,559	1,563	1,567	1,572	1,576	1,580	1,585	1,589	1,594
0,89	1,598	1,603	1,607	1,612	1,616	1,621	1,626	1,630	1,635	1,640
0,90	1,645	1,650	1,655	1,660	1,665	1,670	1,675	1,680	1,685	1,690
0,91	1,695	1,701	1,706	1,711	1,717	1,722	1,728	1,734	1,739	1,745
0,92	1,751	1,757	1,762	1,768	1,774	1,780	1,787	1,793	1,799	1,806
0,93	1,812	1,818	1,825	1,832	1,838	1,845	1,852	1,859	1,866	1,873
0,94	1,881	1,888	1,896	1,903	1,911	1,919	1,927	1,935	1,943	1,951
0,95	1,960	1,969	1,977	1,986	1,995	2,005	2,014	2,024	2,034	2,044
0,96	2,054	2,064	2,075	2,086	2,097	2,108	2,120	2,132	2,144	2,157
0,97	2,170	2,183	2,197	2,212	2,226	2,241	2,257	2,273	2,290	2,308
0,98	2,326	2,346	2,366	2,387	2,409	2,432	2,457	2,484	2,512	2,543
0,99	2,576	2,612	2,652	2,697	2,748	2,807	2,878	2,968	3,090	3,291

Deviation c → Integral

c	0,000	0,001	0,002	0,003	0,004	0,005	0,006	0,007	0,008	0,009
	0,	0,	0,	0,	0,	0,	0,	0,	0,	0,
0,00	00000	00080	00160	00239	00319	00399	00479	00559	00638	00718
0,01	00798	00878	00957	01037	01117	01197	01277	01356	01436	01516
0,02	01596	01675	01755	01835	01915	01995	02074	02154	02234	02314
0,03	02393	02473	02553	02633	02712	02792	02872	02951	03031	03111
0,04	03191	03270	03350	03430	03510	03589	03669	03749	03828	03908
0,05	03988	04067	04147	04227	04306	04386	04466	04545	04625	04705
0,06	04784	04864	04944	05023	05103	05183	05262	05342	05421	05501
0,07	05581	05660	05740	05819	05899	05979	06058	06138	06217	06297
0,08	06376	06456	06535	06615	06694	06774	06853	06933	07012	07092
0,09	07171	07251	07330	07410	07489	07569	07648	07727	07807	07886
0,10	07966	08045	08124	08204	08283	08362	08442	08521	08600	08680
0,11	08759	08838	08918	08997	09076	09155	09235	09314	09393	09472
0,12	09552	09631	09710	09789	09868	09948	10027	10106	10185	10264
0,13	10343	10422	10502	10581	10660	10739	10818	10897	10976	11055
0,14	11134	11213	11292	11371	11450	11529	11608	11687	11766	11845
0,15	11924	12002	12081	12160	12239	12318	12397	12476	12554	12633
0,16	12712	12791	12869	12948	13027	13106	13184	13263	13342	13420
0,17	13499	13578	13656	13735	13813	13892	13971	14049	14128	14206
0,18	14285	14363	14442	14520	14599	14677	14756	14834	14912	14991
0,19	15069	15147	15226	15304	15382	15461	15539	15617	15695	15774
0,20	15852	15930	16008	16086	16165	16243	16321	16399	16477	16555
0,21	16633	16711	16789	16867	16945	17023	17101	17179	17257	17335
0,22	17413	17491	17569	17646	17724	17802	17880	17958	18035	18113
0,23	18191	18269	18346	18424	18502	18579	18657	18734	18812	18889
0,24	18967	19044	19122	19199	19277	19354	19432	19509	19587	19664
0,25	19741	19819	19896	19973	20050	20128	20205	20282	20359	20436
0,26	20514	20591	20668	20745	20822	20899	20976	21053	21130	21207
0,27	21284	21361	21438	21515	21592	21668	21745	21822	21899	21976
0,28	22052	22129	22206	22282	22359	22436	22512	22589	22665	22742
0,29	22818	22895	22971	23048	23124	23201	23277	23353	23430	23506
0,30	23582	23659	23735	23811	23887	23963	24040	24116	24192	24268
0,31	24344	24420	24496	24572	24648	24724	24800	24876	24952	25027
0,32	25103	25179	25255	25330	25406	25482	25558	25633	25709	25784
0,33	25860	25936	26011	26087	26162	26237	26313	26388	26464	26539
0,34	26614	26690	26765	26840	26915	26991	27066	27141	27216	27291
0,35	27366	27441	27516	27591	27666	27741	27816	27891	27966	28040
0,36	28115	28190	28265	28340	28414	28489	28563	28638	28713	28787
0,37	28862	28936	29011	29085	29160	29234	29308	29383	29457	29531
0,38	29605	29680	29754	29828	29902	29976	30050	30124	30198	30272
0,39	30346	30420	30494	30568	30642	30716	30789	30863	30937	31011
0,40	31084	31158	31232	31305	31379	31452	31526	31599	31673	31746
0,41	31819	31893	31966	32039	32113	32186	32259	32332	32405	32478
0,42	32551	32624	32697	32770	32843	32916	32989	33062	33135	33208
0,43	33280	33353	33426	33499	33571	33644	33716	33789	33861	33934
0,44	34006	34079	34151	34223	34296	34368	34440	34512	34585	34657
0,45	34729	34801	34873	34945	35017	35089	35161	35233	35305	35377
0,46	35448	35520	35592	35664	35735	35807	35878	35950	36022	36093
0,47	36164	36236	36307	36379	36450	36521	36593	36664	36735	36806
0,48	36877	36948	37019	37090	37161	37232	37303	37374	37445	37516
0,49	37587	37657	37728	37799	37869	37940	38011	38081	38152	38222
0,50	38292	38363	38433	38504	38574	38644	38714	38785	38855	38925
0,51	38995	39065	39135	39205	39275	39345	39415	39484	39554	39624
0,52	39694	39763	39833	39903	39972	40042	40111	40181	40250	40319
0,53	40389	40458	40527	40597	40666	40735	40804	40873	40942	41011
0,54	41080	41149	41218	41287	41356	41425	41493	41562	41631	41699
0,55	41768	41837	41905	41974	42042	42111	42179	42247	42316	42384
0,56	42452	42520	42588	42657	42725	42793	42861	42929	42997	43064
0,57	43132	43200	43268	43336	43403	43471	43538	43606	43674	43741
0,58	43809	43876	43943	44011	44078	44145	44212	44280	44347	44414
0,59	44481	44548	44615	44682	44749	44816	44882	44949	45016	45083
0,60	45149	45216	45283	45349	45416	45482	45549	45615	45681	45748
0,61	45814	45880	45946	46012	46078	46145	46211	46277	46342	46408
0,62	46474	46540	46606	46672	46737	46803	46869	46934	47000	47065
0,63	47131	47196	47261	47327	47392	47457	47522	47588	47653	47718
0,64	47783	47848	47913	47978	48042	48107	48172	48237	48302	48366
0,65	48431	48495	48560	48624	48689	48753	48818	48882	48946	49010
0,66	49075	49139	49203	49267	49331	49395	49459	49523	49587	49650
0,67	49714	49778	49842	49905	49969	50032	50096	50159	50223	50286
0,68	50350	50413	50476	50539	50602	50666	50729	50792	50855	50918
0,69	50981	51043	51106	51169	51232	51294	51357	51420	51482	51545
0,7	51607	52230	52848	53461	54070	54675	55275	55870	56461	57047
0,8	57629	58206	58778	59346	59909	60467	61021	61570	62114	62653
0,9	63188	63718	64243	64763	65278	65789	66294	66795	67291	67783
1,0	68269	68750	69227	69699	70166	70628	71086	71538	71986	72429
1,1	72867	73300	73729	74152	74571	74986	75395	75800	76200	76595
1,2	76986	77372	77754	78130	78502	78870	79233	79592	79945	80295
1,3	80640	80980	81316	81648	81975	82298	82617	82931	83241	83547
1,4	83849	84146	84439	84728	85013	85294	85571	85844	86113	86378
1,5	86639	86896	87149	87398	87644	87886	88124	88358	88589	88817
1,6	89040	89260	89477	89690	89899	90106	90309	90508	90704	90897
1,7	91087	91273	91457	91637	91814	91988	92159	92327	92492	92655
1,8	92814	92970	93124	93275	93423	93569	93711	93852	93989	94124
1,9	94257	94387	94514	94639	94762	94882	95000	95116	95230	95341
2,0	95450	95557	95662	95764	95865	95964	96060	96155	96247	96338
2,1	96427	96514	96599	96683	96765	96844	96923	96999	97074	97148
2,2	97219	97289	97358	97425	97491	97555	97618	97679	97739	97798
2,3	97855	97911	97966	98019	98072	98123	98173	98221	98269	98315
2,4	98360	98405	98448	98490	98531	98571	98611	98649	98686	98723
2,5	98758	98793	98826	98859	98891	98923	98953	98983	99012	99040
2,6	99068	99095	99121	99146	99171	99195	99219	99241	99264	99285
2,7	99307	99327	99347	99367	99386	99404	99422	99439	99456	99473
2,8	99489	99505	99520	99535	99549	99563	99576	99590	99602	99615
2,9	99627	99639	99650	99661	99672	99682	99692	99702	99712	99721
3,0	99730	99739	99747	99755	99763	99771	99779	99786	99793	99800
3,1	99806	99813	99819	99825	99831	99837	99842	99848	99853	99858
3,2	99863	99867	99872	99876	99880	99885	99889	99892	99896	99900
3,3	99903	99907	99910	99913	99916	99919	99922	99925	99928	99930

3,4: 99933 3,5: 99953 3,6: 99968 3,7: 99978 3,8: 99986 3,891: 99990

[1] Values abridged from *Tables of Normal Probability Functions*, National Bureau of Standards, Applied Mathematics Series 23, Washington, 1953. Reproduction of values on this and the preceding page only by permission of the publishers of the *Geigy Scientific Tables*.

All values conform to the international convention (i.e. 0,1 instead of 0.1).

2 *P* and Integral Between 0 and *c*[1]

where $2P = 1 - 2 \times \int_0^c$

2 P

c	0,000	0,001	0,002	0,003	0,004	0,005	0,006	0,007	0,008	0,009
	0,	0,	0,	0,	0,	0,	0,	0,	0,	0,
0,00	*	99920	99840	99761	99681	99601	99521	99441	99362	99282
0,01	99202	99122	99043	98963	98883	98803	98723	98644	98564	98484
0,02	98404	98325	98245	98165	98085	98005	97926	97846	97766	97686
0,03	97607	97527	97447	97367	97288	97208	97128	97049	96969	96889
0,04	96809	96730	96650	96570	96490	96411	96331	96251	96172	96092
0,05	96012	95933	95853	95773	95694	95614	95534	95455	95375	95295
0,06	95216	95136	95056	94977	94897	94817	94738	94658	94579	94499
0,07	94419	94340	94260	94181	94101	94021	93942	93862	93783	93703
0,08	93624	93544	93465	93385	93306	93226	93147	93067	92988	92908
0,09	92829	92749	92670	92590	92511	92431	92352	92273	92193	92114
0,10	92034	91955	91876	91796	91717	91638	91558	91479	91400	91320
0,11	91241	91162	91082	91003	90924	90845	90765	90686	90607	90528
0,12	90448	90369	90290	90211	90132	90052	89974	89894	89815	89736
0,13	89657	89578	89498	89419	89340	89261	89182	89103	89024	88945
0,14	88866	88787	88708	88629	88550	88471	88392	88313	88234	88155
0,15	88076	87998	87919	87840	87761	87682	87603	87524	87446	87367
0,16	87288	87209	87131	87052	86973	86894	86816	86737	86658	86580
0,17	86501	86422	86344	86265	86187	86108	86029	85951	85872	85794
0,18	85715	85637	85558	85480	85401	85323	85244	85166	85088	85009
0,19	84931	84853	84774	84696	84618	84539	84461	84383	84305	84226
0,20	84148	84070	83992	83914	83835	83757	83679	83601	83523	83445
0,21	83367	83289	83211	83133	83055	82977	82899	82821	82743	82665
0,22	82587	82509	82431	82354	82276	82198	82120	82042	81965	81887
0,23	81809	81731	81654	81576	81498	81421	81343	81266	81188	81111
0,24	81033	80956	80878	80801	80723	80646	80568	80491	80413	80336
0,25	80259	80181	80104	80027	79950	79872	79795	79718	79641	79564
0,26	79486	79409	79332	79255	79178	79101	79024	78947	78870	78793
0,27	78716	78639	78562	78485	78408	78332	78255	78178	78101	78024
0,28	77948	77871	77794	77718	77641	77564	77488	77411	77335	77258
0,29	77182	77105	77029	76952	76876	76799	76723	76647	76570	76494
0,30	76418	76341	76265	76189	76113	76037	75960	75884	75808	75732
0,31	75656	75580	75504	75428	75352	75276	75200	75124	75048	74973
0,32	74897	74821	74745	74670	74594	74518	74442	74367	74291	74216
0,33	74140	74064	73989	73913	73838	73763	73687	73612	73536	73461
0,34	73386	73310	73235	73160	73085	73009	72934	72859	72784	72709
0,35	72634	72559	72484	72409	72334	72259	72184	72109	72034	71960
0,36	71885	71810	71735	71660	71586	71511	71437	71362	71287	71213
0,37	71138	71064	70989	70915	70840	70766	70692	70617	70543	70469
0,38	70395	70320	70246	70172	70098	70024	69950	69876	69802	69728
0,39	69654	69580	69506	69432	69358	69284	69211	69137	69063	68989
0,40	68916	68842	68768	68695	68621	68548	68474	68401	68327	68254
0,41	68181	68107	68034	67961	67887	67814	67741	67668	67595	67522
0,42	67449	67376	67303	67230	67157	67084	67011	66938	66865	66792
0,43	66720	66647	66574	66501	66429	66356	66284	66211	66139	66066
0,44	65994	65921	65849	65777	65704	65632	65560	65488	65415	65343
0,45	65271	65199	65127	65055	64983	64911	64839	64767	64695	64623
0,46	64552	64480	64408	64336	64265	64193	64122	64050	63978	63907
0,47	63836	63764	63693	63621	63550	63479	63407	63336	63265	63194
0,48	63123	63052	62981	62910	62839	62768	62697	62626	62555	62484
0,49	62413	62343	62272	62201	62131	62060	61989	61919	61848	61778
0,50	61708	61637	61567	61496	61426	61356	61286	61215	61145	61075
0,51	61005	60935	60865	60795	60725	60655	60585	60516	60446	60376
0,52	60306	60237	60167	60097	60028	59958	59889	59819	59750	59681
0,53	59611	59542	59473	59403	59334	59265	59196	59127	59058	58989
0,54	58920	58851	58782	58713	58644	58575	58507	58438	58369	58301
0,55	58232	58163	58095	58026	57958	57889	57821	57753	57684	57616
0,56	57548	57480	57412	57343	57275	57207	57139	57071	57003	56936
0,57	56868	56800	56732	56664	56597	56529	56462	56394	56326	56259
0,58	56191	56124	56057	55989	55922	55855	55788	55720	55653	55586
0,59	55519	55452	55385	55318	55251	55184	55118	55051	54984	54917
0,60	54851	54784	54717	54651	54584	54518	54451	54385	54319	54252
0,61	54186	54120	54054	53988	53922	53855	53789	53723	53658	53592
0,62	53526	53460	53394	53328	53263	53197	53131	53066	53000	52935
0,63	52869	52804	52739	52673	52608	52543	52478	52412	52347	52282
0,64	52217	52152	52087	52022	51958	51893	51828	51763	51698	51634
0,65	51569	51505	51440	51376	51311	51247	51182	51118	51054	50990
0,66	50925	50861	50797	50733	50669	50605	50541	50477	50413	50350
0,67	50286	50222	50158	50095	50031	49968	49904	49841	49777	49714
0,68	49650	49587	49524	49461	49398	49334	49271	49208	49145	49082
0,69	49019	48957	48894	48831	48768	48706	48643	48580	48518	48455
0,7	48393	47770	47152	46539	45930	45325	44725	44130	43539	42953
0,8	42371	41794	41222	40654	40091	39533	38979	38430	37886	37347
0,9	36812	36282	35757	35237	34722	34211	33706	33205	32709	32217
1,0	31731	31250	30773	30301	29834	29372	28914	28462	28014	27571
1,1	27133	26700	26271	25848	25429	25014	24605	24200	23800	23405
1,2	23014	22628	22246	21870	21498	21130	20767	20408	20055	19705
1,3	19360	19020	18684	18352	18025	17702	17383	17069	16759	16453
1,4	16151	15854	15561	15272	14987	14706	14429	14156	13887	13622
1,5	13361	13104	12851	12602	12356	12114	11876	11642	11411	11183
1,6	10960	10740	10523	10310	10101	09894	09691	09492	09296	09103
1,7	08913	08727	08543	08363	08186	08012	07841	07673	07508	07345
1,8	07186	07030	06876	06725	06577	06431	06289	06148	06011	05876
1,9	05743	05613	05486	05361	05238	05118	05000	04884	04770	04659
2,0	04550	04443	04338	04236	04135	04036	03940	03845	03753	03662
2,1	03573	03486	03401	03317	03235	03156	03077	03001	02926	02852
2,2	02781	02711	02642	02575	02509	02445	02382	02321	02261	02202
2,3	02145	02089	02034	01981	01928	01877	01827	01779	01731	01685
2,4	01640	01595	01552	01510	01469	01429	01389	01351	01314	01277
2,5	01242	01207	01174	01141	01109	01077	01047	01017	00988	00960
2,6	00932	00905	00879	00854	00829	00805	00781	00759	00736	00715
2,7	00693	00673	00653	00633	00614	00596	00578	00561	00544	00527
2,8	00511	00495	00480	00465	00451	00437	00424	00410	00398	00385
2,9	00373	00361	00350	00339	00328	00318	00308	00298	00288	00279
3,0	00270	00261	00253	00245	00237	00229	00221	00214	00207	00200
3,1	00194	00187	00181	00175	00169	00163	00158	00152	00147	00142
3,2	00137	00133	00128	00124	00120	00115	00111	00108	00104	00100
3,3	00097	00093	00090	00087	00084	00081	00078	00075	00072	00070

3,4: 00067 3,5: 00047 3,6: 00032 3,7: 00022 3,8: 00014 3,891: 00010

$\int_0^c$

c	0,000	0,001	0,002	0,003	0,004	0,005	0,006	0,007	0,008	0,009
	0,	0,	0,	0,	0,	0,	0,	0,	0,	0,
0,00	00000	00040	00080	00120	00160	00200	00240	00280	00319	00359
0,01	00399	00439	00479	00519	00559	00599	00639	00678	00718	00758
0,02	00798	00838	00878	00918	00958	00998	01037	01077	01117	01157
0,03	01197	01237	01277	01317	01356	01396	01436	01476	01516	01556
0,04	01596	01635	01675	01715	01755	01795	01835	01875	01914	01954
0,05	01994	02034	02074	02114	02153	02193	02233	02273	02313	02353
0,06	02392	02432	02472	02512	02552	02592	02631	02671	02711	02751
0,07	02791	02830	02870	02910	02950	02990	03029	03069	03109	03149
0,08	03188	03228	03268	03308	03347	03387	03427	03467	03506	03546
0,09	03586	03626	03665	03705	03745	03785	03824	03864	03904	03943
0,10	03983	04023	04062	04102	04142	04181	04221	04261	04300	04340
0,11	04380	04419	04459	04499	04538	04578	04618	04657	04697	04736
0,12	04776	04816	04855	04895	04934	04974	05013	05053	05093	05132
0,13	05172	05211	05251	05291	05330	05370	05409	05449	05488	05528
0,14	05567	05607	05646	05686	05725	05765	05804	05844	05883	05923
0,15	05962	06001	06041	06080	06120	06159	06199	06238	06277	06317
0,16	06356	06396	06435	06474	06514	06553	06592	06632	06671	06710
0,17	06750	06789	06828	06868	06907	06946	06986	07025	07064	07103
0,18	07143	07182	07221	07260	07300	07339	07378	07417	07456	07496
0,19	07535	07574	07613	07652	07691	07731	07770	07809	07848	07887
0,20	07926	07965	08004	08043	08083	08122	08161	08200	08239	08278
0,21	08317	08356	08395	08434	08473	08512	08551	08590	08629	08668
0,22	08707	08746	08785	08823	08862	08901	08940	08979	09018	09057
0,23	09096	09135	09173	09212	09251	09290	09329	09367	09406	09445
0,24	09484	09522	09561	09600	09639	09677	09716	09755	09794	09832
0,25	09871	09910	09948	09987	10025	10064	10103	10141	10180	10218
0,26	10257	10296	10334	10373	10411	10450	10488	10527	10565	10604
0,27	10642	10681	10719	10758	10796	10834	10873	10911	10950	10988
0,28	11026	11065	11103	11141	11180	11218	11256	11295	11333	11371
0,29	11409	11448	11486	11524	11562	11601	11639	11677	11715	11753
0,30	11791	11830	11868	11906	11944	11982	12020	12058	12096	12134
0,31	12172	12210	12248	12286	12324	12362	12400	12438	12476	12514
0,32	12552	12590	12628	12665	12703	12741	12779	12817	12855	12892
0,33	12930	12968	13006	13044	13081	13119	13157	13194	13232	13270
0,34	13307	13345	13383	13420	13458	13496	13533	13571	13608	13646
0,35	13683	13721	13758	13796	13833	13871	13908	13946	13983	14020
0,36	14058	14095	14133	14170	14207	14245	14282	14319	14357	14394
0,37	14431	14468	14506	14543	14580	14617	14654	14692	14729	14766
0,38	14803	14840	14877	14914	14951	14988	15025	15062	15099	15136
0,39	15173	15210	15247	15284	15321	15358	15395	15432	15469	15506
0,40	15542	15579	15616	15653	15690	15726	15763	15800	15837	15873
0,41	15910	15947	15983	16020	16057	16093	16130	16166	16203	16239
0,42	16276	16312	16349	16385	16422	16458	16495	16531	16568	16604
0,43	16640	16677	16713	16750	16786	16822	16858	16895	16931	16967
0,44	17003	17040	17076	17112	17148	17184	17220	17256	17293	17329
0,45	17365	17401	17437	17473	17509	17545	17581	17617	17653	17689
0,46	17724	17760	17796	17832	17868	17904	17939	17975	18011	18047
0,47	18082	18118	18154	18190	18225	18261	18297	18332	18368	18403
0,48	18439	18474	18510	18545	18581	18616	18652	18687	18723	18758
0,49	18794	18829	18864	18900	18935	18970	19006	19041	19076	19111
0,50	19146	19182	19217	19252	19287	19322	19357	19393	19428	19463
0,51	19498	19533	19568	19603	19638	19673	19708	19742	19777	19812
0,52	19847	19882	19917	19952	19986	20021	20056	20091	20125	20160
0,53	20195	20229	20264	20299	20333	20368	20402	20437	20471	20506
0,54	20540	20575	20609	20644	20678	20713	20747	20781	20816	20850
0,55	20884	20919	20953	20987	21021	21056	21090	21124	21158	21192
0,56	21226	21260	21294	21329	21363	21397	21431	21465	21499	21532
0,57	21566	21600	21634	21668	21702	21736	21769	21803	21837	21871
0,58	21905	21938	21972	22006	22039	22073	22106	22140	22174	22207
0,59	22241	22274	22308	22341	22375	22408	22441	22475	22508	22542
0,60	22575	22608	22642	22675	22708	22741	22775	22808	22841	22874
0,61	22907	22940	22973	23006	23039	23073	23106	23139	23171	23204
0,62	23237	23270	23303	23336	23369	23402	23435	23467	23500	23533
0,63	23566	23598	23631	23664	23696	23729	23761	23794	23827	23859
0,64	23892	23924	23957	23989	24021	24054	24086	24119	24151	24183
0,65	24216	24248	24280	24312	24345	24377	24409	24441	24473	24505
0,66	24538	24570	24602	24634	24666	24698	24730	24762	24794	24825
0,67	24857	24889	24921	24953	24985	25016	25048	25080	25112	25143
0,68	25175	25207	25238	25270	25301	25333	25365	25396	25428	25459
0,69	25491	25522	25553	25585	25616	25647	25679	25710	25741	25773
0,7	25804	26115	26424	26731	27035	27338	27638	27935	28231	28524
0,8	28815	29103	29389	29673	29955	30234	30511	30785	31057	31327
0,9	31594	31859	32122	32382	32639	32895	33147	33398	33646	33892
1,0	34135	34375	34614	34850	35083	35314	35543	35769	35993	36215
1,1	36434	36650	36865	37076	37286	37493	37698	37900	38100	38298
1,2	38493	38686	38877	39065	39251	39435	39617	39796	39973	40148
1,3	40320	40490	40658	40824	40988	41149	41309	41466	41621	41774
1,4	41925	42073	42220	42364	42507	42647	42786	42922	43057	43189
1,5	43320	43448	43575	43699	43822	43943	44062	44179	44295	44409
1,6	44520	44630	44739	44845	44950	45053	45155	45254	45352	45449
1,7	45544	45637	45729	45819	45907	45994	46080	46164	46246	46328
1,8	46407	46485	46562	46638	46712	46785	46856	46926	46995	47062
1,9	47129	47194	47257	47320	47381	47441	47500	47558	47615	47671
2,0	47725	47779	47831	47882	47933	47982	48030	48078	48124	48169
2,1	48214	48257	48300	48342	48383	48422	48462	48500	48537	48574
2,2	48610	48645	48679	48713	48746	48778	48809	48840	48870	48899
2,3	48928	48956	48983	49010	49036	49062	49087	49111	49135	49158
2,4	49180	49203	49224	49245	49266	49286	49306	49325	49343	49362
2,5	49379	49397	49413	49430	49446	49462	49477	49492	49506	49520
2,6	49534	49548	49561	49573	49586	49598	49610	49621	49632	49643
2,7	49654	49664	49674	49684	49693	49702	49711	49720	49728	49737
2,8	49745	49753	49760	49768	49775	49782	49788	49795	49801	49808
2,9	49814	49820	49825	49831	49836	49841	49846	49851	49856	49861
3,0	49865	49870	49874	49878	49882	49886	49890	49893	49897	49900
3,1	49903	49907	49910	49913	49916	49919	49921	49924	49927	49929
3,2	49932	49934	49936	49938	49940	49943	49945	49946	49948	49950
3,3	49952	49954	49955	49957	49958	49960	49961	49963	49964	49965

3,4: 49967 3,5: 49977 3,6: 49984 3,7: 49989 3,8: 49993 3,891: 49995

[1] Calculated from *Tables of Normal Probability Functions*, National Bureau of Standards, Applied Mathematics Series 23, Washington, 1953. Reproduction only by permission of the publishers of the *Geigy Scientific Tables*.

* 1,00000.

All values conform to the international convention (i.e. 0,1 instead of 0.1).

Density function[1] $f(c)$

$\lvert c \rvert$	0,000	0,001	0,002	0,003	0,004	0,005	0,006	0,007	0,008	0,009
	0,	0,	0,	0,	0,	0,	0,	0,	0,	0,
0,00	39894	39894	39894	39894	39894	39894	39894	39893	39893	39893
0,01	39892	39892	39891	39891	39890	39890	39889	39888	39888	39887
0,02	39886	39885	39885	39884	39883	39882	39881	39880	39879	39877
0,03	39876	39875	39874	39873	39871	39870	39868	39867	39865	39864
0,04	39862	39861	39859	39857	39856	39854	39852	39850	39848	39846
0,05	39844	39842	39840	39838	39836	39834	39832	39829	39827	39825
0,06	39822	39820	39818	39815	39813	39810	39807	39805	39802	39799
0,07	39797	39794	39791	39788	39785	39782	39779	39776	39773	39770
0,08	39767	39764	39760	39757	39754	39750	39747	39744	39740	39737
0,09	39733	39729	39726	39722	39718	39715	39711	39707	39703	39699
0,10	39695	39691	39687	39683	39679	39675	39671	39667	39662	39658
0,11	39654	39649	39645	39640	39636	39631	39627	39622	39617	39613
0,12	39608	39603	39598	39594	39589	39584	39579	39574	39569	39564
0,13	39559	39553	39548	39543	39538	39532	39527	39522	39516	39511
0,14	39505	39500	39494	39488	39483	39477	39471	39466	39460	39454
0,15	39448	39442	39436	39430	39424	39418	39412	39406	39399	39393
0,16	39387	39381	39374	39368	39361	39355	39348	39342	39335	39329
0,17	39322	39315	39308	39302	39295	39288	39281	39274	39267	39260
0,18	39253	39246	39239	39232	39225	39217	39210	39203	39195	39188
0,19	39181	39173	39166	39158	39151	39143	39135	39128	39120	39112
0,20	39104	39096	39089	39081	39073	39065	39057	39049	39041	39032
0,21	39024	39016	39008	38999	38991	38983	38974	38966	38957	38949
0,22	38940	38932	38923	38915	38906	38897	38888	38880	38871	38862
0,23	38853	38844	38835	38826	38817	38808	38799	38789	38780	38771
0,24	38762	38752	38743	38734	38724	38715	38705	38696	38686	38676
0,25	38667	38657	38647	38638	38628	38618	38608	38598	38588	38578
0,26	38568	38558	38548	38538	38528	38518	38508	38497	38487	38477
0,27	38466	38456	38445	38435	38424	38414	38403	38393	38382	38371
0,28	38361	38350	38339	38328	38317	38306	38296	38285	38274	38263
0,29	38251	38240	38229	38218	38207	38196	38184	38173	38162	38150
0,30	38139	38127	38116	38104	38093	38081	38070	38058	38046	38034
0,31	38023	38011	37999	37987	37975	37963	37951	37939	37927	37915
0,32	37903	37891	37879	37867	37854	37842	37830	37817	37805	37793
0,33	37780	37768	37755	37743	37730	37717	37705	37692	37679	37667
0,34	37654	37641	37628	37615	37602	37589	37576	37563	37550	37537
0,35	37524	37511	37498	37484	37471	37458	37445	37431	37418	37405
0,36	37391	37378	37364	37351	37337	37323	37310	37296	37282	37269
0,37	37255	37241	37227	37213	37199	37186	37172	37158	37144	37129
0,38	37115	37101	37087	37073	37059	37044	37030	37016	37002	36987
0,39	36973	36958	36944	36929	36915	36900	36886	36871	36856	36842
0,40	36827	36812	36797	36783	36768	36753	36738	36723	36708	36693
0,41	36678	36663	36648	36633	36618	36603	36587	36572	36557	36542
0,42	36526	36511	36496	36480	36465	36449	36434	36418	36403	36387
0,43	36371	36356	36340	36324	36309	36293	36277	36261	36245	36229
0,44	36213	36198	36182	36166	36150	36133	36117	36101	36085	36069
0,45	36053	36036	36020	36004	35988	35971	35955	35938	35922	35906
0,46	35889	35873	35856	35839	35823	35806	35789	35773	35756	35739
0,47	35723	35706	35689	35672	35655	35638	35621	35604	35587	35570
0,48	35553	35536	35519	35502	35485	35468	35450	35433	35416	35399
0,49	35381	35364	35347	35329	35312	35294	35277	35259	35242	35224
0,50	35207	35189	35171	35154	35136	35118	35100	35083	35065	35047
0,51	35029	35011	34993	34975	34958	34940	34922	34904	34885	34867
0,52	34849	34831	34813	34795	34777	34758	34740	34722	34703	34685
0,53	34667	34648	34630	34612	34593	34575	34556	34538	34519	34500
0,54	34482	34463	34445	34426	34407	34388	34370	34351	34332	34313
0,55	34294	34276	34257	34238	34219	34200	34181	34162	34143	34124
0,56	34105	34085	34066	34047	34028	34009	33990	33970	33951	33932
0,57	33912	33893	33874	33854	33835	33815	33796	33777	33757	33738
0,58	33718	33698	33679	33659	33640	33620	33600	33581	33561	33541
0,59	33521	33502	33482	33462	33442	33422	33402	33382	33362	33342
0,60	33322	33302	33282	33262	33242	33222	33202	33182	33162	33142
0,61	33121	33101	33081	33061	33040	33020	33000	32980	32959	32939
0,62	32918	32898	32878	32857	32837	32816	32796	32775	32754	32734
0,63	32713	32693	32672	32651	32631	32610	32589	32569	32548	32527
0,64	32506	32485	32465	32444	32423	32402	32381	32360	32339	32318
0,65	32297	32276	32255	32234	32213	32192	32171	32150	32129	32108
0,66	32086	32065	32044	32023	32002	31980	31959	31938	31916	31895
0,67	31874	31852	31831	31810	31788	31767	31745	31724	31702	31681
0,68	31659	31638	31616	31595	31573	31551	31530	31508	31487	31465
0,69	31443	31421	31400	31378	31356	31334	31313	31291	31269	31247

$\lvert c \rvert$	0,000	0,001	0,002	0,003	0,004	0,005	0,006	0,007	0,008	0,009
	0,	0,	0,	0,	0,	0,	0,	0,	0,	0,
0,70	31225	31204	31182	31160	31138	31116	31094	31072	31050	31028
0,71	31006	30984	30962	30940	30918	30896	30874	30852	30829	30807
0,72	30785	30763	30741	30719	30696	30674	30652	30630	30607	30585
0,73	30563	30540	30518	30496	30473	30451	30429	30406	30384	30361
0,74	30339	30316	30294	30272	30249	30227	30204	30181	30159	30136
0,75	30114	30091	30069	30046	30023	30001	29978	29955	29933	29910
0,76	29887	29865	29842	29819	29796	29774	29751	29728	29705	29682
0,77	29659	29637	29614	29591	29568	29545	29522	29499	29476	29453
0,78	29431	29408	29385	29362	29339	29316	29293	29270	29246	29223
0,79	29200	29177	29154	29131	29108	29085	29062	29039	29015	28992
0,80	28969	28946	28923	28900	28876	28853	28830	28807	28783	28760
0,81	28737	28714	28690	28667	28644	28620	28597	28574	28550	28527
0,82	28504	28480	28457	28433	28410	28387	28363	28340	28316	28293
0,83	28269	28246	28223	28199	28176	28152	28129	28105	28081	28058
0,84	28034	28011	27987	27964	27940	27917	27893	27869	27846	27822
0,85	27798	27775	27751	27728	27704	27680	27657	27633	27609	27586
0,86	27562	27538	27514	27491	27467	27443	27419	27396	27372	27348
0,87	27324	27301	27277	27253	27229	27205	27182	27158	27134	27110
0,88	27086	27063	27039	27015	26991	26967	26943	26919	26896	26872
0,89	26848	26824	26800	26776	26752	26728	26704	26680	26656	26632
0,90	26609	26585	26561	26537	26513	26489	26465	26441	26417	26393
0,91	26369	26345	26321	26297	26273	26249	26225	26201	26177	26153
0,92	26129	26105	26081	26056	26032	26008	25984	25960	25936	25912
0,93	25888	25864	25840	25816	25792	25768	25744	25719	25695	25671
0,94	25647	25623	25599	25575	25551	25527	25502	25478	25454	25430
0,95	25406	25382	25358	25333	25309	25285	25261	25237	25213	25189
0,96	25164	25140	25116	25092	25068	25044	25019	24995	24971	24947
0,97	24923	24899	24874	24850	24826	24802	24778	24754	24729	24705
0,98	24681	24657	24633	24608	24584	24560	24536	24512	24487	24463
0,99	24439	24415	24391	24366	24342	24318	24294	24270	24245	24221
1,00	24197	24173	24149	24124	24100	24076	24052	24028	24003	23979
1,01	23955	23931	23907	23883	23858	23834	23810	23786	23762	23737
1,02	23713	23689	23665	23641	23616	23592	23568	23544	23520	23496
1,03	23471	23447	23423	23399	23375	23351	23326	23302	23278	23254
1,04	23230	23206	23181	23157	23133	23109	23085	23061	23036	23012
1,05	22988	22964	22940	22916	22892	22868	22843	22819	22795	22771
1,06	22747	22723	22699	22675	22651	22626	22602	22578	22554	22530
1,07	22506	22482	22458	22434	22410	22386	22362	22338	22313	22289
1,08	22265	22241	22217	22193	22169	22145	22121	22097	22073	22049
1,09	22025	22001	21977	21953	21929	21905	21881	21857	21833	21809
1,1	21785	21546	21307	21069	20831	20594	20357	20121	19886	19652
1,2	19419	19186	18954	18724	18494	18265	18037	17810	17585	17360
1,3	17137	16915	16694	16474	16256	16038	15822	15608	15395	15183
1,4	14973	14764	14556	14350	14146	13943	13742	13542	13344	13147
1,5	12952	12758	12566	12376	12188	12001	11816	11632	11450	11270
1,6	11092	10915	10741	10567	10396	10226	10059	09893	09728	09566
1,7	09405	09246	09089	08933	08780	08628	08478	08329	08183	08038
1,8	07895	07754	07614	07477	07341	07206	07074	06943	06814	06687
1,9	06562	06438	06316	06195	06077	05959	05844	05730	05618	05508
2,0	05399	05292	05186	05082	04980	04879	04780	04682	04586	04491
2,1	04398	04307	04217	04128	04041	03955	03871	03788	03706	03626
2,2	03547	03470	03394	03319	03246	03174	03103	03034	02965	02898
2,3	02833	02768	02705	02643	02582	02522	02463	02406	02349	02294
2,4	02239	02186	02134	02083	02033	01984	01936	01888	01842	01797
2,5	01753	01709	01667	01625	01585	01545	01506	01468	01431	01394
2,6	01358	01323	01289	01256	01223	01191	01160	01130	01100	01071
2,7	01042	01014	00987	00961	00935	00909	00885	00861	00837	00814
2,8	00792	00770	00748	00727	00707	00687	00668	00649	00631	00613
2,9	00595	00578	00562	00545	00530	00514	00499	00485	00470	00457
3,0	00443	00430	00417	00405	00393	00381	00370	00358	00348	00337
3,1	00327	00317	00307	00298	00288	00279	00271	00262	00254	00246
3,2	00238	00231	00224	00216	00210	00203	00196	00190	00184	00178
3,3	00172	00167	00161	00156	00151	00146	00141	00136	00132	00127
3,4	00123	00119	00115	00111	00107	00104	00100	00097	00094	00090
3,5	00087	00084	00081	00079	00076	00073	00071	00068	00066	00063
3,6	00061	00059	00057	00055	00053	00051	00049	00047	00046	00044
3,7	00042	00041	00039	00038	00037	00035	00034	00033	00031	00030
3,8	00029	00028	00027	00026	00025	00024	00023	00022	00021	00021
3,9	00020	00019	00018	00018	00017	00016	00016	00015	00014	00014
4,0	00013	00013	00012	00012	00011	00011	00011	00010	00010	00009

Probability[2] $2P \rightarrow c$, where $2P = 2 \times \int_c^\infty$

$2P$	0,00	0,01	0,02	0,03	0,04	0,05	0,06	0,07	0,08	0,09
						$\lvert c \rvert$				
0,0	∞	2,575829	2,326348	2,170090	2,053749	1,959964	1,880794	1,811911	1,750686	1,695398
0,1	1,644854	1,598193	1,554774	1,514102	1,475791	1,439531	1,405072	1,372204	1,340755	1,310579
0,2	1,281552	1,253565	1,226528	1,200359	1,174987	1,150349	1,126391	1,103063	1,080319	1,058122
0,3	1,036433	1,015222	0,994458	0,974114	0,954165	0,934589	0,915365	0,896473	0,877896	0,859617
0,4	0,841621	0,823894	0,806421	0,789192	0,772193	0,755415	0,738847	0,722479	0,706303	0,690309
0,5	0,674490	0,658838	0,643345	0,628006	0,612813	0,597760	0,582842	0,568051	0,553385	0,538836
0,6	0,524401	0,510073	0,495850	0,481727	0,467699	0,453762	0,439913	0,426148	0,412463	0,398855
0,7	0,385320	0,371856	0,358459	0,345126	0,331853	0,318639	0,305481	0,292375	0,279319	0,266311
0,8	0,253347	0,240426	0,227545	0,214702	0,201893	0,189118	0,176374	0,163658	0,150969	0,138304
0,9	0,125661	0,113039	0,100434	0,087845	0,075270	0,062707	0,050154	0,037608	0,025069	0,012533

Very small values of P

$2P$	0,004	0,003	0,002	0,001	0,0001	0,00001	0,000001	0,0000001	0,00000001	0,000000001
c	2,878162	2,967738	3,090233	3,290527	3,89059	4,41717	4,89164	5,32672	5,73073	6,10941

[1] Values abridged from *Tables of Normal Probability Functions*, National Bureau of Standards, Applied Mathematics Series 23, Washington, 1953. Reproduction only by permission of the publishers of the *Geigy Scientific Tables.*

[2] Fisher and Yates, *Statistical Tables for Biological, Agricultural and Medical Research*, 6th ed., Longman, Harlow, 1974, page 44. Reprinted by kind permission of the authors and publishers.

All values conform to the international convention (i.e. 0,1 instead of 0.1).

The Student Distribution* $\nu = 1\text{–}50$

P = integral between $-\infty$ and $-t_0$ = integral between t_0 and ∞. The values in the table are the t_0-values

$2P$	0,999	0,998	0,99	0,98	0,95	0,90	0,80	0,70	0,60	0,50	0,40	0,30	0,20	0,10	0,05	0,02	0,01	0,002	0,001
P	0,4995	0,499	0,495	0,49	0,475	0,45	0,40	0,35	0,30	0,25	0,20	0,15	0,10	0,05	0,025	0,01	0,005	0,001	0,0005
ν																			
1	0,0016	0,0031	0,0157	0,0314	0,0787	0,1584	0,3249	0,5095	0,7265	1,0000	1,3764	1,9626	3,0777	6,3138	12,7062	31,8207	63,6574	318,3088	636,6192
2	0,0014	0,0028	0,0141	0,0283	0,0708	0,1421	0,2887	0,4447	0,6172	0,8165	1,0607	1,3862	1,8856	2,9200	4,3027	6,9646	9,9248	22,3271	31,5991
3	0,0014	0,0027	0,0136	0,0272	0,0681	0,1366	0,2767	0,4242	0,5844	0,7649	0,9785	1,2498	1,6377	2,3534	3,1824	4,5407	5,8409	10,2145	12,9240
4	0,0013	0,0027	0,0133	0,0267	0,0667	0,1338	0,2707	0,4142	0,5686	0,7407	0,9410	1,1896	1,5332	2,1318	2,7764	3,7469	4,6041	7,1732	8,6103
5	0,0013	0,0026	0,0132	0,0263	0,0659	0,1322	0,2672	0,4082	0,5594	0,7267	0,9195	1,1558	1,4759	2,0150	2,5706	3,3649	4,0321	5,8934	6,8688
6	0,0013	0,0026	0,0131	0,0261	0,0654	0,1311	0,2648	0,4043	0,5534	0,7176	0,9057	1,1342	1,4398	1,9432	2,4469	3,1427	3,7074	5,2076	5,9588
7	0,0013	0,0026	0,0130	0,0260	0,0650	0,1303	0,2632	0,4015	0,5491	0,7111	0,8960	1,1192	1,4149	1,8946	2,3646	2,9980	3,4995	4,7853	5,4079
8	0,0013	0,0026	0,0129	0,0259	0,0647	0,1297	0,2619	0,3995	0,5459	0,7064	0,8889	1,1081	1,3968	1,8595	2,3060	2,8965	3,3554	4,5008	5,0413
9	0,0013	0,0026	0,0129	0,0258	0,0645	0,1293	0,2610	0,3979	0,5435	0,7027	0,8834	1,0997	1,3839	1,8331	2,2622	2,8214	3,2498	4,2968	4,7809
10	0,0013	0,0026	0,0129	0,0257	0,0643	0,1289	0,2602	0,3966	0,5415	0,6998	0,8791	1,0931	1,3722	1,8125	2,2281	2,7638	3,1693	4,1437	4,5869
11	0,0013	0,0026	0,0128	0,0256	0,0642	0,1286	0,2596	0,3956	0,5399	0,6974	0,8755	1,0877	1,3634	1,7959	2,2010	2,7181	3,1058	4,0247	4,4370
12	0,0013	0,0026	0,0128	0,0256	0,0640	0,1283	0,2590	0,3947	0,5386	0,6955	0,8726	1,0832	1,3562	1,7823	2,1788	2,6810	3,0545	3,9296	4,3178
13	0,0013	0,0026	0,0128	0,0256	0,0639	0,1281	0,2586	0,3940	0,5375	0,6938	0,8702	1,0795	1,3502	1,7709	2,1604	2,6503	3,0123	3,8520	4,2208
14	0,0013	0,0026	0,0128	0,0255	0,0638	0,1280	0,2582	0,3933	0,5366	0,6924	0,8681	1,0763	1,3450	1,7613	2,1448	2,6245	2,9768	3,7874	4,1405
15	0,0013	0,0025	0,0127	0,0255	0,0638	0,1278	0,2579	0,3928	0,5357	0,6912	0,8662	1,0735	1,3406	1,7531	2,1315	2,6025	2,9467	3,7328	4,0728
16	0,0013	0,0025	0,0127	0,0255	0,0637	0,1277	0,2576	0,3923	0,5350	0,6901	0,8647	1,0711	1,3368	1,7459	2,1199	2,5835	2,9208	3,6862	4,0150
17	0,0013	0,0025	0,0127	0,0254	0,0636	0,1276	0,2573	0,3919	0,5344	0,6892	0,8633	1,0690	1,3334	1,7396	2,1098	2,5669	2,8982	3,6458	3,9651
18	0,0013	0,0025	0,0127	0,0254	0,0636	0,1274	0,2571	0,3915	0,5338	0,6884	0,8620	1,0672	1,3304	1,7341	2,1009	2,5524	2,8784	3,6105	3,9216
19	0,0013	0,0025	0,0127	0,0254	0,0635	0,1274	0,2569	0,3912	0,5333	0,6876	0,8610	1,0655	1,3277	1,7291	2,0930	2,5395	2,8609	3,5794	3,8834
20	0,0013	0,0025	0,0127	0,0254	0,0635	0,1273	0,2567	0,3909	0,5329	0,6870	0,8600	1,0640	1,3253	1,7247	2,0860	2,5280	2,8453	3,5518	3,8495
21	0,0013	0,0025	0,0127	0,0254	0,0635	0,1272	0,2566	0,3906	0,5325	0,6864	0,8591	1,0627	1,3232	1,7207	2,0796	2,5176	2,8314	3,5272	3,8193
22	0,0013	0,0025	0,0127	0,0254	0,0634	0,1271	0,2564	0,3904	0,5321	0,6858	0,8583	1,0614	1,3212	1,7171	2,0739	2,5083	2,8188	3,5050	3,7921
23	0,0013	0,0025	0,0127	0,0253	0,0634	0,1271	0,2563	0,3902	0,5317	0,6853	0,8575	1,0603	1,3195	1,7139	2,0687	2,4999	2,8073	3,4850	3,7676
24	0,0013	0,0025	0,0127	0,0253	0,0634	0,1270	0,2562	0,3900	0,5314	0,6848	0,8569	1,0593	1,3178	1,7109	2,0639	2,4922	2,7969	3,4668	3,7454
25	0,0013	0,0025	0,0127	0,0253	0,0633	0,1269	0,2561	0,3898	0,5312	0,6844	0,8562	1,0584	1,3163	1,7081	2,0595	2,4851	2,7874	3,4502	3,7251
26	0,0013	0,0025	0,0127	0,0253	0,0633	0,1269	0,2560	0,3896	0,5309	0,6840	0,8557	1,0575	1,3150	1,7056	2,0555	2,4786	2,7787	3,4350	3,7066
27	0,0013	0,0025	0,0126	0,0253	0,0633	0,1268	0,2559	0,3894	0,5306	0,6837	0,8551	1,0567	1,3137	1,7033	2,0518	2,4727	2,7707	3,4210	3,6896
28	0,0013	0,0025	0,0126	0,0253	0,0633	0,1268	0,2558	0,3893	0,5304	0,6834	0,8546	1,0560	1,3125	1,7011	2,0484	2,4671	2,7633	3,4082	3,6739
29	0,0013	0,0025	0,0126	0,0253	0,0633	0,1268	0,2557	0,3892	0,5302	0,6830	0,8542	1,0553	1,3114	1,6991	2,0452	2,4620	2,7564	3,3962	3,6594
30	0,0013	0,0025	0,0126	0,0253	0,0632	0,1267	0,2556	0,3890	0,5300	0,6828	0,8538	1,0547	1,3104	1,6973	2,0423	2,4573	2,7500	3,3852	3,6460
31	0,0013	0,0025	0,0126	0,0253	0,0632	0,1267	0,2555	0,3889	0,5298	0,6825	0,8534	1,0541	1,3095	1,6955	2,0395	2,4528	2,7440	3,3749	3,6335
32	0,0013	0,0025	0,0126	0,0253	0,0632	0,1267	0,2555	0,3888	0,5297	0,6822	0,8530	1,0535	1,3086	1,6939	2,0369	2,4487	2,7385	3,3653	3,6218
33	0,0013	0,0025	0,0126	0,0253	0,0632	0,1266	0,2554	0,3887	0,5295	0,6820	0,8526	1,0530	1,3077	1,6924	2,0345	2,4448	2,7333	3,3563	3,6109
34	0,0013	0,0025	0,0126	0,0253	0,0632	0,1266	0,2553	0,3886	0,5294	0,6818	0,8523	1,0525	1,3070	1,6909	2,0322	2,4411	2,7284	3,3479	3,6007
35	0,0013	0,0025	0,0126	0,0252	0,0632	0,1266	0,2553	0,3885	0,5292	0,6816	0,8520	1,0520	1,3062	1,6896	2,0301	2,4377	2,7238	3,3400	3,5911
36	0,0013	0,0025	0,0126	0,0252	0,0631	0,1266	0,2552	0,3884	0,5291	0,6814	0,8517	1,0516	1,3055	1,6883	2,0281	2,4345	2,7195	3,3326	3,5821
37	0,0013	0,0025	0,0126	0,0252	0,0631	0,1265	0,2552	0,3883	0,5289	0,6812	0,8514	1,0512	1,3049	1,6871	2,0262	2,4314	2,7154	3,3256	3,5737
38	0,0013	0,0025	0,0126	0,0252	0,0631	0,1265	0,2551	0,3882	0,5288	0,6810	0,8512	1,0508	1,3042	1,6860	2,0244	2,4286	2,7116	3,3190	3,5657
39	0,0013	0,0025	0,0126	0,0252	0,0631	0,1265	0,2551	0,3882	0,5287	0,6808	0,8509	1,0504	1,3036	1,6849	2,0227	2,4258	2,7079	3,3128	3,5581
40	0,0013	0,0025	0,0126	0,0252	0,0631	0,1265	0,2550	0,3881	0,5286	0,6807	0,8507	1,0500	1,3031	1,6839	2,0211	2,4233	2,7045	3,3069	3,5510
41	0,0013	0,0025	0,0126	0,0252	0,0631	0,1264	0,2550	0,3880	0,5285	0,6805	0,8505	1,0497	1,3025	1,6829	2,0195	2,4208	2,7012	3,3013	3,5442
42	0,0013	0,0025	0,0126	0,0252	0,0631	0,1264	0,2550	0,3880	0,5284	0,6804	0,8503	1,0494	1,3020	1,6820	2,0181	2,4185	2,6981	3,2960	3,5377
43	0,0013	0,0025	0,0126	0,0252	0,0631	0,1264	0,2549	0,3879	0,5283	0,6802	0,8501	1,0491	1,3016	1,6811	2,0167	2,4163	2,6951	3,2909	3,5316
44	0,0013	0,0025	0,0126	0,0252	0,0631	0,1264	0,2549	0,3878	0,5282	0,6801	0,8499	1,0488	1,3011	1,6802	2,0154	2,4141	2,6923	3,2861	3,5258
45	0,0013	0,0025	0,0126	0,0252	0,0631	0,1264	0,2549	0,3878	0,5281	0,6800	0,8497	1,0485	1,3006	1,6794	2,0141	2,4121	2,6896	3,2815	3,5203
46	0,0013	0,0025	0,0126	0,0252	0,0630	0,1264	0,2548	0,3877	0,5281	0,6799	0,8495	1,0483	1,3002	1,6787	2,0129	2,4102	2,6870	3,2771	3,5150
47	0,0013	0,0025	0,0126	0,0252	0,0630	0,1263	0,2548	0,3877	0,5280	0,6797	0,8493	1,0480	1,2998	1,6779	2,0117	2,4083	2,6846	3,2729	3,5099
48	0,0013	0,0025	0,0126	0,0252	0,0630	0,1263	0,2548	0,3876	0,5279	0,6796	0,8492	1,0478	1,2994	1,6772	2,0106	2,4066	2,6822	3,2689	3,5051
49	0,0013	0,0025	0,0126	0,0252	0,0630	0,1263	0,2547	0,3876	0,5278	0,6795	0,8490	1,0475	1,2991	1,6766	2,0096	2,4049	2,6800	3,2651	3,5004
50	0,0013	0,0025	0,0126	0,0252	0,0630	0,1263	0,2547	0,3875	0,5278	0,6794	0,8489	1,0473	1,2987	1,6759	2,0086	2,4033	2,6778	3,2614	3,4960

All values conform to the international convention (i.e. 0,1 instead of 0.1).

The Student Distribution* $\nu = 51\text{–}100$

P = integral between $-\infty$ and $-t_0$ = integral between t_0 and ∞. The values in the table are the t_0-values

2 P	0,999	0,998	0,99	0,98	0,95	0,90	0,80	0,70	0,60	0,50	0,40	0,30	0,20	0,10	0,05	0,02	0,01	0,002	0,001
P	0,4995	0,499	0,495	0,49	0,475	0,45	0,40	0,35	0,30	0,25	0,20	0,15	0,10	0,05	0,025	0,01	0,005	0,001	0,0005
ν																			
51	0,0013	0,0025	0,0126	0,0252	0,0630	0,1263	0,2547	0,3875	0,5277	0,6793	0,8487	1,0471	1,2984	1,6753	2,0076	2,4017	2,6757	3,2579	3,4918
52	0,0013	0,0025	0,0126	0,0252	0,0630	0,1263	0,2546	0,3875	0,5276	0,6792	0,8486	1,0469	1,2980	1,6747	2,0066	2,4002	2,6737	3,2545	3,4877
53	0,0013	0,0025	0,0126	0,0252	0,0630	0,1263	0,2546	0,3874	0,5276	0,6791	0,8485	1,0467	1,2977	1,6741	2,0057	2,3988	2,6718	3,2513	3,4838
54	0,0013	0,0025	0,0126	0,0252	0,0630	0,1263	0,2546	0,3874	0,5275	0,6791	0,8483	1,0465	1,2974	1,6736	2,0049	2,3974	2,6700	3,2481	3,4800
55	0,0013	0,0025	0,0126	0,0252	0,0630	0,1262	0,2546	0,3873	0,5275	0,6790	0,8482	1,0463	1,2971	1,6730	2,0040	2,3961	2,6682	3,2451	3,4764
56	0,0013	0,0025	0,0126	0,0252	0,0630	0,1262	0,2546	0,3873	0,5274	0,6789	0,8481	1,0461	1,2969	1,6725	2,0032	2,3948	2,6665	3,2423	3,4729
57	0,0013	0,0025	0,0126	0,0252	0,0630	0,1262	0,2545	0,3873	0,5273	0,6788	0,8480	1,0459	1,2966	1,6720	2,0025	2,3936	2,6649	3,2395	3,4696
58	0,0013	0,0025	0,0126	0,0252	0,0630	0,1262	0,2545	0,3872	0,5273	0,6787	0,8479	1,0458	1,2963	1,6716	2,0017	2,3924	2,6633	3,2368	3,4663
59	0,0013	0,0025	0,0126	0,0252	0,0630	0,1262	0,2545	0,3872	0,5272	0,6787	0,8478	1,0456	1,2961	1,6711	2,0010	2,3912	2,6618	3,2342	3,4632
60	0,0013	0,0025	0,0126	0,0252	0,0630	0,1262	0,2545	0,3872	0,5272	0,6786	0,8477	1,0455	1,2958	1,6706	2,0003	2,3901	2,6603	3,2317	3,4602
61	0,0013	0,0025	0,0126	0,0252	0,0630	0,1262	0,2545	0,3871	0,5272	0,6785	0,8476	1,0453	1,2956	1,6702	1,9996	2,3890	2,6589	3,2293	3,4573
62	0,0013	0,0025	0,0126	0,0252	0,0630	0,1262	0,2544	0,3871	0,5271	0,6785	0,8475	1,0452	1,2954	1,6698	1,9990	2,3880	2,6575	3,2270	3,4545
63	0,0013	0,0025	0,0126	0,0252	0,0630	0,1262	0,2544	0,3871	0,5271	0,6784	0,8474	1,0450	1,2951	1,6694	1,9983	2,3870	2,6561	3,2247	3,4518
64	0,0013	0,0025	0,0126	0,0252	0,0630	0,1262	0,2544	0,3871	0,5270	0,6783	0,8473	1,0449	1,2949	1,6690	1,9977	2,3860	2,6549	3,2225	3,4491
65	0,0013	0,0025	0,0126	0,0252	0,0629	0,1262	0,2544	0,3870	0,5270	0,6783	0,8472	1,0448	1,2947	1,6686	1,9971	2,3851	2,6536	3,2204	3,4466
66	0,0013	0,0025	0,0126	0,0252	0,0629	0,1261	0,2544	0,3870	0,5269	0,6782	0,8471	1,0446	1,2945	1,6683	1,9966	2,3842	2,6524	3,2184	3,4441
67	0,0013	0,0025	0,0126	0,0252	0,0629	0,1261	0,2544	0,3870	0,5269	0,6782	0,8470	1,0445	1,2943	1,6679	1,9960	2,3833	2,6512	3,2164	3,4417
68	0,0013	0,0025	0,0126	0,0252	0,0629	0,1261	0,2543	0,3870	0,5269	0,6781	0,8469	1,0444	1,2941	1,6676	1,9955	2,3824	2,6501	3,2145	3,4394
69	0,0013	0,0025	0,0126	0,0252	0,0629	0,1261	0,2543	0,3869	0,5268	0,6781	0,8469	1,0443	1,2939	1,6672	1,9949	2,3816	2,6490	3,2126	3,4372
70	0,0013	0,0025	0,0126	0,0252	0,0629	0,1261	0,2543	0,3869	0,5268	0,6780	0,8468	1,0442	1,2938	1,6669	1,9944	2,3808	2,6479	3,2108	3,4350
71	0,0013	0,0025	0,0126	0,0252	0,0629	0,1261	0,2543	0,3869	0,5268	0,6780	0,8467	1,0441	1,2936	1,6666	1,9939	2,3800	2,6469	3,2090	3,4329
72	0,0013	0,0025	0,0126	0,0252	0,0629	0,1261	0,2543	0,3869	0,5267	0,6779	0,8466	1,0440	1,2934	1,6663	1,9935	2,3793	2,6459	3,2073	3,4308
73	0,0013	0,0025	0,0126	0,0252	0,0629	0,1261	0,2543	0,3868	0,5267	0,6779	0,8466	1,0438	1,2933	1,6660	1,9930	2,3785	2,6449	3,2057	3,4289
74	0,0013	0,0025	0,0126	0,0252	0,0629	0,1261	0,2543	0,3868	0,5267	0,6778	0,8465	1,0437	1,2931	1,6657	1,9925	2,3778	2,6439	3,2041	3,4269
75	0,0013	0,0025	0,0126	0,0252	0,0629	0,1261	0,2542	0,3868	0,5266	0,6778	0,8464	1,0436	1,2929	1,6654	1,9921	2,3771	2,6430	3,2025	3,4250
76	0,0013	0,0025	0,0126	0,0252	0,0629	0,1261	0,2542	0,3868	0,5266	0,6777	0,8464	1,0436	1,2928	1,6652	1,9917	2,3764	2,6421	3,2010	3,4232
77	0,0013	0,0025	0,0126	0,0252	0,0629	0,1261	0,2542	0,3868	0,5266	0,6777	0,8463	1,0435	1,2926	1,6649	1,9913	2,3758	2,6412	3,1995	3,4214
78	0,0013	0,0025	0,0126	0,0251	0,0629	0,1261	0,2542	0,3867	0,5266	0,6776	0,8463	1,0434	1,2925	1,6646	1,9908	2,3751	2,6403	3,1980	3,4197
79	0,0013	0,0025	0,0126	0,0251	0,0629	0,1261	0,2542	0,3867	0,5265	0,6776	0,8462	1,0433	1,2924	1,6644	1,9905	2,3745	2,6395	3,1966	3,4180
80	0,0013	0,0025	0,0126	0,0251	0,0629	0,1261	0,2542	0,3867	0,5265	0,6776	0,8461	1,0432	1,2922	1,6641	1,9901	2,3739	2,6387	3,1953	3,4163
81	0,0013	0,0025	0,0126	0,0251	0,0629	0,1261	0,2542	0,3867	0,5265	0,6775	0,8461	1,0431	1,2921	1,6639	1,9897	2,3733	2,6379	3,1939	3,4147
82	0,0013	0,0025	0,0126	0,0251	0,0629	0,1261	0,2542	0,3867	0,5264	0,6775	0,8460	1,0430	1,2920	1,6636	1,9893	2,3727	2,6371	3,1926	3,4132
83	0,0013	0,0025	0,0126	0,0251	0,0629	0,1260	0,2542	0,3867	0,5264	0,6775	0,8460	1,0429	1,2918	1,6634	1,9890	2,3721	2,6364	3,1913	3,4116
84	0,0013	0,0025	0,0126	0,0251	0,0629	0,1260	0,2542	0,3866	0,5264	0,6774	0,8459	1,0429	1,2917	1,6632	1,9886	2,3716	2,6356	3,1901	3,4102
85	0,0013	0,0025	0,0126	0,0251	0,0629	0,1260	0,2541	0,3866	0,5264	0,6774	0,8459	1,0428	1,2916	1,6630	1,9883	2,3710	2,6349	3,1889	3,4087
86	0,0013	0,0025	0,0126	0,0251	0,0629	0,1260	0,2541	0,3866	0,5263	0,6774	0,8458	1,0427	1,2915	1,6628	1,9879	2,3705	2,6342	3,1877	3,4073
87	0,0013	0,0025	0,0126	0,0251	0,0629	0,1260	0,2541	0,3866	0,5263	0,6773	0,8458	1,0426	1,2914	1,6626	1,9876	2,3700	2,6335	3,1866	3,4059
88	0,0013	0,0025	0,0126	0,0251	0,0629	0,1260	0,2541	0,3866	0,5263	0,6773	0,8457	1,0426	1,2912	1,6624	1,9873	2,3695	2,6329	3,1854	3,4045
89	0,0013	0,0025	0,0126	0,0251	0,0629	0,1260	0,2541	0,3866	0,5263	0,6773	0,8457	1,0425	1,2911	1,6622	1,9870	2,3690	2,6322	3,1843	3,4032
90	0,0013	0,0025	0,0126	0,0251	0,0629	0,1260	0,2541	0,3866	0,5263	0,6772	0,8456	1,0424	1,2910	1,6620	1,9867	2,3685	2,6316	3,1833	3,4019
91	0,0013	0,0025	0,0126	0,0251	0,0629	0,1260	0,2541	0,3865	0,5262	0,6772	0,8456	1,0424	1,2909	1,6618	1,9864	2,3680	2,6309	3,1822	3,4007
92	0,0013	0,0025	0,0126	0,0251	0,0629	0,1260	0,2541	0,3865	0,5262	0,6772	0,8455	1,0423	1,2908	1,6616	1,9861	2,3676	2,6303	3,1812	3,3994
93	0,0013	0,0025	0,0126	0,0251	0,0629	0,1260	0,2541	0,3865	0,5262	0,6771	0,8455	1,0422	1,2907	1,6614	1,9858	2,3671	2,6297	3,1802	3,3982
94	0,0013	0,0025	0,0126	0,0251	0,0629	0,1260	0,2541	0,3865	0,5262	0,6771	0,8455	1,0422	1,2906	1,6612	1,9855	2,3667	2,6291	3,1792	3,3971
95	0,0013	0,0025	0,0126	0,0251	0,0629	0,1260	0,2541	0,3865	0,5262	0,6771	0,8454	1,0421	1,2905	1,6611	1,9853	2,3662	2,6286	3,1782	3,3959
96	0,0013	0,0025	0,0126	0,0251	0,0629	0,1260	0,2541	0,3865	0,5261	0,6771	0,8454	1,0421	1,2904	1,6609	1,9850	2,3658	2,6280	3,1773	3,3948
97	0,0013	0,0025	0,0126	0,0251	0,0629	0,1260	0,2540	0,3865	0,5261	0,6770	0,8453	1,0420	1,2903	1,6607	1,9847	2,3654	2,6275	3,1764	3,3937
98	0,0013	0,0025	0,0126	0,0251	0,0629	0,1260	0,2540	0,3865	0,5261	0,6770	0,8453	1,0419	1,2902	1,6606	1,9845	2,3650	2,6269	3,1755	3,3926
99	0,0013	0,0025	0,0126	0,0251	0,0629	0,1260	0,2540	0,3864	0,5261	0,6770	0,8453	1,0419	1,2902	1,6604	1,9842	2,3646	2,6264	3,1746	3,3915
100	0,0013	0,0025	0,0126	0,0251	0,0629	0,1260	0,2540	0,3864	0,5261	0,6770	0,8452	1,0418	1,2901	1,6602	1,9840	2,3642	2,6259	3,1737	3,3905

All values conform to the international convention (i.e. 0,1 instead of 0.1).

The Student Distribution* $\nu = 101–150$

P = integral between $-\infty$ and $-t_0$ = integral between t_0 and ∞. The values in the table are the t_0-values

2P	0,999	0,998	0,99	0,98	0,95	0,90	0,80	0,70	0,60	0,50	0,40	0,30	0,20	0,10	0,05	0,02	0,01	0,002	0,001
P	0,4995	0,499	0,495	0,49	0,475	0,45	0,40	0,35	0,30	0,25	0,20	0,15	0,10	0,05	0,025	0,01	0,005	0,001	0,0005
ν																			
101	0,0013	0,0025	0,0126	0,0251	0,0629	0,1260	0,2540	0,3864	0,5261	0,6769	0,8452	1,0418	1,2900	1,6601	1,9837	2,3638	2,6254	3,1729	3,3895
102	0,0013	0,0025	0,0126	0,0251	0,0629	0,1260	0,2540	0,3864	0,5260	0,6769	0,8452	1,0417	1,2899	1,6599	1,9835	2,3635	2,6249	3,1721	3,3885
103	0,0013	0,0025	0,0126	0,0251	0,0629	0,1260	0,2540	0,3364	0,5260	0,6769	0,8451	1,0417	1,2898	1,6598	1,9833	2,3631	2,6244	3,1712	3,3875
104	0,0013	0,0025	0,0126	0,0251	0,0629	0,1260	0,2540	0,3364	0,5260	0,6769	0,8451	1,0416	1,2897	1,6596	1,9830	2,3637	2,6239	3,1705	3,3865
105	0,0013	0,0025	0,0126	0,0251	0,0629	0,1260	0,2540	0,3364	0,5260	0,6768	0,8451	1,0416	1,2897	1,6595	1,9828	2,3634	2,6235	3,1697	3,3856
106	0,0013	0,0025	0,0126	0,0251	0,0629	0,1260	0,2540	0,3364	0,5260	0,6768	0,8450	1,0415	1,2896	1,6594	1,9826	2,3620	2,6230	3,1689	3,3847
107	0,0013	0,0025	0,0126	0,0251	0,0629	0,1260	0,2540	0,3364	0,5260	0,6768	0,8450	1,0415	1,2895	1,6592	1,9824	2,3617	2,6226	3,1682	3,3838
108	0,0013	0,0025	0,0126	0,0251	0,0629	0,1260	0,2540	0,3364	0,5260	0,6768	0,8450	1,0414	1,2894	1,6591	1,9822	2,3614	2,6221	3,1674	3,3829
109	0,0013	0,0025	0,0126	0,0251	0,0629	0,1260	0,2540	0,3863	0,5259	0,6767	0,8449	1,0414	1,2894	1,6590	1,9820	2,3610	2,6217	3,1667	3,3820
110	0,0013	0,0025	0,0126	0,0251	0,0629	0,1260	0,2540	0,3863	0,5259	0,6767	0,8449	1,0413	1,2893	1,6588	1,9818	2,3607	2,6213	3,1660	3,3812
111	0,0013	0,0025	0,0126	0,0251	0,0628	0,1259	0,2540	0,3863	0,5259	0,6767	0,8449	1,0413	1,2892	1,6587	1,9816	2,3604	2,6208	3,1653	3,3803
112	0,0013	0,0025	0,0126	0,0251	0,0628	0,1259	0,2539	0,3863	0,5259	0,6767	0,8448	1,0413	1,2892	1,6586	1,9814	2,3601	2,6204	3,1646	3,3795
113	0,0013	0,0025	0,0126	0,0251	0,0628	0,1259	0,2539	0,3863	0,5259	0,6767	0,8448	1,0412	1,2891	1,6585	1,9812	2,3598	2,6200	3,1639	3,3787
114	0,0013	0,0025	0,0126	0,0251	0,0628	0,1259	0,2539	0,3863	0,5259	0,6766	0,8448	1,0412	1,2890	1,6583	1,9810	2,3595	2,6196	3,1633	3,3779
115	0,0013	0,0025	0,0126	0,0251	0,0628	0,1259	0,2539	0,3863	0,5259	0,6766	0,8448	1,0411	1,2890	1,6582	1,9808	2,3592	2,6193	3,1626	3,3771
116	0,0013	0,0025	0,0126	0,0251	0,0628	0,1259	0,2539	0,3863	0,5258	0,6766	0,8447	1,0411	1,2889	1,6581	1,9806	2,3589	2,6189	3,1620	3,3764
117	0,0013	0,0025	0,0126	0,0251	0,0628	0,1259	0,2539	0,3863	0,5258	0,6766	0,8447	1,0410	1,2888	1,6580	1,9804	2,3586	2,6185	3,1614	3,3756
118	0,0013	0,0025	0,0126	0,0251	0,0628	0,1259	0,2539	0,3863	0,5258	0,6766	0,8447	1,0410	1,2888	1,6579	1,9803	2,3584	2,6181	3,1607	3,3749
119	0,0013	0,0025	0,0126	0,0251	0,0628	0,1259	0,2539	0,3863	0,5258	0,6766	0,8447	1,0410	1,2887	1,6578	1,9801	2,3581	2,6178	3,1601	3,3742
120	0,0013	0,0025	0,0126	0,0251	0,0628	0,1259	0,2539	0,3862	0,5258	0,6765	0,8446	1,0409	1,2886	1,6577	1,9799	2,3578	2,6174	3,1595	3,3735
121	0,0013	0,0025	0,0126	0,0251	0,0628	0,1259	0,2539	0,3862	0,5258	0,6765	0,8446	1,0409	1,2886	1,6575	1,9798	2,3576	2,6171	3,1590	3,3728
122	0,0013	0,0025	0,0126	0,0251	0,0628	0,1259	0,2539	0,3862	0,5258	0,6765	0,8446	1,0409	1,2885	1,6574	1,9796	2,3573	2,6167	3,1584	3,3721
123	0,0013	0,0025	0,0126	0,0251	0,0628	0,1259	0,2539	0,3862	0,5258	0,6765	0,8446	1,0408	1,2885	1,6573	1,9794	2,3570	2,6164	3,1578	3,3714
124	0,0013	0,0025	0,0126	0,0251	0,0628	0,1259	0,2539	0,3862	0,5258	0,6765	0,8445	1,0408	1,2884	1,6572	1,9793	2,3568	2,6161	3,1573	3,3707
125	0,0013	0,0025	0,0126	0,0251	0,0628	0,1259	0,2539	0,3862	0,5257	0,6765	0,8445	1,0408	1,2884	1,6571	1,9791	2,3566	2,6157	3,1567	3,3701
126	0,0013	0,0025	0,0126	0,0251	0,0628	0,1259	0,2539	0,3852	0,5257	0,6764	0,8445	1,0407	1,2883	1,6570	1,9790	2,3563	2,6154	3,1562	3,3694
127	0,0013	0,0025	0,0126	0,0251	0,0628	0,1259	0,2539	0,3852	0,5257	0,6764	0,8445	1,0407	1,2883	1,6569	1,9788	2,3561	2,6151	3,1556	3,3688
128	0,0013	0,0025	0,0126	0,0251	0,0628	0,1259	0,2539	0,3852	0,5257	0,6764	0,8444	1,0406	1,2882	1,6568	1,9787	2,3558	2,6148	3,1551	3,3682
129	0,0013	0,0025	0,0126	0,0251	0,0628	0,1259	0,2539	0,3852	0,5257	0,6764	0,8444	1,0406	1,2881	1,6568	1,9785	2,3556	2,6145	3,1546	3,3675
130	0,0013	0,0025	0,0126	0,0251	0,0628	0,1259	0,2539	0,3862	0,5257	0,6764	0,8444	1,0406	1,2881	1,6567	1,9784	2,3554	2,6142	3,1541	3,3669
131	0,0013	0,0025	0,0126	0,0251	0,0628	0,1259	0,2539	0,3862	0,5257	0,6764	0,8444	1,0406	1,2880	1,6566	1,9782	2,3552	2,6139	3,1536	3,3663
132	0,0013	0,0025	0,0126	0,0251	0,0628	0,1259	0,2539	0,3862	0,5257	0,6764	0,8444	1,0405	1,2880	1,6565	1,9781	2,3549	2,6136	3,1531	3,3658
133	0,0013	0,0025	0,0126	0,0251	0,0628	0,1259	0,2539	0,3862	0,5257	0,6763	0,8443	1,0405	1,2879	1,6564	1,9780	2,3547	2,6133	3,1526	3,3652
134	0,0013	0,0025	0,0126	0,0251	0,0628	0,1259	0,2539	0,3861	0,5257	0,6763	0,8443	1,0405	1,2879	1,6563	1,9778	2,3545	2,6130	3,1522	3,3646
135	0,0013	0,0025	0,0126	0,0251	0,0628	0,1259	0,2538	0,3861	0,5256	0,6763	0,8443	1,0404	1,2879	1,6562	1,9777	2,3543	2,6127	3,1517	3,3641
136	0,0013	0,0025	0,0126	0,0251	0,0628	0,1259	0,2538	0,3861	0,5256	0,6763	0,8443	1,0404	1,2878	1,6561	1,9776	2,3541	2,6125	3,1512	3,3635
137	0,0013	0,0025	0,0126	0,0251	0,0628	0,1259	0,2538	0,3861	0,5256	0,6763	0,8443	1,0404	1,2878	1,6561	1,9774	2,3539	2,6122	3,1508	3,3630
138	0,0013	0,0025	0,0126	0,0251	0,0628	0,1259	0,2538	0,3861	0,5256	0,6763	0,8442	1,0403	1,2877	1,6560	1,9773	2,3537	2,6119	3,1503	3,3624
139	0,0013	0,0025	0,0126	0,0251	0,0628	0,1259	0,2538	0,3861	0,5256	0,6763	0,8442	1,0403	1,2877	1,6559	1,9772	2,3535	2,6117	3,1499	3,3619
140	0,0013	0,0025	0,0126	0,0251	0,0628	0,1259	0,2538	0,3861	0,5256	0,6762	0,8442	1,0403	1,2876	1,6558	1,9771	2,3533	2,6114	3,1495	3,3614
141	0,0013	0,0025	0,0126	0,0251	0,0628	0,1259	0,2538	0,3861	0,5256	0,6762	0,8442	1,0403	1,2876	1,6557	1,9769	2,3531	2,6111	3,1490	3,3609
142	0,0013	0,0025	0,0126	0,0251	0,0628	0,1259	0,2538	0,3861	0,5256	0,6762	0,8442	1,0402	1,2875	1,6557	1,9768	2,3529	2,6109	3,1486	3,3604
143	0,0013	0,0025	0,0126	0,0251	0,0628	0,1259	0,2538	0,3861	0,5256	0,6762	0,8441	1,0402	1,2875	1,6556	1,9767	2,3527	2,6106	3,1482	3,3599
144	0,0013	0,0025	0,0126	0,0251	0,0628	0,1259	0,2538	0,3861	0,5256	0,6762	0,8441	1,0402	1,2875	1,6555	1,9766	2,3525	2,6104	3,1478	3,3594
145	0,0013	0,0025	0,0126	0,0251	0,0628	0,1259	0,2538	0,3861	0,5256	0,6762	0,8441	1,0402	1,2874	1,6554	1,9765	2,3523	2,6102	3,1474	3,3589
146	0,0013	0,0025	0,0126	0,0251	0,0628	0,1259	0,2538	0,3861	0,5255	0,6762	0,8441	1,0401	1,2874	1,6554	1,9763	2,3522	2,6099	3,1470	3,3584
147	0,0013	0,0025	0,0126	0,0251	0,0628	0,1259	0,2538	0,3861	0,5255	0,6762	0,8441	1,0401	1,2873	1,6553	1,9762	2,3520	2,6097	3,1466	3,3579
148	0,0013	0,0025	0,0126	0,0251	0,0628	0,1259	0,2538	0,3861	0,5255	0,6762	0,8441	1,0401	1,2873	1,6552	1,9761	2,3518	2,6095	3,1462	3,3575
149	0,0013	0,0025	0,0126	0,0251	0,0628	0,1259	0,2538	0,3861	0,5255	0,6761	0,8440	1,0401	1,2873	1,6551	1,9760	2,3516	2,6092	3,1458	3,3570
150	0,0013	0,0025	0,0126	0,0251	0,0628	0,1259	0,2538	0,3861	0,5255	0,6761	0,8440	1,0400	1,2872	1,6551	1,9759	2,3515	2,6090	3,1455	3,3566

All values conform to the international convention (i.e. 0,1 instead of 0.1).

The Student Distribution* $\nu = 151-200$

P = integral between $-\infty$ and $-t_0$ = integral between t_0 and ∞. The values in the table are the t_0-values

2P	0,999	0,998	0,99	0,98	0,95	0,90	0,80	0,70	0,60	0,50	0,40	0,30	0,20	0,10	0,05	0,02	0,01	0,002	0,001
P	0,4995	0,499	0,495	0,49	0,475	0,45	0,40	0,35	0,30	0,25	0,20	0,15	0,10	0,05	0,025	0,01	0,005	0,001	0,0005
ν																			
151	0,0013	0,0025	0,0126	0,0251	0,0628	0,1259	0,2538	0,3861	0,5255	0,6761	0,8440	1,0400	1,2872	1,6550	1,9758	2,3513	2,6088	3,1451	3,3561
152	0,0013	0,0025	0,0126	0,0251	0,0628	0,1259	0,2538	0,3860	0,5255	0,6761	0,8440	1,0400	1,2871	1,6549	1,9757	2,3511	2,6086	3,1447	3,3557
153	0,0013	0,0025	0,0126	0,0251	0,0628	0,1259	0,2538	0,3860	0,5255	0,6761	0,8440	1,0400	1,2871	1,6549	1,9756	2,3510	2,6083	3,1444	3,3553
154	0,0013	0,0025	0,0126	0,0251	0,0628	0,1259	0,2538	0,3860	0,5255	0,6761	0,8440	1,0399	1,2871	1,6548	1,9755	2,3508	2,6081	3,1440	3,3548
155	0,0013	0,0025	0,0126	0,0251	0,0628	0,1259	0,2538	0,3860	0,5255	0,6761	0,8439	1,0399	1,2870	1,6547	1,9754	2,3506	2,6079	3,1436	3,3544
156	0,0013	0,0025	0,0126	0,0251	0,0628	0,1259	0,2538	0,3860	0,5255	0,6761	0,8439	1,0399	1,2870	1,6547	1,9753	2,3505	2,6077	3,1433	3,3540
157	0,0013	0,0025	0,0126	0,0251	0,0628	0,1259	0,2538	0,3860	0,5255	0,6761	0,8439	1,0399	1,2870	1,6546	1,9752	2,3503	2,6075	3,1430	3,3536
158	0,0013	0,0025	0,0126	0,0251	0,0628	0,1259	0,2538	0,3860	0,5255	0,6760	0,8439	1,0398	1,2869	1,6546	1,9751	2,3502	2,6073	3,1426	3,3532
159	0,0013	0,0025	0,0126	0,0251	0,0628	0,1259	0,2538	0,3860	0,5255	0,6760	0,8439	1,0398	1,2869	1,6545	1,9750	2,3500	2,6071	3,1423	3,3528
160	0,0013	0,0025	0,0126	0,0251	0,0628	0,1259	0,2538	0,3860	0,5254	0,6760	0,8439	1,0398	1,2869	1,6544	1,9749	2,3499	2,6069	3,1419	3,3524
161	0,0013	0,0025	0,0126	0,0251	0,0628	0,1259	0,2538	0,3860	0,5254	0,6760	0,8439	1,0398	1,2868	1,6544	1,9748	2,3497	2,6067	3,1416	3,3520
162	0,0013	0,0025	0,0126	0,0251	0,0628	0,1259	0,2538	0,3860	0,5254	0,6760	0,8438	1,0398	1,2868	1,6543	1,9747	2,3496	2,6065	3,1413	3,3516
163	0,0013	0,0025	0,0126	0,0251	0,0628	0,1259	0,2538	0,3860	0,5254	0,6760	0,8438	1,0397	1,2868	1,6543	1,9746	2,3494	2,6063	3,1410	3,3512
164	0,0013	0,0025	0,0126	0,0251	0,0628	0,1259	0,2538	0,3860	0,5254	0,6760	0,8438	1,0397	1,2867	1,6542	1,9745	2,3493	2,6061	3,1407	3,3508
165	0,0013	0,0025	0,0126	0,0251	0,0628	0,1259	0,2538	0,3860	0,5254	0,6760	0,8438	1,0397	1,2867	1,6541	1,9744	2,3492	2,6060	3,1404	3,3505
166	0,0013	0,0025	0,0126	0,0251	0,0628	0,1259	0,2538	0,3860	0,5254	0,6760	0,8438	1,0397	1,2867	1,6541	1,9744	2,3490	2,6058	3,1401	3,3501
167	0,0013	0,0025	0,0126	0,0251	0,0628	0,1259	0,2538	0,3860	0,5254	0,6760	0,8438	1,0397	1,2866	1,6540	1,9743	2,3489	2,6056	3,1397	3,3497
168	0,0013	0,0025	0,0126	0,0251	0,0628	0,1259	0,2537	0,3860	0,5254	0,6760	0,8438	1,0396	1,2866	1,6540	1,9742	2,3487	2,6054	3,1395	3,3494
169	0,0013	0,0025	0,0126	0,0251	0,0628	0,1259	0,2537	0,3860	0,5254	0,6759	0,8438	1,0396	1,2866	1,6539	1,9741	2,3486	2,6052	3,1392	3,3490
170	0,0013	0,0025	0,0126	0,0251	0,0628	0,1258	0,2537	0,3860	0,5254	0,6759	0,8437	1,0396	1,2866	1,6539	1,9740	2,3485	2,6051	3,1389	3,3487
171	0,0013	0,0025	0,0126	0,0251	0,0628	0,1258	0,2537	0,3860	0,5254	0,6759	0,8437	1,0396	1,2865	1,6538	1,9739	2,3484	2,6049	3,1386	3,3483
172	0,0013	0,0025	0,0126	0,0251	0,0628	0,1258	0,2537	0,3860	0,5254	0,6759	0,8437	1,0396	1,2865	1,6538	1,9739	2,3482	2,6047	3,1383	3,3480
173	0,0013	0,0025	0,0126	0,0251	0,0628	0,1258	0,2537	0,3860	0,5254	0,6759	0,8437	1,0395	1,2865	1,6537	1,9738	2,3481	2,6045	3,1380	3,3477
174	0,0013	0,0025	0,0126	0,0251	0,0628	0,1258	0,2537	0,3860	0,5254	0,6759	0,8437	1,0395	1,2864	1,6537	1,9737	2,3480	2,6044	3,1377	3,3473
175	0,0013	0,0025	0,0126	0,0251	0,0628	0,1258	0,2537	0,3860	0,5254	0,6759	0,8437	1,0395	1,2864	1,6536	1,9736	2,3478	2,6042	3,1375	3,3470
176	0,0013	0,0025	0,0126	0,0251	0,0628	0,1258	0,2537	0,3859	0,5254	0,6759	0,8437	1,0395	1,2864	1,6536	1,9735	2,3477	2,6041	3,1372	3,3467
177	0,0013	0,0025	0,0126	0,0251	0,0628	0,1258	0,2537	0,3859	0,5253	0,6759	0,8437	1,0395	1,2864	1,6535	1,9735	2,3476	2,6039	3,1369	3,3463
178	0,0013	0,0025	0,0126	0,0251	0,0628	0,1258	0,2537	0,3859	0,5253	0,6759	0,8436	1,0395	1,2863	1,6535	1,9734	2,3475	2,6037	3,1366	3,3460
179	0,0013	0,0025	0,0126	0,0251	0,0628	0,1258	0,2537	0,3859	0,5253	0,6759	0,8436	1,0394	1,2863	1,6534	1,9733	2,3474	2,6036	3,1364	3,3457
180	0,0013	0,0025	0,0126	0,0251	0,0628	0,1258	0,2537	0,3859	0,5253	0,6759	0,8436	1,0394	1,2863	1,6534	1,9732	2,3472	2,6034	3,1361	3,3454
181	0,0013	0,0025	0,0126	0,0251	0,0628	0,1258	0,2537	0,3859	0,5253	0,6758	0,8436	1,0394	1,2862	1,6533	1,9732	2,3471	2,6033	3,1359	3,3451
182	0,0013	0,0025	0,0126	0,0251	0,0628	0,1258	0,2537	0,3859	0,5253	0,6758	0,8436	1,0394	1,2862	1,6533	1,9731	2,3470	2,6031	3,1356	3,3448
183	0,0013	0,0025	0,0126	0,0251	0,0628	0,1258	0,2537	0,3859	0,5253	0,6758	0,8436	1,0394	1,2862	1,6532	1,9730	2,3469	2,6030	3,1354	3,3445
184	0,0013	0,0025	0,0126	0,0251	0,0628	0,1258	0,2537	0,3859	0,5253	0,6758	0,8436	1,0394	1,2862	1,6532	1,9729	2,3468	2,6028	3,1351	3,3442
185	0,0013	0,0025	0,0126	0,0251	0,0628	0,1258	0,2537	0,3859	0,5253	0,6758	0,8436	1,0393	1,2861	1,6531	1,9729	2,3467	2,6027	3,1349	3,3439
186	0,0013	0,0025	0,0126	0,0251	0,0628	0,1258	0,2537	0,3859	0,5253	0,6758	0,8436	1,0393	1,2861	1,6531	1,9728	2,3466	2,6025	3,1346	3,3436
187	0,0013	0,0025	0,0126	0,0251	0,0628	0,1258	0,2537	0,3859	0,5253	0,6758	0,8435	1,0393	1,2861	1,6530	1,9727	2,3465	2,6024	3,1344	3,3433
188	0,0013	0,0025	0,0126	0,0251	0,0628	0,1258	0,2537	0,3859	0,5253	0,6758	0,8435	1,0393	1,2861	1,6530	1,9727	2,3463	2,6022	3,1341	3,3430
189	0,0013	0,0025	0,0126	0,0251	0,0628	0,1258	0,2537	0,3859	0,5253	0,6758	0,8435	1,0393	1,2860	1,6530	1,9726	2,3462	2,6021	3,1339	3,3427
190	0,0013	0,0025	0,0125	0,0251	0,0628	0,1258	0,2537	0,3859	0,5253	0,6758	0,8435	1,0393	1,2860	1,6529	1,9725	2,3461	2,6020	3,1337	3,3425
191	0,0013	0,0025	0,0125	0,0251	0,0628	0,1258	0,2537	0,3859	0,5253	0,6758	0,8435	1,0393	1,2860	1,6529	1,9725	2,3460	2,6018	3,1334	3,3422
192	0,0013	0,0025	0,0125	0,0251	0,0628	0,1258	0,2537	0,3859	0,5253	0,6758	0,8435	1,0392	1,2860	1,6528	1,9724	2,3459	2,6017	3,1332	3,3419
193	0,0013	0,0025	0,0125	0,0251	0,0628	0,1258	0,2537	0,3859	0,5253	0,6758	0,8435	1,0392	1,2860	1,6528	1,9723	2,3458	2,6015	3,1330	3,3416
194	0,0013	0,0025	0,0125	0,0251	0,0628	0,1258	0,2537	0,3859	0,5253	0,6758	0,8435	1,0392	1,2859	1,6527	1,9723	2,3457	2,6014	3,1328	3,3414
195	0,0013	0,0025	0,0125	0,0251	0,0628	0,1258	0,2537	0,3859	0,5253	0,6757	0,8435	1,0392	1,2859	1,6527	1,9722	2,3456	2,6013	3,1326	3,3411
196	0,0013	0,0025	0,0125	0,0251	0,0628	0,1258	0,2537	0,3859	0,5253	0,6757	0,8435	1,0392	1,2859	1,6527	1,9721	2,3455	2,6011	3,1323	3,3409
197	0,0013	0,0025	0,0125	0,0251	0,0628	0,1258	0,2537	0,3859	0,5253	0,6757	0,8434	1,0392	1,2859	1,6526	1,9721	2,3454	2,6010	3,1321	3,3406
198	0,0013	0,0025	0,0125	0,0251	0,0628	0,1258	0,2537	0,3859	0,5252	0,6757	0,8434	1,0392	1,2858	1,6526	1,9720	2,3453	2,6009	3,1319	3,3403
199	0,0013	0,0025	0,0125	0,0251	0,0628	0,1258	0,2537	0,3859	0,5252	0,6757	0,8434	1,0391	1,2858	1,6525	1,9720	2,3452	2,6008	3,1317	3,3401
200	0,0013	0,0025	0,0125	0,0251	0,0628	0,1258	0,2537	0,3859	0,5252	0,6757	0,8434	1,0391	1,2858	1,6525	1,9719	2,3451	2,6006	3,1315	3,3398

All values conform to the international convention (i.e. 0,1 instead of 0.1).

The χ^2-Distribution[1] $\nu = 1-50$

$\int_r$: integral between χ^2 and ∞; $\int_l$: integral between 0 and χ^2

$\int_r$ 1 / ½	0,99950 0,49975	0,9990 0,4995	0,9950 0,4975	0,990 0,495	0,9750 0,4875	0,950 0,475	0,90 0,45	0,80 0,40	0,70 0,35	0,60 0,30	0,50 0,25	0,40 0,20	0,30 0,15	0,20 0,10	0,10 0,05	0,050 0,025	0,0250 0,0125	0,010 0,005	0,0050 0,0025	0,0010 0,0005	0,00050 0,00025
$\int_l$ 1 / ½	0,00050 0,00025	0,0010 0,0005	0,0050 0,0025	0,010 0,005	0,0250 0,0125	0,050 0,025	0,10 0,05	0,20 0,10	0,30 0,15	0,40 0,20	0,50 0,25	0,60 0,30	0,70 0,35	0,80 0,40	0,90 0,45	0,950 0,475	0,9750 0,4875	0,990 0,495	0,9950 0,4975	0,9990 0,4995	0,99950 0,49975
ν																					
1	0,000000393	0,00000157	0,0000393	0,000157	0,000982	0,00393	0,0158	0,0642	0,148	0,275	0,455	0,708	1,074	1,642	2,706	3,841	5,024	6,635	7,879	10,828	12,116
2	0,00100	0,00200	0,0100	0,0201	0,0506	0,103	0,211	0,446	0,713	1,022	1,386	1,833	2,408	3,219	4,605	5,991	7,378	9,210	10,597	13,816	15,202
3	0,0153	0,0243	0,0717	0,115	0,216	0,352	0,584	1,005	1,424	1,869	2,366	2,946	3,665	4,642	6,251	7,815	9,348	11,345	12,838	16,266	17,730
4	0,0639	0,0908	0,207	0,297	0,484	0,711	1,064	1,649	2,195	2,753	3,357	4,045	4,878	5,989	7,779	9,488	11,143	13,277	14,860	18,467	19,997
5	0,158	0,210	0,412	0,554	0,831	1,145	1,610	2,343	3,000	3,655	4,351	5,132	6,064	7,289	9,236	11,070	12,833	15,086	16,750	20,515	22,105
6	0,299	0,381	0,676	0,872	1,237	1,635	2,204	3,070	3,828	4,570	5,348	6,211	7,231	8,558	10,645	12,592	14,449	16,812	18,548	22,458	24,103
7	0,485	0,598	0,989	1,239	1,690	2,167	2,833	3,822	4,671	5,493	6,346	7,283	8,383	9,803	12,017	14,067	16,013	18,475	20,278	24,322	26,018
8	0,710	0,857	1,344	1,646	2,180	2,733	3,490	4,594	5,527	6,423	7,344	8,351	9,524	11,030	13,362	15,507	17,535	20,090	21,955	26,124	27,868
9	0,972	1,152	1,735	2,088	2,700	3,325	4,168	5,380	6,393	7,357	8,343	9,414	10,656	12,242	14,684	16,919	19,023	21,666	23,589	27,877	29,666
10	1,265	1,479	2,156	2,558	3,247	3,940	4,865	6,179	7,267	8,295	9,342	10,473	11,781	13,442	15,987	18,307	20,483	23,209	25,188	29,588	31,420
11	1,587	1,834	2,603	3,053	3,816	4,575	5,578	6,989	8,148	9,237	10,341	11,530	12,899	14,631	17,275	19,675	21,920	24,725	26,757	31,264	33,137
12	1,934	2,214	3,074	3,571	4,404	5,226	6,304	7,807	9,034	10,182	11,340	12,584	14,011	15,812	18,549	21,026	23,337	26,217	28,300	32,909	34,821
13	2,305	2,617	3,565	4,107	5,009	5,892	7,042	8,634	9,926	11,129	12,340	13,636	15,119	16,985	19,812	22,362	24,736	27,688	29,819	34,528	36,478
14	2,697	3,041	4,075	4,660	5,629	6,571	7,790	9,467	10,821	12,078	13,339	14,685	16,222	18,151	21,064	23,685	26,119	29,141	31,319	36,123	38,109
15	3,108	3,483	4,601	5,229	6,262	7,261	8,547	10,307	11,721	13,030	14,339	15,733	17,322	19,311	22,307	24,996	27,488	30,578	32,801	37,697	39,719
16	3,536	3,942	5,142	5,812	6,908	7,962	9,312	11,152	12,624	13,983	15,338	16,780	18,418	20,465	23,542	26,296	28,845	32,000	34,267	39,252	41,308
17	3,980	4,416	5,697	6,408	7,564	8,672	10,085	12,002	13,531	14,937	16,338	17,824	19,511	21,615	24,769	27,587	30,191	33,409	35,718	40,790	42,879
18	4,439	4,905	6,265	7,015	8,231	9,390	10,865	12,857	14,440	15,893	17,338	18,868	20,601	22,760	25,989	28,869	31,526	34,805	37,156	42,312	44,434
19	4,912	5,407	6,844	7,633	8,907	10,117	11,651	13,716	15,352	16,850	18,338	19,910	21,689	23,900	27,204	30,144	32,852	36,191	38,582	43,820	45,973
20	5,398	5,921	7,434	8,260	9,591	10,851	12,443	14,578	16,266	17,809	19,337	20,951	22,775	25,038	28,412	31,410	34,170	37,566	39,997	45,315	47,498
21	5,896	6,447	8,034	8,897	10,283	11,591	13,240	15,445	17,182	18,768	20,337	21,991	23,858	26,171	29,615	32,671	35,479	38,932	41,401	46,797	49,011
22	6,404	6,983	8,643	9,542	10,982	12,338	14,041	16,314	18,101	19,729	21,337	23,031	24,939	27,301	30,813	33,924	36,781	40,289	42,796	48,268	50,511
23	6,924	7,529	9,260	10,196	11,689	13,091	14,848	17,187	19,021	20,690	22,337	24,069	26,018	28,429	32,007	35,172	38,076	41,638	44,181	49,728	52,000
24	7,453	8,085	9,886	10,856	12,401	13,848	15,659	18,062	19,943	21,652	23,337	25,106	27,096	29,553	33,196	36,415	39,364	42,980	45,559	51,179	53,479
25	7,991	8,649	10,520	11,524	13,120	14,611	16,473	18,940	20,867	22,616	24,337	26,143	28,172	30,675	34,382	37,652	40,646	44,314	46,928	52,620	54,947
26	8,538	9,222	11,160	12,198	13,844	15,379	17,292	19,820	21,792	23,579	25,336	27,179	29,246	31,795	35,563	38,885	41,923	45,642	48,290	54,052	56,407
27	9,093	9,803	11,808	12,879	14,573	16,151	18,114	20,703	22,719	24,544	26,336	28,214	30,319	32,912	36,741	40,113	43,195	46,963	49,645	55,476	57,858
28	9,656	10,391	12,461	13,565	15,308	16,928	18,939	21,588	23,647	25,509	27,336	29,249	31,391	34,027	37,916	41,337	44,461	48,278	50,993	56,892	59,300
29	10,227	10,986	13,121	14,256	16,047	17,708	19,768	22,475	24,577	26,475	28,336	30,283	32,461	35,139	39,087	42,557	45,722	49,588	52,336	58,301	60,735
30	10,804	11,588	13,787	14,953	16,791	18,493	20,599	23,364	25,508	27,442	29,336	31,316	33,530	36,250	40,256	43,773	46,979	50,892	53,672	59,703	62,162
31	11,389	12,196	14,458	15,655	17,539	19,281	21,434	24,255	26,440	28,409	30,336	32,349	34,598	37,359	41,422	44,985	48,232	52,191	55,003	61,098	63,582
32	11,979	12,811	15,134	16,362	18,291	20,072	22,271	25,148	27,373	29,376	31,336	33,381	35,665	38,466	42,585	46,194	49,480	53,486	56,328	62,487	64,995
33	12,576	13,431	15,815	17,074	19,047	20,867	23,110	26,042	28,307	30,344	32,336	34,413	36,731	39,572	43,745	47,400	50,725	54,776	57,648	63,870	66,403
34	13,179	14,057	16,501	17,789	19,806	21,664	23,952	26,938	29,242	31,313	33,336	35,444	37,795	40,676	44,903	48,602	51,966	56,061	58,964	65,247	67,803
35	13,787	14,688	17,192	18,509	20,569	22,465	24,797	27,836	30,178	32,282	34,336	36,475	38,859	41,778	46,059	49,802	53,203	57,342	60,275	66,619	69,199
36	14,401	15,324	17,887	19,233	21,336	23,269	25,643	28,735	31,115	33,252	35,336	37,505	39,922	42,879	47,212	50,998	54,437	58,619	61,581	67,985	70,588
37	15,020	15,965	18,586	19,960	22,106	24,075	26,492	29,635	32,053	34,222	36,336	38,535	40,984	43,978	48,363	52,192	55,668	59,893	62,883	69,346	71,972
38	15,644	16,611	19,289	20,691	22,878	24,884	27,343	30,537	32,992	35,192	37,335	39,564	42,045	45,076	49,513	53,384	56,896	61,162	64,181	70,703	73,351
39	16,273	17,262	19,996	21,426	23,654	25,695	28,196	31,441	33,932	36,163	38,335	40,593	43,105	46,173	50,660	54,572	58,120	62,428	65,476	72,055	74,725
40	16,906	17,916	20,707	22,164	24,433	26,509	29,051	32,345	34,872	37,134	39,335	41,622	44,165	47,269	51,805	55,758	59,342	63,691	66,766	73,402	76,095
41	17,544	18,575	21,421	22,906	25,215	27,326	29,907	33,251	35,813	38,105	40,335	42,651	45,224	48,363	52,949	56,942	60,561	64,950	68,053	74,745	77,459
42	18,186	19,239	22,138	23,650	25,999	28,144	30,765	34,157	36,755	39,077	41,335	43,679	46,282	49,456	54,090	58,124	61,777	66,206	69,336	76,084	78,820
43	18,832	19,906	22,859	24,398	26,785	28,965	31,625	35,065	37,698	40,050	42,335	44,706	47,339	50,548	55,230	59,304	62,990	67,459	70,616	77,419	80,176
44	19,483	20,576	23,584	25,148	27,575	29,787	32,487	35,974	38,641	41,022	43,335	45,734	48,396	51,639	56,369	60,481	64,201	68,710	71,893	78,750	81,528
45	20,137	21,251	24,311	25,901	28,366	30,612	33,350	36,884	39,585	41,995	44,335	46,761	49,452	52,729	57,505	61,656	65,410	69,957	73,166	80,077	82,876
46	20,794	21,929	25,041	26,657	29,160	31,439	34,215	37,795	40,529	42,968	45,335	47,787	50,507	53,818	58,641	62,830	66,617	71,201	74,437	81,400	84,220
47	21,456	22,610	25,775	27,416	29,956	32,268	35,081	38,708	41,474	43,942	46,335	48,814	51,562	54,906	59,774	64,001	67,821	72,443	75,704	82,720	85,560
48	22,121	23,295	26,511	28,177	30,755	33,098	35,949	39,621	42,420	44,915	47,335	49,840	52,616	55,993	60,907	65,171	69,023	73,683	76,969	84,037	86,897
49	22,789	23,983	27,249	28,941	31,555	33,930	36,818	40,534	43,366	45,889	48,335	50,866	53,670	57,079	62,038	66,339	70,222	74,919	78,231	85,351	88,231
50	23,461	24,674	27,991	29,707	32,357	34,764	37,689	41,449	44,313	46,864	49,335	51,892	54,723	58,164	63,167	67,505	71,420	76,154	79,490	86,661	89,561

[1] L. Knüsel, Statistics Seminar, University of Mannheim, 1972.

All values conform to the international convention (i.e. 0,1 instead of 0.1).

The χ^2-Distribution[7] $\nu = 51-100$

$\int_r$: integral between χ^2 and ∞; $\int_l$: integral between 0 and χ^2

$\int_r$ 1	0,99950	0,9990	0,9950	0,990	0,9750	0,950	0,90	0,80	0,70	0,60	0,50	0,40	0,30	0,20	0,10	0,050	0,0250	0,010	0,0050	0,0010	0,00050
$\int_r$ ½	0,49975	0,4995	0,4975	0,495	0,4875	0,475	0,45	0,40	0,35	0,30	0,25	0,20	0,15	0,10	0,05	0,025	0,0125	0,005	0,0025	0,0005	0,00025
$\int_l$ 1	0,00050	0,0010	0,0050	0,010	0,0250	0,050	0,10	0,20	0,30	0,40	0,50	0,60	0,70	0,80	0,90	0,950	0,9750	0,990	0,9950	0,9990	0,99950
$\int_l$ ½	0,00025	0,0005	0,0025	0,005	0,0125	0,025	0,05	0,10	0,15	0,20	0,25	0,30	0,35	0,40	0,45	0,475	0,4875	0,495	0,4975	0,4995	0,49975
ν																					
51	24,136	25,368	28,735	30,475	33,162	35,600	38,560	42,365	45,261	47,838	50,335	52,917	55,775	59,248	64,295	68,669	72,616	77,386	80,747	87,968	90,887
52	24,814	26,065	29,481	31,246	33,968	36,437	39,433	43,281	46,209	48,813	51,335	53,942	56,827	60,332	65,422	69,832	73,810	78,616	82,001	89,272	92,211
53	25,495	26,765	30,230	32,018	34,776	37,276	40,308	44,199	47,157	49,788	52,335	54,967	57,879	61,414	66,548	70,993	75,002	79,843	83,253	90,573	93,531
54	26,179	27,468	30,981	32,793	35,586	38,116	41,183	45,117	48,106	50,764	53,335	55,992	58,930	62,496	67,673	72,153	76,192	81,069	84,502	91,872	94,849
55	26,866	28,173	31,735	33,570	36,398	38,958	42,060	46,036	49,055	51,739	54,335	57,016	59,980	63,577	68,796	73,311	77,380	82,292	85,749	93,168	96,163
56	27,555	28,881	32,490	34,350	37,212	39,801	42,937	46,955	50,005	52,715	55,335	58,040	61,031	64,658	69,919	74,468	78,567	83,513	86,994	94,461	97,475
57	28,248	29,592	33,248	35,131	38,027	40,646	43,816	47,876	50,956	53,691	56,335	59,064	62,080	65,737	71,040	75,624	79,752	84,733	88,236	95,751	98,784
58	28,943	30,305	34,008	35,913	38,844	41,492	44,696	48,797	51,906	54,667	57,335	60,088	63,129	66,816	72,160	76,778	80,936	85,950	89,477	97,039	100,090
59	29,640	31,020	34,770	36,698	39,662	42,339	45,577	49,718	52,858	55,643	58,335	61,111	64,178	67,894	73,279	77,931	82,117	87,166	90,715	98,324	101,394
60	30,340	31,738	35,534	37,485	40,482	43,188	46,459	50,641	53,809	56,620	59,335	62,135	65,227	68,972	74,397	79,082	83,298	88,379	91,952	99,607	102,695
61	31,043	32,459	36,301	38,273	41,303	44,038	47,342	51,564	54,761	57,597	60,335	63,158	66,274	70,049	75,514	80,232	84,476	89,591	93,186	100,888	103,993
62	31,748	33,181	37,068	39,063	42,126	44,889	48,226	52,487	55,714	58,574	61,335	64,181	67,322	71,125	76,630	81,381	85,654	90,802	94,419	102,166	105,289
63	32,455	33,906	37,838	39,855	42,950	45,741	49,111	53,412	56,666	59,551	62,335	65,204	68,369	72,201	77,745	82,529	86,830	92,010	95,649	103,442	106,583
64	33,165	34,633	38,610	40,649	43,776	46,595	49,996	54,336	57,620	60,528	63,335	66,226	69,416	73,276	78,860	83,675	88,004	93,217	96,878	104,716	107,875
65	33,877	35,362	39,383	41,444	44,603	47,450	50,883	55,262	58,573	61,506	64,335	67,249	70,462	74,351	79,973	84,821	89,177	94,422	98,105	105,988	109,164
66	34,591	36,093	40,158	42,240	45,431	48,305	51,770	56,188	59,527	62,484	65,335	68,271	71,508	75,424	81,085	85,965	90,349	95,626	99,330	107,258	110,451
67	35,307	36,826	40,935	43,038	46,261	49,162	52,659	57,115	60,481	63,461	66,335	69,293	72,554	76,498	82,197	87,108	91,519	96,828	100,554	108,526	111,736
68	36,025	37,561	41,713	43,838	47,092	50,020	53,548	58,042	61,436	64,440	67,335	70,315	73,600	77,571	83,308	88,250	92,689	98,028	101,776	109,791	113,018
69	36,745	38,298	42,494	44,639	47,924	50,879	54,438	58,970	62,391	65,418	68,334	71,337	74,645	78,643	84,418	89,391	93,856	99,228	102,996	111,055	114,299
70	37,467	39,036	43,275	45,442	48,758	51,739	55,329	59,898	63,346	66,396	69,334	72,358	75,689	79,715	85,527	90,531	95,023	100,425	104,215	112,317	115,578
71	38,192	39,777	44,058	46,246	49,592	52,600	56,221	60,827	64,302	67,375	70,334	73,380	76,734	80,786	86,635	91,670	96,189	101,621	105,432	113,577	116,854
72	38,918	40,519	44,843	47,051	50,428	53,462	57,113	61,756	65,258	68,353	71,334	74,401	77,778	81,857	87,743	92,808	97,353	102,816	106,648	114,835	118,129
73	39,646	41,264	45,629	47,858	51,265	54,325	58,006	62,686	66,214	69,332	72,334	75,422	78,821	82,927	88,850	93,945	98,516	104,010	107,862	116,092	119,402
74	40,376	42,010	46,417	48,666	52,103	55,189	58,900	63,616	67,170	70,311	73,334	76,443	79,865	83,997	89,956	95,081	99,678	105,202	109,074	117,346	120,673
75	41,107	42,757	47,206	49,475	52,942	56,054	59,795	64,547	68,127	71,290	74,334	77,464	80,908	85,066	91,061	96,217	100,839	106,393	110,286	118,599	121,942
76	41,841	43,507	47,997	50,286	53,782	56,920	60,690	65,478	69,084	72,270	75,334	78,485	81,951	86,135	92,166	97,351	101,999	107,583	111,495	119,850	123,209
77	42,576	44,258	48,788	51,097	54,623	57,786	61,586	66,409	70,042	73,249	76,334	79,505	82,994	87,203	93,270	98,484	103,158	108,771	112,704	121,100	124,475
78	43,312	45,010	49,582	51,910	55,466	58,654	62,483	67,341	70,999	74,228	77,334	80,526	84,036	88,271	94,374	99,617	104,316	109,958	113,911	122,348	125,739
79	44,051	45,764	50,376	52,725	56,309	59,522	63,380	68,274	71,957	75,208	78,334	81,546	85,078	89,338	95,476	100,749	105,473	111,144	115,117	123,594	127,001
80	44,791	46,520	51,172	53,540	57,153	60,391	64,278	69,207	72,915	76,188	79,334	82,566	86,120	90,405	96,578	101,879	106,629	112,329	116,321	124,839	128,261
81	45,533	47,277	51,969	54,357	57,998	61,261	65,176	70,140	73,874	77,168	80,334	83,586	87,161	91,472	97,680	103,010	107,783	113,512	117,524	126,083	129,520
82	46,276	48,036	52,767	55,174	58,845	62,132	66,076	71,074	74,833	78,148	81,334	84,606	88,202	92,538	98,780	104,139	108,937	114,695	118,726	127,324	130,778
83	47,021	48,796	53,567	55,993	59,692	63,004	66,976	72,008	75,792	79,128	82,334	85,626	89,243	93,604	99,880	105,267	110,090	115,876	119,927	128,565	132,033
84	47,767	49,557	54,368	56,813	60,540	63,876	67,876	72,943	76,751	80,108	83,334	86,646	90,284	94,669	100,980	106,395	111,242	117,057	121,126	129,804	133,288
85	48,515	50,320	55,170	57,634	61,389	64,749	68,777	73,878	77,710	81,089	84,334	87,665	91,325	95,734	102,079	107,522	112,393	118,236	122,325	131,041	134,540
86	49,264	51,085	55,973	58,456	62,239	65,623	69,679	74,813	78,670	82,069	85,334	88,685	92,365	96,799	103,177	108,648	113,544	119,414	123,522	132,277	135,792
87	50,015	51,850	56,777	59,279	63,089	66,498	70,581	75,749	79,630	83,050	86,334	89,704	93,405	97,863	104,275	109,773	114,693	120,591	124,718	133,512	137,041
88	50,767	52,617	57,582	60,103	63,941	67,373	71,484	76,685	80,590	84,031	87,334	90,723	94,445	98,927	105,372	110,898	115,841	121,767	125,913	134,745	138,290
89	51,521	53,386	58,389	60,928	64,793	68,249	72,387	77,622	81,550	85,012	88,334	91,742	95,484	99,991	106,469	112,022	116,989	122,942	127,106	135,978	139,537
90	52,276	54,155	59,196	61,754	65,647	69,126	73,291	78,558	82,511	85,993	89,334	92,761	96,524	101,054	107,565	113,145	118,136	124,116	128,299	137,208	140,782
91	53,032	54,926	60,005	62,581	66,501	70,003	74,196	79,496	83,472	86,974	90,334	93,780	97,563	102,117	108,661	114,268	119,282	125,289	129,491	138,438	142,027
92	53,790	55,698	60,815	63,409	67,356	70,882	75,100	80,433	84,433	87,955	91,334	94,799	98,602	103,179	109,756	115,390	120,427	126,462	130,681	139,666	143,269
93	54,549	56,472	61,625	64,238	68,211	71,760	76,006	81,371	85,394	88,936	92,334	95,818	99,641	104,241	110,850	116,511	121,571	127,633	131,871	140,893	144,511
94	55,309	57,246	62,437	65,068	69,068	72,640	76,912	82,309	86,356	89,917	93,334	96,836	100,679	105,303	111,944	117,632	122,715	128,803	133,059	142,119	145,751
95	56,070	58,022	63,250	65,898	69,925	73,520	77,818	83,248	87,317	90,899	94,334	97,855	101,717	106,364	113,038	118,752	123,858	129,973	134,247	143,344	146,990
96	56,833	58,799	64,063	66,730	70,783	74,401	78,725	84,187	88,279	91,881	95,334	98,873	102,755	107,425	114,131	119,871	125,000	131,141	135,433	144,567	148,228
97	57,597	59,577	64,878	67,562	71,642	75,282	79,633	85,126	89,241	92,862	96,334	99,892	103,793	108,486	115,223	120,990	126,141	132,309	136,619	145,789	149,465
98	58,362	60,356	65,694	68,396	72,501	76,164	80,541	86,065	90,204	93,844	97,334	100,910	104,831	109,547	116,315	122,108	127,282	133,476	137,803	147,010	150,700
99	59,128	61,137	66,510	69,230	73,361	77,046	81,449	87,005	91,166	94,826	98,334	101,928	105,868	110,607	117,407	123,225	128,422	134,642	138,987	148,230	151,934
100	59,896	61,918	67,328	70,065	74,222	77,929	82,358	87,945	92,129	95,808	99,334	102,946	106,906	111,667	118,498	124,342	129,561	135,807	140,169	149,449	153,167

[7] L. Knüsel, Statistics Seminar, University of Mannheim, 1972.

All values conform to the international convention (i.e. 0,1 instead of 0.1).

The χ^2-Distribution[1] $\nu = 101-150$

$\int_r$: integral between χ^2 and ∞; $\int_l$: integral between 0 and χ^2

$\int_r$ 1	0,99950	0,9990	0,9950	0,990	0,9750	0,950	0,90	0,80	0,70	0,60	0,50	0,40	0,30	0,20	0,10	0,050	0,0250	0,010	0,0050	0,0010	0,00050
$\int_r$ ½	0,49975	0,4995	0,4975	0,495	0,4875	0,475	0,45	0,40	0,35	0,30	0,25	0,20	0,15	0,10	0,05	0,025	0,0125	0,005	0,0025	0,0005	0,00025
$\int_l$ 1	0,00050	0,0010	0,0050	0,010	0,0250	0,050	0,10	0,20	0,30	0,40	0,50	0,60	0,70	0,80	0,90	0,950	0,9750	0,990	0,9950	0,9990	0,99950
$\int_l$ ½	0,00025	0,0005	0,0025	0,005	0,0125	0,025	0,05	0,10	0,15	0,20	0,25	0,30	0,35	0,40	0,45	0,475	0,4875	0,495	0,4975	0,4995	0,49975
ν																					
101	60,664	62,700	68,146	70,901	75,083	78,813	83,267	88,886	93,092	96,790	100,334	103,964	107,943	112,726	119,589	125,458	130,700	136,971	141,351	150,667	154,399
102	61,434	63,484	68,965	71,737	75,946	79,697	84,177	89,826	94,055	97,772	101,334	104,982	108,980	113,786	120,679	126,574	131,838	138,134	142,532	151,884	155,629
103	62,205	64,269	69,785	72,575	76,809	80,582	85,088	90,767	95,018	98,754	102,334	105,999	110,017	114,845	121,769	127,689	132,975	139,297	143,712	153,099	156,859
104	62,977	65,054	70,606	73,413	77,672	81,468	85,998	91,709	95,982	99,737	103,334	107,017	111,053	115,903	122,858	128,804	134,111	140,459	144,891	154,314	158,087
105	63,750	65,841	71,428	74,252	78,536	82,354	86,909	92,650	96,945	100,719	104,334	108,035	112,090	116,962	123,947	129,918	135,247	141,620	146,070	155,528	159,315
106	64,524	66,629	72,251	75,092	79,401	83,240	87,821	93,592	97,909	101,701	105,334	109,052	113,126	118,020	125,035	131,031	136,382	142,780	147,247	156,740	160,541
107	65,299	67,417	73,075	75,932	80,267	84,127	88,733	94,534	98,873	102,684	106,334	110,070	114,162	119,078	126,123	132,144	137,517	143,940	148,424	157,952	161,766
108	66,075	68,207	73,899	76,774	81,133	85,015	89,645	95,477	99,837	103,667	107,334	111,087	115,198	120,135	127,211	133,257	138,651	145,099	149,599	159,162	162,990
109	66,853	68,998	74,724	77,616	82,000	85,903	90,558	96,419	100,801	104,649	108,334	112,104	116,233	121,192	128,298	134,369	139,784	146,257	150,774	160,372	164,213
110	67,631	69,789	75,550	78,458	82,867	86,792	91,471	97,362	101,766	105,632	109,334	113,121	117,269	122,250	129,385	135,480	140,917	147,414	151,948	161,581	165,435
111	68,410	70,582	76,377	79,302	83,735	87,681	92,385	98,306	102,730	106,615	110,334	114,138	118,304	123,306	130,472	136,591	142,049	148,571	153,122	162,788	166,656
112	69,191	71,375	77,204	80,146	84,604	88,570	93,299	99,249	103,695	107,598	111,334	115,156	119,340	124,363	131,558	137,701	143,180	149,727	154,294	163,995	167,876
113	69,972	72,170	78,033	80,991	85,473	89,461	94,213	100,193	104,660	108,581	112,334	116,172	120,375	125,419	132,643	138,811	144,311	150,882	155,466	165,201	169,096
114	70,754	72,965	78,862	81,836	86,342	90,351	95,128	101,137	105,625	109,564	113,334	117,189	121,410	126,475	133,729	139,921	145,441	152,037	156,637	166,406	170,314
115	71,537	73,761	79,692	82,682	87,213	91,242	96,043	102,081	106,590	110,547	114,334	118,206	122,444	127,531	134,813	141,030	146,571	153,191	157,808	167,610	171,531
116	72,321	74,558	80,522	83,529	88,084	92,134	96,958	103,025	107,556	111,531	115,334	119,223	123,479	128,587	135,898	142,138	147,700	154,344	158,977	168,813	172,747
117	73,106	75,356	81,353	84,377	88,955	93,026	97,874	103,970	108,521	112,514	116,334	120,239	124,513	129,642	136,982	143,246	148,829	155,496	160,146	170,016	173,962
118	73,892	76,155	82,185	85,225	89,827	93,918	98,790	104,915	109,487	113,498	117,334	121,256	125,548	130,697	138,066	144,354	149,957	156,648	161,314	171,217	175,177
119	74,679	76,955	83,018	86,074	90,700	94,811	99,707	105,860	110,453	114,481	118,334	122,273	126,582	131,752	139,149	145,461	151,084	157,800	162,481	172,418	176,390
120	75,467	77,755	83,852	86,923	91,573	95,705	100,624	106,806	111,419	115,465	119,334	123,289	127,616	132,806	140,233	146,567	152,211	158,950	163,648	173,617	177,603
121	76,255	78,556	84,686	87,773	92,446	96,598	101,541	107,751	112,385	116,448	120,334	124,305	128,650	133,861	141,315	147,674	153,338	160,100	164,814	174,816	178,815
122	77,045	79,359	85,520	88,624	93,320	97,493	102,458	108,697	113,351	117,432	121,334	125,322	129,684	134,915	142,398	148,779	154,464	161,250	165,980	176,014	180,025
123	77,835	80,161	86,356	89,475	94,195	98,387	103,376	109,643	114,317	118,416	122,334	126,338	130,717	135,969	143,480	149,885	155,589	162,398	167,144	177,212	181,235
124	78,626	80,965	87,192	90,327	95,070	99,283	104,295	110,589	115,284	119,399	123,334	127,354	131,751	137,022	144,562	150,989	156,714	163,546	168,308	178,408	182,445
125	79,418	81,770	88,029	91,180	95,946	100,178	105,213	111,536	116,251	120,383	124,334	128,370	132,784	138,076	145,643	152,094	157,839	164,694	169,471	179,604	183,653
126	80,211	82,575	88,866	92,033	96,822	101,074	106,132	112,483	117,217	121,367	125,334	129,386	133,817	139,129	146,724	153,198	158,962	165,841	170,634	180,799	184,860
127	81,004	83,381	89,704	92,887	97,698	101,971	107,051	113,430	118,184	122,351	126,334	130,402	134,850	140,182	147,805	154,302	160,086	166,987	171,796	181,993	186,067
128	81,799	84,188	90,543	93,741	98,576	102,867	107,971	114,377	119,151	123,335	127,334	131,418	135,883	141,235	148,885	155,405	161,209	168,133	172,957	183,186	187,273
129	82,594	84,995	91,382	94,596	99,453	103,765	108,891	115,324	120,118	124,320	128,334	132,434	136,916	142,288	149,965	156,508	162,331	169,278	174,118	184,379	188,478
130	83,390	85,804	92,222	95,451	100,331	104,662	109,811	116,272	121,086	125,304	129,334	133,450	137,949	143,340	151,045	157,610	163,453	170,423	175,278	185,571	189,682
131	84,187	86,613	93,063	96,307	101,210	105,560	110,732	117,219	122,053	126,288	130,334	134,465	138,981	144,392	152,125	158,712	164,575	171,567	176,438	186,762	190,886
132	84,984	87,422	93,904	97,163	102,089	106,459	111,652	118,167	123,021	127,272	131,334	135,481	140,014	145,444	153,204	159,814	165,696	172,711	177,597	187,953	192,088
133	85,783	88,233	94,746	98,020	102,968	107,357	112,573	119,116	123,989	128,257	132,334	136,497	141,046	146,496	154,283	160,915	166,816	173,854	178,755	189,142	193,290
134	86,582	89,044	95,588	98,878	103,848	108,257	113,495	120,064	124,956	129,241	133,334	137,512	142,078	147,548	155,361	162,016	167,936	174,996	179,913	190,331	194,491
135	87,382	89,856	96,431	99,736	104,729	109,156	114,417	121,012	125,924	130,226	134,334	138,528	143,110	148,599	156,440	163,116	169,056	176,138	181,070	191,520	195,692
136	88,182	90,669	97,275	100,595	105,609	110,056	115,338	121,961	126,892	131,210	135,334	139,543	144,142	149,651	157,518	164,216	170,175	177,280	182,226	192,707	196,891
137	88,983	91,482	98,119	101,454	106,491	110,956	116,261	122,910	127,860	132,195	136,334	140,559	145,174	150,702	158,595	165,316	171,294	178,421	183,382	193,894	198,090
138	89,785	92,296	98,964	102,314	107,372	111,857	117,183	123,859	128,829	133,180	137,334	141,574	146,206	151,753	159,673	166,415	172,412	179,561	184,538	195,080	199,289
139	90,588	93,110	99,809	103,174	108,254	112,758	118,106	124,809	129,797	134,164	138,334	142,589	147,237	152,803	160,750	167,514	173,530	180,701	185,693	196,266	200,486
140	91,391	93,926	100,655	104,034	109,137	113,659	119,029	125,758	130,766	135,149	139,334	143,604	148,269	153,854	161,827	168,613	174,648	181,840	186,847	197,451	201,683
141	92,196	94,742	101,501	104,896	110,020	114,561	119,953	126,708	131,734	136,134	140,334	144,619	149,300	154,904	162,904	169,711	175,765	182,979	188,001	198,635	202,879
142	93,000	95,558	102,348	105,757	110,903	115,463	120,876	127,658	132,703	137,119	141,334	145,635	150,331	155,954	163,980	170,809	176,882	184,118	189,154	199,819	204,074
143	93,806	96,375	103,196	106,619	111,787	116,366	121,800	128,608	133,672	138,104	142,334	146,650	151,362	157,004	165,056	171,907	177,998	185,256	190,306	201,002	205,269
144	94,612	97,193	104,044	107,482	112,671	117,268	122,724	129,558	134,641	139,089	143,334	147,665	152,393	158,054	166,132	173,004	179,114	186,393	191,458	202,184	206,463
145	95,419	98,012	104,892	108,345	113,556	118,171	123,649	130,508	135,610	140,074	144,334	148,680	153,424	159,104	167,207	174,101	180,229	187,530	192,610	203,366	207,656
146	96,226	98,831	105,741	109,209	114,441	119,075	124,574	131,459	136,579	141,059	145,334	149,694	154,455	160,153	168,283	175,198	181,344	188,666	193,761	204,547	208,849
147	97,035	99,651	106,591	110,073	115,326	119,979	125,499	132,409	137,548	142,044	146,334	150,709	155,486	161,202	169,358	176,294	182,459	189,802	194,912	205,727	210,041
148	97,843	100,471	107,441	110,937	116,212	120,883	126,424	133,360	138,518	143,029	147,334	151,724	156,516	162,251	170,432	177,390	183,573	190,938	196,062	206,907	211,233
149	98,653	101,292	108,291	111,802	117,098	121,787	127,349	134,311	139,487	144,015	148,334	152,739	157,547	163,300	171,507	178,485	184,687	192,073	197,211	208,086	212,423
150	99,463	102,113	109,142	112,668	117,985	122,692	128,275	135,263	140,457	145,000	149,334	153,753	158,577	164,349	172,581	179,581	185,800	193,208	198,360	209,265	213,613

[1] L. KNÜSEL, Statistics Seminar, University of Mannheim, 1972.

All values conform to the international convention (i.e. 0,1 instead of 0.1).

The χ^2-Distribution[7] $\nu = 151-200$

$\int_r$: integral between χ^2 and ∞; $\int_l$: integral between 0 and χ^2

$\int_r$ 1 / ½	0,99950 / 0,49975	0,9990 / 0,4995	0,9950 / 0,4975	0,990 / 0,495	0,9750 / 0,4875	0,950 / 0,475	0,90 / 0,45	0,80 / 0,40	0,70 / 0,35	0,60 / 0,30	0,50 / 0,25	0,40 / 0,20	0,30 / 0,15	0,20 / 0,10	0,10 / 0,05	0,050 / 0,025	0,0250 / 0,0125	0,010 / 0,005	0,0050 / 0,0025	0,0010 / 0,0005	0,00050 / 0,00025
$\int_l$ 1 / ½	0,00050 / 0,00025	0,0010 / 0,0005	0,0050 / 0,0025	0,010 / 0,005	0,0250 / 0,0125	0,050 / 0,025	0,10 / 0,05	0,20 / 0,10	0,30 / 0,15	0,40 / 0,20	0,50 / 0,25	0,60 / 0,30	0,70 / 0,35	0,80 / 0,40	0,90 / 0,45	0,950 / 0,475	0,9750 / 0,4875	0,990 / 0,495	0,9950 / 0,4975	0,9990 / 0,4995	0,99950 / 0,49975
ν																					
151	100,274	102,935	109,994	113,533	118,871	123,597	129,201	136,214	141,427	145,985	150,334	154,768	159,608	165,398	173,655	180,676	186,914	194,342	199,509	210,443	214,803
152	101,085	103,758	110,846	114,400	119,759	124,502	130,127	137,165	142,396	146,971	151,334	155,783	160,638	166,446	174,729	181,770	188,026	195,476	200,657	211,620	215,992
153	101,897	104,581	111,698	115,266	120,646	125,408	131,054	138,117	143,366	147,956	152,334	156,797	161,668	167,495	175,803	182,865	189,139	196,609	201,804	212,797	217,180
154	102,709	105,405	112,551	116,134	121,534	126,314	131,980	139,069	144,336	148,942	153,334	157,812	162,698	168,543	176,876	183,959	190,251	197,742	202,951	213,973	218,368
155	103,523	106,230	113,405	117,001	122,423	127,220	132,907	140,021	145,306	149,927	154,334	158,826	163,728	169,591	177,949	185,052	191,362	198,874	204,098	215,149	219,555
156	104,336	107,055	114,259	117,869	123,312	128,127	133,835	140,973	146,277	150,913	155,334	159,841	164,758	170,639	179,022	186,146	192,474	200,006	205,244	216,324	220,741
157	105,151	107,880	115,113	118,738	124,201	129,034	134,762	141,926	147,247	151,898	156,334	160,855	165,787	171,686	180,094	187,239	193,584	201,138	206,390	217,499	221,927
158	105,966	108,706	115,968	119,607	125,090	129,941	135,690	142,878	148,217	152,884	157,334	161,869	166,817	172,734	181,167	188,332	194,695	202,269	207,535	218,673	223,112
159	106,781	109,533	116,823	120,476	125,980	130,848	136,618	143,831	149,188	153,870	158,334	162,883	167,847	173,781	182,239	189,424	195,805	203,400	208,680	219,846	224,297
160	107,597	110,360	117,679	121,346	126,870	131,756	137,546	144,783	150,158	154,856	159,334	163,898	168,876	174,828	183,311	190,516	196,915	204,530	209,824	221,019	225,481
161	108,414	111,188	118,536	122,216	127,761	132,664	138,474	145,736	151,129	155,841	160,334	164,912	169,905	175,875	184,382	191,608	198,025	205,660	210,968	222,191	226,664
162	109,231	112,016	119,392	123,086	128,651	133,572	139,403	146,689	152,100	156,827	161,334	165,926	170,935	176,922	185,454	192,700	199,134	206,790	212,111	223,363	227,847
163	110,049	112,845	120,249	123,957	129,543	134,481	140,331	147,643	153,071	157,813	162,334	166,940	171,964	177,969	186,525	193,791	200,243	207,919	213,254	224,535	229,030
164	110,867	113,674	121,107	124,828	130,434	135,390	141,260	148,596	154,041	158,799	163,334	167,954	172,993	179,016	187,596	194,883	201,351	209,047	214,396	225,705	230,211
165	111,686	114,504	121,965	125,700	131,326	136,299	142,190	149,549	155,012	159,785	164,334	168,968	174,022	180,062	188,667	195,973	202,459	210,176	215,539	226,876	231,393
166	112,506	115,335	122,823	126,572	132,218	137,209	143,119	150,503	155,984	160,771	165,334	169,982	175,051	181,109	189,737	197,064	203,567	211,304	216,680	228,045	232,573
167	113,326	116,166	123,682	127,445	133,111	138,118	144,049	151,457	156,955	161,757	166,334	170,996	176,079	182,155	190,808	198,154	204,675	212,431	217,821	229,215	233,753
168	114,146	116,997	124,541	128,318	134,003	139,028	144,979	152,411	157,926	162,743	167,334	172,010	177,108	183,201	191,878	199,244	205,782	213,558	218,962	230,383	234,933
169	114,967	117,829	125,401	129,191	134,897	139,939	145,909	153,365	158,897	163,729	168,334	173,024	178,137	184,247	192,948	200,334	206,889	214,685	220,102	231,552	236,112
170	115,789	118,661	126,261	130,064	135,790	140,849	146,839	154,319	159,869	164,716	169,334	174,037	179,165	185,293	194,017	201,423	207,995	215,812	221,242	232,719	237,291
171	116,611	119,494	127,122	130,938	136,684	141,760	147,769	155,273	160,840	165,702	170,334	175,051	180,194	186,338	195,087	202,513	209,102	216,938	222,382	233,887	238,469
172	117,434	120,327	127,983	131,813	137,578	142,671	148,700	156,228	161,812	166,688	171,334	176,065	181,222	187,384	196,156	203,602	210,208	218,063	223,521	235,053	239,646
173	118,257	121,161	128,844	132,687	138,472	143,582	149,631	157,182	162,784	167,675	172,334	177,079	182,250	188,429	197,225	204,690	211,313	219,189	224,660	236,220	240,823
174	119,080	121,995	129,706	133,563	139,367	144,494	150,562	158,137	163,756	168,661	173,334	178,092	183,279	189,475	198,294	205,779	212,419	220,314	225,798	237,385	242,000
175	119,904	122,830	130,568	134,438	140,262	145,406	151,493	159,092	164,727	169,647	174,334	179,106	184,307	190,520	199,363	206,867	213,524	221,438	226,936	238,551	243,176
176	120,729	123,665	131,430	135,314	141,157	146,318	152,425	160,047	165,699	170,634	175,334	180,119	185,335	191,565	200,432	207,955	214,628	222,563	228,074	239,716	244,351
177	121,554	124,501	132,293	136,190	142,053	147,230	153,356	161,002	166,671	171,620	176,334	181,133	186,363	192,610	201,500	209,042	215,733	223,687	229,211	240,880	245,526
178	122,380	125,337	133,157	137,066	142,949	148,143	154,288	161,957	167,643	172,607	177,334	182,146	187,391	193,654	202,568	210,130	216,837	224,810	230,347	242,044	246,701
179	123,206	126,174	134,020	137,943	143,845	149,056	155,220	162,913	168,616	173,593	178,334	183,160	188,418	194,699	203,636	211,217	217,941	225,933	231,484	243,207	247,875
180	124,033	127,011	134,884	138,820	144,741	149,969	156,153	163,868	169,588	174,580	179,334	184,173	189,446	195,743	204,704	212,304	219,044	227,056	232,620	244,370	249,048
181	124,860	127,849	135,749	139,698	145,638	150,882	157,085	164,824	170,560	175,567	180,334	185,187	190,474	196,788	205,771	213,391	220,148	228,179	233,755	245,533	250,221
182	125,687	128,687	136,614	140,576	146,535	151,796	158,018	165,780	171,533	176,553	181,334	186,200	191,501	197,832	206,839	214,477	221,251	229,301	234,891	246,695	251,394
183	126,515	129,525	137,479	141,454	147,432	152,709	158,951	166,735	172,505	177,540	182,334	187,213	192,529	198,876	207,906	215,563	222,353	230,423	236,026	247,857	252,566
184	127,344	130,364	138,344	142,332	148,330	153,623	159,883	167,691	173,478	178,527	183,334	188,226	193,556	199,920	208,973	216,649	223,456	231,544	237,160	249,018	253,737
185	128,173	131,203	139,210	143,211	149,228	154,538	160,817	168,647	174,450	179,513	184,334	189,240	194,584	200,964	210,040	217,735	224,558	232,665	238,294	250,179	254,909
186	129,002	132,043	140,077	144,090	150,126	155,452	161,750	169,604	175,423	180,500	185,334	190,253	195,611	202,008	211,106	218,820	225,660	233,786	239,428	251,339	256,079
187	129,832	132,883	140,943	144,970	151,024	156,367	162,684	170,560	176,396	181,487	186,334	191,266	196,638	203,052	212,173	219,906	226,761	234,907	240,561	252,499	257,250
188	130,662	133,724	141,810	145,850	151,923	157,282	163,617	171,517	177,369	182,474	187,334	192,279	197,665	204,095	213,239	220,991	227,863	236,027	241,694	253,659	258,419
189	131,493	134,565	142,678	146,730	152,822	158,197	164,551	172,473	178,342	183,461	188,334	193,292	198,692	205,139	214,305	222,076	228,964	237,147	242,827	254,818	259,589
190	132,324	135,406	143,545	147,610	153,721	159,113	165,485	173,430	179,315	184,448	189,334	194,305	199,719	206,182	215,371	223,160	230,064	238,266	243,959	255,976	260,758
191	133,156	136,248	144,413	148,491	154,621	160,028	166,419	174,387	180,288	185,435	190,334	195,318	200,746	207,225	216,437	224,245	231,165	239,386	245,091	257,135	261,926
192	133,988	137,090	145,282	149,372	155,521	160,944	167,354	175,343	181,261	186,422	191,334	196,331	201,773	208,268	217,502	225,329	232,265	240,505	246,223	258,292	263,094
193	134,821	137,933	146,150	150,254	156,421	161,860	168,288	176,301	182,234	187,409	192,334	197,344	202,800	209,311	218,568	226,413	233,365	241,623	247,354	259,450	264,262
194	135,654	138,776	147,020	151,135	157,321	162,776	169,223	177,258	183,207	188,396	193,334	198,357	203,827	210,354	219,633	227,496	234,465	242,742	248,485	260,607	265,429
195	136,487	139,619	147,889	152,017	158,221	163,693	170,158	178,215	184,181	189,383	194,334	199,370	204,853	211,397	220,698	228,580	235,564	243,860	249,616	261,763	266,595
196	137,321	140,463	148,759	152,900	159,122	164,610	171,093	179,172	185,154	190,370	195,334	200,383	205,880	212,439	221,763	229,663	236,664	244,977	250,746	262,920	267,762
197	138,155	141,308	149,629	153,782	160,023	165,527	172,029	180,130	186,128	191,358	196,334	201,395	206,906	213,482	222,828	230,746	237,763	246,095	251,876	264,075	268,928
198	138,990	142,152	150,499	154,665	160,925	166,444	172,964	181,087	187,101	192,345	197,334	202,408	207,933	214,524	223,892	231,829	238,861	247,212	253,006	265,231	270,093
199	139,825	142,997	151,370	155,548	161,826	167,361	173,900	182,045	188,075	193,332	198,334	203,421	208,959	215,567	224,957	232,912	239,960	248,329	254,135	266,386	271,258
200	140,660	143,843	152,241	156,432	162,728	168,279	174,835	183,003	189,049	194,319	199,334	204,434	209,985	216,609	226,021	233,994	241,058	249,445	255,264	267,541	272,423

[7] L. KNÜSEL, Statistics Seminar, University of Mannheim, 1972.

All values conform to the international convention (i.e. 0,1 instead of 0.1).

The *F*-Distribution* ν_1, ν_2 Degrees of Freedom $P = 0{,}1$

$P = P(\text{right}) =$ integral between F_{ν_1, ν_2} and ∞ (values in the table are the F_{ν_1, ν_2}-values)

ν_2 \ ν_1	1	2	3	4	5	6	7	8	9	10	11	12	13	14	15	16	17	18	19	20
1	39,863	49,500	53,593	55,833	57,240	58,204	58,906	59,439	59,858	60,195	60,473	60,705	60,903	61,073	61,220	61,350	61,464	61,566	61,658	61,740
2	8,5263	9,0000	9,1618	9,2434	9,2926	9,3255	9,3491	9,3668	9,3805	9,3916	9,4006	9,4081	9,4145	9,4200	9,4247	9,4289	9,4325	9,4358	9,4387	9,4413
3	5,5383	5,4624	5,3908	5,3426	5,3092	5,2847	5,2662	5,2517	5,2400	5,2304	5,2224	5,2156	5,2098	5,2047	5,2003	5,1964	5,1929	5,1898	5,1870	5,1845
4	4,5448	4,3246	4,1909	4,1072	4,0506	4,0097	3,9790	3,9549	3,9357	3,9199	3,9067	3,8955	3,8859	3,8776	3,8704	3,8639	3,8582	3,8531	3,8485	3,8443
5	4,0604	3,7797	3,6195	3,5202	3,4530	3,4045	3,3679	3,3393	3,3163	3,2974	3,2816	3,2682	3,2567	3,2468	3,2380	3,2303	3,2234	3,2172	3,2117	3,2067
6	3,7759	3,4633	3,2888	3,1808	3,1075	3,0546	3,0145	2,9830	2,9577	2,9369	2,9195	2,9047	2,8920	2,8809	2,8712	2,8626	2,8550	2,8481	2,8419	2,8363
7	3,5894	3,2574	3,0741	2,9605	2,8833	2,8274	2,7849	2,7516	2,7247	2,7025	2,6839	2,6681	2,6545	2,6426	2,6322	2,6230	2,6148	2,6074	2,6008	2,5947
8	3,4579	3,1131	2,9238	2,8064	2,7264	2,6683	2,6241	2,5893	2,5612	2,5380	2,5186	2,5020	2,4876	2,4752	2,4642	2,4545	2,4458	2,4380	2,4310	2,4246
9	3,3603	3,0065	2,8129	2,6927	2,6106	2,5509	2,5053	2,4694	2,4403	2,4163	2,3961	2,3789	2,3640	2,3510	2,3396	2,3295	2,3205	2,3123	2,3050	2,2983
10	3,2850	2,9245	2,7277	2,6053	2,5216	2,4606	2,4140	2,3772	2,3473	2,3226	2,3018	2,2841	2,2687	2,2553	2,2435	2,2330	2,2237	2,2153	2,2077	2,2007
11	3,2252	2,8595	2,6602	2,5362	2,4512	2,3891	2,3416	2,3040	2,2735	2,2482	2,2269	2,2087	2,1930	2,1792	2,1671	2,1563	2,1467	2,1380	2,1302	2,1230
12	3,1765	2,8068	2,6055	2,4801	2,3940	2,3310	2,2828	2,2446	2,2135	2,1878	2,1660	2,1474	2,1313	2,1173	2,1049	2,0938	2,0839	2,0750	2,0670	2,0597
13	3,1362	2,7632	2,5603	2,4337	2,3467	2,2830	2,2341	2,1953	2,1638	2,1376	2,1155	2,0966	2,0802	2,0658	2,0532	2,0419	2,0318	2,0227	2,0145	2,0070
14	3,1022	2,7265	2,5222	2,3947	2,3069	2,2426	2,1931	2,1539	2,1220	2,0954	2,0730	2,0537	2,0370	2,0224	2,0095	1,9981	1,9878	1,9785	1,9701	1,9625
15	3,0732	2,6952	2,4898	2,3614	2,2730	2,2081	2,1582	2,1185	2,0862	2,0593	2,0366	2,0171	2,0001	1,9853	1,9722	1,9605	1,9501	1,9407	1,9321	1,9243
16	3,0481	2,6682	2,4618	2,3327	2,2438	2,1783	2,1280	2,0880	2,0553	2,0281	2,0051	1,9854	1,9682	1,9532	1,9399	1,9281	1,9175	1,9079	1,8992	1,8913
17	3,0262	2,6446	2,4374	2,3077	2,2183	2,1524	2,1017	2,0613	2,0284	2,0009	1,9777	1,9577	1,9404	1,9252	1,9117	1,8997	1,8889	1,8792	1,8704	1,8624
18	3,0070	2,6239	2,4160	2,2858	2,1958	2,1296	2,0785	2,0379	2,0047	1,9770	1,9535	1,9333	1,9158	1,9004	1,8868	1,8747	1,8638	1,8539	1,8450	1,8368
19	2,9899	2,6056	2,3970	2,2663	2,1760	2,1094	2,0580	2,0171	1,9836	1,9557	1,9321	1,9117	1,8940	1,8785	1,8647	1,8524	1,8414	1,8314	1,8224	1,8142
20	2,9747	2,5893	2,3801	2,2489	2,1582	2,0913	2,0397	1,9985	1,9649	1,9367	1,9129	1,8924	1,8745	1,8588	1,8449	1,8325	1,8214	1,8113	1,8022	1,7938
21	2,9610	2,5746	2,3649	2,2333	2,1423	2,0751	2,0233	1,9819	1,9480	1,9197	1,8956	1,8750	1,8570	1,8412	1,8271	1,8146	1,8034	1,7932	1,7840	1,7756
22	2,9486	2,5613	2,3512	2,2193	2,1279	2,0605	2,0084	1,9668	1,9327	1,9043	1,8801	1,8593	1,8411	1,8252	1,8111	1,7984	1,7871	1,7768	1,7675	1,7590
23	2,9374	2,5493	2,3387	2,2065	2,1149	2,0472	1,9949	1,9531	1,9189	1,8903	1,8659	1,8450	1,8267	1,8107	1,7964	1,7837	1,7723	1,7619	1,7525	1,7439
24	2,9271	2,5383	2,3274	2,1949	2,1030	2,0351	1,9826	1,9407	1,9063	1,8775	1,8530	1,8319	1,8136	1,7974	1,7831	1,7703	1,7587	1,7483	1,7388	1,7302
25	2,9177	2,5283	2,3170	2,1842	2,0922	2,0241	1,9714	1,9292	1,8947	1,8658	1,8412	1,8200	1,8015	1,7853	1,7708	1,7579	1,7463	1,7358	1,7263	1,7175
26	2,9091	2,5191	2,3075	2,1745	2,0822	2,0139	1,9610	1,9188	1,8841	1,8550	1,8303	1,8090	1,7904	1,7741	1,7596	1,7466	1,7349	1,7243	1,7147	1,7059
27	2,9012	2,5106	2,2987	2,1655	2,0730	2,0045	1,9515	1,9091	1,8743	1,8451	1,8203	1,7989	1,7802	1,7638	1,7492	1,7361	1,7243	1,7137	1,7040	1,6951
28	2,8938	2,5028	2,2906	2,1571	2,0645	1,9959	1,9427	1,9001	1,8652	1,8359	1,8110	1,7895	1,7708	1,7542	1,7395	1,7264	1,7146	1,7039	1,6941	1,6852
29	2,8870	2,4955	2,2831	2,1494	2,0566	1,9878	1,9345	1,8918	1,8568	1,8274	1,8024	1,7808	1,7620	1,7454	1,7306	1,7174	1,7055	1,6947	1,6849	1,6759
30	2,8807	2,4887	2,2761	2,1422	2,0492	1,9803	1,9269	1,8841	1,8490	1,8195	1,7944	1,7727	1,7538	1,7371	1,7223	1,7090	1,6970	1,6862	1,6763	1,6673
31	2,8748	2,4824	2,2695	2,1355	2,0424	1,9734	1,9198	1,8769	1,8417	1,8121	1,7869	1,7651	1,7461	1,7294	1,7145	1,7012	1,6891	1,6783	1,6683	1,6593
32	2,8693	2,4765	2,2635	2,1293	2,0360	1,9668	1,9132	1,8702	1,8348	1,8052	1,7799	1,7581	1,7390	1,7222	1,7072	1,6938	1,6818	1,6708	1,6608	1,6517
33	2,8641	2,4710	2,2577	2,1234	2,0300	1,9607	1,9070	1,8639	1,8284	1,7987	1,7733	1,7514	1,7323	1,7154	1,7004	1,6869	1,6748	1,6638	1,6538	1,6446
34	2,8592	2,4658	2,2524	2,1179	2,0244	1,9550	1,9012	1,8580	1,8224	1,7926	1,7672	1,7452	1,7260	1,7091	1,6940	1,6805	1,6683	1,6573	1,6472	1,6380
35	2,8547	2,4609	2,2474	2,1128	2,0191	1,9496	1,8957	1,8524	1,8168	1,7869	1,7614	1,7394	1,7201	1,7031	1,6880	1,6744	1,6622	1,6511	1,6410	1,6317
36	2,8503	2,4563	2,2426	2,1079	2,0141	1,9446	1,8905	1,8471	1,8115	1,7815	1,7559	1,7338	1,7145	1,6974	1,6823	1,6687	1,6564	1,6453	1,6351	1,6258
37	2,8463	2,4520	2,2381	2,1033	2,0094	1,9398	1,8856	1,8422	1,8064	1,7764	1,7508	1,7286	1,7092	1,6921	1,6769	1,6632	1,6509	1,6397	1,6296	1,6202
38	2,8424	2,4479	2,2339	2,0990	2,0050	1,9352	1,8810	1,8375	1,8017	1,7716	1,7459	1,7237	1,7042	1,6871	1,6718	1,6581	1,6457	1,6345	1,6243	1,6149
39	2,8388	2,4440	2,2299	2,0948	2,0008	1,9309	1,8767	1,8331	1,7972	1,7670	1,7413	1,7190	1,6995	1,6823	1,6670	1,6532	1,6408	1,6296	1,6193	1,6099
40	2,8354	2,4404	2,2261	2,0910	1,9968	1,9269	1,8725	1,8289	1,7929	1,7627	1,7369	1,7146	1,6950	1,6778	1,6624	1,6486	1,6362	1,6249	1,6146	1,6052
41	2,8321	2,4369	2,2225	2,0872	1,9930	1,9230	1,8686	1,8249	1,7888	1,7586	1,7327	1,7103	1,6908	1,6735	1,6581	1,6442	1,6318	1,6204	1,6101	1,6006
42	2,8290	2,4336	2,2191	2,0837	1,9894	1,9193	1,8649	1,8211	1,7850	1,7547	1,7288	1,7063	1,6867	1,6694	1,6539	1,6401	1,6276	1,6162	1,6058	1,5963
43	2,8260	2,4304	2,2158	2,0804	1,9860	1,9159	1,8613	1,8175	1,7813	1,7509	1,7250	1,7025	1,6829	1,6655	1,6500	1,6361	1,6235	1,6121	1,6017	1,5922
44	2,8232	2,4274	2,2127	2,0772	1,9828	1,9125	1,8579	1,8140	1,7778	1,7474	1,7214	1,6989	1,6792	1,6618	1,6462	1,6323	1,6197	1,6083	1,5979	1,5883
45	2,8205	2,4245	2,2097	2,0742	1,9796	1,9094	1,8547	1,8107	1,7745	1,7440	1,7180	1,6954	1,6757	1,6582	1,6426	1,6287	1,6161	1,6046	1,5941	1,5846
46	2,8179	2,4218	2,2069	2,0712	1,9767	1,9063	1,8516	1,8076	1,7713	1,7408	1,7147	1,6921	1,6723	1,6548	1,6392	1,6252	1,6126	1,6011	1,5906	1,5810
47	2,8154	2,4192	2,2042	2,0685	1,9738	1,9034	1,8486	1,8046	1,7682	1,7377	1,7115	1,6889	1,6691	1,6516	1,6359	1,6219	1,6092	1,5977	1,5872	1,5776
48	2,8131	2,4167	2,2016	2,0658	1,9711	1,9006	1,8458	1,8017	1,7653	1,7347	1,7085	1,6859	1,6660	1,6485	1,6328	1,6187	1,6060	1,5945	1,5839	1,5743
49	2,8108	2,4143	2,1991	2,0633	1,9685	1,8980	1,8431	1,7989	1,7625	1,7319	1,7057	1,6830	1,6631	1,6455	1,6298	1,6157	1,6030	1,5914	1,5808	1,5711
50	2,8087	2,4120	2,1967	2,0608	1,9660	1,8954	1,8405	1,7963	1,7598	1,7291	1,7029	1,6802	1,6602	1,6426	1,6269	1,6128	1,6000	1,5884	1,5778	1,5681
52	2,8046	2,4076	2,1922	2,0562	1,9613	1,8906	1,8356	1,7913	1,7548	1,7240	1,6977	1,6749	1,6549	1,6372	1,6215	1,6073	1,5945	1,5828	1,5722	1,5624
54	2,8008	2,4036	2,1881	2,0520	1,9570	1,8862	1,8311	1,7867	1,7501	1,7193	1,6929	1,6700	1,6500	1,6323	1,6164	1,6022	1,5893	1,5776	1,5670	1,5572
56	2,7973	2,3999	2,1843	2,0480	1,9529	1,8821	1,8269	1,7825	1,7458	1,7149	1,6885	1,6655	1,6454	1,6276	1,6118	1,5975	1,5846	1,5728	1,5621	1,5523
58	2,7941	2,3965	2,1807	2,0444	1,9492	1,8783	1,8230	1,7785	1,7418	1,7108	1,6843	1,6613	1,6412	1,6233	1,6074	1,5931	1,5802	1,5684	1,5576	1,5477
60	2,7911	2,3933	2,1774	2,0410	1,9457	1,8747	1,8194	1,7748	1,7380	1,7070	1,6805	1,6574	1,6372	1,6193	1,6034	1,5890	1,5760	1,5642	1,5534	1,5435
62	2,7882	2,3903	2,1743	2,0378	1,9425	1,8714	1,8160	1,7714	1,7345	1,7035	1,6769	1,6538	1,6335	1,6156	1,5996	1,5852	1,5722	1,5603	1,5495	1,5395
64	2,7856	2,3875	2,1714	2,0348	1,9394	1,8683	1,8128	1,7682	1,7312	1,7001	1,6735	1,6504	1,6301	1,6121	1,5960	1,5816	1,5685	1,5567	1,5458	1,5358
66	2,7831	2,3848	2,1687	2,0320	1,9366	1,8654	1,8099	1,7651	1,7282	1,6970	1,6703	1,6471	1,6268	1,6088	1,5927	1,5782	1,5651	1,5532	1,5423	1,5323
68	2,7808	2,3823	2,1661	2,0294	1,9339	1,8626	1,8071	1,7623	1,7253	1,6941	1,6673	1,6441	1,6238	1,6057	1,5896	1,5751	1,5619	1,5500	1,5391	1,5290
70	2,7786	2,3800	2,1637	2,0269	1,9313	1,8600	1,8044	1,7596	1,7225	1,6913	1,6645	1,6413	1,6209	1,6028	1,5866	1,5721	1,5589	1,5470	1,5360	1,5259
72	2,7765	2,3778	2,1615	2,0246	1,9290	1,8576	1,8020	1,7571	1,7200	1,6887	1,6619	1,6386	1,6181	1,6000	1,5838	1,5693	1,5561	1,5441	1,5331	1,5230
74	2,7746	2,3757	2,1593	2,0224	1,9267	1,8553	1,7996	1,7547	1,7175	1,6862	1,6594	1,6361	1,6156	1,5974	1,5812	1,5666	1,5534	1,5414	1,5304	1,5202
76	2,7727	2,3738	2,1573	2,0203	1,9246	1,8531	1,7974	1,7524	1,7152	1,6839	1,6570	1,6337	1,6131	1,5950	1,5787	1,5641	1,5509	1,5388	1,5278	1,5176
78	2,7710	2,3719	2,1554	2,0184	1,9226	1,8511	1,7953	1,7503	1,7131	1,6817	1,6548	1,6314	1,6108	1,5926	1,5764	1,5617	1,5484	1,5364	1,5253	1,5151
80	2,7693	2,3701	2,1535	2,0165	1,9206	1,8491	1,7933	1,7483	1,7110	1,6796	1,6526	1,6292	1,6086	1,5904	1,5741	1,5594	1,5461	1,5340	1,5230	1,5128
82	2,7677	2,3685	2,1518	2,0147	1,9188	1,8473	1,7914	1,7463	1,7090	1,6776	1,6506	1,6272	1,6066	1,5883	1,5720	1,5573	1,5440	1,5318	1,5207	1,5105
84	2,7662	2,3669	2,1502	2,0130	1,9171	1,8455	1,7896	1,7445	1,7072	1,6757	1,6487	1,6252	1,6046	1,5863	1,5699	1,5552	1,5419	1,5297	1,5186	1,5084
86	2,7648	2,3654	2,1486	2,0114	1,9154	1,8438	1,7879	1,7427	1,7054	1,6739	1,6468	1,6233	1,6027	1,5844	1,5680	1,5533	1,5399	1,5277	1,5166	1,5063
88	2,7634	2,3639	2,1471	2,0099	1,9139	1,8422	1,7862	1,7411	1,7037	1,6721	1,6451	1,6216	1,6009	1,5826	1,5662	1,5514	1,5380	1,5258	1,5147	1,5044
90	2,7621	2,3625	2,1457	2,0084	1,9123	1,8406	1,7846	1,7395	1,7021	1,6705	1,6434	1,6199	1,5992	1,5808	1,5644	1,5496	1,5362	1,5240	1,5128	1,5025
92	2,7609	2,3612	2,1443	2,0070	1,9109	1,8392	1,7832	1,7379	1,7005	1,6689	1,6418	1,6182	1,5975	1,5791	1,5627	1,5479	1,5345	1,5223	1,5111	1,5008
94	2,7597	2,3599	2,1430	2,0056	1,9095	1,8378	1,7817	1,7365	1,6990	1,6674	1,6403	1,6167	1,5959	1,5775	1,5611	1,5463	1,5328	1,5206	1,5094	1,4990
96	2,7585	2,3587	2,1417	2,0044	1,9082	1,8364	1,7803	1,7351	1,6976	1,6659	1,6388	1,6152	1,5944	1,5760	1,5595	1,5447	1,5312	1,5190	1,5077	1,4974
98	2,7574	2,3575	2,1405	2,0031	1,9070	1,8351	1,7790	1,7337	1,6962	1,6646	1,6374	1,6138	1,5930	1,5745	1,5581	1,5432	1,5297	1,5174	1,5062	1,4959
100	2,7564	2,3564	2,1394	2,0019	1,9057	1,8339	1,7778	1,7324	1,6949	1,6632	1,6360	1,6124	1,5916	1,5731	1,5566	1,5418	1,5283	1,5160	1,5047	1,4943
110	2,7517	2,3515	2,1343	1,9967	1,9004	1,8284	1,7721	1,7267	1,6891	1,6573	1,6300	1,6063	1,5854	1,5669	1,5503	1,5353	1,5218	1,5094	1,4981	1,4877
120	2,7478	2,3473	2,1300	1,9923	1,8959	1,8238	1,7675	1,7220	1,6842	1,6524	1,6250	1,6012	1,5803	1,5617	1,5450	1,5300	1,5164	1,5039	1,4926	1,4821
130	2,7445	2,3439	2,1264	1,9886	1,8921	1,8199	1,7635	1,7179	1,6802	1,6482	1,6208	1,5969	1,5759	1,5572	1,5405	1,5255	1,5118	1,4993	1,4879	1,4773
140	2,7417	2,3409	2,1233	1,9854	1,8889	1,8166	1,7602	1,7145	1,6767	1,6447	1,6172	1,5932	1,5722	1,5535	1,5367	1,5216	1,5079	1,4954	1,4839	1,4733
150	2,7393	2,3383	2,1207	1,9827	1,8861	1,8138	1,7572	1,7115	1,6736	1,6416	1,6140	1,5901	1,5690	1,5502	1,5334	1,5182	1,5045	1,4919	1,4804	1,4698
160	2,7371	2,3360	2,1183	1,9803	1,8836	1,8113	1,7547	1,7089	1,6710	1,6389	1,6113	1,5873	1,5661	1,5473	1,5305	1,5153	1,5015	1,4889	1,4774	1,4667
170	2,7353	2,3341	2,1163	1,9783	1,8815	1,8091	1,7524	1,7066	1,6686	1,6365	1,6089	1,5848	1,5636	1,5448	1,5279	1,5127	1,4989	1,4863	1,4747	1,4640
180	2,7336	2,3323	2,1145	1,9764	1,8795	1,8071	1,7504	1,7046	1,6666	1,6344	1,6067	1,5826	1,5614	1,5426	1,5257	1,5104	1,4966	1,4839	1,4723	1,4616
190	2,7321	2,3307	2,1128	1,9747	1,8778	1,8054	1,7486	1,7028	1,6647	1,6325	1,6048	1,5807	1,5595	1,5406	1,5236	1,5084	1,4945	1,4818	1,4702	1,4595
200	2,7308	2,3293	2,1114	1,9732	1,8763	1,8038	1,7470	1,7011	1,6630	1,6308	1,6031	1,5789	1,5577	1,5388	1,5218	1,5065	1,4926	1,4799	1,4683	1,4575
250	2,7257	2,3239	2,1058	1,9675	1,8704	1,7978	1,7409	1,6949	1,6567	1,6244	1,5965	1,5723	1,5509	1,5319	1,5149	1,4995	1,4855	1,4727	1,4610	1,4501
300	2,7223	2,3203	2,1021	1,9637	1,8666	1,7938	1,7369	1,6908	1,6525	1,6201	1,5922	1,5679	1,5464	1,5273	1,5102	1,4948	1,4807	1,4679	1,4561	1,4452
350	2,7199	2,3178	2,0995	1,9610	1,8638	1,7910	1,7340	1,6878	1,6495	1,6170	1,5891	1,5647	1,5432	1,5241	1,5069	1,4914	1,4773	1,4645	1,4526	1,4417
400	2,7181	2,3159	2,0975	1,9590	1,8617	1,7889	1,7318	1,6856	1,6472	1,6147	1,5867	1,5623	1,5408	1,5216	1,5045	1,4889	1,4748	1,4619	1,4500	1,4391
500	2,7156	2,3132	2,0948	1,9561	1,8588	1,7859	1,7288	1,6825	1,6441	1,6115	1,5835	1,5590	1,5374	1,5182	1,5010	1,4854	1,4712	1,4583	1,4464	1,4354
600	2,7139	2,3114	2,0929	1,9543	1,8569	1,7840	1,7268	1,6805	1,6420	1,6094	1,5813	1,5568	1,5352	1,5160	1,4987	1,4831	1,4689	1,4559	1,4439	1,4329
700	2,7127	2,3102	2,0916	1,9529	1,8555	1,7825	1,7253	1,6790	1,6405	1,6079	1,5797	1,5552	1,5336	1,5143	1,4970	1,4814	1,4672	1,4542	1,4422	1,4312
800	2,7118	2,3092	2,0906	1,9519	1,8545	1,7815	1,7243	1,6779	1,6394	1,6067	1,5786	1,5540	1,5324	1,5131	1,4958	1,4801	1,4659	1,4529	1,4409	1,4298
900	2,7111	2,3085	2,0899	1,9511	1,8537	1,7807	1,7234	1,6770	1,6385	1,6058	1,5777	1,5531	1,5315	1,5122	1,4948	1,4792	1,4649	1,4519	1,4399	1,4288
1000	2,7106	2,3079	2,0893	1,9505	1,8530	1,7800	1,7228	1,6764	1,6378	1,6051	1,5770	1,5524	1,5307	1,5114	1,4941	1,4784	1,4641	1,4511	1,4391	1,4280
2000	2,7081	2,3052	2,0865	1,9477	1,8502	1,7771	1,7197	1,6733	1,6347	1,6019	1,5737	1,5491	1,5274	1,5080	1,4906	1,4749	1,4606	1,4475	1,4354	1,4243
5000	2,7065	2,3036	2,0849	1,9460	1,8484	1,7753	1,7179	1,6714	1,6328	1,6000	1,5718	1,5471	1,5253	1,5059	1,4885	1,4728	1,4584	1,4453	1,4332	1,4221
10000	2,7060	2,3031	2,0843	1,9454	1,8478	1,7747	1,7173	1,6708	1,6321	1,5994	1,5711	1,5464	1,5247	1,5053	1,4878	1,4721	1,4577	1,4446	1,4325	1,4213
∞	2,7055	2,3026	2,0838	1,9449	1,8473	1,7741	1,7167	1,6702	1,6315	1,5987	1,5705	1,5458	1,5240	1,5046	1,4871	1,4714	1,4570	1,4439	1,4318	1,4206

* Reproduction only by permission of the publishers of the *Geigy Scientific Tables*.

All values conform to the international convention (i.e. 0,1 instead of 0.1).

The F-Distribution* ν_1, ν_2 Degrees of Freedom $P = 0{,}1$

$P = P(\text{right}) =$ integral between F_{ν_1,ν_2} and ∞ (values in the table are the F_{ν_1,ν_2}-values)

ν_2 \ ν_1	22	24	26	28	30	32	35	40	45	50	60	70	80	100	120	200	300	500	1000	∞
1	61,883	62,002	62,103	62,190	62,265	62,331	62,416	62,529	62,617	62,688	62,790	62,870	62,927	63,007	63,061	63,167	63,221	63,264	63,296	63,328
2	9,4458	9,4496	9,4528	9,4556	9,4579	9,4600	9,4627	9,4662	9,4690	9,4712	9,4746	9,4769	9,4787	9,4812	9,4829	9,4862	9,4879	9,4892	9,4902	9,4912
3	5,1801	5,1764	5,1732	5,1705	5,1681	5,1660	5,1633	5,1597	5,1569	5,1546	5,1512	5,1487	5,1469	5,1443	5,1425	5,1390	5,1372	5,1358	5,1347	5,1337
4	3,8371	3,8310	3,8258	3,8213	3,8174	3,8140	3,8096	3,8036	3,7990	3,7952	3,7896	3,7855	3,7825	3,7782	3,7753	3,7695	3,7666	3,7642	3,7625	3,7607
5	3,1979	3,1905	3,1842	3,1788	3,1741	3,1699	3,1645	3,1573	3,1517	3,1471	3,1402	3,1353	3,1316	3,1263	3,1228	3,1157	3,1122	3,1093	3,1072	3,1050
6	2,8266	2,8183	2,8113	2,8053	2,8000	2,7953	2,7893	2,7812	2,7748	2,7697	2,7620	2,7564	2,7522	2,7463	2,7423	2,7343	2,7303	2,7270	2,7246	2,7222
7	2,5842	2,5753	2,5677	2,5612	2,5555	2,5504	2,5439	2,5351	2,5282	2,5226	2,5142	2,5082	2,5036	2,4971	2,4928	2,4841	2,4797	2,4761	2,4735	2,4708
8	2,4135	2,4041	2,3961	2,3891	2,3830	2,3777	2,3707	2,3614	2,3540	2,3481	2,3391	2,3326	2,3277	2,3208	2,3162	2,3068	2,3021	2,2983	2,2954	2,2926
9	2,2867	2,2768	2,2684	2,2611	2,2547	2,2491	2,2418	2,2320	2,2242	2,2180	2,2085	2,2017	2,1965	2,1892	2,1843	2,1744	2,1693	2,1653	2,1623	2,1592
10	2,1887	2,1784	2,1697	2,1621	2,1554	2,1496	2,1420	2,1317	2,1236	2,1171	2,1072	2,1000	2,0946	2,0869	2,0818	2,0713	2,0661	2,0618	2,0586	2,0554
11	2,1106	2,1000	2,0909	2,0831	2,0762	2,0701	2,0623	2,0516	2,0432	2,0364	2,0261	2,0187	2,0130	2,0050	1,9997	1,9888	1,9833	1,9788	1,9755	1,9721
12	2,0469	2,0360	2,0267	2,0186	2,0115	2,0052	1,9971	1,9861	1,9774	1,9704	1,9597	1,9520	1,9461	1,9379	1,9323	1,9210	1,9152	1,9106	1,9071	1,9036
13	1,9939	1,9827	1,9732	1,9649	1,9576	1,9511	1,9428	1,9315	1,9225	1,9153	1,9043	1,8963	1,8903	1,8817	1,8759	1,8642	1,8583	1,8535	1,8498	1,8462
14	1,9490	1,9377	1,9279	1,9194	1,9119	1,9053	1,8968	1,8852	1,8760	1,8686	1,8572	1,8490	1,8428	1,8340	1,8280	1,8159	1,8098	1,8048	1,8011	1,7973
15	1,9106	1,8990	1,8891	1,8804	1,8728	1,8660	1,8573	1,8454	1,8360	1,8284	1,8168	1,8083	1,8019	1,7929	1,7867	1,7743	1,7679	1,7628	1,7589	1,7551
16	1,8774	1,8656	1,8554	1,8466	1,8388	1,8319	1,8230	1,8108	1,8012	1,7934	1,7816	1,7729	1,7664	1,7571	1,7507	1,7379	1,7314	1,7262	1,7222	1,7182
17	1,8482	1,8362	1,8259	1,8169	1,8090	1,8020	1,7929	1,7805	1,7707	1,7628	1,7506	1,7418	1,7351	1,7255	1,7191	1,7060	1,6993	1,6939	1,6898	1,6856
18	1,8225	1,8103	1,7999	1,7907	1,7827	1,7756	1,7663	1,7537	1,7437	1,7356	1,7232	1,7142	1,7073	1,6976	1,6910	1,6775	1,6707	1,6651	1,6609	1,6567
19	1,7997	1,7873	1,7767	1,7674	1,7592	1,7520	1,7426	1,7298	1,7196	1,7114	1,6988	1,6896	1,6826	1,6726	1,6659	1,6521	1,6451	1,6394	1,6351	1,6308
20	1,7792	1,7667	1,7559	1,7465	1,7382	1,7309	1,7213	1,7083	1,6980	1,6896	1,6768	1,6674	1,6603	1,6501	1,6433	1,6292	1,6220	1,6162	1,6118	1,6074
21	1,7607	1,7481	1,7372	1,7276	1,7193	1,7118	1,7021	1,6890	1,6785	1,6700	1,6569	1,6474	1,6401	1,6298	1,6228	1,6085	1,6011	1,5952	1,5907	1,5862
22	1,7440	1,7312	1,7202	1,7106	1,7021	1,6946	1,6847	1,6714	1,6608	1,6521	1,6389	1,6292	1,6218	1,6113	1,6041	1,5896	1,5821	1,5760	1,5714	1,5668
23	1,7288	1,7159	1,7047	1,6950	1,6864	1,6788	1,6689	1,6554	1,6446	1,6358	1,6224	1,6125	1,6051	1,5944	1,5871	1,5723	1,5646	1,5585	1,5538	1,5490
24	1,7149	1,7019	1,6906	1,6808	1,6721	1,6644	1,6544	1,6407	1,6298	1,6209	1,6073	1,5973	1,5897	1,5788	1,5715	1,5563	1,5486	1,5423	1,5375	1,5327
25	1,7021	1,6890	1,6776	1,6677	1,6589	1,6512	1,6410	1,6272	1,6161	1,6072	1,5934	1,5833	1,5755	1,5645	1,5570	1,5417	1,5338	1,5274	1,5225	1,5176
26	1,6904	1,6771	1,6657	1,6556	1,6468	1,6390	1,6287	1,6147	1,6036	1,5945	1,5805	1,5703	1,5625	1,5513	1,5437	1,5281	1,5201	1,5136	1,5086	1,5036
27	1,6795	1,6662	1,6546	1,6445	1,6356	1,6277	1,6173	1,6032	1,5919	1,5827	1,5686	1,5582	1,5503	1,5390	1,5313	1,5155	1,5073	1,5007	1,4957	1,4905
28	1,6695	1,6560	1,6444	1,6342	1,6252	1,6172	1,6068	1,5925	1,5811	1,5718	1,5575	1,5470	1,5390	1,5276	1,5198	1,5037	1,4954	1,4887	1,4836	1,4784
29	1,6601	1,6465	1,6348	1,6246	1,6155	1,6075	1,5969	1,5825	1,5710	1,5617	1,5472	1,5366	1,5285	1,5169	1,5090	1,4927	1,4843	1,4775	1,4723	1,4670
30	1,6514	1,6377	1,6259	1,6156	1,6065	1,5984	1,5877	1,5732	1,5616	1,5522	1,5376	1,5269	1,5187	1,5069	1,4989	1,4824	1,4739	1,4670	1,4617	1,4564
31	1,6432	1,6295	1,6176	1,6072	1,5980	1,5899	1,5792	1,5645	1,5528	1,5433	1,5285	1,5177	1,5094	1,4976	1,4895	1,4728	1,4641	1,4571	1,4518	1,4463
32	1,6356	1,6218	1,6098	1,5994	1,5901	1,5819	1,5711	1,5564	1,5446	1,5349	1,5201	1,5091	1,5008	1,4888	1,4806	1,4637	1,4549	1,4478	1,4424	1,4369
33	1,6284	1,6146	1,6025	1,5920	1,5827	1,5744	1,5635	1,5487	1,5368	1,5271	1,5121	1,5011	1,4926	1,4805	1,4722	1,4551	1,4463	1,4390	1,4335	1,4279
34	1,6217	1,6077	1,5957	1,5851	1,5757	1,5674	1,5564	1,5415	1,5295	1,5197	1,5046	1,4934	1,4849	1,4727	1,4643	1,4470	1,4380	1,4307	1,4252	1,4195
35	1,6154	1,6013	1,5892	1,5785	1,5691	1,5607	1,5497	1,5346	1,5226	1,5127	1,4975	1,4862	1,4776	1,4653	1,4568	1,4393	1,4303	1,4229	1,4172	1,4115
36	1,6094	1,5953	1,5831	1,5723	1,5629	1,5544	1,5434	1,5282	1,5161	1,5061	1,4908	1,4794	1,4707	1,4583	1,4497	1,4321	1,4229	1,4154	1,4097	1,4039
37	1,6037	1,5896	1,5773	1,5665	1,5570	1,5485	1,5374	1,5221	1,5099	1,4999	1,4844	1,4730	1,4642	1,4516	1,4430	1,4252	1,4159	1,4083	1,4025	1,3967
38	1,5984	1,5841	1,5718	1,5610	1,5514	1,5429	1,5317	1,5163	1,5040	1,4939	1,4784	1,4669	1,4580	1,4453	1,4366	1,4186	1,4092	1,4016	1,3957	1,3898
39	1,5933	1,5790	1,5666	1,5557	1,5461	1,5375	1,5263	1,5108	1,4985	1,4883	1,4726	1,4610	1,4521	1,4393	1,4305	1,4123	1,4029	1,3951	1,3892	1,3832
40	1,5884	1,5741	1,5617	1,5507	1,5411	1,5325	1,5211	1,5056	1,4932	1,4830	1,4672	1,4555	1,4465	1,4336	1,4248	1,4064	1,3968	1,3890	1,3830	1,3769
41	1,5839	1,5695	1,5570	1,5460	1,5363	1,5276	1,5163	1,5007	1,4881	1,4779	1,4620	1,4502	1,4412	1,4282	1,4192	1,4007	1,3911	1,3831	1,3771	1,3709
42	1,5795	1,5650	1,5525	1,5415	1,5317	1,5230	1,5116	1,4959	1,4833	1,4730	1,4570	1,4452	1,4361	1,4230	1,4140	1,3953	1,3855	1,3775	1,3714	1,3652
43	1,5753	1,5608	1,5482	1,5372	1,5274	1,5186	1,5072	1,4914	1,4788	1,4684	1,4523	1,4404	1,4312	1,4180	1,4089	1,3901	1,3802	1,3722	1,3660	1,3597
44	1,5714	1,5568	1,5442	1,5331	1,5232	1,5145	1,5029	1,4871	1,4744	1,4639	1,4477	1,4358	1,4265	1,4132	1,4041	1,3851	1,3752	1,3670	1,3608	1,3544
45	1,5676	1,5530	1,5403	1,5291	1,5193	1,5105	1,4989	1,4830	1,4702	1,4597	1,4434	1,4313	1,4221	1,4087	1,3995	1,3803	1,3703	1,3621	1,3558	1,3493
46	1,5639	1,5493	1,5366	1,5254	1,5155	1,5066	1,4950	1,4790	1,4662	1,4556	1,4392	1,4271	1,4178	1,4043	1,3950	1,3757	1,3656	1,3573	1,3509	1,3444
47	1,5605	1,5458	1,5330	1,5218	1,5118	1,5030	1,4913	1,4752	1,4623	1,4517	1,4353	1,4231	1,4137	1,4001	1,3908	1,3713	1,3611	1,3527	1,3463	1,3397
48	1,5571	1,5424	1,5296	1,5183	1,5084	1,4994	1,4877	1,4716	1,4586	1,4480	1,4314	1,4192	1,4097	1,3961	1,3867	1,3671	1,3568	1,3483	1,3419	1,3352
49	1,5539	1,5392	1,5263	1,5150	1,5050	1,4961	1,4843	1,4681	1,4551	1,4444	1,4278	1,4154	1,4059	1,3922	1,3827	1,3630	1,3526	1,3441	1,3376	1,3309
50	1,5509	1,5361	1,5232	1,5118	1,5018	1,4928	1,4810	1,4648	1,4517	1,4409	1,4242	1,4119	1,4023	1,3885	1,3789	1,3590	1,3486	1,3400	1,3334	1,3267
52	1,5451	1,5302	1,5173	1,5059	1,4957	1,4867	1,4748	1,4585	1,4453	1,4344	1,4176	1,4051	1,3954	1,3814	1,3718	1,3516	1,3410	1,3323	1,3256	1,3187
54	1,5398	1,5248	1,5118	1,5003	1,4901	1,4811	1,4691	1,4526	1,4393	1,4284	1,4114	1,3988	1,3890	1,3749	1,3651	1,3447	1,3339	1,3251	1,3182	1,3112
56	1,5348	1,5198	1,5067	1,4952	1,4849	1,4758	1,4638	1,4472	1,4338	1,4228	1,4056	1,3929	1,3830	1,3687	1,3589	1,3382	1,3273	1,3183	1,3113	1,3042
58	1,5302	1,5151	1,5019	1,4904	1,4801	1,4709	1,4588	1,4421	1,4286	1,4175	1,4002	1,3874	1,3774	1,3630	1,3530	1,3321	1,3211	1,3119	1,3049	1,2977
60	1,5259	1,5107	1,4975	1,4859	1,4755	1,4663	1,4541	1,4373	1,4238	1,4126	1,3952	1,3822	1,3722	1,3576	1,3476	1,3264	1,3152	1,3060	1,2988	1,2915
62	1,5219	1,5066	1,4934	1,4817	1,4713	1,4620	1,4498	1,4329	1,4193	1,4080	1,3905	1,3774	1,3673	1,3526	1,3424	1,3210	1,3097	1,3003	1,2931	1,2856
64	1,5181	1,5028	1,4895	1,4777	1,4673	1,4580	1,4457	1,4287	1,4150	1,4037	1,3860	1,3729	1,3627	1,3479	1,3376	1,3160	1,3045	1,2950	1,2877	1,2801
66	1,5145	1,4992	1,4858	1,4740	1,4636	1,4542	1,4419	1,4248	1,4110	1,3996	1,3819	1,3686	1,3583	1,3434	1,3330	1,3112	1,2996	1,2900	1,2825	1,2749
68	1,5112	1,4958	1,4824	1,4706	1,4601	1,4506	1,4382	1,4211	1,4072	1,3958	1,3779	1,3646	1,3542	1,3392	1,3287	1,3067	1,2950	1,2852	1,2777	1,2699
70	1,5080	1,4926	1,4791	1,4673	1,4567	1,4473	1,4348	1,4176	1,4037	1,3922	1,3742	1,3608	1,3503	1,3352	1,3246	1,3024	1,2905	1,2807	1,2730	1,2652
72	1,5051	1,4896	1,4761	1,4642	1,4536	1,4441	1,4316	1,4143	1,4003	1,3887	1,3707	1,3572	1,3467	1,3314	1,3208	1,2983	1,2863	1,2764	1,2686	1,2607
74	1,5022	1,4867	1,4732	1,4612	1,4506	1,4411	1,4285	1,4112	1,3971	1,3855	1,3673	1,3537	1,3432	1,3278	1,3171	1,2944	1,2824	1,2723	1,2645	1,2564
76	1,4996	1,4840	1,4704	1,4584	1,4478	1,4382	1,4256	1,4082	1,3941	1,3824	1,3641	1,3505	1,3399	1,3244	1,3136	1,2907	1,2785	1,2684	1,2605	1,2523
78	1,4971	1,4815	1,4678	1,4558	1,4451	1,4355	1,4229	1,4054	1,3912	1,3795	1,3611	1,3474	1,3367	1,3211	1,3102	1,2872	1,2749	1,2646	1,2566	1,2483
80	1,4947	1,4790	1,4653	1,4533	1,4426	1,4330	1,4203	1,4027	1,3885	1,3767	1,3583	1,3444	1,3337	1,3180	1,3071	1,2839	1,2715	1,2611	1,2530	1,2446
82	1,4924	1,4767	1,4630	1,4509	1,4402	1,4305	1,4178	1,4002	1,3859	1,3740	1,3555	1,3416	1,3308	1,3150	1,3040	1,2806	1,2681	1,2577	1,2495	1,2410
84	1,4902	1,4745	1,4607	1,4486	1,4378	1,4282	1,4154	1,3977	1,3834	1,3715	1,3529	1,3390	1,3281	1,3122	1,3011	1,2776	1,2650	1,2544	1,2461	1,2375
86	1,4881	1,4724	1,4586	1,4465	1,4356	1,4260	1,4132	1,3954	1,3810	1,3691	1,3504	1,3364	1,3255	1,3095	1,2984	1,2746	1,2619	1,2512	1,2429	1,2342
88	1,4861	1,4704	1,4566	1,4444	1,4335	1,4238	1,4110	1,3932	1,3788	1,3668	1,3480	1,3339	1,3230	1,3069	1,2957	1,2718	1,2590	1,2482	1,2398	1,2310
90	1,4842	1,4684	1,4546	1,4424	1,4315	1,4218	1,4089	1,3911	1,3766	1,3646	1,3457	1,3316	1,3206	1,3044	1,2932	1,2691	1,2562	1,2453	1,2368	1,2280
92	1,4824	1,4666	1,4527	1,4405	1,4296	1,4199	1,4069	1,3890	1,3745	1,3625	1,3436	1,3294	1,3183	1,3021	1,2907	1,2665	1,2535	1,2425	1,2340	1,2250
94	1,4807	1,4648	1,4509	1,4387	1,4278	1,4180	1,4050	1,3871	1,3725	1,3604	1,3415	1,3272	1,3161	1,2998	1,2884	1,2640	1,2509	1,2399	1,2312	1,2222
96	1,4790	1,4631	1,4492	1,4369	1,4260	1,4162	1,4032	1,3852	1,3706	1,3585	1,3394	1,3251	1,3140	1,2976	1,2861	1,2616	1,2484	1,2373	1,2285	1,2194
98	1,4774	1,4615	1,4476	1,4353	1,4243	1,4145	1,4015	1,3834	1,3688	1,3566	1,3375	1,3231	1,3119	1,2955	1,2840	1,2593	1,2460	1,2348	1,2260	1,2168
100	1,4759	1,4600	1,4460	1,4337	1,4227	1,4128	1,3998	1,3817	1,3670	1,3548	1,3356	1,3212	1,3100	1,2934	1,2819	1,2571	1,2437	1,2324	1,2235	1,2142
110	1,4691	1,4530	1,4389	1,4265	1,4154	1,4055	1,3923	1,3740	1,3591	1,3468	1,3273	1,3127	1,3012	1,2843	1,2725	1,2470	1,2332	1,2215	1,2123	1,2026
120	1,4634	1,4472	1,4331	1,4205	1,4094	1,3993	1,3861	1,3676	1,3526	1,3400	1,3203	1,3055	1,2938	1,2767	1,2646	1,2385	1,2243	1,2122	1,2026	1,1926
130	1,4586	1,4423	1,4281	1,4155	1,4042	1,3941	1,3808	1,3621	1,3470	1,3343	1,3144	1,2993	1,2875	1,2701	1,2578	1,2312	1,2166	1,2042	1,1943	1,1839
140	1,4545	1,4381	1,4238	1,4111	1,3998	1,3897	1,3762	1,3575	1,3422	1,3294	1,3093	1,2941	1,2821	1,2644	1,2519	1,2248	1,2099	1,1972	1,1870	1,1762
150	1,4509	1,4345	1,4201	1,4074	1,3960	1,3858	1,3723	1,3534	1,3380	1,3251	1,3048	1,2895	1,2774	1,2595	1,2468	1,2193	1,2040	1,1910	1,1805	1,1694
160	1,4477	1,4313	1,4169	1,4041	1,3927	1,3824	1,3688	1,3498	1,3343	1,3214	1,3009	1,2854	1,2732	1,2551	1,2423	1,2143	1,1988	1,1854	1,1747	1,1632
170	1,4450	1,4285	1,4140	1,4012	1,3897	1,3794	1,3657	1,3466	1,3311	1,3180	1,2974	1,2818	1,2695	1,2512	1,2383	1,2099	1,1941	1,1805	1,1695	1,1577
180	1,4425	1,4260	1,4114	1,3986	1,3871	1,3767	1,3630	1,3438	1,3282	1,3151	1,2944	1,2786	1,2662	1,2478	1,2347	1,2059	1,1899	1,1760	1,1648	1,1527
190	1,4403	1,4237	1,4092	1,3962	1,3847	1,3743	1,3605	1,3413	1,3256	1,3124	1,2916	1,2757	1,2632	1,2446	1,2314	1,2024	1,1861	1,1720	1,1605	1,1481
200	1,4383	1,4217	1,4071	1,3942	1,3826	1,3722	1,3583	1,3390	1,3232	1,3100	1,2891	1,2731	1,2605	1,2418	1,2285	1,1991	1,1826	1,1683	1,1566	1,1439
250	1,4308	1,4140	1,3993	1,3862	1,3745	1,3640	1,3500	1,3304	1,3143	1,3009	1,2795	1,2632	1,2503	1,2310	1,2172	1,1865	1,1691	1,1537	1,1411	1,1271
300	1,4258	1,4089	1,3941	1,3809	1,3691	1,3585	1,3443	1,3246	1,3083	1,2947	1,2730	1,2565	1,2433	1,2236	1,2095	1,1779	1,1597	1,1435	1,1301	1,1150
350	1,4222	1,4052	1,3903	1,3771	1,3652	1,3545	1,3403	1,3204	1,3040	1,2903	1,2684	1,2516	1,2383	1,2183	1,2039	1,1715	1,1528	1,1360	1,1218	1,1057
400	1,4195	1,4025	1,3875	1,3742	1,3623	1,3516	1,3373	1,3173	1,3008	1,2870	1,2649	1,2480	1,2345	1,2143	1,1997	1,1667	1,1475	1,1301	1,1153	1,0983
500	1,4157	1,3986	1,3836	1,3702	1,3582	1,3474	1,3331	1,3129	1,2963	1,2823	1,2600	1,2428	1,2292	1,2086	1,1936	1,1598	1,1398	1,1216	1,1058	1,0871
600	1,4132	1,3961	1,3810	1,3675	1,3555	1,3447	1,3302	1,3099	1,2932	1,2792	1,2567	1,2394	1,2256	1,2047	1,1896	1,1551	1,1346	1,1156	1,0991	1,0790
700	1,4114	1,3942	1,3791	1,3656	1,3536	1,3427	1,3282	1,3078	1,2910	1,2769	1,2543	1,2369	1,2230	1,2020	1,1867	1,1517	1,1308	1,1113	1,0940	1,0728
800	1,4101	1,3928	1,3777	1,3642	1,3521	1,3412	1,3267	1,3062	1,2894	1,2752	1,2525	1,2350	1,2210	1,1999	1,1845	1,1491	1,1278	1,1079	1,0901	1,0678
900	1,4090	1,3918	1,3766	1,3631	1,3510	1,3401	1,3255	1,3050	1,2881	1,2739	1,2512	1,2336	1,2195	1,1982	1,1827	1,1470	1,1255	1,1053	1,0870	1,0637
1000	1,4082	1,3909	1,3757	1,3622	1,3501	1,3391	1,3245	1,3040	1,2871	1,2729	1,2500	1,2324	1,2183	1,1969	1,1813	1,1454	1,1237	1,1031	1,0845	1,0603
2000	1,4044	1,3870	1,3718	1,3582	1,3460	1,3350	1,3203	1,2996	1,2825	1,2681	1,2450	1,2271	1,2128	1,1910	1,1750	1,1379	1,1150	1,0929	1,0721	1,0420
5000	1,4021	1,3847	1,3694	1,3558	1,3435	1,3324	1,3177	1,2969	1,2797	1,2653	1,2420	1,2240	1,2095	1,1874	1,1712	1,1332	1,1097	1,0864	1,0638	1,0262
10000	1,4014	1,3840	1,3686	1,3549	1,3427	1,3316	1,3168	1,2960	1,2788	1,2643	1,2410	1,2229	1,2083	1,1862	1,1699	1,1317	1,1078	1,0842	1,0608	1,0184
∞	1,4006	1,3832	1,3678	1,3541	1,3419	1,3308	1,3160	1,2951	1,2779	1,2633	1,2400	1,2218	1,2072	1,1850	1,1686	1,1301	1,1060	1,0819	1,0577	1

All values conform to the international convention (i.e. 0,1 instead of 0.1).

The *F*-Distribution* ν_1, ν_2 Degrees of Freedom $P = 0{,}05$

$P = P$ (right) = integral between F_{ν_1, ν_2} and ∞ (values in the table are the F_{ν_1, ν_2}-values)

ν_2 \ ν_1	1	2	3	4	5	6	7	8	9	10	11	12	13	14	15	16	17	18	19	20
1	161,45	199,50	215,71	224,58	230,16	233,99	236,77	238,88	240,54	241,88	242,98	243,91	244,69	245,36	245,95	246,46	246,92	247,32	247,69	248,01
2	18,513	19,000	19,164	19,247	19,296	19,330	19,353	19,371	19,385	19,396	19,405	19,413	19,419	19,424	19,429	19,433	19,437	19,440	19,443	19,446
3	10,128	9,5521	9,2766	9,1172	9,0135	8,9406	8,8868	8,8452	8,8123	8,7855	8,7633	8,7446	8,7287	8,7149	8,7029	8,6923	8,6829	8,6745	8,6670	8,6602
4	7,7086	6,9443	6,5914	6,3882	6,2561	6,1631	6,0942	6,0410	5,9988	5,9644	5,9358	5,9117	5,8911	5,8733	5,8578	5,8441	5,8320	5,8211	5,8114	5,8025
5	6,6079	5,7861	5,4095	5,1922	5,0503	4,9503	4,8759	4,8183	4,7725	4,7351	4,7039	4,6777	4,6552	4,6358	4,6188	4,6038	4,5904	4,5785	4,5678	4,5581
6	5,9874	5,1433	4,7571	4,5337	4,3874	4,2839	4,2067	4,1468	4,0990	4,0600	4,0274	3,9999	3,9764	3,9559	3,9381	3,9223	3,9083	3,8957	3,8844	3,8742
7	5,5914	4,7374	4,3468	4,1203	3,9715	3,8660	3,7870	3,7257	3,6767	3,6365	3,6030	3,5747	3,5503	3,5292	3,5107	3,4944	3,4799	3,4669	3,4551	3,4445
8	5,3177	4,4590	4,0662	3,8379	3,6875	3,5806	3,5005	3,4381	3,3881	3,3472	3,3130	3,2839	3,2590	3,2374	3,2184	3,2016	3,1867	3,1733	3,1613	3,1503
9	5,1174	4,2565	3,8626	3,6331	3,4817	3,3738	3,2927	3,2296	3,1789	3,1373	3,1025	3,0729	3,0475	3,0255	3,0061	2,9890	2,9737	2,9600	2,9477	2,9365
10	4,9646	4,1028	3,7083	3,4780	3,3258	3,2172	3,1355	3,0717	3,0204	2,9782	2,9430	2,9130	2,8872	2,8647	2,8450	2,8276	2,8120	2,7980	2,7854	2,7740
11	4,8443	3,9823	3,5874	3,3567	3,2039	3,0946	3,0123	2,9480	2,8962	2,8536	2,8179	2,7876	2,7614	2,7386	2,7186	2,7009	2,6851	2,6709	2,6581	2,6464
12	4,7472	3,8853	3,4903	3,2592	3,1059	2,9961	2,9134	2,8486	2,7964	2,7534	2,7173	2,6866	2,6602	2,6371	2,6169	2,5989	2,5828	2,5684	2,5554	2,5436
13	4,6672	3,8056	3,4105	3,1791	3,0254	2,9153	2,8321	2,7669	2,7144	2,6710	2,6347	2,6037	2,5769	2,5536	2,5331	2,5149	2,4987	2,4841	2,4709	2,4589
14	4,6001	3,7389	3,3439	3,1122	2,9582	2,8477	2,7642	2,6987	2,6458	2,6022	2,5655	2,5342	2,5073	2,4837	2,4630	2,4446	2,4282	2,4134	2,4000	2,3879
15	4,5431	3,6823	3,2874	3,0556	2,9013	2,7905	2,7066	2,6408	2,5876	2,5437	2,5068	2,4753	2,4481	2,4244	2,4034	2,3849	2,3683	2,3533	2,3398	2,3275
16	4,4940	3,6337	3,2389	3,0069	2,8524	2,7413	2,6572	2,5911	2,5377	2,4935	2,4564	2,4247	2,3973	2,3733	2,3522	2,3335	2,3167	2,3016	2,2880	2,2756
17	4,4513	3,5915	3,1968	2,9647	2,8100	2,6987	2,6143	2,5480	2,4943	2,4499	2,4126	2,3807	2,3531	2,3290	2,3077	2,2888	2,2719	2,2567	2,2429	2,2304
18	4,4139	3,5546	3,1599	2,9277	2,7729	2,6613	2,5767	2,5102	2,4563	2,4117	2,3742	2,3421	2,3143	2,2900	2,2686	2,2496	2,2325	2,2172	2,2033	2,1906
19	4,3807	3,5219	3,1274	2,8951	2,7401	2,6283	2,5435	2,4768	2,4227	2,3779	2,3402	2,3080	2,2800	2,2556	2,2341	2,2149	2,1977	2,1823	2,1683	2,1555
20	4,3512	3,4928	3,0984	2,8661	2,7109	2,5990	2,5140	2,4471	2,3928	2,3479	2,3100	2,2776	2,2495	2,2250	2,2033	2,1840	2,1667	2,1511	2,1370	2,1242
21	4,3248	3,4668	3,0725	2,8401	2,6848	2,5727	2,4876	2,4205	2,3660	2,3210	2,2829	2,2504	2,2222	2,1975	2,1757	2,1563	2,1389	2,1232	2,1090	2,0960
22	4,3009	3,4434	3,0491	2,8167	2,6613	2,5491	2,4638	2,3965	2,3419	2,2967	2,2585	2,2258	2,1975	2,1727	2,1508	2,1313	2,1138	2,0980	2,0837	2,0707
23	4,2793	3,4221	3,0280	2,7955	2,6400	2,5277	2,4422	2,3748	2,3201	2,2747	2,2364	2,2036	2,1752	2,1502	2,1282	2,1086	2,0910	2,0751	2,0608	2,0476
24	4,2597	3,4028	3,0088	2,7763	2,6207	2,5082	2,4226	2,3551	2,3002	2,2547	2,2163	2,1834	2,1548	2,1298	2,1077	2,0880	2,0703	2,0543	2,0399	2,0267
25	4,2417	3,3852	2,9912	2,7587	2,6030	2,4904	2,4047	2,3371	2,2821	2,2365	2,1979	2,1649	2,1362	2,1111	2,0889	2,0691	2,0513	2,0353	2,0207	2,0075
26	4,2252	3,3690	2,9752	2,7426	2,5868	2,4741	2,3883	2,3205	2,2655	2,2197	2,1811	2,1479	2,1192	2,0939	2,0716	2,0518	2,0339	2,0178	2,0032	1,9898
27	4,2100	3,3541	2,9604	2,7278	2,5719	2,4591	2,3732	2,3053	2,2501	2,2043	2,1655	2,1323	2,1035	2,0781	2,0558	2,0358	2,0179	2,0017	1,9870	1,9736
28	4,1960	3,3404	2,9467	2,7141	2,5581	2,4453	2,3593	2,2913	2,2360	2,1900	2,1512	2,1179	2,0889	2,0635	2,0411	2,0210	2,0030	1,9868	1,9720	1,9586
29	4,1830	3,3277	2,9340	2,7014	2,5454	2,4324	2,3463	2,2783	2,2229	2,1768	2,1379	2,1045	2,0755	2,0500	2,0275	2,0073	1,9893	1,9730	1,9581	1,9446
30	4,1709	3,3158	2,9223	2,6896	2,5336	2,4205	2,3343	2,2662	2,2107	2,1646	2,1256	2,0921	2,0630	2,0374	2,0148	1,9946	1,9765	1,9601	1,9452	1,9317
31	4,1596	3,3048	2,9113	2,6787	2,5225	2,4094	2,3232	2,2549	2,1994	2,1532	2,1141	2,0805	2,0513	2,0257	2,0030	1,9828	1,9646	1,9481	1,9332	1,9196
32	4,1491	3,2945	2,9011	2,6684	2,5123	2,3991	2,3127	2,2444	2,1888	2,1425	2,1033	2,0697	2,0404	2,0147	1,9920	1,9717	1,9534	1,9369	1,9219	1,9083
33	4,1393	3,2849	2,8916	2,6589	2,5026	2,3894	2,3030	2,2346	2,1789	2,1325	2,0933	2,0595	2,0302	2,0045	1,9817	1,9613	1,9430	1,9264	1,9114	1,8977
34	4,1300	3,2759	2,8826	2,6499	2,4936	2,3803	2,2938	2,2253	2,1696	2,1231	2,0838	2,0500	2,0207	1,9949	1,9720	1,9516	1,9332	1,9166	1,9015	1,8877
35	4,1213	3,2674	2,8742	2,6415	2,4851	2,3718	2,2852	2,2167	2,1608	2,1143	2,0750	2,0411	2,0117	1,9858	1,9629	1,9424	1,9240	1,9073	1,8922	1,8784
36	4,1132	3,2594	2,8663	2,6335	2,4772	2,3638	2,2771	2,2085	2,1526	2,1061	2,0666	2,0327	2,0032	1,9773	1,9543	1,9338	1,9153	1,8986	1,8834	1,8696
37	4,1055	3,2519	2,8588	2,6261	2,4696	2,3562	2,2695	2,2008	2,1449	2,0982	2,0587	2,0248	1,9952	1,9692	1,9462	1,9256	1,9071	1,8904	1,8752	1,8612
38	4,0982	3,2448	2,8517	2,6190	2,4625	2,3490	2,2623	2,1936	2,1375	2,0909	2,0513	2,0173	1,9877	1,9616	1,9386	1,9179	1,8994	1,8826	1,8673	1,8534
39	4,0913	3,2381	2,8451	2,6123	2,4558	2,3423	2,2555	2,1867	2,1306	2,0839	2,0443	2,0102	1,9805	1,9545	1,9313	1,9107	1,8921	1,8752	1,8599	1,8459
40	4,0847	3,2317	2,8387	2,6060	2,4495	2,3359	2,2490	2,1802	2,1240	2,0772	2,0376	2,0035	1,9738	1,9476	1,9245	1,9037	1,8851	1,8682	1,8529	1,8389
41	4,0785	3,2257	2,8327	2,6000	2,4434	2,3298	2,2429	2,1740	2,1178	2,0710	2,0312	1,9971	1,9673	1,9412	1,9179	1,8972	1,8785	1,8616	1,8462	1,8321
42	4,0727	3,2199	2,8270	2,5943	2,4377	2,3240	2,2371	2,1681	2,1119	2,0650	2,0252	1,9910	1,9612	1,9350	1,9118	1,8910	1,8722	1,8553	1,8399	1,8258
43	4,0670	3,2145	2,8216	2,5888	2,4322	2,3185	2,2315	2,1625	2,1062	2,0593	2,0195	1,9852	1,9554	1,9292	1,9059	1,8850	1,8663	1,8493	1,8338	1,8197
44	4,0617	3,2093	2,8165	2,5837	2,4270	2,3133	2,2263	2,1572	2,1009	2,0539	2,0140	1,9797	1,9499	1,9236	1,9002	1,8794	1,8606	1,8436	1,8281	1,8139
45	4,0566	3,2043	2,8115	2,5787	2,4221	2,3083	2,2212	2,1521	2,0958	2,0487	2,0088	1,9745	1,9446	1,9182	1,8949	1,8740	1,8551	1,8381	1,8226	1,8084
46	4,0517	3,1996	2,8068	2,5740	2,4174	2,3035	2,2164	2,1473	2,0909	2,0438	2,0039	1,9695	1,9395	1,9132	1,8898	1,8688	1,8500	1,8329	1,8173	1,8031
47	4,0471	3,1951	2,8024	2,5695	2,4128	2,2990	2,2118	2,1427	2,0862	2,0391	1,9991	1,9647	1,9347	1,9083	1,8849	1,8639	1,8450	1,8279	1,8123	1,7980
48	4,0427	3,1907	2,7981	2,5652	2,4085	2,2946	2,2074	2,1382	2,0817	2,0346	1,9946	1,9601	1,9301	1,9037	1,8802	1,8592	1,8402	1,8231	1,8075	1,7932
49	4,0384	3,1866	2,7939	2,5611	2,4044	2,2904	2,2032	2,1340	2,0775	2,0303	1,9902	1,9557	1,9257	1,8992	1,8757	1,8546	1,8357	1,8185	1,8029	1,7886
50	4,0343	3,1826	2,7900	2,5572	2,4004	2,2864	2,1992	2,1299	2,0734	2,0261	1,9861	1,9515	1,9214	1,8949	1,8714	1,8503	1,8313	1,8141	1,7985	1,7841
52	4,0266	3,1751	2,7826	2,5498	2,3930	2,2789	2,1916	2,1223	2,0656	2,0184	1,9782	1,9436	1,9135	1,8869	1,8633	1,8422	1,8231	1,8059	1,7902	1,7758
54	4,0195	3,1682	2,7758	2,5429	2,3861	2,2720	2,1846	2,1152	2,0585	2,0112	1,9710	1,9363	1,9061	1,8795	1,8558	1,8346	1,8155	1,7982	1,7825	1,7680
56	4,0130	3,1619	2,7694	2,5366	2,3797	2,2656	2,1782	2,1087	2,0519	2,0045	1,9643	1,9295	1,8993	1,8726	1,8489	1,8276	1,8085	1,7912	1,7753	1,7609
58	4,0069	3,1559	2,7636	2,5307	2,3738	2,2596	2,1721	2,1026	2,0458	1,9983	1,9580	1,9233	1,8929	1,8662	1,8424	1,8212	1,8020	1,7846	1,7687	1,7542
60	4,0012	3,1504	2,7581	2,5252	2,3683	2,2541	2,1665	2,0970	2,0401	1,9926	1,9522	1,9174	1,8870	1,8602	1,8364	1,8151	1,7959	1,7784	1,7625	1,7480
62	3,9959	3,1453	2,7530	2,5201	2,3631	2,2489	2,1613	2,0917	2,0348	1,9872	1,9468	1,9119	1,8815	1,8547	1,8308	1,8095	1,7902	1,7727	1,7568	1,7422
64	3,9909	3,1404	2,7482	2,5153	2,3583	2,2440	2,1564	2,0868	2,0298	1,9822	1,9417	1,9068	1,8763	1,8495	1,8256	1,8042	1,7849	1,7674	1,7514	1,7367
66	3,9863	3,1359	2,7437	2,5108	2,3538	2,2395	2,1518	2,0821	2,0251	1,9775	1,9370	1,9020	1,8715	1,8446	1,8207	1,7992	1,7799	1,7623	1,7463	1,7316
68	3,9819	3,1317	2,7395	2,5066	2,3496	2,2352	2,1475	2,0778	2,0207	1,9730	1,9325	1,8975	1,8669	1,8400	1,8160	1,7946	1,7752	1,7576	1,7415	1,7268
70	3,9778	3,1277	2,7355	2,5027	2,3456	2,2312	2,1435	2,0737	2,0166	1,9689	1,9283	1,8932	1,8627	1,8357	1,8117	1,7902	1,7708	1,7531	1,7371	1,7223
72	3,9739	3,1239	2,7318	2,4989	2,3418	2,2274	2,1397	2,0698	2,0127	1,9649	1,9243	1,8892	1,8586	1,8316	1,8076	1,7860	1,7666	1,7489	1,7328	1,7181
74	3,9702	3,1203	2,7283	2,4954	2,3383	2,2238	2,1360	2,0662	2,0090	1,9612	1,9206	1,8855	1,8548	1,8278	1,8037	1,7821	1,7626	1,7450	1,7288	1,7140
76	3,9668	3,1170	2,7249	2,4920	2,3349	2,2204	2,1326	2,0627	2,0055	1,9577	1,9170	1,8819	1,8512	1,8241	1,8000	1,7784	1,7589	1,7412	1,7250	1,7102
78	3,9635	3,1138	2,7218	2,4889	2,3317	2,2172	2,1294	2,0595	2,0022	1,9544	1,9136	1,8785	1,8478	1,8207	1,7965	1,7749	1,7554	1,7376	1,7214	1,7066
80	3,9604	3,1108	2,7188	2,4859	2,3287	2,2142	2,1263	2,0564	1,9991	1,9512	1,9105	1,8753	1,8445	1,8174	1,7932	1,7716	1,7520	1,7342	1,7180	1,7032
82	3,9574	3,1079	2,7159	2,4830	2,3259	2,2113	2,1234	2,0534	1,9961	1,9482	1,9074	1,8722	1,8414	1,8143	1,7901	1,7684	1,7488	1,7310	1,7148	1,6999
84	3,9546	3,1052	2,7132	2,4803	2,3231	2,2086	2,1206	2,0506	1,9933	1,9454	1,9045	1,8693	1,8385	1,8113	1,7871	1,7654	1,7458	1,7280	1,7117	1,6968
86	3,9519	3,1026	2,7106	2,4777	2,3205	2,2059	2,1180	2,0480	1,9906	1,9426	1,9018	1,8665	1,8357	1,8085	1,7842	1,7625	1,7429	1,7250	1,7088	1,6938
88	3,9493	3,1001	2,7082	2,4753	2,3181	2,2034	2,1155	2,0454	1,9880	1,9400	1,8992	1,8639	1,8330	1,8058	1,7815	1,7598	1,7401	1,7223	1,7060	1,6910
90	3,9469	3,0977	2,7058	2,4729	2,3157	2,2011	2,1131	2,0430	1,9856	1,9376	1,8967	1,8613	1,8305	1,8032	1,7789	1,7571	1,7375	1,7196	1,7033	1,6883
92	3,9445	3,0954	2,7036	2,4707	2,3134	2,1988	2,1108	2,0407	1,9833	1,9352	1,8943	1,8589	1,8280	1,8007	1,7764	1,7546	1,7349	1,7171	1,7007	1,6857
94	3,9423	3,0933	2,7014	2,4685	2,3113	2,1966	2,1086	2,0384	1,9810	1,9329	1,8920	1,8566	1,8257	1,7984	1,7741	1,7522	1,7325	1,7146	1,6983	1,6832
96	3,9402	3,0912	2,6994	2,4665	2,3092	2,1945	2,1065	2,0363	1,9789	1,9308	1,8898	1,8544	1,8235	1,7961	1,7718	1,7500	1,7302	1,7123	1,6959	1,6809
98	3,9381	3,0892	2,6974	2,4645	2,3072	2,1925	2,1044	2,0343	1,9768	1,9287	1,8877	1,8523	1,8213	1,7940	1,7696	1,7478	1,7280	1,7101	1,6937	1,6786
100	3,9361	3,0873	2,6955	2,4626	2,3053	2,1906	2,1025	2,0323	1,9748	1,9267	1,8857	1,8503	1,8193	1,7919	1,7675	1,7456	1,7259	1,7079	1,6915	1,6764
110	3,9274	3,0788	2,6871	2,4542	2,2969	2,1821	2,0939	2,0236	1,9661	1,9178	1,8767	1,8412	1,8101	1,7827	1,7582	1,7363	1,7164	1,6984	1,6819	1,6667
120	3,9201	3,0718	2,6802	2,4472	2,2899	2,1750	2,0868	2,0164	1,9588	1,9105	1,8693	1,8337	1,8026	1,7750	1,7505	1,7285	1,7085	1,6904	1,6739	1,6587
130	3,9140	3,0658	2,6743	2,4414	2,2839	2,1690	2,0807	2,0103	1,9526	1,9042	1,8630	1,8273	1,7961	1,7686	1,7440	1,7219	1,7019	1,6837	1,6671	1,6519
140	3,9087	3,0608	2,6693	2,4363	2,2789	2,1639	2,0756	2,0051	1,9473	1,8989	1,8576	1,8219	1,7907	1,7630	1,7384	1,7162	1,6962	1,6780	1,6613	1,6460
150	3,9042	3,0564	2,6649	2,4320	2,2745	2,1595	2,0711	2,0006	1,9428	1,8943	1,8530	1,8172	1,7859	1,7582	1,7335	1,7113	1,6913	1,6730	1,6563	1,6410
160	3,9002	3,0525	2,6611	2,4282	2,2707	2,1557	2,0672	1,9967	1,9388	1,8903	1,8489	1,8131	1,7818	1,7540	1,7293	1,7071	1,6870	1,6687	1,6519	1,6366
170	3,8967	3,0491	2,6578	2,4248	2,2673	2,1523	2,0638	1,9932	1,9353	1,8868	1,8453	1,8095	1,7781	1,7504	1,7256	1,7033	1,6832	1,6648	1,6481	1,6327
180	3,8936	3,0461	2,6548	2,4218	2,2643	2,1492	2,0608	1,9901	1,9322	1,8836	1,8422	1,8063	1,7749	1,7471	1,7223	1,7000	1,6798	1,6614	1,6446	1,6292
190	3,8909	3,0435	2,6521	2,4192	2,2616	2,1466	2,0580	1,9874	1,9294	1,8808	1,8393	1,8034	1,7720	1,7441	1,7193	1,6970	1,6768	1,6584	1,6416	1,6261
200	3,8884	3,0411	2,6498	2,4168	2,2592	2,1441	2,0556	1,9849	1,9269	1,8783	1,8368	1,8008	1,7694	1,7415	1,7166	1,6943	1,6741	1,6556	1,6388	1,6233
250	3,8789	3,0319	2,6407	2,4078	2,2501	2,1350	2,0463	1,9756	1,9174	1,8687	1,8271	1,7910	1,7595	1,7315	1,7065	1,6841	1,6638	1,6453	1,6283	1,6127
300	3,8726	3,0258	2,6347	2,4017	2,2441	2,1289	2,0402	1,9693	1,9112	1,8623	1,8206	1,7845	1,7529	1,7249	1,6998	1,6773	1,6569	1,6383	1,6213	1,6057
350	3,8682	3,0215	2,6304	2,3975	2,2398	2,1245	2,0358	1,9649	1,9067	1,8578	1,8161	1,7799	1,7482	1,7201	1,6950	1,6725	1,6520	1,6334	1,6163	1,6006
400	3,8648	3,0183	2,6272	2,3942	2,2366	2,1212	2,0325	1,9616	1,9033	1,8544	1,8126	1,7764	1,7447	1,7166	1,6914	1,6688	1,6484	1,6297	1,6126	1,5969
500	3,8601	3,0138	2,6227	2,3898	2,2320	2,1167	2,0279	1,9569	1,8986	1,8496	1,8078	1,7715	1,7398	1,7116	1,6864	1,6638	1,6432	1,6245	1,6074	1,5916
600	3,8570	3,0107	2,6198	2,3868	2,2290	2,1137	2,0248	1,9538	1,8955	1,8465	1,8046	1,7683	1,7365	1,7083	1,6831	1,6604	1,6398	1,6211	1,6039	1,5881
700	3,8548	3,0086	2,6176	2,3847	2,2269	2,1115	2,0226	1,9516	1,8932	1,8442	1,8023	1,7660	1,7341	1,7059	1,6807	1,6580	1,6374	1,6186	1,6014	1,5856
800	3,8531	3,0070	2,6160	2,3831	2,2253	2,1099	2,0210	1,9500	1,8916	1,8425	1,8006	1,7643	1,7324	1,7041	1,6789	1,6562	1,6356	1,6168	1,5995	1,5837
900	3,8518	3,0057	2,6148	2,3818	2,2240	2,1086	2,0197	1,9487	1,8903	1,8412	1,7993	1,7629	1,7310	1,7028	1,6775	1,6548	1,6341	1,6153	1,5981	1,5822
1000	3,8508	3,0047	2,6138	2,3808	2,2231	2,1076	2,0187	1,9476	1,8892	1,8402	1,7982	1,7618	1,7299	1,7017	1,6764	1,6536	1,6330	1,6142	1,5969	1,5811
2000	3,8461	3,0002	2,6094	2,3764	2,2186	2,1031	2,0142	1,9430	1,8846	1,8354	1,7934	1,7570	1,7250	1,6967	1,6714	1,6486	1,6279	1,6090	1,5917	1,5758
5000	3,8433	2,9975	2,6067	2,3737	2,2159	2,1004	2,0114	1,9403	1,8818	1,8326	1,7906	1,7541	1,7221	1,6937	1,6684	1,6455	1,6248	1,6059	1,5886	1,5726
10000	3,8424	2,9966	2,6058	2,3728	2,2150	2,0995	2,0105	1,9393	1,8808	1,8316	1,7896	1,7531	1,7211	1,6928	1,6674	1,6445	1,6238	1,6049	1,5875	1,5716
∞	3,8415	2,9957	2,6049	2,3719	2,2141	2,0986	2,0096	1,9384	1,8799	1,8307	1,7886	1,7522	1,7202	1,6918	1,6664	1,6435	1,6228	1,6038	1,5865	1,5705

All values conform to the international convention (i.e. 0,1 instead of 0.1).

The *F*-Distribution* ν_1, ν_2 Degrees of Freedom $P = 0{,}05$

$P = P(\text{right})$ = integral between F_{ν_1,ν_2} and ∞ (values in the table are the F_{ν_1,ν_2}-values)

ν_2 \ ν_1	22	24	26	28	30	32	35	40	45	50	60	70	80	100	120	200	300	500	1000	∞
1	248,58	249,05	249,45	249,80	250,10	250,36	250,69	251,14	251,49	251,77	252,20	252,50	252,72	253,04	253,25	253,68	253,89	254,06	254,19	254,31
2	19,450	19,454	19,457	19,460	19,462	19,464	19,467	19,471	19,474	19,476	19,479	19,481	19,483	19,486	19,487	19,491	19,492	19,494	19,495	19,496
3	8,6484	8,6385	8,6301	8,6229	8,6166	8,6111	8,6039	8,5944	8,5870	8,5810	8,5720	8,5656	8,5607	8,5539	8,5494	8,5402	8,5356	8,5320	8,5292	8,5265
4	5,7872	5,7744	5,7635	5,7541	5,7459	5,7387	5,7294	5,7170	5,7073	5,6995	5,6877	5,6793	5,6730	5,6641	5,6581	5,6461	5,6401	5,6353	5,6317	5,6281
5	4,5413	4,5272	4,5151	4,5047	4,4957	4,4878	4,4775	4,4638	4,4530	4,4444	4,4314	4,4220	4,4150	4,4051	4,3985	4,3851	4,3784	4,3731	4,3690	4,3650
6	3,8564	3,8415	3,8287	3,8177	3,8082	3,7998	3,7889	3,7743	3,7629	3,7537	3,7398	3,7298	3,7223	3,7117	3,7047	3,6904	3,6833	3,6775	3,6732	3,6689
7	3,4260	3,4105	3,3972	3,3858	3,3758	3,3670	3,3557	3,3404	3,3285	3,3189	3,3043	3,2939	3,2860	3,2749	3,2674	3,2525	3,2449	3,2389	3,2343	3,2298
8	3,1313	3,1152	3,1015	3,0897	3,0794	3,0703	3,0586	3,0428	3,0304	3,0204	3,0053	2,9944	2,9862	2,9747	2,9669	2,9513	2,9434	2,9371	2,9324	2,9276
9	2,9169	2,9005	2,8864	2,8743	2,8637	2,8543	2,8422	2,8259	2,8131	2,8028	2,7872	2,7760	2,7675	2,7556	2,7475	2,7313	2,7232	2,7166	2,7116	2,7067
10	2,7541	2,7372	2,7229	2,7104	2,6996	2,6900	2,6776	2,6609	2,6477	2,6371	2,6211	2,6095	2,6008	2,5884	2,5801	2,5634	2,5549	2,5481	2,5430	2,5379
11	2,6261	2,6090	2,5943	2,5816	2,5705	2,5607	2,5480	2,5309	2,5174	2,5066	2,4901	2,4782	2,4692	2,4566	2,4480	2,4308	2,4221	2,4151	2,4098	2,4045
12	2,5229	2,5055	2,4905	2,4776	2,4663	2,4563	2,4433	2,4259	2,4121	2,4010	2,3842	2,3720	2,3628	2,3498	2,3410	2,3233	2,3143	2,3071	2,3017	2,2962
13	2,4379	2,4202	2,4050	2,3918	2,3803	2,3702	2,3570	2,3392	2,3252	2,3138	2,2966	2,2841	2,2747	2,2614	2,2524	2,2343	2,2251	2,2176	2,2121	2,2064
14	2,3667	2,3487	2,3333	2,3199	2,3082	2,2979	2,2845	2,2664	2,2521	2,2405	2,2229	2,2102	2,2006	2,1870	2,1778	2,1592	2,1498	2,1422	2,1365	2,1307
15	2,3060	2,2878	2,2722	2,2587	2,2468	2,2363	2,2227	2,2043	2,1897	2,1780	2,1601	2,1472	2,1373	2,1234	2,1141	2,0950	2,0854	2,0776	2,0718	2,0658
16	2,2538	2,2354	2,2196	2,2059	2,1938	2,1832	2,1694	2,1507	2,1360	2,1240	2,1058	2,0926	2,0826	2,0684	2,0589	2,0395	2,0296	2,0217	2,0157	2,0096
17	2,2084	2,1898	2,1738	2,1599	2,1477	2,1369	2,1229	2,1040	2,0890	2,0769	2,0584	2,0450	2,0348	2,0204	2,0107	1,9909	1,9808	1,9727	1,9666	1,9604
18	2,1685	2,1497	2,1335	2,1195	2,1071	2,0963	2,0821	2,0629	2,0477	2,0354	2,0166	2,0030	1,9927	1,9780	1,9681	1,9479	1,9377	1,9294	1,9232	1,9168
19	2,1331	2,1141	2,0978	2,0836	2,0712	2,0602	2,0458	2,0264	2,0110	1,9986	1,9795	1,9657	1,9552	1,9403	1,9302	1,9097	1,8993	1,8909	1,8845	1,8780
20	2,1016	2,0825	2,0660	2,0517	2,0391	2,0280	2,0135	1,9938	1,9783	1,9656	1,9464	1,9323	1,9217	1,9066	1,8963	1,8755	1,8648	1,8563	1,8497	1,8432
21	2,0733	2,0540	2,0374	2,0229	2,0102	1,9990	1,9844	1,9645	1,9488	1,9360	1,9165	1,9023	1,8915	1,8761	1,8657	1,8446	1,8338	1,8250	1,8184	1,8117
22	2,0478	2,0283	2,0116	1,9970	1,9842	1,9729	1,9581	1,9380	1,9221	1,9092	1,8894	1,8751	1,8641	1,8486	1,8380	1,8165	1,8055	1,7966	1,7899	1,7831
23	2,0246	2,0050	1,9881	1,9734	1,9605	1,9491	1,9342	1,9139	1,8979	1,8848	1,8648	1,8503	1,8392	1,8234	1,8128	1,7909	1,7798	1,7708	1,7639	1,7570
24	2,0035	1,9838	1,9668	1,9520	1,9390	1,9274	1,9124	1,8920	1,8757	1,8625	1,8424	1,8276	1,8164	1,8005	1,7896	1,7675	1,7562	1,7470	1,7401	1,7330
25	1,9842	1,9643	1,9472	1,9323	1,9192	1,9076	1,8924	1,8718	1,8554	1,8421	1,8217	1,8069	1,7955	1,7794	1,7684	1,7460	1,7345	1,7252	1,7181	1,7110
26	1,9664	1,9464	1,9292	1,9142	1,9010	1,8893	1,8740	1,8533	1,8367	1,8233	1,8027	1,7877	1,7762	1,7599	1,7488	1,7261	1,7145	1,7050	1,6978	1,6906
27	1,9500	1,9299	1,9126	1,8975	1,8842	1,8725	1,8571	1,8361	1,8195	1,8059	1,7851	1,7700	1,7584	1,7419	1,7306	1,7077	1,6959	1,6863	1,6790	1,6717
28	1,9349	1,9147	1,8973	1,8821	1,8687	1,8568	1,8414	1,8203	1,8035	1,7898	1,7689	1,7535	1,7418	1,7251	1,7138	1,6905	1,6786	1,6689	1,6615	1,6541
29	1,9208	1,9005	1,8830	1,8677	1,8543	1,8424	1,8268	1,8055	1,7886	1,7748	1,7537	1,7382	1,7264	1,7096	1,6981	1,6746	1,6625	1,6527	1,6452	1,6376
30	1,9077	1,8874	1,8698	1,8544	1,8409	1,8289	1,8132	1,7918	1,7748	1,7609	1,7396	1,7240	1,7121	1,6950	1,6835	1,6597	1,6474	1,6375	1,6299	1,6223
31	1,8956	1,8751	1,8574	1,8419	1,8283	1,8163	1,8005	1,7790	1,7618	1,7478	1,7264	1,7106	1,6986	1,6814	1,6697	1,6457	1,6333	1,6233	1,6156	1,6078
32	1,8842	1,8636	1,8458	1,8303	1,8166	1,8045	1,7886	1,7670	1,7497	1,7356	1,7140	1,6981	1,6860	1,6687	1,6569	1,6326	1,6201	1,6099	1,6021	1,5943
33	1,8735	1,8528	1,8350	1,8194	1,8056	1,7934	1,7775	1,7557	1,7383	1,7241	1,7024	1,6864	1,6742	1,6567	1,6448	1,6202	1,6076	1,5973	1,5894	1,5815
34	1,8634	1,8427	1,8248	1,8091	1,7953	1,7830	1,7670	1,7451	1,7276	1,7134	1,6914	1,6753	1,6630	1,6454	1,6333	1,6086	1,5958	1,5854	1,5775	1,5694
35	1,8540	1,8332	1,8152	1,7995	1,7856	1,7733	1,7571	1,7351	1,7175	1,7032	1,6811	1,6649	1,6525	1,6347	1,6226	1,5976	1,5847	1,5742	1,5661	1,5580
36	1,8451	1,8242	1,8061	1,7904	1,7764	1,7640	1,7478	1,7257	1,7080	1,6936	1,6714	1,6550	1,6425	1,6246	1,6124	1,5872	1,5741	1,5635	1,5554	1,5471
37	1,8367	1,8157	1,7976	1,7818	1,7678	1,7553	1,7390	1,7168	1,6990	1,6845	1,6621	1,6457	1,6331	1,6151	1,6027	1,5773	1,5641	1,5534	1,5452	1,5369
38	1,8288	1,8077	1,7895	1,7736	1,7596	1,7471	1,7307	1,7084	1,6905	1,6759	1,6534	1,6369	1,6242	1,6060	1,5936	1,5679	1,5547	1,5438	1,5355	1,5271
39	1,8212	1,8001	1,7819	1,7659	1,7518	1,7393	1,7228	1,7004	1,6824	1,6678	1,6451	1,6285	1,6157	1,5974	1,5849	1,5590	1,5456	1,5347	1,5263	1,5178
40	1,8141	1,7929	1,7746	1,7586	1,7444	1,7318	1,7154	1,6928	1,6748	1,6600	1,6373	1,6205	1,6077	1,5892	1,5766	1,5505	1,5370	1,5260	1,5175	1,5089
41	1,8073	1,7861	1,7677	1,7516	1,7374	1,7248	1,7082	1,6856	1,6675	1,6526	1,6298	1,6129	1,6000	1,5814	1,5687	1,5424	1,5288	1,5176	1,5091	1,5004
42	1,8009	1,7796	1,7611	1,7450	1,7308	1,7181	1,7015	1,6787	1,6605	1,6456	1,6226	1,6057	1,5927	1,5740	1,5612	1,5347	1,5210	1,5097	1,5011	1,4923
43	1,7947	1,7734	1,7549	1,7387	1,7244	1,7117	1,6950	1,6722	1,6539	1,6389	1,6158	1,5988	1,5857	1,5669	1,5540	1,5273	1,5135	1,5021	1,4934	1,4846
44	1,7889	1,7675	1,7489	1,7327	1,7184	1,7056	1,6888	1,6659	1,6476	1,6325	1,6093	1,5922	1,5790	1,5601	1,5471	1,5203	1,5063	1,4948	1,4861	1,4771
45	1,7833	1,7618	1,7432	1,7270	1,7126	1,6998	1,6830	1,6599	1,6415	1,6264	1,6031	1,5859	1,5726	1,5536	1,5406	1,5135	1,4994	1,4879	1,4790	1,4700
46	1,7780	1,7564	1,7378	1,7215	1,7070	1,6942	1,6773	1,6542	1,6357	1,6206	1,5971	1,5798	1,5665	1,5474	1,5343	1,5070	1,4928	1,4812	1,4722	1,4632
47	1,7729	1,7513	1,7326	1,7162	1,7017	1,6889	1,6719	1,6488	1,6302	1,6150	1,5914	1,5740	1,5607	1,5414	1,5282	1,5008	1,4865	1,4747	1,4657	1,4566
48	1,7680	1,7464	1,7276	1,7112	1,6967	1,6837	1,6668	1,6435	1,6249	1,6096	1,5859	1,5685	1,5551	1,5357	1,5224	1,4948	1,4804	1,4686	1,4595	1,4502
49	1,7633	1,7416	1,7228	1,7064	1,6918	1,6789	1,6618	1,6385	1,6198	1,6044	1,5807	1,5632	1,5497	1,5302	1,5168	1,4890	1,4745	1,4626	1,4535	1,4441
50	1,7588	1,7371	1,7183	1,7017	1,6872	1,6742	1,6571	1,6337	1,6149	1,5995	1,5757	1,5580	1,5445	1,5249	1,5115	1,4835	1,4689	1,4569	1,4477	1,4383
52	1,7503	1,7285	1,7096	1,6930	1,6784	1,6653	1,6481	1,6246	1,6057	1,5902	1,5661	1,5484	1,5347	1,5149	1,5013	1,4730	1,4582	1,4460	1,4367	1,4271
54	1,7425	1,7206	1,7016	1,6850	1,6702	1,6571	1,6399	1,6162	1,5972	1,5815	1,5573	1,5394	1,5256	1,5056	1,4919	1,4633	1,4483	1,4359	1,4264	1,4167
56	1,7353	1,7133	1,6942	1,6775	1,6627	1,6495	1,6322	1,6084	1,5892	1,5735	1,5491	1,5311	1,5171	1,4970	1,4831	1,4542	1,4390	1,4265	1,4169	1,4070
58	1,7285	1,7065	1,6873	1,6706	1,6557	1,6424	1,6250	1,6011	1,5818	1,5660	1,5415	1,5233	1,5092	1,4889	1,4749	1,4457	1,4303	1,4176	1,4079	1,3979
60	1,7222	1,7001	1,6809	1,6641	1,6491	1,6358	1,6183	1,5943	1,5749	1,5590	1,5343	1,5160	1,5019	1,4814	1,4673	1,4377	1,4222	1,4093	1,3994	1,3893
62	1,7163	1,6942	1,6749	1,6580	1,6430	1,6297	1,6121	1,5879	1,5685	1,5525	1,5276	1,5092	1,4949	1,4743	1,4601	1,4302	1,4145	1,4015	1,3915	1,3812
64	1,7108	1,6886	1,6693	1,6523	1,6373	1,6239	1,6062	1,5819	1,5624	1,5463	1,5213	1,5028	1,4884	1,4676	1,4533	1,4232	1,4073	1,3941	1,3840	1,3735
66	1,7057	1,6834	1,6640	1,6470	1,6319	1,6184	1,6007	1,5763	1,5567	1,5405	1,5154	1,4967	1,4823	1,4614	1,4469	1,4165	1,4005	1,3872	1,3769	1,3663
68	1,7008	1,6785	1,6590	1,6420	1,6268	1,6133	1,5955	1,5711	1,5513	1,5351	1,5098	1,4911	1,4765	1,4554	1,4409	1,4102	1,3940	1,3806	1,3702	1,3594
70	1,6962	1,6738	1,6543	1,6372	1,6220	1,6085	1,5906	1,5661	1,5463	1,5300	1,5046	1,4857	1,4711	1,4498	1,4351	1,4042	1,3879	1,3743	1,3638	1,3529
72	1,6919	1,6695	1,6499	1,6327	1,6175	1,6039	1,5860	1,5614	1,5415	1,5251	1,4996	1,4806	1,4659	1,4445	1,4297	1,3986	1,3821	1,3683	1,3577	1,3467
74	1,6878	1,6653	1,6457	1,6285	1,6133	1,5996	1,5817	1,5569	1,5370	1,5205	1,4949	1,4758	1,4610	1,4395	1,4246	1,3932	1,3765	1,3627	1,3519	1,3408
76	1,6840	1,6614	1,6418	1,6245	1,6092	1,5955	1,5775	1,5527	1,5327	1,5161	1,4904	1,4712	1,4564	1,4347	1,4197	1,3881	1,3713	1,3573	1,3464	1,3352
78	1,6803	1,6577	1,6380	1,6207	1,6054	1,5917	1,5736	1,5487	1,5286	1,5120	1,4862	1,4669	1,4519	1,4302	1,4151	1,3832	1,3663	1,3521	1,3412	1,3298
80	1,6768	1,6542	1,6345	1,6171	1,6017	1,5880	1,5699	1,5449	1,5247	1,5081	1,4821	1,4628	1,4477	1,4259	1,4107	1,3786	1,3615	1,3472	1,3362	1,3247
82	1,6735	1,6508	1,6311	1,6137	1,5983	1,5845	1,5663	1,5413	1,5210	1,5043	1,4783	1,4588	1,4437	1,4217	1,4065	1,3741	1,3569	1,3425	1,3313	1,3198
84	1,6704	1,6476	1,6278	1,6104	1,5950	1,5811	1,5629	1,5378	1,5175	1,5007	1,4746	1,4551	1,4399	1,4178	1,4024	1,3699	1,3525	1,3380	1,3267	1,3150
86	1,6674	1,6446	1,6247	1,6073	1,5918	1,5780	1,5597	1,5345	1,5142	1,4973	1,4711	1,4515	1,4362	1,4140	1,3986	1,3658	1,3484	1,3337	1,3223	1,3105
88	1,6645	1,6417	1,6218	1,6043	1,5888	1,5749	1,5566	1,5314	1,5110	1,4941	1,4677	1,4481	1,4327	1,4104	1,3949	1,3620	1,3443	1,3296	1,3181	1,3062
90	1,6618	1,6389	1,6190	1,6015	1,5859	1,5720	1,5537	1,5284	1,5079	1,4910	1,4645	1,4448	1,4294	1,4070	1,3914	1,3582	1,3405	1,3256	1,3140	1,3020
92	1,6591	1,6363	1,6163	1,5988	1,5832	1,5693	1,5509	1,5255	1,5050	1,4880	1,4615	1,4416	1,4262	1,4037	1,3880	1,3546	1,3368	1,3218	1,3101	1,2979
94	1,6566	1,6337	1,6137	1,5962	1,5806	1,5666	1,5482	1,5227	1,5022	1,4851	1,4585	1,4386	1,4231	1,4005	1,3847	1,3512	1,3332	1,3181	1,3063	1,2941
96	1,6542	1,6313	1,6113	1,5937	1,5780	1,5640	1,5456	1,5201	1,4995	1,4824	1,4557	1,4357	1,4202	1,3975	1,3816	1,3479	1,3298	1,3146	1,3027	1,2903
98	1,6519	1,6289	1,6089	1,5913	1,5756	1,5616	1,5431	1,5176	1,4969	1,4798	1,4530	1,4330	1,4173	1,3945	1,3786	1,3447	1,3265	1,3112	1,2992	1,2867
100	1,6497	1,6267	1,6067	1,5890	1,5733	1,5593	1,5407	1,5151	1,4944	1,4772	1,4504	1,4303	1,4146	1,3917	1,3757	1,3416	1,3233	1,3079	1,2958	1,2832
110	1,6399	1,6167	1,5966	1,5788	1,5630	1,5488	1,5301	1,5043	1,4833	1,4660	1,4388	1,4183	1,4024	1,3791	1,3628	1,3279	1,3090	1,2931	1,2805	1,2674
120	1,6317	1,6084	1,5881	1,5703	1,5543	1,5401	1,5213	1,4952	1,4741	1,4565	1,4290	1,4083	1,3922	1,3685	1,3519	1,3162	1,2968	1,2804	1,2675	1,2539
130	1,6248	1,6014	1,5810	1,5630	1,5470	1,5327	1,5138	1,4875	1,4662	1,4485	1,4207	1,3998	1,3835	1,3595	1,3426	1,3062	1,2864	1,2695	1,2562	1,2421
140	1,6188	1,5954	1,5749	1,5569	1,5408	1,5264	1,5073	1,4809	1,4595	1,4416	1,4136	1,3925	1,3760	1,3517	1,3345	1,2975	1,2773	1,2600	1,2463	1,2318
150	1,6137	1,5902	1,5696	1,5515	1,5354	1,5209	1,5018	1,4752	1,4536	1,4357	1,4074	1,3861	1,3694	1,3448	1,3275	1,2899	1,2693	1,2516	1,2375	1,2226
160	1,6092	1,5856	1,5650	1,5468	1,5306	1,5161	1,4969	1,4702	1,4485	1,4304	1,4020	1,3805	1,3637	1,3388	1,3213	1,2832	1,2622	1,2442	1,2298	1,2144
170	1,6053	1,5816	1,5609	1,5427	1,5264	1,5118	1,4925	1,4657	1,4439	1,4258	1,3972	1,3756	1,3586	1,3335	1,3158	1,2772	1,2559	1,2375	1,2228	1,2070
180	1,6017	1,5780	1,5573	1,5390	1,5227	1,5081	1,4887	1,4618	1,4399	1,4217	1,3929	1,3711	1,3541	1,3288	1,3109	1,2718	1,2502	1,2315	1,2164	1,2002
190	1,5986	1,5748	1,5541	1,5357	1,5194	1,5047	1,4853	1,4583	1,4363	1,4180	1,3891	1,3672	1,3500	1,3245	1,3064	1,2670	1,2450	1,2260	1,2107	1,1941
200	1,5958	1,5720	1,5511	1,5328	1,5164	1,5017	1,4822	1,4551	1,4330	1,4146	1,3856	1,3636	1,3463	1,3206	1,3024	1,2626	1,2404	1,2211	1,2054	1,1885
250	1,5850	1,5610	1,5400	1,5215	1,5049	1,4901	1,4704	1,4430	1,4206	1,4019	1,3723	1,3499	1,3322	1,3058	1,2870	1,2456	1,2221	1,2015	1,1847	1,1661
300	1,5778	1,5537	1,5326	1,5140	1,4973	1,4824	1,4625	1,4349	1,4123	1,3934	1,3634	1,3407	1,3226	1,2958	1,2766	1,2339	1,2095	1,1879	1,1700	1,1500
350	1,5727	1,5485	1,5273	1,5086	1,4919	1,4768	1,4569	1,4291	1,4063	1,3873	1,3571	1,3340	1,3158	1,2885	1,2690	1,2254	1,2003	1,1778	1,1590	1,1377
400	1,5689	1,5446	1,5234	1,5046	1,4878	1,4727	1,4527	1,4247	1,4018	1,3827	1,3522	1,3290	1,3106	1,2831	1,2633	1,2189	1,1932	1,1700	1,1504	1,1279
500	1,5635	1,5392	1,5178	1,4989	1,4821	1,4669	1,4467	1,4186	1,3955	1,3762	1,3455	1,3220	1,3033	1,2753	1,2551	1,2096	1,1829	1,1587	1,1378	1,1132
600	1,5599	1,5355	1,5141	1,4952	1,4782	1,4630	1,4428	1,4145	1,3913	1,3719	1,3409	1,3173	1,2984	1,2701	1,2497	1,2033	1,1760	1,1508	1,1289	1,1026
700	1,5574	1,5329	1,5115	1,4925	1,4755	1,4602	1,4399	1,4116	1,3883	1,3688	1,3377	1,3139	1,2949	1,2664	1,2457	1,1987	1,1709	1,1450	1,1223	1,0944
800	1,5554	1,5310	1,5095	1,4905	1,4735	1,4582	1,4378	1,4094	1,3860	1,3665	1,3353	1,3113	1,2923	1,2635	1,2427	1,1953	1,1670	1,1406	1,1172	1,0879
900	1,5540	1,5294	1,5079	1,4889	1,4719	1,4565	1,4362	1,4077	1,3843	1,3647	1,3334	1,3093	1,2902	1,2613	1,2404	1,1925	1,1639	1,1371	1,1131	1,0826
1000	1,5528	1,5282	1,5067	1,4876	1,4706	1,4552	1,4348	1,4063	1,3829	1,3632	1,3318	1,3078	1,2885	1,2596	1,2385	1,1903	1,1614	1,1342	1,1097	1,0781
2000	1,5474	1,5228	1,5011	1,4820	1,4648	1,4494	1,4289	1,4001	1,3765	1,3567	1,3250	1,3006	1,2811	1,2516	1,2300	1,1803	1,1500	1,1208	1,0935	1,0542
5000	1,5442	1,5195	1,4978	1,4786	1,4614	1,4459	1,4253	1,3964	1,3727	1,3527	1,3208	1,2962	1,2765	1,2467	1,2249	1,1742	1,1429	1,1122	1,0826	1,0338
10000	1,5431	1,5184	1,4967	1,4775	1,4602	1,4447	1,4241	1,3952	1,3714	1,3514	1,3194	1,2948	1,2750	1,2451	1,2231	1,1721	1,1404	1,1093	1,0787	1,0237
∞	1,5420	1,5173	1,4956	1,4763	1,4591	1,4436	1,4229	1,3940	1,3701	1,3501	1,3180	1,2933	1,2735	1,2434	1,2214	1,1700	1,1380	1,1063	1,0747	1

All values conform to the international convention (i.e. 0,1 instead of 0.1).

The *F*-Distribution* ν_1, ν_2 Degrees of Freedom $P = 0{,}025$

$P = P$ (right) = integral between F_{ν_1, ν_2} and ∞ (values in the table are the F_{ν_1, ν_2}-values)

ν_1 / ν_2	1	2	3	4	5	6	7	8	9	10	11	12	13	14	15	16	17	18	19	20
1	647,79	799,50	864,16	899,58	921,85	937,11	948,22	956,66	963,28	968,63	973,03	976,71	979,84	982,53	984,87	986,92	988,73	990,35	991,80	993,10
2	38,506	39,000	39,165	39,248	39,298	39,331	39,355	39,373	39,387	39,398	39,407	39,415	39,421	39,427	39,431	39,435	39,439	39,442	39,445	39,448
3	17,443	16,044	15,439	15,101	14,885	14,735	14,624	14,540	14,473	14,419	14,374	14,337	14,304	14,277	14,253	14,232	14,213	14,196	14,181	14,167
4	12,218	10,649	9,9792	9,6045	9,3645	9,1973	9,0741	8,9796	8,9047	8,8439	8,7935	8,7512	8,7150	8,6838	8,6565	8,6326	8,6113	8,5924	8,5753	8,5599
5	10,007	8,4336	7,7636	7,3879	7,1464	6,9777	6,8531	6,7572	6,6811	6,6192	6,5678	6,5245	6,4876	6,4556	6,4277	6,4032	6,3814	6,3619	6,3444	6,3286
6	8,8131	7,2599	6,5988	6,2272	5,9876	5,8198	5,6955	5,5996	5,5234	5,4613	5,4098	5,3662	5,3290	5,2968	5,2687	5,2439	5,2218	5,2021	5,1844	5,1684
7	8,0727	6,5415	5,8898	5,5226	5,2852	5,1186	4,9949	4,8993	4,8232	4,7611	4,7095	4,6658	4,6285	4,5961	4,5678	4,5428	4,5206	4,5008	4,4829	4,4667
8	7,5709	6,0595	5,4160	5,0526	4,8173	4,6517	4,5286	4,4333	4,3572	4,2951	4,2434	4,1997	4,1622	4,1297	4,1012	4,0761	4,0538	4,0338	4,0158	3,9995
9	7,2093	5,7147	5,0781	4,7181	4,4844	4,3197	4,1970	4,1020	4,0260	3,9639	3,9121	3,8682	3,8306	3,7980	3,7694	3,7441	3,7216	3,7015	3,6833	3,6669
10	6,9367	5,4564	4,8256	4,4683	4,2361	4,0721	3,9498	3,8549	3,7790	3,7168	3,6649	3,6209	3,5832	3,5504	3,5217	3,4963	3,4737	3,4534	3,4351	3,4185
11	6,7241	5,2559	4,6300	4,2751	4,0440	3,8807	3,7586	3,6638	3,5879	3,5257	3,4737	3,4296	3,3917	3,3588	3,3299	3,3044	3,2816	3,2612	3,2428	3,2261
12	6,5538	5,0959	4,4742	4,1212	3,8911	3,7283	3,6065	3,5118	3,4358	3,3736	3,3215	3,2773	3,2393	3,2062	3,1772	3,1515	3,1286	3,1081	3,0896	3,0728
13	6,4143	4,9653	4,3472	3,9959	3,7667	3,6043	3,4827	3,3880	3,3120	3,2497	3,1975	3,1532	3,1150	3,0819	3,0527	3,0269	3,0039	2,9832	2,9646	2,9477
14	6,2979	4,8567	4,2417	3,8919	3,6634	3,5014	3,3799	3,2853	3,2093	3,1469	3,0946	3,0502	3,0119	2,9786	2,9493	2,9234	2,9003	2,8795	2,8607	2,8437
15	6,1995	4,7650	4,1528	3,8043	3,5764	3,4147	3,2934	3,1987	3,1227	3,0602	3,0078	2,9633	2,9249	2,8915	2,8621	2,8360	2,8128	2,7919	2,7730	2,7559
16	6,1151	4,6867	4,0768	3,7294	3,5021	3,3406	3,2194	3,1248	3,0488	2,9862	2,9337	2,8890	2,8506	2,8170	2,7875	2,7614	2,7380	2,7170	2,6980	2,6808
17	6,0420	4,6189	4,0112	3,6648	3,4379	3,2767	3,1556	3,0610	2,9849	2,9222	2,8696	2,8249	2,7863	2,7526	2,7230	2,6968	2,6733	2,6522	2,6331	2,6158
18	5,9781	4,5597	3,9539	3,6083	3,3820	3,2209	3,0999	3,0053	2,9291	2,8664	2,8137	2,7689	2,7302	2,6964	2,6667	2,6404	2,6169	2,5956	2,5764	2,5590
19	5,9216	4,5075	3,9034	3,5587	3,3327	3,1718	3,0509	2,9563	2,8801	2,8172	2,7645	2,7196	2,6808	2,6469	2,6171	2,5907	2,5670	2,5457	2,5265	2,5089
20	5,8715	4,4613	3,8587	3,5147	3,2891	3,1283	3,0074	2,9128	2,8365	2,7737	2,7209	2,6758	2,6369	2,6030	2,5731	2,5465	2,5228	2,5014	2,4821	2,4645
21	5,8266	4,4199	3,8188	3,4754	3,2501	3,0895	2,9686	2,8740	2,7977	2,7348	2,6819	2,6368	2,5978	2,5638	2,5338	2,5071	2,4833	2,4618	2,4424	2,4247
22	5,7863	4,3828	3,7829	3,4401	3,2151	3,0546	2,9338	2,8392	2,7628	2,6998	2,6469	2,6017	2,5626	2,5285	2,4984	2,4717	2,4478	2,4262	2,4067	2,3890
23	5,7498	4,3492	3,7505	3,4083	3,1835	3,0232	2,9023	2,8077	2,7313	2,6682	2,6152	2,5699	2,5308	2,4966	2,4665	2,4396	2,4157	2,3940	2,3745	2,3567
24	5,7166	4,3187	3,7211	3,3794	3,1548	2,9946	2,8738	2,7791	2,7027	2,6396	2,5865	2,5411	2,5019	2,4677	2,4374	2,4105	2,3865	2,3648	2,3452	2,3273
25	5,6864	4,2909	3,6943	3,3530	3,1287	2,9685	2,8478	2,7531	2,6766	2,6135	2,5603	2,5149	2,4756	2,4413	2,4110	2,3840	2,3599	2,3381	2,3184	2,3005
26	5,6586	4,2655	3,6697	3,3289	3,1048	2,9447	2,8240	2,7293	2,6528	2,5896	2,5363	2,4908	2,4515	2,4171	2,3867	2,3597	2,3355	2,3137	2,2939	2,2759
27	5,6331	4,2421	3,6472	3,3067	3,0828	2,9228	2,8021	2,7074	2,6309	2,5676	2,5143	2,4688	2,4293	2,3949	2,3644	2,3373	2,3131	2,2912	2,2713	2,2533
28	5,6096	4,2205	3,6264	3,2863	3,0626	2,9027	2,7820	2,6872	2,6106	2,5473	2,4940	2,4484	2,4089	2,3743	2,3438	2,3167	2,2924	2,2704	2,2505	2,2324
29	5,5878	4,2006	3,6072	3,2674	3,0438	2,8840	2,7633	2,6686	2,5919	2,5286	2,4752	2,4295	2,3900	2,3554	2,3248	2,2976	2,2732	2,2512	2,2313	2,2131
30	5,5675	4,1821	3,5894	3,2499	3,0265	2,8667	2,7460	2,6513	2,5746	2,5112	2,4577	2,4120	2,3724	2,3378	2,3072	2,2799	2,2554	2,2334	2,2134	2,1952
31	5,5487	4,1648	3,5728	3,2336	3,0103	2,8506	2,7299	2,6352	2,5585	2,4950	2,4415	2,3958	2,3561	2,3214	2,2907	2,2634	2,2389	2,2168	2,1967	2,1785
32	5,5311	4,1488	3,5573	3,2185	2,9953	2,8356	2,7150	2,6202	2,5434	2,4799	2,4264	2,3806	2,3409	2,3061	2,2754	2,2480	2,2235	2,2013	2,1812	2,1629
33	5,5147	4,1338	3,5429	3,2043	2,9812	2,8216	2,7009	2,6061	2,5294	2,4658	2,4123	2,3664	2,3266	2,2918	2,2610	2,2336	2,2090	2,1868	2,1667	2,1483
34	5,4993	4,1197	3,5293	3,1910	2,9680	2,8085	2,6878	2,5930	2,5162	2,4526	2,3990	2,3531	2,3133	2,2784	2,2476	2,2201	2,1955	2,1732	2,1531	2,1346
35	5,4848	4,1065	3,5166	3,1785	2,9557	2,7961	2,6755	2,5807	2,5039	2,4403	2,3866	2,3406	2,3008	2,2659	2,2350	2,2075	2,1828	2,1605	2,1403	2,1218
36	5,4712	4,0941	3,5047	3,1668	2,9440	2,7846	2,6639	2,5691	2,4922	2,4286	2,3749	2,3289	2,2890	2,2540	2,2231	2,1956	2,1708	2,1485	2,1282	2,1097
37	5,4584	4,0824	3,4934	3,1557	2,9331	2,7736	2,6530	2,5581	2,4813	2,4176	2,3639	2,3178	2,2779	2,2429	2,2119	2,1843	2,1595	2,1372	2,1169	2,0983
38	5,4463	4,0713	3,4828	3,1453	2,9227	2,7633	2,6427	2,5478	2,4710	2,4072	2,3535	2,3074	2,2674	2,2324	2,2014	2,1737	2,1489	2,1265	2,1061	2,0875
39	5,4348	4,0609	3,4728	3,1354	2,9130	2,7536	2,6330	2,5381	2,4612	2,3974	2,3436	2,2975	2,2575	2,2224	2,1914	2,1637	2,1388	2,1164	2,0960	2,0774
40	5,4239	4,0510	3,4633	3,1261	2,9037	2,7444	2,6238	2,5289	2,4519	2,3882	2,3343	2,2882	2,2481	2,2130	2,1819	2,1542	2,1293	2,1068	2,0864	2,0677
41	5,4136	4,0416	3,4542	3,1173	2,8950	2,7356	2,6150	2,5201	2,4432	2,3794	2,3255	2,2793	2,2392	2,2040	2,1729	2,1452	2,1202	2,0977	2,0772	2,0586
42	5,4039	4,0327	3,4457	3,1089	2,8866	2,7273	2,6068	2,5118	2,4348	2,3710	2,3171	2,2709	2,2307	2,1956	2,1644	2,1366	2,1116	2,0891	2,0686	2,0499
43	5,3946	4,0242	3,4376	3,1009	2,8787	2,7195	2,5989	2,5039	2,4269	2,3631	2,3091	2,2629	2,2227	2,1875	2,1563	2,1285	2,1035	2,0809	2,0603	2,0416
44	5,3857	4,0162	3,4298	3,0933	2,8712	2,7120	2,5914	2,4964	2,4194	2,3555	2,3015	2,2552	2,2151	2,1798	2,1486	2,1207	2,0957	2,0730	2,0525	2,0337
45	5,3773	4,0085	3,4224	3,0860	2,8640	2,7048	2,5842	2,4892	2,4122	2,3483	2,2943	2,2480	2,2078	2,1725	2,1412	2,1133	2,0883	2,0656	2,0450	2,0262
46	5,3692	4,0012	3,4154	3,0791	2,8572	2,6980	2,5774	2,4824	2,4054	2,3414	2,2874	2,2410	2,2008	2,1655	2,1342	2,1063	2,0812	2,0585	2,0379	2,0190
47	5,3615	3,9942	3,4087	3,0725	2,8506	2,6915	2,5709	2,4759	2,3988	2,3348	2,2808	2,2344	2,1941	2,1588	2,1275	2,0995	2,0744	2,0517	2,0310	2,0122
48	5,3541	3,9875	3,4022	3,0662	2,8444	2,6852	2,5646	2,4696	2,3925	2,3286	2,2745	2,2281	2,1878	2,1524	2,1210	2,0931	2,0679	2,0452	2,0245	2,0056
49	5,3471	3,9811	3,3961	3,0602	2,8384	2,6793	2,5587	2,4637	2,3866	2,3226	2,2684	2,2220	2,1817	2,1463	2,1149	2,0869	2,0617	2,0389	2,0182	1,9993
50	5,3403	3,9749	3,3902	3,0544	2,8326	2,6736	2,5530	2,4579	2,3808	2,3168	2,2627	2,2162	2,1758	2,1404	2,1090	2,0810	2,0558	2,0330	2,0122	1,9933
52	5,3276	3,9634	3,3791	3,0436	2,8219	2,6628	2,5422	2,4472	2,3700	2,3060	2,2518	2,2053	2,1649	2,1294	2,0979	2,0699	2,0446	2,0217	2,0010	1,9820
54	5,3159	3,9528	3,3689	3,0335	2,8120	2,6529	2,5323	2,4373	2,3601	2,2960	2,2418	2,1952	2,1548	2,1192	2,0877	2,0596	2,0343	2,0114	1,9906	1,9715
56	5,3051	3,9429	3,3594	3,0243	2,8028	2,6438	2,5232	2,4281	2,3509	2,2868	2,2325	2,1859	2,1454	2,1098	2,0783	2,0501	2,0247	2,0018	1,9809	1,9618
58	5,2950	3,9338	3,3507	3,0157	2,7942	2,6353	2,5147	2,4196	2,3424	2,2782	2,2239	2,1772	2,1367	2,1011	2,0695	2,0413	2,0159	1,9929	1,9720	1,9528
60	5,2856	3,9253	3,3425	3,0077	2,7863	2,6274	2,5068	2,4117	2,3344	2,2702	2,2159	2,1692	2,1286	2,0929	2,0613	2,0330	2,0076	1,9846	1,9636	1,9445
62	5,2769	3,9173	3,3349	3,0002	2,7789	2,6200	2,4994	2,4043	2,3270	2,2628	2,2084	2,1617	2,1211	2,0853	2,0537	2,0254	1,9999	1,9768	1,9558	1,9367
64	5,2687	3,9099	3,3278	2,9932	2,7720	2,6131	2,4925	2,3974	2,3201	2,2558	2,2014	2,1547	2,1140	2,0782	2,0465	2,0182	1,9927	1,9696	1,9486	1,9293
66	5,2610	3,9030	3,3211	2,9867	2,7655	2,6066	2,4861	2,3909	2,3136	2,2493	2,1948	2,1481	2,1074	2,0716	2,0399	2,0115	1,9859	1,9628	1,9417	1,9225
68	5,2538	3,8964	3,3149	2,9805	2,7594	2,6006	2,4800	2,3848	2,3075	2,2431	2,1887	2,1419	2,1012	2,0653	2,0336	2,0052	1,9796	1,9564	1,9353	1,9160
70	5,2470	3,8903	3,3090	2,9748	2,7537	2,5949	2,4743	2,3791	2,3017	2,2374	2,1829	2,1361	2,0953	2,0595	2,0277	1,9992	1,9736	1,9504	1,9293	1,9100
72	5,2406	3,8845	3,3034	2,9693	2,7483	2,5895	2,4689	2,3737	2,2963	2,2320	2,1774	2,1306	2,0898	2,0539	2,0221	1,9936	1,9680	1,9447	1,9236	1,9042
74	5,2346	3,8790	3,2982	2,9642	2,7432	2,5844	2,4638	2,3686	2,2912	2,2268	2,1723	2,1254	2,0846	2,0487	2,0168	1,9883	1,9626	1,9394	1,9182	1,8988
76	5,2289	3,8739	3,2932	2,9593	2,7384	2,5796	2,4590	2,3638	2,2864	2,2220	2,1674	2,1205	2,0797	2,0437	2,0118	1,9833	1,9576	1,9343	1,9131	1,8937
78	5,2235	3,8690	3,2885	2,9547	2,7339	2,5751	2,4545	2,3593	2,2818	2,2174	2,1628	2,1159	2,0750	2,0390	2,0071	1,9786	1,9528	1,9295	1,9083	1,8889
80	5,2184	3,8643	3,2841	2,9504	2,7295	2,5708	2,4502	2,3549	2,2775	2,2130	2,1584	2,1115	2,0706	2,0346	2,0026	1,9741	1,9483	1,9250	1,9037	1,8843
82	5,2135	3,8599	3,2799	2,9462	2,7254	2,5667	2,4461	2,3508	2,2734	2,2089	2,1543	2,1073	2,0664	2,0304	1,9984	1,9698	1,9440	1,9207	1,8994	1,8799
84	5,2088	3,8557	3,2758	2,9423	2,7215	2,5628	2,4422	2,3469	2,2694	2,2050	2,1503	2,1033	2,0624	2,0263	1,9943	1,9657	1,9399	1,9165	1,8952	1,8757
86	5,2044	3,8517	3,2720	2,9385	2,7178	2,5591	2,4385	2,3432	2,2657	2,2012	2,1465	2,0995	2,0585	2,0225	1,9905	1,9618	1,9360	1,9126	1,8913	1,8718
88	5,2002	3,8479	3,2684	2,9350	2,7143	2,5555	2,4350	2,3397	2,2622	2,1976	2,1429	2,0959	2,0549	2,0189	1,9868	1,9581	1,9323	1,9089	1,8875	1,8680
90	5,1962	3,8443	3,2649	2,9315	2,7109	2,5522	2,4316	2,3363	2,2588	2,1942	2,1395	2,0925	2,0515	2,0154	1,9833	1,9546	1,9288	1,9053	1,8840	1,8644
92	5,1924	3,8408	3,2616	2,9283	2,7077	2,5490	2,4284	2,3331	2,2555	2,1910	2,1362	2,0892	2,0481	2,0120	1,9800	1,9513	1,9254	1,9019	1,8805	1,8609
94	5,1887	3,8375	3,2584	2,9252	2,7046	2,5459	2,4253	2,3300	2,2524	2,1879	2,1331	2,0860	2,0450	2,0089	1,9768	1,9480	1,9221	1,8987	1,8773	1,8576
96	5,1852	3,8343	3,2553	2,9222	2,7016	2,5429	2,4223	2,3270	2,2495	2,1849	2,1301	2,0830	2,0419	2,0058	1,9737	1,9449	1,9190	1,8955	1,8741	1,8545
98	5,1818	3,8313	3,2524	2,9193	2,6988	2,5401	2,4195	2,3242	2,2466	2,1820	2,1272	2,0801	2,0390	2,0029	1,9708	1,9420	1,9161	1,8925	1,8711	1,8515
100	5,1786	3,8284	3,2496	2,9166	2,6961	2,5374	2,4168	2,3215	2,2439	2,1793	2,1245	2,0773	2,0363	2,0001	1,9679	1,9391	1,9132	1,8897	1,8682	1,8486
110	5,1642	3,8154	3,2372	2,9044	2,6840	2,5254	2,4048	2,3094	2,2318	2,1671	2,1123	2,0650	2,0239	1,9876	1,9554	1,9265	1,9005	1,8769	1,8554	1,8356
120	5,1523	3,8046	3,2269	2,8943	2,6740	2,5154	2,3948	2,2994	2,2217	2,1570	2,1021	2,0548	2,0136	1,9773	1,9450	1,9161	1,8900	1,8663	1,8447	1,8249
130	5,1423	3,7956	3,2182	2,8858	2,6656	2,5070	2,3864	2,2910	2,2133	2,1485	2,0935	2,0462	2,0049	1,9686	1,9362	1,9072	1,8811	1,8574	1,8357	1,8159
140	5,1337	3,7878	3,2108	2,8785	2,6583	2,4998	2,3792	2,2838	2,2060	2,1412	2,0862	2,0388	1,9975	1,9611	1,9287	1,8997	1,8735	1,8497	1,8280	1,8081
150	5,1263	3,7811	3,2044	2,8722	2,6521	2,4936	2,3730	2,2775	2,1998	2,1349	2,0799	2,0325	1,9911	1,9546	1,9222	1,8931	1,8669	1,8431	1,8213	1,8014
160	5,1198	3,7753	3,1988	2,8667	2,6467	2,4882	2,3675	2,2721	2,1943	2,1294	2,0744	2,0269	1,9855	1,9490	1,9165	1,8874	1,8612	1,8373	1,8155	1,7955
170	5,1141	3,7701	3,1938	2,8619	2,6419	2,4834	2,3628	2,2673	2,1895	2,1246	2,0695	2,0220	1,9806	1,9440	1,9115	1,8824	1,8561	1,8322	1,8104	1,7904
180	5,1090	3,7655	3,1894	2,8576	2,6376	2,4792	2,3585	2,2630	2,1852	2,1203	2,0652	2,0177	1,9762	1,9396	1,9071	1,8779	1,8516	1,8277	1,8058	1,7858
190	5,1045	3,7614	3,1855	2,8538	2,6338	2,4754	2,3547	2,2592	2,1814	2,1165	2,0613	2,0138	1,9723	1,9357	1,9031	1,8739	1,8476	1,8236	1,8018	1,7817
200	5,1004	3,7578	3,1820	2,8503	2,6304	2,4720	2,3513	2,2558	2,1780	2,1130	2,0578	2,0103	1,9688	1,9322	1,8996	1,8704	1,8440	1,8200	1,7981	1,7780
250	5,0850	3,7439	3,1687	2,8373	2,6175	2,4591	2,3384	2,2429	2,1650	2,0999	2,0447	1,9971	1,9555	1,9187	1,8861	1,8567	1,8303	1,8062	1,7842	1,7640
300	5,0747	3,7346	3,1599	2,8286	2,6089	2,4505	2,3299	2,2343	2,1563	2,0913	2,0360	1,9883	1,9466	1,9098	1,8771	1,8477	1,8212	1,7970	1,7750	1,7547
350	5,0674	3,7280	3,1536	2,8225	2,6028	2,4444	2,3238	2,2282	2,1502	2,0851	2,0298	1,9820	1,9403	1,9035	1,8707	1,8413	1,8147	1,7905	1,7684	1,7481
400	5,0619	3,7231	3,1489	2,8179	2,5983	2,4399	2,3192	2,2236	2,1456	2,0805	2,0251	1,9773	1,9356	1,8987	1,8659	1,8364	1,8098	1,7856	1,7635	1,7431
500	5,0543	3,7162	3,1423	2,8114	2,5919	2,4335	2,3129	2,2172	2,1392	2,0740	2,0186	1,9708	1,9290	1,8921	1,8592	1,8297	1,8030	1,7787	1,7566	1,7362
600	5,0492	3,7117	3,1379	2,8071	2,5876	2,4293	2,3086	2,2130	2,1349	2,0697	2,0143	1,9664	1,9246	1,8877	1,8548	1,8252	1,7985	1,7742	1,7520	1,7316
700	5,0456	3,7084	3,1348	2,8041	2,5846	2,4263	2,3056	2,2099	2,1319	2,0666	2,0112	1,9633	1,9215	1,8845	1,8516	1,8220	1,7953	1,7709	1,7487	1,7282
800	5,0429	3,7059	3,1324	2,8018	2,5823	2,4240	2,3033	2,2077	2,1296	2,0643	2,0089	1,9610	1,9191	1,8821	1,8492	1,8196	1,7928	1,7685	1,7462	1,7258
900	5,0407	3,7040	3,1306	2,8000	2,5806	2,4223	2,3016	2,2059	2,1278	2,0626	2,0071	1,9592	1,9173	1,8803	1,8473	1,8177	1,7910	1,7666	1,7443	1,7238
1000	5,0391	3,7025	3,1292	2,7986	2,5792	2,4208	2,3002	2,2045	2,1264	2,0611	2,0056	1,9577	1,9158	1,8788	1,8459	1,8162	1,7895	1,7651	1,7428	1,7223
2000	5,0315	3,6957	3,1227	2,7922	2,5728	2,4145	2,2938	2,1981	2,1200	2,0547	1,9992	1,9512	1,9093	1,8722	1,8392	1,8095	1,7827	1,7583	1,7359	1,7154
5000	5,0269	3,6916	3,1187	2,7884	2,5690	2,4107	2,2901	2,1943	2,1162	2,0509	1,9953	1,9473	1,9054	1,8683	1,8352	1,8055	1,7786	1,7542	1,7318	1,7112
10000	5,0254	3,6902	3,1174	2,7871	2,5678	2,4095	2,2888	2,1931	2,1149	2,0496	1,9940	1,9460	1,9040	1,8670	1,8339	1,8042	1,7773	1,7528	1,7304	1,7099
∞	5,0239	3,6889	3,1161	2,7858	2,5665	2,4082	2,2875	2,1918	2,1136	2,0483	1,9927	1,9447	1,9027	1,8656	1,8326	1,8028	1,7759	1,7515	1,7291	1,7085

All values conform to the international convention (i.e. 0,1 instead of 0.1).

The F-Distribution* ν_1, ν_2 Degrees of Freedom $P = 0{,}025$

$P = P$(right) = integral between F_{ν_1,ν_2} and ∞ (values in the table are the F_{ν_1,ν_2}-values)

ν_2 \ ν_1	22	24	26	28	30	32	35	40	45	50	60	70	80	100	120	200	300	500	1000	∞
1	995,36	997,25	998,85	1000,2	1001,4	1002,5	1003,8	1005,6	1007,0	1008,1	1009,8	1011,0	1011,9	1013,2	1014,0	1015,7	1016,6	1017,2	1017,8	1018,3
2	39,452	39,456	39,459	39,462	39,465	39,467	39,469	39,473	39,476	39,478	39,481	39,484	39,485	39,488	39,490	39,493	39,495	39,496	39,497	39,498
3	14,144	14,124	14,107	14,093	14,081	14,070	14,055	14,037	14,022	14,010	13,992	13,979	13,970	13,956	13,947	13,929	13,920	13,913	13,908	13,902
4	8,5332	8,5109	8,4919	8,4755	8,4613	8,4488	8,4327	8,4111	8,3943	8,3808	8,3604	8,3458	8,3349	8,3195	8,3092	8,2885	8,2781	8,2698	8,2636	8,2573
5	6,3011	6,2780	6,2584	6,2416	6,2269	6,2140	6,1973	6,1750	6,1576	6,1436	6,1225	6,1074	6,0960	6,0800	6,0693	6,0478	6,0370	6,0283	6,0218	6,0153
6	5,1406	5,1172	5,0973	5,0802	5,0652	5,0521	5,0352	5,0125	4,9947	4,9804	4,9589	4,9434	4,9318	4,9154	4,9044	4,8824	4,8713	4,8625	4,8558	4,8491
7	4,4386	4,4150	4,3949	4,3775	4,3624	4,3491	4,3319	4,3089	4,2908	4,2763	4,2544	4,2386	4,2268	4,2101	4,1989	4,1764	4,1651	4,1560	4,1492	4,1423
8	3,9711	3,9472	3,9269	3,9093	3,8940	3,8806	3,8632	3,8398	3,8215	3,8067	3,7844	3,7684	3,7563	3,7393	3,7279	3,7050	3,6934	3,6842	3,6772	3,6702
9	3,6383	3,6142	3,5936	3,5759	3,5604	3,5468	3,5292	3,5055	3,4869	3,4719	3,4493	3,4330	3,4207	3,4034	3,3918	3,3684	3,3566	3,3471	3,3400	3,3329
10	3,3897	3,3654	3,3446	3,3267	3,3110	3,2972	3,2794	3,2554	3,2366	3,2214	3,1984	3,1818	3,1694	3,1517	3,1399	3,1161	3,1040	3,0944	3,0871	3,0798
11	3,1970	3,1725	3,1516	3,1334	3,1176	3,1037	3,0856	3,0613	3,0422	3,0268	3,0035	2,9867	2,9740	2,9561	2,9441	2,9198	2,9075	2,8977	2,8902	2,8828
12	3,0434	3,0187	2,9976	2,9793	2,9633	2,9492	2,9309	2,9063	2,8870	2,8714	2,8478	2,8307	2,8178	2,7996	2,7874	2,7626	2,7502	2,7401	2,7325	2,7249
13	2,9181	2,8932	2,8719	2,8534	2,8372	2,8230	2,8046	2,7797	2,7601	2,7443	2,7204	2,7030	2,6900	2,6715	2,6590	2,6339	2,6212	2,6109	2,6032	2,5955
14	2,8139	2,7888	2,7673	2,7487	2,7324	2,7180	2,6994	2,6742	2,6544	2,6384	2,6142	2,5966	2,5833	2,5646	2,5519	2,5264	2,5134	2,5030	2,4951	2,4872
15	2,7260	2,7006	2,6790	2,6602	2,6437	2,6292	2,6104	2,5850	2,5650	2,5488	2,5242	2,5064	2,4930	2,4739	2,4611	2,4351	2,4220	2,4114	2,4034	2,3953
16	2,6507	2,6252	2,6033	2,5844	2,5678	2,5532	2,5342	2,5085	2,4883	2,4719	2,4471	2,4291	2,4154	2,3961	2,3831	2,3567	2,3434	2,3326	2,3245	2,3163
17	2,5855	2,5598	2,5378	2,5187	2,5020	2,4873	2,4681	2,4422	2,4218	2,4053	2,3801	2,3619	2,3481	2,3285	2,3153	2,2886	2,2750	2,2640	2,2558	2,2474
18	2,5285	2,5027	2,4806	2,4613	2,4445	2,4296	2,4103	2,3842	2,3635	2,3468	2,3214	2,3030	2,2890	2,2692	2,2558	2,2287	2,2149	2,2038	2,1954	2,1869
19	2,4783	2,4523	2,4300	2,4107	2,3937	2,3788	2,3593	2,3329	2,3121	2,2952	2,2696	2,2509	2,2368	2,2167	2,2032	2,1757	2,1617	2,1504	2,1419	2,1333
20	2,4337	2,4076	2,3851	2,3657	2,3486	2,3335	2,3139	2,2873	2,2663	2,2493	2,2234	2,2045	2,1902	2,1699	2,1562	2,1284	2,1142	2,1027	2,0941	2,0853
21	2,3938	2,3675	2,3450	2,3254	2,3082	2,2930	2,2733	2,2465	2,2253	2,2081	2,1819	2,1629	2,1485	2,1280	2,1141	2,0859	2,0715	2,0599	2,0511	2,0422
22	2,3579	2,3315	2,3088	2,2891	2,2718	2,2565	2,2366	2,2097	2,1883	2,1710	2,1446	2,1254	2,1108	2,0901	2,0760	2,0475	2,0329	2,0211	2,0122	2,0032
23	2,3254	2,2989	2,2761	2,2563	2,2389	2,2235	2,2035	2,1763	2,1548	2,1374	2,1107	2,0913	2,0766	2,0557	2,0415	2,0126	1,9978	1,9859	1,9769	1,9677
24	2,2959	2,2693	2,2464	2,2265	2,2090	2,1935	2,1733	2,1460	2,1243	2,1067	2,0799	2,0603	2,0454	2,0243	2,0099	1,9807	1,9658	1,9537	1,9445	1,9353
25	2,2690	2,2422	2,2192	2,1992	2,1816	2,1661	2,1458	2,1183	2,0964	2,0787	2,0516	2,0319	2,0169	1,9955	1,9811	1,9515	1,9364	1,9242	1,9149	1,9055
26	2,2443	2,2174	2,1943	2,1742	2,1565	2,1409	2,1205	2,0928	2,0708	2,0530	2,0257	2,0058	1,9907	1,9691	1,9545	1,9246	1,9094	1,8970	1,8876	1,8781
27	2,2216	2,1946	2,1714	2,1512	2,1334	2,1177	2,0972	2,0693	2,0472	2,0293	2,0018	1,9817	1,9665	1,9447	1,9299	1,8998	1,8843	1,8718	1,8623	1,8527
28	2,2006	2,1735	2,1502	2,1299	2,1121	2,0963	2,0757	2,0477	2,0254	2,0073	1,9797	1,9595	1,9441	1,9221	1,9072	1,8767	1,8611	1,8485	1,8389	1,8291
29	2,1812	2,1540	2,1306	2,1102	2,0923	2,0764	2,0557	2,0276	2,0052	1,9870	1,9591	1,9388	1,9232	1,9011	1,8861	1,8553	1,8396	1,8268	1,8170	1,8072
30	2,1631	2,1359	2,1124	2,0919	2,0739	2,0580	2,0372	2,0089	1,9864	1,9681	1,9400	1,9195	1,9039	1,8816	1,8664	1,8354	1,8194	1,8065	1,7967	1,7867
31	2,1463	2,1190	2,0954	2,0749	2,0568	2,0408	2,0199	1,9914	1,9688	1,9504	1,9222	1,9015	1,8858	1,8633	1,8480	1,8167	1,8006	1,7875	1,7776	1,7675
32	2,1307	2,1032	2,0796	2,0590	2,0408	2,0247	2,0037	1,9752	1,9524	1,9339	1,9055	1,8847	1,8689	1,8462	1,8308	1,7992	1,7830	1,7697	1,7597	1,7495
33	2,1160	2,0885	2,0648	2,0441	2,0259	2,0097	1,9886	1,9599	1,9371	1,9184	1,8899	1,8690	1,8530	1,8302	1,8146	1,7828	1,7664	1,7530	1,7429	1,7326
34	2,1022	2,0747	2,0509	2,0301	2,0118	1,9956	1,9744	1,9456	1,9226	1,9039	1,8752	1,8541	1,8381	1,8151	1,7994	1,7673	1,7508	1,7373	1,7270	1,7166
35	2,0893	2,0617	2,0378	2,0170	1,9986	1,9823	1,9611	1,9321	1,9090	1,8902	1,8613	1,8402	1,8240	1,8009	1,7851	1,7527	1,7360	1,7224	1,7121	1,7016
36	2,0772	2,0494	2,0255	2,0046	1,9862	1,9699	1,9485	1,9194	1,8963	1,8773	1,8483	1,8270	1,8107	1,7874	1,7716	1,7389	1,7221	1,7084	1,6979	1,6873
37	2,0657	2,0379	2,0139	1,9929	1,9745	1,9581	1,9366	1,9074	1,8842	1,8652	1,8360	1,8146	1,7982	1,7748	1,7588	1,7259	1,7089	1,6951	1,6845	1,6738
38	2,0548	2,0270	2,0029	1,9819	1,9634	1,9469	1,9254	1,8961	1,8727	1,8536	1,8243	1,8028	1,7863	1,7627	1,7467	1,7135	1,6964	1,6824	1,6718	1,6609
39	2,0446	2,0166	1,9925	1,9714	1,9529	1,9364	1,9148	1,8854	1,8619	1,8427	1,8133	1,7916	1,7751	1,7513	1,7351	1,7018	1,6845	1,6704	1,6597	1,6487
40	2,0349	2,0069	1,9827	1,9615	1,9429	1,9264	1,9047	1,8752	1,8516	1,8324	1,8028	1,7810	1,7644	1,7405	1,7242	1,6906	1,6732	1,6590	1,6481	1,6371
41	2,0257	1,9976	1,9733	1,9521	1,9335	1,9169	1,8952	1,8655	1,8419	1,8225	1,7928	1,7709	1,7542	1,7302	1,7138	1,6799	1,6624	1,6481	1,6372	1,6260
42	2,0169	1,9888	1,9645	1,9432	1,9245	1,9078	1,8861	1,8563	1,8326	1,8132	1,7833	1,7614	1,7445	1,7204	1,7039	1,6698	1,6521	1,6377	1,6267	1,6155
43	2,0086	1,9804	1,9560	1,9347	1,9159	1,8992	1,8774	1,8476	1,8237	1,8043	1,7743	1,7522	1,7353	1,7110	1,6944	1,6601	1,6423	1,6278	1,6167	1,6054
44	2,0006	1,9724	1,9480	1,9266	1,9078	1,8911	1,8692	1,8392	1,8153	1,7958	1,7656	1,7435	1,7265	1,7021	1,6854	1,6509	1,6330	1,6183	1,6071	1,5957
45	1,9930	1,9647	1,9403	1,9189	1,9000	1,8832	1,8613	1,8313	1,8073	1,7876	1,7574	1,7351	1,7181	1,6935	1,6767	1,6420	1,6240	1,6092	1,5979	1,5864
46	1,9858	1,9575	1,9329	1,9115	1,8926	1,8758	1,8537	1,8236	1,7996	1,7799	1,7495	1,7272	1,7100	1,6853	1,6685	1,6335	1,6154	1,6005	1,5891	1,5775
47	1,9789	1,9505	1,9259	1,9044	1,8855	1,8686	1,8465	1,8164	1,7922	1,7724	1,7420	1,7195	1,7023	1,6775	1,6605	1,6254	1,6071	1,5921	1,5806	1,5690
48	1,9723	1,9438	1,9192	1,8977	1,8787	1,8618	1,8397	1,8094	1,7852	1,7653	1,7347	1,7122	1,6949	1,6700	1,6529	1,6176	1,5992	1,5841	1,5725	1,5607
49	1,9660	1,9375	1,9128	1,8912	1,8722	1,8552	1,8331	1,8027	1,7784	1,7585	1,7278	1,7052	1,6878	1,6628	1,6456	1,6101	1,5916	1,5764	1,5647	1,5528
50	1,9599	1,9313	1,9066	1,8850	1,8659	1,8490	1,8267	1,7963	1,7719	1,7520	1,7211	1,6984	1,6810	1,6558	1,6386	1,6029	1,5842	1,5689	1,5572	1,5452
52	1,9485	1,9198	1,8950	1,8734	1,8542	1,8371	1,8148	1,7842	1,7597	1,7396	1,7086	1,6857	1,6681	1,6428	1,6254	1,5892	1,5704	1,5549	1,5430	1,5308
54	1,9379	1,9092	1,8843	1,8626	1,8433	1,8262	1,8038	1,7730	1,7484	1,7282	1,6970	1,6739	1,6562	1,6307	1,6131	1,5766	1,5575	1,5418	1,5298	1,5174
56	1,9282	1,8994	1,8744	1,8526	1,8333	1,8161	1,7936	1,7627	1,7379	1,7176	1,6862	1,6630	1,6451	1,6194	1,6017	1,5648	1,5455	1,5296	1,5174	1,5049
58	1,9191	1,8902	1,8652	1,8433	1,8239	1,8067	1,7841	1,7530	1,7282	1,7078	1,6762	1,6528	1,6348	1,6089	1,5910	1,5538	1,5343	1,5182	1,5058	1,4932
60	1,9106	1,8817	1,8566	1,8346	1,8152	1,7979	1,7752	1,7440	1,7191	1,6985	1,6668	1,6433	1,6252	1,5990	1,5810	1,5435	1,5238	1,5075	1,4950	1,4821
62	1,9028	1,8737	1,8486	1,8265	1,8071	1,7897	1,7669	1,7356	1,7106	1,6899	1,6580	1,6344	1,6162	1,5898	1,5717	1,5338	1,5139	1,4974	1,4848	1,4718
64	1,8954	1,8663	1,8411	1,8190	1,7994	1,7820	1,7592	1,7278	1,7026	1,6819	1,6498	1,6260	1,6077	1,5812	1,5629	1,5247	1,5046	1,4880	1,4751	1,4620
66	1,8884	1,8593	1,8340	1,8119	1,7923	1,7748	1,7519	1,7204	1,6951	1,6743	1,6421	1,6182	1,5997	1,5730	1,5546	1,5161	1,4958	1,4790	1,4660	1,4527
68	1,8819	1,8527	1,8274	1,8052	1,7855	1,7680	1,7450	1,7134	1,6880	1,6672	1,6348	1,6108	1,5922	1,5654	1,5468	1,5080	1,4875	1,4705	1,4574	1,4440
70	1,8758	1,8466	1,8212	1,7989	1,7792	1,7616	1,7386	1,7069	1,6814	1,6604	1,6279	1,6038	1,5851	1,5581	1,5394	1,5003	1,4796	1,4625	1,4493	1,4357
72	1,8700	1,8407	1,8153	1,7930	1,7732	1,7556	1,7325	1,7007	1,6751	1,6541	1,6214	1,5972	1,5784	1,5512	1,5325	1,4930	1,4722	1,4549	1,4415	1,4278
74	1,8646	1,8352	1,8097	1,7874	1,7676	1,7499	1,7267	1,6948	1,6692	1,6481	1,6153	1,5909	1,5721	1,5447	1,5259	1,4861	1,4651	1,4477	1,4342	1,4203
76	1,8594	1,8300	1,8045	1,7821	1,7622	1,7445	1,7213	1,6893	1,6636	1,6424	1,6094	1,5850	1,5660	1,5386	1,5196	1,4796	1,4584	1,4408	1,4272	1,4131
78	1,8545	1,8250	1,7995	1,7770	1,7571	1,7394	1,7161	1,6840	1,6582	1,6370	1,6039	1,5793	1,5603	1,5327	1,5136	1,4733	1,4520	1,4342	1,4205	1,4063
80	1,8499	1,8204	1,7947	1,7722	1,7523	1,7346	1,7112	1,6790	1,6532	1,6318	1,5987	1,5740	1,5549	1,5271	1,5079	1,4674	1,4459	1,4280	1,4141	1,3997
82	1,8454	1,8159	1,7902	1,7677	1,7477	1,7299	1,7065	1,6743	1,6483	1,6269	1,5937	1,5689	1,5497	1,5218	1,5025	1,4617	1,4401	1,4220	1,4080	1,3935
84	1,8412	1,8117	1,7859	1,7634	1,7434	1,7255	1,7021	1,6698	1,6437	1,6223	1,5889	1,5640	1,5448	1,5168	1,4973	1,4563	1,4345	1,4163	1,4021	1,3875
86	1,8372	1,8076	1,7819	1,7593	1,7392	1,7214	1,6978	1,6655	1,6394	1,6178	1,5843	1,5594	1,5400	1,5119	1,4924	1,4511	1,4291	1,4108	1,3965	1,3818
88	1,8334	1,8038	1,7780	1,7553	1,7353	1,7174	1,6938	1,6613	1,6352	1,6136	1,5800	1,5550	1,5355	1,5073	1,4877	1,4461	1,4240	1,4056	1,3912	1,3763
90	1,8298	1,8001	1,7743	1,7516	1,7315	1,7135	1,6899	1,6574	1,6312	1,6095	1,5758	1,5507	1,5312	1,5028	1,4831	1,4414	1,4191	1,4005	1,3860	1,3710
92	1,8263	1,7966	1,7707	1,7480	1,7279	1,7099	1,6862	1,6536	1,6274	1,6057	1,5719	1,5467	1,5271	1,4986	1,4788	1,4368	1,4144	1,3957	1,3811	1,3659
94	1,8230	1,7932	1,7673	1,7446	1,7244	1,7064	1,6827	1,6500	1,6237	1,6020	1,5681	1,5428	1,5231	1,4945	1,4746	1,4324	1,4099	1,3910	1,3763	1,3610
96	1,8198	1,7900	1,7640	1,7413	1,7211	1,7031	1,6793	1,6466	1,6202	1,5984	1,5644	1,5390	1,5193	1,4906	1,4706	1,4282	1,4056	1,3865	1,3717	1,3563
98	1,8167	1,7869	1,7609	1,7381	1,7179	1,6998	1,6761	1,6433	1,6168	1,5950	1,5609	1,5355	1,5157	1,4869	1,4668	1,4242	1,4014	1,3822	1,3673	1,3517
100	1,8138	1,7839	1,7579	1,7351	1,7148	1,6968	1,6729	1,6401	1,6136	1,5917	1,5575	1,5320	1,5122	1,4833	1,4631	1,4203	1,3973	1,3781	1,3630	1,3473
110	1,8007	1,7707	1,7446	1,7216	1,7013	1,6830	1,6591	1,6259	1,5992	1,5771	1,5425	1,5166	1,4965	1,4671	1,4466	1,4028	1,3792	1,3593	1,3437	1,3274
120	1,7899	1,7597	1,7335	1,7104	1,6899	1,6716	1,6475	1,6141	1,5872	1,5649	1,5299	1,5038	1,4834	1,4536	1,4327	1,3880	1,3639	1,3434	1,3273	1,3104
130	1,7807	1,7505	1,7241	1,7010	1,6804	1,6620	1,6377	1,6042	1,5770	1,5545	1,5193	1,4929	1,4722	1,4420	1,4208	1,3754	1,3507	1,3297	1,3131	1,2957
140	1,7729	1,7425	1,7161	1,6928	1,6722	1,6537	1,6293	1,5956	1,5683	1,5456	1,5101	1,4835	1,4626	1,4321	1,4106	1,3644	1,3392	1,3178	1,3008	1,2828
150	1,7661	1,7356	1,7092	1,6858	1,6651	1,6465	1,6220	1,5882	1,5607	1,5379	1,5022	1,4753	1,4543	1,4234	1,4017	1,3548	1,3292	1,3073	1,2898	1,2714
160	1,7601	1,7296	1,7031	1,6797	1,6589	1,6403	1,6157	1,5817	1,5541	1,5312	1,4952	1,4681	1,4470	1,4158	1,3938	1,3463	1,3203	1,2979	1,2801	1,2611
170	1,7549	1,7244	1,6977	1,6743	1,6534	1,6347	1,6101	1,5759	1,5482	1,5252	1,4890	1,4618	1,4405	1,4090	1,3869	1,3388	1,3123	1,2896	1,2714	1,2519
180	1,7503	1,7197	1,6930	1,6695	1,6485	1,6298	1,6051	1,5708	1,5430	1,5199	1,4835	1,4562	1,4347	1,4030	1,3806	1,3321	1,3052	1,2821	1,2635	1,2436
190	1,7461	1,7154	1,6887	1,6651	1,6442	1,6254	1,6006	1,5663	1,5383	1,5151	1,4786	1,4511	1,4295	1,3976	1,3750	1,3260	1,2988	1,2753	1,2564	1,2360
200	1,7424	1,7117	1,6849	1,6613	1,6403	1,6215	1,5966	1,5621	1,5341	1,5108	1,4742	1,4465	1,4248	1,3927	1,3700	1,3204	1,2929	1,2691	1,2498	1,2290
250	1,7282	1,6973	1,6704	1,6466	1,6254	1,6064	1,5813	1,5465	1,5181	1,4945	1,4573	1,4291	1,4069	1,3739	1,3506	1,2991	1,2702	1,2448	1,2241	1,2014
300	1,7188	1,6878	1,6607	1,6368	1,6155	1,5964	1,5711	1,5360	1,5074	1,4836	1,4459	1,4173	1,3948	1,3613	1,3374	1,2845	1,2545	1,2280	1,2060	1,1815
350	1,7120	1,6809	1,6538	1,6298	1,6084	1,5893	1,5639	1,5286	1,4998	1,4758	1,4378	1,4089	1,3861	1,3522	1,3279	1,2739	1,2430	1,2155	1,1924	1,1664
400	1,7070	1,6758	1,6486	1,6245	1,6031	1,5839	1,5584	1,5230	1,4940	1,4699	1,4317	1,4026	1,3796	1,3453	1,3207	1,2658	1,2342	1,2058	1,1819	1,1545
500	1,7000	1,6687	1,6414	1,6172	1,5957	1,5764	1,5508	1,5151	1,4860	1,4616	1,4231	1,3937	1,3704	1,3356	1,3105	1,2543	1,2216	1,1918	1,1664	1,1365
600	1,6953	1,6639	1,6365	1,6123	1,5907	1,5713	1,5457	1,5099	1,4806	1,4561	1,4173	1,3877	1,3642	1,3290	1,3037	1,2465	1,2129	1,1822	1,1555	1,1236
700	1,6919	1,6605	1,6331	1,6088	1,5872	1,5678	1,5420	1,5061	1,4767	1,4522	1,4132	1,3834	1,3598	1,3243	1,2987	1,2408	1,2066	1,1751	1,1474	1,1136
800	1,6894	1,6580	1,6305	1,6062	1,5845	1,5651	1,5393	1,5033	1,4739	1,4492	1,4101	1,3802	1,3565	1,3208	1,2950	1,2365	1,2019	1,1697	1,1412	1,1057
900	1,6875	1,6560	1,6285	1,6042	1,5825	1,5630	1,5371	1,5011	1,4716	1,4469	1,4077	1,3777	1,3539	1,3180	1,2921	1,2332	1,1981	1,1653	1,1362	1,0992
1000	1,6859	1,6544	1,6269	1,6025	1,5808	1,5613	1,5354	1,4993	1,4698	1,4451	1,4058	1,3757	1,3518	1,3158	1,2898	1,2304	1,1950	1,1618	1,1320	1,0938
2000	1,6789	1,6473	1,6197	1,5952	1,5734	1,5538	1,5278	1,4915	1,4617	1,4368	1,3971	1,3666	1,3424	1,3058	1,2792	1,2181	1,1810	1,1454	1,1123	1,0650
5000	1,6747	1,6430	1,6153	1,5908	1,5689	1,5493	1,5232	1,4867	1,4568	1,4317	1,3918	1,3611	1,3367	1,2997	1,2728	1,2105	1,1722	1,1350	1,0991	1,0404
10000	1,6733	1,6416	1,6139	1,5894	1,5675	1,5478	1,5216	1,4851	1,4552	1,4301	1,3900	1,3593	1,3348	1,2977	1,2706	1,2079	1,1693	1,1314	1,0944	1,0283
∞	1,6719	1,6402	1,6124	1,5879	1,5660	1,5463	1,5201	1,4835	1,4536	1,4284	1,3883	1,3575	1,3329	1,2956	1,2684	1,2053	1,1662	1,1277	1,0895	1

All values conform to the international convention (i.e. 0,1 instead of 0.1).

The *F*-Distribution* ν_1, ν_2 Degrees of Freedom $P = 0{,}01$

$P = P(\text{right})$ = integral between F_{ν_1, ν_2} and ∞ (values in the table are the F_{ν_1, ν_2}-values)

ν_2 \ ν_1	1	2	3	4	5	6	7	8	9	10	11	12	13	14	15	16	17	18	19	20
1	4052,2	4999,5	5403,4	5624,6	5763,6	5859,0	5928,4	5981,1	6022,5	6055,8	6083,3	6106,3	6125,9	6142,7	6157,3	6170,1	6181,4	6191,5	6200,6	6208,7
2	98,503	99,000	99,166	99,249	99,299	99,333	99,356	99,374	99,388	99,399	99,408	99,416	99,422	99,428	99,433	99,437	99,440	99,444	99,447	99,449
3	34,116	30,817	29,457	28,710	28,237	27,911	27,672	27,489	27,345	27,229	27,133	27,052	26,983	26,924	26,872	26,827	26,787	26,751	26,719	26,690
4	21,198	18,000	16,694	15,977	15,522	15,207	14,976	14,799	14,659	14,546	14,452	14,374	14,307	14,249	14,198	14,154	14,115	14,080	14,048	14,020
5	16,258	13,274	12,060	11,392	10,967	10,672	10,456	10,289	10,158	10,051	9,9626	9,8883	9,8248	9,7700	9,7222	9,6802	9,6429	9,6096	9,5797	9,5526
6	13,745	10,925	9,7795	9,1483	8,7459	8,4661	8,2600	8,1017	7,9761	7,8741	7,7896	7,7183	7,6575	7,6049	7,5590	7,5186	7,4827	7,4507	7,4219	7,3958
7	12,246	9,5466	8,4513	7,8466	7,4604	7,1914	6,9928	6,8400	6,7188	6,6201	6,5382	6,4691	6,4100	6,3590	6,3143	6,2750	6,2401	6,2089	6,1808	6,1554
8	11,259	8,6491	7,5910	7,0061	6,6318	6,3707	6,1776	6,0289	5,9106	5,8143	5,7343	5,6667	5,6089	5,5589	5,5151	5,4766	5,4423	5,4116	5,3840	5,3591
9	10,561	8,0215	6,9919	6,4221	6,0569	5,8018	5,6129	5,4671	5,3511	5,2565	5,1779	5,1114	5,0545	5,0052	4,9621	4,9240	4,8902	4,8599	4,8327	4,8080
10	10,044	7,5594	6,5523	5,9943	5,6363	5,3858	5,2001	5,0567	4,9424	4,8491	4,7715	4,7059	4,6496	4,6008	4,5581	4,5204	4,4869	4,4569	4,4299	4,4054
11	9,6460	7,2057	6,2167	5,6683	5,3160	5,0692	4,8861	4,7445	4,6315	4,5393	4,4624	4,3974	4,3416	4,2932	4,2509	4,2134	4,1801	4,1503	4,1234	4,0990
12	9,3302	6,9266	5,9525	5,4120	5,0643	4,8206	4,6395	4,4994	4,3875	4,2961	4,2198	4,1553	4,0999	4,0518	4,0096	3,9724	3,9392	3,9095	3,8827	3,8584
13	9,0738	6,7010	5,7394	5,2053	4,8616	4,6204	4,4410	4,3021	4,1911	4,1003	4,0245	3,9603	3,9052	3,8574	3,8154	3,7783	3,7452	3,7156	3,6888	3,6646
14	8,8616	6,5149	5,5639	5,0354	4,6950	4,4558	4,2779	4,1399	4,0297	3,9394	3,8640	3,8001	3,7452	3,6975	3,6557	3,6187	3,5857	3,5561	3,5294	3,5052
15	8,6831	6,3589	5,4170	4,8932	4,5556	4,3183	4,1415	4,0045	3,8948	3,8049	3,7299	3,6662	3,6115	3,5639	3,5222	3,4852	3,4523	3,4228	3,3961	3,3719
16	8,5310	6,2262	5,2922	4,7726	4,4374	4,2016	4,0259	3,8896	3,7804	3,6909	3,6162	3,5527	3,4981	3,4506	3,4089	3,3720	3,3391	3,3096	3,2829	3,2587
17	8,3997	6,1121	5,1850	4,6690	4,3359	4,1015	3,9267	3,7910	3,6822	3,5931	3,5185	3,4552	3,4007	3,3533	3,3117	3,2748	3,2419	3,2124	3,1857	3,1615
18	8,2854	6,0129	5,0919	4,5790	4,2479	4,0146	3,8406	3,7054	3,5971	3,5082	3,4338	3,3706	3,3162	3,2689	3,2273	3,1904	3,1575	3,1280	3,1013	3,0771
19	8,1849	5,9259	5,0103	4,5003	4,1708	3,9386	3,7653	3,6305	3,5225	3,4338	3,3596	3,2965	3,2422	3,1949	3,1533	3,1165	3,0836	3,0541	3,0274	3,0031
20	8,0960	5,8489	4,9382	4,4307	4,1027	3,8714	3,6987	3,5644	3,4567	3,3682	3,2941	3,2311	3,1769	3,1296	3,0880	3,0512	3,0183	2,9887	2,9620	2,9377
21	8,0166	5,7804	4,8740	4,3688	4,0421	3,8117	3,6396	3,5056	3,3981	3,3098	3,2359	3,1730	3,1187	3,0715	3,0300	2,9931	2,9602	2,9306	2,9039	2,8796
22	7,9454	5,7190	4,8166	4,3134	3,9880	3,7583	3,5867	3,4530	3,3458	3,2576	3,1837	3,1209	3,0667	3,0195	2,9779	2,9411	2,9082	2,8786	2,8518	2,8274
23	7,8811	5,6637	4,7649	4,2636	3,9392	3,7102	3,5390	3,4057	3,2986	3,2106	3,1368	3,0740	3,0199	2,9727	2,9311	2,8943	2,8613	2,8317	2,8049	2,7805
24	7,8229	5,6136	4,7181	4,2184	3,8951	3,6667	3,4959	3,3629	3,2560	3,1681	3,0944	3,0316	2,9775	2,9303	2,8887	2,8519	2,8189	2,7892	2,7624	2,7380
25	7,7698	5,5680	4,6755	4,1774	3,8550	3,6272	3,4568	3,3239	3,2172	3,1294	3,0558	2,9931	2,9389	2,8917	2,8502	2,8133	2,7803	2,7506	2,7238	2,6993
26	7,7213	5,5263	4,6366	4,1400	3,8183	3,5911	3,4210	3,2884	3,1818	3,0941	3,0205	2,9578	2,9038	2,8566	2,8150	2,7781	2,7451	2,7153	2,6885	2,6640
27	7,6767	5,4881	4,6009	4,1056	3,7848	3,5580	3,3882	3,2558	3,1494	3,0618	2,9882	2,9256	2,8715	2,8243	2,7827	2,7458	2,7127	2,6830	2,6561	2,6316
28	7,6356	5,4529	4,5681	4,0740	3,7539	3,5276	3,3581	3,2259	3,1195	3,0320	2,9585	2,8959	2,8418	2,7946	2,7530	2,7160	2,6830	2,6532	2,6263	2,6017
29	7,5977	5,4204	4,5378	4,0449	3,7254	3,4995	3,3303	3,1982	3,0920	3,0045	2,9311	2,8685	2,8144	2,7672	2,7256	2,6886	2,6555	2,6257	2,5987	2,5742
30	7,5625	5,3903	4,5097	4,0179	3,6990	3,4735	3,3045	3,1726	3,0665	2,9791	2,9057	2,8431	2,7890	2,7418	2,7002	2,6632	2,6301	2,6003	2,5732	2,5487
31	7,5298	5,3624	4,4837	3,9928	3,6745	3,4493	3,2806	3,1489	3,0428	2,9555	2,8821	2,8195	2,7655	2,7182	2,6766	2,6396	2,6064	2,5766	2,5496	2,5249
32	7,4993	5,3363	4,4594	3,9695	3,6517	3,4269	3,2583	3,1267	3,0208	2,9335	2,8602	2,7976	2,7435	2,6963	2,6546	2,6176	2,5844	2,5546	2,5275	2,5029
33	7,4708	5,3120	4,4368	3,9477	3,6305	3,4059	3,2376	3,1061	3,0003	2,9130	2,8397	2,7771	2,7231	2,6758	2,6341	2,5971	2,5639	2,5340	2,5069	2,4822
34	7,4441	5,2893	4,4156	3,9273	3,6106	3,3863	3,2182	3,0868	2,9810	2,8938	2,8205	2,7580	2,7039	2,6566	2,6150	2,5779	2,5447	2,5147	2,4876	2,4629
35	7,4191	5,2679	4,3957	3,9082	3,5919	3,3679	3,2000	3,0687	2,9630	2,8758	2,8026	2,7400	2,6859	2,6387	2,5970	2,5599	2,5266	2,4967	2,4695	2,4448
36	7,3956	5,2479	4,3771	3,8903	3,5744	3,3507	3,1829	3,0517	2,9461	2,8589	2,7857	2,7232	2,6691	2,6218	2,5801	2,5430	2,5097	2,4797	2,4526	2,4278
37	7,3734	5,2290	4,3595	3,8734	3,5579	3,3344	3,1668	3,0357	2,9302	2,8431	2,7698	2,7073	2,6532	2,6059	2,5642	2,5270	2,4938	2,4638	2,4366	2,4118
38	7,3525	5,2112	4,3430	3,8575	3,5424	3,3191	3,1516	3,0207	2,9151	2,8281	2,7549	2,6923	2,6382	2,5909	2,5492	2,5120	2,4787	2,4487	2,4215	2,3967
39	7,3328	5,1944	4,3274	3,8425	3,5277	3,3047	3,1373	3,0064	2,9010	2,8139	2,7407	2,6782	2,6241	2,5768	2,5350	2,4978	2,4645	2,4345	2,4072	2,3824
40	7,3141	5,1785	4,3126	3,8283	3,5138	3,2910	3,1238	2,9930	2,8876	2,8005	2,7274	2,6648	2,6107	2,5634	2,5216	2,4844	2,4511	2,4210	2,3937	2,3689
41	7,2964	5,1634	4,2986	3,8148	3,5007	3,2781	3,1109	2,9802	2,8749	2,7879	2,7147	2,6522	2,5981	2,5507	2,5089	2,4717	2,4384	2,4083	2,3810	2,3561
42	7,2796	5,1491	4,2853	3,8021	3,4882	3,2658	3,0988	2,9681	2,8628	2,7758	2,7027	2,6402	2,5860	2,5387	2,4969	2,4596	2,4263	2,3962	2,3688	2,3439
43	7,2636	5,1356	4,2727	3,7899	3,4764	3,2541	3,0872	2,9567	2,8514	2,7644	2,6913	2,6287	2,5746	2,5273	2,4854	2,4482	2,4148	2,3847	2,3573	2,3324
44	7,2484	5,1226	4,2606	3,7784	3,4651	3,2430	3,0762	2,9457	2,8405	2,7536	2,6804	2,6179	2,5638	2,5164	2,4746	2,4373	2,4039	2,3737	2,3463	2,3214
45	7,2339	5,1103	4,2492	3,7674	3,4544	3,2325	3,0658	2,9353	2,8301	2,7432	2,6701	2,6076	2,5534	2,5060	2,4642	2,4269	2,3935	2,3633	2,3359	2,3109
46	7,2200	5,0986	4,2383	3,7570	3,4442	3,2224	3,0558	2,9254	2,8203	2,7334	2,6602	2,5977	2,5436	2,4962	2,4543	2,4170	2,3835	2,3533	2,3259	2,3009
47	7,2068	5,0874	4,2279	3,7470	3,4344	3,2128	3,0463	2,9160	2,8108	2,7240	2,6508	2,5883	2,5342	2,4868	2,4449	2,4075	2,3741	2,3439	2,3164	2,2914
48	7,1942	5,0767	4,2180	3,7374	3,4251	3,2036	3,0372	2,9069	2,8018	2,7150	2,6418	2,5793	2,5252	2,4777	2,4358	2,3985	2,3650	2,3348	2,3073	2,2823
49	7,1821	5,0664	4,2084	3,7283	3,4162	3,1948	3,0285	2,8983	2,7932	2,7064	2,6333	2,5707	2,5166	2,4691	2,4272	2,3899	2,3564	2,3261	2,2986	2,2736
50	7,1706	5,0566	4,1993	3,7195	3,4077	3,1864	3,0202	2,8900	2,7850	2,6981	2,6250	2,5625	2,5083	2,4609	2,4190	2,3816	2,3481	2,3178	2,2903	2,2652
52	7,1489	5,0382	4,1823	3,7031	3,3917	3,1707	3,0045	2,8745	2,7695	2,6827	2,6096	2,5470	2,4929	2,4454	2,4035	2,3661	2,3325	2,3022	2,2747	2,2496
54	7,1288	5,0212	4,1665	3,6880	3,3769	3,1561	2,9901	2,8602	2,7552	2,6685	2,5954	2,5328	2,4786	2,4311	2,3892	2,3517	2,3182	2,2878	2,2603	2,2351
56	7,1103	5,0055	4,1519	3,6740	3,3633	3,1427	2,9768	2,8469	2,7420	2,6553	2,5822	2,5197	2,4654	2,4180	2,3759	2,3385	2,3049	2,2745	2,2469	2,2217
58	7,0931	4,9910	4,1384	3,6611	3,3506	3,1302	2,9645	2,8347	2,7298	2,6431	2,5700	2,5075	2,4532	2,4057	2,3637	2,3262	2,2926	2,2622	2,2346	2,2093
60	7,0771	4,9774	4,1259	3,6490	3,3389	3,1187	2,9530	2,8233	2,7185	2,6318	2,5587	2,4961	2,4419	2,3943	2,3523	2,3148	2,2811	2,2507	2,2230	2,1978
62	7,0622	4,9648	4,1142	3,6378	3,3279	3,1079	2,9424	2,8127	2,7079	2,6212	2,5481	2,4855	2,4313	2,3837	2,3417	2,3042	2,2705	2,2400	2,2123	2,1870
64	7,0483	4,9530	4,1033	3,6273	3,3177	3,0978	2,9324	2,8027	2,6980	2,6113	2,5382	2,4757	2,4214	2,3738	2,3317	2,2942	2,2605	2,2300	2,2023	2,1770
66	7,0352	4,9420	4,0930	3,6175	3,3081	3,0884	2,9230	2,7934	2,6887	2,6021	2,5290	2,4664	2,4121	2,3646	2,3224	2,2849	2,2511	2,2206	2,1929	2,1676
68	7,0229	4,9316	4,0834	3,6083	3,2991	3,0795	2,9143	2,7847	2,6800	2,5934	2,5203	2,4577	2,4035	2,3559	2,3137	2,2761	2,2424	2,2118	2,1841	2,1587
70	7,0114	4,9219	4,0744	3,5996	3,2907	3,0712	2,9060	2,7765	2,6719	2,5852	2,5122	2,4496	2,3953	2,3477	2,3055	2,2679	2,2341	2,2036	2,1758	2,1504
72	7,0005	4,9127	4,0659	3,5915	3,2827	3,0634	2,8983	2,7688	2,6642	2,5775	2,5045	2,4419	2,3876	2,3400	2,2978	2,2602	2,2263	2,1958	2,1680	2,1426
74	6,9903	4,9040	4,0579	3,5838	3,2752	3,0560	2,8909	2,7615	2,6569	2,5703	2,4972	2,4346	2,3803	2,3327	2,2905	2,2528	2,2190	2,1884	2,1606	2,1352
76	6,9806	4,8958	4,0503	3,5765	3,2681	3,0490	2,8840	2,7547	2,6500	2,5634	2,4904	2,4278	2,3735	2,3258	2,2836	2,2459	2,2121	2,1815	2,1536	2,1282
78	6,9714	4,8881	4,0431	3,5696	3,2614	3,0424	2,8775	2,7481	2,6436	2,5570	2,4839	2,4213	2,3670	2,3193	2,2771	2,2394	2,2055	2,1749	2,1470	2,1216
80	6,9627	4,8807	4,0363	3,5631	3,2550	3,0361	2,8713	2,7420	2,6374	2,5508	2,4777	2,4151	2,3608	2,3131	2,2709	2,2332	2,1993	2,1686	2,1408	2,1153
82	6,9544	4,8738	4,0298	3,5569	3,2490	3,0302	2,8654	2,7361	2,6316	2,5450	2,4719	2,4093	2,3549	2,3072	2,2650	2,2273	2,1934	2,1627	2,1348	2,1093
84	6,9466	4,8671	4,0237	3,5510	3,2433	3,0245	2,8598	2,7305	2,6260	2,5394	2,4664	2,4037	2,3494	2,3017	2,2594	2,2217	2,1878	2,1571	2,1292	2,1036
86	6,9391	4,8608	4,0179	3,5454	3,2378	3,0191	2,8544	2,7252	2,6207	2,5342	2,4611	2,3985	2,3441	2,2964	2,2541	2,2164	2,1824	2,1517	2,1238	2,0982
88	6,9319	4,8548	4,0123	3,5401	3,2326	3,0140	2,8494	2,7202	2,6157	2,5291	2,4561	2,3934	2,3390	2,2913	2,2490	2,2113	2,1773	2,1466	2,1186	2,0931
90	6,9251	4,8491	4,0070	3,5350	3,2276	3,0091	2,8445	2,7154	2,6109	2,5243	2,4513	2,3886	2,3342	2,2865	2,2442	2,2064	2,1725	2,1417	2,1137	2,0882
92	6,9186	4,8436	4,0019	3,5301	3,2229	3,0044	2,8399	2,7108	2,6063	2,5197	2,4467	2,3840	2,3296	2,2819	2,2396	2,2018	2,1678	2,1371	2,1091	2,0835
94	6,9124	4,8383	3,9970	3,5255	3,2183	3,0000	2,8355	2,7064	2,6019	2,5154	2,4423	2,3797	2,3252	2,2775	2,2352	2,1974	2,1634	2,1326	2,1046	2,0790
96	6,9065	4,8333	3,9924	3,5210	3,2140	2,9957	2,8312	2,7022	2,5977	2,5112	2,4381	2,3755	2,3210	2,2733	2,2309	2,1931	2,1591	2,1283	2,1003	2,0747
98	6,9008	4,8285	3,9880	3,5168	3,2099	2,9916	2,8272	2,6981	2,5937	2,5072	2,4341	2,3714	2,3170	2,2692	2,2269	2,1891	2,1550	2,1243	2,0962	2,0706
100	6,8953	4,8239	3,9837	3,5127	3,2059	2,9877	2,8233	2,6943	2,5898	2,5033	2,4302	2,3676	2,3132	2,2654	2,2230	2,1852	2,1511	2,1203	2,0923	2,0666
110	6,8710	4,8035	3,9648	3,4946	3,1882	2,9703	2,8061	2,6771	2,5727	2,4862	2,4132	2,3505	2,2960	2,2482	2,2058	2,1679	2,1338	2,1029	2,0748	2,0491
120	6,8509	4,7865	3,9491	3,4795	3,1735	2,9559	2,7918	2,6629	2,5586	2,4721	2,3990	2,3363	2,2818	2,2339	2,1915	2,1536	2,1194	2,0885	2,0604	2,0346
130	6,8339	4,7722	3,9359	3,4669	3,1612	2,9437	2,7797	2,6509	2,5466	2,4602	2,3871	2,3244	2,2698	2,2219	2,1795	2,1415	2,1073	2,0763	2,0481	2,0223
140	6,8194	4,7600	3,9246	3,4561	3,1507	2,9333	2,7695	2,6407	2,5365	2,4500	2,3769	2,3142	2,2596	2,2117	2,1692	2,1312	2,0970	2,0660	2,0377	2,0119
150	6,8069	4,7495	3,9149	3,4467	3,1416	2,9244	2,7606	2,6319	2,5277	2,4412	2,3681	2,3053	2,2508	2,2028	2,1603	2,1223	2,0880	2,0570	2,0287	2,0028
160	6,7960	4,7403	3,9064	3,4386	3,1336	2,9166	2,7528	2,6242	2,5200	2,4335	2,3604	2,2977	2,2431	2,1951	2,1526	2,1145	2,0802	2,0491	2,0208	1,9949
170	6,7863	4,7322	3,8989	3,4314	3,1267	2,9097	2,7460	2,6174	2,5132	2,4268	2,3537	2,2909	2,2363	2,1883	2,1457	2,1076	2,0733	2,0422	2,0139	1,9879
180	6,7778	4,7250	3,8923	3,4251	3,1205	2,9036	2,7400	2,6114	2,5072	2,4208	2,3477	2,2849	2,2303	2,1823	2,1397	2,1016	2,0672	2,0361	2,0077	1,9818
190	6,7702	4,7186	3,8863	3,4194	3,1149	2,8982	2,7346	2,6061	2,5019	2,4154	2,3423	2,2795	2,2249	2,1769	2,1343	2,0961	2,0618	2,0306	2,0021	1,9763
200	6,7633	4,7129	3,8810	3,4143	3,1100	2,8933	2,7298	2,6012	2,4971	2,4106	2,3375	2,2747	2,2201	2,1721	2,1294	2,0913	2,0569	2,0257	1,9973	1,9713
250	6,7373	4,6911	3,8609	3,3950	3,0912	2,8748	2,7114	2,5830	2,4789	2,3925	2,3193	2,2565	2,2018	2,1537	2,1110	2,0728	2,0384	2,0071	1,9786	1,9525
300	6,7201	4,6766	3,8475	3,3823	3,0787	2,8625	2,6993	2,5709	2,4668	2,3804	2,3073	2,2444	2,1897	2,1416	2,0988	2,0606	2,0261	1,9948	1,9662	1,9401
350	6,7078	4,6663	3,8380	3,3732	3,0699	2,8538	2,6906	2,5623	2,4582	2,3718	2,2987	2,2358	2,1811	2,1329	2,0901	2,0518	2,0173	1,9860	1,9574	1,9312
400	6,6987	4,6586	3,8309	3,3664	3,0632	2,8472	2,6842	2,5559	2,4518	2,3654	2,2923	2,2294	2,1746	2,1264	2,0836	2,0453	2,0107	1,9794	1,9508	1,9245
500	6,6858	4,6478	3,8210	3,3569	3,0540	2,8381	2,6751	2,5469	2,4429	2,3565	2,2833	2,2204	2,1656	2,1174	2,0746	2,0362	2,0016	1,9702	1,9415	1,9152
600	6,6773	4,6407	3,8144	3,3505	3,0478	2,8321	2,6691	2,5409	2,4369	2,3505	2,2773	2,2144	2,1596	2,1114	2,0685	2,0301	1,9955	1,9641	1,9354	1,9091
700	6,6712	4,6356	3,8097	3,3460	3,0434	2,8277	2,6649	2,5367	2,4327	2,3463	2,2731	2,2102	2,1554	2,1071	2,0642	2,0258	1,9912	1,9597	1,9310	1,9047
800	6,6667	4,6318	3,8062	3,3427	3,0401	2,8245	2,6617	2,5335	2,4295	2,3431	2,2699	2,2070	2,1522	2,1039	2,0610	2,0226	1,9879	1,9564	1,9277	1,9013
900	6,6631	4,6288	3,8034	3,3400	3,0376	2,8220	2,6592	2,5310	2,4270	2,3406	2,2674	2,2045	2,1497	2,1014	2,0585	2,0201	1,9854	1,9539	1,9251	1,8988
1000	6,6603	4,6264	3,8012	3,3380	3,0355	2,8200	2,6572	2,5290	2,4250	2,3386	2,2655	2,2025	2,1477	2,0994	2,0565	2,0180	1,9834	1,9519	1,9231	1,8967
2000	6,6476	4,6158	3,7914	3,3285	3,0264	2,8110	2,6482	2,5201	2,4162	2,3298	2,2566	2,1936	2,1388	2,0905	2,0475	2,0090	1,9743	1,9427	1,9139	1,8875
5000	6,6400	4,6094	3,7855	3,3229	3,0209	2,8056	2,6429	2,5148	2,4109	2,3245	2,2513	2,1883	2,1334	2,0851	2,0421	2,0036	1,9688	1,9373	1,9084	1,8820
10000	6,6374	4,6073	3,7836	3,3210	3,0191	2,8038	2,6411	2,5130	2,4091	2,3227	2,2495	2,1865	2,1316	2,0833	2,0403	2,0018	1,9670	1,9354	1,9066	1,8801
∞	6,6349	4,6052	3,7816	3,3192	3,0173	2,8020	2,6393	2,5113	2,4073	2,3209	2,2477	2,1847	2,1299	2,0815	2,0385	2,0000	1,9652	1,9336	1,9048	1,8783

All values conform to the international convention (i.e. 0,1 instead of 0.1).

The *F*-Distribution* ν_1, ν_2 Degrees of Freedom $P = 0{,}01$

$P = P(\text{right})$ = integral between F_{ν_1,ν_2} and ∞ (values in the table are the F_{ν_1,ν_2}-values)

ν_2 \ ν_1	22	24	26	28	30	32	35	40	45	50	60	70	80	100	120	200	300	500	1000	∞
1	6222,8	6234,6	6244,6	6253,2	6260,6	6267,2	6275,6	6286,8	6295,5	6302,5	6313,0	6320,5	6326,2	6334,1	6339,4	6349,9	6355,3	6359,4	6362,7	6365,9
2	99,454	99,458	99,461	99,463	99,466	99,468	99,471	99,474	99,477	99,479	99,483	99,485	99,487	99,489	99,491	99,494	99,496	99,497	99,498	99,499
3	26,640	26,598	26,562	26,531	26,505	26,481	26,451	26,411	26,379	26,354	26,316	26,289	26,269	26,240	26,221	26,183	26,164	26,148	26,137	26,125
4	13,970	13,929	13,894	13,864	13,838	13,815	13,785	13,745	13,714	13,690	13,652	13,625	13,605	13,577	13,558	13,520	13,501	13,486	13,475	13,463
5	9,5058	9,4665	9,4331	9,4043	9,3793	9,3574	9,3291	9,2912	9,2616	9,2378	9,2020	9,1763	9,1570	9,1299	9,1118	9,0754	9,0571	9,0424	9,0314	9,0204
6	7,3506	7,3127	7,2805	7,2527	7,2285	7,2073	7,1799	7,1432	7,1145	7,0915	7,0567	7,0318	7,0130	6,9867	6,9690	6,9336	6,9158	6,9015	6,8908	6,8800
7	6,1113	6,0743	6,0428	6,0157	5,9920	5,9712	5,9444	5,9084	5,8803	5,8577	5,8236	5,7991	5,7806	5,7547	5,7373	5,7024	5,6848	5,6707	5,6601	5,6495
8	5,3157	5,2793	5,2482	5,2214	5,1981	5,1776	5,1512	5,1156	5,0878	5,0654	5,0316	5,0073	4,9890	4,9633	4,9461	4,9114	4,8939	4,8799	4,8694	4,8588
9	4,7651	4,7290	4,6982	4,6717	4,6486	4,6282	4,6020	4,5666	4,5390	4,5167	4,4831	4,4589	4,4407	4,4150	4,3978	4,3631	4,3457	4,3317	4,3211	4,3105
10	4,3628	4,3269	4,2963	4,2700	4,2469	4,2267	4,2005	4,1653	4,1377	4,1155	4,0819	4,0577	4,0394	4,0137	3,9965	3,9617	3,9442	3,9302	3,9196	3,9090
11	4,0566	4,0209	3,9904	3,9641	3,9411	3,9209	3,8948	3,8596	3,8320	3,8097	3,7761	3,7518	3,7335	3,7077	3,6904	3,6555	3,6379	3,6238	3,6131	3,6024
12	3,8161	3,7805	3,7500	3,7237	3,7008	3,6806	3,6544	3,6192	3,5915	3,5692	3,5355	3,5111	3,4928	3,4668	3,4494	3,4143	3,3966	3,3823	3,3716	3,3608
13	3,6224	3,5868	3,5563	3,5300	3,5070	3,4868	3,4606	3,4253	3,3976	3,3752	3,3413	3,3168	3,2984	3,2723	3,2548	3,2194	3,2015	3,1871	3,1763	3,1654
14	3,4630	3,4274	3,3969	3,3706	3,3476	3,3273	3,3010	3,2656	3,2378	3,2153	3,1813	3,1567	3,1381	3,1118	3,0942	3,0585	3,0405	3,0260	3,0150	3,0040
15	3,3297	3,2940	3,2635	3,2372	3,2141	3,1938	3,1674	3,1319	3,1039	3,0814	3,0471	3,0224	3,0037	2,9772	2,9595	2,9235	2,9053	2,8906	2,8795	2,8684
16	3,2165	3,1808	3,1503	3,1238	3,1007	3,0803	3,0539	3,0182	2,9902	2,9675	2,9330	2,9082	2,8893	2,8627	2,8447	2,8084	2,7901	2,7752	2,7641	2,7528
17	3,1192	3,0835	3,0529	3,0264	3,0032	2,9828	2,9563	2,9205	2,8922	2,8694	2,8348	2,8097	2,7908	2,7639	2,7459	2,7092	2,6907	2,6757	2,6644	2,6530
18	3,0348	2,9990	2,9683	2,9418	2,9185	2,8980	2,8714	2,8354	2,8071	2,7841	2,7493	2,7241	2,7050	2,6779	2,6597	2,6227	2,6040	2,5889	2,5775	2,5660
19	2,9607	2,9249	2,8941	2,8675	2,8442	2,8236	2,7969	2,7608	2,7323	2,7093	2,6742	2,6488	2,6296	2,6023	2,5839	2,5467	2,5277	2,5124	2,5009	2,4893
20	2,8953	2,8594	2,8286	2,8019	2,7785	2,7578	2,7310	2,6947	2,6661	2,6430	2,6077	2,5822	2,5628	2,5353	2,5168	2,4792	2,4600	2,4446	2,4329	2,4212
21	2,8370	2,8010	2,7702	2,7434	2,7200	2,6992	2,6723	2,6359	2,6071	2,5838	2,5484	2,5227	2,5032	2,4755	2,4568	2,4189	2,3996	2,3840	2,3722	2,3603
22	2,7849	2,7488	2,7179	2,6910	2,6675	2,6467	2,6197	2,5831	2,5542	2,5308	2,4951	2,4693	2,4496	2,4217	2,4029	2,3646	2,3452	2,3294	2,3175	2,3055
23	2,7378	2,7017	2,6707	2,6438	2,6202	2,5993	2,5722	2,5355	2,5065	2,4829	2,4471	2,4210	2,4013	2,3732	2,3542	2,3156	2,2959	2,2800	2,2680	2,2558
24	2,6953	2,6591	2,6280	2,6010	2,5773	2,5564	2,5292	2,4923	2,4632	2,4395	2,4035	2,3773	2,3573	2,3291	2,3100	2,2710	2,2512	2,2351	2,2230	2,2107
25	2,6565	2,6203	2,5891	2,5620	2,5383	2,5173	2,4900	2,4530	2,4237	2,3999	2,3637	2,3373	2,3173	2,2888	2,2696	2,2303	2,2103	2,1941	2,1818	2,1694
26	2,6211	2,5848	2,5536	2,5264	2,5026	2,4816	2,4542	2,4170	2,3876	2,3637	2,3273	2,3008	2,2806	2,2519	2,2325	2,1930	2,1728	2,1564	2,1440	2,1315
27	2,5887	2,5522	2,5209	2,4937	2,4699	2,4487	2,4213	2,3840	2,3544	2,3304	2,2938	2,2672	2,2469	2,2180	2,1985	2,1586	2,1382	2,1217	2,1092	2,0965
28	2,5587	2,5223	2,4909	2,4636	2,4397	2,4185	2,3909	2,3535	2,3238	2,2997	2,2629	2,2361	2,2157	2,1867	2,1670	2,1268	2,1063	2,0896	2,0769	2,0642
29	2,5311	2,4946	2,4631	2,4358	2,4118	2,3906	2,3629	2,3253	2,2956	2,2714	2,2344	2,2074	2,1869	2,1577	2,1379	2,0974	2,0766	2,0598	2,0471	2,0342
30	2,5055	2,4689	2,4374	2,4100	2,3860	2,3647	2,3369	2,2992	2,2693	2,2450	2,2079	2,1808	2,1601	2,1307	2,1108	2,0700	2,0491	2,0321	2,0192	2,0062
31	2,4818	2,4451	2,4135	2,3861	2,3619	2,3406	2,3127	2,2749	2,2449	2,2205	2,1832	2,1559	2,1352	2,1056	2,0855	2,0444	2,0234	2,0063	1,9933	1,9801
32	2,4596	2,4229	2,3912	2,3637	2,3395	2,3181	2,2902	2,2523	2,2221	2,1976	2,1601	2,1328	2,1119	2,0821	2,0619	2,0206	1,9993	1,9821	1,9690	1,9557
33	2,4389	2,4021	2,3704	2,3428	2,3186	2,2971	2,2691	2,2311	2,2008	2,1762	2,1386	2,1111	2,0901	2,0602	2,0398	1,9982	1,9768	1,9594	1,9462	1,9328
34	2,4195	2,3827	2,3509	2,3233	2,2990	2,2775	2,2494	2,2112	2,1809	2,1562	2,1184	2,0908	2,0697	2,0396	2,0191	1,9772	1,9556	1,9381	1,9248	1,9113
35	2,4014	2,3645	2,3327	2,3050	2,2806	2,2590	2,2309	2,1926	2,1622	2,1374	2,0994	2,0716	2,0505	2,0202	1,9996	1,9574	1,9357	1,9180	1,9046	1,8910
36	2,3843	2,3473	2,3155	2,2877	2,2633	2,2417	2,2135	2,1751	2,1445	2,1197	2,0815	2,0537	2,0324	2,0019	1,9812	1,9387	1,9169	1,8991	1,8855	1,8718
37	2,3682	2,3312	2,2993	2,2715	2,2470	2,2254	2,1971	2,1585	2,1279	2,1030	2,0647	2,0367	2,0153	1,9847	1,9639	1,9211	1,8991	1,8812	1,8675	1,8537
38	2,3531	2,3160	2,2840	2,2562	2,2317	2,2099	2,1816	2,1430	2,1122	2,0872	2,0488	2,0206	1,9991	1,9684	1,9475	1,9045	1,8823	1,8642	1,8505	1,8365
39	2,3387	2,3016	2,2696	2,2417	2,2171	2,1954	2,1669	2,1282	2,0974	2,0723	2,0337	2,0055	1,9839	1,9530	1,9319	1,8887	1,8663	1,8481	1,8343	1,8202
40	2,3252	2,2880	2,2559	2,2280	2,2034	2,1816	2,1531	2,1142	2,0833	2,0581	2,0194	1,9911	1,9694	1,9383	1,9172	1,8737	1,8512	1,8329	1,8189	1,8047
41	2,3123	2,2751	2,2430	2,2150	2,1903	2,1685	2,1399	2,1010	2,0700	2,0447	2,0059	1,9774	1,9556	1,9244	1,9032	1,8594	1,8368	1,8183	1,8042	1,7900
42	2,3001	2,2629	2,2307	2,2026	2,1780	2,1560	2,1274	2,0884	2,0573	2,0319	1,9930	1,9644	1,9425	1,9112	1,8898	1,8458	1,8231	1,8045	1,7903	1,7759
43	2,2885	2,2512	2,2190	2,1909	2,1662	2,1442	2,1155	2,0764	2,0453	2,0198	1,9807	1,9520	1,9301	1,8986	1,8771	1,8329	1,8100	1,7913	1,7770	1,7625
44	2,2775	2,2401	2,2079	2,1797	2,1550	2,1330	2,1042	2,0650	2,0338	2,0083	1,9690	1,9402	1,9182	1,8866	1,8650	1,8205	1,7975	1,7786	1,7643	1,7496
45	2,2670	2,2296	2,1973	2,1691	2,1443	2,1222	2,0934	2,0542	2,0228	1,9972	1,9579	1,9290	1,9069	1,8751	1,8535	1,8087	1,7855	1,7666	1,7521	1,7374
46	2,2570	2,2195	2,1872	2,1590	2,1341	2,1120	2,0832	2,0438	2,0124	1,9867	1,9472	1,9182	1,8960	1,8642	1,8424	1,7974	1,7741	1,7550	1,7404	1,7256
47	2,2474	2,2099	2,1775	2,1493	2,1244	2,1022	2,0733	2,0339	2,0024	1,9766	1,9371	1,9080	1,8857	1,8537	1,8318	1,7866	1,7631	1,7440	1,7293	1,7143
48	2,2383	2,2007	2,1683	2,1400	2,1150	2,0929	2,0639	2,0244	1,9928	1,9670	1,9273	1,8981	1,8757	1,8436	1,8217	1,7762	1,7526	1,7333	1,7186	1,7035
49	2,2295	2,1919	2,1594	2,1311	2,1061	2,0839	2,0549	2,0153	1,9837	1,9578	1,9180	1,8887	1,8662	1,8340	1,8119	1,7663	1,7426	1,7231	1,7083	1,6931
50	2,2211	2,1835	2,1510	2,1226	2,0976	2,0754	2,0463	2,0066	1,9749	1,9490	1,9090	1,8797	1,8571	1,8248	1,8026	1,7567	1,7329	1,7133	1,6984	1,6831
52	2,2054	2,1677	2,1351	2,1066	2,0815	2,0593	2,0301	1,9902	1,9584	1,9323	1,8922	1,8626	1,8399	1,8073	1,7850	1,7387	1,7146	1,6948	1,6797	1,6642
54	2,1908	2,1531	2,1204	2,0919	2,0667	2,0444	2,0151	1,9751	1,9431	1,9170	1,8766	1,8469	1,8241	1,7912	1,7687	1,7220	1,6976	1,6777	1,6623	1,6467
56	2,1774	2,1396	2,1068	2,0783	2,0530	2,0306	2,0013	1,9611	1,9290	1,9027	1,8622	1,8323	1,8093	1,7763	1,7536	1,7064	1,6819	1,6617	1,6461	1,6303
58	2,1649	2,1270	2,0942	2,0656	2,0403	2,0178	1,9884	1,9481	1,9159	1,8895	1,8488	1,8187	1,7956	1,7623	1,7395	1,6920	1,6671	1,6467	1,6310	1,6150
60	2,1533	2,1154	2,0825	2,0538	2,0285	2,0059	1,9764	1,9360	1,9037	1,8772	1,8363	1,8061	1,7828	1,7493	1,7263	1,6784	1,6534	1,6327	1,6169	1,6006
62	2,1425	2,1045	2,0716	2,0428	2,0174	1,9948	1,9652	1,9247	1,8923	1,8657	1,8246	1,7942	1,7709	1,7372	1,7140	1,6657	1,6405	1,6196	1,6036	1,5872
64	2,1324	2,0943	2,0614	2,0325	2,0071	1,9845	1,9548	1,9141	1,8816	1,8549	1,8136	1,7831	1,7596	1,7257	1,7024	1,6538	1,6283	1,6073	1,5911	1,5745
66	2,1229	2,0848	2,0518	2,0229	1,9974	1,9747	1,9450	1,9042	1,8716	1,8448	1,8033	1,7727	1,7491	1,7150	1,6916	1,6426	1,6169	1,5956	1,5793	1,5625
68	2,1140	2,0758	2,0428	2,0139	1,9883	1,9656	1,9358	1,8949	1,8621	1,8353	1,7937	1,7629	1,7392	1,7049	1,6813	1,6320	1,6061	1,5847	1,5681	1,5512
70	2,1057	2,0674	2,0343	2,0053	1,9797	1,9570	1,9271	1,8861	1,8533	1,8263	1,7846	1,7537	1,7298	1,6954	1,6717	1,6220	1,5959	1,5743	1,5576	1,5404
72	2,0978	2,0595	2,0263	1,9973	1,9717	1,9488	1,9189	1,8778	1,8449	1,8178	1,7760	1,7449	1,7210	1,6864	1,6625	1,6125	1,5862	1,5644	1,5476	1,5303
74	2,0903	2,0520	2,0188	1,9897	1,9641	1,9412	1,9112	1,8700	1,8370	1,8099	1,7678	1,7367	1,7126	1,6779	1,6539	1,6036	1,5770	1,5551	1,5381	1,5206
76	2,0833	2,0449	2,0117	1,9826	1,9568	1,9339	1,9039	1,8626	1,8295	1,8023	1,7601	1,7289	1,7047	1,6698	1,6457	1,5950	1,5683	1,5462	1,5290	1,5114
78	2,0766	2,0382	2,0049	1,9758	1,9500	1,9271	1,8969	1,8556	1,8224	1,7951	1,7528	1,7215	1,6972	1,6621	1,6379	1,5869	1,5600	1,5377	1,5204	1,5026
80	2,0703	2,0318	1,9985	1,9693	1,9435	1,9205	1,8904	1,8489	1,8157	1,7883	1,7459	1,7144	1,6901	1,6548	1,6305	1,5792	1,5521	1,5296	1,5122	1,4942
82	2,0643	2,0258	1,9924	1,9632	1,9374	1,9143	1,8841	1,8426	1,8093	1,7818	1,7393	1,7077	1,6833	1,6479	1,6234	1,5719	1,5446	1,5219	1,5043	1,4862
84	2,0586	2,0201	1,9867	1,9574	1,9315	1,9084	1,8782	1,8366	1,8032	1,7757	1,7330	1,7013	1,6768	1,6413	1,6167	1,5649	1,5374	1,5146	1,4968	1,4785
86	2,0532	2,0146	1,9811	1,9518	1,9259	1,9028	1,8725	1,8308	1,7974	1,7698	1,7270	1,6952	1,6706	1,6349	1,6102	1,5582	1,5305	1,5075	1,4897	1,4712
88	2,0480	2,0094	1,9759	1,9466	1,9206	1,8975	1,8671	1,8254	1,7918	1,7642	1,7213	1,6894	1,6647	1,6289	1,6041	1,5518	1,5240	1,5008	1,4828	1,4642
90	2,0430	2,0044	1,9709	1,9415	1,9155	1,8924	1,8619	1,8201	1,7865	1,7588	1,7158	1,6838	1,6591	1,6231	1,5982	1,5456	1,5177	1,4943	1,4762	1,4574
92	2,0383	1,9996	1,9661	1,9367	1,9107	1,8875	1,8570	1,8151	1,7815	1,7537	1,7106	1,6785	1,6537	1,6176	1,5926	1,5397	1,5116	1,4881	1,4698	1,4509
94	2,0338	1,9951	1,9615	1,9321	1,9060	1,8828	1,8523	1,8104	1,7766	1,7488	1,7056	1,6734	1,6485	1,6123	1,5872	1,5341	1,5058	1,4822	1,4637	1,4446
96	2,0295	1,9907	1,9571	1,9277	1,9016	1,8783	1,8478	1,8058	1,7720	1,7441	1,7008	1,6686	1,6436	1,6072	1,5820	1,5287	1,5002	1,4764	1,4579	1,4386
98	2,0253	1,9866	1,9529	1,9234	1,8973	1,8741	1,8435	1,8014	1,7675	1,7396	1,6962	1,6639	1,6388	1,6024	1,5770	1,5234	1,4948	1,4709	1,4522	1,4328
100	2,0214	1,9826	1,9489	1,9194	1,8933	1,8699	1,8393	1,7972	1,7633	1,7353	1,6918	1,6594	1,6342	1,5977	1,5723	1,5184	1,4897	1,4656	1,4468	1,4272
110	2,0037	1,9648	1,9310	1,9013	1,8751	1,8517	1,8209	1,7784	1,7443	1,7160	1,6721	1,6393	1,6139	1,5767	1,5509	1,4960	1,4665	1,4417	1,4223	1,4020
120	1,9891	1,9500	1,9161	1,8864	1,8600	1,8365	1,8055	1,7628	1,7284	1,7000	1,6557	1,6226	1,5968	1,5592	1,5330	1,4770	1,4469	1,4215	1,4015	1,3805
130	1,9767	1,9375	1,9036	1,8737	1,8473	1,8236	1,7925	1,7497	1,7151	1,6865	1,6418	1,6084	1,5824	1,5443	1,5178	1,4609	1,4301	1,4041	1,3835	1,3620
140	1,9661	1,9269	1,8928	1,8629	1,8364	1,8127	1,7815	1,7384	1,7036	1,6748	1,6299	1,5962	1,5700	1,5315	1,5046	1,4469	1,4156	1,3890	1,3679	1,3457
150	1,9570	1,9177	1,8836	1,8536	1,8270	1,8032	1,7719	1,7286	1,6937	1,6648	1,6195	1,5856	1,5592	1,5204	1,4932	1,4347	1,4029	1,3757	1,3542	1,3314
160	1,9491	1,9097	1,8755	1,8454	1,8187	1,7949	1,7635	1,7201	1,6850	1,6559	1,6105	1,5764	1,5497	1,5106	1,4832	1,4240	1,3916	1,3640	1,3419	1,3185
170	1,9420	1,9026	1,8683	1,8382	1,8115	1,7876	1,7561	1,7125	1,6773	1,6482	1,6025	1,5682	1,5414	1,5020	1,4743	1,4144	1,3816	1,3535	1,3310	1,3070
180	1,9358	1,8963	1,8620	1,8318	1,8050	1,7811	1,7495	1,7059	1,6705	1,6413	1,5954	1,5609	1,5339	1,4942	1,4663	1,4057	1,3726	1,3440	1,3211	1,2966
190	1,9302	1,8907	1,8563	1,8261	1,7993	1,7753	1,7436	1,6999	1,6644	1,6351	1,5890	1,5544	1,5272	1,4873	1,4592	1,3982	1,3645	1,3355	1,3122	1,2872
200	1,9252	1,8857	1,8512	1,8210	1,7941	1,7700	1,7383	1,6945	1,6590	1,6295	1,5833	1,5485	1,5212	1,4811	1,4527	1,3912	1,3571	1,3277	1,3040	1,2785
250	1,9063	1,8665	1,8319	1,8015	1,7744	1,7502	1,7183	1,6740	1,6381	1,6083	1,5614	1,5260	1,4982	1,4571	1,4280	1,3643	1,3286	1,2974	1,2720	1,2442
300	1,8937	1,8538	1,8191	1,7885	1,7614	1,7371	1,7049	1,6604	1,6242	1,5942	1,5468	1,5110	1,4828	1,4410	1,4114	1,3459	1,3090	1,2764	1,2495	1,2196
350	1,8847	1,8448	1,8100	1,7793	1,7521	1,7276	1,6954	1,6507	1,6143	1,5840	1,5363	1,5002	1,4717	1,4295	1,3993	1,3326	1,2946	1,2609	1,2327	1,2011
400	1,8780	1,8380	1,8031	1,7724	1,7451	1,7206	1,6883	1,6434	1,6068	1,5764	1,5285	1,4921	1,4634	1,4207	1,3902	1,3225	1,2837	1,2489	1,2197	1,1864
500	1,8686	1,8285	1,7936	1,7627	1,7353	1,7108	1,6783	1,6332	1,5964	1,5658	1,5174	1,4807	1,4517	1,4084	1,3774	1,3081	1,2680	1,2317	1,2007	1,1644
600	1,8624	1,8222	1,7872	1,7563	1,7288	1,7042	1,6716	1,6263	1,5895	1,5587	1,5101	1,4731	1,4438	1,4001	1,3688	1,2983	1,2573	1,2198	1,1873	1,1486
700	1,8580	1,8177	1,7826	1,7517	1,7242	1,6995	1,6668	1,6215	1,5845	1,5536	1,5048	1,4676	1,4382	1,3942	1,3626	1,2913	1,2495	1,2110	1,1774	1,1365
800	1,8546	1,8144	1,7792	1,7483	1,7207	1,6960	1,6633	1,6178	1,5808	1,5498	1,5008	1,4635	1,4340	1,3897	1,3579	1,2860	1,2436	1,2043	1,1698	1,1269
900	1,8520	1,8117	1,7766	1,7456	1,7180	1,6933	1,6605	1,6150	1,5778	1,5468	1,4978	1,4603	1,4307	1,3863	1,3543	1,2818	1,2389	1,1990	1,1636	1,1191
1000	1,8500	1,8096	1,7745	1,7435	1,7158	1,6911	1,6583	1,6127	1,5755	1,5445	1,4953	1,4578	1,4280	1,3835	1,3513	1,2784	1,2351	1,1947	1,1586	1,1125
2000	1,8406	1,8002	1,7650	1,7338	1,7061	1,6812	1,6483	1,6025	1,5651	1,5338	1,4842	1,4462	1,4161	1,3708	1,3380	1,2630	1,2178	1,1746	1,1346	1,0777
5000	1,8351	1,7946	1,7592	1,7281	1,7003	1,6754	1,6423	1,5964	1,5588	1,5274	1,4775	1,4393	1,4089	1,3632	1,3300	1,2536	1,2070	1,1619	1,1186	1,0481
10000	1,8332	1,7927	1,7573	1,7261	1,6983	1,6734	1,6403	1,5943	1,5567	1,5252	1,4752	1,4370	1,4065	1,3606	1,3273	1,2504	1,2034	1,1575	1,1129	1,0337
∞	1,8313	1,7908	1,7554	1,7242	1,6964	1,6714	1,6383	1,5923	1,5546	1,5231	1,4730	1,4346	1,4041	1,3581	1,3246	1,2472	1,1997	1,1530	1,1070	1

All values conform to the international convention (i.e. 0,1 instead of 0.1).

The *F*-Distribution* ν_1, ν_2 Degrees of Freedom $P = 0{,}005$

$P = P$ (right) = integral between F_{ν_1,ν_2} and ∞ (values in the table are the F_{ν_1,ν_2}-values)

ν_2 \ ν_1	1	2	3	4	5	6	7	8	9	10	11	12	13	14	15	16	17	18	19	20
1	16211	20000	21615	22500	23056	23437	23715	23925	24091	24224	24334	24426	24505	24572	24630	24681	24727	24767	24803	24836
2	198,50	199,00	199,17	199,25	199,30	199,33	199,36	199,37	199,39	199,40	199,41	199,42	199,42	199,43	199,43	199,44	199,44	199,45	199,45	199,45
3	55,552	49,799	47,467	46,195	45,392	44,838	44,434	44,126	43,882	43,686	43,524	43,387	43,271	43,171	43,085	43,008	42,941	42,880	42,826	42,778
4	31,333	26,284	24,259	23,155	22,456	21,975	21,622	21,352	21,139	20,967	20,824	20,705	20,603	20,515	20,438	20,371	20,311	20,258	20,210	20,167
5	22,758	18,314	16,530	15,556	14,940	14,513	14,200	13,961	13,772	13,618	13,491	13,384	13,293	13,215	13,146	13,086	13,033	12,985	12,942	12,903
6	18,635	14,544	12,917	12,028	11,464	11,073	10,786	10,566	10,391	10,250	10,133	10,034	9,9501	9,8774	9,8140	9,7582	9,7086	9,6644	9,6247	9,5888
7	16,236	12,404	10,882	10,050	9,5221	9,1553	8,8854	8,6781	8,5138	8,3803	8,2697	8,1764	8,0967	8,0279	7,9678	7,9148	7,8678	7,8258	7,7881	7,7540
8	14,688	11,042	9,5965	8,8051	8,3018	7,9520	7,6941	7,4959	7,3386	7,2106	7,1045	7,0149	6,9384	6,8721	6,8143	6,7633	6,7180	6,6775	6,6411	6,6082
9	13,614	10,107	8,7171	7,9559	7,4712	7,1339	6,8849	6,6933	6,5411	6,4172	6,3142	6,2274	6,1530	6,0887	6,0325	5,9829	5,9388	5,8994	5,8639	5,8318
10	12,826	9,4270	8,0807	7,3428	6,8724	6,5446	6,3025	6,1159	5,9676	5,8467	5,7462	5,6613	5,5887	5,5257	5,4707	5,4221	5,3789	5,3403	5,3055	5,2740
11	12,226	8,9122	7,6004	6,8809	6,4217	6,1016	5,8648	5,6821	5,5368	5,4183	5,3197	5,2363	5,1649	5,1031	5,0489	5,0011	4,9586	4,9205	4,8863	4,8552
12	11,754	8,5096	7,2258	6,5211	6,0711	5,7570	5,5245	5,3451	5,2021	5,0855	4,9884	4,9062	4,8358	4,7748	4,7213	4,6741	4,6321	4,5945	4,5606	4,5299
13	11,374	8,1865	6,9258	6,2335	5,7910	5,4819	5,2529	5,0761	4,9351	4,8199	4,7240	4,6429	4,5733	4,5129	4,4600	4,4132	4,3716	4,3344	4,3008	4,2703
14	11,060	7,9216	6,6804	5,9984	5,5623	5,2574	5,0313	4,8566	4,7173	4,6034	4,5085	4,4281	4,3591	4,2993	4,2468	4,2005	4,1592	4,1221	4,0888	4,0585
15	10,798	7,7008	6,4760	5,8029	5,3721	5,0708	4,8473	4,6744	4,5364	4,4235	4,3295	4,2497	4,1813	4,1219	4,0698	4,0237	3,9827	3,9459	3,9127	3,8826
16	10,575	7,5138	6,3034	5,6378	5,2117	4,9134	4,6920	4,5207	4,3838	4,2719	4,1785	4,0994	4,0314	3,9723	3,9205	3,8747	3,8338	3,7972	3,7641	3,7342
17	10,384	7,3536	6,1556	5,4967	5,0746	4,7789	4,5594	4,3894	4,2535	4,1424	4,0496	3,9709	3,9033	3,8445	3,7929	3,7473	3,7066	3,6701	3,6372	3,6073
18	10,218	7,2148	6,0278	5,3746	4,9560	4,6627	4,4448	4,2759	4,1410	4,0305	3,9382	3,8599	3,7926	3,7341	3,6827	3,6373	3,5967	3,5603	3,5275	3,4977
19	10,073	7,0935	5,9161	5,2681	4,8526	4,5614	4,3448	4,1770	4,0428	3,9329	3,8410	3,7631	3,6961	3,6378	3,5866	3,5412	3,5008	3,4645	3,4318	3,4020
20	9,9439	6,9865	5,8177	5,1743	4,7616	4,4721	4,2569	4,0900	3,9564	3,8470	3,7555	3,6779	3,6111	3,5530	3,5020	3,4568	3,4164	3,3802	3,3475	3,3178
21	9,8295	6,8914	5,7304	5,0911	4,6809	4,3931	4,1789	4,0128	3,8799	3,7709	3,6798	3,6024	3,5358	3,4779	3,4270	3,3818	3,3416	3,3054	3,2728	3,2431
22	9,7271	6,8064	5,6524	5,0168	4,6088	4,3225	4,1094	3,9440	3,8116	3,7030	3,6122	3,5350	3,4686	3,4108	3,3600	3,3150	3,2748	3,2387	3,2060	3,1764
23	9,6348	6,7300	5,5823	4,9500	4,5441	4,2591	4,0469	3,8822	3,7502	3,6420	3,5515	3,4745	3,4083	3,3506	3,2999	3,2549	3,2148	3,1787	3,1461	3,1165
24	9,5513	6,6610	5,5190	4,8898	4,4857	4,2019	3,9905	3,8264	3,6949	3,5870	3,4967	3,4199	3,3538	3,2962	3,2456	3,2007	3,1606	3,1246	3,0920	3,0624
25	9,4753	6,5982	5,4615	4,8351	4,4327	4,1500	3,9394	3,7758	3,6447	3,5370	3,4470	3,3704	3,3044	3,2469	3,1963	3,1515	3,1114	3,0754	3,0429	3,0133
26	9,4059	6,5408	5,4091	4,7852	4,3844	4,1027	3,8928	3,7297	3,5989	3,4916	3,4017	3,3252	3,2594	3,2020	3,1515	3,1067	3,0666	3,0306	2,9981	2,9685
27	9,3423	6,4885	5,3611	4,7396	4,3402	4,0594	3,8501	3,6875	3,5571	3,4499	3,3602	3,2839	3,2182	3,1608	3,1104	3,0656	3,0256	2,9896	2,9571	2,9275
28	9,2838	6,4403	5,3170	4,6977	4,2996	4,0197	3,8110	3,6487	3,5186	3,4117	3,3222	3,2460	3,1803	3,1231	3,0727	3,0279	2,9879	2,9520	2,9194	2,8899
29	9,2297	6,3958	5,2764	4,6591	4,2622	3,9831	3,7749	3,6131	3,4832	3,3765	3,2871	3,2110	3,1454	3,0882	3,0379	2,9932	2,9532	2,9173	2,8847	2,8551
30	9,1797	6,3547	5,2388	4,6234	4,2276	3,9492	3,7416	3,5801	3,4505	3,3440	3,2547	3,1787	3,1132	3,0560	3,0057	2,9611	2,9211	2,8852	2,8526	2,8230
31	9,1332	6,3165	5,2039	4,5902	4,1955	3,9178	3,7106	3,5495	3,4201	3,3138	3,2247	3,1488	3,0833	3,0262	2,9759	2,9313	2,8913	2,8554	2,8229	2,7933
32	9,0899	6,2810	5,1715	4,5594	4,1657	3,8886	3,6819	3,5210	3,3919	3,2857	3,1967	3,1209	3,0555	2,9984	2,9482	2,9036	2,8636	2,8277	2,7952	2,7656
33	9,0495	6,2478	5,1412	4,5307	4,1379	3,8615	3,6551	3,4945	3,3656	3,2596	3,1707	3,0949	3,0296	2,9726	2,9223	2,8777	2,8378	2,8019	2,7693	2,7397
34	9,0117	6,2169	5,1130	4,5039	4,1119	3,8360	3,6301	3,4698	3,3410	3,2351	3,1463	3,0707	3,0054	2,9484	2,8982	2,8536	2,8137	2,7777	2,7452	2,7156
35	8,9763	6,1878	5,0865	4,4787	4,0876	3,8123	3,6066	3,4466	3,3180	3,2123	3,1235	3,0480	2,9827	2,9258	2,8756	2,8310	2,7911	2,7551	2,7226	2,6930
36	8,9430	6,1606	5,0616	4,4552	4,0648	3,7899	3,5847	3,4248	3,2965	3,1908	3,1022	3,0267	2,9614	2,9045	2,8543	2,8098	2,7699	2,7339	2,7014	2,6717
37	8,9117	6,1350	5,0383	4,4330	4,0433	3,7689	3,5640	3,4044	3,2762	3,1706	3,0821	3,0065	2,9414	2,8845	2,8344	2,7898	2,7499	2,7140	2,6814	2,6518
38	8,8821	6,1108	5,0163	4,4121	4,0231	3,7492	3,5445	3,3851	3,2570	3,1516	3,0632	2,9877	2,9226	2,8657	2,8156	2,7710	2,7311	2,6952	2,6626	2,6330
39	8,8542	6,0880	4,9955	4,3924	4,0041	3,7305	3,5262	3,3670	3,2390	3,1337	3,0453	2,9699	2,9048	2,8480	2,7979	2,7533	2,7134	2,6774	2,6449	2,6152
40	8,8279	6,0664	4,9758	4,3738	3,9860	3,7129	3,5088	3,3498	3,2220	3,1167	3,0284	2,9531	2,8880	2,8312	2,7811	2,7365	2,6966	2,6607	2,6281	2,5984
41	8,8029	6,0460	4,9572	4,3561	3,9690	3,6962	3,4924	3,3335	3,2059	3,1007	3,0124	2,9372	2,8721	2,8153	2,7652	2,7207	2,6808	2,6448	2,6122	2,5825
42	8,7791	6,0266	4,9396	4,3394	3,9528	3,6804	3,4768	3,3181	3,1906	3,0855	2,9973	2,9221	2,8571	2,8003	2,7502	2,7056	2,6657	2,6297	2,5972	2,5675
43	8,7566	6,0083	4,9229	4,3236	3,9375	3,6654	3,4620	3,3035	3,1761	3,0711	2,9829	2,9077	2,8428	2,7860	2,7359	2,6913	2,6514	2,6155	2,5829	2,5531
44	8,7352	5,9908	4,9070	4,3085	3,9229	3,6511	3,4480	3,2896	3,1623	3,0574	2,9693	2,8941	2,8292	2,7724	2,7223	2,6778	2,6378	2,6019	2,5693	2,5395
45	8,7148	5,9741	4,8918	4,2941	3,9090	3,6376	3,4346	3,2764	3,1492	3,0443	2,9563	2,8811	2,8162	2,7595	2,7094	2,6648	2,6249	2,5889	2,5563	2,5266
46	8,6953	5,9583	4,8774	4,2804	3,8958	3,6246	3,4219	3,2638	3,1367	3,0319	2,9439	2,8688	2,8039	2,7471	2,6971	2,6525	2,6126	2,5766	2,5440	2,5142
47	8,6767	5,9431	4,8636	4,2674	3,8832	3,6123	3,4097	3,2518	3,1247	3,0200	2,9321	2,8570	2,7921	2,7354	2,6853	2,6408	2,6009	2,5649	2,5322	2,5025
48	8,6590	5,9287	4,8505	4,2549	3,8711	3,6005	3,3981	3,2403	3,1133	3,0087	2,9208	2,8458	2,7809	2,7242	2,6741	2,6297	2,5896	2,5536	2,5210	2,4912
49	8,6420	5,9148	4,8379	4,2430	3,8956	3,5893	3,3871	3,2294	3,1025	2,9979	2,9100	2,8350	2,7701	2,7134	2,6634	2,6188	2,5789	2,5429	2,5102	2,4805
50	8,6258	5,9016	4,8259	4,2316	3,8486	3,5785	3,3765	3,2189	3,0920	2,9875	2,8997	2,8247	2,7599	2,7032	2,6531	2,6086	2,5686	2,5326	2,4999	2,4702
52	8,5952	5,8768	4,8033	4,2103	3,8279	3,5583	3,3566	3,1992	3,0725	2,9681	2,8803	2,8054	2,7406	2,6839	2,6338	2,5893	2,5494	2,5133	2,4806	2,4508
54	8,5671	5,8539	4,7825	4,1906	3,8089	3,5397	3,3382	3,1811	3,0545	2,9502	2,8625	2,7876	2,7228	2,6662	2,6161	2,5716	2,5316	2,4956	2,4629	2,4330
56	8,5411	5,8328	4,7633	4,1724	3,7913	3,5225	3,3213	3,1643	3,0379	2,9337	2,8460	2,7712	2,7064	2,6498	2,5997	2,5552	2,5152	2,4792	2,4464	2,4166
58	8,5170	5,8132	4,7455	4,1555	3,7751	3,5066	3,3057	3,1488	3,0226	2,9184	2,8308	2,7560	2,6912	2,6346	2,5846	2,5400	2,5000	2,4640	2,4312	2,4014
60	8,4946	5,7950	4,7290	4,1399	3,7599	3,4918	3,2911	3,1344	3,0083	2,9042	2,8167	2,7419	2,6771	2,6205	2,5705	2,5259	2,4859	2,4498	2,4171	2,3872
62	8,4737	5,7780	4,7136	4,1253	3,7459	3,4781	3,2776	3,1210	2,9950	2,8909	2,8035	2,7287	2,6640	2,6074	2,5573	2,5128	2,4728	2,4367	2,4039	2,3740
64	8,4542	5,7622	4,6992	4,1117	3,7327	3,4652	3,2649	3,1085	2,9825	2,8786	2,7911	2,7164	2,6517	2,5951	2,5451	2,5005	2,4605	2,4244	2,3916	2,3617
66	8,4359	5,7474	4,6858	4,0990	3,7204	3,4532	3,2531	3,0968	2,9709	2,8670	2,7796	2,7049	2,6402	2,5836	2,5336	2,4890	2,4490	2,4129	2,3801	2,3501
68	8,4188	5,7334	4,6731	4,0870	3,7089	3,4419	3,2420	3,0858	2,9600	2,8562	2,7688	2,6941	2,6295	2,5729	2,5228	2,4782	2,4382	2,4021	2,3693	2,3393
70	8,4027	5,7204	4,6613	4,0758	3,6980	3,4313	3,2315	3,0755	2,9498	2,8460	2,7587	2,6840	2,6193	2,5627	2,5127	2,4681	2,4281	2,3919	2,3591	2,3291
72	8,3875	5,7081	4,6501	4,0652	3,6878	3,4213	3,2217	3,0658	2,9401	2,8364	2,7491	2,6745	2,6098	2,5532	2,5032	2,4586	2,4185	2,3824	2,3495	2,3196
74	8,3731	5,6964	4,6396	4,0553	3,6782	3,4119	3,2125	3,0566	2,9310	2,8273	2,7401	2,6655	2,6008	2,5442	2,4942	2,4496	2,4095	2,3734	2,3405	2,3105
76	8,3596	5,6855	4,6296	4,0459	3,6691	3,4030	3,2037	3,0480	2,9224	2,8188	2,7316	2,6570	2,5923	2,5357	2,4857	2,4411	2,4010	2,3649	2,3320	2,3020
78	8,3468	5,6751	4,6202	4,0369	3,6605	3,3946	3,1954	3,0398	2,9143	2,8107	2,7235	2,6489	2,5843	2,5277	2,4777	2,4330	2,3930	2,3568	2,3239	2,2939
80	8,3346	5,6652	4,6113	4,0285	3,6524	3,3867	3,1876	3,0320	2,9066	2,8031	2,7159	2,6413	2,5767	2,5201	2,4700	2,4254	2,3854	2,3492	2,3163	2,2862
82	8,3231	5,6559	4,6028	4,0205	3,6446	3,3791	3,1801	3,0247	2,8993	2,7958	2,7086	2,6341	2,5695	2,5129	2,4628	2,4182	2,3781	2,3419	2,3090	2,2789
84	8,3121	5,6470	4,5947	4,0129	3,6373	3,3719	3,1731	3,0177	2,8924	2,7889	2,7017	2,6272	2,5626	2,5060	2,4560	2,4113	2,3712	2,3350	2,3021	2,2720
86	8,3017	5,6386	4,5871	4,0056	3,6303	3,3651	3,1664	3,0110	2,8858	2,7823	2,6952	2,6207	2,5561	2,4995	2,4494	2,4048	2,3647	2,3285	2,2955	2,2655
88	8,2917	5,6305	4,5798	3,9987	3,6236	3,3586	3,1599	3,0047	2,8795	2,7760	2,6889	2,6144	2,5499	2,4933	2,4432	2,3986	2,3585	2,3222	2,2893	2,2592
90	8,2822	5,6228	4,5728	3,9922	3,6173	3,3524	3,1538	2,9986	2,8735	2,7701	2,6830	2,6085	2,5439	2,4873	2,4373	2,3926	2,3525	2,3163	2,2833	2,2532
92	8,2732	5,6155	4,5662	3,9859	3,6112	3,3465	3,1480	2,9929	2,8678	2,7644	2,6773	2,6028	2,5383	2,4817	2,4316	2,3869	2,3468	2,3106	2,2776	2,2475
94	8,2645	5,6085	4,5598	3,9799	3,6054	3,3408	3,1424	2,9874	2,8623	2,7589	2,6719	2,5974	2,5328	2,4763	2,4262	2,3815	2,3414	2,3051	2,2722	2,2420
96	8,2562	5,6018	4,5538	3,9741	3,5999	3,3354	3,1371	2,9821	2,8570	2,7537	2,6667	2,5922	2,5277	2,4711	2,4210	2,3763	2,3362	2,2999	2,2669	2,2368
98	8,2483	5,5954	4,5480	3,9686	3,5946	3,3302	3,1320	2,9770	2,8520	2,7487	2,6617	2,5873	2,5227	2,4661	2,4160	2,3714	2,3312	2,2949	2,2620	2,2318
100	8,2406	5,5892	4,5424	3,9634	3,5895	3,3252	3,1271	2,9722	2,8472	2,7440	2,6570	2,5825	2,5180	2,4614	2,4113	2,3666	2,3265	2,2902	2,2572	2,2270
110	8,2068	5,5619	4,5177	3,9400	3,5669	3,3032	3,1054	2,9507	2,8259	2,7228	2,6358	2,5614	2,4969	2,4403	2,3902	2,3455	2,3053	2,2690	2,2359	2,2057
120	8,1788	5,5393	4,4972	3,9207	3,5482	3,2849	3,0874	2,9330	2,8083	2,7052	2,6183	2,5439	2,4794	2,4228	2,3727	2,3280	2,2878	2,2514	2,2183	2,1881
130	8,1552	5,5202	4,4799	3,9044	3,5325	3,2696	3,0723	2,9180	2,7934	2,6904	2,6036	2,5292	2,4647	2,4081	2,3580	2,3133	2,2730	2,2366	2,2035	2,1733
140	8,1351	5,5040	4,4652	3,8905	3,5191	3,2565	3,0594	2,9052	2,7808	2,6778	2,5910	2,5167	2,4522	2,3956	2,3455	2,3007	2,2604	2,2240	2,1909	2,1606
150	8,1177	5,4900	4,4525	3,8785	3,5075	3,2452	3,0438	2,8942	2,7698	2,6669	2,5802	2,5059	2,4413	2,3847	2,3346	2,2898	2,2496	2,2131	2,1800	2,1496
160	8,1025	5,4777	4,4414	3,8680	3,4974	3,2353	3,0386	2,8846	2,7603	2,6575	2,5707	2,4961	2,4319	2,3753	2,3252	2,2804	2,2401	2,2036	2,1704	2,1401
170	8,0891	5,4669	4,4317	3,8588	3,4886	3,2266	3,0301	2,8762	2,7519	2,6491	2,5624	2,4881	2,4236	2,3670	2,3168	2,2720	2,2317	2,1953	2,1621	2,1317
180	8,0773	5,4574	4,4231	3,8507	3,4807	3,2190	3,0225	2,8687	2,7445	2,6417	2,5550	2,4807	2,4162	2,3596	2,3095	2,2647	2,2243	2,1878	2,1546	2,1242
190	8,0667	5,4489	4,4154	3,8434	3,4737	3,2121	3,0157	2,8620	2,7379	2,6351	2,5484	2,4742	2,4097	2,3531	2,3029	2,2581	2,2177	2,1812	2,1480	2,1176
200	8,0572	5,4412	4,4084	3,8368	3,4674	3,2059	3,0097	2,8560	2,7319	2,6292	2,5425	2,4683	2,4038	2,3472	2,2970	2,2521	2,2118	2,1753	2,1420	2,1116
250	8,0212	5,4122	4,3822	3,8121	3,4435	3,1826	2,9867	2,8333	2,7094	2,6068	2,5202	2,4459	2,3814	2,3248	2,2746	2,2297	2,1894	2,1528	2,1194	2,0889
300	7,9973	5,3930	4,3649	3,7957	3,4277	3,1672	2,9716	2,8183	2,6945	2,5919	2,5054	2,4311	2,3667	2,3100	2,2598	2,2149	2,1745	2,1378	2,1045	2,0739
350	7,9803	5,3793	4,3525	3,7841	3,4164	3,1562	2,9608	2,8076	2,6839	2,5814	2,4948	2,4206	2,3561	2,2995	2,2493	2,2043	2,1639	2,1272	2,0938	2,0633
400	7,9676	5,3691	4,3433	3,7754	3,4081	3,1480	2,9527	2,7996	2,6759	2,5735	2,4870	2,4128	2,3483	2,2916	2,2414	2,1964	2,1560	2,1193	2,0859	2,0553
500	7,9498	5,3549	4,3304	3,7632	3,3963	3,1366	2,9414	2,7885	2,6649	2,5625	2,4760	2,4018	2,3373	2,2806	2,2304	2,1854	2,1449	2,1082	2,0748	2,0441
600	7,9380	5,3454	4,3219	3,7551	3,3886	3,1290	2,9339	2,7811	2,6575	2,5551	2,4687	2,3945	2,3300	2,2733	2,2231	2,1781	2,1376	2,1008	2,0674	2,0367
700	7,9296	5,3386	4,3158	3,7494	3,3830	3,1236	2,9286	2,7758	2,6523	2,5499	2,4635	2,3893	2,3248	2,2681	2,2178	2,1729	2,1323	2,0956	2,0621	2,0314
800	7,9234	5,3336	4,3112	3,7451	3,3788	3,1195	2,9246	2,7719	2,6483	2,5460	2,4596	2,3854	2,3209	2,2642	2,2139	2,1689	2,1284	2,0917	2,0581	2,0274
900	7,9185	5,3296	4,3076	3,7417	3,3756	3,1164	2,9215	2,7688	2,6453	2,5430	2,4565	2,3824	2,3179	2,2612	2,2109	2,1659	2,1254	2,0886	2,0551	2,0244
1000	7,9145	5,3265	4,3048	3,7390	3,3730	3,1138	2,9190	2,7663	2,6429	2,5405	2,4541	2,3800	2,3155	2,2588	2,2085	2,1635	2,1229	2,0862	2,0526	2,0219
2000	7,8969	5,3124	4,2921	3,7270	3,3615	3,1025	2,9079	2,7553	2,6319	2,5297	2,4433	2,3691	2,3046	2,2479	2,1976	2,1526	2,1120	2,0752	2,0416	2,0109
5000	7,8873	5,3039	4,2845	3,7198	3,3545	3,0958	2,9012	2,7488	2,6254	2,5232	2,4368	2,3626	2,2981	2,2414	2,1911	2,1460	2,1054	2,0686	2,0350	2,0042
10000	7,8829	5,3011	4,2819	3,7175	3,3522	3,0935	2,8990	2,7466	2,6232	2,5210	2,4346	2,3605	2,2960	2,2393	2,1889	2,1439	2,1033	2,0664	2,0328	2,0020
∞	7,8794	5,2983	4,2794	3,7151	3,3499	3,0913	2,8968	2,7444	2,6210	2,5188	2,4324	2,3583	2,2938	2,2371	2,1868	2,1417	2,1011	2,0642	2,0306	1,9998

All values conform to the international convention (i.e. 0,1 instead of 0.1).

The *F*-Distribution* ν_1, ν_2 Degrees of Freedom $P = 0{,}005$

$P = P(\text{right})$ = integral between F_{ν_1,ν_2} and ∞ (values in the table are the F_{ν_1,ν_2}-values)

ν_1 / ν_2	22	24	26	28	30	32	35	40	45	50	60	70	80	100	120	200	300	500	1000	∞
1	24892	24940	24980	25014	25044	25070	25103	25148	25183	25211	25253	25283	25306	25337	25359	25401	25422	25440	25452	25464
2	199,45	199,46	199,46	199,46	199,47	199,47	199,47	199,47	199,48	199,48	199,48	199,49	199,49	199,49	199,49	199,49	199,50	199,50	199,50	199,50
3	42,693	42,622	42,562	42,511	42,466	42,427	42,376	42,308	42,255	42,213	42,149	42,104	42,070	42,022	41,989	41,925	41,893	41,867	41,848	41,828
4	20,093	20,030	19,977	19,931	19,892	19,857	19,812	19,752	19,705	19,667	19,611	19,570	19,540	19,497	19,468	19,411	19,382	19,359	19,342	19,325
5	12,836	12,780	12,732	12,691	12,656	12,624	12,584	12,530	12,487	12,454	12,402	12,366	12,338	12,300	12,274	12,222	12,196	12,174	12,159	12,144
6	9,5264	9,4742	9,4297	9,3915	9,3582	9,3290	9,2913	9,2408	9,2014	9,1697	9,1219	9,0877	9,0619	9,0257	9,0015	8,9528	8,9284	8,9088	8,8941	8,8793
7	7,6947	7,6450	7,6027	7,5662	7,5345	7,5066	7,4707	7,4224	7,3847	7,3544	7,3088	7,2760	7,2513	7,2165	7,1933	7,1466	7,1232	7,1044	7,0902	7,0760
8	6,5510	6,5029	6,4620	6,4268	6,3961	6,3691	6,3343	6,2875	6,2510	6,2215	6,1772	6,1453	6,1213	6,0875	6,0649	6,0194	5,9965	5,9782	5,9644	5,9506
9	5,7760	5,7292	5,6892	5,6548	5,6248	5,5984	5,5643	5,5186	5,4827	5,4539	5,4104	5,3791	5,3555	5,3223	5,3001	5,2554	5,2328	5,2148	5,2012	5,1875
10	5,2192	5,1732	5,1339	5,1001	5,0706	5,0446	5,0110	4,9659	4,9306	4,9022	4,8592	4,8283	4,8050	4,7721	4,7501	4,7058	4,6835	4,6656	4,6521	4,6385
11	4,8012	4,7557	4,7170	4,6835	4,6543	4,6287	4,5955	4,5508	4,5158	4,4876	4,4450	4,4143	4,3912	4,3585	4,3367	4,2926	4,2703	4,2525	4,2390	4,2255
12	4,4765	4,4314	4,3930	4,3599	4,3309	4,3054	4,2725	4,2282	4,1934	4,1653	4,1229	4,0924	4,0693	4,0368	4,0149	3,9709	3,9488	3,9309	3,9174	3,9039
13	4,2173	4,1726	4,1344	4,1015	4,0727	4,0474	4,0146	3,9704	3,9358	3,9078	3,8655	3,8350	3,8120	3,7795	3,7577	3,7136	3,6914	3,6735	3,6601	3,6465
14	4,0058	3,9614	3,9234	3,8906	3,8619	3,8367	3,8040	3,7600	3,7254	3,6975	3,6552	3,6248	3,6017	3,5692	3,5473	3,5032	3,4809	3,4630	3,4494	3,4359
15	3,8301	3,7859	3,7480	3,7153	3,6867	3,6616	3,6289	3,5850	3,5504	3,5225	3,4803	3,4498	3,4267	3,3941	3,3722	3,3279	3,3055	3,2875	3,2739	3,2602
16	3,6819	3,6378	3,6000	3,5674	3,5389	3,5137	3,4811	3,4372	3,4026	3,3747	3,3324	3,3018	3,2787	3,2460	3,2240	3,1796	3,1571	3,1389	3,1253	3,1115
17	3,5552	3,5112	3,4735	3,4409	3,4124	3,3873	3,3547	3,3107	3,2762	3,2482	3,2058	3,1752	3,1520	3,1192	3,0971	3,0524	3,0298	3,0116	2,9978	2,9839
18	3,4456	3,4017	3,3641	3,3315	3,3030	3,2779	3,2453	3,2014	3,1667	3,1387	3,0962	3,0655	3,0422	3,0093	2,9871	2,9421	2,9194	2,9010	2,8871	2,8732
19	3,3500	3,3062	3,2685	3,2360	3,2075	3,1824	3,1498	3,1058	3,0711	3,0430	3,0004	2,9695	2,9462	2,9131	2,8908	2,8456	2,8227	2,8042	2,7902	2,7762
20	3,2659	3,2220	3,1845	3,1519	3,1234	3,0983	3,0656	3,0215	2,9868	2,9586	2,9159	2,8849	2,8614	2,8282	2,8058	2,7603	2,7373	2,7186	2,7046	2,6904
21	3,1912	3,1474	3,1098	3,0771	3,0488	3,0236	2,9909	2,9467	2,9119	2,8837	2,8408	2,8097	2,7861	2,7527	2,7302	2,6845	2,6612	2,6425	2,6283	2,6140
22	3,1246	3,0807	3,0432	3,0106	2,9821	2,9569	2,9241	2,8799	2,8449	2,8167	2,7736	2,7424	2,7187	2,6852	2,6625	2,6165	2,5931	2,5742	2,5599	2,5455
23	3,0647	3,0208	2,9833	2,9507	2,9221	2,8969	2,8641	2,8197	2,7847	2,7564	2,7132	2,6818	2,6581	2,6243	2,6015	2,5552	2,5317	2,5126	2,4982	2,4837
24	3,0106	2,9667	2,9291	2,8965	2,8679	2,8426	2,8098	2,7654	2,7303	2,7018	2,6585	2,6270	2,6031	2,5692	2,5463	2,4997	2,4760	2,4568	2,4423	2,4276
25	2,9615	2,9176	2,8800	2,8473	2,8187	2,7934	2,7605	2,7160	2,6808	2,6522	2,6088	2,5772	2,5532	2,5191	2,4961	2,4492	2,4253	2,4059	2,3913	2,3765
26	2,9167	2,8728	2,8352	2,8025	2,7738	2,7485	2,7155	2,6709	2,6356	2,6070	2,5633	2,5316	2,5075	2,4733	2,4501	2,4029	2,3788	2,3594	2,3446	2,3297
27	2,8757	2,8318	2,7941	2,7614	2,7327	2,7073	2,6743	2,6296	2,5942	2,5655	2,5217	2,4898	2,4656	2,4312	2,4079	2,3604	2,3362	2,3166	2,3017	2,2867
28	2,8380	2,7941	2,7564	2,7236	2,6949	2,6695	2,6364	2,5916	2,5561	2,5273	2,4834	2,4514	2,4270	2,3925	2,3690	2,3213	2,2969	2,2771	2,2621	2,2469
29	2,8033	2,7594	2,7216	2,6888	2,6600	2,6346	2,6015	2,5565	2,5209	2,4921	2,4479	2,4158	2,3914	2,3566	2,3331	2,2850	2,2605	2,2405	2,2254	2,2102
30	2,7712	2,7272	2,6894	2,6566	2,6278	2,6023	2,5691	2,5241	2,4884	2,4594	2,4151	2,3829	2,3584	2,3234	2,2998	2,2514	2,2267	2,2066	2,1914	2,1760
31	2,7414	2,6974	2,6596	2,6267	2,5978	2,5723	2,5390	2,4939	2,4581	2,4291	2,3847	2,3523	2,3277	2,2926	2,2688	2,2201	2,1952	2,1750	2,1597	2,1442
32	2,7137	2,6696	2,6318	2,5989	2,5700	2,5444	2,5111	2,4658	2,4300	2,4008	2,3563	2,3238	2,2990	2,2638	2,2399	2,1909	2,1659	2,1455	2,1301	2,1144
33	2,6878	2,6438	2,6059	2,5729	2,5440	2,5183	2,4850	2,4396	2,4037	2,3745	2,3298	2,2972	2,2723	2,2369	2,2128	2,1636	2,1384	2,1179	2,1023	2,0866
34	2,6636	2,6196	2,5816	2,5486	2,5197	2,4940	2,4606	2,4151	2,3791	2,3498	2,3049	2,2722	2,2473	2,2117	2,1875	2,1380	2,1126	2,0920	2,0763	2,0604
35	2,6410	2,5969	2,5589	2,5259	2,4969	2,4712	2,4377	2,3922	2,3560	2,3266	2,2816	2,2488	2,2237	2,1880	2,1637	2,1140	2,0884	2,0676	2,0518	2,0359
36	2,6197	2,5756	2,5376	2,5045	2,4755	2,4497	2,4162	2,3706	2,3344	2,3049	2,2597	2,2268	2,2016	2,1657	2,1413	2,0913	2,0656	2,0447	2,0288	2,0127
37	2,5998	2,5556	2,5175	2,4844	2,4553	2,4296	2,3959	2,3502	2,3139	2,2844	2,2391	2,2060	2,1808	2,1447	2,1202	2,0699	2,0441	2,0230	2,0070	1,9908
38	2,5809	2,5367	2,4986	2,4655	2,4364	2,4105	2,3769	2,3311	2,2947	2,2651	2,2197	2,1865	2,1611	2,1249	2,1003	2,0497	2,0237	2,0025	1,9864	1,9700
39	2,5631	2,5189	2,4808	2,4476	2,4184	2,3926	2,3588	2,3130	2,2765	2,2468	2,2013	2,1680	2,1425	2,1062	2,0814	2,0306	2,0044	1,9831	1,9669	1,9504
40	2,5463	2,5020	2,4639	2,4307	2,4015	2,3756	2,3418	2,2958	2,2593	2,2295	2,1838	2,1504	2,1249	2,0844	2,0636	2,0125	1,9862	1,9647	1,9483	1,9318
41	2,5304	2,4861	2,4479	2,4147	2,3854	2,3595	2,3257	2,2796	2,2430	2,2131	2,1673	2,1338	2,1082	2,0715	2,0466	1,9952	1,9688	1,9472	1,9307	1,9140
42	2,5153	2,4710	2,4328	2,3995	2,3702	2,3442	2,3103	2,2642	2,2275	2,1976	2,1517	2,1180	2,0923	2,0555	2,0305	1,9789	1,9523	1,9305	1,9140	1,8972
43	2,5010	2,4566	2,4184	2,3850	2,3557	2,3297	2,2958	2,2496	2,2128	2,1828	2,1367	2,1030	2,0772	2,0403	2,0151	1,9633	1,9365	1,9147	1,8980	1,8811
44	2,4873	2,4429	2,4047	2,3713	2,3420	2,3159	2,2819	2,2356	2,1988	2,1687	2,1225	2,0887	2,0628	2,0258	2,0005	1,9484	1,9215	1,8995	1,8827	1,8657
45	2,4744	2,4299	2,3916	2,3582	2,3288	2,3028	2,2687	2,2224	2,1854	2,1553	2,1090	2,0751	2,0491	2,0119	1,9865	1,9342	1,9072	1,8850	1,8682	1,8510
46	2,4620	2,4175	2,3792	2,3458	2,3164	2,2903	2,2562	2,2097	2,1727	2,1425	2,0961	2,0621	2,0360	1,9987	1,9732	1,9206	1,8935	1,8712	1,8542	1,8370
47	2,4502	2,4057	2,3673	2,3339	2,3044	2,2783	2,2442	2,1976	2,1606	2,1303	2,0838	2,0496	2,0235	1,9861	1,9605	1,9077	1,8803	1,8580	1,8409	1,8235
48	2,4389	2,3944	2,3560	2,3225	2,2930	2,2669	2,2327	2,1861	2,1489	2,1186	2,0720	2,0378	2,0115	1,9740	1,9483	1,8952	1,8678	1,8453	1,8281	1,8106
49	2,4281	2,3836	2,3451	2,3116	2,2821	2,2559	2,2217	2,1750	2,1378	2,1074	2,0607	2,0264	2,0001	1,9624	1,9366	1,8833	1,8557	1,8331	1,8158	1,7982
50	2,4178	2,3732	2,3348	2,3012	2,2717	2,2455	2,2112	2,1644	2,1272	2,0967	2,0499	2,0155	1,9891	1,9512	1,9254	1,8719	1,8441	1,8214	1,8040	1,7863
52	2,3984	2,3538	2,3153	2,2817	2,2521	2,2258	2,1914	2,1446	2,1071	2,0766	2,0295	1,9949	1,9684	1,9303	1,9043	1,8503	1,8223	1,7993	1,7818	1,7638
54	2,3806	2,3359	2,2973	2,2637	2,2340	2,2077	2,1732	2,1262	2,0887	2,0580	2,0107	1,9760	1,9493	1,9110	1,8848	1,8304	1,8021	1,7789	1,7611	1,7430
56	2,3641	2,3194	2,2808	2,2470	2,2173	2,1909	2,1564	2,1093	2,0716	2,0408	1,9934	1,9584	1,9316	1,8931	1,8667	1,8119	1,7833	1,7599	1,7419	1,7236
58	2,3488	2,3040	2,2654	2,2316	2,2018	2,1754	2,1408	2,0935	2,0557	2,0248	1,9772	1,9421	1,9152	1,8764	1,8498	1,7946	1,7658	1,7422	1,7240	1,7055
60	2,3346	2,2898	2,2511	2,2172	2,1874	2,1609	2,1263	2,0789	2,0410	2,0100	1,9622	1,9269	1,8998	1,8609	1,8341	1,7785	1,7495	1,7256	1,7073	1,6885
62	2,3214	2,2765	2,2377	2,2039	2,1740	2,1475	2,1127	2,0652	2,0272	1,9961	1,9481	1,9127	1,8855	1,8463	1,8194	1,7634	1,7342	1,7101	1,6915	1,6726
64	2,3090	2,2641	2,2253	2,1914	2,1615	2,1349	2,1000	2,0524	2,0144	1,9832	1,9350	1,8995	1,8721	1,8327	1,8057	1,7493	1,7198	1,6955	1,6768	1,6576
66	2,2974	2,2525	2,2136	2,1797	2,1497	2,1231	2,0882	2,0405	2,0023	1,9710	1,9227	1,8870	1,8595	1,8199	1,7927	1,7360	1,7063	1,6817	1,6628	1,6435
68	2,2866	2,2416	2,2027	2,1687	2,1387	2,1120	2,0770	2,0292	1,9909	1,9596	1,9111	1,8753	1,8477	1,8079	1,7806	1,7234	1,6935	1,6688	1,6497	1,6302
70	2,2764	2,2313	2,1924	2,1583	2,1283	2,1016	2,0666	2,0186	1,9803	1,9488	1,9002	1,8642	1,8365	1,7966	1,7691	1,7116	1,6815	1,6565	1,6373	1,6176
72	2,2667	2,2217	2,1827	2,1486	2,1185	2,0918	2,0567	2,0087	1,9702	1,9387	1,8899	1,8538	1,8260	1,7859	1,7582	1,7004	1,6700	1,6449	1,6255	1,6056
74	2,2577	2,2126	2,1735	2,1394	2,1093	2,0825	2,0474	1,9993	1,9607	1,9291	1,8802	1,8440	1,8161	1,7758	1,7480	1,6898	1,6592	1,6339	1,6143	1,5942
76	2,2491	2,2039	2,1649	2,1307	2,1006	2,0737	2,0386	1,9904	1,9517	1,9200	1,8710	1,8347	1,8067	1,7662	1,7383	1,6798	1,6490	1,6235	1,6037	1,5834
78	2,2410	2,1958	2,1567	2,1225	2,0923	2,0654	2,0302	1,9819	1,9432	1,9115	1,8623	1,8258	1,7977	1,7571	1,7290	1,6702	1,6392	1,6135	1,5936	1,5732
80	2,2333	2,1881	2,1489	2,1147	2,0845	2,0576	2,0223	1,9739	1,9352	1,9033	1,8540	1,8174	1,7892	1,7484	1,7203	1,6611	1,6300	1,6041	1,5840	1,5634
82	2,2260	2,1807	2,1416	2,1073	2,0771	2,0501	2,0148	1,9663	1,9275	1,8956	1,8461	1,8095	1,7812	1,7402	1,7119	1,6525	1,6211	1,5950	1,5748	1,5540
84	2,2190	2,1738	2,1346	2,1003	2,0700	2,0430	2,0076	1,9591	1,9202	1,8882	1,8386	1,8019	1,7735	1,7324	1,7040	1,6442	1,6127	1,5864	1,5660	1,5450
86	2,2124	2,1671	2,1279	2,0936	2,0633	2,0362	2,0008	1,9522	1,9132	1,8812	1,8315	1,7946	1,7662	1,7249	1,6964	1,6364	1,6046	1,5783	1,5576	1,5365
88	2,2061	2,1608	2,1216	2,0872	2,0568	2,0298	1,9943	1,9457	1,9066	1,8745	1,8247	1,7877	1,7592	1,7178	1,6891	1,6288	1,5969	1,5703	1,5496	1,5282
90	2,2001	2,1548	2,1155	2,0811	2,0507	2,0237	1,9881	1,9394	1,9003	1,8681	1,8182	1,7811	1,7525	1,7109	1,6822	1,6216	1,5895	1,5627	1,5419	1,5204
92	2,1944	2,1490	2,1097	2,0753	2,0449	2,0178	1,9822	1,9334	1,8942	1,8620	1,8120	1,7748	1,7461	1,7044	1,6755	1,6147	1,5824	1,5554	1,5345	1,5128
94	2,1889	2,1435	2,1042	2,0697	2,0393	2,0122	1,9766	1,9277	1,8884	1,8561	1,8060	1,7688	1,7400	1,6982	1,6692	1,6081	1,5756	1,5485	1,5274	1,5055
96	2,1837	2,1382	2,0989	2,0644	2,0339	2,0068	1,9711	1,9222	1,8829	1,8506	1,8003	1,7630	1,7341	1,6922	1,6631	1,6017	1,5691	1,5418	1,5205	1,4985
98	2,1786	2,1332	2,0938	2,0593	2,0288	2,0016	1,9660	1,9170	1,8776	1,8452	1,7949	1,7575	1,7285	1,6864	1,6572	1,5956	1,5628	1,5353	1,5139	1,4918
100	2,1738	2,1283	2,0889	2,0544	2,0239	1,9967	1,9610	1,9119	1,8725	1,8400	1,7896	1,7521	1,7231	1,6809	1,6516	1,5897	1,5567	1,5291	1,5076	1,4853
110	2,1525	2,1069	2,0673	2,0327	2,0021	1,9747	1,9389	1,8895	1,8499	1,8172	1,7663	1,7284	1,6990	1,6562	1,6265	1,5634	1,5297	1,5013	1,4791	1,4560
120	2,1347	2,0890	2,0494	2,0147	1,9840	1,9565	1,9205	1,8709	1,8310	1,7981	1,7469	1,7086	1,6789	1,6357	1,6055	1,5413	1,5068	1,4778	1,4550	1,4311
130	2,1198	2,0740	2,0343	1,9995	1,9687	1,9412	1,9050	1,8553	1,8151	1,7820	1,7304	1,6919	1,6619	1,6182	1,5877	1,5225	1,4874	1,4576	1,4342	1,4096
140	2,1071	2,0612	2,0214	1,9865	1,9556	1,9281	1,8918	1,8418	1,8015	1,7683	1,7163	1,6775	1,6473	1,6032	1,5723	1,5063	1,4705	1,4401	1,4161	1,3909
150	2,0961	2,0501	2,0103	1,9753	1,9444	1,9167	1,8803	1,8302	1,7898	1,7563	1,7041	1,6651	1,6347	1,5901	1,5590	1,4921	1,4557	1,4248	1,4003	1,3744
160	2,0864	2,0405	2,0006	1,9655	1,9345	1,9068	1,8703	1,8201	1,7795	1,7459	1,6935	1,6542	1,6236	1,5787	1,5472	1,4796	1,4427	1,4112	1,3862	1,3596
170	2,0780	2,0320	1,9920	1,9569	1,9258	1,8981	1,8615	1,8111	1,7704	1,7367	1,6841	1,6446	1,6138	1,5686	1,5369	1,4685	1,4311	1,3991	1,3736	1,3464
180	2,0705	2,0244	1,9844	1,9493	1,9181	1,8903	1,8537	1,8032	1,7623	1,7286	1,6757	1,6360	1,6050	1,5596	1,5276	1,4586	1,4207	1,3882	1,3622	1,3345
190	2,0638	2,0177	1,9776	1,9425	1,9113	1,8834	1,8467	1,7961	1,7551	1,7212	1,6682	1,6284	1,5972	1,5515	1,5193	1,4497	1,4113	1,3784	1,3519	1,3236
200	2,0578	2,0116	1,9715	1,9363	1,9051	1,8772	1,8404	1,7897	1,7487	1,7147	1,6614	1,6215	1,5902	1,5442	1,5118	1,4416	1,4028	1,3694	1,3426	1,3137
250	2,0350	1,9887	1,9484	1,9131	1,8817	1,8536	1,8166	1,7655	1,7241	1,6897	1,6358	1,5952	1,5633	1,5163	1,4831	1,4105	1,3700	1,3347	1,3059	1,2745
300	2,0199	1,9735	1,9331	1,8976	1,8661	1,8380	1,8008	1,7494	1,7077	1,6731	1,6187	1,5776	1,5453	1,4976	1,4638	1,3894	1,3475	1,3106	1,2802	1,2466
350	2,0091	1,9627	1,9222	1,8866	1,8551	1,8268	1,7895	1,7379	1,6960	1,6612	1,6064	1,5650	1,5325	1,4842	1,4499	1,3741	1,3310	1,2929	1,2611	1,2255
400	2,0011	1,9546	1,9140	1,8784	1,8468	1,8184	1,7811	1,7293	1,6872	1,6523	1,5972	1,5556	1,5228	1,4741	1,4394	1,3624	1,3185	1,2792	1,2463	1,2088
500	1,9899	1,9432	1,9026	1,8669	1,8352	1,8068	1,7692	1,7172	1,6750	1,6398	1,5843	1,5423	1,5091	1,4598	1,4245	1,3459	1,3005	1,2596	1,2247	1,1840
600	1,9824	1,9357	1,8951	1,8593	1,8275	1,7990	1,7614	1,7092	1,6668	1,6315	1,5757	1,5334	1,5000	1,4502	1,4146	1,3347	1,2883	1,2460	1,2095	1,1661
700	1,9771	1,9303	1,8896	1,8538	1,8220	1,7934	1,7558	1,7035	1,6609	1,6255	1,5696	1,5271	1,4935	1,4434	1,4074	1,3266	1,2794	1,2361	1,1983	1,1525
800	1,9731	1,9263	1,8856	1,8497	1,8178	1,7893	1,7515	1,6992	1,6566	1,6211	1,5650	1,5223	1,4886	1,4382	1,4020	1,3205	1,2727	1,2285	1,1897	1,1417
900	1,9700	1,9232	1,8824	1,8465	1,8146	1,7860	1,7483	1,6958	1,6532	1,6176	1,5614	1,5186	1,4848	1,4342	1,3978	1,3157	1,2674	1,2225	1,1827	1,1328
1000	1,9675	1,9207	1,8799	1,8440	1,8121	1,7835	1,7457	1,6932	1,6504	1,6148	1,5585	1,5156	1,4817	1,4310	1,3945	1,3119	1,2631	1,2176	1,1771	1,1254
2000	1,9564	1,9095	1,8686	1,8326	1,8006	1,7718	1,7339	1,6812	1,6382	1,6023	1,5455	1,5022	1,4679	1,4164	1,3792	1,2943	1,2434	1,1949	1,1500	1,0865
5000	1,9497	1,9027	1,8618	1,8257	1,7937	1,7649	1,7268	1,6740	1,6308	1,5948	1,5377	1,4942	1,4596	1,4076	1,3699	1,2836	1,2312	1,1804	1,1320	1,0535
10000	1,9475	1,9005	1,8596	1,8235	1,7914	1,7626	1,7245	1,6716	1,6284	1,5923	1,5351	1,4915	1,4568	1,4046	1,3668	1,2800	1,2270	1,1755	1,1256	1,0374
∞	1,9453	1,8983	1,8573	1,8212	1,7891	1,7603	1,7221	1,6691	1,6259	1,5898	1,5325	1,4888	1,4540	1,4017	1,3637	1,2763	1,2228	1,1704	1,1189	1

All values conform to the international convention (i.e. 0,1 instead of 0.1).

The *F*-Distribution* ν_1, ν_2 Degrees of Freedom $P = 0{,}001$

$P = P$ (right) = integral between F_{ν_1,ν_2} and ∞ (values in the table are the F_{ν_1,ν_2}-values)

ν_2 \ ν_1	1	2	3	4	5	6	7	8	9	10	11	12	13	14	15	16	17	18	19	20
1	405280	500000	540380	562500	576410	585940	592870	598140	602280	605620	608370	610670	612620	614300	615760	617050	618180	619190	620090	620910
2	998,50	999,00	999,17	999,25	999,30	999,33	999,36	999,37	999,39	999,40	999,41	999,42	999,42	999,43	999,43	999,44	999,44	999,44	999,45	999,45
3	167,03	148,50	141,11	137,10	134,58	132,85	131,58	130,62	129,86	129,25	128,74	128,32	127,96	127,64	127,37	127,14	126,93	126,74	126,57	126,42
4	74,140	61,246	56,177	53,436	51,712	50,525	49,658	48,996	48,475	48,053	47,704	47,412	47,163	46,948	46,761	46,597	46,451	46,322	46,205	46,100
5	47,181	37,122	33,202	31,085	29,752	28,834	28,163	27,649	27,244	26,917	26,646	26,418	26,224	26,057	25,911	25,783	25,669	25,568	25,477	25,395
6	35,507	27,000	23,703	21,921	20,803	20,030	19,463	19,030	18,688	18,411	18,182	17,989	17,824	17,682	17,559	17,450	17,353	17,267	17,190	17,120
7	29,245	21,689	18,772	17,198	16,206	15,521	15,019	14,634	14,329	14,083	13,879	13,707	13,561	13,434	13,324	13,226	13,140	13,063	12,994	12,932
8	25,415	18,494	15,829	14,392	13,485	12,858	12,398	12,046	11,767	11,540	11,352	11,194	11,060	10,943	10,841	10,752	10,672	10,601	10,537	10,480
9	22,857	16,387	13,902	12,560	11,714	11,128	10,698	10,368	10,107	9,8943	9,7183	9,5700	9,4433	9,3337	9,2381	9,1538	9,0790	9,0121	8,9520	8,8976
10	21,040	14,905	12,553	11,283	10,481	9,9256	9,5174	9,2042	8,9558	8,7539	8,5864	8,4452	8,3245	8,2200	8,1288	8,0484	7,9770	7,9131	7,8557	7,8037
11	19,687	13,812	11,561	10,346	9,5784	9,0466	8,6553	8,3548	8,1163	7,9224	7,7614	7,6256	7,5094	7,4089	7,3210	7,2435	7,1747	7,1131	7,0577	7,0076
12	18,643	12,974	10,804	9,6327	8,8921	8,3788	8,0009	7,7104	7,4797	7,2920	7,1362	7,0046	6,8920	6,7945	6,7092	6,6340	6,5672	6,5074	6,4535	6,4048
13	17,815	12,313	10,209	9,0727	8,3541	7,8557	7,4886	7,2061	6,9818	6,7992	6,6474	6,5192	6,4094	6,3144	6,2312	6,1578	6,0926	6,0342	5,9816	5,9340
14	17,143	11,779	9,7293	8,6223	7,9218	7,4358	7,0775	6,8017	6,5826	6,4041	6,2556	6,1302	6,0228	5,9297	5,8483	5,7764	5,7124	5,6551	5,6035	5,5568
15	16,587	11,339	9,3353	8,2527	7,5674	7,0917	6,7408	6,4707	6,2559	6,0808	5,9352	5,8121	5,7066	5,6151	5,5351	5,4644	5,4015	5,3452	5,2944	5,2484
16	16,120	10,971	9,0059	7,9442	7,2719	6,8049	6,4604	6,1950	5,9839	5,8117	5,6684	5,5473	5,4434	5,3533	5,2745	5,2048	5,1428	5,0872	5,0372	4,9918
17	15,722	10,658	8,7269	7,6831	7,0219	6,5625	6,2234	5,9620	5,7541	5,5844	5,4431	5,3237	5,2212	5,1323	5,0544	4,9856	4,9244	4,8695	4,8200	4,7751
18	15,379	10,390	8,4875	7,4593	6,8078	6,3550	6,0206	5,7628	5,5575	5,3900	5,2505	5,1324	5,0312	4,9433	4,8663	4,7982	4,7376	4,6833	4,6343	4,5899
19	15,081	10,157	8,2799	7,2655	6,6225	6,1754	5,8452	5,5904	5,3876	5,2219	5,0840	4,9672	4,8669	4,7799	4,7037	4,6362	4,5762	4,5223	4,4738	4,4297
20	14,819	9,9526	8,0984	7,0960	6,4606	6,0186	5,6920	5,4400	5,2392	5,0752	4,9386	4,8229	4,7236	4,6374	4,5618	4,4949	4,4353	4,3819	4,3337	4,2900
21	14,587	9,7723	7,9383	6,9467	6,3179	5,8805	5,5571	5,3076	5,1087	4,9462	4,8107	4,6960	4,5975	4,5119	4,4369	4,3705	4,3114	4,2583	4,2104	4,1670
22	14,380	9,6120	7,7960	6,8142	6,1914	5,7580	5,4376	5,1901	4,9929	4,8317	4,6973	4,5835	4,4857	4,4007	4,3262	4,2602	4,2015	4,1487	4,1011	4,0579
23	14,195	9,4685	7,6688	6,6957	6,0783	5,6486	5,3308	5,0853	4,8896	4,7296	4,5962	4,4831	4,3859	4,3015	4,2274	4,1618	4,1034	4,0509	4,0036	3,9606
24	14,028	9,3394	7,5545	6,5892	5,9768	5,5504	5,2349	4,9912	4,7968	4,6379	4,5053	4,3929	4,2963	4,2124	4,1387	4,0735	4,0154	3,9631	3,9160	3,8732
25	13,877	9,2225	7,4511	6,4931	5,8851	5,4617	5,1484	4,9063	4,7131	4,5551	4,4233	4,3116	4,2155	4,1320	4,0587	3,9938	3,9359	3,8839	3,8370	3,7944
26	13,739	9,1163	7,3572	6,4057	5,8018	5,3812	5,0698	4,8292	4,6372	4,4801	4,3490	4,2378	4,1422	4,0591	3,9861	3,9215	3,8638	3,8120	3,7653	3,7228
27	13,613	9,0194	7,2715	6,3261	5,7259	5,3078	4,9983	4,7590	4,5680	4,4117	4,2812	4,1706	4,0754	3,9926	3,9200	3,8556	3,7981	3,7466	3,7000	3,6576
28	13,498	8,9305	7,1931	6,2532	5,6565	5,2407	4,9328	4,6947	4,5047	4,3491	4,2193	4,1091	4,0143	3,9319	3,8595	3,7953	3,7381	3,6867	3,6402	3,5980
29	13,391	8,8488	7,1209	6,1863	5,5927	5,1791	4,8727	4,6358	4,4466	4,2917	4,1624	4,0526	3,9582	3,8761	3,8039	3,7400	3,6829	3,6316	3,5853	3,5432
30	13,293	8,7734	7,0545	6,1245	5,5339	5,1223	4,8173	4,5814	4,3930	4,2388	4,1100	4,0006	3,9065	3,8247	3,7527	3,6890	3,6321	3,5810	3,5348	3,4928
31	13,202	8,7036	6,9929	6,0674	5,4796	5,0697	4,7661	4,5312	4,3436	4,1899	4,0615	3,9526	3,8588	3,7772	3,7055	3,6419	3,5851	3,5341	3,4880	3,4461
32	13,117	8,6388	6,9359	6,0145	5,4291	5,0211	4,7186	4,4846	4,2977	4,1446	4,0166	3,9080	3,8145	3,7331	3,6616	3,5982	3,5416	3,4907	3,4447	3,4029
33	13,039	8,5785	6,8828	5,9652	5,3823	4,9758	4,6745	4,4414	4,2551	4,1024	3,9749	3,8666	3,7734	3,6922	3,6209	3,5576	3,5011	3,4504	3,4044	3,3627
34	12,965	8,5223	6,8333	5,9193	5,3386	4,9336	4,6334	4,4010	4,2153	4,0632	3,9360	3,8280	3,7350	3,6541	3,5829	3,5198	3,4634	3,4127	3,3669	3,3253
35	12,896	8,4697	6,7870	5,8764	5,2978	4,8942	4,5950	4,3634	4,1782	4,0265	3,8997	3,7920	3,6992	3,6185	3,5474	3,4845	3,4282	3,3776	3,3319	3,2903
36	12,832	8,4204	6,7436	5,8362	5,2596	4,8573	4,5590	4,3281	4,1435	3,9922	3,8657	3,7583	3,6657	3,5851	3,5143	3,4514	3,3952	3,3447	3,2990	3,2575
37	12,771	8,3741	6,7029	5,7985	5,2237	4,8227	4,5253	4,2950	4,1109	3,9600	3,8338	3,7266	3,6343	3,5539	3,4831	3,4204	3,3643	3,3139	3,2682	3,2268
38	12,714	8,3305	6,6646	5,7631	5,1900	4,7901	4,4936	4,2639	4,0803	3,9298	3,8039	3,6969	3,6047	3,5245	3,4538	3,3912	3,3352	3,2849	3,2393	3,1979
39	12,660	8,2895	6,6286	5,7297	5,1582	4,7595	4,4637	4,2347	4,0515	3,9013	3,7756	3,6689	3,5769	3,4968	3,4263	3,3637	3,3078	3,2575	3,2120	3,1707
40	12,609	8,2508	6,5945	5,6981	5,1283	4,7306	4,4355	4,2070	4,0243	3,8744	3,7490	3,6425	3,5507	3,4707	3,4003	3,3378	3,2820	3,2318	3,1863	3,1450
41	12,561	8,2141	6,5624	5,6683	5,1000	4,7032	4,4089	4,1809	3,9986	3,8490	3,7239	3,6175	3,5259	3,4460	3,3757	3,3133	3,2576	3,2074	3,1620	3,1207
42	12,516	8,1794	6,5319	5,6402	5,0732	4,6774	4,3837	4,1563	3,9742	3,8250	3,7001	3,5939	3,5024	3,4227	3,3525	3,2902	3,2345	3,1844	3,1390	3,0978
43	12,472	8,1465	6,5030	5,6134	5,0478	4,6529	4,3599	4,1329	3,9512	3,8022	3,6775	3,5715	3,4802	3,4005	3,3304	3,2682	3,2126	3,1625	3,1172	3,0760
44	12,431	8,1152	6,4756	5,5880	5,0236	4,6296	4,3372	4,1106	3,9293	3,7806	3,6561	3,5503	3,4591	3,3795	3,3095	3,2474	3,1918	3,1418	3,0966	3,0554
45	12,392	8,0855	6,4495	5,5639	5,0007	4,6075	4,3157	4,0895	3,9086	3,7601	3,6358	3,5301	3,4390	3,3596	3,2897	3,2276	3,1721	3,1221	3,0769	3,0357
46	12,355	8,0572	6,4247	5,5410	4,9789	4,5865	4,2952	4,0695	3,8888	3,7405	3,6165	3,5109	3,4199	3,3406	3,2708	3,2088	3,1533	3,1034	3,0582	3,0171
47	12,319	8,0303	6,4011	5,5191	4,9582	4,5665	4,2757	4,0503	3,8700	3,7219	3,5980	3,4926	3,4018	3,3225	3,2528	3,1908	3,1354	3,0855	3,0404	2,9993
48	12,285	8,0045	6,3785	5,4982	4,9383	4,5474	4,2571	4,0321	3,8520	3,7042	3,5805	3,4752	3,3844	3,3053	3,2356	3,1737	3,1183	3,0685	3,0234	2,9823
49	12,253	7,9799	6,3570	5,4783	4,9194	4,5291	4,2393	4,0147	3,8348	3,6872	3,5637	3,4585	3,3679	3,2888	3,2192	3,1574	3,1021	3,0522	3,0071	2,9661
50	12,222	7,9564	6,3364	5,4593	4,9013	4,5117	4,2224	3,9980	3,8185	3,6711	3,5476	3,4426	3,3521	3,2731	3,2035	3,1418	3,0865	3,0367	2,9916	2,9506
52	12,164	7,9124	6,2978	5,4236	4,8675	4,4790	4,1906	3,9669	3,7878	3,6407	3,5176	3,4128	3,3225	3,2436	3,1742	3,1125	3,0573	3,0076	2,9626	2,9216
54	12,111	7,8718	6,2623	5,3908	4,8364	4,4490	4,1613	3,9382	3,7596	3,6129	3,4900	3,3855	3,2953	3,2166	3,1472	3,0856	3,0305	2,9809	2,9359	2,8949
56	12,061	7,8345	6,2296	5,3606	4,8077	4,4214	4,1344	3,9119	3,7336	3,5872	3,4646	3,3602	3,2702	3,1916	3,1224	3,0609	3,0058	2,9562	2,9113	2,8704
58	12,015	7,7999	6,1993	5,3326	4,7811	4,3958	4,1095	3,8875	3,7096	3,5635	3,4411	3,3369	3,2470	3,1685	3,0994	3,0380	2,9830	2,9334	2,8885	2,8476
60	11,973	7,7678	6,1712	5,3067	4,7565	4,3721	4,0864	3,8648	3,6873	3,5415	3,4193	3,3153	3,2255	3,1472	3,0781	3,0167	2,9618	2,9123	2,8674	2,8266
62	11,933	7,7379	6,1451	5,2826	4,7336	4,3500	4,0649	3,8438	3,6666	3,5210	3,3990	3,2952	3,2055	3,1273	3,0583	2,9970	2,9421	2,8926	2,8478	2,8069
64	11,897	7,7100	6,1207	5,2601	4,7123	4,3294	4,0449	3,8242	3,6473	3,5019	3,3801	3,2764	3,1869	3,1087	3,0398	2,9786	2,9237	2,8743	2,8295	2,7887
66	11,862	7,6839	6,0979	5,2390	4,6923	4,3102	4,0262	3,8058	3,6292	3,4841	3,3625	3,2589	3,1695	3,0914	3,0225	2,9613	2,9065	2,8571	2,8124	2,7716
68	11,830	7,6595	6,0766	5,2193	4,6736	4,2922	4,0087	3,7887	3,6123	3,4674	3,3459	3,2425	3,1531	3,0751	3,0064	2,9452	2,8905	2,8411	2,7963	2,7556
70	11,799	7,6366	6,0566	5,2008	4,6561	4,2753	3,9922	3,7725	3,5964	3,4517	3,3304	3,2271	3,1378	3,0599	2,9912	2,9301	2,8754	2,8260	2,7813	2,7405
72	11,771	7,6150	6,0377	5,1835	4,6396	4,2594	3,9768	3,7574	3,5815	3,4370	3,3158	3,2126	3,1234	3,0456	2,9769	2,9159	2,8612	2,8119	2,7671	2,7264
74	11,744	7,5947	6,0199	5,1671	4,6241	4,2444	3,9622	3,7431	3,5675	3,4231	3,3021	3,1989	3,1099	3,0321	2,9635	2,9025	2,8478	2,7985	2,7538	2,7131
76	11,718	7,5754	6,0032	5,1516	4,6094	4,2303	3,9485	3,7297	3,5542	3,4100	3,2891	3,1861	3,0971	3,0194	2,9508	2,8898	2,8352	2,7859	2,7412	2,7005
78	11,694	7,5573	5,9873	5,1370	4,5955	4,2169	3,9355	3,7169	3,5417	3,3976	3,2768	3,1739	3,0850	3,0073	2,9388	2,8779	2,8233	2,7740	2,7293	2,6886
80	11,671	7,5401	5,9723	5,1231	4,5824	4,2043	3,9232	3,7049	3,5298	3,3859	3,2652	3,1624	3,0735	2,9959	2,9274	2,8665	2,8120	2,7627	2,7181	2,6774
82	11,650	7,5238	5,9581	5,1100	4,5700	4,1923	3,9115	3,6934	3,5186	3,3748	3,2542	3,1515	3,0627	2,9851	2,9167	2,8558	2,8013	2,7520	2,7074	2,6667
84	11,629	7,5083	5,9445	5,0975	4,5581	4,1809	3,9004	3,6826	3,5079	3,3643	3,2438	3,1411	3,0524	2,9749	2,9065	2,8456	2,7911	2,7419	2,6973	2,6566
86	11,610	7,4935	5,9317	5,0857	4,5469	4,1701	3,8899	3,6723	3,4977	3,3542	3,2338	3,1312	3,0426	2,9651	2,8967	2,8359	2,7814	2,7322	2,6876	2,6470
88	11,591	7,4795	5,9195	5,0744	4,5362	4,1598	3,8799	3,6625	3,4881	3,3447	3,2244	3,1218	3,0332	2,9558	2,8875	2,8267	2,7722	2,7231	2,6785	2,6378
90	11,573	7,4661	5,9078	5,0636	4,5260	4,1500	3,8703	3,6531	3,4789	3,3356	3,2154	3,1129	3,0244	2,9470	2,8787	2,8179	2,7634	2,7143	2,6697	2,6291
92	11,556	7,4534	5,8967	5,0534	4,5163	4,1406	3,8612	3,6442	3,4701	3,3269	3,2068	3,1044	3,0159	2,9385	2,8703	2,8095	2,7551	2,7060	2,6614	2,6207
94	11,540	7,4412	5,8860	5,0436	4,5070	4,1317	3,8525	3,6357	3,4617	3,3186	3,1986	3,0962	3,0078	2,9305	2,8623	2,8015	2,7471	2,6980	2,6534	2,6128
96	11,524	7,4295	5,8759	5,0342	4,4981	4,1231	3,8442	3,6275	3,4537	3,3107	3,1907	3,0885	3,0000	2,9228	2,8546	2,7939	2,7395	2,6904	2,6458	2,6051
98	11,510	7,4184	5,8661	5,0253	4,4896	4,1150	3,8362	3,6197	3,4460	3,3031	3,1832	3,0810	2,9926	2,9154	2,8472	2,7865	2,7321	2,6831	2,6385	2,5979
100	11,495	7,4077	5,8568	5,0167	4,4815	4,1071	3,8286	3,6123	3,4387	3,2959	3,1760	3,0739	2,9855	2,9083	2,8402	2,7795	2,7251	2,6761	2,6315	2,5909
110	11,432	7,3603	5,8155	4,9786	4,4455	4,0724	3,7949	3,5792	3,4061	3,2637	3,1442	3,0423	2,9541	2,8771	2,8090	2,7485	2,6941	2,6451	2,6006	2,5600
120	11,380	7,3211	5,7814	4,9472	4,4157	4,0437	3,7670	3,5519	3,3792	3,2372	3,1179	3,0162	2,9282	2,8512	2,7833	2,7228	2,6685	2,6195	2,5750	2,5344
130	11,336	7,2882	5,7527	4,9207	4,3907	4,0197	3,7436	3,5289	3,3567	3,2149	3,0958	2,9942	2,9064	2,8295	2,7617	2,7012	2,6470	2,5980	2,5535	2,5130
140	11,299	7,2601	5,7282	4,8982	4,3693	3,9992	3,7236	3,5094	3,3374	3,1959	3,0770	2,9756	2,8878	2,8110	2,7432	2,6828	2,6286	2,5797	2,5352	2,4947
150	11,267	7,2359	5,7072	4,8788	4,3510	3,9815	3,7064	3,4926	3,3209	3,1795	3,0608	2,9595	2,8718	2,7951	2,7274	2,6670	2,6128	2,5639	2,5195	2,4789
160	11,238	7,2148	5,6888	4,8619	4,3350	3,9661	3,6914	3,4779	3,3064	3,1652	3,0467	2,9454	2,8579	2,7812	2,7135	2,6532	2,5991	2,5502	2,5057	2,4652
170	11,214	7,1962	5,6726	4,8471	4,3209	3,9525	3,6783	3,4650	3,2937	3,1527	3,0343	2,9331	2,8456	2,7690	2,7014	2,6411	2,5870	2,5381	2,4937	2,4531
180	11,192	7,1798	5,6583	4,8339	4,3084	3,9406	3,6666	3,4536	3,2825	3,1416	3,0233	2,9222	2,8348	2,7582	2,6906	2,6304	2,5763	2,5274	2,4830	2,4424
190	11,172	7,1651	5,6456	4,8222	4,2973	3,9299	3,6562	3,4434	3,2725	3,1317	3,0135	2,9125	2,8251	2,7486	2,6810	2,6208	2,5667	2,5178	2,4734	2,4328
200	11,155	7,1519	5,6341	4,8116	4,2874	3,9203	3,6469	3,4343	3,2635	3,1228	3,0047	2,9038	2,8164	2,7400	2,6724	2,6122	2,5581	2,5093	2,4648	2,4243
250	11,088	7,1022	5,5909	4,7719	4,2497	3,8841	3,6117	3,3998	3,2296	3,0893	2,9715	2,8708	2,7837	2,7074	2,6399	2,5797	2,5257	2,4769	2,4325	2,3920
300	11,044	7,0693	5,5623	4,7456	4,2249	3,8601	3,5884	3,3771	3,2072	3,0672	2,9495	2,8490	2,7620	2,6858	2,6184	2,5583	2,5043	2,4555	2,4111	2,3706
350	11,013	7,0459	5,5420	4,7269	4,2072	3,8431	3,5719	3,3609	3,1913	3,0515	2,9340	2,8336	2,7466	2,6705	2,6031	2,5431	2,4891	2,4403	2,3959	2,3554
400	10,989	7,0284	5,5268	4,7129	4,1940	3,8305	3,5596	3,3488	3,1794	3,0397	2,9224	2,8220	2,7352	2,6591	2,5917	2,5317	2,4778	2,4290	2,3846	2,3440
500	10,957	7,0041	5,5057	4,6935	4,1756	3,8128	3,5424	3,3320	3,1628	3,0234	2,9061	2,8060	2,7192	2,6431	2,5759	2,5159	2,4619	2,4132	2,3688	2,3282
600	10,935	6,9879	5,4916	4,6806	4,1634	3,8010	3,5310	3,3208	3,1518	3,0125	2,8954	2,7953	2,7085	2,6326	2,5653	2,5053	2,4514	2,4027	2,3583	2,3177
700	10,920	6,9764	5,4816	4,6714	4,1547	3,7927	3,5229	3,3129	3,1440	3,0048	2,8877	2,7877	2,7010	2,6250	2,5578	2,4978	2,4439	2,3952	2,3508	2,3103
800	10,908	6,9677	5,4741	4,6645	4,1482	3,7864	3,5168	3,3069	3,1381	2,9990	2,8820	2,7820	2,6953	2,6194	2,5522	2,4922	2,4383	2,3896	2,3452	2,3047
900	10,899	6,9610	5,4683	4,6592	4,1432	3,7816	3,5121	3,3023	3,1336	2,9945	2,8776	2,7776	2,6909	2,6150	2,5478	2,4879	2,4340	2,3852	2,3409	2,3003
1000	10,892	6,9557	5,4637	4,6549	4,1391	3,7777	3,5083	3,2986	3,1300	2,9909	2,8740	2,7740	2,6874	2,6115	2,5443	2,4844	2,4305	2,3818	2,3374	2,2968
2000	10,860	6,9317	5,4428	4,6358	4,1210	3,7603	3,4914	3,2820	3,1137	2,9748	2,8581	2,7582	2,6717	2,5958	2,5287	2,4688	2,4149	2,3662	2,3218	2,2812
5000	10,840	6,9173	5,4304	4,6243	4,1102	3,7499	3,4813	3,2721	3,1039	2,9652	2,8485	2,7487	2,6623	2,5865	2,5194	2,4595	2,4056	2,3569	2,3125	2,2719
10000	10,834	6,9125	5,4262	4,6205	4,1066	3,7464	3,4779	3,2688	3,1007	2,9620	2,8454	2,7456	2,6591	2,5834	2,5163	2,4564	2,4025	2,3538	2,3094	2,2688
∞	10,828	6,9078	5,4221	4,6167	4,1030	3,7430	3,4746	3,2656	3,0975	2,9588	2,8422	2,7426	2,6560	2,5802	2,5132	2,4533	2,3994	2,3507	2,3063	2,2657

All values conform to the international convention (i.e. 0,1 instead of 0.1).

The *F*-Distribution* ν_1, ν_2 Degrees of Freedom $P = 0{,}001$

$P = P(\text{right})$ = integral between F_{ν_1,ν_2} and ∞ (values in the table are the F_{ν_1,ν_2}-values)

ν_2 \ ν_1	22	24	26	28	30	32	35	40	45	50	60	70	80	100	120	200	300	500	1000	∞
1	622320	623500	624500	625350	626100	626750	627590	628710	629590	630290	631340	632090	632650	633440	633970	635030	635560	635980	636300	636620
2	999,45	999,46	999,46	999,46	999,47	999,47	999,47	999,47	999,48	999,48	999,48	999,49	999,49	999,49	999,49	999,49	999,50	999,50	999,50	999,50
3	126,15	125,93	125,75	125,59	125,45	125,33	125,17	124,96	124,79	124,66	124,47	124,32	124,22	124,07	123,97	123,77	123,67	123,59	123,53	123,47
4	45,918	45,766	45,636	45,525	45,429	45,344	45,235	45,089	44,975	44,883	44,746	44,647	44,573	44,469	44,400	44,261	44,191	44,135	44,093	44,051
5	25,252	25,133	25,032	24,945	24,869	24,802	24,717	24,602	24,513	24,441	24,333	24,255	24,197	24,115	24,060	23,951	23,896	23,852	23,819	23,785
6	16,999	16,897	16,811	16,737	16,672	16,616	16,542	16,445	16,368	16,307	16,214	16,148	16,098	16,028	15,981	15,887	15,840	15,802	15,774	15,745
7	12,823	12,732	12,655	12,588	12,530	12,480	12,414	12,326	12,257	12,202	12,119	12,059	12,014	11,951	11,909	11,824	11,782	11,747	11,722	11,696
8	10,379	10,295	10,224	10,162	10,109	10,062	10,001	9,9194	9,8556	9,8044	9,7272	9,6718	9,6300	9,5714	9,5321	9,4531	9,4135	9,3817	9,3577	9,3337
9	8,8031	8,7239	8,6564	8,5982	8,5476	8,5031	8,4456	8,3685	8,3082	8,2597	8,1865	8,1340	8,0944	8,0387	8,0014	7,9264	7,8887	7,8584	7,8357	7,8128
10	7,7134	7,6376	7,5730	7,5173	7,4688	7,4262	7,3711	7,2971	7,2393	7,1927	7,1224	7,0719	7,0338	6,9802	6,9443	6,8720	6,8357	6,8065	6,7845	6,7625
11	6,9204	6,8471	6,7847	6,7309	6,6839	6,6427	6,5894	6,5178	6,4616	6,4165	6,3483	6,2993	6,2623	6,2102	6,1753	6,1050	6,0696	6,0412	6,0198	5,9983
12	6,3200	6,2488	6,1880	6,1355	6,0898	6,0496	5,9976	5,9278	5,8730	5,8290	5,7623	5,7144	5,6782	5,6272	5,5931	5,5242	5,4895	5,4616	5,4406	5,4195
13	5,8511	5,7814	5,7219	5,6706	5,6258	5,5864	5,5355	5,4670	5,4133	5,3700	5,3046	5,2575	5,2219	5,1718	5,1381	4,0703	5,0361	5,0086	4,9879	4,9671
14	5,4755	5,4070	5,3486	5,2982	5,2542	5,2154	5,1653	5,0979	5,0450	5,0023	4,9378	4,8913	4,8562	4,8067	4,7735	4,7064	4,6726	4,6453	4,6248	4,6042
15	5,1683	5,1009	5,0433	4,9936	4,9502	4,9120	4,8625	4,7959	4,7437	4,7015	4,6377	4,5917	4,5569	4,5079	4,4750	4,4084	4,3749	4,3478	4,3275	4,3070
16	4,9128	4,8462	4,7893	4,7401	4,6972	4,6594	4,6105	4,5446	4,4928	4,4511	4,3878	4,3422	4,3077	4,2590	4,2263	4,1602	4,1268	4,0999	4,0796	4,0592
17	4,6969	4,6311	4,5748	4,5261	4,4836	4,4461	4,3976	4,3323	4,2809	4,2395	4,1767	4,1313	4,0970	4,0486	4,0160	3,9502	3,9169	3,8901	3,8699	3,8496
18	4,5124	4,4471	4,3913	4,3430	4,3009	4,2637	4,2156	4,1507	4,0996	4,0584	3,9960	3,9508	3,9167	3,8685	3,8360	3,7703	3,7371	3,7103	3,6901	3,6698
19	4,3529	4,2881	4,2327	4,1848	4,1429	4,1060	4,0581	3,9936	3,9428	3,9018	3,8396	3,7946	3,7606	3,7125	3,6801	3,6146	3,5814	3,5546	3,5344	3,5141
20	4,2137	4,1493	4,0943	4,0466	4,0050	3,9683	3,9207	3,8564	3,8059	3,7650	3,7030	3,6582	3,6242	3,5762	3,5438	3,4783	3,4451	3,4183	3,3981	3,3778
21	4,0912	4,0272	3,9724	3,9250	3,8836	3,8470	3,7996	3,7357	3,6853	3,6445	3,5827	3,5379	3,5040	3,4560	3,4237	3,3582	3,3249	3,2981	3,2779	3,2575
22	3,9825	3,9189	3,8644	3,8172	3,7759	3,7395	3,6923	3,6285	3,5783	3,5376	3,4759	3,4312	3,3973	3,3493	3,3170	3,2514	3,2181	3,1913	3,1710	3,1505
23	3,8856	3,8222	3,7679	3,7209	3,6798	3,6435	3,5964	3,5328	3,4827	3,4421	3,3804	3,3358	3,3019	3,2539	3,2216	3,1559	3,1226	3,0956	3,0753	3,0548
24	3,7985	3,7354	3,6813	3,6345	3,5935	3,5573	3,5103	3,4468	3,3968	3,3562	3,2946	3,2500	3,2161	3,1681	3,1357	3,0700	3,0365	3,0095	2,9891	2,9685
25	3,7199	3,6570	3,6031	3,5564	3,5155	3,4794	3,4325	3,3692	3,3192	3,2787	3,2171	3,1724	3,1386	3,0905	3,0581	2,9922	2,9587	2,9315	2,9111	2,8904
26	3,6486	3,5859	3,5321	3,4856	3,4448	3,4087	3,3619	3,2987	3,2487	3,2083	3,1467	3,1020	3,0681	3,0200	2,9875	2,9215	2,8878	2,8606	2,8401	2,8193
27	3,5837	3,5211	3,4675	3,4210	3,3803	3,3443	3,2976	3,2344	3,1845	3,1440	3,0825	3,0378	3,0038	2,9557	2,9231	2,8569	2,8231	2,7958	2,7752	2,7543
28	3,5242	3,4618	3,4083	3,3619	3,3213	3,2853	3,2387	3,1755	3,1256	3,0852	3,0236	2,9789	2,9449	2,8967	2,8640	2,7976	2,7638	2,7364	2,7156	2,6947
29	3,4696	3,4074	3,3540	3,3076	3,2671	3,2312	3,1846	3,1215	3,0716	3,0311	2,9695	2,9247	2,8907	2,8424	2,8097	2,7431	2,7091	2,6816	2,6607	2,6397
30	3,4194	3,3572	3,3039	3,2576	3,2171	3,1813	3,1347	3,0716	3,0217	2,9813	2,9196	2,8748	2,8407	2,7923	2,7595	2,6927	2,6586	2,6310	2,6100	2,5889
31	3,3729	3,3108	3,2576	3,2114	3,1709	3,1351	3,0885	3,0255	2,9756	2,9352	2,8734	2,8286	2,7944	2,7459	2,7131	2,6460	2,6118	2,5841	2,5630	2,5418
32	3,3298	3,2678	3,2147	3,1685	3,1280	3,0923	3,0457	2,9827	2,9328	2,8923	2,8306	2,7856	2,7514	2,7028	2,6699	2,6027	2,5683	2,5404	2,5193	2,4979
33	3,2897	3,2278	3,1747	3,1286	3,0882	3,0525	3,0059	2,9429	2,8930	2,8525	2,7907	2,7457	2,7114	2,6627	2,6297	2,5622	2,5277	2,4997	2,4785	2,4570
34	3,2523	3,1906	3,1375	3,0915	3,0511	3,0153	2,9688	2,9058	2,8559	2,8154	2,7535	2,7084	2,6741	2,6252	2,5921	2,5245	2,4898	2,4617	2,4404	2,4188
35	3,2174	3,1557	3,1028	3,0567	3,0163	2,9806	2,9341	2,8711	2,8212	2,7806	2,7187	2,6735	2,6391	2,5902	2,5570	2,4891	2,4543	2,4261	2,4046	2,3829
36	3,1848	3,1231	3,0702	3,0242	2,9838	2,9481	2,9017	2,8386	2,7886	2,7481	2,6860	2,6408	2,6064	2,5573	2,5240	2,4559	2,4210	2,3926	2,3710	2,3492
37	3,1541	3,0925	3,0396	2,9937	2,9533	2,9176	2,8712	2,8081	2,7581	2,7175	2,6554	2,6101	2,5756	2,5264	2,4930	2,4247	2,3896	2,3611	2,3395	2,3175
38	3,1253	3,0638	3,0109	2,9650	2,9246	2,8890	2,8425	2,7794	2,7294	2,6887	2,6265	2,5812	2,5466	2,4973	2,4638	2,3952	2,3601	2,3314	2,3097	2,2876
39	3,0982	3,0367	2,9839	2,9379	2,8976	2,8619	2,8154	2,7523	2,7023	2,6616	2,5993	2,5539	2,5193	2,4699	2,4363	2,3675	2,3321	2,3034	2,2815	2,2593
40	3,0726	3,0111	2,9583	2,9124	2,8721	2,8364	2,7899	2,7268	2,6767	2,6360	2,5737	2,5282	2,4934	2,4439	2,4103	2,3412	2,3057	2,2768	2,2549	2,2326
41	3,0484	2,9870	2,9342	2,8883	2,8480	2,8123	2,7658	2,7027	2,6526	2,6118	2,5494	2,5038	2,4690	2,4194	2,3856	2,3163	2,2807	2,2517	2,2296	2,2072
42	3,0255	2,9641	2,9114	2,8655	2,8252	2,7895	2,7430	2,6798	2,6297	2,5889	2,5264	2,4807	2,4458	2,3961	2,3622	2,2927	2,2570	2,2278	2,2056	2,1831
43	3,0038	2,9424	2,8897	2,8438	2,8035	2,7679	2,7213	2,6581	2,6080	2,5671	2,5045	2,4588	2,4239	2,3740	2,3400	2,2703	2,2344	2,2051	2,1828	2,1602
44	2,9832	2,9219	2,8691	2,8233	2,7830	2,7473	2,7008	2,6376	2,5873	2,5464	2,4838	2,4380	2,4030	2,3530	2,3189	2,2490	2,2129	2,1835	2,1611	2,1384
45	2,9636	2,9023	2,8496	2,8038	2,7635	2,7278	2,6812	2,6180	2,5677	2,5268	2,4640	2,4182	2,3831	2,3330	2,2989	2,2287	2,1925	2,1629	2,1404	2,1176
46	2,9449	2,8837	2,8310	2,7852	2,7449	2,7092	2,6626	2,5993	2,5490	2,5081	2,4452	2,3993	2,3641	2,3139	2,2797	2,2093	2,1730	2,1433	2,1207	2,0977
47	2,9272	2,8660	2,8133	2,7675	2,7272	2,6915	2,6449	2,5816	2,5312	2,4902	2,4273	2,3813	2,3461	2,2957	2,2614	2,1908	2,1543	2,1245	2,1018	2,0787
48	2,9102	2,8491	2,7964	2,7506	2,7103	2,6746	2,6280	2,5646	2,5142	2,4732	2,4102	2,3641	2,3288	2,2784	2,2440	2,1731	2,1365	2,1066	2,0837	2,0605
49	2,8941	2,8329	2,7803	2,7344	2,6941	2,6584	2,6118	2,5484	2,4980	2,4569	2,3938	2,3476	2,3123	2,2617	2,2273	2,1562	2,1194	2,0894	2,0664	2,0431
50	2,8786	2,8175	2,7648	2,7190	2,6787	2,6430	2,5964	2,5329	2,4825	2,4413	2,3782	2,3319	2,2965	2,2458	2,2113	2,1399	2,1031	2,0729	2,0499	2,0264
52	2,8497	2,7885	2,7359	2,6901	2,6498	2,6140	2,5674	2,5039	2,4534	2,4121	2,3488	2,3024	2,2669	2,2160	2,1812	2,1095	2,0723	2,0419	2,0187	1,9950
54	2,8231	2,7620	2,7094	2,6635	2,6232	2,5874	2,5408	2,4772	2,4266	2,3853	2,3218	2,2753	2,2396	2,1885	2,1536	2,0814	2,0440	2,0133	1,9898	1,9659
56	2,7985	2,7375	2,6848	2,6390	2,5987	2,5629	2,5162	2,4526	2,4019	2,3605	2,2969	2,2502	2,2144	2,1630	2,1280	2,0553	2,0177	1,9868	1,9631	1,9390
58	2,7758	2,7148	2,6622	2,6163	2,5760	2,5402	2,4935	2,4297	2,3790	2,3375	2,2737	2,2269	2,1910	2,1395	2,1042	2,0312	1,9932	1,9621	1,9382	1,9139
60	2,7548	2,6938	2,6412	2,5953	2,5549	2,5191	2,4724	2,4086	2,3577	2,3162	2,2523	2,2053	2,1693	2,1175	2,0821	2,0087	1,9705	1,9391	1,9150	1,8905
62	2,7352	2,6742	2,6216	2,5757	2,5354	2,4995	2,4527	2,3889	2,3379	2,2963	2,2323	2,1852	2,1490	2,0971	2,0615	1,9876	1,9492	1,9176	1,8933	1,8685
64	2,7170	2,6559	2,6033	2,5575	2,5171	2,4812	2,4344	2,3705	2,3195	2,2778	2,2136	2,1663	2,1301	2,0779	2,0422	1,9680	1,9293	1,8974	1,8730	1,8480
66	2,6999	2,6389	2,5863	2,5404	2,5000	2,4641	2,4172	2,3532	2,3022	2,2604	2,1961	2,1487	2,1123	2,0600	2,0241	1,9495	1,9106	1,8785	1,8538	1,8286
68	2,6839	2,6229	2,5703	2,5244	2,4840	2,4481	2,4012	2,3371	2,2860	2,2441	2,1797	2,1322	2,0957	2,0432	2,0071	1,9322	1,8930	1,8607	1,8358	1,8104
70	2,6689	2,6079	2,5553	2,5094	2,4689	2,4330	2,3861	2,3220	2,2708	2,2289	2,1643	2,1167	2,0801	2,0274	1,9912	1,9158	1,8764	1,8439	1,8188	1,7932
72	2,6548	2,5938	2,5412	2,4953	2,4548	2,4189	2,3719	2,3077	2,2564	2,2145	2,1497	2,1020	2,0653	2,0124	1,9761	1,9004	1,8607	1,8280	1,8028	1,7769
74	2,6415	2,5805	2,5279	2,4819	2,4415	2,4055	2,3585	2,2943	2,2429	2,2009	2,1360	2,0882	2,0514	1,9983	1,9619	1,8858	1,8459	1,8130	1,7876	1,7615
76	2,6289	2,5679	2,5153	2,4694	2,4289	2,3929	2,3459	2,2816	2,2302	2,1881	2,1231	2,0751	2,0382	1,9850	1,9484	1,8720	1,8319	1,7987	1,7731	1,7469
78	2,6170	2,5561	2,5034	2,4575	2,4170	2,3810	2,3339	2,2695	2,2181	2,1759	2,1108	2,0628	2,0258	1,9724	1,9356	1,8589	1,8186	1,7852	1,7594	1,7329
80	2,6058	2,5448	2,4922	2,4462	2,4057	2,3697	2,3226	2,2582	2,2066	2,1644	2,0992	2,0510	2,0139	1,9604	1,9235	1,8464	1,8059	1,7723	1,7464	1,7197
82	2,5952	2,5342	2,4815	2,4355	2,3950	2,3590	2,3118	2,2474	2,1958	2,1535	2,0882	2,0399	2,0027	1,9490	1,9120	1,8346	1,7938	1,7601	1,7339	1,7071
84	2,5850	2,5241	2,4714	2,4254	2,3849	2,3488	2,3016	2,2371	2,1855	2,1431	2,0777	2,0293	1,9920	1,9382	1,9011	1,8233	1,7824	1,7484	1,7221	1,6950
86	2,5754	2,5144	2,4618	2,4158	2,3752	2,3391	2,2919	2,2273	2,1756	2,1333	2,0677	2,0193	1,9819	1,9279	1,8906	1,8126	1,7714	1,7372	1,7108	1,6835
88	2,5662	2,5053	2,4526	2,4066	2,3660	2,3299	2,2827	2,2180	2,1663	2,1238	2,0582	2,0096	1,9722	1,9180	1,8807	1,8023	1,7609	1,7266	1,6999	1,6725
90	2,5575	2,4965	2,4439	2,3978	2,3572	2,3211	2,2739	2,2092	2,1574	2,1149	2,0491	2,0005	1,9629	1,9086	1,8712	1,7925	1,7509	1,7164	1,6895	1,6619
92	2,5492	2,4882	2,4355	2,3895	2,3489	2,3128	2,2655	2,2007	2,1489	2,1063	2,0405	1,9917	1,9541	1,8997	1,8621	1,7831	1,7413	1,7066	1,6796	1,6518
94	2,5412	2,4802	2,4275	2,3815	2,3409	2,3048	2,2574	2,1926	2,1407	2,0981	2,0322	1,9834	1,9457	1,8911	1,8534	1,7741	1,7321	1,6972	1,6701	1,6420
96	2,5336	2,4726	2,4199	2,3739	2,3332	2,2971	2,2497	2,1849	2,1329	2,0903	2,0242	1,9753	1,9376	1,8829	1,8450	1,7655	1,7233	1,6882	1,6609	1,6327
98	2,5263	2,4653	2,4126	2,3666	2,3259	2,2898	2,2424	2,1775	2,1255	2,0828	2,0167	1,9677	1,9298	1,8750	1,8370	1,7572	1,7149	1,6796	1,6521	1,6237
100	2,5194	2,4584	2,4056	2,3596	2,3189	2,2827	2,2353	2,1704	2,1183	2,0756	2,0094	1,9603	1,9224	1,8674	1,8294	1,7493	1,7067	1,6713	1,6436	1,6150
110	2,4885	2,4274	2,3747	2,3286	2,2878	2,2516	2,2041	2,1389	2,0866	2,0437	1,9770	1,9276	1,8893	1,8337	1,7952	1,7138	1,6704	1,6340	1,6057	1,5762
120	2,4629	2,4019	2,3491	2,3029	2,2621	2,2258	2,1782	2,1128	2,0604	2,0172	1,9502	1,9004	1,8618	1,8057	1,7667	1,6841	1,6399	1,6028	1,5737	1,5433
130	2,4415	2,3804	2,3276	2,2813	2,2405	2,2041	2,1564	2,0909	2,0383	1,9949	1,9276	1,8775	1,8386	1,7820	1,7426	1,6589	1,6140	1,5761	1,5463	1,5151
140	2,4232	2,3621	2,3092	2,2630	2,2221	2,1857	2,1378	2,0722	2,0194	1,9759	1,9083	1,8579	1,8187	1,7617	1,7220	1,6373	1,5916	1,5530	1,5225	1,4905
150	2,4074	2,4363	2,2934	2,2471	2,2062	2,1697	2,1218	2,0560	2,0031	1,9595	1,8915	1,8409	1,8015	1,7441	1,7040	1,6184	1,5721	1,5328	1,5017	1,4690
160	2,3937	2,3325	2,2796	2,2333	2,1923	2,1558	2,1078	2,0419	1,9889	1,9451	1,8769	1,8261	1,7865	1,7287	1,6883	1,6018	1,5549	1,5149	1,4833	1,4498
170	2,3816	2,3204	2,2675	2,2211	2,1801	2,1436	2,0955	2,0295	1,9763	1,9325	1,8641	1,8130	1,7732	1,7151	1,6744	1,5871	1,5396	1,4991	1,4669	1,4327
180	2,3709	2,3097	2,2568	2,2104	2,1693	2,1327	2,0846	2,0185	1,9652	1,9212	1,8527	1,8014	1,7615	1,7030	1,6621	1,5740	1,5260	1,4849	1,4521	1,4172
190	2,3613	2,3002	2,2472	2,2008	2,1597	2,1231	2,0749	2,0087	1,9553	1,9112	1,8425	1,7910	1,7509	1,6922	1,6510	1,5623	1,5137	1,4721	1,4388	1,4032
200	2,3528	2,2916	2,2386	2,1921	2,1510	2,1144	2,0662	1,9999	1,9464	1,9022	1,8333	1,7817	1,7414	1,6824	1,6410	1,5516	1,5026	1,4604	1,4266	1,3904
250	2,3204	2,2592	2,2061	2,1595	2,1183	2,0815	2,0332	1,9665	1,9127	1,8681	1,7985	1,7462	1,7054	1,6453	1,6030	1,5109	1,4598	1,4154	1,3793	1,3401
300	2,2990	2,2377	2,1846	2,1379	2,0967	2,0598	2,0113	1,9444	1,8903	1,8455	1,7754	1,7226	1,6814	1,6205	1,5774	1,4833	1,4306	1,3844	1,3464	1,3046
350	2,2838	2,2225	2,1693	2,1226	2,0813	2,0443	1,9957	1,9286	1,8743	1,8294	1,7589	1,7058	1,6642	1,6027	1,5591	1,4634	1,4093	1,3616	1,3221	1,2778
400	2,2724	2,2111	2,1579	2,1111	2,0697	2,0328	1,9841	1,9168	1,8624	1,8173	1,7465	1,6932	1,6513	1,5893	1,5453	1,4483	1,3932	1,3442	1,3032	1,2568
500	2,2565	2,1952	2,1419	2,0952	2,0537	2,0166	1,9678	1,9004	1,8457	1,8004	1,7292	1,6755	1,6332	1,5705	1,5259	1,4269	1,3702	1,3191	1,2759	1,2256
600	2,2461	2,1847	2,1314	2,0845	2,0430	2,0059	1,9570	1,8894	1,8347	1,7892	1,7177	1,6637	1,6211	1,5579	1,5129	1,4125	1,3545	1,3019	1,2568	1,2033
700	2,2386	2,1772	2,1238	2,0770	2,0354	1,9983	1,9493	1,8816	1,8268	1,7812	1,7095	1,6552	1,6125	1,5489	1,5035	1,4021	1,3432	1,2894	1,2427	1,1863
800	2,2330	2,1715	2,1182	2,0713	2,0297	1,9926	1,9436	1,8758	1,8208	1,7752	1,7033	1,6489	1,6060	1,5422	1,4965	1,3942	1,3346	1,2798	1,2318	1,1729
900	2,2286	2,1672	2,1138	2,0669	2,0253	1,9881	1,9391	1,8712	1,8162	1,7705	1,6985	1,6440	1,6010	1,5369	1,4911	1,3881	1,3278	1,2722	1,2232	1,1619
1000	2,2252	2,1637	2,1103	2,0634	2,0218	1,9846	1,9355	1,8676	1,8125	1,7668	1,6947	1,6400	1,5969	1,5327	1,4867	1,3832	1,3224	1,2661	1,2161	1,1528
2000	2,2095	2,1480	2,0946	2,0476	2,0059	1,9686	1,9194	1,8513	1,7960	1,7500	1,6774	1,6223	1,5787	1,5137	1,4668	1,3607	1,2974	1,2375	1,1823	1,1048
5000	2,2002	2,1387	2,0852	2,0382	1,9964	1,9591	1,9098	1,8415	1,7861	1,7399	1,6670	1,6116	1,5678	1,5022	1,4547	1,3470	1,2819	1,2194	1,1600	1,0646
10000	2,1971	2,1356	2,0820	2,0350	1,9933	1,9559	1,9066	1,8383	1,7828	1,7366	1,6636	1,6081	1,5641	1,4983	1,4508	1,3424	1,2767	1,2132	1,1521	1,0451
∞	2,1940	2,1324	2,0789	2,0319	1,9901	1,9527	1,9034	1,8350	1,7795	1,7332	1,6601	1,6045	1,5605	1,4945	1,4468	1,3377	1,2714	1,2069	1,1439	1

All values conform to the international convention (i.e. 0,1 instead of 0.1).

Confidence Factors* for the Mean μ

Confidence limits for μ: $\bar{x} \pm k_2 s$ (k_2 is given in the table); N: size of the sample from which $\bar{x}$ and s are calculated

$100(1-2\alpha) = 95\%$

N	0	1	2	3	4	5	6	7	8	9
0	–	–	8,9845	2,4842	1,5913	1,2416	1,0494	0,9248	0,8360	0,7687
10	0,7154	0,6718	0,6354	0,6043	0,5774	0,5538	0,5329	5142	4973	4820
20	4680	4552	4434	4324	4223	4128	4039	3956	3878	3804
30	3734	3668	3605	3546	3489	3435	3384	3334	3287	3242
40	3198	3156	3116	3078	3040	3004	2970	2936	2904	2872
50	0,2842	0,2813	0,2784	0,2756	0,2730	0,2703	0,2678	0,2653	0,2629	0,2606
60	2583	2561	2540	2519	2498	2478	2458	2439	2421	2402
70	2385	2367	2350	2333	2317	2301	2285	2270	2255	2240
80	2225	2211	2197	2184	2170	2157	2144	2131	2119	2107
90	2095	2083	2071	2060	2048	2037	2026	2016	2005	1995
100	0,1984	0,1974	0,1964	0,1954	0,1945	0,1935	0,1926	0,1917	0,1908	0,1899
110	1890	1881	1872	1864	1856	1847	1839	1831	1823	1815
120	1808	1800	1792	1785	1778	1770	1763	1756	1749	1742
130	1735	1729	1722	1715	1709	1702	1696	1690	1683	1677
140	1671	1665	1659	1653	1647	1642	1636	1630	1625	1619
150	0,1614	0,1608	0,1603	0,1597	0,1592	0,1587	0,1582	0,1577	0,1571	0,1566
160	1561	1556	1552	1547	1542	1537	1533	1528	1523	1519
170	1514	1510	1505	1501	1496	1492	1488	1483	1479	1475
180	1471	1467	1463	1459	1455	1451	1447	1443	1439	1435
190	1431	1427	1424	1420	1416	1412	1409	1405	1402	1398
200	0,1394	0,1391	0,1379	0,1376	0,1372	0,1369	0,1366	0,1362	0,1359	0,1356
210	1353	1349	1346	1343	1340	1337	1334	1331	1328	1324
220	1321	1318	1315	1313	1310	1307	1304	1301	1298	1295
230	1292	1290	1287	1284	1281	1279	1276	1273	1271	1268
240	1265	1263	1260	1257	1255	1252	1250	1247	1245	1242
250	0,1240	0,1237	0,1235	0,1232	0,1230	0,1227	0,1225	0,1223	0,1220	0,1218
260	1216	1213	1211	1209	1206	1204	1202	1200	1197	1195
270	1193	1191	1188	1186	1184	1182	1180	1178	1176	1173
280	1171	1169	1167	1165	1163	1161	1159	1157	1155	1153
290	1151	1149	1147	1145	1143	1141	1139	1138	1135	1134
300	0,1132	0,1130	0,1128	0,1126	0,1124	0,1122	0,1120	0,1119	0,1117	0,1115
310	1113	1111	1110	1108	1106	1104	1103	1101	1099	1097
320	1096	1094	1092	1091	1089	1087	1086	1084	1082	1081
330	1079	1077	1076	1074	1072	1071	1069	1068	1066	1065
340	1063	1061	1060	1058	1057	1055	1054	1052	1051	1049
350	0,1048	0,1046	0,1045	0,1043	0,1042	0,1040	0,1039	0,1037	0,1036	0,1034
360	1033	1032	1030	1029	1027	1026	1025	1023	1022	1020
370	1019	1018	1016	1015	1014	1012	1011	1009	1008	1007
380	1005	1004	1003	1002	1000	0999	0998	0996	0995	0994
390	0993	0991	0990	0989	0987	0986	0985	0984	0982	0981
400	0,0980	0,0979	0,0978	0,0976	0,0975	0,0974	0,0973	0,0972	0,0970	0,0969
410	0968	0967	0966	0964	0963	0962	0961	0960	0959	0958
420	0956	0955	0954	0953	0952	0951	0950	0949	0947	0946
430	0945	0944	0943	0942	0941	0940	0939	0938	0937	0935
440	0934	0933	0932	0931	0930	0929	0928	0927	0926	0925
450	0,0924	0,0923	0,0922	0,0921	0,0920	0,0919	0,0918	0,0917	0,0916	0,0915
460	0914	0913	0912	0911	0910	0909	0908	0907	0906	0905
470	0904	0903	0902	0901	0900	0899	0898	0897	0897	0896
480	0895	0894	0893	0892	0891	0890	0889	0888	0887	0886
490	0885	0885	0884	0883	0882	0881	0880	0879	0878	0877
500	0,0877	0,0876	0,0875	0,0874	0,0873	0,0872	0,0871	0,0871	0,0870	0,0869
510	0868	0867	0866	0865	0865	0864	0863	0862	0861	0860
520	0860	0859	0858	0857	0856	0855	0855	0854	0853	0852
530	0851	0851	0850	0849	0848	0847	0847	0846	0845	0844
540	0843	0843	0842	0841	0840	0840	0839	0838	0837	0837
550	0,0836	0,0835	0,0834	0,0834	0,0833	0,0832	0,0831	0,0831	0,0830	0,0829
560	0828	0828	0827	0826	0825	0825	0824	0823	0822	0822
570	0821	0820	0820	0819	0818	0817	0817	0816	0815	0815
580	0814	0813	0812	0812	0811	0810	0810	0809	0808	0808
590	0807	0806	0806	0805	0804	0804	0803	0802	0802	0801
600	0,0800	0,0800	0,0799	0,0798	0,0798	0,0797	0,0796	0,0796	0,0795	0,0794
610	0794	0793	0792	0792	0791	0790	0790	0789	0788	0788
620	0787	0787	0786	0785	0785	0784	0783	0783	0782	0782
630	0781	0780	0780	0779	0778	0778	0777	0777	0776	0775
640	0775	0774	0774	0773	0772	0772	0771	0771	0770	0769
650	0,0769	0,0768	0,0768	0,0767	0,0766	0,0766	0,0765	0,0765	0,0764	0,0764
660	0763	0762	0762	0761	0761	0760	0760	0759	0758	0758
670	0757	0757	0756	0756	0755	0754	0754	0753	0753	0752
680	0752	0751	0751	0750	0749	0749	0748	0748	0747	0747
690	0746	0746	0745	0745	0744	0744	0743	0742	0742	0741
700	0,0741	0,0740	0,0740	0,0739	0,0739	0,0738	0,0738	0,0737	0,0737	0,0736
710	0736	0735	0735	0734	0734	0733	0733	0732	0732	0731
720	0730	0730	0729	0729	0728	0728	0727	0727	0726	0726
730	0725	0725	0724	0724	0723	0723	0723	0722	0722	0721
740	0721	0720	0720	0719	0719	0718	0718	0717	0717	0716
750	0,0716	0,0715	0,0715	0,0714	0,0714	0,0713	0,0713	0,0712	0,0712	0,0711
760	0711	0711	0710	0710	0709	0709	0708	0708	0707	0707
770	0706	0706	0705	0705	0705	0704	0704	0703	0703	0702
780	0702	0701	0701	0700	0700	0700	0699	0699	0698	0698
790	0697	0697	0696	0696	0696	0695	0695	0694	0694	0693
800	0,0693	0,0693	0,0692	0,0692	0,0691	0,0691	0,0690	0,0690	0,0690	0,0689
810	0689	0688	0688	0687	0687	0687	0686	0686	0685	0685
820	0684	0684	0684	0683	0683	0682	0682	0682	0681	0681
830	0680	0680	0680	0679	0679	0678	0678	0678	0677	0677
840	0676	0676	0675	0675	0675	0674	0674	0674	0673	0673
850	0,0672	0,0672	0,0672	0,0671	0,0671	0,0670	0,0670	0,0670	0,0669	0,0669
860	0668	0668	0668	0667	0667	0666	0666	0666	0665	0665
870	0665	0664	0664	0663	0663	0663	0662	0662	0662	0661
880	0661	0660	0660	0660	0659	0659	0659	0658	0658	0657
890	0657	0657	0656	0656	0656	0655	0655	0654	0654	0654
900	0,0653	0,0653	0,0653	0,0652	0,0652	0,0652	0,0651	0,0651	0,0650	0,0650
910	0650	0649	0649	0649	0648	0648	0648	0647	0647	0647
920	0646	0646	0645	0645	0644	0644	0644	0643	0643	0643
930	0643	0642	0642	0642	0641	0641	0641	0640	0640	0640
940	0639	0639	0639	0638	0638	0638	0637	0637	0637	0636
950	0,0636	0,0636	0,0635	0,0635	0,0635	0,0634	0,0634	0,0634	0,0633	0,0633
960	0633	0632	0632	0632	0631	0631	0631	0630	0630	0630
970	0629	0629	0629	0628	0628	0628	0627	0627	0627	0626
980	0626	0626	0625	0625	0625	0625	0624	0624	0624	0623
990	0623	0623	0622	0622	0622	0621	0621	0621	0620	0620
1000	0,0620									

$100(1-2\alpha) = 99\%$

N	0	1	2	3	4	5	6	7	8	9
0	–	–	45,012	5,7301	2,9205	2,0590	1,6461	1,4013	1,2373	1,1185
10	1,0277	0,9556	0,8966	0,8472	0,8051	0,7686	0,7367	0,7084	0,6831	0,6604
20	0,6397	6209	6037	5878	5730	5594	5467	5348	5236	5131
30	5033	4939	4851	4767	4688	4612	4540	4471	4405	4342
40	4282	4224	4168	4115	4063	4013	3966	3919	3875	3832
50	0,3790	0,3750	0,3711	0,3673	0,3636	0,3600	0,3566	0,3532	0,3499	0,3467
60	3436	3406	3377	3348	3320	3293	3267	3241	3215	3190
70	3166	3143	3120	3097	3075	3053	3032	3011	2991	2971
80	2951	2932	2913	2895	2877	2859	2841	2824	2807	2791
90	2775	2759	2743	2728	2712	2698	2683	2668	2654	2640
100	0,2627	0,2613	0,2600	0,2586	0,2574	0,2561	0,2548	0,2536	0,2524	0,2512
110	2500	2488	2477	2465	2454	2443	2432	2421	2411	2400
120	2390	2380	2370	2360	2350	2340	2330	2321	2312	2302
130	2293	2284	2275	2266	2258	2249	2241	2232	2224	2216
140	2207	2199	2191	2183	2176	2168	2160	2153	2145	2138
150	0,2131	0,2123	0,2116	0,2109	0,2102	0,2095	0,2088	0,2081	0,2074	0,2068
160	2061	2055	2048	2042	2035	2029	2023	2016	2010	2004
170	1998	1992	1986	1980	1975	1969	1963	1957	1952	1946
180	1941	1935	1930	1924	1919	1914	1909	1903	1898	1893
190	1888	1883	1878	1873	1868	1863	1858	1853	1849	1844
200	0,1839	0,1834	0,1812	0,1808	0,1803	0,1799	0,1795	0,1790	0,1786	0,1782
210	1778	1773	1769	1765	1761	1757	1753	1749	1745	1741
220	1737	1733	1729	1725	1721	1717	1713	1710	1706	1702
230	1699	1695	1691	1688	1684	1680	1677	1673	1670	1666
240	1663	1659	1656	1652	1649	1646	1642	1639	1636	1632
250	0,1629	0,1626	0,1623	0,1619	0,1616	0,1613	0,1610	0,1607	0,1604	0,1601
260	1598	1594	1591	1588	1585	1582	1579	1576	1573	1571
270	1568	1565	1562	1559	1556	1553	1551	1548	1545	1542
280	1539	1537	1534	1531	1529	1526	1523	1521	1518	1515
290	1513	1510	1507	1505	1502	1500	1497	1495	1492	1490
300	0,1487	0,1485	0,1482	0,1480	0,1477	0,1475	0,1473	0,1470	0,1468	0,1465
310	1463	1461	1458	1456	1454	1451	1449	1447	1445	1442
320	1440	1438	1436	1433	1431	1429	1427	1424	1422	1420
330	1418	1416	1414	1412	1409	1407	1405	1403	1401	1399
340	1397	1395	1393	1391	1389	1387	1385	1383	1381	1379
350	0,1377	0,1375	0,1373	0,1371	0,1369	0,1367	0,1365	0,1363	0,1361	0,1360
360	1358	1356	1354	1352	1350	1348	1346	1345	1343	1341
370	1339	1337	1336	1334	1332	1330	1328	1327	1325	1323
380	1321	1320	1318	1316	1315	1313	1311	1309	1308	1306
390	1304	1303	1301	1299	1298	1296	1294	1293	1291	1290
400	0,1288	0,1286	0,1285	0,1283	0,1282	0,1280	0,1278	0,1277	0,1275	0,1274
410	1272	1271	1269	1268	1266	1264	1263	1261	1260	1258
420	1257	1255	1254	1252	1251	1250	1248	1247	1245	1244
430	1242	1241	1239	1238	1236	1235	1234	1232	1231	1229
440	1228	1227	1225	1224	1222	1221	1220	1218	1217	1216
450	0,1214	0,1213	0,1212	0,1210	0,1209	0,1208	0,1206	0,1205	0,1204	0,1202
460	1201	1200	1198	1197	1196	1195	1193	1192	1191	1189
470	1188	1187	1186	1184	1183	1182	1181	1179	1178	1177
480	1176	1175	1173	1172	1171	1170	1168	1167	1166	1165
490	1164	1163	1161	1160	1159	1158	1157	1155	1154	1153
500	0,1152	0,1151	0,1150	0,1149	0,1147	0,1146	0,1145	0,1144	0,1143	0,1142
510	1141	1140	1138	1137	1136	1135	1134	1133	1132	1131
520	1130	1129	1127	1126	1125	1124	1123	1122	1121	1120
530	1119	1118	1117	1116	1115	1114	1113	1112	1111	1110
540	1109	1107	1106	1105	1104	1103	1102	1101	1100	1099
550	0,1098	0,1097	0,1096	0,1095	0,1094	0,1093	0,1092	0,1091	0,1090	0,1090
560	1089	1088	1087	1086	1085	1084	1083	1082	1081	1080
570	1079	1078	1077	1076	1075	1074	1073	1072	1071	1071
580	1070	1069	1068	1067	1066	1065	1064	1063	1062	1061
590	1061	1060	1059	1058	1057	1056	1055	1054	1053	1053
600	0,1052	0,1051	0,1050	0,1049	0,1048	0,1047	0,1046	0,1046	0,1045	0,1044
610	1043	1042	1041	1040	1040	1039	1038	1037	1036	1035
620	1035	1034	1033	1032	1031	1030	1030	1029	1028	1027
630	1026	1025	1025	1024	1023	1022	1021	1021	1020	1019
640	1018	1017	1017	1016	1015	1014	1013	1013	1012	1011
650	0,1010	0,1010	0,1009	0,1008	0,1007	0,1007	0,1006	0,1005	0,1004	0,1003
660	1003	1002	1001	1000	1000	0999	0998	0997	0997	0996
670	0995	0994	0994	0993	0992	0991	0991	0990	0989	0989
680	0988	0987	0986	0986	0985	0984	0984	0983	0982	0981
690	0981	0980	0979	0979	0978	0977	0976	0976	0975	0974
700	0,0974	0,0973	0,0972	0,0972	0,0971	0,0970	0,0969	0,0969	0,0968	0,0967
710	0967	0966	0965	0965	0964	0963	0963	0962	0961	0961
720	0960	0959	0959	0958	0957	0957	0956	0955	0955	0954
730	0953	0953	0952	0951	0951	0950	0950	0949	0948	0948
740	0947	0946	0946	0945	0944	0944	0943	0942	0942	0941
750	0,0941	0,0940	0,0939	0,0939	0,0938	0,0937	0,0937	0,0936	0,0936	0,0935
760	0934	0934	0933	0933	0932	0931	0931	0930	0930	0929
770	0928	0928	0927	0927	0926	0925	0925	0924	0924	0923
780	0922	0922	0921	0921	0920	0919	0919	0918	0918	0917
790	0916	0916	0915	0915	0914	0914	0913	0912	0912	0911
800	0,0911	0,0910	0,0910	0,0909	0,0908	0,0908	0,0907	0,0907	0,0906	0,0906
810	0905	0905	0904	0903	0903	0902	0902	0901	0901	0900
820	0900	0899	0898	0898	0897	0897	0896	0896	0895	0895
830	0894	0894	0893	0893	0892	0891	0891	0890	0890	0889
840	0889	0888	0888	0887	0887	0886	0886	0885	0885	0884
850	0,0884	0,0883	0,0883	0,0882	0,0881	0,0881	0,0880	0,0880	0,0879	0,0879
860	0878	0878	0877	0877	0876	0876	0875	0875	0874	0874
870	0873	0873	0872	0872	0871	0871	0870	0870	0869	0869
880	0868	0868	0867	0867	0866	0866	0865	0865	0864	0864
890	0863	0863	0863	0862	0862	0861	0861	0860	0860	0859
900	0,0859	0,0858	0,0858	0,0857	0,0857	0,0856	0,0856	0,0855	0,0855	0,0854
910	0854	0853	0853	0853	0852	0852	0851	0851	0850	0850
920	0849	0849	0848	0848	0847	0847	0847	0846	0846	0845
930	0845	0844	0844	0843	0843	0842	0842	0842	0841	0841
940	0840	0840	0839	0839	0838	0838	0838	0837	0837	0836
950	0,0836	0,0835	0,0835	0,0834	0,0834	0,0834	0,0833	0,0833	0,0832	0,0832
960	0831	0831	0831	0830	0830	0829	0829	0828	0828	0828
970	0827	0827	0826	0826	0825	0825	0825	0824	0824	0823
980	0823	0822	0822	0822	0821	0821	0820	0820	0820	0819
990	0819	0818	0818	0817	0817	0817	0816	0816	0815	0815
1000	0,0815									

All values conform to the international convention (i.e. 0,1 instead of 0.1).

$\beta_p = 1 - 2\,\alpha_p$: tolerance probability; $\beta_t = 1 - 2\,\alpha_t$: confidence probability; N: size of the sample from which $\bar{x}$ and s are calculated

	A									B									
	k_3 for $(\bar{x} \pm k_3\,\sigma)$				k_4 for $(\bar{x} \pm k_4\,s)$				$\sqrt{\frac{N+1}{N}}$	k_5 for $(\bar{x} \pm k_5\,\sigma)$				k_6 for $(\mu \pm k_6\,s)$					
										$\beta_t = 0{,}95$		$\beta_t = 0{,}99$		$\beta_t = 0{,}95$		$\sqrt{\frac{N-1}{\chi^2_{N-1;\,0{,}05}}}$	$\beta_t = 0{,}99$		$\sqrt{\frac{N-1}{\chi^2_{N-1;\,0{,}01}}}$
β_p / N	0,90	0,95	0,98	0,99	0,90	0,95	0,98	0,99		0,90	0,95	0,95	0,99	0,90	0,95		0,95	0,99	
2	2,0145	2,4005	2,8492	3,1547	7,7328	15,562	38,973	77,964	1,224745	2,667	3,031	3,466	4,147	26,231	31,256	15,947	156,38	205,52	79,789
3	1,8993	2,2632	2,6862	2,9743	3,3717	4,9683	8,042	11,460	154701	2,415	2,776	3,132	3,813	7,263	8,654	4,4155	19,550	25,694	9,9749
4	1,8390	2,1913	2,6009	2,8799	2,6312	3,5581	5,077	6,5303	118034	2,265	2,626	2,933	3,614	4,803	5,723	2,9199	10,018	13,166	5,1113
5	1,8018	2,1470	2,5484	2,8217	2,3353	3,0414	4,105	5,0435	1,095445	2,165	2,525	2,797	3,478	3,902	4,650	2,3724	7,191	9,451	3,6692
6	7766	1170	5127	7822	2,1764	2,7766	3,635	4,3552	080123	2,093	450	698	3,370	3,437	4,095	2,0893	5,887	7,736	3,0034
7	7584	0953	4870	7537	2,0774	2,6158	3,360	3,9634	069045	2,038	394	620	3,301	3,151	3,754	1,9154	5,141	6,756	2,6230
8	7446	0789	4675	7321	2,0095	2,5080	3,180	3,7118	060660	1,995	349	558	3,238	2,956	3,522	1,7971	4,659	6,122	2,3769
9	7338	0660	4522	7152	1,9601	2,4307	3,053	3,5369	054092	1,961	313	507	3,186	2,814	3,354	1,7110	4,320	5,678	2,2043
10	1,7251	2,0556	2,4399	2,7016	1,9226	2,3726	2,959	3,4084	1,048809	1,932	2,283	2,465	3,143	2,706	3,225	1,6452	4,069	5,348	2,0762
11	7180	0471	4298	6904	8931	3272	887	3,3102	044466	909	258	428	3,105	620	3,122	5931	3,875	5,093	1,9771
12	7120	0400	4213	6810	8692	2909	829	3,2326	040833	889	236	397	3,073	551	3,039	5506	3,720	4,889	1,8980
13	7069	0340	4142	6731	8496	2610	782	3,1698	037749	872	218	369	3,044	492	2,970	5153	3,593	4,722	1,8332
14	7026	0288	4080	6662	8331	2362	743	3,1180	035098	856	201	345	3,018	443	2,911	4854	3,487	4,583	1,7792
15	1,6988	2,0242	2,4026	2,6603	1,8191	2,2151	2,710	3,0744	1,032796	1,843	2,186	2,324	2,996	2,401	2,861	1,4597	3,397	4,464	1,7332
16	6955	0203	3979	6551	8070	1971	682	3,0374	030776	832	174	309	976	364	817	4373	3,319	4,361	6936
17	6925	0168	3938	6505	7965	1814	658	3,0055	028991	821	162	287	958	332	778	4176	3,252	4,274	6592
18	6899	0137	3901	6464	7873	1676	637	2,9776	027402	812	153	272	941	303	744	4001	3,192	4,196	6288
19	6876	0109	3868	6427	7791	1555	618	2,9532	025978	804	143	258	926	277	714	3845	3,140	4,126	6019
20	1,6855	2,0084	2,3838	2,6394	1,7718	2,1447	2,602	2,9315	1,024695	1,796	2,134	2,245	2,912	2,254	2,686	1,3704	3,092	4,064	1,5777
21	6836	0061	3811	6364	7653	1351	587	9123	023533	789	127	233	899	233	661	3576	3,050	4,008	5560
22	6818	0040	3786	6337	7594	1263	575	8950	022475	783	120	222	887	214	638	3460	3,011	3,957	5363
23	6802	0021	3764	6312	7540	1185	562	8794	021508	777	113	212	876	196	617	3353	2,976	3,911	5184
24	6788	0004	3743	6289	7492	1114	552	8652	020621	772	107	202	866	180	598	3255	2,944	3,869	5020
25	1,6774	1,9988	2,3724	2,6268	1,7448	2,1048	2,541	2,8523	1,019804	1,767	2,101	2,193	2,856	2,165	2,580	1,3165	2,914	3,830	1,4868
26	6762	9973	3707	6249	7406	0987	532	8405	019049	762	096	185	847	152	564	3081	887	794	4729
27	6750	9959	3690	6231	7369	0932	524	8297	018350	758	092	178	839	139	548	3002	861	761	4600
28	6740	9947	3675	6214	7334	0881	517	8197	017700	754	087	171	831	127	534	2929	838	730	4479
29	6730	9935	3661	6199	7302	0834	509	8105	017095	751	083	164	823	115	521	2861	816	701	4367
30	1,6720	1,9924	2,3648	2,6184	1,7272	2,0790	2,503	2,8020	1,016530	1,747	2,079	2,158	2,816	2,105	2,508	1,2797	2,795	3,674	1,4262
31	6712	9913	3636	6170	7245	0750	496	7940	016001	744	075	153	810	095	496	2737	776	648	4164
32	6704	9904	3624	6158	7218	0711	491	7866	015505	741	072	147	803	086	485	2680	758	625	4072
33	6696	9894	3613	6146	7194	0676	486	7797	015039	738	069	142	797	077	475	2626	741	602	3985
34	6689	9886	3603	6134	7171	0642	481	7732	014599	736	066	137	792	069	465	2576	725	581	3903
35	1,6682	1,9878	2,3593	2,6124	1,7149	2,0611	2,476	2,7671	1,014185	1,733	2,063	2,132	2,786	2,061	2,455	1,2528	2,710	3,561	1,3825
36	6675	9870	3584	6114	7129	0581	472	7615	013794	731	060	127	781	053	446	2482	695	542	3751
37	6669	9863	3576	6104	7110	0553	467	7560	013423	728	057	123	776	046	438	2438	682	524	3681
38	6664	9856	3568	6095	7092	0527	463	7510	013072	726	055	119	772	039	430	2397	669	507	3615
39	6658	9849	3560	6086	7075	0502	459	7461	012740	724	053	115	767	033	422	2358	656	491	3552
40	1,6653	1,9843	2,3552	2,6078	1,7058	2,0478	2,456	2,7415	1,012423	1,722	2,051	2,112	2,763	2,026	2,415	1,2320	2,644	3,475	1,3492
41	6648	9837	3545	6071	7043	0456	452	7373	012122	720	048	108	759	020	408	2284	633	460	3434
42	6643	9832	3539	6063	7028	0435	450	7332	011835	718	046	105	755	015	401	2249	622	446	3379
43	6639	9826	3532	6056	7014	0414	446	7293	011561	717	044	102	752	009	394	2216	612	433	3326
44	6634	9821	3526	6049	7001	0395	443	7257	011300	715	042	099	748	004	388	2184	602	420	3276
45	1,6630	1,9816	2,3521	2,6043	1,6988	2,0377	2,441	2,7220	1,011050	1,714	2,040	2,096	2,745	1,999	2,382	1,2154	2,593	3,407	1,3227
46	6626	9812	3515	6037	6976	0359	438	7187	010811	712	039	093	742	994	376	2124	583	395	3181
47	6623	9807	3510	6031	6965	0342	436	7154	010582	711	037	091	738	990	371	2096	575	384	3136
48	6619	9803	3505	6025	6953	0326	433	7124	010363	710	036	088	735	985	365	2069	566	373	3093
49	6616	9799	3500	6020	6942	0310	430	7094	010152	708	034	086	732	981	360	2043	558	361	3052
50	1,6612	1,9795	2,3495	2,6015	1,6933	2,0296	2,429	2,7066	1,009951	1,707	2,033	2,083	2,729	1,977	2,355	1,2017	2,550	3,352	1,3012
51	6609	9791	3490	6010	6923	0282	426	7039	009756	706	031	081	727	973	351	1993	543	342	2974
52	6606	9787	3486	6005	6913	0269	425	7014	009569	705	030	079	724	969	346	1969	536	332	2936
53	6603	9784	3482	6000	6904	0255	423	6989	009390	704	029	077	722	965	341	1946	528	323	2900
54	6600	9780	3478	5996	6896	0243	421	6965	009217	703	028	075	719	961	337	1924	522	314	2866
55	1,6597	1,9777	2,3474	2,5991	1,6887	2,0230	2,419	2,6942	1,009050	1,702	2,026	2,073	2,717	1,958	2,333	1,1903	2,515	3,305	1,2832
56	6595	9774	3470	5987	6879	0219	417	6920	008889	701	025	071	714	954	329	1882	509	297	2800
57	6592	9771	3467	5983	6871	0208	416	6899	008734	700	024	069	712	951	325	1862	503	289	2768
58	6590	9768	3463	5979	6864	0197	414	6878	008584	699	023	067	710	948	321	1842	497	281	2738
59	6587	9765	3460	5976	6857	0186	412	6858	008439	698	022	065	708	945	317	1823	491	273	2708
60	1,6585	1,9762	2,3457	2,5972	1,6850	2,0176	2,411	2,6839	1,008299	1,697	2,021	2,064	2,706	1,942	2,314	1,1805	2,485	3,266	1,2680
61	6583	9760	3453	5969	6843	0166	410	6820	008164	696	020	062	704	939	310	1787	480	259	2652
62	6581	9757	3450	5965	6837	0157	408	6803	008032	695	019	060	702	936	307	1769	474	252	2625
63	6579	9755	3447	5962	6830	0148	407	6785	007906	694	018	059	700	933	303	1752	469	245	2598
64	6577	9752	3445	5959	6824	0139	406	6769	007782	694	017	057	698	930	300	1736	464	239	2573
65	1,6575	1,9750	2,3442	2,5956	1,6818	2,0130	2,404	2,6753	1,007663	1,693	2,016	2,056	2,696	1,928	2,297	1,1720	2,459	3,232	1,2548
66	6573	9748	3439	5953	6813	0122	403	6737	007547	692	016	055	695	925	294	1704	455	226	2524
67	6571	9745	3436	5950	6807	0114	402	6722	007435	691	015	053	693	923	291	1689	450	220	2500
68	6569	9743	3434	5947	6802	0107	400	6707	007326	691	014	052	692	920	288	1674	445	214	2477
69	6567	9741	3431	5944	6796	0099	399	6692	007221	690	013	051	690	918	285	1660	441	208	2455
70	1,6566	1,9739	2,3429	2,5942	1,6791	2,0092	2,398	2,6679	1,007118	1,689	2,012	2,049	2,689	1,916	2,282	1,1645	2,437	3,203	1,2433
71	6564	9737	3427	5939	6786	0085	398	6666	007018	689	012	048	687	913	280	1632	433	197	2411
72	6562	9735	3424	5937	6781	0078	396	6653	006920	688	011	047	686	911	277	1618	429	192	2391
73	6561	9733	3422	5934	6777	0071	395	6640	006826	688	010	046	684	909	275	1605	425	186	2370
74	6559	9732	3420	5932	6772	0065	394	6628	006734	687	010	045	683	907	272	1592	421	181	2350
75	1,6558	1,9730	2,3418	2,5929	1,6768	2,0058	2,394	2,6616	1,006645	1,686	2,009	2,044	2,681	1,905	2 270	1,1579	2,417	3,176	1,2331
76	6556	9728	3416	5927	6764	0052	393	6604	006558	686	009	043	680	903	267	1567	413	171	2312
77	6555	9727	3414	5925	6760	0046	391	6592	006473	685	008	042	679	901	265	1555	410	167	2294
78	6554	9725	3412	5923	6755	0040	391	6582	006390	685	007	041	678	899	263	1543	406	162	2276
79	6552	9723	3410	5921	6751	0035	390	6571	006309	685	007	040	677	897	260	1532	403	158	2258
80	1,6551	1,9722	2,3408	2,5919	1,6747	2,0029	2,389	2,6560	1,006231	1,684	2,006	2,039	2,676	1,895	2,258	1,1521	2,399	3,153	1,2241
81	6550	9720	3407	5917	6743	0023	389	6550	006154	684	006	038	674	893	256	1509	396	149	2224
82	6549	9719	3405	5915	6740	0018	387	6540	006079	683	005	037	673	891	254	1499	393	144	2207
83	6547	9717	3403	5913	6737	0012	386	6530	006006	683	004	036	672	890	252	1488	389	140	2191
84	6546	9716	3402	5911	6734	0007	386	6521	005934	682	004	035	671	888	250	1478	386	136	2175
85	1,6545	1,9715	2,3400	2,5909	1,6730	2,0003	2,385	2,6512	1,005865	1,682	2,004	2,034	2,670	1,886	2,248	1,1468	2,383	3,132	1,2159
86	6544	9713	3398	5908	6726	1,9998	385	6503	005797	681	003	033	669	885	246	1458	380	128	2144
87	6543	9712	3397	5906	6723	9994	384	6494	005731	681	002	032	668	883	244	1448	377	124	2129
88	6542	9711	3395	5904	6720	9989	383	6485	005666	680	002	032	667	881	242	1438	374	121	2115
89	6541	9709	3394	5903	6717	9985	382	6476	005602	680	002	031	666	880	240	1429	372	117	2100
90	1,6540	1,9708	2,3392	2,5901	1,6714	1,9980	2,382	2,6468	1,005541	1,680	2,001	2,030	2,665	1,878	2,238	1,1419	2,369	3,113	1,2086
91	6539	9707	3391	5899	6711	9976	381	6460	005480	679	000	029	664	877	236	1410	366	110	2072
92	6538	9706	3390	5898	6708	9972	381	6452	005420	679	000	029	664	875	235	1401	363	106	2059
93	6537	9705	3388	5896	6705	9968	380	6444	005362	678	000	028	663	874	233	1393	361	103	2045
94	6536	9704	3387	5895	6702	9964	380	6437	005305	678	1,999	027	662	873	231	1384	358	099	2032
95	1,6535	1,9703	2,3386	2,5893	1,6699	1,9960	2,378	2,6430	1,005249	1,678	1,999	2,026	2,661	1,871	2,230	1,1376	2,356	3,096	1,2019
96	6534	9701	3384	5892	6697	9956	378	6423	005195	677	999	026	660	870	228	1367	353	093	2007
97	6533	9700	3383	5891	6694	9952	378	6416	005141	677	998	025	659	868	226	1359	351	090	1994
98	6532	9699	3382	5889	6692	9949	377	6409	005090	677	998	024	658	867	225	1351	348	086	1982
99	6531	9698	3381	5888	6689	9945	377	6402	005038	677	997	024	657	866	223	1343	346	083	1970
100	1,6531	1,9697	2,3380	2,5887	1,6687	1,9942	2,376	2,6396	1,004988	1,676	1,997	2,023	2,657	1,865	2,222	1,1336	2,344	3,080	1,1958
∞	1,6449	1,9600	2,3263	2,5758	1,6449	1,9600	2,326	2,5758	1,000000	1,645	1,960	1,960	2,576	1,645	1,960	1,0000	1,960	2,576	1,0000

All values conform to the international convention (i.e. 0,1 instead of 0.1).

Tolerance factor[1] k_7 for determination of the tolerance interval $\bar{x} \pm k_7 s$; $\beta_p = 1 - 2\alpha_p$: tolerance probability; $\beta_t = 1 - 2\alpha_t$: confidence probability; N: size of the sample from which $\bar{x}$ and s are calculated

	$\beta_t = 0{,}75$					$\beta_t = 0{,}90$					$\beta_t = 0{,}95$					$\beta_t = 0{,}99$				
β_p	0,75	0,90	0,95	0,99	0,999	0,75	0,90	0,95	0,99	0,999	0,75	0,90	0,95	0,99	0,999	0,75	0,90	0,95	0,99	0,999
N																				
2	4,498	6,301	7,414	9,531	11,920	11,407	15,978	18,800	24,167	30,227	22,858	32,019	37,674	48,430	60,573	114,363	160,193	188,491	242,300	303,054
3	2,501	3,538	4,187	5,431	6,844	4,132	5,847	6,919	8,974	11,309	5,922	8,380	9,916	12,861	16,208	13,378	18,930	22,401	29,055	36,616
4	2,035	2,892	3,431	4,471	5,657	2,932	4,166	4,943	6,440	8,149	3,779	5,369	6,370	8,299	10,502	6,614	9,398	11,150	14,527	18,383
5	1,825	2,599	3,088	4,033	5,117	2,454	3,494	4,152	5,423	6,879	3,002	4,275	5,079	6,634	8,415	4,643	6,612	7,855	10,260	13,015
6	1,704	2,429	2,889	3,779	4,802	2,196	3,131	3,723	4,870	6,188	2,604	3,712	4,414	5,775	7,337	3,743	5,337	6,345	8,301	10,548
7	1,624	2,318	2,757	3,611	4,593	2,034	2,902	3,452	4,521	5,750	2,361	3,369	4,007	5,248	6,676	3,233	4,613	5,488	7,187	9,142
8	1,568	2,238	2,663	3,491	4,444	1,921	2,743	3,264	4,278	5,446	2,197	3,136	3,732	4,891	6,226	2,905	4,147	4,936	6,468	8,234
9	1,525	2,178	2,593	3,400	4,330	1,839	2,626	3,125	4,098	5,220	2,078	2,967	3,532	4,631	5,899	2,677	3,822	4,550	5,966	7,600
10	1,492	2,131	2,537	3,328	4,241	1,775	2,535	3,018	3,959	5,046	1,987	2,839	3,379	4,433	5,649	2,508	3,582	4,265	5,594	7,129
11	1,465	2,093	2,493	3,271	4,169	1,724	2,463	2,933	3,849	4,906	1,916	2,737	3,259	4,277	5,452	2,378	3,397	4,045	5,308	6,766
12	1,443	2,062	2,456	3,223	4,110	1,683	2,404	2,863	3,758	4,792	1,858	2,655	3,162	4,150	5,291	2,274	3,250	3,870	5,079	6,477
13	1,425	2,036	2,424	3,183	4,059	1,648	2,355	2,805	3,682	4,697	1,810	2,587	3,081	4,044	5,158	2,190	3,130	3,727	4,893	6,240
14	1,409	2,013	2,398	3,148	4,016	1,619	2,314	2,756	3,618	4,615	1,770	2,529	3,012	3,955	5,045	2,120	3,029	3,608	4,737	6,043
15	1,395	1,994	2,375	3,118	3,979	1,594	2,278	2,713	3,562	4,545	1,735	2,480	2,954	3,878	4,949	2,060	2,945	3,507	4,605	5,876
16	1,383	1,977	2,355	3,092	3,946	1,572	2,246	2,676	3,514	4,484	1,705	2,437	2,903	3,812	4,865	2,009	2,872	3,421	4,492	5,732
17	1,372	1,962	2,337	3,069	3,917	1,552	2,219	2,643	3,471	4,430	1,679	2,400	2,858	3,754	4,791	1,965	2,808	3,345	4,393	5,607
18	1,363	1,948	2,321	3,048	3,891	1,535	2,194	2,614	3,433	4,382	1,655	2,366	2,819	3,702	4,725	1,926	2,753	3,279	4,307	5,497
19	1,355	1,936	2,307	3,030	3,867	1,520	2,172	2,588	3,399	4,339	1,635	2,337	2,784	3,656	4,667	1,891	2,703	3,221	4,230	5,399
20	1,347	1,925	2,294	3,013	3,846	1,506	2,152	2,564	3,368	4,300	1,616	2,310	2,752	3,615	4,614	1,860	2,659	3,168	4,161	5,312
21	1,340	1,915	2,282	2,998	3,827	1,493	2,135	2,543	3,340	4,264	1,599	2,286	2,723	3,577	4,567	1,833	2,620	3,121	4,100	5,234
22	1,334	1,906	2,271	2,984	3,809	1,482	2,118	2,524	3,315	4,232	1,584	2,264	2,697	3,543	4,523	1,808	2,584	3,078	4,044	5,163
23	1,328	1,898	2,261	2,971	3,793	1,471	2,103	2,506	3,292	4,203	1,570	2,244	2,673	3,512	4,484	1,785	2,551	3,040	3,993	5,098
24	1,322	1,891	2,252	2,959	3,778	1,462	2,089	2,489	3,270	4,176	1,557	2,225	2,651	3,483	4,447	1,764	2,522	3,004	3,947	5,039
25	1,317	1,883	2,244	2,948	3,764	1,453	2,077	2,474	3,251	4,151	1,545	2,208	2,631	3,457	4,413	1,745	2,494	2,972	3,904	4,985
26	1,313	1,877	2,236	2,938	3,751	1,444	2,065	2,460	3,232	4,127	1,534	2,193	2,612	3,432	4,382	1,727	2,469	2,941	3,865	4,935
27	1,309	1,871	2,229	2,929	3,740	1,437	2,054	2,447	3,215	4,106	1,523	2,178	2,595	3,409	4,353	1,711	2,446	2,914	3,828	4,888
28	1,305	1,865	2,222	2,920	3,728	1,430	2,044	2,435	3,199	4,085	1,514	2,164	2,579	3,388	4,326	1,695	2,424	2,888	3,794	4,845
29	1,301	1,860	2,216	2,911	3,718	1,423	2,034	2,424	3,184	4,066	1,505	2,152	2,564	3,368	4,301	1,681	2,404	2,864	3,763	4,805
30	1,297	1,855	2,210	2,904	3,708	1,417	2,025	2,413	3,170	4,049	1,497	2,140	2,549	3,350	4,278	1,668	2,385	2,841	3,733	4,768
31	1,294	1,850	2,204	2,896	3,699	1,411	2,017	2,403	3,157	4,032	1,489	2,129	2,536	3,332	4,256	1,656	2,367	2,820	3,706	4,732
32	1,291	1,846	2,199	2,890	3,690	1,405	2,009	2,393	3,145	4,016	1,481	2,118	2,524	3,316	4,235	1,644	2,351	2,801	3,680	4,699
33	1,288	1,842	2,194	2,883	3,682	1,400	2,001	2,385	3,133	4,001	1,475	2,108	2,512	3,300	4,215	1,633	2,335	2,782	3,655	4,668
34	1,285	1,838	2,189	2,877	3,674	1,395	1,994	2,376	3,122	3,987	1,468	2,099	2,501	3,286	4,197	1,623	2,320	2,764	3,632	4,639
35	1,283	1,834	2,185	2,871	3,667	1,390	1,988	2,368	3,112	3,974	1,462	2,090	2,490	3,272	4,179	1,613	2,306	2,748	3,611	4,611
36	1,280	1,830	2,181	2,866	3,660	1,386	1,981	2,361	3,102	3,961	1,455	2,081	2,479	3,258	4,161	1,604	2,293	2,732	3,590	4,585
37	1,278	1,827	2,177	2,860	3,653	1,381	1,975	2,353	3,092	3,949	1,450	2,073	2,470	3,246	4,146	1,595	2,281	2,717	3,571	4,560
38	1,275	1,824	2,173	2,855	3,647	1,377	1,969	2,346	3,083	3,938	1,446	2,068	2,464	3,237	4,134	1,587	2,269	2,703	3,552	4,537
39	1,273	1,821	2,169	2,850	3,641	1,374	1,964	2,340	3,075	3,927	1,441	2,060	2,455	3,226	4,120	1,579	2,257	2,690	3,534	4,514
40	1,271	1,818	2,166	2,846	3,635	1,370	1,959	2,334	3,066	3,917	1,435	2,052	2,445	3,213	4,104	1,571	2,247	2,677	3,518	4,493
41	1,269	1,815	2,162	2,841	3,629	1,366	1,954	2,328	3,059	3,907	1,430	2,045	2,437	3,202	4,090	1,564	2,236	2,665	3,502	4,472
42	1,267	1,812	2,159	2,837	3,624	1,363	1,949	2,322	3,051	3,897	1,426	2,039	2,429	3,192	4,077	1,557	2,227	2,653	3,486	4,453
43	1,266	1,810	2,156	2,833	3,619	1,360	1,944	2,316	3,044	3,888	1,422	2,033	2,422	3,183	4,065	1,551	2,217	2,642	3,472	4,434
44	1,264	1,807	2,153	2,829	3,614	1,357	1,940	2,311	3,037	3,879	1,418	2,027	2,415	3,173	4,053	1,545	2,208	2,631	3,458	4,416
45	1,262	1,805	2,150	2,826	3,609	1,354	1,935	2,306	3,030	3,871	1,414	2,021	2,408	3,165	4,042	1,539	2,200	2,621	3,444	4,399
46	1,261	1,802	2,148	2,822	3,605	1,351	1,931	2,301	3,024	3,863	1,410	2,016	2,402	3,156	4,031	1,533	2,192	2,611	3,431	4,383
47	1,259	1,800	2,145	2,819	3,600	1,348	1,927	2,297	3,018	3,855	1,406	2,011	2,396	3,148	4,021	1,527	2,184	2,602	3,419	4,367
48	1,258	1,798	2,143	2,815	3,596	1,345	1,924	2,292	3,012	3,847	1,403	2,006	2,390	3,140	4,011	1,522	2,176	2,593	3,407	4,352
49	1,256	1,796	2,140	2,812	3,592	1,343	1,920	2,288	3,006	3,840	1,399	2,001	2,384	3,133	4,002	1,517	2,169	2,584	3,396	4,337
50	1,255	1,794	2,138	2,809	3,588	1,340	1,916	2,284	3,001	3,833	1,396	1,996	2,379	3,126	3,993	1,512	2,162	2,576	3,385	4,323
51	1,253	1,792	2,135	2,806	3,584	1,338	1,913	2,279	2,995	3,826	1,393	1,992	2,373	3,119	3,984	1,507	2,155	2,568	3,374	4,310
52	1,252	1,790	2,133	2,803	3,581	1,336	1,910	2,276	2,990	3,820	1,390	1,988	2,368	3,112	3,975	1,503	2,148	2,560	3,364	4,297
53	1,251	1,789	2,131	2,801	3,577	1,334	1,907	2,272	2,985	3,813	1,387	1,984	2,363	3,106	3,967	1,498	2,142	2,552	3,354	4,284
54	1,250	1,787	2,129	2,798	3,574	1,331	1,904	2,268	2,981	3,807	1,384	1,980	2,359	3,100	3,959	1,494	2,136	2,545	3,344	4,272
55	1,249	1,785	2,127	2,795	3,571	1,329	1,901	2,265	2,976	3,801	1,382	1,976	2,354	3,094	3,951	1,490	2,130	2,538	3,335	4,260
56	1,247	1,784	2,125	2,793	3,567	1,327	1,898	2,261	2,972	3,796	1,379	1,972	2,350	3,088	3,944	1,486	2,124	2,531	3,326	4,249
57	1,246	1,782	2,123	2,790	3,564	1,325	1,895	2,258	2,967	3,790	1,377	1,968	2,345	3,082	3,937	1,482	2,119	2,524	3,318	4,238
58	1,245	1,781	2,122	2,788	3,561	1,323	1,892	2,255	2,963	3,785	1,374	1,965	2,341	3,076	3,930	1,478	2,113	2,518	3,309	4,227
59	1,244	1,779	2,120	2,786	3,558	1,322	1,890	2,252	2,959	3,779	1,372	1,961	2,337	3,071	3,923	1,474	2,108	2,512	3,301	4,216
60	1,243	1,778	2,118	2,784	3,556	1,320	1,887	2,248	2,955	3,774	1,369	1,958	2,333	3,066	3,916	1,471	2,103	2,506	3,293	4,206
61	1,242	1,776	2,117	2,781	3,553	1,318	1,885	2,245	2,951	3,769	1,367	1,955	2,329	3,061	3,909	1,467	2,098	2,500	3,285	4,196
62	1,241	1,775	2,115	2,779	3,550	1,316	1,882	2,243	2,947	3,765	1,365	1,951	2,325	3,056	3,903	1,464	2,093	2,494	3,278	4,187
63	1,240	1,774	2,113	2,777	3,548	1,315	1,880	2,240	2,944	3,760	1,363	1,948	2,322	3,051	3,897	1,461	2,089	2,489	3,271	4,178
64	1,240	1,772	2,112	2,775	3,545	1,313	1,878	2,237	2,940	3,755	1,361	1,945	2,318	3,046	3,891	1,458	2,084	2,483	3,264	4,169
65	1,239	1,771	2,110	2,773	3,543	1,312	1,875	2,235	2,937	3,751	1,359	1,943	2,315	3,042	3,886	1,455	2,080	2,478	3,257	4,160
66	1,238	1,770	2,109	2,771	3,540	1,310	1,873	2,232	2,933	3,747	1,357	1,940	2,311	3,037	3,880	1,452	2,076	2,473	3,250	4,152
67	1,237	1,769	2,108	2,770	3,538	1,309	1,871	2,229	2,930	3,742	1,355	1,937	2,308	3,033	3,874	1,449	2,071	2,468	3,244	4,143
68	1,236	1,768	2,106	2,768	3,536	1,307	1,869	2,227	2,927	3,738	1,353	1,934	2,305	3,029	3,869	1,446	2,067	2,463	3,237	4,135
69	1,235	1,766	2,105	2,766	3,533	1,306	1,867	2,225	2,923	3,734	1,351	1,932	2,302	3,025	3,864	1,443	2,063	2,459	3,231	4,127
70	1,235	1,765	2,104	2,764	3,531	1,304	1,865	2,222	2,920	3,730	1,349	1,929	2,299	3,021	3,859	1,440	2,060	2,454	3,225	4,120
71	1,234	1,764	2,102	2,763	3,529	1,303	1,863	2,220	2,917	3,727	1,347	1,927	2,296	3,017	3,854	1,438	2,056	2,450	3,219	4,112
72	1,233	1,763	2,101	2,761	3,527	1,302	1,861	2,218	2,915	3,723	1,346	1,924	2,293	3,013	3,849	1,435	2,052	2,445	3,214	4,105
73	1,233	1,762	2,100	2,760	3,525	1,300	1,859	2,216	2,912	3,719	1,344	1,922	2,290	3,009	3,844	1,433	2,049	2,441	3,208	4,098
74	1,232	1,761	2,099	2,758	3,523	1,299	1,858	2,214	2,909	3,716	1,343	1,920	2,287	3,006	3,840	1,430	2,045	2,437	3,203	4,091
75	1,231	1,760	2,098	2,757	3,521	1,298	1,856	2,211	2,906	3,712	1,341	1,917	2,285	3,002	3,835	1,428	2,042	2,433	3,197	4,084
76	1,230	1,759	2,096	2,755	3,519	1,297	1,854	2,209	2,904	3,709	1,339	1,915	2,282	2,999	3,831	1,426	2,039	2,429	3,192	4,078
77	1,230	1,758	2,095	2,754	3,517	1,296	1,853	2,207	2,901	3,706	1,338	1,913	2,279	2,996	3,826	1,423	2,035	2,425	3,187	4,071
78	1,229	1,758	2,094	2,752	3,516	1,295	1,851	2,206	2,898	3,702	1,336	1,911	2,277	2,992	3,822	1,421	2,032	2,421	3,182	4,065
79	1,229	1,757	2,093	2,751	3,514	1,293	1,849	2,204	2,896	3,699	1,335	1,909	2,274	2,989	3,818	1,419	2,029	2,418	3,177	4,059
80	1,228	1,756	2,092	2,749	3,512	1,292	1,848	2,202	2,894	3,696	1,334	1,907	2,272	2,986	3,814	1,417	2,026	2,414	3,173	4,053
81	1,227	1,755	2,091	2,748	3,510	1,291	1,846	2,200	2,891	3,693	1,332	1,905	2,270	2,983	3,810	1,415	2,023	2,411	3,168	4,047
82	1,227	1,754	2,090	2,747	3,509	1,290	1,845	2,198	2,889	3,690	1,331	1,903	2,267	2,980	3,806	1,413	2,020	2,407	3,163	4,041
83	1,226	1,753	2,089	2,746	3,507	1,289	1,843	2,196	2,887	3,687	1,329	1,901	2,265	2,977	3,803	1,411	2,017	2,404	3,159	4,035
84	1,226	1,753	2,088	2,744	3,506	1,288	1,842	2,195	2,884	3,684	1,328	1,899	2,263	2,974	3,799	1,409	2,014	2,400	3,155	4,030
85	1,225	1,752	2,087	2,743	3,504	1,287	1,841	2,193	2,882	3,682	1,327	1,897	2,261	2,971	3,795	1,407	2,012	2,397	3,150	4,024
86	1,225	1,751	2,086	2,742	3,503	1,286	1,839	2,191	2,880	3,679	1,326	1,896	2,259	2,968	3,792	1,405	2,009	2,394	3,146	4,019
87	1,224	1,750	2,086	2,741	3,501	1,285	1,838	2,190	2,878	3,676	1,324	1,894	2,257	2,966	3,788	1,403	2,007	2,391	3,142	4,014
88	1,224	1,749	2,085	2,740	3,500	1,284	1,837	2,188	2,876	3,674	1,323	1,892	2,255	2,963	3,785	1,402	2,004	2,388	3,138	4,009
89	1,223	1,749	2,084	2,738	3,498	1,284	1,835	2,187	2,874	3,671	1,322	1,890	2,253	2,960	3,781	1,400	2,001	2,385	3,134	4,004
90	1,223	1,748	2,083	2,737	3,497	1,283	1,834	2,185	2,872	3,669	1,321	1,889	2,251	2,958	3,778	1,398	1,999	2,382	3,130	3,999
91	1,222	1,747	2,082	2,736	3,495	1,282	1,833	2,184	2,870	3,666	1,320	1,887	2,249	2,955	3,775	1,396	1,997	2,379	3,127	3,994
92	1,222	1,747	2,081	2,735	3,494	1,281	1,832	2,182	2,868	3,664	1,319	1,886	2,247	2,953	3,772	1,395	1,994	2,376	3,123	3,989
93	1,221	1,746	2,081	2,734	3,493	1,280	1,830	2,181	2,866	3,661	1,318	1,884	2,245	2,950	3,769	1,393	1,992	2,373	3,119	3,985
94	1,221	1,745	2,080	2,733	3,491	1,279	1,829	2,180	2,864	3,659	1,317	1,882	2,243	2,948	3,766	1,392	1,990	2,371	3,116	3,980
95	1,220	1,745	2,079	2,732	3,490	1,278	1,828	2,178	2,863	3,657	1,315	1,881	2,241	2,945	3,763	1,390	1,987	2,368	3,112	3,976
96	1,220	1,744	2,078	2,731	3,489	1,278	1,827	2,177	2,861	3,654	1,314	1,880	2,240	2,943	3,760	1,388	1,985	2,366	3,109	3,971
97	1,219	1,743	2,077	2,730	3,488	1,277	1,826	2,175	2,859	3,652	1,313	1,878	2,238	2,941	3,757	1,387	1,983	2,363	3,105	3,967
98	1,219	1,743	2,077	2,729	3,486	1,276	1,825	2,174	2,857	3,650	1,312	1,877	2,236	2,939	3,754	1,385	1,981	2,360	3,102	3,963
99	1,219	1,742	2,076	2,728	3,485	1,275	1,824	2,173	2,856	3,648	1,311	1,875	2,234	2,936	3,751	1,384	1,979	2,358	3,099	3,958

[1] BOWKER, A. H., in EISENHART et al. (Eds.), *Selected Techniques of Statistical Analysis for Scientific and Industrial Research and Production and Management Engineering*, McGraw-Hill, New York, 1947, page 102. Reprinted by kind permission of the author and publishers.

All values conform to the international convention (i.e. 0,1 instead of 0.1).

Tolerance factor[1] k_7 for determination of the tolerance interval $\bar{x} \pm k_7 s$; $\beta_p = 1 - 2\alpha_p$: tolerance probability;
$\beta_t = 1 - 2\alpha_t$: confidence probability; N: size of the sample from which $\bar{x}$ and s are calculated

	$\beta_t = 0{,}75$					$\beta_t = 0{,}90$					$\beta_t = 0{,}95$					$\beta_t = 0{,}99$				
β_p	0,75	0,90	0,95	0,99	0,999	0,75	0,90	0,95	0,99	0,999	0,75	0,90	0,95	0,99	0,999	0,75	0,90	0,95	0,99	0,999
N																				
100	1,218	1,742	2,075	2,727	3,484	1,275	1,822	2,172	2,854	3,646	1,311	1,874	2,233	2,934	3,748	1,383	1,977	2,355	3,096	3,954
101	1,218	1,741	2,075	2,726	3,483	1,274	1,821	2,170	2,852	3,644	1,310	1,872	2,231	2,932	3,746	1,381	1,975	2,353	3,092	3,950
102	1,217	1,741	2,074	2,726	3,482	1,273	1,820	2,169	2,851	3,642	1,309	1,871	2,230	2,930	3,743	1,380	1,973	2,351	3,089	3,946
104	1,217	1,739	2,073	2,724	3,480	1,272	1,818	2,167	2,848	3,638	1,307	1,869	2,227	2,926	3,738	1,377	1,969	2,346	3,083	3,939
106	1,216	1,738	2,071	2,722	3,477	1,270	1,816	2,164	2,845	3,634	1,305	1,866	2,224	2,922	3,733	1,374	1,965	2,342	3,077	3,931
108	1,215	1,737	2,070	2,721	3,475	1,269	1,815	2,162	2,842	3,630	1,303	1,864	2,221	2,918	3,728	1,372	1,962	2,337	3,072	3,924
110	1,214	1,736	2,069	2,719	3,473	1,268	1,813	2,160	2,839	3,626	1,302	1,861	2,218	2,915	3,723	1,369	1,958	2,333	3,066	3,917
112	1,214	1,735	2,068	2,717	3,471	1,267	1,811	2,158	2,836	3,623	1,300	1,859	2,215	2,911	3,719	1,367	1,955	2,329	3,061	3,910
114	1,213	1,734	2,067	2,716	3,469	1,265	1,809	2,156	2,833	3,619	1,299	1,857	2,212	2,908	3,714	1,365	1,951	2,325	3,056	3,904
116	1,212	1,733	2,065	2,714	3,468	1,264	1,808	2,154	2,831	3,616	1,297	1,855	2,210	2,904	3,710	1,363	1,948	2,321	3,051	3,897
118	1,212	1,733	2,064	2,713	3,466	1,263	1,806	2,152	2,828	3,613	1,296	1,852	2,207	2,901	3,706	1,360	1,945	2,318	3,046	3,891
120	1,211	1,732	2,063	2,712	3,464	1,262	1,804	2,150	2,826	3,610	1,294	1,850	2,205	2,898	3,702	1,358	1,942	2,314	3,041	3,885
122	1,210	1,731	2,062	2,710	3,462	1,261	1,803	2,148	2,823	3,607	1,293	1,848	2,203	2,895	3,698	1,356	1,939	2,311	3,037	3,879
124	1,210	1,730	2,061	2,709	3,461	1,260	1,801	2,147	2,821	3,604	1,291	1,847	2,200	2,892	3,694	1,354	1,936	2,307	3,032	3,873
126	1,209	1,729	2,060	2,708	3,459	1,259	1,800	2,145	2,819	3,601	1,290	1,845	2,198	2,889	3,690	1,352	1,934	2,304	3,028	3,868
128	1,209	1,728	2,060	2,707	3,458	1,258	1,799	2,143	2,816	3,598	1,289	1,843	2,196	2,886	3,686	1,350	1,931	2,301	3,024	3,862
130	1,208	1,728	2,059	2,705	3,456	1,257	1,797	2,141	2,814	3,595	1,288	1,841	2,194	2,883	3,683	1,349	1,928	2,298	3,019	3,857
132	1,208	1,727	2,058	2,704	3,455	1,256	1,796	2,140	2,812	3,592	1,286	1,839	2,192	2,880	3,679	1,347	1,926	2,295	3,015	3,852
134	1,207	1,726	2,057	2,703	3,453	1,255	1,795	2,138	2,810	3,590	1,285	1,838	2,190	2,878	3,676	1,345	1,923	2,292	3,012	3,847
136	1,207	1,725	2,056	2,702	3,452	1,254	1,793	2,137	2,808	3,587	1,284	1,836	2,188	2,875	3,673	1,343	1,921	2,289	3,008	3,842
138	1,206	1,725	2,055	2,701	3,450	1,253	1,792	2,135	2,806	3,585	1,283	1,834	2,186	2,873	3,669	1,342	1,918	2,286	3,004	3,837
140	1,206	1,724	2,054	2,700	3,449	1,252	1,791	2,134	2,804	3,582	1,282	1,833	2,184	2,870	3,666	1,340	1,916	2,283	3,000	3,833
142	1,205	1,723	2,054	2,699	3,448	1,252	1,790	2,132	2,802	3,580	1,281	1,831	2,182	2,868	3,663	1,338	1,914	2,280	2,997	3,828
144	1,205	1,723	2,053	2,698	3,446	1,251	1,788	2,131	2,801	3,578	1,280	1,830	2,180	2,865	3,660	1,337	1,912	2,278	2,993	3,824
146	1,204	1,722	2,052	2,697	3,445	1,250	1,787	2,130	2,799	3,575	1,279	1,828	2,178	2,863	3,657	1,335	1,909	2,275	2,990	3,820
148	1,204	1,722	2,051	2,696	3,444	1,249	1,786	2,128	2,797	3,573	1,278	1,827	2,177	2,861	3,654	1,334	1,907	2,273	2,987	3,815
150	1,204	1,721	2,051	2,695	3,443	1,248	1,785	2,127	2,795	3,571	1,277	1,825	2,175	2,859	3,652	1,332	1,905	2,270	2,983	3,811
152	1,203	1,720	2,050	2,694	3,441	1,248	1,784	2,126	2,794	3,569	1,276	1,824	2,173	2,856	3,649	1,331	1,903	2,268	2,980	3,807
154	1,203	1,720	2,049	2,693	3,440	1,247	1,783	2,125	2,792	3,567	1,275	1,823	2,172	2,854	3,646	1,330	1,901	2,265	2,977	3,803
156	1,202	1,719	2,049	2,692	3,439	1,246	1,782	2,123	2,791	3,565	1,274	1,821	2,170	2,852	3,644	1,328	1,899	2,263	2,974	3,799
158	1,202	1,719	2,048	2,691	3,438	1,246	1,781	2,122	2,789	3,563	1,273	1,820	2,169	2,850	3,641	1,327	1,897	2,261	2,971	3,796
160	1,202	1,718	2,047	2,691	3,437	1,245	1,780	2,121	2,787	3,561	1,272	1,819	2,167	2,848	3,638	1,326	1,896	2,259	2,968	3,792
162	1,201	1,718	2,047	2,690	3,436	1,244	1,779	2,120	2,786	3,559	1,271	1,818	2,166	2,846	3,636	1,324	1,894	2,256	2,965	3,788
164	1,201	1,717	2,046	2,689	3,435	1,244	1,778	2,119	2,785	3,557	1,270	1,816	2,164	2,844	3,634	1,323	1,892	2,254	2,963	3,785
166	1,201	1,717	2,045	2,688	3,434	1,243	1,777	2,118	2,783	3,555	1,269	1,815	2,163	2,843	3,631	1,322	1,890	2,252	2,960	3,781
168	1,200	1,716	2,045	2,687	3,433	1,242	1,776	2,117	2,782	3,553	1,269	1,814	2,162	2,841	3,629	1,321	1,888	2,250	2,957	3,778
170	1,200	1,716	2,044	2,687	3,432	1,242	1,775	2,116	2,780	3,552	1,268	1,813	2,160	2,839	3,627	1,320	1,887	2,248	2,955	3,774
172	1,199	1,715	2,044	2,686	3,431	1,241	1,775	2,115	2,779	3,550	1,267	1,812	2,159	2,837	3,624	1,318	1,885	2,246	2,952	3,771
174	1,199	1,715	2,043	2,685	3,430	1,240	1,774	2,114	2,778	3,548	1,266	1,811	2,158	2,835	3,622	1,317	1,884	2,244	2,950	3,768
176	1,199	1,714	2,043	2,684	3,429	1,240	1,773	2,113	2,776	3,547	1,266	1,810	2,156	2,834	3,620	1,316	1,882	2,243	2,947	3,765
178	1,199	1,714	2,042	2,684	3,428	1,239	1,772	2,112	2,775	3,545	1,265	1,809	2,155	2,832	3,618	1,315	1,880	2,241	2,945	3,762
180	1,198	1,713	2,042	2,683	3,427	1,239	1,771	2,111	2,774	3,543	1,264	1,808	2,154	2,831	3,616	1,314	1,879	2,239	2,942	3,759
185	1,197	1,712	2,040	2,681	3,425	1,237	1,769	2,108	2,771	3,539	1,262	1,805	2,151	2,827	3,611	1,311	1,875	2,234	2,937	3,751
190	1,197	1,711	2,039	2,680	3,423	1,236	1,767	2,106	2,768	3,536	1,261	1,803	2,148	2,823	3,606	1,309	1,872	2,230	2,931	3,744
195	1,196	1,710	2,038	2,678	3,421	1,235	1,766	2,104	2,765	3,532	1,259	1,800	2,145	2,819	3,601	1,307	1,868	2,226	2,926	3,738
200	1,195	1,709	2,037	2,677	3,419	1,234	1,764	2,102	2,762	3,529	1,258	1,798	2,143	2,816	3,597	1,304	1,865	2,222	2,921	3,731
205	1,195	1,708	2,036	2,675	3,418	1,233	1,762	2,100	2,760	3,526	1,256	1,796	2,140	2,812	3,593	1,302	1,862	2,219	2,916	3,725
210	1,194	1,708	2,035	2,674	3,416	1,231	1,761	2,098	2,757	3,522	1,255	1,794	2,138	2,809	3,589	1,300	1,859	2,215	2,911	3,719
215	1,194	1,707	2,034	2,673	3,414	1,230	1,759	2,096	2,755	3,519	1,253	1,792	2,135	2,806	3,585	1,298	1,856	2,212	2,907	3,713
220	1,193	1,706	2,033	2,671	3,413	1,229	1,758	2,095	2,753	3,516	1,252	1,790	2,133	2,803	3,581	1,296	1,854	2,209	2,903	3,708
225	1,192	1,705	2,032	2,670	3,411	1,228	1,756	2,093	2,750	3,514	1,251	1,788	2,131	2,800	3,577	1,294	1,851	2,205	2,898	3,703
230	1,192	1,704	2,031	2,669	3,409	1,227	1,755	2,091	2,748	3,511	1,249	1,787	2,129	2,798	3,574	1,293	1,848	2,202	2,894	3,697
235	1,191	1,704	2,030	2,668	3,408	1,226	1,754	2,090	2,746	3,508	1,248	1,785	2,127	2,795	3,571	1,291	1,846	2,199	2,890	3,692
240	1,191	1,703	2,029	2,667	3,407	1,226	1,752	2,088	2,744	3,506	1,247	1,783	2,125	2,792	3,567	1,289	1,843	2,197	2,887	3,688
245	1,190	1,702	2,028	2,666	3,405	1,225	1,751	2,087	2,742	3,503	1,246	1,782	2,123	2,790	3,564	1,288	1,841	2,194	2,883	3,683
250	1,190	1,702	2,028	2,665	3,404	1,224	1,750	2,085	2,740	3,501	1,245	1,780	2,121	2,788	3,561	1,286	1,839	2,191	2,880	3,678
255	1,190	1,701	2,027	2,664	3,403	1,223	1,749	2,084	2,739	3,499	1,244	1,779	2,119	2,785	3,558	1,284	1,837	2,189	2,876	3,674
260	1,189	1,700	2,026	2,663	3,401	1,222	1,748	2,083	2,737	3,496	1,243	1,777	2,118	2,783	3,555	1,283	1,835	2,186	2,873	3,670
265	1,189	1,700	2,025	2,662	3,400	1,222	1,747	2,081	2,735	3,494	1,242	1,776	2,116	2,781	3,552	1,282	1,833	2,184	2,870	3,666
270	1,188	1,699	2,025	2,661	3,399	1,221	1,746	2,080	2,734	3,492	1,241	1,774	2,114	2,779	3,550	1,280	1,831	2,181	2,867	3,662
275	1,188	1,699	2,024	2,660	3,398	1,220	1,745	2,079	2,732	3,490	1,240	1,773	2,113	2,777	3,547	1,279	1,829	2,179	2,864	3,658
280	1,188	1,698	2,023	2,659	3,397	1,219	1,744	2,078	2,730	3,488	1,239	1,772	2,111	2,775	3,544	1,278	1,827	2,177	2,861	3,655
285	1,187	1,698	2,023	2,658	3,396	1,219	1,743	2,076	2,729	3,486	1,238	1,771	2,110	2,773	3,542	1,276	1,825	2,175	2,858	3,651
290	1,187	1,697	2,022	2,658	3,395	1,218	1,742	2,075	2,727	3,484	1,237	1,769	2,108	2,771	3,540	1,275	1,823	2,173	2,855	3,647
295	1,186	1,697	2,022	2,657	3,394	1,217	1,741	2,074	2,726	3,482	1,237	1,768	2,107	2,769	3,537	1,274	1,822	2,170	2,853	3,644
300	1,186	1,696	2,021	2,656	3,393	1,217	1,740	2,073	2,725	3,481	1,236	1,767	2,106	2,767	3,535	1,273	1,820	2,169	2,850	3,641
310	1,185	1,695	2,020	2,655	3,391	1,216	1,738	2,071	2,722	3,477	1,234	1,765	2,103	2,764	3,531	1,271	1,817	2,165	2,845	3,634
320	1,185	1,694	2,019	2,653	3,389	1,215	1,737	2,069	2,719	3,474	1,233	1,763	2,100	2,760	3,526	1,268	1,814	2,161	2,840	3,628
330	1,184	1,693	2,018	2,652	3,388	1,213	1,735	2,067	2,717	3,471	1,231	1,761	2,098	2,757	3,522	1,266	1,811	2,158	2,836	3,623
340	1,184	1,693	2,017	2,651	3,386	1,212	1,734	2,066	2,715	3,468	1,230	1,759	2,096	2,754	3,519	1,265	1,808	2,154	2,831	3,617
350	1,183	1,692	2,016	2,649	3,384	1,211	1,732	2,064	2,713	3,465	1,229	1,757	2,094	2,752	3,515	1,263	1,805	2,151	2,827	3,612
360	1,183	1,691	2,015	2,648	3,383	1,210	1,731	2,062	2,710	3,463	1,228	1,755	2,092	2,749	3,512	1,261	1,803	2,148	2,823	3,607
370	1,182	1,690	2,014	2,647	3,382	1,210	1,730	2,061	2,708	3,460	1,227	1,754	2,090	2,746	3,508	1,259	1,801	2,146	2,820	3,602
380	1,182	1,690	2,013	2,646	3,380	1,209	1,728	2,059	2,707	3,458	1,225	1,752	2,088	2,744	3,505	1,258	1,798	2,143	2,816	3,598
390	1,181	1,689	2,013	2,645	3,379	1,208	1,727	2,058	2,705	3,455	1,224	1,751	2,086	2,742	3,502	1,256	1,796	2,140	2,813	3,593
400	1,181	1,688	2,012	2,644	3,378	1,207	1,726	2,057	2,703	3,453	1,223	1,749	2,084	2,739	3,499	1,255	1,794	2,138	2,809	3,589
425	1,180	1,687	2,010	2,642	3,375	1,205	1,723	2,054	2,699	3,448	1,221	1,746	2,080	2,734	3,492	1,251	1,789	2,132	2,802	3,579
450	1,179	1,686	2,009	2,640	3,372	1,204	1,721	2,051	2,695	3,443	1,219	1,743	2,077	2,729	3,486	1,248	1,785	2,127	2,795	3,570
475	1,178	1,685	2,007	2,638	3,370	1,202	1,719	2,048	2,692	3,438	1,217	1,740	2,073	2,725	3,481	1,245	1,781	2,122	2,788	3,562
500	1,177	1,683	2,006	2,636	3,368	1,201	1,717	2,046	2,689	3,434	1,215	1,737	2,070	2,721	3,475	1,243	1,777	2,117	2,783	3,555
525	1,177	1,682	2,005	2,635	3,366	1,199	1,715	2,043	2,686	3,431	1,213	1,735	2,067	2,717	3,471	1,240	1,773	2,113	2,777	3,548
550	1,176	1,681	2,004	2,633	3,364	1,198	1,713	2,041	2,683	3,427	1,212	1,733	2,065	2,713	3,466	1,238	1,770	2,109	2,772	3,541
575	1,175	1,681	2,003	2,632	3,362	1,197	1,712	2,039	2,680	3,424	1,210	1,731	2,062	2,710	3,462	1,236	1,767	2,106	2,767	3,535
600	1,175	1,680	2,002	2,631	3,360	1,196	1,710	2,038	2,678	3,421	1,209	1,729	2,060	2,707	3,458	1,234	1,764	2,102	2,763	3,530
625	1,174	1,679	2,001	2,629	3,359	1,195	1,709	2,036	2,676	3,418	1,208	1,727	2,058	2,704	3,455	1,232	1,762	2,099	2,759	3,525
650	1,174	1,678	2,000	2,628	3,357	1,194	1,707	2,034	2,674	3,416	1,207	1,725	2,056	2,702	3,451	1,230	1,759	2,096	2,755	3,520
675	1,173	1,678	1,999	2,627	3,356	1,193	1,706	2,033	2,672	3,413	1,205	1,724	2,054	2,699	3,448	1,229	1,757	2,094	2,752	3,515
700	1,173	1,677	1,998	2,626	3,355	1,192	1,705	2,032	2,670	3,411	1,204	1,722	2,052	2,697	3,445	1,227	1,755	2,091	2,748	3,511
725	1,172	1,676	1,998	2,625	3,354	1,192	1,704	2,030	2,668	3,408	1,203	1,721	2,050	2,694	3,442	1,226	1,753	2,089	2,745	3,507
750	1,172	1,676	1,997	2,624	3,352	1,191	1,703	2,029	2,667	3,406	1,202	1,719	2,049	2,692	3,439	1,225	1,751	2,086	2,742	3,503
800	1,171	1,675	1,996	2,623	3,350	1,189	1,701	2,027	2,663	3,402	1,201	1,717	2,046	2,688	3,434	1,222	1,747	2,082	2,736	3,495
850	1,171	1,674	1,994	2,621	3,348	1,188	1,699	2,025	2,661	3,399	1,199	1,714	2,043	2,685	3,430	1,220	1,744	2,078	2,731	3,489
900	1,170	1,673	1,993	2,620	3,347	1,187	1,697	2,023	2,658	3,396	1,198	1,712	2,040	2,682	3,426	1,218	1,741	2,075	2,726	3,483
950	1,169	1,672	1,992	2,619	3,345	1,186	1,696	2,021	2,656	3,393	1,196	1,710	2,038	2,679	3,422	1,216	1,738	2,071	2,722	3,477
1000	1,169	1,671	1,992	2,617	3,344	1,185	1,695	2,019	2,654	3,390	1,195	1,709	2,036	2,676	3,418	1,214	1,736	2,068	2,718	3,472
∞	1,150	1,645	1,960	2,576	3,291	1,150	1,645	1,960	2,576	3,291	1,150	1,645	1,960	2,576	3,291	1,150	1,645	1,960	2,576	3,291

[1] Bowker, A.H., in Eisenhart et al. (Eds.), *Selected Techniques of Statistical Analysis for Scientific and Industrial Research and Production and Management Engineering*, McGraw-Hill, New York, 1947, page 102. Reprinted by kind permission of the author and publishers.

All values conform to the international convention (i.e. 0,1 instead of 0.1).

For explanation see next page

Correction factors[1] and confidence factors[2] for σ

v	k_s	$1-2\alpha=0{,}90$	$1-2\alpha=0{,}95$	$1-2\alpha=0{,}98$	$1-2\alpha=0{,}99$
1	1,2533	0,5102–15,947	0,4463–31,910	0,3882–79,789	0,3562–159,58
2	1284	0,5777– 4,416	0,5207– 6,285	0,4660– 9,974	0,4344– 14,124
3	0854	0,6196– 2,920	0,5665– 3,729	0,5142– 5,111	0,4834– 6,468
4	0638	0,6493– 2,372	0,5991– 2,874	0,5489– 3,669	0,5188– 4,396
5	1,0509	0,6720– 2,089	0,6242– 2,453	0,5757– 3,003	0,5464– 3,485
6	0424	0,6903– 1,915	0,6444– 2,202	0,5974– 2,623	0,5688– 2,980
7	0362	0,7054– 1,797	0,6612– 2,035	0,6155– 2,377	0,5875– 2,660
8	0317	0,7183– 1,711	0,6755– 1,916	0,6310– 2,204	0,6036– 2,439
9	0281	0,7293– 1,645	0,6878– 1,826	0,6445– 2,076	0,6177– 2,278
10	1,0253	0,7391– 1,593	0,6987– 1,755	0,6564– 1,977	0,6301– 2,154
11	0230	0,7477– 1,551	0,7084– 1,698	0,6670– 1,898	0,6412– 2,056
12	0210	0,7555– 1,515	0,7171– 1,651	0,6765– 1,833	0,6512– 1,976
13	0194	0,7625– 1,485	0,7250– 1,611	0,6852– 1,779	0,6603– 1,910
14	0180	0,7688– 1,460	0,7321– 1,577	0,6931– 1,733	0,6686– 1,854
15	1,0168	0,7747– 1,437	0,7387– 1,548	0,7004– 1,694	0,6762– 1,806
16	0157	0,7800– 1,418	0,7448– 1,522	0,7071– 1,659	0,6833– 1,764
17	0148	0,7850– 1,400	0,7504– 1,499	0,7133– 1,629	0,6899– 1,727
18	0140	0,7896– 1,384	0,7556– 1,479	0,7191– 1,602	0,6960– 1,695
19	0132	0,7939– 1,370	0,7604– 1,461	0,7246– 1,578	0,7018– 1,666
20	1,0126	0,7980– 1,358	0,7651– 1,444	0,7297– 1,556	0,7071– 1,640
21	0120	0,8017– 1,346	0,7694– 1,429	0,7344– 1,536	0,7122– 1,617
22	0114	0,8053– 1,335	0,7734– 1,415	0,7390– 1,518	0,7170– 1,596
23	0109	0,8087– 1,326	0,7772– 1,403	0,7432– 1,502	0,7215– 1,576
24	0105	0,8118– 1,316	0,7808– 1,391	0,7473– 1,487	0,7258– 1,558
25	1,0100	0,8148– 1,308	0,7843– 1,380	0,7511– 1,473	0,7299– 1,542
26	0097	0,8177– 1,300	0,7875– 1,370	0,7548– 1,460	0,7338– 1,526
27	0093	0,8204– 1,293	0,7906– 1,361	0,7582– 1,448	0,7375– 1,512
28	0090	0,8230– 1,286	0,7936– 1,352	0,7616– 1,437	0,7410– 1,499
29	0087	0,8255– 1,280	0,7964– 1,344	0,7647– 1,426	0,7444– 1,487
30	1,0084	0,8279– 1,274	0,7991– 1,337	0,7678– 1,416	0,7476– 1,475
31	0081	0,8301– 1,268	0,8017– 1,329	0,7707– 1,407	0,7507– 1,464
32	0078	0,8323– 1,263	0,8042– 1,323	0,7735– 1,399	0,7537– 1,454
33	0076	0,8344– 1,258	0,8066– 1,316	0,7762– 1,390	0,7566– 1,445
34	0074	0,8364– 1,253	0,8089– 1,310	0,7788– 1,382	0,7594– 1,435
35	1,0072	0,8383– 1,248	0,8111– 1,304	0,7813– 1,375	0,7620– 1,427
36	0070	0,8402– 1,244	0,8132– 1,299	0,7837– 1,368	0,7646– 1,419
37	0068	0,8420– 1,240	0,8153– 1,294	0,7860– 1,362	0,7671– 1,411
38	0066	0,8437– 1,236	0,8172– 1,289	0,7882– 1,355	0,7695– 1,404
39	0064	0,8454– 1,232	0,8192– 1,284	0,7904– 1,349	0,7718– 1,397
40	1,0063	0,8470– 1,228	0,8210– 1,279	0,7925– 1,343	0,7740– 1,390
41	0061	0,8485– 1,225	0,8228– 1,275	0,7945– 1,338	0,7762– 1,383
42	0060	0,8501– 1,222	0,8245– 1,271	0,7965– 1,333	0,7783– 1,377
43	0058	0,8515– 1,218	0,8262– 1,267	0,7984– 1,328	0,7803– 1,372
44	0057	0,8529– 1,215	0,8279– 1,263	0,8002– 1,323	0,7823– 1,366
45	1,0056	0,8543– 1,212	0,8294– 1,260	0,8020– 1,318	0,7842– 1,361
46	0055	0,8556– 1,210	0,8310– 1,256	0,8038– 1,314	0,7861– 1,355
47	0053	0,8569– 1,207	0,8325– 1,253	0,8055– 1,309	0,7879– 1,350
48	0052	0,8582– 1,204	0,8339– 1,249	0,8071– 1,305	0,7897– 1,346
49	0051	0,8594– 1,202	0,8353– 1,246	0,8087– 1,301	0,7914– 1,341
50	1,0050	0,8606– 1,199	0,8367– 1,243	0,8103– 1,297	0,7931– 1,337
51	0049	0,8618– 1,197	0,8380– 1,240	0,8118– 1,294	0,7947– 1,332
52	0048	0,8629– 1,195	0,8394– 1,237	0,8133– 1,290	0,7963– 1,328
53	0047	0,8640– 1,192	0,8406– 1,235	0,8147– 1,287	0,7979– 1,324
54	0046	0,8651– 1,190	0,8419– 1,232	0,8161– 1,283	0,7994– 1,320
55	1,0046	0,8662– 1,188	0,8431– 1,229	0,8175– 1,280	0,8009– 1,316
56	0045	0,8672– 1,186	0,8443– 1,227	0,8189– 1,277	0,8023– 1,313
57	0044	0,8682– 1,184	0,8454– 1,224	0,8202– 1,274	0,8037– 1,309
58	0043	0,8692– 1,182	0,8465– 1,222	0,8215– 1,271	0,8051– 1,306
59	0043	0,8701– 1,180	0,8476– 1,220	0,8227– 1,268	0,8065– 1,303
60	1,0042	0,8710– 1,179	0,8487– 1,217	0,8239– 1,265	0,8078– 1,299
61	0041	0,8719– 1,177	0,8498– 1,215	0,8251– 1,262	0,8091– 1,296
62	0040	0,8728– 1,175	0,8508– 1,213	0,8263– 1,260	0,8103– 1,293
63	0040	0,8737– 1,174	0,8518– 1,211	0,8275– 1,257	0,8116– 1,290
64	0039	0,8746– 1,172	0,8528– 1,209	0,8286– 1,255	0,8128– 1,287
65	1,0039	0,8754– 1,170	0,8537– 1,207	0,8297– 1,252	0,8140– 1,285
66	0038	0,8762– 1,169	0,8547– 1,205	0,8308– 1,250	0,8151– 1,282
67	0037	0,8770– 1,167	0,8556– 1,203	0,8318– 1,248	0,8163– 1,279
68	0037	0,8778– 1,166	0,8565– 1,202	0,8329– 1,245	0,8174– 1,277
69	0036	0,8786– 1,165	0,8574– 1,200	0,8339– 1,243	0,8185– 1,274
70	1,0036	0,8793– 1,163	0,8583– 1,198	0,8349– 1,241	0,8196– 1,272
71	0035	0,8801– 1,162	0,8591– 1,197	0,8359– 1,239	0,8206– 1,269
72	0035	0,8808– 1,160	0,8600– 1,195	0,8368– 1,237	0,8217– 1,267
73	0034	0,8815– 1,159	0,8608– 1,193	0,8378– 1,235	0,8227– 1,265
74	0034	0,8822– 1,158	0,8616– 1,192	0,8387– 1,233	0,8237– 1,263
75	1,0033	0,8829– 1,157	0,8624– 1,190	0,8396– 1,231	0,8247– 1,260
76	0033	0,8836– 1,156	0,8632– 1,189	0,8405– 1,229	0,8256– 1,258
77	0033	0,8842– 1,154	0,8640– 1,187	0,8414– 1,228	0,8266– 1,256
78	0032	0,8849– 1,153	0,8647– 1,186	0,8422– 1,226	0,8275– 1,254
79	0032	0,8855– 1,152	0,8655– 1,184	0,8431– 1,224	0,8284– 1,252
80	1,0031	0,8861– 1,151	0,8662– 1,183	0,8439– 1,222	0,8293– 1,250
81	0031	0,8868– 1,150	0,8669– 1,182	0,8447– 1,221	0,8302– 1,248
82	0031	0,8874– 1,149	0,8676– 1,180	0,8455– 1,219	0,8311– 1,247
83	0030	0,8880– 1,148	0,8683– 1,179	0,8463– 1,218	0,8319– 1,245
84	0030	0,8885– 1,147	0,8690– 1,178	0,8471– 1,216	0,8328– 1,243
85	1,0030	0,8891– 1,146	0,8696– 1,177	0,8479– 1,214	0,8336– 1,241
86	0029	0,8897– 1,145	0,8703– 1,175	0,8486– 1,213	0,8344– 1,240
87	0029	0,8902– 1,144	0,8709– 1,174	0,8494– 1,211	0,8352– 1,238
88	0029	0,8908– 1,143	0,8716– 1,173	0,8501– 1,210	0,8360– 1,236
89	0028	0,8913– 1,142	0,8722– 1,172	0,8508– 1,209	0,8368– 1,235
90	1,0028	0,8919– 1,141	0,8728– 1,171	0,8515– 1,207	0,8375– 1,233
91	0028	0,8924– 1,140	0,8734– 1,170	0,8522– 1,206	0,8383– 1,231
92	0027	0,8929– 1,139	0,8740– 1,169	0,8529– 1,205	0,8390– 1,230
93	0027	0,8934– 1,138	0,8746– 1,168	0,8536– 1,203	0,8398– 1,228
94	0027	0,8939– 1,138	0,8752– 1,167	0,8543– 1,202	0,8405– 1,227
95	1,0026	0,8944– 1,137	0,8758– 1,166	0,8549– 1,201	0,8412– 1,226
96	0026	0,8949– 1,136	0,8764– 1,165	0,8556– 1,199	0,8419– 1,224
97	0026	0,8954– 1,135	0,8769– 1,164	0,8562– 1,198	0,8426– 1,223
98	0026	0,8959– 1,134	0,8775– 1,163	0,8569– 1,197	0,8433– 1,221
99	0025	0,8963– 1,134	0,8780– 1,162	0,8575– 1,196	0,8440– 1,220
100	1,0025	0,8968– 1,133	0,8785– 1,161	0,8581– 1,195	0,8446– 1,219
∞	1,0000	1,0000	1,0000	1,0000	1,0000

[1–4] For footnotes see next page.

Mean extreme range[3] as a multiple of σ

n	0	1	2	3	4	5	6	7	8	9
0	–	–	1,1284	1,6926	2,0588	2,3259	2,5344	2,7044	2,8472	2,9700
10	3,0775	3,1729	3,2585	3,3360	3,4068	3,4718	3,5320	3,5879	3,6401	3,6890
20	3,7350	3,7783	3,8194	3,8583	3,8954	3,9306	3,9643	3,9965	4,0274	4,0570
30	4,0855	4,1129	4,1393	4,1648	4,1894	4,2132	4,2363	4,2586	4,2802	4,3012
40	4,3216	4,3414	4,3606	4,3794	4,3976	4,4154	4,4328	4,4497	4,4662	4,4824
50	4,4982	4,5136	4,5286	4,5434	4,5578	4,5720	4,5858	4,5994	4,6127	4,6258
60	4,6386	4,6511	4,6635	4,6756	4,6875	4,6992	4,7107	4,7219	4,7331	4,7440
70	4,7547	4,7653	4,7757	4,7860	4,7960	4,8060	4,8158	4,8254	4,8349	4,8443
80	4,8536	4,8627	4,8717	4,8805	4,8893	4,8979	4,9064	4,9148	4,9231	4,9313
90	4,9394	4,9474	4,9553	4,9631	4,9708	4,9784	4,9859	4,9934	5,0007	5,0080
100	5,0152	5,0223	5,0293	5,0363	5,0432	5,0500	5,0567	5,0634	5,0700	5,0765
110	5,0830	5,0893	5,0957	5,1020	5,1082	5,1143	5,1204	5,1264	5,1324	5,1383
120	5,1442	5,1500	5,1557	5,1614	5,1671	5,1727	5,1782	5,1837	5,1892	5,1946
130	5,2000	5,2053	5,2106	5,2158	5,2210	5,2261	5,2312	5,2363	5,2413	5,2462
140	5,2512	5,2561	5,2609	5,2658	5,2705	5,2753	5,2800	5,2847	5,2893	5,2939
150	5,2985	5,3030	5,3075	5,3120	5,3165	5,3209	5,3252	5,3296	5,3339	5,3382
160	5,3424	5,3467	5,3509	5,3550	5,3592	5,3633	5,3674	5,3714	5,3755	5,3795
170	5,3834	5,3874	5,3913	5,3952	5,3991	5,4030	5,4068	5,4106	5,4144	5,4181
180	5,4219	5,4256	5,4293	5,4329	5,4366	5,4402	5,4438	5,4474	5,4509	5,4545
190	5,4580	5,4615	5,4650	5,4684	5,4719	5,4753	5,4787	5,4821	5,4854	5,4888
200	5,4921	5,4954	5,4987	5,5020	5,5052	5,5084	5,5117	5,5149	5,5180	5,5212
210	5,5244	5,5275	5,5306	5,5337	5,5368	5,5399	5,5429	5,5459	5,5490	5,5520
220	5,5550	5,5579	5,5609	5,5639	5,5668	5,5697	5,5726	5,5755	5,5784	5,5812
230	5,5841	5,5869	5,5898	5,5926	5,5954	5,5981	5,6009	5,6037	5,6064	5,6091
240	5,6119	5,6146	5,6173	5,6199	5,6226	5,6253	5,6279	5,6305	5,6332	5,6358
250	5,6384	5,6410	5,6435	5,6461	5,6487	5,6512	5,6537	5,6563	5,6588	5,6613
260	5,6638	5,6662	5,6687	5,6712	5,6736	5,6760	5,6785	5,6809	5,6833	5,6857
270	5,6881	5,6905	5,6928	5,6952	5,6975	5,6999	5,7022	5,7045	5,7068	5,7091
280	5,7114	5,7137	5,7160	5,7183	5,7205	5,7228	5,7250	5,7273	5,7295	5,7317
290	5,7339	5,7361	5,7383	5,7405	5,7427	5,7448	5,7470	5,7491	5,7513	5,7534
300	5,7555	5,7577	5,7598	5,7619	5,7640	5,7661	5,7681	5,7702	5,7723	5,7743
310	5,7764	5,7784	5,7805	5,7825	5,7845	5,7865	5,7886	5,7906	5,7926	5,7945
320	5,7965	5,7985	5,8005	5,8024	5,8044	5,8063	5,8083	5,8102	5,8121	5,8141
330	5,8160	5,8179	5,8198	5,8217	5,8236	5,8255	5,8273	5,8292	5,8311	5,8329
340	5,8348	5,8367	5,8385	5,8403	5,8422	5,8440	5,8458	5,8476	5,8494	5,8512
350	5,8530	5,8548	5,8566	5,8584	5,8602	5,8619	5,8637	5,8655	5,8672	5,8690
360	5,8707	5,8724	5,8742	5,8759	5,8776	5,8793	5,8810	5,8827	5,8844	5,8861
370	5,8878	5,8895	5,8912	5,8929	5,8945	5,8962	5,8979	5,8995	5,9012	5,9028
380	5,9045	5,9061	5,9077	5,9094	5,9110	5,9126	5,9142	5,9158	5,9174	5,9190
390	5,9206	5,9222	5,9238	5,9254	5,9270	5,9286	5,9301	5,9317	5,9333	5,9348

n	0	10	20	30	40	50	60	70	80	90
400	5,9364	5,9517	5,9666	5,9811	5,9952	6,0090	6,0225	6,0357	6,0485	6,0611
500	6,0734	6,0854	6,0972	6,1087	6,1200	6,1311	6,1420	6,1526	6,1631	6,1733
600	6,1834	6,1933	6,2030	6,2126	6,2219	6,2312	6,2402	6,2492	6,2579	6,2666
700	6,2751	6,2835	6,2917	6,2999	6,3079	6,3158	6,3235	6,3312	6,3388	6,3462
800	6,3536	6,3608	6,3680	6,3751	6,3820	6,3889	6,3957	6,4025	6,4091	6,4156
900	6,4221	6,4285	6,4348	6,4411	6,4473	6,4534	6,4594	6,4754	6,4713	6,4771

σ as fraction of the mean extreme range[4]

n	0	1	2	3	4	5	6	7	8	9
	0,	0,	0,	0,	0,	0,	0,	0,	0,	0,
0	–	–	88623	59082	48573	42994	39457	36977	35122	33670
10	32494	31517	30689	29976	29353	28803	28313	27872	27472	27108
20	26774	26467	26182	25918	25672	25441	25225	25022	24830	24649
30	24477	24314	24158	24011	23870	23735	23606	23482	23364	23249
40	23140	23034	22932	22834	22739	22648	22559	22473	22390	22310
50	22231	22155	22082	22010	21940	21872	21806	21742	21679	21618
60	21558	21500	21443	21388	21333	21280	21228	21178	21128	21079
70	21032	20985	20939	20894	20851	20807	20765	20724	20683	20643
80	20603	20565	20527	20490	20453	20417	20382	20347	20312	20279
90	20245	20213	20180	20149	20118	20087	20056	20027	19997	19968
100	19939	19911	19883	19856	19829	19802	19776	19750	19724	19699
110	19674	19649	19624	19600	19577	19553	19530	19507	19484	19462
120	19439	19418	19396	19374	19353	19332	19312	19291	19271	19251
130	19231	19211	19192	19173	19154	19135	19116	19098	19079	19061
140	19043	19026	19008	18991	18973	18956	18939	18923	18906	18890
150	18873	18857	18841	18825	18810	18794	18779	18763	18748	18733
160	18718	18703	18689	18674	18660	18645	18631	18617	18603	18589
170	18575	18562	18548	18535	18522	18508	18495	18482	18469	18457
180	18444	18431	18419	18406	18394	18382	18370	18357	18345	18334
190	18322	18310	18298	18287	18275	18264	18253	18241	18230	18219
200	18208	18197	18186	18175	18165	18154	18143	18133	18122	18112
210	18102	18091	18081	18071	18061	18051	18041	18031	18021	18012
220	18002	17992	17983	17973	17964	17954	17945	17936	17926	17917
230	17908	17899	17890	17881	17872	17863	17854	17845	17837	17828
240	17819	17811	17802	17794	17785	17777	17769	17760	17752	17744
250	17736	17727	17719	17711	17703	17695	17687	17680	17672	17664
260	17656	17648	17641	17633	17625	17618	17610	17603	17595	17588
270	17581	17573	17566	17559	17551	17544	17537	17530	17523	17516
280	17509	17502	17495	17488	17481	17474	17467	17460	17454	17447
290	17440	17433	17427	17420	17414	17407	17400	17394	17387	17381
300	17375	17368	17362	17355	17349	17343	17337	17330	17324	17318
310	17312	17306	17300	17294	17287	17281	17275	17270	17264	17258
320	17252	17246	17240	17234	17228	17223	17217	17211	17205	17200
330	17194	17188	17183	17177	17172	17166	17160	17155	17149	17144
340	17139	17133	17128	17122	17117	17112	17106	17101	17096	17090
350	17085	17080	17075	17070	17064	17059	17054	17049	17044	17039
360	17034	17029	17024	17019	17014	17009	17004	16999	16994	16989
370	16984	16979	16974	16970	16965	16960	16955	16951	16946	16941
380	16936	16932	16927	16922	16918	16913	16908	16904	16899	16895
390	16890	16886	16881	16876	16872	16868	16863	16859	16854	16850

n	0	10	20	30	40	50	60	70	80	90
	0,	0,	0,	0,	0,	0,	0,	0,	0,	0,
400	16845	16802	16760	16719	16680	16642	16604	16568	16533	16499
500	16465	16433	16401	16370	16340	16310	16281	16253	16226	16199
600	16172	16146	16121	16096	16072	16048	16025	16002	15980	15958
700	15936	15915	15894	15873	15853	15833	15814	15795	15776	15757
800	15739	15721	15704	15686	15669	15652	15636	15619	15603	15587
900	15571	15556	15540	15525	15510	15496	15481	15443	15453	15439

All values conform to the international convention (i.e. 0,1 instead of 0.1).

$\sigma_{\bar{x}}$ as fraction of the mean extreme range[4] (for explanation see below)

n	2	3	4	5	6	7	8	9	10	11	12	13	14	15	16	17	18	19	20
m	*0,* 0,0	*0,* 0,0	*0,* 0,0	*0,* 0,0	*0,* 0,0	*0,* 0,0	*0,* 0,0	*0,* 0,0	*0,* 0,0	0,0	0,0	0,0	0,0	0,0	0,0	0,0 *0,00*	0,0 *0,00*	0,0 *0,00*	0,0 *0,00*
1	*62666*	*34111*	*24287*	*19227*	*16108*	*13976*	*12418*	*11223*	*10275*	95027	88592	83139	78450	74370	70782	67599	64752	62190	59869
2	*44311*	*24120*	*17173*	*13596*	*11390*	98826	87806	79360	72658	67195	62644	58788	55473	52587	50050	47799	45787	43975	42334
3	*36180*	*19694*	*14022*	*11101*	93001	80691	71693	64797	59325	54864	51149	48000	45293	42937	40866	39028	37385	35905	34565
4	*31333*	*17055*	*12143*	96137	80541	69548	62088	56116	51377	47514	44296	41569	39225	37185	35391	33799	32376	31095	29934
5	*28025*	*15255*	*10861*	85987	72038	62503	55533	50192	45953	42498	39620	37181	35084	33259	31655	30231	28958	27812	26774
6	*25583*	*13926*	99150	78495	65762	57057	50695	45819	41949	38795	36168	33941	32027	30361	28897	27597	26435	25389	24441
7	*23685*	*12893*	91795	72672	60883	52825	46934	42420	38838	35917	33485	31424	29651	28109	26753	25550	24474	23506	22628
8	*22156*	*12060*	85866	67979	56951	49413	43903	39680	36329	33597	31322	29394	27736	26294	25025	23900	22893	21987	21167
9	*20889*	*11370*	80955	64091	53694	46587	41392	37411	34251	31676	29531	27713	26150	24790	23594	22533	21584	20730	19956
10	*19817*	*10787*	76801	60802	50939	44196	39268	35491	32494	30050	28015	26291	24808	23518	22383	21377	20476	19666	18932
11	*18894*	*10285*	73227	57973	48568	42140	37440	33839	30982	28652	26712	25067	23654	22423	21342	20382	19524	18751	18051
12	*18090*	98470	70109	55504	46500	40346	35846	32399	29663	27432	25574	24000	22647	21469	20433	19514	18692	17953	17283
13	*17380*	94607	67359	53327	44676	38763	34440	31128	28499	26356	24571	23059	21758	20626	19631	18748	17959	17248	16605
14	*16748*	91165	64909	51387	43051	37353	33187	29995	27462	25397	23677	22220	20967	19876	18917	18066	17306	16621	16001
15	*16180*	88074	62708	49645	41591	36086	32062	28978	26531	24536	22874	21466	20256	19202	18276	17454	16719	16057	15458
16	*15666*	85277	60716	48068	40271	34940	31044	28058	25689	23757	22148	20785	19613	18592	17695	16900	16188	15547	14967
17	*15199*	82731	58904	46633	39068	33897	30117	27220	24922	23048	21487	20164	19027	18037	17167	16395	15705	15083	14520
18	*14770*	80400	57244	45319	37967	32942	29269	26453	24219	22398	20881	19596	18491	17529	16683	15933	15262	14658	14111
19	*14376*	78256	55717	44110	36955	32063	28488	25748	23573	21801	20325	19073	17998	17062	16238	15508	14855	14267	13735
20	*14012*	76274	54306	42994	36019	31252	27767	25096	22977	21249	19810	18590	17542	16630	15827	15115	14479	13906	13387
21	*13675*	74436	52998	41957	35151	30498	27097	24491	22423	20737	19332	18142	17119	16229	15446	14751	14130	13571	13064
22	*13360*	72725	51779	40993	34343	29797	26474	23928	21907	20260	18888	17725	16726	15856	15091	14412	13805	13259	12764
23	*13067*	71126	50641	40092	33588	29142	25892	23402	21426	19815	18473	17336	16358	15507	14759	14095	13502	12967	12483
24	*12792*	69628	49575	39248	32881	28529	25347	22909	20975	19397	18084	16971	16014	15181	14448	13799	13218	12694	12220
25	*12533*	68222	48573	38455	32216	27952	24835	22446	20551	19006	17718	16628	15690	14874	14156	13520	12950	12438	11974
26	*12290*	66897	47630	37708	31591	27409	24353	22011	20152	18637	17374	16305	15385	14585	13881	13257	12699	12196	11741
27	*12060*	65646	46740	37003	31000	26897	23898	21599	19775	18288	17050	16000	15098	14312	13622	13009	12462	11968	11522
28	*11843*	64463	45897	36336	30442	26412	23467	21210	19419	17959	16742	15712	14826	14055	13377	12775	12237	11753	11314
29	*11637*	63342	45099	35704	29912	25953	23059	20841	19081	17646	16451	15439	14568	13810	13144	12553	12024	11548	11117
30	*11441*	62278	44341	35104	29409	25517	22671	20491	18760	17350	16175	15179	14323	13578	12923	12342	11822	11354	10930
31	*11255*	61265	43620	34533	28931	25102	22303	20158	18455	17068	15912	14932	14090	13357	12713	12141	11630	11170	10753
32	*11078*	60300	42932	33989	28476	24707	21951	19840	18165	16799	15661	14697	13868	13147	12513	11950	11447	10994	10583
33	*10909*	59379	42277	33470	28041	24329	21616	19537	17887	16542	15422	14473	13656	12946	12322	11767	11272	10826	10422
34	*10747*	58500	41651	32975	27625	23969	21296	19248	17622	16297	15193	14258	13454	12754	12139	11593	11105	10665	10267
35	*10592*	57658	41052	32500	27228	23624	20990	18971	17369	16063	14975	14053	13261	12571	11964	11426	10945	10512	10120
36	*10444*	56851	40478	32046	26847	23294	20696	18705	17126	15838	14765	13856	13075	12395	11797	11266	10792	10365	*99781*
37	*10302*	56078	39927	31610	26482	22977	20414	18451	16893	15623	14565	13668	12897	12226	11636	11113	10645	10224	*98424*
38	*10166*	55335	39398	31191	26131	22672	20144	18206	16669	15416	14372	13487	12726	12064	11482	10966	10504	10089	*97120*
39	*10035*	54621	38890	30788	25794	22380	19884	17972	16454	15217	14186	13313	12562	11909	11334	10824	10369	*99583*	*95867*
40	99083	53934	38400	30401	25469	22098	19634	17745	16247	15025	14008	13145	12404	11759	11192	10688	10238	*98331*	*94661*
41	97867	53272	37929	30028	25157	21827	19393	17528	16048	14841	13836	12984	12252	11615	11054	10557	10113	*97124*	*93499*
42	96695	52634	37475	29668	24856	21566	19161	17318	15855	14663	13670	12829	12105	11476	10922	10431	*99915*	*95961*	*92380*
43	95564	52019	37037	29321	24565	21313	18937	17115	15670	14492	13510	12679	11964	11341	10794	10309	*98746*	*94839*	*91299*
44	94472	51424	36613	28986	24284	21070	18720	16920	15491	14326	13356	12534	11827	11212	10671	10191	*97618*	*93755*	*90256*
45	93416	50849	36204	28662	24013	20834	18511	16731	15318	14166	13207	12394	11695	11086	10552	10077	*96527*	*92707*	*89247*
46	92395	50294	35809	28349	23750	20607	18309	16548	15150	14011	13062	12258	11567	10965	10436	*99668*	*95472*	*91694*	*88272*
47	91407	49756	35426	28046	23496	20386	18113	16371	14988	13861	12923	12127	11443	10848	10325	*98603*	*94451*	*90713*	*87328*
48	90450	49235	35055	27752	23250	20173	17923	16199	14831	13716	12787	12000	11323	10734	10216	*97570*	*93462*	*89763*	*86413*
49	89522	48730	34695	27468	23012	19966	17739	16033	14679	13575	12656	11877	11207	10624	10112	*96569*	*92503*	*88843*	*85527*
50	88623	48240	34346	27192	22780	19765	17561	15872	14532	13439	12529	11758	11095	10517	10010	*95599*	*91574*	*87950*	*84667*

Explanation to the pages 54–56:

Correction factors[1] and confidence factors[2] for σ

(a) The estimate s^2 of σ^2 is unbiased, but s is not an unbiased estimator of σ. This bias is eliminated by multiplying s by the factor k_s.

(b) Confidence limits for σ. Columns 3–6 give the confidence factors by which s must be multiplied in order to obtain the confidence limits that include σ with a probability of $1-2\alpha$.

Extreme range

If x_1 is the lowest and x_n the highest value of a sample of size n, then $x_n - x_1$ is the extreme range w_n of this sample.
The standardized extreme range of a sample of size n from a population with standard deviation σ is

$$W_n = \frac{w_n}{\sigma} = \frac{x_n - x_1}{\sigma}$$

The mean extreme range of m samples of size n from the same population is

$$\bar{w}_{m,n} = \frac{\sum\limits_1^m w_n}{m} = \frac{\sum\limits_1^m (x_n - x_1)}{m}$$

The standardized mean extreme range is

$$\overline{W}_{m,n} = \frac{\bar{w}_{m,n}}{\sigma} = \frac{\sum\limits_1^m w_n}{m\,\sigma} = \frac{\sum\limits_1^m (x_n - x_1)}{m\,\sigma}$$

Since the extreme range w_n is merely a special case of the mean extreme range $\bar{w}_{m,n}$ with $m = 1$, only the mean extreme range will be referred to in the text that follows.

Mean extreme range[3] as a multiple of σ

The expected value $\mathbf{W}_n$ of the extreme range of random samples of size n from a normally distributed population with unit standard deviation satisfies the relation

$$\overline{W}_{m,n} \underset{(m\to\infty)}{\to} \mathbf{W}_n$$

The table gives values of $\mathbf{W}_n$ for the standardized normal distribution as multiples of σ. (Many authors use d_n instead of $\mathbf{W}_n$.)

σ as a fraction of the mean extreme range[4]

The quotient $\dfrac{\bar{w}_{m,n}}{\mathbf{W}_n} = \bar{w}_{m,n} \times \mathbf{A}_n$

gives an unbiased estimate of σ that improves as m increases but rapidly worsens as the size n of the individual samples increases. Its variance is also greater than s.
With small samples (n between 5 and 10), however, there is practically no difference between the accuracy of the two estimates, even for $m = 1$.

$\sigma_{\bar{x}}$ as a fraction of the mean extreme range[4]

The quotient $\dfrac{\bar{w}_{m,n}}{\mathbf{W}_n\sqrt{m\,n}} = \bar{w}_{m,n} \times \mathbf{A}_{m,n}$

where $m\,n$ = sample size N, gives an unbiased estimate of the standard deviation $\sigma_{\bar{x}}$ of the estimate $\bar{x}$. See remarks in the previous paragraph. Values of the factor $\mathbf{A}_{m,n}$ are given in the table above.

Significance limits for the difference between two means based on the extreme range

The table on page 56 gives the 2α significance limits for u (where $m = m' + m''$):

$$u = \frac{(\bar{x} - \mu)\,m}{[\Sigma(x_n - x_1)]\,\mathbf{A}_{m,n}}$$

when $m = 1$, the test is much simpler (see page 60),

$$u = \frac{(\bar{x}' - \bar{x}'')\sqrt{m'\,m''}}{[\Sigma(x_n' - x_1') + \Sigma(x_n'' - x_1'')]\,\mathbf{A}_{m,n}}$$

when $m' = m'' = 1$, the test is much simpler [see page 60 and also (**622**), page 209].

[1] Calculated from values in PEARSON and HARTLEY (Eds.), *Biometrika Tables for Statisticians*, 3rd ed., volume 1, Cambridge University Press, Cambridge, 1970.

[2] Calculated from χ^2-values in PEARSON and HARTLEY[1] and from data of HALD and SINKBÆK, *Skand. Aktuar Tidskr.*, **33**, 168 (1950). Reproduction only by permission of the publishers of the *Geigy Scientific Tables*.

[3] TIPPETT, L.H., *Biometrika*, **17**, 364 (1925). Reprinted by kind permission of the author and publishers.

[4] Calculated from values of TIPPETT, L.H., *Biometrika*, **17**, 364 (1925). Reproduction only by permission of the publishers of the *Geigy Scientific Tables*.

All values conform to the international convention (i.e. 0,1 instead of 0.1).

The Extreme Range Test[1]: The Difference Between Two Means*

n / m	2	3	4	5	6	7	8	9	10	11	12	13	14	15	16	17	18	19	20
	$2\alpha=0,10$																		
1	5,04	2,59	2,18	2,02	1,94	1,88	1,85	1,82	1,81	1,79	1,78	1,77	1,76	1,75	1,75	1,74	1,74	1,73	1,73
2	2,62	02	1,88	1,81	78	76	74	73	72	71	71	71	70	70	70	69	69	69	69
3	20	1,88	79	75	73	72	71	70	70	69	69	69	68	68	68	68	68	67	67
4	03	81	75	73	71	70	69	69	68	68	68	68	67	67	67	67	67	67	67
5	1,94	1,77	1,73	1,71	1,70	1,69	1,68	1,68	1,68	1,68	1,67	1,67	1,67	1,67	1,67	1,67	1,66	1,66	1,66
6	89	75	72	70	69	68	68	67	67	67	67	67	66	66	66	66	66	66	66
7	85	73	71	69	68	67	67	67	66	66	66	66	66	66	66	66	66	66	66
8	82	72	70	68	68	67	67	67	66	66	66	66	66	66	66	66	66	66	66
9	80	71	69	68	67	67	67	66	66	66	66	66	66	66	66	66	66	66	66
10	1,78	1,71	1,69	1,68	1,67	1,67	1,66	1,66	1,66	1,66	1,66	1,66	1,66	1,66	1,65	1,65	1,65	1,65	1,65
11	77	71	68	68	67	67	66	66	66	66	66	66	66	66	65	65	65	65	65
12	76	70	68	68	66	66	66	66	65	65	65	65	65	65	65	65	65	65	65
13	75	70	67	67	66	66	66	66	65	65	65	65	65	65	65	65	65	65	65
14	74	69	67	67	66	66	66	66	65	65	65	65	65	65	65	65	65	65	65
15	1,73	1,69	1,67	1,67	1,66	1,66	1,66	1,66	1,65	1,65	1,65	1,65	1,65	1,65	1,65	1,65	1,65	1,65	1,65
16	72	69	67	67	66	66	66	66	65	65	65	65	65	65	65	65	65	65	65
17	72	68	67	67	66	66	66	66	65	65	65	65	65	65	65	65	65	65	65
18	72	68	67	66	66	66	65	65	65	65	65	65	65	65	65	65	65	65	65
19	71	67	67	66	66	66	65	65	65	65	65	65	65	65	65	65	65	65	65
20	1,71	1,67	1,67	1,66	1,66	1,66	1,65	1,65	1,65	1,65	1,65	1,65	1,65	1,65	1,65	1,65	1,65	1,65	1,65
30	69	66	66	66	65	65	65	65	65	65	65	65	65	65	65	65	65	65	65
60	67	66	65	65	65	65	65	65	65	65	65	65	65	65	65	65	65	65	65
120	66	65	65	65	65	65	65	65	65	65	65	65	65	65	65	65	65	65	65
	$2\alpha=0,05$																		
1	10,14	3,82	2,95	2,63	2,48	2,38	2,32	2,27	2,24	2,21	2,19	2,17	2,16	2,15	2,14	2,13	2,12	2,11	2,11
2	3,87	2,64	37	25	19	15	13	11	09	08	07	06	06	05	05	04	04	03	03
3	2,98	37	22	15	11	09	07	06	05	04	03	02	02	02	02	01	01	01	01
4	66	25	15	10	07	05	04	03	02	01	01	01	01	00	00	00	00	00	00
5	2,49	2,19	2,11	2,07	2,05	2,03	2,02	2,02	2,01	2,01	2,00	2,00	2,00	1,99	1,99	1,99	1,99	1,99	1,99
6	38	14	08	05	03	02	01	01	00	00	00	00	1,99	99	99	99	99	99	99
7	31	11	06	04	02	02	01	00	1,99	1,99	1,99	1,99	99	98	98	98	98	98	98
8	26	09	05	03	01	01	00	00	99	99	99	99	98	98	98	98	98	98	98
9	23	08	04	02	01	00	1,99	1,99	99	99	98	98	98	98	98	98	98	98	98
10	2,20	2,07	2,03	2,01	2,00	2,00	1,99	1,99	1,98	1,98	1,98	1,98	1,98	1,98	1,98	1,98	1,98	1,97	1,97
11	17	06	02	01	00	1,99	99	99	98	98	98	98	98	98	98	98	98	97	97
12	15	05	02	01	00	99	98	99	98	98	97	97	97	97	97	97	97	97	97
13	14	04	02	00	1,99	98	98	98	98	98	97	97	97	97	97	97	97	97	97
14	12	04	01	00	99	98	98	98	98	98	97	97	97	97	97	97	97	97	97
15	2,11	2,03	2,01	2,00	1,99	1,98	1,98	1,98	1,98	1,98	1,97	1,97	1,97	1,97	1,97	1,97	1,97	1,97	1,97
16	10	03	01	00	99	98	98	98	98	98	97	97	97	97	97	97	97	97	97
17	09	02	01	00	99	98	98	98	98	98	97	97	97	97	97	97	97	97	97
18	08	02	00	1,99	98	98	98	97	97	97	97	97	97	97	97	97	97	97	97
19	08	01	00	99	98	98	98	97	97	97	97	97	97	97	97	97	97	97	97
20	2,07	2,01	2,00	1,99	1,98	1,98	1,98	1,97	1,97	1,97	1,97	1,97	1,97	1,97	1,97	1,97	1,97	1,97	1,97
30	03	1,99	1,98	98	97	97	97	97	97	97	97	97	97	97	97	97	97	96	96
60	00	98	97	97	97	97	97	96	96	96	96	96	96	96	96	96	96	96	96
120	1,98	97	97	96	96	96	96	96	96	96	96	96	96	96	96	96	96	96	96
	$2\alpha=0,02$																		
1	25,39	6,19	4,21	3,56	3,25	3,07	2,95	2,87	2,81	2,76	2,72	2,69	2,67	2,65	2,63	2,61	2,60	2,59	2,58
2	6,27	3,56	3,05	2,84	2,73	2,66	61	58	55	53	51	50	49	48	47	46	46	45	45
3	4,27	05	2,77	65	58	54	51	49	47	46	45	44	43	43	42	42	41	41	41
4	3,60	2,84	65	56	51	48	46	45	44	43	42	42	41	41	40	40	39	39	39
5	3,27	2,72	2,58	2,51	2,47	2,45	2,43	2,42	2,41	2,41	2,40	2,40	2,39	2,39	2,38	2,38	2,38	2,37	2,37
6	08	65	53	48	45	43	42	41	40	39	39	38	38	38	37	37	37	37	37
7	2,95	60	50	46	43	41	40	40	39	38	38	37	37	37	36	36	36	36	36
8	86	56	48	44	42	40	39	39	38	38	37	37	37	37	36	36	36	36	36
9	79	53	46	43	41	39	38	38	37	37	37	36	36	36	35	35	35	35	35
10	2,73	2,51	2,45	2,42	2,40	2,39	2,38	2,37	2,37	2,37	2,36	2,36	2,36	2,36	2,35	2,35	2,35	2,35	2,35
11	69	49	44	41	39	38	37	37	36	36	36	36	36	36	35	35	35	35	35
12	66	48	43	41	38	38	37	37	36	36	36	36	36	36	35	35	35	35	34
13	63	47	42	40	38	38	37	36	36	36	35	35	35	35	35	34	34	34	34
14	61	46	42	40	37	37	36	36	35	35	35	35	35	35	35	34	34	34	34
15	2,59	2,45	2,41	2,39	2,37	2,37	2,36	2,36	2,35	2,35	2,35	2,35	2,35	2,35	2,35	2,34	2,34	2,34	2,34
16	57	44	41	39	37	37	36	36	35	35	35	35	35	35	35	34	34	34	34
17	56	44	40	38	36	37	36	36	35	35	35	35	35	35	35	34	34	34	34
18	54	43	40	38	36	36	35	35	35	34	34	34	34	34	34	34	34	34	34
19	53	42	39	37	36	36	35	35	35	34	34	34	34	34	34	34	34	34	34
20	2,52	2,42	2,39	2,37	2,36	2,36	2,35	2,35	2,35	2,34	2,34	2,34	2,34	2,34	2,34	2,34	2,34	2,34	2,34
30	45	39	37	36	35	35	34	34	34	34	34	34	34	34	34	33	33	33	33
60	39	36	35	34	34	34	33	33	33	33	33	33	33	33	33	33	33	33	33
120	36	34	34	33	33	33	33	33	33	33	33	33	33	33	33	33	33	33	33
	$2\alpha=0,01$																		
1	50,79	8,82	5,42	4,38	3,90	3,63	3,45	3,33	3,24	3,17	3,12	3,08	3,05	3,02	2,99	2,97	2,95	2,93	2,92
2	8,93	4,34	3,60	3,29	13	03	2,97	2,92	2,88	2,85	2,83	2,81	2,80	2,79	78	77	76	75	74
3	5,49	3,60	20	02	2,93	2,87	83	80	78	76	74	73	72	71	71	70	70	69	69
4	4,43	30	02	2,90	83	79	76	74	72	71	70	69	69	68	67	66	66	66	66
5	3,93	3,14	2,92	2,83	2,78	2,75	2,72	2,71	2,69	2,68	2,68	2,67	2,66	2,66	2,65	2,65	2,65	2,64	2,64
6	64	03	86	79	74	72	70	68	67	66	66	65	65	64	64	64	63	63	63
7	46	2,96	82	75	72	70	68	67	66	65	65	64	64	63	63	63	62	62	62
8	32	91	79	73	70	68	67	66	65	64	64	63	63	62	62	62	62	62	62
9	21	87	77	71	68	67	66	65	64	63	63	63	62	62	62	62	61	61	61
10	3,14	2,84	2,74	2,70	2,67	2,66	2,65	2,64	2,63	2,63	2,62	2,62	2,62	2,62	2,61	2,61	2,61	2,61	2,61
11	08	82	72	69	66	65	64	64	63	62	62	62	62	61	61	61	61	61	61
12	03	80	71	68	66	64	63	63	62	62	62	62	61	61	61	61	61	61	61
13	2,99	78	70	67	65	64	63	63	62	62	61	61	61	60	60	60	60	60	60
14	96	76	69	67	65	63	62	62	61	61	61	61	60	60	60	60	60	60	60
15	2,93	2,75	2,68	2,66	2,64	2,63	2,62	2,62	2,61	2,61	2,61	2,61	2,60	2,60	2,60	2,60	2,60	2,60	2,60
16	91	74	68	66	64	63	62	62	61	61	61	61	60	60	60	60	60	60	60
17	89	73	67	65	63	63	61	62	61	61	61	61	60	60	60	60	60	60	60
18	87	72	67	65	63	62	61	61	60	60	60	60	60	60	60	59	59	59	59
19	85	71	66	64	62	62	61	61	60	60	60	60	60	60	60	59	59	59	59
20	2,84	2,70	2,66	2,64	2,62	2,62	2,61	2,61	2,60	2,60	2,60	2,60	2,60	2,60	2,60	2,59	2,59	2,59	2,59
30	75	66	63	62	61	60	60	60	59	59	59	59	59	59	59	59	59	59	59
60	66	62	60	60	59	59	59	59	59	58	58	58	58	58	58	58	58	58	58
120	62	60	59	59	58	58	58	58	58	58	58	58	58	58	58	58	58	58	58

* For explanation see page 55.

[1] Values from LORD, E., *Biometrika*, **34**, 41 (1947) (with interpolations). Reprinted by kind permission of the author and publishers.

All values conform to the international convention (i.e. 0,1 instead of 0.1).

Duncan's Multiple Comparison Test[1]

For explanation see page 210

n / ν	2	3	4	5	6	7	8	9	10	11	12	13	14	15	16	17	18	19	20	22	24	26	28	30	32	34	36	38	40	50	60
	α = 0,05																														
1	17,97	17,97	17,97	17,97	17,97	17,97	17,97	17,97	17,97	17,97	17,97	17,97	17,97	17,97	17,97	17,97	17,97	17,97	17,97	17,97	17,97	17,97	17,97	17,97	17,97	17,97	17,97	17,97	17,97	17,97	17,97
2	6,085	6,085	6,085	6,085	6,085	6,085	6,085	6,085	6,085	6,085	6,085	6,085	6,085	6,085	6,085	6,085	6,085	6,085	6,085	6,085	6,085	6,085	6,085	6,085	6,085	6,085	6,085	6,085	6,085	6,085	6,085
3	4,501	4,516	4,516	4,516	4,516	4,516	4,516	4,516	4,516	4,516	4,516	4,516	4,516	4,516	4,516	4,516	4,516	4,516	4,516	4,516	4,516	4,516	4,516	4,516	4,516	4,516	4,516	4,516	4,516	4,516	4,516
4	3,927	4,013	4,033	4,033	4,033	4,033	4,033	4,033	4,033	4,033	4,033	4,033	4,033	4,033	4,033	4,033	4,033	4,033	4,033	4,033	4,033	4,033	4,033	4,033	4,033	4,033	4,033	4,033	4,033	4,033	4,033
5	3,635	3,749	3,797	3,814	3,814	3,814	3,814	3,814	3,814	3,814	3,814	3,814	3,814	3,814	3,814	3,814	3,814	3,814	3,814	3,814	3,814	3,814	3,814	3,814	3,814	3,814	3,814	3,814	3,814	3,814	3,814
6	3,461	3,587	3,649	3,680	3,694	3,697	3,697	3,697	3,697	3,697	3,697	3,697	3,697	3,697	3,697	3,697	3,697	3,697	3,697	3,697	3,697	3,697	3,697	3,697	3,697	3,697	3,697	3,697	3,697	3,697	3,697
7	3,344	3,477	3,548	3,588	3,611	3,622	3,626	3,626	3,626	3,626	3,626	3,626	3,626	3,626	3,626	3,626	3,626	3,626	3,626	3,626	3,626	3,626	3,626	3,626	3,626	3,626	3,626	3,626	3,626	3,626	3,626
8	3,261	3,399	3,475	3,521	3,549	3,566	3,575	3,579	3,579	3,579	3,579	3,579	3,579	3,579	3,579	3,579	3,579	3,579	3,579	3,579	3,579	3,579	3,579	3,579	3,579	3,579	3,579	3,579	3,579	3,579	3,579
9	3,199	3,339	3,420	3,470	3,502	3,523	3,536	3,544	3,547	3,547	3,547	3,547	3,547	3,547	3,547	3,547	3,547	3,547	3,547	3,547	3,547	3,547	3,547	3,547	3,547	3,547	3,547	3,547	3,547	3,547	3,547
10	3,151	3,293	3,376	3,430	3,465	3,489	3,505	3,516	3,522	3,525	3,526	3,526	3,526	3,526	3,526	3,526	3,526	3,526	3,526	3,526	3,526	3,526	3,526	3,526	3,526	3,526	3,526	3,526	3,526	3,526	3,526
11	3,113	3,256	3,342	3,397	3,435	3,462	3,480	3,493	3,501	3,506	3,509	3,510	3,510	3,510	3,510	3,510	3,510	3,510	3,510	3,510	3,510	3,510	3,510	3,510	3,510	3,510	3,510	3,510	3,510	3,510	3,510
12	3,082	3,225	3,313	3,370	3,410	3,439	3,459	3,474	3,484	3,491	3,496	3,498	3,499	3,499	3,499	3,499	3,499	3,499	3,499	3,499	3,499	3,499	3,499	3,499	3,499	3,499	3,499	3,499	3,499	3,499	3,499
13	3,055	3,200	3,289	3,348	3,389	3,419	3,442	3,458	3,470	3,478	3,484	3,488	3,490	3,490	3,490	3,490	3,490	3,490	3,490	3,490	3,490	3,490	3,490	3,490	3,490	3,490	3,490	3,490	3,490	3,490	3,490
14	3,033	3,178	3,268	3,329	3,372	3,403	3,426	3,444	3,457	3,467	3,474	3,479	3,482	3,484	3,484	3,485	3,485	3,485	3,485	3,485	3,485	3,485	3,485	3,485	3,485	3,485	3,485	3,485	3,485	3,485	3,485
15	3,014	3,160	3,250	3,312	3,356	3,389	3,413	3,432	3,446	3,457	3,465	3,471	3,476	3,478	3,480	3,481	3,481	3,481	3,481	3,481	3,481	3,481	3,481	3,481	3,481	3,481	3,481	3,481	3,481	3,481	3,481
16	2,998	3,144	3,235	3,298	3,343	3,376	3,402	3,422	3,437	3,449	3,458	3,465	3,470	3,473	3,477	3,478	3,478	3,478	3,478	3,478	3,478	3,478	3,478	3,478	3,478	3,478	3,478	3,478	3,478	3,478	3,478
17	2,984	3,130	3,222	3,285	3,331	3,366	3,392	3,412	3,429	3,441	3,451	3,459	3,465	3,469	3,473	3,475	3,476	3,476	3,476	3,476	3,476	3,476	3,476	3,476	3,476	3,476	3,476	3,476	3,476	3,476	3,476
18	2,971	3,118	3,210	3,274	3,321	3,356	3,383	3,405	3,421	3,435	3,445	3,454	3,460	3,465	3,470	3,472	3,474	3,474	3,474	3,474	3,474	3,474	3,474	3,474	3,474	3,474	3,474	3,474	3,474	3,474	3,474
19	2,960	3,107	3,199	3,264	3,311	3,347	3,375	3,397	3,415	3,429	3,440	3,449	3,456	3,462	3,467	3,470	3,472	3,473	3,474	3,474	3,474	3,474	3,474	3,474	3,474	3,474	3,474	3,474	3,474	3,474	3,474
20	2,950	3,097	3,190	3,255	3,303	3,339	3,368	3,391	3,409	3,424	3,436	3,445	3,453	3,459	3,464	3,467	3,470	3,472	3,473	3,474	3,474	3,474	3,474	3,474	3,474	3,474	3,474	3,474	3,474	3,474	3,474
24	2,919	3,066	3,160	3,226	3,276	3,315	3,345	3,370	3,390	3,406	3,420	3,432	3,441	3,449	3,456	3,461	3,465	3,469	3,471	3,475	3,477	3,477	3,477	3,477	3,477	3,477	3,477	3,477	3,477	3,477	3,477
30	2,888	3,035	3,131	3,199	3,250	3,290	3,322	3,349	3,371	3,389	3,405	3,418	3,430	3,439	3,447	3,454	3,460	3,466	3,470	3,477	3,481	3,484	3,486	3,486	3,486	3,486	3,486	3,486	3,486	3,486	3,486
40	2,858	3,006	3,102	3,171	3,224	3,266	3,300	3,328	3,352	3,373	3,390	3,405	3,418	3,429	3,439	3,448	3,456	3,463	3,469	3,479	3,486	3,492	3,497	3,500	3,503	3,504	3,504	3,504	3,504	3,504	3,504
60	2,829	2,976	3,073	3,143	3,198	3,241	3,277	3,307	3,333	3,355	3,374	3,391	3,406	3,419	3,431	3,442	3,451	3,460	3,467	3,481	3,492	3,501	3,509	3,515	3,521	3,525	3,529	3,531	3,534	3,537	3,537
120	2,800	2,947	3,045	3,116	3,172	3,217	3,254	3,287	3,314	3,337	3,359	3,377	3,394	3,409	3,423	3,435	3,446	3,457	3,466	3,483	3,498	3,511	3,522	3,532	3,541	3,548	3,555	3,561	3,566	3,585	3,596
∞	2,772	2,918	3,017	3,089	3,146	3,193	3,232	3,265	3,294	3,320	3,343	3,363	3,382	3,399	3,414	3,428	3,442	3,454	3,466	3,486	3,505	3,522	3,536	3,550	3,562	3,574	3,584	3,594	3,603	3,640	3,668
	α = 0,01																														
1	90,03	90,03	90,03	90,03	90,03	90,03	90,03	90,03	90,03	90,03	90,03	90,03	90,03	90,03	90,03	90,03	90,03	90,03	90,03	90,03	90,03	90,03	90,03	90,03	90,03	90,03	90,03	90,03	90,03	90,03	90,03
2	14,04	14,04	14,04	14,04	14,04	14,04	14,04	14,04	14,04	14,04	14,04	14,04	14,04	14,04	14,04	14,04	14,04	14,04	14,04	14,04	14,04	14,04	14,04	14,04	14,04	14,04	14,04	14,04	14,04	14,04	14,04
3	8,261	8,321	8,321	8,321	8,321	8,321	8,321	8,321	8,321	8,321	8,321	8,321	8,321	8,321	8,321	8,321	8,321	8,321	8,321	8,321	8,321	8,321	8,321	8,321	8,321	8,321	8,321	8,321	8,321	8,321	8,321
4	6,512	6,677	6,740	6,756	6,756	6,756	6,756	6,756	6,756	6,756	6,756	6,756	6,756	6,756	6,756	6,756	6,756	6,756	6,756	6,756	6,756	6,756	6,756	6,756	6,756	6,756	6,756	6,756	6,756	6,756	6,756
5	5,702	5,893	5,989	6,040	6,065	6,074	6,074	6,074	6,074	6,074	6,074	6,074	6,074	6,074	6,074	6,074	6,074	6,074	6,074	6,074	6,074	6,074	6,074	6,074	6,074	6,074	6,074	6,074	6,074	6,074	6,074
6	5,243	5,439	5,549	5,614	5,655	5,680	5,694	5,701	5,703	5,703	5,703	5,703	5,703	5,703	5,703	5,703	5,703	5,703	5,703	5,703	5,703	5,703	5,703	5,703	5,703	5,703	5,703	5,703	5,703	5,703	5,703
7	4,949	5,145	5,260	5,334	5,383	5,416	5,439	5,454	5,464	5,470	5,472	5,472	5,472	5,472	5,472	5,472	5,472	5,472	5,472	5,472	5,472	5,472	5,472	5,472	5,472	5,472	5,472	5,472	5,472	5,472	5,472
8	4,746	4,939	5,057	5,135	5,189	5,227	5,256	5,276	5,291	5,302	5,309	5,314	5,316	5,317	5,317	5,317	5,317	5,317	5,317	5,317	5,317	5,317	5,317	5,317	5,317	5,317	5,317	5,317	5,317	5,317	5,317
9	4,596	4,787	4,906	4,986	5,043	5,086	5,118	5,142	5,160	5,174	5,185	5,193	5,199	5,203	5,205	5,206	5,206	5,206	5,206	5,206	5,206	5,206	5,206	5,206	5,206	5,206	5,206	5,206	5,206	5,206	5,206
10	4,482	4,671	4,790	4,871	4,931	4,975	5,010	5,037	5,058	5,074	5,088	5,098	5,106	5,112	5,117	5,120	5,122	5,124	5,124	5,124	5,124	5,124	5,124	5,124	5,124	5,124	5,124	5,124	5,124	5,124	5,124
11	4,392	4,579	4,697	4,780	4,841	4,887	4,924	4,952	4,975	4,994	5,009	5,021	5,031	5,039	5,045	5,050	5,054	5,057	5,059	5,061	5,061	5,061	5,061	5,061	5,061	5,061	5,061	5,061	5,061	5,061	5,061
12	4,320	4,504	4,622	4,706	4,767	4,815	4,852	4,883	4,907	4,927	4,944	4,958	4,969	4,978	4,986	4,993	4,998	5,002	5,006	5,010	5,011	5,011	5,011	5,011	5,011	5,011	5,011	5,011	5,011	5,011	5,011
13	4,260	4,442	4,560	4,644	4,706	4,755	4,793	4,824	4,850	4,872	4,889	4,904	4,917	4,928	4,937	4,944	4,950	4,956	4,960	4,966	4,970	4,972	4,972	4,972	4,972	4,972	4,972	4,972	4,972	4,972	4,972
14	4,210	4,391	4,508	4,591	4,654	4,704	4,743	4,775	4,802	4,824	4,843	4,859	4,872	4,884	4,894	4,902	4,910	4,916	4,921	4,929	4,935	4,938	4,940	4,940	4,940	4,940	4,940	4,940	4,940	4,940	4,940
15	4,168	4,347	4,463	4,547	4,610	4,660	4,700	4,733	4,760	4,783	4,803	4,820	4,834	4,846	4,857	4,866	4,874	4,881	4,887	4,897	4,904	4,909	4,912	4,914	4,914	4,914	4,914	4,914	4,914	4,914	4,914
16	4,131	4,309	4,425	4,509	4,572	4,622	4,663	4,696	4,724	4,748	4,768	4,786	4,800	4,813	4,825	4,835	4,844	4,851	4,858	4,869	4,877	4,883	4,887	4,890	4,892	4,892	4,892	4,892	4,892	4,892	4,892
17	4,099	4,275	4,391	4,475	4,539	4,589	4,630	4,664	4,693	4,717	4,738	4,756	4,771	4,785	4,797	4,807	4,816	4,824	4,832	4,844	4,853	4,860	4,865	4,869	4,872	4,873	4,874	4,874	4,874	4,874	4,874
18	4,071	4,246	4,362	4,445	4,509	4,560	4,601	4,635	4,664	4,689	4,711	4,729	4,745	4,759	4,772	4,783	4,792	4,801	4,808	4,821	4,832	4,839	4,846	4,850	4,854	4,856	4,857	4,858	4,858	4,858	4,858
19	4,046	4,220	4,335	4,419	4,483	4,534	4,575	4,610	4,639	4,665	4,686	4,705	4,722	4,736	4,749	4,761	4,771	4,780	4,788	4,802	4,812	4,821	4,828	4,833	4,838	4,841	4,843	4,844	4,845	4,845	4,845
20	4,024	4,197	4,312	4,395	4,459	4,510	4,552	4,587	4,617	4,642	4,664	4,684	4,701	4,716	4,729	4,741	4,751	4,761	4,769	4,784	4,795	4,805	4,813	4,818	4,823	4,827	4,830	4,832	4,833	4,833	4,833
24	3,956	4,126	4,239	4,322	4,386	4,437	4,480	4,516	4,546	4,573	4,596	4,616	4,634	4,651	4,665	4,678	4,690	4,700	4,710	4,727	4,741	4,752	4,762	4,770	4,777	4,783	4,788	4,791	4,794	4,802	4,802
30	3,889	4,056	4,168	4,250	4,314	4,366	4,409	4,445	4,477	4,504	4,528	4,550	4,569	4,586	4,601	4,615	4,628	4,640	4,650	4,669	4,685	4,699	4,711	4,721	4,730	4,738	4,744	4,750	4,755	4,772	4,777
40	3,825	3,988	4,098	4,180	4,244	4,296	4,339	4,376	4,408	4,436	4,461	4,483	4,503	4,521	4,537	4,553	4,566	4,579	4,591	4,611	4,630	4,645	4,659	4,671	4,682	4,692	4,700	4,708	4,715	4,740	4,754
60	3,762	3,922	4,031	4,111	4,174	4,226	4,270	4,307	4,340	4,368	4,394	4,417	4,438	4,456	4,474	4,490	4,504	4,518	4,530	4,553	4,573	4,591	4,607	4,620	4,633	4,645	4,655	4,665	4,673	4,707	4,730
120	3,702	3,858	3,965	4,044	4,107	4,158	4,202	4,239	4,272	4,301	4,327	4,351	4,372	4,392	4,410	4,426	4,442	4,456	4,469	4,494	4,516	4,535	4,552	4,568	4,583	4,596	4,609	4,619	4,630	4,673	4,703
∞	3,643	3,796	3,900	3,978	4,040	4,091	4,135	4,172	4,205	4,235	4,261	4,285	4,307	4,327	4,345	4,363	4,379	4,394	4,408	4,434	4,457	4,478	4,497	4,514	4,530	4,545	4,559	4,572	4,584	4,635	4,675

[1] HARTER, H. L., *Biometrics*, **16**, 671 (1960). Reprinted by kind permission of the author and publishers.

All values conform to the international convention (i.e. 0,1 instead of 0.1).

Test quotient: $\frac{x_{N_1} - x_1}{s}$, where x_{N_1} is the highest and x_1 the lowest value of the sample of size N_1 to be tested; s: standard deviation with degrees of freedom $\nu = N_2 - 1$ of a sample of size N_2 *independent* of the sample of size N_1

N_1 / ν	2	3	4	5	6	7	8	9	10	11	12	13	14	15	16	17	18	19	20
	$\alpha = 0{,}05$																		
1	17,969	26,98	32,82	37,08	40,41	43,12	45,40	47,36	49,07	50,59	51,96	53,20	54,33	55,36	56,32	57,22	58,04	58,83	59,56
2	6,085	8,33	9,80	10,88	11,74	12,44	13,03	13,54	13,99	14,39	14,75	15,08	15,38	15,65	15,91	16,14	16,37	16,57	16,77
3	4,501	5,91	6,82	7,50	8,04	8,48	8,85	9,18	9,46	9,72	9,95	10,15	10,35	10,52	10,69	10,84	10,98	11,11	11,24
4	3,927	5,04	5,76	6,29	6,71	7,05	7,35	7,60	7,83	8,03	8,21	8,37	8,52	8,66	8,79	8,91	9,03	9,13	9,23
5	3,635	4,60	5,22	5,67	6,03	6,33	6,58	6,80	6,99	7,17	7,32	7,47	7,60	7,72	7,83	7,93	8,03	8,12	8,21
6	461	34	4,90	30	5,63	5,90	12	32	49	6,65	6,79	6,92	03	14	24	34	7,43	7,51	7,59
7	344	16	68	06	36	61	5,82	00	16	30	43	55	6,66	6,76	6,85	6,94	02	10	17
8	261	04	53	4,89	17	40	60	5,77	5,92	05	18	29	39	48	57	65	6,73	6,80	6,87
9	199	3,95	41	76	02	24	43	59	74	5,87	5,98	09	19	28	36	44	51	58	64
10	3,151	3,88	4,33	4,65	4,91	5,12	5,30	5,46	5,60	5,72	5,83	5,93	6,03	6,11	6,19	6,27	6,34	6,40	6,47
11	113	82	26	57	82	03	20	35	49	61	71	81	5,90	5,98	06	13	20	27	33
12	082	77	20	51	75	4,95	12	27	39	51	61	71	80	88	5,95	02	09	15	21
13	055	73	15	45	69	88	05	19	32	43	53	63	71	79	86	5,93	5,99	05	11
14	033	70	11	41	64	83	4,99	13	25	36	46	55	64	71	79	85	91	5,97	03
15	3,014	3,67	4,08	4,37	4,59	4,78	4,94	5,08	5,20	5,31	5,40	5,49	5,57	5,65	5,72	5,78	5,85	5,90	5,96
16	2,998	65	05	33	56	74	90	03	15	26	35	44	52	59	66	73	79	84	90
17	984	63	02	30	52	70	86	4,99	11	21	31	39	47	54	61	67	73	79	84
18	971	61	00	28	49	67	82	96	07	17	27	35	43	50	57	63	69	74	79
19	960	59	3,98	25	47	65	79	92	04	14	23	31	39	46	53	59	65	70	75
20	2,950	3,58	3,96	4,23	4,45	4,62	4,77	4,90	5,01	5,11	5,20	5,28	5,36	5,43	5,49	5,55	5,61	5,66	5,71
21	941	56	94	21	43	60	74	87	4,98	08	17	25	33	40	46	52	58	62	67
22	933	55	93	20	41	58	72	85	96	05	15	23	30	37	43	49	55	59	64
23	926	54	91	18	39	56	70	83	94	03	12	20	27	34	40	46	52	57	62
24	919	53	90	17	37	54	68	81	92	01	10	18	25	32	38	44	49	55	59
25	2,913	3,52	3,89	4,16	4,36	4,52	4,66	4,79	4,90	4,99	5,08	5,16	5,23	5,30	5,36	5,42	5,48	5,52	5,57
26	907	51	88	14	34	51	65	78	89	97	06	14	21	28	34	40	46	50	55
27	902	51	87	13	33	50	63	76	87	96	04	12	19	26	32	38	43	48	53
28	897	50	86	12	32	48	62	75	86	94	03	11	18	24	30	36	42	46	51
29	892	49	85	11	31	47	61	73	84	93	01	09	16	23	29	35	40	44	49
30	2,888	3,49	3,85	4,10	4,30	4,46	4,60	4,72	4,82	4,92	5,00	5,08	5,15	5,21	5,27	5,33	5,38	5,43	5,47
31	884	48	83	09	29	45	59	71	82	91	4,99	07	14	20	26	32	37	41	46
32	881	48	83	09	28	44	58	70	81	89	98	06	13	19	24	30	35	40	45
33	877	47	82	08	27	44	57	69	80	88	97	04	11	17	23	29	34	39	44
34	874	47	82	07	27	43	56	68	79	87	96	03	10	16	22	28	33	37	42
35	2,871	3,46	3,81	4,07	4,26	4,42	4,55	4,67	4,78	4,86	4,95	5,02	5,09	5,15	5,21	5,27	5,32	5,36	5,41
36	868	46	81	06	25	41	55	66	77	85	94	01	08	14	20	26	31	35	40
37	865	45	80	05	25	41	54	65	76	84	93	00	08	14	19	25	30	34	39
38	863	45	80	05	24	40	53	64	75	84	92	00	07	13	18	24	29	33	38
39	861	44	79	04	24	40	53	64	75	83	92	4,99	06	12	17	23	28	32	37
40	2,858	3,44	3,79	4,04	4,23	4,39	4,52	4,63	4,73	4,82	4,90	4,98	5,04	5,11	5,16	5,22	5,27	5,31	5,36
50	841	41	76	00	19	34	47	58	69	76	85	92	4,99	05	10	15	20	24	29
60	829	40	74	3,98	16	31	44	55	65	73	81	88	94	00	06	11	15	20	24
120	800	36	68	92	10	24	36	47	56	64	71	78	84	4,90	4,95	00	04	09	13
∞	772	31	63	86	03	17	29	39	47	55	62	68	74	80	85	4,89	4,93	4,97	01
	$\alpha = 0{,}01$																		
1	90,025	135,0	164,3	185,6	202,2	215,8	227,2	237,0	245,6	253,2	260,0	266,2	271,8	277,0	281,8	286,3	290,4	294,3	298,0
2	14,036	19,02	22,29	24,72	26,63	28,20	29,53	30,68	31,69	32,59	33,40	34,13	34,81	35,43	36,00	36,53	37,03	37,50	37,95
3	8,261	10,62	12,17	13,33	14,24	15,00	15,64	16,20	16,69	17,13	17,53	17,89	18,22	18,52	18,81	19,07	19,32	19,55	19,77
4	6,512	8,12	9,17	9,96	10,58	11,10	11,55	11,93	12,27	12,57	12,84	13,09	13,32	13,53	13,73	13,91	14,08	14,24	14,40
5	5,702	6,98	7,80	8,42	8,91	9,32	9,67	9,97	10,24	10,48	10,70	10,89	11,08	11,24	11,40	11,55	11,68	11,81	11,93
6	243	33	03	7,56	7,97	8,32	8,61	8,87	9,10	9,30	9,48	9,65	9,81	9,95	10,08	10,21	10,32	10,43	10,54
7	4,949	5,92	6,54	01	37	7,68	7,94	17	8,37	8,55	8,71	8,86	00	12	9,24	9,35	9,46	9,55	9,65
8	746	64	20	6,62	6,96	24	47	7,68	7,86	03	18	31	8,44	8,55	8,66	8,76	8,85	8,94	03
9	596	43	5,96	35	66	6,91	13	33	49	7,65	7,78	7,91	03	13	23	33	41	49	8,57
10	4,482	5,27	5,77	6,14	6,43	6,67	6,87	7,05	7,21	7,36	7,49	7,60	7,71	7,81	7,91	7,99	8,08	8,15	8,23
11	392	15	62	5,97	25	48	67	6,84	6,99	13	25	36	46	56	65	73	7,81	7,88	7,95
12	320	05	50	84	10	32	51	67	81	6,94	06	17	26	36	44	52	59	66	73
13	260	4,96	40	73	5,98	19	37	53	67	79	6,90	01	10	19	27	35	42	48	55
14	210	89	32	63	88	08	26	41	54	66	77	6,87	6,96	05	13	20	27	33	39
15	4,168	4,84	5,25	5,56	5,80	5,99	6,16	6,31	6,44	6,55	6,66	6,76	6,84	6,93	7,00	7,07	7,14	7,20	7,26
16	131	79	19	49	72	92	08	22	35	46	56	66	74	82	6,90	6,97	03	09	15
17	099	74	14	43	66	85	01	15	27	38	48	57	66	73	81	87	6,94	00	05
18	071	70	09	38	60	79	5,94	08	20	31	41	50	58	65	73	79	85	6,91	6,97
19	046	67	05	33	55	73	89	02	14	25	34	43	51	58	65	72	78	84	89
20	4,024	4,64	5,02	5,29	5,51	5,69	5,84	5,97	6,09	6,19	6,28	6,37	6,45	6,52	6,59	6,65	6,71	6,77	6,82
21	004	61	4,99	26	47	65	80	92	04	14	24	32	39	47	53	59	65	70	76
22	3,986	58	96	22	43	61	76	88	00	10	19	27	35	42	48	54	60	65	70
23	970	56	93	20	40	57	72	84	5,96	06	15	23	30	37	43	49	55	60	65
24	956	55	91	17	37	54	69	81	92	02	11	19	26	33	39	45	51	56	61
25	3,942	4,52	4,89	5,15	5,34	5,51	5,66	5,78	5,89	5,99	6,07	6,15	6,22	6,29	6,35	6,41	6,47	6,52	6,57
26	930	50	87	12	32	49	63	75	86	95	04	12	19	26	32	38	43	48	53
27	918	49	85	10	30	46	61	72	83	93	01	09	16	22	28	34	40	45	50
28	908	47	83	08	28	44	58	70	80	90	5,98	06	13	19	25	31	37	42	47
29	898	46	82	07	26	42	56	67	78	87	95	03	10	17	23	29	34	39	44
30	3,889	4,45	4,80	5,05	5,24	5,40	5,54	5,65	5,76	5,85	5,93	6,01	6,08	6,14	6,20	6,26	6,31	6,36	6,41
31	881	44	79	03	22	38	52	63	74	83	91	5,99	06	12	18	23	29	34	38
32	873	43	78	02	21	37	50	61	72	81	89	97	03	09	16	21	26	31	36
33	865	42	76	01	19	35	48	59	70	79	87	95	01	07	13	19	24	29	34
34	859	41	75	4,99	18	34	47	58	68	77	86	93	5,99	05	12	17	22	27	31
35	3,852	4,41	4,74	4,98	5,16	5,33	5,45	5,56	5,67	5,76	5,84	5,91	5,98	6,04	6,10	6,15	6,20	6,25	6,29
36	846	40	73	97	15	31	44	55	65	74	82	90	96	02	08	13	18	23	28
37	841	39	72	96	14	30	43	54	64	73	81	88	94	00	06	12	17	22	26
38	835	38	72	95	13	29	41	52	62	72	80	87	93	5,99	05	10	15	20	24
39	830	38	71	94	12	28	40	51	61	70	78	85	91	97	03	08	13	18	23
40	3,825	4,37	4,70	4,93	5,11	5,26	5,39	5,50	5,60	5,69	5,76	5,83	5,90	5,96	6,02	6,07	6,12	6,16	6,21
50	787	32	64	86	04	19	30	41	51	59	67	74	80	86	5,91	5,96	01	06	09
60	762	28	59	82	4,99	13	25	36	45	53	60	67	73	78	84	89	5,93	5,97	01
120	702	20	50	71	87	01	12	21	30	37	44	50	56	61	66	71	75	79	5,83
∞	643	12	40	60	76	4,88	4,99	08	16	23	29	35	40	45	49	54	57	61	65

[7] Values from MAY, J.M., *Biometrika*, **39**, 192 (1952), with corrections from PEARSON and HARTLEY (Eds.), *Biometrika Tables for Statisticians*, 3rd ed., volume 1, Cambridge University Press, Cambridge, 1970, page 192, from PACHARES, J., *Biometrika*, **46**, 461 (1959), and from HARTER, H.L., *Biometrics*, **16**, 671 (1960). Completed with calculated (column 2) and interpolated values. Reprinted by kind permission of the authors and publishers.

All values conform to the international convention (i.e. 0,1 instead of 0.1).

The standardized extreme deviation*

Test quotient: $\frac{x_N-\mu}{\sigma}$ or $\frac{\mu-x_1}{\sigma}$, where x_N is the highest and x_1 the lowest value of the sample

N \ α	0,10	0,05	0,025	0,01	0,005	0,001	0,0005
1	1,282	1,645	1,960	2,326	2,576	3,090	3,291
2	632	955	2,239	575	807	290	481
3	818	2,121	391	712	935	403	588
4	943	234	494	806	3,023	481	662
5	2,036	2,319	2,572	2,877	3,090	3,540	3,719
6	111	386	635	934	143	588	765
7	172	442	687	981	188	628	803
8	224	490	731	3,022	227	662	836
9	269	531	769	057	260	692	865
10	2,309	2,568	2,803	3,089	3,290	3,719	3,891
11	344	601	834	117	317	743	914
12	376	630	862	143	341	765	935
13	406	657	887	166	363	785	954
14	432	682	910	187	383	803	971
15	2,457	2,705	2,932	3,207	3,402	3,820	3,988
16	480	726	952	226	420	836	4,003
17	502	746	970	243	436	851	017
18	522	765	988	259	452	865	031
19	541	783	3,004	275	466	878	044
20	2,559	2,799	3,020	3,289	3,480	3,890	4,056
21	576	815	034	303	493	902	067
22	592	830	048	316	506	914	078
23	607	844	062	328	517	924	088
24	621	858	075	340	529	934	098
25	2,635	2,870	3,087	3,351	3,539	3,944	4,107
26	648	883	098	362	550	954	116
27	661	895	109	373	560	963	125
28	673	906	120	383	569	971	134
29	685	917	130	392	578	980	142
30	2,696	2,928	3,140	3,402	3,587	3,988	4,149
31	707	938	150	411	596	996	157
32	718	948	159	419	604	4,003	164
33	728	957	168	428	612	010	171
34	738	966	177	436	620	017	178
35	2,747	2,975	3,185	3,444	3,627	4,024	4,185
36	756	984	193	451	635	031	191
37	765	992	201	459	642	037	197
38	774	3,000	209	466	648	044	203
39	782	008	216	473	655	050	209

N \ α	0,10	0,05	0,025	0,01	0,005	0,001	0,0005
40	2,791	3,016	3,224	3,479	3,662	4,056	4,215
41	799	023	231	486	668	061	220
42	806	031	238	493	674	067	226
43	814	038	244	499	680	072	231
44	821	045	251	505	686	078	236
45	2,828	3,051	3,257	3,511	3,692	4,083	4,241
46	835	058	263	517	697	088	246
47	842	064	270	522	703	093	251
48	849	071	276	528	708	098	256
49	856	077	281	533	713	103	260
50	2,862	3,083	3,287	3,539	3,718	4,107	4,265
51	868	089	293	544	723	112	269
52	875	094	298	549	728	116	274
53	880	100	303	554	733	121	278
54	886	106	309	559	738	125	282
55	2,892	3,111	3,314	3,564	3,742	4,129	4,286
56	898	116	319	569	747	134	290
57	903	122	324	573	751	138	294
58	909	127	329	578	756	142	298
59	914	132	333	582	760	146	302
60	2,919	3,137	3,338	3,587	3,764	4,149	4,305
61	924	141	343	591	768	153	309
62	929	146	347	595	772	157	313
63	934	151	352	599	776	160	316
64	939	155	356	603	780	164	320
65	2,944	3,160	3,360	3,607	3,784	4,168	4,323
66	949	164	364	611	788	171	326
67	953	169	369	615	792	175	330
68	958	173	373	619	795	178	333
69	962	177	377	623	799	181	336
70	2,967	3,182	3,381	3,627	3,803	4,184	4,339
71	971	186	384	630	806	188	342
72	976	190	388	634	810	191	346
73	980	194	392	637	813	194	349
74	984	198	396	641	816	197	352
75	2,988	3,201	3,400	3,644	3,820	4,200	4,355
76	992	205	403	648	823	203	357
77	996	209	407	651	826	206	360
78	3,000	213	410	655	829	209	363
79	004	216	414	658	832	212	366

N \ α	0,10	0,05	0,025	0,01	0,005	0,001	0,0005
80	3,008	3,220	3,417	3,661	3,835	4,215	4,369
81	011	224	421	664	839	217	371
82	015	227	424	667	842	220	374
83	019	231	427	670	845	223	377
84	022	234	430	673	847	226	379
85	3,026	3,237	3,434	3,676	3,850	4,228	4,382
86	030	241	437	679	853	231	384
87	033	244	440	682	856	234	387
88	037	247	443	685	859	236	389
89	040	250	446	688	862	239	392
90	3,043	3,254	3,449	3,691	3,864	4,241	4,394
91	047	257	452	694	867	244	397
92	050	260	455	697	870	246	399
93	053	263	458	699	872	249	401
94	056	266	461	702	875	251	404
95	3,060	3,269	3,464	3,705	3,878	4,253	4,406
96	063	272	466	707	880	256	408
97	066	275	469	710	883	258	411
98	069	278	472	713	885	260	413
99	072	281	475	715	888	263	415
100	3,075	3,283	3,477	3,718	3,890	4,265	4,417
200	276	474	659	889	4,055	417	565
300	389	581.	762	987	149	504	649
400	467	656	833	4,054	214	565	708
500	3,526	3,713	3,888	4,106	4,264	4,611	4,754
600	574	758	932	148	305	649	790
700	614	797	968	183	339	681	821
800	649	830	4,000	214	368	708	848
900	679	859	028	240	394	732	871
1000	3,706	3,884	4,053	4,264	4,417	4,754	4,892

The studentized extreme deviation[7]

Test quotients: $\frac{x_{N_1}-\bar{x}}{s}$ or $\frac{\bar{x}-x_1}{s}$ $[\nu<\infty]$

$\frac{x_{N_1}-\bar{x}}{\sigma}$ or $\frac{\bar{x}-x_1}{\sigma}$ $[\nu=\infty]$

where x_{N_1} is the highest value, x_1 the lowest value and $\bar{x}$ the mean of the sample of size N_1 to be tested; s: standard deviation with degrees of freedom $\nu=N_2-1$ of a sample of size N_2 *independent* of the sample of size N_1

N_1	3	4	5	6	7	8	9	3	4	5	6	7	8	9	3	4	5	6	7	8	9
ν	α = 0,1							α = 0,05							α = 0,025						
10	1,68	1,92	2,09	2,23	2,33	2,42	2,50	2,01	2,27	2,46	2,60	2,72	2,81	2,89	2,34	2,63	2,83	2,98	3,10	3,20	3,29
11	1,66	1,90	2,07	2,20	2,30	2,39	2,46	1,98	2,24	2,42	2,56	2,67	2,76	2,84	2,30	2,58	2,77	2,92	3,03	3,13	3,22
12	1,65	1,88	2,05	2,17	2,28	2,36	2,44	1,96	2,21	2,39	2,52	2,63	2,72	2,80	2,27	2,54	2,73	2,87	2,98	3,08	3,16
13	1,63	1,86	2,03	2,16	2,26	2,34	2,41	1,94	2,19	2,36	2,50	2,60	2,69	2,76	2,24	2,51	2,69	2,83	2,94	3,03	3,11
14	1,62	1,85	2,01	2,14	2,24	2,32	2,39	1,93	2,17	2,34	2,47	2,57	2,66	2,74	2,22	2,48	2,66	2,79	2,90	2,99	3,07
15	1,61	1,84	2,00	2,12	2,22	2,31	2,38	1,91	2,15	2,32	2,45	2,55	2,64	2,71	2,20	2,45	2,63	2,76	2,87	2,96	3,04
16	1,61	1,83	1,99	2,11	2,21	2,29	2,36	1,90	2,14	2,31	2,43	2,53	2,62	2,69	2,18	2,43	2,61	2,74	2,84	2,93	3,01
17	1,60	1,82	1,98	2,10	2,20	2,28	2,35	1,89	2,13	2,29	2,42	2,52	2,60	2,67	2,17	2,42	2,59	2,72	2,82	2,91	2,98
18	1,59	1,82	1,97	2,09	2,19	2,27	2,34	1,88	2,11	2,28	2,40	2,50	2,58	2,65	2,15	2,40	2,57	2,70	2,80	2,89	2,96
19	1,59	1,81	1,96	2,08	2,18	2,26	2,33	1,87	2,11	2,27	2,39	2,49	2,57	2,64	2,14	2,39	2,56	2,68	2,78	2,87	2,94
20	1,58	1,80	1,96	2,08	2,17	2,25	2,32	1,87	2,10	2,26	2,38	2,47	2,56	2,63	2,13	2,37	2,54	2,67	2,77	2,85	2,92
24	1,57	1,78	1,94	2,05	2,15	2,22	2,29	1,84	2,07	2,23	2,34	2,44	2,52	2,58	2,10	2,34	2,50	2,62	2,72	2,80	2,87
30	1,55	1,77	1,92	2,03	2,12	2,20	2,26	1,82	2,04	2,20	2,31	2,40	2,48	2,54	2,07	2,30	2,46	2,58	2,67	2,75	2,81
40	1,54	1,75	1,90	2,01	2,10	2,17	2,23	1,80	2,02	2,17	2,28	2,37	2,44	2,50	2,04	2,27	2,42	2,53	2,62	2,70	2,76
60	1,52	1,73	1,87	1,98	2,07	2,14	2,20	1,78	1,99	2,14	2,25	2,33	2,41	2,47	2,01	2,23	2,38	2,49	2,58	2,65	2,71
120	1,51	1,71	1,85	1,96	2,05	2,12	2,18	1,76	1,96	2,11	2,22	2,30	2,37	2,43	1,98	2,20	2,34	2,45	2,53	2,60	2,66
∞	1,50	1,70	1,83	1,94	2,02	2,09	2,15	1,74	1,94	2,08	2,18	2,27	2,33	2,39	1,95	2,16	2,30	2,41	2,49	2,56	2,61
	α = 0,01							α = 0,005							α = 0,001						
10	2,78	3,10	3,32	3,48	3,62	3,73	3,82	3,12	3,46	3,70	3,87	4,02	4,14	4,24	4,0	4,3	4,6	4,8	5,0	5,2	5,3
11	2,72	3,02	3,24	3,39	3,52	3,63	3,72	3,04	3,37	3,59	3,76	3,90	4,01	4,11	3,8	4,2	4,5	4,7	4,8	5,0	5,1
12	2,67	2,96	3,17	3,32	3,45	3,55	3,64	2,98	3,29	3,51	3,67	3,80	3,91	4,00	3,7	4,1	4,3	4,5	4,7	4,8	4,9
13	2,63	2,92	3,12	3,27	3,38	3,48	3,57	2,93	3,23	3,44	3,60	3,72	3,83	3,92	3,6	4,0	4,2	4,4	4,5	4,6	4,7
14	2,60	2,88	3,07	3,22	3,33	3,43	3,51	2,88	3,18	3,38	3,54	3,66	3,76	3,85	3,5	3,9	4,1	4,3	4,4	4,5	4,6
15	2,57	2,84	3,03	3,17	3,29	3,38	3,46	2,84	3,13	3,33	3,48	3,60	3,70	3,78	3,5	3,8	4,0	4,2	4,3	4,4	4,5
16	2,54	2,81	3,00	3,14	3,25	3,34	3,42	2,81	3,10	3,29	3,44	3,56	3,65	3,73	3,4	3,7	4,0	4,1	4,3	4,4	4,5
17	2,52	2,79	2,97	3,11	3,22	3,31	3,38	2,78	3,07	3,26	3,40	3,52	3,61	3,68	3,4	3,7	3,9	4,1	4,2	4,3	4,4
18	2,50	2,77	2,95	3,08	3,19	3,28	3,35	2,76	3,04	3,23	3,37	3,48	3,57	3,64	3,3	3,6	3,9	4,0	4,1	4,2	4,3
19	2,49	2,75	2,93	3,06	3,16	3,25	3,33	2,74	3,01	3,20	3,34	3,45	3,54	3,61	3,3	3,6	3,8	4,0	4,1	4,2	4,3
20	2,47	2,73	2,91	3,04	3,14	3,23	3,30	2,72	2,99	3,17	3,31	3,42	3,51	3,58	3,3	3,6	3,8	3,9	4,0	4,1	4,2
24	2,42	2,68	2,84	2,97	3,07	3,16	3,23	2,66	2,92	3,10	3,23	3,33	3,42	3,49	3,2	3,5	3,7	3,8	3,9	4,0	4,1
30	2,38	2,62	2,79	2,91	3,01	3,08	3,15	2,60	2,86	3,03	3,15	3,25	3,33	3,40	3,1	3,4	3,6	3,7	3,8	3,9	4,0
40	2,34	2,57	2,73	2,85	2,94	3,02	3,08	2,55	2,79	2,96	3,08	3,17	3,25	3,31	3,0	3,3	3,5	3,6	3,7	3,7	3,8
60	2,29	2,52	2,68	2,79	2,88	2,95	3,01	2,50	2,73	2,89	3,01	3,10	3,17	3,23	2,9	3,2	3,4	3,5	3,6	3,6	3,7
120	2,25	2,48	2,62	2,73	2,82	2,89	2,95	2,45	2,67	2,83	2,94	3,02	3,09	3,15	2,9	3,1	3,3	3,4	3,5	3,5	3,6
∞	2,22	2,43	2,57	2,68	2,76	2,83	2,88	2,40	2,62	2,76	2,87	2,95	3,02	3,07	2,8	3,0	3,2	3,3	3,4	3,4	3,5

*Reproduction only by permission of the publishers of the *Geigy Scientific Tables*.

[7] NAIR, K.R., *Biometrika*, **39**, 189 (1952), and DAVID, H.A., *Biometrika*, **43**, 449 (1956). Reprinted by kind permission of the authors and publishers.

All values conform to the international convention (i.e. 0,1 instead of 0.1).

Significance limits[1] for testing extreme values of a sample

$x_1 \leq x_2 \leq x_3 \ldots \leq x_N$

α / N	0,30	0,20	0,10	0,05	0,02	0,01	0,005	Test quotient
3	0,684	0,781	0,886	0,941	0,976	0,988	0,994	$\frac{x_N - x_{N-1}}{x_N - x_1}$
4	471	560	679	765	846	889	926	
5	373	451	557	642	729	780	821	
6	318	386	482	560	644	698	740	
7	281	344	434	507	586	637	680	
8	0,318	0,385	0,479	0,554	0,631	0,683	0,725	$\frac{x_N - x_{N-1}}{x_N - x_2}$
9	288	352	441	512	587	635	677	
10	265	325	409	477	551	597	639	
11	0,391	0,442	0,517	0,576	0,638	0,679	0,713	$\frac{x_N - x_{N-2}}{x_N - x_2}$
12	370	419	490	546	605	642	675	
13	351	399	467	521	578	615	649	
14	0,370	0,421	0,492	0,546	0,602	0,641	0,674	$\frac{x_N - x_{N-2}}{x_N - x_3}$
15	0,353	0,402	0,472	0,525	0,579	0,616	0,647	
16	338	386	454	507	559	595	624	
17	325	373	438	490	542	577	605	
18	314	361	424	475	527	561	589	
19	304	350	412	462	514	547	575	
20	0,295	0,340	0,401	0,450	0,502	0,535	0,562	
21	287	331	391	440	491	524	551	
22	280	323	382	430	481	514	541	
23	274	316	374	421	472	505	532	
24	268	310	367	413	464	497	524	
25	0,262	0,304	0,360	0,406	0,457	0,489	0,516	

Significance limits[2] for the difference between the mean of a sample and a hypothetical mean μ

Test quotient: $\frac{|\bar{x} - \mu|}{x_N - x_1}$

x_N is the highest, x_1 the lowest value of a sample of size N

2α / N	0,10	0,05	0,02	0,01	0,002	0,001
2	3,157	6,353	15,910	31,828	159,16	318,31
3	0,885	1,304	2,111	3,008	6,77	9,58
4	0,529	0,717	1,023	1,316	2,29	2,85
5	0,388	0,507	0,685	0,843	1,32	1,58
6	0,312	0,399	0,523	0,628	0,92	1,07
7	0,263	0,333	0,429	0,507	0,71	0,82
8	0,230	0,288	0,366	0,429	0,59	0,67
9	0,205	0,255	0,322	0,374	0,50	0,57
10	0,186	0,230	0,288	0,333	0,44	0,50
11	0,170	0,210	0,262	0,302	0,40	0,44
12	0,158	0,194	0,241	0,277	0,36	0,40
13	0,147	0,181	0,224	0,256	0,33	0,37
14	0,138	0,170	0,209	0,239	0,31	0,34
15	0,131	0,160	0,197	0,224	0,29	0,32
16	0,124	0,151	0,186	0,212	0,27	0,30
17	0,118	0,144	0,177	0,201	0,26	0,28
18	0,113	0,137	0,168	0,191	0,24	0,26
19	0,108	0,131	0,161	0,182	0,23	0,25
20	0,104	0,126	0,154	0,175	0,22	0,24

Significance limits[2] for the difference between the means of two samples of the same size

Test quotient: $\frac{|\bar{x}' - \bar{x}''|}{x'_N - x'_1 + x''_N - x''_1}$

x_N is the highest, x_1 the lowest value of the two samples of size $N' = N'' = N$

2α / N	0,10	0,05	0,02	0,01	0,002	0,001
2	1,161	1,714	2,777	3,958	8,91	12,62
3	0,487	0,636	0,857	1,047	1,64	2,09
4	0,322	0,407	0,524	0,619	0,87	1,00
5	0,247	0,307	0,386	0,448	0,61	0,68
6	0,203	0,250	0,311	0,357	0,47	0,52
7	0,174	0,213	0,263	0,300	0,39	0,43
8	0,153	0,187	0,230	0,261	0,34	0,37
9	0,137	0,167	0,205	0,232	0,30	0,32
10	0,125	0,152	0,186	0,210	0,27	0,29
11	0,117	0,140	0,170	0,192	0,24	0,26
12	0,107	0,130	0,158	0,178	0,22	0,24
13	0,101	0,122	0,147	0,166	0,21	0,22
14	0,095	0,114	0,138	0,156	0,20	0,21
15	0,090	0,108	0,131	0,147	0,18	0,20
16	0,085	0,103	0,124	0,139	0,17	0,19
17	0,081	0,098	0,118	0,132	0,17	0,18
18	0,078	0,094	0,113	0,126	0,16	0,17
19	0,075	0,090	0,108	0,121	0,15	0,16
20	0,072	0,086	0,104	0,116	0,15	0,16

Significance limits for the difference between the mean of a sample and a hypothetical mean μ

$\bar{x}$ does not need to be calculated in these tests. The values x are so arranged that $x_1 \leq x_2 \leq x_3 \ldots \leq x_N$. Test **B** is also suitable for symmetrical distributions that are not normal distributions

A[3] Test quotient: $\frac{|x_N + x_1 - 2\mu|}{x_N - x_1}$

2α / N	0,10	0,05	0,02	0,01
2	6,32	12,70	31,82	63,66
3	1,80	2,60	4,22	6,04
4	1,11	1,48	2,08	2,74
5	0,85	1,04	1,42	1,70
6	0,70	0,86	1,12	1,32
7	0,60	0,75	0,95	1,10
8	0,53	0,66	0,84	0,95
9	0,48	0,60	0,76	0,85
10	0,45	0,55	0,70	0,78

B[3, 4]

N	$\bar{x} \neq \mu$ [significance 2α], when — either: $\bar{x} < \mu$ [significance α], when	or: $\bar{x} > \mu$ [significance α], when	2α
4	$1{,}055\,x_4 - 0{,}055\,x_1 < \mu$	$1{,}055\,x_1 - 0{,}055\,x_4 > \mu$	0,10
5	$0{,}63\,x_5 + 0{,}37\,x_4 < \mu$	$0{,}63\,x_1 + 0{,}37\,x_2 > \mu$	0,10
	$1{,}02\,x_5 - 0{,}02\,x_1 < \mu$	$1{,}02\,x_1 - 0{,}02\,x_5 > \mu$	0,05
6	$0{,}63\,x_6 + 0{,}37\,x_5 < \mu$	$0{,}63\,x_1 + 0{,}37\,x_2 > \mu$	0,05
	$1{,}06\,x_6 - 0{,}06\,x_1 < \mu$	$1{,}06\,x_1 - 0{,}06\,x_6 > \mu$	0,02
7	$0{,}785\,x_7 + 0{,}215\,x_6 < \mu$	$0{,}785\,x_1 + 0{,}215\,x_2 > \mu$	0,02
	$1{,}05\,x_7 - 0{,}05\,x_1 < \mu$	$1{,}05\,x_1 - 0{,}05\,x_7 > \mu$	0,01
8	the *greater* of the values x_7 or $(0{,}5\,x_8 + 0{,}28\,x_6 + 0{,}22\,x_7) < \mu$	the *smaller* of the values x_2 or $(0{,}5\,x_1 + 0{,}28\,x_3 + 0{,}22\,x_2) > \mu$	$\simeq 0{,}02$
	$0{,}785\,x_6 + 0{,}215\,x_7 < \mu$	$0{,}785\,x_1 + 0{,}215\,x_2 > \mu$	0,01
9	the *greater* of the values x_8 or $0{,}5\,(x_5 + x_9) < \mu$	the *smaller* of the values x_2 or $0{,}5\,(x_1 + x_5) > \mu$	0,02
	the *greater* of the values x_8 or $(0{,}5\,x_9 + 0{,}28\,x_7 + 0{,}22\,x_8) < \mu$	the *smaller* of the values x_2 or $(0{,}5\,x_1 + 0{,}28\,x_3 + 0{,}22\,x_2) > \mu$	$\simeq 0{,}01$
10	the *greater* of the values x_9 or $0{,}5\,(x_6 + x_{10}) < \mu$	the *smaller* of the values x_2 or $0{,}5\,(x_1 + x_5) > \mu$	0,01
11	the *greater* of the values x_7 or $0{,}5\,(x_4 + x_{11}) < \mu$	the *smaller* of the values x_5 or $0{,}5\,(x_1 + x_8) > \mu$	$\simeq 0{,}10$
	the *greater* of the values x_9 or $0{,}5\,(x_7 + x_{11}) < \mu$	the *smaller* of the values x_3 or $0{,}5\,(x_1 + x_5) > \mu$	$\simeq 0{,}01$
12	the *greater* of the values x_9 or $0{,}5\,(x_6 + x_{12}) < \mu$	the *smaller* of the values x_4 or $0{,}5\,(x_1 + x_7) > \mu$	0,02
13	the *greater* of the values x_{10} or $0{,}5\,(x_7 + x_{13}) < \mu$	the *smaller* of the values x_4 or $0{,}5\,(x_1 + x_7) > \mu$	0,01
14	the *greater* of the values x_{10} or $0{,}5\,(x_6 + x_{14}) < \mu$	the *smaller* of the values x_5 or $0{,}5\,(x_1 + x_9) > \mu$	0,02
15	the *greater* of the values x_{11} or $0{,}5\,(x_7 + x_{15}) < \mu$	the *smaller* of the values x_5 or $0{,}5\,(x_1 + x_9) > \mu$	0,01

[1] DIXON, W.J., *Biometrics*, **9**, 74 (1953).

[2] Values from LORD, E., *Biometrika*, **34**, 41 (1947), but recalculated from the simplified test quotient given.

[3] WALSH, J.E., *Ann. math. Statist.*, **20**, 257 (1949).

[4] WALSH, J.E., *J. Amer. statist. Ass.*, **44**, 342 (1949).

[1–4] Reprinted by kind permission of the authors and publishers.

All values conform to the international convention (i.e. 0,1 instead of 0.1).

Functions of the Correlation Coefficient r: $\sqrt{1-r^2}$; $1-r^2$*

$\sqrt{1-r^2}$

r	0,000	0,001	0,002	0,003	0,004	0,005	0,006	0,007	0,008	0,009
	0,	0,	0,	0,	0,	0,	0,	0,	0,	0,
0,000	◊	◊	◊	◊	99999	99999	99998	99998	99997	99996
010	99995	99994	99993	99992	99990	99989	99987	99986	99984	99982
020	99980	99978	99976	99974	99971	99969	99966	99964	99961	99958
030	99955	99952	99949	99946	99942	99939	99935	99932	99928	99924
040	99920	99916	99912	99908	99903	99899	99894	99889	99885	99880
0,050	99875	99870	99865	99859	99854	99849	99843	99837	99832	99826
060	99820	99814	99808	99801	99795	99789	99782	99775	99769	99762
070	99755	99748	99740	99733	99726	99718	99711	99703	99695	99687
080	99679	99671	99663	99655	99647	99638	99630	99621	99612	99603
090	99594	99585	99576	99567	99557	99548	99538	99528	99519	99509
0,100	99499	99489	99478	99468	99458	99447	99437	99426	99415	99404
110	99393	99382	99371	99359	99348	99337	99325	99313	99301	99289
120	99277	99265	99253	99241	99228	99216	99203	99190	99177	99164
130	99151	99138	99125	99112	99098	99085	99071	99057	99043	99029
140	99015	99001	98987	98972	98958	98943	98928	98914	98899	98884
0,150	98869	98853	98838	98823	98807	98791	98776	98760	98744	98728
160	98712	98695	98679	98663	98646	98629	98613	98596	98579	98562
170	98544	98527	98510	98492	98475	98457	98439	98421	98403	98385
180	98367	98348	98330	98311	98293	98274	98255	98236	98217	98198
190	98178	98159	98139	98120	98100	98080	98060	98040	98020	98000
0,200	97980	97959	97939	97918	97897	97876	97855	97834	97813	97792
210	97770	97749	97727	97705	97683	97661	97639	97617	97595	97572
220	97550	97527	97505	97482	97459	97436	97413	97389	97366	97343
230	97319	97295	97272	97248	97224	97200	97175	97151	97127	97102
240	97077	97053	97028	97003	96978	96952	96927	96902	96876	96850
0,250	96825	96799	96773	96747	96720	96694	96668	96641	96614	96588
260	96561	96534	96507	96480	96452	96425	96397	96370	96342	96314
270	96286	96258	96230	96201	96173	96144	96116	96087	96058	96029
280	96000	95971	95941	95912	95882	95853	95823	95793	95763	95733
290	95703	95672	95642	95611	95581	95550	95519	95488	95457	95425
0,300	95394	95362	95331	95299	95267	95235	95203	95171	95139	95106
310	95074	95041	95008	94975	94942	94909	94876	94843	94809	94775
320	94742	94708	94674	94640	94606	94571	94537	94502	94468	94433
330	94398	94363	94328	94293	94257	94222	94186	94150	94115	94079
340	94043	94006	93970	93934	93897	93860	93823	93787	93749	93712
0,350	93675	93638	93600	93562	93525	93487	93449	93410	93372	93334
360	93295	93257	93218	93179	93140	93101	93061	93022	92983	92943
370	92903	92863	92823	92783	92743	92702	92662	92621	92581	92540
380	92499	92458	92416	92375	92333	92292	92250	92208	92166	92124
390	92081	92039	91997	91954	91911	91868	91825	91782	91739	91695
0,400	91652	91608	91564	91520	91476	91432	91387	91343	91298	91253
410	91209	91164	91118	91073	91028	90982	90936	90891	90845	90799
420	90752	90706	90660	90613	90566	90519	90472	90425	90378	90330
430	90283	90235	90187	90139	90091	90043	89995	89946	89897	89849
440	89800	89751	89702	89652	89603	89553	89503	89453	89403	89353
0,450	89303	89252	89202	89151	89100	89049	88998	88947	88895	88844
460	88792	88740	88688	88636	88584	88531	88478	88426	88373	88320
470	88267	88213	88160	88106	88052	87999	87945	87890	87836	87781
480	87727	87672	87617	87562	87507	87451	87396	87340	87284	87228
490	87172	87116	87060	87003	86946	86889	86832	86775	86718	86660
0,500	86603	86545	86487	86429	86370	86312	86253	86195	86136	86077
510	86017	85958	85899	85839	85779	85719	85659	85599	85538	85477
520	85417	85356	85295	85233	85172	85110	85048	84987	84924	84862
530	84800	84737	84674	84612	84548	84485	84422	84358	84294	84231
540	84167	84102	84038	83973	83909	83844	83779	83713	83648	83582
0,550	83516	83451	83384	83318	83252	83185	83118	83051	82984	82917
560	82849	82782	82714	82646	82577	82509	82441	82372	82303	82234
570	82164	82095	82025	81956	81886	81815	81745	81674	81604	81533
580	81462	81390	81319	81247	81175	81103	81031	80959	80886	80813
590	80740	80667	80594	80520	80447	80373	80298	80224	80150	80075
0,600	80000	79925	79850	79774	79698	79623	79546	79470	79394	79317
610	79240	79163	79086	79008	78931	78853	78775	78696	78618	78539
620	78460	78381	78302	78222	78142	78062	77982	77902	77821	77741
630	77660	77578	77497	77415	77333	77251	77169	77086	77004	76921
640	76837	76754	76670	76587	76503	76418	76334	76249	76164	76079
0,650	75993	75908	75822	75736	75649	75563	75476	75389	75302	75214
660	75127	75039	74950	74862	74773	74684	74595	74506	74416	74326
670	74236	74146	74055	73964	73873	73782	73690	73598	73506	73414
680	73321	73228	73135	73042	72948	72854	72760	72666	72571	72476
690	72381	72285	72190	72094	71997	71901	71804	71707	71610	71512
0,700	71414	71316	71218	71119	71020	70921	70821	70721	70621	70521
710	70420	70319	70218	70116	70015	69912	69810	69707	69604	69501
720	69397	69294	69189	69085	68980	68875	68769	68664	68558	68451
730	68345	68238	68130	68023	67915	67807	67698	67589	67480	67371
740	67261	67151	67040	66929	66818	66706	66595	66482	66370	66257
0,750	66144	66030	65916	65802	65687	65572	65457	65341	65225	65109
760	64992	64875	64758	64640	64522	64403	64284	64165	64045	63925
770	63804	63684	63562	63441	63319	63196	63073	62950	62826	62702
780	62578	62453	62328	62202	62076	61950	61823	61695	61568	61439
790	61311	61182	61052	60922	60792	60661	60530	60398	60266	60133
0,800	60000	59866	59732	59598	59463	59327	59192	59055	58918	58781
810	58643	58505	58366	58226	58086	57946	57805	57664	57522	57379
820	57236	57093	56949	56804	56659	56513	56367	56220	56073	55925
830	55776	55627	55478	55327	55176	55025	54873	54720	54567	54413
840	54259	54104	53948	53791	53634	53477	53318	53159	53000	52839
0,850	52678	52517	52354	52191	52027	51863	51698	51532	51365	51198
860	51029	50860	50691	50520	50349	50177	50004	49831	49656	49481
870	49305	49128	48951	48772	48593	48412	48231	48049	47866	47682
880	47497	47312	47125	46937	46749	46559	46369	46177	45984	45791
890	45596	45400	45204	45006	44807	44607	44405	44203	44000	43795
0,900	43589	43382	43174	42964	42753	42541	42328	42113	41897	41680
910	41461	41241	41019	40796	40571	40345	40118	39889	39658	39426
920	39192	38956	38719	38480	38239	37997	37752	37506	37258	37008
930	36756	36502	36246	35988	35727	35465	35200	34933	34664	34392
940	34117	33841	33561	33279	32995	32707	32417	32123	31827	31528
0,950	31225	30919	30610	30297	29981	29661	29337	29009	28677	28341
960	28000	27655	27305	26950	26590	26225	25854	25478	25095	24706
970	24310	23908	23498	23081	22655	22220	21777	21324	20860	20386
980	19900	19401	18888	18361	17817	17255	16675	16072	15445	14792
990	14107	13386	12624	11811	10938	09987	08935	07740	06321	04471

$1-r^2$

r	0,000	0,001	0,002	0,003	0,004	0,005	0,006	0,007	0,008	0,009
	0,	0,	0,	0,	0,	0,	0,	0,	0,	0,
0,000	◊	◊	◊	99999	99998	99998	99996	99995	99994	99992
010	99990	99988	99986	99983	99980	99978	99974	99971	99968	99964
020	99960	99956	99952	99947	99942	99938	99932	99927	99922	99916
030	99910	99904	99898	99891	99884	99878	99870	99863	99856	99848
040	99840	99832	99824	99815	99806	99798	99788	99779	99770	99760
0,050	99750	99740	99730	99719	99708	99698	99686	99675	99664	99652
060	99640	99628	99616	99603	99590	99578	99564	99551	99538	99524
070	99510	99496	99482	99467	99452	99438	99422	99407	99392	99376
080	99360	99344	99328	99311	99294	99278	99260	99243	99226	99208
090	99190	99172	99154	99135	99116	99098	99078	99059	99040	99020
0,100	99000	98980	98960	98939	98918	98898	98876	98855	98834	98812
110	98790	98768	98746	98723	98700	98678	98654	98631	98608	98584
120	98560	98536	98512	98487	98462	98438	98412	98387	98362	98336
130	98310	98284	98258	98231	98204	98178	98150	98123	98096	98068
140	98040	98012	97984	97955	97926	97898	97868	97839	97810	97780
0,150	97750	97720	97690	97659	97628	97598	97566	97535	97504	97472
160	97440	97408	97376	97343	97310	97278	97244	97211	97178	97144
170	97110	97076	97042	97007	96972	96938	96902	96867	96832	96796
180	96760	96724	96688	96651	96614	96578	96540	96503	96466	96428
190	96390	96352	96314	96275	96236	96198	96158	96119	96080	96040
0,200	96000	95960	95920	95879	95838	95798	95756	95715	95674	95632
210	95590	95548	95506	95463	95420	95378	95334	95291	95248	95204
220	95160	95116	95072	95027	94982	94938	94892	94847	94802	94756
230	94710	94664	94618	94571	94524	94478	94430	94383	94336	94288
240	94240	94192	94144	94095	94046	93998	93948	93899	93850	93800
0,250	93750	93700	93650	93599	93548	93498	93446	93395	93344	93292
260	93240	93188	93136	93083	93030	92978	92924	92871	92818	92764
270	92710	92656	92602	92547	92492	92438	92382	92327	92272	92216
280	92160	92104	92048	91991	91934	91878	91820	91763	91706	91648
290	91590	91532	91474	91415	91356	91298	91238	91179	91120	91060
0,300	91000	90940	90880	90819	90758	90698	90636	90575	90514	90452
310	90390	90328	90266	90203	90140	90078	90014	89951	89888	89824
320	89760	89696	89632	89567	89502	89438	89372	89307	89242	89176
330	89110	89044	88978	88911	88844	88778	88710	88643	88576	88508
340	88440	88372	88304	88235	88166	88098	88028	87959	87890	87820
0,350	87750	87680	87610	87539	87468	87398	87326	87255	87184	87112
360	87040	86968	86896	86823	86750	86678	86604	86531	86458	86384
370	86310	86236	86162	86087	86012	85938	85862	85787	85712	85636
380	85560	85484	85408	85331	85254	85178	85100	85023	84946	84868
390	84790	84712	84634	84555	84476	84398	84318	84239	84160	84080
0,400	84000	83920	83840	83759	83678	83598	83516	83435	83354	83272
410	83190	83108	83026	82943	82860	82778	82694	82611	82528	82444
420	82360	82276	82192	82107	82022	81938	81852	81767	81682	81596
430	81510	81424	81338	81251	81164	81078	80990	80903	80816	80728
440	80640	80552	80464	80375	80286	80198	80108	80019	79930	79840
0,450	79750	79660	79570	79479	79388	79298	79206	79115	79024	78932
460	78840	78748	78656	78563	78470	78378	78284	78191	78098	78004
470	77910	77816	77722	77627	77532	77438	77342	77247	77152	77056
480	76960	76864	76768	76671	76574	76478	76380	76283	76186	76088
490	75990	75892	75794	75695	75596	75498	75398	75299	75200	75100
0,500	75000	74900	74800	74699	74598	74498	74396	74295	74194	74092
510	73990	73888	73786	73683	73580	73478	73374	73271	73168	73064
520	72960	72856	72752	72647	72542	72438	72332	72227	72122	72016
530	71910	71804	71698	71591	71484	71378	71270	71163	71056	70948
540	70840	70732	70624	70515	70406	70298	70188	70079	69970	69860
0,550	69750	69640	69530	69419	69308	69198	69086	68975	68864	68752
560	68640	68528	68416	68303	68190	68078	67964	67851	67738	67624
570	67510	67396	67282	67167	67052	66938	66822	66707	66592	66476
580	66360	66244	66128	66011	65894	65778	65660	65543	65426	65308
590	65190	65072	64954	64835	64716	64598	64478	64359	64240	64120
0,600	64000	63880	63760	63639	63518	63398	63276	63155	63034	62912
610	62790	62668	62546	62423	62300	62178	62054	61931	61808	61684
620	61560	61436	61312	61187	61062	60938	60812	60687	60562	60436
630	60310	60184	60058	59931	59804	59678	59550	59423	59296	59168
640	59040	58912	58784	58655	58526	58398	58268	58139	58010	57880
0,650	57750	57620	57490	57359	57228	57098	56966	56835	56704	56572
660	56440	56308	56176	56043	55910	55778	55644	55511	55378	55244
670	55110	54976	54842	54707	54572	54438	54302	54167	54032	53896
680	53760	53624	53488	53351	53214	53078	52940	52803	52666	52528
690	52390	52252	52114	51975	51836	51698	51558	51419	51280	51140
0,700	51000	50860	50720	50579	50438	50298	50156	50015	49874	49732
710	49590	49448	49306	49163	49020	48878	48734	48591	48448	48304
720	48160	48016	47872	47727	47582	47438	47292	47147	47002	46856
730	46710	46564	46418	46271	46124	45978	45830	45683	45536	45388
740	45240	45092	44944	44795	44646	44498	44348	44199	44050	43900
0,750	43750	43600	43450	43299	43148	42998	42846	42695	42544	42392
760	42240	42088	41936	41783	41630	41478	41324	41171	41018	40864
770	40710	40556	40402	40247	40092	39938	39782	39627	39472	39316
780	39160	39004	38848	38691	38534	38378	38220	38063	37906	37748
790	37590	37432	37274	37115	36956	36798	36638	36479	36320	36160
0,800	36000	35840	35680	35519	35358	35198	35036	34875	34714	34552
810	34390	34228	34066	33903	33740	33578	33414	33251	33088	32924
820	32760	32596	32432	32267	32102	31938	31772	31607	31442	31276
830	31110	30944	30778	30611	30444	30278	30110	29943	29776	29608
840	29440	29272	29104	28935	28766	28598	28428	28259	28090	27920
0,850	27750	27580	27410	27239	27068	26898	26726	26555	26384	26212
860	26040	25868	25696	25523	25350	25178	25004	24831	24658	24484
870	24310	24136	23962	23787	23612	23438	23262	23087	22912	22736
880	22560	22384	22208	22031	21854	21678	21500	21323	21146	20968
890	20790	20612	20434	20255	20076	19898	19718	19539	19360	19180
0,900	19000	18820	18640	18459	18278	18098	17916	17735	17554	17372
910	17190	17008	16826	16643	16460	16278	16094	15911	15728	15544
920	15360	15176	14992	14807	14622	14438	14252	14067	13882	13696
930	13510	13324	13138	12951	12764	12578	12390	12203	12016	11828
940	11640	11452	11264	11075	10886	10698	10508	10319	10130	09940
0,950	09750	09560	09370	09179	08988	08798	08606	08415	08224	08032
960	07840	07648	07456	07263	07070	06878	06684	06491	06298	06104
970	05910	05716	05522	05327	05132	04938	04742	04547	04352	04156
980	03960	03764	03568	03371	03174	02978	02780	02583	02386	02188
990	01990	01792	01594	01395	01196	00998	00798	00599	00400	00200

 ◊1,00000.

All values conform to the international convention (i.e. 0,1 instead of 0.1).

n	$\sqrt{\frac{n-1}{n-2}}$	$\frac{n-1}{n-2}$	n	$\sqrt{\frac{n-1}{n-2}}$	$\frac{n-1}{n-2}$	n	$\sqrt{\frac{n-1}{n-2}}$	$\frac{n-1}{n-2}$	n	$\sqrt{\frac{n-1}{n-2}}$	$\frac{n-1}{n-2}$	n	$\sqrt{\frac{n-1}{n-2}}$	$\frac{n-1}{n-2}$
	1,	1,		1,	1,		1,	1,		1,	1,		1,	1,
0	–	–	**50**	01036	02083	**100**	00509	01020	**150**	00337	00676	**200**	00252	00505
1	–	–	51	01015	02041	101	00504	01010	151	00335	00671	201	00251	00503
2	–	–	52	00995	02000	102	00499	01000	152	00333	00667	202	00250	00500
3	41421	◊	53	00976	01961	103	00494	00990	153	00331	00662	203	00248	00498
4	22474	50000	54	00957	01923	104	00489	00980	154	00328	00658	204	00247	00495
5	15470	33333	**55**	00939	01887	**105**	00484	00971	**155**	00326	00654	**205**	00246	00493
6	11803	25000	56	00922	01852	106	00480	00962	156	00324	00649	206	00245	00490
7	09545	20000	57	00905	01818	107	00475	00952	157	00322	00645	207	00244	00488
8	08012	16667	58	00889	01786	108	00471	00943	158	00320	00641	208	00242	00485
9	06904	14286	59	00873	01754	109	00466	00935	159	00318	00637	209	00241	00483
10	06066	12500	**60**	00858	01724	**110**	00462	00926	**160**	00316	00633	**210**	00240	00481
11	05409	11111	61	00844	01695	111	00458	00917	161	00314	00629	211	00239	00478
12	04881	10000	62	00830	01667	112	00454	00909	162	00312	00625	212	00238	00476
13	04447	09091	63	00816	01639	113	00449	00901	163	00310	00621	213	00237	00474
14	04083	08333	64	00803	01613	114	00445	00893	164	00308	00617	214	00236	00472
15	03775	07692	**65**	00791	01587	**115**	00442	00885	**165**	00306	00613	**215**	00234	00469
16	03510	07143	66	00778	01563	116	00438	00877	166	00304	00610	216	00233	00467
17	03280	06667	67	00766	01538	117	00434	00870	167	00303	00606	217	00232	00465
18	03078	06250	68	00755	01515	118	00430	00862	168	00301	00602	218	00231	00463
19	02899	05882	69	00744	01493	119	00426	00855	169	00299	00599	219	00230	00461
20	02740	05556	**70**	00733	01471	**120**	00423	00847	**170**	00297	00595	**220**	00229	00459
21	02598	05263	71	00722	01449	121	00419	00840	171	00295	00592	221	00228	00457
22	02470	05000	72	00712	01429	122	00416	00833	172	00294	00588	222	00227	00455
23	02353	04762	73	00702	01408	123	00412	00826	173	00292	00585	223	00226	00452
24	02247	04545	74	00692	01389	124	00409	00820	174	00290	00581	224	00225	00450
25	02151	04348	**75**	00683	01370	**125**	00406	00813	**175**	00289	00578	**225**	00224	00448
26	02062	04167	76	00673	01351	126	00402	00806	176	00287	00575	226	00223	00446
27	01980	04000	77	00664	01333	127	00399	00800	177	00285	00571	227	00222	00444
28	01905	03846	78	00656	01316	128	00396	00794	178	00284	00568	228	00221	00442
29	01835	03704	79	00647	01299	129	00393	00787	179	00282	00565	229	00220	00441
30	01770	03571	**80**	00639	01282	**130**	00390	00781	**180**	00281	00562	**230**	00219	00439
31	01710	03448	81	00631	01266	131	00387	00775	181	00279	00559	231	00218	00437
32	01653	03333	82	00623	01250	132	00384	00769	182	00277	00556	232	00217	00435
33	01600	03226	83	00615	01235	133	00381	00763	183	00276	00552	233	00216	00433
34	01550	03125	84	00608	01220	134	00378	00758	184	00274	00549	234	00215	00431
35	01504	03030	**85**	00601	01205	**135**	00375	00752	**185**	00273	00546	**235**	00214	00429
36	01460	02941	86	00593	01190	136	00372	00746	186	00271	00543	236	00213	00427
37	01419	02857	87	00587	01176	137	00370	00741	187	00270	00541	237	00213	00426
38	01379	02778	88	00580	01163	138	00367	00735	188	00268	00538	238	00212	00424
39	01342	02703	89	00573	01149	139	00364	00730	189	00267	00535	239	00211	00422
40	01307	02632	**90**	00567	01136	**140**	00362	00725	**190**	00266	00532	**240**	00210	00420
41	01274	02564	91	00560	01124	141	00359	00719	191	00264	00529	241	00209	00418
42	01242	02500	92	00554	01111	142	00357	00714	192	00263	00526	242	00208	00417
43	01212	02439	93	00548	01099	143	00354	00709	193	00261	00524	243	00207	00415
44	01183	02381	94	00542	01087	144	00351	00704	194	00260	00521	244	00206	00413
45	01156	02326	**95**	00536	01075	**145**	00349	00699	**195**	00259	00518	**245**	00206	00412
46	01130	02273	96	00531	01064	146	00347	00694	196	00257	00515	246	00205	00410
47	01105	02222	97	00525	01053	147	00344	00690	197	00256	00513	247	00204	00408
48	01081	02174	98	00519	01042	148	00342	00685	198	00255	00510	248	00203	00407
49	01058	02128	99	00514	01031	149	00340	00680	199	00253	00508	249	00202	00405
50	01036	02083	**100**	00509	01020	**150**	00337	00676	**200**	00252	00505	**250**	00202	00403

Examples: $s_{y.x} = s_y\sqrt{1-r^2}\sqrt{\frac{n-1}{n-2}}$; $s^2_{y.x} = s^2_y(1-r^2)\frac{n-1}{n-2}$, etc.

 ◊2,00000.

Explanation of the table on page 63

The table gives the values of

$$|r| = \frac{t_{2\alpha}}{\sqrt{\nu + t^2_{2\alpha}}} \quad [\nu\text{: degrees of freedom of } t]$$

for testing whether a correlation coefficient differs significantly from 0. The table also allows the corresponding regression coefficients to be tested automatically in the same way. If, for example, $r_{xy} \neq 0$, then b_{xy} and b_{yx} are not equal to 0.

All values conform to the international convention (i.e. 0,1 instead of 0.1).

The degrees of freedom are found as follows: subtract 2 from the number n of pairs of observations. In the case of partial correlation coefficients the number of excluded variables is also subtracted. Examples:

r_{12} (ordinary correlation coefficient): $\nu = n-2$

$r_{12.3}$ (partial correlation coefficient excluding one variable): $\nu = n-2-1$

$r_{12.34}$ (partial correlation coefficient excluding two variables): $\nu = n-2-2$

2α	0,1	0,05	0,01	0,001	2α	0,1	0,05	0,01	0,001
ν					ν				
1	0,9877	0,9969	0,9999	1,0000	101	0,1630	0,1937	0,2528	0,3196
2	9000	9500	9900	0,9990	102	1622	1927	2515	3181
3	8054	8783	9587	9911	103	1614	1918	2504	3166
4	7293	8114	9172	9741	104	1606	1909	2492	3152
5	0,6694	0,7545	0,8745	0,9509	**105**	0,1599	0,1900	0,2480	0,3138
6	6215	7067	8343	9249	106	1591	1891	2469	3123
7	5822	6664	7977	8983	107	1584	1882	2458	3109
8	5494	6319	7646	8721	108	1577	1874	2447	3095
9	5214	6021	7348	8471	109	1569	1865	2436	3082
10	0,4973	0,5760	0,7079	0,8233	**110**	0,1562	0,1857	0,2425	0,3069
11	4762	5529	6835	8010	111	1555	1848	2414	3055
12	4575	5324	6614	7800	112	1548	1840	2404	3042
13	4409	5139	6411	7604	113	1542	1832	2393	3029
14	4259	4973	6226	7419	114	1535	1824	2383	3017
15	0,4124	0,4821	0,6055	0,7247	**115**	0,1528	0,1816	0,2373	0,3004
16	4000	4683	5897	7084	116	1522	1809	2363	2992
17	3887	4555	5751	6932	117	1515	1801	2353	2979
18	3783	4438	5614	6788	118	1509	1793	2343	2967
19	3687	4329	5487	6652	119	1502	1786	2334	2955
20	0,3598	0,4227	0,5368	0,6524	**120**	0,1496	0,1779	0,2324	0,2943
21	3515	4132	5256	6402	121	1490	1771	2315	2932
22	3438	4044	5151	6287	122	1484	1764	2305	2920
23	3365	3961	5052	6177	123	1478	1757	2296	2909
24	3297	3882	4958	6073	124	1472	1750	2287	2897
25	0,3233	0,3809	0,4869	0,5974	**125**	0,1466	0,1743	0,2278	0,2886
26	3172	3739	4785	5880	126	1460	1736	2269	2875
27	3115	3673	4705	5790	127	1455	1730	2261	2864
28	3061	3610	4629	5703	128	1449	1723	2252	2854
29	3009	3550	4556	5620	129	1443	1716	2243	2843
30	0,2960	0,3494	0,4487	0,5541	**130**	0,1438	0,1710	0,2235	0,2832
31	2913	3440	4421	5465	131	1432	1703	2226	2822
32	2869	3388	4357	5392	132	1427	1697	2218	2812
33	2826	3338	4297	5322	133	1422	1690	2210	2801
34	2785	3291	4238	5255	134	1416	1684	2202	2791
35	0,2746	0,3246	0,4182	0,5189	**135**	0,1411	0,1678	0,2194	0,2781
36	2709	3202	4128	5126	136	1406	1672	2186	2771
37	2673	3160	4076	5066	137	1401	1666	2178	2762
38	2638	3120	4026	5007	138	1396	1660	2170	2752
39	2605	3081	3978	4951	139	1391	1654	2163	2742
40	0,2573	0,3044	0,3932	0,4896	**140**	0,1386	0,1648	0,2155	0,2733
41	2542	3008	3887	4843	141	1381	1642	2148	2724
42	2512	2973	3843	4792	142	1376	1637	2140	2714
43	2483	2940	3802	4742	143	1371	1631	2133	2705
44	2455	2907	3761	4694	144	1367	1625	2126	2696
45	0,2428	0,2875	0,3721	0,4647	**145**	0,1362	0,1620	0,2118	0,2687
46	2403	2845	3683	4602	146	1357	1614	2111	2678
47	2377	2816	3646	4558	147	1353	1609	2104	2669
48	2353	2787	3610	4515	148	1348	1603	2097	2660
49	2329	2759	3575	4473	149	1344	1598	2090	2652
50	0,2306	0,2732	0,3541	0,4433	**150**	0,1339	0,1593	0,2083	0,2643
51	2284	2706	3509	4393	151	1335	1587	2077	2635
52	2262	2681	3477	4355	152	1330	1582	2070	2626
53	2241	2656	3445	4317	153	1326	1577	2063	2618
54	2221	2632	3415	4281	154	1322	1572	2057	2610
55	0,2201	0,2609	0,3385	0,4245	**155**	0,1318	0,1567	0,2050	0,2602
56	2181	2586	3357	4210	156	1313	1562	2044	2594
57	2162	2564	3329	4176	157	1309	1557	2037	2586
58	2144	2542	3301	4143	158	1305	1552	2031	2578
59	2126	2521	3274	4111	159	1301	1547	2025	2570
60	0,2108	0,2500	0,3248	0,4079	**160**	0,1297	0,1543	0,2019	0,2562
61	2091	2480	3223	4048	161	1293	1538	2012	2554
62	2075	2461	3198	4018	162	1289	1533	2006	2547
63	2058	2442	3174	3988	163	1285	1529	2000	2539
64	2042	2423	3150	3959	164	1281	1524	1994	2532
65	0,2027	0,2405	0,3127	0,3931	**165**	0,1277	0,1519	0,1988	0,2524
66	2012	2387	3104	3904	166	1273	1515	1982	2517
67	1997	2369	3081	3877	167	1270	1510	1977	2510
68	1982	2352	3060	3850	168	1266	1506	1971	2502
69	1968	2335	3038	3824	169	1262	1501	1965	2495
70	0,1954	0,2319	0,3017	0,3798	**170**	0,1258	0,1497	0,1959	0,2488
71	1940	2303	2997	3773	171	1255	1493	1954	2481
72	1927	2287	2977	3749	172	1251	1488	1948	2474
73	1914	2272	2957	3725	173	1248	1484	1943	2467
74	1901	2257	2938	3701	174	1244	1480	1937	2460
75	0,1889	0,2242	0,2919	0,3678	**175**	0,1240	0,1476	0,1932	0,2453
76	1876	2227	2900	3655	176	1237	1471	1926	2446
77	1864	2213	2882	3633	177	1233	1467	1921	2440
78	1852	2199	2864	3611	178	1230	1463	1915	2433
79	1841	2185	2847	3590	179	1227	1459	1910	2426
80	0,1829	0,2172	0,2830	0,3569	**180**	0,1223	0,1455	0,1905	0,2420
81	1818	2159	2813	3548	181	1220	1451	1900	2413
82	1807	2146	2796	3527	182	1216	1447	1895	2407
83	1796	2133	2780	3507	183	1213	1443	1890	2400
84	1786	2120	2764	3488	184	1210	1439	1885	2394
85	0,1775	0,2108	0,2748	0,3468	**185**	0,1207	0,1435	0,1880	0,2388
86	1765	2096	2733	3449	186	1203	1432	1874	2381
87	1755	2084	2717	3430	187	1200	1428	1870	2375
88	1745	2072	2702	3412	188	1197	1424	1865	2369
89	1735	2061	2688	3394	189	1194	1420	1860	2363
90	0,1726	0,2050	0,2673	0,3376	**190**	0,1191	0,1417	0,1855	0,2357
91	1716	2039	2659	3358	191	1188	1413	1850	2351
92	1707	2028	2645	3341	192	1184	1409	1845	2345
93	1698	2017	2631	3324	193	1181	1406	1841	2339
94	1689	2006	2617	3307	194	1178	1402	1836	2333
95	0,1680	0,1996	0,2604	0,3291	**195**	0,1175	0,1399	0,1831	0,2327
96	1671	1986	2591	3274	196	1172	1395	1827	2321
97	1663	1976	2578	3258	197	1169	1391	1822	2316
98	1654	1966	2565	3242	198	1166	1388	1818	2310
99	1646	1956	2552	3227	199	1164	1384	1813	2304
100	0,1638	0,1946	0,2540	0,3211	**200**	0,1161	0,1381	0,1809	0,2299

All values conform to the international convention (i.e. 0,1 instead of 0.1).

r	0,000	0,001	0,002	0,003	0,004	0,005	0,006	0,007	0,008	0,009
0,000	0,00000	0,00100	0,00200	0,00300	0,00400	0,00500	0,00600	0,00700	0,00800	0,00900
010	01000	01100	01200	01300	01400	01500	01600	01700	01800	01900
020	02000	02100	02200	02300	02400	02501	02601	02701	02801	02901
030	03001	03101	03201	03301	03401	03501	03602	03702	03802	03902
040	04002	04102	04202	04303	04403	04503	04603	04703	04804	04904
0,050	0,05004	0,05104	0,05205	0,05305	0,05405	0,05506	0,05606	0,05706	0,05806	0,05907
060	06007	06108	06208	06308	06409	06509	06610	06710	06810	06911
070	07011	07112	07212	07313	07414	07514	07615	07715	07816	07916
080	08017	08118	08218	08319	08420	08521	08621	08722	08823	08924
090	09024	09125	09226	09327	09428	09529	09630	09731	09832	09933
0,100	0,10034	0,10135	0,10236	0,10337	0,10438	0,10539	0,10640	0,10741	0,10842	0,10943
110	11045	11146	11247	11348	11450	11551	11652	11754	11855	11957
120	12058	12160	12261	12363	12464	12566	12667	12769	12871	12972
130	13074	13176	13277	13379	13481	13583	13685	13787	13889	13991
140	14093	14195	14297	14399	14501	14603	14705	14807	14910	15012
0,150	0,15114	0,15216	0,15319	0,15421	0,15524	0,15626	0,15728	0,15831	0,15934	0,16036
160	16139	16241	16344	16447	16549	16652	16755	16858	16961	17064
170	17167	17270	17373	17476	17579	17682	17785	17888	17992	18095
180	18198	18302	18405	18509	18612	18716	18819	18923	19026	19130
190	19234	19338	19441	19545	19649	19753	19857	19961	20065	20169
0,200	0,20273	0,20377	0,20482	0,20586	0,20690	0,20795	0,20899	0,21004	0,21108	0,21213
210	21317	21422	21526	21631	21736	21841	21946	22051	22156	22261
220	22366	22471	22576	22681	22786	22892	22997	23102	23208	23313
230	23419	23525	23630	23736	23842	23948	24053	24159	24265	24371
240	24477	24584	24690	24796	24902	25009	25115	25222	25328	25435
0,250	0,25541	0,25648	0,25755	0,25862	0,25968	0,26075	0,26182	0,26289	0,26396	0,26504
260	26611	26718	26825	26933	27040	27148	27255	27363	27471	27579
270	27686	27794	27902	28010	28118	28226	28335	28443	28551	28660
280	28768	28877	28985	29094	29203	29312	29420	29529	29638	29747
290	29857	29966	30075	30184	30294	30403	30513	30623	30732	30842
0,300	0,30952	0,31062	0,31172	0,31282	0,31392	0,31502	0,31613	0,31723	0,31833	0,31944
310	32055	32165	32276	32387	32498	32609	32720	32831	32942	33053
320	33165	33276	33388	33499	33611	33723	33835	33947	34059	34171
330	34283	34395	34507	34620	34732	34845	34958	35070	35183	35296
340	35409	35522	35636	35749	35862	35976	36089	36203	36317	36430
0,350	0,36544	0,36658	0,36772	0,36887	0,37001	0,37115	0,37230	0,37344	0,37459	0,37574
360	37689	37804	37919	38034	38149	38264	38380	38495	38611	38726
370	38842	38958	39074	39190	39307	39423	39539	39656	39772	39889
380	40006	40123	40240	40357	40474	40592	40709	40827	40944	41062
390	41180	41298	41416	41534	41653	41771	41890	42008	42127	42246
0,400	0,42365	0,42484	0,42603	0,42723	0,42842	0,42962	0,43081	0,43201	0,43321	0,43441
410	43561	43681	43802	43922	44043	44164	44284	44405	44527	44648
420	44769	44891	45012	45134	45256	45378	45500	45622	45745	45867
430	45990	46112	46235	46358	46481	46605	46728	46852	46975	47099
440	47223	47347	47471	47596	47720	47845	47970	48094	48220	48345
0,450	0,48470	0,48595	0,48721	0,48847	0,48973	0,49099	0,49225	0,49351	0,49478	0,49604
460	49731	49858	49985	50112	50240	50367	50495	50623	50751	50879
470	51007	51135	51264	51393	51522	51651	51780	51909	52039	52169
480	52298	52428	52559	52689	52819	52950	53081	53212	53343	53475
490	53606	53738	53870	54002	54134	54266	54399	54531	54664	54797
0,500	0,54931	0,55064	0,55198	0,55331	0,55465	0,55600	0,55734	0,55868	0,56003	0,56138
510	56273	56408	56544	56679	56815	56951	57087	57224	57360	57497
520	57634	57771	57908	58046	58184	58322	58460	58598	58737	58876
530	59015	59154	59293	59433	59572	59712	59853	59993	60134	60274
540	60416	60557	60698	60840	60982	61124	61266	61409	61552	61695
0,550	0,61838	0,61982	0,62125	0,62269	0,62413	0,62558	0,62702	0,62847	0,62992	0,63138
560	63283	63429	63575	63721	63868	64015	64162	64309	64457	64604
570	64752	64901	65049	65198	65347	65496	65646	65795	65945	66096
580	66246	66397	66548	66700	66851	67003	67155	67308	67460	67613
590	67767	67920	68074	68228	68382	68537	68692	68847	69003	69159
0,600	0,69315	0,69471	0,69628	0,69785	0,69942	0,70100	0,70258	0,70416	0,70574	0,70733
610	70892	71052	71211	71371	71532	71692	71853	72015	72176	72338
620	72500	72663	72826	72989	73153	73317	73481	73646	73811	73976
630	74142	74308	74474	74641	74808	74975	75143	75311	75479	75648
640	75817	75987	76157	76327	76498	76669	76840	77012	77184	77357
0,650	0,77530	0,77703	0,77877	0,78051	0,78226	0,78401	0,78576	0,78752	0,78928	0,79104
660	79281	79459	79637	79815	79993	80172	80352	80532	80712	80893
670	81074	81256	81438	81621	81804	81987	82171	82355	82540	82726
680	82911	83098	83284	83472	83659	83847	84036	84225	84415	84605
690	84796	84987	85178	85370	85563	85756	85950	86144	86339	86534
0,700	0,86730	0,86926	0,87123	0,87321	0,87519	0,87717	0,87916	0,88116	0,88316	0,88517
710	88718	88920	89123	89326	89530	89734	89939	90144	90350	90557
720	90765	90972	91181	91390	91600	91811	92022	92233	92446	92659
730	92873	93087	93302	93518	93735	93952	94169	94388	94607	94827
740	95048	95269	95491	95714	95938	96162	96387	96613	96840	97067
0,750	0,97296	0,97524	0,97754	0,97985	0,98216	0,98448	0,98681	0,98915	0,99150	0,99385
760	99622	99859	1,00097	1,00336	1,00575	1,00816	1,01058	1,01300	1,01543	1,01788
770	1,02033	1,02279	02526	02774	03023	03273	03524	03775	04028	04282
780	04537	04793	05050	05308	05567	05827	06088	06350	06613	06878
790	07143	07410	07677	07946	08216	08488	08760	09033	09308	09584
0,800	1,09861	1,10140	1,10419	1,10700	1,10982	1,11266	1,11551	1,11837	1,12124	1,12413
810	12703	12994	13287	13581	13877	14174	14473	14773	15074	15377
820	15682	15988	16295	16604	16915	17227	17541	17857	18174	18493
830	18814	19136	19460	19786	20113	20443	20774	21107	21442	21779
840	22117	22458	22801	23145	23492	23840	24191	24544	24899	25256
0,850	1,25615	1,25977	1,26340	1,26706	1,27075	1,27445	1,27818	1,28194	1,28571	1,28952
860	29334	29720	30108	30498	30891	31287	31686	32087	32491	32898
870	33308	33721	34137	34555	34977	35403	35831	36262	36697	37135
880	37577	38022	38470	38922	39378	39838	40301	40768	41239	41714
890	42193	42676	43163	43654	44150	44651	45156	45665	46179	46698
0,900	1,47222	1,47751	1,48285	1,48824	1,49368	1,49918	1,50473	1,51034	1,51601	1,52174
910	52752	53337	53928	54526	55130	55741	56359	56984	57616	58256
920	58903	59558	60221	60892	61571	62260	62957	63663	64379	65104
930	65839	66584	67340	68107	68885	69674	70475	71288	72114	72953
940	73805	74671	75552	76447	77358	78284	79227	80188	81166	82162
0,950	1,83178	1,84214	1,85270	1,86349	1,87450	1,88574	1,89723	1,90898	1,92100	1,93331
960	94591	95882	97207	98566	99961	2,01395	2,02870	2,04388	2,05952	2,07565
970	2,09230	2,10950	2,12730	2,14574	2,16486	18472	20539	22692	24940	27291
980	29756	32346	35075	37958	41014	44266	47741	51472	55499	59875
990	64665	69958	75873	82574	90307	99448	3,10630	3,25039	3,45338	3,80020

z-Transformation

When the population correlation coefficient ϱ differs from 0, the distribution of the sample correlation coefficient is complicated. However, its distribution can be approximated to a normal distribution by the z-transformation. The approximation improves as n (the number of pairs of observations) increases and is better the greater the absolute value of r.

$$z = \tfrac{1}{2}\ln\frac{1+r}{1-r}$$

[z: values in the table on this page]

and

$$r = \frac{e^{2z}-1}{e^{2z}+1} = \tanh z$$

[tanh z: see pages 66 and 67]

The variance of z is

$$\sigma_z^2 = \frac{1}{n-p-3} = \frac{1}{n'-3}$$

where n = number of pairs of observations, p = number of excluded variables. In the case of the correlation coefficient r_{xy}, for example, $p = 0$, whence $n' = n$; in the case of the partial correlation coefficient $r_{xy.z}$, $p = 1$, whence $n' = n-1$.

The approximate expected value $\boldsymbol{z}$ of z (see page 216) is

$$\boldsymbol{z} \approx \tfrac{1}{2}\ln\frac{1+\varrho}{1-\varrho}$$

where ϱ is the population value of r.

$\boldsymbol{z}$ is estimated by z, with k correlation coefficients by $\bar{z}$ (see footnote):

$$\bar{z} = \frac{\sum_{1}^{k}(n_i'-3)\,z_i}{\sum_{1}^{k}(n_i'-3)}$$

with the variance

$$\sigma_{\bar{z}}^2 = \frac{1}{\sum_{1}^{k}(n_i'-3)}$$

The confidence interval for $\boldsymbol{z}$ is

$$z \pm \frac{|c_\alpha|}{\sqrt{n'-3}} \quad \text{or} \quad \bar{z} \pm |c_\alpha|\,\sigma_{\bar{z}}$$

[$|c_\alpha|/\sqrt{n'-3}$ see table on next page]

The confidence interval for ϱ is

$$\tanh\left(z-\frac{|c_\alpha|}{\sqrt{n'-3}}\right) \le \boldsymbol{r} \le \tanh\left(z+\frac{|c_\alpha|}{\sqrt{n'-3}}\right)$$

$$\text{or } \tanh(\bar{z}-|c_\alpha|\,\sigma_{\bar{z}}) \le \varrho \le \tanh(\bar{z}+|c_\alpha|\,\sigma_{\bar{z}})$$

Tests

Testing for $\boldsymbol{r} = r_0$

$$c = (z-\boldsymbol{z}_0)\sqrt{n'-3}$$

Testing for $\boldsymbol{r}_1 = \boldsymbol{r}_2$

$$c = \frac{z_1-z_2}{\sqrt{\dfrac{1}{n_1'-3}+\dfrac{1}{n_2'-3}}}$$

For other tests see pages 215 and 216.

$\bar{z}$ can be used for estimating $\boldsymbol{z}$ only when χ^2 is not significant, i.e., when

$$\chi^2 = \sum_{1}^{k}(n_i'-3)(z_i-\bar{z})^2$$

does not exceed a chosen upper significance limit with degrees of freedom $\nu = k-1$.

All values conform to the international convention (i.e. 0,1 instead of 0.1).

Confidence Limits* for the Correlation Coefficient r

Confidence limits for $\mathfrak{z} = z \pm |c_{\alpha}| / \sqrt{n'-3}$. The table gives the values for $|c_{\alpha}| / \sqrt{n'-3}$. See page 216

95% limits $(1-2\alpha = 0{,}95)$

n'	0	1	2	3	4	5	6	7	8	9
	0,	0,	0,	0,	0,	0,	0,	0,	0,	0,
10	74080	69295	65332	61980	59095	56579	54360	52382	50606	48999
20	47536	46197	44965	43826	42770	41787	40868	40008	39199	38438
30	37720	37040	36396	35784	35202	34648	34119	33613	33129	32666
40	32222	31795	31385	30990	30609	30243	29889	29548	29217	28898
50	28589	28290	27999	27718	27445	27180	26922	26672	26428	26191
60	25960	25736	25517	25303	25095	24892	24693	24500	24310	24125
70	23945	23768	23595	23426	23260	23098	22940	22784	22632	22482
80	22336	22192	22051	21913	21777	21644	21513	21385	21259	21135
90	21013	20893	20776	20660	20546	20434	20324	20215	20109	20004
100	19900	19799	19698	19600	19502	19407	19312	19219	19127	19037
110	18948	18860	18773	18688	18603	18520	18438	18357	18277	18198
120	18120	18043	17967	17892	17818	17745	17672	17601	17530	17461
130	17392	17324	17257	17190	17124	17059	16995	16932	16869	16807
140	16745	16684	16624	16565	16506	16448	16390	16333	16277	16221
150	16166	16111	16057	16003	15950	15897	15845	15794	15743	15692
160	15642	15593	15544	15495	15447	15399	15352	15305	15258	15212
170	15167	15121	15077	15032	14988	14945	14901	14858	14816	14774
180	14732	14691	14649	14609	14568	14528	14488	14449	14410	14371
190	14333	14295	14257	14219	14182	14145	14108	14072	14036	14000
200	13964	13929	13894	13859	13825	13790	13756	13722	13689	13656
210	13623	13590	13557	13525	13493	13461	13429	13398	13367	13336
220	13305	13275	13244	13214	13184	13154	13125	13096	13066	13037
230	13009	12980	12952	12924	12896	12868	12840	12813	12785	12758
240	12731	12705	12678	12652	12625	12599	12573	12547	12522	12496
250	12471	12446	12421	12396	12371	12347	12322	12298	12274	12250
260	12226	12202	12179	12155	12132	12109	12086	12063	12040	12017
270	11995	11972	11950	11928	11906	11884	11862	11841	11819	11798
280	11776	11755	11734	11713	11692	11671	11651	11630	11610	11590
290	11569	11549	11529	11509	11490	11470	11450	11431	11411	11392
300	11373	11354	11335	11316	11297	11278	11260	11241	11223	11204
310	11186	11168	11150	11132	11114	11096	11078	11061	11043	11026
320	11008	10991	10974	10957	10939	10922	10906	10889	10872	10855
330	10839	10822	10806	10789	10773	10757	10741	10724	10708	10692
340	10677	10661	10645	10629	10614	10598	10583	10567	10552	10537
350	10522	10507	10491	10476	10462	10447	10432	10417	10402	10388
360	10373	10359	10344	10330	10316	10301	10287	10273	10259	10245
370	10231	10217	10203	10189	10176	10162	10148	10135	10121	10108
380	10094	10081	10068	10054	10041	10028	10015	10002	09989	09976
390	09963	09950	09937	09925	09912	09899	09887	09874	09862	09849
400	09837	09824	09812	09800	09788	09775	09763	09751	09739	09727
410	09715	09703	09691	09680	09668	09656	09644	09633	09621	09610
420	09598	09586	09575	09564	09552	09541	09530	09518	09507	09496
430	09485	09474	09463	09452	09441	09430	09419	09408	09397	09387
440	09376	09365	09354	09344	09333	09323	09312	09302	09291	09281
450	09270	09260	09250	09239	09229	09219	09209	09199	09188	09178
460	09168	09158	09148	09138	09128	09119	09109	09099	09089	09079
470	09070	09060	09050	09041	09031	09021	09012	09002	08993	08983
480	08974	08965	08955	08946	08937	08927	08918	08909	08900	08891
490	08881	08872	08863	08854	08845	08836	08827	08818	08809	08800
500	08792	08783	08774	08765	08756	08748	08739	08730	08722	08713
510	08705	08696	08687	08679	08670	08662	08653	08645	08637	08628
520	08620	08612	08603	08595	08587	08579	08570	08562	08554	08546
530	08538	08530	08522	08514	08506	08498	08490	08482	08474	08466
540	08458	08450	08442	08434	08427	08419	08411	08403	08396	08388
550	08380	08373	08365	08357	08350	08342	08335	08327	08320	08312
560	08305	08297	08290	08282	08275	08268	08260	08253	08246	08238
570	08231	08224	08217	08209	08202	08195	08188	08181	08174	08167
580	08159	08152	08145	08138	08131	08124	08117	08110	08103	08097
590	08090	08083	08076	08069	08062	08055	08049	08042	08035	08028
600	08022	08015	08008	08002	07995	07988	07982	07975	07968	07962
610	07955	07949	07942	07936	07929	07923	07916	07910	07903	07897
620	07891	07884	07878	07871	07865	07859	07852	07846	07840	07834
630	07827	07821	07815	07809	07802	07796	07790	07784	07778	07772
640	07766	07760	07753	07747	07741	07735	07729	07723	07717	07711
650	07705	07699	07694	07688	07682	07676	07670	07664	07658	07652
660	07647	07641	07635	07629	07623	07618	07612	07606	07600	07595
670	07589	07583	07578	07572	07566	07561	07555	07549	07544	07538
680	07533	07527	07522	07516	07511	07505	07500	07494	07489	07483
690	07478	07472	07467	07461	07456	07451	07445	07440	07435	07429
700	07424	07419	07413	07408	07403	07397	07392	07387	07382	07376
710	07371	07366	07361	07356	07350	07345	07340	07335	07330	07325
720	07320	07315	07309	07304	07299	07294	07289	07284	07279	07274
730	07269	07264	07259	07254	07249	07244	07239	07234	07229	07225
740	07220	07215	07210	07205	07200	07195	07190	07186	07181	07176
750	07171	07166	07162	07157	07152	07147	07143	07138	07133	07128
760	07124	07119	07114	07110	07105	07100	07096	07091	07086	07082
770	07077	07072	07068	07063	07059	07054	07050	07045	07040	07036
780	07031	07027	07022	07018	07013	07009	07004	07000	06995	06991
790	06987	06982	06978	06973	06969	06964	06960	06956	06951	06947
800	06943	06938	06934	06930	06925	06921	06917	06912	06908	06904
810	06899	06895	06891	06887	06882	06878	06874	06870	06865	06861
820	06857	06853	06849	06844	06840	06836	06832	06828	06824	06820
830	06815	06811	06807	06803	06799	06795	06791	06787	06783	06779
840	06775	06771	06767	06763	06758	06754	06750	06746	06742	06738
850	06735	06731	06727	06723	06719	06715	06711	06707	06703	06699
860	06695	06691	06687	06683	06680	06676	06672	06668	06664	06660
870	06656	06653	06649	06645	06641	06637	06633	06630	06626	06622
880	06618	06615	06611	06607	06603	06600	06596	06592	06588	06585
890	06581	06577	06574	06570	06566	06562	06559	06555	06551	06548
900	06544	06540	06537	06533	06530	06526	06522	06519	06515	06512
910	06508	06504	06501	06497	06494	06490	06487	06483	06479	06476
920	06472	06469	06465	06462	06458	06455	06451	06448	06444	06441
930	06437	06434	06430	06427	06424	06420	06417	06413	06410	06406
940	06403	06400	06396	06393	06389	06386	06383	06379	06376	06372
950	06369	06366	06362	06359	06356	06352	06349	06346	06342	06339
960	06336	06332	06329	06326	06322	06319	06316	06313	06309	06306
970	06303	06300	06296	06293	06290	06287	06283	06280	06277	06274
980	06270	06267	06264	06261	06258	06254	06251	06248	06245	06242
990	06239	06235	06232	06229	06226	06223	06220	06217	06214	06210
1000	06207									

99% limits $(1-2\alpha = 0{,}99)$

n'	0	1	2	3	4	5	6	7	8	9
	0,	0,	0,	0,	0,	0,	0,	0,	0,	0,
10	97357	91069	85861	81455	77664	74358	71441	68842	66508	64396
20	62473	60713	59094	57597	56209	54917	53710	52579	51517	50516
30	49572	48679	47832	47028	46263	45535	44839	44175	43539	42930
40	42346	41785	41246	40727	40228	39746	39281	38832	38398	37979
50	37572	37179	36798	36428	36069	35720	35382	35053	34732	34421
60	34118	33822	33534	33254	32980	32713	32452	32198	31949	31706
70	31469	31237	31009	30787	30569	30356	30148	29943	29743	29547
80	29354	29166	28980	28799	28620	28445	28273	28105	27939	27776
90	27616	27458	27304	27152	27002	26855	26710	26568	26427	26289
100	26154	26020	25888	25758	25630	25505	25380	25258	25138	25019
110	24901	24786	24672	24560	24449	24339	24231	24125	24020	23916
120	23814	23712	23613	23514	23417	23320	23225	23132	23039	22947
130	22857	22767	22679	22592	22505	22420	22335	22252	22169	22088
140	22007	21927	21848	21770	21692	21616	21540	21465	21391	21318
150	21245	21173	21102	21032	20962	20893	20824	20757	20690	20623
160	20557	20492	20428	20364	20300	20238	20175	20114	20053	19992
170	19932	19873	19814	19756	19698	19641	19584	19527	19471	19416
180	19361	19307	19253	19199	19146	19093	19041	18989	18938	18887
190	18836	18786	18736	18687	18638	18589	18541	18493	18446	18399
200	18352	18306	18260	18214	18168	18123	18079	18034	17990	17947
210	17903	17860	17817	17775	17733	17691	17649	17608	17567	17526
220	17486	17446	17406	17366	17327	17288	17249	17210	17172	17134
230	17096	17059	17022	16985	16948	16911	16875	16839	16803	16767
240	16732	16697	16662	16627	16592	16558	16524	16490	16456	16423
250	16390	16357	16324	16291	16258	16226	16194	16162	16130	16099
260	16068	16036	16005	15975	15944	15914	15883	15853	15823	15793
270	15764	15734	15705	15676	15647	15618	15590	15561	15533	15505
280	15477	15449	15421	15394	15366	15339	15312	15285	15258	15231
290	15205	15178	15152	15126	15100	15074	15048	15023	14997	14972
300	14946	14921	14896	14872	14847	14822	14798	14773	14749	14725
310	14701	14677	14653	14630	14606	14583	14559	14536	14513	14490
320	14467	14445	14422	14399	14377	14355	14332	14310	14288	14266
330	14244	14223	14201	14179	14158	14137	14115	14094	14073	14052
340	14031	14011	13990	13969	13949	13928	13908	13888	13868	13848
350	13828	13808	13788	13768	13749	13729	13710	13690	13671	13652
360	13633	13614	13595	13576	13557	13538	13520	13501	13483	13464
370	13446	13427	13409	13391	13373	13355	13337	13319	13302	13284
380	13266	13249	13231	13214	13196	13179	13162	13145	13128	13111
390	13094	13077	13060	13043	13027	13010	12993	12977	12960	12944
400	12928	12911	12895	12879	12863	12847	12831	12815	12799	12784
410	12768	12752	12737	12721	12706	12690	12675	12660	12644	12629
420	12614	12599	12584	12569	12554	12539	12524	12509	12495	12480
430	12465	12451	12436	12422	12407	12393	12379	12364	12350	12336
440	12322	12308	12294	12280	12266	12252	12238	12224	12211	12197
450	12183	12170	12156	12143	12129	12116	12102	12089	12076	12062
460	12049	12036	12023	12010	11997	11984	11971	11958	11945	11932
470	11920	11907	11894	11881	11869	11856	11844	11831	11819	11806
480	11794	11782	11769	11757	11745	11733	11720	11708	11696	11684
490	11672	11660	11648	11636	11625	11613	11601	11589	11577	11566
500	11554	11543	11531	11519	11508	11496	11485	11474	11462	11451
510	11440	11428	11417	11406	11395	11384	11373	11361	11350	11339
520	11328	11318	11307	11296	11285	11274	11263	11253	11242	11231
530	11220	11210	11199	11189	11178	11168	11157	11147	11136	11126
540	11116	11105	11095	11085	11074	11064	11054	11044	11034	11024
550	11013	11003	10993	10983	10973	10963	10954	10944	10934	10924
560	10914	10904	10895	10885	10875	10865	10856	10846	10837	10827
570	10817	10808	10798	10789	10780	10770	10761	10751	10742	10733
580	10723	10714	10705	10696	10686	10677	10668	10659	10650	10641
590	10632	10623	10614	10605	10596	10587	10578	10569	10560	10551
600	10542	10533	10525	10516	10507	10498	10490	10481	10472	10464
610	10455	10446	10438	10429	10421	10412	10404	10395	10387	10378
620	10370	10362	10353	10345	10336	10328	10320	10312	10303	10295
630	10287	10279	10271	10262	10254	10246	10238	10230	10222	10214
640	10206	10198	10190	10182	10174	10166	10158	10150	10142	10134
650	10127	10119	10111	10103	10095	10088	10080	10072	10065	10057
660	10049	10042	10034	10026	10019	10011	10004	09996	09989	09981
670	09974	09966	09959	09951	09944	09936	09929	09922	09914	09907
680	09900	09892	09885	09878	09871	09863	09856	09849	09842	09835
690	09827	09820	09813	09806	09799	09792	09785	09778	09771	09764
700	09757	09750	09743	09736	09729	09722	09715	09708	09701	09694
710	09687	09681	09674	09667	09660	09653	09647	09640	09633	09626
720	09620	09613	09606	09600	09593	09586	09580	09573	09566	09560
730	09553	09547	09540	09534	09527	09521	09514	09508	09501	09495
740	09488	09482	09475	09469	09463	09456	09450	09443	09437	09431
750	09424	09418	09412	09406	09399	09393	09387	09381	09374	09368
760	09362	09356	09350	09344	09337	09331	09325	09319	09313	09307
770	09301	09295	09289	09283	09277	09271	09265	09259	09253	09247
780	09241	09235	09229	09223	09217	09211	09205	09199	09194	09188
790	09182	09176	09170	09164	09159	09153	09147	09141	09136	09130
800	09124	09118	09113	09107	09101	09096	09090	09084	09079	09073
810	09067	09062	09056	09051	09045	09039	09034	09028	09023	09017
820	09012	09006	09001	08995	08990	08984	08979	08973	08968	08962
830	08957	08952	08946	08941	08935	08930	08925	08919	08914	08909
840	08903	08898	08893	08887	08882	08877	08872	08866	08861	08856
850	08851	08845	08840	08835	08830	08825	08819	08814	08809	08804
860	08799	08794	08789	08784	08778	08773	08768	08763	08758	08753
870	08748	08743	08738	08733	08728	08723	08718	08713	08708	08703
880	08698	08693	08688	08683	08678	08673	08668	08663	08659	08654
890	08649	08644	08639	08634	08629	08625	08620	08615	08610	08605
900	08600	08596	08591	08586	08581	08577	08572	08567	08562	08558
910	08553	08548	08543	08539	08534	08529	08525	08520	08515	08511
920	08506	08502	08497	08492	08488	08483	08478	08474	08469	08465
930	08460	08456	08451	08446	08442	08437	08433	08428	08424	08419
940	08415	08410	08406	08401	08397	08393	08388	08384	08379	08375
950	08370	08366	08361	08357	08353	08348	08344	08340	08335	08331
960	08326	08322	08318	08313	08309	08305	08300	08296	08292	08288
970	08283	08279	08275	08270	08266	08262	08258	08253	08249	08245
980	08241	08237	08232	08228	08224	08220	08216	08211	08207	08203
990	08199	08195	08191	08187	08182	08178	08174	08170	08166	08162
1000	08158									

All values conform to the international convention (i.e. 0,1 instead of 0.1).

$z = \tanh^{-1} r$

z	0,000	0,001	0,002	0,003	0,004	0,005	0,006	0,007	0,008	0,009
0,000	0,00000	0,00100	0,00200	0,00300	0,00400	0,00500	0,00600	0,00700	0,00800	0,00900
010	01000	01100	01200	01300	01400	01500	01600	01700	01800	01900
020	02000	02100	02200	02300	02400	02499	02599	02699	02799	02899
030	02999	03099	03199	03299	03399	03499	03598	03698	03798	03898
040	03998	04098	04198	04297	04397	04497	04597	04697	04796	04896
0,050	0,04996	0,05096	0,05195	0,05295	0,05395	0,05494	0,05594	0,05694	0,05794	0,05893
060	05993	06092	06192	06292	06391	06491	06590	06690	06790	06889
070	06989	07088	07188	07287	07387	07486	07585	07685	07784	07884
080	07983	08082	08182	08281	08380	08480	08579	08678	08777	08877
090	08976	09075	09174	09273	09372	09472	09571	09670	09769	09868
0,100	0,09967	0,10066	0,10165	0,10264	0,10363	0,10462	0,10560	0,10659	0,10758	0,10857
110	10956	11055	11153	11252	11351	11450	11548	11647	11746	11844
120	11943	12041	12140	12238	12337	12435	12534	12632	12731	12829
130	12927	13026	13124	13222	13320	13419	13517	13615	13713	13811
140	13909	14007	14105	14203	14301	14399	14497	14595	14693	14791
0,150	0,14889	0,14986	0,15084	0,15182	0,15279	0,15377	0,15475	0,15572	0,15670	0,15767
160	15865	15962	16060	16157	16255	16352	16449	16546	16644	16741
170	16838	16935	17032	17129	17227	17324	17420	17517	17614	17711
180	17808	17905	18002	18098	18195	18292	18388	18485	18582	18678
190	18775	18871	18967	19064	19160	19257	19353	19449	19545	19641
0,200	0,19738	0,19834	0,19930	0,20026	0,20122	0,20218	0,20313	0,20409	0,20505	0,20601
210	20697	20792	20888	20984	21079	21175	21270	21366	21461	21556
220	21652	21747	21842	21938	22033	22128	22223	22318	22413	22508
230	22603	22698	22793	22887	22982	23077	23171	23266	23361	23455
240	23550	23644	23738	23833	23927	24021	24115	24210	24304	24398
0,250	0,24492	0,24586	0,24680	0,24774	0,24868	0,24961	0,25055	0,25149	0,25242	0,25336
260	25430	25523	25617	25710	25803	25897	25990	26083	26176	26269
270	26362	26456	26548	26641	26734	26827	26920	27013	27105	27198
280	27291	27383	27476	27568	27660	27753	27845	27937	28029	28121
290	28213	28305	28397	28489	28581	28673	28765	28856	28948	29040
0,300	0,29131	0,29223	0,29314	0,29406	0,29497	0,29588	0,29679	0,29771	0,29862	0,29953
310	30044	30135	30226	30316	30407	30498	30589	30679	30770	30860
320	30951	31041	31131	31222	31312	31402	31492	31582	31672	31762
330	31852	31942	32032	32121	32211	32301	32390	32480	32569	32658
340	32748	32837	32926	33015	33104	33193	33282	33371	33460	33549
0,350	0,33638	0,33726	0,33815	0,33903	0,33992	0,34080	0,34169	0,34257	0,34345	0,34433
360	34521	34609	34697	34785	34873	34961	35049	35136	35224	35312
370	35399	35487	35574	35661	35749	35836	35923	36010	36097	36184
380	36271	36358	36444	36531	36618	36704	36791	36877	36963	37050
390	37136	37222	37308	37394	37480	37566	37652	37738	37824	37909
0,400	0,37995	0,38080	0,38166	0,38251	0,38337	0,38422	0,38507	0,38592	0,38677	0,38762
410	38847	38932	39017	39102	39186	39271	39356	39440	39524	39609
420	39693	39777	39861	39945	40029	40113	40197	40281	40365	40449
430	40532	40616	40699	40783	40866	40949	41032	41115	41199	41282
440	41364	41447	41530	41613	41695	41778	41861	41943	42025	42108
0,450	0,42190	0,42272	0,42354	0,42436	0,42518	0,42600	0,42682	0,42764	0,42845	0,42927
460	43008	43090	43171	43253	43334	43415	43496	43577	43658	43739
470	43820	43901	43981	44062	44143	44223	44303	44384	44464	44544
480	44624	44704	44784	44864	44944	45024	45104	45183	45263	45342
490	45422	45501	45580	45659	45739	45818	45897	45975	46054	46133
0,500	0,46212	0,46290	0,46369	0,46447	0,46526	0,46604	0,46682	0,46760	0,46839	0,46917
510	46995	47072	47150	47228	47306	47383	47461	47538	47615	47693
520	47770	47847	47924	48001	48078	48155	48232	48308	48385	48462
530	48538	48615	48691	48767	48843	48919	48995	49071	49147	49223
540	49299	49374	49450	49526	49601	49676	49752	49827	49902	49977
0,550	0,50052	0,50127	0,50202	0,50277	0,50351	0,50426	0,50500	0,50575	0,50649	0,50724
560	50798	50872	50946	51020	51094	51168	51242	51315	51389	51462
570	51536	51609	51683	51756	51829	51902	51975	52048	52121	52194
580	52267	52339	52412	52484	52557	52629	52701	52773	52846	52918
590	52990	53061	53133	53205	53277	53348	53420	53491	53562	53634
0,600	0,53705	0,53776	0,53847	0,53918	0,53989	0,54060	0,54131	0,54201	0,54272	0,54342
610	54413	54483	54553	54624	54694	54764	54834	54904	54973	55043
620	55113	55182	55252	55321	55391	55460	55529	55598	55667	55736
630	55805	55874	55943	56011	56080	56149	56217	56285	56354	56422
640	56490	56558	56626	56694	56762	56829	56897	56965	57032	57100
0,650	0,57167	0,57234	0,57301	0,57369	0,57436	0,57503	0,57570	0,57636	0,57703	0,57770
660	57836	57903	57969	58036	58102	58168	58234	58300	58366	58432
670	58498	58564	58629	58695	58760	58826	58891	58957	59022	59087
680	59152	59217	59282	59347	59411	59476	59541	59605	59670	59734
690	59798	59862	59927	59991	60055	60118	60182	60246	60310	60373
0,700	0,60437	0,60500	0,60564	0,60627	0,60690	0,60753	0,60816	0,60879	0,60942	0,61005
710	61068	61130	61193	61255	61318	61380	61443	61505	61567	61629
720	61691	61753	61815	61876	61938	62000	62061	62123	62184	62245
730	62307	62368	62429	62490	62551	62611	62672	62733	62794	62854
740	62915	62975	63035	63095	63156	63216	63276	63336	63395	63455
0,750	0,63515	0,63575	0,63634	0,63694	0,63753	0,63812	0,63871	0,63931	0,63990	0,64049
760	64108	64167	64225	64284	64343	64401	64460	64518	64576	64635
770	64693	64751	64809	64867	64925	64983	65040	65098	65156	65213
780	65271	65328	65385	65443	65500	65557	65614	65671	65727	65784
790	65841	65898	65954	66011	66067	66123	66179	66236	66292	66348
0,800	0,66404	0,66460	0,66515	0,66571	0,66627	0,66682	0,66738	0,66793	0,66849	0,66904
810	66959	67014	67069	67124	67179	67234	67289	67343	67398	67453
820	67507	67561	67616	67670	67724	67778	67832	67886	67940	67994
830	68048	68101	68155	68208	68262	68315	68368	68422	68475	68528
840	68581	68634	68687	68739	68792	68845	68897	68950	69002	69055
0,850	0,69107	0,69159	0,69211	0,69263	0,69315	0,69367	0,69419	0,69471	0,69523	0,69574
860	69626	69677	69729	69780	69831	69882	69934	69985	70036	70087
870	70137	70188	70239	70290	70340	70391	70441	70491	70542	70592
880	70642	70692	70742	70792	70842	70892	70941	70991	71040	71090
890	71139	71189	71238	71287	71336	71385	71434	71483	71532	71581
0,900	0,71630	0,71678	0,71727	0,71776	0,71824	0,71872	0,71921	0,71969	0,72017	0,72065
910	72113	72161	72209	72257	72305	72352	72400	72448	72495	72542
920	72590	72637	72684	72731	72778	72825	72872	72919	72966	73013
930	73059	73106	73153	73199	73245	73292	73338	73384	73430	73476
940	73522	73568	73614	73660	73705	73751	73797	73842	73888	73933
0,950	0,73978	0,74024	0,74069	0,74114	0,74159	0,74204	0,74249	0,74294	0,74338	0,74383
960	74428	74472	74517	74561	74606	74650	74694	74738	74782	74826
970	74870	74914	74958	75002	75046	75089	75133	75176	75220	75263
980	75307	75350	75393	75436	75479	75522	75565	75608	75651	75694
990	75736	75779	75821	75864	75906	75949	75991	76033	76075	76117
1,000	0,76159	0,76201	0,76243	0,76285	0,76327	0,76369	0,76410	0,76452	0,76493	0,76535
010	76576	76618	76659	76700	76741	76782	76823	76864	76905	76946
020	76987	77027	77068	77109	77149	77190	77230	77270	77310	77351
030	77391	77431	77471	77511	77551	77591	77630	77670	77710	77749
040	77789	77828	77868	77907	77946	77985	78025	78064	78103	78142

[1] Values abridged from *Table of Circular and Hyperbolic Tangents and Cotangents for Radian Arguments*, New York, 1947. Reprinted by kind permission of the National Bureau of Standards and the Columbia University Press.

All values conform to the international convention (i.e. 0,1 instead of 0.1).

z-Transformation[1] of the Correlation Coefficient r

$z = \tanh^{-1} r$

z	0,000	0,001	0,002	0,003	0,004	0,005	0,006	0,007	0,008	0,009
1,050	0,78181	0,78219	0,78258	0,78297	0,78336	0,78374	0,78413	0,78451	0,78490	0,78528
060	78566	78605	78643	78681	78719	78757	78795	78833	78871	78908
070	78946	78984	79021	79059	79096	79134	79171	79208	79246	79283
080	79320	79357	79394	79431	79468	79505	79541	79578	79615	79651
090	79688	79724	79761	79797	79833	79870	79906	79942	79978	80014
1,100	0,80050	0,80086	0,80122	0,80157	0,80193	0,80229	0,80264	0,80300	0,80335	0,80371
110	80406	80442	80477	80512	80547	80582	80617	80652	80687	80722
120	80757	80792	80826	80861	80896	80930	80965	80999	81033	81068
130	81102	81136	81170	81204	81238	81272	81306	81340	81374	81408
140	81441	81475	81509	81542	81576	81609	81642	81676	81709	81742
1,150	0,81775	0,81809	0,81842	0,81875	0,81907	0,81940	0,81973	0,82006	0,82039	0,82071
160	82104	82137	82169	82202	82234	82266	82299	82331	82363	82395
170	82427	82459	82491	82523	82555	82587	82619	82650	82682	82714
180	82745	82777	82808	82840	82871	82902	82933	82965.	82996	83027
190	83058	83089	83120	83151	83182	83212	83243	83274	83304	83335
1,200	0,83365	0,83396	0,83426	0,83457	0,83487	0,83517	0,83548	0,83578	0,83608	0,83638
210	83668	83698	83728	83758	83788	83817	83847	83877	83906	83936
220	83965	83995	84024	84054	84083	84112	84142	84171	84200	84229
230	84258	84287	84316	84345	84374	84402	84431	84460	84488	84517
240	84546	84574	84603	84631	84659	84688	84716	84744	84772	84800
1,250	0,84828	0,84856	0,84884	0,84912	0,84940	0,84968	0,84996	0,85023	0,85051	0,85079
260	85106	85134	85161	85189	85216	85244	85271	85298	85325	85353
270	85380	85407	85434	85461	85488	85515	85542	85568	85595	85622
280	85648	85675	85702	85728	85755	85781	85808	85834	85860	85886
290	85913	85939	85965	85991	86017	86043	86069	86095	86121	86147
1,300	0,86172	0,86198	0,86224	0,86249	0,86275	0,86300	0,86326	0,86351	0,86377	0,86402
310	86428	86453	86478	86503	86528	86554	86579	86604	86629	86654
320	86678	86703	86728	86753	86778	86802	86827	86851	86876	86900
330	86925	86949	86974	86998	87022	87047	87071	87095	87119	87143
340	87167	87191	87215	87239	87263	87287	87311	87334	87358	87382
1,350	0,87405	0,87429	0,87452	0,87476	0,87499	0,87523	0,87546	0,87570	0,87593	0,87616
360	87639	87662	87686	87709	87732	87755	87778	87801	87824	87846
370	87869	87892	87915	87937	87960	87983	88005	88028	88050	88073
380	88095	88118	88140	88162	88184	88207	88229	88251	88273	88295
390	88317	88339	88361	88383	88405	88427	88448	88470	88492	88514
1,400	0,88535	0,88557	0,88578	0,88600	0,88621	0,88643	0,88664	0,88686	0,88707	0,88728
410	88749	88771	88792	88813	88834	88855	88876	88897	88918	88939
420	88960	88981	89002	89022	89043	89064	89084	89105	89126	89146
430	89167	89187	89208	89228	89248	89269	89289	89309	89329	89350
440	89370	89390	89410	89430	89450	89470	89490	89510	89530	89549
1,450	0,89569	0,89589	0,89609	0,89628	0,89648	0,89668	0,89687	0,89707	0,89726	0,89746
460	89765	89785	89804	89823	89843	89862	89881	89900	89920	89939
470	89958	89977	89996	90015	90034	90053	90072	90090	90109	90128
480	90147	90166	90184	90203	90221	90240	90259	90277	90296	90314
490	90332	90351	90369	90388	90406	90424	90442	90460	90479	90497
1,500	0,90515	0,90533	0,90551	0,90569	0,90587	0,90605	0,90623	0,90641	0,90658	0,90676
510	90694	90712	90729	90747	90765	90782	90800	90817	90835	90852
520	90870	90887	90905	90922	90939	90957	90974	90991	91008	91025
530	91042	91060	91077	91094	91111	91128	91145	91161	91178	91195
540	91212	91229	91246	91262	91279	91296	91312	91329	91345	91362
1,550	0,91379	0,91395	0,91411	0,91428	0,91444	0,91461	0,91477	0,91493	0,91510	0,91526
560	91542	91558	91574	91591	91607	91623	91639	91655	91671	91687
570	91703	91718	91734	91750	91766	91782	91797	91813	91829	91845
580	91860	91876	91891	91907	91922	91938	91953	91969	91984	92000
590	92015	92030	92046	92061	92076	92091	92106	92122	92137	92152
1,600	0,92167	0,92182	0,92197	0,92212	0,92227	0,92242	0,92257	0,92272	0,92286	0,92301
610	92316	92331	92346	92360	92375	92390	92404	92419	92433	92448
620	92462	92477	92491	92506	92520	92535	92549	92563	92578	92592
630	92606	92620	92635	92649	92663	92677	92691	92705	92719	92733
640	92747	92761	92775	92789	92803	92817	92831	92844	92858	92872
1,650	0,92886	0,92899	0,92913	0,92927	0,92940	0,92954	0,92968	0,92981	0,92995	0,93008
660	93022	93035	93049	93062	93075	93089	93102	93115	93129	93142
670	93155	93168	93182	93195	93208	93221	93234	93247	93260	93273
680	93286	93299	93312	93325	93338	93351	93364	93376	93389	93402
690	93415	93427	93440	93453	93465	93478	93491	93503	93516	93528
1,700	0,93541	0,93553	0,93566	0,93578	0,93591	0,93603	0,93615	0,93628	0,93640	0,93652
710	93665	93677	93689	93701	93714	93726	93738	93750	93762	93774
720	93786	93798	93810	93822	93834	93846	93858	93870	93882	93894
730	93906	93917	93929	93941	93953	93964	93976	93988	93999	94011
740	94023	94034	94046	94057	94069	94080	94092	94103	94115	94126
1,750	0,94138	0,94149	0,94160	0,94172	0,94183	0,94194	0,94205	0,94217	0,94228	0,94239
760	94250	94261	94273	94284	94295	94306	94317	94328	94339	94350
770	94361	94372	94383	94394	94405	94415	94426	94437	94448	94459
780	94470	94480	94491	94502	94512	94523	94534	94544	94555	94565
790	94576	94587	94597	94608	94618	94629	94639	94649	94660	94670
1,800	0,94681	0,94691	0,94701	0,94712	0,94722	0,94732	0,94742	0,94753	0,94763	0,94773
810	94783	94793	94803	94814	94824	94834	94844	94854	94864	94874
820	94884	94894	94904	94914	94924	94933	94943	94953	94963	94973
830	94983	94992	95002	95012	95022	95031	95041	95051	95060	95070
840	95080	95089	95099	95108	95118	95127	95137	95146	95156	95165
1,850	0,95175	0,95184	0,95193	0,95203	0,95212	0,95221	0,95231	0,95240	0,95249	0,95259
860	95268	95277	95286	95296	95305	95314	95323	95332	95341	95350
870	95359	95368	95378	95387	95396	95405	95413	95422	95431	95440
880	95449	95458	95467	95476	95485	95493	95502	95511	95520	95529
890	95537	95546	95555	95563	95572	95581	95589	95598	95607	95615
1,900	0,95624	0,95632	0,95641	0,95649	0,95658	0,95666	0,95675	0,95683	0,95692	0,95700
910	95709	95717	95725	95734	95742	95750	95759	95767	95775	95783
920	95792	95800	95808	95816	95825	95833	95841	95849	95857	95865
930	95873	95881	95889	95898	95906	95914	95922	95930	95938	95945
940	95953	95961	95969	95977	95985	95993	96001	96009	96016	96024
1,950	0,96032	0,96040	0,96047	0,96055	0,96063	0,96071	0,96078	0,96086	0,96094	0,96101
960	96109	96117	96124	96132	96139	96147	96155	96162	96170	96177
970	96185	96192	96200	96207	96214	96222	96229	96237	96244	96251
980	96259	96266	96273	96281	96288	96295	96303	96310	96317	96324
990	96331	96339	96346	96353	96360	96367	96374	96382	96389	96396

z	0,0	0,1	0,2	0,3	0,4	0,5	0,6	0,7	0,8	0,9
0,0	0,0000000000	0,0996679946	0,1973753202	0,2913126125	0,3799489623	0,4621171573	0,5370495670	0,6043677771	0,6640367703	0,7162978702
1,0	7615941560	8004990218	8336546070	8617231593	8853516482	9051482536	9216685544	9354090706	9468060128	9562374581
2,0	9640275801	9704519366	9757431300	9800963963	9836748577	9866142982	9890274022	9910074537	9926315202	9939631674
3,0	9950547537	9959493592	9966823978	9972829601	9977749279	9981778976	9985079423	9987782413	9989995978	9991808657
4,0	9993292997	9994508437	9995503665	9996318562	9996985793	9997532108	9997979416	9998345656	9998645517	9998891030
5,0	0,9999092043	0,9999256621	0,9999391369	0,9999501692	0,9999592018	0,9999665972	0,9999726520	0,9999776093	0,9999816680	0,9999849910
6,0	9999877117	9999899391	9999917629	9999932560	9999944785	9999954794	9999962988	9999969697	9999975190	9999979687
7,0	9999983369	9999986384	9999988852	9999990873	9999992527	9999993882	9999994991	9999995899	9999996642	9999997251
8,0	9999997749	9999998157	9999998491	9999998765	9999998989	9999999172	9999999322	9999999445	9999999546	9999999628
9,0	9999999695	9999999751	9999999796	9999999833	9999999863	9999999888	9999999908	9999999925	9999999939	9999999950

[1] See footnote on previous page.

All values conform to the international convention (i.e. 0,1 instead of 0.1).

The percentages correspond to 100 times the normal integral from $-\infty$ to c. The probits are equal to $c+5$

%	0,0	0,1	0,2	0,3	0,4	0,5	0,6	0,7	0,8	0,9	1	2	3	4	5
	Probits														
0		1,9098	2,1218	2,2522	2,3479	2,4242	2,4879	2,5427	2,5911	2,6344					
1	2,6737	2,7096	2,7429	2,7738	2,8027	2,8299	2,8556	2,8799	2,9031	2,9251					
2	2,9463	2,9665	2,9859	3,0046	3,0226	3,0400	3,0569	3,0732	3,0890	3,1043					
3	3,1192	3,1337	3,1478	3,1616	3,1750	3,1881	3,2009	3,2134	3,2256	3,2376					
4	3,2493	3,2608	3,2721	3,2831	3,2940	3,3046	3,3151	3,3253	3,3354	3,3454					
5	3,3551	3,3648	3,3742	3,3836	3,3928	3,4018	3,4107	3,4195	3,4282	3,4368	9	18	27	36	45
6	3,4452	3,4536	3,4618	3,4699	3,4780	3,4859	3,4937	3,5015	3,5091	3,5167	8	16	24	32	40
7	3,5242	3,5316	3,5389	3,5462	3,5534	3,5605	3,5675	3,5745	3,5813	3,5882	7	14	21	28	36
8	3,5949	3,6016	3,6083	3,6148	3,6213	3,6278	3,6342	3,6405	3,6468	3,6531	6	13	19	26	32
9	3,6592	3,6654	3,6715	3,6775	3,6835	3,6894	3,6953	3,7012	3,7070	3,7127	6	12	18	24	30
10	3,7184	3,7241	3,7298	3,7354	3,7409	3,7464	3,7519	3,7574	3,7628	3,7681	6	11	17	22	28
11	3,7735	3,7788	3,7840	3,7893	3,7945	3,7996	3,8048	3,8099	3,8150	3,8200	5	10	16	21	26
12	3,8250	3,8300	3,8350	3,8399	3,8448	3,8497	3,8545	3,8593	3,8641	3,8689	5	10	15	20	24
13	3,8736	3,8783	3,8830	3,8877	3,8923	3,8969	3,9015	3,9061	3,9107	3,9152	5	9	14	18	23
14	3,9197	3,9242	3,9286	3,9331	3,9375	3,9419	3,9463	3,9506	3,9550	3,9593	4	9	13	18	22
15	3,9636	3,9678	3,9721	3,9763	3,9806	3,9848	3,9890	3,9931	3,9973	4,0014	4	8	13	17	21
16	4,0055	4,0096	4,0137	4,0178	4,0218	4,0259	4,0299	4,0339	4,0379	4,0419	4	8	12	16	20
17	4,0458	4,0498	4,0537	4,0576	4,0615	4,0654	4,0693	4,0731	4,0770	4,0808	4	8	12	16	19
18	4,0846	4,0884	4,0922	4,0960	4,0998	4,1035	4,1073	4,1110	4,1147	4,1184	4	8	11	15	19
19	4,1221	4,1258	4,1295	4,1331	4,1367	4,1404	4,1440	4,1476	4,1512	4,1548	4	7	11	15	18
20	4,1584	4,1619	4,1655	4,1690	4,1726	4,1761	4,1796	4,1831	4,1866	4,1901	4	7	11	14	18
21	4,1936	4,1970	4,2005	4,2039	4,2074	4,2108	4,2142	4,2176	4,2210	4,2244	3	7	10	14	17
22	4,2278	4,2312	4,2345	4,2379	4,2412	4,2446	4,2479	4,2512	4,2546	4,2579	3	7	10	13	17
23	4,2612	4,2644	4,2677	4,2710	4,2743	4,2775	4,2808	4,2840	4,2872	4,2905	3	7	10	13	16
24	4,2937	4,2969	4,3001	4,3033	4,3065	4,3097	4,3129	4,3160	4,3192	4,3224	3	6	10	13	16
25	4,3255	4,3287	4,3318	4,3349	4,3380	4,3412	4,3443	4,3474	4,3505	4,3536	3	6	9	12	16
26	4,3567	4,3597	4,3628	4,3659	4,3689	4,3720	4,3750	4,3781	4,3811	4,3842	3	6	9	12	15
27	4,3872	4,3902	4,3932	4,3962	4,3992	4,4022	4,4052	4,4082	4,4112	4,4142	3	6	9	12	15
28	4,4172	4,4201	4,4231	4,4260	4,4290	4,4319	4,4349	4,4378	4,4408	4,4437	3	6	9	12	15
29	4,4466	4,4495	4,4524	4,4554	4,4583	4,4612	4,4641	4,4670	4,4698	4,4727	3	6	9	12	14
30	4,4756	4,4785	4,4813	4,4842	4,4871	4,4899	4,4928	4,4956	4,4985	4,5013	3	6	9	11	14
31	4,5041	4,5070	4,5098	4,5126	4,5155	4,5183	4,5211	4,5239	4,5267	4,5295	3	6	8	11	14
32	4,5323	4,5351	4,5379	4,5407	4,5435	4,5462	4,5490	4,5518	4,5546	4,5573	3	6	8	11	14
33	4,5601	4,5628	4,5656	4,5684	4,5711	4,5739	4,5766	4,5793	4,5821	4,5848	3	5	8	11	14
34	4,5875	4,5903	4,5930	4,5957	4,5984	4,6011	4,6039	4,6066	4,6093	4,6120	3	5	8	11	14
35	4,6147	4,6174	4,6201	4,6228	4,6255	4,6281	4,6308	4,6335	4,6362	4,6389	3	5	8	11	13
36	4,6415	4,6442	4,6469	4,6495	4,6522	4,6549	4,6575	4,6602	4,6628	4,6655	3	5	8	11	13
37	4,6681	4,6708	4,6734	4,6761	4,6787	4,6814	4,6840	4,6866	4,6893	4,6919	3	5	8	11	13
38	4,6945	4,6971	4,6998	4,7024	4,7050	4,7076	4,7102	4,7129	4,7155	4,7181	3	5	8	10	13
39	4,7207	4,7233	4,7259	4,7285	4,7311	4,7337	4,7363	4,7389	4,7415	4,7441	3	5	8	10	13
40	4,7467	4,7492	4,7518	4,7544	4,7570	4,7596	4,7622	4,7647	4,7673	4,7699	3	5	8	10	13
41	4,7725	4,7750	4,7776	4,7802	4,7827	4,7853	4,7879	4,7904	4,7930	4,7955	3	5	8	10	13
42	4,7981	4,8007	4,8032	4,8058	4,8083	4,8109	4,8134	4,8160	4,8185	4,8211	3	5	8	10	13
43	4,8236	4,8262	4,8287	4,8313	4,8338	4,8363	4,8389	4,8414	4,8440	4,8465	3	5	8	10	13
44	4,8490	4,8516	4,8541	4,8566	4,8592	4,8617	4,8642	4,8668	4,8693	4,8718	3	5	8	10	13
45	4,8743	4,8769	4,8794	4,8819	4,8844	4,8870	4,8895	4,8920	4,8945	4,8970	3	5	8	10	13
46	4,8996	4,9021	4,9046	4,9071	4,9096	4,9122	4,9147	4,9172	4,9197	4,9222	3	5	8	10	13
47	4,9247	4,9272	4,9298	4,9323	4,9348	4,9373	4,9398	4,9423	4,9448	4,9473	3	5	8	10	13
48	4,9498	4,9524	4,9549	4,9574	4,9599	4,9624	4,9649	4,9674	4,9699	4,9724	3	5	8	10	13
49	4,9749	4,9774	4,9799	4,9825	4,9850	4,9875	4,9900	4,9925	4,9950	4,9975	3	5	8	10	13
50	5,0000	5,0025	5,0050	5,0075	5,0100	5,0125	5,0150	5,0175	5,0201	5,0226	3	5	8	10	13
51	5,0251	5,0276	5,0301	5,0326	5,0351	5,0376	5,0401	5,0426	5,0451	5,0476	3	5	8	10	13
52	5,0502	5,0527	5,0552	5,0577	5,0602	5,0627	5,0652	5,0677	5,0702	5,0728	3	5	8	10	13
53	5,0753	5,0778	5,0803	5,0828	5,0853	5,0878	5,0904	5,0929	5,0954	5,0979	3	5	8	10	13
54	5,1004	5,1030	5,1055	5,1080	5,1105	5,1130	5,1156	5,1181	5,1206	5,1231	3	5	8	10	13
55	5,1257	5,1282	5,1307	5,1332	5,1358	5,1383	5,1408	5,1434	5,1459	5,1484	3	5	8	10	13
56	5,1510	5,1535	5,1560	5,1586	5,1611	5,1637	5,1662	5,1687	5,1713	5,1738	3	5	8	10	13
57	5,1764	5,1789	5,1815	5,1840	5,1866	5,1891	5,1917	5,1942	5,1968	5,1993	3	5	8	10	13
58	5,2019	5,2045	5,2070	5,2096	5,2121	5,2147	5,2173	5,2198	5,2224	5,2250	3	5	8	10	13
59	5,2275	5,2301	5,2327	5,2353	5,2378	5,2404	5,2430	5,2456	5,2482	5,2508	3	5	8	10	13
60	5,2533	5,2559	5,2585	5,2611	5,2637	5,2663	5,2689	5,2715	5,2741	5,2767	3	5	8	10	13
61	5,2793	5,2819	5,2845	5,2871	5,2898	5,2924	5,2950	5,2976	5,3002	5,3029	3	5	8	10	13
62	5,3055	5,3081	5,3107	5,3134	5,3160	5,3186	5,3213	5,3239	5,3266	5,3292	3	5	8	11	13
63	5,3319	5,3345	5,3372	5,3398	5,3425	5,3451	5,3478	5,3505	5,3531	5,3558	3	5	8	11	13
64	5,3585	5,3611	5,3638	5,3665	5,3692	5,3719	5,3745	5,3772	5,3799	5,3826	3	5	8	11	13
65	5,3853	5,3880	5,3907	5,3934	5,3961	5,3989	5,4016	5,4043	5,4070	5,4097	3	5	8	11	14
66	5,4125	5,4152	5,4179	5,4207	5,4234	5,4261	5,4289	5,4316	5,4344	5,4372	3	5	8	11	14
67	5,4399	5,4427	5,4454	5,4482	5,4510	5,4538	5,4565	5,4593	5,4621	5,4649	3	6	8	11	14
68	5,4677	5,4705	5,4733	5,4761	5,4789	5,4817	5,4845	5,4874	5,4902	5,4930	3	6	8	11	14
69	5,4959	5,4987	5,5015	5,5044	5,5072	5,5101	5,5129	5,5158	5,5187	5,5215	3	6	9	11	14
70	5,5244	5,5273	5,5302	5,5330	5,5359	5,5388	5,5417	5,5446	5,5476	5,5505	3	6	9	12	14
71	5,5534	5,5563	5,5592	5,5622	5,5651	5,5681	5,5710	5,5740	5,5769	5,5799	3	6	9	12	15
72	5,5828	5,5858	5,5888	5,5918	5,5948	5,5978	5,6008	5,6038	5,6068	5,6098	3	6	9	12	15
73	5,6128	5,6158	5,6189	5,6219	5,6250	5,6280	5,6311	5,6341	5,6372	5,6403	3	6	9	12	15
74	5,6433	5,6464	5,6495	5,6526	5,6557	5,6588	5,6620	5,6651	5,6682	5,6713	3	6	9	12	16
75	5,6745	5,6776	5,6808	5,6840	5,6871	5,6903	5,6935	5,6967	5,6999	5,7031	3	6	10	13	16
76	5,7063	5,7095	5,7128	5,7160	5,7192	5,7225	5,7257	5,7290	5,7323	5,7356	3	7	10	13	16
77	5,7388	5,7421	5,7454	5,7488	5,7521	5,7554	5,7588	5,7621	5,7655	5,7688	3	7	10	13	17
78	5,7722	5,7756	5,7790	5,7824	5,7858	5,7892	5,7926	5,7961	5,7995	5,8030	3	7	10	14	17
79	5,8064	5,8099	5,8134	5,8169	5,8204	5,8239	5,8274	5,8310	5,8345	5,8381	4	7	11	14	18
80	5,8416	5,8452	5,8488	5,8524	5,8560	5,8596	5,8633	5,8669	5,8705	5,8742	4	7	11	14	18
81	5,8779	5,8816	5,8853	5,8890	5,8927	5,8965	5,9002	5,9040	5,9078	5,9116	4	7	11	15	19
82	5,9154	5,9192	5,9230	5,9269	5,9307	5,9346	5,9385	5,9424	5,9463	5,9502	4	8	12	15	19
83	5,9542	5,9581	5,9621	5,9661	5,9701	5,9741	5,9782	5,9822	5,9863	5,9904	4	8	12	16	20
84	5,9945	5,9986	6,0027	6,0069	6,0110	6,0152	6,0194	6,0237	6,0279	6,0322	4	8	13	17	21
85	6,0364	6,0407	6,0450	6,0494	6,0537	6,0581	6,0625	6,0669	6,0714	6,0758	4	9	13	18	22
86	6,0803	6,0848	6,0893	6,0939	6,0985	6,1031	6,1077	6,1123	6,1170	6,1217	5	9	14	18	23
87	6,1264	6,1311	6,1359	6,1407	6,1455	6,1503	6,1552	6,1601	6,1650	6,1700	5	10	15	19	24
88	6,1750	6,1800	6,1850	6,1901	6,1952	6,2004	6,2055	6,2107	6,2160	6,2212	5	10	15	21	26
89	6,2265	6,2319	6,2372	6,2426	6,2481	6,2536	6,2591	6,2646	6,2702	6,2759	5	11	16	22	27
90	6,2816	6,2873	6,2930	6,2988	6,3047	6,3106	6,3165	6,3225	6,3285	6,3346	6	12	18	24	29
91	6,3408	6,3469	6,3532	6,3595	6,3658	6,3722	6,3787	6,3852	6,3917	6,3984	6	13	19	26	32
92	6,4051	6,4118	6,4187	6,4255	6,4325	6,4395	6,4466	6,4538	6,4611	6,4684	7	14	21	28	35
93	6,4758	6,4833	6,4909	6,4985	6,5063	6,5141	6,5220	6,5301	6,5382	6,5464	8	16	24	31	39
94	6,5548	6,5632	6,5718	6,5805	6,5893	6,5982	6,6072	6,6164	6,6258	6,6352	9	18	27	36	45

[7] FISHER and YATES, *Statistical Tables for Biological, Agricultural and Medical Research,* 6th ed., Longman, Harlow, 1974, page 68. Reprinted by kind permission of the authors and publishers.

All values conform to the international convention (i.e. 0,1 instead of 0.1).

Probits[1]

(Continuation of table on page 68)

%	0,0	0,1	0,2	0,3	0,4	0,5	0,6	0,7	0,8	0,9	1	2	3	4	5
	Probits														
95	6,6449	6,6546	6,6646	6,6747	6,6849	6,6954	6,7060	6,7169	6,7279	6,7392					
	97	100	101	102	105	106	109	110	113	115					
96	6,7507	6,7624	6,7744	6,7866	6,7991	6,8119	6,8250	6,8384	6,8522	6,8663					
	117	120	122	125	128	131	134	138	141	145					
97	6,8808	6,8957	6,9110	6,9268	6,9431	6,9600	6,9774	6,9954	7,0141	7,0335					
	149	153	158	163	169	174	180	187	194	202					
%	0,00	0,01	0,02	0,03	0,04	0,05	0,06	0,07	0,08	0,09					
	Probits														
98,0	7,0537	7,0558	7,0579	7,0600	7,0621	7,0642	7,0663	7,0684	7,0706	7,0727	2	4	6	8	11
98,1	7,0749	7,0770	7,0792	7,0814	7,0836	7,0858	7,0880	7,0902	7,0924	7,0947	2	4	7	9	11
98,2	7,0969	7,0992	7,1015	7,1038	7,1061	7,1084	7,1107	7,1130	7,1154	7,1177	2	5	7	9	12
98,3	7,1201	7,1224	7,1248	7,1272	7,1297	7,1321	7,1345	7,1370	7,1394	7,1419	2	5	7	10	12
98,4	7,1444	7,1469	7,1494	7,1520	7,1545	7,1571	7,1596	7,1622	7,1648	7,1675	3	5	8	10	13
98,5	7,1701	7,1727	7,1754	7,1781	7,1808	7,1835	7,1862	7,1890	7,1917	7,1945	3	5	8	11	14
98,6	7,1973	7,2001	7,2029	7,2058	7,2086	7,2115	7,2144	7,2173	7,2203	7,2232	3	6	9	12	14
98,7	7,2262	7,2292	7,2322	7,2353	7,2383	7,2414	7,2445	7,2476	7,2508	7,2539	3	6	9	12	15
98,8	7,2571	7,2603	7,2636	7,2668	7,2701	7,2734	7,2768	7,2801	7,2835	7,2869	3	7	10	13	17
98,9	7,2904	7,2938	7,2973	7,3009	7,3044	7,3080	7,3116	7,3152	7,3189	7,3226	4	7	11	14	18
99,0	7,3263	7,3301	7,3339	7,3378	7,3416	7,3455	7,3495	7,3535	7,3575	7,3615	4	8	12	16	20
99,1	7,3656	7,3698	7,3739	7,3781	7,3824	7,3867	7,3911	7,3954	7,3999	7,4044	4	9	13	17	22
99,2	7,4089	7,4135	7,4181	7,4228	7,4276	7,4324	7,4372	7,4422	7,4471	7,4522	5	10	14	19	24
99,3	7,4573	7,4624	7,4677	7,4730	7,4783	7,4838	7,4893	7,4949	7,5006	7,5063	5	11	16	22	27
99,4	7,5121	7,5181	7,5241	7,5302	7,5364	7,5427	7,5491	7,5556	7,5622	7,5690	6	13	19	25	32
99,5	7,5758	7,5828	7,5899	7,5972	7,6045	7,6121	7,6197	7,6276	7,6356	7,6437					
99,6	7,6521	7,6606	7,6693	7,6783	7,6874	7,6968	7,7065	7,7164	7,7266	7,7370					
99,7	7,7478	7,7589	7,7703	7,7822	7,7944	7,8070	7,8202	7,8338	7,8480	7,8627					
99,8	7,8782	7,8943	7,9112	7,9290	7,9478	7,9677	7,9889	8,0115	8,0357	8,0618					
99,9	8,0902	8,1214	8,1559	8,1947	8,2389	8,2905	8,3528	8,4316	8,5401	8,7190					

Weighting coefficients and probit values to be used for final adjustments[1]

Expected probit Y	Minimum working probit $Y-P/Z$	Range $1/Z$	Maximum working probit $Y+Q/Z$	Weighting coefficient Z^2/PQ	Expected probit Y	Minimum working probit $Y-P/Z$	Range $1/Z$	Maximum working probit $Y+Q/Z$	Weighting coefficient Z^2/PQ
					5,0	3,7467	2,5066	6,2533	0,63662
1,1	0,8579	5034	5035	0,00082	5,1	3,7401	2,5192	6,2593	63431
1,2	0,9522	3425	3426	00118	5,2	3,7186	2,5573	6,2759	62742
1,3	1,0462	2354	2355	00167	5,3	3,6798	2,6220	6,3018	61609
1,4	1,1400	1634	1635	00235	5,4	3,6203	2,7154	6,3357	60052
1,5	1,2335	1146	1147	0,00327	**5,5**	3,5360	2,8404	6,3764	0,58099
1,6	1,3266	811,5	812,8	00451	5,6	3,4220	3,0010	6,4230	55788
1,7	1,4194	580,5	581,9	00614	5,7	3,2724	3,2025	6,4749	53159
1,8	1,5118	419,4	420,9	00828	5,8	3,0794	3,4519	6,5313	50260
1,9	1,6038	306,1	307,7	01104	5,9	2,8335	3,7582	6,5917	47144
2,0	1,6954	225,6	227,3	0,01457	**6,0**	2,5230	4,1327	6,6557	0,43863
2,1	1,7866	168,00	169,79	01903	6,1	2,1324	4,5903	6,7227	40474
2,2	1,8772	126,34	128,22	02459	6,2	1,6429	5,1497	6,7926	37031
2,3	1,9673	95,96	97,93	03143	6,3	1,0295	5,8354	6,8649	33589
2,4	2,0568	73,62	75,68	03977	6,4	0,2606	6,6788	6,9394	30199
2,5	2,1457	57,05	59,20	0,04979	**6,5**	− 0,705	7,721	7,0158	0,26907
2,6	2,2340	44,654	46,888	06169	6,6	− 1,921	9,015	7,0940	23753
2,7	2,3214	35,302	37,623	07563	6,7	− 3,459	10,633	7,1739	20774
2,8	2,4081	28,189	30,597	09179	6,8	− 5,411	12,666	7,2551	17994
2,9	2,4938	22,736	25,230	11026	6,9	− 7,902	15,240	7,3376	15436
3,0	2,5786	18,522	21,101	0,13112	**7,0**	− 11,101	18,522	7,4214	0,13112
3,1	2,6624	15,240	17,902	15436	7,1	− 15,230	22,736	7,5062	11026
3,2	2,7449	12,666	15,411	17994	7,2	− 20,597	28,189	7,5919	09179
3,3	2,8261	10,633	13,459	20774	7,3	− 27,623	35,302	7,6786	07564
3,4	2,9060	9,015	11,921	23753	7,4	− 36,888	44,654	7,7661	06168
3,5	2,9842	7,721	10,705	0,26907	**7,5**	− 49,20	57,05	7,8543	0,04979
3,6	3,0606	6,6788	9,7394	30199	7,6	− 65,68	73,62	7,9432	03977
3,7	3,1351	5,8354	8,9705	33589	7,7	− 87,93	95,96	8,0327	03143
3,8	3,2074	5,1497	8,3571	37031	7,8	− 118,22	126,34	8,1228	02458
3,9	3,2773	4,5903	7,8676	40474	7,9	− 159,79	168,00	8,2134	01903
4,0	3,3443	4,1327	7,4770	0,43863	**8,0**	− 217,3	225,6	8,3046	0,01457
4,1	3,4083	3,7582	7,1665	47144	8,1	− 297,7	306,1	8,3962	01104
4,2	3,4687	3,4519	6,9206	50260	8,2	− 410,9	419,4	8,4882	00828
4,3	3,5251	3,2025	6,7276	53159	8,3	− 571,9	580,5	8,5806	00614
4,4	3,5770	3,0010	6,5780	55788	8,4	− 802,8	811,5	8,6734	00451
4,5	3,6236	2,8404	6,4640	0,58099	**8,5**	− 1137	1146	8,7666	0,00327
4,6	3,6643	2,7154	6,3797	60052	8,6	− 1625	1634	8,8600	00235
4,7	3,6982	2,6220	6,3202	61609	8,7	− 2345	2354	8,9538	00167
4,8	3,7241	2,5573	6,2814	62741	8,8	− 3416	3425	9,0478	00118
4,9	3,7407	2,5192	6,2599	63481	8,9	− 5025	5034	9,1421	00082

[1] FISHER and YATES, *Statistical Tables for Biological, Agricultural and Medical Research*, 6th ed., Longman, Harlow, 1974, pages 68 and 71. Reprinted by kind permission of the authors and publishers.

Logits and Antilogits[1]

Numbers in *italics* are negative values

p	0,000	0,001	0,002	0,003	0,004	0,005	0,006	0,007	0,008	0,009
0,00		*6,90675*	*6,21261*	*5,80614*	*5,51745*	*5,29330*	*5,10998*	*4,95482*	*4,82028*	*4,70149*
0,01	*4,59512*	*4,49880*	*4,41078*	*4,32972*	*4,25460*	*4,18459*	*4,11904*	*4,05740*	*3,99922*	*3,94413*
0,02	*3,89182*	*3,84201*	*3,79447*	*3,74899*	*3,70541*	*3,66356*	*3,62331*	*3,58455*	*3,54715*	*3,51103*
0,03	*3,47610*	*3,44228*	*3,40950*	*3,37769*	*3,34680*	*3,31678*	*3,28757*	*3,25914*	*3,23143*	*3,20441*
0,04	*3,17805*	*3,15232*	*3,12718*	*3,10260*	*3,07857*	*3,05505*	*3,03202*	*3,00947*	*2,98736*	*2,96569*
0,05	*2,94444*	*2,92358*	*2,90311*	*2,88301*	*2,86326*	*2,84385*	*2,82477*	*2,80601*	*2,78756*	*2,76941*
0,06	*2,75154*	*2,73394*	*2,71662*	*2,69955*	*2,68273*	*2,66616*	*2,64982*	*2,63371*	*2,61783*	*2,60215*
0,07	*2,58669*	*2,57143*	*2,55637*	*2,54149*	*2,52681*	*2,51231*	*2,49798*	*2,48382*	*2,46984*	*2,45601*
0,08	*2,44235*	*2,42884*	*2,41548*	*2,40227*	*2,38920*	*2,37627*	*2,36348*	*2,35083*	*2,33830*	*2,32591*
0,09	*2,31363*	*2,30149*	*2,28946*	*2,27754*	*2,26574*	*2,25406*	*2,24248*	*2,23101*	*2,21965*	*2,20839*
0,10	*2,19722*	*2,18616*	*2,17520*	*2,16433*	*2,15355*	*2,14286*	*2,13227*	*2,12176*	*2,11133*	*2,10100*
0,11	*2,09074*	*2,08057*	*2,07047*	*2,06046*	*2,05052*	*2,04066*	*2,03087*	*2,02115*	*2,01151*	*2,00193*
0,12	*1,99243*	*1,98299*	*1,97363*	*1,96432*	*1,95508*	*1,94591*	*1,93680*	*1,92775*	*1,91876*	*1,90983*
0,13	*1,90096*	*1,89215*	*1,88339*	*1,87469*	*1,86605*	*1,85745*	*1,84892*	*1,84043*	*1,83200*	*1,82362*
0,14	*1,81529*	*1,80701*	*1,79878*	*1,79059*	*1,78246*	*1,77437*	*1,76632*	*1,75833*	*1,75037*	*1,74247*
0,15	*1,73460*	*1,72678*	*1,71900*	*1,71126*	*1,70357*	*1,69591*	*1,68830*	*1,68072*	*1,67318*	*1,66569*
0,16	*1,65823*	*1,65081*	*1,64342*	*1,63607*	*1,62876*	*1,62149*	*1,61425*	*1,60704*	*1,59987*	*1,59273*
0,17	*1,58563*	*1,57856*	*1,57152*	*1,56451*	*1,55754*	*1,55060*	*1,54369*	*1,53681*	*1,52996*	*1,52314*
0,18	*1,51635*	*1,50959*	*1,50286*	*1,49615*	*1,48948*	*1,48283*	*1,47621*	*1,46962*	*1,46306*	*1,45652*
0,19	*1,45001*	*1,44353*	*1,43707*	*1,43063*	*1,42423*	*1,41784*	*1,41148*	*1,40515*	*1,39884*	*1,39256*
0,20	*1,38629*	*1,38006*	*1,37384*	*1,36765*	*1,36148*	*1,35533*	*1,34921*	*1,34310*	*1,33702*	*1,33096*
0,21	*1,32493*	*1,31891*	*1,31291*	*1,30694*	*1,30098*	*1,29505*	*1,28913*	*1,28324*	*1,27736*	*1,27150*
0,22	*1,26567*	*1,25985*	*1,25405*	*1,24827*	*1,24251*	*1,23676*	*1,23104*	*1,22533*	*1,21964*	*1,21397*
0,23	*1,20831*	*1,20267*	*1,19705*	*1,19145*	*1,18586*	*1,18029*	*1,17474*	*1,16920*	*1,16368*	*1,15817*
0,24	*1,15268*	*1,14720*	*1,14175*	*1,13630*	*1,13087*	*1,12546*	*1,12006*	*1,11468*	*1,10931*	*1,10395*
0,25	*1,09861*	*1,09329*	*1,08797*	*1,08268*	*1,07739*	*1,07212*	*1,06686*	*1,06162*	*1,05639*	*1,05117*
0,26	*1,04597*	*1,04078*	*1,03560*	*1,03043*	*1,02528*	*1,02014*	*1,01501*	*1,00990*	*1,00479*	*0,99970*
0,27	*0,99462*	*0,98955*	*0,98450*	*0,97945*	*0,97442*	*0,96940*	*0,96439*	*0,95939*	*0,95440*	*0,94943*
0,28	*0,94446*	*0,93951*	*0,93456*	*0,92963*	*0,92471*	*0,91979*	*0,91489*	*0,91000*	*0,90512*	*0,90025*
0,29	*0,89538*	*0,89053*	*0,88569*	*0,88086*	*0,87604*	*0,87122*	*0,86642*	*0,86162*	*0,85684*	*0,85206*
0,30	*0,84730*	*0,84254*	*0,83779*	*0,83305*	*0,82832*	*0,82360*	*0,81889*	*0,81418*	*0,80949*	*0,80480*
0,31	*0,80012*	*0,79545*	*0,79079*	*0,78613*	*0,78148*	*0,77685*	*0,77222*	*0,76759*	*0,76298*	*0,75837*
0,32	*0,75377*	*0,74918*	*0,74460*	*0,74002*	*0,73545*	*0,73089*	*0,72633*	*0,72179*	*0,71724*	*0,71271*
0,33	*0,70819*	*0,70367*	*0,69915*	*0,69465*	*0,69015*	*0,68566*	*0,68117*	*0,67669*	*0,67222*	*0,66775*
0,34	*0,66329*	*0,65884*	*0,65439*	*0,64995*	*0,64552*	*0,64109*	*0,63667*	*0,63225*	*0,62784*	*0,62344*
0,35	*0,61904*	*0,61465*	*0,61026*	*0,60588*	*0,60150*	*0,59713*	*0,59277*	*0,58841*	*0,58406*	*0,57971*
0,36	*0,57536*	*0,57103*	*0,56669*	*0,56237*	*0,55804*	*0,55373*	*0,54942*	*0,54511*	*0,54081*	*0,53651*
0,37	*0,53222*	*0,52793*	*0,52365*	*0,51937*	*0,51509*	*0,51083*	*0,50656*	*0,50230*	*0,49805*	*0,49379*
0,38	*0,48955*	*0,48531*	*0,48107*	*0,47683*	*0,47260*	*0,46838*	*0,46416*	*0,45994*	*0,45573*	*0,45152*
0,39	*0,44731*	*0,44311*	*0,43891*	*0,43472*	*0,43053*	*0,42634*	*0,42216*	*0,41798*	*0,41381*	*0,40963*
0,40	*0,40547*	*0,40130*	*0,39714*	*0,39298*	*0,38883*	*0,38467*	*0,38053*	*0,37638*	*0,37224*	*0,36810*
0,41	*0,36397*	*0,35983*	*0,35570*	*0,35158*	*0,34745*	*0,34333*	*0,33922*	*0,33510*	*0,33099*	*0,32688*
0,42	*0,32277*	*0,31867*	*0,31457*	*0,31047*	*0,30637*	*0,30228*	*0,29819*	*0,29410*	*0,29002*	*0,28593*
0,43	*0,28185*	*0,27777*	*0,27370*	*0,26962*	*0,26555*	*0,26148*	*0,25741*	*0,25335*	*0,24928*	*0,24522*
0,44	*0,24116*	*0,23710*	*0,23305*	*0,22900*	*0,22494*	*0,22089*	*0,21685*	*0,21280*	*0,20875*	*0,20471*
0,45	*0,20067*	*0,19663*	*0,19259*	*0,18856*	*0,18452*	*0,18049*	*0,17646*	*0,17243*	*0,16840*	*0,16437*
0,46	*0,16034*	*0,15632*	*0,15229*	*0,14827*	*0,14425*	*0,14023*	*0,13621*	*0,13219*	*0,12818*	*0,12416*
0,47	*0,12014*	*0,11613*	*0,11212*	*0,10811*	*0,10409*	*0,10008*	*0,09607*	*0,09206*	*0,08806*	*0,08405*
0,48	*0,08004*	*0,07604*	*0,07203*	*0,06803*	*0,06402*	*0,06002*	*0,05601*	*0,05201*	*0,04801*	*0,04401*
0,49	*0,04001*	*0,03600*	*0,03200*	*0,02800*	*0,02400*	*0,02000*	*0,01600*	*0,01200*	*0,00800*	*0,00400*
0,50	0,00000	0,00400	0,00800	0,01200	0,01600	0,02000	0,02400	0,02800	0,03200	0,03600
0,51	0,04001	0,04401	0,04801	0,05201	0,05601	0,06002	0,06402	0,06803	0,07203	0,07604
0,52	0,08004	0,08405	0,08806	0,09206	0,09607	0,10008	0,10409	0,10811	0,11212	0,11613
0,53	0,12014	0,12416	0,12818	0,13219	0,13621	0,14023	0,14425	0,14827	0,15229	0,15632
0,54	0,16034	0,16437	0,16840	0,17243	0,17646	0,18049	0,18452	0,18856	0,19259	0,19663
0,55	0,20067	0,20471	0,20875	0,21280	0,21685	0,22089	0,22494	0,22900	0,23305	0,23710
0,56	0,24116	0,24522	0,24928	0,25335	0,25741	0,26148	0,26555	0,26962	0,27370	0,27777
0,57	0,28185	0,28593	0,29002	0,29410	0,29819	0,30228	0,30637	0,31047	0,31457	0,31867
0,58	0,32277	0,32688	0,33099	0,33510	0,33922	0,34333	0,34745	0,35158	0,35570	0,35983
0,59	0,36397	0,36810	0,37224	0,37638	0,38053	0,38467	0,38883	0,39298	0,39714	0,40130
0,60	0,40547	0,40963	0,41381	0,41798	0,42216	0,42634	0,43053	0,43472	0,43891	0,44311
0,61	0,44731	0,45152	0,45573	0,45994	0,46416	0,46838	0,47260	0,47683	0,48107	0,48531
0,62	0,48955	0,49379	0,49805	0,50230	0,50656	0,51083	0,51509	0,51937	0,52365	0,52793
0,63	0,53222	0,53651	0,54081	0,54511	0,54942	0,55373	0,55804	0,56237	0,56669	0,57103
0,64	0,57536	0,57971	0,58406	0,58841	0,59277	0,59713	0,60150	0,60588	0,61026	0,61465
0,65	0,61904	0,62344	0,62784	0,63225	0,63667	0,64109	0,64552	0,64995	0,65439	0,65884
0,66	0,66329	0,66775	0,67222	0,67669	0,68117	0,68566	0,69015	0,69465	0,69915	0,70367
0,67	0,70819	0,71271	0,71724	0,72179	0,72633	0,73089	0,73545	0,74002	0,74460	0,74918
0,68	0,75377	0,75837	0,76298	0,76759	0,77222	0,77685	0,78148	0,78613	0,79079	0,79545
0,69	0,80012	0,80480	0,80949	0,81418	0,81889	0,82360	0,82832	0,83305	0,83779	0,84254
0,70	0,84730	0,85206	0,85684	0,86162	0,86642	0,87122	0,87604	0,88086	0,88569	0,89053
0,71	0,89538	0,90025	0,90512	0,91000	0,91489	0,91979	0,92471	0,92963	0,93456	0,93951
0,72	0,94446	0,94943	0,95440	0,95939	0,96439	0,96940	0,97442	0,97945	0,98450	0,98955
0,73	0,99462	0,99970	1,00479	1,00990	1,01501	1,02014	1,02528	1,03043	1,03560	1,04078
0,74	1,04597	1,05117	1,05639	1,06162	1,06686	1,07212	1,07739	1,08268	1,08797	1,09329
0,75	1,09861	1,10395	1,10931	1,11468	1,12006	1,12546	1,13087	1,13630	1,14175	1,14720
0,76	1,15268	1,15817	1,16368	1,16920	1,17474	1,18029	1,18586	1,19145	1,19705	1,20267
0,77	1,20831	1,21397	1,21964	1,22533	1,23104	1,23676	1,24251	1,24827	1,25405	1,25985
0,78	1,26567	1,27150	1,27736	1,28324	1,28913	1,29505	1,30098	1,30694	1,31291	1,31891
0,79	1,32493	1,33096	1,33702	1,34310	1,34921	1,35533	1,36148	1,36765	1,37384	1,38006
0,80	1,38629	1,39256	1,39884	1,40515	1,41148	1,41784	1,42423	1,43063	1,43707	1,44353
0,81	1,45001	1,45652	1,46306	1,46962	1,47621	1,48283	1,48948	1,49615	1,50286	1,50959
0,82	1,51635	1,52314	1,52996	1,53681	1,54369	1,55060	1,55754	1,56451	1,57152	1,57856
0,83	1,58563	1,59273	1,59987	1,60704	1,61425	1,62149	1,62876	1,63607	1,64342	1,65081
0,84	1,65823	1,66569	1,67318	1,68072	1,68830	1,69591	1,70357	1,71126	1,71900	1,72678
0,85	1,73460	1,74247	1,75037	1,75833	1,76632	1,77437	1,78246	1,79059	1,79878	1,80701
0,86	1,81529	1,82362	1,83200	1,84043	1,84892	1,85745	1,86605	1,87469	1,88339	1,89215
0,87	1,90096	1,90983	1,91876	1,92775	1,93680	1,94591	1,95508	1,96432	1,97363	1,98299
0,88	1,99243	2,00193	2,01151	2,02115	2,03087	2,04066	2,05052	2,06046	2,07047	2,08057
0,89	2,09074	2,10100	2,11133	2,12176	2,13227	2,14286	2,15355	2,16433	2,17520	2,18616
0,90	2,19722	2,20839	2,21965	2,23101	2,24248	2,25406	2,26574	2,27754	2,28946	2,30149
0,91	2,31363	2,32591	2,33830	2,35083	2,36348	2,37627	2,38920	2,40227	2,41548	2,42884
0,92	2,44235	2,45601	2,46984	2,48382	2,49798	2,51231	2,52681	2,54149	2,55637	2,57143
0,93	2,58669	2,60215	2,61783	2,63371	2,64982	2,66616	2,68273	2,69955	2,71662	2,73394
0,94	2,75154	2,76941	2,78756	2,80601	2,82477	2,84385	2,86326	2,88301	2,90311	2,92358
0,95	2,94444	2,96569	2,98736	3,00947	3,03202	3,05505	3,07857	3,10260	3,12718	3,15232
0,96	3,17805	3,20441	3,23143	3,25914	3,28757	3,31678	3,34680	3,37769	3,40950	3,44228
0,97	3,47610	3,51103	3,54715	3,58455	3,62331	3,66356	3,70541	3,74899	3,79447	3,84201
0,98	3,89182	3,94413	3,99922	4,05740	4,11904	4,18459	4,25460	4,32972	4,41078	4,49880
0,99	4,59512	4,70149	4,82028	4,95482	5,10998	5,29330	5,51745	5,80614	6,21261	6,90675

l	0,00	0,01	0,02	0,03	0,04	0,05	0,06	0,07	0,08	0,09
	0,	0,	0,	0,	0,	0,	0,	0,	0,	0,
−4,9	00739	00732	00725	00717	00710	00703	00696	00690	00683	00676
−4,8	00816	00808	00800	00792	00785	00777	00769	00761	00754	00747
−4,7	00901	00892	00884	00875	00866	00858	00849	00841	00833	00824
−4,6	00995	00985	00976	00966	00957	00947	00938	00929	00919	00910
−4,5	01099	01088	01077	01067	01056	01046	01035	01025	01015	01005
−4,4	01213	01201	01189	01177	01166	01154	01143	01132	01121	01110
−4,3	01339	01326	01313	01300	01287	01274	01262	01249	01237	01225
−4,2	01477	01463	01449	01434	01420	01406	01393	01379	01365	01352
−4,1	01630	01614	01598	01583	01567	01552	01537	01522	01507	01492
−4,0	01799	01781	01764	01746	01729	01712	01696	01679	01663	01646
−3,9	01984	01965	01946	01927	01908	01889	01871	01852	01834	01816
−3,8	02188	02167	02146	02125	02104	02084	02063	02043	02023	02004
−3,7	02413	02389	02366	02343	02320	02298	02275	02253	02231	02210
−3,6	02660	02634	02608	02583	02558	02533	02509	02484	02460	02436
−3,5	02931	02903	02875	02847	02820	02792	02765	02738	02712	02686
−3,4	03230	03198	03168	03137	03107	03077	03047	03018	02989	02960
−3,3	03557	03523	03489	03456	03422	03390	03357	03325	03293	03261
−3,2	03917	03879	03842	03805	03769	03733	03697	03661	03626	03592
−3,1	04311	04270	04229	04189	04149	04109	04070	04031	03993	03954
−3,0	04743	04698	04653	04609	04565	04522	04479	04436	04394	04352
−2,9	05215	05166	05117	05069	05021	04974	04927	04880	04834	04788
−2,8	05732	05679	05625	05572	05520	05468	05417	05366	05315	05265
−2,7	06297	06239	06180	06123	06065	06009	05952	05897	05841	05787
−2,6	06914	06850	06786	06723	06661	06599	06538	06477	06416	06357
−2,5	07586	07516	07447	07378	07310	07243	07176	07109	07044	06978
−2,4	08317	08241	08166	08091	08017	07944	07871	07799	07727	07656
−2,3	09112	09030	08948	08867	08786	08707	08627	08549	08471	08394
−2,2	09975	09886	09797	09709	09622	09535	09449	09364	09279	09195
−2,1	10910	10813	10717	10621	10527	10433	10340	10248	10156	10065
−2,0	11920	11816	11712	11609	11507	11405	11305	11205	11106	11007
−1,9	13011	12898	12786	12675	12565	12455	12347	12239	12132	12026
−1,8	14185	14064	13943	13824	13705	13587	13470	13354	13239	13124
−1,7	15447	15316	15187	15059	14931	14805	14679	14554	14430	14307
−1,6	16798	16659	16520	16383	16247	16111	15976	15842	15710	15578
−1,5	18243	18094	17946	17799	17654	17509	17365	17222	17080	16938
−1,4	19782	19623	19466	19310	19155	19000	18847	18694	18543	18392
−1,3	21417	21249	21082	20916	20751	20587	20424	20262	20101	19941
−1,2	23148	22970	22794	22618	22444	22270	22097	21926	21755	21585
−1,1	24974	24787	24601	24416	24232	24049	23867	23685	23505	23326
−1,0	26894	26698	26503	26308	26115	25923	25731	25540	25351	25162
−0,9	28905	28700	28496	28292	28090	27888	27688	27488	27289	27091
−0,8	31003	30789	30576	30365	30153	29943	29734	29525	29318	29111
−0,7	33181	32960	32739	32519	32300	32082	31865	31648	31432	31217
−0,6	35434	35206	34978	34751	34525	34299	34074	33850	33626	33403
−0,5	37754	37519	37285	37052	36819	36586	36355	36124	35893	35663
−0,4	40131	39891	39652	39413	39174	38936	38699	38462	38225	37989
−0,3	42556	42311	42068	41824	41581	41338	41096	40854	40613	40372
−0,2	45017	44769	44522	44275	44029	43782	43536	43291	43045	42800
−0,1	47502	47253	47004	46755	46506	46257	46009	45760	45512	45264
−0,0	50000	49750	49500	49250	49000	48750	48500	48251	48001	47752
+0,0	50000	50250	50500	50750	51000	51250	51500	51749	51999	52248
+0,1	52498	52747	52996	53245	53494	53743	53991	54240	54488	54736
+0,2	54983	55231	55478	55725	55971	56218	56464	56709	56955	57200
+0,3	57444	57689	57932	58176	58419	58662	58904	59146	59387	59628
+0,4	59869	60109	60348	60587	60826	61064	61301	61538	61775	62011
+0,5	62246	62481	62715	62948	63181	63414	63645	63876	64107	64337
+0,6	64566	64794	65022	65249	65475	65701	65926	66150	66374	66597
+0,7	66819	67040	67261	67481	67700	67918	68135	68352	68568	68783
+0,8	68997	69211	69424	69635	69847	70057	70266	70475	70682	70889
+0,9	71095	71300	71504	71708	71910	72112	72312	72512	72711	72909
+1,0	73106	73302	73497	73692	73885	74077	74269	74460	74649	74838
+1,1	75026	75213	75399	75584	75768	75951	76133	76315	76495	76674
+1,2	76852	77030	77206	77382	77556	77730	77903	78074	78245	78415
+1,3	78583	78751	78918	79084	79249	79413	79576	79738	79899	80059
+1,4	80218	80377	80534	80690	80845	81000	81153	81306	81457	81608
+1,5	81757	81906	82054	82201	82346	82491	82635	82778	82920	83062
+1,6	83202	83341	83480	83617	83753	83889	84024	84158	84290	84422
+1,7	84553	84684	84813	84941	85069	85195	85321	85446	85570	85693
+1,8	85815	85936	86057	86176	86295	86413	86530	86646	86761	86876
+1,9	86989	87102	87214	87325	87435	87545	87653	87761	87868	87974
+2,0	88080	88184	88288	88391	88493	88595	88695	88795	88894	88993
+2,1	89090	89187	89283	89379	89473	89567	89660	89752	89844	89935
+2,2	90025	90114	90203	90291	90378	90465	90551	90636	90721	90805
+2,3	90888	90970	91052	91133	91214	91293	91373	91451	91529	91606
+2,4	91683	91759	91834	91909	91983	92056	92129	92201	92273	92344
+2,5	92414	92484	92553	92622	92690	92757	92824	92891	92956	93022
+2,6	93086	93150	93214	93277	93339	93401	93462	93523	93584	93643
+2,7	93703	93761	93820	93877	93935	93991	94048	94103	94159	94213
+2,8	94268	94321	94375	94428	94480	94532	94583	94634	94685	94735
+2,9	94785	94834	94883	94931	94979	95026	95073	95120	95166	95212
+3,0	95257	95302	95347	95391	95435	95478	95521	95564	95606	95648
+3,1	95689	95730	95771	95811	95851	95891	95930	95969	96007	96046
+3,2	96083	96121	96158	96195	96231	96267	96303	96339	96374	96408
+3,3	96443	96477	96511	96544	96578	96610	96643	96675	96707	96739
+3,4	96770	96802	96832	96863	96893	96923	96953	96982	97011	97040
+3,5	97069	97097	97125	97153	97180	97208	97235	97262	97288	97314
+3,6	97340	97366	97392	97417	97442	97467	97491	97516	97540	97564
+3,7	97587	97611	97634	97657	97680	97702	97725	97747	97769	97790
+3,8	97812	97833	97854	97875	97896	97916	97937	97957	97977	97996
+3,9	98016	98035	98054	98073	98092	98111	98129	98148	98166	98184
+4,0	98201	98219	98236	98254	98271	98288	98304	98321	98337	98354
+4,1	98370	98386	98402	98417	98433	98448	98463	98478	98493	98508
+4,2	98523	98537	98551	98566	98580	98594	98607	98621	98635	98648
+4,3	98661	98674	98687	98700	98713	98726	98738	98751	98763	98775
+4,4	98787	98799	98811	98823	98834	98846	98857	98868	98879	98890
+4,5	98901	98912	98923	98933	98944	98954	98965	98975	98985	98995
+4,6	99005	99015	99024	99034	99043	99053	99062	99071	99081	99090
+4,7	99099	99108	99116	99125	99134	99142	99151	99159	99167	99176
+4,8	99184	99192	99200	99208	99215	99223	99231	99239	99246	99253
+4,9	99261	99268	99275	99283	99290	99297	99304	99310	99317	99324

[1] BERKSON, J., *J. Amer. statist. Ass.*, **48**, 565 (1953). Reprinted by kind permission of the author and publishers.

All values conform to the international convention (i.e. 0,1 instead of 0.1).

Logistic Weights[1]

In the upper line are values of $w = p\,q$, in the lower line those of $w\,l = p\,q\,l$. Numbers in *italics* are negative values

p	0,000	0,001	0,002	0,003	0,004	0,005	0,006	0,007	0,008	0,009
	0,	0,	0,	0,	0,	0,	0,	0,	0,	0,
0,00	0000	0010	0020	0030	0040	0050	0060	0070	0079	0089
	–	*0069*	*0124*	*0174*	*0220*	*0263*	*0305*	*0344*	*0383*	*0419*
0,01	0099	0109	0119	0128	0138	0148	0157	0167	0177	0186
	0455	*0489*	*0523*	*0556*	*0587*	*0618*	*0649*	*0678*	*0707*	*0735*
0,02	0196	0206	0215	0225	0234	0244	0253	0263	0272	0282
	0763	*0790*	*0816*	*0842*	*0868*	*0893*	*0918*	*0942*	*0965*	*0989*
0,03	0291	0300	0310	0319	0328	0338	0347	0356	0366	0375
	1012	*1034*	*1056*	*1078*	*1099*	*1120*	*1141*	*1161*	*1181*	*1201*
0,04	0384	0393	0402	0412	0421	0430	0439	0448	0457	0466
	1220	*1239*	*1258*	*1277*	*1295*	*1313*	*1331*	*1348*	*1365*	*1382*
0,05	0475	0484	0493	0502	0511	0520	0529	0538	0546	0555
	1399	*1415*	*1431*	*1447*	*1463*	*1478*	*1493*	*1508*	*1523*	*1538*
0,06	0564	0573	0582	0590	0599	0608	0616	0625	0634	0642
	1552	*1566*	*1580*	*1594*	*1607*	*1620*	*1633*	*1646*	*1659*	*1672*
0,07	0651	0660	0668	0677	0685	0694	0702	0711	0719	0728
	1684	*1696*	*1708*	*1720*	*1731*	*1743*	*1754*	*1765*	*1776*	*1787*
0,08	0736	0744	0753	0761	0769	0778	0786	0794	0803	0811
	1798	*1808*	*1818*	*1828*	*1838*	*1848*	*1858*	*1867*	*1877*	*1886*
0,09	0819	0827	0835	0844	0852	0860	0868	0876	0884	0892
	1895	*1904*	*1913*	*1921*	*1930*	*1938*	*1946*	*1954*	*1962*	*1970*
0,10	0900	0908	0916	0924	0932	0940	0948	0956	0963	0971
	1977	*1985*	*1992*	*2000*	*2007*	*2014*	*2021*	*2027*	*2034*	*2040*
0,11	0979	0987	0995	1002	1010	1018	1025	1033	1041	1048
	2047	*2053*	*2059*	*2065*	*2071*	*2077*	*2083*	*2088*	*2093*	*2099*
0,12	1056	1064	1071	1079	1086	1094	1101	1109	1116	1124
	2104	*2109*	*2114*	*2119*	*2124*	*2128*	*2133*	*2137*	*2142*	*2146*
0,13	1131	1138	1146	1153	1160	1168	1175	1182	1190	1197
	2150	*2154*	*2158*	*2162*	*2165*	*2169*	*2173*	*2176*	*2179*	*2182*
0,14	1204	1211	1218	1226	1233	1240	1247	1254	1261	1268
	2186	*2189*	*2192*	*2194*	*2197*	*2200*	*2202*	*2205*	*2207*	*2209*
0,15	1275	1282	1289	1296	1303	1310	1317	1324	1330	1337
	2212	*2214*	*2216*	*2218*	*2219*	*2221*	*2223*	*2224*	*2226*	*2227*
0,16	1344	1351	1358	1364	1371	1378	1384	1391	1398	1404
	2229	*2230*	*2231*	*2232*	*2233*	*2234*	*2235*	*2236*	*2236*	*2237*
0,17	1411	1418	1424	1431	1437	1444	1450	1457	1463	1470
	2237	*2238*	*2238*	*2238*	*2239*	*2239*	*2239*	*2239*	*2239*	*2238*
0,18	1476	1482	1489	1495	1501	1508	1514	1520	1527	1533
	2238	*2238*	*2237*	*2237*	*2236*	*2236*	*2235*	*2234*	*2233*	*2233*
0,19	1539	1545	1551	1558	1564	1570	1576	1582	1588	1594
	2232	*2231*	*2229*	*2228*	*2227*	*2226*	*2224*	*2223*	*2221*	*2220*
0,20	1600	1606	1612	1618	1624	1630	1636	1642	1647	1653
	2218	*2216*	*2215*	*2213*	*2211*	*2209*	*2207*	*2205*	*2203*	*2200*
0,21	1659	1665	1671	1676	1682	1688	1693	1699	1705	1710
	2198	*2196*	*2193*	*2191*	*2188*	*2186*	*2183*	*2180*	*2178*	*2175*
0,22	1716	1722	1727	1733	1738	1744	1749	1755	1760	1766
	2172	*2169*	*2166*	*2163*	*2160*	*2157*	*2153*	*2150*	*2147*	*2143*
0,23	1771	1776	1782	1787	1792	1798	1803	1808	1814	1819
	2140	*2136*	*2133*	*2129*	*2126*	*2122*	*2118*	*2114*	*2110*	*2106*
0,24	1824	1829	1834	1840	1845	1850	1855	1860	1865	1870
	2102	*2098*	*2094*	*2090*	*2086*	*2082*	*2078*	*2073*	*2069*	*2064*
0,25	1875	1880	1885	1890	1895	1900	1905	1910	1914	1919
	2060	*2055*	*2051*	*2046*	*2041*	*2037*	*2032*	*2027*	*2022*	*2017*
0,26	1924	1929	1934	1938	1943	1948	1952	1957	1962	1966
	2012	*2007*	*2002*	*1997*	*1992*	*1987*	*1982*	*1976*	*1971*	*1966*
0,27	1971	1976	1980	1985	1989	1994	1998	2003	2007	2012
	1960	*1955*	*1949*	*1944*	*1938*	*1933*	*1927*	*1921*	*1916*	*1910*
0,28	2016	2020	2025	2029	2033	2038	2042	2046	2051	2055
	1904	*1898*	*1892*	*1886*	*1880*	*1874*	*1868*	*1862*	*1856*	*1850*
0,29	2059	2063	2067	2072	2076	2080	2084	2088	2092	2096
	1844	*1837*	*1831*	*1825*	*1818*	*1812*	*1805*	*1799*	*1792*	*1786*
0,30	2100	2104	2108	2112	2116	2120	2124	2128	2131	2135
	1779	*1773*	*1766*	*1759*	*1753*	*1746*	*1739*	*1732*	*1725*	*1718*
0,31	2139	2143	2147	2150	2154	2158	2161	2165	2169	2172
	1711	*1704*	*1697*	*1690*	*1683*	*1676*	*1669*	*1662*	*1655*	*1647*
0,32	2176	2180	2183	2187	2190	2194	2197	2201	2204	2208
	1640	*1633*	*1626*	*1618*	*1611*	*1603*	*1596*	*1588*	*1581*	*1573*
0,33	2211	2214	2218	2221	2224	2228	2231	2234	2238	2241
	1566	*1558*	*1551*	*1543*	*1535*	*1527*	*1520*	*1512*	*1504*	*1496*
0,34	2244	2247	2250	2254	2257	2260	2263	2266	2269	2272
	1488	*1481*	*1473*	*1465*	*1457*	*1449*	*1441*	*1433*	*1425*	*1416*
0,35	2275	2278	2281	2284	2287	2290	2293	2296	2298	2301
	1408	*1400*	*1392*	*1384*	*1376*	*1367*	*1359*	*1351*	*1342*	*1334*
0,36	2304	2307	2310	2312	2315	2318	2320	2323	2326	2328
	1326	*1317*	*1309*	*1300*	*1292*	*1283*	*1275*	*1266*	*1258*	*1249*
0,37	2331	2334	2336	2339	2341	2344	2346	2349	2351	2354
	1241	*1232*	*1223*	*1215*	*1206*	*1197*	*1189*	*1180*	*1171*	*1162*
0,38	2356	2358	2361	2363	2365	2368	2370	2372	2375	2377
	1153	*1145*	*1136*	*1127*	*1118*	*1109*	*1100*	*1091*	*1082*	*1073*
0,39	2379	2381	2383	2386	2388	2390	2392	2394	2396	2398
	1064	*1055*	*1046*	*1037*	*1028*	*1019*	*1010*	*1001*	*0991*	*0982*
0,40	2400	2402	2404	2406	2408	2410	2412	2414	2415	2417
	0973	*0964*	*0955*	*0945*	*0936*	*0927*	*0918*	*0908*	*0899*	*0890*
0,41	2419	2421	2423	2424	2426	2428	2429	2431	2433	2434
	0880	*0871*	*0862*	*0852*	*0843*	*0834*	*0824*	*0815*	*0805*	*0796*
0,42	2436	2438	2439	2441	2442	2444	2445	2447	2448	2450
	0786	*0777*	*0767*	*0758*	*0748*	*0739*	*0729*	*0720*	*0710*	*0700*
0,43	2451	2452	2454	2455	2456	2458	2459	2460	2462	2463
	0691	*0681*	*0672*	*0662*	*0652*	*0643*	*0633*	*0623*	*0614*	*0604*
0,44	2464	2465	2466	2468	2469	2470	2471	2472	2473	2474
	0594	*0584*	*0575*	*0565*	*0555*	*0546*	*0536*	*0526*	*0516*	*0506*
0,45	2475	2476	2477	2478	2479	2480	2481	2482	2482	2483
	0497	*0487*	*0477*	*0467*	*0457*	*0448*	*0438*	*0428*	*0418*	*0408*
0,46	2484	2485	2486	2486	2487	2488	2488	2489	2490	2490
	0398	*0388*	*0379*	*0369*	*0359*	*0349*	*0339*	*0329*	*0319*	*0309*
0,47	2491	2492	2492	2493	2493	2494	2494	2495	2495	2496
	0299	*0289*	*0279*	*0269*	*0260*	*0250*	*0240*	*0230*	*0220*	*0210*
0,48	2496	2496	2497	2497	2497	2498	2498	2498	2499	2499
	0200	*0190*	*0180*	*0170*	*0160*	*0150*	*0140*	*0130*	*0120*	*0110*
0,49	2499	2499	2499	2500	2500	2500	2500	2500	2500	2500
	0100	*0090*	*0080*	*0070*	*0060*	*0050*	*0040*	*0030*	*0020*	*0010*

p	0,000	0,001	0,002	0,003	0,004	0,005	0,006	0,007	0,008	0,009
	0,	0,	0,	0,	0,	0,	0,	0,	0,	0,
0,50	2500	2500	2500	2500	2500	2500	2500	2500	2499	2499
	0000	0010	0020	0030	0040	0050	0060	0070	0080	0090
0,51	2499	2499	2499	2498	2498	2498	2497	2497	2497	2496
	0100	0110	0120	0130	0140	0150	0160	0170	0180	0190
0,52	2496	2496	2495	2495	2494	2494	2493	2493	2492	2492
	0200	0210	0220	0230	0240	0250	0260	0269	0279	0289
0,53	2491	2490	2490	2489	2488	2488	2487	2486	2486	2485
	0299	0309	0319	0329	0339	0349	0359	0369	0379	0388
0,54	2484	2483	2482	2482	2481	2480	2479	2478	2477	2476
	0398	0408	0418	0428	0438	0448	0457	0467	0477	0487
0,55	2475	2474	2473	2472	2471	2470	2469	2468	2466	2465
	0497	0506	0516	0526	0536	0546	0555	0565	0575	0584
0,56	2464	2463	2462	2460	2459	2458	2456	2455	2454	2552
	0594	0604	0614	0623	0633	0643	0652	0662	0672	0681
0,57	2451	2450	2448	2447	2445	2444	2442	2441	2439	2438
	0691	0700	0710	0720	0729	0739	0748	0758	0767	0777
0,58	2436	2434	2433	2431	2429	2428	2426	2424	2423	2421
	0786	0796	0805	0815	0824	0834	0843	0852	0862	0871
0,59	2419	2417	2415	2414	2412	2410	2408	2406	2404	2402
	0880	0890	0899	0908	0918	0927	0936	0945	0955	0964
0,60	2400	2398	2396	2394	2392	2390	2388	2386	2383	2381
	0973	0982	0991	1001	1010	1019	1028	1037	1046	1055
0,61	2379	2377	2375	2372	2370	2368	2365	2363	2361	2358
	1064	1073	1082	1091	1100	1109	1118	1127	1136	1145
0,62	2356	2354	2351	2349	2346	2344	2341	2339	2336	2334
	1153	1162	1171	1180	1189	1197	1206	1215	1223	1232
0,63	2331	2328	2326	2323	2320	2318	2315	2312	2310	2307
	1241	1249	1258	1266	1275	1283	1292	1300	1309	1317
0,64	2304	2301	2298	2296	2293	2290	2287	2284	2281	2278
	1326	1334	1342	1351	1359	1367	1376	1384	1392	1400
0,65	2275	2272	2269	2266	2263	2260	2257	2254	2250	2247
	1408	1416	1425	1433	1441	1449	1457	1465	1473	1481
0,66	2244	2241	2238	2234	2231	2228	2224	2221	2218	2214
	1488	1496	1504	1512	1520	1527	1535	1543	1551	1558
0,67	2211	2208	2204	2201	2197	2194	2190	2187	2183	2180
	1566	1573	1581	1588	1596	1603	1611	1618	1626	1633
0,68	2176	2172	2169	2165	2161	2158	2154	2150	2147	2143
	1640	1647	1655	1662	1669	1676	1683	1690	1697	1704
0,69	2139	2135	2131	3128	2124	2120	2116	2112	2108	2104
	1711	1718	1725	1732	1739	1746	1753	1759	1766	1773
0,70	2100	2096	2092	2088	2084	2080	2076	2072	2067	2063
	1779	1786	1792	1799	1805	1812	1818	1825	1831	1837
0,71	2059	2055	2051	2046	2042	2038	2033	2029	2025	2020
	1844	1850	1856	1862	1868	1874	1880	1886	1892	1898
0,72	2016	2012	2007	2003	1998	1994	1989	1985	1980	1976
	1904	1910	1916	1921	1927	1933	1938	1944	1949	1955
0,73	1971	1966	1962	1957	1952	1948	1943	1938	1934	1929
	1960	1966	1971	1976	1982	1987	1992	1997	2002	2007
0,74	1924	1919	1914	1910	1905	1900	1895	1890	1885	1880
	2012	2017	2022	2027	2032	2037	2041	2046	2051	2055
0,75	1875	1870	1865	1860	1855	1850	1845	1840	1834	1829
	2060	2064	2069	2073	2078	2082	2086	2090	2094	2098
0,76	1824	1819	1814	1808	1803	1798	1792	1787	1782	1776
	2102	2106	2110	2114	2118	2122	2126	2129	2133	2136
0,77	1771	1766	1760	1755	1749	1744	1738	1733	1727	1722
	2140	2143	2147	2150	2153	2157	2160	2163	2166	2169
0,78	1716	1710	1705	1699	1693	1688	1682	1676	1671	1665
	2172	2175	2178	2180	2183	2186	2188	2191	2193	2196
0,79	1659	1653	1647	1642	1636	1630	1624	1618	1612	1606
	2198	2200	2203	2205	2207	2209	2211	2213	2215	2216
0,80	1600	1594	1588	1582	1576	1570	1564	1558	1551	1545
	2218	2220	2221	2223	2224	2226	2227	2228	2229	2231
0,81	1539	1533	1527	1520	1514	1508	1501	1495	1489	1482
	2232	2233	2233	2234	2235	2236	2236	2237	2237	2238
0,82	1476	1470	1463	1457	1450	1444	1437	1431	1424	1418
	2238	2238	2239	2239	2239	2239	2239	2238	2238	2238
0,83	1411	1404	1398	1391	1384	1378	1371	1364	1358	1351
	2237	2237	2236	2236	2235	2234	2233	2232	2231	2230
0,84	1344	1337	1330	1324	1317	1310	1303	1296	1289	1282
	2229	2227	2226	2224	2223	2221	2219	2218	2216	2214
0,85	1275	1268	1261	1254	1247	1240	1233	1226	1218	1211
	2212	2209	2207	2205	2202	2200	2197	2194	2192	2189
0,86	1204	1197	1190	1182	1175	1168	1160	1153	1146	1138
	2186	2182	2179	2176	2173	2169	2165	2162	2158	2154
0,87	1131	1124	1116	1109	1101	1094	1086	1079	1071	1064
	2150	2146	2142	2137	2133	2128	2124	2119	2114	2109
0,88	1056	1048	1041	1033	1025	1018	1010	1002	0995	0987
	2104	2099	2093	2088	2083	2077	2071	2065	2059	2053
0,89	0979	0971	0963	0956	0948	0940	0932	0924	0916	0908
	2047	2040	2034	2027	2021	2014	2007	2000	1992	1985
0,90	0900	0892	0884	0876	0868	0860	0852	0844	0835	0827
	1977	1970	1962	1954	1946	1938	1930	1921	1913	1904
0,91	0819	0811	0803	0794	0786	0778	0769	0761	0753	0744
	1895	1886	1877	1867	1858	1848	1838	1828	1818	1808
0,92	0736	0728	0719	0711	0702	0694	0685	0677	0668	0660
	1798	1787	1776	1765	1754	1743	1731	1720	1708	1696
0,93	0651	0642	0634	0625	0616	0608	0599	0590	0582	0573
	1684	1672	1659	1646	1633	1620	1607	1594	1580	1566
0,94	0564	0555	0546	0538	0529	0520	0511	0502	0493	0484
	1552	1538	1523	1508	1493	1478	1463	1447	1431	1415
0,95	0475	0466	0457	0448	0439	0430	0421	0412	0402	0393
	1399	1382	1365	1348	1331	1313	1295	1277	1258	1239
0,96	0384	0375	0366	0356	0347	0338	0328	0319	0310	0300
	1220	1201	1181	1161	1141	1120	1099	1078	1056	1034
0,97	0291	0282	0272	0263	0253	0244	0234	0225	0215	0206
	1012	0989	0965	0942	0918	0893	0868	0842	0816	0790
0,98	0196	0186	0177	0167	0157	0148	0138	0128	0119	0109
	0763	0735	0707	0678	0649	0618	0587	0556	0523	0489
0,99	0099	0089	0079	0070	0060	0050	0040	0030	0020	0010
	0455	0419	0383	0344	0305	0263	0220	0174	0124	0069

[1] BERKSON, J., *J. Amer. statist. Ass.*, **48**, 565 (1953). Reprinted by kind permission of the author and publishers.

All values conform to the international convention (i.e. 0,1 instead of 0.1).

Significance Limits for Mean Square Successive Difference and for Serial Correlation

Mean square successive difference[1,3]

N: size of sample. For interpretation of the test ratio see **(880)**, page 232

N	2α=0,10	2α=0,02	N	2α=0,10	2α=0,02
4	0,780–3,220	0,626–3,374	103	1,679–2,321	1,546–2,454
5	0,820–3,180	0,538–3,462	104	1,680–2,320	1,548–2,452
6	0,890–3,110	0,561–3,439	**105**	1,682–2,318	1,550–2,450
7	0,936–3,064	0,614–3,386	106	1,683–2,317	1,552–2,448
8	0,982–3,018	0,663–3,337	107	1,685–2,315	1,554–2,446
9	1,024–2,976	0,709–3,291	108	1,686–2,314	1,556–2,444
10	1,062–2,938	0,752–3,248	109	1,688–2,312	1,558–2,442
11	1,096–2,904	0,791–3,209	**110**	1,689–2,311	1,560–2,440
12	1,128–2,872	0,828–3,172	111	1,691–2,309	1,562–2,438
13	1,156–2,844	0,862–3,138	112	1,692–2,308	1,564–2,436
14	1,182–2,818	0,893–3,107	113	1,693–2,307	1,566–2,434
15	1,205–2,795	0,922–3,078	114	1,695–2,305	1,568–2,432
16	1,227–2,773	0,949–3,051	**115**	1,696–2,304	1,570–2,430
17	1,247–2,753	0,974–3,026	116	1,697–2,303	1,572–2,428
18	1,266–2,734	0,998–3,002	117	1,698–2,302	1,573–2,427
19	1,283–2,717	1,020–2,980	118	1,700–2,300	1,575–2,425
20	1,300–2,700	1,041–2,959	119	1,701–2,299	1,577–2,423
21	1,315–2,685	1,060–2,940	**120**	1,702–2,298	1,579–2,421
22	1,329–2,671	1,078–2,922	121	1,703–2,297	1,580–2,420
23	1,342–2,658	1,096–2,904	122	1,705–2,295	1,582–2,418
24	1,355–2,645	1,112–2,888	123	1,706–2,294	1,584–2,416
25	1,367–2,633	1,128–2,872	124	1,707–2,293	1,585–2,415
26	1,378–2,622	1,142–2,858	**125**	1,708–2,292	1,587–2,413
27	1,389–2,611	1,157–2,843	126	1,709–2,291	1,589–2,411
28	1,399–2,601	1,170–2,830	127	1,710–2,290	1,590–2,410
29	1,409–2,591	1,183–2,817	128	1,711–2,289	1,592–2,408
30	1,418–2,582	1,195–2,805	129	1,713–2,287	1,593–2,407
31	1,426–2,574	1,207–2,793	**130**	1,714–2,286	1,595–2,405
32	1,435–2,565	1,218–2,782	131	1,715–2,285	1,597–2,403
33	1,443–2,557	1,228–2,772	132	1,716–2,284	1,598–2,402
34	1,451–2,549	1,239–2,761	133	1,717–2,283	1,600–2,400
35	1,458–2,542	1,248–2,752	134	1,718–2,282	1,601–2,399
36	1,466–2,534	1,258–2,742	**135**	1,719–2,281	1,602–2,398
37	1,472–2,528	1,267–2,733	136	1,720–2,280	1,604–2,396
38	1,479–2,521	1,276–2,724	137	1,721–2,279	1,605–2,395
39	1,486–2,514	1,285–2,715	138	1,722–2,278	1,607–2,393
40	1,492–2,508	1,293–2,707	139	1,723–2,277	1,608–2,392
41	1,498–2,502	1,302–2,698	**140**	1,724–2,276	1,610–2,390
42	1,504–2,496	1,310–2,690	141	1,725–2,275	1,611–2,389
43	1,510–2,490	1,317–2,683	142	1,726–2,274	1,612–2,388
44	1,515–2,485	1,325–2,675	143	1,727–2,273	1,614–2,386
45	1,521–2,479	1,332–2,668	144	1,728–2,272	1,615–2,385
46	1,526–2,474	1,339–2,661	**145**	1,729–2,271	1,616–2,384
47	1,530–2,470	1,345–2,655	146	1,730–2,270	1,618–2,382
48	1,535–2,465	1,351–2,649	147	1,730–2,270	1,619–2,381
49	1,539–2,461	1,357–2,643	148	1,731–2,269	1,620–2,380
50	1,544–2,456	1,363–2,637	149	1,732–2,268	1,621–2,379
51	1,548–2,452	1,368–2,632	**150**	1,733–2,267	1,623–2,377
52	1,552–2,448	1,374–2,626	151	1,734–2,266	1,624–2,376
53	1,556–2,444	1,379–2,621	152	1,735–2,265	1,625–2,375
54	1,559–2,441	1,384–2,616	153	1,736–2,264	1,626–2,374
55	1,563–2,437	1,390–2,610	154	1,737–2,263	1,627–2,373
56	1,567–2,433	1,395–2,605	**155**	1,737–2,263	1,629–2,371
57	1,571–2,429	1,400–2,600	156	1,738–2,262	1,630–2,370
58	1,574–2,426	1,405–2,595	157	1,739–2,261	1,631–2,369
59	1,578–2,422	1,410–2,590	158	1,740–2,260	1,632–2,368
60	1,581–2,419	1,414–2,586	159	1,741–2,259	1,633–2,367
61	1,584–2,416	1,419–2,581	**160**	1,742–2,258	1,634–2,366
62	1,587–2,413	1,423–2,577	161	1,742–2,258	1,636–2,364
63	1,590–2,410	1,427–2,573	162	1,743–2,257	1,637–2,363
64	1,593–2,407	1,431–2,569	163	1,744–2,256	1,638–2,362
65	1,596–2,404	1,435–2,565	164	1,745–2,255	1,639–2,361
66	1,599–2,401	1,439–2,561	**165**	1,745–2,255	1,640–2,360
67	1,602–2,398	1,443–2,557	166	1,746–2,254	1,641–2,359
68	1,605–2,395	1,447–2,553	167	1,747–2,253	1,642–2,358
69	1,608–2,392	1,451–2,549	168	1,748–2,252	1,643–2,357
70	1,611–2,389	1,454–2,546	169	1,748–2,252	1,644–2,356
71	1,614–2,386	1,458–2,542	**170**	1,749–2,251	1,645–2,355
72	1,617–2,383	1,461–2,539	171	1,750–2,250	1,646–2,354
73	1,620–2,380	1,465–2,535	172	1,751–2,249	1,647–2,353
74	1,623–2,377	1,468–2,532	173	1,751–2,249	1,648–2,352
75	1,625–2,375	1,471–2,529	174	1,752–2,248	1,649–2,351
76	1,628–2,372	1,474–2,526	**175**	1,753–2,247	1,650–2,350
77	1,630–2,370	1,477–2,523	176	1,753–2,247	1,651–2,349
78	1,632–2,368	1,480–2,520	177	1,754–2,246	1,652–2,348
79	1,635–2,365	1,483–2,517	178	1,755–2,245	1,653–2,347
80	1,637–2,363	1,486–2,514	179	1,755–2,245	1,654–2,346
81	1,639–2,361	1,489–2,511	**180**	1,756–2,244	1,655–2,345
82	1,641–2,359	1,492–2,508	181	1,757–2,243	1,656–2,344
83	1,643–2,357	1,495–2,505	182	1,757–2,243	1,657–2,343
84	1,645–2,355	1,498–2,502	183	1,758–2,242	1,658–2,342
85	1,647–2,353	1,501–2,499	184	1,759–2,241	1,659–2,341
86	1,649–2,351	1,504–2,496	**185**	1,759–2,241	1,660–2,340
87	1,651–2,349	1,507–2,493	186	1,760–2,240	1,661–2,339
88	1,653–2,347	1,510–2,490	187	1,761–2,239	1,662–2,338
89	1,655–2,345	1,512–2,488	188	1,761–2,239	1,662–2,338
90	1,657–2,343	1,515–2,485	189	1,762–2,238	1,663–2,337
91	1,659–2,341	1,518–2,482	**190**	1,763–2,237	1,664–2,336
92	1,661–2,339	1,520–2,480	191	1,763–2,237	1,665–2,335
93	1,662–2,338	1,523–2,477	192	1,764–2,236	1,666–2,334
94	1,664–2,336	1,525–2,475	193	1,764–2,236	1,667–2,333
95	1,666–2,334	1,528–2,472	194	1,765–2,235	1,668–2,332
96	1,668–2,332	1,530–2,470	**195**	1,766–2,234	1,668–2,332
97	1,669–2,331	1,532–2,468	196	1,766–2,234	1,669–2,331
98	1,671–2,329	1,535–2,465	197	1,767–2,233	1,670–2,330
99	1,673–2,327	1,537–2,463	198	1,767–2,233	1,671–2,329
100	1,674–2,326	1,539–2,461	199	1,768–2,232	1,672–2,328
101	1,676–2,324	1,542–2,458	**200**	1,768–2,232	1,673–2,327
102	1,677–2,323	1,544–2,456	∞	2,000–2,000	2,000–2,000

Serial correlation[2,3]

Testing the null hypothesis of $r_h = 0$, when h is the lag and is assumed equal to 1. For other values of h and the interpretation of the test ratio see **(883)**, page 232

N	2α=0,10	2α=0,02	N	2α=0,10	2α=0,02
			103	−0,172–+0,152	−0,239–+0,219
5	−0,753–+0,253	−0,798–+0,297	104	171– 152	238– 218
6	708– 345	863– 447	**105**	−0,170–+0,151	−0,237–+0,217
7	674– 370	799– 510	106	169– 150	236– 216
8	625– 371	764– 531	107	168– 150	234– 216
9	593– 366	737– 533	108	167– 149	233– 215
10	−0,564–+0,360	−0,705–+0,525	109	167– 148	232– 214
11	539– 353	679– 515	**110**	−0,166–+0,148	−0,231–+0,213
12	516– 348	655– 505	111	165– 147	230– 212
13	497– 341	634– 495	112	164– 146	229– 211
14	479– 335	615– 485	113	164– 146	228– 210
15	−0,462–+0,328	−0,597–+0,475	114	163– 145	227– 209
16	447– 322	580– 465	**115**	−0,162–+0,145	−0,226–+0,208
17	434– 316	564– 456	116	161– 144	225– 207
18	421– 310	550– 448	117	161– 143	224– 206
19	410– 304	536– 440	118	160– 143	223– 206
20	−0,399–+0,299	−0,524–+0,432	119	159– 142	222– 205
21	389– 294	512– 424	**120**	−0,159–+0,142	−0,221–+0,204
22	380– 289	502– 417	121	158– 141	220– 203
23	372– 285	491– 411	122	157– 141	219– 202
24	364– 280	482– 404	123	157– 140	218– 202
25	−0,356–+0,276	−0,473–+0,398	124	156– 140	217– 201
26	349– 272	464– 392	**125**	−0,155–+0,139	−0,216–+0,200
27	343– 268	456– 386	126	155– 139	215– 199
28	336– 264	448– 380	127	154– 138	214– 199
29	331– 260	440– 375	128	153– 138	214– 198
30	−0,325–+0,257	−0,433–+0,370	129	153– 137	213– 197
31	319– 254	426– 365	**130**	−0,152–+0,137	−0,212–+0,196
32	314– 251	420– 361	131	151– 136	211– 196
33	309– 248	413– 356	132	151– 136	210– 195
34	304– 245	408– 352	133	150– 135	209– 194
35	−0,300–+0,242	−0,402–+0,348	134	150– 135	209– 193
36	295– 239	396– 344	**135**	−0,149–+0,134	−0,208–+0,193
37	291– 236	391– 340	136	148– 134	207– 192
38	287– 234	386– 336	137	148– 133	206– 191
39	283– 231	381– 333	138	147– 133	205– 191
40	−0,279–+0,229	−0,377–+0,330	139	147– 132	205– 190
41	275– 227	372– 326	**140**	−0,146–+0,132	−0,204–+0,189
42	272– 224	368– 323	141	146– 131	203– 189
43	268– 222	364– 320	142	145– 131	202– 188
44	265– 220	360– 317	143	145– 131	202– 188
45	−0,262–+0,218	−0,356–+0,314	144	144– 130	201– 187
46	259– 216	352– 311	**145**	−0,144–+0,130	−0,200–+0,186
47	256– 214	348– 308	146	143– 129	199– 186
48	253– 212	345– 305	147	143– 129	199– 185
49	250– 210	341– 302	148	142– 128	198– 184
50	−0,248–+0,208	−0,338–+0,300	149	142– 128	197– 184
51	245– 206	334– 297	**150**	−0,141–+0,128	−0,197–+0,183
52	242– 205	331– 295	151	141– 127	196– 183
53	240– 203	328– 292	152	140– 127	195– 182
54	238– 201	325– 290	153	140– 126	195– 182
55	−0,235–+0,199	−0,322–+0,287	154	139– 126	194– 181
56	233– 198	319– 285	**155**	−0,139–+0,126	−0,193–+0,180
57	231– 196	316– 283	156	138– 125	193– 180
58	229– 195	314– 281	157	138– 125	192– 179
59	227– 193	311– 279	158	137– 125	191– 179
60	−0,225–+0,192	−0,308–+0,276	159	137– 124	191– 178
61	223– 190	306– 274	**160**	−0,136–+0,124	−0,190–+0,178
62	221– 189	303– 272	161	136– 123	190– 177
63	219– 188	301– 270	162	135– 123	189– 177
64	217– 186	299– 269	163	135– 122	188– 176
65	−0,215–+0,185	−0,296–+0,267	164	135– 122	188– 176
66	213– 184	294– 265	**165**	−0,134–+0,122	−0,187–+0,175
67	212– 182	292– 263	166	134– 122	187– 175
68	210– 181	290– 261	167	133– 121	186– 174
69	208– 180	288– 260	168	133– 121	186– 174
70	−0,207–+0,179	−0,286–+0,258	169	133– 121	185– 173
71	205– 177	284– 256	**170**	−0,132–+0,120	−0,184–+0,173
72	203– 176	282– 255	171	132– 120	184– 172
73	202– 175	280– 253	172	131– 120	183– 172
74	200– 174	278– 252	173	131– 119	183– 171
75	−0,199–+0,173	−0,276–+0,250	174	131– 119	182– 171
76	198– 172	275– 249	**175**	−0,130–+0,119	−0,182–+0,170
77	197– 172	273– 248	176	130– 118	181– 170
78	196– 171	272– 247	177	129– 118	181– 169
79	195– 170	271– 246	178	129– 118	180– 169
80	−0,194–+0,169	−0,269–+0,245	179	129– 117	180– 168
81	193– 169	268– 243	**180**	−0,128–+0,117	−0,179–+0,168
82	192– 168	267– 242	181	128– 117	179– 167
83	191– 167	265– 241	182	127– 116	178– 167
84	190– 166	264– 240	183	127– 116	178– 167
85	−0,189–+0,166	−0,263–+0,239	184	127– 116	177– 166
86	188– 165	261– 238	**185**	−0,126–+0,116	−0,177–+0,166
87	187– 164	260– 237	186	126– 115	176– 165
88	186– 163	259– 236	187	126– 115	176– 165
89	185– 163	257– 234	188	125– 115	175– 164
90	−0,184–+0,162	−0,256–+0,233	189	125– 114	175– 164
91	183– 161	255– 232	**190**	−0,125–+0,114	−0,174–+0,164
92	182– 160	254– 231	191	124– 114	174– 163
93	181– 160	252– 230	192	124– 114	173– 163
94	180– 159	251– 229	193	124– 113	173– 162
95	−0,179–+0,158	−0,249–+0,228	194	123– 113	172– 162
96	178– 157	248– 227	**195**	−0,123–+0,113	−0,172–+0,161
97	177– 157	247– 226	196	123– 112	171– 161
98	177– 156	245– 224	197	122– 112	171– 161
99	176– 155	244– 223	198	122– 112	170– 160
100	−0,175–+0,154	−0,243–+0,222	199	122– 112	170– 160
101	174– 154	242– 221	**200**	−0,121–+0,111	−0,170–+0,160
102	173– 153	240– 220	1000	−0,053–+0,051	−0,075–+0,073

[1] Values up to $N = 60$ obtained by converting the exact values of HART, B.I., *Ann. math. Statist.*, **13**, 445 (1942), by use of the factor $(N-1)/N$. Reprinted by kind permission of the author and publishers.

[2] Values up to $N = 75$ from the exact values of ANDERSON, R.L., *Ann. math. Statist.*, **13**, 1 (1942), with interpolated values from $N = 16$ to $N = 75$. Reprinted by kind permission of the author and publishers.

[3] Empirical approximation at transition values, then normal approximation.

All values conform to the international convention (i.e. 0,1 instead of 0.1).

Arc Sin x[1]

(for arc-sine transformations)

x	0,000	0,001	0,002	0,003	0,004	0,005	0,006	0,007	0,008	0,009
0,000	0,00000	0,00100	0,00200	0,00300	0,00400	0,00500	0,00600	0,00700	0,00800	0,00900
010	01000	01100	01200	01300	01400	01500	01600	01700	01800	01900
020	02000	02100	02200	02300	02400	02500	02600	02700	02800	02900
030	03000	03100	03201	03301	03401	03501	03601	03701	03801	03901
040	04001	04101	04201	04301	04401	04502	04602	04702	04802	04902
0,050	0,05002	0,05102	0,05202	0,05302	0,05403	0,05503	0,05603	0,05703	0,05803	0,05903
060	06004	06104	06204	06304	06404	06505	06605	06705	06805	06905
070	07006	07106	07206	07306	07407	07507	07607	07708	07808	07908
080	08009	08109	08209	08310	08410	08510	08611	08711	08811	08912
090	09012	09113	09213	09313	09414	09514	09615	09715	09816	09916
0,100	0,10017	0,10117	0,10218	0,10318	0,10419	0,10519	0,10620	0,10721	0,10821	0,10922
110	11022	11123	11224	11324	11425	11525	11626	11727	11828	11928
120	12029	12130	12230	12331	12432	12533	12634	12734	12835	12936
130	13037	13138	13239	13340	13440	13541	13642	13743	13844	13945
140	14046	14147	14248	14349	14450	14551	14652	14753	14855	14956
0,150	0,15057	0,15158	0,15259	0,15360	0,15462	0,15563	0,15664	0,15765	0,15866	0,15968
160	16069	16170	16272	16373	16474	16576	16677	16779	16880	16981
170	17083	17184	17286	17387	17489	17591	17692	17794	17895	17997
180	18099	18200	18302	18404	18505	18607	18709	18811	18913	19014
190	19116	19218	19320	19422	19524	19626	19728	19830	19932	20034
0,200	0,20136	0,20238	0,20340	0,20442	0,20544	0,20646	0,20749	0,20851	0,20953	0,21055
210	21157	21260	21362	21464	21567	21669	21772	21874	21976	22079
220	22181	22284	22387	22489	22592	22694	22797	22900	23002	23105
230	23208	23311	23413	23516	23619	23722	23825	23928	24031	24134
240	24237	24340	24443	24546	24649	24752	24855	24958	25062	25165
0,250	0,25268	0,25371	0,25475	0,25578	0,25681	0,25785	0,25888	0,25992	0,26095	0,26199
260	26302	26406	26509	26613	26717	26820	26924	27028	27132	27235
270	27339	27443	27547	27651	27755	27859	27963	28067	28171	28275
280	28379	28484	28588	28692	28796	28901	29005	29109	29214	29318
290	29423	29527	29632	29736	29841	29946	30050	30155	30260	30364
0,300	0,30469	0,30574	0,30679	0,30784	0,30889	0,30994	0,31099	0,31204	0,31309	0,31414
310	31519	31625	31730	31835	31940	32046	32151	32256	32362	32467
320	32573	32679	32784	32890	32995	33101	33207	33313	33419	33524
330	33630	33736	33842	33948	34054	34161	34267	34373	34479	34585
340	34692	34798	34904	35011	35117	35224	35330	35437	35544	35650
0,350	0,35757	0,35864	0,35971	0,36078	0,36184	0,36291	0,36398	0,36505	0,36613	0,36720
360	36827	36934	37041	37149	37256	37363	37471	37578	37686	37793
370	37901	38009	38116	38224	38332	38440	38548	38656	38764	38872
380	38980	39088	39196	39304	39412	39521	39629	39738	39846	39955
390	40063	40172	40280	40389	40498	40607	40716	40825	40934	41043
0,400	0,41152	0,41261	0,41370	0,41479	0,41589	4,41698	0,41807	0,41917	0,42026	0,42136
410	42245	42355	42465	42575	42684	42794	42904	43014	43124	43234
420	43345	43455	43565	43675	43786	43896	44007	44117	44228	44339
430	44449	44560	44671	44782	44893	45004	45115	45226	45337	45449
440	45560	45671	45783	45894	46006	46117	46229	46341	46453	46565
0,450	0,46677	0,46789	0,46901	0,47013	0,47125	0,47237	0,47350	0,47462	0,47574	0,47687
460	47800	47912	48025	48138	48251	48363	48476	48590	48703	48816
470	48929	49042	49156	49269	49383	49496	49610	49724	49838	49952
480	50065	50179	50294	50408	50522	50636	50751	50865	50980	51094
490	51209	51324	51439	51553	51668	51783	51899	52014	52129	52244
0,500	0,52360	0,52475	0,52591	0,52707	0,52822	0,52938	0,53054	0,53170	0,53286	0,53402
510	53518	53635	53751	53868	53984	54101	54217	54334	54451	54568
520	54685	54802	54919	55037	55154	55272	55389	55507	55624	55742
530	55860	55978	56096	56214	56332	56451	56569	56688	56806	56925
540	57044	57163	57282	57401	57520	57639	57758	57878	57997	58117
0,550	0,58236	0,58356	0,58476	0,58596	0,58716	0,58836	0,58957	0,59077	0,59197	0,59318
560	59439	59559	59680	59801	59922	60043	60165	60286	60407	60529
570	60651	60772	60894	61016	61138	61260	61383	61505	61628	61750
580	61873	61996	62119	62242	62365	62488	62611	62735	62858	62982
590	63106	63230	63354	63478	63602	63727	63851	63976	64100	64225
0,600	0,64350	0,64475	0,64600	0,64726	0,64851	0,64977	0,65102	0,65228	0,65354	0,65480
610	65606	65732	65859	65985	66112	66239	66365	66492	66620	66747
620	66874	67002	67129	67257	67385	67513	67641	67770	67898	68027
630	68155	68284	68413	68542	68671	68801	68930	69060	69190	69320
640	69450	69580	69710	69841	69972	70102	70233	70364	70496	70627
0,650	0,70758	0,70890	0,71022	0,71154	0,71286	0,71418	0,71551	0,71683	0,71816	0,71949
660	72082	72215	72348	72482	72616	72749	72883	73017	73152	73286
670	73421	73556	73691	73826	73961	74096	74232	74368	74504	74640
680	74776	74913	75049	75186	75323	75460	75598	75735	75873	76011
690	76149	76287	76426	76564	76703	76842	76981	77121	77260	77400
0,700	0,77540	0,77680	0,77820	0,77961	0,78101	0,78242	0,78383	0,78525	0,78666	0,78808
710	78950	79092	79234	79377	79519	79662	79806	79949	80092	80236
720	80380	80524	80669	80813	80958	81103	81249	81394	81540	81686
730	81832	81979	82125	82272	82419	82567	82714	82862	83010	83158
740	83307	83456	83605	83754	83904	84053	84204	84354	84504	84655
0,750	0,84806	0,84958	0,85109	0,85261	0,85413	0,85565	0,85718	0,85871	0,86024	0,86178
760	86331	86485	86640	86794	86949	87104	87260	87415	87571	87728
770	87884	88041	88198	88356	88513	88672	88830	88989	89148	89307
780	89467	89627	89787	89947	90108	90270	90431	90593	90755	90918
790	91081	91244	91408	91572	91736	91901	92066	92231	92397	92563
0,800	0,92730	0,92896	0,93064	0,93231	0,93399	0,93568	0,93736	0,93905	0,94075	0,94245
810	94415	94586	94757	94929	95101	95273	95446	95619	95793	95967
820	96141	96316	96491	96667	96843	97020	97197	97375	97553	97732
830	97911	98090	98270	98451	98632	98813	98995	99178	99361	99544
840	99728	99913	1,00098	1,00284	1,00470	1,00657	1,00844	1,01032	1,01220	1,01409
0,850	1,01599	1,01789	1,01979	1,02171	1,02363	1,02555	1,02748	1,02942	1,03136	1,03331
860	03527	03723	03920	04118	04316	04515	04715	04915	05116	05318
870	05520	05723	05927	06132	06337	06544	06751	06958	07167	07376
880	07586	07797	08009	08222	08435	08649	08865	09081	09298	09516
890	09735	09954	10175	10397	10619	10843	11068	11294	11520	11748
0,900	1,11977	1,12207	1,12438	1,12670	1,12903	1,13138	1,13374	1,13610	1,13849	1,14088
910	14328	14570	14813	15058	15304	15551	15799	16049	16301	16554
920	16808	17064	17321	17581	17841	18104	18368	18633	18901	19170
930	19441	19714	19989	20266	20545	20826	21109	21394	21681	21971
940	22263	22557	22854	23153	23455	23759	24067	24376	24689	25005
0,950	1,25324	1,25645	1,25970	1,26299	1,26631	1,26966	1,27305	1,27648	1,27994	1,28345
960	28700	29060	29423	29792	30166	30544	30928	31318	31713	32115
970	32523	32938	33360	33789	34226	34672	35127	35591	36065	36550
980	37046	37555	38077	38614	39167	39737	40327	40938	41572	42234
990	42926	43653	44422	45241	46120	47075	48132	49332	50754	52607
1,000	1,57080									

[1] Abridged from *Table of Arc Sin X*, New York, 1945. Reprinted by kind permission of the National Bureau of Standards and the Columbia University Press.

All values conform to the international convention (i.e. 0,1 instead of 0.1).

Common Logarithms of the Binomial Coefficient C and Their Reciprocals* $N=2–33$

Exponent of p (q)	Exponent of q (p)	log C	log 1/C
N = 2			
0	2	0,00000	0 00000
1	1	0,30103	1 69897
N = 3			
0	3	0,00000	0 00000
1	2	0,47712	1 52288
N = 4			
0	4	0,00000	0 00000
1	3	0,60206	1 39794
2	2	0,77815	1 22185
N = 5			
0	5	0,00000	0 00000
1	4	0,69897	1 30103
2	3	1,00000	2 00000
N = 6			
0	6	0,00000	0 00000
1	5	0,77815	1 22185
2	4	1,17609	2 82391
3	3	1,30103	2 69897
N = 7			
0	7	0,00000	0 00000
1	6	0,84510	1 15490
2	5	1,32222	2 67778
3	4	1,54407	2 45593
N = 8			
0	8	0,00000	0 00000
1	7	0,90309	1 09691
2	6	1,44716	2 55284
3	5	1,74819	2 25181
4	4	1,84510	2 15490
N = 9			
0	9	0,00000	0 00000
1	8	0,95424	1 04576
2	7	1,55630	2 44370
3	6	1,92428	2 07572
4	5	2,10037	3 89963
N = 10			
0	10	0,00000	0 00000
1	9	1,00000	2 00000
2	8	1,65321	2 34679
3	7	2,07918	3 92082
4	6	2,32222	3 67778
5	5	2,40140	3 59860
N = 11			
0	11	0,00000	0 00000
1	10	1,04139	2 95861
2	9	1,74036	2 25964
3	8	2,21748	3 78252
4	7	2,51851	3 48149
5	6	2,66464	3 33536
N = 12			
0	12	0,00000	0 00000
1	11	1,07918	2 92082
2	10	1,81954	2 18046
3	9	2,34242	3 65758
4	8	2,69461	3 30539
5	7	2,89873	3 10127
6	6	2,96567	3 03433
N = 13			
0	13	0,00000	0 00000
1	12	1,11394	2 88606
2	11	1,89209	2 10791
3	10	2,45637	3 54363
4	9	2,85431	3 14569
5	8	3,10958	4 89042
6	7	3,23452	4 76548
N = 14			
0	14	0,00000	0 00000
1	13	1,14613	2 85387
2	12	1,95904	2 04096
3	11	2,56110	3 43890
4	10	3,00043	4 99957
5	9	3,30146	4 69854
6	8	3,47756	4 52244
7	7	3,53555	4 46445
N = 15			
0	15	0,00000	0 00000
1	14	1,17609	2 82391
2	13	2,02119	3 97881
3	12	2,65801	3 34199
4	11	3,13513	4 86487
5	10	3,47756	4 52244
6	9	3,69940	4 30060
7	8	3,80855	4 19145
N = 16			
0	16	0,00000	0 00000
1	15	1,20412	2 79588
2	14	2,07918	3 92082
3	13	2,74819	3 25181
4	12	3,26007	4 73993
5	11	3,64028	4 35972
6	10	3,90352	4 09648
7	9	4,05843	5 94157
8	8	4,10958	5 89042
N = 17			
0	17	0,00000	0 00000
1	16	1,23045	2 76955
2	15	2,13354	3 86646
3	14	2,83251	3 16749
4	13	3,37658	4 62342
5	12	3,79155	4 20845
6	11	4,09258	5 90742
7	10	4,28887	5 71113
8	9	4,38578	5 61422
N = 18			
0	18	0,00000	0 00000
1	17	1,25527	2 74473
2	16	2,18469	3 81531
3	15	2,91169	3 08831
4	14	3,48572	4 51428
5	13	3,93288	4 06712
6	12	4,26867	5 73133
7	11	4,50275	5 49725
8	10	4,64106	5 35894
9	9	4,68681	5 31319
N = 19			
0	19	0,00000	0 00000
1	18	1,27875	2 72125
2	17	2,23300	3 76700
3	16	2,98632	3 01368
4	15	3,58838	4 41162
5	14	4,06551	5 93449
6	13	4,43348	5 56652
7	12	4,70233	5 29767
8	11	4,87842	5 12158
9	10	4,96557	5 03443
N = 20			
0	20	0,00000	0 00000
1	19	1,30103	2 69897
2	18	2,27875	3 72125
3	17	3,05690	4 94310
4	16	3,68529	4 31471
5	15	4,19044	5 80956
6	14	4,58838	5 41162
7	13	4,88941	5 11059
8	12	5,10027	6 89973
9	11	5,22521	6 77479
10	10	5,26660	6 73340
N = 21			
0	21	0,00000	0 00000
1	20	1,32222	2 67778
2	19	2,32222	3 67778
3	18	3,12385	4 87615
4	17	3,77706	4 22294
5	16	4,30854	5 69146
6	15	4,73451	5 26549
7	14	5,06551	6 93449
8	13	5,30854	6 69146
9	12	5,46824	6 53176
10	11	5,54743	6 45257
N = 22			
0	22	0,00000	0 00000
1	21	1,34242	2 65758
2	20	2,36361	3 63639
3	19	3,18752	4 81248
4	18	3,86421	4 13579
5	17	4,42052	5 57948
6	16	4,87281	5 12719
7	15	5,23184	6 76816
N = 22 (continued)			
8	14	5,50484	6 49516
9	13	5,69672	6 30328
10	12	5,81067	6 18933
11	11	5,84846	6 15154
N = 23			
0	23	0,00000	0 00000
1	22	1,36173	2 63827
2	21	2,40312	3 59688
3	20	3,24822	4 75178
4	19	3,94719	4 05281
5	18	4,52697	5 47303
6	17	5,00409	6 99591
7	16	5,38944	6 61056
8	15	5,69047	6 30953
9	14	5,91232	6 08768
10	13	6,05845	7 94155
11	12	6,13100	7 86900
N = 24			
0	24	0,00000	0 00000
1	23	1,38021	2 61979
2	22	2,44091	3 55909
3	21	3,30621	4 69379
4	20	4,02637	5 97363
5	19	4,62843	5 37157
6	18	5,12903	6 87097
7	17	5,53921	6 46079
8	16	5,86657	6 13343
9	15	6,11644	7 88356
10	14	6,29253	7 70747
11	13	6,39727	7 60273
12	12	6,43203	7 56797
N = 25			
0	25	0,00000	0 00000
1	24	1,39794	2 60206
2	23	2,47712	3 52288
3	22	3,36173	4 63827
4	21	4,10209	5 89791
5	20	4,72534	5 27466
6	19	5,24822	6 75178
7	18	5,68187	6 31813
8	17	6,03406	7 96594
9	16	6,31026	7 68974
10	15	6,51438	7 48562
11	14	6,64908	7 35092
12	13	6,71603	7 28397
N = 26			
0	26	0,00000	0 00000
1	25	1,41497	2 58503
2	24	2,51188	3 48812
3	23	3,41497	4 58503
4	22	4,17464	5 82536
5	21	4,81809	5 18191
6	20	5,36216	6 63784
7	19	5,81809	6 18191
8	18	6,19376	7 80624
9	17	6,49479	7 50521
10	16	6,72524	7 27476
11	15	6,88796	7 11204
12	14	6,98487	7 01513
13	13	7,01706	8 98294
N = 27			
0	27	0,00000	0 00000
1	26	1,43136	2 56864
2	25	2,54531	3 45469
3	24	3,46613	4 53387
4	23	4,24428	5 75572
5	22	4,90703	5 09297
6	21	5,47131	6 52869
7	20	5,94843	6 05157
8	19	6,34637	7 65363
9	18	6,67088	7 32912
10	17	6,92615	7 07385
11	16	7,11521	8 88479
12	15	7,24015	8 75985
13	14	7,30229	8 69771
N = 28			
0	28	0,00000	0 00000
1	27	1,44716	2 55284
2	26	2,57749	3 42251
3	25	3,51534	4 48466
4	24	4,31122	5 68878
5	23	4,99247	5 00753
6	22	5,57604	6 42396
7	21	6,07337	7 92663
N = 28 (continued)			
8	20	6,49250	7 50750
9	19	6,83928	7 16072
10	18	7,11804	8 88196
11	17	7,33192	8 66808
12	16	7,48318	8 51682
13	15	7,57336	8 42664
14	14	7,60332	8 39668
N = 29			
0	29	0,00000	0 00000
1	28	1,46240	2 53760
2	27	2,60853	3 39147
3	26	3,56277	4 43723
4	25	4,37568	5 62432
5	24	5,07465	6 92535
6	23	5,67671	6 32329
7	22	6,19334	7 80666
8	21	6,63267	7 36733
9	20	7,00065	8 99935
10	19	7,30168	8 69832
11	18	7,53904	8 46096
12	17	7,71513	8 28487
13	16	7,83164	8 16836
14	15	7,88963	8 11037
N = 30			
0	30	0,00000	0 00000
1	29	1,47712	2 52288
2	28	2,63849	3 36151
3	27	3,60853	4 39147
4	26	4,43783	5 56217
5	25	5,15383	6 84617
6	24	5,77362	6 22638
7	23	6,30874	7 69126
8	22	6,76737	7 23263
9	21	7,15555	8 84445
10	20	7,47777	8 52223
11	19	7,73741	8 26259
12	18	7,93698	8 06302
13	17	8,07831	9 92169
14	16	8,16263	9 83737
15	15	8,19066	9 80934
N = 31			
0	31	0,00000	0 00000
1	30	1,49136	2 50864
2	29	2,66745	3 33255
3	28	3,65273	4 34727
4	27	4,49783	5 50217
5	26	5,23022	6 76978
6	25	5,86704	6 13296
7	24	6,41989	7 58011
8	23	6,89701	7 10299
9	22	7,30449	8 69551
10	21	7,64691	8 35309
11	20	7,92774	8 07226
12	19	8,14959	9 85041
13	18	8,31440	9 68560
14	17	8,42354	9 57646
15	16	8,47790	9 52210
N = 32			
0	32	0,00000	0 00000
1	31	1,50515	2 49485
2	30	2,69548	3 30452
3	29	3,69548	4 30452
4	28	4,55582	5 44418
5	27	5,30401	6 69599
6	26	5,95722	6 04278
7	25	6,52710	7 47290
8	24	7,02195	8 97805
9	23	7,44791	8 55209
10	22	7,80964	8 19036
11	21	8,11067	9 88933
12	20	8,35371	9 64629
13	19	8,54080	9 45920
14	18	8,67342	9 32658
15	17	8,75260	9 24740
16	16	8,77893	9 22107
N = 33			
0	33	0,00000	0 00000
1	32	1,51851	2 48149
2	31	2,72263	3 27737
3	30	3,73687	4 26313
4	29	4,61194	5 38806
5	28	5,37536	6 62464
6	27	6,04437	7 95563
7	26	6,63064	7 36936
8	25	7,14252	8 85748
9	24	7,58622	8 41378

* For explanation see page 81. –

All values conform to the international convention (i.e. 0,1 instead of 0.1).

Common Logarithms of the Binomial Coefficient C and Their Reciprocals* N=33–49

N = 33 (continued)

Exponent of p (q)	q (p)	log C	log 1/C
10	23	7,96643	8 03357
11	22	8,28676	9 71324
12	21	8,55000	9 45000
13	20	8,75828	9 24172
14	19	8,91318	9 08682
15	18	9,01585	10 98415
16	17	9,06700	10 93300

N = 34

Exponent of p (q)	q (p)	log C	log 1/C
0	34	0,00000	0 00000
1	33	1,53148	2 46852
2	32	2,74896	3 25104
3	31	3,77699	4 22301
4	30	4,66629	5 33371
5	29	5,44444	6 55556
6	28	6,12869	7 87131
7	27	6,73075	7 26925
8	26	7,25903	8 74097
9	25	7,71976	8 28024
10	24	8,11770	9 88230
11	23	8,45651	9 54349
12	22	8,73906	9 26094
13	21	8,96754	9 03246
14	20	9,14363	10 85637
15	19	9,26857	10 73143
16	18	9,34320	10 65680
17	17	9,36803	10 63197

N = 35

Exponent of p (q)	q (p)	log C	log 1/C
0	35	0,00000	0 00000
1	34	1,54407	2 45593
2	33	2,77452	3 22548
3	32	3,81591	4 18409
4	31	4,71900	5 28100
5	30	5,51139	6 48861
6	29	6,21036	7 78964
7	28	6,82766	7 17234
8	27	7,37173	8 62827
9	26	7,84885	8 15115
10	25	8,26382	9 73618
11	24	8,62037	9 37963
12	23	8,92140	9 07860
13	22	9,16919	10 83081
14	21	9,36548	10 63452
15	20	9,51161	10 48839
16	19	9,60852	10 39148
17	18	9,65682	10 34318

N = 36

Exponent of p (q)	q (p)	log C	log 1/C
0	36	0,00000	0 00000
1	35	1,55630	2 44370
2	34	2,79934	3 20066
3	33	3,85370	4 14630
4	32	4,77015	5 22985
5	31	5,57633	6 42367
6	30	6,28954	7 71046
7	29	6,92157	7 07843
8	28	7,48087	8 51913
9	27	7,97379	8 02621
10	26	8,40515	9 59485
11	25	8,77873	9 22127
12	24	9,09749	10 90251
13	23	9,36376	10 63624
14	22	9,57936	10 42064
15	21	9,74569	10 25431
16	20	9,86379	10 13621
17	19	9,93437	10 06563
18	18	9,95785	10 04215

N = 37

Exponent of p (q)	q (p)	log C	log 1/C
0	37	0,00000	000000
1	36	1,56820	243180
2	35	2,82347	317653
3	34	3,89042	410958
4	33	4,81984	518016
5	32	5,63938	636062
6	31	6,36638	763362
7	30	7,01265	898735
8	29	7,58668	841332
9	28	8,09483	990517
10	27	8,54199	945801
11	26	8,93196	906804
12	25	9,26775	1073225
13	24	9,55175	1044825
14	23	9,78583	1021417
15	22	9,97147	1002853
16	21	10,10977	11 89023
17	20	10,20154	11 79846
18	19	10,24730	11 75270

N = 38

Exponent of p (q)	q (p)	log C	log 1/C
0	38	0,00000	000000
1	37	1,57978	242022
2	36	2,84696	315304
3	35	3,92614	407386
4	34	4,86814	513186
5	33	5,70065	629935
6	32	6,44102	755898
7	31	7,10107	889893
8	30	7,68934	831066
9	29	8,21222	978778
10	28	8,67642	932538
11	27	9,08038	1091962
12	26	9,43256	1056744
13	25	9,73359	1026641
14	24	9,98541	1001459
15	23	10,18953	1181047
16	22	10,34713	1165287
17	21	10,45911	1154089
18	20	10,52605	1147395
19	19	10,54833	1145167

N = 39

Exponent of p (q)	q (p)	log C	log 1/C
0	39	0,00000	0 00000
1	38	1,59106	2 40894
2	37	2,86982	3 13018
3	36	3,96090	4 03910
4	35	4,91514	5 08486
5	34	5,76024	6 23976
6	33	6,51357	7 48643
7	32	7,18698	8 81302
8	31	7,78904	8 21096
9	30	8,32616	9 67384
10	29	8,80328	9 19672
11	28	9,22429	10 77571
12	27	9,59227	10 40773
13	26	9,90969	10 09031
14	25	10,17853	11 82147
15	24	10,40038	11 59962
16	23	10,57647	11 42353
17	22	10,70775	11 29225
18	21	10,79490	11 20510
19	20	10,83837	11 16163

N = 40

Exponent of p (q)	q (p)	log C	log 1/C
0	40	0,00000	0 00000
1	39	1,60206	2 39794
2	38	2,89209	3 10791
3	37	3,99476	4 00524
4	36	4,96090	5 03910
5	35	5,81823	6 18177
6	34	6,58415	7 41585
7	33	7,27053	8 72947
8	32	7,88595	8 11405
9	31	8,43686	9 56314
10	30	8,92822	9 07178
11	29	9,36395	10 63605
12	28	9,74717	10 25283
13	27	10,08038	11 91962
14	26	10,36562	11 63438
15	25	10,60450	11 39550
16	24	10,79832	11 20168
17	23	10,94808	11 05192
18	22	11,05454	12 94546
19	21	11,11821	12 88179
20	20	11,13940	12 86060

N = 41

Exponent of p (q)	q (p)	log C	log 1/C
0	41	0,00000	0 00000
1	40	1,61278	2 38722
2	39	2,91381	3 08619
3	38	4,02776	5 97224
4	37	5,00548	6 99452
5	36	5,87471	6 12529
6	35	6,65286	7 34714
7	34	7,35183	8 64817
8	33	7,98022	8 01978
9	32	8,54449	9 45551
10	31	9,04964	10 95036
11	30	9,49961	10 50039
12	29	9,89755	10 10245
13	28	10,24601	11 75399
14	27	10,54704	11 45296
15	26	10,80231	11 19769
16	25	11,01316	12 98684
17	24	11,18065	12 81935
18	23	11,30559	12 69441
19	22	11,38857	12 61143
20	21	11,42996	12 57004

N = 42

Exponent of p (q)	q (p)	log C	log 1/C
0	42	0,00000	0 00000
1	41	1,62325	2 37675
2	40	2,93500	3 06500
3	39	4,05994	5 94006
4	38	5,04895	6 95105
5	37	5,92976	6 07024
6	36	6,71981	7 28019
7	35	7,43102	8 56898
8	34	8,07199	9 92801
9	33	8,64923	9 35077
10	32	9,16774	10 83226
11	31	9,63150	10 36850
12	30	10,04368	11 95632
13	29	10,40686	11 59314
14	28	10,72313	11 27687
15	27	10,99420	11 00580
16	26	11,22144	12 77856
17	25	11,40596	12 59404
18	24	11,54863	12 45137
19	23	11,65009	12 34991
20	22	11,71079	12 28921
21	21	11,73099	12 26901

N = 43

Exponent of p (q)	q (p)	log C	log 1/C
0	43	0,00000	0 00000
1	42	1,63347	2 36653
2	41	2,95569	3 04431
3	40	4,09135	5 90865
4	39	5,09135	6 90865
5	38	5,98344	6 01656
6	37	6,78508	7 21492
7	36	7,50818	8 49182
8	35	8,16139	9 83861
9	34	8,75122	9 24878
10	33	9,28270	10 71730
11	32	9,75982	10 24018
12	31	10,18579	11 81421
13	30	10,56321	11 43679
14	29	10,89420	11 10580
15	28	11,18051	12 81949
16	27	11,42354	12 57646
17	26	11,62446	12 37554
18	25	11,78416	12 21584
19	24	11,90335	12 09665
20	23	11,98253	12 01747
21	22	12,02204	13 97796

N = 44

Exponent of p (q)	q (p)	log C	log 1/C
0	44	0,00000	0 00000
1	43	1,64345	2 35655
2	42	2,97589	3 02411
3	41	4,12202	5 87798
4	40	5,13274	6 86726
5	39	6,03583	7 96417
6	38	6,84875	7 15125
7	37	7,58343	8 41657
8	36	8,24854	9 75146
9	35	8,85060	9 14940
10	34	9,39467	10 60533
11	33	9,88476	10 11524
12	32	10,32409	11 67591
13	31	10,71530	11 28470
14	30	11,06053	12 93947
15	29	11,36156	12 63844
16	28	11,61984	12 38016
17	27	11,83655	12 16345
18	26	12,01264	13 98736
19	25	12,14886	13 85114
20	24	12,24577	13 75423
21	23	12,30376	13 69624
22	22	12,32307	13 67693

N = 45

Exponent of p (q)	q (p)	log C	log 1/C
0	45	0,00000	0 00000
1	44	1,65321	2 34679
2	43	2,99564	3 00436
3	42	4,15198	5 84802
4	41	5,17317	6 82683
5	40	6,08699	7 91301
6	39	6,91089	7 08911
7	38	7,65686	8 34314
8	37	8,33355	9 66645
9	36	8,94751	9 05249
10	35	9,50382	10 49618
11	34	10,00649	11 99351
12	33	10,45879	11 54121
13	32	10,86336	11 13664
14	31	11,22238	12 77762
15	30	11,53765	12 46235
16	29	11,81065	12 18935
17	28	12,04260	13 95740
18	27	12,23449	13 76551
19	26	12,38710	13 61290
20	25	12,50104	13 49896
21	24	12,57676	13 42324
22	23	12,61455	13 38545

N = 46

Exponent of p (q)	q (p)	log C	log 1/C
0	46	0,00000	0 00000
1	45	1,66276	2 33724
2	44	3,01494	4 98506
3	43	4,18127	5 81873
4	42	5,21268	6 78732
5	41	6,13696	7 86304
6	40	6,97159	7 02841
7	39	7,72855	8 27145
8	38	8,41653	9 58347
9	37	9,04207	10 95793
10	36	9,61027	10 38973
11	35	10,12518	11 87482
12	34	10,59007	11 40993
13	33	11,00760	12 99240
14	32	11,37999	12 62001
15	31	11,70905	12 29095
16	30	11,99629	12 00371
17	29	12,24296	13 75704
18	28	12,45009	13 54991
19	27	12,61849	13 38151
20	26	12,74883	13 25117
21	25	12,84158	13 15842
22	24	12,89710	13 10290
23	23	12,91558	13 08442

N = 47

Exponent of p (q)	q (p)	log C	log 1/C
0	47	0,00000	0 00000
1	46	1,67210	2 32790
2	45	3,03383	4 96617
3	44	4,20992	5 79008
4	43	5,25131	6 74869
5	42	6,18581	7 81419
6	41	7,03091	8 96909
7	40	7,79859	8 20141
8	39	8,49756	9 50244
9	38	9,13438	10 86562
10	37	9,71417	10 28583
11	36	10,24098	11 75902
12	35	10,71810	11 28190
13	34	11,14822	12 85178
14	33	11,53357	12 46643
15	32	11,87600	12 12400
16	31	12,17703	13 82297
17	30	12,43794	13 56206
18	29	12,65979	13 34021
19	28	12,84343	13 15657
20	27	12,98956	13 01044
21	26	13,09870	14 90130
22	25	13,17126	14 82874
23	24	13,20747	14 79253

N = 48

Exponent of p (q)	q (p)	log C	log 1/C
0	48	0,00000	0 00000
1	47	1,68124	2 31876
2	46	3,05231	4 94769
3	45	4,23795	5 76205
4	44	5,28910	6 71090
5	43	6,23358	7 76642
6	42	7,08890	8 91110
7	41	7,86705	8 13295
8	40	8,57674	9 42326
9	39	9,22456	10 77544
10	38	9,81563	10 18437
11	37	10,35402	11 64598
12	36	10,84304	11 15696
13	35	11,28540	12 71460
14	34	11,68334	12 31666
15	33	12,03872	13 96128
16	32	12,35312	13 64688
17	31	12,62782	13 37218
18	30	12,86391	13 13609
19	29	13,06228	14 93772
20	28	13,22364	14 77636
21	27	13,34858	14 65142
22	26	13,43752	14 56248
23	25	13,49077	14 50923
24	24	13,50850	14 49150

N = 49

Exponent of p (q)	q (p)	log C	log 1/C
0	49	0,00000	0 00000
1	48	1,69020	2 30980
2	47	3,07041	4 92959
3	46	4,26538	5 73462
4	45	5,32608	6 67392
5	44	6,28032	7 71968
6	43	7,14563	8 85437
7	42	7,93400	8 06600
8	41	8,65416	9 34584
9	40	9,31270	10 68730
10	39	9,91476	10 08524
11	38	10,46443	11 53557
12	37	10,96503	11 03497
13	36	11,41929	12 58071
14	35	11,82946	12 17054

* For explanation see page 81. –

All values conform to the international convention (i.e. 0,1 instead of 0.1).

Common Logarithms of the Binomial Coefficient C and Their Reciprocals* N=49–61

N = 49 (continued)

Exponent of p (q)	Exponent of q (p)	log C	log 1/C
15	34	12,19744	13 80256
16	33	12,52480	13 47520
17	32	12,81286	13 18714
18	31	13,06274	14 93726
19	30	13,27535	14 72465
20	29	13,45144	14 54856
21	28	13,59162	14 40838
22	27	13,69636	14 30364
23	26	13,76599	14 23401
24	25	13,80075	14 19925

N = 50

Exponent of p (q)	Exponent of q (p)	log C	log 1/C
0	50	0,00000	0 00000
1	49	1,69897	2 30103
2	48	3,08814	4 91186
3	47	4,29226	5 70774
4	46	5,36229	6 63771
5	45	6,32608	7 67392
6	44	7,20114	8 79886
7	43	7,99950	8 00050
8	42	8,72988	9 27012
9	41	9,39888	10 60112
10	40	10,01167	11 98833
11	39	10,57233	11 42767
12	38	11,08422	12 91578
13	37	11,55006	12 44994
14	36	11,97213	12 02787
15	35	12,35234	13 64766
16	34	12,69229	13 30771
17	33	12,99332	13 00668
18	32	13,25656	14 74344
19	31	13,48296	14 51704
20	30	13,67329	14 32671
21	29	13,82819	14 17181
22	28	13,94817	14 05183
23	27	14,03360	15 96640
24	26	14,08475	15 91525
25	25	14,10178	15 89822

N = 51

Exponent of p (q)	Exponent of q (p)	log C	log 1/C
0	51	0,00000	0 00000
1	50	1,70757	2 29243
2	49	3,10551	4 89449
3	48	4,31859	5 68141
4	47	5,39777	6 60223
5	46	6,37089	7 62911
6	45	7,25550	8 74450
7	44	8,06362	9 93638
8	43	8,80398	9 19602
9	42	9,48320	10 51680
10	41	10,10645	11 89355
11	40	10,67784	11 32216
12	39	11,20072	12 79928
13	38	11,67784	12 32216
14	37	12,11150	13 88850
15	36	12,50361	13 49639
16	35	12,85579	13 14421
17	34	13,16941	14 83059
18	33	13,44562	14 55438
19	32	13,68538	14 31462
20	31	13,88950	14 11050
21	30	14,05864	15 94136
22	29	14,19334	15 80666
23	28	14,29401	15 70599
24	27	14,36096	15 63904
25	26	14,39438	15 60562

N = 52

Exponent of p (q)	Exponent of q (p)	log C	log 1/C
0	52	0,00000	0 00000
1	51	1,71600	2 28400
2	50	3,12254	4 87746
3	49	4,34439	5 65561
4	48	5,43253	6 56747
5	47	6,41480	7 58520
6	46	7,30875	8 69125
7	45	8,12641	9 87359
8	44	8,87653	9 12347
9	43	9,56574	10 43426
10	42	10,19921	11 80079
11	41	10,78106	11 21894
12	40	11,31467	12 68533
13	39	11,80278	12 19722
14	38	12,24772	13 75228
15	37	12,65141	13 34859
16	36	13,01549	14 98451
17	35	13,34135	14 65865
18	34	13,63014	14 36986
19	33	13,88287	14 11713
20	32	14,10035	15 89965
21	31	14,28328	15 71672
22	30	14,43222	15 56778
23	29	14,54762	15 45238
24	28	14,62980	15 37020

N = 52 (continued)

Exponent of p (q)	Exponent of q (p)	log C	log 1/C
25	27	14,67902	15 32098
26	26	14,69541	15 30459

N = 53

Exponent of p (q)	Exponent of q (p)	log C	log 1/C
0	53	0,00000	0 00000
1	52	1,72428	2 27572
2	51	3,13925	4 86075
3	50	4,36970	5 63030
4	49	5,46661	6 53339
5	48	6,45783	7 54217
6	47	7,36092	8 63908
7	46	8,18792	9 81208
8	45	8,94759	9 05241
9	44	9,64656	10 35344
10	43	10,29001	11 70999
11	42	10,88209	11 11791
12	41	11,42616	12 57384
13	40	11,92500	12 07500
14	39	12,38093	13 61907
15	38	12,79590	13 20410
16	37	13,17157	14 82843
17	36	13,50932	14 49068
18	35	13,81035	14 18965
19	34	14,07567	15 92433
20	33	14,30611	15 69389
21	32	14,50241	15 49759
22	31	14,66514	15 33486
23	30	14,79477	15 20523
24	29	14,89168	15 10832
25	28	14,95614	15 04386
26	27	14,98832	15 01168

N = 54

Exponent of p (q)	Exponent of q (p)	log C	log 1/C
0	54	0,00000	0 00000
1	53	1,73239	2 26761
2	52	3,15564	4 84436
3	51	4,39452	5 60548
4	50	5,50003	6 49997
5	49	6,50003	7 49997
6	48	7,41208	8 58792
7	47	8,24822	9 75178
8	46	9,01723	10 98277
9	45	9,72574	10 27426
10	44	10,37896	11 62104
11	43	10,98102	11 01898
12	42	11,53530	12 46470
13	41	12,04461	13 95539
14	40	12,51126	13 48874
15	39	12,93723	13 06277
16	38	13,32418	14 67582
17	37	13,67351	14 32649
18	36	13,98644	14 01356
19	35	14,26399	15 73601
20	34	14,50703	15 49297
21	33	14,71629	15 28371
22	32	14,89238	15 10762
23	31	15,03580	16 96420
24	30	15,14695	16 85305
25	29	15,22613	16 77387
26	28	15,27356	16 72644
27	27	15,28935	16 71065

N = 55

Exponent of p (q)	Exponent of q (p)	log C	log 1/C
0	55	0,00000	0 00000
1	54	1,74036	2 25964
2	53	3,17173	4 82827
3	52	4,41888	5 58112
4	51	5,53282	6 46718
5	50	6,54142	7 45858
6	49	7,46224	8 53776
7	48	8,30734	9 69266
8	47	9,08549	10 91451
9	46	9,80335	10 19665
10	45	10,46611	11 53389
11	44	11,07793	12 92207
12	43	11,64220	12 35780
13	42	12,16172	13 83828
14	41	12,63884	13 36116
15	40	13,07554	14 92446
16	39	13,47348	14 52652
17	38	13,83409	14 16591
18	37	14,15860	15 84140
19	36	14,44805	15 55195
20	35	14,70332	15 29668
21	34	14,92517	15 07483
22	33	15,11423	16 88577
23	32	15,27101	16 72899
24	31	15,39595	16 60405
25	30	15,48937	16 51063
26	29	15,55152	16 44848
27	28	15,58256	16 41744

N = 56

Exponent of p (q)	Exponent of q (p)	log C	log 1/C
0	56	0,00000	0 00000
1	55	1,74819	2 25181
2	54	3,18752	4 81248
3	53	4,44279	5 55721
4	52	5,56501	6 43499
5	51	6,58204	7 41796
6	50	7,51146	8 48854
7	49	8,36533	9 63467
8	48	9,15244	10 84756
9	47	9,87944	10 12056
10	46	10,55154	11 44846
11	45	11,17290	12 82710
12	44	11,74693	12 25307
13	43	12,27644	13 72356
14	42	12,76378	13 23622
15	41	13,21094	14 78906
16	40	13,61960	14 38040
17	39	13,99122	14 00878
18	38	14,32701	15 67299
19	37	14,62804	15 37196
20	36	14,89521	15 10479
21	35	15,12929	16 87071
22	34	15,33094	16 66906
23	33	15,50069	16 49931
24	32	15,63899	16 36101
25	31	15,74620	16 25380
26	30	15,82259	16 17741
27	29	15,86835	16 13165
28	28	15,88359	16 11641

N = 57

Exponent of p (q)	Exponent of q (p)	log C	log 1/C
0	57	0,00000	0 00000
1	56	1,75587	2 24413
2	55	3,20303	4 79697
3	54	4,46627	5 53373
4	53	5,59661	6 40339
5	52	6,62191	7 37809
6	51	7,55977	8 44023
7	50	8,42224	9 57776
8	49	9,21812	10 78188
9	48	9,95407	10 04593
10	47	10,63531	11 36469
11	46	11,26602	12 73398
12	45	11,84959	12 15041
13	44	12,38886	13 61114
14	43	12,88619	13 11381
15	42	13,34357	14 65643
16	41	13,76270	14 23730
17	40	14,14503	15 85497
18	39	14,49182	15 50818
19	38	14,80413	15 19587
20	37	15,08288	16 91712
21	36	15,32886	16 67114
22	35	15,54274	16 45726
23	34	15,72508	16 27492
24	33	15,87635	16 12365
25	32	15,99693	16 00307
26	31	16,08710	17 91290
27	30	16,14710	17 85290
28	29	16,17706	17 82294

N = 58

Exponent of p (q)	Exponent of q (p)	log C	log 1/C
0	58	0,00000	0 00000
1	57	1,76343	2 23657
2	56	3,21827	4 78173
3	55	4,48934	5 51066
4	54	5,62764	6 37236
5	53	6,66107	7 33893
6	52	7,60719	8 39281
7	51	8,47810	9 52190
8	50	9,28258	10 71742
9	49	10,02730	11 97270
10	48	10,71750	11 28250
11	47	11,35735	12 64265
12	46	11,95026	12 04974
13	45	12,49908	13 50092
14	44	13,00616	14 99384
15	43	13,47353	14 52647
16	42	13,90287	14 09713
17	41	14,29567	15 70433
18	40	14,65319	15 34681
19	39	14,97649	15 02351
20	38	15,26653	16 73347
21	37	15,52409	16 47591
22	36	15,74987	16 25013
23	35	15,94444	16 05556
24	34	16,10830	17 89170
25	33	16,24184	17 75816
26	32	16,34538	17 65462
27	31	16,41917	17 58083
28	30	16,46337	17 53663
29	29	16,47809	17 52191

N = 59

Exponent of p (q)	Exponent of q (p)	log C	log 1/C
0	59	0,00000	0 00000
1	58	1,77085	2 22915
2	57	3,23325	4 76675
3	56	4,51200	5 48800
4	55	5,65813	6 34187
5	54	6,69952	7 30048
6	53	7,65377	8 34623
7	52	8,53294	9 46706
8	51	9,34586	10 65414
9	50	10,09919	11 90081
10	49	10,79816	11 20184
11	48	11,44696	12 55304
12	47	12,04902	13 95098
13	46	12,60717	13 39283
14	45	13,12380	14 87620
15	44	13,60092	14 39908
16	43	14,04026	15 95974
17	42	14,44328	15 55672
18	41	14,81125	15 18875
19	40	15,14528	16 85472
20	39	15,44631	16 55369
21	38	15,71516	16 28484
22	37	15,95252	16 04748
23	36	16,15899	17 84101
24	35	16,33509	17 66491
25	34	16,48121	17 51879
26	33	16,59772	17 40228
27	32	16,68487	17 31513
28	31	16,74286	17 25714
29	30	16,77182	17 22818

N = 60

Exponent of p (q)	Exponent of q (p)	log C	log 1/C
0	60	0,00000	0 00000
1	59	1,77815	2 22185
2	58	3,24797	4 75203
3	57	4,53428	5 46572
4	56	5,68809	6 31191
5	55	6,73731	7 26269
6	54	7,69952	8 30048
7	53	8,58682	9 41318
8	52	9,40801	10 59199
9	51	10,16977	11 83023
10	50	10,87734	11 12266
11	49	11,53491	12 46509
12	48	12,14593	13 85407
13	47	12,71323	13 28677
14	46	13,23920	14 76080
15	45	13,72586	14 27414
16	44	14,17496	15 82504
17	43	14,58796	15 41204
18	42	14,96616	15 03384
19	41	15,31065	16 68935
20	40	15,62241	16 37759
21	39	15,90225	16 09775
22	38	16,15089	17 84911
23	37	16,36894	17 63106
24	36	16,55693	17 44307
25	35	16,71530	17 28470
26	34	16,84439	17 15561
27	33	16,94451	17 05549
28	32	17,01586	18 98414
29	31	17,05861	18 94139
30	30	17,07285	18 92715

N = 61

Exponent of p (q)	Exponent of q (p)	log C	log 1/C
0	61	0,00000	0 00000
1	60	1,78533	2 21467
2	59	3,26245	4 73755
3	58	4,55618	5 44382
4	57	5,71755	6 28245
5	56	6,77445	7 22555
6	55	7,74449	8 25551
7	54	8,63976	9 36024
8	53	9,46906	10 53094
9	52	10,23909	11 76091
10	51	10,95510	11 04490
11	50	11,62127	12 37873
12	49	12,24106	13 75894
13	48	12,81732	13 18268
14	47	13,35243	14 64757
15	46	13,84844	14 15156
16	45	14,30707	15 69293
17	44	14,72984	15 27016
18	43	15,11802	16 88198
19	42	15,47273	16 52727
20	41	15,79495	16 20505
21	40	16,08552	17 91448
22	39	16,34515	17 65485
23	38	16,57449	17 42551
24	37	16,77406	17 22594
25	36	16,94432	17 05568
26	35	17,08565	18 91435
27	34	17,19836	18 80164
28	33	17,28268	18 71732

* For explanation see page 81. – Reproduction only by permission of the publishers of the *Geigy Scientific Tables.*

All values conform to the international convention (i.e. 0,1 instead of 0.1).

Common Logarithms of the Binomial Coefficient C and Their Reciprocals* N=61–72

Exponent of p (q)	Exponent of q (p)	log C	log 1/C
N = 61 (continued)			
29	32	17,33879	18 66121
30	31	17,36682	18 63318
N = 62			
0	62	0,00000	0 00000
1	61	1,79239	2 20761
2	60	3,27669	4 72331
3	59	4,57772	5 42228
4	58	5,74651	6 25349
5	57	6,81097	7 18903
6	56	7,78870	8 21130
7	55	8,69179	9 30821
8	54	9,52906	10 47094
9	53	10,30721	11 69279
10	52	11,03148	12 96852
11	51	11,70610	12 29390
12	50	12,33448	13 66552
13	49	12,91951	13 08049
14	48	13,46358	14 53642
15	47	13,96873	14 03127
16	46	14,43671	15 56329
17	45	14,86902	15 13098
18	44	15,26696	16 73304
19	43	15,63166	16 36834
20	42	15,96409	16 03591
21	41	16,26512	17 73488
22	40	16,53548	17 46452
23	39	16,77582	17 22418
24	38	16,98667	17 01333
25	37	17,16851	18 83149
26	36	17,32174	18 67826
27	35	17,44668	18 55332
28	34	17,54359	18 45641
29	33	17,61267	18 38733
30	32	17,65406	18 34594
31	31	17,66785	18 33215
N = 63			
0	63	0,00000	0 00000
1	62	1,79934	2 20066
2	61	3,29070	4 70930
3	60	4,59891	5 40109
4	59	5,77500	6 22500
5	58	6,84688	7 15312
6	57	7,83216	8 16784
7	56	8,74294	9 25706
8	55	9,58804	10 41196
9	54	10,37416	11 62584
10	53	11,10655	12 89345
11	52	11,78943	12 21057
12	51	12,42625	13 57375
13	50	13,01988	14 98012
14	49	13,57272	14 42728
15	48	14,08683	15 91317
16	47	14,56395	15 43605
17	46	15,00560	16 99440
18	45	15,41308	16 58692
19	44	15,78754	16 21246
20	43	16,12997	17 87003
21	42	16,44121	17 55879
22	41	16,72204	17 27796
23	40	16,97310	17 02690
24	39	17,19495	18 80505
25	38	17,38807	18 61193
26	37	17,55288	18 44712
27	36	17,68972	18 31028
28	35	17,79886	18 20114
29	34	17,88053	18 11947
30	33	17,93489	18 06511
31	32	17,96204	18 03796
N = 64			
0	64	0,00000	0 00000
1	63	1,80618	2 19382
2	62	3,30449	4 69551
3	61	4,61976	5 38024
4	60	5,80303	6 19697
5	59	6,88221	7 11779
6	58	7,87491	8 12509
7	57	8,79324	9 20676
8	56	9,64603	10 35397
9	55	10,43997	11 56003
10	54	11,18034	12 81966
11	53	11,87134	12 12866
12	52	12,51643	13 48357
13	51	13,11849	14 88151
14	50	13,67993	14 32007
15	49	14,20281	15 79719
16	48	14,68889	15 31111
17	47	15,13968	16 86032
18	46	15,55651	16 44349
19	45	15,94051	16 05949

Exponent of p (q)	Exponent of q (p)	log C	log 1/C
N = 64 (continued)			
20	44	16,29269	17 70731
21	43	16,61393	17 38607
22	42	16,90497	17 09503
23	41	17,16649	18 83351
24	40	17,39907	18 60093
25	39	17,60319	18 39681
26	38	17,77928	18 22072
27	37	17,92770	18 07230
28	36	18,04874	19 95126
29	35	18,14265	19 85735
30	34	18,20959	19 79041
31	33	18,24971	19 75029
32	32	18,26307	19 73693
N = 65			
0	65	0,00000	0 00000
1	64	1,81291	2 18709
2	63	3,31806	4 68194
3	62	4,64028	5 35972
4	61	5,83061	6 16939
5	60	6,91697	7 08303
6	59	7,91697	8 08303
7	58	8,84273	9 15727
8	57	9,70307	10 29693
9	56	10,50470	11 49530
10	55	11,25289	12 74711
11	54	11,95186	12 04814
12	53	12,60507	13 39493
13	52	13,21540	14 78460
14	51	13,78528	14 21472
15	50	14,31676	15 68324
16	49	14,81161	15 18839
17	48	15,27135	16 72865
18	47	15,69732	16 30268
19	46	16,09067	17 90933
20	45	16,45239	17 54761
21	44	16,78339	17 21661
22	43	17,08442	18 91558
23	42	17,35616	18 64384
24	41	17,59920	18 40080
25	40	17,81404	18 18596
26	39	18,00113	19 99887
27	38	18,16083	19 83917
28	37	18,29345	19 70655
29	36	18,39926	19 60074
30	35	18,47844	19 52156
31	34	18,53114	19 46886
32	33	18,55747	19 44253
N = 66			
0	66	0,00000	0 00000
1	65	1,81954	2 18046
2	64	3,33143	4 66857
3	63	4,66049	5 33951
4	62	5,85777	6 14223
5	61	6,95119	7 04881
6	60	7,95837	8 04163
7	59	8,89142	9 10858
8	58	9,75918	10 24082
9	57	10,56837	11 43163
10	56	11,32424	12 67576
11	55	12,03104	13 96896
12	54	12,69222	13 30778
13	53	13,31067	14 68933
14	52	13,88882	14 11118
15	51	14,42873	15 57127
16	50	14,93218	15 06782
17	49	15,40070	16 59930
18	48	15,83562	16 16438
19	47	16,23811	17 76189
20	46	16,60918	17 39082
21	45	16,94972	17 05028
22	44	17,26051	18 73949
23	43	17,54223	18 45777
24	42	17,79549	18 20451
25	41	18,02080	19 97920
26	40	18,21861	19 78139
27	39	18,38931	19 61069
28	38	18,53321	19 46679
29	37	18,65060	19 34940
30	36	18,74168	19 25832
31	35	18,80662	19 19338
32	34	18,84554	19 15446
33	33	18,85850	19 14150
N = 67			
0	67	0,00000	0 00000
1	66	1,82607	2 17393
2	65	3,34459	4 65541
3	64	4,68038	5 31962
4	63	5,88450	6 11550
5	62	6,98487	7 01513
6	61	7,99911	8 00089

Exponent of p (q)	Exponent of q (p)	log C	log 1/C
N = 67 (continued)			
7	60	8,93934	9 06066
8	59	9,81440	10 18560
9	58	10,63101	11 36899
10	57	11,39444	12 60556
11	56	12,10892	13 89108
12	55	12,77793	13 22207
13	54	13,40435	14 59565
14	53	13,99062	14 00938
15	52	14,53880	15 46120
16	51	15,05068	16 94932
17	50	15,52781	16 47219
18	49	15,97150	16 02850
19	48	16,38295	17 61705
20	47	16,76316	17 23684
21	46	17,11304	18 88696
22	45	17,43337	18 56663
23	44	17,72486	18 27514
24	43	17,98810	18 01190
25	42	18,22363	19 77637
26	41	18,43190	19 56810
27	40	18,61332	19 38668
28	39	18,76822	19 23178
29	38	18,89689	19 10311
30	37	18,99955	19 00045
31	36	19,07639	20 92361
32	35	19,12754	20 87246
33	34	19,15310	20 84690
N = 68			
0	68	0,00000	0 00000
1	67	1,83251	2 16749
2	66	3,35755	4 64245
3	65	4,69998	5 30002
4	64	5,91083	6 08917
5	63	7,01804	8 98196
6	62	8,03923	9 96077
7	61	8,98652	9 01348
8	60	9,86876	10 13124
9	59	10,69267	11 30733
10	58	11,46352	12 53648
11	57	12,18556	13 81444
12	56	12,86225	13 13775
13	55	13,49650	14 50350
14	54	14,09073	15 90927
15	53	14,64703	15 35297
16	52	15,16719	16 83281
17	51	15,65274	16 34726
18	50	16,10504	17 89496
19	49	16,52526	17 47474
20	48	16,91442	17 08558
21	47	17,27345	18 72655
22	46	17,60312	18 39688
23	45	17,90415	18 09585
24	44	18,17715	19 82285
25	43	18,42267	19 57733
26	42	18,64116	19 35884
27	41	18,83305	19 16695
28	40	18,99867	19 00133
29	39	19,13833	20 86167
30	38	19,25228	20 74772
31	37	19,34070	20 65930
32	36	19,40375	20 59625
33	35	19,44154	20 55846
34	34	19,45413	20 54587
N = 69			
0	69	0,00000	0 00000
1	68	1,83885	2 16115
2	67	3,37033	4 62967
3	66	4,71928	5 28072
4	65	5,93677	6 06323
5	64	7,05071	8 94929
6	63	8,07874	9 92126
7	62	9,03298	10 96702
8	61	9,92228	10 07772
9	60	10,75337	11 24663
10	59	11,53152	12 46848
11	58	12,26098	13 73902
12	57	12,94523	13 05477
13	56	13,58716	14 41284
14	55	14,18922	15 81078
15	54	14,75349	15 24651
16	53	15,28176	16 71824
17	52	15,77559	16 22441
18	51	16,23632	17 76368
19	50	16,66514	17 33486
20	49	17,06308	18 93692
21	48	17,43105	18 56895
22	47	17,76987	18 23013
23	46	18,08024	19 91976
24	45	18,36279	19 63721
25	44	18,61806	19 38194
26	43	18,84654	19 15346
27	42	19,04865	20 95135

Exponent of p (q)	Exponent of q (p)	log C	log 1/C
N = 69 (continued)			
28	41	19,22474	20 77526
29	40	19,37512	20 62488
30	39	19,50006	20 49994
31	38	19,59976	20 40024
32	37	19,67440	20 32560
33	36	19,72409	20 27591
34	35	19,74891	20 25109
N = 70			
0	70	0,00000	0 00000
1	69	1,84510	2 15490
2	68	3,38292	4 61708
3	67	4,73830	5 26170
4	66	5,96232	6 03768
5	65	7,08289	8 91711
6	64	8,11766	9 88234
7	63	9,07874	10 92126
8	62	9,97499	10 02501
9	61	10,81314	11 18686
10	60	11,59847	12 40153
11	59	12,33523	13 66477
12	58	13,02690	14 97310
13	57	13,67638	14 32362
14	56	14,28613	15 71387
15	55	14,85822	15 14178
16	54	15,39447	16 60553
17	53	15,89641	16 10359
18	52	16,36542	17 63458
19	51	16,80267	17 19733
20	50	17,20921	18 79079
21	49	17,58596	18 41404
22	48	17,93373	18 06627
23	47	18,25324	19 74676
24	46	18,54513	19 45487
25	45	18,80995	19 19005
26	44	19,04819	20 95181
27	43	19,26028	20 73972
28	42	19,44659	20 55341
29	41	19,60744	20 39256
30	40	19,74310	20 25690
31	39	19,85380	20 14620
32	38	19,93971	20 06029
33	37	20,00098	21 99902
34	36	20,03771	21 96229
35	35	20,04994	21 95006
N = 71			
0	71	0,00000	0 00000
1	70	1,85126	2 14874
2	69	3,39533	4 60467
3	68	4,75705	5 24295
4	67	5,98750	6 01250
5	66	7,11461	8 88539
6	65	8,15600	9 84400
7	64	9,12382	10 87618
8	63	10,02691	11 97309
9	62	10,87200	11 12800
10	61	11,66440	12 33560
11	60	12,40833	13 59167
12	59	13,10730	14 89270
13	58	13,76421	14 23579
14	57	14,38151	15 61849
15	56	14,96130	15 03870
16	55	15,50536	16 49464
17	54	16,01528	17 98472
18	53	16,49240	17 50760
19	52	16,93792	17 06208
20	51	17,35289	18 64711
21	50	17,73824	18 26176
22	49	18,09479	19 90521
23	48	18,42326	19 57674
24	47	18,72429	19 27571
25	46	18,99845	19 00155
26	45	19,24623	20 75377
27	44	19,46808	20 53192
28	43	19,66438	20 33562
29	42	19,83545	20 16455
30	41	19,98157	20 01843
31	40	20,10300	21 89700
32	39	20,19991	21 80009
33	38	20,27246	21 72754
34	37	20,32076	21 67924
35	36	20,34490	21 65510
N = 72			
0	72	0,00000	0 00000
1	71	1,85733	2 14267
2	70	3,40756	4 59244
3	69	4,77554	5 22446
4	68	6,01233	7 98767
5	67	7,14587	8 85413
6	66	8,19379	9 80621

* For explanation see page 81. –

All values conform to the international convention (i.e. 0,1 instead of 0.1).

Common Logarithms of the Binomial Coefficient C and Their Reciprocals* N=72–81

Exponent of p (q)	Exponent of q (p)	log C	log 1/C
N = 72 (continued)			
7	65	9,16824	10 83176
8	64	10,07806	11 92194
9	63	10,93000	11 07000
10	62	11,72934	12 27066
11	61	12,48034	13 51966
12	60	13,18648	14 81352
13	59	13,85069	14 14931
14	58	14,47542	15 52458
15	57	15,06275	16 93725
16	56	15,61451	16 38549
17	55	16,13225	17 86775
18	54	16,61734	17 38266
19	53	17,07098	18 92902
20	52	17,49422	18 50578
21	51	17,88801	18 11199
22	50	18,25315	19 74685
23	49	18,59040	19 40960
24	48	18,90038	19 09962
25	47	19,18368	20 81632
26	46	19,44081	20 55919
27	45	19,67220	20 32780
28	44	19,87826	20 12174
29	43	20,05931	21 94069
30	42	20,21566	21 78434
31	41	20,34755	21 65245
32	40	20,45518	21 54482
33	39	20,53873	21 46127
34	38	20,59831	21 40169
35	37	20,63403	21 36597
36	36	20,64593	21 35407
N = 73			
0	73	0,00000	0 00000
1	72	1,86332	2 13668
2	71	3,41963	4 58037
3	70	4,79376	5 20624
4	69	6,03680	7 96320
5	68	7,17668	8 82332
6	67	8,23104	9 76896
7	66	9,21201	10 78799
8	65	10,12847	11 87153
9	64	10,98714	11 01286
10	63	11,79332	12 20668
11	62	12,55127	13 44873
12	61	13,26448	14 73552
13	60	13,93586	14 06414
14	59	14,56789	15 43211
15	58	15,16265	16 83735
16	57	15,72196	16 27804
17	56	16,24738	17 75262
18	55	16,74030	17 25970
19	54	17,20191	18 79809
20	53	17,63327	18 36673
21	52	18,03533	19 96467
22	51	18,40891	19 59109
23	50	18,75475	19 24525
24	49	19,07351	20 92649
25	48	19,36576	20 63424
26	47	19,63203	20 36797
27	46	19,87277	20 12723
28	45	20,08837	21 91163
29	44	20,27918	21 72082
30	43	20,44551	21 55449
31	42	20,58762	21 41238
32	41	20,70572	21 29428
33	40	20,79999	21 20001
34	39	20,87057	21 12943
35	38	20,91757	21 08243
36	37	20,94105	21 05895
N = 74			
0	74	0,00000	0 00000
1	73	1,86923	2 13077
2	72	3,43152	4 56848
3	71	4,81174	5 18826
4	70	6,06093	7 93907
5	69	7,20706	8 79294
6	68	8,26776	9 73224
7	67	9,25517	10 74483
8	66	10,17816	11 82184
9	65	11,04346	12 95654
10	64	11,85637	12 14363
11	63	12,62116	13 37884
12	62	13,34132	14 65868
13	61	14,01977	15 98023
14	60	14,65897	15 34103
15	59	15,26103	16 73897
16	58	15,82776	16 17224
17	57	16,36074	17 63926
18	56	16,86134	17 13866
19	55	17,33078	18 66922
20	54	17,77011	18 22989
21	53	18,18028	19 81972
22	52	18,56214	19 43786
23	51	18,91641	19 08359
24	50	19,24377	20 75623
25	49	19,54480	20 45520
26	48	19,82002	20 17998
27	47	20,06990	21 93010
28	46	20,29484	21 70516
29	45	20,49520	21 50480
30	44	20,67129	21 32871
31	43	20,82338	21 17662
32	42	20,95170	21 04830
33	41	21,05644	22 94356
34	40	21,13774	22 86226
35	39	21,19573	22 80427
36	38	21,23049	22 76951
37	37	21,24208	22 75792
N = 75			
0	75	0,00000	0 00000
1	74	1,87506	2 12494
2	73	3,44326	4 55674
3	72	4,82946	5 17054
4	71	6,08474	7 91526
5	70	7,23703	8 76297
6	69	8,30397	9 69603
7	68	9,29772	10 70228
8	67	10,22714	11 77286
9	66	11,09897	12 90103
10	65	11,91852	12 08148
11	64	12,69004	13 30996
12	63	13,41704	14 58296
13	62	14,10244	15 89756
14	61	14,74870	15 25130
15	60	15,35794	16 64206
16	59	15,93197	16 06803
17	58	16,47237	17 52763
18	57	16,98053	17 01947
19	56	17,45765	18 54235
20	55	17,90481	18 09519
21	54	18,32295	19 67705
22	53	18,71292	19 28708
23	52	19,07547	20 92453
24	51	19,41126	20 58874
25	50	19,72089	20 27911
26	49	20,00489	21 99511
27	48	20,26372	21 73628
28	47	20,49780	21 50220
29	46	20,70750	21 29250
30	45	20,89314	21 10686
31	44	21,05499	22 94501
32	43	21,19329	22 80671
33	42	21,30825	22 69175
34	41	21,40002	22 59998
35	40	21,46873	22 53127
36	39	21,51449	22 48551
37	38	21,53735	22 46265
N = 76			
0	76	0,00000	0 00000
1	75	1,88081	2 11919
2	74	3,45484	4 54516
3	73	4,84696	5 15304
4	72	6,10822	7 89178
5	71	7,26658	8 73342
6	70	8,33969	9 66031
7	69	9,33969	10 66031
8	68	10,27545	11 72455
9	67	11,15371	12 84629
10	66	11,97979	12 02021
11	65	12,75794	13 24206
12	64	13,49167	14 50833
13	63	14,18391	15 81609
14	62	14,83712	15 16288
15	61	15,45342	16 54658
16	60	16,03463	17 96537
17	59	16,58233	17 41767
18	58	17,09791	18 90209
19	57	17,58259	18 41741
20	56	18,03743	19 96257
21	55	18,46340	19 53660
22	54	18,86134	19 13866
23	53	19,23201	20 76799
24	52	19,57607	20 42393
25	51	19,89413	20 10587
26	50	20,18673	21 81327
27	49	20,45434	21 54566
28	48	20,69738	21 30262
29	47	20,91622	21 08378
30	46	21,11120	22 88880
31	45	21,28259	22 71741
32	44	21,43065	22 56935
33	43	21,55559	22 44441
34	42	21,65758	22 34242
35	41	21,73676	22 26324
36	40	21,79325	22 20675
37	39	21,82710	22 17290
38	38	21,83838	22 16162
N = 77			
0	77	0,00000	0 00000
1	76	1,88649	2 11351
2	75	3,46627	4 53373
3	74	4,86421	5 13579
4	73	6,13139	7 86861
5	72	7,29574	8 70426
6	71	8,37492	9 62508
7	70	9,38108	10 61892
8	69	10,32309	11 67691
9	68	11,20770	12 79230
10	67	12,04020	13 95980
11	66	12,82489	13 17511
12	65	13,56525	14 43475
13	64	14,26422	15 73578
14	63	14,92427	15 07573
15	62	15,54752	16 45248
16	61	16,13579	17 86421
17	60	16,69067	17 30933
18	59	17,21355	18 78645
19	58	17,70565	18 29435
20	57	18,16805	19 83195
21	56	18,60170	19 39830
22	55	19,00747	20 99253
23	54	19,38610	20 61390
24	53	19,73829	20 26171
25	52	20,06462	21 93538
26	51	20,36565	21 63435
27	50	20,64186	21 35814
28	49	20,89367	21 10633
29	48	21,12147	22 87853
30	47	21,32559	22 67441
31	46	21,50632	22 49368
32	45	21,66393	22 33607
33	44	21,79863	22 20137
34	43	21,91060	22 08940
35	42	22,00001	23 99999
36	41	22,06695	23 93305
37	40	22,11153	23 88847
38	39	22,13381	23 86619
N = 78			
0	78	0,00000	0 00000
1	77	1,89209	2 10791
2	76	3,47756	4 52244
3	75	4,88125	5 11875
4	74	6,15425	7 84575
5	73	7,32451	8 67549
6	72	8,40968	9 59032
7	71	9,42192	10 57808
8	70	10,37009	11 62991
9	69	11,26094	12 73906
10	68	12,09979	13 90021
11	67	12,89091	13 10909
12	66	13,63780	14 36220
13	65	14,34340	15 65660
14	64	15,01019	16 98981
15	63	15,64027	16 35973
16	62	16,23549	17 76451
17	61	16,79744	17 20256
18	60	17,32749	18 67251
19	59	17,82689	18 17311
20	58	18,29671	19 70329
21	57	18,73792	19 26208
22	56	19,15138	20 84862
23	55	19,53784	20 46216
24	54	19,89799	20 10201
25	53	20,23244	21 76756
26	52	20,54174	21 45826
27	51	20,82638	21 17362
28	50	21,08679	22 91321
29	49	21,32337	22 67663
30	48	21,53644	22 46356
31	47	21,72632	22 27368
32	46	21,89327	22 10673
33	45	22,03751	23 96249
34	44	22,15925	23 84075
35	43	22,25863	23 74137
36	42	22,33580	23 66420
37	41	22,39084	23 60916
38	40	22,42385	23 57615
39	39	22,43484	23 56516
N = 79			
0	79	0,00000	0 00000
1	78	1,89763	2 10237
2	77	3,48869	4 51131
3	76	4,89806	5 10194
4	75	6,17681	7 82319
5	74	7,35291	8 64709
6	73	8,44399	9 55601
7	72	9,46221	10 53779
8	71	10,41645	11 58355
9	70	11,31347	12 68653
10	69	12,15857	13 84143
11	68	12,95602	13 04398
12	67	13,70935	14 29065
13	66	14,42148	15 57852
14	65	15,09490	16 90510
15	64	15,73172	16 26828
16	63	16,33378	17 66622
17	62	16,90267	17 09733
18	61	17,43979	18 56021
19	60	17,94637	18 05363
20	59	18,42349	19 57651
21	58	18,87212	19 12788
22	57	19,29313	20 70687
23	56	19,68727	20 31273
24	55	20,05525	21 94475
25	54	20,39767	21 60233
26	53	20,71509	21 28491
27	52	21,00801	22 99199
28	51	21,27685	22 72315
29	50	21,52202	22 47798
30	49	21,74387	22 25613
31	48	21,94271	22 05729
32	47	22,11880	23 88120
33	46	22,27238	23 72762
34	45	22,40366	23 59634
35	44	22,51281	23 48719
36	43	22,59996	23 40004
37	42	22,66522	23 33478
38	41	22,70869	23 29131
39	40	22,73041	23 26959
N = 80			
0	80	0,00000	0 00000
1	79	1,90309	2 09691
2	78	3,49969	4 50031
3	77	4,91466	5 08534
4	76	6,19909	7 80091
5	75	7,38093	8 61907
6	74	8,47784	9 52216
7	73	9,50198	10 49802
8	72	10,46221	11 53779
9	71	11,36530	12 63470
10	70	12,21656	13 78344
11	69	13,02027	14 97973
12	68	13,77993	14 22007
13	67	14,49850	15 50150
14	66	15,17845	16 82155
15	65	15,82190	16 17810
16	64	16,43069	17 56931
17	63	17,00642	18 99358
18	62	17,55049	18 44951
19	61	18,06413	19 93587
20	60	18,54843	19 45157
21	59	19,00436	20 99564
22	58	19,43279	20 56721
23	57	19,83449	20 16551
24	56	20,21015	21 78985
25	55	20,56040	21 43960
26	54	20,88579	21 11421
27	53	21,18682	22 81318
28	52	21,46394	22 53606
29	51	21,71754	22 28246
30	50	21,94799	22 05201
31	49	22,15560	23 84440
32	48	22,34065	23 65935
33	47	22,50337	23 49663
34	46	22,64399	23 35601
35	45	22,76268	23 23732
36	44	22,85959	23 14041
37	43	22,93484	23 06516
38	42	22,98853	23 01147
39	41	23,02071	24 97929
40	40	23,03144	24 96856
N = 81			
0	81	0,00000	0 00000
1	80	1,90849	2 09151
2	79	3,51055	4 48945
3	78	4,93105	5 06895
4	77	6,22109	7 77891
5	76	7,40861	8 59139
6	75	8,51127	9 48873
7	74	9,54123	10 45877
8	73	10,50737	11 49263
9	72	11,41645	12 58355
10	71	12,27379	13 72621
11	70	13,08365	14 91635
12	69	13,84957	14 15043
13	68	14,57447	15 42553
14	67	15,26086	16 73914

* For explanation see page 81. –

All values conform to the international convention (i.e. 0,1 instead of 0.1).

Common Logarithms of the Binomial Coefficient C and Their Reciprocals* N=81–89

N = 81 (continued)

Exponent of p (q)	q (p)	log C	log 1/C
15	66	15,91084	16 08916
16	65	16,52626	17 47374
17	64	17,10873	18 89127
18	63	17,65963	18 34037
19	62	18,18022	19 81978
20	61	18,67158	19 32842
21	60	19,13469	20 86531
22	59	19,57042	20 42958
23	58	19,97955	20 02045
24	57	20,36276	21 63724
25	56	20,72070	21 27930
26	55	21,05391	22 94609
27	54	21,36291	22 63709
28	53	21,64815	22 35185
29	52	21,91003	22 08997
30	51	22,14891	23 85109
31	50	22,36512	23 63488
32	49	22,55894	23 44106
33	48	22,73062	23 26938
34	47	22,88038	23 11962
35	46	23,00841	24 99159
36	45	23,11487	24 88513
37	44	23,19988	24 80012
38	43	23,26355	24 73645
39	42	23,30595	24 69405
40	41	23,32714	24 67286

N = 82

Exponent of p (q)	q (p)	log C	log 1/C
0	82	0,00000	0 00000
1	81	1,91381	2 08619
2	80	3,52127	4 47873
3	79	4,94724	5 05276
4	78	6,24280	7 75720
5	77	7,43593	8 56407
6	76	8,54427	9 45573
7	75	9,57998	10 42002
8	74	10,55196	11 44804
9	73	11,46694	12 53306
10	72	12,33027	13 66973
11	71	13,14621	14 85379
12	70	13,91828	14 08172
13	69	14,64944	15 35056
14	68	15,34216	16 65784
15	67	15,99858	16 00142
16	66	16,62053	17 37947
17	65	17,20963	18 79037
18	64	17,76727	18 23273
19	63	18,29470	19 70530
20	62	18,79301	19 20699
21	61	19,26318	20 73682
22	60	19,70609	20 29391
23	59	20,12251	21 87749
24	58	20,51315	21 48685
25	57	20,87864	21 12136
26	56	21,21954	22 78046
27	55	21,53636	22 46364
28	54	21,82957	22 17043
29	53	22,09956	23 90044
30	52	22,34672	23 65328
31	51	22,57136	23 42864
32	50	22,77378	23 22622
33	49	22,95424	23 04576
34	48	23,11295	24 88705
35	47	23,25013	24 74987
36	46	23,36592	24 63408
37	45	23,46048	24 53952
38	44	23,53391	24 46609
39	43	23,58629	24 41371
40	42	23,61770	24 38230
41	41	23,62817	24 37183

N = 83

Exponent of p (q)	q (p)	log C	log 1/C
0	83	0,00000	0 00000
1	82	1,91908	2 08092
2	81	3,53186	4 46814
3	80	4,96323	5 03677
4	79	6,26426	7 73574
5	78	7,46291	8 53709
6	77	8,57686	9 42314
7	76	9,61825	10 38175
8	75	10,59597	11 40403
9	74	11,51679	12 48321
10	73	12,38602	13 61398
11	72	13,20795	14 79205
12	71	13,98610	14 01390
13	70	14,72342	15 27658
14	69	15,42239	16 57761
15	68	16,08515	17 91485
16	67	16,71354	17 28646
17	66	17,30916	18 69084
18	65	17,87343	18 12657
19	64	18,40759	19 59241
20	63	18,91274	19 08726
21	62	19,38986	20 61014
22	61	19,83983	20 16017
23	60	20,26344	21 73656
24	59	20,66138	21 33862
25	58	21,03429	22 96571
26	57	21,38274	22 61726
27	56	21,70725	22 29275
28	55	22,00828	23 99172
29	54	22,28625	23 71375
30	53	22,54152	23 45848
31	52	22,77443	23 22557
32	51	22,98529	23 01471
33	50	23,17434	24 82566
34	49	23,34184	24 65816
35	48	23,48796	24 51204
36	47	23,61290	24 38710
37	46	23,71680	24 28320
38	45	23,79977	24 20023
39	44	23,86192	24 13808
40	43	23,90331	24 09669
41	42	23,92400	24 07600

N = 84

Exponent of p (q)	q (p)	log C	log 1/C
0	84	0,00000	0 00000
1	83	1,92428	2 07572
2	82	3,54233	4 45767
3	81	4,97902	5 02098
4	80	6,28545	7 71455
5	79	7,48956	8 51044
6	78	8,60904	9 39096
7	77	9,65604	10 34396
8	76	10,63944	11 36056
9	75	11,56601	12 43399
10	74	12,44107	13 55893
11	73	13,26891	14 73109
12	72	14,05305	15 94695
13	71	14,79644	15 20356
14	70	15,50157	16 49843
15	69	16,17058	17 82942
16	68	16,80531	17 19469
17	67	17,40737	18 59263
18	66	17,97817	18 02183
19	65	18,51896	19 48104
20	64	19,03084	20 96916
21	63	19,51480	20 48520
22	62	19,97172	20 02828
23	61	20,40238	21 59762
24	60	20,80750	21 19250
25	59	21,18771	22 81229
26	58	21,54359	22 45641
27	57	21,87566	22 12434
28	56	22,18437	23 81563
29	55	22,47016	23 52984
30	54	22,73341	23 26659
31	53	22,97444	23 02556
32	52	23,19356	24 80644
33	51	23,39105	24 60895
34	50	23,56714	24 43286
35	49	23,72205	24 27795
36	48	23,85594	24 14406
37	47	23,96898	24 03102
38	46	24,06129	25 93871
39	45	24,13299	25 86701
40	44	24,18414	25 81586
41	43	24,21481	25 78519
42	42	24,22503	25 77497

N = 85

Exponent of p (q)	q (p)	log C	log 1/C
0	85	0,00000	0 00000
1	84	1,92942	2 07058
2	83	3,55267	4 44733
3	82	4,99463	5 00537
4	81	6,30638	7 69362
5	80	7,51589	8 48411
6	79	8,64083	9 35917
7	78	9,69336	10 30664
8	77	10,68237	11 31763
9	76	11,61461	12 38539
10	75	12,49543	13 50457
11	74	13,32910	14 67090
12	73	14,11915	15 88085
13	72	14,86853	15 13147
14	71	15,57973	16 42027
15	70	16,25490	17 74510
16	69	16,89588	17 10412
17	68	17,50428	18 49572
18	67	18,08151	19 91849
19	66	18,62883	19 37117
20	65	19,14735	20 85265
21	64	19,63804	20 36196
22	63	20,10180	21 89820
23	62	20,53941	21 46059
24	61	20,95159	21 04841
25	60	21,33898	22 66102
26	59	21,70216	22 29784
27	58	22,04165	23 95835
28	57	22,35792	23 64208
29	56	22,65140	23 34860
30	55	22,92246	23 07754
31	54	23,17146	24 82854
32	53	23,39871	24 60129
33	52	23,60447	24 39553
34	51	23,78899	24 21101
35	50	23,95250	24 04750
36	49	24,09516	25 90484
37	48	24,21716	25 78284
38	47	24,31861	25 68139
39	46	24,39965	25 60035
40	45	24,46035	25 53965
41	44	24,50077	25 49923
42	43	24,52098	25 47902

N = 86

Exponent of p (q)	q (p)	log C	log 1/C
0	86	0,00000	0 00000
1	85	1,93450	2 06550
2	84	3,56289	4 43711
3	83	5,01005	6 98995
4	82	6,32706	7 67294
5	81	7,54191	8 45809
6	80	8,67224	9 32776
7	79	9,73023	10 26977
8	78	10,72477	11 27523
9	77	11,66262	12 33738
10	76	12,54911	13 45089
11	75	13,38853	14 61147
12	74	14,18441	15 81559
13	73	14,93970	15 06030
14	72	15,65690	16 34310
15	71	16,33814	17 66186
16	70	16,98528	17 01472
17	69	17,59993	18 40007
18	68	18,18350	19 81650
19	67	18,73726	19 26274
20	66	19,26230	20 73770
21	65	19,75963	20 24037
22	64	20,23012	21 76988
23	63	20,67457	21 32543
24	62	21,09370	22 90630
25	61	21,48815	22 51185
26	60	21,85851	22 14149
27	59	22,20529	23 79471
28	58	22,52899	23 47101
29	57	22,83002	23 16998
30	56	23,10877	24 89123
31	55	23,36560	24 63440
32	54	23,60081	24 39919
33	53	23,81469	24 18531
34	52	24,00749	25 99251
35	51	24,17942	25 82058
36	50	24,33069	25 66931
37	49	24,46146	25 53854
38	48	24,57187	25 42813
39	47	24,66205	25 33795
40	46	24,73209	25 26791
41	45	24,78206	25 21794
42	44	24,81202	25 18798
43	43	24,82201	25 17799

N = 87

Exponent of p (q)	q (p)	log C	log 1/C
0	87	0,00000	0 00000
1	86	1,93952	2 06048
2	85	3,57299	4 42701
3	84	5,02529	6 97471
4	83	6,34750	7 65250
5	82	7,56761	8 43239
6	81	8,70328	9 29672
7	80	9,76666	10 23334
8	79	10,76666	11 23334
9	78	11,71005	12 28995
10	77	12,60214	13 39786
11	76	13,44724	14 55276
12	75	14,24887	15 75113
13	74	15,00999	16 99001
14	73	15,73309	16 26691
15	72	16,42033	17 57967
16	71	17,07354	18 92646
17	70	17,69435	18 30565
18	69	18,28417	19 71583
19	68	18,84427	19 15573
20	67	19,37575	20 62425
21	66	19,87960	20 12040
22	65	20,35672	21 64328
23	64	20,80791	21 19209
24	63	21,23388	22 76612
25	62	21,63528	22 36472
26	61	22,01270	23 98730
27	60	22,36666	23 63334
28	59	22,69766	23 30234
29	58	23,00611	24 99389
30	57	23,29242	24 70758
31	56	23,55693	24 44307
32	55	23,79997	24 20003
33	54	24,02182	25 97818
34	53	24,22273	25 77727
35	52	24,40294	25 59706
36	51	24,56264	25 43736
37	50	24,70201	25 29799
38	49	24,82120	25 17880
39	48	24,92033	25 07967
40	47	24,99951	25 00049
41	46	25,05882	26 94118
42	45	25,09833	26 90167
43	44	25,11807	26 88193

N = 88

Exponent of p (q)	q (p)	log C	log 1/C
0	88	0,00000	0 00000
1	87	1,94448	2 05552
2	86	3,58297	4 41703
3	85	5,04035	6 95965
4	84	6,36771	7 63229
5	83	7,59302	8 40698
6	82	8,73394	9 26606
7	81	9,80266	10 19734
8	80	10,80806	11 19194
9	79	11,75690	12 24310
10	78	12,65453	13 34547
11	77	13,50523	14 49477
12	76	14,31254	15 68746
13	75	15,07941	16 92059
14	74	15,80834	16 19166
15	73	16,50148	17 49852
16	72	17,16069	18 83931
17	71	17,78757	18 21243
18	70	18,38356	19 61644
19	69	18,94990	19 05010
20	68	19,48772	20 51228
21	67	19,99801	20 00199
22	66	20,48166	21 51834
23	65	20,93948	21 06052
24	64	21,37218	22 62782
25	63	21,78042	22 21958
26	62	22,16479	23 83521
27	61	22,52582	23 47418
28	60	22,86399	23 13601
29	59	23,17974	24 82026
30	58	23,47347	24 52653
31	57	23,74554	24 25446
32	56	23,99626	24 00374
33	55	24,22594	25 77406
34	54	24,43482	25 56518
35	53	24,62315	25 37685
36	52	24,79112	25 20888
37	51	24,93892	25 06108
38	50	25,06671	26 93329
39	49	25,17461	26 82539
40	48	25,26275	26 73725
41	47	25,33121	26 66879
42	46	25,38006	26 61994
43	45	25,40934	26 59066
44	44	25,41910	26 58090

N = 89

Exponent of p (q)	q (p)	log C	log 1/C
0	89	0,00000	0 00000
1	88	1,94939	2 05061
2	87	3,59284	4 40716
3	86	5,05524	6 94476
4	85	6,38768	7 61232
5	84	7,61813	8 38187
6	83	8,76426	9 23574
7	82	9,83824	10 16176
8	81	10,84896	11 15104
9	80	11,80320	12 19680
10	79	12,70629	13 29371
11	78	13,56253	14 43747
12	77	14,37544	15 62456
13	76	15,14799	16 85201
14	75	15,88267	16 11733
15	74	16,58164	17 41836
16	73	17,24675	18 75325
17	72	17,87963	18 12037
18	71	18,48169	19 51831
19	70	19,05419	20 94581
20	69	19,59826	20 40174
21	68	20,11489	21 88511
22	67	20,60498	21 39502
23	66	21,06932	22 93068
24	65	21,50866	22 49134
25	64	21,92363	22 07637
26	63	22,31484	23 68516
27	62	22,68281	23 31719
28	61	23,02805	24 97195
29	60	23,35098	24 64902
30	59	23,65201	24 34799
31	58	23,93150	24 06850

* For explanation see page 81. – Reproduction only by permission of the publishers of the *Geigy Scientific Tables*.

All values conform to the international convention (i.e. 0,1 instead of 0.1).

Common Logarithms of the Binomial Coefficient C and Their Reciprocals* N=89–97

N = 89 (continued)

Exponent of p (q)	q (p)	log C	log 1/C
32	57	24,18978	25 81022
33	56	24,42714	25 57286
34	55	24,64385	25 35615
35	54	24,84014	25 15986
36	53	25,01623	26 98377
37	52	25,17231	26 82769
38	51	25,30853	26 69147
39	50	25,42503	26 57497
40	49	25,52194	26 47806
41	48	25,59936	26 40064
42	47	25,65735	26 34265
43	46	25,69598	26 30402
44	45	25,71528	26 28472

N = 90

Exponent of p (q)	q (p)	log C	log 1/C
0	90	0,00000	0 00000
1	89	1,95424	2 04576
2	88	3,60260	4 39740
3	87	5,06996	6 93004
4	86	6,40742	7 59258
5	85	7,64295	8 35705
6	84	8,79422	9 20578
7	83	9,87340	10 12660
8	82	10,88939	11 11061
9	81	11,84896	12 15104
10	80	12,75745	13 24255
11	79	13,61914	14 38086
12	78	14,43759	15 56241
13	77	15,21574	16 78426
14	76	15,95610	16 04390
15	75	16,66082	17 33918
16	74	17,33177	18 66823
17	73	17,97055	18 02945
18	72	18,57860	19 42140
19	71	19,15718	20 84282
20	70	19,70741	20 29259
21	69	20,23028	21 76972
22	68	20,72671	21 27329
23	67	21,19749	22 80251
24	66	21,64336	22 35664
25	65	22,06496	23 93504
26	64	22,46290	23 53710
27	63	22,83772	23 16228
28	62	23,18990	24 81010
29	61	23,51989	24 48011
30	60	23,82810	24 17190
31	59	24,11489	25 88511
32	58	24,38059	25 61941
33	57	24,62551	25 37449
34	56	24,84990	25 15010
35	55	25,05402	26 94598
36	54	25,23808	26 76192
37	53	25,40227	26 59773
38	52	25,54677	26 45323
39	51	25,67171	26 32829
40	50	25,77722	26 22278
41	49	25,86340	26 13660
42	48	25,93035	26 06965
43	47	25,97812	26 02188
44	46	26,00677	27 99323
45	45	26,01631	27 98369

N = 91

Exponent of p (q)	q (p)	log C	log 1/C
0	91	0,00000	0 00000
1	90	1,95904	2 04096
2	89	3,61225	4 38775
3	88	5,08452	6 91548
4	87	6,42695	7 57305
5	86	7,66749	8 33251
6	85	8,82384	9 17616
7	84	9,90816	10 09184
8	83	10,92935	11 07065
9	82	11,89419	12 10581
10	81	12,80800	13 19200
11	80	13,67509	14 32491
12	79	14,49900	15 50100
13	78	15,28269	16 71731
14	77	16,02865	17 97135
15	76	16,73905	17 26095
16	75	17,41575	18 58425
17	74	18,06036	19 93964
18	73	18,67432	19 32568
19	72	19,25889	20 74111
20	71	19,81519	20 18481
21	70	20,34423	21 65577
22	69	20,84690	21 15310
23	68	21,32402	22 67598
24	67	21,77632	22 22368
25	66	22,20446	23 79554
26	65	22,60903	23 39097
27	64	22,99058	23 00942
28	63	23,34960	24 65040
29	62	23,68654	24 31346
30	61	24,00181	25 99819

N = 91 (continued)

Exponent of p (q)	q (p)	log C	log 1/C
31	60	24,29578	25 70422
32	59	24,56878	25 43122
33	58	24,82112	25 17888
34	57	25,05307	26 94693
35	56	25,26488	26 73512
36	55	25,45676	26 54324
37	54	25,62892	26 37108
38	53	25,78153	26 21847
39	52	25,91474	26 08526
40	51	26,02869	27 97131
41	50	26,12347	27 87653
42	49	26,19919	27 80081
43	48	26,25592	27 74408
44	47	26,29371	27 70629
45	46	26,31260	27 68740

N = 92

Exponent of p (q)	q (p)	log C	log 1/C
0	92	0,00000	0 00000
1	91	1,96379	2 03621
2	90	3,62180	4 37820
3	89	5,09892	6 90108
4	88	6,44625	7 55375
5	87	7,69176	8 30824
6	86	8,85313	9 14687
7	85	9,94253	10 05747
8	84	10,96886	11 03114
9	83	11,93890	12 06110
10	82	12,85798	13 14202
11	81	13,73040	14 26960
12	80	14,55970	15 44030
13	79	15,34885	16 65115
14	78	16,10035	17 89965
15	77	16,81635	17 18365
16	76	17,49872	18 50128
17	75	18,14908	19 85092
18	74	18,76887	19 23113
19	73	19,35935	20 64065
20	72	19,92164	20 07836
21	71	20,45676	21 54324
22	70	20,96559	21 03441
23	69	21,44896	22 55104
24	68	21,90760	22 09240
25	67	22,34217	23 65783
26	66	22,75327	23 24673
27	65	23,14145	24 85855
28	64	23,50721	24 49279
29	63	23,85099	24 14901
30	62	24,17321	25 82679
31	61	24,47424	25 52576
32	60	24,75442	25 24558
33	59	25,01406	26 98594
34	58	25,25343	26 74657
35	57	25,47279	26 52721
36	56	25,67236	26 32764
37	55	25,85235	26 14765
38	54	26,01293	27 98707
39	53	26,15426	27 84574
40	52	26,27647	27 72353
41	51	26,37969	27 62031
42	50	26,46401	27 53599
43	49	26,52951	27 47049
44	48	26,57626	27 42374
45	47	26,60429	27 39571
46	46	26,61363	27 38637

N = 93

Exponent of p (q)	q (p)	log C	log 1/C
0	93	0,00000	0 00000
1	92	1,96848	2 03152
2	91	3,63124	4 36876
3	90	5,11316	6 88684
4	89	6,46534	7 53466
5	88	7,71576	8 28424
6	87	8,88209	9 11791
7	86	9,97652	10 02348
8	85	11,00792	12 99208
9	84	11,98310	12 01690
10	83	12,90738	13 09262
11	82	13,78507	14 21493
12	81	14,61970	15 38030
13	80	15,41424	16 58576
14	79	16,17120	17 82880
15	78	16,89274	17 10726
16	77	17,58071	18 41929
17	76	18,23675	19 76325
18	75	18,86230	19 13770
19	74	19,45860	20 54140
20	73	20,02680	21 97320
21	72	20,56791	21 43209
22	71	21,08282	22 91718
23	70	21,57235	22 42765
24	69	22,03724	23 96276
25	68	22,47814	23 52186
26	67	22,89568	23 10432
27	66	23,29039	24 70961

N = 93 (continued)

Exponent of p (q)	q (p)	log C	log 1/C
28	65	23,66278	24 33722
29	64	24,01329	25 98671
30	63	24,34235	25 65765
31	62	24,65033	25 34967
32	61	24,93757	25 06243
33	60	25,20439	26 79561
34	59	25,45106	26 54894
35	58	25,67784	26 32216
36	57	25,88497	26 11503
37	56	26,07264	27 92736
38	55	26,24105	27 75895
39	54	26,39034	27 60966
40	53	26,52068	27 47932
41	52	26,63217	27 36783
42	51	26,72492	27 27508
43	50	26,79903	27 20097
44	49	26,85454	27 14546
45	48	26,89153	27 10847
46	47	26,91001	27 08999

N = 94

Exponent of p (q)	q (p)	log C	log 1/C
0	94	0,00000	0 00000
1	93	1,97313	2 02687
2	92	3,64058	4 35942
3	91	5,12725	6 87275
4	90	6,48423	7 51577
5	89	7,73950	8 26050
6	88	8,91074	9 08926
7	87	10,01012	11 98988
8	86	11,04655	12 95345
9	85	12,02681	13 97319
10	84	12,95623	13 04377
11	83	13,83912	14 16088
12	82	14,67901	15 32099
13	81	15,47888	16 52112
14	80	16,24124	17 75876
15	79	16,96824	17 03176
16	78	17,66175	18 33825
17	77	18,32339	19 67661
18	76	18,95461	19 04539
19	75	19,55667	20 44333
20	74	20,13070	21 86930
21	73	20,67771	21 32229
22	72	21,19861	22 80139
23	71	21,69422	22 30578
24	70	22,16527	23 83473
25	69	22,61242	23 38758
26	68	23,03630	24 96370
27	67	23,43744	24 56256
28	66	23,81636	24 18364
29	65	24,17351	25 82649
30	64	24,50930	25 49070
31	63	24,82412	25 17588
32	62	25,11831	26 88169
33	61	25,39219	26 60781
34	60	25,64604	26 35396
35	59	25,88012	26 11988
36	58	26,09467	27 90533
37	57	26,28990	27 71010
38	56	26,46599	27 53401
39	55	26,62311	27 37689
40	54	26,76141	27 23859
41	53	26,88102	27 11898
42	52	26,98205	27 01795
43	51	27,06458	28 93542
44	50	27,12870	28 87130
45	49	27,17446	28 82554
46	48	27,20190	28 79810
47	47	27,21104	28 78896

N = 95

Exponent of p (q)	q (p)	log C	log 1/C
0	95	0,00000	0 00000
1	94	1,97772	2 02228
2	93	3,64982	4 35018
3	92	5,14118	6 85882
4	91	6,50291	7 49709
5	90	7,76298	8 23702
6	89	8,93907	9 06093
7	88	10,04337	11 95663
8	87	11,08476	12 91524
9	86	12,07004	13 92996
10	85	13,00453	14 99547
11	84	13,89256	14 10744
12	83	14,73766	15 26234
13	82	15,54279	16 45721
14	81	16,31048	17 68952
15	80	17,04287	18 95713
16	79	17,74184	18 25816
17	78	18,40902	19 59098
18	77	19,04584	20 95416
19	76	19,65358	20 34642
20	75	20,23336	21 76664
21	74	20,78621	21 21379
22	73	21,31301	22 68699

N = 95 (continued)

Exponent of p (q)	q (p)	log C	log 1/C
23	72	21,81461	22 18539
24	71	22,29173	23 70827
25	70	22,74505	23 25495
26	69	23,17517	24 82483
27	68	23,58266	24 41734
28	67	23,96801	24 03199
29	66	24,33169	25 66831
30	65	24,67411	25 32589
31	64	24,99566	25 00434
32	63	25,29669	26 70331
33	62	25,57752	26 42248
34	61	25,83843	26 16157
35	60	26,07969	27 92031
36	59	26,30154	27 69846
37	58	26,50419	27 49581
38	57	26,68784	27 31216
39	56	26,85265	27 14735
40	55	26,99877	27 00123
41	54	27,12635	28 87365
42	53	27,23550	28 76450
43	52	27,32630	28 67370
44	51	27,39886	28 60114
45	50	27,45321	28 54679
46	49	27,48942	28 51058
47	48	27,50752	28 49248

N = 96

Exponent of p (q)	q (p)	log C	log 1/C
0	96	0,00000	0 00000
1	95	1,98227	2 01773
2	94	3,65896	4 34104
3	93	5,15497	6 84503
4	92	6,52139	7 47861
5	91	7,78621	8 21379
6	90	8,96710	9 03290
7	89	10,07625	11 92375
8	88	11,12255	12 87745
9	87	12,11279	13 88721
10	86	13,05231	14 94769
11	85	13,94541	14 05459
12	84	14,79565	15 20435
13	83	15,60599	16 39401
14	82	16,37894	17 62106
15	81	17,11666	18 88334
16	80	17,82102	18 17898
17	79	18,49366	19 50634
18	78	19,13602	20 86398
19	77	19,74936	20 25064
20	76	20,33482	21 66518
21	75	20,89342	21 10658
22	74	21,42605	22 57395
23	73	21,93356	22 06644
24	72	22,41667	23 58333
25	71	22,87606	23 12394
26	70	23,31235	24 68765
27	69	23,72608	24 27392
28	68	24,11777	25 88223
29	67	24,48788	25 51212
30	66	24,83684	25 16316
31	65	25,16502	26 83498
32	64	25,47278	26 52722
33	63	25,76045	26 23955
34	62	26,02831	27 97169
35	61	26,27663	27 72337
36	60	26,50566	27 49434
37	59	26,71561	27 28439
38	58	26,90668	27 09332
39	57	27,07904	28 92096
40	56	27,23286	28 76714
41	55	27,36826	28 63174
42	54	27,48537	28 51463
43	53	27,58430	28 41570
44	52	27,66512	28 33488
45	51	27,72791	28 27209
46	50	27,77273	28 22727
47	49	27,79960	28 20040
48	48	27,80855	28 19145

N = 97

Exponent of p (q)	q (p)	log C	log 1/C
0	97	0,00000	0 00000
1	96	1,98677	2 01323
2	95	3,66801	4 33199
3	94	5,16862	6 83138
4	93	6,53968	7 46032
5	92	7,80920	8 19080
6	91	8,99483	9 00517
7	90	10,10878	11 89122
8	89	11,15993	12 84007
9	88	12,15508	13 84492
10	87	13,09956	14 90044
11	86	13,99769	14 00231
12	85	14,85300	15 14700
13	84	15,66848	16 33152
14	83	16,44663	17 55337
15	82	17,18962	18 81038

* For explanation see page 81. –

All values conform to the international convention (i.e. 0,1 instead of 0.1).

Common Logarithms of the Binomial Coefficient C and Their Reciprocals* N=97–100

Exponent of p (q)	q (p)	log C	log 1/C
N = 97 (continued)			
16	81	17,89931	18 10069
17	80	18,57735	19 42265
18	79	19,22516	20 77484
19	78	19,84404	20 15596
20	77	20,43510	21 56490
21	76	20,99937	21 00063
22	75	21,53776	22 46224
23	74	22,05110	23 94890
24	73	22,54012	23 45988
25	72	23,00550	24 99450
26	71	23,44786	24 55214
27	70	23,86775	24 13225
28	69	24,26569	25 73431
29	68	24,64215	25 35785
30	67	24,99753	25 00247
31	66	25,33225	26 66775
32	65	25,64664	26 35336
33	64	25,94104	26 05896
34	63	26,21574	27 78426
35	62	26,47101	27 52899
36	61	26,70710	27 29290
37	60	26,92423	27 07577
38	59	27,12260	28 87740
39	58	27,30239	28 69761
40	57	27,46375	28 53625
41	56	27,60684	28 39316
42	55	27,73178	28 26822
43	54	27,83868	28 16132
44	53	27,92762	28 07238
45	52	27,99868	28 00132
46	51	28,05193	29 94807
47	50	28,08740	29 91260
48	49	28,10513	29 89487
N = 98			
0	98	0,00000	0 00000
1	97	1,99123	2 00877
2	96	3,67697	4 32303
3	95	5,18212	6 81788
4	94	6,55778	7 44222
5	93	7,83194	8 16806
6	92	9,02227	10 97773
7	91	10,14096	11 85904
8	90	11,19691	12 80309
9	89	12,19691	13 80309
10	88	13,14630	14 85370
11	87	14,04939	15 95061
12	86	14,90973	15 09027
13	85	15,73029	16 26971
14	84	16,51358	17 48642
15	83	17,26176	18 73824
16	82	17,97672	18 02328
17	81	18,66009	19 33991
18	80	19,31330	20 68670
19	79	19,93764	20 06236
20	78	20,53423	21 46577
21	77	21,10411	22 89589
22	76	21,64818	22 35182
23	75	22,16726	23 83274
24	74	22,66211	23 33789
25	73	23,13340	24 86660
26	72	23,58175	24 41825
27	71	24,00772	25 99228
28	70	24,41182	25 58818
29	69	24,79452	25 20548
30	68	25,15625	26 84375
31	67	25,49740	26 50260
32	66	25,81832	26 18168
33	65	26,11935	27 88065
34	64	26,40079	27 59921
35	63	26,66290	27 33710
36	62	26,90594	27 09406
37	61	27,13013	28 86987
38	60	27,33567	28 66433
39	59	27,52276	28 47724
40	58	27,69155	28 30845
41	57	27,84220	28 15780
42	56	27,97482	28 02518
43	55	28,08954	29 91046
44	54	28,18645	29 81355
45	53	28,26563	29 73437
46	52	28,32715	29 67285
47	51	28,37106	29 62894
48	50	28,39738	29 60262
49	49	28,40616	29 59384
N = 99			
0	99	0,00000	0 00000
1	98	1,99564	2 00436
2	97	3,68583	4 31417
3	96	5,19548	6 80452
4	95	6,57569	7 42431
5	94	7,85445	8 14555
6	93	9,04942	10 95058
N = 99 (continued)			
7	92	10,17281	11 82719
8	91	11,23351	12 76649
9	90	12,23830	13 76170
10	89	13,19255	14 80745
11	88	14,10054	15 89946
12	87	14,96585	15 03415
13	86	15,79142	16 20858
14	85	16,57979	17 42021
15	84	17,33312	18 66688
16	83	18,05328	19 94672
17	82	18,74191	19 25809
18	81	19,40045	20 59955
19	80	20,03018	21 96982
20	79	20,63224	21 36776
21	78	21,20765	22 79235
22	77	21,75732	22 24268
23	76	22,28208	23 71792
24	75	22,78269	23 21731
25	74	23,25981	24 74019
26	73	23,71407	24 28593
27	72	24,14602	25 85398
28	71	24,55620	25 44380
29	70	24,94506	25 05494
30	69	25,31304	26 68696
31	68	25,66052	26 33948
32	67	25,98788	26 01212
33	66	26,29544	27 70456
34	65	26,58351	27 41649
35	64	26,85235	27 14765
36	63	27,10223	28 89777
37	62	27,33337	28 66663
38	61	27,54598	28 45402
39	60	27,74024	28 25976
40	59	27,91633	28 08367
41	58	28,07440	29 92560
42	57	28,21458	29 78542
43	56	28,33699	29 66301
44	55	28,44172	29 55828
45	54	28,52887	29 47113
46	53	28,59851	29 40149
47	52	28,65069	29 34931
48	51	28,68545	29 31455
49	50	28,70282	29 29718
N = 100			
0	100	0,00000	0 00000
1	99	2,00000	3 00000
2	98	3,69461	4 30539
3	97	5,20871	6 79129
4	96	6,59342	7 40658
5	95	7,87672	8 12328
6	94	9,07630	10 92370
7	93	10,20433	11 79567
8	92	11,26972	12 73028
9	91	12,27926	13 72074
10	90	13,23830	14 76170
11	89	14,15115	15 84885
12	88	15,02136	16 97864
13	87	15,85190	16 14810
14	86	16,64529	17 35471
15	85	17,40370	18 59630
16	84	18,12900	19 87100
17	83	18,82283	19 17717
18	82	19,48664	20 51336
19	81	20,12170	21 87830
20	80	20,72915	21 27085
21	79	21,31002	22 68998
22	78	21,86523	22 13477
23	77	22,39559	23 60441
24	76	22,90187	23 09813
25	75	23,38475	24 61525
26	74	23,84483	24 15517
27	73	24,28270	25 71730
28	72	24,69887	25 30113
29	71	25,09380	26 90620
30	70	25,46794	26 53206
31	69	25,82167	26 17833
32	68	26,15537	27 84463
33	67	26,46937	27 53063
34	66	26,76396	27 23604
35	65	27,03944	28 96056
36	64	27,29605	28 70395
37	63	27,53403	28 46597
38	62	27,75359	28 24641
39	61	27,95491	28 04509
40	60	28,13818	29 86182
41	59	28,30355	29 69645
42	58	28,45115	29 54885
43	57	28,58111	29 41889
44	56	28,69354	29 30646
45	55	28,78851	29 21149
46	54	28,86612	29 13388
47	53	28,92641	29 07359
48	52	28,96945	29 03055
49	51	28,99525	29 00475
50	50	29,00385	30 99615

Explanation of the tables on pages 74–88

The **bold figures** in the tables are negative characteristics. The mantissae are all positive.

Binomial coefficient $C(N,x)=\binom{N}{x}=\dfrac{N!}{x!\,(N-x)!}$

For N between 2 and 100 use the tables on pages 74–81. For N between 100 and 1000 values of C can be calculated using the tables of factorials on pages 24 and 25.

Example:

$\log\binom{54}{6}=7{,}41208 \qquad C(54,6)=2{,}583\times 10^{7}$

$\log 1\Big/\binom{54}{6}=-8+0{,}58792 \qquad 1/C(54,6)=3{,}872\times 10^{-8}$

Calculation of individual probabilities $\mathrm{Prob}(x_1\,|\,N,N_1,X)$ **in the hypergeometric distribution**

Given are:

x_1	N_1-x_1	N_1
x_2	N_2-x_2	N_2
X	$N-X$	N

Required is: $\mathrm{Prob}(x_1\,|\,N,N_1,X)=\dfrac{N_1!\,N_2!\,X!\,(N-X)!}{x_1!\,(N_1-x_1)!\,x_2!\,(N_2-x_2)!\,N!}$

$=\dot P(x_1)=\binom{N_1}{x_1}\times\binom{N_2}{x_2}\times 1\Big/\binom{N}{X}$

Solution: $\log\dot P(x_1)=\underbrace{\log C(N_1,x_1)+\log C(N_2,x_2)+\log 1/C(N,X)}_{\text{from pages 74–81}}$

Example:

2	5	7
3	2	5
5	7	12

$\log C(7,2)=+1+0{,}32222$

$\log C(5,3)=+1+0{,}00000$

$\log 1/C(12,5)=-3+0{,}10127$

$\log\dot P(x_1)=-1+0{,}42349$

$\dot P(x_1)=0{,}2653$

Calculation of individual probabilities $\dot P(x)$ **in the binomial distribution**

Required is: $\dot P(x)=\binom{N}{x}p^{x}q^{N-x}$

Solution: $\log\dot P(x)=\underbrace{\log C(N,x)}_{\text{pages 74–81}}+\underbrace{\log p^{x}+\log q^{N-x}}_{\text{pages 82–88}}$

Example:

$N=32;\ p=0{,}06;\ x_1=2;\ x_2=30$

$\dot P_2$		$\dot P_{30}$	
$\log C(32,2)$	$=+2+0{,}69548$	$\log C(32,30)$	$=+\ 2+0{,}69548$
$\log p^{2}$	$=-3+0{,}55630$	$\log p^{30}$	$=-37+0{,}34454$
$\log q^{30}$	$=-1+0{,}19384$	$\log q^{2}$	$=-\ 1+0{,}94626$
$\log\dot P_2$	$=-2+1{,}44562$	$\log\dot P_{30}$	$=-36+1{,}98628$
	$=-1+0{,}44562$		$=-35+0{,}98628$
$\dot P_2$	$=0{,}2790$	$\dot P_{30}$	$=9{,}690\times 10^{-35}$

All values conform to the international convention (i.e. 0,1 instead of 0.1).

n	p (q) 0,01	q (p) 0,99	p (q) 0,02	q (p) 0,98	p (q) 0,03	q (p) 0,97	p (q) 0,04	q (p) 0,96	p (q) 0,05	q (p) 0,95	p (q) 0,06	q (p) 0,94	p (q) 0,07	q (p) 0,93
0	0 00000	0 00000	0 00000	0 00000	0 00000	0 00000	0 00000	0 00000	0 00000	0 00000	0 00000	0 00000	0 00000	0 00000
1	2 00000	1 99564	2 30103	1 99123	2 47712	1 98677	2 60206	1 98227	2 69897	1 97772	2 77815	1 97313	2 84510	1 96848
2	4 00000	1 99127	4 60206	1 98245	4 95424	1 97354	3 20412	1 96454	3 39794	1 95545	3 55630	1 94626	3 69020	1 93697
3	6 00000	1 98691	6 90309	1 97368	5 43136	1 96032	5 80618	1 94681	4 09691	1 93317	4 33445	1 91938	4 53529	1 90545
4	8 00000	1 98254	7 20412	1 96490	7 90849	1 94709	6 40824	1 92908	6 79588	1 91089	5 11261	1 89251	5 38039	1 87393
5	10 00000	1 97818	9 50515	1 95613	8 38561	1 93386	7 01030	1 91136	7 49485	1 88862	7 89076	1 86564	6 22549	1 84241
6	12 00000	1 97381	11 80618	1 94736	10 86273	1 92063	9 61236	1 89363	8 19382	1 86634	8 66891	1 83877	7 07059	1 81090
7	14 00000	1 96945	12 10721	1 93858	11 33985	1 90740	10 21442	1 87590	10 89279	1 84407	9 44706	1 81189	9 91569	1 77938
8	16 00000	1 96508	14 40824	1 92981	13 81697	1 89417	12 81648	1 85817	11 59176	1 82179	10 22521	1 78502	10 76078	1 74786
9	18 00000	1 96072	16 70927	1 92103	14 29409	1 88095	13 41854	1 84044	12 29073	1 79951	11 00336	1 75815	11 60588	1 71635
10	20 00000	1 95635	17 01030	1 91226	16 77121	1 86772	14 02060	1 82271	14 98970	1 77724	13 78151	1 73128	12 45098	1 68483
11	22 00000	1 95199	19 31133	1 90349	17 24833	1 85449	16 62266	1 80498	15 68867	1 75496	14 55966	1 70441	13 29608	1 65331
12	24 00000	1 94762	21 61236	1 89471	19 72546	1 84126	17 22472	1 78725	16 38764	1 73268	15 33782	1 67753	14 14118	1 62180
13	26 00000	1 94326	23 91339	1 88594	20 20258	1 82803	19 82678	1 76953	17 08661	1 71041	16 11597	1 65066	16 98627	1 59028
14	28 00000	1 93889	24 21442	1 87717	22 67970	1 81480	20 42884	1 75180	19 78558	1 68813	18 89412	1 62379	17 83137	1 55876
15	30 00000	1 93453	26 51545	1 86839	23 15682	1 80158	21 03090	1 73407	20 48455	1 66585	19 67227	1 59692	18 67647	1 52724
16	32 00000	1 93016	28 81648	1 85962	25 63394	1 78835	23 63296	1 71634	21 18352	1 64358	20 45042	1 57005	19 52157	1 49573
17	34 00000	1 92580	29 11751	1 85084	26 11106	1 77512	24 23502	1 69861	23 88249	1 62130	21 22857	1 54317	20 36667	1 46421
18	36 00000	1 92143	31 41854	1 84207	28 58818	1 76189	26 83708	1 68088	24 58146	1 59902	22 00672	1 51630	21 21176	1 43269
19	38 00000	1 91707	33 71957	1 83330	29 06530	1 74866	27 43914	1 66315	25 28043	1 57675	24 78487	1 48943	22 05686	1 40118
20	40 00000	1 91270	34 02060	1 82452	31 54243	1 73543	28 04120	1 64542	27 97940	1 55447	25 56303	1 46256	24 90196	1 36966
21	42 00000	1 90834	36 32163	1 81575	32 01955	1 72221	30 64326	1 62770	28 67837	1 53220	26 34118	1 43568	25 74706	1 33814
22	44 00000	1 90397	38 62266	1 80697	34 49667	1 70898	31 24532	1 60997	29 37734	1 50992	27 11933	1 40881	26 59216	1 30662
23	46 00000	1 89961	40 92369	1 79820	36 97379	1 69575	33 84738	1 59224	30 07631	1 48764	29 89748	1 38194	27 43725	1 27511
24	48 00000	1 89524	41 22472	1 78943	37 45091	1 68252	34 44944	1 57451	32 77528	1 46537	30 67563	1 35507	28 28235	1 24359
25	50 00000	1 89088	43 52575	1 78065	39 92803	1 66929	35 05150	1 55678	33 47425	1 44309	31 45378	1 32820	29 12745	1 21207
26	52 00000	1 88652	45 82678	1 77188	40 40515	1 65607	37 65356	1 53905	34 17322	1 42081	32 23193	1 30132	31 97255	1 18056
27	54 00000	1 88215	46 12781	1 76310	42 88227	1 64284	38 25562	1 52132	36 87219	1 39854	33 01008	1 27445	32 81765	1 14904
28	56 00000	1 87779	48 42884	1 75433	43 35940	1 62961	40 85768	1 50359	37 57116	1 37626	35 78824	1 24758	33 66275	1 11752
29	58 00000	1 87342	50 72987	1 74556	45 83652	1 61638	41 45974	1 48587	38 27013	1 35398	36 56639	1 22071	34 50784	1 08601
30	60 00000	1 86906	51 03090	1 73678	46 31364	1 60315	42 06180	1 46814	40 96910	1 33171	37 34454	1 19384	35 35294	1 05449
31	62 00000	1 86469	53 33193	1 72801	48 79076	1 58992	44 66386	1 45041	41 66807	1 30943	38 12269	1 16696	36 19804	1 02297
32	64 00000	1 86033	55 63296	1 71923	49 26788	1 57670	45 26592	1 43268	42 36704	1 28716	40 90084	1 14009	37 04314	2 99145
33	66 00000	1 85596	57 93399	1 71046	51 74500	1 56347	47 86798	1 41495	43 06601	1 26488	41 67899	1 11322	39 88824	2 95994
34	68 00000	1 85160	58 23502	1 70169	52 22212	1 55024	48 47004	1 39722	45 76498	1 24260	42 45714	1 08635	40 73333	2 92842
35	70 00000	1 84723	60 53605	1 69291	54 69924	1 53701	49 07210	1 37949	46 46395	1 22033	43 23529	1 05947	41 57843	2 89690
36	72 00000	1 84287	62 83708	1 68414	55 17637	1 52378	51 67416	1 36176	47 16292	1 19805	44 01345	1 03260	42 42353	2 86539
37	74 00000	1 83850	63 13811	1 67536	57 65349	1 51055	52 27622	1 34404	49 86189	1 17577	46 79160	1 00573	43 26863	2 83387
38	76 00000	1 83414	65 43914	1 66659	58 13061	1 49733	54 87828	1 32631	50 56086	1 15350	47 56975	2 97886	44 11373	2 80235
39	78 00000	1 82977	67 74017	1 65782	60 60773	1 48410	55 48034	1 30858	51 25983	1 13122	48 34790	2 95199	46 95882	2 77083
40	80 00000	1 82541	68 04120	1 64904	61 08485	1 47087	56 08240	1 29085	53 95880	1 10894	49 12605	2 92511	47 80392	2 73932
41	82 00000	1 82104	70 34223	1 64027	63 56197	1 45764	58 68446	1 27312	54 65777	1 08667	51 90420	2 89824	48 64902	2 70780
42	84 00000	1 81668	72 64326	1 63150	64 03909	1 44441	59 28652	1 25539	55 35674	1 06439	52 68235	2 87137	49 49412	2 67628
43	86 00000	1 81231	74 94429	1 62272	66 51621	1 43118	61 88858	1 23766	56 05571	1 04212	53 46050	2 84450	50 33922	2 64477
44	88 00000	1 80795	75 24532	1 61395	68 99334	1 41796	62 49064	1 21993	58 75468	1 01984	54 23866	2 81763	51 18431	2 61325
45	90 00000	1 80358	77 54635	1 60517	69 47046	1 40473	63 09270	1 20221	59 45365	2 99756	55 01681	2 79075	52 02941	2 58173
46	92 00000	1 79922	79 84738	1 59640	71 94758	1 39150	65 69476	1 18448	60 15262	2 97529	57 79496	2 76388	54 87451	2 55022
47	94 00000	1 79485	80 14841	1 58763	72 42470	1 37827	66 29682	1 16675	62 85159	2 95301	58 57311	2 73701	55 71961	2 51870
48	96 00000	1 79049	82 44944	1 57885	74 90182	1 36504	68 89888	1 14902	63 55056	2 93073	59 35126	2 71014	56 56471	2 48718
49	98 00000	1 78612	84 75047	1 57008	75 37894	1 35181	69 50094	1 13129	64 24953	2 90846	60 12941	2 68326	57 40980	2 45566
50	100 00000	1 78176	85 05150	1 56130	77 85606	1 33859	70 10300	1 11356	66 94850	2 88618	62 90756	2 65639	58 25490	2 42415
51	102 00000	1 77739	87 35253	1 55253	78 33318	1 32536	72 70506	1 09583	67 64747	2 86390	63 68571	2 62952	59 10000	2 39263
52	104 00000	1 77303	89 65356	1 54376	80 81031	1 31213	73 30712	1 07810	68 34644	2 84163	64 46387	2 60265	61 94510	2 36111
53	106 00000	1 76867	91 95459	1 53498	81 28743	1 29890	75 90918	1 06038	69 04541	2 81935	65 24202	2 57578	62 79020	2 32960
54	108 00000	1 76430	92 25562	1 52621	83 76455	1 28567	76 51124	1 04265	71 74438	2 79707	66 02017	2 54890	63 63529	2 29808
55	110 00000	1 75994	94 55665	1 51743	84 24167	1 27245	77 11330	1 02492	72 44335	2 77480	68 79832	2 52203	64 48039	2 26656
56	112 00000	1 75557	96 85768	1 50866	86 71879	1 25922	79 71536	1 00719	73 14232	2 75252	69 57647	2 49516	65 32549	2 23505
57	114 00000	1 75121	97 15871	1 49989	87 19591	1 24599	80 31742	2 98946	75 84129	2 73025	70 35462	2 46829	66 17059	2 20353
58	116 00000	1 74684	99 45974	1 49111	89 67303	1 23276	82 91948	2 97173	76 54026	2 70797	71 13277	2 44142	67 01569	2 17201
59	118 00000	1 74248	101 76077	1 48234	90 15015	1 21953	83 52154	2 95400	77 23923	2 68569	73 91092	2 41454	69 86078	2 14049
60	120 00000	1 73811	102 06180	1 47356	92 62728	1 20630	84 12360	2 93627	79 93820	2 66342	74 68908	2 38767	70 70588	2 10898
61	122 00000	1 73375	104 36283	1 46479	93 10440	1 19308	86 72566	2 91855	80 63717	2 64114	75 46723	2 36080	71 55098	2 07746
62	124 00000	1 72938	106 66386	1 45602	95 58152	1 17985	87 32772	2 90082	81 33614	2 61886	76 24538	2 33393	72 39608	2 04594
63	126 00000	1 72502	108 96489	1 44724	96 05864	1 16662	89 92978	2 88309	82 03511	2 59659	77 02353	2 30705	73 24118	2 01443
64	128 00000	1 72065	109 26592	1 43847	98 53576	1 15339	90 53184	2 86536	84 73408	2 57431	79 80168	2 28018	74 08627	3 98291
65	130 00000	1 71629	111 56695	1 42969	99 01288	1 14016	91 13390	2 84763	85 43305	2 55203	80 57983	2 25331	76 93137	3 95139
66	132 00000	1 71192	113 86798	1 42092	101 49000	1 12693	93 73596	2 82990	86 13202	2 52976	81 35798	2 22644	77 77647	3 91987
67	134 00000	1 70756	114 16901	1 41215	103 96712	1 11371	94 33802	2 81217	88 83099	2 50748	82 13613	2 19957	78 62157	3 88836
68	136 00000	1 70319	116 47004	1 40337	104 44425	1 10048	96 94008	2 79444	89 52996	2 48521	84 91429	2 17269	79 46667	3 85684
69	138 00000	1 69883	118 77107	1 39460	106 92137	1 08725	97 54214	2 77672	90 22893	2 46293	85 69244	2 14582	80 31176	3 82532
70	140 00000	1 69446	119 07210	1 38583	107 39849	1 07402	98 14420	2 75899	92 92790	2 44065	86 47059	2 11895	81 15686	3 79381
71	142 00000	1 69010	121 37313	1 37705	109 87561	1 06079	100 74626	2 74126	93 62687	2 41838	87 24874	2 09208	82 00196	3 76229
72	144 00000	1 68573	123 67416	1 36828	110 35273	1 04756	101 34832	2 72353	94 32584	2 39610	88 02689	2 06521	84 84706	3 73077
73	146 00000	1 68137	125 97519	1 35950	112 82985	1 03434	103 95038	2 70580	95 02481	2 37382	90 80504	2 03833	85 69216	3 69926
74	148 00000	1 67700	126 27622	1 35073	113 30697	1 02111	104 55244	2 68807	97 72378	2 35155	91 58319	2 01146	86 53725	3 66774
75	150 00000	1 67264	128 57725	1 34196	115 78409	1 00788	105 15450	2 67034	98 42275	2 32927	92 36134	3 98459	87 38235	3 63622
76	152 00000	1 66827	130 87828	1 33318	116 26122	2 99465	107 75656	2 65261	99 12172	2 30699	93 13950	3 95772	88 22745	3 60470
77	154 00000	1 66391	131 17931	1 32441	118 73834	2 98142	108 35862	2 63488	101 82069	2 28472	95 91765	3 93084	89 07255	3 57319
78	156 00000	1 65955	133 48034	1 31563	119 21546	2 96820	110 96068	2 61716	102 51966	2 26244	96 69580	3 90397	91 91765	3 54167
79	158 00000	1 65518	135 78137	1 30686	121 69258	2 95497	111 56274	2 59943	103 21863	2 24016	97 47395	3 87710	92 76275	3 51015
80	160 00000	1 65082	136 08240	1 29809	122 16970	2 94174	112 16480	2 58170	105 91760	2 21789	98 25210	3 85023	93 60784	3 47864
81	162 00000	1 64645	138 38343	1 28931	124 64682	2 92851	114 76686	2 56397	106 61657	2 19561	99 03025	3 82336	94 45294	3 44712
82	164 00000	1 64209	140 68446	1 28054	125 12394	2 91528	115 36892	2 54624	107 31554	2 17334	101 80840	3 79648	95 29804	3 41560
83	166 00000	1 63772	142 98549	1 27176	127 60106	2 90205	117 97098	2 52851	108 01451	2 15106	102 58655	3 76961	96 14314	3 38408
84	168 00000	1 63336	143 28652	1 26299	128 07819	2 88883	118 57304	2 51078	110 71348	2 12878	103 36471	3 74274	98 98824	3 35257
85	170 00000	1 62899	145 58755	1 25422	130 55531	2 87560	119 17510	2 49305	111 41245	2 10651	104 14286	3 71587	99 83333	3 32105
86	172 00000	1 62463	147 88858	1 24544	131 03243	2 86237	121 77716	2 47533	112 11142	2 08423	106 92101	3 68900	100 67843	3 28953
87	174 00000	1 62026	148 18961	1 23667	133 50955	2 84914	122 37922	2 45760	114 81039	2 06195	107 69916	3 66212	101 52353	3 25802
88	176 00000	1 61590	150 49064	1 22789	135 98667	2 83591	124 98128	2 43987	115 50936	2 03968	108 47731	3 63525	102 36863	3 22650
89	178 00000	1 61153	152 79167	1 21912	136 46379	2 82268	125 58334	2 42214	116 20833	2 01740	109 25546	3 60838	103 21373	3 19498
90	180 00000	1 60717	153 09270	1 21035	138 94091	2 80946	126 18540	2 40441	118 90730	3 99512	110 03361	3 58151	104 05882	3 16347
91	182 00000	1 60280	155 39373	1 20157	139 41803	2 79623	128 78746	2 38668	119 60627	3 97285	112 81176	3 55463	106 90392	3 13195
92	184 00000	1 59844	157 69476	1 19280	141 89516	2 78300	129 38952	2 36895	120 30524	3 95057	113 58992	3 52776	107 74902	3 10043
93	186 00000	1 59407	159 99579	1 18403	142 37228	2 76977	131 99158	2 35122	121 00421	3 92830	114 36807	3 50089	108 59412	3 06891
94	188 00000	1 58971	160 29682	1 17525	144 84940	2 75654	132 59364	2 33350	123 70318	3 90602	115 14622	3 47402	109 43922	3 03740
95	190 00000	1 58534	162 59785	1 16648	145 32652	2 74331	133 19570	2 31577	124 40215	3 88374	117 92437	3 44715	110 28431	3 00588
96	192 00000	1 58098	164 89888	1 15770	147 80364	2 73009	135 79776	2 29804	125 10112	3 86147	118 70252	3 42027	111 12941	4 97436
97	194 00000	1 57661	165 19991	1 14893	148 28076	2 71686	136 39982	2 28031	127 80009	3 83919	119 48067	3 39340	113 97451	4 94285
98	196 00000	1 57225	167 50094	1 14016	150 75788	2 70363	137 00188	2 26258	128 49906	3 81691	120 25882	3 36653	114 81961	4 91133
99	198 00000	1 56788	169 80197	1 13138	151 23500	2 69040	139 60394	2 24485	129 19803	3 79464	121 03697	3 33966	115 66471	4 87981
100	200 00000	1 56352	170 10300	1 12261	153 71213	2 67717	140 20600	2 22712	131 89700	3 77236	123 81513	3 31279	116 50980	4 84829

* For explanation see page 81. – Reproduction only by permission of the publishers of the *Geigy Scientific Tables.*

All values conform to the international convention (i.e. 0,1 instead of 0.1).

Common Logarithms* of p^n and q^n $q=1-p$

n	p (q) 0,08	q (p) 0,92	p (q) 0,09	q (p) 0,91	p (q) 0,10	q (p) 0,90	p (q) 0,11	q (p) 0,89	p (q) 0,12	q (p) 0,88	p (q) 0,13	q (p) 0,87	p (q) 0,14	q (p) 0,86
0	0 00000	0 00000	0 00000	0 00000	0 00000	0 00000	0 00000	0 00000	0 00000	0 00000	0 00000	0 00000	0 00000	0 00000
1	2 90309	1 96379	2 95424	1 95904	1 00000	1 95424	1 04139	1 94939	1 07918	1 94448	1 11394	1 93952	1 14613	1 93450
2	3 80618	1 92758	3 90849	1 91808	2 00000	1 90849	2 08279	1 89878	2 15836	1 88897	2 22789	1 87904	2 29226	1 86900
3	4 70927	1 89136	4 86273	1 87712	3 00000	1 86273	3 12418	1 84817	3 23754	1 83345	3 34183	1 81856	3 43838	1 80350
4	5 61236	1 85515	5 81697	1 83617	4 00000	1 81697	4 16557	1 79756	4 31672	1 77793	4 45577	1 75808	4 58451	1 73799
5	6 51545	1 81894	6 77121	1 79521	5 00000	1 77121	5 20696	1 74695	5 39591	1 72241	5 56972	1 69760	5 73064	1 67249
6	7 41854	1 78273	7 72546	1 75425	6 00000	1 72546	6 24836	1 69634	6 47509	1 66690	6 68366	1 63712	6 87677	1 60699
7	8 32163	1 74651	8 67970	1 71329	7 00000	1 67970	7 28975	1 64573	7 55427	1 61138	7 79760	1 57663	6 02290	1 54149
8	9 22472	1 71030	9 63394	1 67233	8 00000	1 63394	8 33114	1 59512	8 63345	1 55586	8 91155	1 51615	7 16902	1 47599
9	10 12781	1 67409	10 58818	1 63137	9 00000	1 58818	9 37253	1 54451	9 71263	1 50034	8 02549	1 45567	8 31515	1 41049
10	11 03090	1 63788	11 54243	1 59041	10 00000	1 54243	10 41393	1 49390	10 79181	1 44483	9 13943	1 39519	9 46128	1 34498
11	13 93399	1 60167	12 49667	1 54946	11 00000	1 49667	11 45532	1 44329	11 87099	1 38931	10 25338	1 33471	10 60741	1 27948
12	14 83708	1 56545	13 45091	1 50850	12 00000	1 45091	12 49671	1 39268	12 95017	1 33379	11 36732	1 27423	11 75354	1 21398
13	15 74017	1 52924	14 40515	1 46754	13 00000	1 40515	13 53810	1 34207	12 02936	1 27827	12 48126	1 21375	12 89966	1 14848
14	16 64326	1 49303	15 35940	1 42658	14 00000	1 35940	14 57950	1 29146	13 10854	1 22276	13 59521	1 15327	12 04579	1 08298
15	17 54635	1 45682	16 31364	1 38562	15 00000	1 31364	15 62089	1 24085	14 18772	1 16724	14 70915	1 09279	13 19192	1 01748
16	18 44944	1 42061	17 26788	1 34466	16 00000	1 26788	16 66228	1 19024	15 26690	1 11172	15 82309	1 03231	14 33805	2 95198
17	19 35253	1 38439	18 22212	1 30370	17 00000	1 22212	17 70368	1 13963	16 34608	1 05621	16 93704	2 97183	15 48418	2 88647
18	20 25562	1 34818	19 17637	1 26275	18 00000	1 17637	18 74507	1 08902	17 42526	1 00069	16 05098	2 91135	16 63030	2 82097
19	21 15871	1 31197	20 13061	1 22179	19 00000	1 13061	19 78646	1 03841	18 50444	2 94517	17 16492	2 85087	17 77643	2 75547
20	22 06180	1 27576	21 08485	1 18083	20 00000	1 08485	20 82785	2 98780	19 58362	2 88965	18 27887	2 79039	18 92256	2 68997
21	24 96489	1 23954	22 03909	1 13987	21 00000	1 03909	21 86925	2 93719	20 66281	2 83414	19 39281	2 72990	18 06869	2 62447
22	25 86798	1 20333	24 99334	1 09891	22 00000	2 99334	22 91064	2 88658	21 74199	2 77862	20 50675	2 66942	19 21482	2 55897
23	26 77107	1 16712	25 94758	1 05795	23 00000	2 94758	23 95203	2 83597	22 82117	2 72310	21 62070	2 60894	20 36094	2 49346
24	27 67416	1 13091	26 90182	1 01699	24 00000	2 90182	24 99342	2 78536	23 90035	2 66758	22 73464	2 54846	21 50707	2 42796
25	28 57725	1 09470	27 85606	2 97603	25 00000	2 85606	24 03482	2 73475	24 97953	2 61207	23 84858	2 48798	22 65320	2 36246
26	29 48034	1 05848	28 81031	2 93508	26 00000	2 81031	25 07621	2 68414	24 05871	2 55655	24 96253	2 42750	23 79933	2 29696
27	30 38343	1 02227	29 76455	2 89412	27 00000	2 76455	26 11760	2 63353	25 13789	2 50103	24 07647	2 36702	24 94546	2 23146
28	31 28652	2 98606	30 71879	2 85316	28 00000	2 71879	27 15900	2 58292	26 21707	2 44551	25 19041	2 30654	24 09159	2 16596
29	32 18961	2 94985	31 67303	2 81220	29 00000	2 67303	28 20039	2 53231	27 29626	2 39000	26 30436	2 24606	25 23771	2 10046
30	33 09270	2 91363	32 62728	2 77124	30 00000	2 62728	29 24178	2 48170	28 37544	2 33448	27 41830	2 18558	26 38384	2 03495
31	35 99579	2 87742	33 58152	2 73028	31 00000	2 58152	30 28317	2 43109	29 45462	2 27896	28 53224	2 12510	27 52997	3 96945
32	36 89888	2 84121	34 53576	2 68932	32 00000	2 53576	31 32457	2 38048	30 53380	2 22345	29 64619	2 06462	28 67610	3 90395
33	37 80197	2 80500	35 49000	2 64837	33 00000	2 49000	32 36596	2 32987	31 61298	2 16793	30 76013	2 00414	29 82223	3 83845
34	38 70506	2 76879	36 44425	2 60741	34 00000	2 44425	33 40735	2 27926	32 69216	2 11241	31 87407	3 94365	30 96835	3 77295
35	39 60815	2 73257	37 39849	2 56645	35 00000	2 39849	34 44874	2 22865	33 77134	2 05689	32 98802	3 88317	30 11448	3 70745
36	40 51124	2 69636	38 35273	2 52549	36 00000	2 35273	35 49014	2 17804	34 85052	2 00138	32 10196	3 82269	31 26061	3 64194
37	41 41433	2 66015	39 30697	2 48453	37 00000	2 30697	36 53153	2 12743	35 92971	3 94586	33 21590	3 76221	32 40674	3 57644
38	42 31742	2 62394	40 26122	2 44357	38 00000	2 26122	37 57292	2 07682	35 00889	3 89034	34 32985	3 70173	33 55287	3 51094
39	43 22051	2 58773	41 21546	2 40261	39 00000	2 21546	38 61431	2 02621	36 08807	3 83482	35 44379	3 64125	34 69899	3 44544
40	44 12360	2 55151	42 16970	2 36166	40 00000	2 16970	39 65571	3 97560	37 16725	3 77931	36 55773	3 58077	35 84512	3 37994
41	45 02669	2 51530	43 12394	2 32070	41 00000	2 12394	40 69710	3 92499	38 24643	3 72379	37 67168	3 52029	36 99125	3 31444
42	47 92978	2 47909	44 07819	2 27974	42 00000	2 07819	41 73849	3 87438	39 32561	3 66827	38 78562	3 45981	36 13738	3 24893
43	48 83287	2 44288	45 03243	2 23878	43 00000	2 03243	42 77989	3 82377	40 40479	3 61275	39 89956	3 39933	37 28351	3 18343
44	49 73596	2 40666	47 98667	2 19782	44 00000	3 98667	43 82128	3 77316	41 48397	3 55724	39 01351	3 33885	38 42963	3 11793
45	50 63905	2 37045	48 94091	2 15686	45 00000	3 94091	44 86267	3 72255	42 56316	3 50172	40 12745	3 27837	39 57576	3 05243
46	51 54214	2 33424	49 89516	2 11590	46 00000	3 89516	45 90406	3 67194	43 64234	3 44620	41 24139	3 21789	40 72189	4 98693
47	52 44523	2 29803	50 84940	2 07495	47 00000	3 84940	46 94546	3 62133	44 72152	3 39069	42 35534	3 15740	41 86802	4 92143
48	53 34832	2 26182	51 80364	2 03399	48 00000	3 80364	47 98685	3 57072	45 80070	3 33517	43 46928	3 09692	41 01415	4 85593
49	54 25141	2 22560	52 75788	3 99303	49 00000	3 75788	47 02824	3 52011	46 87988	3 27965	44 58322	3 03644	42 16027	4 79042
50	55 15450	2 18939	53 71213	3 95207	50 00000	3 71213	48 06963	3 46950	47 95906	3 22413	45 69717	4 97596	43 30640	4 72492
51	56 05759	2 15318	54 66637	3 91111	51 00000	3 66637	49 11103	3 41889	47 03824	3 16862	46 81111	4 91548	44 45253	4 65942
52	58 96068	2 11697	55 62061	3 87015	52 00000	3 62061	50 15242	3 36828	48 11742	3 11310	47 92505	4 85500	45 59866	4 59392
53	59 86377	2 08075	56 57485	3 82919	53 00000	3 57485	51 19381	3 31767	49 19661	3 05758	47 03900	4 79452	46 74479	4 52842
54	60 76686	2 04454	57 52910	3 78824	54 00000	3 52910	52 23521	3 26706	50 27579	3 00206	48 15294	4 73404	47 89091	4 46292
55	61 66995	2 00833	58 48334	3 74728	55 00000	3 48334	53 27660	3 21645	51 35497	4 94655	49 26688	4 67356	47 03704	4 39741
56	62 57304	3 97212	59 43758	3 70632	56 00000	3 43758	54 31799	3 16584	52 43415	4 89103	50 38083	4 61308	48 18317	4 33191
57	63 47613	3 93591	60 39182	3 66536	57 00000	3 39182	55 35938	3 11523	53 51333	4 83551	51 49477	4 55260	49 32930	4 26641
58	64 37922	3 89969	61 34607	3 62440	58 00000	3 34607	56 40078	3 06462	54 59251	4 77999	52 60871	4 49212	50 47543	4 20091
59	65 28231	3 86348	62 30031	3 58344	59 00000	3 30031	57 44217	3 01401	55 67169	4 72448	53 72266	4 43164	51 62155	4 13541
60	66 18540	3 82727	63 25455	3 54248	60 00000	3 25455	58 48356	4 96340	56 75087	4 66896	54 83660	4 37116	52 76768	4 06991
61	67 08849	3 79106	64 20879	3 50152	61 00000	3 20879	59 52495	4 91279	57 83006	4 61344	55 95054	4 31067	53 91381	4 00441
62	69 99158	3 75485	65 16304	3 46057	62 00000	3 16304	60 56635	4 86218	58 90924	4 55793	55 06449	4 25019	53 05994	5 93890
63	70 89467	3 71863	66 11728	3 41961	63 00000	3 11728	61 60774	4 81157	59 98842	4 50241	56 17843	4 18971	54 20607	5 87340
64	71 79776	3 68242	67 07152	3 37865	64 00000	3 07152	62 64913	4 76096	59 06760	4 44689	57 29237	4 12923	55 35219	5 80790
65	72 70085	3 64621	68 02576	3 33769	65 00000	3 02576	63 69052	4 71035	60 14678	4 39137	58 40632	4 06875	56 49832	5 74240
66	73 60394	3 61000	70 98001	3 29673	66 00000	4 98001	64 73192	4 65974	61 22596	4 33586	59 52026	4 00827	57 64445	5 67690
67	74 50703	3 57378	71 93425	3 25577	67 00000	4 93425	65 77331	4 60913	62 30514	4 28034	60 63420	5 94779	58 79058	5 61140
68	75 41012	3 53757	72 88849	3 21481	68 00000	4 88849	66 81470	4 55852	63 38432	4 22482	61 74815	5 88731	59 93671	5 54589
69	76 31321	3 50136	73 84273	3 17386	69 00000	4 84273	67 85610	4 50791	64 46351	4 16930	62 86209	5 82683	59 08283	5 48039
70	77 21630	3 46515	74 79698	3 13290	70 00000	4 79698	68 89749	4 45730	65 54269	4 11379	63 97603	5 76635	60 22896	5 41489
71	78 11939	3 42894	75 75122	3 09194	71 00000	4 75122	69 93888	4 40669	66 62187	4 05827	63 08998	5 70587	61 37509	5 34939
72	79 02248	3 39272	76 70546	3 05098	72 00000	4 70546	70 98027	4 35608	67 70105	4 00275	64 20392	5 64539	62 52122	5 28389
73	81 92557	3 35651	77 65970	3 01002	73 00000	4 65970	70 02167	4 30547	68 78023	5 94724	65 31786	5 58491	63 66735	5 21839
74	82 82866	3 32030	78 61395	4 96906	74 00000	4 61395	71 06306	4 25486	69 85941	5 89172	66 43181	5 52442	64 81347	5 15289
75	83 73175	3 28409	79 56819	4 92810	75 00000	4 56819	72 10445	4 20425	70 93859	5 83620	67 54575	5 46394	65 95960	5 08738
76	84 63484	3 24787	80 52243	4 88715	76 00000	4 52243	73 14584	4 15364	70 01777	5 78068	68 65969	5 40346	65 10573	5 02188
77	85 53793	3 21166	81 47667	4 84619	77 00000	4 47667	74 18724	4 10303	71 09696	5 72517	69 77364	5 34298	66 25186	6 95638
78	86 44102	3 17545	82 43092	4 80523	78 00000	4 43092	75 22863	4 05242	72 17614	5 66965	70 88758	5 28250	67 39799	6 89088
79	87 34411	3 13924	83 38516	4 76427	79 00000	4 38516	76 27002	4 00181	73 25532	5 61413	70 00152	5 22202	68 54411	6 82538
80	88 24720	3 10303	84 33940	4 72331	80 00000	4 33940	77 31141	5 95120	74 33450	5 55861	71 11547	5 16154	69 69024	6 75988
81	89 15029	3 06681	85 29364	4 68235	81 00000	4 29364	78 35281	5 90059	75 41368	5 50310	72 22941	5 10106	70 83637	6 69437
82	90 05338	3 03060	86 24789	4 64139	82 00000	4 24789	79 39420	5 84998	76 49286	5 44758	73 34335	5 04058	71 98250	6 62887
83	92 95647	4 99439	87 20213	4 60044	83 00000	4 20213	80 43559	5 79937	77 57204	5 39206	74 45730	6 98010	71 12863	6 56337
84	93 85956	4 95818	88 15637	4 55948	84 00000	4 15637	81 47699	5 74876	78 65122	5 33654	75 57124	6 91962	72 27476	6 49787
85	94 76265	4 92197	89 11061	4 51852	85 00000	4 11061	82 51838	5 69815	79 73041	5 28103	76 68518	6 85914	73 42088	6 43237
86	95 66574	4 88575	90 06486	4 47756	86 00000	4 06486	83 55977	5 64754	80 80959	5 22551	77 79913	6 79866	74 56701	6 36687
87	96 56883	4 84954	91 01910	4 43660	87 00000	4 01910	84 60116	5 59693	81 88877	5 16999	78 91307	6 73817	75 71314	6 30137
88	97 47192	4 81333	93 97334	4 39564	88 00000	5 97334	85 64256	5 54632	82 96795	5 11448	78 02702	6 67769	76 85927	6 23586
89	98 37501	4 77712	94 92758	4 35468	89 00000	5 92758	86 68395	5 49571	82 04713	5 05896	79 14096	6 61721	76 00540	6 17036
90	99 27810	4 74090	95 88183	4 31373	90 00000	5 88183	87 72534	5 44510	83 12631	5 00344	80 25490	6 55673	77 15152	6 10486
91	100 18119	4 70469	96 83607	4 27277	91 00000	5 83607	88 76673	5 39449	84 20549	6 94792	81 36885	6 49625	78 29765	6 03936
92	101 08428	4 66848	97 79031	4 23181	92 00000	5 79031	89 80813	5 34388	85 28467	6 89241	82 48279	6 43577	79 44378	7 97386
93	103 98737	4 63227	98 74455	4 19085	93 00000	5 74455	90 84952	5 29327	86 36386	6 83689	83 59673	6 37529	80 58991	7 90836
94	104 89046	4 59606	99 69880	4 14989	94 00000	5 69880	91 89091	5 24266	87 44304	6 78137	84 71068	6 31481	81 73604	7 84285
95	105 79355	4 55984	100 65304	4 10893	95 00000	5 65304	92 93231	5 19205	88 52222	6 72585	85 82462	6 25433	82 88216	7 77735
96	106 69664	4 52363	101 60728	4 06797	96 00000	5 60728	93 97370	5 14144	89 60140	6 67034	86 93856	6 19385	82 02829	7 71185
97	107 59973	4 48742	102 56152	4 02702	97 00000	5 56152	93 01509	5 09083	90 68058	6 61482	86 05251	6 13337	83 17442	7 64635
98	108 50282	4 45121	103 51577	5 98606	98 00000	5 51577	94 05648	5 04022	91 75976	6 55930	87 16645	6 07289	84 32055	7 58085
99	109 40591	4 41499	104 47001	5 94510	99 00000	5 47001	95 09788	6 98961	92 83894	6 50378	88 28039	6 01241	85 46668	7 51535
100	110 30900	4 37878	105 42425	5 90414	100 00000	5 42425	96 13927	6 93900	93 91812	6 44827	89 39434	7 95193	86 61280	7 44985

* For explanation see page 81. –

All values conform to the international convention (i.e. 0,1 instead of 0.1).

n	p (q) 0,15	q (p) 0,85	p (q) 0,16	q (p) 0,84	p (q) 0,17	q (p) 0,83	p (q) 0,18	q (p) 0,82	p (q) 0,19	q (p) 0,81	p (q) 0,20	q (p) 0,80	p (q) 0,21	q (p) 0,79
0	0 00000	0 00000	0 00000	0 00000	0 00000	0 00000	0 00000	0 00000	0 00000	0 00000	0 00000	0 00000	0 00000	0 00000
1	1 17609	1 92942	1 20412	1 92428	1 23045	1 91908	1 25527	1 91381	1 27875	1 90849	1 30103	1 90309	1 32222	1 89763
2	2 35218	1 85884	2 40824	1 84856	2 46090	1 83816	2 51055	1 82763	2 55751	1 81697	2 60206	1 80618	2 64444	1 79525
3	3 52827	1 78826	3 61236	1 77284	3 69135	1 75723	3 76582	1 74144	3 83626	1 72546	3 90309	1 70927	3 96666	1 69288
4	4 70437	1 71768	4 81648	1 69712	4 92180	1 67631	3 02109	1 65526	3 11501	1 63394	3 20412	1 61236	3 28888	1 59051
5	5 88046	1 64709	4 02060	1 62140	4 15224	1 59539	4 27636	1 56907	4 39377	1 54243	4 50515	1 51545	4 61110	1 48814
6	5 05655	1 57651	5 22472	1 54568	5 38269	1 51447	5 53164	1 48288	5 67252	1 45091	5 80618	1 41854	5 93332	1 38576
7	6 23264	1 50593	6 42884	1 46996	6 61314	1 43355	6 78691	1 39670	6 95128	1 35940	5 10721	1 32163	5 25554	1 28339
8	7 40873	1 43535	7 63296	1 39423	7 84359	1 35262	6 04218	1 31051	6 23003	1 26788	6 40824	1 22472	6 57775	1 18102
9	8 58482	1 36477	8 83708	1 31851	7 07404	1 27170	7 29745	1 22432	7 50878	1 17637	7 70927	1 12781	7 89997	1 07864
10	9 76091	1 29419	8 04120	1 24279	8 30449	1 19078	8 55273	1 13814	8 78754	1 08485	7 01030	1 03090	7 22219	2 97627
11	10 93700	1 22361	9 24532	1 16707	9 53494	1 10986	9 80800	1 05195	8 06629	2 99334	8 31133	2 93399	8 54441	2 87390
12	10 11310	1 15303	10 44944	1 09135	10 76539	1 02894	9 06327	2 96577	9 34504	2 90182	9 61236	2 83708	9 86663	2 77153
13	11 28919	1 08245	11 65356	1 01563	11 99584	2 94802	10 31854	2 87958	10 62380	2 81031	10 91339	2 74017	9 18885	2 66915
14	12 46528	1 01186	12 85768	2 93991	11 22628	2 86709	11 57382	2 79339	11 90255	2 71879	10 21442	2 64326	10 51107	2 56678
15	13 64137	2 94128	12 06180	2 86419	12 45673	2 78617	12 82909	2 70721	11 18130	2 62728	11 51545	2 54635	11 83329	2 46441
16	14 81746	2 87070	13 26592	2 78847	13 68718	2 70525	12 08436	2 62102	12 46006	2 53576	12 81648	2 44944	11 15551	2 36203
17	15 99355	2 80012	14 47004	2 71275	14 91763	2 62433	13 33963	2 53484	13 73881	2 44425	12 11751	2 35253	12 47773	2 25966
18	15 16964	2 72954	15 67416	2 63703	14 14808	2 54341	14 59491	2 44865	13 01756	2 35273	13 41854	2 25562	13 79995	2 15729
19	16 34573	2 65896	16 87828	2 56131	15 37853	2 46248	15 85018	2 36246	14 29632	2 26122	14 71957	2 15871	13 12217	2 05491
20	17 52183	2 58838	16 08240	2 48559	16 60898	2 38156	15 10545	2 27628	15 57507	2 16970	14 02060	2 06180	14 44439	3 95254
21	18 69792	2 51780	17 28652	2 40987	17 83943	2 30064	16 36072	2 19009	16 85383	2 07819	15 32163	3 96489	15 76661	3 85017
22	19 87401	2 44722	18 49064	2 33414	17 06988	2 21972	17 61600	2 10390	16 13258	3 98667	16 62266	3 86798	15 08882	3 74780
23	19 05010	2 37664	19 69476	2 25842	18 30033	2 13880	18 87127	2 01772	17 41133	3 89516	17 92369	3 77107	16 41104	3 64542
24	20 22619	2 30605	20 89888	2 18270	19 53077	2 05787	18 12654	3 93153	18 69009	3 80364	17 22472	3 67416	17 73326	3 54305
25	21 40228	2 23547	20 10300	2 10698	20 76122	3 97695	19 38181	3 84535	19 96884	3 71213	18 52575	3 57725	17 05548	3 44068
26	22 57837	2 16489	21 30712	2 03126	21 99167	3 89603	20 63709	3 75916	19 24759	3 62061	19 82678	3 48034	18 37770	3 33830
27	23 75446	2 09431	22 51124	3 95554	21 22212	3 81511	21 89236	3 67297	20 52635	3 52910	19 12781	3 38343	19 69992	3 23593
28	24 93056	2 02373	23 71536	3 87982	22 45257	3 73419	21 14763	3 58679	21 80510	3 43758	20 42884	3 28652	19 02214	3 13356
29	24 10665	3 95315	24 91948	3 80410	23 68302	3 65326	22 40290	3 50060	21 08385	3 34607	21 72987	3 18961	20 34436	3 03119
30	25 28274	3 88257	24 12360	3 72838	24 91347	3 57234	23 65818	3 41442	22 36261	3 25455	21 03090	3 09270	21 66658	4 92881
31	26 45883	3 81199	25 32772	3 65266	24 14392	3 49142	24 91345	3 32823	23 64136	3 16304	22 33193	4 99579	22 98880	4 82644
32	27 63492	3 74141	26 53184	3 57694	25 37437	3 41050	24 16872	3 24204	24 92012	3 07152	23 63296	4 89888	22 31102	4 72407
33	28 81101	3 67082	27 73596	3 50122	26 60481	3 32958	25 42399	3 15586	24 19887	4 98001	24 93399	4 80197	23 63324	4 62169
34	29 98710	3 60024	28 94008	3 42550	27 83526	3 24866	26 67927	3 06967	25 47762	4 88849	24 23502	4 70506	24 95546	4 51932
35	29 16319	3 52966	28 14420	3 34978	27 06571	3 16773	27 93454	4 98348	26 75638	4 79698	25 53605	4 60815	24 27768	4 41695
36	30 33929	3 45908	29 34832	3 27405	28 29616	3 08681	27 18981	4 89730	26 03513	4 70546	26 83708	4 51124	25 59989	4 31458
37	31 51538	3 38850	30 55244	3 19833	29 52661	3 00589	28 44508	4 81111	27 31388	4 61395	26 13811	4 41433	26 92211	4 21220
38	32 69147	3 31792	31 75656	3 12261	30 75706	4 92497	29 70036	4 72493	28 59264	4 52243	27 43914	4 31742	26 24433	4 10983
39	33 86756	3 24734	32 96068	3 04689	31 98751	4 84405	30 95563	4 63874	29 87139	4 43092	28 74017	4 22051	27 56655	4 00746
40	33 04365	3 17676	32 16480	4 97117	31 21796	4 76312	30 21090	4 55255	29 15014	4 33940	28 04120	4 12360	28 88877	5 90508
41	34 21974	3 10618	33 36892	4 89545	32 44841	4 68220	31 46617	4 46637	30 42890	4 24789	29 34223	4 02669	28 21099	5 80271
42	35 39583	3 03559	34 57304	4 81973	33 67885	4 60128	32 72145	4 38018	31 70765	4 15637	30 64326	5 92978	29 53321	5 70034
43	36 57192	4 96501	35 77716	4 74401	34 90930	4 52036	33 97672	4 29400	32 98640	4 06486	31 94429	5 83287	30 85543	5 59796
44	37 74802	4 89443	36 98128	4 66829	34 13975	4 43944	33 23199	4 20781	32 26516	5 97334	31 24532	5 73596	30 17765	5 49559
45	38 92411	4 82385	36 18540	4 59257	35 37020	4 35851	34 48726	4 12162	33 54391	5 88183	32 54635	5 63905	31 49987	5 39322
46	38 10020	4 75327	37 38952	4 51685	36 60065	4 27759	35 74254	4 03544	34 82267	5 79031	33 84738	5 54214	32 82209	5 29085
47	39 27629	4 68269	38 59364	4 44113	37 83110	4 19667	36 99781	5 94925	34 10142	5 69880	33 14841	5 44523	32 14431	5 18847
48	40 45238	4 61211	39 79776	4 36541	37 06155	4 11575	36 25308	5 86306	35 38017	5 60728	34 44944	5 34832	33 46653	5 08610
49	41 62847	4 54153	39 00188	4 28969	38 29200	4 03483	37 50835	5 77688	36 65893	5 51577	35 75047	5 25141	34 78875	6 98373
50	42 80456	4 47095	40 20600	4 21396	39 52245	5 95390	38 76363	5 69069	37 93768	5 42425	35 05150	5 15450	34 11096	6 88135
51	43 98065	4 40037	41 41012	4 13824	40 75290	5 87298	38 01890	5 60451	37 21643	5 33274	36 35253	5 05759	35 43318	6 77898
52	43 15675	4 32978	42 61424	4 06252	41 98334	5 79206	39 27417	5 51832	38 49519	5 24122	37 65356	6 96068	36 75540	6 67661
53	44 33284	4 25920	43 81836	5 98680	41 21379	5 71114	40 52944	5 43213	39 77394	5 14971	38 95459	6 86377	36 07762	6 57424
54	45 50893	4 18862	43 02248	5 91108	42 44424	5 63022	41 78472	5 34595	39 05269	5 05819	38 25562	6 76686	37 39984	6 47186
55	46 68502	4 11804	44 22660	5 83536	43 67469	5 54930	41 03999	5 25976	40 33145	6 96668	39 55665	6 66995	38 72206	6 36949
56	47 86111	4 04746	45 43072	5 75964	44 90514	5 46837	42 29526	5 17358	41 61020	6 87516	40 85768	6 57304	38 04428	6 26712
57	47 03720	5 97688	46 63484	5 68392	44 13559	5 38745	43 55053	5 08739	42 88896	6 78365	40 15871	6 47613	39 36650	6 16474
58	48 21329	5 90630	47 83896	5 60820	45 36604	5 30653	44 80581	5 00120	42 16771	6 69213	41 45974	6 37922	40 68872	6 06237
59	49 38938	5 83572	47 04308	5 53248	46 59649	5 22561	44 06108	6 91502	43 44646	6 60062	42 76077	6 28231	40 01094	7 96000
60	50 56548	5 76514	48 24720	5 45676	47 82694	5 14469	45 31635	6 82883	44 72522	6 50910	42 06180	6 18540	41 33316	7 85763
61	51 74157	5 69455	49 45132	5 38104	47 05738	5 06376	46 57162	6 74264	44 00397	6 41759	43 36283	6 08849	42 65538	7 75525
62	52 91766	5 62397	50 65544	5 30532	48 28783	6 98284	47 82690	6 65646	45 28272	6 32607	44 66386	7 99158	43 97760	7 65288
63	52 09375	5 55339	51 85956	5 22960	49 51828	6 90192	47 08217	6 57027	46 56148	6 23456	45 96489	7 89467	43 29982	7 55051
64	53 26984	5 48281	51 06368	5 15387	50 74873	6 82100	48 33744	6 48409	47 84023	6 14304	45 26592	7 79776	44 62203	7 44813
65	54 44593	5 41223	52 26780	5 07815	51 97918	6 74008	49 59271	6 39790	47 11898	6 05153	46 56695	7 70085	45 94425	7 34576
66	55 62202	5 34165	53 47192	5 00243	51 20963	6 65915	50 84799	6 31171	48 39774	7 96001	47 86798	7 60394	45 26647	7 24339
67	56 79811	5 27107	54 67604	6 92671	52 44008	6 57823	50 10326	6 22553	49 67649	7 86850	47 16901	7 50703	46 58869	7 14102
68	57 97421	5 20049	55 88016	6 85099	53 67053	6 49731	51 35853	6 13934	50 95524	7 77698	48 47004	7 41012	47 91091	7 03864
69	57 15030	5 12991	55 08428	6 77527	54 90098	6 41639	52 61380	6 05316	50 23400	7 68547	49 77107	7 31321	47 23313	8 93627
70	58 32639	5 05932	56 28840	6 69955	54 13142	6 33547	53 86908	7 96697	51 51275	7 59395	49 07210	7 21630	48 55535	8 83390
71	59 50248	6 98874	57 49252	6 62383	55 36187	6 25454	53 12435	7 88078	52 79151	7 50244	50 37313	7 11939	49 87757	8 73152
72	60 67857	6 91816	58 69664	6 54811	56 59232	6 17362	54 37962	7 79460	52 07026	7 41092	51 67416	7 02248	49 19979	8 62915
73	61 85466	6 84758	59 90076	6 47239	57 82277	6 09270	55 63489	7 70841	53 34901	7 31941	52 97519	8 92557	50 52201	8 52678
74	61 03075	6 77700	59 10488	6 39667	57 05322	6 01178	56 89017	7 62223	54 62777	7 22789	52 27622	8 82866	51 84423	8 42440
75	62 20684	6 70642	60 30900	6 32095	58 28367	7 93086	56 14544	7 53604	55 90652	7 13638	53 57725	8 73175	51 16645	8 32203
76	63 38294	6 63584	61 51312	6 24523	59 51412	7 84994	57 40071	7 44985	55 18527	7 04486	54 87828	8 63484	52 48867	8 21966
77	64 55903	6 56526	62 71724	6 16951	60 74457	7 76901	58 65598	7 36367	56 46403	8 95335	54 17931	8 53793	53 81089	8 11729
78	65 73512	6 49468	63 92136	6 09378	61 97502	7 68809	59 91126	7 27748	57 74278	8 86183	55 48034	8 44102	53 13311	8 01491
79	66 91121	6 42410	63 12548	6 01806	61 20546	7 60717	59 16653	7 19129	57 02153	8 77032	56 78137	8 34411	54 45532	9 91254
80	66 08730	6 35351	64 32960	7 94234	62 43591	7 52625	60 42180	7 10511	58 30029	8 67880	56 08240	8 24720	55 77754	9 81017
81	67 26339	6 28293	65 53372	7 86662	63 66636	7 44533	61 67707	7 01892	59 57904	8 58729	57 38343	8 15029	55 09976	9 70779
82	68 43948	6 21235	66 73784	7 79090	64 89681	7 36440	62 93235	8 93274	60 85780	8 49577	58 68446	8 05338	56 42198	9 60542
83	69 61557	6 14177	67 94196	7 71518	64 12726	7 28348	62 18762	8 84655	60 13655	8 40426	59 98549	9 95647	57 74420	9 50305
84	70 79167	6 07119	67 14608	7 63946	65 35771	7 20256	63 44289	8 76036	61 41530	8 31274	59 28652	9 85956	57 06642	9 40068
85	71 96776	6 00061	68 35020	7 56374	66 58816	7 12164	64 69816	8 67418	62 69406	8 22123	60 58755	9 76265	58 38864	9 29830
86	71 14385	7 93003	69 55432	7 48802	67 81861	7 04072	65 95344	8 58799	63 97281	8 12971	61 88858	9 66574	59 71086	9 19593
87	72 31994	7 85945	70 75844	7 41230	67 04906	8 95979	65 20871	8 50181	63 25156	8 03820	61 18961	9 56883	59 03308	9 09356
88	73 49603	7 78887	71 96256	7 33658	68 27951	8 87887	66 46398	8 41562	64 53032	9 94668	62 49064	9 47192	60 35530	10 99118
89	74 67212	7 71828	71 16668	7 26086	69 50995	8 79795	67 71925	8 32943	65 80907	9 85517	63 79167	9 37501	61 67752	10 88881
90	75 84821	7 64770	72 37080	7 18514	70 74040	8 71703	68 97453	8 24325	65 08782	9 76365	63 09270	9 27810	62 99974	10 78644
91	75 02430	7 57712	73 57492	7 10942	71 97085	8 63611	68 22980	8 15706	66 36658	9 67214	64 39373	9 18119	62 32196	10 68407
92	76 20040	7 50654	74 77904	7 03369	71 20130	8 55518	69 48507	8 07087	67 64533	9 58062	65 69476	9 08428	63 64418	10 58169
93	77 37649	7 43596	75 98316	8 95797	72 43175	8 47426	70 74034	9 98469	68 92408	9 48911	66 99579	10 98737	64 96639	10 47932
94	78 55258	7 36538	75 18728	8 88225	73 66220	8 39334	71 99562	9 89850	68 20284	9 39759	66 29682	10 89046	64 28861	10 37695
95	79 72867	7 29480	76 39140	8 80653	74 89265	8 31242	71 25089	9 81232	69 48159	9 30608	67 59785	10 79355	65 61083	10 27457
96	80 90476	7 22422	77 59552	8 73081	74 12310	8 23150	72 50616	9 72613	70 76035	9 21456	68 89888	10 69664	66 93305	10 17220
97	80 08085	7 15364	78 79964	8 65509	75 35355	8 15057	73 76143	9 63994	70 03910	9 12305	68 19991	10 59973	66 25527	10 06983
98	81 25694	7 08305	78 00376	8 57937	76 58399	8 06965	73 01671	9 55376	71 31785	9 03153	69 50094	10 50282	67 57749	11 96745
99	82 43303	7 01247	79 20788	8 50365	77 81444	9 98873	74 27198	9 46757	72 59661	10 94002	70 80197	10 40591	68 89971	11 86508
100	83 60913	8 94189	80 41200	8 42793	77 04489	9 90781	75 52725	9 38139	73 87536	10 84850	70 10300	10 30900	68 22193	11 76271

*For explanation see page 81. – Reproduction only by permission of the publishers of the *Geigy Scientific Tables.*

All values conform to the international convention (i.e. 0,1 instead of 0.1).

n	p (q) 0,22	q (p) 0,78	p (q) 0,23	q (p) 0,77	p (q) 0,24	q (p) 0,76	p (q) 0,25	q (p) 0,75	p (q) 0,26	q (p) 0,74	p (q) 0,27	q (p) 0,73	p (q) 0,28	q (p) 0,72
0	0 00000	0 00000	0 00000	0 00000	0 00000	0 00000	0 00000	0 00000	0 00000	0 00000	0 00000	0 00000	0 00000	0 00000
1	1 34242	1 89209	1 36173	1 88649	1 38021	1 88081	1 39794	1 87506	1 41497	1 86923	1 43136	1 86332	1 44716	1 85733
2	2 68485	1 78419	2 72346	1 77298	2 76042	1 76163	2 79588	1 75012	2 82995	1 73846	2 86273	1 72665	2 89432	1 71466
3	2 02727	1 67628	2 08518	1 65947	2 14063	1 64244	2 19382	1 62518	2 24492	1 60770	2 29409	1 58997	2 34147	1 57200
4	3 36969	1 56838	3 44691	1 54596	3 52084	1 52325	3 59176	1 50025	3 65989	1 47693	3 72546	1 45329	3 78863	1 42933
5	4 71211	1 46047	4 80864	1 43245	4 90106	1 40407	4 98970	1 37531	3 07487	1 34616	3 15682	1 31661	3 23579	1 28666
6	4 05454	1 35257	4 17037	1 31894	4 28127	1 28488	4 38764	1 25037	4 48984	1 21539	4 58818	1 17994	4 68295	1 14399
7	5 39696	1 24466	5 53209	1 20544	5 66148	1 16570	5 78558	1 12543	5 90481	1 08462	4 01955	1 04326	4 13011	1 00133
8	6 73938	1 13676	6 89382	1 09193	5 04169	1 04651	5 18352	1 00049	5 31979	2 95385	5 45091	2 90658	5 57726	2 85866
9	6 08180	1 02885	6 25555	2 97842	6 42190	2 92732	6 58146	2 87555	6 73476	2 82309	6 88227	2 76991	5 02442	2 71599
10	7 42423	2 92095	7 61728	2 86491	7 80211	2 80814	7 97940	2 75061	6 14973	2 69232	6 31364	2 63323	6 47158	2 57332
11	8 76665	2 81304	8 97901	2 75140	7 18232	2 68895	7 37734	2 62567	7 56471	2 56155	7 74500	2 49655	7 91874	2 43066
12	8 10907	2 70514	8 34073	2 63789	8 56253	2 56976	8 77528	2 50074	8 97968	2 43078	7 17637	2 35987	7 36590	2 28799
13	9 45149	2 59723	9 70246	2 52438	9 94275	2 45058	8 17322	2 37580	8 39465	2 30001	8 60773	2 22320	8 81305	2 14532
14	10 79392	2 48932	9 06419	2 41087	9 32296	2 33139	9 57116	2 25086	9 80963	2 16924	8 03909	2 08652	8 26021	2 00265
15	10 13634	2 38142	10 42592	2 29736	10 70317	2 21220	10 96910	2 12592	9 22460	2 03848	9 47046	3 94984	9 70737	3 85999
16	11 47876	2 27351	11 78765	2 18385	10 08338	2 09302	10 36704	2 00098	10 63957	3 90771	10 90182	3 81317	9 15453	3 71732
17	12 82119	2 16561	11 14937	2 07034	11 46359	3 97383	11 76498	3 87604	10 05455	3 77694	10 33318	3 67649	10 60169	3 57465
18	12 16361	2 05770	12 51110	3 95683	12 84380	3 85464	11 16292	3 75110	11 46952	3 64617	11 76455	3 53981	10 04884	3 43198
19	13 50603	3 94980	13 87283	3 84332	12 22401	3 73546	12 56086	3 62616	12 88449	3 51540	11 19591	3 40313	11 49600	3 28932
20	14 84845	3 84189	13 23456	3 72981	13 60422	3 61627	13 95880	3 50123	12 29947	3 38463	12 62728	3 26646	12 94316	3 14665
21	14 19088	3 73399	14 59628	3 61631	14 98444	3 49709	13 35674	3 37629	13 71444	3 25387	12 05864	3 12978	12 39032	3 00398
22	15 53330	3 62608	15 95801	3 50280	14 36465	3 37790	14 75468	3 25135	13 12941	3 12310	13 49000	4 99310	13 83748	4 86131
23	16 87572	3 51818	15 31974	3 38929	15 74486	3 25871	14 15262	3 12641	14 54439	4 99233	14 92137	4 85643	13 28463	4 71865
24	16 21814	3 41027	16 68147	3 27578	15 12507	3 13953	15 55056	3 00147	15 95936	4 86156	14 35273	4 71975	14 73179	4 57598
25	17 56057	3 30237	16 04320	3 16227	16 50528	3 02034	16 94850	4 87653	15 37433	4 73079	15 78409	4 58307	14 17895	4 43331
26	18 90299	3 19446	17 40492	3 04876	17 88549	4 90115	16 34644	4 75159	16 78931	4 60002	15 21546	4 44639	15 62611	4 29064
27	18 24541	3 08655	18 76665	4 93525	17 26570	4 78197	17 74438	4 62665	16 20428	4 46926	16 64682	4 30972	15 07327	4 14798
28	19 58784	4 97865	18 12838	4 82174	18 64591	4 66278	17 14232	4 50172	17 61925	4 33849	16 07819	4 17304	16 52042	4 00531
29	20 93026	4 87074	19 49011	4 70823	18 02613	4 54359	18 54026	4 37678	17 03423	4 20772	17 50955	4 03636	17 96758	5 86264
30	20 27268	4 76284	20 85184	4 59472	19 40634	4 42441	19 93820	4 25184	18 44920	4 07695	18 94091	5 89969	17 41474	5 71997
31	21 61510	4 65493	20 21356	4 48121	20 78655	4 30522	19 33614	4 12690	19 86417	5 94618	18 37228	5 76301	18 86190	5 57731
32	22 95753	4 54703	21 57529	4 36770	20 16676	4 18603	20 73408	4 00196	19 27915	5 81542	19 80364	5 62633	18 30906	5 43464
33	22 29995	4 43912	22 93702	4 25419	21 54697	4 06685	20 13202	5 87702	20 69412	5 68465	19 23500	5 48965	19 75622	5 29197
34	23 64237	4 33122	22 29875	4 14068	22 92718	5 94766	21 52996	5 75208	20 10909	5 55388	20 66637	5 35298	19 20337	5 14930
35	24 98479	4 22331	23 66047	4 02718	22 30739	5 82848	22 92790	5 62714	21 52407	5 42311	20 09773	5 21630	20 65053	5 00664
36	24 32722	4 11541	23 02220	5 91367	23 68760	5 70929	22 32584	5 50221	22 93904	5 29234	21 52910	5 07962	20 09769	6 86397
37	25 66964	4 00750	24 38393	5 80016	23 06782	5 59010	23 72378	5 37727	22 35401	5 16157	22 96046	6 94295	21 54485	6 72130
38	25 01206	5 89959	25 74566	5 68665	24 44803	5 47092	23 12172	5 25233	23 76899	5 03081	22 39182	6 80627	22 99201	6 57863
39	26 35448	5 79169	25 10739	5 57314	25 82824	5 35173	24 51966	5 12739	23 18396	6 90004	23 82319	6 66959	22 43916	6 43597
40	27 69691	5 68378	26 46911	5 45963	25 20845	5 23254	25 91760	5 00245	24 59893	6 76927	23 25455	6 53291	23 88632	6 29330
41	27 03933	5 57588	27 83084	5 34612	26 58866	5 11336	25 31554	6 87751	24 01391	6 63850	24 68591	6 39624	23 33348	6 15063
42	28 38175	5 46797	27 19257	5 23261	27 96887	6 99417	26 71348	6 75257	25 42888	6 50773	24 11728	6 25956	24 78064	6 00796
43	29 72418	5 36007	28 55430	5 11910	27 34908	6 87498	26 11142	6 62763	26 84385	6 37696	25 54864	6 12288	24 22780	7 86530
44	29 06660	5 25216	29 91602	5 00559	28 72929	6 75580	27 50936	6 50270	26 25883	6 24620	26 98001	7 98621	25 67495	7 72263
45	30 40902	5 14426	29 27775	6 89208	28 10951	6 63661	28 90730	6 37776	27 67380	6 11543	26 41137	7 84953	25 12211	7 57996
46	31 75144	5 03635	30 63948	6 77857	29 48972	6 51743	28 30524	6 25282	27 08877	7 98466	27 84273	7 71285	26 56927	7 43729
47	31 09387	6 92845	30 00121	6 66506	30 86993	6 39824	29 70318	6 12788	28 50375	7 85389	27 27410	7 57617	26 01643	7 29463
48	32 43629	6 82054	31 36294	6 55155	30 25014	6 27905	29 10112	6 00294	29 91872	7 72312	28 70546	7 43950	27 46359	7 15196
49	33 77871	6 71264	32 72466	6 43805	31 63035	6 15987	30 49906	7 87800	29 33369	7 59235	28 13682	7 30282	28 91074	7 00929
50	33 12113	6 60473	32 08639	6 32454	31 01056	6 04068	31 89700	7 75306	30 74867	7 46159	29 56819	7 16614	28 35790	8 86662
51	34 46356	6 49682	33 44812	6 21103	32 39077	7 92149	31 29494	7 62812	30 16364	7 33082	30 99955	7 02947	29 80506	8 72396
52	35 80598	6 38892	34 80985	6 09752	33 77098	7 80231	32 69288	7 50319	31 57861	7 20005	30 43092	8 89279	29 25222	8 58129
53	35 14840	6 28101	34 17158	7 98401	33 15120	7 68312	32 09082	7 37825	32 99359	7 06928	31 86228	8 75611	30 69938	8 43862
54	36 49082	6 17311	35 53330	7 87050	34 53141	7 56393	33 48876	7 25331	32 40856	8 93851	31 29364	8 61943	30 14653	8 29595
55	37 83325	6 06520	36 89503	7 75699	35 91162	7 44475	34 88670	7 12837	33 82353	8 80774	32 72501	8 48276	31 59369	8 15329
56	37 17567	7 95730	36 25676	7 64348	35 29183	7 32556	34 28464	7 00343	33 23851	8 67698	32 15637	8 34608	31 04085	8 01062
57	38 51809	7 84939	37 61849	7 52997	36 67204	7 20637	35 68258	8 87849	34 65348	8 54621	33 58773	8 20940	32 48801	9 86795
58	39 86052	7 74149	38 98021	7 41646	36 05225	7 08719	35 08052	8 75355	34 06845	8 41544	33 01910	8 07273	33 93517	9 72528
59	39 20294	7 63358	38 34194	7 30295	37 43246	8 96800	36 47846	8 62861	35 48343	8 28467	34 45046	9 93605	33 38232	9 58262
60	40 54536	7 52568	39 70367	7 18944	38 81267	8 84882	37 87640	8 50368	36 89840	8 15390	35 88183	9 79937	34 82948	9 43995
61	41 88778	7 41777	39 06540	7 07593	38 19289	8 72963	37 27434	8 37874	36 31337	8 02313	35 31319	9 66269	34 27664	9 29728
62	41 23021	7 30987	40 42713	8 96242	39 57310	8 61044	38 67228	8 25380	37 72835	9 89237	36 74455	9 52602	35 72380	9 15461
63	42 57263	7 20196	41 78885	8 84892	40 95331	8 49126	38 07022	8 12886	37 14332	9 76160	36 17592	9 38934	35 17096	9 01195
64	43 91505	7 09405	41 15058	8 73541	40 33352	8 37207	39 46816	8 00392	38 55829	9 63083	37 60728	9 25266	36 61811	10 86928
65	43 25747	8 98615	42 51231	8 62190	41 71373	8 25288	40 86610	9 87898	39 97327	9 50006	37 03864	9 11599	36 06527	10 72661
66	44 59990	8 87824	43 87404	8 50839	41 09394	8 13370	40 26404	9 75404	39 38824	9 36929	38 47001	10 97931	37 51243	10 58394
67	45 94232	8 77034	43 23577	8 39488	42 47415	8 01451	41 66198	9 62910	40 80321	9 23853	39 90137	10 84263	38 95959	10 44128
68	45 28474	8 66243	44 59749	8 28137	43 85436	9 89532	41 05992	9 50417	40 21819	9 10776	39 33274	10 70595	38 40675	10 29861
69	46 62716	8 55453	45 95922	8 16786	43 23458	9 77614	42 45786	9 37923	41 63316	10 97699	40 76410	10 56928	39 85390	10 15594
70	47 96959	8 44662	45 32095	8 05435	44 61479	9 65695	43 85580	9 25429	41 04813	10 84622	40 19546	10 43260	39 30106	10 01327
71	47 31201	8 33872	46 68268	9 94084	45 99500	9 53777	43 25374	9 12935	42 46311	10 71545	41 62683	10 29592	40 74822	11 87061
72	48 65443	8 23081	46 04440	9 82733	45 37521	9 41858	44 65168	9 00441	43 87808	10 58468	41 05819	10 15925	40 19538	11 72794
73	49 99686	8 12291	47 40613	9 71382	46 75542	9 29939	44 04962	10 87947	43 29305	10 45392	42 48955	10 02257	41 64254	11 58527
74	49 33928	8 01500	48 76786	9 60031	46 13563	9 18021	45 44756	10 75453	44 70803	10 32315	43 92092	11 88589	41 08969	11 44260
75	50 68170	9 90710	48 12959	9 48680	47 51584	9 06102	46 84550	10 62959	44 12300	10 19238	43 35228	11 74921	42 53685	11 29994
76	50 02412	9 79919	49 49132	9 37330	48 89605	10 94183	46 24344	10 50466	45 53797	10 06161	44 78365	11 61254	43 98401	11 15727
77	51 36655	9 69128	50 85304	9 25979	48 27627	10 82265	47 64138	10 37972	46 95295	11 93084	44 21501	11 47586	43 43117	11 01460
78	52 70897	9 58338	50 21477	9 14628	49 65648	10 70346	47 03932	10 25478	46 36792	11 80007	45 64637	11 33918	44 87833	12 87193
79	52 05139	9 47547	51 57650	9 03277	49 03669	10 58427	48 43726	10 12984	47 78289	11 66931	45 07774	11 20251	44 32548	12 72927
80	53 39381	9 36757	52 93823	10 91926	50 41690	10 46509	49 83520	10 00490	47 19787	11 53854	46 50910	11 06583	45 77264	12 58660
81	54 73624	9 25966	52 29995	10 80575	51 79711	10 34590	49 23314	11 87996	48 61284	11 40777	47 94046	12 92915	45 21980	12 44393
82	54 07866	9 15176	53 66168	10 69224	51 17732	10 22671	50 63108	11 75502	48 02781	11 27700	47 37183	12 79247	46 66696	12 30126
83	55 42108	9 04385	53 02341	10 57873	52 55753	10 10753	50 02902	11 63008	49 44279	11 14623	48 80319	12 65580	46 11412	12 15860
84	56 76351	10 93595	54 38514	10 46522	53 93774	11 98834	51 42696	11 50515	50 85776	11 01546	48 23456	12 51912	47 56127	12 01593
85	56 10593	10 82804	55 74687	10 35171	53 31796	11 86916	52 82490	11 38021	50 27273	12 88470	49 66592	12 38244	47 00843	13 87326
86	57 44835	10 72014	55 10859	10 23820	54 69817	11 74997	52 22284	11 25527	51 68771	12 75393	49 09728	12 24577	48 45559	13 73059
87	58 79077	10 61223	56 47032	10 12469	54 07838	11 63078	53 62078	11 13033	51 10268	12 62316	50 52865	12 10909	49 90275	13 58793
88	58 13320	10 50433	57 83205	10 01118	55 45859	11 51160	53 01872	11 00539	52 51765	12 49239	51 96001	13 97241	49 34991	13 44526
89	59 47562	10 39642	57 19378	11 89767	56 83880	11 39241	54 41666	12 88045	53 93263	12 36162	51 39138	13 83573	50 79706	13 30259
90	60 81804	10 28851	58 55551	11 78417	56 21901	11 27322	55 81460	12 75551	53 34760	12 23085	52 82274	13 69906	50 24422	13 15992
91	60 16046	10 18061	59 91723	11 67066	57 59922	11 15404	55 21254	12 63057	54 76257	12 10009	52 25410	13 56238	51 69138	13 01726
92	61 50289	10 07270	59 27896	11 55715	58 97943	11 03485	56 61048	12 50564	54 17755	13 96932	53 68547	13 42570	51 13854	14 87459
93	62 84531	11 96480	60 64069	11 44364	58 35965	12 91566	56 00842	12 38070	55 59252	13 83855	53 11683	13 28903	52 58570	14 73192
94	62 18773	11 85689	60 00242	11 33013	59 73986	12 79648	57 40636	12 25576	55 00749	13 70778	54 54819	13 15235	52 03285	14 58925
95	63 53015	11 74899	61 36414	11 21662	59 12007	12 67729	58 80430	12 13082	56 42247	13 57701	55 97956	13 01567	53 48001	14 44659
96	64 87258	11 64108	62 72587	11 10311	60 50028	12 55810	58 20224	12 00588	57 83744	13 44625	55 41092	14 87899	54 92717	14 30392
97	64 21500	11 53318	62 08760	12 98960	61 88049	12 43892	59 60018	13 88094	57 25241	13 31548	56 84229	14 74232	54 37433	14 16125
98	65 55742	11 42527	63 44933	12 87609	61 26070	12 31973	60 99812	13 75600	58 66739	13 18471	56 27365	14 60564	55 82149	14 01858
99	66 89985	11 31737	64 81106	12 76258	62 64091	12 20055	60 39606	13 63107	58 08236	13 05394	57 70501	14 46896	55 26865	15 87592
100	66 24227	11 20946	64 17278	12 64907	62 02112	12 08136	61 79400	13 50613	59 49733	14 92317	57 13638	14 33229	56 71580	15 73325

* For explanation see page 81. –

All values conform to the international convention (i.e. 0,1 instead of 0.1).

n	p (q) 0,29	q (p) 0,71	p (q) 0,30	q (p) 0,70	p (q) 0,31	q (p) 0,69	p (q) 0,32	q (p) 0,68	p (q) 0,33	q (p) 0,67	p (q) 0,34	q (p) 0,66	p (q) 0,35	q (p) 0,65
0	0 00000	0 00000	0 00000	0 00000	0 00000	0 00000	0 00000	0 00000	0 00000	0 00000	0 00000	0 00000	0 00000	0 00000
1	1 46240	1 85126	1 47712	1 84510	1 49136	1 83885	1 50515	1 83251	1 51851	1 82607	1 53148	1 81954	1 54407	1 81291
2	2 92480	1 70252	2 95424	1 69020	2 98272	1 67770	1 01030	1 66502	1 03703	1 65215	1 06296	1 63909	1 08814	1 62583
3	2 38719	1 55378	2 43136	1 53529	2 47409	1 51655	2 51545	1 49753	2 55554	1 47822	2 59444	1 45863	2 63220	1 43874
4	3 84959	1 40503	3 90849	1 38039	3 96545	1 35540	2 02060	1 33004	2 07406	1 30430	2 12592	1 27818	2 17627	1 25165
5	3 31199	1 25629	3 38561	1 22549	3 45681	1 19425	3 52575	1 16254	3 59257	1 13037	3 65739	1 09772	3 72034	1 06457
6	4 77439	1 10755	4 86273	1 07059	4 94817	1 03309	3 03090	2 99505	3 11108	2 95645	3 18887	2 91726	3 26441	2 87748
7	4 23679	2 95881	4 33985	2 91569	4 43953	2 87194	4 53605	2 82756	4 62960	2 78252	4 72035	2 73681	4 80848	2 69039
8	5 69918	2 81007	5 81697	2 76078	5 93089	2 71079	4 04120	2 66007	4 14811	2 60860	4 25183	2 55635	4 35254	2 50331
9	5 16158	2 66133	5 29409	2 60588	5 42226	2 54964	5 54635	2 49258	5 66663	2 43467	5 78331	2 37590	5 89661	2 31622
10	6 62398	2 51258	6 77121	2 45098	6 91362	2 38849	5 05150	2 32509	5 18514	2 26075	5 31479	2 19544	5 44068	2 12913
11	6 08638	2 36384	6 24833	2 29608	6 40498	2 22734	6 55665	2 15760	6 70365	2 08682	6 84627	2 01498	6 98475	3 94205
12	7 54878	2 21510	7 72546	2 14118	7 89634	2 06619	6 06180	3 99011	6 22217	3 91290	6 37775	3 83453	6 52882	3 75496
13	7 01117	2 06636	7 20258	3 98627	7 38770	3 90504	7 56695	3 82262	7 74068	3 73897	7 90923	3 65407	6 07288	3 56787
14	8 47357	3 91762	8 67970	3 83137	8 87906	3 74389	7 07210	3 65512	7 25920	3 56505	7 44070	3 47362	7 61695	3 38079
15	9 93597	3 76888	8 15682	3 67647	8 37043	3 58274	8 57725	3 48763	8 77771	3 39112	8 97218	3 29316	7 16102	3 19370
16	9 39837	3 62013	9 63394	3 52157	9 86179	3 42159	8 08240	3 32014	8 29622	3 21720	8 50366	3 11270	8 70509	3 00661
17	10 86077	3 47139	9 11106	3 36667	9 35315	3 26043	9 58755	3 15265	9 81474	3 04327	8 03514	4 93225	8 24916	4 81953
18	10 32316	3 32265	10 58818	3 21176	10 84451	3 09928	9 09270	4 98516	9 33325	4 86935	9 56662	4 75179	9 79322	4 63244
19	11 78556	3 17391	10 06530	3 05686	10 33587	4 93813	10 59785	4 81767	10 85176	4 69542	9 09810	4 57133	9 33729	4 44535
20	11 24796	3 02517	11 54243	4 90196	11 82723	4 77698	10 10300	4 65018	10 37028	4 52150	10 62958	4 39088	10 88136	4 25827
21	12 71036	4 87643	11 01955	4 74706	11 31860	4 61583	11 60815	4 48269	11 88879	4 34757	10 16106	4 21042	10 42543	4 07118
22	12 17276	4 72768	12 49667	4 59216	12 80996	4 45468	11 11330	4 31520	11 40731	4 17365	11 69254	4 02997	11 96950	5 88409
23	13 63515	4 57894	13 97379	4 43725	12 30132	4 29353	12 61845	4 14770	12 92582	5 99972	11 22402	5 84951	11 51357	5 69701
24	13 09755	4 43020	13 45091	4 28235	13 79268	4 13238	12 12360	5 98021	12 44433	5 82580	12 75549	5 66905	11 05763	5 50992
25	14 55995	4 28146	14 92803	4 12745	13 28404	5 97123	13 62875	5 81272	13 96285	5 65187	12 28697	5 48860	12 60170	5 32283
26	14 02235	4 13272	14 40515	5 97255	14 77540	5 81008	13 13390	5 64523	13 48136	5 47794	13 81845	5 30814	12 14577	5 13575
27	15 48475	5 98398	15 88227	5 81765	14 26677	5 64893	14 63905	5 47774	14 99988	5 30402	13 34993	5 12769	13 68984	6 94866
28	16 94714	5 83523	15 35940	5 66275	15 75813	5 48777	14 14420	5 31025	14 51839	5 13009	14 88141	6 94723	13 23391	6 76157
29	16 40954	5 68649	16 83652	5 50784	15 24949	5 32662	15 64935	5 14276	14 03690	6 95617	14 41289	6 76677	14 77797	6 57449
30	17 87194	5 53775	16 31364	5 35294	16 74085	5 16547	15 15450	6 97527	15 55542	6 78224	15 94437	6 58632	14 32204	6 38740
31	17 33434	5 38901	17 79076	5 19804	16 23221	5 00432	16 65965	6 80778	15 07393	6 60832	15 47585	6 40586	15 86611	6 20031
32	18 79674	5 24027	17 26788	5 04314	17 72357	6 84317	16 16480	6 64029	16 59245	6 43439	15 00733	6 22541	15 41018	6 01323
33	18 25913	5 09153	18 74500	6 88824	17 21494	6 68202	17 66995	6 47279	16 11096	6 26047	16 53880	6 04495	16 95425	7 82614
34	19 72153	6 94278	18 22212	6 73333	18 70630	6 52087	17 17510	6 30530	17 62947	6 08654	16 07028	7 86449	16 49831	7 63905
35	19 18393	6 79404	19 69924	6 57843	18 19766	6 35972	18 68025	6 13781	17 14799	7 91262	17 60176	7 68404	16 04238	7 45197
36	20 64633	6 64530	19 17637	6 42353	19 68902	6 19857	18 18540	7 97032	18 66650	7 73869	17 13324	7 50358	17 58645	7 26488
37	20 10873	6 49656	20 65349	6 26863	19 18038	6 03742	19 69055	7 80283	18 18502	7 56477	18 66472	7 32313	17 13052	7 07779
38	21 57112	6 34782	20 13061	6 11373	20 67174	7 87627	19 19570	7 63534	19 70353	7 39084	18 19620	7 14267	18 67459	8 89071
39	21 03352	6 19908	21 60773	7 95882	20 16311	7 71511	20 70085	7 46785	19 22204	7 21692	19 72768	8 96221	18 21865	8 70362
40	22 49592	6 05033	21 08485	7 80392	21 65447	7 55396	20 20600	7 30036	20 74056	7 04299	19 25916	8 78176	19 76272	8 51653
41	23 95832	7 90159	22 56197	7 64902	21 14583	7 39281	21 71115	7 13287	20 25907	8 86907	20 79064	8 60130	19 30679	8 32945
42	23 42072	7 75285	22 03909	7 49412	22 63719	7 23166	21 21630	8 96537	21 77759	8 69514	20 32211	8 42085	20 85086	8 14236
43	24 88311	7 60411	23 51621	7 33922	22 12855	7 07051	22 72145	8 79788	21 29610	8 52122	21 85359	8 24039	20 39493	9 95527
44	24 34551	7 45537	24 99334	7 18431	23 61991	8 90936	22 22660	8 63039	22 81461	8 34729	21 38507	8 05993	21 93899	9 76819
45	25 80791	7 30663	24 47046	7 02941	23 11128	8 74821	23 73175	8 46290	22 33313	8 17337	22 91655	9 87948	21 48306	9 58110
46	25 27031	7 15788	25 94758	8 87451	24 60264	8 58706	23 23690	8 29541	23 85164	9 99944	22 44803	9 69902	21 02713	9 39401
47	26 73271	7 00914	25 42470	8 71961	24 09400	8 42591	24 74205	8 12792	23 37016	9 82552	23 97951	9 51856	22 57120	9 20693
48	26 19510	8 86040	26 90182	8 56471	25 58536	8 26476	24 24720	9 96043	24 88867	9 65159	23 51099	9 33811	22 11527	9 01984
49	27 65750	8 71166	26 37894	8 40980	25 07672	8 10361	25 75235	9 79294	24 40718	9 47767	23 04247	9 15765	23 65933	10 83275
50	27 11990	8 56292	27 85606	8 25490	26 56808	9 94245	25 25750	9 62545	25 92570	9 30374	24 57395	10 97720	23 20340	10 64567
51	28 58230	8 41418	27 33318	8 10000	26 05945	9 78130	26 76265	9 45795	25 44421	9 12981	24 10542	10 79674	24 74747	10 45858
52	28 04470	8 26543	28 81031	9 94510	27 55081	9 62015	26 26780	9 29046	26 96272	10 95589	25 63690	10 61628	24 29154	10 27149
53	29 50709	8 11669	28 28743	9 79020	27 04217	9 45900	27 77295	9 12297	26 48124	10 78196	25 16838	10 43583	25 83561	10 08441
54	30 96949	9 96795	29 76455	9 63529	28 53353	9 29785	27 27810	10 95548	27 99975	10 60804	26 69986	10 25537	25 37967	11 89732
55	30 43189	9 81921	29 24167	9 48039	28 02489	9 13670	28 78325	10 78799	27 51827	10 43411	26 23134	10 07492	26 92374	11 71023
56	31 89429	9 67047	30 71879	9 32549	29 51625	10 97555	28 28840	10 62050	27 03678	10 26019	27 76282	11 89446	26 46781	11 52315
57	31 35669	9 52173	30 19591	9 17059	29 00762	10 81440	29 79355	10 45301	28 55529	10 08626	27 29430	11 71400	26 01188	11 33606
58	32 81908	9 37298	31 67303	9 01569	30 49898	10 65325	29 29870	10 28552	28 07381	11 91234	28 82578	11 53355	27 55595	11 14897
59	32 28148	9 22424	31 15015	10 86078	31 99034	10 49210	30 80385	10 11803	29 59232	11 73841	28 35726	11 35309	27 10001	12 96189
60	33 74388	9 07550	32 62728	10 70588	31 48170	10 33095	30 30900	11 95053	29 11084	11 56449	29 88874	11 17264	28 64408	12 77480
61	33 20628	10 92676	32 10440	10 55098	32 97306	10 16979	31 81415	11 78304	30 62935	11 39056	29 42021	12 99218	28 18815	12 58771
62	34 66868	10 77802	33 58152	10 39608	32 46443	10 00864	31 31930	11 61555	30 14786	11 21664	30 95169	12 81172	29 73222	12 40063
63	34 13107	10 62928	33 05864	10 24118	33 95579	11 84749	32 82445	11 44806	31 66638	11 04271	30 48317	12 63127	29 27629	12 21354
64	35 59347	10 48053	34 53576	10 08627	33 44715	11 68634	32 32960	11 28057	31 18489	12 86879	30 01465	12 45081	30 82035	12 02645
65	35 05587	10 33179	34 01288	11 93137	34 93851	11 52519	33 83475	11 11308	32 70341	12 69486	31 54613	12 27036	30 36442	13 83937
66	36 51827	10 18305	35 49000	11 77647	34 42987	11 36404	33 33990	12 94559	32 22192	12 52094	31 07761	12 08990	31 90849	13 65228
67	37 98067	10 03431	36 96712	11 62157	35 92123	11 20289	34 84505	12 77810	33 74043	12 34701	32 60909	13 90944	31 45256	13 46519
68	37 44306	11 88557	36 44425	11 46667	35 41260	11 04174	34 35020	12 61061	33 25895	12 17309	32 14057	13 72899	32 99663	13 27811
69	38 90546	11 73683	37 92137	11 31176	36 90396	12 88059	35 85535	12 44311	34 77746	13 99916	33 67205	13 54853	32 54070	13 09102
70	38 36786	11 58808	37 39849	11 15686	36 39532	12 71944	35 36050	12 27562	34 29598	13 82524	33 20352	13 36808	32 08476	14 90393
71	39 83026	11 43934	38 87561	11 00196	37 88668	12 55829	36 86565	12 10813	35 81449	13 65131	34 73500	13 18762	33 62883	14 71685
72	39 29266	11 29060	38 35273	12 84706	37 37804	12 39713	36 37080	13 94064	35 33300	13 47739	34 26648	13 00716	33 17290	14 52976
73	40 75505	11 14186	39 82985	12 69216	38 86940	12 23598	37 87595	13 77315	36 85152	13 30346	35 79796	14 82671	34 71697	14 34268
74	40 21745	12 99312	39 30697	12 53725	38 36077	12 07483	37 38110	13 60566	36 37003	13 12954	35 32944	14 64625	34 26104	14 15559
75	41 67985	12 84438	40 78409	12 38235	39 85213	13 91368	38 88625	13 43817	37 88855	14 95561	36 86092	14 46580	35 80510	15 96850
76	41 14225	12 69563	40 26122	12 22745	39 34349	13 75253	38 39140	13 27068	37 40706	14 78169	36 39240	14 28534	35 34917	15 78142
77	42 60465	12 54689	41 73834	12 07255	40 83485	13 59138	39 89655	13 10319	38 92557	14 60776	37 92388	14 10488	36 89324	15 59433
78	42 06704	12 39815	41 21546	13 91765	40 32621	13 43023	39 40170	14 93570	38 44409	14 43383	37 45536	15 92443	36 43731	15 40724
79	43 52944	12 24941	42 69258	13 76275	41 81757	13 26908	40 90685	14 76820	39 96260	14 25991	38 98683	15 74397	37 98138	15 22016
80	44 99184	12 10067	42 16970	13 60784	41 30894	13 10793	40 41200	14 60071	39 48112	14 08598	38 51831	15 56351	37 52544	15 03307
81	44 45424	13 95193	43 64682	13 45294	42 80030	14 94678	41 91715	14 43322	40 99963	15 91206	38 04979	15 38306	37 06951	16 84598
82	45 91664	13 80318	43 12394	13 29804	42 29166	14 78563	41 42230	14 26573	40 51814	15 73813	39 58127	15 20260	38 61358	16 65890
83	45 37903	13 65444	44 60106	13 14314	43 78302	14 62447	42 92745	14 09824	40 03666	15 56421	39 11275	15 02215	38 15765	16 47181
84	46 84143	13 50570	44 07819	14 98824	43 27438	14 46332	42 43260	15 93075	41 55517	15 39028	40 64423	16 84169	39 70172	16 28472
85	46 30383	13 35696	45 55531	14 83333	44 76574	14 30217	43 93775	15 76326	41 07368	15 21636	40 17571	16 66123	39 24578	16 09764
86	47 76623	13 20822	45 03243	14 67843	44 25711	14 14102	43 44290	15 59577	42 59220	15 04243	41 70719	16 48078	40 78985	17 91055
87	47 22863	13 05948	46 50955	14 52353	45 74847	15 97987	44 94805	15 42828	42 11071	16 86851	41 23867	16 30032	40 33392	17 72346
88	48 69102	14 91073	47 98667	14 36863	45 23983	15 81872	44 45320	15 26078	43 62923	16 69458	42 77014	16 11987	41 87799	17 53638
89	48 15342	14 76199	47 46379	14 21373	46 73119	15 65757	45 95835	15 09329	43 14774	16 52066	42 30162	17 93941	41 42206	17 34929
90	49 61582	14 61325	48 94091	14 05882	46 22255	15 49642	45 46350	16 92580	44 66625	16 34673	43 83310	17 75895	42 96612	17 16220
91	49 07822	14 46451	48 41803	15 90392	47 71391	15 33527	46 96865	16 75831	44 18477	16 17281	43 36458	17 57850	42 51019	18 97512
92	50 54062	14 31577	49 89516	15 74902	47 20528	15 17412	46 47380	16 59082	45 70328	17 99888	44 89606	17 39804	42 05426	18 78803
93	50 00301	14 16703	49 37228	15 59412	48 69664	15 01297	47 97895	16 42333	45 22180	17 82496	44 42754	17 21759	43 59833	18 60094
94	51 46541	14 01828	50 84940	15 43922	48 18800	16 85181	47 48410	16 25584	46 74031	17 65103	45 95902	17 03713	43 14240	18 41386
95	52 92781	15 86954	50 32652	15 28431	49 67936	16 69066	48 98925	16 08835	46 25882	17 47711	45 49050	18 85667	44 68646	18 22677
96	52 39021	15 72080	51 80364	15 12941	49 17072	16 52951	48 49440	17 92086	47 77734	17 30318	45 02198	18 67622	44 23053	18 03968
97	53 85261	15 57206	51 28076	16 97451	50 66208	16 36836	49 99955	17 75336	47 29585	17 12926	46 55345	18 49576	45 77460	19 85260
98	53 31500	15 42332	52 75788	16 81961	50 15345	16 20721	49 50470	17 58587	48 81437	18 95533	46 08493	18 31531	45 31867	19 66551
99	54 77740	15 27458	52 23500	16 66471	51 64481	16 04606	49 00985	17 41838	48 33288	18 78141	47 61641	18 13485	46 86274	19 47842
100	54 23980	15 12583	53 71213	16 50980	51 13617	17 88491	50 51500	17 25089	49 85139	18 60748	47 14789	19 95439	46 40680	19 29134

* For explanation see page 81. –

All values conform to the international convention (i.e. 0,1 instead of 0.1).

n	p (q) 0,36	q (p) 0,64	p (q) 0,37	q (p) 0,63	p (q) 0,38	q (p) 0,62	p (q) 0,39	q (p) 0,61	p (q) 0,40	q (p) 0,60	p (q) 0,41	q (p) 0,59	p (q) 0,42	q (p) 0,58
0	0 00000	0 00000	0 00000	0 00000	0 00000	0 00000	0 00000	0 00000	0 00000	0 00000	0 00000	0 00000	0 00000	0 00000
1	1 55630	1 80618	1 56820	1 79934	1 57978	1 79239	1 59106	1 78533	1 60206	1 77815	1 61278	1 77085	1 62325	1 76343
2	1 11261	1 61236	1 13640	1 59868	1 15957	1 58478	1 18213	1 57066	1 20412	1 55630	1 22557	1 54170	1 24650	1 52686
3	2 66891	1 41854	2 70461	1 39802	2 73935	1 37718	2 77319	1 35599	2 80618	1 33445	2 83835	1 31256	2 86975	1 29028
4	2 22521	1 22472	2 27281	1 19736	2 31913	1 16957	2 36426	1 14132	2 40824	1 11261	2 45114	1 08341	2 49300	1 05371
5	3 78151	1 03090	3 84101	2 99670	3 89892	2 96196	3 95532	2 92665	2 01030	2 89076	2 06392	2 85426	2 11625	2 81714
6	3 33782	2 83708	3 40921	2 79604	3 47870	2 75435	3 54639	2 71198	3 61236	2 66891	3 67670	2 62511	3 73950	2 58057
7	4 89412	2 64326	4 97741	2 59538	3 05849	2 54674	3 13745	2 49731	3 21442	2 44706	3 28949	2 39596	3 36275	2 34400
8	4 45042	2 44944	4 54561	2 39472	4 63827	2 33913	4 72852	2 28264	4 81648	2 22521	4 90227	2 16682	4 98599	2 10742
9	4 00672	2 25562	4 11382	2 19406	4 21805	2 13153	4 31958	2 06797	4 41854	2 00336	4 51505	3 93767	4 60924	3 87085
10	5 56303	2 06180	5 68202	3 99341	5 79784	3 92392	5 91065	3 85330	4 02060	3 78151	4 12784	3 70852	4 23249	3 63428
11	5 11933	3 86798	5 25022	3 79275	5 37762	3 71631	5 50171	3 63863	5 62266	3 55966	5 74062	3 47937	5 85574	3 39771
12	6 67563	3 67416	6 81842	3 59209	6 95740	3 50870	5 09278	3 42396	5 22472	3 33782	5 35341	3 25022	5 47899	3 16114
13	6 23193	3 48034	6 38662	3 39143	6 53719	3 30109	6 68384	3 20929	6 82678	3 11597	6 96619	3 02108	5 10224	4 92456
14	7 78824	3 28652	7 95482	3 19077	6 11697	3 09348	6 27490	4 99462	6 42884	4 89412	6 57897	4 79193	6 72549	4 68799
15	7 34454	3 09270	7 52303	4 99011	7 69675	4 88588	7 86597	4 77995	6 03090	4 67227	6 19176	4 56278	6 34874	4 45142
16	8 90084	4 89888	7 09123	4 78945	7 27654	4 67827	7 45703	4 56528	7 63296	4 45042	7 80454	4 33363	7 97199	4 21485
17	8 45714	4 70506	8 65943	4 58879	8 85632	4 47066	7 04810	4 35061	7 23502	4 22857	7 41733	4 10448	7 59524	5 97828
18	8 01345	4 51124	8 22763	4 38813	8 43610	4 26305	8 63916	4 13594	8 83708	4 00672	7 03011	5 87534	7 21849	5 74170
19	9 56975	4 31742	9 79583	4 18747	8 01589	4 05544	8 23023	5 92127	8 43914	5 78487	8 64289	5 64619	8 84174	5 50513
20	9 12605	4 12360	9 36403	5 98681	9 59567	5 84783	9 82129	5 70660	8 04120	5 56303	8 25568	5 41704	8 46499	5 26856
21	10 68235	5 92978	10 93224	5 78615	9 17546	5 64023	9 41236	5 49193	9 64326	5 34118	9 86846	5 18789	8 08824	5 03199
22	10 23866	5 73596	10 50044	5 58549	10 75524	5 43262	9 00342	5 27726	9 24532	5 11933	9 48124	6 95874	9 71148	6 79542
23	11 79496	5 54214	10 06864	5 38483	10 33502	5 22501	10 59449	5 06259	10 84738	6 89748	9 09403	6 72960	9 33473	6 55884
24	11 35126	5 34832	11 63684	5 18417	11 91481	5 01740	10 18555	6 84792	10 44944	6 67563	10 70681	6 50045	10 95798	6 32227
25	12 90756	5 15450	11 20504	6 98351	11 49459	6 80979	11 77662	6 63325	10 05150	6 45378	10 31960	6 27130	10 58123	6 08570
26	12 46387	6 96068	12 77324	6 78285	11 07437	6 60218	11 36768	6 41858	11 65356	6 23193	11 93238	6 04215	10 20448	7 84913
27	12 02017	6 76686	12 34145	6 58219	12 65416	6 39458	12 95874	6 20391	11 25562	6 01008	11 54516	7 81300	11 82773	7 61256
28	13 57647	6 57304	13 90965	6 38154	12 23394	6 18697	12 54981	7 98924	12 85768	7 78824	11 15795	7 58386	11 45098	7 37598
29	13 13277	6 37922	13 47785	6 18088	13 81372	7 97936	12 14087	7 77457	12 45974	7 56639	12 77073	7 35471	11 07423	7 13941
30	14 68908	6 18540	13 04605	7 98022	13 39351	7 77175	13 73194	7 55990	12 06180	7 34454	12 38352	7 12556	12 69748	8 90284
31	14 24538	7 99158	14 61425	7 77956	14 97329	7 56414	13 32300	7 34522	13 66386	7 12269	13 99630	8 89641	12 32073	8 66627
32	15 80168	7 79776	14 18246	7 57890	14 55308	7 35653	14 91407	7 13055	13 26592	8 90084	13 60908	8 66726	13 94398	8 42970
33	15 35798	7 60394	15 75066	7 37824	14 13286	7 14893	14 50513	8 91588	14 86798	8 67899	13 22187	8 43812	13 56723	8 19312
34	16 91429	7 41012	15 31886	7 17758	15 71264	8 94132	14 09620	8 70121	14 47004	8 45714	14 83465	8 20897	13 19048	9 95655
35	16 47059	7 21630	16 88706	8 97692	15 29243	8 73371	15 68726	8 48654	14 07210	8 23529	14 44743	9 97982	14 81373	9 71998
36	16 02689	7 02248	16 45526	8 77626	16 87221	8 52610	15 27833	8 27187	15 67416	8 01345	14 06022	9 75067	14 43697	9 48341
37	17 58319	8 82866	16 02346	8 57560	16 45199	8 31849	16 86939	8 05720	15 27622	9 79160	15 67300	9 52152	14 06022	9 24684
38	17 13950	8 63484	17 59167	8 37494	16 03178	8 11088	16 46046	9 84253	16 87828	9 56975	15 28579	9 29238	15 68347	9 01026
39	18 69580	8 44102	17 15987	8 17428	17 61156	9 90328	16 05152	9 62786	16 48034	9 34790	16 89857	9 06323	15 30672	10 77369
40	18 25210	8 24720	18 72807	9 97362	17 19134	9 69567	17 64258	9 41319	16 08240	9 12605	16 51135	10 83408	16 92997	10 53712
41	19 80840	8 05338	18 29627	9 77296	18 77113	9 48806	17 23365	9 19852	17 68446	10 90420	16 12414	10 60493	16 55322	10 30055
42	19 36471	9 85956	19 86447	9 57230	18 35091	9 28045	18 82471	10 98385	17 28652	10 68235	17 73692	10 37578	16 17647	10 06398
43	20 92101	9 66574	19 43267	9 37164	19 93069	9 07284	18 41578	10 76918	18 88858	10 46050	17 34971	10 14664	17 79972	11 82740
44	20 47731	9 47192	19 00088	9 17098	19 51048	10 86523	18 00684	10 55451	18 49064	10 23866	18 96249	11 91749	17 42297	11 59083
45	20 03361	9 27810	20 56908	10 97032	19 09026	10 65763	19 59791	10 33984	18 09270	10 01681	18 57527	11 68834	17 04622	11 35426
46	21 58992	9 08428	20 13728	10 76967	20 67005	10 45002	19 18897	10 12517	19 69476	11 79496	18 18806	11 45919	18 66947	11 11769
47	21 14622	10 89046	21 70548	10 56901	20 24983	10 24241	20 78004	11 91050	19 29682	11 57311	19 80084	11 23004	18 29272	12 88112
48	22 70252	10 69664	21 27368	10 36835	21 82961	10 03480	20 37110	11 69583	20 89888	11 35126	19 41363	11 00090	19 91597	12 64454
49	22 25882	10 50282	22 84188	10 16769	21 40940	11 82719	21 96217	11 48116	20 50094	11 12941	19 02641	12 77175	19 53922	12 40797
50	23 81513	10 30900	22 41009	11 96703	22 98918	11 61958	21 55323	11 26649	20 10300	12 90756	20 63919	12 54260	19 16246	12 17140
51	23 37143	10 11518	23 97829	11 76637	22 56896	11 41198	21 14429	11 05182	21 70506	12 68571	20 25198	12 31345	20 78571	13 93483
52	24 92773	11 92136	23 54649	11 56571	22 14875	11 20437	22 73536	12 83715	21 30712	12 46387	21 86476	12 08430	20 40896	13 69826
53	24 48403	11 72754	23 11469	11 36505	23 72853	12 99676	22 32642	12 62248	22 90918	12 24202	21 47754	13 85516	20 03221	13 46168
54	24 04034	11 53372	24 68289	11 16439	23 30831	12 78915	23 91749	12 40781	22 51124	12 02017	21 09033	13 62601	21 65546	13 22511
55	25 59664	11 33990	24 25109	12 96373	24 88810	12 58154	23 50855	12 19314	22 11330	13 79832	22 70311	13 39686	21 27871	14 98854
56	25 15294	11 14608	25 81930	12 76307	24 46788	12 37393	23 09962	13 97847	23 71536	13 57647	22 31590	13 16771	22 90196	14 75197
57	26 70924	12 95226	25 38750	12 56241	24 04767	12 16633	24 69068	13 76380	23 31742	13 35462	23 92868	14 93856	22 52521	14 51540
58	26 26555	12 75844	26 95570	12 36175	25 62745	13 95872	24 28175	13 54913	24 91948	13 13277	23 54146	14 70942	22 14846	14 27882
59	27 82185	12 56462	26 52390	12 16109	25 20723	13 75111	25 87281	13 33446	24 52154	14 91092	23 15425	14 48027	23 77171	14 04225
60	27 37815	12 37080	26 09210	13 96043	26 78702	13 54350	25 46388	13 11979	24 12360	14 68908	24 76703	14 25112	23 39496	15 80568
61	28 93445	12 17698	27 66031	13 75977	26 36680	13 33589	25 05494	14 90512	25 72566	14 46723	24 37982	14 02197	23 01821	15 56911
62	28 49076	13 98316	27 22851	13 55911	27 94658	13 12828	26 64601	14 69045	25 32772	14 24538	25 99260	15 79282	24 64146	15 33254
63	28 04706	13 78934	28 79671	13 35845	27 52637	14 92068	26 23707	14 47578	26 92978	14 02353	25 60538	15 56368	24 26471	15 09596
64	29 60336	13 59552	28 36491	13 15780	27 10615	14 71307	27 82813	14 26111	26 53184	15 80168	25 21817	15 33453	25 88795	16 85939
65	29 15966	13 40170	29 93311	14 95714	28 68593	14 50546	27 41920	14 04644	26 13390	15 57983	26 83095	15 10538	25 51120	16 62282
66	30 71597	13 20788	29 50131	14 75648	28 26572	14 29785	27 01026	15 83177	27 73596	15 35798	26 44373	16 87623	25 13445	16 38625
67	30 27227	13 01406	29 06952	14 55582	29 84550	14 09024	28 60133	15 61710	27 33802	15 13613	26 05652	16 64708	26 75770	16 14968
68	31 82857	14 82024	30 63772	14 35516	29 42528	15 88263	28 19239	15 40243	28 94008	16 91429	27 66930	16 41794	26 38095	17 91310
69	31 38487	14 62642	30 20592	14 15450	29 00507	15 67503	29 78346	15 18776	28 54214	16 69244	27 28209	16 18879	26 00420	17 67653
70	32 94118	14 43260	31 77412	15 95384	30 58485	15 46742	29 37452	16 97309	28 14420	16 47059	28 89487	17 95964	27 62745	17 43996
71	32 49748	14 23878	31 34232	15 75318	30 16464	15 25981	30 96559	16 75842	29 74626	16 24874	28 50765	17 73049	27 25070	17 20339
72	32 05378	14 04496	32 91052	15 55252	31 74442	15 05220	30 55665	16 54375	29 34832	16 02689	28 12044	17 50134	28 87395	18 96682
73	33 61008	15 85114	32 47873	15 35186	31 32420	16 84459	30 14772	16 32908	30 95038	17 80504	29 73322	17 27220	28 49720	18 73024
74	33 16639	15 65732	32 04693	15 15120	32 90399	16 63699	31 73878	16 11441	30 55244	17 58319	29 34601	17 04305	28 12045	18 49367
75	34 72269	15 46350	33 61513	16 95054	32 48377	16 42938	31 32985	17 89974	30 15450	17 36134	30 95879	18 81390	29 74370	18 25710
76	34 27899	15 26968	33 18333	16 74988	32 06355	16 22177	32 92091	17 68507	31 75656	17 13950	30 57157	18 58475	29 36695	18 02053
77	35 83529	15 07586	34 75153	16 54922	33 64334	16 01416	32 51197	17 47040	31 35862	18 91765	30 18436	18 35560	30 99020	19 78396
78	35 39160	16 88204	34 31973	16 34856	33 22312	17 80655	32 10304	17 25573	32 96068	18 69580	31 79714	18 12646	30 61344	19 54738
79	36 94790	16 68822	35 88794	16 14790	34 80290	17 59894	33 69410	17 04106	32 56274	18 47395	31 40992	19 89731	30 23669	19 31081
80	36 50420	16 49440	35 45614	17 94724	34 38269	17 39134	33 28517	18 82639	32 16480	18 25210	31 02271	19 66816	31 85994	19 07424
81	36 06050	16 30058	35 02434	17 74658	35 96247	17 18373	34 87623	18 61172	33 76686	18 03025	32 63549	19 43901	31 48319	20 83767
82	37 61681	16 10676	36 59254	17 54593	35 54225	18 97612	34 46730	18 39705	33 36892	19 80840	32 24828	19 20986	31 10644	20 60110
83	37 17311	17 91294	36 16074	17 34527	35 12204	18 76851	34 05836	18 18238	34 97098	19 58655	33 86106	20 98072	32 72969	20 36452
84	38 72941	17 71912	37 72894	17 14461	36 70182	18 56090	35 64943	19 96771	34 57304	19 36471	33 47384	20 75157	32 35294	20 12795
85	38 28571	17 52530	37 29715	18 94395	36 28161	18 35329	35 24049	19 75304	34 17510	19 14286	33 08663	20 52242	33 97619	21 89138
86	39 84202	17 33148	38 86535	18 74329	37 86139	18 14569	36 83156	19 53837	35 77716	20 92101	34 69941	20 29327	33 59944	21 65481
87	39 39832	17 13766	38 43355	18 54263	37 44117	19 93808	36 42262	19 32370	35 37922	20 69916	34 31220	20 06413	33 22269	21 41824
88	40 95462	18 94384	38 00175	18 34197	37 02096	19 73047	36 01369	19 10903	36 98128	20 47731	35 92498	21 83498	34 84594	21 18166
89	40 51092	18 75002	39 56995	18 14131	38 60074	19 52286	37 60475	20 89436	36 58334	20 25546	35 53776	21 60583	34 46919	22 94509
90	40 06723	18 55620	39 13816	19 94065	38 18052	19 31525	37 19581	20 67969	36 18540	20 03361	35 15055	21 37668	34 09244	22 70852
91	41 62353	18 36238	40 70636	19 73999	39 76031	19 10764	38 78688	20 46501	37 78746	21 81176	36 76333	21 14753	35 71569	22 47195
92	41 17983	18 16856	40 27456	19 53933	39 34009	20 90004	38 37794	20 25034	37 38952	21 58992	36 37611	22 91839	35 33893	22 23538
93	42 73613	19 97474	41 84276	19 33867	40 91987	20 69243	39 96901	20 03567	38 99158	21 36807	37 98890	22 68924	36 96218	23 99880
94	42 29244	19 78092	41 41096	19 13801	40 49966	20 48482	39 56007	21 82100	38 59364	21 14622	37 60168	22 46009	36 58543	23 76223
95	43 84874	19 58710	42 97916	20 93735	40 07944	20 27721	39 15114	21 60633	38 19570	22 92437	37 21447	22 23094	36 20868	23 52566
96	43 40504	19 39328	42 54737	20 73669	41 65923	20 06960	40 74220	21 39166	39 79776	22 70252	38 82725	22 00179	37 83193	23 28909
97	44 96134	19 19946	42 11557	20 53603	41 23901	21 86199	40 33327	21 17699	39 39982	22 48067	38 44003	23 77265	37 45518	23 05252
98	44 51765	19 00564	43 68377	20 33537	42 81879	21 65439	41 92433	22 96232	39 00188	22 25882	38 05282	23 54350	37 07843	24 81594
99	44 07395	20 81182	43 25197	20 13471	42 39858	21 44678	41 51540	22 74765	40 60394	22 03697	39 66560	23 31435	38 70168	24 57937
100	45 63025	20 61800	44 82017	21 93405	43 97836	21 23917	41 10646	22 53298	40 20600	23 81513	39 27839	23 08520	38 32493	24 34280

* For explanation see page 81. –

All values conform to the international convention (i.e. 0,1 instead of 0.1).

n	p (q) 0,43	q (p) 0,57	p (q) 0,44	q (p) 0,56	p (q) 0,45	q (p) 0,55	p (q) 0,46	q (p) 0,54	p (q) 0,47	q (p) 0,53	p (q) 0,48	q (p) 0,52	p (q) 0,49	q (p) 0,51	p (q) 0,50	q (p) 0,50
0	0 00000	0 00000	0 00000	0 00000	0 00000	0 00000	0 00000	0 00000	0 00000	0 00000	0 00000	0 00000	0 00000	0 00000	0 00000	0 00000
1	1 63347	1 75587	1 64345	1 74819	1 65321	1 74036	1 66276	1 73239	1 67210	1 72428	1 68124	1 71600	1 69020	1 70757	1 69897	1 69897
2	1 26694	1 51175	1 28691	1 49638	1 30643	1 48073	1 32552	1 46479	1 34420	1 44855	1 36248	1 43201	1 38039	1 41514	1 39794	1 39794
3	2 90041	1 26762	2 93036	1 24456	2 95964	1 22109	2 98827	1 19718	1 01629	1 17283	1 04372	1 14801	1 07059	1 12271	1 09691	1 09691
4	2 53387	1 02350	2 57381	2 99275	2 61285	2 96145	2 65103	2 92958	2 68839	2 89710	2 72496	2 86401	2 76078	2 83028	2 79588	2 79588
5	2 16734	2 77937	2 21726	2 74094	2 26606	2 70181	2 31379	2 66197	2 36049	2 62138	2 40621	2 58002	2 45098	2 53785	2 49485	2 49485
6	3 80081	2 53525	3 86072	2 48913	3 91928	2 44218	3 97655	2 39436	2 03259	2 34566	2 08745	2 29602	2 14118	2 24542	2 19382	2 19382
7	3 43428	2 29112	3 50417	2 23732	3 57249	2 18254	3 63930	2 12676	3 70469	2 06993	3 76869	2 01202	3 83137	3 95299	3 89279	3 89279
8	3 06775	2 04700	3 14762	3 98550	3 22570	3 92290	3 30206	3 85915	3 37678	3 79421	3 44993	3 72803	3 52157	3 66056	3 59176	3 59176
9	4 70122	3 80287	4 79107	3 73369	4 87891	3 66326	4 96482	3 59154	3 04888	3 51848	3 13117	3 44403	3 21176	3 36813	3 29073	3 29073
10	4 33468	3 55875	4 43453	3 48188	4 53213	3 40363	4 62758	3 32394	4 72098	3 24276	4 81241	3 16003	4 90196	3 07570	4 98970	4 98970
11	5 96815	3 31462	4 07798	3 23007	4 18534	3 14399	4 29034	3 05633	4 39308	4 96703	4 49365	4 87604	4 59216	4 78327	4 68867	4 68867
12	5 60162	3 07050	5 72143	4 97826	5 83855	4 88435	5 95309	4 78873	4 06517	4 69131	4 17489	4 59204	4 28235	4 49084	4 38764	4 38764
13	5 23509	4 82637	5 36488	4 72644	5 49176	4 62471	5 61585	4 52112	5 73727	4 41559	5 85614	4 30804	5 97255	4 19841	4 08661	4 08661
14	6 86856	4 58225	5 00834	4 47463	5 14498	4 36508	5 27861	4 25351	5 40937	4 13986	5 53738	4 02405	5 66275	5 90598	5 78558	5 78558
15	6 50203	4 33812	6 65179	4 22282	6 79819	4 10544	6 94137	5 98591	5 08147	5 86414	5 21862	5 74005	5 35294	5 61355	5 48455	5 48455
16	6 13550	4 09400	6 29524	5 97101	6 45140	5 84580	6 60413	5 71830	6 75357	5 58841	6 89986	5 45605	5 04314	5 32112	5 18352	5 18352
17	7 76896	5 84987	7 93870	5 71920	6 10461	5 58617	6 26688	5 45069	6 42566	5 31269	6 58110	5 17206	6 73333	5 02869	6 88249	6 88249
18	7 40243	5 60575	7 58215	5 46738	7 75783	5 32653	7 92964	5 18309	6 09776	5 03697	6 26234	6 88806	6 42353	6 73626	6 58146	6 58146
19	7 03590	5 36162	7 22560	5 21557	7 41104	5 06689	7 59240	6 91548	7 76986	6 76124	7 94358	6 60406	6 11373	6 44383	6 28043	6 28043
20	8 66937	5 11750	8 86905	6 96376	7 06425	6 80725	7 25516	6 64788	7 44196	6 48552	7 62482	6 32007	7 80392	6 15140	7 97940	7 97940
21	8 30284	6 87337	8 51251	6 71195	8 71746	6 54762	8 91791	6 38027	7 11406	6 20979	7 30607	6 03607	7 49412	7 85897	7 67837	7 67837
22	9 93631	6 62925	8 15596	6 46014	8 37068	6 28798	8 58067	6 11266	8 78615	7 93407	8 98731	7 75207	7 18431	7 56654	7 37734	7 37734
23	9 56977	6 38512	9 79941	6 20832	8 02389	6 02834	8 24343	7 84506	8 45825	7 65835	8 66855	7 46808	8 87451	7 27411	7 07631	7 07631
24	9 20324	6 14100	9 44286	7 95651	9 67710	7 76870	9 90619	7 57745	8 13035	7 38262	8 34979	7 18408	8 56471	8 98168	8 77528	8 77528
25	10 83671	7 89687	9 08632	7 70470	9 33031	7 50907	9 56895	7 30984	9 80245	7 10690	8 03103	8 90008	8 25490	8 68925	8 47425	8 47425
26	10 47018	7 65275	10 72977	7 45289	10 98353	7 24943	9 23170	7 04224	9 47454	8 83117	9 71227	8 61609	9 94510	8 39682	8 17322	8 17322
27	10 10365	7 40862	10 37322	7 20108	10 63674	8 98979	10 89446	8 77463	9 14664	8 55545	9 39351	8 33209	9 63529	8 10439	9 87219	9 87219
28	11 73712	7 16450	10 01667	8 94926	10 28995	8 73016	10 55722	8 50703	10 81874	8 27972	9 07475	8 04809	9 32549	9 81196	9 57116	9 57116
29	11 37059	8 92037	11 66013	8 69745	11 94316	8 47052	10 21998	8 23942	10 49084	8 00400	10 75600	9 76410	9 01569	9 51954	9 27013	9 27013
30	11 00405	8 67625	11 30358	8 44564	11 59638	8 21088	11 88273	9 97181	10 16294	9 72828	10 43724	9 48010	10 70588	9 22711	10 96910	10 96910
31	12 63752	8 43212	12 94703	8 19383	11 24959	9 95124	11 54549	9 70421	11 83503	9 45255	10 11848	9 19610	10 39608	10 93468	10 66807	10 66807
32	12 27099	8 18800	12 59049	9 94202	12 90280	9 69161	11 20825	9 43660	11 50713	9 17683	11 79972	10 91211	10 08627	10 64225	10 36704	10 36704
33	13 90446	9 94387	12 23394	9 69020	12 55601	9 43197	12 87101	9 16899	11 17923	10 90110	11 48096	10 62811	11 77647	10 34982	10 06601	10 06601
34	13 53793	9 69975	13 87739	9 43839	12 20923	9 17233	12 53377	10 90139	12 85133	10 62538	11 16220	10 34411	11 46667	10 05739	11 76498	11 76498
35	13 17140	9 45562	13 52084	9 18658	13 86244	10 91269	12 19652	10 63378	12 52343	10 34966	12 84344	10 06012	11 15686	11 76496	11 46395	11 46395
36	14 80486	9 21149	13 16430	10 93477	13 51565	10 65306	13 85928	10 36618	12 19552	10 07393	12 52468	11 77612	12 84706	11 47253	11 16292	11 16292
37	14 43833	10 96737	14 80775	10 68296	13 16886	10 39342	13 52204	10 09857	13 86762	11 79821	12 20593	11 49212	12 53725	11 18010	12 86189	12 86189
38	14 07180	10 72324	14 45120	10 43115	14 82208	10 13378	13 18480	11 83096	13 53972	11 52248	13 88717	11 20813	12 22745	12 88767	12 56086	12 56086
39	15 70527	10 47912	14 09465	10 17933	14 47529	11 87414	14 84756	11 56336	13 21182	11 24676	13 56841	12 92413	13 91765	12 59524	12 25983	12 25983
40	15 33874	10 23499	15 73811	11 92752	14 12850	11 61451	14 51031	11 29575	14 88391	12 97103	13 24965	12 64013	13 60784	12 30281	13 95880	13 95880
41	16 97221	11 99087	15 38156	11 67571	15 78171	11 35487	14 17307	11 02814	14 55601	12 69531	14 93089	12 35614	13 29804	12 01038	13 65777	13 65777
42	16 60568	11 74674	15 02501	11 42390	15 43493	11 09523	15 83583	12 76054	14 22811	12 41959	14 61213	12 07214	14 98824	13 71795	13 35674	13 35674
43	16 23914	11 50262	16 66847	11 17209	15 08814	12 83560	15 49859	12 49293	15 90021	12 14386	14 29337	13 78814	14 67843	13 42552	13 05571	13 05571
44	17 87261	11 25849	16 31192	12 92027	16 74135	12 57596	15 16134	12 22533	15 57231	13 86814	15 97461	13 50415	14 36863	13 13309	14 75468	14 75468
45	17 50608	11 01437	17 95537	12 66846	16 39456	12 31632	16 82410	13 95772	15 24440	13 59241	15 65586	13 22015	14 05882	14 84066	14 45365	14 45365
46	17 13955	12 77024	17 59882	12 41665	16 04778	12 05668	16 48686	13 69011	16 91650	13 31669	15 33710	14 93615	15 74902	14 54823	14 15262	14 15262
47	18 77302	12 52612	17 24228	12 16484	17 70099	13 79705	16 14962	13 42251	16 58860	13 04097	15 01834	14 65216	15 43922	14 25580	15 85159	15 85159
48	18 40649	12 28199	18 88573	13 91303	17 35420	13 53741	17 81238	13 15490	16 26070	14 76524	16 69958	14 36816	15 12941	15 96337	15 55056	15 55056
49	18 03995	12 03787	18 52918	13 66121	17 00741	13 27777	17 47513	14 88729	17 93280	14 48952	16 38082	14 08416	16 81961	15 67094	15 24953	15 24953
50	19 67342	13 79374	18 17263	13 40940	18 66063	13 01813	17 13789	14 61969	17 60489	14 21379	16 06206	15 80017	16 50980	15 37851	16 94850	16 94850
51	19 30689	13 54962	19 81609	13 15759	18 31384	14 75850	18 80065	14 35208	17 27699	15 93807	17 74330	15 51617	16 20000	15 08608	16 64747	16 64747
52	20 94036	13 30549	19 45954	14 90578	19 96705	14 49886	18 46341	14 08448	18 94909	15 66235	17 42454	15 23217	17 89020	16 79365	16 34644	16 34644
53	20 57383	13 06137	19 10299	14 65397	19 62026	14 23922	18 12617	15 81687	18 62119	15 38662	17 10579	16 94818	17 58039	16 50122	16 04541	16 04541
54	20 20730	14 81724	20 74644	14 40215	19 27348	15 97959	19 78892	15 54926	18 29328	15 11090	18 78703	16 66418	17 27059	16 20879	17 74438	17 74438
55	21 84077	14 57312	20 38990	14 15034	20 92669	15 71995	19 45168	15 28166	19 96538	16 83517	18 46827	16 38018	18 96078	17 91636	17 44335	17 44335
56	21 47423	14 32899	20 03335	15 89853	20 57990	15 46031	19 11444	15 01405	19 63748	16 55945	18 14951	16 09619	18 65098	17 62393	17 14232	17 14232
57	21 10770	14 08487	21 67680	15 64672	20 23311	15 20067	20 77720	16 74644	19 30958	16 28372	19 83075	17 81219	18 34118	17 33150	18 84129	18 84129
58	22 74117	15 84074	21 32026	15 39491	21 88633	16 94104	20 43995	16 47884	20 98168	16 00800	19 51199	17 52819	18 03137	17 03907	18 54026	18 54026
59	22 37464	15 59662	22 96371	15 14309	21 53954	16 68140	20 10271	16 21123	20 65377	17 73228	19 19323	17 24420	19 72157	18 74664	18 23923	18 23923
60	22 00811	15 35249	22 60716	16 89128	21 19275	16 42176	21 76547	17 94363	20 32587	17 45655	20 87447	18 96020	19 41176	18 45421	19 93820	19 93820
61	23 64158	15 10837	22 25061	16 63947	22 84596	16 16212	21 42823	17 67602	21 99797	17 18083	20 55572	18 67620	19 10196	18 16178	19 63717	19 63717
62	23 27504	16 86424	23 89407	16 38766	22 49918	17 90249	21 09099	17 40841	21 67007	18 90510	20 23696	18 39221	20 79216	19 86935	19 33614	19 33614
63	24 90851	16 62012	23 53752	16 13585	22 15239	17 64285	22 75374	17 14081	21 34217	18 62938	21 91820	18 10821	20 48235	19 57692	19 03511	19 03511
64	24 54198	16 37599	23 18097	17 88403	23 80560	17 38321	22 41650	18 87320	21 01426	18 35366	21 59944	19 82421	20 17255	19 28449	20 73408	20 73408
65	24 17545	16 13187	24 82442	17 63222	23 45881	17 12357	22 07926	18 60559	22 68636	18 07793	21 28068	19 54022	21 86275	20 99206	20 43305	20 43305
66	25 80892	17 88774	24 46788	17 38041	23 11203	18 86394	23 74202	18 33799	22 35846	19 80221	22 96192	19 25622	21 55294	20 69963	20 13202	20 13202
67	25 44239	17 64362	24 11133	17 12860	24 76524	18 60430	23 40477	18 07038	22 03056	19 52648	22 64316	20 97222	21 24314	20 40720	21 83099	21 83099
68	25 07585	17 39949	25 75478	18 87679	24 41845	18 34466	23 06753	19 80278	23 70265	19 25076	22 32440	20 68823	22 93333	20 11477	21 52996	21 52996
69	26 70932	17 15537	25 39823	18 62497	24 07166	18 08503	24 73029	19 53517	23 37475	20 97504	22 00565	20 40423	22 62353	21 82234	21 22893	21 22893
70	26 34279	18 91124	25 04169	18 37316	25 72488	19 82539	24 39305	19 26756	23 04685	20 69931	23 68689	20 12023	22 31373	21 52991	22 92790	22 92790
71	27 97626	18 66711	26 68514	18 12135	25 37809	19 56575	24 05581	20 99996	24 71895	20 42359	23 36813	21 83624	22 00392	21 23748	22 62687	22 62687
72	27 60973	18 42299	26 32859	19 86954	25 03130	19 30611	25 71856	20 73235	24 39105	20 14786	23 04937	21 55224	23 69412	22 94505	22 32584	22 32584
73	27 24320	18 17886	27 97205	19 61773	26 68451	19 04648	25 38132	20 46474	24 06314	21 87214	24 73061	21 26824	23 38431	22 65262	22 02481	22 02481
74	28 87667	19 93474	27 61550	19 36591	26 33773	20 78684	25 04408	20 19714	25 73524	21 59641	24 41185	22 98425	23 07451	22 36019	23 72378	23 72378
75	28 51013	19 69061	27 25895	19 11410	27 99094	20 52720	26 70684	21 92953	25 40734	21 32069	24 09309	22 70025	24 76471	22 06776	23 42275	23 42275
76	28 14360	19 44649	28 90240	20 86229	27 64415	20 26756	26 36960	21 66193	25 07944	21 04497	25 77433	22 41625	24 45490	23 77533	23 12172	23 12172
77	29 77707	19 20236	28 54586	20 61048	27 29736	20 00793	26 03235	21 39432	26 75154	22 76924	25 45558	22 13226	24 14510	23 48290	24 82069	24 82069
78	29 41054	20 95824	28 18931	20 35867	28 95058	21 74829	27 69511	21 12671	26 42363	22 49352	25 13682	23 84826	25 83529	23 19047	24 51966	24 51966
79	29 04401	20 71411	29 83276	20 10685	28 60379	21 48865	27 35787	22 85911	26 09573	22 21779	26 81806	23 56426	25 52549	24 89804	24 21863	24 21863
80	30 67748	20 46999	29 47621	21 85504	28 25700	21 22902	27 02063	22 59150	27 76783	23 94207	26 49930	23 28027	25 21569	24 60561	25 91760	25 91760
81	30 31094	20 22586	29 11967	21 60323	29 91021	22 96938	28 68338	22 32389	27 43993	23 66635	26 18054	24 99627	26 90588	24 31318	25 61657	25 61657
82	31 94441	21 98174	30 76312	21 35142	29 56343	22 70974	28 34614	22 05629	27 11202	23 39062	27 86178	24 71227	26 59608	24 02075	25 31554	25 31554
83	31 57788	21 73761	30 40657	21 09961	29 21664	22 45010	28 00890	23 78868	28 78412	23 11490	27 54302	24 42828	26 28627	25 72832	25 01451	25 01451
84	31 21135	21 49349	30 05002	22 84779	30 86985	22 19047	29 67166	23 52108	28 45622	24 83917	27 22426	24 14428	27 97647	25 43589	26 71348	26 71348
85	32 84482	21 24936	31 69348	22 59598	30 52306	23 93083	29 33442	23 25347	28 12832	24 56345	28 90551	25 86028	27 66667	25 14347	26 41245	26 41245
86	32 47829	21 00524	31 33693	22 34417	30 17628	23 67119	30 99717	24 98586	29 80042	24 28772	28 58675	25 57629	27 35686	26 85104	26 11142	26 11142
87	32 11176	22 76111	32 98038	22 09236	31 82949	23 41155	30 65993	24 71826	29 47251	24 01200	28 26799	25 29229	27 04706	26 55861	27 81039	27 81039
88	33 74522	22 51699	32 62384	23 84055	31 48270	23 15192	30 32269	24 45065	29 14461	25 73628	29 94923	25 00829	28 73726	26 26618	27 50936	27 50936
89	33 37869	22 27286	32 26729	23 58873	31 13591	24 89228	31 98545	24 18304	30 81671	25 46055	29 63047	26 72430	28 42745	27 97375	27 20833	27 20833
90	33 01216	22 02874	33 91074	23 33692	32 78913	24 63264	31 64820	25 91544	30 48881	25 18483	29 31171	26 44030	28 11765	27 68132	28 90730	28 90730
91	34 64563	23 78461	33 55419	23 08511	32 44234	24 37300	31 31096	25 64783	30 16091	26 90910	30 99295	26 15630	29 80784	27 38889	28 60627	28 60627
92	34 27910	23 54049	33 19765	24 83330	32 09555	24 11337	32 97372	25 38023	31 83300	26 63338	30 67419	27 87231	29 49804	27 09646	28 30524	28 30524
93	35 91257	23 29636	34 84110	24 58149	33 74876	25 85373	32 63648	25 11262	31 50510	26 35766	30 35544	27 58831	29 18824	28 80403	28 00421	28 00421
94	35 54603	23 05224	34 48455	24 32967	33 40198	25 59409	32 29924	26 84501	31 17720	26 08193	30 03668	27 30431	30 87843	28 51160	29 70318	29 70318
95	35 17950	24 80811	34 12800	24 07786	33 05519	25 33446	33 96199	26 57741	32 84930	27 80621	31 71792	27 02032	30 56863	28 21917	29 40215	29 40215
96	36 81297	24 56399	35 77146	25 82605	34 70840	25 07482	33 62475	26 30980	32 52139	27 53048	31 39916	28 73632	30 25882	29 92674	29 10112	29 10112
97	36 44644	24 31986	35 41491	25 57424	34 36161	26 81518	33 28751	26 04219	32 19349	27 25476	31 08040	28 45232	31 94902	29 63431	30 80009	30 80009
98	36 07991	24 07574	35 05836	25 32243	34 01483	26 55554	34 95027	27 77459	33 86559	28 97904	32 76164	28 16833	31 63922	29 34188	30 49906	30 49906
99	37 71338	25 83161	36 70182	25 07061	35 66804	26 29591	34 61303	27 50698	33 53769	28 70331	32 44288	29 88433	31 32941	29 04945	30 19803	30 19803
100	37 34685	25 58749	36 34527	26 81880	35 32125	26 03627	34 27578	27 23938	33 20979	28 42759	32 12412	29 60033	31 01961	30 75702	31 89700	31 89700

* For explanation see page 81. –

All values conform to the international convention (i.e. 0,1 instead of 0.1).

N: number of trials; x: number of successes, etc.; $100\,p_x = 100\,x/N$

x	$100\,p_x$	$100(1-2\alpha)$ limits 95% $100\,p_l$ – $100\,p_r$	$100(1-2\alpha)$ limits 99% $100\,p_l$ – $100\,p_r$
$N = 2$			
0	0,00	0,00– 84,19	0,00– 92,93
1	50,00	1,26– 98,74	0,25– 99,75
2	100,00	15,81–100,00	7,07–100,00
$N = 3$			
0	0,00	0,00– 70,76	0,00– 82,90
1	33,33	0,84– 90,57	0,17– 95,86
2	66,67	9,43– 99,16	4,14– 99,83
3	100,00	29,24–100,00	17,10–100,00
$N = 4$			
0	0,00	0,00– 60,24	0,00– 73,41
1	25,00	0,63– 80,59	0,13– 88,91
2	50,00	6,76– 93,24	2,94– 97,06
3	75,00	19,41– 99,37	11,09– 99,87
4	100,00	39,76–100,00	26,59–100,00
$N = 5$			
0	0,00	0,00– 52,18	0,00– 65,34
1	20,00	0,51– 71,64	0,10– 81,49
2	40,00	5,27– 85,34	2,29– 91,72
3	60,00	14,66– 94,73	8,28– 97,71
4	80,00	28,36– 99,49	18,51– 99,90
5	100,00	47,82–100,00	34,66–100,00
$N = 6$			
0	0,00	0,00– 45,93	0,00– 58,65
1	16,67	0,42– 64,12	0,08– 74,60
2	33,33	4,33– 77,72	1,87– 85,64
3	50,00	11,81– 88,19	6,63– 93,37
4	66,67	22,28– 95,67	14,36– 98,13
5	83,33	35,88– 99,58	25,40– 99,92
6	100,00	54,07–100,00	41,35–100,00
$N = 7$			
0	0,00	0,00– 40,96	0,00– 53,09
1	14,29	0,36– 57,87	0,07– 68,49
2	28,57	3,67– 70,96	1,58– 79,70
3	42,86	9,90– 81,59	5,53– 88,23
4	57,14	18,41– 90,10	11,77– 94,47
5	71,43	29,04– 96,33	20,30– 98,42
6	85,71	42,13– 99,64	31,51– 99,93
7	100,00	59,04–100,00	46,91–100,00
$N = 8$			
0	0,00	0,00– 36,94	0,00– 48,43
1	12,50	0,32– 52,65	0,06– 63,15
2	25,00	3,19– 65,09	1,37– 74,22
3	37,50	8,52– 75,51	4,75– 83,03
4	50,00	15,70– 84,30	9,99– 90,01
5	62,50	24,49– 91,48	16,97– 95,25
6	75,00	34,91– 96,81	25,78– 98,63
7	87,50	47,35– 99,68	36,85– 99,94
8	100,00	63,06–100,00	51,57–100,00
$N = 9$			
0	0,00	0,00– 33,63	0,00– 44,50
1	11,11	0,28– 48,25	0,06– 58,50
2	22,22	2,81– 60,01	1,21– 69,26
3	33,33	7,49– 70,07	4,16– 78,09
4	44,44	13,70– 78,80	8,68– 85,39
5	55,56	21,20– 86,30	14,61– 91,32
6	66,67	29,93– 92,51	21,91– 95,84
7	77,78	39,99– 97,19	30,74– 98,79
8	88,89	51,75– 99,72	41,50– 99,94
9	100,00	66,37–100,00	55,50–100,00
$N = 10$			
0	0,00	0,00– 30,85	0,00– 41,13
1	10,00	0,25– 44,50	0,05– 54,43
2	20,00	2,52– 55,61	1,09– 64,82
3	30,00	6,67– 65,25	3,70– 73,51
4	40,00	12,16– 73,76	7,68– 80,91
5	50,00	18,71– 81,29	12,83– 87,17
6	60,00	26,24– 87,84	19,09– 92,32
7	70,00	34,75– 93,33	26,49– 96,30
8	80,00	44,39– 97,48	35,18– 98,91
9	90,00	55,50– 99,75	45,57– 99,95
10	100,00	69,15–100,00	58,87–100,00
$N = 11$			
0	0,00	0,00– 28,49	0,00– 38,22
1	9,09	0,23– 41,28	0,05– 50,86
2	18,18	2,28– 51,78	0,98– 60,85
3	27,27	6,02– 60,97	3,33– 69,33
4	36,36	10,93– 69,21	6,88– 76,68
5	45,45	16,75– 76,62	11,45– 83,07
6	54,55	23,38– 83,25	16,93– 88,55
7	63,64	30,79– 89,07	23,32– 93,12
8	72,73	39,03– 93,98	30,67– 96,67
9	81,82	48,22– 97,72	39,15– 99,02
$N = 11$ (continued)			
10	90,91	58,72– 99,77	49,14– 99,95
11	100,00	71,51–100,00	61,78–100,00
$N = 12$			
0	0,00	0,00– 26,46	0,00– 35,69
1	8,33	0,21– 38,48	0,04– 47,70
2	16,67	2,09– 48,41	0,90– 57,29
3	25,00	5,49– 57,19	3,03– 65,52
4	33,33	9,92– 65,11	6,24– 72,75
5	41,67	15,17– 72,33	10,34– 79,15
6	50,00	21,09– 78,91	15,22– 84,78
7	58,33	27,67– 84,83	20,85– 89,66
8	66,67	34,89– 90,08	27,25– 93,76
9	75,00	42,81– 94,51	34,48– 96,97
10	83,33	51,59– 97,91	42,71– 99,10
11	91,67	61,52– 99,79	52,30– 99,96
12	100,00	73,54–100,00	64,31–100,00
$N = 13$			
0	0,00	0,00– 24,71	0,00– 33,47
1	7,69	0,19– 36,03	0,04– 44,90
2	15,38	1,92– 45,45	0,83– 54,10
3	23,08	5,04– 53,81	2,78– 62,06
4	30,77	9,09– 61,43	5,71– 69,13
5	38,46	13,86– 68,42	9,42– 75,46
6	46,15	19,22– 74,87	13,83– 81,13
7	53,85	25,13– 80,78	18,87– 86,17
8	61,54	31,58– 86,14	24,54– 90,58
9	69,23	38,57– 90,91	30,87– 94,29
10	76,92	46,19– 94,96	37,94– 97,22
11	84,62	54,55– 98,08	45,90– 99,17
12	92,31	63,97– 99,81	55,10– 99,96
13	100,00	75,29–100,00	66,53–100,00
$N = 14$			
0	0,00	0,00– 23,16	0,00– 31,51
1	7,14	0,18– 33,87	0,04– 42,40
2	14,29	1,78– 42,81	0,76– 51,23
3	21,43	4,66– 50,80	2,57– 58,92
4	28,57	8,39– 58,10	5,26– 65,79
5	35,71	12,76– 64,86	8,66– 72,01
6	42,86	17,66– 71,14	12,67– 77,66
7	50,00	23,04– 76,96	17,24– 82,76
8	57,14	28,86– 82,34	22,34– 87,33
9	64,29	35,14– 87,24	27,99– 91,34
10	71,43	41,90– 91,61	34,21– 94,74
11	78,57	49,20– 95,34	41,08– 97,43
12	85,71	57,19– 98,22	48,77– 99,24
13	92,86	66,13– 99,82	57,60– 99,96
14	100,00	76,84–100,00	68,49–100,00
$N = 15$			
0	0,00	0,00– 21,80	0,00– 29,76
1	6,67	0,17– 31,95	0,03– 40,16
2	13,33	1,66– 40,46	0,71– 48,63
3	20,00	4,33– 48,09	2,39– 56,05
4	26,67	7,79– 55,10	4,88– 62,73
5	33,33	11,82– 61,62	8,01– 68,82
6	40,00	16,34– 67,71	11,70– 74,39
7	46,67	21,27– 73,41	15,87– 79,49
8	53,33	26,59– 78,73	20,51– 84,13
9	60,00	32,29– 83,66	25,61– 88,30
10	66,67	38,38– 88,18	31,18– 91,99
11	73,33	44,90– 92,21	37,27– 95,12
12	80,00	51,91– 95,67	43,95– 97,61
13	86,67	59,54– 98,34	51,37– 99,29
14	93,33	68,05– 99,83	59,84– 99,97
15	100,00	78,20–100,00	70,24–100,00
$N = 16$			
0	0,00	0,00– 20,59	0,00– 28,19
1	6,25	0,16– 30,23	0,03– 38,14
2	12,50	1,55– 38,35	0,67– 46,28
3	18,75	4,05– 45,65	2,23– 53,44
4	25,00	7,27– 52,38	4,55– 59,91
5	31,25	11,02– 58,66	7,45– 65,85
6	37,50	15,20– 64,57	10,86– 71,32
7	43,75	19,75– 70,12	14,71– 76,38
8	50,00	24,65– 75,35	18,97– 81,03
9	56,25	29,88– 80,25	23,62– 85,29
10	62,50	35,43– 84,80	28,68– 89,14
11	68,75	41,34– 88,98	34,15– 92,55
12	75,00	47,62– 92,73	40,09– 95,45
13	81,25	54,35– 95,95	46,56– 97,77
14	87,50	61,65– 98,45	53,72– 99,33
15	93,75	69,77– 99,84	61,86– 99,97
16	100,00	79,41–100,00	71,81–100,00
$N = 17$			
0	0,00	0,00– 19,51	0,00– 26,78
1	5,88	0,15– 28,69	0,03– 36,30
2	11,76	1,46– 36,44	0,63– 44,13
3	17,65	3,80– 43,43	2,09– 51,04
4	23,53	6,81– 49,90	4,26– 57,32
$N = 17$ (continued)			
5	29,41	10,31– 55,96	6,97– 63,10
6	35,29	14,21– 61,67	10,14– 68,46
7	41,18	18,44– 67,08	13,71– 73,44
8	47,06	22,98– 72,19	17,64– 78,07
9	52,94	27,81– 77,02	21,93– 82,36
10	58,82	32,92– 81,56	26,56– 86,29
11	64,71	38,33– 85,79	31,54– 89,86
12	70,59	44,04– 89,69	36,90– 93,03
13	76,47	50,10– 93,19	42,68– 95,74
14	82,35	56,57– 96,20	48,96– 97,91
15	88,24	63,56– 98,54	55,87– 99,37
16	94,12	71,31– 99,85	63,70– 99,97
17	100,00	80,49–100,00	73,22–100,00
$N = 18$			
0	0,00	0,00– 18,53	0,00– 25,50
1	5,56	0,14– 27,29	0,03– 34,63
2	11,11	1,38– 34,71	0,59– 42,17
3	16,67	3,58– 41,42	1,97– 48,84
4	22,22	6,41– 47,64	4,00– 54,92
5	27,78	9,69– 53,48	6,54– 60,55
6	33,33	13,34– 59,01	9,51– 65,79
7	38,89	17,30– 64,25	12,84– 70,68
8	44,44	21,53– 69,24	16,49– 75,26
9	50,00	26,02– 73,98	20,47– 79,53
10	55,56	30,76– 78,47	24,74– 83,51
11	61,11	35,75– 82,70	29,32– 87,16
12	66,67	40,99– 86,66	34,21– 90,49
13	72,22	46,52– 90,31	39,45– 93,46
14	77,78	52,36– 93,59	45,08– 96,00
15	83,33	58,58– 96,42	51,16– 98,03
16	88,89	65,29– 98,62	57,83– 99,41
17	94,44	72,71– 99,86	65,37– 99,97
18	100,00	81,47–100,00	74,50–100,00
$N = 19$			
0	0,00	0,00– 17,65	0,00– 24,34
1	5,26	0,13– 26,03	0,03– 33,11
2	10,53	1,30– 33,14	0,56– 40,37
3	15,79	3,38– 39,58	1,86– 46,82
4	21,05	6,05– 45,57	3,78– 52,71
5	26,32	9,15– 51,20	6,17– 58,18
6	31,58	12,58– 56,55	8,95– 63,29
7	36,84	16,29– 61,64	12,07– 68,09
8	42,11	20,25– 66,50	15,49– 72,60
9	47,37	24,45– 71,14	19,19– 76,84
10	52,63	28,86– 75,55	23,16– 80,81
11	57,89	33,50– 79,75	27,40– 84,51
12	63,16	38,36– 83,71	31,91– 87,93
13	68,42	43,45– 87,42	36,71– 91,05
14	73,68	48,80– 90,85	41,82– 93,83
15	78,95	54,43– 93,95	47,29– 96,22
16	84,21	60,42– 96,62	53,18– 98,14
17	89,47	66,86– 98,70	59,63– 99,44
18	94,74	73,97– 99,87	66,89– 99,97
19	100,00	82,35–100,00	75,66–100,00
$N = 20$			
0	0,00	0,00– 16,84	0,00– 23,27
1	5,00	0,13– 24,87	0,03– 31,71
2	10,00	1,23– 31,70	0,53– 38,71
3	15,00	3,21– 37,89	1,76– 44,95
4	20,00	5,73– 43,66	3,58– 50,66
5	25,00	8,66– 49,10	5,83– 55,98
6	30,00	11,89– 54,28	8,46– 60,96
7	35,00	15,39– 59,22	11,39– 65,66
8	40,00	19,12– 63,95	14,60– 70,09
9	45,00	23,06– 68,47	18,06– 74,28
10	50,00	27,20– 72,80	21,77– 78,23
11	55,00	31,53– 76,94	25,72– 81,94
12	60,00	36,05– 80,88	29,91– 85,40
13	65,00	40,78– 84,61	34,34– 88,61
14	70,00	45,72– 88,11	39,04– 91,54
15	75,00	50,90– 91,34	44,02– 94,17
16	80,00	56,34– 94,27	49,34– 96,42
17	85,00	62,11– 96,79	55,05– 98,24
18	90,00	68,30– 98,77	61,29– 99,47
19	95,00	75,13– 99,87	68,29– 99,97
20	100,00	83,16–100,00	76,73–100,00
$N = 21$			
0	0,00	0,00– 16,11	0,00– 22,30
1	4,76	0,12– 23,82	0,02– 30,43
2	9,52	1,17– 30,38	0,50– 37,18
3	14,29	3,05– 36,34	1,68– 43,22
4	19,05	5,45– 41,91	3,39– 48,76
5	23,81	8,22– 47,17	5,53– 53,92
6	28,57	11,28– 52,18	8,01– 58,78
7	33,33	14,59– 56,97	10,78– 63,37
8	38,10	18,11– 61,56	13,81– 67,72
9	42,86	21,82– 65,98	17,07– 71,85
10	47,62	25,71– 70,22	20,55– 75,76
11	52,38	29,78– 74,29	24,24– 79,45
12	57,14	34,02– 78,18	28,15– 82,93
13	61,90	38,44– 81,89	32,28– 86,19
14	66,67	43,03– 85,41	36,63– 89,22
$N = 21$ (continued)			
15	71,43	47,82– 88,72	41,22– 91,99
16	76,19	52,83– 91,78	46,08– 94,47
17	80,95	58,09– 94,55	51,24– 96,61
18	85,71	63,66– 96,95	56,78– 98,32
19	90,48	69,62– 98,83	62,82– 99,50
20	95,24	76,18– 99,88	69,57– 99,98
21	100,00	83,89–100,00	77,70–100,00
$N = 22$			
0	0,00	0,00– 15,44	0,00– 21,40
1	4,55	0,12– 22,84	0,02– 29,24
2	9,09	1,12– 29,16	0,48– 35,77
3	13,64	2,91– 34,91	1,60– 41,61
4	18,18	5,19– 40,28	3,23– 46,99
5	22,73	7,82– 45,37	5,26– 52,01
6	27,27	10,73– 50,22	7,61– 56,74
7	31,82	13,86– 54,87	10,24– 61,23
8	36,36	17,20– 59,34	13,10– 65,49
9	40,91	20,71– 63,65	16,18– 69,54
10	45,45	24,39– 67,79	19,46– 73,40
11	50,00	28,22– 71,78	22,93– 77,07
12	54,55	32,21– 75,61	26,60– 80,54
13	59,09	36,35– 79,29	30,46– 83,82
14	63,64	40,66– 82,80	34,51– 86,90
15	68,18	45,13– 86,14	38,77– 89,76
16	72,73	49,78– 89,27	43,26– 92,39
17	77,27	54,63– 92,18	47,99– 94,74
18	81,82	59,72– 94,81	53,01– 96,77
19	86,36	65,09– 97,09	58,39– 98,40
20	90,91	70,84– 98,88	64,23– 99,52
21	95,45	77,16– 99,88	70,76– 99,98
22	100,00	84,56–100,00	78,60–100,00
$N = 23$			
0	0,00	0,00– 14,82	0,00– 20,58
1	4,35	0,11– 21,95	0,02– 28,14
2	8,70	1,07– 28,04	0,46– 34,46
3	13,04	2,78– 33,59	1,53– 40,12
4	17,39	4,95– 38,78	3,08– 45,34
5	21,74	7,46– 43,70	5,02– 50,22
6	26,09	10,23– 48,41	7,25– 54,83
7	30,43	13,21– 52,92	9,74– 59,21
8	34,78	16,38– 57,27	12,46– 63,38
9	39,13	19,71– 61,46	15,37– 67,36
10	43,48	23,19– 65,51	18,48– 71,16
11	47,83	26,82– 69,41	21,76– 74,79
12	52,17	30,59– 73,18	25,21– 78,24
13	56,52	34,49– 76,81	28,84– 81,52
14	60,87	38,54– 80,29	32,64– 84,63
15	65,22	42,73– 83,62	36,62– 87,54
16	69,57	47,08– 86,79	40,79– 90,26
17	73,91	51,59– 89,77	45,17– 92,75
18	78,26	56,30– 92,54	49,78– 94,98
19	82,61	61,22– 95,05	54,66– 96,92
20	86,96	66,41– 97,22	59,88– 98,47
21	91,30	71,96– 98,93	65,54– 99,54
22	95,65	78,05– 99,89	71,86– 99,98
23	100,00	85,18–100,00	79,42–100,00
$N = 24$			
0	0,00	0,00– 14,25	0,00– 19,81
1	4,17	0,11– 21,12	0,02– 27,13
2	8,33	1,03– 27,00	0,44– 33,24
3	12,50	2,66– 32,36	1,46– 38,73
4	16,67	4,74– 37,38	2,95– 43,79
5	20,83	7,13– 42,15	4,79– 48,55
6	25,00	9,77– 46,71	6,92– 53,04
7	29,17	12,62– 51,09	9,30– 57,32
8	33,33	15,63– 55,32	11,88– 61,40
9	37,50	18,80– 59,41	14,65– 65,30
10	41,67	22,11– 63,36	17,59– 69,04
11	45,83	25,55– 67,18	20,70– 72,62
12	50,00	29,12– 70,88	23,96– 76,04
13	54,17	32,82– 74,45	27,38– 79,30
14	58,33	36,64– 77,89	30,96– 82,41
15	62,50	40,59– 81,20	34,70– 85,35
16	66,67	44,68– 84,37	38,60– 88,12
17	70,83	48,91– 87,38	42,68– 90,70
18	75,00	53,29– 90,23	46,96– 93,08
19	79,17	57,85– 92,87	51,45– 95,21
20	83,33	62,62– 95,26	56,21– 97,05
21	87,50	67,64– 97,34	61,27– 98,54
22	91,67	73,00– 98,97	66,76– 99,56
23	95,83	78,88– 99,89	72,87– 99,98
24	100,00	85,75–100,00	80,19–100,00
$N = 25$			
0	0,00	0,00– 13,72	0,00– 19,10
1	4,00	0,10– 20,35	0,02– 26,18
2	8,00	0,98– 26,03	0,42– 32,10
3	12,00	2,55– 31,22	1,40– 37,43
4	16,00	4,54– 36,08	2,82– 42,35
5	20,00	6,83– 40,70	4,59– 46,98
6	24,00	9,36– 45,13	6,63– 51,36
7	28,00	12,07– 49,39	8,89– 55,53
8	32,00	14,95– 53,50	11,35– 59,52

All values conform to the international convention (i.e. 0,1 instead of 0.1).

N: number of trials; x: number of successes, etc.; $100\,p_x = 100\,x/N$

$N=25$ (continued)

x	$100\,p_x$	95%: $100\,p_l$ – $100\,p_r$	99%: $100\,p_l$ – $100\,p_r$
9	36,00	17,97–57,48	13,99–63,35
10	40,00	21,13–61,33	16,79–67,02
11	44,00	24,40–65,07	19,74–70,54
12	48,00	27,80–68,69	22,83–73,93
13	52,00	31,31–72,20	26,07–77,17
14	56,00	34,93–75,60	29,46–80,26
15	60,00	38,67–78,87	32,98–83,21
16	64,00	42,52–82,03	36,65–86,01
17	68,00	46,50–85,05	40,48–88,65
18	72,00	50,61–87,93	44,47–91,11
19	76,00	54,87–90,64	48,64–93,37
20	80,00	59,30–93,17	53,02–95,41
21	84,00	63,92–95,46	57,65–97,18
22	88,00	68,78–97,45	62,57–98,60
23	92,00	73,97–99,02	67,90–99,58
24	96,00	79,65–99,90	73,82–99,98
25	100,00	86,28–100,00	80,90–100,00

$N=26$

x	$100\,p_x$	95%: $100\,p_l$ – $100\,p_r$	99%: $100\,p_l$ – $100\,p_r$
0	0,00	0,00–13,23	0,00–18,44
1	3,85	0,10–19,64	0,02–25,29
2	7,69	0,95–25,13	0,41–31,04
3	11,54	2,45–30,15	1,34–36,21
4	15,38	4,36–34,87	2,71–41,00
5	19,23	6,55–39,35	4,40–45,50
6	23,08	8,97–43,65	6,35–49,77
7	26,92	11,57–47,79	8,52–53,85
8	30,77	14,33–51,79	10,87–57,75
9	34,62	17,21–55,67	13,38–61,50
10	38,46	20,23–59,43	16,05–65,10
11	42,31	23,35–63,08	18,86–68,57
12	46,15	26,59–66,63	21,81–71,91
13	50,00	29,93–70,07	24,89–75,11
14	53,85	33,37–73,41	28,09–78,19
15	57,69	36,92–76,65	31,43–81,14
16	61,54	40,57–79,77	34,90–83,95
17	65,38	44,33–82,79	38,50–86,62
18	69,23	48,21–85,67	42,25–89,13
19	73,08	52,21–88,43	46,15–91,48
20	76,92	56,35–91,03	50,23–93,65
21	80,77	60,65–93,45	54,50–95,60
22	84,62	65,13–95,64	59,00–97,29
23	88,46	69,85–97,55	63,79–98,66
24	92,31	74,87–99,05	68,96–99,59
25	96,15	80,36–99,90	74,71–99,98
26	100,00	86,77–100,00	81,56–100,00

$N=27$

x	$100\,p_x$	95%: $100\,p_l$ – $100\,p_r$	99%: $100\,p_l$ – $100\,p_r$
0	0,00	0,00–12,77	0,00–17,82
1	3,70	0,09–18,97	0,02–24,46
2	7,41	0,91–24,29	0,39–30,04
3	11,11	2,35–29,16	1,29–35,07
4	14,81	4,19–33,73	2,60–39,73
5	18,52	6,30–38,08	4,23–44,11
6	22,22	8,62–42,26	6,10–48,28
7	25,93	11,11–46,28	8,17–52,26
8	29,63	13,75–50,18	10,42–56,08
9	33,33	16,52–53,96	12,83–59,75
10	37,04	19,40–57,63	15,38–63,28
11	40,74	22,39–61,20	18,07–66,69
12	44,44	25,48–64,67	20,88–69,98
13	48,15	28,67–68,05	23,81–73,14
14	51,85	31,95–71,33	26,86–76,19
15	55,56	35,33–74,52	30,02–79,12
16	59,26	38,80–77,61	33,31–81,93
17	62,96	42,37–80,60	36,72–84,62
18	66,67	46,04–83,48	40,25–87,17
19	70,37	49,82–86,25	43,92–89,58
20	74,07	53,72–88,89	47,74–91,83
21	77,78	57,74–91,38	51,72–93,90
22	81,48	61,92–93,70	55,89–95,77
23	85,19	66,27–95,81	60,27–97,40
24	88,89	70,84–97,65	64,93–98,71
25	92,59	75,71–99,09	69,96–99,61
26	96,30	81,03–99,91	75,54–99,98
27	100,00	87,23–100,00	82,18–100,00

$N=28$

x	$100\,p_x$	95%: $100\,p_l$ – $100\,p_r$	99%: $100\,p_l$ – $100\,p_r$
0	0,00	0,00–12,34	0,00–17,24
1	3,57	0,09–18,35	0,02–23,69
2	7,14	0,88–23,50	0,38–29,11
3	10,71	2,27–28,23	1,25–33,99
4	14,29	4,03–32,67	2,51–38,53
5	17,86	6,06–36,89	4,07–42,80
6	21,43	8,30–40,95	5,86–46,87
7	25,00	10,69–44,87	7,86–50,76
8	28,57	13,22–48,67	10,02–54,49
9	32,14	15,88–52,35	12,32–58,08
10	35,71	18,64–55,93	14,77–61,55
11	39,29	21,50–59,42	17,33–64,90
12	42,86	24,46–62,82	20,02–68,14
13	46,43	27,51–66,13	22,82–71,26
14	50,00	30,65–69,35	25,72–74,28
15	53,57	33,87–72,49	28,74–77,18
16	57,14	37,18–75,54	31,86–79,98
17	60,71	40,58–78,50	35,10–82,67
18	64,29	44,07–81,36	38,45–85,23
19	67,86	47,65–84,12	41,92–87,68
20	71,43	51,33–86,78	45,51–89,98
21	75,00	55,13–89,31	49,24–92,14
22	78,57	59,05–91,70	53,13–94,14
23	82,14	63,11–93,94	57,20–95,93
24	85,71	67,33–95,97	61,47–97,49
25	89,29	71,77–97,73	66,01–98,75
26	92,86	76,50–99,12	70,89–99,62
27	96,43	81,65–99,91	76,31–99,98
28	100,00	87,66–100,00	82,76–100,00

$N=29$

x	$100\,p_x$	95%: $100\,p_l$ – $100\,p_r$	99%: $100\,p_l$ – $100\,p_r$
0	0,00	0,00–11,94	0,00–16,70
1	3,45	0,09–17,76	0,02–22,96
2	6,90	0,85–22,77	0,36–28,23
3	10,34	2,19–27,35	1,20–32,98
4	13,79	3,89–31,66	2,42–37,40
5	17,24	5,85–35,77	3,92–41,57
6	20,69	7,99–39,72	5,65–45,54
7	24,14	10,30–43,54	7,56–49,33
8	27,59	12,73–47,24	9,64–52,99
9	31,03	15,28–50,83	11,85–56,51
10	34,48	17,94–54,33	14,20–59,91
11	37,93	20,69–57,74	16,66–63,20
12	41,38	23,52–61,06	19,23–66,38
13	44,83	26,45–64,31	21,91–69,46
14	48,28	29,45–67,47	24,69–72,43
15	51,72	32,53–70,55	27,57–75,31
16	55,17	35,69–73,55	30,54–78,09
17	58,62	38,94–76,48	33,62–80,77
18	62,07	42,26–79,31	36,80–83,34
19	65,52	45,67–82,06	40,09–85,80
20	68,97	49,17–84,72	43,49–88,15
21	72,41	52,76–87,27	47,01–90,36
22	75,86	56,46–89,70	50,67–92,44
23	79,31	60,28–92,01	54,46–94,35
24	82,76	64,23–94,15	58,43–96,08
25	86,21	68,34–96,11	62,60–97,58
26	89,66	72,65–97,81	67,02–98,80
27	93,10	77,23–99,15	71,77–99,64
28	96,55	82,24–99,91	77,04–99,98
29	100,00	88,06–100,00	83,30–100,00

$N=30$

x	$100\,p_x$	95%: $100\,p_l$ – $100\,p_r$	99%: $100\,p_l$ – $100\,p_r$
0	0,00	0,00–11,57	0,00–16,19
1	3,33	0,08–17,22	0,02–22,27
2	6,67	0,82–22,07	0,35–27,40
3	10,00	2,11–26,53	1,16–32,03
4	13,33	3,76–30,72	2,33–36,34
5	16,67	5,64–34,72	3,78–40,40
6	20,00	7,71–38,57	5,45–44,28
7	23,33	9,93–42,28	7,29–47,99
8	26,67	12,28–45,89	9,29–51,56
9	30,00	14,73–49,40	11,42–55,01
10	33,33	17,29–52,81	13,67–58,34
11	36,67	19,93–56,14	16,04–61,57
12	40,00	22,66–59,40	18,50–64,70
13	43,33	25,46–62,57	21,07–67,73
14	46,67	28,34–65,67	23,73–70,67
15	50,00	31,30–68,70	26,48–73,52
16	53,33	34,33–71,66	29,33–76,27
17	56,67	37,43–74,54	32,27–78,93
18	60,00	40,60–77,34	35,30–81,50
19	63,33	43,86–80,07	38,43–83,96
20	66,67	47,19–82,71	41,66–86,33
21	70,00	50,60–85,27	44,99–88,58
22	73,33	54,11–87,72	48,44–90,71
23	76,67	57,72–90,07	52,01–92,71
24	80,00	61,43–92,29	55,72–94,55
25	83,33	65,28–94,36	59,60–96,22
26	86,67	69,28–96,24	63,66–97,67
27	90,00	73,47–97,89	67,97–98,84
28	93,33	77,93–99,18	72,60–99,65
29	96,67	82,78–99,92	77,73–99,98
30	100,00	88,43–100,00	83,81–100,00

$N=31$

x	$100\,p_x$	95%: $100\,p_l$ – $100\,p_r$	99%: $100\,p_l$ – $100\,p_r$
0	0,00	0,00–11,22	0,00–15,71
1	3,23	0,08–16,70	0,02–21,63
2	6,45	0,79–21,42	0,34–26,62
3	9,68	2,04–25,75	1,12–31,13
4	12,90	3,63–29,83	2,25–35,33
5	16,13	5,45–33,73	3,65–39,30
6	19,35	7,45–37,47	5,26–43,08
7	22,58	9,59–41,10	7,04–46,71
8	25,81	11,86–44,61	8,96–50,21
9	29,03	14,22–48,04	11,02–53,58
10	32,26	16,68–51,37	13,18–56,85
11	35,48	19,23–54,63	15,46–60,02
12	38,71	21,85–57,81	17,83–63,09
13	41,94	24,55–60,92	20,29–66,08
14	45,16	27,32–63,97	22,85–68,98
15	48,39	30,15–66,94	25,49–71,79
16	51,61	33,06–69,85	28,21–74,51
17	54,84	36,03–72,68	31,02–77,15
18	58,06	39,08–75,45	33,92–79,71
19	61,29	42,19–78,15	36,91–82,17
20	64,52	45,37–80,77	39,98–84,54
21	67,74	48,63–83,32	43,15–86,82
22	70,97	51,96–85,78	46,42–88,98
23	74,19	55,39–88,14	49,79–91,04
24	77,42	58,90–90,41	53,29–92,96
25	80,65	62,53–92,55	56,92–94,74
26	83,87	66,27–94,55	60,70–96,35
27	87,10	70,17–96,37	64,67–97,75
28	90,32	74,25–97,96	68,87–98,88
29	93,55	78,58–99,21	73,38–99,66
30	96,77	83,30–99,92	78,37–99,98
31	100,00	88,78–100,00	84,29–100,00

$N=32$

x	$100\,p_x$	95%: $100\,p_l$ – $100\,p_r$	99%: $100\,p_l$ – $100\,p_r$
0	0,00	0,00–10,89	0,00–15,26
1	3,13	0,08–16,22	0,02–21,02
2	6,25	0,77–20,81	0,33–25,88
3	9,38	1,98–25,02	1,09–30,28
4	12,50	3,51–28,99	2,18–34,38
5	15,63	5,28–32,79	3,53–38,25
6	18,75	7,21–36,44	5,09–41,95
7	21,88	9,28–39,97	6,80–45,50
8	25,00	11,46–43,40	8,66–48,92
9	28,13	13,75–46,75	10,64–52,22
10	31,25	16,12–50,01	12,73–55,43
11	34,38	18,57–53,19	14,92–58,54
12	37,50	21,10–56,31	17,20–61,56
13	40,63	23,70–59,36	19,57–64,50
14	43,75	26,36–62,34	22,03–67,35
15	46,88	29,09–65,26	24,56–70,13
16	50,00	31,89–68,11	27,18–72,82
17	53,13	34,74–70,91	29,87–75,44
18	56,25	37,66–73,64	32,65–77,97
19	59,38	40,64–76,30	35,50–80,43
20	62,50	43,69–78,90	38,44–82,80
21	65,63	46,81–81,43	41,46–85,08
22	68,75	49,99–83,88	44,57–87,27
23	71,88	53,25–86,25	47,78–89,36
24	75,00	56,60–88,54	51,08–91,34
25	78,13	60,03–90,72	54,50–93,20
26	81,25	63,56–92,79	58,05–94,91
27	84,38	67,21–94,72	61,75–96,47
28	87,50	71,01–96,49	65,62–97,82
29	90,63	74,98–98,02	69,72–98,91
30	93,75	79,19–99,23	74,12–99,67
31	96,88	83,78–99,92	78,98–99,98
32	100,00	89,11–100,00	84,74–100,00

$N=33$

x	$100\,p_x$	95%: $100\,p_l$ – $100\,p_r$	99%: $100\,p_l$ – $100\,p_r$
0	0,00	0,00–10,58	0,00–14,83
1	3,03	0,08–15,76	0,02–20,44
2	6,06	0,74–20,23	0,32–25,18
3	9,09	1,92–24,33	1,05–29,47
4	12,12	3,40–28,20	2,11–33,47
5	15,15	5,11–31,90	3,42–37,26
6	18,18	6,98–35,46	4,92–40,87
7	21,21	8,98–38,91	6,58–44,34
8	24,24	11,09–42,26	8,38–47,69
9	27,27	13,30–45,52	10,29–50,93
10	30,30	15,59–48,71	12,31–54,08
11	33,33	17,96–51,83	14,42–57,13
12	36,36	20,40–54,88	16,62–60,10
13	39,39	22,91–57,86	18,90–62,98
14	42,42	25,48–60,78	21,27–65,79
15	45,45	28,11–63,65	23,71–68,53
16	48,48	30,80–66,46	26,22–71,19
17	51,52	33,54–69,20	28,81–73,78
18	54,55	36,35–71,89	31,47–76,29
19	57,58	39,22–74,52	34,21–78,73
20	60,61	42,14–77,09	37,02–81,10
21	63,64	45,12–79,60	39,90–83,38
22	66,67	48,17–82,04	42,87–85,58
23	69,70	51,29–84,41	45,92–87,69
24	72,73	54,48–86,70	49,07–89,71
25	75,76	57,74–88,91	52,31–91,62
26	78,79	61,09–91,02	55,66–93,42
27	81,82	64,54–93,02	59,13–95,08
28	84,85	68,10–94,89	62,74–96,58
29	87,88	71,80–96,60	66,53–97,89
30	90,91	75,67–98,08	70,53–98,95
31	93,94	79,77–99,26	74,82–99,68
32	96,97	84,24–99,92	79,56–99,98
33	100,00	89,42–100,00	85,17–100,00

$N=34$

x	$100\,p_x$	95%: $100\,p_l$ – $100\,p_r$	99%: $100\,p_l$ – $100\,p_r$
0	0,00	0,00–10,28	0,00–14,43
1	2,94	0,07–15,33	0,01–19,90
2	5,88	0,72–19,68	0,31–24,52
3	8,82	1,86–23,68	1,02–28,71
4	11,76	3,30–27,45	2,05–32,62
5	14,71	4,95–31,06	3,32–36,31
6	17,65	6,76–34,53	4,77–39,85
7	20,59	8,70–37,90	6,38–43,24
8	23,53	10,75–41,17	8,11–46,52
9	26,47	12,88–44,36	9,96–49,70
10	29,41	15,10–47,48	11,91–52,78
11	32,35	17,39–50,53	13,95–55,78
12	35,29	19,75–53,51	16,07–58,69
13	38,24	22,17–56,44	18,28–61,53
14	41,18	24,65–59,30	20,56–64,30
15	44,12	27,19–62,11	22,91–67,00
16	47,06	29,78–64,87	25,33–69,62
17	50,00	32,43–67,57	27,82–72,18
18	52,94	35,13–70,22	30,38–74,67
19	55,88	37,89–72,81	33,00–77,09
20	58,82	40,70–75,35	35,70–79,44
21	61,76	43,56–77,83	38,47–81,72
22	64,71	46,49–80,25	41,31–83,93
23	67,65	49,47–82,61	44,22–86,05
24	70,59	52,52–84,90	47,22–88,09
25	73,53	55,64–87,12	50,30–90,04
26	76,47	58,83–89,25	53,48–91,89
27	79,41	62,10–91,30	56,76–93,62
28	82,35	65,47–93,24	60,15–95,23
29	85,29	68,94–95,05	63,69–96,68
30	88,24	72,55–96,70	67,38–97,95
31	91,18	76,32–98,14	71,29–98,98
32	94,12	80,32–99,28	75,48–99,69
33	97,06	84,67–99,93	80,10–99,99
34	100,00	89,72–100,00	85,57–100,00

$N=35$

x	$100\,p_x$	95%: $100\,p_l$ – $100\,p_r$	99%: $100\,p_l$ – $100\,p_r$
0	0,00	0,00–10,00	0,00–14,05
1	2,86	0,07–14,92	0,01–19,38
2	5,71	0,70–19,16	0,30–23,89
3	8,57	1,80–23,06	0,99–27,98
4	11,43	3,20–26,74	1,99–31,80
5	14,29	4,81–30,26	3,22–35,42
6	17,14	6,56–33,65	4,63–38,87
7	20,00	8,44–36,94	6,18–42,20
8	22,86	10,42–40,14	7,86–45,41
9	25,71	12,49–43,26	9,65–48,52
10	28,57	14,64–46,30	11,54–51,55
11	31,43	16,85–49,29	13,51–54,49
12	34,29	19,13–52,21	15,56–57,35
13	37,14	21,47–55,08	17,69–60,14
14	40,00	23,87–57,89	19,89–62,87
15	42,86	26,32–60,65	22,16–65,52
16	45,71	28,83–63,35	24,50–68,11
17	48,57	31,38–66,01	26,90–70,64
18	51,43	33,99–68,62	29,36–73,10
19	54,29	36,65–71,17	31,89–75,50
20	57,14	39,35–73,68	34,48–77,84
21	60,00	42,11–76,13	37,13–80,11
22	62,86	44,92–78,53	39,86–82,31
23	65,71	47,79–80,87	42,65–84,44
24	68,57	50,71–83,15	45,51–86,49
25	71,43	53,70–85,36	48,45–88,46
26	74,29	56,74–87,51	51,48–90,35
27	77,14	59,86–89,58	54,59–92,14
28	80,00	63,06–91,56	57,80–93,82
29	82,86	66,35–93,44	61,13–95,37
30	85,71	69,74–95,19	64,58–96,78
31	88,57	73,26–96,80	68,20–98,01
32	91,43	76,94–98,20	72,02–99,01
33	94,29	80,84–99,30	76,11–99,70
34	97,14	85,08–99,93	80,62–99,99
35	100,00	90,00–100,00	85,95–100,00

$N=36$

x	$100\,p_x$	95%: $100\,p_l$ – $100\,p_r$	99%: $100\,p_l$ – $100\,p_r$
0	0,00	0,00–9,74	0,00–13,69
1	2,78	0,07–14,53	0,01–18,89
2	5,56	0,68–18,66	0,29–23,29
3	8,33	1,75–22,47	0,96–27,29
4	11,11	3,11–26,06	1,93–31,02
5	13,89	4,67–29,50	3,12–34,56
6	16,67	6,37–32,81	4,49–37,94
7	19,44	8,19–36,02	6,00–41,20
8	22,22	10,12–39,15	7,63–44,35
9	25,00	12,12–42,20	9,36–47,40
10	27,78	14,20–45,19	11,19–50,37
11	30,56	16,35–48,11	13,10–53,25
12	33,33	18,56–50,97	15,09–56,07
13	36,11	20,82–53,78	17,14–58,81
14	38,89	23,14–56,54	19,27–61,49
15	41,67	25,51–59,24	21,46–64,11
16	44,44	27,94–61,90	23,72–66,66
17	47,22	30,41–64,51	26,03–69,16
18	50,00	32,92–67,08	28,41–71,59
19	52,78	35,49–69,59	30,84–73,97
20	55,56	38,10–72,06	33,34–76,28
21	58,33	40,76–74,49	35,89–78,54
22	61,11	43,46–76,86	38,51–80,73
23	63,89	46,22–79,18	41,19–82,86
24	66,67	49,03–81,44	43,93–84,91
25	69,44	51,89–83,65	46,75–86,90
26	72,22	54,81–85,80	49,63–88,81
27	75,00	57,80–87,88	52,60–90,64
28	77,78	60,85–89,88	55,65–92,37
29	80,56	63,98–91,81	58,80–94,00

All values conform to the international convention (i.e. 0,1 instead of 0.1).

N: number of trials; x: number of successes, etc.; $100\,p_x = 100\,x/N$

$N = 36$ (continued)

x	$100\,p_x$	95% $100\,p_l$	95% $100\,p_r$	99% $100\,p_l$	99% $100\,p_r$
30	83,33	67,19	93,63	62,06	95,51
31	86,11	70,50	95,33	65,44	96,88
32	88,89	73,94	96,89	68,98	98,07
33	91,67	77,53	98,25	72,71	99,04
34	94,44	81,34	99,32	76,71	99,71
35	97,22	85,47	99,93	81,11	99,99
36	100,00	90,26	100,00	86,31	100,00

$N = 37$

x	$100\,p_x$	95% $100\,p_l$	95% $100\,p_r$	99% $100\,p_l$	99% $100\,p_r$
0	0,00	0,00	9,49	0,00	13,34
1	2,70	0,07	14,16	0,01	18,42
2	5,41	0,66	18,19	0,28	22,73
3	8,11	1,70	21,91	0,94	26,63
4	10,81	3,03	25,42	1,88	30,28
5	13,51	4,54	28,77	3,04	33,75
6	16,22	6,19	32,01	4,36	37,06
7	18,92	7,96	35,16	5,83	40,25
8	21,62	9,83	38,21	7,41	43,33
9	24,32	11,77	41,20	9,09	46,32
10	27,03	13,79	44,12	10,86	49,24
11	29,73	15,87	46,98	12,71	52,07
12	32,43	18,01	49,79	14,64	54,83
13	35,14	20,21	52,54	16,63	57,53
14	37,84	22,46	55,24	18,69	60,17
15	40,54	24,75	57,90	20,81	62,75
16	43,24	27,10	60,51	22,99	65,26
17	45,95	29,49	63,08	25,22	67,73
18	48,65	31,92	65,60	27,52	70,13
19	51,35	34,40	68,08	29,87	72,48
20	54,05	36,92	70,51	32,27	74,78
21	56,76	39,49	72,90	34,74	77,01
22	59,46	42,10	75,25	37,25	79,19
23	62,16	44,76	77,54	39,83	81,31
24	64,86	47,46	79,79	42,47	83,37
25	67,57	50,21	81,99	45,17	85,36
26	70,27	53,02	84,13	47,93	87,29
27	72,97	55,88	86,21	50,76	89,14
28	75,68	58,80	88,23	53,68	90,91
29	78,38	61,79	90,17	56,67	92,59
30	81,08	64,84	92,04	59,75	94,17
31	83,78	67,99	93,81	62,94	95,64
32	86,49	71,23	95,46	66,25	96,96
33	89,19	74,58	96,97	69,72	98,12
34	91,89	78,09	98,30	73,37	99,06
35	94,59	81,81	99,34	77,27	99,72
36	97,30	85,84	99,93	81,58	99,99
37	100,00	90,51	100,00	86,66	100,00

$N = 38$

x	$100\,p_x$	95% $100\,p_l$	95% $100\,p_r$	99% $100\,p_l$	99% $100\,p_r$
0	0,00	0,00	9,25	0,00	13,01
1	2,63	0,07	13,81	0,01	17,98
2	5,26	0,64	17,75	0,28	22,19
3	7,89	1,66	21,38	0,91	26,01
4	10,53	2,94	24,80	1,83	29,58
5	13,16	4,41	28,09	2,95	32,97
6	15,79	6,02	31,25	4,24	36,21
7	18,42	7,74	34,33	5,67	39,34
8	21,05	9,55	37,32	7,20	42,36
9	23,68	11,44	40,24	8,83	45,30
10	26,32	13,40	43,10	10,55	48,15
11	28,95	15,42	45,90	12,35	50,94
12	31,58	17,50	48,65	14,21	53,65
13	34,21	19,63	51,35	16,14	56,31
14	36,84	21,81	54,01	18,14	58,90
15	39,47	24,04	56,61	20,19	61,44
16	42,11	26,31	59,18	22,30	63,92
17	44,74	28,62	61,70	24,47	66,35
18	47,37	30,98	64,18	26,68	68,72
19	50,00	33,38	66,62	28,95	71,05
20	52,63	35,82	69,02	31,28	73,32
21	55,26	38,30	71,38	33,65	75,53
22	57,89	40,82	73,69	36,08	77,70
23	60,53	43,39	75,96	38,56	79,81
24	63,16	45,99	78,19	41,10	81,86
25	65,79	48,65	80,37	43,69	83,86
26	68,42	51,35	82,50	46,35	85,79
27	71,05	54,10	84,58	49,06	87,65
28	73,68	56,90	86,60	51,85	89,45
29	76,32	59,76	88,56	54,70	91,17
30	78,95	62,68	90,45	57,64	92,80
31	81,58	65,67	92,26	60,66	94,33
32	84,21	68,75	93,98	63,79	95,76
33	86,84	71,91	95,59	67,03	97,05
34	89,47	75,20	97,06	70,42	98,17
35	92,11	78,62	98,34	73,99	99,09
36	94,74	82,25	99,36	77,81	99,72
37	97,37	86,19	99,93	82,02	99,99
38	100,00	90,75	100,00	86,99	100,00

$N = 39$

x	$100\,p_x$	95% $100\,p_l$	95% $100\,p_r$	99% $100\,p_l$	99% $100\,p_r$
0	0,00	0,00	9,03	0,00	12,70
1	2,56	0,06	13,48	0,01	17,56
2	5,13	0,63	17,32	0,27	21,67
3	7,69	1,62	20,87	0,89	25,41
4	10,26	2,87	24,22	1,78	28,90
5	12,82	4,30	27,43	2,87	32,22
6	15,38	5,86	30,53	4,13	35,40
7	17,95	7,54	33,54	5,51	38,47
8	20,51	9,30	36,46	7,01	41,43
9	23,08	11,13	39,33	8,59	44,31
10	25,64	13,04	42,13	10,26	47,12
11	28,21	15,00	44,87	12,00	49,85
12	30,77	17,02	47,57	13,81	52,52
13	33,33	19,09	50,22	15,69	55,13
14	35,90	21,20	52,82	17,62	57,68
15	38,46	23,36	55,38	19,61	60,18
16	41,03	25,57	57,90	21,66	62,62
17	43,59	27,81	60,38	23,75	65,02
18	46,15	30,09	62,82	25,90	67,36
19	48,72	32,42	65,22	28,10	69,66
20	51,28	34,78	67,58	30,34	71,90
21	53,85	37,18	69,91	32,64	74,10
22	56,41	39,62	72,19	34,98	76,25
23	58,97	42,10	74,43	37,38	78,34
24	61,54	44,62	76,64	39,82	80,39
25	64,10	47,18	78,80	42,32	82,38
26	66,67	49,78	80,91	44,87	84,31
27	69,23	52,43	82,98	47,48	86,19
28	71,79	55,13	85,00	50,15	88,00
29	74,36	57,87	86,96	52,88	89,74
30	76,92	60,67	88,87	55,69	91,41
31	79,49	63,54	90,70	58,57	92,99
32	82,05	66,46	92,46	61,53	94,49
33	84,62	69,47	94,14	64,60	95,87
34	87,18	72,57	95,70	67,78	97,13
35	89,74	75,78	97,13	71,10	98,22
36	92,31	79,13	98,38	74,59	99,11
37	94,87	82,68	99,37	78,33	99,73
38	97,44	86,52	99,94	82,44	99,99
39	100,00	90,97	100,00	87,30	100,00

$N = 40$

x	$100\,p_x$	95% $100\,p_l$	95% $100\,p_r$	99% $100\,p_l$	99% $100\,p_r$
0	0,00	0,00	8,81	0,00	12,41
1	2,50	0,06	13,16	0,01	17,15
2	5,00	0,61	16,92	0,26	21,18
3	7,50	1,57	20,39	0,86	24,84
4	10,00	2,79	23,66	1,73	28,26
5	12,50	4,19	26,80	2,80	31,51
6	15,00	5,71	29,84	4,02	34,63
7	17,50	7,34	32,78	5,37	37,63
8	20,00	9,05	35,65	6,82	40,54
9	22,50	10,84	38,45	8,36	43,37
10	25,00	12,69	41,20	9,98	46,12
11	27,50	14,60	43,89	11,68	48,81
12	30,00	16,56	46,53	13,44	51,43
13	32,50	18,57	49,13	15,26	54,00
14	35,00	20,63	51,68	17,13	56,51
15	37,50	22,73	54,20	19,06	58,97
16	40,00	24,86	56,67	21,05	61,38
17	42,50	27,04	59,11	23,08	63,74
18	45,00	29,26	61,51	25,16	66,05
19	47,50	31,51	63,87	27,29	68,32
20	50,00	33,80	66,20	29,46	70,54
21	52,50	36,13	68,49	31,68	72,71
22	55,00	38,49	70,74	33,95	74,84
23	57,50	40,89	72,96	36,26	76,92
24	60,00	43,33	75,14	38,62	78,95
25	62,50	45,80	77,27	41,03	80,94
26	65,00	48,32	79,37	43,49	82,87
27	67,50	50,87	81,43	46,00	84,74
28	70,00	53,47	83,44	48,57	86,56
29	72,50	56,11	85,40	51,19	88,32
30	75,00	58,80	87,31	53,88	90,02
31	77,50	61,55	89,16	56,63	91,64
32	80,00	64,35	90,95	59,46	93,18
33	82,50	67,22	92,66	62,37	94,63
34	85,00	70,16	94,29	65,37	95,98
35	87,50	73,20	95,81	68,49	97,20
36	90,00	76,34	97,21	71,74	98,27
37	92,50	79,61	98,43	75,16	99,14
38	95,00	83,08	99,39	78,82	99,74
39	97,50	86,84	99,94	82,85	99,99
40	100,00	91,19	100,00	87,59	100,00

$N = 41$

x	$100\,p_x$	95% $100\,p_l$	95% $100\,p_r$	99% $100\,p_l$	99% $100\,p_r$
0	0,00	0,00	8,60	0,00	12,12
1	2,44	0,06	12,86	0,01	16,77
2	4,88	0,60	16,53	0,26	20,71
3	7,32	1,54	19,92	0,84	24,29
4	9,76	2,72	23,13	1,69	27,64
5	12,20	4,08	26,20	2,73	30,83
6	14,63	5,57	29,17	3,92	33,89
7	17,07	7,15	32,06	5,23	36,83
8	19,51	8,82	34,87	6,64	39,69
9	21,95	10,56	37,61	8,14	42,46
10	24,39	12,36	40,30	9,72	45,17
11	26,83	14,22	42,94	11,37	47,81
12	29,27	16,13	45,54	13,08	50,38
13	31,71	18,08	48,09	14,85	52,91
14	34,15	20,08	50,59	16,67	55,38
15	36,59	22,12	53,06	18,55	57,80
16	39,02	24,20	55,50	20,47	60,17
17	41,46	26,32	57,89	22,44	62,50
18	43,90	28,47	60,25	24,46	64,78
19	46,34	30,66	62,58	26,53	67,02
20	48,78	32,88	64,87	28,63	69,22
21	51,22	35,13	67,12	30,78	71,37
22	53,66	37,42	69,34	32,98	73,47
23	56,10	39,75	71,53	35,22	75,54
24	58,54	42,11	73,68	37,50	77,56
25	60,98	44,50	75,80	39,83	79,53
26	63,41	46,94	77,88	42,20	81,45
27	65,85	49,41	79,92	44,62	83,33
28	68,29	51,91	81,92	47,09	85,15
29	70,73	54,46	83,87	49,62	86,92
30	73,17	57,06	85,78	52,19	88,63
31	75,61	59,70	87,64	54,83	90,28
32	78,05	62,39	89,44	57,54	91,86
33	80,49	65,13	91,18	60,31	93,36
34	82,93	67,94	92,85	63,17	94,77
35	85,37	70,83	94,43	66,11	96,08
36	87,80	73,80	95,92	69,17	97,27
37	90,24	76,87	97,28	72,36	98,31
38	92,68	80,08	98,46	75,71	99,16
39	95,12	83,47	99,40	79,29	99,74
40	97,56	87,14	99,94	83,23	99,99
41	100,00	91,40	100,00	87,88	100,00

$N = 42$

x	$100\,p_x$	95% $100\,p_l$	95% $100\,p_r$	99% $100\,p_l$	99% $100\,p_r$
0	0,00	0,00	8,41	0,00	11,85
1	2,38	0,06	12,57	0,01	16,40
2	4,76	0,58	16,16	0,25	20,26
3	7,14	1,50	19,48	0,82	23,77
4	9,52	2,66	22,62	1,65	27,05
5	11,90	3,98	25,63	2,66	30,18
6	14,29	5,43	28,54	3,82	33,18
7	16,67	6,97	31,36	5,10	36,07
8	19,05	8,60	34,12	6,47	38,87
9	21,43	10,30	36,81	7,94	41,59
10	23,81	12,05	39,45	9,47	44,25
11	26,19	13,86	42,04	11,08	46,84
12	28,57	15,72	44,58	12,74	49,38
13	30,95	17,62	47,09	14,46	51,86
14	33,33	19,57	49,55	16,23	54,29
15	35,71	21,55	51,97	18,06	56,68
16	38,10	23,57	54,36	19,93	59,02
17	40,48	25,63	56,72	21,84	61,31
18	42,86	27,72	59,04	23,80	63,55
19	45,24	29,85	61,33	25,81	65,77
20	47,62	32,00	63,58	27,85	67,94
21	50,00	34,19	65,81	29,93	70,07
22	52,38	36,42	68,00	32,06	72,15
23	54,76	38,67	70,15	34,23	74,19
24	57,14	40,96	72,28	36,44	76,20
25	59,52	43,28	74,37	38,69	78,16
26	61,90	45,64	76,43	40,98	80,07
27	64,29	48,03	78,45	43,32	81,94
28	66,67	50,45	80,43	45,71	83,77
29	69,05	52,91	82,38	48,14	85,54
30	71,43	55,42	84,28	50,62	87,26
31	73,81	57,96	86,14	53,16	88,92
32	76,19	60,55	87,95	55,75	90,53
33	78,57	63,19	89,70	58,41	92,06
34	80,95	65,88	91,40	61,13	93,53
35	83,33	68,64	93,03	63,93	94,90
36	85,71	71,46	94,57	66,82	96,18
37	88,10	74,37	96,02	69,82	97,34
38	90,48	77,38	97,34	72,95	98,35
39	92,86	80,52	98,50	76,23	99,18
40	95,24	83,84	99,42	79,74	99,75
41	97,62	87,43	99,94	83,60	99,99
42	100,00	91,59	100,00	88,15	100,00

$N = 43$

x	$100\,p_x$	95% $100\,p_l$	95% $100\,p_r$	99% $100\,p_l$	99% $100\,p_r$
0	0,00	0,00	8,22	0,00	11,59
1	2,33	0,06	12,29	0,01	16,04
2	4,65	0,57	15,81	0,24	19,82
3	6,98	1,46	19,06	0,80	23,27
4	9,30	2,59	22,14	1,61	26,49
5	11,63	3,89	25,08	2,60	29,55
6	13,95	5,30	27,93	3,73	32,49
7	16,28	6,81	30,70	4,97	35,33
8	18,60	8,39	33,40	6,32	38,08
9	20,93	10,04	36,04	7,74	40,76
10	23,26	11,76	38,63	9,24	43,37
11	25,58	13,52	41,17	10,80	45,92
12	27,91	15,33	43,67	12,42	48,41
13	30,23	17,18	46,13	14,09	50,85
14	32,56	19,08	48,54	15,82	53,25
15	34,88	21,01	50,93	17,59	55,59
16	37,21	22,98	53,27	19,41	57,90
17	39,53	24,98	55,59	21,27	60,16
18	41,86	27,01	57,87	23,18	62,38
19	44,19	29,08	60,12	25,12	64,56
20	46,51	31,18	62,35	27,11	66,70
21	48,84	33,31	64,54	29,13	68,80
22	51,16	35,46	66,69	31,20	70,87
23	53,49	37,65	68,82	33,30	72,89
24	55,81	39,88	70,92	35,44	74,88
25	58,14	42,13	72,99	37,62	76,82
26	60,47	44,41	75,02	39,84	78,73
27	62,79	46,73	77,02	42,10	80,59
28	65,12	49,07	78,99	44,41	82,41
29	67,44	51,46	80,92	46,75	84,18
30	69,77	53,87	82,82	49,15	85,91
31	72,09	56,33	84,67	51,59	87,58
32	74,42	58,83	86,48	54,08	89,20
33	76,74	61,37	88,24	56,63	90,76
34	79,07	63,96	89,96	59,24	92,26
35	81,40	66,60	91,61	61,92	93,68
36	83,72	69,30	93,19	64,67	95,03
37	86,05	72,07	94,70	67,51	96,27
38	88,37	74,92	96,11	70,45	97,40
39	90,70	77,86	97,41	73,51	98,39
40	93,02	80,94	98,54	76,73	99,20
41	95,35	84,19	99,43	80,18	99,76
42	97,67	87,71	99,94	83,96	99,99
43	100,00	91,78	100,00	88,41	100,00

$N = 44$

x	$100\,p_x$	95% $100\,p_l$	95% $100\,p_r$	99% $100\,p_l$	99% $100\,p_r$
0	0,00	0,00	8,04	0,00	11,34
1	2,27	0,06	12,02	0,01	15,70
2	4,55	0,56	15,47	0,24	19,41
3	6,82	1,43	18,66	0,78	22,79
4	9,09	2,53	21,67	1,57	25,95
5	11,36	3,79	24,56	2,54	28,95
6	13,64	5,17	27,35	3,64	31,84
7	15,91	6,64	30,07	4,85	34,62
8	18,18	8,19	32,71	6,16	37,33
9	20,45	9,80	35,30	7,55	39,96
10	22,73	11,47	37,84	9,01	42,52
11	25,00	13,19	40,34	10,53	45,03
12	27,27	14,96	42,79	12,11	47,48
13	29,55	16,76	45,20	13,74	49,88
14	31,82	18,61	47,58	15,43	52,24
15	34,09	20,49	49,92	17,15	54,55
16	36,36	22,41	52,23	18,92	56,82
17	38,64	24,36	54,50	20,73	59,05
18	40,91	26,34	56,75	22,59	61,24
19	43,18	28,35	58,97	24,48	63,39
20	45,45	30,39	61,15	26,41	65,50
21	47,73	32,46	63,31	28,37	67,58
22	50,00	34,56	65,44	30,38	69,62
23	52,27	36,69	67,54	32,42	71,63
24	54,55	38,85	69,61	34,50	73,59
25	56,82	41,03	71,65	36,61	75,52
26	59,09	43,25	73,66	38,76	77,41
27	61,36	45,50	75,64	40,95	79,27
28	63,64	47,77	77,59	43,18	81,08
29	65,91	50,08	79,51	45,45	82,85
30	68,18	52,42	81,39	47,76	84,57
31	70,45	54,80	83,24	50,12	86,26
32	72,73	57,21	85,04	52,52	87,89
33	75,00	59,66	86,81	54,97	89,47
34	77,27	62,16	88,53	57,48	90,99
35	79,55	64,70	90,20	60,04	92,45
36	81,82	67,29	91,81	62,67	93,84
37	84,09	69,93	93,36	65,38	95,15
38	86,36	72,65	94,83	68,16	96,36
39	88,64	75,44	96,21	71,05	97,46
40	90,91	78,33	97,47	74,05	98,43
41	93,18	81,34	98,57	77,21	99,22
42	95,45	84,53	99,44	80,59	99,76
43	97,73	87,98	99,94	84,30	99,99
44	100,00	91,96	100,00	88,66	100,00

$N = 45$

x	$100\,p_x$	95% $100\,p_l$	95% $100\,p_r$	99% $100\,p_l$	99% $100\,p_r$
0	0,00	0,00	7,87	0,00	11,11
1	2,22	0,06	11,77	0,01	15,38
2	4,44	0,54	15,15	0,23	19,01
3	6,67	1,40	18,27	0,77	22,32
4	8,89	2,48	21,22	1,54	25,43
5	11,11	3,71	24,05	2,48	28,38
6	13,33	5,05	26,79	3,56	31,21
7	15,56	6,49	29,46	4,74	33,95
8	17,78	8,00	32,05	6,02	36,60
9	20,00	9,58	34,60	7,37	39,18
10	22,22	11,20	37,09	8,80	41,71
11	24,44	12,88	39,54	10,28	44,17
12	26,67	14,60	41,94	11,82	46,58
13	28,89	16,37	44,31	13,41	48,95
14	31,11	18,17	46,65	15,05	51,27
15	33,33	20,00	48,95	16,73	53,54
16	35,56	21,87	51,22	18,46	55,78
17	37,78	23,77	53,46	20,22	57,98
18	40,00	25,70	55,67	22,02	60,14
19	42,22	27,66	57,85	23,86	62,26
20	44,44	29,64	60,00	25,74	64,35
21	46,67	31,66	62,13	27,65	66,40
22	48,89	33,70	64,23	29,60	68,42
23	51,11	35,77	66,30	31,58	70,40
24	53,33	37,87	68,34	33,60	72,35
25	55,56	40,00	70,36	35,65	74,26
26	57,78	42,15	72,34	37,74	76,14
27	60,00	44,33	74,30	39,86	77,98

All values conform to the international convention (i.e. 0,1 instead of 0.1).

N: number of trials; x: number of successes, etc.; $100\,p_x = 100\,x/N$

x	$100\,p_x$	100(1 − 2α) limits 95% $100\,p_l$	95% $100\,p_r$	99% $100\,p_l$	99% $100\,p_r$
		$N = 45$ (continued)			
28	62,22	46,54	76,23	42,02	79,78
29	64,44	48,78	78,13	44,22	81,54
30	66,67	51,05	80,00	46,46	83,27
31	68,89	53,35	81,83	48,73	84,95
32	71,11	55,69	83,63	51,05	86,59
33	73,33	58,06	85,40	53,42	88,18
34	75,56	60,46	87,12	55,83	89,72
35	77,78	62,91	88,80	58,29	91,20
36	80,00	65,40	90,42	60,82	92,63
37	82,22	67,95	92,00	63,40	93,98
38	84,44	70,54	93,51	66,05	95,26
39	86,67	73,21	94,95	68,79	96,44
40	88,89	75,95	96,29	71,62	97,52
41	91,11	78,78	97,52	74,57	98,46
42	93,33	81,73	98,60	77,68	99,23
43	95,56	84,85	99,46	80,99	99,77
44	97,78	88,23	99,94	84,62	99,99
45	100,00	92,13	100,00	88,89	100,00
		$N = 46$			
0	0,00	0,00	7,71	0,00	10,88
1	2,17	0,06	11,53	0,01	15,07
2	4,35	0,53	14,84	0,23	18,63
3	6,52	1,37	17,90	0,75	21,88
4	8,70	2,42	20,79	1,50	24,93
5	10,87	3,62	23,57	2,42	27,82
6	13,04	4,94	26,26	3,47	30,60
7	15,22	6,34	28,87	4,63	33,29
8	17,39	7,82	31,42	5,88	35,90
9	19,57	9,36	33,91	7,20	38,44
10	21,74	10,95	36,36	8,59	40,92
11	23,91	12,59	38,77	10,04	43,34
12	26,09	14,27	41,13	11,54	45,72
13	28,26	15,99	43,46	13,10	48,04
14	30,43	17,74	45,75	14,69	50,33
15	32,61	19,53	48,02	16,33	52,57
16	34,78	21,35	50,25	18,01	54,77
17	36,96	23,21	52,45	19,73	56,94
18	39,13	25,09	54,63	21,49	59,07
19	41,30	27,00	56,77	23,28	61,16
20	43,48	28,93	58,89	25,11	63,23
21	45,65	30,90	60,99	26,97	65,25
22	47,83	32,89	63,05	28,86	67,25
23	50,00	34,90	65,10	30,79	69,21
24	52,17	36,95	67,11	32,75	71,14
25	54,35	39,01	69,10	34,75	73,03
26	56,52	41,11	71,07	36,77	74,89
27	58,70	43,23	73,00	38,84	76,72
28	60,87	45,37	74,91	40,93	78,51
29	63,04	47,55	76,79	43,06	80,27
30	65,22	49,75	78,65	45,23	81,99
31	67,39	51,98	80,47	47,43	83,67
32	69,57	54,25	82,26	49,67	85,31
33	71,74	56,54	84,01	51,96	86,90
34	73,91	58,87	85,73	54,28	88,46
35	76,09	61,23	87,41	56,66	89,96
36	78,26	63,64	89,05	59,08	91,41
37	80,43	66,09	90,64	61,56	92,80
38	82,61	68,58	92,18	64,10	94,12
39	84,78	71,13	93,66	66,71	95,37
40	86,96	73,74	95,06	69,40	96,53
41	89,13	76,43	96,38	72,18	97,58
42	91,30	79,21	97,58	75,07	98,50
43	93,48	82,10	98,63	78,12	99,25
44	95,65	85,16	99,47	81,37	99,77
45	97,83	88,47	99,94	84,93	99,99
46	100,00	92,29	100,00	89,12	100,00
		$N = 47$			
0	0,00	0,00	7,55	0,00	10,66
1	2,13	0,05	11,29	0,01	14,77
2	4,26	0,52	14,54	0,22	18,27
3	6,38	1,34	17,54	0,73	21,45
4	8,51	2,37	20,38	1,47	24,44
5	10,64	3,55	23,10	2,37	27,29
6	12,77	4,83	25,74	3,40	30,02
7	14,89	6,20	28,31	4,53	32,66
8	17,02	7,65	30,81	5,75	35,23
9	19,15	9,15	33,26	7,04	37,72
10	21,28	10,70	35,66	8,40	40,16
11	23,40	12,30	38,03	9,81	42,55
12	25,53	13,94	40,35	11,28	44,88
13	27,66	15,62	42,64	12,79	47,17
14	29,79	17,34	44,89	14,35	49,42
15	31,91	19,09	47,12	15,95	51,63
16	34,04	20,86	49,31	17,59	53,80
17	36,17	22,67	51,48	19,27	55,94
18	38,30	24,51	53,62	20,98	58,04
19	40,43	26,37	55,73	22,73	60,11
20	42,55	28,26	57,82	24,51	62,14
21	44,68	30,17	59,88	26,32	64,14
22	46,81	32,11	61,92	28,16	66,11
23	48,94	34,08	63,94	30,04	68,05
24	51,06	36,06	65,92	31,95	69,96
25	53,19	38,08	67,89	33,89	71,84
26	55,32	40,12	69,83	35,86	73,68
27	57,45	42,18	71,74	37,86	75,49
		$N = 47$ (continued)			
28	59,57	44,27	73,63	39,89	77,27
29	61,70	46,38	75,49	41,96	79,02
30	63,83	48,52	77,33	44,06	80,73
31	65,96	50,69	79,14	46,20	82,41
32	68,09	52,88	80,91	48,37	84,05
33	70,21	55,11	82,66	50,58	85,65
34	72,34	57,36	84,38	52,83	87,21
35	74,47	59,65	86,06	55,12	88,72
36	76,60	61,97	87,70	57,45	90,19
37	78,72	64,34	89,30	59,84	91,60
38	80,85	66,74	90,85	62,28	92,96
39	82,98	69,19	92,35	64,77	94,25
40	85,11	71,69	93,80	67,34	95,47
41	87,23	74,26	95,17	69,98	96,60
42	89,36	76,90	96,45	72,71	97,63
43	91,49	79,62	97,63	75,56	98,53
44	93,62	82,46	98,66	78,55	99,27
45	95,74	85,46	99,48	81,73	99,78
46	97,87	88,71	99,95	85,23	99,99
47	100,00	92,45	100,00	89,34	100,00
		$N = 48$			
0	0,00	0,00	7,40	0,00	10,45
1	2,08	0,05	11,07	0,01	14,48
2	4,17	0,51	14,25	0,22	17,91
3	6,25	1,31	17,20	0,72	21,04
4	8,33	2,32	19,98	1,44	23,98
5	10,42	3,47	22,66	2,32	26,78
6	12,50	4,73	25,25	3,32	29,46
7	14,58	6,07	27,76	4,43	32,06
8	16,67	7,48	30,22	5,62	34,58
9	18,75	8,95	32,63	6,89	37,03
10	20,83	10,47	34,99	8,21	39,43
11	22,92	12,03	37,31	9,59	41,78
12	25,00	13,64	39,60	11,03	44,08
13	27,08	15,28	41,85	12,51	46,33
14	29,17	16,95	44,06	14,03	48,55
15	31,25	18,66	46,25	15,59	50,72
16	33,33	20,40	48,41	17,19	52,86
17	35,42	22,16	50,54	18,83	54,97
18	37,50	23,95	52,65	20,50	57,04
19	39,58	25,77	54,73	22,20	59,08
20	41,67	27,61	56,79	23,93	61,09
21	43,75	29,48	58,82	25,70	63,07
22	45,83	31,37	60,83	27,50	65,01
23	47,92	33,29	62,81	29,33	66,93
24	50,00	35,23	64,77	31,18	68,82
25	52,08	37,19	66,71	33,07	70,67
26	54,17	39,17	68,63	34,99	72,50
27	56,25	41,18	70,52	36,93	74,30
28	58,33	43,21	72,39	38,91	76,07
29	60,42	45,27	74,23	40,92	77,80
30	62,50	47,35	76,05	42,96	79,50
31	64,58	49,46	77,84	45,03	81,17
32	66,67	51,59	79,60	47,14	82,81
33	68,75	53,75	81,34	49,28	84,41
34	70,83	55,94	83,05	51,45	85,97
35	72,92	58,15	84,72	53,67	87,49
36	75,00	60,40	86,36	55,92	88,97
37	77,08	62,69	87,97	58,22	90,41
38	79,17	65,01	89,53	60,57	91,79
39	81,25	67,37	91,05	62,97	93,11
40	83,33	69,78	92,52	65,42	94,38
41	85,42	72,24	93,93	67,94	95,57
42	87,50	74,75	95,27	70,54	96,68
43	89,58	77,34	96,53	73,22	97,68
44	91,67	80,02	97,68	76,02	98,56
45	93,75	82,80	98,69	78,96	99,28
46	95,83	85,75	99,49	82,09	99,78
47	97,92	88,93	99,95	85,52	99,99
48	100,00	92,60	100,00	89,55	100,00
		$N = 49$			
0	0,00	0,00	7,25	0,00	10,25
1	2,04	0,05	10,85	0,01	14,21
2	4,08	0,50	13,98	0,21	17,58
3	6,12	1,28	16,87	0,70	20,65
4	8,16	2,27	19,60	1,41	23,53
5	10,20	3,40	22,23	2,27	26,28
6	12,24	4,63	24,77	3,25	28,92
7	14,29	5,94	27,24	4,34	31,47
8	16,33	7,32	29,66	5,50	33,95
9	18,37	8,76	32,02	6,74	36,37
10	20,41	10,24	34,34	8,03	38,73
11	22,45	11,77	36,62	9,39	41,04
12	24,49	13,34	38,87	10,79	43,30
13	26,53	14,95	41,08	12,23	45,52
14	28,57	16,58	43,26	13,72	47,70
15	30,61	18,25	45,42	15,24	49,85
16	32,65	19,95	47,54	16,81	51,96
17	34,69	21,67	49,64	18,40	54,03
18	36,73	23,42	51,71	20,03	56,07
19	38,78	25,20	53,76	21,69	58,09
20	40,82	27,00	55,79	23,39	60,07
21	42,86	28,82	57,79	25,11	62,02
22	44,90	30,67	59,77	26,86	63,95
23	46,94	32,53	61,73	28,64	65,84
		$N = 49$ (continued)			
24	48,98	34,42	63,66	30,45	67,71
25	51,02	36,34	65,58	32,29	69,55
26	53,06	38,27	67,47	34,16	71,36
27	55,10	40,23	69,33	36,05	73,14
28	57,14	42,21	71,18	37,98	74,89
29	59,18	44,21	73,00	39,93	76,61
30	61,22	46,24	74,80	41,91	78,31
31	63,27	48,29	76,58	43,93	79,97
32	65,31	50,36	78,33	45,97	81,60
33	67,35	52,46	80,05	48,04	83,19
34	69,39	54,58	81,75	50,15	84,76
35	71,43	56,74	83,42	52,30	86,28
36	73,47	58,92	85,05	54,48	87,77
37	75,51	61,13	86,66	56,70	89,21
38	77,55	63,38	88,23	58,96	90,61
39	79,59	65,66	89,76	61,27	91,97
40	81,63	67,98	91,24	63,63	93,26
41	83,67	70,34	92,68	66,05	94,50
42	85,71	72,76	94,06	68,53	95,66
43	87,76	75,23	95,37	71,08	96,75
44	89,80	77,77	96,60	73,72	97,73
45	91,84	80,40	97,73	76,47	98,59
46	93,88	83,13	98,72	79,35	99,30
47	95,92	86,02	99,50	82,42	99,79
48	97,96	89,15	99,95	85,79	99,99
49	100,00	92,75	100,00	89,75	100,00
		$N = 50$			
0	0,00	0,00	7,11	0,00	10,05
1	2,00	0,05	10,65	0,01	13,94
2	4,00	0,49	13,71	0,21	17,25
3	6,00	1,25	16,55	0,69	20,27
4	8,00	2,22	19,23	1,38	23,11
5	10,00	3,33	21,81	2,22	25,80
6	12,00	4,53	24,31	3,19	28,40
7	14,00	5,82	26,74	4,25	30,91
8	16,00	7,17	29,11	5,39	33,35
9	18,00	8,58	31,44	6,60	35,73
10	20,00	10,03	33,72	7,86	38,05
11	22,00	11,53	35,96	9,19	40,32
12	24,00	13,06	38,17	10,56	42,55
13	26,00	14,63	40,34	11,97	44,74
14	28,00	16,23	42,49	13,42	46,89
15	30,00	17,86	44,61	14,91	49,00
16	32,00	19,52	46,70	16,44	51,08
17	34,00	21,21	48,77	18,00	53,12
18	36,00	22,92	50,81	19,59	55,14
19	38,00	24,65	52,83	21,21	57,13
20	40,00	26,41	54,82	22,87	59,08
21	42,00	28,19	56,79	24,55	61,01
22	44,00	29,99	58,75	26,26	62,91
23	46,00	31,81	60,68	27,99	64,78
24	48,00	33,66	62,58	29,76	66,63
25	50,00	35,53	64,47	31,55	68,45
26	52,00	37,42	66,34	33,37	70,24
27	54,00	39,32	68,19	35,22	72,01
28	56,00	41,25	70,01	37,09	73,74
29	58,00	43,21	71,81	38,99	75,45
30	60,00	45,18	73,59	40,92	77,13
31	62,00	47,17	75,35	42,87	78,79
32	64,00	49,19	77,08	44,86	80,41
33	66,00	51,23	78,79	46,88	82,00
34	68,00	53,30	80,48	48,92	83,56
35	70,00	55,39	82,14	51,00	85,09
36	72,00	57,51	83,77	53,11	86,58
37	74,00	59,66	85,37	55,26	88,03
38	76,00	61,83	86,94	57,45	89,44
39	78,00	64,04	88,47	59,68	90,81
40	80,00	66,28	89,97	61,95	92,14
41	82,00	68,56	91,42	64,27	93,40
42	84,00	70,89	92,83	66,65	94,61
43	86,00	73,26	94,18	69,09	95,75
44	88,00	75,69	95,47	71,60	96,81
45	90,00	78,19	96,67	74,20	97,78
46	92,00	80,77	97,78	76,89	98,62
47	94,00	83,45	98,75	79,73	99,31
48	96,00	86,29	99,51	82,75	99,79
49	98,00	89,35	99,95	86,06	99,99
50	100,00	92,89	100,00	89,95	100,00
		$N = 51$			
0	0,00	0,00	6,98	0,00	9,87
1	1,96	0,05	10,45	0,01	13,68
2	3,92	0,48	13,46	0,20	16,94
3	5,88	1,23	16,24	0,67	19,90
4	7,84	2,18	18,88	1,35	22,69
5	9,80	3,26	21,41	2,18	25,35
6	11,76	4,44	23,87	3,12	27,90
7	13,73	5,70	26,26	4,16	30,37
8	15,69	7,02	28,59	5,28	32,77
9	17,65	8,40	30,87	6,46	35,11
10	19,61	9,82	33,12	7,70	37,39
11	21,57	11,29	35,32	8,99	39,63
12	23,53	12,79	37,49	10,33	41,82
13	25,49	14,33	39,63	11,72	43,98
14	27,45	15,89	41,74	13,14	46,09
15	29,41	17,49	43,83	14,59	48,18
		$N = 51$ (continued)			
16	31,37	19,11	45,89	16,09	50,23
17	33,33	20,76	47,92	17,61	52,25
18	35,29	22,43	49,93	19,17	54,23
19	37,25	24,13	51,92	20,75	56,19
20	39,22	25,84	53,89	22,37	58,12
21	41,18	27,58	55,83	24,01	60,03
22	43,14	29,35	57,75	25,68	61,91
23	45,10	31,13	59,66	27,37	63,76
24	47,06	32,93	61,54	29,10	65,58
25	49,02	34,75	63,40	30,84	67,38
26	50,98	36,60	65,25	32,62	69,16
27	52,94	38,46	67,07	34,42	70,90
28	54,90	40,34	68,87	36,24	72,63
29	56,86	42,25	70,65	38,09	74,32
30	58,82	44,17	72,42	39,97	75,99
31	60,78	46,11	74,16	41,88	77,63
32	62,75	48,08	75,87	43,81	79,25
33	64,71	50,07	77,57	45,77	80,83
34	66,67	52,08	79,24	47,75	82,39
35	68,63	54,11	80,89	49,77	83,91
36	70,59	56,17	82,51	51,82	85,41
37	72,55	58,26	84,11	53,91	86,86
38	74,51	60,37	85,67	56,02	88,28
39	76,47	62,51	87,21	58,18	89,67
40	78,43	64,68	88,71	60,37	91,01
41	80,39	66,88	90,18	62,61	92,30
42	82,35	69,13	91,60	64,89	93,54
43	84,31	71,41	92,98	67,23	94,72
44	86,27	73,74	94,30	69,63	95,84
45	88,24	76,13	95,56	72,10	96,88
46	90,20	78,59	96,74	74,65	97,82
47	92,16	81,12	97,82	77,31	98,65
48	94,12	83,76	98,77	80,10	99,33
49	96,08	86,54	99,52	83,06	99,80
50	98,04	89,55	99,95	86,32	99,99
51	100,00	93,02	100,00	90,13	100,00
		$N = 52$			
0	0,00	0,00	6,85	0,00	9,69
1	1,92	0,05	10,26	0,01	13,44
2	3,85	0,47	13,21	0,20	16,63
3	5,77	1,21	15,95	0,66	19,55
4	7,69	2,14	18,54	1,32	22,29
5	9,62	3,20	21,03	2,13	24,90
6	11,54	4,35	23,44	3,06	27,41
7	13,46	5,59	25,79	4,08	29,84
8	15,38	6,88	28,08	5,17	32,20
9	17,31	8,23	30,33	6,33	34,51
10	19,23	9,63	32,53	7,54	36,76
11	21,15	11,06	34,70	8,81	38,96
12	23,08	12,53	36,84	10,12	41,12
13	25,00	14,03	38,95	11,47	43,24
14	26,92	15,57	41,02	12,86	45,33
15	28,85	17,13	43,08	14,29	47,38
16	30,77	18,72	45,10	15,75	49,40
17	32,69	20,33	47,11	17,24	51,39
18	34,62	21,97	49,09	18,76	53,36
19	36,54	23,62	51,04	20,31	55,29
20	38,46	25,30	52,98	21,89	57,20
21	40,38	27,01	54,90	23,49	59,08
22	42,31	28,73	56,80	25,12	60,93
23	44,23	30,47	58,67	26,78	62,76
24	46,15	32,23	60,53	28,46	64,57
25	48,08	34,01	62,37	30,17	66,35
26	50,00	35,81	64,19	31,90	68,10
27	51,92	37,63	65,99	33,65	69,83
28	53,85	39,47	67,77	35,43	71,54
29	55,77	41,33	69,53	37,24	73,22
30	57,69	43,20	71,27	39,07	74,88
31	59,62	45,10	72,99	40,92	76,51
32	61,54	47,02	74,70	42,80	78,11
33	63,46	48,96	76,38	44,71	79,69
34	65,38	50,91	78,03	46,64	81,24
35	67,31	52,89	79,67	48,61	82,76
36	69,23	54,90	81,28	50,60	84,25
37	71,15	56,92	82,87	52,62	85,71
38	73,08	58,98	84,43	54,67	87,14
39	75,00	61,05	85,97	56,76	88,53
40	76,92	63,16	87,47	58,88	89,88
41	78,85	65,30	88,94	61,04	91,19
42	80,77	67,47	90,37	63,24	92,46
43	82,69	69,67	91,77	65,49	93,67
44	84,62	71,92	93,12	67,80	94,83
45	86,54	74,21	94,41	70,16	95,92
46	88,46	76,56	95,65	72,59	96,94
47	90,38	78,97	96,80	75,10	97,87
48	92,31	81,46	97,86	77,71	98,68
49	94,23	84,05	98,79	80,45	99,34
50	96,15	86,79	99,53	83,37	99,80
51	98,08	89,74	99,95	86,56	99,99
52	100,00	93,15	100,00	90,31	100,00
		$N = 53$			
0	0,00	0,00	6,72	0,00	9,51
1	1,89	0,05	10,07	0,01	13,20
2	3,77	0,46	12,98	0,20	16,34
3	5,66	1,18	15,66	0,65	19,21

All values conform to the international convention (i.e. 0,1 instead of 0.1).

N: number of trials; x: number of successes, etc.; $100\,p_x = 100\,x/N$

$N=53$ (continued)

x	$100\,p_x$	95% $100\,p_l$	95% $100\,p_r$	99% $100\,p_l$	99% $100\,p_r$
4	7,55	2,09–	18,21	1,30–	21,90
5	9,43	3,13–	20,66	2,09–	24,47
6	11,32	4,27–	23,03	3,00–	26,94
7	13,21	5,48–	25,34	4,00–	29,33
8	15,09	6,75–	27,59	5,07–	31,66
9	16,98	8,07–	29,80	6,20–	33,93
10	18,87	9,44–	31,97	7,39–	36,14
11	20,75	10,84–	34,11	8,63–	38,31
12	22,64	12,28–	36,21	9,92–	40,44
13	24,53	13,76–	38,28	11,24–	42,53
14	26,42	15,26–	40,33	12,60–	44,59
15	28,30	16,79–	42,35	14,00–	46,61
16	30,19	18,34–	44,34	15,43–	48,61
17	32,08	19,92–	46,32	16,89–	50,57
18	33,96	21,52–	48,27	18,37–	52,51
19	35,85	23,14–	50,20	19,89–	54,41
20	37,74	24,79–	52,11	21,43–	56,30
21	39,62	26,45–	54,00	23,00–	58,15
22	41,51	28,14–	55,87	24,59–	59,99
23	43,40	29,84–	57,72	26,21–	61,79
24	45,28	31,56–	59,55	27,86–	63,58
25	47,17	33,30–	61,36	29,52–	65,34
26	49,06	35,06–	63,16	31,21–	67,07
27	50,94	36,84–	64,94	32,93–	68,79
28	52,83	38,64–	66,70	34,66–	70,48
29	54,72	40,45–	68,44	36,42–	72,14
30	56,60	42,28–	70,16	38,21–	73,79
31	58,49	44,13–	71,86	40,01–	75,41
32	60,38	46,00–	73,55	41,85–	77,00
33	62,26	47,89–	75,21	43,70–	78,57
34	64,15	49,80–	76,86	45,59–	80,11
35	66,04	51,73–	78,48	47,49–	81,63
36	67,92	53,68–	80,08	49,43–	83,11
37	69,81	55,66–	81,66	51,39–	84,57
38	71,70	57,65–	83,21	53,39–	86,00
39	73,58	59,67–	84,74	55,41–	87,40
40	75,47	61,72–	86,24	57,47–	88,76
41	77,36	63,79–	87,72	59,56–	90,08
42	79,25	65,89–	89,16	61,69–	91,37
43	81,13	68,03–	90,56	63,86–	92,61
44	83,02	70,20–	91,93	66,07–	93,80
45	84,91	72,41–	93,25	68,34–	94,93
46	86,79	74,66–	94,52	70,67–	96,00
47	88,68	76,97–	95,73	73,06–	97,00
48	90,57	79,34–	96,87	75,53–	97,91
49	92,45	81,79–	97,91	78,10–	98,70
50	94,34	84,34–	98,82	80,79–	99,35
51	96,23	87,02–	99,54	83,66–	99,80
52	98,11	89,93–	99,95	86,80–	99,99
53	100,00	93,28–	100,00	90,49–	100,00

$N=54$

x	$100\,p_x$	95% $100\,p_l$	95% $100\,p_r$	99% $100\,p_l$	99% $100\,p_r$
0	0,00	0,00–	6,60	0,00–	9,35
1	1,85	0,05–	9,89	0,01–	12,97
2	3,70	0,45–	12,75	0,19–	16,06
3	5,56	1,16–	15,39	0,64–	18,88
4	7,41	2,06–	17,89	1,27–	21,53
5	9,26	3,08–	20,30	2,05–	24,06
6	11,11	4,19–	22,63	2,94–	26,49
7	12,96	5,37–	24,90	3,92–	28,84
8	14,81	6,62–	27,12	4,97–	31,13
9	16,67	7,92–	29,29	6,08–	33,36
10	18,52	9,25–	31,43	7,25–	35,55
11	20,37	10,63–	33,53	8,46–	37,69
12	22,22	12,04–	35,60	9,72–	39,78
13	24,07	13,49–	37,64	11,02–	41,85
14	25,93	14,96–	39,65	12,35–	43,87
15	27,78	16,46–	41,64	13,72–	45,87
16	29,63	17,98–	43,61	15,12–	47,83
17	31,48	19,52–	45,55	16,55–	49,77
18	33,33	21,09–	47,47	18,00–	51,68
19	35,19	22,68–	49,38	19,49–	53,56
20	37,04	24,29–	51,26	20,99–	55,42
21	38,89	25,92–	53,12	22,53–	57,26
22	40,74	27,57–	54,97	24,09–	59,07
23	42,59	29,23–	56,79	25,67–	60,85
24	44,44	30,92–	58,60	27,27–	62,62
25	46,30	32,62–	60,39	28,90–	64,36
26	48,15	34,34–	62,16	30,55–	66,08
27	50,00	36,08–	63,92	32,23–	67,77
28	51,85	37,84–	65,66	33,92–	69,45
29	53,70	39,61–	67,38	35,64–	71,10
30	55,56	41,40–	69,08	37,38–	72,73
31	57,41	43,21–	70,77	39,15–	74,33
32	59,26	45,03–	72,43	40,93–	75,91
33	61,11	46,88–	74,08	42,74–	77,47
34	62,96	48,74–	75,71	44,58–	79,01
35	64,81	50,62–	77,32	46,44–	80,51
36	66,67	52,53–	78,91	48,32–	82,00
37	68,52	54,45–	80,48	50,23–	83,45
38	70,37	56,39–	82,02	52,17–	84,88
39	72,22	58,36–	83,54	54,13–	86,28
40	74,07	60,35–	85,04	56,13–	87,65
41	75,93	62,36–	86,51	58,15–	88,98
42	77,78	64,40–	87,96	60,22–	90,28
43	79,63	66,47–	89,37	62,31–	91,54
44	81,48	68,57–	90,75	64,45–	92,75
45	83,33	70,71–	92,08	66,64–	93,92

$N=54$ (continued)

x	$100\,p_x$	95% $100\,p_l$	95% $100\,p_r$	99% $100\,p_l$	99% $100\,p_r$
46	85,19	72,88–	93,38	68,87–	95,03
47	87,04	75,10–	94,63	71,16–	96,08
48	88,89	77,37–	95,81	73,51–	97,06
49	90,74	79,70–	96,92	75,94–	97,95
50	92,59	82,11–	97,94	78,47–	98,73
51	94,44	84,61–	98,84	81,12–	99,36
52	96,30	87,25–	99,55	83,94–	99,81
53	98,15	90,11–	99,95	87,03–	99,99
54	100,00	93,40–	100,00	90,65–	100,00

$N=55$

x	$100\,p_x$	95% $100\,p_l$	95% $100\,p_r$	99% $100\,p_l$	99% $100\,p_r$
0	0,00	0,00–	6,49	0,00–	9,18
1	1,82	0,05–	9,72	0,01–	12,75
2	3,64	0,44–	12,53	0,19–	15,79
3	5,45	1,14–	15,12	0,62–	18,56
4	7,27	2,02–	17,59	1,25–	21,17
5	9,09	3,02–	19,95	2,01–	23,66
6	10,91	4,11–	22,25	2,89–	26,05
7	12,73	5,27–	24,48	3,85–	28,37
8	14,55	6,50–	26,66	4,88–	30,62
9	16,36	7,77–	28,80	5,97–	32,82
10	18,18	9,08–	30,90	7,11–	34,97
11	20,00	10,43–	32,97	8,30–	37,08
12	21,82	11,81–	35,01	9,53–	39,15
13	23,64	13,23–	37,02	10,81–	41,18
14	25,45	14,67–	39,00	12,11–	43,18
15	27,27	16,14–	40,96	13,45–	45,15
16	29,09	17,63–	42,90	14,82–	47,08
17	30,91	19,14–	44,81	16,22–	49,00
18	32,73	20,68–	46,71	17,64–	50,88
19	34,55	22,24–	48,58	19,10–	52,74
20	36,36	23,81–	50,44	20,57–	54,57
21	38,18	25,41–	52,27	22,07–	56,39
22	40,00	27,02–	54,09	23,60–	58,17
23	41,82	28,65–	55,89	25,15–	59,94
24	43,64	30,30–	57,68	26,72–	61,68
25	45,45	31,97–	59,45	28,31–	63,40
26	47,27	33,65–	61,20	29,92–	65,10
27	49,09	35,35–	62,93	31,56–	66,78
28	50,91	37,07–	64,65	33,22–	68,44
29	52,73	38,80–	66,35	34,90–	70,08
30	54,55	40,55–	68,03	36,60–	71,69
31	56,36	42,32–	69,70	38,32–	73,28
32	58,18	44,11–	71,35	40,06–	74,85
33	60,00	45,91–	72,98	41,83–	76,40
34	61,82	47,73–	74,59	43,61–	77,93
35	63,64	49,56–	76,19	45,43–	79,43
36	65,45	51,42–	77,76	47,26–	80,90
37	67,27	53,29–	79,32	49,12–	82,36
38	69,09	55,19–	80,86	51,00–	83,78
39	70,91	57,10–	82,37	52,92–	85,18
40	72,73	59,04–	83,86	54,85–	86,55
41	74,55	61,00–	85,33	56,82–	87,89
42	76,36	62,98–	86,77	58,82–	89,19
43	78,18	64,99–	88,19	60,85–	90,47
44	80,00	67,03–	89,57	62,92–	91,70
45	81,82	69,10–	90,92	65,03–	92,89
46	83,64	71,20–	92,23	67,18–	94,03
47	85,45	73,34–	93,50	69,38–	95,12
48	87,27	75,52–	94,73	71,63–	96,15
49	89,09	77,75–	95,89	73,95–	97,11
50	90,91	80,05–	96,98	76,34–	97,99
51	92,73	82,41–	97,98	78,83–	98,75
52	94,55	84,88–	98,86	81,44–	99,38
53	96,36	87,47–	99,56	84,21–	99,81
54	98,18	90,28–	99,95	87,25–	99,99
55	100,00	93,51–	100,00	90,82–	100,00

$N=56$

x	$100\,p_x$	95% $100\,p_l$	95% $100\,p_r$	99% $100\,p_l$	99% $100\,p_r$
0	0,00	0,00–	6,38	0,00–	9,03
1	1,79	0,05–	9,55	0,01–	12,53
2	3,57	0,44–	12,31	0,19–	15,52
3	5,36	1,12–	14,87	0,61–	18,25
4	7,14	1,98–	17,29	1,23–	20,82
5	8,93	2,96–	19,62	1,98–	23,27
6	10,71	4,03–	21,88	2,83–	25,63
7	12,50	5,18–	24,07	3,77–	27,91
8	14,29	6,38–	26,22	4,79–	30,13
9	16,07	7,62–	28,33	5,86–	32,30
10	17,86	8,91–	30,40	6,98–	34,42
11	19,64	10,23–	32,43	8,14–	36,49
12	21,43	11,59–	34,44	9,35–	38,53
13	23,21	12,98–	36,42	10,60–	40,53
14	25,00	14,39–	38,37	11,88–	42,50
15	26,79	15,83–	40,30	13,19–	44,45
16	28,57	17,30–	42,21	14,53–	46,36
17	30,36	18,78–	44,10	15,90–	48,24
18	32,14	20,29–	45,96	17,30–	50,10
19	33,93	21,81–	47,81	18,72–	51,94
20	35,71	23,36–	49,64	20,17–	53,75
21	37,50	24,92–	51,45	21,64–	55,54
22	39,29	26,50–	53,25	23,13–	57,31
23	41,07	28,10–	55,02	24,65–	59,05
24	42,86	29,71–	56,78	26,18–	60,77
25	44,64	31,34–	58,53	27,74–	62,48
26	46,43	32,99–	60,26	29,32–	64,16
27	48,21	34,66–	61,97	30,92–	65,82

$N=56$ (continued)

x	$100\,p_x$	95% $100\,p_l$	95% $100\,p_r$	99% $100\,p_l$	99% $100\,p_r$
28	50,00	36,34–	63,66	32,54–	67,46
29	51,79	38,03–	65,34	34,18–	69,08
30	53,57	39,74–	67,01	35,84–	70,68
31	55,36	41,47–	68,66	37,52–	72,26
32	57,14	43,22–	70,29	39,23–	73,82
33	58,93	44,98–	71,90	40,95–	75,35
34	60,71	46,75–	73,50	42,69–	76,87
35	62,50	48,55–	75,08	44,46–	78,36
36	64,29	50,36–	76,64	46,25–	79,83
37	66,07	52,19–	78,19	48,06–	81,28
38	67,86	54,04–	79,71	49,90–	82,70
39	69,64	55,90–	81,22	51,76–	84,10
40	71,43	57,79–	82,70	53,64–	85,47
41	73,21	59,70–	84,17	55,55–	86,81
42	75,00	61,63–	85,61	57,50–	88,12
43	76,79	63,58–	87,02	59,47–	89,40
44	78,57	65,56–	88,41	61,47–	90,65
45	80,36	67,57–	89,77	63,51–	91,86
46	82,14	69,60–	91,09	65,58–	93,02
47	83,93	71,67–	92,38	67,70–	94,14
48	85,71	73,78–	93,62	69,87–	95,21
49	87,50	75,93–	94,82	72,09–	96,23
50	89,29	78,12–	95,97	74,37–	97,17
51	91,07	80,38–	97,04	76,73–	98,02
52	92,86	82,71–	98,02	79,18–	98,77
53	94,64	85,13–	98,88	81,75–	99,39
54	96,43	87,69–	99,56	84,48–	99,81
55	98,21	90,45–	99,95	87,47–	99,99
56	100,00	93,62–	100,00	90,97–	100,00

$N=57$

x	$100\,p_x$	95% $100\,p_l$	95% $100\,p_r$	99% $100\,p_l$	99% $100\,p_r$
0	0,00	0,00–	6,27	0,00–	8,88
1	1,75	0,04–	9,39	0,01–	12,32
2	3,51	0,43–	12,11	0,18–	15,27
3	5,26	1,10–	14,62	0,60–	17,96
4	7,02	1,95–	17,00	1,21–	20,48
5	8,77	2,91–	19,30	1,94–	22,90
6	10,53	3,96–	21,52	2,78–	25,22
7	12,28	5,08–	23,68	3,71–	27,47
8	14,04	6,26–	25,79	4,70–	29,65
9	15,79	7,48–	27,87	5,75–	31,79
10	17,54	8,75–	29,91	6,85–	33,88
11	19,30	10,05–	31,91	7,99–	35,92
12	21,05	11,38–	33,89	9,18–	37,93
13	22,81	12,74–	35,84	10,40–	39,91
14	24,56	14,13–	37,76	11,66–	41,85
15	26,32	15,54–	39,66	12,94–	43,77
16	28,07	16,97–	41,54	14,26–	45,65
17	29,82	18,43–	43,40	15,60–	47,51
18	31,58	19,91–	45,24	16,97–	49,35
19	33,33	21,40–	47,06	18,36–	51,16
20	35,09	22,91–	48,87	19,78–	52,95
21	36,84	24,45–	50,66	21,22–	54,72
22	38,60	26,00–	52,43	22,68–	56,46
23	40,35	27,56–	54,18	24,17–	58,19
24	42,11	29,14–	55,92	25,67–	59,89
25	43,86	30,74–	57,64	27,20–	61,57
26	45,61	32,36–	59,34	28,74–	63,24
27	47,37	33,98–	61,03	30,31–	64,88
28	49,12	35,63–	62,71	31,89–	66,51
29	50,88	37,29–	64,37	33,49–	68,11
30	52,63	38,97–	66,02	35,12–	69,69
31	54,39	40,66–	67,64	36,76–	71,26
32	56,14	42,36–	69,26	38,43–	72,80
33	57,89	44,08–	70,86	40,11–	74,33
34	59,65	45,82–	72,44	41,81–	75,83
35	61,40	47,57–	74,00	43,54–	77,32
36	63,16	49,34–	75,55	45,28–	78,78
37	64,91	51,13–	77,09	47,05–	80,22
38	66,67	52,94–	78,60	48,84–	81,64
39	68,42	54,76–	80,09	50,65–	83,03
40	70,18	56,60–	81,57	52,49–	84,40
41	71,93	58,46–	83,03	54,35–	85,74
42	73,68	60,34–	84,46	56,23–	87,06
43	75,44	62,24–	85,87	58,15–	88,34
44	77,19	64,16–	87,26	60,09–	89,60
45	78,95	66,11–	88,62	62,07–	90,82
46	80,70	68,09–	89,95	64,08–	92,01
47	82,46	70,09–	91,25	66,12–	93,15
48	84,21	72,13–	92,52	68,21–	94,25
49	85,96	74,21–	93,74	70,35–	95,30
50	87,72	76,32–	94,92	72,53–	96,29
51	89,47	78,48–	96,04	74,78–	97,22
52	91,23	80,70–	97,09	77,10–	98,06
53	92,98	83,00–	98,05	79,52–	98,79
54	94,74	85,38–	98,90	82,04–	99,40
55	96,49	87,89–	99,57	84,73–	99,82
56	98,25	90,61–	99,96	87,68–	99,99
57	100,00	93,73–	100,00	91,12–	100,00

$N=58$

x	$100\,p_x$	95% $100\,p_l$	95% $100\,p_r$	99% $100\,p_l$	99% $100\,p_r$
0	0,00	0,00–	6,16	0,00–	8,73
1	1,72	0,04–	9,24	0,01–	12,12
2	3,45	0,42–	11,91	0,18–	15,02
3	5,17	1,08–	14,38	0,59–	17,67
4	6,90	1,91–	16,73	1,18–	20,16

$N=58$ (continued)

x	$100\,p_x$	95% $100\,p_l$	95% $100\,p_r$	99% $100\,p_l$	99% $100\,p_r$
5	8,62	2,86–	18,98	1,91–	22,53
6	10,34	3,89–	21,17	2,73–	24,82
7	12,07	4,99–	23,30	3,64–	27,03
8	13,79	6,15–	25,38	4,61–	29,19
9	15,52	7,35–	27,42	5,64–	31,29
10	17,24	8,59–	29,43	6,72–	33,35
11	18,97	9,87–	31,41	7,85–	35,37
12	20,69	11,17–	33,35	9,01–	37,35
13	22,41	12,51–	35,27	10,21–	39,30
14	24,14	13,87–	37,17	11,44–	41,22
15	25,86	15,26–	39,04	12,70–	43,11
16	27,59	16,66–	40,90	13,99–	44,97
17	29,31	18,09–	42,73	15,31–	46,80
18	31,03	19,54–	44,54	16,65–	48,62
19	32,76	21,01–	46,34	18,02–	50,41
20	34,48	22,49–	48,12	19,41–	52,17
21	36,21	23,99–	49,88	20,82–	53,92
22	37,93	25,51–	51,63	22,25–	55,64
23	39,66	27,05–	53,36	23,70–	57,35
24	41,38	28,60–	55,07	25,18–	59,03
25	43,10	30,16–	56,77	26,67–	60,70
26	44,83	31,74–	58,46	28,18–	62,34
27	46,55	33,34–	60,13	29,72–	63,97
28	48,28	34,95–	61,78	31,27–	65,57
29	50,00	36,58–	63,42	32,84–	67,16
30	51,72	38,22–	65,05	34,43–	68,73
31	53,45	39,87–	66,66	36,03–	70,28
32	55,17	41,54–	68,26	37,66–	71,82
33	56,90	43,23–	69,84	39,30–	73,33
34	58,62	44,93–	71,40	40,97–	74,82
35	60,34	46,64–	72,95	42,65–	76,30
36	62,07	48,37–	74,49	44,36–	77,75
37	63,79	50,12–	76,01	46,08–	79,18
38	65,52	51,88–	77,51	47,83–	80,59
39	67,24	53,66–	78,99	49,59–	81,98
40	68,97	55,46–	80,46	51,38–	83,35
41	70,69	57,27–	81,91	53,20–	84,69
42	72,41	59,10–	83,34	55,03–	86,01
43	74,14	60,96–	84,74	56,89–	87,30
44	75,86	62,83–	86,13	58,78–	88,56
45	77,59	64,73–	87,49	60,70–	89,79
46	79,31	66,65–	88,83	62,65–	90,99
47	81,03	68,59–	90,13	64,63–	92,15
48	82,76	70,57–	91,41	66,65–	93,28
49	84,48	72,58–	92,65	68,71–	94,36
50	86,21	74,62–	93,85	70,81–	95,39
51	87,93	76,70–	95,01	72,97–	96,36
52	89,66	78,83–	96,11	75,18–	97,27
53	91,38	81,02–	97,14	77,47–	98,09
54	93,10	83,27–	98,09	79,84–	98,82
55	94,83	85,62–	98,92	82,33–	99,41
56	96,55	88,09–	99,58	84,98–	99,82
57	98,28	90,76–	99,96	87,88–	99,99
58	100,00	93,84–	100,00	91,27–	100,00

$N=59$

x	$100\,p_x$	95% $100\,p_l$	95% $100\,p_r$	99% $100\,p_l$	99% $100\,p_r$
0	0,00	0,00–	6,06	0,00–	8,59
1	1,69	0,04–	9,09	0,01–	11,93
2	3,39	0,41–	11,71	0,18–	14,78
3	5,08	1,06–	14,15	0,58–	17,39
4	6,78	1,88–	16,46	1,16–	19,84
5	8,47	2,81–	18,68	1,87–	22,18
6	10,17	3,82–	20,83	2,69–	24,43
7	11,86	4,91–	22,93	3,58–	26,62
8	13,56	6,04–	24,98	4,53–	28,74
9	15,25	7,22–	26,99	5,54–	30,82
10	16,95	8,44–	28,97	6,60–	32,84
11	18,64	9,69–	30,91	7,71–	34,83
12	20,34	10,98–	32,83	8,85–	36,79
13	22,03	12,29–	34,73	10,03–	38,71
14	23,73	13,62–	36,60	11,24–	40,60
15	25,42	14,98–	38,44	12,47–	42,47
16	27,12	16,36–	40,27	13,74–	44,30
17	28,81	17,76–	42,08	15,03–	46,12
18	30,51	19,19–	43,87	16,35–	47,91
19	32,20	20,62–	45,64	17,69–	49,67
20	33,90	22,08–	47,39	19,05–	51,42
21	35,59	23,55–	49,13	20,43–	53,14
22	37,29	25,04–	50,85	21,84–	54,84
23	38,98	26,55–	52,56	23,26–	56,53
24	40,68	28,07–	54,25	24,70–	58,19
25	42,37	29,61–	55,93	26,17–	59,84
26	44,07	31,16–	57,60	27,65–	61,47
27	45,76	32,72–	59,25	29,15–	63,08
28	47,46	34,30–	60,88	30,67–	64,67
29	49,15	35,89–	62,50	32,20–	66,24
30	50,85	37,50–	64,11	33,76–	67,80
31	52,54	39,12–	65,70	35,33–	69,33
32	54,24	40,75–	67,28	36,92–	70,85
33	55,93	42,40–	68,84	38,53–	72,35
34	57,63	44,07–	70,39	40,16–	73,83
35	59,32	45,75–	71,93	41,81–	75,30
36	61,02	47,44–	73,45	43,47–	76,74
37	62,71	49,15–	74,96	45,16–	78,16
38	64,41	50,87–	76,45	46,86–	79,57
39	66,10	52,61–	77,92	48,58–	80,95
40	67,80	54,36–	79,38	50,33–	82,31
41	69,49	56,13–	80,81	52,09–	83,65

All values conform to the international convention (i.e. 0,1 instead of 0.1).

N: number of trials; x: number of successes, etc.; $100\,p_x = 100\,x/N$

$N=59$ (continued)

x	$100\,p_x$	95% $100\,p_l$	95% $100\,p_r$	99% $100\,p_l$	99% $100\,p_r$
42	71,19	57,92	82,24	53,88	84,97
43	72,88	59,73	83,64	55,70	86,26
44	74,58	61,56	85,02	57,53	87,53
45	76,27	63,40	86,38	59,40	88,76
46	77,97	65,27	87,71	61,29	89,97
47	79,66	67,17	89,02	63,21	91,15
48	81,36	69,09	90,31	65,17	92,29
49	83,05	71,03	91,56	67,16	93,40
50	84,75	73,01	92,78	69,18	94,46
51	86,44	75,02	93,96	71,26	95,47
52	88,14	77,07	95,09	73,38	96,42
53	89,83	79,17	96,18	75,57	97,31
54	91,53	81,32	97,19	77,82	98,13
55	93,22	83,54	98,12	80,16	98,84
56	94,92	85,85	98,94	82,61	99,42
57	96,61	88,29	99,59	85,22	99,82
58	98,31	90,91	99,96	88,07	99,99
59	100,00	93,94	100,00	91,41	100,00

$N=60$

x	$100\,p_x$	95% $100\,p_l$	95% $100\,p_r$	99% $100\,p_l$	99% $100\,p_r$
0	0,00	0,00	5,96	0,00	8,45
1	1,67	0,04	8,94	0,01	11,74
2	3,33	0,41	11,53	0,17	14,55
3	5,00	1,04	13,92	0,57	17,12
4	6,67	1,85	16,20	1,14	19,53
5	8,33	2,76	18,39	1,84	21,84
6	10,00	3,76	20,51	2,64	24,06
7	11,67	4,82	22,57	3,51	26,21
8	13,33	5,94	24,59	4,45	28,31
9	15,00	7,10	26,57	5,45	30,35
10	16,67	8,29	28,52	6,49	32,35
11	18,33	9,52	30,44	7,57	34,31
12	20,00	10,78	32,33	8,69	36,24
13	21,67	12,07	34,20	9,85	38,14
14	23,33	13,38	36,04	11,04	40,00
15	25,00	14,72	37,86	12,25	41,84
16	26,67	16,07	39,66	13,49	43,66
17	28,33	17,45	41,44	14,76	45,45
18	30,00	18,85	43,21	16,05	47,21
19	31,67	20,26	44,96	17,37	48,96
20	33,33	21,69	46,69	18,70	50,68
21	35,00	23,13	48,40	20,06	52,39
22	36,67	24,59	50,10	21,44	54,07
23	38,33	26,07	51,79	22,83	55,73
24	40,00	27,56	53,46	24,25	57,38
25	41,67	29,07	55,12	25,68	59,01
26	43,33	30,59	56,76	27,13	60,62
27	45,00	32,12	58,39	28,60	62,21
28	46,67	33,67	60,00	30,09	63,78
29	48,33	35,23	61,61	31,60	65,34
30	50,00	36,81	63,19	33,12	66,88
31	51,67	38,39	64,77	34,66	68,40
32	53,33	40,00	66,33	36,22	69,91
33	55,00	41,61	67,88	37,79	71,40
34	56,67	43,24	69,41	39,38	72,87
35	58,33	44,88	70,93	40,99	74,32
36	60,00	46,54	72,44	42,62	75,75
37	61,67	48,21	73,93	44,27	77,17
38	63,33	49,90	75,41	45,93	78,56
39	65,00	51,60	76,87	47,61	79,94
40	66,67	53,31	78,31	49,32	81,30
41	68,33	55,04	79,74	51,04	82,63
42	70,00	56,79	81,15	52,79	83,95
43	71,67	58,56	82,55	54,55	85,24
44	73,33	60,34	83,93	56,34	86,51
45	75,00	62,14	85,28	58,16	87,75
46	76,67	63,96	86,62	60,00	88,96
47	78,33	65,80	87,93	61,86	90,15
48	80,00	67,67	89,22	63,76	91,31
49	81,67	69,56	90,48	65,69	92,43
50	83,33	71,48	91,71	67,65	93,51
51	85,00	73,43	92,90	69,65	94,55
52	86,67	75,41	94,06	71,69	95,55
53	88,33	77,43	95,18	73,79	96,49
54	90,00	79,49	96,24	75,94	97,36
55	91,67	81,61	97,24	78,16	98,16
56	93,33	83,80	98,15	80,47	98,86
57	95,00	86,08	98,96	82,88	99,43
58	96,67	88,47	99,59	85,45	99,83
59	98,33	91,06	99,96	88,26	99,99
60	100,00	94,04	100,00	91,55	100,00

$N=61$

x	$100\,p_x$	95% $100\,p_l$	95% $100\,p_r$	99% $100\,p_l$	99% $100\,p_r$
0	0,00	0,00	5,87	0,00	8,32
1	1,64	0,04	8,80	0,01	11,56
2	3,28	0,40	11,35	0,17	14,33
3	4,92	1,03	13,71	0,56	16,86
4	6,56	1,82	15,95	1,12	19,24
5	8,20	2,72	18,10	1,81	21,51
6	9,84	3,70	20,19	2,59	23,70
7	11,48	4,74	22,22	3,45	25,82
8	13,11	5,84	24,22	4,38	27,88
9	14,75	6,98	26,17	5,35	29,90
10	16,39	8,15	28,09	6,38	31,87
11	18,03	9,36	29,98	7,44	33,81
12	19,67	10,60	31,84	8,54	35,71
13	21,31	11,86	33,68	9,68	37,58

$N=61$ (continued)

x	$100\,p_x$	95% $100\,p_l$	95% $100\,p_r$	99% $100\,p_l$	99% $100\,p_r$
14	22,95	13,15	35,50	10,84	39,42
15	24,59	14,46	37,29	12,04	41,24
16	26,23	15,80	39,07	13,26	43,03
17	27,87	17,15	40,83	14,50	44,80
18	29,51	18,52	42,57	15,77	46,54
19	31,15	19,90	44,29	17,06	48,26
20	32,79	21,31	46,00	18,37	49,97
21	34,43	22,73	47,69	19,70	51,65
22	36,07	24,16	49,37	21,05	53,31
23	37,70	25,61	51,04	22,42	54,96
24	39,34	27,07	52,69	23,81	56,59
25	40,98	28,55	54,32	25,21	58,20
26	42,62	30,04	55,94	26,64	59,79
27	44,26	31,55	57,55	28,08	61,36
28	45,90	33,06	59,15	29,54	62,92
29	47,54	34,60	60,73	31,01	64,46
30	49,18	36,14	62,30	32,50	65,99
31	50,82	37,70	63,86	34,01	67,50
32	52,46	39,27	65,40	35,54	68,99
33	54,10	40,85	66,94	37,08	70,46
34	55,74	42,45	68,45	38,64	71,92
35	57,38	44,06	69,96	40,21	73,36
36	59,02	45,68	71,45	41,80	74,79
37	60,66	47,31	72,93	43,41	76,19
38	62,30	48,96	74,39	45,04	77,58
39	63,93	50,63	75,84	46,69	78,95
40	65,57	52,31	77,27	48,35	80,30
41	67,21	54,00	78,69	50,03	81,63
42	68,85	55,71	80,10	51,74	82,94
43	70,49	57,43	81,48	53,46	84,23
44	72,13	59,17	82,85	55,20	85,50
45	73,77	60,93	84,20	56,97	86,74
46	75,41	62,71	85,54	58,76	87,96
47	77,05	64,50	86,85	60,58	89,16
48	78,69	66,32	88,14	62,42	90,32
49	80,33	68,16	89,40	64,29	91,46
50	81,97	70,02	90,64	66,19	92,56
51	83,61	71,91	91,85	68,13	93,62
52	85,25	73,83	93,02	70,10	94,65
53	86,89	75,78	94,16	72,12	95,62
54	88,52	77,78	95,26	74,18	96,55
55	90,16	79,81	96,30	76,30	97,41
56	91,80	81,90	97,28	78,49	98,19
57	93,44	84,05	98,18	80,76	98,88
58	95,08	86,29	98,97	83,14	99,44
59	96,72	88,65	99,60	85,67	99,83
60	98,36	91,20	99,96	88,44	99,99
61	100,00	94,13	100,00	91,68	100,00

$N=62$

x	$100\,p_x$	95% $100\,p_l$	95% $100\,p_r$	99% $100\,p_l$	99% $100\,p_r$
0	0,00	0,00	5,78	0,00	8,19
1	1,61	0,04	8,66	0,01	11,38
2	3,23	0,39	11,17	0,17	14,11
3	4,84	1,01	13,50	0,55	16,60
4	6,45	1,79	15,70	1,11	18,95
5	8,06	2,67	17,83	1,78	21,19
6	9,68	3,63	19,88	2,55	23,35
7	11,29	4,66	21,89	3,40	25,44
8	12,90	5,74	23,85	4,30	27,47
9	14,52	6,86	25,78	5,26	29,46
10	16,13	8,02	27,67	6,27	31,41
11	17,74	9,20	29,53	7,32	33,32
12	19,35	10,42	31,37	8,40	35,20
13	20,97	11,66	33,18	9,51	37,04
14	22,58	12,93	34,97	10,66	38,86
15	24,19	14,22	36,74	11,83	40,65
16	25,81	15,53	38,50	13,03	42,42
17	27,42	16,85	40,23	14,25	44,16
18	29,03	18,20	41,95	15,49	45,89
19	30,65	19,56	43,65	16,76	47,59
20	32,26	20,94	45,34	18,05	49,27
21	33,87	22,33	47,01	19,35	50,93
22	35,48	23,74	48,66	20,68	52,58
23	37,10	25,16	50,31	22,02	54,21
24	38,71	26,60	51,93	23,38	55,81
25	40,32	28,05	53,55	24,76	57,41
26	41,94	29,51	55,15	26,16	58,98
27	43,55	30,99	56,74	27,57	60,54
28	45,16	32,48	58,32	29,00	62,08
29	46,77	33,98	59,88	30,45	63,61
30	48,39	35,50	61,44	31,91	65,12
31	50,00	37,02	62,98	33,39	66,61
32	51,61	38,56	64,50	34,88	68,09
33	53,23	40,12	66,02	36,39	69,55
34	54,84	41,68	67,52	37,92	71,00
35	56,45	43,26	69,01	39,46	72,43
36	58,06	44,85	70,49	41,02	73,84
37	59,68	46,45	71,95	42,59	75,24
38	61,29	48,07	73,40	44,19	76,62
39	62,90	49,69	74,84	45,79	77,98
40	64,52	51,34	76,26	47,42	79,32
41	66,13	52,99	77,67	49,07	80,65
42	67,74	54,66	79,06	50,73	81,95
43	69,35	56,35	80,44	52,41	83,24
44	70,97	58,05	81,80	54,11	84,51
45	72,58	59,77	83,15	55,84	85,75
46	74,19	61,50	84,47	57,58	86,97
47	75,81	63,26	85,78	59,35	88,17

$N=62$ (continued)

x	$100\,p_x$	95% $100\,p_l$	95% $100\,p_r$	99% $100\,p_l$	99% $100\,p_r$
48	77,42	65,03	87,07	61,14	89,34
49	79,03	66,82	88,34	62,96	90,49
50	80,65	68,63	89,58	64,80	91,60
51	82,26	70,47	90,80	66,68	92,68
52	83,87	72,33	91,98	68,59	93,73
53	85,48	74,22	93,14	70,54	94,74
54	87,10	76,15	94,26	72,53	95,70
55	88,71	78,11	95,34	74,56	96,60
56	90,32	80,12	96,37	76,65	97,45
57	91,94	82,17	97,33	78,81	98,22
58	93,55	84,30	98,21	81,05	98,89
59	95,16	86,50	98,99	83,40	99,45
60	96,77	88,83	99,61	85,89	99,83
61	98,39	91,34	99,96	88,62	99,99
62	100,00	94,22	100,00	91,81	100,00

$N=63$

x	$100\,p_x$	95% $100\,p_l$	95% $100\,p_r$	99% $100\,p_l$	99% $100\,p_r$
0	0,00	0,00	5,69	0,00	8,07
1	1,59	0,04	8,53	0,01	11,21
2	3,17	0,39	11,00	0,17	13,90
3	4,76	0,99	13,29	0,54	16,36
4	6,35	1,76	15,47	1,09	18,67
5	7,94	2,63	17,56	1,75	20,88
6	9,52	3,58	19,59	2,51	23,00
7	11,11	4,59	21,56	3,34	25,07
8	12,70	5,65	23,50	4,23	27,08
9	14,29	6,75	25,39	5,18	29,04
10	15,87	7,88	27,26	6,17	30,96
11	17,46	9,05	29,10	7,19	32,84
12	19,05	10,25	30,91	8,26	34,70
13	20,63	11,47	32,70	9,35	36,52
14	22,22	12,72	34,46	10,48	38,31
15	23,81	13,98	36,21	11,63	40,08
16	25,40	15,27	37,94	12,81	41,83
17	26,98	16,57	39,65	14,01	43,55
18	28,57	17,89	41,35	15,23	45,25
19	30,16	19,23	43,02	16,47	46,93
20	31,75	20,58	44,69	17,74	48,59
21	33,33	21,95	46,34	19,02	50,24
22	34,92	23,34	47,97	20,32	51,86
23	36,51	24,73	49,60	21,64	53,47
24	38,10	26,15	51,20	22,98	55,06
25	39,68	27,57	52,80	24,33	56,64
26	41,27	29,01	54,38	25,70	58,19
27	42,86	30,46	55,95	27,08	59,74
28	44,44	31,92	57,51	28,49	61,26
29	46,03	33,39	59,06	29,90	62,77
30	47,62	34,88	60,59	31,34	64,27
31	49,21	36,38	62,11	32,79	65,75
32	50,79	37,89	63,62	34,25	67,21
33	52,38	39,41	65,12	35,73	68,66
34	53,97	40,94	66,61	37,23	70,10
35	55,56	42,49	68,08	38,74	71,51
36	57,14	44,05	69,54	40,26	72,92
37	58,73	45,62	70,99	41,81	74,30
38	60,32	47,20	72,43	43,36	75,67
39	61,90	48,80	73,85	44,94	77,02
40	63,49	50,40	75,27	46,53	78,36
41	65,08	52,03	76,66	48,14	79,68
42	66,67	53,66	78,05	49,76	80,98
43	68,25	55,31	79,42	51,41	82,26
44	69,84	56,98	80,77	53,07	83,53
45	71,43	58,65	82,11	54,75	84,77
46	73,02	60,35	83,43	56,45	85,99
47	74,60	62,06	84,73	58,17	87,19
48	76,19	63,79	86,02	59,92	88,37
49	77,78	65,54	87,28	61,69	89,52
50	79,37	67,30	88,53	63,48	90,65
51	80,95	69,09	89,75	65,30	91,74
52	82,54	70,90	90,95	67,16	92,81
53	84,13	72,74	92,12	69,04	93,83
54	85,71	74,61	93,25	70,96	94,82
55	87,30	76,50	94,35	72,92	95,77
56	88,89	78,44	95,41	74,93	96,66
57	90,48	80,41	96,42	77,00	97,49
58	92,06	82,44	97,37	79,12	98,25
59	93,65	84,53	98,24	81,33	98,91
60	95,24	86,71	99,01	83,64	99,46
61	96,83	89,00	99,61	86,10	99,83
62	98,41	91,47	99,96	88,79	99,99
63	100,00	94,31	100,00	91,93	100,00

$N=64$

x	$100\,p_x$	95% $100\,p_l$	95% $100\,p_r$	99% $100\,p_l$	99% $100\,p_r$
0	0,00	0,00	5,60	0,00	7,95
1	1,56	0,04	8,40	0,01	11,04
2	3,13	0,38	10,84	0,16	13,69
3	4,69	0,98	13,09	0,54	16,12
4	6,25	1,73	15,24	1,07	18,40
5	7,81	2,59	17,30	1,72	20,57
6	9,38	3,52	19,30	2,47	22,67
7	10,94	4,51	21,25	3,29	24,71
8	12,50	5,55	23,15	4,17	26,69
9	14,06	6,64	25,02	5,09	28,62
10	15,63	7,76	26,86	6,07	30,52
11	17,19	8,90	28,68	7,08	32,38
12	18,75	10,08	30,46	8,12	34,21
13	20,31	11,28	32,23	9,20	36,01

$N=64$ (continued)

x	$100\,p_x$	95% $100\,p_l$	95% $100\,p_r$	99% $100\,p_l$	99% $100\,p_r$
14	21,88	12,51	33,97	10,30	37,78
15	23,44	13,75	35,69	11,44	39,53
16	25,00	15,02	37,40	12,59	41,25
17	26,56	16,30	39,09	13,77	42,95
18	28,13	17,60	40,76	14,97	44,63
19	29,69	18,91	42,42	16,19	46,29
20	31,25	20,24	44,06	17,43	47,94
21	32,81	21,59	45,69	18,69	49,56
22	34,38	22,95	47,30	19,97	51,17
23	35,94	24,32	48,90	21,27	52,76
24	37,50	25,70	50,49	22,58	54,33
25	39,06	27,10	52,07	23,91	55,89
26	40,63	28,51	53,63	25,25	57,43
27	42,19	29,94	55,18	26,61	58,95
28	43,75	31,37	56,72	27,99	60,46
29	45,31	32,82	58,25	29,38	61,96
30	46,88	34,28	59,77	30,79	63,44
31	48,44	35,75	61,27	32,21	64,90
32	50,00	37,23	62,77	33,64	66,36
33	51,56	38,73	64,25	35,10	67,79
34	53,13	40,23	65,72	36,56	69,21
35	54,69	41,75	67,18	38,04	70,62
36	56,25	43,28	68,63	39,54	72,01
37	57,81	44,82	70,06	41,05	73,39
38	59,38	46,37	71,49	42,57	74,75
39	60,94	47,93	72,90	44,11	76,09
40	62,50	49,51	74,30	45,67	77,42
41	64,06	51,10	75,68	47,24	78,73
42	65,63	52,70	77,05	48,83	80,03
43	67,19	54,31	78,41	50,44	81,31
44	68,75	55,94	79,76	52,06	82,57
45	70,31	57,58	81,09	53,71	83,81
46	71,88	59,24	82,40	55,37	85,03
47	73,44	60,91	83,70	57,05	86,23
48	75,00	62,60	84,98	58,75	87,41
49	76,56	64,31	86,25	60,47	88,56
50	78,13	66,03	87,49	62,22	89,70
51	79,69	67,77	88,72	63,99	90,80
52	81,25	69,54	89,92	65,79	91,88
53	82,81	71,32	91,10	67,62	92,92
54	84,38	73,14	92,24	69,48	93,93
55	85,94	74,98	93,36	71,38	94,91
56	87,50	76,85	94,45	73,31	95,83
57	89,06	78,75	95,49	75,29	96,71
58	90,63	80,70	96,48	77,33	97,53
59	92,19	82,70	97,41	79,43	98,28
60	93,75	84,76	98,27	81,60	98,93
61	95,31	86,91	99,02	83,88	99,46
62	96,88	89,16	99,62	86,31	99,84
63	98,44	91,60	99,96	88,96	99,99
64	100,00	94,40	100,00	92,05	100,00

$N=65$

x	$100\,p_x$	95% $100\,p_l$	95% $100\,p_r$	99% $100\,p_l$	99% $100\,p_r$
0	0,00	0,00	5,52	0,00	7,83
1	1,54	0,04	8,28	0,01	10,88
2	3,08	0,37	10,68	0,16	13,49
3	4,62	0,96	12,90	0,53	15,88
4	6,15	1,70	15,01	1,05	18,13
5	7,69	2,54	17,05	1,70	20,28
6	9,23	3,46	19,02	2,43	22,35
7	10,77	4,44	20,94	3,24	24,36
8	12,31	5,47	22,82	4,10	26,31
9	13,85	6,53	24,66	5,01	28,22
10	15,38	7,63	26,48	5,97	30,09
11	16,92	8,76	28,27	6,96	31,93
12	18,46	9,92	30,03	7,99	33,73
13	20,00	11,10	31,77	9,05	35,51
14	21,54	12,31	33,49	10,14	37,26
15	23,08	13,53	35,19	11,25	38,98
16	24,62	14,77	36,87	12,38	40,69
17	26,15	16,03	38,54	13,54	42,37
18	27,69	17,31	40,19	14,72	44,03
19	29,23	18,60	41,83	15,93	45,67
20	30,77	19,91	43,45	17,14	47,29
21	32,31	21,23	45,05	18,38	48,90
22	33,85	22,57	46,65	19,64	50,49
23	35,38	23,92	48,23	20,91	52,06
24	36,92	25,28	49,80	22,20	53,61
25	38,46	26,65	51,36	23,50	55,15
26	40,00	28,04	52,90	24,82	56,68
27	41,54	29,44	54,44	26,16	58,19
28	43,08	30,85	55,96	27,51	59,68
29	44,62	32,27	57,47	28,88	61,16
30	46,15	33,70	58,97	30,26	62,63
31	47,69	35,15	60,46	31,65	64,08
32	49,23	36,60	61,93	33,06	65,52
33	50,77	38,07	63,40	34,48	66,94
34	52,31	39,54	64,85	35,92	68,35
35	53,85	41,03	66,30	37,37	69,74
36	55,38	42,53	67,73	38,84	71,12
37	56,92	44,04	69,15	40,32	72,49
38	58,46	45,56	70,56	41,81	73,84
39	60,00	47,10	71,96	43,32	75,18
40	61,54	48,64	73,35	44,85	76,50
41	63,08	50,20	74,72	46,39	77,80
42	64,62	51,77	76,08	47,94	79,09
43	66,15	53,35	77,43	49,51	80,36
44	67,69	54,95	78,77	51,10	81,62

All values conform to the international convention (i.e. 0,1 instead of 0.1).

N: number of trials; x: number of successes, etc.; $100\,p_x = 100\;x/N$

$N=65$ (continued)

x	$100\,p_x$	95% $100\,p_l$	95% $100\,p_r$	99% $100\,p_l$	99% $100\,p_r$
45	69,23	56,55	80,09	52,71	82,86
46	70,77	58,17	81,40	54,33	84,07
47	72,31	59,81	82,69	55,97	85,28
48	73,85	61,46	83,97	57,63	86,46
49	75,38	63,13	85,23	59,31	87,62
50	76,92	64,81	86,47	61,02	88,75
51	78,46	66,51	87,69	62,74	89,86
52	80,00	68,23	88,90	64,49	90,95
53	81,54	69,97	90,08	66,27	92,01
54	83,08	71,73	91,24	68,07	93,04
55	84,62	73,52	92,37	69,91	94,03
56	86,15	75,34	93,47	71,78	94,99
57	87,69	77,18	94,53	73,69	95,90
58	89,23	79,06	95,56	75,64	96,76
59	90,77	80,98	96,54	77,65	97,57
60	92,31	82,95	97,46	79,72	98,30
61	93,85	84,99	98,30	81,87	98,95
62	95,38	87,10	99,04	84,12	99,47
63	96,92	89,32	99,63	86,51	99,84
64	98,46	91,72	99,96	89,12	99,99
65	100,00	94,48	100,00	92,17	100,00

$N=66$

x	$100\,p_x$	95% $100\,p_l$	95% $100\,p_r$	99% $100\,p_l$	99% $100\,p_r$
0	0,00	0,00	5,44	0,00	7,71
1	1,52	0,04	8,16	0,01	10,72
2	3,03	0,37	10,52	0,16	13,30
3	4,55	0,95	12,71	0,52	15,66
4	6,06	1,68	14,80	1,04	17,88
5	7,58	2,51	16,80	1,67	19,99
6	9,09	3,41	18,74	2,39	22,04
7	10,61	4,37	20,64	3,19	24,02
8	12,12	5,38	22,49	4,03	25,95
9	13,64	6,43	24,31	4,93	27,83
10	15,15	7,51	26,10	5,87	29,68
11	16,67	8,62	27,87	6,85	31,49
12	18,18	9,76	29,61	7,86	33,27
13	19,70	10,93	31,32	8,90	35,03
14	21,21	12,11	33,02	9,97	36,75
15	22,73	13,31	34,70	11,07	38,46
16	24,24	14,54	36,36	12,18	40,14
17	25,76	15,78	38,01	13,32	41,80
18	27,27	17,03	39,64	14,49	43,44
19	28,79	18,30	41,25	15,67	45,06
20	30,30	19,59	42,85	16,86	46,67
21	31,82	20,89	44,44	18,08	48,25
22	33,33	22,20	46,01	19,31	49,82
23	34,85	23,53	47,58	20,56	51,38
24	36,36	24,87	49,13	21,83	52,92
25	37,88	26,22	50,66	23,11	54,44
26	39,39	27,58	52,19	24,41	55,95
27	40,91	28,95	53,71	25,72	57,44
28	42,42	30,34	55,21	27,05	58,92
29	43,94	31,74	56,70	28,39	60,39
30	45,45	33,14	58,19	29,74	61,84
31	46,97	34,56	59,66	31,11	63,28
32	48,48	35,99	61,12	32,49	64,70
33	50,00	37,43	62,57	33,89	66,11
34	51,52	38,88	64,01	35,30	67,51
35	53,03	40,34	65,44	36,72	68,89
36	54,55	41,81	66,86	38,16	70,26
37	56,06	43,30	68,26	39,61	71,61
38	57,58	44,79	69,66	41,08	72,95
39	59,09	46,29	71,05	42,56	74,28
40	60,61	47,81	72,42	44,05	75,59
41	62,12	49,34	73,78	45,56	76,89
42	63,64	50,87	75,13	47,08	78,17
43	65,15	52,42	76,47	48,62	79,44
44	66,67	53,99	77,80	50,18	80,69
45	68,18	55,56	79,11	51,75	81,92
46	69,70	57,15	80,41	53,33	83,14
47	71,21	58,75	81,70	54,94	84,33
48	72,73	60,36	82,97	56,56	85,51
49	74,24	61,99	84,22	58,20	86,68
50	75,76	63,64	85,46	59,86	87,82
51	77,27	65,30	86,69	61,54	88,93
52	78,79	66,98	87,89	63,25	90,03
53	80,30	68,68	89,07	64,97	91,10
54	81,82	70,39	90,24	66,73	92,14
55	83,33	72,13	91,38	68,51	93,15
56	84,85	73,90	92,49	70,32	94,13
57	86,36	75,69	93,57	72,17	95,07
58	87,88	77,51	94,62	74,05	95,97
59	89,39	79,36	95,63	75,98	96,81
60	90,91	81,26	96,59	77,96	97,61
61	92,42	83,20	97,49	80,01	98,33
62	93,94	85,20	98,32	82,12	98,96
63	95,45	87,29	99,05	84,34	99,48
64	96,97	89,48	99,63	86,70	99,84
65	98,48	91,84	99,96	89,28	99,99
66	100,00	94,56	100,00	92,29	100,00

$N=67$

x	$100\,p_x$	95% $100\,p_l$	95% $100\,p_r$	99% $100\,p_l$	99% $100\,p_r$
0	0,00	0,00	5,36	0,00	7,60
1	1,49	0,04	8,04	0,01	10,57
2	2,99	0,36	10,37	0,16	13,11
3	4,48	0,93	12,53	0,51	15,44
4	5,97	1,65	14,59	1,02	17,63
5	7,46	2,47	16,56	1,65	19,72
6	8,96	3,36	18,48	2,36	21,73
7	10,45	4,31	20,35	3,14	23,69
8	11,94	5,30	22,18	3,97	25,59
9	13,43	6,33	23,97	4,86	27,45
10	14,93	7,40	25,74	5,78	29,28
11	16,42	8,49	27,48	6,74	31,07
12	17,91	9,61	29,20	7,74	32,82
13	19,40	10,76	30,89	8,76	34,56
14	20,90	11,92	32,57	9,82	36,26
15	22,39	13,11	34,22	10,89	37,95
16	23,88	14,31	35,86	11,99	39,61
17	25,37	15,53	37,49	13,11	41,25
18	26,87	16,76	39,10	14,25	42,87
19	28,36	18,01	40,69	15,41	44,47
20	29,85	19,28	42,27	16,59	46,06
21	31,34	20,56	43,84	17,79	47,63
22	32,84	21,85	45,40	19,00	49,18
23	34,33	23,15	46,94	20,23	50,72
24	35,82	24,47	48,47	21,47	52,24
25	37,31	25,80	49,99	22,73	53,74
26	38,81	27,14	51,50	24,01	55,24
27	40,30	28,49	53,00	25,30	56,72
28	41,79	29,85	54,48	26,60	58,18
29	43,28	31,22	55,96	27,92	59,63
30	44,78	32,60	57,42	29,25	61,07
31	46,27	34,00	58,88	30,59	62,49
32	47,76	35,40	60,33	31,95	63,90
33	49,25	36,82	61,76	33,32	65,30
34	50,75	38,24	63,18	34,70	66,68
35	52,24	39,67	64,60	36,10	68,05
36	53,73	41,12	66,00	37,51	69,41
37	55,22	42,58	67,40	38,93	70,75
38	56,72	44,04	68,78	40,37	72,08
39	58,21	45,52	70,15	41,82	73,40
40	59,70	47,00	71,51	43,28	74,70
41	61,19	48,50	72,86	44,76	75,99
42	62,69	50,01	74,20	46,26	77,27
43	64,18	51,53	75,53	47,76	78,53
44	65,67	53,06	76,85	49,28	79,77
45	67,16	54,60	78,15	50,82	81,00
46	68,66	56,16	79,44	52,37	82,21
47	70,15	57,73	80,72	53,94	83,41
48	71,64	59,31	81,99	55,53	84,59
49	73,13	60,90	83,24	57,13	85,75
50	74,63	62,51	84,47	58,75	86,89
51	76,12	64,14	85,69	60,39	88,01
52	77,61	65,78	86,89	62,05	89,11
53	79,10	67,43	88,08	63,74	90,18
54	80,60	69,11	89,24	65,44	91,24
55	82,09	70,80	90,39	67,18	92,26
56	83,58	72,52	91,51	68,93	93,26
57	85,07	74,26	92,60	70,72	94,22
58	86,57	76,03	93,67	72,55	95,14
59	88,06	77,82	94,70	74,41	96,03
60	89,55	79,65	95,69	76,31	96,86
61	91,04	81,52	96,64	78,27	97,64
62	92,54	83,44	97,53	80,28	98,35
63	94,03	85,41	98,35	82,37	98,98
64	95,52	87,47	99,07	84,56	99,49
65	97,01	89,63	99,64	86,89	99,84
66	98,51	91,96	99,96	89,43	99,99
67	100,00	94,64	100,00	92,40	100,00

$N=68$

x	$100\,p_x$	95% $100\,p_l$	95% $100\,p_r$	99% $100\,p_l$	99% $100\,p_r$
0	0,00	0,00	5,28	0,00	7,50
1	1,47	0,04	7,92	0,01	10,42
2	2,94	0,36	10,22	0,15	12,93
3	4,41	0,92	12,36	0,50	15,22
4	5,88	1,63	14,38	1,01	17,38
5	7,35	2,43	16,33	1,62	19,45
6	8,82	3,31	18,22	2,32	21,44
7	10,29	4,24	20,07	3,09	23,37
8	11,76	5,22	21,87	3,91	25,25
9	13,24	6,23	23,64	4,78	27,08
10	14,71	7,28	25,39	5,69	28,88
11	16,18	8,36	27,10	6,64	30,65
12	17,65	9,46	28,80	7,62	32,39
13	19,12	10,59	30,47	8,63	34,10
14	20,59	11,74	32,12	9,66	35,78
15	22,06	12,90	33,76	10,72	37,45
16	23,53	14,09	35,38	11,80	39,09
17	25,00	15,29	36,98	12,91	40,71
18	26,47	16,50	38,57	14,03	42,31
19	27,94	17,73	40,15	15,17	43,90
20	29,41	18,98	41,71	16,33	45,46
21	30,88	20,24	43,26	17,51	47,02
22	32,35	21,51	44,79	18,70	48,55
23	33,82	22,79	46,32	19,91	50,07
24	35,29	24,08	47,83	21,13	51,57
25	36,76	25,39	49,33	22,37	53,07
26	38,24	26,71	50,82	23,62	54,54
27	39,71	28,03	52,30	24,89	56,00
28	41,18	29,37	53,77	26,17	57,45
29	42,65	30,72	55,23	27,46	58,89
30	44,12	32,08	56,68	28,77	60,31
31	45,59	33,45	58,12	30,09	61,72
32	47,06	34,83	59,55	31,42	63,12
33	48,53	36,22	60,97	32,77	64,50
34	50,00	37,62	62,38	34,12	65,88
35	51,47	39,03	63,78	35,50	67,23
36	52,94	40,45	65,17	36,88	68,58
37	54,41	41,88	66,55	38,28	69,91
38	55,88	43,32	67,92	39,69	71,23
39	57,35	44,77	69,28	41,11	72,54
40	58,82	46,23	70,63	42,55	73,83
41	60,29	47,70	71,97	44,00	75,11
42	61,76	49,18	73,29	45,46	76,38
43	63,24	50,67	74,61	46,93	77,63
44	64,71	52,17	75,92	48,43	78,87
45	66,18	53,68	77,21	49,93	80,09
46	67,65	55,21	78,49	51,45	81,30
47	69,12	56,74	79,76	52,98	82,49
48	70,59	58,29	81,02	54,54	83,67
49	72,06	59,85	82,27	56,10	84,83
50	73,53	61,43	83,50	57,69	85,97
51	75,00	63,02	84,71	59,29	87,09
52	76,47	64,62	85,91	60,91	88,20
53	77,94	66,24	87,10	62,55	89,28
54	79,41	67,88	88,26	64,22	90,34
55	80,88	69,53	89,41	65,90	91,37
56	82,35	71,20	90,54	67,61	92,38
57	83,82	72,90	91,64	69,35	93,36
58	85,29	74,61	92,72	71,12	94,31
59	86,76	76,36	93,77	72,92	95,22
60	88,24	78,13	94,78	74,75	96,09
61	89,71	79,93	95,76	76,63	96,91
62	91,18	81,78	96,69	78,56	97,68
63	92,65	83,67	97,57	80,55	98,38
64	94,12	85,62	98,37	82,62	98,99
65	95,59	87,64	99,08	84,78	99,50
66	97,06	89,78	99,64	87,07	99,85
67	98,53	92,08	99,96	89,58	99,99
68	100,00	94,72	100,00	92,50	100,00

$N=69$

x	$100\,p_x$	95% $100\,p_l$	95% $100\,p_r$	99% $100\,p_l$	99% $100\,p_r$
0	0,00	0,00	5,21	0,00	7,39
1	1,45	0,04	7,81	0,01	10,28
2	2,90	0,35	10,08	0,15	12,75
3	4,35	0,91	12,18	0,50	15,02
4	5,80	1,60	14,18	0,99	17,15
5	7,25	2,39	16,11	1,60	19,18
6	8,70	3,26	17,97	2,29	21,15
7	10,14	4,18	19,79	3,04	23,05
8	11,59	5,14	21,57	3,85	24,91
9	13,04	6,14	23,32	4,71	26,72
10	14,49	7,17	25,04	5,61	28,50
11	15,94	8,24	26,74	6,54	30,25
12	17,39	9,32	28,41	7,50	31,96
13	18,84	10,43	30,06	8,50	33,65
14	20,29	11,56	31,69	9,51	35,32
15	21,74	12,71	33,31	10,56	36,96
16	23,19	13,87	34,91	11,62	38,58
17	24,64	15,06	36,49	12,71	40,19
18	26,09	16,25	38,06	13,81	41,77
19	27,54	17,46	39,62	14,93	43,34
20	28,99	18,69	41,16	16,07	44,88
21	30,43	19,92	42,69	17,23	46,42
22	31,88	21,17	44,21	18,40	47,94
23	33,33	22,44	45,71	19,59	49,44
24	34,78	23,71	47,21	20,80	50,93
25	36,23	25,00	48,69	22,01	52,40
26	37,68	26,29	50,16	23,24	53,86
27	39,13	27,60	51,63	24,49	55,31
28	40,58	28,91	53,08	25,75	56,75
29	42,03	30,24	54,52	27,02	58,17
30	43,48	31,58	55,96	28,30	59,58
31	44,93	32,92	57,38	29,60	60,97
32	46,38	34,28	58,80	30,91	62,36
33	47,83	35,65	60,20	32,23	63,73
34	49,28	37,02	61,59	33,57	65,09
35	50,72	38,41	62,98	34,91	66,43
36	52,17	39,80	64,35	36,27	67,77
37	53,62	41,20	65,72	37,64	69,09
38	55,07	42,62	67,08	39,03	70,40
39	56,52	44,04	68,42	40,42	71,70
40	57,97	45,48	69,76	41,83	72,98
41	59,42	46,92	71,09	43,25	74,25
42	60,87	48,37	72,40	44,69	75,51
43	62,32	49,84	73,71	46,14	76,76
44	63,77	51,31	75,00	47,60	77,99
45	65,22	52,79	76,29	49,07	79,20
46	66,67	54,29	77,56	50,56	80,41
47	68,12	55,79	78,83	52,06	81,60
48	69,57	57,31	80,08	53,58	82,77
49	71,01	58,84	81,31	55,12	83,93
50	72,46	60,38	82,54	56,66	85,07
51	73,91	61,94	83,75	58,23	86,19
52	75,36	63,51	84,94	59,81	87,29
53	76,81	65,09	86,13	61,42	88,38
54	78,26	66,69	87,29	63,04	89,44
55	79,71	68,31	88,44	64,68	90,49
56	81,16	69,94	89,57	66,35	91,50
57	82,61	71,59	90,68	68,04	92,50
58	84,06	73,26	91,76	69,75	93,46
59	85,51	74,96	92,83	71,50	94,39
60	86,96	76,68	93,86	73,28	95,29
61	88,41	78,43	94,86	75,09	96,15
62	89,86	80,21	95,82	76,95	96,96
63	91,30	82,03	96,74	78,85	97,71
64	92,75	83,89	97,61	80,82	98,40
65	94,20	85,82	98,40	82,85	99,01
66	95,65	87,82	99,09	84,98	99,50
67	97,10	89,92	99,65	87,25	99,85
68	98,55	92,19	99,96	89,72	99,99
69	100,00	94,79	100,00	92,61	100,00

$N=70$

x	$100\,p_x$	95% $100\,p_l$	95% $100\,p_r$	99% $100\,p_l$	99% $100\,p_r$
0	0,00	0,00	5,13	0,00	7,29
1	1,43	0,04	7,70	0,01	10,14
2	2,86	0,35	9,94	0,15	12,58
3	4,29	0,89	12,02	0,49	14,81
4	5,71	1,58	13,99	0,98	16,92
5	7,14	2,36	15,89	1,57	18,93
6	8,57	3,21	17,73	2,25	20,87
7	10,00	4,12	19,52	3,00	22,75
8	11,43	5,07	21,28	3,80	24,58
9	12,86	6,05	23,01	4,64	26,37
10	14,29	7,07	24,71	5,52	28,13
11	15,71	8,11	26,38	6,44	29,85
12	17,14	9,18	28,03	7,39	31,55
13	18,57	10,28	29,66	8,37	33,22
14	20,00	11,39	31,27	9,37	34,86
15	21,43	12,52	32,87	10,40	36,49
16	22,86	13,67	34,45	11,45	38,09
17	24,29	14,83	36,01	12,51	39,67
18	25,71	16,01	37,56	13,60	41,24
19	27,14	17,20	39,10	14,71	42,79
20	28,57	18,40	40,62	15,83	44,32
21	30,00	19,62	42,13	16,97	45,84
22	31,43	20,85	43,63	18,12	47,34
23	32,86	22,09	45,12	19,29	48,82
24	34,29	23,35	46,60	20,47	50,30
25	35,71	24,61	48,07	21,67	51,76
26	37,14	25,89	49,52	22,88	53,20
27	38,57	27,17	50,97	24,11	54,63
28	40,00	28,47	52,41	25,34	56,05
29	41,43	29,77	53,83	26,59	57,46
30	42,86	31,09	55,25	27,85	58,86
31	44,29	32,41	56,66	29,13	60,24
32	45,71	33,74	58,06	30,42	61,61
33	47,14	35,09	59,45	31,72	62,97
34	48,57	36,44	60,83	33,03	64,32
35	50,00	37,80	62,20	34,35	65,65
36	51,43	39,17	63,56	35,68	66,97
37	52,86	40,55	64,91	37,03	68,28
38	54,29	41,94	66,26	38,39	69,58
39	55,71	43,34	67,59	39,76	70,87
40	57,14	44,75	68,91	41,14	72,15
41	58,57	46,17	70,23	42,54	73,41
42	60,00	47,59	71,53	43,95	74,66
43	61,43	49,03	72,83	45,37	75,89
44	62,86	50,48	74,11	46,80	77,12
45	64,29	51,93	75,39	48,24	78,33
46	65,71	53,40	76,65	49,70	79,53
47	67,14	54,88	77,91	51,18	80,71
48	68,57	56,37	79,15	52,66	81,88
49	70,00	57,87	80,38	54,16	83,03
50	71,43	59,38	81,60	55,68	84,17
51	72,86	60,90	82,80	57,21	85,29
52	74,29	62,44	83,99	58,76	86,40
53	75,71	63,99	85,17	60,33	87,49
54	77,14	65,55	86,33	61,91	88,55
55	78,57	67,13	87,48	63,51	89,60
56	80,00	68,73	88,61	65,14	90,63
57	81,43	70,34	89,72	66,78	91,63
58	82,86	71,97	90,82	68,45	92,61
59	84,29	73,62	91,89	70,15	93,56
60	85,71	75,29	92,93	71,87	94,48
61	87,14	76,99	93,95	73,63	95,36
62	88,57	78,72	94,93	75,42	96,20
63	90,00	80,48	95,88	77,25	97,00
64	91,43	82,27	96,79	79,13	97,75
65	92,86	84,11	97,64	81,07	98,43
66	94,29	86,01	98,42	83,08	99,02
67	95,71	87,98	99,11	85,19	99,51
68	97,14	90,06	99,65	87,42	99,85
69	98,57	92,30	99,96	89,86	99,99
70	100,00	94,87	100,00	92,71	100,00

$N=71$

x	$100\,p_x$	95% $100\,p_l$	95% $100\,p_r$	99% $100\,p_l$	99% $100\,p_r$
0	0,00	0,00	5,06	0,00	7,19
1	1,41	0,04	7,60	0,01	10,00
2	2,82	0,34	9,81	0,15	12,41
3	4,23	0,88	11,86	0,48	14,62
4	5,63	1,56	13,80	0,96	16,69
5	7,04	2,33	15,67	1,55	18,68
6	8,45	3,17	17,49	2,22	20,59
7	9,86	4,06	19,26	2,95	22,45
8	11,27	4,99	21,00	3,74	24,26
9	12,68	5,96	22,70	4,57	26,03
10	14,08	6,97	24,38	5,44	27,77
11	15,49	8,00	26,03	6,35	29,47
12	16,90	9,05	27,66	7,28	31,14

All values conform to the international convention (i.e. 0,1 instead of 0.1).

N: number of trials; x: number of successes, etc.; $100\,p_x = 100\,x/N$

$N = 71$ (continued)

x	$100\,p_x$	95% $100\,p_l$	95% $100\,p_r$	99% $100\,p_l$	99% $100\,p_r$
13	18,31	10,13	29,27	8,24	32,79
14	19,72	11,22	30,87	9,23	34,42
15	21,13	12,33	32,44	10,24	36,02
16	22,54	13,46	34,00	11,27	37,61
17	23,94	14,61	35,54	12,33	39,17
18	25,35	15,77	37,08	13,40	40,72
19	26,76	16,94	38,59	14,48	42,25
20	28,17	18,13	40,10	15,59	43,77
21	29,58	19,33	41,59	16,71	45,27
22	30,99	20,54	43,08	17,84	46,75
23	32,39	21,76	44,55	18,99	48,22
24	33,80	23,00	46,01	20,16	49,68
25	35,21	24,24	47,46	21,34	51,12
26	36,62	25,50	48,90	22,53	52,55
27	38,03	26,76	50,33	23,73	53,97
28	39,44	28,03	51,75	24,95	55,38
29	40,85	29,32	53,16	26,18	56,77
30	42,25	30,61	54,56	27,42	58,15
31	43,66	31,91	55,95	28,67	59,52
32	45,07	33,23	57,34	29,94	60,88
33	46,48	34,55	58,71	31,22	62,23
34	47,89	35,88	60,08	32,50	63,56
35	49,30	37,22	61,44	33,80	64,88
36	50,70	38,56	62,78	35,12	66,20
37	52,11	39,92	64,12	36,44	67,50
38	53,52	41,29	65,45	37,77	68,78
39	54,93	42,66	66,77	39,12	70,06
40	56,34	44,05	68,09	40,48	71,33
41	57,75	45,44	69,39	41,85	72,58
42	59,15	46,84	70,68	43,23	73,82
43	60,56	48,25	71,97	44,62	75,05
44	61,97	49,67	73,24	46,03	76,27
45	63,38	51,10	74,50	47,45	77,47
46	64,79	52,54	75,76	48,88	78,66
47	66,20	53,99	77,00	50,32	79,84
48	67,61	55,45	78,24	51,78	81,01
49	69,01	56,92	79,46	53,25	82,16
50	70,42	58,41	80,67	54,73	83,29
51	71,83	59,90	81,87	56,23	84,41
52	73,24	61,41	83,06	57,75	85,52
53	74,65	62,92	84,23	59,28	86,60
54	76,06	64,46	85,39	60,83	87,67
55	77,46	66,00	86,54	62,39	88,73
56	78,87	67,56	87,67	63,98	89,76
57	80,28	69,13	88,78	65,58	90,77
58	81,69	70,73	89,87	67,21	91,76
59	83,10	72,34	90,95	68,86	92,72
60	84,51	73,97	92,00	70,53	93,65
61	85,92	75,62	93,03	72,23	94,56
62	87,32	77,30	94,04	73,97	95,43
63	88,73	79,00	95,01	75,74	96,26
64	90,14	80,74	95,94	77,55	97,05
65	91,55	82,51	96,83	79,41	97,78
66	92,96	84,33	97,67	81,32	98,45
67	94,37	86,20	98,44	83,31	99,04
68	95,77	88,14	99,12	85,38	99,52
69	97,18	90,19	99,66	87,59	99,85
70	98,59	92,40	99,96	90,00	99,99
71	100,00	94,94	100,00	92,81	100,00

$N = 72$

x	$100\,p_x$	95% $100\,p_l$	95% $100\,p_r$	99% $100\,p_l$	99% $100\,p_r$
0	0,00	0,00	4,99	0,00	7,09
1	1,39	0,04	7,50	0,01	9,87
2	2,78	0,34	9,68	0,14	12,25
3	4,17	0,87	11,70	0,48	14,42
4	5,56	1,53	13,62	0,95	16,48
5	6,94	2,29	15,47	1,53	18,44
6	8,33	3,12	17,26	2,19	20,33
7	9,72	4,00	19,01	2,91	22,16
8	11,11	4,92	20,72	3,69	23,95
9	12,50	5,88	22,41	4,51	25,70
10	13,89	6,87	24,06	5,36	27,41
11	15,28	7,88	25,69	6,26	29,09
12	16,67	8,92	27,30	7,18	30,75
13	18,06	9,98	28,89	8,12	32,38
14	19,44	11,06	30,47	9,10	33,99
15	20,83	12,16	32,02	10,09	35,57
16	22,22	13,27	33,56	11,11	37,14
17	23,61	14,40	35,09	12,14	38,69
18	25,00	15,54	36,60	13,20	40,22
19	26,39	16,70	38,10	14,27	41,73
20	27,78	17,86	39,59	15,36	43,23
21	29,17	19,05	41,07	16,46	44,71
22	30,56	20,24	42,53	17,58	46,18
23	31,94	21,44	43,99	18,71	47,64
24	33,33	22,66	45,43	19,86	49,08
25	34,72	23,88	46,86	21,01	50,51
26	36,11	25,12	48,29	22,19	51,92
27	37,50	26,36	49,70	23,37	53,33
28	38,89	27,62	51,11	24,57	54,72
29	40,28	28,88	52,50	25,78	56,10
30	41,67	30,15	53,89	27,00	57,47
31	43,06	31,43	55,27	28,23	58,82
32	44,44	32,72	56,64	29,48	60,17
33	45,83	34,02	58,00	30,73	61,50
34	47,22	35,33	59,35	32,00	62,82
35	48,61	36,65	60,69	33,28	64,13
36	50,00	37,98	62,02	34,57	65,43

$N = 72$ (continued)

x	$100\,p_x$	95% $100\,p_l$	95% $100\,p_r$	99% $100\,p_l$	99% $100\,p_r$
37	51,39	39,31	63,35	35,87	66,72
38	52,78	40,65	64,67	37,18	68,00
39	54,17	42,00	65,98	38,50	69,27
40	55,56	43,36	67,28	39,83	70,52
41	56,94	44,73	68,57	41,18	71,77
42	58,33	46,11	69,85	42,53	73,00
43	59,72	47,50	71,12	43,90	74,22
44	61,11	48,89	72,38	45,28	75,43
45	62,50	50,30	73,64	46,67	76,63
46	63,89	51,71	74,88	48,08	77,81
47	65,28	53,14	76,12	49,49	78,99
48	66,67	54,57	77,34	50,92	80,14
49	68,06	56,01	78,56	52,36	81,29
50	69,44	57,47	79,76	53,82	82,42
51	70,83	58,93	80,95	55,29	83,54
52	72,22	60,41	82,14	56,77	84,64
53	73,61	61,90	83,30	58,27	85,73
54	75,00	63,40	84,46	59,78	86,80
55	76,39	64,91	85,60	61,31	87,86
56	77,78	66,44	86,73	62,86	88,89
57	79,17	67,98	87,84	64,43	89,91
58	80,56	69,53	88,94	66,01	90,90
59	81,94	71,11	90,02	67,62	91,88
60	83,33	72,70	91,08	69,25	92,82
61	84,72	74,31	92,12	70,91	93,74
62	86,11	75,94	93,13	72,59	94,64
63	87,50	77,59	94,12	74,30	95,49
64	88,89	79,28	95,08	76,05	96,31
65	90,28	80,99	96,00	77,84	97,09
66	91,67	82,74	96,88	79,67	97,81
67	93,06	84,53	97,71	81,56	98,47
68	94,44	86,38	98,47	83,52	99,05
69	95,83	88,30	99,13	85,58	99,52
70	97,22	90,32	99,66	87,75	99,86
71	98,61	92,50	99,96	90,13	99,99
72	100,00	95,01	100,00	92,91	100,00

$N = 73$

x	$100\,p_x$	95% $100\,p_l$	95% $100\,p_r$	99% $100\,p_l$	99% $100\,p_r$
0	0,00	0,00	4,93	0,00	7,00
1	1,37	0,03	7,40	0,01	9,74
2	2,74	0,33	9,55	0,14	12,09
3	4,11	0,86	11,54	0,47	14,24
4	5,48	1,51	13,44	0,94	16,26
5	6,85	2,26	15,26	1,51	18,20
6	8,22	3,08	17,04	2,16	20,07
7	9,59	3,94	18,76	2,87	21,88
8	10,96	4,85	20,46	3,63	23,65
9	12,33	5,80	22,12	4,44	25,37
10	13,70	6,77	23,75	5,29	27,07
11	15,07	7,77	25,36	6,17	28,73
12	16,44	8,79	26,95	7,07	30,37
13	17,81	9,84	28,53	8,01	31,98
14	19,18	10,90	30,08	8,97	33,57
15	20,55	11,98	31,62	9,95	35,13
16	21,92	13,08	33,14	10,95	36,68
17	23,29	14,19	34,65	11,97	38,21
18	24,66	15,32	36,14	13,01	39,73
19	26,03	16,45	37,62	14,06	41,22
20	27,40	17,61	39,09	15,13	42,71
21	28,77	18,77	40,55	16,22	44,17
22	30,14	19,94	42,00	17,32	45,63
23	31,51	21,13	43,44	18,43	47,06
24	32,88	22,33	44,87	19,56	48,49
25	34,25	23,53	46,28	20,70	49,90
26	35,62	24,75	47,69	21,86	51,31
27	36,99	25,97	49,09	23,02	52,70
28	38,36	27,21	50,48	24,20	54,07
29	39,73	28,45	51,86	25,39	55,44
30	41,10	29,71	53,23	26,59	56,79
31	42,47	30,97	54,59	27,80	58,14
32	43,84	32,24	55,95	29,03	59,47
33	45,21	33,52	57,30	30,26	60,79
34	46,58	34,80	58,63	31,51	62,10
35	47,95	36,10	59,96	32,77	63,40
36	49,32	37,40	61,28	34,03	64,69
37	50,68	38,72	62,60	35,31	65,97
38	52,05	40,04	63,90	36,60	67,23
39	53,42	41,37	65,20	37,90	68,49
40	54,79	42,70	66,48	39,21	69,74
41	56,16	44,05	67,76	40,53	70,97
42	57,53	45,41	69,03	41,86	72,20
43	58,90	46,77	70,29	43,21	73,41
44	60,27	48,14	71,55	44,56	74,61
45	61,64	49,52	72,79	45,93	75,80
46	63,01	50,91	74,03	47,30	76,98
47	64,38	52,31	75,25	48,69	78,14
48	65,75	53,72	76,47	50,10	79,30
49	67,12	55,13	77,67	51,51	80,44
50	68,49	56,56	78,87	52,94	81,57
51	69,86	58,00	80,06	54,37	82,68
52	71,23	59,45	81,23	55,83	83,78
53	72,60	60,91	82,39	57,29	84,87
54	73,97	62,38	83,55	58,78	85,94
55	75,34	63,86	84,68	60,27	86,99
56	76,71	65,35	85,81	61,79	88,03
57	78,08	66,86	86,92	63,32	89,05
58	79,45	68,38	88,02	64,87	90,05
59	80,82	69,92	89,10	66,43	91,03

$N = 73$ (continued)

x	$100\,p_x$	95% $100\,p_l$	95% $100\,p_r$	99% $100\,p_l$	99% $100\,p_r$
60	82,19	71,47	90,16	68,02	91,99
61	83,56	73,05	91,21	69,63	92,93
62	84,93	74,64	92,23	71,27	93,83
63	86,30	76,25	93,23	72,93	94,71
64	87,67	77,88	94,20	74,63	95,56
65	89,04	79,54	95,15	76,35	96,37
66	90,41	81,24	96,06	78,12	97,13
67	91,78	82,96	96,92	79,93	97,84
68	93,15	84,74	97,74	81,80	98,49
69	94,52	86,56	98,49	83,74	99,06
70	95,89	88,46	99,14	85,76	99,53
71	97,26	90,45	99,67	87,91	99,86
72	98,63	92,60	99,97	90,26	99,99
73	100,00	95,07	100,00	93,00	100,00

$N = 74$

x	$100\,p_x$	95% $100\,p_l$	95% $100\,p_r$	99% $100\,p_l$	99% $100\,p_r$
0	0,00	0,00	4,86	0,00	6,91
1	1,35	0,03	7,30	0,01	9,62
2	2,70	0,33	9,42	0,14	11,93
3	4,05	0,84	11,39	0,46	14,06
4	5,41	1,49	13,27	0,92	16,06
5	6,76	2,23	15,07	1,49	17,97
6	8,11	3,03	16,82	2,13	19,81
7	9,46	3,89	18,52	2,83	21,60
8	10,81	4,78	20,19	3,58	23,35
9	12,16	5,71	21,84	4,38	25,06
10	13,51	6,68	23,45	5,21	26,73
11	14,86	7,66	25,04	6,08	28,37
12	16,22	8,67	26,61	6,97	29,99
13	17,57	9,70	28,17	7,89	31,58
14	18,92	10,75	29,70	8,84	33,15
15	20,27	11,81	31,22	9,80	34,70
16	21,62	12,89	32,72	10,79	36,24
17	22,97	13,99	34,21	11,80	37,75
18	24,32	15,10	35,69	12,82	39,25
19	25,68	16,22	37,16	13,86	40,73
20	27,03	17,35	38,61	14,91	42,19
21	28,38	18,50	40,05	15,98	43,64
22	29,73	19,66	41,48	17,07	45,08
23	31,08	20,83	42,90	18,16	46,51
24	32,43	22,00	44,32	19,27	47,92
25	33,78	23,19	45,72	20,40	49,32
26	35,14	24,39	47,11	21,53	50,70
27	36,49	25,60	48,49	22,68	52,08
28	37,84	26,81	49,87	23,84	53,44
29	39,19	28,04	51,23	25,01	54,79
30	40,54	29,27	52,59	26,20	56,14
31	41,89	30,51	53,94	27,39	57,47
32	43,24	31,77	55,28	28,59	58,79
33	44,59	33,02	56,61	29,81	60,10
34	45,95	34,29	57,93	31,03	61,39
35	47,30	35,57	59,25	32,27	62,68
36	48,65	36,85	60,56	33,52	63,96
37	50,00	38,14	61,86	34,77	65,23
38	51,35	39,44	63,15	36,04	66,48
39	52,70	40,75	64,43	37,32	67,73
40	54,05	42,07	65,71	38,61	68,97
41	55,41	43,39	66,98	39,90	70,19
42	56,76	44,72	68,23	41,21	71,41
43	58,11	46,06	69,49	42,53	72,61
44	59,46	47,41	70,73	43,86	73,80
45	60,81	48,77	71,96	45,21	74,99
46	62,16	50,13	73,19	46,56	76,16
47	63,51	51,51	74,40	47,92	77,32
48	64,86	52,89	75,61	49,30	78,47
49	66,22	54,28	76,81	50,68	79,60
50	67,57	55,68	78,00	52,08	80,73
51	68,92	57,10	79,17	53,49	81,84
52	70,27	58,52	80,34	54,92	82,93
53	71,62	59,95	81,50	56,36	84,02
54	72,97	61,39	82,65	57,81	85,09
55	74,32	62,84	83,78	59,27	86,14
56	75,68	64,31	84,90	60,75	87,18
57	77,03	65,79	86,01	62,25	88,20
58	78,38	67,28	87,11	63,76	89,21
59	79,73	68,78	88,19	65,30	90,20
60	81,08	70,30	89,25	66,85	91,16
61	82,43	71,83	90,30	68,42	92,11
62	83,78	73,39	91,33	70,01	93,03
63	85,14	74,96	92,34	71,63	93,92
64	86,49	76,55	93,32	73,27	94,79
65	87,84	78,16	94,29	74,94	95,62
66	89,19	79,81	95,22	76,65	96,42
67	90,54	81,48	96,11	78,40	97,17
68	91,89	83,18	96,97	80,19	97,87
69	93,24	84,93	97,77	82,03	98,51
70	94,59	86,73	98,51	83,94	99,08
71	95,95	88,61	99,16	85,94	99,54
72	97,30	90,58	99,67	88,07	99,86
73	98,65	92,70	99,97	90,38	99,99
74	100,00	95,14	100,00	93,09	100,00

$N = 75$

x	$100\,p_x$	95% $100\,p_l$	95% $100\,p_r$	99% $100\,p_l$	99% $100\,p_r$
0	0,00	0,00	4,80	0,00	6,82
1	1,33	0,03	7,21	0,01	9,49
2	2,67	0,32	9,30	0,14	11,78
3	4,00	0,83	11,25	0,46	13,88
4	5,33	1,47	13,10	0,91	15,85

$N = 75$ (continued)

x	$100\,p_x$	95% $100\,p_l$	95% $100\,p_r$	99% $100\,p_l$	99% $100\,p_r$
5	6,67	2,20	14,88	1,47	17,74
6	8,00	2,99	16,60	2,10	19,57
7	9,33	3,84	18,29	2,79	21,34
8	10,67	4,72	19,94	3,53	23,06
9	12,00	5,64	21,56	4,32	24,75
10	13,33	6,58	23,16	5,14	26,40
11	14,67	7,56	24,73	5,99	28,03
12	16,00	8,55	26,28	6,88	29,63
13	17,33	9,57	27,81	7,78	31,20
14	18,67	10,60	29,33	8,71	32,75
15	20,00	11,65	30,83	9,67	34,29
16	21,33	12,71	32,32	10,64	35,80
17	22,67	13,79	33,79	11,63	37,30
18	24,00	14,89	35,25	12,64	38,78
19	25,33	15,99	36,70	13,66	40,24
20	26,67	17,11	38,14	14,70	41,69
21	28,00	18,24	39,56	15,75	43,13
22	29,33	19,38	40,98	16,82	44,55
23	30,67	20,53	42,38	17,90	45,96
24	32,00	21,69	43,78	19,00	47,36
25	33,33	22,86	45,17	20,10	48,74
26	34,67	24,04	46,54	21,22	50,11
27	36,00	25,23	47,91	22,35	51,48
28	37,33	26,43	49,27	23,49	52,83
29	38,67	27,64	50,62	24,65	54,16
30	40,00	28,85	51,96	25,81	55,49
31	41,33	30,08	53,30	26,99	56,81
32	42,67	31,31	54,62	28,17	58,12
33	44,00	32,55	55,94	29,37	59,42
34	45,33	33,79	57,25	30,57	60,70
35	46,67	35,05	58,55	31,79	61,98
36	48,00	36,31	59,85	33,02	63,25
37	49,33	37,58	61,14	34,25	64,50
38	50,67	38,86	62,42	35,50	65,75
39	52,00	40,15	63,69	36,75	66,98
40	53,33	41,45	64,95	38,02	68,21
41	54,67	42,75	66,21	39,30	69,43
42	56,00	44,06	67,45	40,58	70,63
43	57,33	45,38	68,69	41,88	71,83
44	58,67	46,70	69,92	43,19	73,01
45	60,00	48,04	71,15	44,51	74,19
46	61,33	49,38	72,36	45,84	75,35
47	62,67	50,73	73,57	47,17	76,51
48	64,00	52,09	74,77	48,52	77,65
49	65,33	53,46	75,96	49,89	78,78
50	66,67	54,83	77,14	51,26	79,90
51	68,00	56,22	78,31	52,64	81,00
52	69,33	57,62	79,47	54,04	82,10
53	70,67	59,02	80,62	55,45	83,18
54	72,00	60,44	81,76	56,87	84,25
55	73,33	61,86	82,89	58,31	85,30
56	74,67	63,30	84,01	59,76	86,34
57	76,00	64,75	85,11	61,22	87,36
58	77,33	66,21	86,21	62,70	88,37
59	78,67	67,68	87,29	64,20	89,36
60	80,00	69,17	88,35	65,71	90,33
61	81,33	70,67	89,40	67,25	91,29
62	82,67	72,19	90,43	68,80	92,22
63	84,00	73,72	91,45	70,37	93,12
64	85,33	75,27	92,44	71,97	94,01
65	86,67	76,84	93,42	73,60	94,86
66	88,00	78,44	94,36	75,25	95,68
67	89,33	80,06	95,28	76,94	96,47
68	90,67	81,71	96,16	78,66	97,21
69	92,00	83,40	97,01	80,43	97,90
70	93,33	85,12	97,80	82,26	98,53
71	94,67	86,90	98,53	84,15	99,09
72	96,00	88,75	99,17	86,12	99,54
73	97,33	90,70	99,68	88,22	99,86
74	98,67	92,79	99,97	90,51	99,99
75	100,00	95,20	100,00	93,18	100,00

$N = 76$

x	$100\,p_x$	95% $100\,p_l$	95% $100\,p_r$	99% $100\,p_l$	99% $100\,p_r$
0	0,00	0,00	4,74	0,00	6,73
1	1,32	0,03	7,11	0,01	9,37
2	2,63	0,32	9,18	0;14	11,63
3	3,95	0,82	11,11	0,45	13,71
4	5,26	1,45	12,93	0,90	15,66
5	6,58	2,17	14,69	1,45	17,52
6	7,89	2,95	16,40	2,07	19,33
7	9,21	3,78	18,06	2,76	21,07
8	10,53	4,66	19,69	3,49	22,78
9	11,84	5,56	21,29	4,26	24,45
10	13,16	6,49	22,87	5,07	26,08
11	14,47	7,45	24,42	5,91	27,69
12	15,79	8,43	25,96	6,78	29,27
13	17,11	9,43	27,47	7,68	30,83
14	18,42	10,45	28,97	8,59	32,36
15	19,74	11,49	30,46	9,53	33,88
16	21,05	12,54	31,92	10,49	35,37
17	22,37	13,60	33,38	11,47	36,85
18	23,68	14,68	34,82	12,46	38,32
19	25,00	15,77	36,26	13,47	39,77
20	26,32	16,87	37,68	14,49	41,20
21	27,63	17,99	39,09	15,53	42,62
22	28,95	19,11	40,49	16,58	44,03
23	30,26	20,25	41,87	17,65	45,43
24	31,58	21,39	43,25	18,73	46,81

All values conform to the international convention (i.e. 0,1 instead of 0.1).

'Exact' Confidence Limits* for p $N=76–81$

N: number of trials; x: number of successes, etc.; $100\,p_x = 100\,x/N$

$N=76$ (continued)

x	$100\,p_x$	95% $100\,p_l$	95% $100\,p_r$	99% $100\,p_l$	99% $100\,p_r$
25	32,89	22,54–	44,63	19,82–	48,18
26	34,21	23,71–	45,99	20,92–	49,54
27	35,53	24,88–	47,34	22,03–	50,89
28	36,84	26,06–	48,69	23,16–	52,22
29	38,16	27,25–	50,02	24,29–	53,55
30	39,47	28,44–	51,35	25,44–	54,86
31	40,79	29,65–	52,67	26,59–	56,17
32	42,11	30,86–	53,98	27,76–	57,46
33	43,42	32,08–	55,29	28,94–	58,75
34	44,74	33,31–	56,59	30,13–	60,02
35	46,05	34,55–	57,87	31,32–	61,29
36	47,37	35,79–	59,16	32,53–	62,55
37	48,68	37,04–	60,43	33,75–	63,79
38	50,00	38,30–	61,70	34,97–	65,03
39	51,32	39,57–	62,96	36,21–	66,25
40	52,63	40,84–	64,21	37,45–	67,47
41	53,95	42,13–	65,45	38,71–	68,68
42	55,26	43,41–	66,69	39,98–	69,87
43	56,58	44,71–	67,92	41,25–	71,06
44	57,89	46,02–	69,14	42,54–	72,24
45	59,21	47,33–	70,35	43,83–	73,41
46	60,53	48,65–	71,56	45,14–	74,56
47	61,84	49,98–	72,75	46,45–	75,71
48	63,16	51,31–	73,94	47,78–	76,84
49	64,47	52,66–	75,12	49,11–	77,97
50	65,79	54,01–	76,29	50,46–	79,08
51	67,11	55,37–	77,46	51,82–	80,18
52	68,42	56,75–	78,61	53,19–	81,27
53	69,74	58,13–	79,75	54,57–	82,35
54	71,05	59,51–	80,89	55,97–	83,42
55	72,37	60,91–	82,01	57,38–	84,47
56	73,68	62,32–	83,13	58,80–	85,51
57	75,00	63,74–	84,23	60,23–	86,53
58	76,32	65,18–	85,32	61,68–	87,54
59	77,63	66,62–	86,40	63,15–	88,53
60	78,95	68,08–	87,46	64,63–	89,51
61	80,26	69,54–	88,51	66,12–	90,47
62	81,58	71,03–	89,55	67,64–	91,41
63	82,89	72,53–	90,57	69,17–	92,32
64	84,21	74,04–	91,57	70,73–	93,22
65	85,53	75,58–	92,55	72,31–	94,09
66	86,84	77,13–	93,51	73,92–	94,93
67	88,16	78,71–	94,44	75,55–	95,74
68	89,47	80,31–	95,34	77,22–	96,51
69	90,79	81,94–	96,22	78,93–	97,24
70	92,11	83,60–	97,05	80,67–	97,93
71	93,42	85,31–	97,83	82,48–	98,55
72	94,74	87,07–	98,55	84,34–	99,10
73	96,05	88,89–	99,18	86,29–	99,55
74	97,37	90,82–	99,68	88,37–	99,86
75	98,68	92,89–	99,97	90,63–	99,99
76	100,00	95,26–	100,00	93,27–	100,00

$N=77$

x	$100\,p_x$	95% $100\,p_l$	95% $100\,p_r$	99% $100\,p_l$	99% $100\,p_r$
0	0,00	0,00–	4,68	0,00–	6,65
1	1,30	0,03–	7,02	0,01–	9,26
2	2,60	0,32–	9,07	0,14–	11,49
3	3,90	0,81–	10,97	0,44–	13,54
4	5,19	1,43–	12,77	0,89–	15,47
5	6,49	2,14–	14,51	1,43–	17,31
6	7,79	2,91–	16,19	2,04–	19,09
7	9,09	3,73–	17,84	2,72–	20,82
8	10,39	4,59–	19,45	3,44–	22,50
9	11,69	5,49–	21,03	4,20–	24,15
10	12,99	6,41–	22,59	5,00–	25,77
11	14,29	7,35–	24,13	5,83–	27,36
12	15,58	8,32–	25,64	6,69–	28,92
13	16,88	9,31–	27,14	7,57–	30,46
14	18,18	10,31–	28,62	8,48–	31,98
15	19,48	11,33–	30,09	9,40–	33,48
16	20,78	12,37–	31,54	10,35–	34,96
17	22,08	13,42–	32,98	11,31–	36,42
18	23,38	14,48–	34,41	12,29–	37,87
19	24,68	15,56–	35,82	13,28–	39,31
20	25,97	16,64–	37,23	14,29–	40,72
21	27,27	17,74–	38,62	15,32–	42,13
22	28,57	18,85–	40,00	16,35–	43,52
23	29,87	19,97–	41,38	17,40–	44,90
24	31,17	21,09–	42,74	18,46–	46,27
25	32,47	22,23–	44,10	19,54–	47,63
26	33,77	23,38–	45,45	20,62–	48,97
27	35,06	24,53–	46,78	21,72–	50,31
28	36,36	25,70–	48,12	22,83–	51,63
29	37,66	26,87–	49,44	23,95–	52,95
30	38,96	28,05–	50,75	25,08–	54,25
31	40,26	29,23–	52,06	26,21–	55,54
32	41,56	30,43–	53,36	27,36–	56,82
33	42,86	31,63–	54,65	28,52–	58,10
34	44,16	32,84–	55,93	29,69–	59,36
35	45,45	34,06–	57,21	30,87–	60,62
36	46,75	35,29–	58,48	32,06–	61,86
37	48,05	36,52–	59,74	33,26–	63,10
38	49,35	37,76–	61,00	34,46–	64,32
39	50,65	39,00–	62,24	35,68–	65,54
40	51,95	40,26–	63,48	36,90–	66,74
41	53,25	41,52–	64,71	38,14–	67,94
42	54,55	42,79–	65,94	39,38–	69,13
43	55,84	44,07–	67,16	40,64–	70,31

$N=77$ (continued)

x	$100\,p_x$	95% $100\,p_l$	95% $100\,p_r$	99% $100\,p_l$	99% $100\,p_r$
44	57,14	45,35–	68,37	41,90–	71,48
45	58,44	46,64–	69,57	43,18–	72,64
46	59,74	47,94–	70,77	44,46–	73,79
47	61,04	49,25–	71,95	45,75–	74,92
48	62,34	50,56–	73,13	47,05–	76,05
49	63,64	51,88–	74,30	48,37–	77,17
50	64,94	53,22–	75,47	49,69–	78,28
51	66,23	54,55–	76,62	51,03–	79,38
52	67,53	55,90–	77,77	52,37–	80,46
53	68,83	57,26–	78,91	53,73–	81,54
54	70,13	58,62–	80,03	55,10–	82,60
55	71,43	60,00–	81,15	56,48–	83,65
56	72,73	61,38–	82,26	57,87–	84,68
57	74,03	62,77–	83,36	59,28–	85,71
58	75,32	64,18–	84,44	60,69–	86,72
59	76,62	65,59–	85,52	62,13–	87,71
60	77,92	67,02–	86,58	63,58–	88,69
61	79,22	68,46–	87,63	65,04–	89,65
62	80,52	69,91–	88,67	66,52–	90,60
63	81,82	71,38–	89,69	68,02–	91,52
64	83,12	72,86–	90,69	69,54–	92,43
65	84,42	74,36–	91,68	71,08–	93,31
66	85,71	75,87–	92,65	72,64–	94,17
67	87,01	77,41–	93,59	74,23–	95,00
68	88,31	78,97–	94,51	75,85–	95,80
69	89,61	80,55–	95,41	77,50–	96,56
70	90,91	82,16–	96,27	79,18–	97,28
71	92,21	83,81–	97,09	80,91–	97,96
72	93,51	85,49–	97,86	82,69–	98,57
73	94,81	87,23–	98,57	84,53–	99,11
74	96,10	89,03–	99,19	86,46–	99,56
75	97,40	90,93–	99,68	88,51–	99,86
76	98,70	92,98–	99,97	90,74–	99,99
77	100,00	95,32–	100,00	93,35–	100,00

$N=78$

x	$100\,p_x$	95% $100\,p_l$	95% $100\,p_r$	99% $100\,p_l$	99% $100\,p_r$
0	0,00	0,00–	4,62	0,00–	6,57
1	1,28	0,03–	6,94	0,01–	9,14
2	2,56	0,31–	8,96	0,13–	11,35
3	3,85	0,80–	10,83	0,44–	13,37
4	5,13	1,41–	12,61	0,88–	15,28
5	6,41	2,11–	14,33	1,41–	17,10
6	7,69	2,88–	15,99	2,02–	18,86
7	8,97	3,68–	17,62	2,68–	20,57
8	10,26	4,53–	19,21	3,39–	22,24
9	11,54	5,41–	20,78	4,15–	23,87
10	12,82	6,32–	22,32	4,94–	25,46
11	14,10	7,26–	23,83	5,76–	27,03
12	15,38	8,21–	25,33	6,60–	28,58
13	16,67	9,18–	26,81	7,47–	30,10
14	17,95	10,17–	28,28	8,36–	31,60
15	19,23	11,18–	29,73	9,28–	33,09
16	20,51	12,20–	31,16	10,21–	34,55
17	21,79	13,24–	32,59	11,16–	36,00
18	23,08	14,29–	34,00	12,12–	37,43
19	24,36	15,35–	35,40	13,10–	38,85
20	25,64	16,42–	36,79	14,10–	40,26
21	26,92	17,50–	38,16	15,11–	41,65
22	28,21	18,59–	39,53	16,13–	43,03
23	29,49	19,70–	40,89	17,16–	44,39
24	30,77	20,81–	42,24	18,21–	45,75
25	32,05	21,93–	43,58	19,27–	47,09
26	33,33	23,06–	44,92	20,34–	48,42
27	34,62	24,20–	46,24	21,42–	49,74
28	35,90	25,34–	47,56	22,51–	51,05
29	37,18	26,50–	48,87	23,61–	52,36
30	38,46	27,66–	50,17	24,72–	53,65
31	39,74	28,83–	51,46	25,85–	54,93
32	41,03	30,01–	52,75	26,98–	56,20
33	42,31	31,19–	54,02	28,12–	57,46
34	43,59	32,39–	55,30	29,27–	58,71
35	44,87	33,59–	56,56	30,43–	59,96
36	46,15	34,79–	57,82	31,60–	61,19
37	47,44	36,01–	59,07	32,78–	62,41
38	48,72	37,23–	60,31	33,97–	63,63
39	50,00	38,46–	61,54	35,16–	64,84
40	51,28	39,69–	62,77	36,37–	66,03
41	52,56	40,93–	63,99	37,59–	67,22
42	53,85	42,18–	65,21	38,81–	68,40
43	55,13	43,44–	66,41	40,04–	69,57
44	56,41	44,70–	67,61	41,29–	70,73
45	57,69	45,98–	68,81	42,54–	71,88
46	58,97	47,25–	69,99	43,80–	73,02
47	60,26	48,54–	71,17	45,07–	74,15
48	61,54	49,83–	72,34	46,35–	75,28
49	62,82	51,13–	73,50	47,64–	76,39
50	64,10	52,44–	74,66	48,95–	77,49
51	65,38	53,76–	75,80	50,26–	78,58
52	66,67	55,08–	76,94	51,58–	79,66
53	67,95	56,42–	78,07	52,91–	80,73
54	69,23	57,76–	79,19	54,25–	81,79
55	70,51	59,11–	80,30	55,61–	82,84
56	71,79	60,47–	81,41	56,97–	83,87
57	73,08	61,84–	82,50	58,35–	84,89
58	74,36	63,21–	83,58	59,74–	85,90
59	75,64	64,60–	84,65	61,15–	86,90
60	76,92	66,00–	85,71	62,57–	87,88
61	78,21	67,41–	86,76	64,00–	88,84

$N=78$ (continued)

x	$100\,p_x$	95% $100\,p_l$	95% $100\,p_r$	99% $100\,p_l$	99% $100\,p_r$
62	79,49	68,84–	87,80	65,45–	89,79
63	80,77	70,27–	88,82	66,91–	90,72
64	82,05	71,72–	89,83	68,40–	91,64
65	83,33	73,19–	90,82	69,90–	92,53
66	84,62	74,67–	91,79	71,42–	93,40
67	85,90	76,17–	92,74	72,97–	94,24
68	87,18	77,68–	93,68	74,54–	95,06
69	88,46	79,22–	94,59	76,13–	95,85
70	89,74	80,79–	95,47	77,76–	96,61
71	91,03	82,38–	96,32	79,43–	97,32
72	92,31	84,01–	97,12	81,14–	97,98
73	93,59	85,67–	97,89	82,90–	98,59
74	94,87	87,39–	98,59	84,72–	99,12
75	96,15	89,17–	99,20	86,63–	99,56
76	97,44	91,04–	99,69	88,65–	99,87
77	98,72	93,06–	99,97	90,86–	99,99
78	100,00	95,38–	100,00	93,43–	100,00

$N=79$

x	$100\,p_x$	95% $100\,p_l$	95% $100\,p_r$	99% $100\,p_l$	99% $100\,p_r$
0	0,00	0,00–	4,56	0,00–	6,49
1	1,27	0,03–	6,85	0,01–	9,03
2	2,53	0,31–	8,85	0,13–	11,21
3	3,80	0,79–	10,70	0,43–	13,21
4	5,06	1,40–	12,46	0,86–	15,10
5	6,33	2,09–	14,16	1,39–	16,90
6	7,59	2,84–	15,80	1,99–	18,64
7	8,86	3,64–	17,41	2,65–	20,33
8	10,13	4,47–	18,98	3,35–	21,97
9	11,39	5,34–	20,53	4,09–	23,59
10	12,66	6,24–	22,05	4,87–	25,17
11	13,92	7,16–	23,55	5,68–	26,72
12	15,19	8,10–	25,03	6,51–	28,25
13	16,46	9,06–	26,49	7,37–	29,75
14	17,72	10,04–	27,94	8,25–	31,24
15	18,99	11,03–	29,38	9,15–	32,71
16	20,25	12,04–	30,80	10,07–	34,16
17	21,52	13,06–	32,20	11,01–	35,59
18	22,78	14,10–	33,60	11,96–	37,01
19	24,05	15,14–	34,98	12,93–	38,41
20	25,32	16,20–	36,36	13,91–	39,80
21	26,58	17,27–	37,72	14,90–	41,18
22	27,85	18,35–	39,07	15,91–	42,54
23	29,11	19,43–	40,42	16,93–	43,89
24	30,38	20,53–	41,75	17,96–	45,23
25	31,65	21,63–	43,08	19,00–	46,56
26	32,91	22,75–	44,40	20,06–	47,88
27	34,18	23,87–	45,71	21,12–	49,19
28	35,44	25,00–	47,01	22,20–	50,49
29	36,71	26,14–	48,31	23,29–	51,78
30	37,97	27,28–	49,59	24,38–	53,06
31	39,24	28,44–	50,87	25,49–	54,33
32	40,51	29,60–	52,15	26,60–	55,59
33	41,77	30,77–	53,41	27,73–	56,84
34	43,04	31,94–	54,67	28,86–	58,08
35	44,30	33,12–	55,92	30,00–	59,31
36	45,57	34,31–	57,17	31,16–	60,53
37	46,84	35,51–	58,40	32,32–	61,75
38	48,10	36,71–	59,64	33,49–	62,95
39	49,37	37,92–	60,86	34,66–	64,15
40	50,63	39,14–	62,08	35,85–	65,34
41	51,90	40,36–	63,29	37,05–	66,51
42	53,16	41,60–	64,49	38,25–	67,68
43	54,43	42,83–	65,69	39,47–	68,84
44	55,70	44,08–	66,88	40,69–	70,00
45	56,96	45,33–	68,06	41,92–	71,14
46	58,23	46,59–	69,23	43,16–	72,27
47	59,49	47,85–	70,40	44,41–	73,40
48	60,76	49,13–	71,56	45,67–	74,51
49	62,03	50,41–	72,72	46,94–	75,62
50	63,29	51,69–	73,86	48,22–	76,71
51	64,56	52,99–	75,00	49,51–	77,80
52	65,82	54,29–	76,13	50,81–	78,88
53	67,09	55,60–	77,25	52,12–	79,94
54	68,35	56,92–	78,37	53,44–	81,00
55	69,62	58,25–	79,47	54,77–	82,04
56	70,89	59,58–	80,57	56,11–	83,07
57	72,15	60,93–	81,65	57,46–	84,09
58	73,42	62,28–	82,73	58,82–	85,10
59	74,68	63,64–	83,80	60,20–	86,09
60	75,95	65,02–	84,86	61,59–	87,07
61	77,22	66,40–	85,90	62,99–	88,04
62	78,48	67,80–	86,94	64,41–	88,99
63	79,75	69,20–	87,96	65,84–	89,93
64	81,01	70,62–	88,97	67,29–	90,85
65	82,28	72,06–	89,96	68,76–	91,75
66	83,54	73,51–	90,94	70,25–	92,63
67	84,81	74,97–	91,90	71,75–	93,49
68	86,08	76,45–	92,84	73,28–	94,32
69	87,34	77,95–	93,76	74,83–	95,13
70	88,61	79,47–	94,66	76,41–	95,91
71	89,87	81,02–	95,53	78,03–	96,65
72	91,14	82,59–	96,36	79,67–	97,35
73	92,41	84,20–	97,16	81,36–	98,01
74	93,67	85,84–	97,91	83,10–	98,61
75	94,94	87,54–	98,60	84,90–	99,14
76	96,20	89,30–	99,21	86,79–	99,57
77	97,47	91,15–	99,69	88,79–	99,87
78	98,73	93,15–	99,97	90,97–	99,99
79	100,00	95,44–	100,00	93,51–	100,00

$N=80$

x	$100\,p_x$	95% $100\,p_l$	95% $100\,p_r$	99% $100\,p_l$	99% $100\,p_r$
0	0,00	0,00–	4,51	0,00–	6,41
1	1,25	0,03–	6,77	0,01–	8,92
2	2,50	0,30–	8,74	0,13–	11,08
3	3,75	0,78–	10,57	0,43–	13,05
4	5,00	1,38–	12,31	0,85–	14,92
5	6,25	2,06–	13,99	1,37–	16,70
6	7,50	2,80–	15,61	1,96–	18,42
7	8,75	3,59–	17,20	2,61–	20,09
8	10,00	4,42–	18,76	3,31–	21,72
9	11,25	5,28–	20,28	4,04–	23,31
10	12,50	6,16–	21,79	4,81–	24,87
11	13,75	7,07–	23,27	5,61–	26,41
12	15,00	8,00–	24,74	6,43–	27,92
13	16,25	8,95–	26,18	7,28–	29,41
14	17,50	9,91–	27,62	8,14–	30,88
15	18,75	10,89–	29,03	9,03–	32,33
16	20,00	11,89–	30,44	9,94–	33,77
17	21,25	12,89–	31,83	10,86–	35,19
18	22,50	13,91–	33,21	11,80–	36,59
19	23,75	14,95–	34,58	12,75–	37,98
20	25,00	15,99–	35,94	13,72–	39,35
21	26,25	17,04–	37,29	14,70–	40,72
22	27,50	18,10–	38,62	15,70–	42,07
23	28,75	19,18–	39,95	16,70–	43,41
24	30,00	20,26–	41,28	17,72–	44,73
25	31,25	21,35–	42,59	18,75–	46,05
26	32,50	22,45–	43,89	19,79–	47,36
27	33,75	23,55–	45,19	20,84–	48,65
28	35,00	24,67–	46,48	21,90–	49,94
29	36,25	25,79–	47,76	22,97–	51,21
30	37,50	26,92–	49,04	24,05–	52,48
31	38,75	28,06–	50,30	25,14–	53,74
32	40,00	29,20–	51,56	26,24–	54,99
33	41,25	30,35–	52,82	27,35–	56,22
34	42,50	31,51–	54,06	28,46–	57,45
35	43,75	32,68–	55,30	29,59–	58,68
36	45,00	33,85–	56,53	30,72–	59,89
37	46,25	35,03–	57,76	31,87–	61,09
38	47,50	36,21–	58,98	33,02–	62,29
39	48,75	37,41–	60,19	34,18–	63,47
40	50,00	38,60–	61,40	35,35–	64,65
41	51,25	39,81–	62,59	36,53–	65,82
42	52,50	41,02–	63,79	37,71–	66,98
43	53,75	42,24–	64,97	38,91–	68,13
44	55,00	43,47–	66,15	40,11–	69,28
45	56,25	44,70–	67,32	41,32–	70,41
46	57,50	45,94–	68,49	42,55–	71,54
47	58,75	47,18–	69,65	43,78–	72,65
48	60,00	48,44–	70,80	45,01–	73,76
49	61,25	49,70–	71,94	46,26–	74,86
50	62,50	50,96–	73,08	47,52–	75,95
51	63,75	52,24–	74,21	48,79–	77,03
52	65,00	53,52–	75,33	50,06–	78,10
53	66,25	54,81–	76,45	51,35–	79,16
54	67,50	56,11–	77,55	52,64–	80,21
55	68,75	57,41–	78,65	53,95–	81,25
56	70,00	58,72–	79,74	55,27–	82,28
57	71,25	60,05–	80,82	56,59–	83,30
58	72,50	61,38–	81,90	57,93–	84,30
59	73,75	62,71–	82,96	59,28–	85,30
60	75,00	64,06–	84,01	60,65–	86,28
61	76,25	65,42–	85,05	62,02–	87,25
62	77,50	66,79–	86,09	63,41–	88,20
63	78,75	68,17–	87,11	64,81–	89,14
64	80,00	69,56–	88,11	66,23–	90,06
65	81,25	70,97–	89,11	67,67–	90,97
66	82,50	72,38–	90,09	69,12–	91,86
67	83,75	73,82–	91,05	70,59–	92,72
68	85,00	75,26–	92,00	72,08–	93,57
69	86,25	76,73–	92,93	73,59–	94,39
70	87,50	78,21–	93,84	75,13–	95,19
71	88,75	79,72–	94,72	76,69–	95,96
72	90,00	81,24–	95,58	78,28–	96,69
73	91,25	82,80–	96,41	79,91–	97,39
74	92,50	84,39–	97,20	81,58–	98,04
75	93,75	86,01–	97,94	83,30–	98,63
76	95,00	87,69–	98,62	85,08–	99,15
77	96,25	89,43–	99,22	86,95–	99,57
78	97,50	91,26–	99,70	88,92–	99,87
79	98,75	93,23–	99,97	91,08–	99,99
80	100,00	95,49–	100,00	93,59–	100,00

$N=81$

x	$100\,p_x$	95% $100\,p_l$	95% $100\,p_r$	99% $100\,p_l$	99% $100\,p_r$
0	0,00	0,00–	4,45	0,00–	6,33
1	1,23	0,03–	6,69	0,01–	8,82
2	2,47	0,30–	8,64	0,13–	10,95
3	3,70	0,77–	10,44	0,42–	12,90
4	4,94	1,36–	12,16	0,84–	14,74
5	6,17	2,03–	13,82	1,36–	16,50
6	7,41	2,77–	15,43	1,94–	18,21
7	8,64	3,55–	17,00	2,58–	19,86
8	9,88	4,36–	18,54	3,27–	21,47
9	11,11	5,21–	20,05	3,99–	23,04
10	12,35	6,08–	21,53	4,75–	24,59
11	13,58	6,98–	23,00	5,53–	26,11
12	14,81	7,90–	24,45	6,35–	27,60
13	16,05	8,83–	25,88	7,18–	29,08
14	17,28	9,78–	27,30	8,04–	30,53

All values conform to the international convention (i.e. 0,1 instead of 0.1).

N: number of trials; x: number of successes, etc.; $100\,p_x = 100\,x/N$

$N = 81$ (continued)

x	$100\,p_x$	95% $100\,p_l$	95% $100\,p_r$	99% $100\,p_l$	99% $100\,p_r$
15	18,52	10,75	28,70	8,92	31,97
16	19,75	11,73	30,09	9,81	33,39
17	20,99	12,73	31,46	10,72	34,79
18	22,22	13,73	32,83	11,65	36,18
19	23,46	14,75	34,18	12,59	37,55
20	24,69	15,78	35,53	13,54	38,92
21	25,93	16,82	36,86	14,51	40,27
22	27,16	17,87	38,19	15,49	41,60
23	28,40	18,93	39,50	16,48	42,93
24	29,63	19,99	40,81	17,49	44,24
25	30,86	21,07	42,11	18,50	45,55
26	32,10	22,15	43,40	19,52	46,84
27	33,33	23,24	44,68	20,56	48,12
28	34,57	24,34	45,96	21,61	49,40
29	35,80	25,45	47,23	22,66	50,66
30	37,04	26,56	48,49	23,73	51,92
31	38,27	27,69	49,74	24,80	53,16
32	39,51	28,81	50,99	25,88	54,40
33	40,74	29,95	52,23	26,97	55,62
34	41,98	31,09	53,46	28,08	56,84
35	43,21	32,24	54,69	29,18	58,05
36	44,44	33,40	55,91	30,30	59,26
37	45,68	34,56	57,13	31,43	60,45
38	46,91	35,73	58,33	32,56	61,64
39	48,15	36,90	59,53	33,71	62,81
40	49,38	38,08	60,73	34,86	63,98
41	50,62	39,27	61,92	36,02	65,14
42	51,85	40,47	63,10	37,19	66,29
43	53,09	41,67	64,27	38,36	67,44
44	54,32	42,87	65,44	39,55	68,57
45	55,56	44,09	66,60	40,74	69,70
46	56,79	45,31	67,76	41,95	70,82
47	58,02	46,54	68,91	43,16	71,92
48	59,26	47,77	70,05	44,38	73,03
49	60,49	49,01	71,19	45,60	74,12
50	61,73	50,26	72,31	46,84	75,20
51	62,96	51,51	73,44	48,08	76,27
52	64,20	52,77	74,55	49,34	77,34
53	65,43	54,04	75,66	50,60	78,39
54	66,67	55,32	76,76	51,88	79,44
55	67,90	56,60	77,85	53,16	80,48
56	69,14	57,89	78,93	54,45	81,50
57	70,37	59,19	80,01	55,76	82,51
58	71,60	60,50	81,07	57,07	83,52
59	72,84	61,81	82,13	58,40	84,51
60	74,07	63,14	83,18	59,73	85,49
61	75,31	64,47	84,22	61,08	86,46
62	76,54	65,82	85,25	62,45	87,41
63	77,78	67,17	86,27	63,82	88,35
64	79,01	68,54	87,27	65,21	89,28
65	80,25	69,91	88,27	66,61	90,19
66	81,48	71,30	89,25	68,03	91,08
67	82,72	72,70	90,22	69,47	91,96
68	83,95	74,12	91,17	70,92	92,82
69	85,19	75,55	92,10	72,40	93,65
70	86,42	77,00	93,02	73,89	94,47
71	87,65	78,47	93,92	75,41	95,25
72	88,89	79,95	94,79	76,96	96,01
73	90,12	81,46	95,64	78,53	96,73
74	91,36	83,00	96,45	80,14	97,42
75	92,59	84,57	97,23	81,79	98,06
76	93,83	86,18	97,97	83,50	98,64
77	95,06	87,84	98,64	85,26	99,16
78	96,30	89,56	99,23	87,10	99,58
79	97,53	91,36	99,70	89,05	99,87
80	98,77	93,31	99,97	91,18	99,99
81	100,00	95,55	100,00	93,67	100,00

$N = 82$

x	$100\,p_x$	95% $100\,p_l$	95% $100\,p_r$	99% $100\,p_l$	99% $100\,p_r$
0	0,00	0,00	4,40	0,00	6,26
1	1,22	0,03	6,61	0,01	8,71
2	2,44	0,30	8,53	0,13	10,82
3	3,66	0,76	10,32	0,42	12,75
4	4,88	1,34	12,02	0,83	14,57
5	6,10	2,01	13,66	1,34	16,31
6	7,32	2,73	15,25	1,92	18,00
7	8,54	3,50	16,80	2,55	19,63
8	9,76	4,31	18,32	3,22	21,22
9	10,98	5,14	19,82	3,94	22,78
10	12,20	6,01	21,29	4,69	24,31
11	13,41	6,89	22,74	5,46	25,81
12	14,63	7,80	24,17	6,27	27,29
13	15,85	8,72	25,58	7,09	28,75
14	17,07	9,66	26,98	7,94	30,19
15	18,29	10,62	28,37	8,80	31,61
16	19,51	11,58	29,74	9,68	33,02
17	20,73	12,57	31,11	10,58	34,41
18	21,95	13,56	32,46	11,50	35,78
19	23,17	14,56	33,80	12,42	37,14
20	24,39	15,58	35,12	13,37	38,49
21	25,61	16,60	36,45	14,32	39,82
22	26,83	17,64	37,76	15,29	41,15
23	28,05	18,68	39,06	16,27	42,46
24	29,27	19,74	40,35	17,26	43,76
25	30,49	20,80	41,64	18,26	45,05
26	31,71	21,87	42,92	19,27	46,33
27	32,93	22,94	44,19	20,29	47,61
28	34,15	24,03	45,45	21,32	48,87

$N = 82$ (continued)

x	$100\,p_x$	95% $100\,p_l$	95% $100\,p_r$	99% $100\,p_l$	99% $100\,p_r$
29	35,37	25,12	46,70	22,36	50,12
30	36,59	26,22	47,95	23,41	51,36
31	37,80	27,32	49,19	24,47	52,60
32	39,02	28,44	50,43	25,54	53,82
33	40,24	29,56	51,66	26,61	55,04
34	41,46	30,68	52,88	27,70	56,25
35	42,68	31,82	54,09	28,79	57,45
36	43,90	32,95	55,30	29,89	58,64
37	45,12	34,10	56,51	31,00	59,82
38	46,34	35,25	57,70	32,12	61,00
39	47,56	36,41	58,89	33,25	62,16
40	48,78	37,58	60,08	34,38	63,32
41	50,00	38,75	61,25	35,53	64,47
42	51,22	39,92	62,42	36,68	65,62
43	52,44	41,11	63,59	37,84	66,75
44	53,66	42,30	64,75	39,00	67,88
45	54,88	43,49	65,90	40,18	69,00
46	56,10	44,70	67,05	41,36	70,11
47	57,32	45,91	68,18	42,55	71,21
48	58,54	47,12	69,32	43,75	72,30
49	59,76	48,34	70,44	44,96	73,39
50	60,98	49,57	71,56	46,18	74,46
51	62,20	50,81	72,68	47,40	75,53
52	63,41	52,05	73,78	48,64	76,59
53	64,63	53,30	74,88	49,88	77,64
54	65,85	54,55	75,97	51,13	78,68
55	67,07	55,81	77,06	52,39	79,71
56	68,29	57,08	78,13	53,67	80,73
57	69,51	58,36	79,20	54,95	81,74
58	70,73	59,65	80,26	56,24	82,74
59	71,95	60,94	81,32	57,54	83,73
60	73,17	62,24	82,36	58,85	84,71
61	74,39	63,55	83,40	60,18	85,68
62	75,61	64,88	84,42	61,51	86,63
63	76,83	66,20	85,44	62,86	87,58
64	78,05	67,54	86,44	64,22	88,50
65	79,27	68,89	87,43	65,59	89,42
66	80,49	70,26	88,42	66,98	90,32
67	81,71	71,63	89,38	68,39	91,20
68	82,93	73,02	90,34	69,81	92,06
69	84,15	74,42	91,28	71,25	92,91
70	85,37	75,83	92,20	72,71	93,73
71	86,59	77,26	93,11	74,19	94,54
72	87,80	78,71	93,99	75,69	95,31
73	89,02	80,18	94,86	77,22	96,06
74	90,24	81,68	95,69	78,78	96,78
75	91,46	83,20	96,50	80,37	97,45
76	92,68	84,75	97,27	82,00	98,08
77	93,90	86,34	97,99	83,69	98,66
78	95,12	87,98	98,66	85,43	99,17
79	96,34	89,68	99,24	87,25	99,58
80	97,56	91,47	99,70	89,18	99,87
81	98,78	93,39	99,97	91,29	99,99
82	100,00	95,60	100,00	93,74	100,00

$N = 83$

x	$100\,p_x$	95% $100\,p_l$	95% $100\,p_r$	99% $100\,p_l$	99% $100\,p_r$
0	0,00	0,00	4,35	0,00	6,18
1	1,20	0,03	6,53	0,01	8,61
2	2,41	0,29	8,43	0,13	10,70
3	3,61	0,75	10,20	0,41	12,61
4	4,82	1,33	11,88	0,82	14,41
5	6,02	1,98	13,50	1,32	16,13
6	7,23	2,70	15,07	1,89	17,79
7	8,43	3,46	16,61	2,52	19,41
8	9,64	4,25	18,11	3,18	20,98
9	10,84	5,08	19,59	3,89	22,53
10	12,05	5,93	21,04	4,63	24,04
11	13,25	6,81	22,48	5,40	25,53
12	14,46	7,70	23,89	6,19	26,99
13	15,66	8,61	25,29	7,00	28,43
14	16,87	9,54	26,68	7,84	29,86
15	18,07	10,48	28,05	8,69	31,26
16	19,28	11,44	29,41	9,56	32,65
17	20,48	12,41	30,76	10,45	34,03
18	21,69	13,39	32,09	11,35	35,39
19	22,89	14,38	33,42	12,27	36,74
20	24,10	15,38	34,73	13,20	38,07
21	25,30	16,39	36,04	14,14	39,39
22	26,51	17,42	37,34	15,09	40,70
23	27,71	18,45	38,62	16,06	42,00
24	28,92	19,48	39,91	17,03	43,29
25	30,12	20,53	41,18	18,02	44,57
26	31,33	21,59	42,44	19,02	45,84
27	32,53	22,65	43,70	20,03	47,10
28	33,73	23,72	44,95	21,04	48,35
29	34,94	24,80	46,19	22,07	49,59
30	36,14	25,88	47,43	23,10	50,82
31	37,35	26,97	48,66	24,15	52,04
32	38,55	28,07	49,88	25,20	53,26
33	39,76	29,17	51,10	26,26	54,46
34	40,96	30,28	52,31	27,33	55,66
35	42,17	31,40	53,51	28,41	56,85
36	43,37	32,53	54,71	29,50	58,03
37	44,58	33,66	55,90	30,59	59,20
38	45,78	34,79	57,08	31,69	60,37
39	46,99	35,93	58,26	32,80	61,53
40	48,19	37,08	59,44	33,92	62,68
41	49,40	38,24	60,60	35,05	63,82

$N = 83$ (continued)

x	$100\,p_x$	95% $100\,p_l$	95% $100\,p_r$	99% $100\,p_l$	99% $100\,p_r$
42	50,60	39,40	61,76	36,18	64,95
43	51,81	40,56	62,92	37,32	66,08
44	53,01	41,74	64,07	38,47	67,20
45	54,22	42,92	65,21	39,63	68,31
46	55,42	44,10	66,34	40,80	69,41
47	56,63	45,29	67,47	41,97	70,50
48	57,83	46,49	68,60	43,15	71,59
49	59,04	47,69	69,72	44,34	72,67
50	60,24	48,90	70,83	45,54	73,74
51	61,45	50,12	71,93	46,74	74,80
52	62,65	51,34	73,03	47,96	75,85
53	63,86	52,57	74,12	49,18	76,90
54	65,06	53,81	75,20	50,41	77,93
55	66,27	55,05	76,28	51,65	78,96
56	67,47	56,30	77,35	52,90	79,97
57	68,67	57,56	78,41	54,16	80,98
58	69,88	58,82	79,47	55,43	81,98
59	71,08	60,09	80,52	56,71	82,97
60	72,29	61,38	81,55	58,00	83,94
61	73,49	62,66	82,58	59,30	84,91
62	74,70	63,96	83,61	60,61	85,86
63	75,90	65,27	84,62	61,93	86,80
64	77,11	66,58	85,62	63,26	87,73
65	78,31	67,91	86,61	64,61	88,65
66	79,52	69,24	87,59	65,97	89,55
67	80,72	70,59	88,56	67,35	90,44
68	81,93	71,95	89,52	68,74	91,31
69	83,13	73,32	90,46	70,14	92,16
70	84,34	74,71	91,39	71,57	93,00
71	85,54	76,11	92,30	73,01	93,81
72	86,75	77,52	93,19	74,47	94,60
73	87,95	78,96	94,07	75,96	95,37
74	89,16	80,41	94,92	77,47	96,11
75	90,36	81,89	95,75	79,02	96,82
76	91,57	83,39	96,54	80,59	97,48
77	92,77	84,93	97,30	82,21	98,11
78	93,98	86,50	98,02	83,87	98,68
79	95,18	88,12	98,67	85,59	99,18
80	96,39	89,80	99,25	87,39	99,59
81	97,59	91,57	99,71	89,30	99,87
82	98,80	93,47	99,97	91,39	99,99
83	100,00	95,65	100,00	93,82	100,00

$N = 84$

x	$100\,p_x$	95% $100\,p_l$	95% $100\,p_r$	99% $100\,p_l$	99% $100\,p_r$
0	0,00	0,00	4,30	0,00	6,11
1	1,19	0,03	6,46	0,01	8,51
2	2,38	0,29	8,34	0,12	10,57
3	3,57	0,74	10,08	0,41	12,46
4	4,76	1,31	11,75	0,81	14,24
5	5,95	1,96	13,35	1,31	15,95
6	7,14	2,67	14,90	1,87	17,59
7	8,33	3,42	16,42	2,49	19,19
8	9,52	4,20	17,91	3,15	20,75
9	10,71	5,02	19,37	3,84	22,28
10	11,90	5,86	20,81	4,57	23,77
11	13,10	6,72	22,22	5,33	25,25
12	14,29	7,61	23,62	6,11	26,69
13	15,48	8,51	25,01	6,91	28,12
14	16,67	9,42	26,38	7,74	29,53
15	17,86	10,35	27,74	8,58	30,92
16	19,05	11,30	29,08	9,44	32,30
17	20,24	12,25	30,41	10,32	33,66
18	21,43	13,22	31,74	11,21	35,01
19	22,62	14,20	33,05	12,11	36,34
20	23,81	15,19	34,35	13,03	37,66
21	25,00	16,19	35,64	13,96	38,97
22	26,19	17,20	36,93	14,90	40,27
23	27,38	18,21	38,20	15,85	41,56
24	28,57	19,24	39,47	16,82	42,83
25	29,76	20,27	40,73	17,79	44,10
26	30,95	21,31	41,98	18,77	45,35
27	32,14	22,36	43,22	19,77	46,60
28	33,33	23,42	44,46	20,77	47,84
29	34,52	24,48	45,69	21,78	49,07
30	35,71	25,55	46,92	22,81	50,29
31	36,90	26,63	48,13	23,84	51,50
32	38,10	27,71	49,34	24,87	52,70
33	39,29	28,80	50,55	25,92	53,90
34	40,48	29,90	51,75	26,98	55,09
35	41,67	31,00	52,94	28,04	56,27
36	42,86	32,11	54,12	29,11	57,44
37	44,05	33,22	55,30	30,19	58,60
38	45,24	34,34	56,48	31,28	59,76
39	46,43	35,47	57,65	32,37	60,90
40	47,62	36,60	58,81	33,47	62,04
41	48,81	37,74	59,96	34,58	63,18
42	50,00	38,88	61,12	35,70	64,30
43	51,19	40,04	62,26	36,82	65,42
44	52,38	41,19	63,40	37,96	66,53
45	53,57	42,35	64,53	39,10	67,63
46	54,76	43,52	65,66	40,24	68,72
47	55,95	44,70	66,78	41,40	69,81
48	57,14	45,88	67,89	42,56	70,89
49	58,33	47,06	69,00	43,73	71,96
50	59,52	48,25	70,10	44,91	73,02
51	60,71	49,45	71,20	46,10	74,08
52	61,90	50,66	72,29	47,30	75,13
53	63,10	51,87	73,37	48,50	76,16

$N = 84$ (continued)

x	$100\,p_x$	95% $100\,p_l$	95% $100\,p_r$	99% $100\,p_l$	99% $100\,p_r$
54	64,29	53,08	74,45	49,71	77,19
55	65,48	54,31	75,52	50,93	78,22
56	66,67	55,54	76,58	52,16	79,23
57	67,86	56,78	77,64	53,40	80,23
58	69,05	58,02	78,69	54,65	81,23
59	70,24	59,27	79,73	55,90	82,21
60	71,43	60,53	80,76	57,17	83,18
61	72,62	61,80	81,79	58,44	84,15
62	73,81	63,07	82,80	59,73	85,10
63	75,00	64,36	83,81	61,03	86,04
64	76,19	65,65	84,81	62,34	86,97
65	77,38	66,95	85,80	63,66	87,89
66	78,57	68,26	86,78	64,99	88,79
67	79,76	69,59	87,75	66,34	89,68
68	80,95	70,92	88,70	67,70	90,56
69	82,14	72,26	89,65	69,08	91,42
70	83,33	73,62	90,58	70,47	92,26
71	84,52	74,99	91,49	71,88	93,09
72	85,71	76,38	92,39	73,31	93,89
73	86,90	77,78	93,28	74,75	94,67
74	88,10	79,19	94,14	76,23	95,43
75	89,29	80,63	94,98	77,72	96,16
76	90,48	82,09	95,80	79,25	96,85
77	91,67	83,58	96,58	80,81	97,51
78	92,86	85,10	97,33	82,41	98,13
79	94,05	86,65	98,04	84,05	98,69
80	95,24	88,25	98,69	85,76	99,19
81	96,43	89,92	99,26	87,54	99,59
82	97,62	91,66	99,71	89,43	99,88
83	98,81	93,54	99,97	91,49	99,99
84	100,00	95,70	100,00	93,89	100,00

$N = 85$

x	$100\,p_x$	95% $100\,p_l$	95% $100\,p_r$	99% $100\,p_l$	99% $100\,p_r$
0	0,00	0,00	4,25	0,00	6,04
1	1,18	0,03	6,38	0,01	8,42
2	2,35	0,29	8,24	0,12	10,45
3	3,53	0,74	9,97	0,40	12,32
4	4,71	1,30	11,61	0,80	14,08
5	5,88	1,94	13,20	1,29	15,77
6	7,06	2,64	14,73	1,85	17,40
7	8,24	3,38	16,23	2,46	18,98
8	9,41	4,15	17,71	3,11	20,52
9	10,59	4,96	19,15	3,80	22,03
10	11,76	5,79	20,57	4,52	23,51
11	12,94	6,64	21,98	5,26	24,97
12	14,12	7,51	23,36	6,04	26,40
13	15,29	8,40	24,73	6,83	27,82
14	16,47	9,31	26,09	7,64	29,21
15	17,65	10,23	27,43	8,48	30,59
16	18,82	11,16	28,76	9,33	31,95
17	20,00	12,10	30,08	10,19	33,30
18	21,18	13,06	31,39	11,07	34,63
19	22,35	14,03	32,69	11,96	35,95
20	23,53	15,00	33,97	12,87	37,26
21	24,71	15,99	35,25	13,78	38,56
22	25,88	16,99	36,52	14,71	39,84
23	27,06	17,99	37,79	15,65	41,12
24	28,24	19,00	39,04	16,61	42,38
25	29,41	20,02	40,29	17,57	43,63
26	30,59	21,05	41,53	18,54	44,88
27	31,76	22,08	42,76	19,52	46,12
28	32,94	23,13	43,98	20,51	47,34
29	34,12	24,18	45,20	21,51	48,56
30	35,29	25,23	46,41	22,51	49,77
31	36,47	26,29	47,62	23,53	50,97
32	37,65	27,36	48,82	24,55	52,16
33	38,82	28,44	50,01	25,59	53,35
34	40,00	29,52	51,20	26,63	54,52
35	41,18	30,61	52,38	27,68	55,69
36	42,35	31,70	53,55	28,73	56,85
37	43,53	32,80	54,72	29,80	58,01
38	44,71	33,91	55,89	30,87	59,15
39	45,88	35,02	57,04	31,95	60,29
40	47,06	36,13	58,19	33,03	61,42
41	48,24	37,26	59,34	34,13	62,55
42	49,41	38,39	60,48	35,23	63,66
43	50,59	39,52	61,61	36,34	64,77
44	51,76	40,66	62,74	37,45	65,87
45	52,94	41,81	63,87	38,58	66,97
46	54,12	42,96	64,98	39,71	68,05
47	55,29	44,11	66,09	40,85	69,13
48	56,47	45,28	67,20	41,99	70,20
49	57,65	46,45	68,30	43,15	71,27
50	58,82	47,62	69,39	44,31	72,32
51	60,00	48,80	70,48	45,48	73,37
52	61,18	49,99	71,56	46,65	74,41
53	62,35	51,18	72,64	47,84	75,45
54	63,53	52,38	73,71	49,03	76,47
55	64,71	53,59	74,77	50,23	77,49
56	65,88	54,80	75,82	51,44	78,49
57	67,06	56,02	76,87	52,66	79,49
58	68,24	57,24	77,92	53,88	80,48
59	69,41	58,47	78,95	55,12	81,46
60	70,59	59,71	79,98	56,37	82,43
61	71,76	60,96	81,00	57,62	83,39
62	72,94	62,21	82,01	58,88	84,35
63	74,12	63,48	83,01	60,16	85,29
64	75,29	64,75	84,01	61,44	86,22

All values conform to the international convention (i.e. 0,1 instead of 0.1).

N: number of trials; x: number of successes, etc.; $100\,p_x = 100\,x/N$

N = 85 (continued)

x	100 p_x	95% 100 p_l	95% 100 p_r	99% 100 p_l	99% 100 p_r
65	76,47	66,03	85,00	62,74	87,13
66	77,65	67,31	85,97	64,05	88,04
67	78,82	68,61	86,94	65,37	88,93
68	80,00	69,92	87,90	66,70	89,81
69	81,18	71,24	88,84	68,05	90,67
70	82,35	72,57	89,77	69,41	91,52
71	83,53	73,91	90,69	70,79	92,36
72	84,71	75,27	91,60	72,18	93,17
73	85,88	76,64	92,49	73,60	93,96
74	87,06	78,02	93,36	75,03	94,74
75	88,24	79,43	94,21	76,49	95,48
76	89,41	80,85	95,04	77,97	96,20
77	90,59	82,29	95,85	79,48	96,89
78	91,76	83,77	96,62	81,02	97,54
79	92,94	85,27	97,36	82,60	98,15
80	94,12	86,80	98,06	84,23	98,71
81	95,29	88,39	98,70	85,92	99,20
82	96,47	90,03	99,26	87,68	99,60
83	97,65	91,76	99,71	89,55	99,88
84	98,82	93,62	99,97	91,58	99,99
85	100,00	95,75	100,00	93,96	100,00

N = 86

x	100 p_x	95% 100 p_l	95% 100 p_r	99% 100 p_l	99% 100 p_r
0	0,00	0,00	4,20	0,00	5,97
1	1,16	0,03	6,31	0,01	8,32
2	2,33	0,28	8,15	0,12	10,34
3	3,49	0,73	9,86	0,40	12,19
4	4,65	1,28	11,48	0,79	13,93
5	5,81	1,91	13,05	1,28	15,60
6	6,98	2,60	14,57	1,82	17,21
7	8,14	3,34	16,05	2,43	18,77
8	9,30	4,10	17,51	3,07	20,30
9	10,47	4,90	18,94	3,75	21,79
10	11,63	5,72	20,35	4,46	23,26
11	12,79	6,56	21,73	5,20	24,70
12	13,95	7,42	23,11	5,96	26,12
13	15,12	8,30	24,46	6,75	27,52
14	16,28	9,20	25,80	7,55	28,90
15	17,44	10,10	27,13	8,37	30,26
16	18,60	11,02	28,45	9,21	31,61
17	19,77	11,96	29,75	10,07	32,94
18	20,93	12,90	31,05	10,93	34,27
19	22,09	13,86	32,33	11,81	35,57
20	23,26	14,82	33,61	12,71	36,87
21	24,42	15,80	34,87	13,61	38,15
22	25,58	16,78	36,13	14,53	39,42
23	26,74	17,77	37,38	15,46	40,69
24	27,91	18,77	38,62	16,40	41,94
25	29,07	19,78	39,86	17,35	43,18
26	30,23	20,79	41,08	18,31	44,41
27	31,40	21,81	42,30	19,27	45,64
28	32,56	22,84	43,52	20,25	46,85
29	33,72	23,88	44,72	21,24	48,06
30	34,88	24,92	45,92	22,23	49,26
31	36,05	25,97	47,12	23,23	50,45
32	37,21	27,02	48,30	24,24	51,63
33	38,37	28,08	49,49	25,26	52,80
34	39,53	29,15	50,66	26,29	53,97
35	40,70	30,22	51,83	27,32	55,13
36	41,86	31,30	52,99	28,37	56,28
37	43,02	32,39	54,15	29,41	57,43
38	44,19	33,48	55,30	30,47	58,56
39	45,35	34,58	56,45	31,54	59,69
40	46,51	35,68	57,59	32,61	60,81
41	47,67	36,79	58,73	33,69	61,93
42	48,84	37,90	59,86	34,77	63,03
43	50,00	39,02	60,98	35,86	64,14
44	51,16	40,14	62,10	36,97	65,23
45	52,33	41,27	63,21	38,07	66,31
46	53,49	42,41	64,32	39,19	67,39
47	54,65	43,55	65,42	40,31	68,46
48	55,81	44,70	66,52	41,44	69,53
49	56,98	45,85	67,61	42,57	70,59
50	58,14	47,01	68,70	43,72	71,63
51	59,30	48,17	69,78	44,87	72,68
52	60,47	49,34	70,85	46,03	73,71
53	61,63	50,51	71,92	47,20	74,74
54	62,79	51,70	72,98	48,37	75,76
55	63,95	52,88	74,03	49,55	76,77
56	65,12	54,08	75,08	50,74	77,77
57	66,28	55,28	76,12	51,94	78,76
58	67,44	56,48	77,16	53,15	79,75
59	68,60	57,70	78,19	54,36	80,73
60	69,77	58,92	79,21	55,59	81,69
61	70,93	60,14	80,22	56,82	82,65
62	72,09	61,38	81,23	58,06	83,60
63	73,26	62,62	82,23	59,31	84,54
64	74,42	63,87	83,22	60,58	85,47
65	75,58	65,13	84,20	61,85	86,39
66	76,74	66,39	85,18	63,13	87,29
67	77,91	67,67	86,14	64,43	88,19
68	79,07	68,95	87,10	65,73	89,07
69	80,23	70,25	88,04	67,06	89,93
70	81,40	71,55	88,98	68,39	90,79
71	82,56	72,87	89,90	69,74	91,63
72	83,72	74,20	90,80	71,10	92,45
73	84,88	75,54	91,70	72,48	93,25
74	86,05	76,89	92,58	73,88	94,04

N = 86 (continued)

x	100 p_x	95% 100 p_l	95% 100 p_r	99% 100 p_l	99% 100 p_r
75	87,21	78,27	93,44	75,30	94,80
76	88,37	79,65	94,28	76,74	95,54
77	89,53	81,06	95,10	78,21	96,25
78	90,70	82,49	95,90	79,70	96,93
79	91,86	83,95	96,66	81,23	97,57
80	93,02	85,43	97,40	82,79	98,18
81	94,19	86,95	98,09	84,40	98,72
82	95,35	88,52	98,72	86,07	99,21
83	96,51	90,14	99,27	87,81	99,60
84	97,67	91,85	99,72	89,66	99,88
85	98,84	93,69	99,97	91,68	99,99
86	100,00	95,80	100,00	94,03	100,00

N = 87

x	100 p_x	95% 100 p_l	95% 100 p_r	99% 100 p_l	99% 100 p_r
0	0,00	0,00	4,15	0,00	5,91
1	1,15	0,03	6,24	0,01	8,23
2	2,30	0,28	8,06	0,12	10,22
3	3,45	0,72	9,75	0,39	12,05
4	4,60	1,27	11,36	0,78	13,78
5	5,75	1,89	12,90	1,26	15,43
6	6,90	2,57	14,41	1,80	17,02
7	8,05	3,30	15,88	2,40	18,57
8	9,20	4,05	17,32	3,03	20,08
9	10,34	4,84	18,73	3,71	21,56
10	11,49	5,65	20,12	4,41	23,01
11	12,64	6,48	21,50	5,14	24,44
12	13,79	7,34	22,85	5,89	25,84
13	14,94	8,20	24,20	6,67	27,23
14	16,09	9,09	25,52	7,46	28,59
15	17,24	9,98	26,84	8,27	29,94
16	18,39	10,89	28,14	9,10	31,28
17	19,54	11,81	29,43	9,94	32,60
18	20,69	12,75	30,71	10,80	33,91
19	21,84	13,69	31,98	11,67	35,20
20	22,99	14,64	33,25	12,55	36,48
21	24,14	15,60	34,50	13,45	37,75
22	25,29	16,58	35,75	14,35	39,02
23	26,44	17,55	36,98	15,27	40,27
24	27,59	18,54	38,21	16,20	41,51
25	28,74	19,54	39,43	17,13	42,74
26	29,89	20,54	40,65	18,08	43,96
27	31,03	21,55	41,86	19,04	45,17
28	32,18	22,56	43,06	20,00	46,38
29	33,33	23,58	44,25	20,97	47,57
30	34,48	24,61	45,44	21,95	48,76
31	35,63	25,65	46,62	22,94	49,94
32	36,78	26,69	47,80	23,94	51,11
33	37,93	27,74	48,97	24,95	52,27
34	39,08	28,79	50,13	25,96	53,43
35	40,23	29,85	51,29	26,98	54,58
36	41,38	30,92	52,45	28,01	55,72
37	42,53	31,99	53,59	29,04	56,85
38	43,68	33,06	54,74	30,09	57,98
39	44,83	34,15	55,87	31,13	59,10
40	45,98	35,23	57,00	32,19	60,21
41	47,13	36,33	58,13	33,26	61,32
42	48,28	37,42	59,25	34,33	62,42
43	49,43	38,53	60,36	35,40	63,51
44	50,57	39,64	61,47	36,49	64,60
45	51,72	40,75	62,58	37,58	65,67
46	52,87	41,87	63,67	38,68	66,74
47	54,02	43,00	64,77	39,79	67,81
48	55,17	44,13	65,85	40,90	68,87
49	56,32	45,26	66,94	42,02	69,91
50	57,47	46,41	68,01	43,15	70,96
51	58,62	47,55	69,08	44,28	71,99
52	59,77	48,71	70,15	45,42	73,02
53	60,92	49,87	71,21	46,57	74,04
54	62,07	51,03	72,26	47,73	75,05
55	63,22	52,20	73,31	48,89	76,06
56	64,37	53,38	74,35	50,06	77,06
57	65,52	54,56	75,39	51,24	78,05
58	66,67	55,75	76,42	52,43	79,03
59	67,82	56,94	77,44	53,62	80,00
60	68,97	58,14	78,45	54,83	80,96
61	70,11	59,35	79,46	56,04	81,92
62	71,26	60,57	80,46	57,26	82,87
63	72,41	61,79	81,46	58,49	83,80
64	73,56	63,02	82,45	59,73	84,73
65	74,71	64,25	83,42	60,98	85,65
66	75,86	65,50	84,40	62,25	86,55
67	77,01	66,75	85,36	63,52	87,45
68	78,16	68,02	86,31	64,80	88,33
69	79,31	69,29	87,25	66,09	89,20
70	80,46	70,57	88,19	67,40	90,06
71	81,61	71,86	89,11	68,72	90,90
72	82,76	73,16	90,02	70,06	91,73
73	83,91	74,48	90,91	71,41	92,54
74	85,06	75,80	91,80	72,77	93,33
75	86,21	77,15	92,66	74,16	94,11
76	87,36	78,50	93,52	75,56	94,86
77	88,51	79,88	94,35	76,99	95,59
78	89,66	81,27	95,16	78,44	96,29
79	90,80	82,68	95,95	79,92	96,97
80	91,95	84,12	96,70	81,43	97,60
81	93,10	85,59	97,43	82,98	98,20
82	94,25	87,10	98,11	84,57	98,74
83	95,40	88,64	98,73	86,22	99,22

N = 87 (continued)

x	100 p_x	95% 100 p_l	95% 100 p_r	99% 100 p_l	99% 100 p_r
84	96,55	90,25	99,28	87,95	99,61
85	97,70	91,94	99,72	89,78	99,88
86	98,85	93,76	99,97	91,77	99,99
87	100,00	95,85	100,00	94,09	100,00

N = 88

x	100 p_x	95% 100 p_l	95% 100 p_r	99% 100 p_l	99% 100 p_r
0	0,00	0,00	4,11	0,00	5,84
1	1,14	0,03	6,17	0,01	8,14
2	2,27	0,28	7,97	0,12	10,11
3	3,41	0,71	9,64	0,39	11,92
4	4,55	1,25	11,23	0,77	13,63
5	5,68	1,87	12,76	1,25	15,26
6	6,82	2,54	14,25	1,78	16,84
7	7,95	3,26	15,70	2,37	18,37
8	9,09	4,01	17,13	3,00	19,87
9	10,23	4,78	18,53	3,66	21,33
10	11,36	5,59	19,91	4,36	22,77
11	12,50	6,41	21,27	5,08	24,18
12	13,64	7,25	22,61	5,82	25,57
13	14,77	8,11	23,94	6,59	26,94
14	15,91	8,98	25,25	7,37	28,29
15	17,05	9,87	26,55	8,17	29,63
16	18,18	10,76	27,84	8,99	30,95
17	19,32	11,68	29,12	9,82	32,26
18	20,45	12,60	30,39	10,67	33,55
19	21,59	13,53	31,65	11,53	34,84
20	22,73	14,47	32,89	12,40	36,11
21	23,86	15,42	34,14	13,29	37,37
22	25,00	16,38	35,37	14,18	38,61
23	26,14	17,34	36,59	15,09	39,85
24	27,27	18,32	37,81	16,00	41,08
25	28,41	19,30	39,02	16,93	42,30
26	29,55	20,29	40,22	17,86	43,51
27	30,68	21,29	41,42	18,80	44,71
28	31,82	22,29	42,61	19,76	45,91
29	32,95	23,30	43,79	20,72	47,09
30	34,09	24,32	44,97	21,68	48,27
31	35,23	25,34	46,14	22,66	49,44
32	36,36	26,37	47,31	23,65	50,60
33	37,50	27,40	48,47	24,64	51,75
34	38,64	28,44	49,62	25,64	52,90
35	39,77	29,49	50,77	26,64	54,04
36	40,91	30,54	51,91	27,66	55,17
37	42,05	31,60	53,05	28,68	56,29
38	43,18	32,66	54,18	29,71	57,41
39	44,32	33,73	55,30	30,74	58,52
40	45,45	34,80	56,42	31,79	59,63
41	46,59	35,88	57,54	32,84	60,72
42	47,73	36,96	58,65	33,89	61,81
43	48,86	38,05	59,75	34,96	62,90
44	50,00	39,15	60,85	36,03	63,97
45	51,14	40,25	61,95	37,10	65,04
46	52,27	41,35	63,04	38,19	66,11
47	53,41	42,46	64,12	39,28	67,16
48	54,55	43,58	65,20	40,37	68,21
49	55,68	44,70	66,27	41,48	69,26
50	56,82	45,82	67,34	42,59	70,29
51	57,95	46,95	68,40	43,71	71,32
52	59,09	48,09	69,46	44,83	72,34
53	60,23	49,23	70,51	45,96	73,36
54	61,36	50,38	71,56	47,10	74,36
55	62,50	51,53	72,60	48,25	75,36
56	63,64	52,69	73,63	49,40	76,35
57	64,77	53,86	74,66	50,56	77,34
58	65,91	55,03	75,68	51,73	78,32
59	67,05	56,21	76,70	52,91	79,28
60	68,18	57,39	77,71	54,09	80,24
61	69,32	58,58	78,71	55,29	81,20
62	70,45	59,78	79,71	56,49	82,14
63	71,59	60,98	80,70	57,70	83,07
64	72,73	62,19	81,68	58,92	84,00
65	73,86	63,41	82,66	60,15	84,91
66	75,00	64,63	83,62	61,39	85,82
67	76,14	65,86	84,58	62,63	86,71
68	77,27	67,11	85,53	63,89	87,60
69	78,41	68,35	86,47	65,16	88,47
70	79,55	69,61	87,40	66,45	89,33
71	80,68	70,88	88,32	67,74	90,18
72	81,82	72,16	89,24	69,05	91,01
73	82,95	73,45	90,13	70,37	91,83
74	84,09	74,75	91,02	71,71	92,63
75	85,23	76,06	91,89	73,06	93,41
76	86,36	77,39	92,75	74,43	94,18
77	87,50	78,73	93,59	75,82	94,92
78	88,64	80,09	94,41	77,23	95,64
79	89,77	81,47	95,22	78,67	96,34
80	90,91	82,87	95,99	80,13	97,00
81	92,05	84,30	96,74	81,63	97,63
82	93,18	85,75	97,46	83,16	98,22
83	94,32	87,24	98,13	84,74	98,75
84	95,45	88,77	98,75	86,37	99,23
85	96,59	90,36	99,29	88,08	99,61
86	97,73	92,03	99,72	89,89	99,88
87	98,86	93,83	99,97	91,86	99,99
88	100,00	95,89	100,00	94,16	100,00

N = 89

x	100 p_x	95% 100 p_l	95% 100 p_r	99% 100 p_l	99% 100 p_r
0	0,00	0,00	4,06	0,00	5,78
1	1,12	0,03	6,10	0,01	8,05

N = 89 (continued)

x	100 p_x	95% 100 p_l	95% 100 p_r	99% 100 p_l	99% 100 p_r
2	2,25	0,27	7,88	0,12	10,00
3	3,37	0,70	9,54	0,38	11,79
4	4,49	1,24	11,11	0,77	13,48
5	5,62	1,85	12,63	1,23	15,10
6	6,74	2,51	14,10	1,76	16,66
7	7,87	3,22	15,54	2,34	18,18
8	8,99	3,96	16,95	2,96	19,66
9	10,11	4,73	18,33	3,62	21,11
10	11,24	5,52	19,69	4,31	22,53
11	12,36	6,33	21,04	5,02	23,92
12	13,48	7,17	22,37	5,75	25,30
13	14,61	8,01	23,68	6,51	26,66
14	15,73	8,88	24,98	7,29	28,00
15	16,85	9,75	26,27	8,08	29,32
16	17,98	10,64	27,55	8,89	30,63
17	19,10	11,54	28,81	9,71	31,93
18	20,22	12,45	30,07	10,55	33,21
19	21,35	13,37	31,31	11,39	34,48
20	22,47	14,30	32,55	12,26	35,74
21	23,60	15,24	33,78	13,13	36,99
22	24,72	16,19	35,00	14,01	38,22
23	25,84	17,14	36,21	14,91	39,45
24	26,97	18,10	37,42	15,81	40,67
25	28,09	19,07	38,62	16,72	41,87
26	29,21	20,05	39,81	17,65	43,07
27	30,34	21,03	40,99	18,58	44,27
28	31,46	22,03	42,17	19,52	45,45
29	32,58	23,02	43,34	20,47	46,62
30	33,71	24,03	44,51	21,42	47,79
31	34,83	25,04	45,67	22,39	48,95
32	35,96	26,05	46,82	23,36	50,10
33	37,08	27,07	47,97	24,34	51,24
34	38,20	28,10	49,11	25,32	52,38
35	39,33	29,13	50,25	26,32	53,51
36	40,45	30,17	51,38	27,32	54,63
37	41,57	31,21	52,51	28,33	55,75
38	42,70	32,26	53,63	29,34	56,85
39	43,82	33,32	54,75	30,36	57,96
40	44,94	34,38	55,86	31,39	59,05
41	46,07	35,44	56,96	32,43	60,14
42	47,19	36,51	58,06	33,47	61,22
43	48,31	37,59	59,16	34,52	62,30
44	49,44	38,67	60,25	35,57	63,36
45	50,56	39,75	61,33	36,64	64,43
46	51,69	40,84	62,41	37,70	65,48
47	52,81	41,94	63,49	38,78	66,53
48	53,93	43,04	64,56	39,86	67,57
49	55,06	44,14	65,62	40,95	68,61
50	56,18	45,25	66,68	42,04	69,64
51	57,30	46,37	67,74	43,15	70,66
52	58,43	47,49	68,79	44,25	71,67
53	59,55	48,62	69,83	45,37	72,68
54	60,67	49,75	70,87	46,49	73,68
55	61,80	50,89	71,90	47,62	74,68
56	62,92	52,03	72,93	48,76	75,66
57	64,04	53,18	73,95	49,90	76,64
58	65,17	54,33	74,96	51,05	77,61
59	66,29	55,49	75,97	52,21	78,58
60	67,42	56,66	76,98	53,38	79,53
61	68,54	57,83	77,97	54,55	80,48
62	69,66	59,01	78,97	55,73	81,42
63	70,79	60,19	79,95	56,93	82,35
64	71,91	61,38	80,93	58,13	83,28
65	73,03	62,58	81,90	59,33	84,19
66	74,16	63,79	82,86	60,55	85,09
67	75,28	65,00	83,81	61,78	85,99
68	76,40	66,22	84,76	63,01	86,87
69	77,53	67,45	85,70	64,26	87,74
70	78,65	68,69	86,63	65,52	88,61
71	79,78	69,93	87,55	66,79	89,45
72	80,90	71,19	88,46	68,07	90,29
73	82,02	72,45	89,36	69,37	91,11
74	83,15	73,73	90,25	70,68	91,92
75	84,27	75,02	91,12	72,00	92,71
76	85,39	76,32	91,99	73,34	93,49
77	86,52	77,63	92,83	74,70	94,25
78	87,64	78,96	93,67	76,08	94,98
79	88,76	80,31	94,48	77,47	95,69
80	89,89	81,67	95,27	78,89	96,38
81	91,01	83,05	96,04	80,34	97,04
82	92,13	84,46	96,78	81,82	97,66
83	93,26	85,90	97,49	83,34	98,24
84	94,38	87,37	98,15	84,90	98,77
85	95,51	88,89	98,76	86,52	99,23
86	96,63	90,46	99,30	88,21	99,62
87	97,75	92,12	99,73	90,00	99,88
88	98,88	93,90	99,97	91,95	99,99
89	100,00	95,94	100,00	94,22	100,00

N = 90

x	100 p_x	95% 100 p_l	95% 100 p_r	99% 100 p_l	99% 100 p_r
0	0,00	0,00	4,02	0,00	5,72
1	1,11	0,03	6,04	0,01	7,97
2	2,22	0,27	7,80	0,12	9,90
3	3,33	0,69	9,43	0,38	11,67
4	4,44	1,22	10,99	0,76	13,34
5	5,56	1,83	12,49	1,22	14,94
6	6,67	2,49	13,95	1,74	16,48
7	7,78	3,18	15,37	2,32	17,99
8	8,89	3,92	16,77	2,93	19,45

All values conform to the international convention (i.e. 0,1 instead of 0.1).

N: number of trials; x: number of successes, etc.; $100\,p_x = 100\,x/N$

N = 90 (continued)

x	$100\,p_x$	95% $100\,p_l$	95% $100\,p_r$	99% $100\,p_l$	99% $100\,p_r$
9	10,00	4,68	18,14	3,58	20,89
10	11,11	5,46	19,49	4,26	22,29
11	12,22	6,26	20,82	4,96	23,68
12	13,33	7,08	22,13	5,69	25,04
13	14,44	7,92	23,43	6,44	26,38
14	15,56	8,77	24,72	7,20	27,71
15	16,67	9,64	26,00	7,98	29,02
16	17,78	10,52	27,26	8,78	30,32
17	18,89	11,41	28,51	9,60	31,60
18	20,00	12,31	29,75	10,42	32,87
19	21,11	13,22	30,99	11,26	34,13
20	22,22	14,13	32,21	12,11	35,38
21	23,33	15,06	33,43	12,97	36,61
22	24,44	16,00	34,64	13,85	37,84
23	25,56	16,94	35,84	14,73	39,05
24	26,67	17,89	37,03	15,62	40,26
25	27,78	18,85	38,22	16,53	41,46
26	28,89	19,82	39,40	17,44	42,65
27	30,00	20,79	40,57	18,36	43,83
28	31,11	21,77	41,74	19,28	45,00
29	32,22	22,75	42,90	20,22	46,16
30	33,33	23,74	44,05	21,16	47,32
31	34,44	24,74	45,20	22,12	48,47
32	35,56	25,74	46,35	23,08	49,61
33	36,67	26,75	47,49	24,04	50,74
34	37,78	27,77	48,62	25,02	51,87
35	38,89	28,79	49,74	26,00	52,99
36	40,00	29,81	50,87	26,99	54,10
37	41,11	30,84	51,98	27,98	55,21
38	42,22	31,88	53,09	28,98	56,31
39	43,33	32,92	54,20	29,99	57,40
40	44,44	33,96	55,30	31,01	58,49
41	45,56	35,02	56,40	32,03	59,57
42	46,67	36,07	57,49	33,06	60,64
43	47,78	37,13	58,57	34,09	61,71
44	48,89	38,20	59,65	35,13	62,77
45	50,00	39,27	60,73	36,18	63,82
46	51,11	40,35	61,80	37,23	64,87
47	52,22	41,43	62,87	38,29	65,91
48	53,33	42,51	63,93	39,36	66,94
49	54,44	43,60	64,98	40,43	67,97
50	55,56	44,70	66,04	41,51	68,99
51	56,67	45,80	67,08	42,60	70,01
52	57,78	46,91	68,12	43,69	71,02
53	58,89	48,02	69,16	44,79	72,02
54	60,00	49,13	70,19	45,90	73,01
55	61,11	50,26	71,21	47,01	74,00
56	62,22	51,38	72,23	48,13	74,98
57	63,33	52,51	73,25	49,26	75,96
58	64,44	53,65	74,26	50,39	76,92
59	65,56	54,80	75,26	51,53	77,88
60	66,67	55,95	76,26	52,68	78,84
61	67,78	57,10	77,25	53,84	79,78
62	68,89	58,26	78,23	55,00	80,72
63	70,00	59,43	79,21	56,17	81,64
64	71,11	60,60	80,18	57,35	82,56
65	72,22	61,78	81,15	58,54	83,47
66	73,33	62,97	82,11	59,74	84,38
67	74,44	64,16	83,06	60,95	85,27
68	75,56	65,36	84,00	62,16	86,15
69	76,67	66,57	84,94	63,39	87,03
70	77,78	67,79	85,87	64,62	87,89
71	78,89	69,01	86,78	65,87	88,74
72	80,00	70,25	87,69	67,13	89,58
73	81,11	71,49	88,59	68,40	90,40
74	82,22	72,74	89,48	69,68	91,22
75	83,33	74,00	90,36	70,98	92,02
76	84,44	75,28	91,23	72,29	92,80
77	85,56	76,57	92,08	73,62	93,56
78	86,67	77,87	92,92	74,96	94,31
79	87,78	79,18	93,74	76,32	95,04
80	88,89	80,51	94,54	77,71	95,74
81	90,00	81,86	95,32	79,11	96,42
82	91,11	83,23	96,08	80,55	97,07
83	92,22	84,63	96,82	82,01	97,68
84	93,33	86,05	97,51	83,52	98,26
85	94,44	87,51	98,17	85,06	98,78
86	95,56	89,01	98,78	86,66	99,24
87	96,67	90,57	99,31	88,33	99,62
88	97,78	92,20	99,73	90,10	99,88
89	98,89	93,96	99,97	92,03	99,99
90	100,00	95,98	100,00	94,28	100,00

N = 91

x	$100\,p_x$	95% $100\,p_l$	95% $100\,p_r$	99% $100\,p_l$	99% $100\,p_r$
0	0,00	0,00	3,97	0,00	5,66
1	1,10	0,03	5,97	0,01	7,88
2	2,20	0,27	7,71	0,11	9,79
3	3,30	0,69	9,33	0,38	11,55
4	4,40	1,21	10,87	0,75	13,20
5	5,49	1,81	12,36	1,20	14,78
6	6,59	2,46	13,80	1,72	16,31
7	7,69	3,15	15,21	2,29	17,80
8	8,79	3,87	16,59	2,90	19,25
9	9,89	4,62	17,95	3,54	20,67
10	10,99	5,40	19,28	4,21	22,06
11	12,09	6,19	20,60	4,91	23,43
12	13,19	7,00	21,90	5,62	24,78
13	14,29	7,83	23,19	6,36	26,12

N = 91 (continued)

x	$100\,p_x$	95% $100\,p_l$	95% $100\,p_r$	99% $100\,p_l$	99% $100\,p_r$
14	15,38	8,67	24,46	7,12	27,43
15	16,48	9,53	25,73	7,89	28,73
16	17,58	10,40	26,98	8,68	30,01
17	18,68	11,28	28,22	9,49	31,28
18	19,78	12,17	29,45	10,30	32,54
19	20,88	13,06	30,67	11,13	33,79
20	21,98	13,97	31,88	11,97	35,02
21	23,08	14,89	33,09	12,82	36,25
22	24,18	15,81	34,28	13,69	37,46
23	25,27	16,75	35,47	14,56	38,66
24	26,37	17,69	36,65	15,44	39,86
25	27,47	18,63	37,83	16,33	41,05
26	28,57	19,59	39,00	17,23	42,22
27	29,67	20,55	40,16	18,14	43,39
28	30,77	21,51	41,32	19,06	44,56
29	31,87	22,49	42,47	19,98	45,71
30	32,97	23,47	43,61	20,91	46,85
31	34,07	24,45	44,75	21,85	47,99
32	35,16	25,44	45,88	22,80	49,12
33	36,26	26,44	47,01	23,76	50,25
34	37,36	27,44	48,13	24,72	51,37
35	38,46	28,45	49,25	25,69	52,48
36	39,56	29,46	50,36	26,66	53,58
37	40,66	30,48	51,47	27,65	54,68
38	41,76	31,50	52,57	28,63	55,77
39	42,86	32,53	53,66	29,63	56,85
40	43,96	33,56	54,75	30,63	57,93
41	45,05	34,60	55,84	31,64	59,00
42	46,15	35,64	56,92	32,65	60,07
43	47,25	36,69	58,00	33,68	61,12
44	48,35	37,74	59,07	34,70	62,18
45	49,45	38,80	60,14	35,74	63,22
46	50,55	39,86	61,20	36,78	64,26
47	51,65	40,93	62,26	37,82	65,30
48	52,75	42,00	63,31	38,88	66,32
49	53,85	43,08	64,36	39,93	67,35
50	54,95	44,16	65,40	41,00	68,36
51	56,04	45,25	66,44	42,07	69,37
52	57,14	46,34	67,47	43,15	70,37
53	58,24	47,43	68,50	44,23	71,37
54	59,34	48,53	69,52	45,32	72,35
55	60,44	49,64	70,54	46,42	73,34
56	61,54	50,75	71,55	47,52	74,31
57	62,64	51,87	72,56	48,63	75,28
58	63,74	52,99	73,56	49,75	76,24
59	64,84	54,12	74,56	50,88	77,20
60	65,93	55,25	75,55	52,01	78,15
61	67,03	56,39	76,53	53,15	79,09
62	68,13	57,53	77,51	54,29	80,02
63	69,23	58,68	78,49	55,44	80,94
64	70,33	59,84	79,45	56,61	81,86
65	71,43	61,00	80,41	57,78	82,77
66	72,53	62,17	81,37	58,95	83,67
67	73,63	63,35	82,31	60,14	84,56
68	74,73	64,53	83,25	61,34	85,44
69	75,82	65,72	84,19	62,54	86,31
70	76,92	66,91	85,11	63,75	87,18
71	78,02	68,12	86,03	64,98	88,03
72	79,12	69,33	86,94	66,21	88,87
73	80,22	70,55	87,83	67,46	89,70
74	81,32	71,78	88,72	68,72	90,51
75	82,42	73,02	89,60	69,99	91,32
76	83,52	74,27	90,47	71,27	92,11
77	84,62	75,54	91,33	72,57	92,88
78	85,71	76,81	92,17	73,88	93,64
79	86,81	78,10	93,00	75,22	94,38
80	87,91	79,40	93,81	76,57	95,09
81	89,01	80,72	94,60	77,94	95,79
82	90,11	82,05	95,38	79,33	96,46
83	91,21	83,41	96,13	80,75	97,10
84	92,31	84,79	96,85	82,20	97,71
85	93,41	86,20	97,54	83,69	98,28
86	94,51	87,64	98,19	85,22	98,80
87	95,60	89,13	98,79	86,80	99,25
88	96,70	90,67	99,31	88,45	99,62
89	97,80	92,29	99,73	90,21	99,89
90	98,90	94,03	99,97	92,12	99,99
91	100,00	96,03	100,00	94,34	100,00

N = 92

x	$100\,p_x$	95% $100\,p_l$	95% $100\,p_r$	99% $100\,p_l$	99% $100\,p_r$
0	0,00	0,00	3,93	0,00	5,60
1	1,09	0,03	5,91	0,01	7,80
2	2,17	0,26	7,63	0,11	9,69
3	3,26	0,68	9,24	0,37	11,43
4	4,35	1,20	10,76	0,74	13,06
5	5,43	1,79	12,23	1,19	14,63
6	6,52	2,43	13,66	1,70	16,15
7	7,61	3,11	15,05	2,27	17,62
8	8,70	3,83	16,42	2,87	19,05
9	9,78	4,57	17,76	3,50	20,46
10	10,87	5,34	19,08	4,16	21,84
11	11,96	6,12	20,39	4,85	23,20
12	13,04	6,93	21,68	5,56	24,53
13	14,13	7,74	22,95	6,29	25,85
14	15,22	8,58	24,21	7,04	27,15
15	16,30	9,42	25,46	7,80	28,44
16	17,39	10,28	26,70	8,58	29,71
17	18,48	11,15	27,93	9,38	30,97

N = 92 (continued)

x	$100\,p_x$	95% $100\,p_l$	95% $100\,p_r$	99% $100\,p_l$	99% $100\,p_r$
18	19,57	12,03	29,15	10,18	32,22
19	20,65	12,92	30,36	11,00	33,45
20	21,74	13,81	31,56	11,83	34,67
21	22,83	14,72	32,75	12,68	35,89
22	23,91	15,63	33,94	13,53	37,09
23	25,00	16,55	35,11	14,39	38,28
24	26,09	17,48	36,29	15,26	39,47
25	27,17	18,42	37,45	16,14	40,64
26	28,26	19,36	38,61	17,03	41,81
27	29,35	20,31	39,76	17,93	42,97
28	30,43	21,27	40,90	18,83	44,12
29	31,52	22,23	42,04	19,75	45,27
30	32,61	23,20	43,18	20,67	46,40
31	33,70	24,17	44,30	21,60	47,53
32	34,78	25,15	45,43	22,53	48,65
33	35,87	26,13	46,54	23,48	49,77
34	36,96	27,12	47,66	24,43	50,87
35	38,04	28,12	48,76	25,38	51,98
36	39,13	29,12	49,86	26,35	53,07
37	40,22	30,12	50,96	27,32	54,16
38	41,30	31,13	52,05	28,29	55,24
39	42,39	32,15	53,14	29,28	56,32
40	43,48	33,17	54,22	30,27	57,38
41	44,57	34,19	55,30	31,26	58,45
42	45,65	35,22	56,37	32,26	59,50
43	46,74	36,26	57,44	33,27	60,55
44	47,83	37,30	58,50	34,28	61,60
45	48,91	38,34	59,56	35,30	62,64
46	50,00	39,39	60,61	36,33	63,67
47	51,09	40,44	61,66	37,36	64,70
48	52,17	41,50	62,70	38,40	65,72
49	53,26	42,56	63,74	39,45	66,73
50	54,35	43,63	64,78	40,50	67,74
51	55,43	44,70	65,81	41,55	68,74
52	56,52	45,78	66,83	42,62	69,73
53	57,61	46,86	67,85	43,68	70,72
54	58,70	47,95	68,87	44,76	71,71
55	59,78	49,04	69,88	45,84	72,68
56	60,87	50,14	70,88	46,93	73,65
57	61,96	51,24	71,88	48,02	74,62
58	63,04	52,34	72,88	49,13	75,57
59	64,13	53,46	73,87	50,23	76,52
60	65,22	54,57	74,85	51,35	77,47
61	66,30	55,70	75,83	52,47	78,40
62	67,39	56,82	76,80	53,60	79,33
63	68,48	57,96	77,77	54,73	80,25
64	69,57	59,10	78,73	55,88	81,17
65	70,65	60,24	79,69	57,03	82,07
66	71,74	61,39	80,64	58,19	82,97
67	72,83	62,55	81,58	59,36	83,86
68	73,91	63,71	82,52	60,53	84,74
69	75,00	64,89	83,45	61,72	85,61
70	76,09	66,06	84,37	62,91	86,47
71	77,17	67,25	85,28	64,11	87,32
72	78,26	68,44	86,19	65,33	88,17
73	79,35	69,64	87,08	66,55	89,00
74	80,43	70,85	87,97	67,78	89,82
75	81,52	72,07	88,85	69,03	90,62
76	82,61	73,30	89,72	70,29	91,42
77	83,70	74,54	90,58	71,56	92,20
78	84,78	75,79	91,42	72,85	92,96
79	85,87	77,05	92,26	74,15	93,71
80	86,96	78,32	93,07	75,47	94,44
81	88,04	79,61	93,88	76,80	95,15
82	89,13	80,92	94,66	78,16	95,84
83	90,22	82,24	95,43	79,54	96,50
84	91,30	83,58	96,17	80,95	97,13
85	92,39	84,95	96,89	82,38	97,73
86	93,48	86,34	97,57	83,85	98,30
87	94,57	87,77	98,21	85,37	98,81
88	95,65	89,24	98,80	86,94	99,26
89	96,74	90,76	99,32	88,57	99,63
90	97,83	92,37	99,74	90,31	99,89
91	98,91	94,09	99,97	92,20	99,99
92	100,00	96,07	100,00	94,40	100,00

N = 93

x	$100\,p_x$	95% $100\,p_l$	95% $100\,p_r$	99% $100\,p_l$	99% $100\,p_r$
0	0,00	0,00	3,89	0,00	5,54
1	1,08	0,03	5,85	0,01	7,72
2	2,15	0,26	7,55	0,11	9,59
3	3,23	0,67	9,14	0,37	11,31
4	4,30	1,18	10,65	0,73	12,93
5	5,38	1,77	12,10	1,18	14,48
6	6,45	2,41	13,52	1,68	15,98
7	7,53	3,08	14,90	2,24	17,44
8	8,60	3,79	16,25	2,83	18,86
9	9,68	4,52	17,58	3,46	20,25
10	10,75	5,28	18,89	4,12	21,62
11	11,83	6,05	20,18	4,80	22,96
12	12,90	6,85	21,45	5,50	24,29
13	13,98	7,66	22,72	6,22	25,59
14	15,05	8,48	23,97	6,96	26,88
15	16,13	9,32	25,20	7,72	28,16
16	17,20	10,17	26,43	8,49	29,42
17	18,28	11,02	27,65	9,27	30,66
18	19,35	11,89	28,85	10,07	31,90
19	20,43	12,77	30,05	10,88	33,12
20	21,51	13,66	31,24	11,70	34,33

N = 93 (continued)

x	$100\,p_x$	95% $100\,p_l$	95% $100\,p_r$	99% $100\,p_l$	99% $100\,p_r$
21	22,58	14,55	32,42	12,53	35,54
22	23,66	15,46	33,60	13,37	36,73
23	24,73	16,37	34,76	14,23	37,91
24	25,81	17,29	35,92	15,09	39,08
25	26,88	18,21	37,08	15,96	40,25
26	27,96	19,14	38,22	16,84	41,41
27	29,03	20,08	39,36	17,72	42,56
28	30,11	21,03	40,50	18,62	43,70
29	31,18	21,98	41,63	19,52	44,83
30	32,26	22,93	42,75	20,43	45,96
31	33,33	23,89	43,87	21,35	47,08
32	34,41	24,86	44,98	22,27	48,19
33	35,48	25,83	46,09	23,20	49,29
34	36,56	26,81	47,19	24,14	50,39
35	37,63	27,79	48,28	25,09	51,48
36	38,71	28,78	49,38	26,04	52,57
37	39,78	29,78	50,46	27,00	53,65
38	40,86	30,77	51,54	27,96	54,72
39	41,94	31,78	52,62	28,93	55,79
40	43,01	32,78	53,69	29,91	56,85
41	44,09	33,80	54,76	30,89	57,90
42	45,16	34,81	55,83	31,88	58,95
43	46,24	35,84	56,88	32,87	59,99
44	47,31	36,86	57,94	33,88	61,03
45	48,39	37,89	58,99	34,88	62,06
46	49,46	38,93	60,03	35,90	63,09
47	50,54	39,97	61,07	36,91	64,10
48	51,61	41,01	62,11	37,94	65,12
49	52,69	42,06	63,14	38,97	66,12
50	53,76	43,12	64,16	40,01	67,13
51	54,84	44,17	65,19	41,05	68,12
52	55,91	45,24	66,20	42,10	69,11
53	56,99	46,31	67,22	43,15	70,09
54	58,06	47,38	68,22	44,21	71,07
55	59,14	48,46	69,23	45,28	72,04
56	60,22	49,54	70,22	46,35	73,00
57	61,29	50,62	71,22	47,43	73,96
58	62,37	51,72	72,21	48,52	74,91
59	63,44	52,81	73,19	49,61	75,86
60	64,52	53,91	74,17	50,71	76,80
61	65,59	55,02	75,14	51,81	77,73
62	66,67	56,13	76,11	52,92	78,65
63	67,74	57,25	77,07	54,04	79,57
64	68,82	58,37	78,02	55,17	80,48
65	69,89	59,50	78,97	56,30	81,38
66	70,97	60,64	79,92	57,44	82,28
67	72,04	61,78	80,86	58,59	83,16
68	73,12	62,92	81,79	59,75	84,04
69	74,19	64,08	82,71	60,92	84,91
70	75,27	65,24	83,63	62,09	85,77
71	76,34	66,40	84,54	63,27	86,63
72	77,42	67,58	85,45	64,46	87,47
73	78,49	68,76	86,34	65,67	88,30
74	79,57	69,95	87,23	66,88	89,12
75	80,65	71,15	88,11	68,10	89,93
76	81,72	72,35	88,98	69,34	90,73
77	82,80	73,57	89,83	70,58	91,51
78	83,87	74,80	90,68	71,84	92,28
79	84,95	76,03	91,52	73,12	93,04
80	86,02	77,28	92,34	74,41	93,78
81	87,10	78,55	93,15	75,71	94,50
82	88,17	79,82	93,95	77,04	95,20
83	89,25	81,11	94,72	78,38	95,88
84	90,32	82,42	95,48	79,75	96,54
85	91,40	83,75	96,21	81,14	97,17
86	92,47	85,10	96,92	82,56	97,76
87	93,55	86,48	97,59	84,02	98,32
88	94,62	87,90	98,23	85,52	98,82
89	95,70	89,35	98,82	87,07	99,27
90	96,77	90,86	99,33	88,69	99,63
91	97,85	92,45	99,74	90,41	99,89
92	98,92	94,15	99,97	92,28	99,99
93	100,00	96,11	100,00	94,46	100,00

N = 94

x	$100\,p_x$	95% $100\,p_l$	95% $100\,p_r$	99% $100\,p_l$	99% $100\,p_r$
0	0,00	0,00	3,85	0,00	5,48
1	1,06	0,03	5,79	0,01	7,64
2	2,13	0,26	7,48	0,11	9,49
3	3,19	0,66	9,04	0,36	11,19
4	4,26	1,17	10,54	0,72	12,80
5	5,32	1,75	11,98	1,17	14,33
6	6,38	2,38	13,38	1,67	15,82
7	7,45	3,05	14,74	2,22	17,26
8	8,51	3,75	16,08	2,80	18,67
9	9,57	4,47	17,40	3,42	20,05
10	10,64	5,22	18,70	4,07	21,40
11	11,70	5,99	19,97	4,74	22,74
12	12,77	6,77	21,24	5,44	24,05
13	13,83	7,57	22,49	6,15	25,34
14	14,89	8,39	23,72	6,88	26,62
15	15,96	9,22	24,95	7,63	27,88
16	17,02	10,05	26,16	8,39	29,13
17	18,09	10,90	27,37	9,17	30,36
18	19,15	11,76	28,56	9,96	31,59
19	20,21	12,63	29,75	10,76	32,80
20	21,28	13,51	30,93	11,57	34,00
21	22,34	14,39	32,10	12,39	35,19
22	23,40	15,29	33,26	13,22	36,37

All values conform to the international convention (i.e. 0,1 instead of 0.1).

N: number of trials; x: number of successes, etc.; $100\,p_x = 100\,x/N$

N=94 (continued)

x	$100\,p_x$	95% $100\,p_l$	95% $100\,p_r$	99% $100\,p_l$	99% $100\,p_r$
23	24,47	16,19	34,42	14,07	37,54
24	25,53	17,09	35,57	14,92	38,71
25	26,60	18,01	36,71	15,78	39,86
26	27,66	18,93	37,85	16,65	41,01
27	28,72	19,86	38,98	17,52	42,15
28	29,79	20,79	40,10	18,41	43,28
29	30,85	21,73	41,22	19,30	44,40
30	31,91	22,67	42,33	20,20	45,52
31	32,98	23,62	43,44	21,10	46,63
32	34,04	24,58	44,54	22,02	47,73
33	35,11	25,54	45,64	22,94	48,83
34	36,17	26,51	46,73	23,86	49,92
35	37,23	27,48	47,82	24,80	51,00
36	38,30	28,46	48,90	25,74	52,08
37	39,36	29,44	49,98	26,68	53,15
38	40,43	30,42	51,05	27,64	54,21
39	41,49	31,41	52,12	28,59	55,27
40	42,55	32,41	53,18	29,56	56,32
41	43,62	33,41	54,24	30,53	57,37
42	44,68	34,41	55,29	31,51	58,41
43	45,74	35,42	56,34	32,49	59,44
44	46,81	36,44	57,39	33,48	60,47
45	47,87	37,46	58,43	34,47	61,50
46	48,94	38,48	59,46	35,47	62,51
47	50,00	39,51	60,49	36,48	63,52
48	51,06	40,54	61,52	37,49	64,53
49	52,13	41,57	62,54	38,50	65,53
50	53,19	42,61	63,56	39,53	66,52
51	54,26	43,66	64,58	40,56	67,51
52	55,32	44,71	65,59	41,59	68,49
53	56,38	45,76	66,59	42,63	69,47
54	57,45	46,82	67,59	43,68	70,44
55	58,51	47,88	68,59	44,73	71,41
56	59,57	48,95	69,58	45,79	72,36
57	60,64	50,02	70,56	46,85	73,32
58	61,70	51,10	71,54	47,92	74,26
59	62,77	52,18	72,52	49,00	75,20
60	63,83	53,27	73,49	50,08	76,14
61	64,89	54,36	74,46	51,17	77,06
62	65,96	55,46	75,42	52,27	77,98
63	67,02	56,56	76,38	53,37	78,90
64	68,09	57,67	77,33	54,48	79,80
65	69,15	58,78	78,27	55,60	80,70
66	70,21	59,90	79,21	56,72	81,59
67	71,28	61,02	80,14	57,85	82,48
68	72,34	62,15	81,07	58,99	83,35
69	73,40	63,29	81,99	60,14	84,22
70	74,47	64,43	82,91	61,29	85,08
71	75,53	65,58	83,81	62,46	85,93
72	76,60	66,74	84,71	63,63	86,78
73	77,66	67,90	85,61	64,81	87,61
74	78,72	69,07	86,49	66,00	88,43
75	79,79	70,25	87,37	67,20	89,24
76	80,85	71,44	88,24	68,41	90,04
77	81,91	72,63	89,10	69,64	90,83
78	82,98	73,84	89,95	70,87	91,61
79	84,04	75,05	90,78	72,12	92,37
80	85,11	76,28	91,61	73,38	93,12
81	86,17	77,51	92,43	74,66	93,85
82	87,23	78,76	93,23	75,95	94,56
83	88,30	80,03	94,01	77,26	95,26
84	89,36	81,30	94,78	78,60	95,93
85	90,43	82,60	95,53	79,95	96,58
86	91,49	83,92	96,25	81,33	97,20
87	92,55	85,26	96,95	82,74	97,78
88	93,62	86,62	97,62	84,18	98,33
89	94,68	88,02	98,25	85,67	98,83
90	95,74	89,46	98,83	87,20	99,28
91	96,81	90,96	99,34	88,81	99,64
92	97,87	92,52	99,74	90,51	99,89
93	98,94	94,21	99,97	92,36	99,99
94	100,00	96,15	100,00	94,52	100,00

N=95

x	$100\,p_x$	95% $100\,p_l$	95% $100\,p_r$	99% $100\,p_l$	99% $100\,p_r$
0	0,00	0,00	3,81	0,00	5,42
1	1,05	0,03	5,73	0,01	7,56
2	2,11	0,26	7,40	0,11	9,40
3	3,16	0,66	8,95	0,36	11,08
4	4,21	1,16	10,43	0,72	12,67
5	5,26	1,73	11,86	1,15	14,19
6	6,32	2,35	13,24	1,65	15,66
7	7,37	3,01	14,59	2,19	17,09
8	8,42	3,71	15,92	2,77	18,49
9	9,47	4,42	17,22	3,39	19,85
10	10,53	5,16	18,51	4,03	21,19
11	11,58	5,92	19,77	4,69	22,51
12	12,63	6,70	21,03	5,38	23,81
13	13,68	7,49	22,26	6,08	25,09
14	14,74	8,30	23,49	6,81	26,36
15	15,79	9,12	24,70	7,55	27,61
16	16,84	9,94	25,90	8,30	28,84
17	17,89	10,78	27,10	9,07	30,07
18	18,95	11,63	28,28	9,85	31,28
19	20,00	12,49	29,46	10,64	32,48
20	21,05	13,36	30,62	11,44	33,67
21	22,11	14,23	31,78	12,25	34,85
22	23,16	15,12	32,94	13,08	36,02
23	24,21	16,01	34,08	13,91	37,18

N=95 (continued)

x	$100\,p_x$	95% $100\,p_l$	95% $100\,p_r$	99% $100\,p_l$	99% $100\,p_r$
24	25,26	16,91	35,22	14,75	38,34
25	26,32	17,81	36,35	15,60	39,48
26	27,37	18,72	37,48	16,46	40,62
27	28,42	19,64	38,60	17,33	41,75
28	29,47	20,56	39,71	18,20	42,87
29	30,53	21,49	40,82	19,08	43,98
30	31,58	22,42	41,92	19,97	45,09
31	32,63	23,36	43,02	20,86	46,19
32	33,68	24,31	44,11	21,77	47,28
33	34,74	25,26	45,20	22,68	48,37
34	35,79	26,21	46,28	23,59	49,45
35	36,84	27,17	47,36	24,51	50,53
36	37,89	28,14	48,43	25,44	51,59
37	38,95	29,11	49,50	26,38	52,66
38	40,00	30,08	50,56	27,32	53,71
39	41,05	31,06	51,62	28,27	54,76
40	42,11	32,04	52,67	29,22	55,81
41	43,16	33,03	53,72	30,18	56,84
42	44,21	34,02	54,77	31,14	57,88
43	45,26	35,02	55,81	32,11	58,90
44	46,32	36,02	56,85	33,09	59,92
45	47,37	37,03	57,88	34,07	60,94
46	48,42	38,04	58,90	35,06	61,95
47	49,47	39,05	59,93	36,05	62,95
48	50,53	40,07	60,95	37,05	63,95
49	51,58	41,10	61,96	38,05	64,94
50	52,63	42,12	62,97	39,06	65,93
51	53,68	43,15	63,98	40,08	66,91
52	54,74	44,19	64,98	41,10	67,89
53	55,79	45,23	65,98	42,12	68,86
54	56,84	46,28	66,97	43,16	69,82
55	57,89	47,33	67,96	44,19	70,78
56	58,95	48,38	68,94	45,24	71,73
57	60,00	49,44	69,92	46,29	72,68
58	61,05	50,50	70,89	47,34	73,62
59	62,11	51,57	71,86	48,41	74,56
60	63,16	52,64	72,83	49,47	75,49
61	64,21	53,72	73,79	50,55	76,41
62	65,26	54,80	74,74	51,63	77,32
63	66,32	55,89	75,69	52,72	78,23
64	67,37	56,98	76,64	53,81	79,14
65	68,42	58,08	77,58	54,91	80,03
66	69,47	59,18	78,51	56,02	80,92
67	70,53	60,29	79,44	57,13	81,80
68	71,58	61,40	80,36	58,25	82,67
69	72,63	62,52	81,28	59,38	83,54
70	73,68	63,65	82,19	60,52	84,40
71	74,74	64,78	83,09	61,66	85,25
72	75,79	65,92	83,99	62,82	86,09
73	76,84	67,06	84,88	63,98	86,92
74	77,89	68,22	85,77	65,15	87,75
75	78,95	69,38	86,64	66,33	88,56
76	80,00	70,55	87,51	67,52	89,36
77	81,05	71,72	88,37	68,72	90,15
78	82,11	72,90	89,22	69,93	90,93
79	83,16	74,10	90,06	71,16	91,70
80	84,21	75,30	90,88	72,39	92,45
81	85,26	76,51	91,70	73,64	93,19
82	86,32	77,74	92,51	74,91	93,92
83	87,37	78,97	93,30	76,19	94,62
84	88,42	80,23	94,08	77,49	95,31
85	89,47	81,49	94,84	78,81	95,97
86	90,53	82,78	95,58	80,15	96,61
87	91,58	84,08	96,29	81,51	97,23
88	92,63	85,41	96,99	82,91	97,81
89	93,68	86,76	97,65	84,34	98,35
90	94,74	88,14	98,27	85,81	98,85
91	95,79	89,57	98,84	87,33	99,28
92	96,84	91,05	99,34	88,92	99,64
93	97,89	92,60	99,74	90,60	99,89
94	98,95	94,27	99,97	92,44	99,99
95	100,00	96,19	100,00	94,58	100,00

N=96

x	$100\,p_x$	95% $100\,p_l$	95% $100\,p_r$	99% $100\,p_l$	99% $100\,p_r$
0	0,00	0,00	3,77	0,00	5,37
1	1,04	0,03	5,67	0,01	7,49
2	2,08	0,25	7,32	0,11	9,30
3	3,13	0,65	8,86	0,36	10,97
4	4,17	1,15	10,33	0,71	12,54
5	5,21	1,71	11,74	1,14	14,05
6	6,25	2,33	13,11	1,63	15,51
7	7,29	2,98	14,45	2,17	16,92
8	8,33	3,67	15,76	2,74	18,30
9	9,38	4,38	17,05	3,35	19,66
10	10,42	5,11	18,32	3,98	20,99
11	11,46	5,86	19,58	4,64	22,29
12	12,50	6,63	20,82	5,32	23,58
13	13,54	7,41	22,04	6,02	24,85
14	14,58	8,21	23,26	6,73	26,10
15	15,63	9,02	24,46	7,47	27,34
16	16,67	9,84	25,65	8,21	28,57
17	17,71	10,67	26,83	8,97	29,78
18	18,75	11,51	28,00	9,74	30,98
19	19,79	12,36	29,17	10,52	32,17
20	20,83	13,21	30,33	11,32	33,35
21	21,88	14,08	31,47	12,12	34,52
22	22,92	14,95	32,62	12,93	35,68
23	23,96	15,83	33,75	13,76	36,83

N=96 (continued)

x	$100\,p_x$	95% $100\,p_l$	95% $100\,p_r$	99% $100\,p_l$	99% $100\,p_r$
24	25,00	16,72	34,88	14,59	37,98
25	26,04	17,62	36,00	15,43	39,11
26	27,08	18,52	37,11	16,28	40,24
27	28,13	19,42	38,22	17,13	41,36
28	29,17	20,33	39,33	18,00	42,47
29	30,21	21,25	40,43	18,87	43,57
30	31,25	22,18	41,52	19,75	44,67
31	32,29	23,10	42,61	20,63	45,76
32	33,33	24,04	43,69	21,52	46,85
33	34,38	24,98	44,77	22,42	47,92
34	35,42	25,92	45,84	23,33	48,99
35	36,46	26,87	46,91	24,24	50,06
36	37,50	27,82	47,97	25,16	51,12
37	38,54	28,78	49,03	26,08	52,17
38	39,58	29,75	50,08	27,01	53,22
39	40,63	30,71	51,13	27,94	54,26
40	41,67	31,68	52,18	28,88	55,30
41	42,71	32,66	53,22	29,83	56,33
42	43,75	33,64	54,25	30,78	57,35
43	44,79	34,63	55,29	31,74	58,37
44	45,83	35,62	56,31	32,71	59,38
45	46,88	36,61	57,34	33,68	60,39
46	47,92	37,61	58,36	34,65	61,39
47	48,96	38,61	59,37	35,63	62,39
48	50,00	39,62	60,38	36,62	63,38
49	51,04	40,63	61,39	37,61	64,37
50	52,08	41,64	62,39	38,61	65,35
51	53,13	42,66	63,39	39,61	66,32
52	54,17	43,69	64,38	40,62	67,29
53	55,21	44,71	65,37	41,63	68,26
54	56,25	45,75	66,36	42,65	69,22
55	57,29	46,78	67,34	43,67	70,17
56	58,33	47,82	68,32	44,70	71,12
57	59,38	48,87	69,29	45,74	72,06
58	60,42	49,92	70,25	46,78	72,99
59	61,46	50,97	71,22	47,83	73,92
60	62,50	52,03	72,18	48,88	74,84
61	63,54	53,09	73,13	49,94	75,76
62	64,58	54,16	74,08	51,01	76,67
63	65,63	55,23	75,02	52,08	77,58
64	66,67	56,31	75,96	53,15	78,48
65	67,71	57,39	76,90	54,24	79,37
66	68,75	58,48	77,82	55,33	80,25
67	69,79	59,57	78,75	56,43	81,13
68	70,83	60,67	79,67	57,53	82,00
69	71,88	61,78	80,58	58,64	82,87
70	72,92	62,89	81,48	59,76	83,72
71	73,96	64,00	82,38	60,89	84,57
72	75,00	65,12	83,28	62,02	85,41
73	76,04	66,25	84,17	63,17	86,24
74	77,08	67,38	85,05	64,32	87,07
75	78,13	68,53	85,92	65,48	87,88
76	79,17	69,67	86,79	66,65	88,68
77	80,21	70,83	87,64	67,83	89,48
78	81,25	72,00	88,49	69,02	90,26
79	82,29	73,17	89,33	70,22	91,03
80	83,33	74,35	90,16	71,43	91,79
81	84,38	75,54	90,98	72,66	92,53
82	85,42	76,74	91,79	73,90	93,27
83	86,46	77,96	92,59	75,15	93,98
84	87,50	79,18	93,37	76,42	94,68
85	88,54	80,42	94,14	77,71	95,36
86	89,58	81,68	94,89	79,01	96,02
87	90,63	82,95	95,62	80,34	96,65
88	91,67	84,24	96,33	81,70	97,26
89	92,71	85,55	97,02	83,08	97,83
90	93,75	86,89	97,67	84,49	98,37
91	94,79	88,26	98,29	85,95	98,86
92	95,83	89,67	98,85	87,46	99,29
93	96,88	91,14	99,35	89,03	99,64
94	97,92	92,68	99,75	90,70	99,89
95	98,96	94,33	99,97	92,51	99,99
96	100,00	96,23	100,00	94,63	100,00

N=97

x	$100\,p_x$	95% $100\,p_l$	95% $100\,p_r$	99% $100\,p_l$	99% $100\,p_r$
0	0,00	0,00	3,73	0,00	5,32
1	1,03	0,03	5,61	0,01	7,41
2	2,06	0,25	7,25	0,11	9,21
3	3,09	0,64	8,77	0,35	10,86
4	4,12	1,13	10,22	0,70	12,42
5	5,15	1,69	11,62	1,13	13,91
6	6,19	2,30	12,98	1,61	15,35
7	7,22	2,95	14,30	2,15	16,76
8	8,25	3,63	15,61	2,71	18,13
9	9,28	4,33	16,88	3,31	19,47
10	10,31	5,06	18,14	3,94	20,78
11	11,34	5,80	19,39	4,59	22,08
12	12,37	6,56	20,61	5,26	23,35
13	13,40	7,33	21,83	5,95	24,61
14	14,43	8,12	23,03	6,66	25,85
15	15,46	8,92	24,22	7,39	27,08
16	16,49	9,73	25,40	8,12	28,29
17	17,53	10,55	26,57	8,87	29,50
18	18,56	11,38	27,73	9,63	30,69
19	19,59	12,22	28,89	10,41	31,87
20	20,62	13,07	30,03	11,19	33,03
21	21,65	13,93	31,17	11,99	34,19
22	22,68	14,79	32,30	12,79	35,34

N=97 (continued)

x	$100\,p_x$	95% $100\,p_l$	95% $100\,p_r$	99% $100\,p_l$	99% $100\,p_r$
23	23,71	15,66	33,42	13,61	36,49
24	24,74	16,54	34,54	14,43	37,62
25	25,77	17,42	35,65	15,26	38,74
26	26,80	18,32	36,76	16,10	39,86
27	27,84	19,21	37,86	16,94	40,97
28	28,87	20,11	38,95	17,80	42,07
29	29,90	21,02	40,04	18,66	43,17
30	30,93	21,93	41,12	19,53	44,26
31	31,96	22,85	42,20	20,40	45,34
32	32,99	23,78	43,27	21,28	46,41
33	34,02	24,70	44,34	22,17	47,48
34	35,05	25,64	45,41	23,07	48,55
35	36,08	26,58	46,46	23,97	49,60
36	37,11	27,52	47,52	24,87	50,65
37	38,14	28,47	48,57	25,79	51,70
38	39,18	29,42	49,61	26,71	52,74
39	40,21	30,37	50,65	27,63	53,77
40	41,24	31,33	51,69	28,56	54,80
41	42,27	32,30	52,72	29,49	55,82
42	43,30	33,27	53,75	30,44	56,84
43	44,33	34,24	54,77	31,38	57,85
44	45,36	35,22	55,79	32,33	58,85
45	46,39	36,20	56,81	33,29	59,86
46	47,42	37,19	57,82	34,26	60,85
47	48,45	38,18	58,82	35,22	61,84
48	49,48	39,17	59,83	36,20	62,82
49	50,52	40,17	60,83	37,18	63,80
50	51,55	41,18	61,82	38,16	64,78
51	52,58	42,18	62,81	39,15	65,74
52	53,61	43,19	63,80	40,14	66,71
53	54,64	44,21	64,78	41,15	67,67
54	55,67	45,23	65,76	42,15	68,62
55	56,70	46,25	66,73	43,16	69,56
56	57,73	47,28	67,70	44,18	70,51
57	58,76	48,31	68,67	45,20	71,44
58	59,79	49,35	69,63	46,23	72,37
59	60,82	50,39	70,58	47,26	73,29
60	61,86	51,43	71,53	48,30	74,21
61	62,89	52,48	72,48	49,35	75,13
62	63,92	53,54	73,42	50,40	76,03
63	64,95	54,59	74,36	51,45	76,93
64	65,98	55,66	75,30	52,52	77,83
65	67,01	56,73	76,22	53,59	78,72
66	68,04	57,80	77,15	54,66	79,60
67	69,07	58,88	78,07	55,74	80,47
68	70,10	59,96	78,98	56,83	81,34
69	71,13	61,05	79,89	57,93	82,20
70	72,16	62,14	80,79	59,03	83,06
71	73,20	63,24	81,68	60,14	83,90
72	74,23	64,35	82,58	61,26	84,74
73	75,26	65,46	83,46	62,38	85,57
74	76,29	66,58	84,34	63,51	86,39
75	77,32	67,70	85,21	64,66	87,21
76	78,35	68,83	86,07	65,81	88,01
77	79,38	69,97	86,93	66,97	88,81
78	80,41	71,11	87,78	68,13	89,59
79	81,44	72,27	88,62	69,31	90,37
80	82,47	73,43	89,45	70,50	91,13
81	83,51	74,60	90,27	71,71	91,88
82	84,54	75,78	91,08	72,92	92,61
83	85,57	76,97	91,88	74,15	93,34
84	86,60	78,17	92,67	75,39	94,05
85	87,63	79,39	93,44	76,65	94,74
86	88,66	80,61	94,20	77,92	95,41
87	89,69	81,86	94,94	79,22	96,06
88	90,72	83,12	95,67	80,53	96,69
89	91,75	84,39	96,37	81,87	97,29
90	92,78	85,70	97,05	83,24	97,85
91	93,81	87,02	97,70	84,65	98,39
92	94,85	88,38	98,31	86,09	98,87
93	95,88	89,78	98,87	87,58	99,30
94	96,91	91,23	99,36	89,14	99,65
95	97,94	92,75	99,75	90,79	99,89
96	98,97	94,39	99,97	92,59	99,99
97	100,00	96,27	100,00	94,68	100,00

N=98

x	$100\,p_x$	95% $100\,p_l$	95% $100\,p_r$	99% $100\,p_l$	99% $100\,p_r$
0	0,00	0,00	3,69	0,00	5,26
1	1,02	0,03	5,55	0,01	7,34
2	2,04	0,25	7,18	0,11	9,12
3	3,06	0,64	8,69	0,35	10,75
4	4,08	1,12	10,12	0,69	12,30
5	5,10	1,68	11,51	1,12	13,78
6	6,12	2,28	12,85	1,60	15,21
7	7,14	2,92	14,16	2,12	16,60
8	8,16	3,59	15,45	2,69	17,95
9	9,18	4,29	16,72	3,28	19,28
10	10,20	5,00	17,97	3,90	20,58
11	11,22	5,74	19,20	4,54	21,87
12	12,24	6,49	20,41	5,21	23,13
13	13,27	7,26	21,62	5,89	24,38
14	14,29	8,04	22,81	6,59	25,61
15	15,31	8,83	23,99	7,31	26,82
16	16,33	9,63	25,16	8,04	28,03
17	17,35	10,44	26,31	8,78	29,22
18	18,37	11,26	27,47	9,53	30,40
19	19,39	12,10	28,61	10,30	31,57
20	20,41	12,93	29,74	11,07	32,73

All values conform to the international convention (i.e. 0,1 instead of 0.1).

N: number of trials; x: number of successes, etc.; $100\,p_x = 100\,x/N$

x	$100\,p_x$	100(1 − 2α) limits 95% $100\,p_l$	$100\,p_r$	99% $100\,p_l$	$100\,p_r$
		$N=98$ (continued)			
21	21,43	13,78–	30,87	11,86–	33,87
22	22,45	14,64–	31,99	12,65–	35,01
23	23,47	15,50–	33,11	13,46–	36,15
24	24,49	16,36–	34,21	14,27–	37,27
25	25,51	17,24–	35,31	15,09–	38,38
26	26,53	18,12–	36,41	15,92–	39,49
27	27,55	19,01–	37,50	16,76–	40,59
28	28,57	19,90–	38,58	17,60–	41,69
29	29,59	20,79–	39,66	18,46–	42,77
30	30,61	21,70–	40,74	19,31–	43,85
31	31,63	22,61–	41,80	20,18–	44,92
32	32,65	23,52–	42,87	21,05–	45,99
33	33,67	24,44–	43,93	21,93–	47,05
34	34,69	25,36–	44,98	22,81–	48,11
35	35,71	26,29–	46,03	23,70–	49,15
36	36,73	27,22–	47,07	24,60–	50,20
37	37,76	28,16–	48,12	25,50–	51,23
38	38,78	29,10–	49,15	26,41–	52,26
39	39,80	30,04–	50,18	27,32–	53,29
40	40,82	30,99–	51,21	28,24–	54,31
41	41,84	31,95–	52,23	29,17–	55,32
42	42,86	32,90–	53,25	30,10–	56,33
43	43,88	33,87–	54,27	31,03–	57,34
44	44,90	34,83–	55,28	31,97–	58,33
45	45,92	35,80–	56,29	32,92–	59,33
46	46,94	36,78–	57,29	33,87–	60,31
47	47,96	37,76–	58,29	34,82–	61,30
48	48,98	38,74–	59,28	35,79–	62,27
49	50,00	39,73–	60,27	36,75–	63,25
50	51,02	40,72–	61,26	37,73–	64,21
51	52,04	41,71–	62,24	38,70–	65,18
52	53,06	42,71–	63,22	39,69–	66,13
53	54,08	43,71–	64,20	40,67–	67,08
54	55,10	44,72–	65,17	41,67–	68,03
55	56,12	45,73–	66,13	42,66–	68,97
56	57,14	46,75–	67,10	43,67–	69,90
57	58,16	47,77–	68,05	44,68–	70,83
58	59,18	48,79–	69,01	45,69–	71,76
59	60,20	49,82–	69,96	46,71–	72,68
60	61,22	50,85–	70,90	47,74–	73,59
61	62,24	51,88–	71,84	48,77–	74,50
62	63,27	52,93–	72,78	49,80–	75,40
63	64,29	53,97–	73,71	50,85–	76,30
64	65,31	55,02–	74,64	51,89–	77,19
65	66,33	56,07–	75,56	52,95–	78,07
66	67,35	57,13–	76,48	54,01–	78,95
67	68,37	58,20–	77,39	55,08–	79,82
68	69,39	59,26–	78,30	56,15–	80,69
69	70,41	60,34–	79,21	57,23–	81,54
70	71,43	61,42–	80,10	58,31–	82,40
71	72,45	62,50–	80,99	59,41–	83,24
72	73,47	63,59–	81,88	60,51–	84,08
73	74,49	64,69–	82,76	61,62–	84,91
74	75,51	65,79–	83,64	62,73–	85,73
75	76,53	66,89–	84,50	63,85–	86,54
76	77,55	68,01–	85,36	64,99–	87,35
77	78,57	69,13–	86,22	66,13–	88,14
78	79,59	70,26–	87,07	67,27–	88,93
79	80,61	71,39–	87,90	68,43–	89,70
80	81,63	72,53–	88,74	69,60–	90,47
81	82,65	73,69–	89,56	70,78–	91,22
82	83,67	74,84–	90,37	71,97–	91,96
83	84,69	76,01–	91,17	73,18–	92,69
84	85,71	77,19–	91,96	74,39–	93,41
85	86,73	78,38–	92,74	75,62–	94,11
86	87,76	79,59–	93,51	76,87–	94,79
87	88,78	80,80–	94,26	78,13–	95,46
88	89,80	82,03–	95,00	79,42–	96,10
89	90,82	83,28–	95,71	80,72–	96,72
90	91,84	84,55–	96,41	82,05–	97,31
91	92,86	85,84–	97,08	83,40–	97,88

x	$100\,p_x$	100(1 − 2α) limits 95% $100\,p_l$	$100\,p_r$	99% $100\,p_l$	$100\,p_r$
		$N=98$ (continued)			
92	93,88	87,15–	97,72	84,79–	98,40
93	94,90	88,49–	98,32	86,22–	98,88
94	95,92	89,88–	98,88	87,70–	99,31
95	96,94	91,31–	99,36	89,25–	99,65
96	97,96	92,82–	99,75	90,88–	99,89
97	98,98	94,45–	99,97	92,66–	99,99
98	100,00	96,31–	100,00	94,74–	100,00
		$N=99$			
0	0,00	0,00–	3,66	0,00–	5,21
1	1,01	0,03–	5,50	0,01–	7,27
2	2,02	0,25–	7,11	0,11–	9,03
3	3,03	0,63–	8,60	0,34–	10,65
4	4,04	1,11–	10,02	0,69–	12,18
5	5,05	1,66–	11,39	1,11–	13,64
6	6,06	2,26–	12,73	1,58–	15,06
7	7,07	2,89–	14,03	2,10–	16,44
8	8,08	3,55–	15,30	2,66–	17,78
9	9,09	4,24–	16,56	3,25–	19,10
10	10,10	4,95–	17,79	3,86–	20,39
11	11,11	5,68–	19,01	4,50–	21,66
12	12,12	6,42–	20,22	5,15–	22,91
13	13,13	7,18–	21,41	5,83–	24,15
14	14,14	7,95–	22,59	6,52–	25,36
15	15,15	8,74–	23,76	7,23–	26,57
16	16,16	9,53–	24,91	7,95–	27,76
17	17,17	10,33–	26,06	8,69–	28,94
18	18,18	11,15–	27,20	9,43–	30,11
19	19,19	11,97–	28,34	10,19–	31,27
20	20,20	12,80–	29,46	10,96–	32,42
21	21,21	13,64–	30,58	11,73–	33,56
22	22,22	14,48–	31,69	12,52–	34,69
23	23,23	15,33–	32,79	13,32–	35,81
24	24,24	16,19–	33,89	14,12–	36,93
25	25,25	17,06–	34,98	14,93–	38,03
26	26,26	17,93–	36,07	15,75–	39,13
27	27,27	18,80–	37,15	16,58–	40,22
28	28,28	19,69–	38,22	17,42–	41,31
29	29,29	20,57–	39,29	18,26–	42,38
30	30,30	21,47–	40,36	19,11–	43,45
31	31,31	22,36–	41,41	19,96–	44,52
32	32,32	23,27–	42,47	20,82–	45,57
33	33,33	24,18–	43,52	21,69–	46,63
34	34,34	25,09–	44,56	22,56–	47,67
35	35,35	26,01–	45,60	23,44–	48,71
36	36,36	26,93–	46,64	24,33–	49,75
37	37,37	27,85–	47,67	25,22–	50,77
38	38,38	28,78–	48,70	26,12–	51,80
39	39,39	29,72–	49,72	27,02–	52,81
40	40,40	30,66–	50,74	27,93–	53,83
41	41,41	31,60–	51,76	28,84–	54,83
42	42,42	32,55–	52,77	29,76–	55,83
43	43,43	33,50–	53,77	30,69–	56,83
44	44,44	34,45–	54,78	31,62–	57,82
45	45,45	35,41–	55,77	32,55–	58,81
46	46,46	36,38–	56,77	33,49–	59,79
47	47,47	37,34–	57,76	34,44–	60,76
48	48,48	38,32–	58,75	35,39–	61,73
49	49,49	39,29–	59,73	36,34–	62,70
50	50,51	40,27–	60,71	37,30–	63,66
51	51,52	41,25–	61,68	38,27–	64,61
52	52,53	42,24–	62,66	39,24–	65,56
53	53,54	43,23–	63,62	40,21–	66,51
54	54,55	44,23–	64,59	41,19–	67,45
55	55,56	45,22–	65,55	42,18–	68,38
56	56,57	46,23–	66,50	43,17–	69,31
57	57,58	47,23–	67,45	44,17–	70,24
58	58,59	48,24–	68,40	45,17–	71,16
59	59,60	49,26–	69,34	46,17–	72,07
60	60,61	50,28–	70,28	47,19–	72,98
61	61,62	51,30–	71,22	48,20–	73,88

x	$100\,p_x$	100(1 − 2α) limits 95% $100\,p_l$	$100\,p_r$	99% $100\,p_l$	$100\,p_r$
		$N=99$ (continued)			
62	62,63	52,33–	72,15	49,23–	74,78
63	63,64	53,36–	73,07	50,25–	75,67
64	64,65	54,40–	73,99	51,29–	76,56
65	65,66	55,44–	74,91	52,33–	77,44
66	66,67	56,48–	75,82	53,37–	78,31
67	67,68	57,53–	76,73	54,43–	79,18
68	68,69	58,59–	77,64	55,48–	80,04
69	69,70	59,64–	78,53	56,55–	80,89
70	70,71	60,71–	79,43	57,62–	81,74
71	71,72	61,78–	80,31	58,69–	82,58
72	72,73	62,85–	81,20	59,78–	83,42
73	73,74	63,93–	82,07	60,87–	84,25
74	74,75	65,02–	82,94	61,97–	85,07
75	75,76	66,11–	83,81	63,07–	85,88
76	76,77	67,21–	84,67	64,19–	86,68
77	77,78	68,31–	85,52	65,31–	87,48
78	78,79	69,42–	86,36	66,44–	88,27
79	79,80	70,54–	87,20	67,58–	89,04
80	80,81	71,66–	88,03	68,73–	89,81
81	81,82	72,80–	88,85	69,89–	90,57
82	82,83	73,94–	89,67	71,06–	91,31
83	83,84	75,09–	90,47	72,24–	92,05
84	84,85	76,24–	91,26	73,43–	92,77
85	85,86	77,41–	92,05	74,64–	93,48
86	86,87	78,59–	92,82	75,85–	94,17
87	87,88	79,78–	93,58	77,09–	94,85
88	88,89	80,99–	94,32	78,34–	95,50
89	89,90	82,21–	95,05	79,61–	96,14
90	90,91	83,44–	95,76	80,90–	96,75
91	91,92	84,70–	96,45	82,22–	97,34
92	92,93	85,97–	97,11	83,56–	97,90
93	93,94	87,27–	97,74	84,94–	98,42
94	94,95	88,61–	98,34	86,36–	98,89
95	95,96	89,98–	98,89	87,82–	99,31
96	96,97	91,40–	99,37	89,35–	99,66
97	97,98	92,89–	99,75	90,97–	99,89
98	98,99	94,50–	99,97	92,73–	99,99
99	100,00	96,34–	100,00	94,79–	100,00
		$N=100$			
0	0,00	0,00–	3,62	0,00–	5,16
1	1,00	0,03–	5,45	0,01–	7,20
2	2,00	0,24–	7,04	0,10–	8,94
3	3,00	0,62–	8,52	0,34–	10,55
4	4,00	1,10–	9,93	0,68–	12,06
5	5,00	1,64–	11,28	1,09–	13,51
6	6,00	2,23–	12,60	1,56–	14,92
7	7,00	2,86–	13,89	2,08–	16,28
8	8,00	3,52–	15,16	2,63–	17,61
9	9,00	4,20–	16,40	3,21–	18,92
10	10,00	4,90–	17,62	3,82–	20,20
11	11,00	5,62–	18,83	4,45–	21,45
12	12,00	6,36–	20,02	5,10–	22,70
13	13,00	7,11–	21,20	5,77–	23,92
14	14,00	7,87–	22,37	6,45–	25,13
15	15,00	8,65–	23,53	7,15–	26,32
16	16,00	9,43–	24,68	7,87–	27,51
17	17,00	10,23–	25,82	8,59–	28,68
18	18,00	11,03–	26,95	9,33–	29,84
19	19,00	11,84–	28,07	10,08–	30,98
20	20,00	12,67–	29,18	10,84–	32,12
21	21,00	13,49–	30,29	11,61–	33,25
22	22,00	14,33–	31,39	12,39–	34,37
23	23,00	15,17–	32,49	13,18–	35,49
24	24,00	16,02–	33,57	13,97–	36,59
25	25,00	16,88–	34,66	14,77–	37,69
26	26,00	17,74–	35,73	15,59–	38,77
27	27,00	18,61–	36,80	16,40–	39,86
28	28,00	19,48–	37,87	17,23–	40,93
29	29,00	20,36–	38,93	18,06–	42,00

x	$100\,p_x$	100(1 − 2α) limits 95% $100\,p_l$	$100\,p_r$	99% $100\,p_l$	$100\,p_r$
		$N=100$ (continued)			
30	30,00	21,24–	39,98	18,90–	43,06
31	31,00	22,13–	41,03	19,75–	44,12
32	32,00	23,02–	42,08	20,60–	45,17
33	33,00	23,92–	43,12	21,46–	46,21
34	34,00	24,82–	44,15	22,32–	47,25
35	35,00	25,73–	45,18	23,19–	48,28
36	36,00	26,64–	46,21	24,07–	49,30
37	37,00	27,56–	47,24	24,95–	50,32
38	38,00	28,48–	48,25	25,84–	51,34
39	39,00	29,40–	49,27	26,73–	52,35
40	40,00	30,33–	50,28	27,63–	53,35
41	41,00	31,26–	51,29	28,53–	54,35
42	42,00	32,20–	52,29	29,44–	55,35
43	43,00	33,14–	53,29	30,35–	56,33
44	44,00	34,08–	54,28	31,27–	57,32
45	45,00	35,03–	55,27	32,19–	58,30
46	46,00	35,98–	56,26	33,12–	59,27
47	47,00	36,94–	57,24	34,06–	60,24
48	48,00	37,90–	58,22	34,99–	61,20
49	49,00	38,86–	59,20	35,94–	62,16
50	50,00	39,83–	60,17	36,89–	63,11
51	51,00	40,80–	61,14	37,84–	64,06
53	52,00	41,78–	62,10	38,80–	65,01
53	53,00	42,76–	63,06	39,76–	65,94
54	54,00	43,74–	64,02	40,73–	66,88
55	55,00	44,73–	64,97	41,70–	67,81
56	56,00	45,72–	65,92	42,68–	68,73
57	57,00	46,71–	66,86	43,67–	69,65
58	58,00	47,71–	67,80	44,65–	70,56
59	59,00	48,71–	68,74	45,65–	71,47
60	60,00	49,72–	69,67	46,65–	72,37
61	61,00	50,73–	70,60	47,65–	73,27
62	62,00	51,75–	71,52	48,66–	74,16
63	63,00	52,76–	72,44	49,68–	75,05
64	64,00	53,79–	73,36	50,70–	75,93
65	65,00	54,82–	74,27	51,72–	76,81
66	66,00	55,85–	75,18	52,75–	77,68
67	67,00	56,88–	76,08	53,79–	78,54
68	68,00	57,92–	76,98	54,83–	79,40
69	69,00	58,97–	77,87	55,88–	80,25
70	70,00	60,02–	78,76	56,94–	81,10
71	71,00	61,07–	79,64	58,00–	81,94
72	72,00	62,13–	80,52	59,07–	82,77
73	73,00	63,20–	81,39	60,14–	83,60
74	74,00	64,27–	82,26	61,23–	84,41
75	75,00	65,34–	83,12	62,31–	85,23
76	76,00	66,43–	83,98	63,41–	86,03
77	77,00	67,51–	84,83	64,51–	86,82
78	78,00	68,61–	85,67	65,63–	87,61
79	79,00	69,71–	86,51	66,75–	88,39
80	80,00	70,82–	87,33	67,88–	89,16
81	81,00	71,93–	88,16	69,02–	89,92
82	82,00	73,05–	88,97	70,16–	90,67
83	83,00	74,18–	89,77	71,32–	91,41
84	84,00	75,32–	90,57	72,49–	92,13
85	85,00	76,47–	91,35	73,68–	92,85
86	86,00	77,63–	92,13	74,87–	93,55
87	87,00	78,80–	92,89	76,08–	94,23
88	88,00	79,98–	93,64	77,30–	94,90
89	89,00	81,17–	94,38	78,55–	95,55
90	90,00	82,38–	95,10	79,80–	96,18
91	91,00	83,60–	95,80	81,08–	96,79
92	92,00	84,84–	96,48	82,39–	97,37
93	93,00	86,11–	97,14	83,72–	97,92
94	94,00	87,40–	97,77	85,08–	98,44
95	95,00	88,72–	98,36	86,49–	98,91
96	96,00	90,07–	98,90	87,94–	99,32
97	97,00	91,48–	99,38	89,45–	99,66
98	98,00	92,96–	99,76	91,06–	99,90
99	99,00	94,55–	99,97	92,80–	99,99
100	100,00	96,38–	100,00	94,84–	100,00

All values conform to the international convention (i.e. 0,1 instead of 0.1).

Confidence Limits* for $N\boldsymbol{p}$

N: number of trials

Confidence limits for binomial distribution: $\text{Prob}[x_l < N\boldsymbol{p} < x_r] \geq 1 - 2\alpha$; for quantiles of continuous distributions: $\text{Prob}[(x_l + 1) < N\boldsymbol{p} < x_r] \geq 1 - 2\alpha$

A point (•) indicates the absence of a lower and/or upper limit

$\boldsymbol{p}$	0,05		0,10		0,15		0,20		0,25		0,30		0,35		0,40		0,45		0,50	
2α	0,05	0,01	0,05	0,01	0,05	0,01	0,05	0,01	0,05	0,01	0,05	0,01	0,05	0,01	0,05	0,01	0,05	0,01	0,05	0,01
N	x_l x_r	x_l x_r	x_l x_r	x_l x_r	x_l x_r	x_l x_r	x_l x_r	x_l x_r	x_l x_r	x_l x_r	x_l x_r	x_l x_r	x_l x_r	x_l x_r	x_l x_r	x_l x_r	x_l x_r	x_l x_r	x_l x_r	x_l x_r
5	•–2	•–3	•–3	•–4	•–4	•–4	•–4	•–5	•–4	•–5	•–5	•–5	•–5	•–•	•–5	•–•	•–5	•–•	•–•	•–•
6	•–3	•–3	•–3	•–4	•–4	•–5	•–4	•–5	•–5	•–5	•–5	•–6	•–5	•–6	•–6	•–6	•–6	•–•	0–6	•–•
7	•–3	•–3	•–4	•–4	•–4	•–5	•–5	•–5	•–5	•–6	•–6	•–6	•–6	•–7	•–6	•–7	0–7	•–7	0–7	•–•
8	•–3	•–4	•–4	•–5	•–4	•–5	•–5	•–6	•–6	•–6	•–6	•–7	•–7	•–7	0–7	•–8	0–7	•–8	0–8	0–8
9	•–3	•–4	•–4	•–5	•–5	•–6	•–5	•–6	•–6	•–7	•–7	•–7	0–7	•–8	0–8	•–8	0–8	0–9	1–8	0–9
10	•–3	•–4	•–4	•–5	•–5	•–6	•–6	•–7	•–6	•–7	•–7	•–8	0–8	•–8	0–8	•–9	1–9	0–9	1–9	0–10
11	•–3	•–4	•–4	•–5	•–5	•–6	•–6	•–7	•–7	•–8	0–7	•–8	0–8	•–9	0–9	0–10	1–9	0–10	1–10	0–11
12	•–3	•–4	•–5	•–5	•–5	•–6	•–6	•–7	•–7	•–8	0–8	•–9	0–9	•–10	1–9	0–10	1–10	0–11	2–10	1–11
13	•–3	•–4	•–5	•–6	•–6	•–7	•–7	•–8	0–7	•–9	0–8	•–9	0–9	0–10	1–10	0–11	1–10	1–11	2–11	1–12
14	•–4	•–4	•–5	•–6	•–6	•–7	•–7	•–8	0–8	•–9	0–9	•–10	1–9	0–11	1–10	0–11	2–11	1–12	2–12	1–13
15	•–4	•–5	•–5	•–6	•–6	•–7	•–7	•–8	0–8	•–9	0–9	0–10	1–10	0–11	1–11	0–12	2–12	1–13	3–12	2–13
16	•–4	•–5	•–5	•–6	•–6	•–8	•–8	•–9	0–9	•–10	0–10	0–11	1–10	0–12	2–11	1–12	2–12	1–13	3–13	2–14
17	•–4	•–5	•–5	•–6	•–7	•–8	0–8	•–9	0–9	•–10	1–10	0–11	1–11	0–12	2–12	1–13	3–13	2–14	4–13	2–15
18	•–4	•–5	•–6	•–7	•–7	•–8	0–8	•–9	0–9	•–11	1–10	0–12	2–11	1–13	2–12	1–14	3–13	2–14	4–14	3–15
19	•–4	•–5	•–6	•–7	•–7	•–8	0–8	•–10	0–10	0–11	1–11	0–12	2–12	1–13	3–13	1–14	3–14	2–15	4–15	3–16
20	•–4	•–5	•–6	•–7	•–7	•–9	0–9	•–10	1–10	0–11	1–11	0–13	2–12	1–14	3–13	2–15	4–14	3–16	5–15	3–17
21	•–4	•–5	•–6	•–7	•–8	•–9	0–9	•–10	1–10	0–12	1–12	0–13	2–13	1–14	3–14	2–15	4–15	3–16	5–16	4–17
22	•–4	•–5	•–6	•–7	•–8	•–9	0–9	•–11	1–11	0–12	2–12	1–13	3–13	1–15	3–14	2–16	4–15	3–17	5–17	4–18
23	•–5	•–5	•–6	•–8	0–8	•–9	0–10	•–11	1–11	0–12	2–12	1–14	3–14	2–15	4–15	2–16	5–16	3–17	6–17	4–19
24	•–5	•–6	•–7	•–8	0–8	•–10	0–10	0–11	1–11	0–13	2–13	1–14	3–14	2–16	4–15	3–17	5–17	4–18	6–18	5–19
25	•–5	•–6	•–7	•–8	0–9	•–10	0–10	0–12	1–12	0–13	2–13	1–15	3–15	2–16	4–16	3–17	5–17	4–19	7–18	5–20
26	•–5	•–6	•–7	•–8	0–9	•–10	1–10	0–12	1–12	0–14	2–14	1–15	4–15	2–17	5–16	3–18	6–18	4–19	7–19	6–20
27	•–5	•–6	•–7	•–8	0–9	•–10	1–11	0–12	2–12	1–14	3–14	1–15	4–15	2–17	5–17	4–18	6–18	5–20	7–20	6–21
28	•–5	•–6	•–7	•–8	0–9	•–11	1–11	0–12	2–13	1–14	3–14	2–16	4–16	3–17	5–17	4–19	7–19	5–20	8–20	6–22
29	•–5	•–6	•–7	•–9	0–9	•–11	1–11	0–13	2–13	1–15	3–15	2–16	4–16	3–18	6–18	4–19	7–19	5–21	8–21	7–22
30	•–5	•–6	•–8	•–9	0–10	•–11	1–12	0–13	2–13	1–15	3–15	2–17	5–17	3–18	6–18	4–20	7–20	6–22	9–21	7–23
31	•–5	•–6	•–8	•–9	0–10	•–11	1–12	0–13	2–14	1–15	4–15	2–17	5–17	3–19	6–19	5–21	8–20	6–22	9–22	7–24
32	•–5	•–6	•–8	•–9	0–10	•–12	1–12	0–14	2–14	1–16	4–16	2–18	5–18	4–19	7–19	5–21	8–21	6–23	9–23	8–24
33	•–5	•–7	•–8	•–9	0–10	0–12	1–12	0–14	3–14	1–16	4–16	3–18	5–18	4–20	7–20	5–22	8–21	7–23	10–23	8–25
34	•–6	•–7	•–8	•–10	0–10	0–12	2–13	1–14	3–15	2–16	4–17	3–18	6–18	4–20	7–20	6–22	9–22	7–24	10–24	9–25
35	•–6	•–7	•–8	•–10	1–11	0–12	2–13	1–15	3–15	2–17	4–17	3–19	6–19	4–21	7–21	6–23	9–23	7–24	11–24	9–26
36	•–6	•–7	0–8	•–10	1–11	0–12	2–13	1–15	3–15	2–17	5–17	3–19	6–19	5–21	8–21	6–23	9–23	8–25	11–25	9–27
37	•–6	•–7	0–9	•–10	1–11	0–13	2–13	1–15	3–16	2–17	5–18	3–20	6–20	5–22	8–22	6–24	10–24	8–25	12–25	10–27
38	•–6	•–7	0–9	•–10	1–11	0–13	2–14	1–15	4–16	2–18	5–18	4–20	7–20	5–22	8–22	7–24	10–24	8–26	12–26	10–28
39	•–6	•–7	0–9	•–10	1–11	0–13	2–14	1–16	4–16	2–18	5–18	4–20	7–21	5–23	9–23	7–25	11–25	9–27	12–27	11–28
40	•–6	•–7	0–9	•–11	1–12	0–13	2–14	1–16	4–17	3–18	6–19	4–21	7–21	6–23	9–23	7–25	11–25	9–27	13–27	11–29
41	•–6	•–7	0–9	•–11	1–12	0–14	3–14	1–16	4–17	3–19	6–19	4–21	8–21	6–23	9–24	8–26	11–26	9–28	13–28	11–30
42	•–6	•–7	0–9	•–11	1–12	0–14	3–15	1–17	4–17	3–19	6–20	4–22	8–22	6–24	10–24	8–26	12–26	10–28	14–28	12–30
43	•–6	•–8	0–9	•–11	1–12	0–14	3–15	2–17	4–18	3–19	6–20	5–22	8–22	6–24	10–25	8–27	12–27	10–29	14–29	12–31
44	•–6	•–8	0–10	•–11	1–13	0–14	3–15	2–17	5–18	3–20	6–20	5–22	8–23	7–25	10–25	9–27	12–27	10–29	15–29	13–31
45	•–6	•–8	0–10	•–11	1–13	0–14	3–15	2–17	5–18	3–20	7–21	5–23	9–23	7–25	11–25	9–28	13–28	11–30	15–30	13–32
46	•–7	•–8	0–10	•–11	2–13	0–15	3–16	2–18	5–18	4–20	7–21	5–23	9–24	7–26	11–26	9–28	13–28	11–30	15–31	13–33
47	•–7	•–8	0–10	•–12	2–13	1–15	3–16	2–18	5–19	4–21	7–21	5–23	9–24	7–26	11–26	9–29	14–29	12–31	16–31	14–33
48	•–7	•–8	0–10	•–12	2–13	1–15	4–16	2–18	5–19	4–21	7–22	6–24	10–24	8–27	12–27	10–29	14–29	12–31	16–32	14–34
49	•–7	•–8	0–10	•–12	2–14	1–15	4–17	2–18	6–19	4–21	8–22	6–24	10–25	8–27	12–27	10–30	14–30	12–32	17–32	15–34
50	•–7	•–8	0–10	•–12	2–14	1–16	4–17	2–19	6–20	4–22	8–23	6–25	10–25	8–27	12–28	10–30	15–30	13–33	17–33	15–35
51	•–7	•–8	0–11	0–12	2–14	1–16	4–17	3–19	6–20	4–22	8–23	6–25	10–26	8–28	13–28	11–31	15–31	13–33	18–33	15–36
52	•–7	•–8	0–11	0–12	2–14	1–16	4–17	3–19	6–20	5–22	8–23	7–25	11–26	9–28	13–29	11–31	15–31	13–34	18–34	16–36
53	•–7	•–8	0–11	0–13	2–14	1–16	4–18	3–20	6–21	5–23	9–24	7–26	11–26	9–29	13–29	11–31	16–32	14–34	18–35	16–37
54	•–7	•–9	1–11	0–13	2–15	1–16	4–18	3–20	7–21	5–23	9–24	7–26	11–27	9–29	14–30	12–32	16–32	14–35	19–35	17–37
55	•–7	•–9	1–11	0–13	2–15	1–17	5–18	3–20	7–21	5–23	9–24	7–27	11–27	10–30	14–30	12–32	17–33	14–35	19–36	17–38
56	•–7	•–9	1–11	0–13	3–15	1–17	5–18	3–20	7–22	5–24	9–25	7–27	12–28	10–30	14–31	12–33	17–34	15–36	20–36	17–39
57	•–7	•–9	1–11	0–13	3–15	1–17	5–19	3–21	7–22	5–24	10–25	8–27	12–28	10–30	15–31	13–33	17–34	15–36	20–37	18–39
58	•–8	•–9	1–12	0–13	3–15	1–17	5–19	3–21	7–22	6–24	10–25	8–28	12–29	10–31	15–32	13–34	18–35	16–37	21–37	18–40
59	•–8	•–9	1–12	0–13	3–16	2–17	5–19	4–21	8–22	6–25	10–26	8–28	13–29	11–31	15–32	13–34	18–35	16–37	21–38	19–40
60	•–8	•–9	1–12	0–14	3–16	2–18	5–19	4–21	8–23	6–25	10–26	8–28	13–29	11–32	16–32	13–35	19–36	16–38	21–39	19–41
61	•–8	•–9	1–12	0–14	3–16	2–18	5–20	4–22	8–23	6–25	11–26	9–29	13–30	11–32	16–33	14–35	19–36	17–38	22–39	20–41
62	•–8	•–9	1–12	0–14	3–16	2–18	6–20	4–22	8–23	6–26	11–27	9–29	14–30	11–33	16–33	14–36	19–37	17–39	22–40	20–42
63	•–8	•–9	1–12	0–14	3–16	2–18	6–20	4–22	8–24	6–26	11–27	9–30	14–31	12–33	17–34	14–36	20–37	17–40	23–40	20–43
64	•–8	•–9	1–12	0–14	3–16	2–19	6–20	4–23	8–24	7–26	11–28	9–30	14–31	12–33	17–34	15–37	20–38	18–40	23–41	21–43
65	•–8	•–9	1–13	0–14	3–17	2–19	6–21	4–23	9–24	7–27	11–28	9–30	14–31	12–34	17–35	15–37	20–38	18–41	24–41	21–44
66	•–8	•–10	1–13	0–15	4–17	2–19	6–21	5–23	9–25	7–27	12–28	10–31	15–32	12–34	18–35	15–38	21–39	18–41	24–42	22–44
67	•–8	•–10	1–13	0–15	4–17	2–19	6–21	5–23	9–25	7–27	12–29	10–31	15–32	13–35	18–36	16–38	21–39	19–42	25–42	22–45
68	•–8	•–10	1–13	0–15	4–17	2–19	6–21	5–24	9–25	7–28	12–29	10–31	15–33	13–35	18–36	16–39	22–40	19–42	25–43	22–46
69	•–8	•–10	1–13	0–15	4–17	2–20	7–22	5–24	9–26	8–28	12–29	10–32	16–33	13–36	19–37	16–39	22–40	20–43	25–44	23–46
70	•–8	•–10	2–13	0–15	4–18	3–20	7–22	5–24	10–26	8–28	13–30	11–32	16–33	14–36	19–37	17–40	22–41	20–43	26–44	23–47
71	•–9	•–10	2–13	0–15	4–18	3–20	7–22	5–24	10–26	8–29	13–30	11–33	16–34	14–36	19–38	17–40	23–41	20–44	26–45	24–47
72	0–9	•–10	2–14	1–15	4–18	3–20	7–22	5–25	10–26	8–29	13–30	11–33	16–34	14–37	20–38	17–41	23–42	21–44	27–45	24–48
73	0–9	•–10	2–14	1–16	4–18	3–20	7–23	5–25	10–27	8–29	13–31	11–33	17–35	14–37	20–38	18–41	24–42	21–45	27–46	25–48
74	0–9	•–10	2–14	1–16	4–18	3–21	7–23	6–25	10–27	8–29	14–31	12–34	17–35	15–38	20–39	18–42	24–43	21–45	28–46	25–49
75	0–9	•–10	2–14	1–16	5–19	3–21	8–23	6–25	11–27	9–30	14–31	12–34	17–35	15–38	21–39	18–42	24–43	22–46	28–47	25–50
76	0–9	•–10	2–14	1–16	5–19	3–21	8–23	6–26	11–28	9–30	14–32	12–34	18–36	15–39	21–40	19–43	25–44	22–46	28–48	26–50
77	0–9	•–10	2–14	1–16	5–19	3–21	8–24	6–26	11–28	9–30	14–32	12–35	18–36	16–39	21–40	19–43	25–44	23–47	29–48	26–51
78	0–9	•–11	2–14	1–16	5–19	3–21	8–24	6–26	11–28	9–31	15–32	12–35	18–37	16–39	22–41	19–43	26–45	23–47	29–49	27–51
79	0–9	•–11	2–14	1–16	5–19	3–22	8–24	6–26	11–28	9–31	15–33	13–35	19–37	16–40	22–41	20–44	26–45	23–48	30–49	27–52
80	0–9	•–11	2–15	1–17	5–20	4–22	8–24	6–27	12–29	10–31	15–33	13–36	19–37	16–40	23–42	20–44	26–46	24–48	30–50	28–52
81	0–9	•–11	2–15	1–17	5–20	4–22	8–25	7–27	12–29	10–32	15–34	13–36	19–38	17–41	23–42	20–45	27–46	24–49	31–50	28–53
82	0–9	•–11	2–15	1–17	5–20	4–22	9–25	7–27	12–29	10–32	16–34	13–37	19–38	17–41	23–43	21–45	27–47	24–50	31–51	28–54
83	0–9	•–11	2–15	1–17	5–20	4–22	9–25	7–27	12–30	10–32	16–34	14–37	20–39	17–41	24–43	21–46	28–47	25–50	32–51	29–54
84	0–9	•–11	2–15	1–17	6–20	4–23	9–25	7–28	12–30	10–33	16–35	14–37	20–39	17–42	24–43	21–46	28–48	25–51	32–52	29–55
85	0–10	•–11	3–15	1–17	6–20	4–23	9–25	7–28	13–30	11–33	16–35	14–38	20–39	18–42	24–44	22–47	28–48	26–51	32–53	30–55
86	0–10	•–11	3–15	1–17	6–21	4–23	9–26	7–28	13–31	11–33	17–35	14–38	21–40	18–43	25–44	22–47	29–49	26–52	33–53	30–56
87	0–10	•–11	3–16	1–18	6–21	4–23	9–26	7–28	13–31	11–34	17–36	15–38	21–40	18–43	25–45	22–48	29–49	26–52	33–54	31–56
88	0–10	•–11	3–16	1–18	6–21	4–23	10–26	8–29	13–31	11–34	17–36	15–39	21–41	19–44	25–45	23–48	30–50	27–53	34–54	31–57
89	0–10	•–11	3–16	1–18	6–21	4–24	10–26	8–29	14–31	11–34	17–36	15–39	21–41	19–44	26–46	23–49	30–50	27–53	34–55	31–58
90	0–10	•–12	3–16	2–18	6–21	5–24	10–27	8–29	14–32	11–34	18–37	15–40	22–41	19–44	26–46	23–49	30–51	27–54	35–55	32–58
91	0–10	•–12	3–16	2–18	6–22	5–24	10–27	8–30	14–32	12–35	18–37	15–40	22–42	19–45	26–47	24–50	31–51	28–54	35–56	32–59
92	0–10	•–12	3–16	2–18	6–22	5–24	10–27	8–30	14–32	12–35	18–37	16–40	22–42	20–45	27–47	24–50	31–52	28–55	36–56	33–59
93	0–10	•–12	3–16	2–18	7–22	5–24	10–27	8–30	14–33	12–35	18–38	16–41	23–43	20–46	27–48	24–50	32–52	29–55	36–57	33–60
94	0–10	•–12	3–16	2–19	7–22	5–25	11–28	8–30	15–33	12–36	19–38	16–41	23–43	20–46	27–48	25–51	32–53	29–56	37–57	34–60
95	0–10	•–12	3–17	2–19	7–22	5–25	11–28	9–31	15–33	12–36	19–38	16–41	23–43	21–46	28–48	25–51	32–53	29–56	37–58	34–61
96	0–10	•–12	3–17	2–19	7–23	5–25	11–28	9–31	15–34	13–36	19–39	17–42	24–44	21–47	28–49	25–52	33–54	30–57	37–59	34–62
97	0–10	•–12	3–17	2–19	7–23	5–25	11–28	9–31	15–34	13–37	19–39	17–42	24–44	21–47	28–49	26–52	33–54	30–57	38–59	35–62
98	0–11	•–12	3–17	2–19	7–23	5–25	11–29	9–31	15–34	13–37	20–39	17–42	24–45	21–48	29–50	26–53	34–55	31–58	38–60	35–63
99	0–11	•–12	3–17	2–19	7–23	5–26	11–29	9–32	16–34	13–37	20–40	17–43	25–45	22–48	29–50	26–53	34–55	31–58	39–60	36–63
100	0–11	•–12	4–17	2–19	7–23	6–26	11–29	9–32	16–35	13–38	20–40	18–43	25–45	22–49	30–51	27–54	34–56	31–59	39–61	36–64

All values conform to the international convention (i.e. 0,1 instead of 0.1).

'Exact' Confidence Limits* for Np $p=0,5$; $N=0–499$

Top half of table: $2\alpha = 0,2$; bottom half of table: $2\alpha = 0,1$ (see also page 103)

N	0	1	2	3	4	5	6	7	8	9
0	•–•	•–•	•–•	•–•	0–4	0–5	0–6	1–6	1–7	2–7
10	2–8	2–9	3–9	3–10	4–10	4–11	4–12	5–12	5–13	6–13
20	6–14	7–14	7–15	7–16	8–16	8–17	9–17	9–18	10–18	10–19
30	10–20	11–20	11–21	12–21	12–22	13–22	13–23	14–23	14–24	15–24
40	15–25	15–26	16–26	16–27	17–27	17–28	18–28	18–29	19–29	19–30
50	19–31	20–31	20–32	21–32	21–33	22–33	22–34	23–34	23–35	24–35
60	24–36	24–37	25–37	25–38	26–38	26–39	27–39	27–40	28–40	28–41
70	29–41	29–42	30–42	30–43	30–44	31–44	31–45	32–45	32–46	33–46
80	33–47	34–47	34–48	35–48	35–49	36–49	36–50	37–50	37–51	37–52
90	38–52	38–53	39–53	39–54	40–54	40–55	41–55	41–56	42–56	42–57
100	43–57	43–58	44–58	44–59	44–60	45–60	45–61	46–61	46–62	47–62
110	47–63	48–63	48–64	49–64	49–65	50–65	50–66	51–66	51–67	52–67
120	52–68	52–69	53–69	53–70	54–70	54–71	55–71	55–72	56–72	56–73
130	57–73	57–74	58–74	58–75	59–75	59–76	60–76	60–77	60–78	61–78
140	61–79	62–79	62–80	63–80	63–81	64–81	64–82	65–82	65–83	66–83
150	66–84	67–84	67–85	68–85	68–86	69–86	69–87	69–88	70–88	70–89
160	71–89	71–90	72–90	72–91	73–91	73–92	74–92	74–93	75–93	75–94
170	76–94	76–95	77–95	77–96	78–96	78–97	79–97	79–98	79–99	80–99
180	80–100	81–100	81–101	82–101	82–102	83–102	83–103	84–103	84–104	85–104
190	85–105	86–105	86–106	87–106	87–107	88–107	88–108	89–108	89–109	89–110
200	90–110	90–111	91–111	91–112	92–112	92–113	93–113	93–114	94–114	94–115
210	95–115	95–116	96–116	96–117	97–117	97–118	98–118	98–119	99–119	99–120
220	99–121	100–121	100–122	101–122	101–123	102–123	102–124	103–124	103–125	104–125
230	104–126	105–126	105–127	106–127	106–128	107–128	107–129	108–129	108–130	109–130
240	109–131	110–131	110–132	111–132	111–133	111–134	112–134	112–135	113–135	113–136
250	114–136	114–137	115–137	115–138	116–138	116–139	117–139	117–140	118–140	118–141
260	119–141	119–142	120–142	120–143	121–143	121–144	122–144	122–145	123–145	123–146
270	123–147	124–147	124–148	125–148	125–149	126–149	126–150	127–150	127–151	128–151
280	128–152	129–152	129–153	130–153	130–154	131–154	131–155	132–155	132–156	133–156
290	133–157	134–157	134–158	135–158	135–159	135–160	136–160	136–161	137–161	137–162
300	138–162	138–163	139–163	139–164	140–164	140–165	141–165	141–166	142–166	142–167
310	143–167	143–168	144–168	144–169	145–169	145–170	146–170	146–171	147–171	147–172
320	148–172	148–173	149–173	149–174	149–175	150–175	150–176	151–176	151–177	152–177
330	152–178	153–178	153–179	154–179	154–180	155–180	155–181	156–181	156–182	157–182
340	157–183	158–183	158–184	159–184	159–185	160–185	160–186	161–186	161–187	162–187
350	162–188	162–189	163–189	163–190	164–190	164–191	165–191	165–192	166–192	166–193
360	167–193	167–194	168–194	168–195	169–195	169–196	170–196	170–197	171–197	171–198
370	172–198	172–199	173–199	173–200	174–200	174–201	175–201	175–202	176–202	176–203
380	177–203	177–204	177–205	178–205	178–206	179–206	179–207	180–207	180–208	181–208
390	181–209	182–209	182–210	183–210	183–211	184–211	184–212	185–212	185–213	186–213
400	186–214	187–214	187–215	188–215	188–216	189–216	189–217	190–217	190–218	191–218
410	191–219	192–219	192–220	192–221	193–221	193–222	194–222	194–223	195–223	195–224
420	196–224	196–225	197–225	197–226	198–226	198–227	199–227	199–228	200–228	200–229
430	201–229	201–230	202–230	202–231	203–231	203–232	204–232	204–233	205–233	205–234
440	206–234	206–235	207–235	207–236.	207–237	208–237	208–238	209–238	209–239	210–239
450	210–240	211–240	211–241	212–241	212–242	213–242	213–243	214–243	214–244	215–244
460	215–245	216–245	216–246	217–246	217–247	218–247	218–248	219–248	219–249	220–249
470	220–250	221–250	221–251	222–251	222–252	223–252	223–253	224–253	224–254	224–255
480	225–255	225–256	226–256	226–257	227–257	227–258	228–258	228–259	229–259	229–260
490	230–260	230–261	231–261	231–262	232–262	232–263	233–263	233–264	234–264	234–265

N	0	1	2	3	4	5	6	7	8	9
0	•–•	•–•	•–•	•–•	•–•	0–5	0–6	0–7	1–7	1–8
10	1–9	2–9	2–10	3–10	3–11	3–12	4–12	4–13	5–13	5–14
20	5–15	6–15	6–16	7–16	7–17	7–18	8–18	8–19	9–19	9–20
30	10–20	10–21	10–22	11–22	11–23	12–23	12–24	13–24	13–25	13–26
40	14–26	14–27	15–27	15–28	16–28	16–29	16–30	17–30	17–31	18–31
50	18–32	19–32	19–33	20–33	20–34	20–35	21–35	21–36	22–36	22–37
60	23–37	23–38	24–38	24–39	24–40	25–40	25–41	26–41	26–42	27–42
70	27–43	28–43	28–44	28–45	29–45	29–46	30–46	30–47	31–47	31–48
80	32–48	32–49	33–49	33–50	33–51	34–51	34–52	35–52	35–53	36–53
90	36–54	37–54	37–55	38–55	38–56	38–57	39–57	39–58	40–58	40–59
100	41–59	41–60	42–60	42–61	43–61	43–62	44–62	44–63	44–64	45–64
110	45–65	46–65	46–66	47–66	47–67	48–67	48–68	49–68	49–69	50–69
120	50–70	50–71	51–71	51–72	52–72	52–73	53–73	53–74	54–74	54–75
130	55–75	55–76	56–76	56–77	56–78	57–78	57–79	58–79	58–80	59–80
140	59–81	60–81	60–82	61–82	61–83	62–83	62–84	63–84	63–85	63–86
150	64–86	64–87	65–87	65–88	66–88	66–89	67–89	67–90	68–90	68–91
160	69–91	69–92	70–92	70–93	70–94	71–94	71–95	72–95	72–96	73–96
170	73–97	74–97	74–98	75–98	75–99	76–99	76–100	77–100	77–101	78–101
180	78–102	78–103	79–103	79–104	80–104	80–105	81–105	81–106	82–106	82–107
190	83–107	83–108	84–108	84–109	85–109	85–110	85–111	86–111	86–112	87–112
200	87–113	88–113	88–114	89–114	89–115	90–115	90–116	91–116	91–117	92–117
210	92–118	93–118	93–119	94–119	94–120	94–121	95–121	95–122	96–122	96–123
220	97–123	97–124	98–124	98–125	99–125	99–126	100–126	100–127	101–127	101–128
230	102–128	102–129	102–130	103–130	103–131	104–131	104–132	105–132	105–133	106–133
240	106–134	107–134	107–135	108–135	108–136	109–136	109–137	110–137	110–138	111–138
250	111–139	111–140	112–140	112–141	113–141	113–142	114–142	114–143	115–143	115–144
260	116–144	116–145	117–145	117–146	118–146	118–147	119–147	119–148	120–148	120–149
270	120–150	121–150	121–151	122–151	122–152	123–152	123–153	124–153	124–154	125–154
280	125–155	126–155	126–156	127–156	127–157	128–157	128–158	129–158	129–159	130–159
290	130–160	130–161	131–161	131–162	132–162	132–163	133–163	133–164	134–164	134–165
300	135–165	135–166	136–166	136–167	137–167	137–168	138–168	138–169	139–169	139–170
310	140–170	140–171	140–172	141–172	141–173	142–173	142–174	143–174	143–175	144–175
320	144–176	145–176	145–177	146–177	146–178	147–178	147–179	148–179	148–180	149–180
330	149–181	150–181	150–182	150–183	151–183	151–184	152–184	152–185	153–185	153–186
340	154–186	154–187	155–187	155–188	156–188	156–189	157–189	157–190	158–190	158–191
350	159–191	159–192	160–192	160–193	161–193	161–194	161–195	162–195	162–196	163–196
360	163–197	164–197	164–198	165–198	165–199	166–199	166–200	167–200	167–201	168–201
370	168–202	169–202	169–203	170–203	170–204	171–204	171–205	172–205	172–206	172–207
380	173–207	173–208	174–208	174–209	175–209	175–210	176–210	176–211	177–211	177–212
390	178–212	178–213	179–213	179–214	180–214	180–215	181–215	181–216	182–216	182–217
400	183–217	183–218	184–218	184–219	184–220	185–220	185–221	186–221	186–222	187–222
410	187–223	188–223	188–224	189–224	189–225	190–225	190–226	191–226	191–227	192–227
420	192–228	193–228	193–229	194–229	194–230	195–230	195–231	196–231	196–232	196–233
430	197–233	197–234	198–234	198–235	199–235	199–236	200–236	200–237	201–237	201–238
440	202–238	202–239	203–239	203–240	204–240	204–241	205–241	205–242	206–242	206–243
450	207–243	207–244	208–244	208–245	208–246	209–246	209–247	210–247	210–248	211–248
460	211–249	212–249	212–250	213–250	213–251	214–251	214–252	215–252	215–253	216–253
470	216–254	217–254	217–255	218–255	218–256	219–256	219–257	220–257	220–258	221–258
480	221–259	221–260	222–260	222–261	223–261	223–262	224–262	224–263	225–263	225–264
490	226–264	226–265	227–265	227–266	228–266	228–267	229–267	229–268	230–268	230–269

All values conform to the international convention (i.e. 0,1 instead of 0.1).

'Exact' Confidence Limits* for Np $p=0,5$; $N=0–499$

Top half of table: $2\alpha = 0,05$; bottom half of table: $2\alpha = 0,02$ (see also page 103)

N	0	1	2	3	4	5	6	7	8	9
0	•–•	•–•	•–•	•–•	•–•	•–•	0– 6	0– 7	0– 8	1– 8
10	1– 9	1– 10	2– 10	2– 11	2– 12	3– 12	3– 13	4– 13	4– 14	4– 15
20	5– 15	5– 16	5– 17	6– 17	6– 18	7– 18	7– 19	7– 20	8– 20	8– 21
30	9– 21	9– 22	9– 23	10– 23	10– 24	11– 24	11– 25	12– 25	12– 26	12– 27
40	13– 27	13– 28	14– 28	14– 29	15– 29	15– 30	15– 31	16– 31	16– 32	17– 32
50	17– 33	18– 33	18– 34	18– 35	19– 35	19– 36	20– 36	20– 37	21– 37	21– 38
60	21– 39	22– 39	22– 40	23– 40	23– 41	24– 41	24– 42	25– 42	25– 43	25– 44
70	26– 44	26– 45	27– 45	27– 46	28– 46	28– 47	28– 48	29– 48	29– 49	30– 49
80	30– 50	31– 50	31– 51	32– 51	32– 52	32– 53	33– 53	33– 54	34– 54	34– 55
90	35– 55	35– 56	36– 56	36– 57	37– 57	37– 58	37– 59	38– 59	38– 60	39– 60
100	39– 61	40– 61	40– 62	41– 62	41– 63	41– 64	42– 64	42– 65	43– 65	43– 66
110	44– 66	44– 67	45– 67	45– 68	46– 68	46– 69	46– 70	47– 70	47– 71	48– 71
120	48– 72	49– 72	49– 73	50– 73	50– 74	51– 74	51– 75	51– 76	52– 76	52– 77
130	53– 77	53– 78	54– 78	54– 79	55– 79	55– 80	56– 80	56– 81	57– 81	57– 82
140	57– 83	58– 83	58– 84	59– 84	59– 85	60– 85	60– 86	61– 86	61– 87	62– 87
150	62– 88	62– 89	63– 89	63– 90	64– 90	64– 91	65– 91	65– 92	66– 92	66– 93
160	67– 93	67– 94	68– 94	68– 95	68– 96	69– 96	69– 97	70– 97	70– 98	71– 98
170	71– 99	72– 99	72–100	73–100	73–101	74–101	74–102	74–103	75–103	75–104
180	76–104	76–105	77–105	77–106	78–106	78–107	79–107	79–108	80–108	80–109
190	81–109	81–110	81–111	82–111	82–112	83–112	83–113	84–113	84–114	85–114
200	85–115	86–115	86–116	87–116	87–117	87–118	88–118	88–119	89–119	89–120
210	90–120	90–121	91–121	91–122	92–122	92–123	93–123	93–124	94–124	94–125
220	94–126	95–126	95–127	96–127	96–128	97–128	97–129	98–129	98–130	99–130
230	99–131	100–131	100–132	101–132	101–133	101–134	102–134	102–135	103–135	103–136
240	104–136	104–137	105–137	105–138	106–138	106–139	107–139	107–140	108–140	108–141
250	109–141	109–142	109–143	110–143	110–144	111–144	111–145	112–145	112–146	113–146
260	113–147	114–147	114–148	115–148	115–149	116–149	116–150	117–150	117–151	117–152
270	118–152	118–153	119–153	119–154	120–154	120–155	121–155	121–156	122–156	122–157
280	123–157	123–158	124–158	124–159	124–160	125–160	125–161	126–161	126–162	127–162
290	127–163	128–163	128–164	129–164	129–165	130–165	130–166	131–166	131–167	132–167
300	132–168	133–168	133–169	133–170	134–170	134–171	135–171	135–172	136–172	136–173
310	137–173	137–174	138–174	138–175	139–175	139–176	140–176	140–177	141–177	141–178
320	141–179	142–179	142–180	143–180	143–181	144–181	144–182	145–182	145–183	146–183
330	146–184	147–184	147–185	148–185	148–186	149–186	149–187	150–187	150–188	150–189
340	151–189	151–190	152–190	152–191	153–191	153–192	154–192	154–193	155–193	155–194
350	156–194	156–195	157–195	157–196	158–196	158–197	159–197	159–198	159–199	160–199
360	160–200	161–200	161–201	162–201	162–202	163–202	163–203	164–203	164–204	165–204
370	165–205	166–205	166–206	167–206	167–207	168–207	168–208	168–209	169–209	169–210
380	170–210	170–211	171–211	171–212	172–212	172–213	173–213	173–214	174–214	174–215
390	175–215	175–216	176–216	176–217	177–217	177–218	178–218	178–219	178–220	179–220
400	179–221	180–221	180–222	181–222	181–223	182–223	182–224	183–224	183–225	184–225
410	184–226	185–226	185–227	186–227	186–228	187–228	187–229	187–230	188–230	188–231
420	189–231	189–232	190–232	190–233	191–233	191–234	192–234	192–235	193–235	193–236
430	194–236	194–237	195–237	195–238	196–238	196–239	197–239	197–240	198–240	198–241
440	198–242	199–242	199–243	200–243	200–244	201–244	201–245	202–245	202–246	203–246
450	203–247	204–247	204–248	205–248	205–249	206–249	206–250	207–250	207–251	208–251
460	208–252	208–253	209–253	209–254	210–254	210–255	211–255	211–256	212–256	212–257
470	213–257	213–258	214–258	214–259	215–259	215–260	216–260	216–261	217–261	217–262
480	218–262	218–263	218–264	219–264	219–265	220–265	220–266	221–266	221–267	222–267
490	222–268	223–268	223–269	224–269	224–270	225–270	225–271	226–271	226–272	227–272

N	0	1	2	3	4	5	6	7	8	9
0	•–•	•–•	•–•	•–•	•–•	•–•	•–•	0– 7	0– 8	0– 9
10	0– 10	1– 10	1– 11	1– 12	2– 12	2– 13	2– 14	3– 14	3– 15	4– 15
20	4– 16	4– 17	5– 17	5– 18	5– 19	6– 19	6– 20	7– 20	7– 21	7– 22
30	8– 22	8– 23	8– 24	9– 24	9– 25	10– 25	10– 26	10– 27	11– 27	11– 28
40	12– 28	12– 29	13– 29	13– 30	13– 31	14– 31	14– 32	15– 32	15– 33	15– 34
50	16– 34	16– 35	17– 35	17– 36	18– 36	18– 37	18– 38	19– 38	19– 39	20– 39
60	20– 40	20– 41	21– 41	21– 42	22– 42	22– 43	23– 43	23– 44	23– 45	24– 45
70	24– 46	25– 46	25– 47	26– 47	26– 48	26– 49	27– 49	27– 50	28– 50	28– 51
80	29– 51	29– 52	30– 52	30– 53	30– 54	31– 54	31– 55	32– 55	32– 56	33– 56
90	33– 57	33– 58	34– 58	34– 59	35– 59	35– 60	36– 60	36– 61	37– 61	37– 62
100	37– 63	38– 63	38– 64	39– 64	39– 65	40– 65	40– 66	41– 66	41– 67	41– 68
110	42– 68	42– 69	43– 69	43– 70	44– 70	44– 71	45– 71	45– 72	45– 73	46– 73
120	46– 74	47– 74	47– 75	48– 75	48– 76	49– 76	49– 77	49– 78	50– 78	50– 79
130	51– 79	51– 80	52– 80	52– 81	53– 81	53– 82	53– 83	54– 83	54– 84	55– 84
140	55– 85	56– 85	56– 86	57– 86	57– 87	58– 87	58– 88	58– 89	59– 89	59– 90
150	60– 90	60– 91	61– 91	61– 92	62– 92	62– 93	63– 93	63– 94	63– 95	64– 95
160	64– 96	65– 96	65– 97	66– 97	66– 98	67– 98	67– 99	68– 99	68–100	68–101
170	69–101	69–102	70–102	70–103	71–103	71–104	72–104	72–105	73–105	73–106
180	73–107	74–107	74–108	75–108	75–109	76–109	76–110	77–110	77–111	78–111
190	78–112	78–113	79–113	79–114	80–114	80–115	81–115	81–116	82–116	82–117
200	83–117	83–118	83–119	84–119	84–120	85–120	85–121	86–121	86–122	87–122
210	87–123	88–123	88–124	89–124	89–125	89–126	90–126	90–127	91–127	91–128
220	92–128	92–129	93–129	93–130	94–130	94–131	95–131	95–132	95–133	96–133
230	96–134	97–134	97–135	98–135	98–136	99–136	99–137	100–137	100–138	101–138
240	101–139	101–140	102–140	102–141	103–141	103–142	104–142	104–143	105–143	105–144
250	106–144	106–145	107–145	107–146	107–147	108–147	108–148	109–148	109–149	110–149
260	110–150	111–150	111–151	112–151	112–152	113–152	113–153	114–153	114–154	114–155
270	115–155	115–156	116–156	116–157	117–157	117–158	118–158	118–159	119–159	119–160
280	120–160	120–161	120–162	121–162	121–163	122–163	122–164	123–164	123–165	124–165
290	124–166	125–166	125–167	126–167	126–168	127–168	127–169	127–170	128–170	128–171
300	129–171	129–172	130–172	130–173	131–173	131–174	132–174	132–175	133–175	133–176
310	134–176	134–177	134–178	135–178	135–179	136–179	136–180	137–180	137–181	138–181
320	138–182	139–182	139–183	140–183	140–184	141–184	141–185	141–186	142–186	142–187
330	143–187	143–188	144–188	144–189	145–189	145–190	146–190	146–191	147–191	147–192
340	148–192	148–193	149–193	149–194	149–195	150–195	150–196	151–196	151–197	152–197
350	152–198	153–198	153–199	154–199	154–200	155–200	155–201	156–201	156–202	156–203
360	157–203	157–204	158–204	158–205	159–205	159–206	160–206	160–207	161–207	161–208
370	162–208	162–209	163–209	163–210	164–210	164–211	164–212	165–212	165–213	166–213
380	166–214	167–214	167–215	168–215	168–216	169–216	169–217	170–217	170–218	171–218
390	171–219	172–219	172–220	172–221	173–221	173–222	174–222	174–223	175–223	175–224
400	176–224	176–225	177–225	177–226	178–226	178–227	179–227	179–228	180–228	180–229
410	180–230	181–230	181–231	182–231	182–232	183–232	183–233	184–233	184–234	185–234
420	185–235	186–235	186–236	187–236	187–237	188–237	188–238	188–239	189–239	189–240
430	190–240	190–241	191–241	191–242	192–242	192–243	193–243	193–244	194–244	194–245
440	195–245	195–246	196–246	196–247	197–247	197–248	197–249	198–249	198–250	199–250
450	199–251	200–251	200–252	201–252	201–253	202–253	202–254	203–254	203–255	204–255
460	204–256	205–256	205–257	205–258	206–258	206–259	207–259	207–260	208–260	208–261
470	209–261	209–262	210–262	210–263	211–263	211–264	212–264	212–265	213–265	213–266
480	214–266	214–267	214–268	215–268	215–269	216–269	216–270	217–270	217–271	218–271
490	218–272	219–272	219–273	220–273	220–274	221–274	221–275	222–275	222–276	223–276

All values conform to the international convention (i.e. 0,1 instead of 0.1).

'Exact' Confidence Limits* for Np $p = 0{,}5$; $N = 0–499$

Top half of table: $2\alpha = 0{,}01$; bottom half of table: $2\alpha = 0{,}002$ (see also page 103)

N	0	1	2	3	4	5	6	7	8	9
0	•–•	•–•	•–•	•–•	•–•	•–•	•–•	•–•	0– 8	0– 9
10	0– 10	0– 11	1– 11	1– 12	1– 13	2– 13	2– 14	2– 15	3– 15	3– 16
20	3– 17	4– 17	4– 18	4– 19	5– 19	5– 20	6– 20	6– 21	6– 22	7– 22
30	7– 23	7– 24	8– 24	8– 25	9– 25	9– 26	9– 27	10– 27	10– 28	11– 28
40	11– 29	11– 30	12– 30	12– 31	13– 31	13– 32	13– 33	14– 33	14– 34	15– 34
50	15– 35	15– 36	16– 36	16– 37	17– 37	17– 38	17– 39	18– 39	18– 40	19– 40
60	19– 41	20– 41	20– 42	20– 43	21– 43	21– 44	22– 44	22– 45	22– 46	23– 46
70	23– 47	24– 47	24– 48	25– 48	25– 49	25– 50	26– 50	26– 51	27– 51	27– 52
80	28– 52	28– 53	28– 54	29– 54	29– 55	30– 55	30– 56	31– 56	31– 57	31– 58
90	32– 58	32– 59	33– 59	33– 60	34– 60	34– 61	34– 62	35– 62	35– 63	36– 63
100	36– 64	37– 64	37– 65	37– 66	38– 66	38– 67	39– 67	39– 68	40– 68	40– 69
110	41– 69	41– 70	41– 71	42– 71	42– 72	43– 72	43– 73	44– 73	44– 74	45– 74
120	45– 75	45– 76	46– 76	46– 77	47– 77	47– 78	48– 78	48– 79	48– 80	49– 80
130	49– 81	50– 81	50– 82	51– 82	51– 83	52– 83	52– 84	52– 85	53– 85	53– 86
140	54– 86	54– 87	55– 87	55– 88	56– 88	56– 89	56– 90	57– 90	57– 91	58– 91
150	58– 92	59– 92	59– 93	60– 93	60– 94	61– 94	61– 95	61– 96	62– 96	62– 97
160	63– 97	63– 98	64– 98	64– 99	65– 99	65–100	65–101	66–101	66–102	67–102
170	67–103	68–103	68–104	69–104	69–105	70–105	70–106	70–107	71–107	71–108
180	72–108	72–109	73–109	73–110	74–110	74–111	74–112	75–112	75–113	76–113
190	76–114	77–114	77–115	78–115	78–116	79–116	79–117	79–118	80–118	80–119
200	81–119	81–120	82–120	82–121	83–121	83–122	84–122	84–123	84–124	85–124
210	85–125	86–125	86–126	87–126	87–127	88–127	88–128	89–128	89–129	89–130
220	90–130	90–131	91–131	91–132	92–132	92–133	93–133	93–134	94–134	94–135
230	95–135	95–136	95–137	96–137	96–138	97–138	97–139	98–139	98–140	99–140
240	99–141	100–141	100–142	100–143	101–143	101–144	102–144	102–145	103–145	103–146
250	104–146	104–147	105–147	105–148	106–148	106–149	106–150	107–150	107–151	108–151
260	108–152	109–152	109–153	110–153	110–154	111–154	111–155	111–156	112–156	112–157
270	113–157	113–158	114–158	114–159	115–159	115–160	116–160	116–161	117–161	117–162
280	117–163	118–163	118–164	119–164	119–165	120–165	120–166	121–166	121–167	122–167
290	122–168	123–168	123–169	123–170	124–170	124–171	125–171	125–172	126–172	126–173
300	127–173	127–174	128–174	128–175	129–175	129–176	130–176	130–177	130–178	131–178
310	131–179	132–179	132–180	133–180	133–181	134–181	134–182	135–182	135–183	136–183
320	136–184	136–185	137–185	137–186	138–186	138–187	139–187	139–188	140–188	140–189
330	141–189	141–190	142–190	142–191	142–192	143–192	143–193	144–193	144–194	145–194
340	145–195	146–195	146–196	147–196	147–197	148–197	148–198	149–198	149–199	149–200
350	150–200	150–201	151–201	151–202	152–202	152–203	153–203	153–204	154–204	154–205
360	155–205	155–206	156–206	156–207	156–208	157–208	157–209	158–209	158–210	159–210
370	159–211	160–211	160–212	161–212	161–213	162–213	162–214	163–214	163–215	163–216
380	164–216	164–217	165–217	165–218	166–218	166–219	167–219	167–220	168–220	168–221
390	169–221	169–222	170–222	170–223	170–224	171–224	171–225	172–225	172–226	173–226
400	173–227	174–227	174–228	175–228	175–229	176–229	176–230	177–230	177–231	177–232
410	178–232	178–233	179–233	179–234	180–234	180–235	181–235	181–236	182–236	182–237
420	183–237	183–238	184–238	184–239	185–239	185–240	185–241	186–241	186–242	187–242
430	187–243	188–243	188–244	189–244	189–245	190–245	190–246	191–246	191–247	192–247
440	192–248	192–249	193–249	193–250	194–250	194–251	195–251	195–252	196–252	196–253
450	197–253	197–254	198–254	198–255	199–255	199–256	200–256	200–257	200–258	201–258
460	201–259	202–259	202–260	203–260	203–261	204–261	204–262	205–262	205–263	206–263
470	206–264	207–264	207–265	208–265	208–266	208–267	209–267	209–268	210–268	210–269
480	211–269	211–270	212–270	212–271	213–271	213–272	214–272	214–273	215–273	215–274
490	216–274	216–275	216–276	217–276	217–277	218–277	218–278	219–278	219–279	220–279

N	0	1	2	3	4	5	6	7	8	9
0	•–•	•–•	•–•	•–•	•–•	•–•	•–•	•–•	•–•	•–•
10	0– 10	0– 11	0– 12	0– 13	1– 13	1– 14	1– 15	1– 16	2– 16	2– 17
20	2– 18	3– 18	3– 19	3– 20	4– 20	4– 21	4– 22	5– 22	5– 23	5– 24
30	6– 24	6– 25	6– 26	7– 26	7– 27	8– 27	8– 28	8– 29	9– 29	9– 30
40	9– 31	10– 31	10– 32	11– 32	11– 33	11– 34	12– 34	12– 35	12– 36	13– 36
50	13– 37	14– 37	14– 38	14– 39	15– 39	15– 40	16– 40	16– 41	16– 42	17– 42
60	17– 43	18– 43	18– 44	18– 45	19– 45	19– 46	20– 46	20– 47	20– 48	21– 48
70	21– 49	22– 49	22– 50	22– 51	23– 51	23– 52	24– 52	24– 53	24– 54	25– 54
80	25– 55	26– 55	26– 56	27– 56	27– 57	27– 58	28– 58	28– 59	29– 59	29– 60
90	29– 61	30– 61	30– 62	31– 62	31– 63	32– 63	32– 64	32– 65	33– 65	33– 66
100	34– 66	34– 67	35– 67	35– 68	35– 69	36– 69	36– 70	37– 70	37– 71	37– 72
110	38– 72	38– 73	39– 73	39– 74	40– 74	40– 75	40– 76	41– 76	41– 77	42– 77
120	42– 78	43– 78	43– 79	43– 80	44– 80	44– 81	45– 81	45– 82	46– 82	46– 83
130	46– 84	47– 84	47– 85	48– 85	48– 86	49– 86	49– 87	50– 87	50– 88	50– 89
140	51– 89	51– 90	52– 90	52– 91	53– 91	53– 92	53– 93	54– 93	54– 94	55– 94
150	55– 95	56– 95	56– 96	56– 97	57– 97	57– 98	58– 98	58– 99	59– 99	59–100
160	60–100	60–101	60–102	61–102	61–103	62–103	62–104	63–104	63–105	63–106
170	64–106	64–107	65–107	65–108	66–108	66–109	67–109	67–110	67–111	68–111
180	68–112	69–112	69–113	70–113	70–114	71–114	71–115	71–116	72–116	72–117
190	73–117	73–118	74–118	74–119	75–119	75–120	75–121	76–121	76–122	77–122
200	77–123	78–123	78–124	79–124	79–125	79–126	80–126	80–127	81–127	81–128
210	82–128	82–129	83–129	83–130	83–131	84–131	84–132	85–132	85–133	86–133
220	86–134	87–134	87–135	88–135	88–136	88–137	89–137	89–138	90–138	90–139
230	91–139	91–140	92–140	92–141	92–142	93–142	93–143	94–143	94–144	95–144
240	95–145	96–145	96–146	96–147	97–147	97–148	98–148	98–149	99–149	99–150
250	100–150	100–151	101–151	101–152	101–153	102–153	102–154	103–154	103–155	104–155
260	104–156	105–156	105–157	106–157	106–158	106–159	107–159	107–160	108–160	108–161
270	109–161	109–162	110–162	110–163	110–164	111–164	111–165	112–165	112–166	113–166
280	113–167	114–167	114–168	115–168	115–169	115–170	116–170	116–171	117–171	117–172
290	118–172	118–173	119–173	119–174	120–174	120–175	120–176	121–176	121–177	122–177
300	122–178	123–178	123–179	124–179	124–180	125–180	125–181	125–182	126–182	126–183
310	127–183	127–184	128–184	128–185	129–185	129–186	130–186	130–187	131–187	131–188
320	131–189	132–189	132–190	133–190	133–191	134–191	134–192	135–192	135–193	136–193
330	136–194	136–195	137–195	137–196	138–196	138–197	139–197	139–198	140–198	140–199
340	141–199	141–200	141–201	142–201	142–202	143–202	143–203	144–203	144–204	145–204
350	145–205	146–205	146–206	147–206	147–207	147–208	148–208	148–209	149–209	149–210
360	150–210	150–211	151–211	151–212	152–212	152–213	152–214	153–214	153–215	154–215
370	154–216	155–216	155–217	156–217	156–218	157–218	157–219	158–219	158–220	158–221
380	159–221	159–222	160–222	160–223	161–223	161–224	162–224	162–225	163–225	163–226
390	164–226	164–227	164–228	165–228	165–229	166–229	166–230	167–230	167–231	168–231
400	168–232	169–232	169–233	170–233	170–234	170–235	171–235	171–236	172–236	172–237
410	173–237	173–238	174–238	174–239	175–239	175–240	176–240	176–241	176–242	177–242
420	177–243	178–243	178–244	179–244	179–245	180–245	180–246	181–246	181–247	182–247
430	182–248	182–249	183–249	183–250	184–250	184–251	185–251	185–252	186–252	186–253
440	187–253	187–254	188–254	188–255	188–256	189–256	189–257	190–257	190–258	191–258
450	191–259	192–259	192–260	193–260	193–261	194–261	194–262	195–262	195–263	195–264
460	196–264	196–265	197–265	197–266	198–266	198–267	199–267	199–268	200–268	200–269
470	201–269	201–270	201–271	202–271	202–272	203–272	203–273	204–273	204–274	205–274
480	205–275	206–275	206–276	207–276	207–277	208–277	208–278	208–279	209–279	209–280
490	210–280	210–281	211–281	211–282	212–282	212–283	213–283	213–284	214–284	214–285

All values conform to the international convention (i.e. 0,1 instead of 0.1).

'Exact' Confidence Limits* for Np $p = 0{,}5$; $N = 0$–499

Top half of table: $2\alpha = 0{,}001$; bottom half of table: $2\alpha = 0{,}0001$ (see also page 103)

N	0	1	2	3	4	5	6	7	8	9
0	•–•	•–•	•–•	•–•	•–•	•–•	•–•	•–•	•–•	•–•
10	•–•	0–11	0–12	0–13	0–14	1–14	1–15	1–16	1–17	2–17
20	2–18	2–19	3–19	3–20	3–21	4–21	4–22	4–23	5–23	5–24
30	5–25	6–25	6–26	6–27	7–27	7–28	7–29	8–29	8–30	8–31
40	9–31	9–32	10–32	10–33	10–34	11–34	11–35	11–36	12–36	12–37
50	13–37	13–38	13–39	14–39	14–40	14–41	15–41	15–42	16–42	16–43
60	16–44	17–44	17–45	18–45	18–46	18–47	19–47	19–48	20–48	20–49
70	20–50	21–50	21–51	22–51	22–52	22–53	23–53	23–54	24–54	24–55
80	24–56	25–56	25–57	26–57	26–58	26–59	27–59	27–60	28–60	28–61
90	29–61	29–62	29–63	30–63	30–64	31–64	31–65	31–66	32–66	32–67
100	33–67	33–68	34–68	34–69	34–70	35–70	35–71	36–71	36–72	36–73
110	37–73	37–74	38–74	38–75	39–75	39–76	39–77	40–77	40–78	41–78
120	41–79	42–79	42–80	42–81	43–81	43–82	44–82	44–83	45–83	45–84
130	45–85	46–85	46–86	47–86	47–87	48–87	48–88	48–89	49–89	49–90
140	50–90	50–91	51–91	51–92	51–93	52–93	52–94	53–94	53–95	54–95
150	54–96	54–97	55–97	55–98	56–98	56–99	57–99	57–100	57–101	58–101
160	58–102	59–102	59–103	60–103	60–104	60–105	61–105	61–106	62–106	62–107
170	63–107	63–108	64–108	64–109	64–110	65–110	65–111	66–111	66–112	67–112
180	67–113	67–114	68–114	68–115	69–115	69–116	70–116	70–117	71–117	71–118
190	71–119	72–119	72–120	73–120	73–121	74–121	74–122	75–122	75–123	75–124
200	76–124	76–125	77–125	77–126	78–126	78–127	78–128	79–128	79–129	80–129
210	80–130	81–130	81–131	82–131	82–132	82–133	83–133	83–134	84–134	84–135
220	85–135	85–136	86–136	86–137	86–138	87–138	87–139	88–139	88–140	89–140
230	89–141	90–141	90–142	90–143	91–143	91–144	92–144	92–145	93–145	93–146
240	94–146	94–147	94–148	95–148	95–149	96–149	96–150	97–150	97–151	98–151
250	98–152	99–152	99–153	99–154	100–154	100–155	101–155	101–156	102–156	102–157
260	103–157	103–158	103–159	104–159	104–160	105–160	105–161	106–161	106–162	107–162
270	107–163	107–164	108–164	108–165	109–165	109–166	110–166	110–167	111–167	111–168
280	112–168	112–169	112–170	113–170	113–171	114–171	114–172	115–172	115–173	116–173
290	116–174	117–174	117–175	117–176	118–176	118–177	119–177	119–178	120–178	120–179
300	121–179	121–180	121–181	122–181	122–182	123–182	123–183	124–183	124–184	125–184
310	125–185	126–185	126–186	126–187	127–187	127–188	128–188	128–189	129–189	129–190
320	130–190	130–191	131–191	131–192	131–193	132–193	132–194	133–194	133–195	134–195
330	134–196	135–196	135–197	136–197	136–198	136–199	137–199	137–200	138–200	138–201
340	139–201	139–202	140–202	140–203	141–203	141–204	141–205	142–205	142–206	143–206
350	143–207	144–207	144–208	145–208	145–209	146–209	146–210	146–211	147–211	147–212
360	148–212	148–213	149–213	149–214	150–214	150–215	151–215	151–216	152–216	152–217
370	152–218	153–218	153–219	154–219	154–220	155–220	155–221	156–221	156–222	157–222
380	157–223	157–224	158–224	158–225	159–225	159–226	160–226	160–227	161–227	161–228
390	162–228	162–229	162–230	163–230	163–231	164–231	164–232	165–232	165–233	166–233
400	166–234	167–234	167–235	168–235	168–236	168–237	169–237	169–238	170–238	170–239
410	171–239	171–240	172–240	172–241	173–241	173–242	174–242	174–243	174–244	175–244
420	175–245	176–245	176–246	177–246	177–247	178–247	178–248	179–248	179–249	179–250
430	180–250	180–251	181–251	181–252	182–252	182–253	183–253	183–254	184–254	184–255
440	185–255	185–256	185–257	186–257	186–258	187–258	187–259	188–259	188–260	189–260
450	189–261	190–261	190–262	191–262	191–263	191–264	192–264	192–265	193–265	193–266
460	194–266	194–267	195–267	195–268	196–268	196–269	197–269	197–270	197–271	198–271
470	198–272	199–272	199–273	200–273	200–274	201–274	201–275	202–275	202–276	203–276
480	203–277	203–278	204–278	204–279	205–279	205–280	206–280	206–281	207–281	207–282
490	208–282	208–283	209–283	209–284	209–285	210–285	210–286	211–286	211–287	212–287

N	0	1	2	3	4	5	6	7	8	9
0	•–•	•–•	•–•	•–•	•–•	•–•	•–•	•–•	•–•	•–•
10	•–•	•–•	•–•	•–•	•–•	0–15	0–16	0–17	0–18	1–18
20	1–19	1–20	1–21	2–21	2–22	2–23	3–23	3–24	3–25	3–26
30	4–26	4–27	4–28	5–28	5–29	5–30	6–30	6–31	6–32	7–32
40	7–33	7–34	8–34	8–35	8–36	9–36	9–37	10–37	10–38	10–39
50	11–39	11–40	11–41	12–41	12–42	12–43	13–43	13–44	13–45	14–45
60	14–46	15–46	15–47	15–48	16–48	16–49	16–50	17–50	17–51	18–51
70	18–52	18–53	19–53	19–54	20–54	20–55	20–56	21–56	21–57	21–58
80	22–58	22–59	23–59	23–60	23–61	24–61	24–62	25–62	25–63	25–64
90	26–64	26–65	27–65	27–66	27–67	28–67	28–68	29–68	29–69	29–70
100	30–70	30–71	31–71	31–72	31–73	32–73	32–74	33–74	33–75	33–76
110	34–76	34–77	35–77	35–78	35–79	36–79	36–80	37–80	37–81	37–82
120	38–82	38–83	39–83	39–84	40–84	40–85	40–86	41–86	41–87	42–87
130	42–88	42–89	43–89	43–90	44–90	44–91	45–91	45–92	45–93	46–93
140	46–94	47–94	47–95	47–96	48–96	48–97	49–97	49–98	50–98	50–99
150	50–100	51–100	51–101	52–101	52–102	52–103	53–103	53–104	54–104	54–105
160	55–105	55–106	55–107	56–107	56–108	57–108	57–109	58–109	58–110	58–111
170	59–111	59–112	60–112	60–113	61–113	61–114	61–115	62–115	62–116	63–116
180	63–117	63–118	64–118	64–119	65–119	65–120	66–120	66–121	66–122	67–122
190	67–123	68–123	68–124	69–124	69–125	70–125	70–126	70–127	71–127	71–128
200	72–128	72–129	73–129	73–130	73–131	74–131	74–132	75–132	75–133	76–133
210	76–134	76–135	77–135	77–136	78–136	78–137	79–137	79–138	79–139	80–139
220	80–140	81–140	81–141	82–141	82–142	82–143	83–143	83–144	84–144	84–145
230	85–145	85–146	86–146	86–147	86–148	87–148	87–149	88–149	88–150	89–150
240	89–151	89–152	90–152	90–153	91–153	91–154	92–154	92–155	93–155	93–156
250	93–157	94–157	94–158	95–158	95–159	96–159	96–160	96–161	97–161	97–162
260	98–162	98–163	99–163	99–164	100–164	100–165	100–166	101–166	101–167	102–167
270	102–168	103–168	103–169	103–170	104–170	104–171	105–171	105–172	106–172	106–173
280	107–173	107–174	107–175	108–175	108–176	109–176	109–177	110–177	110–178	111–178
290	111–179	111–180	112–180	112–181	113–181	113–182	114–182	114–183	115–183	115–184
300	115–185	116–185	116–186	117–186	117–187	118–187	118–188	119–188	119–189	119–190
310	120–190	120–191	121–191	121–192	122–192	122–193	123–193	123–194	123–195	124–195
320	124–196	125–196	125–197	126–197	126–198	127–198	127–199	127–200	128–200	128–201
330	129–201	129–202	130–202	130–203	131–203	131–204	131–205	132–205	132–206	133–206
340	133–207	134–207	134–208	135–208	135–209	135–210	136–210	136–211	137–211	137–212
350	138–212	138–213	139–213	139–214	140–214	140–215	140–216	141–216	141–217	142–217
360	142–218	143–218	143–219	144–219	144–220	144–221	145–221	145–222	146–222	146–223
370	147–223	147–224	148–224	148–225	148–226	149–226	149–227	150–227	150–228	151–228
380	151–229	152–229	152–230	153–230	153–231	153–232	154–232	154–233	155–233	155–234
390	156–234	156–235	157–235	157–236	158–236	158–237	158–238	159–238	159–239	160–239
400	160–240	161–240	161–241	162–241	162–242	162–243	163–243	163–244	164–244	164–245
410	165–245	165–246	166–246	166–247	167–247	167–248	167–249	168–249	168–250	169–250
420	169–251	170–251	170–252	171–252	171–253	172–253	172–254	172–255	173–255	173–256
430	174–256	174–257	175–257	175–258	176–258	176–259	176–260	177–260	177–261	178–261
440	178–262	179–262	179–263	180–263	180–264	181–264	181–265	181–266	182–266	182–267
450	183–267	183–268	184–268	184–269	185–269	185–270	186–270	186–271	186–272	187–272
460	187–273	188–273	188–274	189–274	189–275	190–275	190–276	191–276	191–277	191–278
470	192–278	192–279	193–279	193–280	194–280	194–281	195–281	195–282	196–282	196–283
480	196–284	197–284	197–285	198–285	198–286	199–286	199–287	200–287	200–288	201–288
490	201–289	201–290	202–290	202–291	203–291	203–292	204–292	204–293	205–293	205–294

All values conform to the international convention (i.e. 0,1 instead of 0.1).

Distribution-Free Tolerance Limits* $\beta_t = 0{,}80$

$l+r = 1$–20, $N = 2(1)50(2)150$. The values in the table are those of β_p

$l+r$	1	2	3	4	5	6	7	8	9	10	11	12	13	14	15	16	17	18	19	20
N	0,	0,	0,	0,	0,	0,	0,	0,	0,	0,	0,	0,	0,	0,	0,	0,	0,	0,	0,	0,
2	4472	1056																		
3	5848	2871	0717																	
4	6687	4175	2123	0543																
5	7248	5098	3266	1686	0436															
6	7647	5776	4146	2686	1399	0365														
7	7946	6291	4832	3501	2283	1195	0314													
8	8178	6696	5379	4163	3032	1986	1044	0275												
9	8363	7022	5823	4709	3661	2675	1757	0926	0245											
10	8513	7290	6191	5163	4191	3268	2394	1576	0833	0221										
11	8639	7514	6499	5548	4643	3779	2953	2167	1429	0756	0201									
12	8745	7704	6762	5876	5032	4221	3441	2693	1979	1307	0693	0184								
13	8836	7867	6989	6161	5369	4606	3870	3160	2476	1822	1204	0639	0170							
14	8914	8008	7186	6408	5664	4945	4249	3574	2921	2291	1688	1117	0593	0158						
15	8983	8133	7359	6627	5924	5244	4585	3944	3321	2716	2132	1571	1041	0553	0148					
16	9043	8242	7512	6820	6155	5511	4884	4274	3680	3101	2539	1994	1471	0975	0518	0138				
17	9097	8339	7648	6992	6361	5749	5154	4572	4004	3450	2909	2383	1873	1382	0916	0488	0130			
18	9145	8426	7770	7147	6547	5964	5396	4841	4298	3767	3247	2740	2245	1765	1304	0865	0460	0123		
19	9188	8505	7880	7287	6715	6159	5616	5085	4565	4056	3556	3067	2589	2123	1670	1233	0818	0436	0117	
20	9227	8576	7980	7414	6867	6335	5816	5308	4809	4320	3840	3368	2906	2454	2013	1584	1170	0777	0414	0111
21	9262	8640	8071	7529	7006	6497	5999	5511	5033	4562	4100	3646	3199	2762	2333	1914	1507	1114	0740	0394
22	9295	8699	8154	7635	7133	6645	6167	5698	5238	4785	4340	3902	3471	3047	2631	2223	1824	1436	1062	0706
23	9324	8753	8230	7732	7250	6780	6321	5870	5427	4991	4562	4139	3722	3312	2908	2512	2123	1742	1372	1015
24	9351	8803	8300	7821	7358	6906	6463	6029	5602	5181	4767	4358	3955	3558	3167	2782	2403	2031	1668	1314
25	9377	8849	8365	7904	7457	7022	6595	6177	5764	5358	4958	4562	4173	3788	3408	3034	2666	2303	1947	1599
26	9400	8892	8425	7980	7550	7130	6718	6313	5915	5522	5135	4753	4375	4002	3634	3271	2912	2559	2212	1870
27	9421	8931	8481	8052	7636	7230	6832	6441	6056	5676	5301	4930	4564	4203	3845	3492	3144	2800	2461	2127
28	9441	8968	8533	8118	7716	7323	6938	6560	6187	5819	5456	5097	4742	4391	4044	3701	3361	3026	2696	2370
29	9460	9002	8582	8180	7791	7411	7038	6671	6310	5953	5601	5252	4908	4567	4230	3896	3566	3240	2918	2599
30	9478	9035	8627	8238	7861	7493	7131	6776	6425	6079	5737	5399	5064	4733	4405	4081	3759	3442	3127	2816
31	9494	9065	8670	8292	7927	7569	7219	6874	6533	6197	5865	5537	5211	4889	4570	4254	3942	3632	3325	3022
32	9509	9093	8710	8344	7989	7642	7301	6966	6635	6309	5986	5666	5350	5037	4726	4419	4114	3812	3513	3217
33	9524	9120	8748	8392	8047	7710	7379	7053	6732	6414	6100	5789	5481	5176	4874	4574	4277	3982	3691	3401
34	9538	9145	8783	8437	8102	7774	7452	7135	6822	6513	6207	5905	5605	5308	5013	4721	4431	4144	3859	3577
35	9551	9169	8817	8480	8154	7835	7522	7213	6908	6607	6309	6014	5722	5432	5145	4860	4578	4297	4019	3743
36	9563	9191	8849	8521	8203	7893	7587	7287	6990	6696	6406	6118	5833	5551	5271	4993	4717	4443	4171	3902
37	9574	9212	8879	8560	8250	7947	7650	7357	7067	6781	6498	6217	5939	5663	5390	5118	4849	4582	4316	4053
38	9585	9232	8907	8596	8294	7999	7709	7423	7141	6861	6585	6311	6040	5770	5503	5238	4975	4713	4454	4196
39	9596	9252	8935	8631	8337	8048	7765	7486	7210	6938	6668	6401	6135	5872	5611	5352	5095	4839	4586	4333
40	9606	9270	8960	8664	8377	8095	7819	7546	7277	7011	6747	6486	6227	5969	5714	5461	5209	4959	4711	4464
41	9615	9287	8985	8696	8415	8140	7870	7604	7341	7080	6822	6567	6314	6062	5813	5565	5319	5074	4831	4590
42	9624	9304	9009	8726	8451	8183	7919	7658	7401	7147	6895	6645	6397	6151	5907	5664	5423	5184	4946	4709
43	9633	9320	9031	8755	8486	8224	7965	7711	7459	7210	6963	6719	6476	6236	5996	5759	5523	5289	5055	4824
44	9641	9335	9052	8782	8520	8263	8010	7761	7514	7271	7029	6790	6552	6317	6082	5850	5619	5389	5161	4934
45	9649	9349	9073	8808	8551	8300	8052	7808	7567	7329	7092	6858	6625	6394	6165	5937	5710	5485	5261	5039
46	9656	9363	9093	8834	8582	8336	8093	7854	7618	7384	7153	6923	6695	6469	6244	6021	5799	5578	5358	5140
47	9663	9376	9111	8858	8611	8370	8133	7898	7667	7438	7211	6986	6762	6540	6320	6101	5883	5667	5451	5237
48	9670	9389	9130	8881	8639	8403	8170	7941	7714	7489	7266	7046	6827	6609	6393	6178	5964	5752	5541	5330
49	9677	9401	9147	8903	8666	8434	8206	7981	7759	7538	7320	7103	6888	6675	6463	6252	6042	5834	5627	5420
50	9683	9413	9164	8925	8692	8465	8241	8020	7802	7586	7371	7159	6948	6738	6530	6323	6117	5913	5709	5507
52	9695	9435	9195	8965	8741	8522	8307	8094	7883	7675	7469	7264	7061	6858	6658	6458	6260	6062	5866	5670
54	9706	9456	9224	9002	8787	8575	8367	8162	7959	7758	7559	7361	7165	6970	6776	6583	6392	6201	6011	5822
56	9717	9475	9251	9037	8829	8625	8424	8226	8030	7836	7643	7452	7262	7074	6887	6700	6515	6330	6147	5964
58	9726	9493	9277	9070	8868	8671	8477	8285	8096	7908	7722	7537	7353	7171	6990	6809	6630	6451	6274	6097
60	9735	9509	9300	9100	8905	8714	8526	8341	8157	7975	7795	7616	7438	7262	7086	6911	6738	6565	6392	6221
62	9744	9525	9322	9128	8940	8755	8573	8393	8215	8039	7864	7691	7518	7347	7177	7007	6839	6671	6504	6338
64	9752	9539	9343	9155	8972	8793	8616	8442	8269	8098	7929	7761	7593	7427	7262	7097	6934	6771	6609	6447
66	9759	9553	9363	9180	9003	8829	8657	8488	8320	8154	7990	7826	7664	7502	7342	7182	7023	6865	6708	6551
68	9766	9566	9381	9204	9031	8862	8696	8531	8368	8207	8047	7888	7730	7574	7418	7262	7108	6954	6801	6648
70	9773	9578	9399	9226	9058	8894	8732	8572	8414	8257	8101	7947	7793	7641	7489	7338	7188	7038	6889	6740
72	9779	9590	9415	9247	9084	8924	8767	8611	8457	8304	8153	8002	7853	7704	7557	7409	7263	7117	6972	6828
74	9785	9601	9431	9267	9109	8953	8799	8648	8498	8349	8201	8055	7909	7765	7621	7477	7335	7193	7051	6910
76	9790	9611	9445	9286	9131	8980	8830	8682	8536	8391	8248	8105	7963	7822	7681	7542	7403	7264	7126	6989
78	9796	9621	9459	9304	9153	9005	8859	8715	8573	8432	8291	8152	8014	7876	7739	7603	7467	7332	7197	7063
80	9801	9630	9473	9321	9174	9030	8887	8747	8608	8470	8333	8197	8062	7928	7794	7661	7529	7397	7265	7134
82	9806	9639	9485	9338	9194	9053	8914	8777	8641	8506	8373	8240	8108	7977	7846	7717	7587	7458	7330	7202
84	9810	9648	9497	9353	9213	9075	8939	8805	8673	8541	8411	8281	8152	8024	7896	7769	7643	7517	7392	7267
86	9815	9656	9509	9368	9231	9096	8964	8833	8703	8574	8447	8320	8194	8069	7944	7820	7696	7573	7451	7328
88	9819	9664	9520	9382	9248	9116	8987	8859	8732	8606	8481	8357	8234	8112	7990	7868	7747	7627	7507	7387
90	9823	9671	9531	9396	9264	9136	9009	8884	8759	8636	8514	8393	8272	8152	8033	7914	7796	7678	7561	7444
92	9827	9678	9541	9409	9280	9154	9030	8907	8786	8665	8546	8427	8309	8192	8075	7959	7843	7727	7612	7498
94	9830	9685	9550	9421	9295	9172	9050	8930	8811	8693	8576	8460	8344	8229	8115	8001	7887	7774	7662	7550
96	9834	9691	9560	9433	9310	9189	9070	8952	8836	8720	8605	8491	8378	8265	8153	8042	7930	7820	7709	7599
98	9837	9698	9568	9444	9324	9205	9088	8973	8859	8746	8633	8522	8411	8300	8190	8081	7972	7863	7755	7647
100	9840	9704	9577	9455	9337	9221	9106	8993	8881	8770	8660	8551	8442	8333	8226	8118	8011	7905	7799	7693
102	9843	9709	9585	9466	9350	9236	9124	9013	8903	8794	8686	8578	8472	8365	8260	8154	8049	7945	7841	7737
104	9846	9715	9593	9476	9362	9250	9140	9031	8924	8817	8711	8605	8500	8396	8292	8189	8086	7984	7881	7779
106	9849	9720	9601	9486	9374	9264	9156	9049	8944	8839	8735	8631	8528	8426	8324	8222	8121	8021	7920	7820
108	9852	9725	9608	9495	9386	9278	9172	9067	8963	8860	8758	8656	8555	8454	8354	8255	8155	8057	7958	7860
110	9855	9730	9615	9504	9397	9291	9187	9083	8981	8880	8780	8680	8581	8482	8384	8286	8188	8091	7994	7898
112	9857	9735	9622	9513	9407	9303	9201	9100	8999	8900	8801	8703	8606	8509	8412	8316	8220	8125	8029	7935
114	9860	9740	9628	9522	9417	9315	9215	9115	9017	8919	8822	8725	8630	8534	8439	8345	8251	8157	8063	7970
116	9862	9744	9635	9530	9427	9327	9228	9130	9033	8937	8842	8747	8653	8559	8466	8373	8280	8188	8096	8004
118	9865	9748	9641	9538	9437	9338	9241	9145	9049	8955	8861	8768	8675	8583	8491	8400	8309	8218	8128	8037
120	9867	9753	9647	9545	9446	9349	9253	9159	9065	8972	8880	8788	8697	8606	8516	8426	8336	8247	8158	8069
122	9869	9757	9653	9553	9455	9360	9266	9172	9080	8989	8898	8808	8718	8629	8540	8451	8363	8275	8188	8100
124	9871	9760	9658	9560	9464	9370	9277	9186	9095	9005	8915	8827	8738	8650	8563	8476	8389	8303	8216	8130
126	9873	9764	9663	9567	9472	9380	9289	9198	9109	9020	8932	8845	8758	8671	8585	8500	8414	8329	8244	8160
128	9875	9768	9669	9573	9480	9389	9300	9211	9123	9035	8949	8863	8777	8692	8607	8523	8438	8355	8271	8188
130	9877	9771	9674	9580	9488	9399	9310	9223	9136	9050	8965	8880	8796	8712	8628	8545	8462	8379	8297	8215
132	9879	9775	9679	9586	9496	9408	9320	9234	9149	9064	8980	8897	8814	8731	8649	8567	8485	8404	8322	8242
134	9881	9778	9683	9592	9504	9416	9331	9246	9162	9078	8995	8913	8831	8750	8668	8588	8507	8427	8347	8267
136	9882	9781	9688	9598	9511	9425	9340	9257	9174	9092	9010	8929	8848	8768	8688	8608	8529	8450	8371	8292
138	9884	9785	9692	9604	9518	9433	9350	9267	9186	9104	9024	8944	8864	8785	8706	8628	8550	8472	8394	8317
140	9886	9788	9697	9610	9525	9441	9359	9278	9197	9117	9038	8959	8880	8802	8725	8647	8570	8493	8417	8340
142	9887	9791	9701	9615	9531	9449	9368	9288	9208	9129	9051	8973	8896	8819	8742	8666	8590	8514	8439	8363
144	9889	9793	9705	9620	9538	9457	9377	9297	9219	9141	9064	8987	8911	8835	8760	8684	8609	8534	8460	8386
146	9890	9796	9709	9626	9544	9464	9385	9307	9230	9153	9077	9001	8926	8851	8776	8702	8628	8554	8481	8407
148	9892	9799	9713	9631	9550	9471	9393	9316	9240	9164	9089	9014	8940	8866	8793	8719	8646	8573	8501	8429
150	9893	9802	9717	9635	9556	9478	9401	9325	9250	9175	9101	9027	8954	8881	8808	8736	8664	8592	8521	8449

All values conform to the international convention (i.e. 0,1 instead of 0.1).

Distribution-Free Tolerance Limits* $\beta_t = 0{,}80$

Top: $l+r = 21$–40, $N = 21(1)50(2)150$; bottom: $l+r = 41$–60, $N = 41(1)50(2)58$. The values in the table are those of β_p

$l+r$	21	22	23	24	25	26	27	28	29	30	31	32	33	34	35	36	37	38	39	40
N	0,	0,	0,	0,	0,	0,	0,	0,	0,	0,	0,	0,	0,	0,	0,	0,	0,	0,	0,	0,
21	0106																			
22	0376	0101																		
23	0675	0360	0097																	
24	0972	0646	0345	0093																
25	1260	0933	0620	0331	0089															
26	1536	1211	0896	0596	0318	0085														
27	1799	1478	1165	0862	0574	0306	0082													
28	2049	1733	1424	1123	0831	0553	0295	0079												
29	2285	1976	1672	1374	1083	0802	0534	0285	0077											
30	2509	2207	1908	1615	1327	1047	0775	0516	0276	0074										
31	2722	2426	2133	1845	1561	1283	1012	0750	0499	0267	0072									
32	2924	2634	2347	2064	1786	1511	1243	0980	0726	0483	0258	0069								
33	3115	2832	2551	2274	2000	1730	1464	1204	0950	0704	0469	0251	0067							
34	3297	3020	2745	2473	2205	1939	1678	1420	1168	0922	0683	0455	0243	0065						
35	3470	3199	2930	2664	2400	2140	1883	1629	1379	1134	0895	0663	0442	0236	0064					
36	3634	3369	3106	2845	2587	2332	2079	1829	1582	1340	1102	0870	0645	0429	0230	0062				
37	3791	3532	3274	3019	2766	2515	2267	2021	1778	1539	1303	1072	0846	0627	0418	0223	0060			
38	3940	3687	3435	3184	2936	2690	2447	2205	1966	1730	1497	1268	1043	0823	0610	0407	0217	0059		
39	4083	3835	3588	3343	3100	2858	2619	2382	2147	1914	1685	1458	1235	1016	0802	0594	0396	0212	0057	
40	4219	3976	3734	3494	3256	3019	2784	2551	2320	2092	1865	1642	1421	1204	0990	0782	0579	0386	0207	0056
41	4350	4111	3874	3639	3405	3173	2943	2714	2487	2262	2039	1819	1601	1386	1174	0966	0762	0565	0377	0202
42	4474	4241	4008	3778	3549	3321	3095	2870	2647	2426	2207	1989	1774	1562	1352	1145	0942	0744	0552	0368
43	4594	4365	4137	3911	3686	3463	3241	3020	2801	2584	2368	2154	1942	1732	1525	1320	1118	0920	0726	0539
44	4708	4483	4260	4038	3818	3599	3381	3164	2949	2735	2523	2312	2104	1897	1692	1489	1289	1092	0899	0710
45	4818	4597	4379	4161	3944	3729	3515	3303	3091	2881	2672	2465	2260	2056	1854	1653	1456	1260	1068	0879
46	4923	4707	4492	4279	4066	3855	3645	3436	3228	3022	2816	2612	2410	2209	2010	1812	1617	1423	1232	1044
47	5024	4812	4601	4392	4183	3976	3769	3564	3360	3157	2955	2754	2555	2357	2161	1966	1773	1582	1392	1206
48	5121	4913	4706	4501	4296	4092	3889	3687	3487	3287	3089	2891	2695	2500	2307	2115	1924	1735	1548	1363
49	5215	5011	4808	4605	4404	4204	4004	3806	3609	3413	3217	3023	2830	2638	2448	2258	2070	1884	1699	1516
50	5305	5104	4905	4706	4508	4312	4116	3921	3727	3534	3342	3151	2961	2772	2584	2397	2212	2028	1845	1664
52	5476	5282	5089	4897	4706	4516	4327	4138	3950	3764	3578	3393	3209	3025	2843	2662	2482	2303	2125	1948
54	5634	5447	5261	5075	4890	4706	4523	4341	4159	3978	3798	3619	3440	3262	3086	2910	2735	2560	2387	2215
56	5782	5601	5421	5241	5062	4884	4707	4530	4354	4179	4004	3830	3657	3485	3313	3142	2972	2802	2634	2466
58	5921	5745	5571	5397	5223	5051	4879	4707	4537	4367	4197	4028	3860	3693	3526	3360	3195	3030	2866	2703
60	6050	5880	5711	5542	5374	5207	5040	4874	4708	4543	4378	4215	4051	3889	3727	3565	3404	3244	3085	2926
62	6172	6007	5843	5679	5516	5353	5191	5030	4869	4709	4549	4390	4231	4073	3915	3758	3602	3446	3291	3136
64	6286	6126	5967	5808	5649	5491	5334	5177	5021	4865	4709	4555	4400	4247	4093	3941	3788	3637	3485	3335
66	6394	6239	6083	5929	5775	5621	5468	5316	5164	5012	4861	4710	4560	4411	4261	4113	3964	3817	3669	3522
68	6496	6345	6194	6043	5894	5744	5595	5447	5299	5151	5004	4858	4711	4566	4420	4275	4131	3987	3843	3700
70	6592	6445	6298	6152	6006	5860	5715	5571	5427	5283	5140	4997	4854	4712	4571	4430	4289	4148	4008	3869
72	6683	6540	6397	6254	6112	5970	5829	5688	5548	5408	5268	5129	4990	4852	4713	4576	4438	4301	4165	4029
74	6770	6630	6490	6351	6213	6075	5937	5800	5663	5526	5390	5254	5119	4984	4849	4715	4581	4447	4314	4181
76	6852	6715	6579	6444	6309	6174	6040	5906	5772	5639	5506	5373	5241	5109	4978	4847	4716	4585	4455	4325
78	6930	6797	6664	6532	6400	6268	6137	6006	5876	5746	5616	5487	5357	5229	5100	4972	4844	4717	4590	4463
80	7004	6874	6744	6615	6486	6358	6230	6102	5975	5848	5721	5594	5468	5343	5217	5092	4967	4842	4718	4594
82	7075	6948	6821	6695	6569	6444	6318	6194	6069	5945	5821	5697	5574	5451	5328	5206	5084	4962	4840	4719
84	7142	7018	6894	6771	6648	6525	6403	6281	6159	6038	5916	5796	5675	5555	5435	5315	5196	5076	4957	4839
86	7207	7085	6964	6844	6723	6603	6484	6364	6245	6126	6008	5890	5772	5654	5536	5419	5302	5186	5069	4953
88	7268	7149	7031	6913	6795	6678	6561	6444	6327	6211	6095	5979	5864	5749	5634	5519	5405	5290	5176	5063
90	7327	7211	7095	6979	6864	6749	6635	6520	6406	6292	6179	6065	5952	5839	5727	5615	5502	5391	5279	5167
92	7384	7270	7156	7043	6930	6818	6705	6593	6482	6370	6259	6148	6037	5926	5816	5706	5596	5487	5377	5268
94	7438	7326	7215	7104	6993	6883	6773	6663	6554	6445	6336	6227	6118	6010	5902	5794	5686	5579	5472	5364
96	7490	7380	7271	7163	7054	6946	6838	6731	6623	6516	6409	6303	6196	6090	5984	5878	5773	5667	5562	5457
98	7540	7432	7325	7219	7113	7007	6901	6795	6690	6585	6480	6376	6271	6167	6063	5959	5856	5752	5649	5546
100	7587	7482	7378	7273	7169	7065	6961	6857	6754	6651	6548	6446	6343	6241	6139	6037	5936	5834	5733	5632
102	7634	7530	7428	7325	7223	7121	7019	6917	6816	6715	6614	6513	6413	6312	6212	6112	6012	5913	5814	5714
104	7678	7577	7476	7375	7275	7174	7075	6975	6875	6776	6677	6578	6479	6381	6283	6184	6087	5989	5891	5794
106	7721	7621	7522	7423	7325	7226	7128	7030	6933	6835	6738	6641	6544	6447	6350	6254	6158	6062	5966	5870
108	7762	7664	7567	7470	7373	7276	7180	7084	6988	6892	6796	6701	6606	6511	6416	6321	6227	6132	6038	5944
110	7802	7706	7610	7515	7419	7325	7230	7135	7041	6947	6853	6759	6666	6572	6479	6386	6293	6200	6108	6015
112	7840	7746	7652	7558	7464	7371	7278	7185	7092	7000	6908	6815	6723	6632	6540	6448	6357	6266	6175	6084
114	7877	7784	7692	7600	7508	7416	7325	7233	7142	7051	6960	6870	6779	6689	6599	6509	6419	6329	6240	6150
116	7913	7822	7731	7640	7550	7460	7370	7280	7190	7101	7011	6922	6833	6744	6656	6567	6479	6391	6303	6215
118	7947	7858	7768	7679	7590	7502	7413	7325	7236	7148	7061	6973	6885	6798	6711	6624	6537	6450	6363	6277
120	7981	7893	7805	7717	7630	7542	7455	7368	7281	7195	7108	7022	6936	6850	6764	6678	6593	6507	6422	6337
122	8013	7927	7840	7754	7668	7582	7496	7410	7325	7240	7154	7070	6985	6900	6816	6731	6647	6563	6479	6395
124	8045	7959	7874	7789	7704	7620	7535	7451	7367	7283	7199	7116	7032	6949	6866	6783	6700	6617	6534	6452
126	8075	7991	7907	7823	7740	7657	7573	7491	7408	7325	7243	7160	7078	6996	6914	6832	6751	6669	6588	6506
128	8105	8022	7939	7857	7774	7692	7611	7529	7447	7366	7285	7204	7123	7042	6961	6880	6800	6720	6640	6559
130	8133	8052	7970	7889	7808	7727	7646	7566	7486	7405	7325	7245	7166	7086	7007	6927	6848	6769	6690	6611
132	8161	8081	8000	7920	7840	7761	7681	7602	7523	7444	7365	7286	7208	7129	7051	6973	6894	6816	6739	6661
134	8188	8109	8030	7951	7872	7794	7715	7637	7559	7481	7403	7326	7248	7171	7094	7017	6940	6863	6786	6709
136	8214	8136	8058	7980	7903	7825	7748	7671	7594	7517	7441	7364	7288	7212	7135	7059	6984	6908	6832	6756
138	8239	8162	8086	8009	7933	7856	7780	7704	7628	7553	7477	7402	7326	7251	7176	7101	7026	6951	6877	6802
140	8264	8188	8112	8037	7961	7886	7811	7736	7661	7587	7512	7438	7364	7289	7215	7141	7068	6994	6920	6847
142	8288	8213	8139	8064	7990	7915	7841	7767	7694	7620	7547	7473	7400	7327	7254	7181	7108	7035	6963	6890
144	8312	8238	8164	8090	8017	7944	7871	7798	7725	7652	7580	7507	7435	7363	7291	7219	7147	7075	7004	6932
146	8334	8261	8189	8116	8044	7971	7899	7827	7756	7684	7612	7541	7470	7398	7327	7256	7185	7115	7044	6973
148	8356	8284	8213	8141	8070	7998	7927	7856	7785	7715	7644	7573	7503	7433	7363	7292	7222	7153	7083	7013
150	8378	8307	8236	8165	8095	8025	7954	7884	7814	7744	7675	7605	7536	7466	7397	7328	7259	7190	7121	7052

$l+r$	41	42	43	44	45	46	47	48	49	50	51	52	53	54	55	56	57	58	59	60
N	0,	0,	0,	0,	0,	0,	0,	0,	0,	0,	0,	0,	0,	0,	0,	0,	0,	0,		
41	0054																			
42	0197	0053																		
43	0359	0192	0052																	
44	0526	0351	0188	0051																
45	0694	0515	0343	0184	0049															
46	0859	0679	0503	0335	0180	0048														
47	1022	0841	0664	0492	0328	0176	0047													
48	1180	1000	0823	0650	0482	0321	0172	0046												
49	1335	1156	0979	0806	0637	0472	0315	0169	0045											
50	1485	1307	1132	0959	0790	0624	0463	0308	0165	0045										
52	1773	1599	1427	1256	1088	0922	0759	0600	0445	0297	0159	0043								
54	2044	1874	1706	1538	1373	1209	1047	0887	0731	0577	0428	0286	0153	0041						
56	2300	2134	1969	1806	1643	1482	1323	1165	1009	0855	0704	0556	0413	0275	0147	0040				
58	2541	2379	2218	2059	1900	1742	1586	1430	1277	1124	0974	0826	0680	0537	0398	0266	0142	0038		

All values conform to the international convention (i.e. 0,1 instead of 0.1).

Distribution-Free Tolerance Limits* $\beta_t = 0{,}80$

Top: $l+r$ = 41–60, N = 60(2)150; bottom: $l+r$ = 61–80, N = 62(2)150. The values in the table are those of β_p

$l+r$	41	42	43	44	45	46	47	48	49	50	51	52	53	54	55	56	57	58	59	60
N	0,	0,	0,	0,	0,	0,	0,	0,	0,	0,	0,	0,	0,	0,	0,	0,	0,	0,	0,	0,
60	2768	2610	2454	2298	2143	1988	1835	1683	1532	1382	1233	1086	0941	0798	0657	0519	0385	0257	0138	0037
62	2982	2829	2676	2524	2372	2222	2072	1923	1775	1628	1482	1337	1193	1051	0910	0772	0635	0502	0373	0249
64	3185	3035	2886	2738	2590	2443	2296	2151	2006	1861	1718	1576	1434	1294	1155	1017	0881	0747	0615	0486
66	3376	3230	3085	2940	2796	2652	2509	2367	2225	2084	1944	1804	1665	1527	1390	1254	1120	0986	0854	0724
68	3558	3415	3274	3132	2991	2851	2711	2572	2434	2296	2158	2021	1885	1750	1615	1481	1349	1217	1086	0957
70	3730	3591	3452	3315	3177	3040	2904	2767	2632	2497	2362	2228	2095	1962	1830	1699	1568	1438	1310	1182
72	3893	3757	3622	3488	3353	3220	3086	2953	2821	2689	2557	2426	2295	2165	2036	1907	1778	1651	1524	1398
74	4048	3916	3784	3652	3521	3390	3260	3130	3000	2871	2742	2614	2486	2359	2232	2105	1979	1854	1729	1605
76	4196	4066	3937	3809	3681	3553	3425	3298	3172	3045	2919	2793	2668	2543	2419	2295	2172	2049	1926	1804
78	4336	4210	4084	3958	3833	3708	3583	3459	3335	3211	3088	2965	2842	2720	2598	2477	2356	2235	2115	1995
80	4470	4347	4224	4101	3978	3856	3734	3612	3491	3370	3249	3129	3008	2889	2769	2650	2532	2413	2295	2178
82	4598	4477	4357	4237	4117	3997	3878	3759	3640	3521	3403	3285	3167	3050	2933	2816	2700	2584	2468	2353
84	4720	4602	4484	4367	4249	4132	4015	3899	3782	3666	3550	3435	3320	3205	3090	2975	2861	2748	2634	2521
86	4837	4722	4606	4491	4376	4261	4147	4033	3919	3805	3691	3578	3465	3352	3240	3128	3016	2904	2793	2682
88	4949	4836	4723	4610	4497	4385	4273	4161	4049	3938	3827	3716	3605	3494	3384	3274	3164	3055	2946	2837
90	5056	4945	4835	4724	4614	4503	4394	4284	4174	4065	3956	3847	3739	3630	3522	3414	3307	3199	3092	2985
92	5159	5050	4942	4833	4725	4617	4509	4402	4295	4187	4081	3974	3867	3761	3655	3549	3443	3338	3233	3128
94	5258	5151	5045	4938	4832	4726	4621	4515	4410	4305	4200	4095	3991	3886	3782	3678	3575	3471	3368	3265
96	5352	5248	5143	5039	4935	4831	4728	4624	4521	4418	4315	4212	4109	4007	3905	3803	3701	3600	3498	3397
98	5443	5341	5238	5136	5034	4932	4830	4729	4627	4526	4425	4324	4224	4123	4023	3923	3823	3723	3623	3524
100	5531	5430	5330	5229	5129	5029	4929	4829	4730	4631	4531	4432	4334	4235	4136	4038	3940	3842	3744	3646
102	5615	5516	5418	5319	5221	5122	5024	4926	4829	4731	4634	4536	4439	4342	4246	4149	4053	3956	3860	3764
104	5696	5599	5502	5406	5309	5212	5116	5020	4924	4828	4732	4637	4541	4446	4351	4256	4161	4067	3972	3878
106	5775	5679	5584	5489	5394	5299	5205	5110	5016	4921	4827	4734	4640	4546	4453	4359	4266	4173	4080	3987
108	5850	5756	5663	5569	5476	5383	5290	5197	5104	5012	4919	4827	4735	4643	4551	4459	4367	4276	4184	4093
110	5923	5831	5739	5647	5555	5464	5372	5281	5190	5099	5008	4917	4826	4736	4645	4555	4465	4375	4285	4196
112	5993	5903	5812	5722	5632	5542	5452	5362	5272	5183	5093	5004	4915	4826	4737	4648	4560	4471	4383	4294
114	6061	5972	5883	5794	5706	5617	5529	5440	5352	5264	5176	5088	5001	4913	4825	4738	4651	4564	4477	4390
116	6127	6039	5952	5864	5777	5690	5603	5516	5429	5343	5256	5170	5083	4997	4911	4825	4739	4654	4568	4482
118	6191	6104	6018	5932	5846	5760	5675	5589	5504	5419	5333	5248	5163	5079	4994	4909	4825	4740	4656	4572
120	6252	6167	6082	5998	5913	5829	5744	5660	5576	5492	5408	5325	5241	5158	5074	4991	4908	4824	4741	4659
122	6312	6228	6145	6061	5978	5895	5812	5729	5646	5564	5481	5399	5316	5234	5152	5070	4988	4906	4824	4743
124	6369	6287	6205	6123	6041	5959	5877	5796	5714	5633	5551	5470	5389	5308	5227	5146	5066	4985	4904	4824
126	6425	6344	6263	6182	6102	6021	5941	5860	5780	5700	5620	5540	5460	5380	5300	5220	5141	5062	4982	4903
128	6479	6400	6320	6240	6161	6081	6002	5923	5844	5765	5686	5607	5528	5449	5371	5292	5214	5136	5058	4980
130	6532	6453	6375	6296	6218	6140	6062	5983	5906	5828	5750	5672	5595	5517	5440	5362	5285	5208	5131	5054
132	6583	6506	6428	6351	6274	6196	6119	6042	5966	5889	5812	5736	5659	5583	5506	5430	5354	5278	5202	5126
134	6633	6556	6480	6404	6328	6252	6176	6100	6024	5948	5873	5797	5722	5646	5571	5496	5421	5346	5271	5196
136	6681	6606	6530	6455	6380	6305	6230	6155	6081	6006	5932	5857	5783	5708	5634	5560	5486	5412	5338	5264
138	6728	6653	6579	6505	6431	6357	6383	6209	6136	6062	5989	5915	5842	5769	5695	5622	5549	5476	5403	5331
140	6773	6700	6627	6554	6481	6408	6335	6262	6189	6117	6044	5972	5899	5827	5755	5683	5611	5539	5467	5395
142	6818	6745	6673	6601	6529	6457	6385	6313	6242	6170	6098	6027	5955	5884	5813	5742	5671	5600	5529	5458
144	6861	6789	6718	6647	6576	6505	6434	6363	6292	6222	6151	6080	6010	5940	5869	5799	5729	5659	5589	5519
146	6903	6832	6762	6692	6622	6551	6481	6411	6342	6272	6202	6133	6063	5994	5924	5855	5786	5716	5647	5578
148	6944	6874	6805	6735	6666	6597	6528	6459	6390	6321	6252	6183	6115	6046	5978	5909	5841	5773	5704	5636
150	6983	6915	6846	6778	6709	6641	6573	6505	6437	6369	6301	6233	6165	6097	6030	5962	5895	5827	5760	5693

$l+r$	61	62	63	64	65	66	67	68	69	70	71	72	73	74	75	76	77	78	79	80
N	0,	0,	0,	0,	0,	0,	0,	0,	0,	0,	0,	0,	0,	0,	0,	0,	0,	0,	0,	0,
62	0133	0036																		
64	0361	0241	0129	0035																
66	0597	0471	0350	0233	0125	0034														
68	0829	0703	0579	0457	0340	0227	0121	0033												
70	1055	0929	0805	0683	0562	0444	0330	0220	0118	0032										
72	1273	1148	1025	0903	0782	0663	0546	0432	0321	0214	0115	0031								
74	1482	1359	1238	1117	0997	0878	0761	0645	0532	0420	0312	0208	0112	0030						
76	1683	1562	1442	1323	1205	1087	0970	0855	0741	0628	0517	0409	0304	0203	0109	0029				
78	1876	1757	1639	1522	1405	1289	1173	1059	0945	0833	0722	0612	0504	0398	0296	0197	0106	0029		
80	2061	1944	1828	1712	1597	1483	1369	1256	1144	1032	0921	0812	0703	0597	0491	0388	0288	0192	0103	0028
82	2238	2124	2009	1896	1783	1670	1558	1446	1335	1225	1115	1007	0899	0792	0686	0582	0479	0379	0281	0188
84	2408	2296	2184	2072	1961	1850	1739	1630	1520	1411	1303	1195	1088	0982	0877	0773	0670	0568	0468	0370
86	2571	2461	2351	2241	2132	2023	1914	1806	1698	1591	1484	1378	1272	1167	1063	0959	0856	0755	0654	0555
88	2728	2620	2511	2404	2296	2189	2082	1976	1870	1764	1659	1554	1450	1346	1243	1140	1038	0937	0837	0737
90	2878	2772	2666	2560	2454	2349	2244	2140	2035	1931	1828	1724	1622	1519	1417	1316	1215	1115	1015	0916
92	3023	2919	2814	2710	2607	2503	2400	2297	2194	2092	1990	1888	1787	1686	1586	1486	1386	1287	1188	1090
94	3162	3059	2957	2855	2753	2651	2550	2449	2348	2247	2147	2047	1947	1848	1748	1650	1551	1454	1356	1259
96	3296	3195	3094	2994	2894	2794	2694	2595	2496	2397	2298	2199	2101	2003	1906	1808	1711	1615	1519	1423
98	3425	3326	3227	3128	3030	2931	2833	2736	2638	2541	2443	2347	2250	2154	2057	1962	1866	1771	1676	1581
100	3549	3451	3354	3257	3161	3064	2968	2871	2775	2680	2584	2489	2394	2299	2204	2110	2016	1922	1828	1735
102	3668	3573	3477	3382	3287	3192	3097	3002	2908	2814	2720	2626	2532	2439	2346	2253	2160	2067	1975	1883
104	3784	3690	3596	3502	3408	3315	3222	3129	3036	2943	2851	2758	2666	2574	2482	2391	2300	2209	2118	2027
106	3895	3802	3710	3618	3526	3434	3342	3251	3159	3068	2977	2886	2796	2705	2615	2525	2435	2345	2255	2166
108	4002	3911	3820	3730	3639	3549	3459	3369	3279	3189	3099	3010	2921	2832	2743	2654	2565	2477	2389	2301
110	4106	4017	3927	3838	3749	3660	3571	3483	3394	3306	3218	3130	3042	2954	2866	2779	2692	2605	2518	2431
112	4206	4118	4030	3943	3855	3767	3680	3593	3506	3419	3332	3245	3159	3072	2986	2900	2814	2728	2643	2557
114	4303	4217	4130	4044	3957	3871	3785	3699	3614	3528	3443	3357	3272	3187	3102	3017	2932	2848	2764	2679
116	4397	4312	4227	4142	4057	3972	3887	3803	3718	3634	3550	3466	3382	3298	3214	3131	3047	2964	2881	2798
118	4488	4404	4320	4236	4153	4069	3986	3903	3819	3736	3653	3571	3488	3405	3323	3241	3158	3076	2994	2912
120	4576	4493	4411	4328	4246	4164	4081	3999	3917	3836	3754	3672	3591	3510	3428	3347	3266	3185	3104	3024
122	4661	4580	4498	4417	4336	4255	4174	4093	4013	3932	3851	3771	3691	3611	3530	3450	3371	3291	3211	3132
124	4744	4663	4583	4503	4423	4344	4264	4184	4105	4025	3946	3867	3788	3708	3630	3551	3472	3393	3315	3236
126	4824	4745	4666	4587	4508	4430	4351	4272	4194	4116	4038	3959	3881	3804	3726	3648	3570	3493	3415	3338
128	4902	4824	4746	4668	4590	4513	4435	4358	4281	4204	4127	4050	3973	3896	3819	3742	3666	3590	3513	3437
130	4977	4900	4824	4747	4670	4594	4518	4441	4365	4289	4213	4137	4061	3985	3910	3834	3759	3683	3608	3533
132	5050	4975	4899	4823	4748	4673	4597	4522	4447	4372	4297	4222	4147	4073	3998	3923	3849	3775	3700	3626
134	5121	5047	4972	4898	4823	4749	4675	4601	4526	4452	4378	4305	4231	4157	4084	4010	3937	3863	3790	3717
136	5191	5117	5043	4970	4897	4823	4750	4677	4604	4531	4458	4385	4312	4239	4167	4094	4022	3949	3877	3805
138	5258	5185	5113	5040	4968	4895	4823	4751	4679	4607	4535	4463	4391	4319	4248	4176	4105	4033	3962	3891
140	5323	5252	5180	5109	5037	4966	4894	4823	4752	4681	4610	4539	4468	4397	4327	4256	4185	4115	4044	3974
142	5387	5316	5246	5175	5105	5034	4964	4893	4823	4753	4683	4613	4543	4473	4403	4334	4264	4194	4125	4055
144	5449	5379	5309	5240	5170	5101	5031	4962	4892	4823	4754	4685	4616	4547	4478	4409	4340	4272	4203	4134
146	5509	5440	5372	5303	5234	5165	5097	5028	4960	4892	4823	4755	4687	4619	4551	4483	4415	4347	4279	4211
148	5568	5500	5432	5364	5296	5229	5161	5093	5026	4958	4891	4823	4756	4689	4621	4554	4487	4420	4353	4286
150	5625	5558	5491	5424	5357	5290	5223	5156	5090	5023	4956	4890	4823	4757	4691	4624	4558	4492	4426	4360

All values conform to the international convention (i.e. 0,1 instead of 0.1).

Distribution-Free Tolerance Limits* $\beta_t = 0{,}80$

Top: $l+r = 81$–100, $N = 82(2)150$; middle: $l+r = 101$–120, $N = 102(2)150$; bottom: $l+r = 121$–140, $N = 122(2)150$. The values in the table are those of β_p

$l+r$	81	82	83	84	85	86	87	88	89	90	91	92	93	94	95	96	97	98	99	100
N	0,	0,	0,	0,	0,	0,	0,	0,	0,	0,	0,	0,	0,	0,	0,	0,	0,	0,	0,	0,
82	0101	0027																		
84	0275	0183	0098	0027																
86	0457	0361	0268	0179	0096	0026														
88	0639	0542	0446	0353	0262	0175	0094	0025												
90	0818	0721	0625	0530	0436	0345	0256	0171	0092	0025										
92	0993	0896	0800	0705	0611	0518	0427	0338	0251	0167	0090	0024								
94	1163	1067	0971	0877	0783	0690	0598	0507	0418	0330	0245	0164	0088	0024						
96	1327	1232	1138	1044	0951	0858	0766	0675	0585	0496	0409	0323	0240	0160	0086	0023				
98	1487	1393	1300	1207	1115	1023	0931	0841	0751	0661	0573	0486	0401	0317	0235	0157	0084	0023		
100	1642	1549	1457	1365	1274	1183	1092	1002	0912	0824	0735	0648	0562	0476	0393	0310	0230	0154	0083	0022
102	1792	1700	1609	1518	1428	1338	1248	1159	1070	0982	0894	0807	0721	0635	0551	0467	0385	0304	0226	0151
104	1937	1846	1757	1667	1578	1489	1400	1312	1224	1136	1049	0963	0877	0792	0707	0623	0540	0458	0377	0298
106	2077	1988	1899	1811	1723	1635	1548	1460	1373	1287	1201	1115	1029	0945	0860	0776	0693	0611	0530	0449
108	2213	2125	2038	1951	1864	1777	1690	1604	1518	1433	1348	1263	1178	1094	1010	0927	0844	0762	0680	0600
110	2344	2258	2172	2086	2000	1915	1829	1744	1659	1575	1490	1406	1323	1239	1156	1074	0992	0910	0829	0748
112	2472	2387	2302	2217	2132	2048	1964	1880	1796	1712	1629	1546	1463	1381	1299	1217	1135	1054	0974	0893
114	2595	2511	2428	2344	2260	2177	2094	2011	1929	1846	1764	1682	1600	1519	1437	1356	1276	1195	1115	1036
116	2715	2632	2550	2467	2385	2303	2221	2139	2057	1976	1895	1814	1733	1653	1572	1492	1412	1333	1253	1174
118	2831	2749	2668	2587	2505	2424	2344	2263	2182	2102	2022	1942	1862	1783	1703	1624	1545	1466	1388	1310
120	2943	2863	2783	2702	2622	2543	2463	2383	2304	2225	2145	2066	1988	1909	1831	1752	1674	1597	1519	1442
122	3052	2973	2894	2815	2736	2657	2579	2500	2422	2343	2265	2187	2110	2032	1955	1877	1800	1723	1647	1570
124	3158	3080	3002	2924	2846	2768	2691	2613	2536	2459	2382	2305	2228	2151	2075	1999	1923	1847	1771	1695
126	3261	3184	3107	3030	2953	2877	2800	2724	2647	2571	2495	2419	2343	2268	2192	2117	2041	1966	1891	1817
128	3361	3285	3209	3133	3057	2982	2906	2831	2755	2680	2605	2530	2455	2381	2306	2232	2157	2083	2009	1935
130	3458	3383	3308	3233	3158	3084	3009	2935	2860	2786	2712	2638	2564	2490	2417	2343	2270	2197	2123	2050
132	3552	3478	3404	3330	3256	3183	3109	3036	2963	2889	2816	2743	2670	2597	2525	2452	2379	2307	2235	2163
134	3644	3571	3498	3425	3352	3279	3207	3134	3062	2990	2917	2845	2773	2701	2629	2558	2486	2415	2343	2272
136	3733	3661	3589	3517	3445	3373	3302	3230	3158	3087	3016	2945	2874	2802	2732	2661	2590	2519	2449	2379
138	3819	3748	3677	3606	3535	3465	3394	3323	3253	3182	3112	3041	2971	2901	2831	2761	2691	2621	2552	2482
140	3904	3834	3763	3693	3623	3553	3484	3414	3344	3275	3205	3136	3066	2997	2928	2859	2790	2721	2652	2583
142	3986	3917	3847	3778	3709	3640	3571	3502	3433	3365	3296	3227	3159	3090	3022	2954	2886	2818	2750	2682
144	4066	3997	3929	3861	3792	3724	3656	3588	3520	3452	3384	3317	3249	3182	3114	3047	2979	2912	2845	2778
146	4144	4076	4009	3941	3874	3806	3739	3672	3605	3538	3471	3404	3337	3270	3204	3137	3070	3004	2938	2871
148	4220	4153	4086	4020	3953	3886	3820	3754	3687	3621	3555	3489	3423	3357	3291	3225	3159	3094	3028	2963
150	4294	4228	4162	4096	4030	3964	3899	3833	3768	3702	3637	3572	3506	3441	3376	3311	3246	3181	3116	3052

$l+r$	101	102	103	104	105	106	107	108	109	110	111	112	113	114	115	116	117	118	119	120
N	0,	0,	0,	0,	0,	0,	0,	0,	0,	0,	0,	0,	0,	0,	0,	0,	0,	0,	0,	0,
102	0081	0022																		
104	0222	0148	0079	0021																
106	0370	0292	0217	0145	0078	0021														
108	0520	0441	0363	0287	0213	0142	0076	0021												
110	0668	0589	0510	0433	0357	0282	0209	0140	0075	0020										
112	0814	0735	0656	0578	0501	0425	0350	0277	0206	0137	0074	0020								
114	0956	0878	0799	0722	0644	0568	0492	0418	0344	0272	0202	0135	0072	0020						
116	1096	1018	0940	0862	0785	0709	0633	0558	0484	0410	0338	0267	0199	0133	0071	0019				
118	1232	1154	1077	1000	0924	0848	0772	0697	0622	0549	0475	0403	0332	0263	0195	0130	0070	0019		
120	1365	1288	1211	1135	1059	0983	0908	0833	0759	0685	0612	0539	0468	0397	0327	0258	0192	0128	0069	0019
122	1494	1418	1342	1266	1191	1116	1041	0967	0893	0820	0746	0674	0602	0530	0460	0390	0321	0254	0189	0126
124	1620	1544	1469	1395	1320	1246	1172	1098	1024	0951	0879	0806	0734	0663	0592	0522	0452	0384	0316	0250
126	1742	1668	1594	1520	1446	1372	1299	1226	1153	1080	1008	0936	0864	0793	0723	0652	0583	0513	0445	0378
128	1861	1788	1715	1641	1568	1495	1423	1350	1278	1206	1135	1063	0992	0921	0851	0781	0711	0642	0573	0505
130	1978	1905	1832	1760	1688	1616	1544	1472	1401	1329	1258	1188	1117	1047	0977	0907	0838	0769	0700	0632
132	2091	2019	1947	1876	1804	1733	1662	1591	1520	1450	1379	1309	1239	1169	1100	1031	0962	0893	0825	0757
134	2201	2130	2059	1988	1918	1847	1777	1707	1637	1567	1497	1428	1358	1289	1220	1152	1083	1015	0947	0880
136	2308	2238	2168	2098	2028	1959	1889	1820	1750	1681	1612	1543	1475	1406	1338	1270	1202	1135	1067	1000
138	2413	2343	2274	2205	2136	2067	1998	1930	1861	1793	1725	1657	1589	1521	1453	1386	1318	1251	1185	1118
140	2515	2446	2378	2309	2241	2173	2105	2037	1969	1902	1834	1767	1700	1633	1566	1499	1432	1366	1299	1233
142	2614	2546	2479	2411	2344	2276	2209	2142	2075	2008	1941	1875	1808	1742	1675	1609	1543	1477	1412	1346
144	2711	2644	2577	2510	2443	2377	2310	2244	2178	2112	2046	1980	1914	1848	1783	1717	1652	1587	1522	1457
146	2805	2739	2673	2607	2541	2475	2409	2344	2278	2213	2147	2082	2017	1952	1887	1822	1758	1693	1629	1565
148	2897	2832	2766	2701	2636	2571	2506	2441	2376	2312	2247	2182	2118	2054	1989	1925	1861	1797	1734	1670
150	2987	2922	2858	2793	2729	2664	2600	2536	2472	2408	2344	2280	2216	2153	2089	2026	1963	1899	1836	1773

$l+r$	121	122	123	124	125	126	127	128	129	130	131	132	133	134	135	136	137	138	139	140
N	0,	0,	0,	0,	0,	0,	0,	0,	0,	0,	0,	0,	0,	0,	0,	0,	0,	0,	0,	0,
122	0068	0018																		
124	0186	0124	0067	0018																
126	0311	0246	0183	0122	0065	0018														
128	0438	0372	0306	0242	0180	0120	0064	0017												
130	0565	0498	0431	0366	0302	0239	0177	0118	0063	0017										
132	0689	0622	0556	0490	0425	0360	0297	0235	0174	0116	0062	0017								
134	0812	0746	0679	0613	0548	0483	0418	0355	0293	0231	0172	0115	0062	0017						
136	0933	0867	0800	0734	0669	0604	0539	0475	0412	0350	0288	0228	0169	0113	0061	0016				
138	1052	0985	0920	0854	0789	0724	0659	0595	0532	0469	0406	0345	0284	0225	0167	0111	0060	0016		
140	1167	1102	1036	0971	0906	0842	0777	0713	0650	0587	0524	0462	0400	0340	0280	0221	0164	0110	0059	0016
142	1281	1216	1151	1086	1022	0957	0893	0830	0766	0703	0641	0578	0517	0455	0395	0335	0276	0218	0162	0108
144	1392	1327	1263	1199	1135	1071	1007	0944	0881	0818	0756	0693	0632	0570	0509	0449	0389	0330	0272	0215
146	1500	1436	1373	1309	1245	1182	1119	1056	0993	0931	0869	0807	0745	0684	0623	0562	0502	0443	0384	0326
148	1607	1543	1480	1417	1354	1291	1228	1166	1104	1042	0980	0918	0857	0796	0735	0674	0614	0555	0495	0437
150	1710	1647	1585	1522	1460	1398	1336	1274	1212	1150	1089	1028	0967	0906	0845	0785	0725	0665	0606	0547

All values conform to the international convention (i.e. 0,1 instead of 0.1).

Distribution-Free Tolerance Limits* $\beta_t = 0{,}90$

$l + r = 1$–20, $N = 2(1)50(2)150$. The values in the table are those of β_p

$l+r$	1	2	3	4	5	6	7	8	9	10	11	12	13	14	15	16	17	18	19	20
N	0,	0,	0,	0,	0,	0,	0,	0,	0,	0,	0,	0,	0,	0,	0,	0,	0,	0,	0,	0,
2	3162	0513																		
3	4642	1958	0345																	
4	5623	3205	1426	0260																
5	6310	4160	2466	1122	0209															
6	6813	4897	3332	2009	0926	0174														
7	7196	5474	4038	2786	1696	0788	0149													
8	7499	5938	4618	3446	2397	1468	0686	0131												
9	7743	6315	5099	4005	3010	2104	1295	0608	0116											
10	7943	6631	5504	4483	3542	2673	1875	1158	0545	0105										
11	8111	6897	5848	4892	4005	3177	2405	1692	1048	0494	0095									
12	8254	7125	6145	5247	4410	3623	2882	2187	1542	0956	0452	0087								
13	8377	7322	6402	5557	4766	4017	3308	2637	2005	1416	0880	0417	0081							
14	8483	7493	6628	5830	5080	4369	3691	3045	2431	1851	1309	0815	0387	0075						
15	8577	7644	6827	6072	5360	4683	4035	3415	2822	2256	1719	1218	0759	0360	0070					
16	8660	7778	7004	6288	5611	4965	4345	3750	3178	2629	2104	1605	1138	0710	0337	0066				
17	8733	7898	7163	6481	5836	5219	4626	4055	3504	2972	2461	1971	1506	1068	0667	0317	0062			
18	8799	8006	7306	6656	6040	5450	4881	4333	3802	3288	2792	2314	1855	1418	1006	0629	0299	0058		
19	8859	8102	7435	6814	6225	5659	5114	4587	4075	3579	3098	2633	2183	1751	1339	0951	0595	0283	0055	
20	8913	8190	7552	6958	6393	5851	5327	4820	4327	3847	3381	2929	2490	2066	1659	1269	0902	0564	0269	0053
21	8962	8270	7659	7090	6548	6027	5523	5034	4558	4095	3644	3205	2778	2363	1962	1575	1206	0858	0537	0256
22	9006	8344	7758	7210	6689	6188	5703	5231	4772	4325	3888	3462	3046	2641	2248	1867	1500	1149	0817	0512
23	9047	8411	7848	7322	6820	6337	5869	5414	4971	4538	4114	3701	3297	2902	2518	2144	1781	1432	1097	0781
24	9085	8474	7931	7424	6941	6475	6023	5584	5155	4736	4326	3924	3531	3147	2772	2406	2049	1703	1369	1050
25	9120	8531	8008	7520	7053	6603	6167	5742	5326	4920	4523	4133	3751	3377	3011	2653	2303	1962	1632	1312
26	9152	8585	8080	7608	7157	6722	6300	5889	5486	5093	4707	4328	3957	3593	3236	2886	2543	2209	1883	1566
27	9183	8634	8147	7690	7254	6833	6425	6026	5636	5254	4879	4512	4151	3796	3448	3106	2771	2443	2122	1809
28	9211	8680	8209	7767	7345	6937	6541	6154	5776	5405	5041	4684	4333	3987	3648	3314	2986	2665	2350	2042
29	9237	8724	8267	7839	7430	7035	6650	6275	5908	5547	5194	4846	4504	4167	3836	3511	3190	2876	2567	2264
30	9261	8764	8322	7907	7510	7126	6753	6388	6031	5681	5337	4998	4665	4338	4015	3697	3384	3076	2773	2476
31	9284	8802	8373	7970	7585	7212	6849	6495	6148	5807	5472	5143	4818	4498	4183	3873	3567	3266	2969	2678
32	9306	8838	8421	8030	7655	7293	6940	6596	6258	5926	5600	5279	4962	4651	4343	4040	3741	3446	3156	2870
33	9326	8872	8467	8086	7722	7370	7026	6691	6362	6039	5721	5408	5099	4795	4495	4198	3906	3618	3334	3053
34	9345	8903	8509	8139	7785	7442	7108	6781	6460	6145	5835	5530	5229	4932	4638	4349	4063	3781	3503	3228
35	9363	8934	8550	8190	7845	7510	7185	6866	6553	6246	5944	5646	5352	5062	4775	4492	4213	3937	3664	3395
36	9380	8962	8588	8237	7901	7575	7258	6947	6642	6342	6047	5756	5469	5185	4905	4629	4355	4085	3818	3554
37	9397	8989	8625	8283	7955	7637	7327	7024	6726	6433	6145	5861	5580	5303	5029	4758	4491	4226	3965	3706
38	9412	9014	8659	8326	8006	7695	7393	7097	6806	6520	6238	5960	5686	5415	5147	4882	4621	4361	4105	3852
39	9427	9039	8692	8367	8054	7751	7456	7166	6882	6603	6327	6056	5787	5522	5260	5001	4744	4491	4239	3991
40	9441	9062	8724	8405	8100	7804	7515	7233	6955	6682	6412	6146	5884	5624	5368	5114	4863	4614	4368	4124
41	9454	9084	8754	8443	8144	7855	7572	7296	7024	6757	6493	6233	5976	5722	5471	5222	4976	4732	4491	4252
42	9467	9105	8782	8478	8186	7903	7627	7356	7091	6829	6571	6316	6064	5816	5569	5326	5084	4845	4609	4374
43	9479	9125	8809	8512	8226	7949	7679	7414	7154	6898	6645	6396	6149	5905	5664	5425	5188	4954	4722	4492
44	9490	9144	8835	8545	8265	7994	7729	7470	7215	6964	6716	6472	6230	5991	5754	5520	5288	5058	4830	4604
45	9501	9163	8860	8575	8302	8036	7777	7523	7273	7027	6784	6545	6308	6073	5841	5611	5384	5158	4934	4713
46	9512	9180	8884	8605	8337	8077	7823	7574	7329	7088	6850	6615	6382	6152	5925	5699	5476	5254	5035	4817
47	9522	9197	8907	8633	8371	8116	7867	7623	7382	7146	6913	6682	6454	6228	6005	5784	5564	5347	5131	4917
48	9532	9214	8929	8661	8403	8153	7909	7669	7434	7202	6973	6747	6523	6301	6082	5865	5649	5436	5224	5014
49	9541	9229	8950	8687	8434	8189	7950	7715	7484	7256	7031	6809	6589	6372	6156	5943	5731	5521	5313	5107
50	9550	9244	8970	8712	8464	8224	7989	7758	7531	7308	7087	6869	6653	6439	6228	6018	5810	5604	5399	5196
52	9567	9272	9009	8760	8521	8289	8063	7840	7621	7406	7193	6982	6774	6568	6363	6161	5960	5760	5563	5366
54	9583	9299	9044	8804	8574	8350	8131	7916	7705	7497	7291	7088	6886	6687	6489	6294	6099	5906	5715	5525
56	9597	9323	9077	8846	8623	8407	8195	7988	7783	7582	7383	7186	6991	6798	6607	6417	6229	6042	5857	5673
58	9611	9346	9108	8884	8669	8459	8255	8054	7856	7661	7469	7278	7089	6902	6717	6533	6351	6170	5990	5811
60	9624	9367	9137	8920	8712	8505	8311	8116	7925	7736	7549	7364	7181	7000	6820	6642	6465	6290	6115	5942
62	9635	9387	9164	8954	8752	8555	8363	8174	7989	7806	7624	7445	7268	7092	6917	6744	6573	6402	6233	6064
64	9647	9406	9190	8986	8790	8599	8412	8229	8049	7871	7695	7521	7349	7178	7009	6841	6674	6508	6343	6179
66	9657	9423	9214	9016	8825	8640	8459	8281	8106	7933	7762	7593	7425	7259	7095	6931	6769	6608	6448	6288
68	9667	9440	9236	9044	8859	8679	8503	8329	8159	7991	7825	7661	7498	7336	7176	7017	6859	6702	6546	6391
70	9676	9456	9258	9070	8890	8715	8544	8376	8210	8046	7885	7725	7566	7409	7253	7098	6944	6791	6639	6488
72	9685	9470	9278	9096	8920	8750	8583	8419	8258	8098	7941	7785	7631	7477	7325	7175	7025	6876	6728	6581
74	9694	9484	9297	9119	8949	8783	8620	8460	8303	8148	7994	7843	7692	7543	7395	7247	7101	6956	6812	6668
76	9702	9498	9315	9142	8976	8814	8655	8500	8346	8195	8045	7897	7750	7605	7460	7317	7174	7032	6891	6751
78	9709	9510	9332	9164	9001	8843	8689	8537	8387	8240	8094	7949	7806	7663	7522	7382	7243	7105	6967	6831
80	9716	9522	9348	9184	9026	8871	8721	8572	8426	8282	8140	7998	7858	7720	7582	7445	7309	7174	7040	6906
82	9723	9534	9364	9203	9049	8898	8751	8606	8464	8323	8183	8045	7909	7773	7638	7505	7372	7240	7108	6978
84	9730	9545	9379	9222	9071	8924	8780	8638	8499	8361	8225	8090	7957	7824	7692	7562	7432	7303	7174	7047
86	9736	9555	9393	9240	9092	8948	8808	8669	8533	8398	8265	8133	8002	7873	7744	7616	7489	7363	7237	7112
88	9742	9565	9406	9257	9112	8972	8834	8699	8565	8434	8303	8174	8046	7919	7793	7668	7544	7420	7297	7175
90	9747	9575	9419	9273	9131	8994	8859	8727	8596	8467	8340	8213	8088	7964	7841	7718	7596	7475	7355	7235
92	9753	9584	9432	9288	9150	9015	8883	8754	8626	8500	8375	8251	8128	8007	7886	7766	7647	7528	7410	7293
94	9758	9592	9444	9303	9168	9036	8907	8780	8654	8531	8408	8287	8167	8048	7929	7812	7695	7579	7463	7348
96	9763	9601	9455	9317	9184	9055	8929	8804	8682	8560	8440	8322	8204	8087	7971	7856	7741	7627	7514	7401
98	9768	9609	9466	9331	9201	9074	8950	8828	8708	8589	8471	8355	8239	8125	8011	7898	7786	7674	7563	7452
100	9772	9617	9477	9344	9216	9092	8971	8851	8733	8616	8501	8387	8274	8161	8050	7939	7828	7719	7610	7501
102	9777	9624	9487	9357	9232	9110	8990	8873	8757	8643	8530	8418	8306	8196	8087	7978	7869	7762	7655	7548
104	9781	9631	9496	9369	9246	9126	9009	8894	8781	8668	8557	8447	8338	8230	8122	8015	7909	7803	7698	7594
106	9785	9638	9506	9381	9260	9143	9028	8914	8803	8693	8584	8476	8369	8262	8157	8052	7947	7844	7740	7638
108	9789	9645	9515	9392	9273	9158	9045	8934	8825	8716	8609	8503	8398	8293	8190	8087	7984	7882	7781	7680
110	9793	9651	9523	9403	9286	9173	9062	8953	8845	8739	8634	8530	8426	8324	8222	8120	8020	7919	7820	7721
112	9797	9657	9532	9413	9299	9188	9079	8971	8866	8761	8658	8555	8454	8353	8253	8153	8054	7955	7857	7760
114	9800	9663	9540	9423	9311	9202	9094	8989	8885	8782	8681	8580	8480	8381	8282	8184	8087	7990	7894	7798
116	9803	9669	9548	9433	9323	9215	9110	9006	8904	8803	8703	8604	8506	8408	8311	8215	8119	8024	7929	7835
118	9807	9674	9555	9443	9334	9228	9124	9023	8922	8823	8724	8627	8530	8434	8339	8244	8150	8056	7963	7870
120	9810	9680	9563	9452	9345	9241	9139	9039	8940	8842	8745	8649	8554	8460	8366	8273	8180	8088	7996	7905
122	9813	9685	9570	9461	9355	9253	9153	9054	8957	8860	8765	8671	8577	8484	8392	8300	8209	8118	8028	7938
124	9816	9690	9576	9469	9366	9265	9166	9069	8973	8878	8785	8692	8600	8508	8417	8327	8237	8148	8059	7970
126	9819	9695	9583	9477	9376	9276	9179	9083	8989	8896	8804	8712	8621	8531	8442	8353	8264	8176	8089	8002
128	9822	9699	9590	9485	9385	9287	9192	9097	9005	8913	8822	8732	8642	8554	8465	8378	8291	8204	8118	8032
130	9824	9704	9596	9493	9394	9298	9204	9111	9020	8929	8840	8751	8663	8575	8488	8402	8316	8231	8146	8061
132	9827	9709	9602	9501	9403	9309	9216	9124	9034	8945	8857	8769	8683	8596	8511	8426	8341	8257	8173	8090
134	9830	9713	9608	9508	9412	9319	9227	9137	9048	8960	8873	8787	8702	8617	8533	8449	8365	8282	8200	8118
136	9832	9717	9613	9515	9421	9329	9238	9150	9062	8975	8890	8805	8720	8637	8554	8471	8389	8307	8226	8145
138	9835	9721	9619	9522	9429	9338	9249	9162	9075	8990	8905	8822	8739	8656	8574	8493	8411	8331	8251	8171
140	9837	9725	9624	9529	9437	9348	9260	9174	9088	9004	8921	8838	8756	8675	8594	8514	8434	8354	8275	8196
142	9839	9729	9630	9536	9445	9357	9270	9185	9101	9018	8936	8854	8773	8693	8613	8534	8455	8377	8299	8221
144	9841	9733	9635	9542	9453	9365	9280	9196	9113	9031	8950	8870	8790	8711	8632	8554	8476	8399	8322	8245
146	9844	9736	9640	9548	9460	9374	9290	9207	9125	9044	8964	8885	8806	8728	8650	8573	8496	8420	8344	8268
148	9846	9740	9644	9554	9467	9382	9299	9217	9137	9057	8978	8900	8822	8745	8668	8592	8516	8441	8366	8291
150	9848	9743	9649	9560	9474	9390	9308	9228	9148	9069	8991	8914	8837	8761	8686	8610	8536	8461	8387	8313

All values conform to the international convention (i.e. 0,1 instead of 0.1).

Top: $l+r = 21$–40, $N = 21(1)50(2)150$; bottom: $l+r = 41$–60, $N = 41(1)50(2)58$. The values in the table are those of β_p

$l+r$	21	22	23	24	25	26	27	28	29	30	31	32	33	34	35	36	37	38	39	40
N	0,	0,	0,	0,	0,	0,	0,	0,	0,	0,	0,	0,	0,	0,	0,	0,	0,	0,	0,	0,
21	0050																			
22	0244	0048																		
23	0489	0234	0046																	
24	0747	0468	0224	0044																
25	1006	0717	0449	0215	0042															
26	1260	0966	0688	0432	0206	0040														
27	1505	1211	0929	0662	0415	0199	0039													
28	1741	1449	1166	0895	0638	0400	0192	0038												
29	1968	1678	1397	1125	0863	0615	0386	0185	0036											
30	2184	1899	1620	1348	1086	0833	0594	0373	0179	0035										
31	2391	2110	1834	1565	1303	1049	0806	0575	0361	0173	0034									
32	2588	2312	2040	1774	1514	1261	1016	0780	0555	0349	0167	0033								
33	2777	2505	2238	1975	1718	1466	1221	0984	0756	0539	0339	0162	0032							
34	2957	2690	2427	2168	1914	1665	1421	1184	0954	0733	0523	0329	0157	0031						
35	3129	2867	2608	2354	2103	1857	1615	1379	1149	0926	0711	0508	0319	0153	0030					
36	3294	3036	2782	2532	2285	2042	1803	1569	1339	1116	0899	0691	0493	0310	0149	0029				
37	3451	3198	2949	2702	2459	2220	1984	1752	1524	1302	1085	0874	0672	0480	0302	0145	0028			
38	3601	3353	3108	2866	2627	2391	2158	1929	1704	1483	1266	1055	0851	0654	0467	0294	0141	0028		
39	3745	3502	3261	3023	2788	2555	2326	2100	1877	1658	1443	1233	1028	0828	0637	0455	0286	0137	0027	
40	3883	3644	3408	3174	2943	2714	2488	2265	2045	1828	1615	1406	1201	1001	0807	0621	0443	0279	0134	0026
41	4015	3781	3548	3319	3091	2866	2644	2424	2207	1993	1782	1574	1370	1171	0976	0787	0605	0432	0272	0130
42	4142	3912	3684	3458	3234	3013	2794	2577	2363	2152	1943	1737	1535	1336	1142	0952	0768	0590	0422	0265
43	4263	4037	3814	3592	3372	3154	2938	2725	2514	2305	2099	1896	1695	1498	1304	1115	0929	0750	0576	0412
44	4380	4158	3938	3720	3504	3290	3078	2868	2660	2454	2250	2049	1851	1655	1463	1274	1088	0908	0732	0563
45	4493	4275	4058	3844	3632	3421	3212	3005	2800	2597	2397	2198	2002	1808	1617	1429	1244	1064	0887	0716
46	4601	4387	4174	3963	3754	3547	3341	3138	2936	2736	2538	2342	2148	1956	1767	1581	1397	1217	1040	0867
47	4705	4494	4285	4078	3873	3669	3466	3266	3067	2870	2674	2481	2290	2100	1913	1728	1546	1366	1190	1017
48	4805	4598	4393	4189	3987	3786	3587	3389	3193	2999	2807	2616	2427	2240	2054	1871	1691	1512	1337	1164
49	4902	4698	4496	4296	4097	3899	3703	3509	3316	3124	2934	2746	2560	2375	2192	2011	1832	1655	1480	1309
50	4995	4795	4596	4399	4203	4009	3816	3624	3434	3245	3058	2872	2688	2506	2325	2146	1969	1793	1620	1450
52	5171	4977	4785	4594	4405	4216	4029	3843	3659	3475	3294	3113	2934	2756	2580	2405	2231	2060	1890	1722
54	5336	5148	4962	4777	4593	4410	4229	4048	3869	3691	3514	3339	3164	2991	2819	2649	2479	2311	2145	1980
56	5490	5308	5127	4948	4769	4592	4416	4241	4067	3894	3722	3551	3381	3212	3045	2879	2713	2549	2387	2225
58	5634	5458	5282	5108	4935	4763	4592	4421	4252	4084	3917	3751	3585	3421	3258	3095	2934	2774	2615	2457
60	5769	5598	5428	5259	5091	4923	4757	4591	4427	4263	4100	3939	3778	3618	3458	3300	3143	2987	2831	2677
62	5897	5730	5565	5401	5237	5074	4912	4752	4591	4432	4274	4116	3959	3803	3648	3494	3340	3188	3036	2885
64	6017	5855	5694	5534	5375	5217	5059	4903	4747	4592	4437	4284	4131	3979	3828	3677	3527	3378	3230	3083
66	6130	5973	5816	5660	5505	5351	5198	5045	4894	4742	4592	4442	4293	4145	3997	3851	3704	3559	3414	3270
68	6237	6084	5931	5780	5629	5479	5329	5180	5032	4885	4738	4592	4447	4302	4158	4015	3872	3730	3589	3448
70	6338	6189	6040	5893	5746	5599	5454	5309	5164	5020	4877	4735	4593	4452	4311	4171	4032	3893	3755	3618
72	6435	6289	6144	6000	5856	5714	5572	5430	5289	5149	5009	4870	4732	4594	4457	4320	4184	4048	3913	3779
74	6525	6383	6242	6102	5962	5822	5684	5545	5408	5271	5135	4999	4864	4729	4595	4461	4328	4195	4063	3932
76	6612	6473	6336	6198	6062	5926	5790	5655	5521	5387	5254	5121	4989	4857	4726	4596	4466	4336	4207	4078
78	6695	6559	6424	6290	6157	6024	5892	5760	5629	5498	5368	5238	5109	4980	4852	4724	4597	4470	4344	4218
80	6773	6641	6509	6378	6248	6118	5988	5860	5731	5603	5476	5345	5223	5097	4971	4846	4722	4598	4474	4351
82	6848	6719	6590	6462	6334	6207	6081	5955	5829	5704	5580	5455	5332	5209	5086	4963	4842	4720	4599	4478
84	6919	6793	6667	6542	6417	6293	6169	6046	5923	5800	5679	5557	5436	5315	5195	5075	4956	4837	4718	4600
86	6988	6864	6741	6618	6496	6374	6253	6133	6012	5893	5773	5654	5536	5418	5300	5182	5065	4949	4833	4717
88	7053	6932	6811	6691	6572	6453	6334	6216	6098	5981	5864	5747	5631	5515	5400	5285	5170	5056	4942	4829
90	7116	6997	6879	6761	6644	6528	6411	6296	6180	6065	5951	5836	5723	5609	5496	5383	5271	5159	5047	4936
92	7176	7060	6944	6829	6714	6599	6486	6372	6259	6146	6034	5922	5810	5699	5588	5478	5368	5258	5148	5039
94	7233	7120	7006	6893	6781	6668	6557	6445	6335	6224	6114	6004	5895	5786	5677	5568	5460	5352	5245	5138
96	7289	7177	7066	6955	6845	6735	6625	6516	6407	6299	6191	6083	5976	5869	5762	5656	5549	5444	5338	5233
98	7342	7232	7123	7014	6906	6798	6691	6584	6477	6371	6265	6159	6054	5948	5844	5739	5635	5531	5428	5324
100	7393	7285	7178	7072	6965	6860	6754	6649	6544	6440	6336	6232	6128	6025	5923	5820	5718	5616	5514	5413
102	7442	7337	7232	7127	7022	6919	6815	6712	6609	6506	6404	6302	6201	6099	5998	5898	5797	5697	5597	5497
104	7490	7386	7283	7180	7077	6975	6874	6772	6671	6571	6470	6370	6270	6171	6071	5972	5874	5775	5677	5579
106	7535	7433	7332	7231	7130	7030	6930	6831	6731	6623	6534	6435	6337	6239	6142	6045	5948	5851	5754	5658
108	7579	7479	7380	7280	7181	7083	6985	6887	6789	6692	6595	6498	6402	6306	6210	6114	6019	5924	5829	5734
110	7622	7523	7425	7328	7231	7134	7037	6941	6845	6750	6654	6559	6464	6370	6276	6182	6088	5994	5901	5808
112	7663	7566	7470	7374	7278	7183	7088	6994	6899	6805	6711	6618	6525	6432	6339	6247	6154	6062	5971	5879
114	7702	7607	7513	7418	7324	7231	7137	7044	6951	6859	6767	6675	6583	6492	6400	6309	6219	6128	6038	5948
116	7741	7647	7554	7461	7369	7277	7185	7093	7002	6911	6820	6730	6640	6550	6460	6370	6281	6192	6103	6014
118	7778	7686	7594	7503	7412	7321	7231	7141	7051	6961	6872	6783	6694	6606	6517	6429	6341	6253	6166	6079
120	7814	7723	7633	7543	7453	7364	7275	7187	7098	7010	6922	6834	6747	6660	6573	6486	6399	6313	6227	6114
122	7848	7759	7670	7582	7494	7406	7318	7231	7144	7057	6971	6884	6798	6712	6627	6541	6456	6371	6286	6201
124	7882	7794	7707	7620	7533	7446	7360	7274	7188	7103	7018	6933	6848	6763	6679	6595	6511	6427	6343	6260
126	7915	7828	7742	7656	7571	7486	7401	7316	7231	7147	7063	6979	6896	6813	6729	6647	6564	6481	6399	6317
128	7946	7861	7776	7692	7607	7524	7440	7356	7273	7190	7107	7025	6943	6860	6779	6697	6615	6534	6453	6372
130	7977	7893	7809	7726	7643	7560	7478	7396	7314	7232	7150	7069	6988	6907	6826	6746	6665	6585	6505	6425
132	8007	7924	7842	7760	7678	7596	7515	7434	7353	7272	7192	7112	7032	6952	6873	6793	6714	6635	6556	6477
134	8036	7954	7873	7792	7711	7631	7551	7471	7391	7312	7232	7153	7075	6996	6917	6839	6761	6683	6605	6528
136	8064	7983	7903	7824	7744	7665	7586	7507	7428	7350	7272	7194	7116	7039	6961	6884	6807	6730	6653	6577
138	8091	8012	7933	7854	7776	7698	7620	7542	7464	7387	7310	7233	7156	7080	7004	6927	6852	6776	6700	6625
140	8118	8039	7962	7884	7807	7729	7653	7576	7499	7423	7347	7271	7196	7120	7045	6970	6895	6820	6745	6671
142	8143	8066	7989	7913	7837	7760	7685	7609	7534	7458	7383	7309	7234	7159	7085	7011	6937	6863	6790	6716
144	8169	8092	8017	7941	7866	7791	7716	7641	7567	7493	7419	7345	7271	7198	7124	7051	6978	6905	6833	6760
146	8193	8118	8043	7968	7894	7820	7746	7673	7599	7526	7453	7380	7307	7235	7162	7090	7018	6946	6874	6803
148	8217	8143	8069	7995	7922	7849	7776	7703	7631	7558	7486	7414	7342	7271	7199	7128	7057	6986	6915	6844
150	8240	8167	8094	8021	7949	7877	7805	7733	7661	7590	7518	7448	7377	7306	7236	7165	7095	7025	6955	6885

$l+r$	41	42	43	44	45	46	47	48	49	50	51	52	53	54	55	56	57	58	59	60
N	0,	0,	0,	0,	0,	0,	0,	0,	0,	0,	0,	0,	0,	0,	0,	0,	0,	0,		
41	0026																			
42	0127	0025																		
43	0259	0124	0024																	
44	0402	0253	0121	0024																
45	0550	0393	0247	0119	0023															
46	0700	0538	0385	0242	0116	0023														
47	0848	0684	0527	0376	0237	0114	0022													
48	0995	0830	0670	0515	0368	0232	0111	0022												
49	1140	0974	0813	0656	0505	0361	0227	0109	0021											
50	1282	1116	0954	0796	0643	0494	0353	0222	0107	0021										
52	1556	1392	1231	1072	0917	0765	0617	0475	0340	0214	0103	0020								
54	1817	1656	1496	1339	1184	1032	0882	0736	0594	0457	0327	0206	0099	0019						
56	2065	1907	1750	1594	1441	1290	1140	0994	0850	0709	0572	0441	0315	0198	0095	0019				
58	2301	2145	1991	1838	1687	1538	1390	1244	1100	0959	0820	0684	0552	0425	0304	0191	0092	0018		

All values conform to the international convention (i.e. 0,1 instead of 0.1).

Distribution-Free Tolerance Limits* $\beta_t = 0{,}90$

Top: $l+r = 41$–60, $N = 60(2)150$; bottom: $l+r = 61$–80, $N = 62(2)150$. The values in the table are those of β_p

$l+r$	41	42	43	44	45	46	47	48	49	50	51	52	53	54	55	56	57	58	59	60
N	0,	0,	0,	0,	0,	0,	0,	0,	0,	0,	0,	0,	0,	0,	0,	0,	0,	0,	0,	0,
60	2524	2372	2221	2071	1922	1775	1629	1485	1342	1201	1062	0926	0792	0661	0534	0411	0294	0185	0090	0018
62	2736	2587	2439	2292	2146	2001	1858	1716	1575	1435	1298	1161	1027	0895	0766	0639	0516	0397	0284	0179
64	2936	2791	2646	2502	2359	2217	2076	1936	1798	1660	1524	1389	1256	1124	0995	0867	0741	0619	0500	0385
66	3127	2985	2843	2702	2562	2423	2285	2147	2011	1876	1741	1608	1476	1346	1217	1089	0964	0840	0719	0600
68	3309	3169	3030	2893	2755	2619	2483	2349	2215	2082	1950	1818	1688	1559	1432	1305	1180	1057	0935	0815
70	3481	3344	3209	3074	2940	2806	2673	2541	2410	2279	2149	2020	1892	1765	1639	1514	1390	1267	1146	1026
72	3645	3511	3379	3247	3115	2984	2854	2724	2596	2467	2340	2213	2087	1962	1838	1714	1592	1470	1350	1231
74	3801	3671	3541	3411	3238	3154	3027	2900	2773	2648	2522	2398	2274	2151	2029	1907	1786	1666	1547	1429
76	3950	3822	3695	3569	3443	3317	3192	3067	2943	2820	2697	2575	2453	2332	2212	2092	1973	1855	1738	1621
78	4092	3967	3843	3719	3595	3472	3350	3228	3106	2985	2864	2744	2625	2506	2388	2270	2153	2037	1921	1806
80	4228	4106	3984	3862	3741	3621	3501	3381	3262	3143	3025	2907	2790	2673	2557	2441	2326	2211	2097	1984
82	4358	4238	4119	4000	3881	3763	3645	3528	3411	3294	3178	3063	2948	2833	2719	2605	2492	2379	2267	2155
84	4482	4365	4248	4131	4015	3899	3784	3668	3554	3439	3326	3212	3099	2986	2874	2763	2651	2540	2430	2320
86	4601	4486	4371	4257	4143	4029	3916	3803	3691	3579	3467	3356	3245	3134	3024	2914	2805	2696	2587	2479
88	4715	4603	4490	4378	4266	4155	4044	3933	3822	3712	3603	3493	3384	3276	3167	3059	2952	2845	2738	2632
90	4825	4714	4604	4494	4384	4275	4166	4057	3949	3841	3733	3626	3518	3412	3305	3199	3094	2988	2884	2779
92	4930	4821	4713	4605	4498	4390	4283	4176	4070	3964	3858	3753	3648	3543	3438	3334	3230	3127	3024	2921
94	5031	4924	4818	4712	4607	4501	4396	4291	4187	4083	3979	3875	3772	3669	3566	3464	3362	3260	3158	3057
96	5128	5023	4919	4815	4711	4608	4505	4402	4299	4197	4095	3993	3891	3790	3689	3589	3488	3388	3288	3189
98	5221	5119	5016	4914	4812	4711	4609	4508	4407	4307	4206	4106	4007	3907	3808	3709	3610	3512	3414	3316
100	5311	5211	5110	5010	4909	4810	4710	4611	4512	4413	4314	4216	4118	4020	3922	3825	3728	3631	3535	3438
102	5398	5299	5200	5101	5003	4905	4807	4709	4612	4515	4418	4321	4225	4129	4033	3937	3841	3746	3651	3557
104	5482	5384	5287	5190	5093	4997	4901	4805	4709	4613	4518	4423	4328	4234	4139	4045	3951	3857	3764	3671
106	5562	5466	5371	5276	5181	5086	4991	4897	4802	4709	4615	4521	4428	4335	4242	4149	4057	3965	3873	3781
108	5640	5546	5452	5358	5265	5171	5078	4985	4893	4800	4708	4616	4524	4433	4341	4250	4159	4069	3978	3888
110	5715	5622	5530	5438	5346	5254	5163	5071	4980	4889	4798	4708	4618	4527	4437	4348	4258	4169	4080	3991
112	5788	5697	5606	5515	5425	5334	5244	5154	5065	4975	4886	4797	4708	4619	4530	4442	4354	4266	4178	4091
114	5858	5768	5679	5590	5500	5412	5323	5234	5146	5058	4970	4882	4795	4708	4620	4533	4447	4360	4273	4187
116	5926	5838	5750	5662	5574	5487	5399	5312	5225	5138	5052	4966	4879	4793	4707	4622	4536	4451	4366	4281
118	5992	5905	5818	5732	5645	5559	5473	5387	5302	5216	5131	5046	4961	4876	4792	4707	4623	4539	4455	4371
120	6055	5970	5884	5799	5714	5629	5545	5460	5376	5292	5208	5124	5040	4957	4873	4790	4707	4625	4542	4459
122	6117	6033	5949	5865	5781	5697	5614	5531	5448	5365	5282	5200	5117	5035	4953	4871	4789	4707	4626	4545
124	6177	6094	6011	5928	5846	5763	5681	5599	5517	5436	5354	5273	5192	5111	5030	4949	4868	4788	4707	4627
126	6235	6153	6071	5990	5909	5827	5746	5666	5585	5504	5424	5344	5264	5184	5105	5025	4945	4866	4787	4708
128	6291	6210	6130	6050	5970	5890	5810	5730	5651	5571	5492	5413	5334	5255	5177	5098	5020	4941	4863	4785
130	6346	6266	6187	6108	6029	5950	5871	5793	5714	5636	5558	5480	5402	5324	5247	5169	5092	5015	4938	4861
132	6399	6320	6242	6164	6086	6009	5931	5853	5776	5699	5622	5545	5468	5392	5315	5239	5163	5087	5011	4935
134	6450	6373	6296	6219	6142	6065	5989	5913	5836	5760	5684	5609	5533	5457	5382	5306	5231	5156	5081	5006
136	6500	6424	6348	6272	6196	6121	6045	5970	5895	5820	5745	5670	5595	5521	5446	5372	5298	5224	5150	5076
138	6549	6474	6399	6324	6249	6175	6100	6026	5952	5878	5804	5730	5656	5582	5509	5436	5362	5289	5216	5143
140	6597	6522	6448	6374	6301	6227	6154	6080	6007	5934	5861	5788	5715	5643	5570	5498	5425	5353	5281	5209
142	6643	6569	6496	6423	6351	6278	6205	6133	6061	5989	5917	5845	5773	5701	5630	5558	5487	5416	5344	5273
144	6688	6615	6543	6471	6399	6328	6256	6185	6113	6042	5971	5900	5829	5758	5688	5617	5547	5476	5406	5336
146	6731	6660	6589	6518	6447	6376	6305	6235	6164	6094	6024	5954	5884	5814	5744	5674	5605	5535	5466	5397
148	6774	6703	6633	6563	6493	6423	6353	6283	6214	6144	6075	6006	5937	5868	5799	5730	5661	5593	5524	5456
150	6815	6746	6676	6607	6538	6469	6400	6331	6262	6194	6125	6057	5989	5921	5852	5785	5717	5649	5581	5514

$l+r$	61	62	63	64	65	66	67	68	69	70	71	72	73	74	75	76	77	78	79	80
N	0,	0,	0,	0,	0,	0,	0,	0,	0,	0,	0,	0,	0,	0,	0,	0,	0,	0,	0,	0,
62	0086	0017																		
64	0275	0173	0083	0016																
66	0484	0373	0267	0168	0081	0016														
68	0697	0582	0470	0362	0259	0163	0078	0015												
70	0907	0791	0677	0565	0456	0352	0252	0158	0076	0015										
72	1113	0996	0882	0769	0658	0549	0444	0342	0244	0154	0074	0015								
74	1312	1197	1082	0969	0857	0747	0640	0534	0431	0332	0238	0150	0072	0014						
76	1505	1391	1277	1164	1053	0943	0834	0727	0622	0520	0420	0323	0231	0146	0070	0014				
78	1692	1578	1466	1354	1243	1134	1025	0918	0812	0708	0606	0506	0409	0315	0225	0142	0068	0013		
80	1871	1759	1648	1538	1428	1319	1212	1105	0999	0895	0792	0690	0591	0493	0399	0307	0220	0139	0067	0013
82	2044	1934	1824	1715	1607	1499	1392	1286	1181	1077	0974	0872	0772	0673	0576	0481	0389	0300	0214	0135
84	2211	2102	1994	1887	1780	1673	1568	1463	1358	1255	1153	1051	0951	0851	0753	0657	0562	0470	0379	0292
86	2372	2264	2158	2052	1946	1841	1737	1633	1530	1428	1326	1225	1125	1026	0928	0831	0736	0641	0549	0459
88	2526	2421	2316	2211	2107	2004	1901	1798	1696	1595	1494	1394	1295	1197	1099	1002	0907	0812	0719	0627
90	2675	2571	2468	2365	2262	2160	2059	1958	1857	1757	1658	1559	1460	1363	1266	1169	1074	0979	0886	0794
92	2818	2716	2614	2513	2412	2312	2211	2112	2013	1914	1815	1718	1620	1524	1428	1332	1237	1143	1050	0958
94	2956	2856	2756	2656	2557	2458	2359	2261	2163	2065	1968	1872	1776	1680	1585	1491	1397	1303	1211	1119
96	3090	2991	2892	2794	2696	2599	2501	2405	2308	2212	2116	2021	1926	1832	1738	1644	1551	1459	1367	1275
98	3218	3121	3024	2927	2831	2735	2639	2544	2449	2354	2259	2165	2072	1978	1886	1793	1701	1610	1519	1428
100	3342	3247	3151	3056	2961	2866	2772	2678	2584	2491	2398	2305	2213	2121	2029	1938	1847	1756	1666	1577
102	3462	3368	3274	3180	3087	2993	2901	2808	2716	2624	2532	2440	2349	2258	2168	2078	1988	1899	1810	1721
104	3578	3485	3392	3300	3208	3116	3025	2934	2843	2752	2661	2571	2481	2392	2303	2214	2125	2037	1949	1861
106	3689	3598	3507	3416	3326	3235	3145	3055	2965	2876	2787	2698	2609	2521	2433	2345	2258	2170	2084	1997
108	3798	3708	3618	3528	3439	3350	3261	3173	3084	2996	2908	2821	2733	2646	2559	2473	2386	2300	2215	2129
110	3902	3814	3725	3637	3549	3461	3374	3287	3200	3113	3026	2940	2853	2768	2682	2596	2511	2426	2342	2257
112	4003	3916	3829	3742	3656	3569	3483	3397	3311	3225	3140	3055	2970	2885	2801	2716	2632	2548	2465	2381
114	4101	4015	3930	3844	3759	3673	3589	3504	3419	3335	3251	3167	3083	2999	2916	2833	2750	2667	2584	2502
116	4196	4111	4027	3943	3859	3775	3691	3607	3524	3441	3358	3275	3192	3110	3028	2946	2864	2782	2701	2619
118	4288	4204	4121	4038	3955	3873	3790	3708	3625	3543	3462	3380	3298	3217	3136	3055	2974	2894	2813	2733
120	4377	4295	4213	4131	4049	3968	3886	3805	3724	3643	3562	3482	3401	3321	3241	3161	3082	3002	2923	2844
122	4463	4382	4302	4221	4140	4060	3980	3900	3820	3740	3660	3581	3501	3422	3343	3265	3186	3108	3029	2951
124	4547	4467	4388	4308	4229	4149	4070	3991	3912	3834	3755	3677	3599	3521	3443	3365	3287	3210	3133	3056
126	4629	4550	4471	4393	4314	4236	4158	4080	4003	3925	3847	3770	3693	3616	3539	3462	3387	3309	3233	3157
128	4708	4630	4552	4475	4398	4321	4244	4167	4090	4014	3937	3861	3785	3709	3633	3557	3481	3406	3331	3256
130	4784	4708	4631	4555	4479	4403	4327	4251	4175	4100	4024	3949	3874	3799	3724	3649	3575	3500	3426	3352
132	4859	4783	4708	4633	4557	4482	4407	4333	4258	4183	4109	4035	3961	3886	3813	3739	3665	3592	3518	3445
134	4932	4857	4783	4708	4634	4560	4486	4412	4338	4265	4191	4118	4045	3972	3899	3826	3753	3681	3608	3536
136	5002	4929	4855	4782	4708	4635	4562	4489	4417	4344	4272	4199	4127	4055	3983	3911	3839	3767	3696	3624
138	5071	4998	4926	4853	4781	4709	4637	4565	4493	4421	4350	4278	4207	4135	4064	3993	3922	3852	3781	3710
140	5138	5066	4994	4923	4851	4780	4709	4638	4567	4496	4426	4355	4285	4214	4144	4074	4004	3934	3864	3794
142	5203	5132	5061	4991	4920	4850	4779	4709	4639	4569	4500	4430	4360	4291	4221	4152	4083	4014	3945	3876
144	5266	5196	5126	5057	4987	4917	4848	4779	4710	4641	4572	4503	4434	4365	4297	4228	4160	4092	4024	3956
146	5328	5259	5190	5121	5052	4983	4915	4847	4778	4710	4642	4574	4506	4438	4370	4303	4235	4168	4100	4033
148	5388	5320	5251	5183	5116	5048	4980	4913	4845	4778	4710	4643	4576	4509	4442	4375	4309	4242	4175	4109
150	5446	5379	5312	5245	5177	5111	5044	4977	4910	4844	4777	4711	4644	4578	4512	4446	4380	4314	4248	4183

All values conform to the international convention (i.e. 0,1 instead of 0.1).

Distribution-Free Tolerance Limits* $\beta_t = 0{,}90$

Top: $l+r = 81$–100, $N = 82(2)150$; middle: $l+r = 101$–120, $N = 102(2)150$; bottom: $l+r = 121$–140, $N = 122(2)150$. The values in the table are those of β_p

$l+r$	81	82	83	84	85	86	87	88	89	90	91	92	93	94	95	96	97	98	99	100
N	0,	0,	0,	0,	0,	0,	0,	0,	0,	0,	0,	0,	0,	0,	0,	0,	0,	0,	0,	0,
82	0065	0013																		
84	0209	0132	0063	0013																
86	0371	0285	0204	0129	0062	0012														
88	0536	0448	0362	0279	0200	0126	0061	0012												
90	0702	0613	0524	0438	0354	0273	0195	0123	0059	0012										
92	0866	0776	0687	0599	0513	0428	0346	0267	0191	0120	0058	0011								
94	1027	0937	0848	0759	0672	0586	0502	0419	0339	0261	0187	0118	0057	0011						
96	1185	1095	1006	0917	0830	0743	0658	0574	0491	0410	0332	0255	0183	0115	0056	0011				
98	1338	1249	1160	1072	0985	0898	0812	0728	0644	0562	0481	0402	0325	0250	0179	0113	0054	0011		
100	1488	1399	1311	1223	1136	1050	0965	0880	0796	0713	0631	0550	0471	0394	0318	0245	0176	0111	0053	0011
102	1633	1545	1458	1371	1284	1199	1114	1029	0945	0862	0780	0699	0618	0540	0462	0386	0312	0240	0172	0109
104	1774	1687	1601	1514	1429	1344	1259	1175	1092	1009	0927	0845	0765	0685	0606	0529	0453	0378	0306	0236
106	1911	1825	1739	1654	1570	1485	1401	1318	1235	1153	1071	0990	0909	0829	0750	0672	0595	0519	0444	0371
108	2044	1959	1874	1790	1706	1623	1540	1457	1375	1293	1212	1131	1050	0971	0892	0814	0736	0659	0584	0509
110	2173	2089	2006	1922	1839	1757	1675	1593	1511	1430	1349	1269	1189	1110	1031	0953	0875	0799	0722	0647
112	2298	2216	2133	2051	1969	1887	1806	1725	1644	1563	1483	1404	1325	1246	1167	1090	1012	0936	0859	0784
114	2420	2338	2257	2176	2094	2014	1933	1853	1773	1694	1614	1535	1457	1379	1301	1223	1146	1070	0994	0919
116	2538	2458	2377	2297	2217	2137	2057	1978	1899	1820	1742	1664	1586	1508	1431	1354	1278	1202	1126	1051
118	2653	2573	2494	2415	2336	2257	2178	2100	2021	1944	1866	1789	1711	1635	1558	1482	1406	1331	1256	1181
120	2765	2686	2608	2529	2451	2373	2295	2218	2141	2064	1987	1910	1834	1758	1682	1607	1532	1457	1382	1308
122	2873	2795	2718	2641	2563	2486	2410	2333	2257	2180	2105	2029	1953	1878	1803	1728	1654	1580	1506	1432
124	2979	2902	2825	2749	2673	2596	2521	2445	2369	2294	2219	2144	2070	1995	1921	1847	1773	1700	1627	1554
126	3081	3005	2930	2854	2779	2704	2629	2554	2479	2405	2331	2257	2183	2109	2036	1963	1890	1817	1744	1672
128	3181	3106	3031	2957	2882	2808	2734	2660	2586	2513	2439	2366	2293	2220	2148	2075	2003	1931	1859	1788
130	3277	3204	3130	3056	2983	2909	2836	2763	2690	2618	2545	2473	2401	2329	2257	2185	2114	2043	1971	1901
132	3372	3299	3226	3153	3081	3008	2936	2864	2792	2720	2648	2577	2505	2434	2363	2292	2222	2151	2081	2011
134	3464	3391	3319	3248	3176	3104	3033	2962	2891	2820	2749	2678	2608	2537	2467	2397	2327	2257	2188	2118
136	3553	3482	3411	3340	3269	3198	3128	3057	2987	2917	2847	2777	2707	2637	2568	2499	2429	2360	2292	2223
138	3640	3570	3499	3429	3359	3289	3220	3150	3081	3011	2942	2873	2804	2735	2666	2598	2530	2461	2393	2325
140	3725	3655	3586	3516	3447	3378	3309	3241	3172	3103	3035	2967	2899	2830	2763	2695	2627	2560	2492	2425
142	3807	3738	3670	3602	3533	3465	3397	3329	3261	3193	3126	3058	2991	2923	2856	2789	2722	2656	2589	2523
144	3888	3820	3752	3684	3617	3550	3482	3415	3348	3281	3214	3147	3081	3014	2948	2882	2815	2749	2683	2618
146	3966	3899	3832	3765	3699	3632	3565	3499	3433	3366	3300	3234	3168	3103	3037	2971	2906	2841	2776	2710
148	4043	3976	3910	3844	3778	3712	3647	3581	3515	3450	3385	3319	3254	3189	3124	3059	2995	2930	2865	2801
150	4117	4052	3986	3921	3856	3791	3726	3661	3596	3531	3467	3402	3338	3273	3209	3145	3081	3017	2953	2890

$l+r$	101	102	103	104	105	106	107	108	109	110	111	112	113	114	115	116	117	118	119	120
N	0,	0,	0,	0,	0,	0,	0,	0,	0,	0,	0,	0,	0,	0,	0,	0,	0,	0,	0,	0,
102	0052	0010																		
104	0169	0106	0051	0010																
106	0300	0231	0166	0104	0050	0010														
108	0436	0364	0294	0227	0162	0102	0049	0010												
110	0573	0500	0428	0358	0289	0223	0160	0101	0048	0010										
112	0709	0635	0563	0491	0420	0351	0284	0219	0156	0099	0048	0009								
114	0844	0770	0697	0624	0553	0482	0413	0345	0279	0215	0154	0097	0047	0009						
116	0977	0903	0829	0757	0684	0613	0543	0474	0406	0339	0274	0211	0151	0095	0046	0009				
118	1107	1033	0960	0887	0815	0744	0673	0603	0534	0465	0399	0333	0269	0208	0149	0094	0045	0009		
120	1234	1161	1088	1016	0944	0872	0801	0731	0661	0593	0525	0458	0392	0327	0265	0204	0146	0092	0044	0009
122	1359	1286	1214	1142	1070	0999	0928	0858	0788	0719	0650	0583	0516	0450	0385	0322	0260	0201	0144	0091
124	1481	1409	1337	1265	1194	1123	1052	0982	0913	0844	0775	0707	0640	0573	0507	0443	0379	0317	0256	0197
126	1600	1528	1457	1386	1315	1245	1174	1105	1035	0966	0898	0830	0762	0696	0629	0564	0499	0436	0373	0312
128	1716	1645	1575	1504	1434	1364	1294	1225	1156	1087	1019	0951	0884	0817	0750	0685	0620	0555	0491	0429
130	1830	1760	1689	1619	1550	1480	1411	1342	1274	1206	1137	1070	1003	0936	0870	0804	0739	0674	0610	0546
132	1941	1871	1802	1732	1663	1594	1526	1457	1389	1322	1254	1187	1120	1054	0987	0922	0856	0792	0727	0664
134	2049	1980	1911	1842	1774	1706	1638	1570	1502	1435	1368	1301	1235	1169	1103	1038	0972	0908	0843	0780
136	2154	2086	2018	1950	1882	1815	1747	1680	1613	1546	1480	1414	1348	1282	1216	1151	1087	1022	0958	0894
138	2257	2190	2122	2055	1988	1921	1854	1788	1721	1655	1589	1523	1458	1393	1328	1263	1199	1134	1071	1007
140	2358	2291	2224	2158	2091	2025	1959	1893	1827	1762	1696	1631	1566	1501	1437	1372	1308	1245	1181	1118
142	2456	2390	2324	2258	2192	2126	2061	1996	1931	1866	1801	1736	1672	1607	1543	1480	1416	1352	1290	1227
144	2552	2486	2421	2356	2291	2226	2161	2096	2032	1967	1903	1839	1775	1711	1648	1585	1522	1459	1396	1334
146	2645	2581	2516	2451	2387	2323	2258	2194	2130	2067	2003	1940	1876	1813	1750	1687	1625	1562	1500	1438
148	2737	2673	2609	2545	2481	2417	2354	2290	2227	2164	2101	2038	1975	1913	1850	1788	1726	1664	1602	1541
150	2826	2763	2699	2636	2573	2510	2447	2384	2321	2259	2196	2134	2072	2010	1948	1887	1825	1764	1702	1641

$l+r$	121	122	123	124	125	126	127	128	129	130	131	132	133	134	135	136	137	138	139	140
N	0,	0,	0,	0,	0,	0,	0,	0,	0,	0,	0,	0,	0,	0,	0,	0,	0,	0,	0,	0,
122	0044	0009																		
124	0141	0089	0043	0008																
126	0252	0194	0139	0088	0042	0008														
128	0367	0307	0248	0191	0137	0086	0042	0008												
130	0484	0422	0361	0302	0244	0188	0135	0085	0041	0008										
132	0600	0538	0476	0416	0356	0297	0240	0185	0133	0084	0040	0008								
134	0716	0654	0591	0530	0469	0409	0351	0293	0237	0183	0131	0083	0040	0008						
136	0831	0768	0706	0644	0583	0522	0462	0403	0345	0289	0233	0180	0129	0081	0039	0008				
138	0944	0881	0819	0757	0695	0634	0574	0514	0455	0397	0340	0284	0230	0177	0127	0080	0039	0008		
140	1055	0992	0930	0868	0807	0746	0685	0625	0566	0507	0449	0392	0335	0280	0227	0175	0125	0079	0038	0008
142	1164	1102	1040	0978	0917	0856	0795	0735	0675	0616	0558	0500	0443	0386	0331	0276	0223	0172	0123	0078
144	1271	1209	1148	1086	1025	0964	0904	0844	0784	0725	0666	0608	0550	0492	0436	0380	0326	0272	0220	0170
146	1376	1315	1254	1193	1132	1071	1011	0951	0891	0832	0773	0715	0657	0599	0542	0486	0430	0375	0322	0269
148	1480	1418	1358	1297	1236	1176	1116	1056	0997	0938	0879	0821	0763	0705	0648	0591	0535	0479	0424	0370
150	1581	1520	1459	1399	1339	1279	1220	1160	1101	1042	0983	0925	0867	0810	0752	0695	0639	0583	0528	0473

All values conform to the international convention (i.e. 0,1 instead of 0.1).

Distribution-Free Tolerance Limits* $\beta_t = 0{,}95$

$l+r$ = 1–20, N = 2(1)50(2)150. The values in the table are those of β_p

$l+r$	1	2	3	4	5	6	7	8	9	10	11	12	13	14	15	16	17	18	19	20
N	0,	0,	0,	0,	0,	0,	0,	0,	0,	0,	0,	0,	0,	0,	0,	0,	0,	0,	0,	0,
2	2236	0253																		
3	3684	1353	0170																	
4	4729	2486	0976	0127																
5	5493	3426	1893	0764	0102															
6	6070	4182	2713	1532	0628	0085														
7	6518	4793	3432	2253	1288	0534	0073													
8	6877	5293	4003	2892	1929	1111	0464	0064												
9	7169	5709	4504	3449	2514	1687	0977	0410	0057											
10	7411	6058	4931	3934	3035	2224	1500	0873	0368	0051										
11	7616	6356	5299	4356	3498	2712	1996	1351	0788	0333	0047									
12	7791	6613	5619	4727	3909	3152	2453	1810	1229	0718	0305	0043								
13	7942	6837	5899	5053	4274	3548	2870	2240	1657	1127	0660	0281	0039							
14	8074	7033	6146	5343	4600	3904	3250	2636	2061	1527	1041	0611	0260	0037						
15	8190	7206	6366	5602	4892	4226	3596	3000	2437	1909	1417	0967	0568	0242	0034					
16	8293	7360	6562	5834	5156	4516	3910	3334	2786	2267	1778	1321	0903	0531	0227	0032				
17	8384	7499	6738	6044	5394	4781	4197	3640	3108	2601	2119	1664	1238	0846	0499	0213	0030			
18	8467	7623	6897	6233	5611	5022	4460	3922	3406	2912	2440	1989	1563	1164	0797	0470	0201	0028		
19	8541	7736	7042	6406	5809	5242	4700	4181	3681	3201	2739	2297	1875	1475	1099	0753	0445	0190	0027	
20	8609	7839	7174	6563	5990	5444	4922	4420	3936	3469	3020	2586	2171	1773	1396	1041	0713	0422	0181	0026
21	8671	7933	7294	6708	6156	5630	5126	4641	4172	3719	3281	2858	2450	2057	1682	1324	0988	0678	0401	0172
22	8727	8019	7405	6841	6309	5802	5315	4845	4391	3952	3525	3113	2713	2327	1956	1599	1260	0941	0646	0382
23	8779	8098	7507	6964	6451	5961	5490	5036	4595	4168	3754	3351	2961	2582	2216	1863	1525	1202	0898	0617
24	8827	8171	7602	7077	6582	6109	5653	5213	4786	4371	3968	3576	3194	2824	2464	2116	1780	1457	1149	0859
25	8871	8239	7690	7183	6704	6246	5805	5378	4964	4561	4168	3786	3414	3051	2699	2356	2024	1703	1395	1101
26	8912	8302	7771	7281	6818	6374	5946	5532	5130	4738	4357	3984	3621	3266	2921	2584	2257	1940	1633	1338
27	8950	8360	7847	7373	6924	6494	6079	5677	5286	4905	4534	4171	3816	3470	3131	2801	2479	2166	1862	1568
28	8985	8415	7918	7458	7023	6606	6203	5813	5433	5062	4700	4346	4000	3662	3331	3007	2691	2383	2082	1791
29	9019	8466	7984	7539	7116	6711	6320	5940	5571	5210	4857	4512	4175	3844	3520	3203	2893	2589	2293	2005
30	9050	8514	8047	7614	7204	6810	6430	6061	5701	5349	5006	4669	4339	4016	3699	3389	3085	2787	2495	2211
31	9079	8559	8105	7685	7286	6904	6533	6174	5823	5481	5146	4817	4496	4179	3870	3566	3267	2975	2688	2408
32	9106	8602	8161	7752	7364	6992	6631	6281	5939	5606	5279	4958	4644	4335	4032	3734	3441	3154	2873	2597
33	9132	8641	8213	7815	7437	7075	6724	6382	6049	5724	5404	5091	4784	4482	4186	3894	3607	3326	3049	2777
34	9157	8679	8262	7875	7507	7154	6811	6478	6153	5835	5524	5218	4918	4622	4332	4047	3766	3489	3218	2951
35	9180	8715	8308	7931	7573	7228	6894	6569	6252	5942	5637	5338	5045	4756	4472	4192	3917	3646	3379	3117
36	9202	8749	8353	7985	7635	7299	6973	6656	6346	6043	5745	5453	5166	4883	4605	4331	4061	3795	3533	3275
37	9222	8781	8395	8036	7695	7366	7048	6738	6436	6139	5848	5562	5281	5004	4732	4463	4199	3938	3681	3428
38	9242	8811	8434	8084	7751	7430	7120	6817	6521	6231	5946	5667	5391	5120	4853	4590	4331	4075	3822	3574
39	9261	8840	8472	8130	7805	7491	7188	6892	6602	6318	6040	5766	5497	5231	4969	4711	4457	4206	3958	3714
40	9278	8868	8508	8174	7856	7550	7253	6963	6680	6402	6129	5861	5597	5337	5081	4828	4578	4331	4088	3848
41	9295	8894	8543	8216	7905	7605	7315	7031	6754	6482	6215	5952	5693	5438	5187	4939	4694	4452	4213	3977
42	9312	8920	8576	8256	7952	7658	7374	7096	6825	6558	6297	6039	5786	5536	5289	5045	4805	4567	4333	4101
43	9327	8944	8607	8294	7996	7709	7431	7159	6893	6632	6375	6123	5874	5629	5387	5148	4912	4678	4448	4220
44	9342	8967	8637	8331	8039	7758	7485	7219	6958	6702	6450	6203	5959	5718	5481	5246	5014	4785	4559	4335
45	9356	8989	8666	8366	8080	7805	7537	7276	7020	6769	6523	6280	6040	5804	5571	5341	5113	4888	4665	4445
46	9370	9010	8694	8400	8120	7849	7587	7331	7080	6834	6592	6354	6119	5887	5658	5431	5208	4987	4768	4551
47	9382	9030	8720	8432	8157	7892	7635	7384	7138	6896	6659	6425	6194	5966	5741	5519	5299	5082	4867	4654
48	9395	9049	8746	8463	8194	7934	7681	7435	7193	6956	6723	6493	6266	6043	5822	5603	5387	5173	4962	4752
49	9407	9068	8770	8493	8229	7973	7726	7484	7246	7014	6785	6559	6336	6116	5899	5684	5472	5262	5054	4848
50	9418	9086	8794	8522	8262	8012	7768	7531	7298	7069	6844	6622	6403	6187	5974	5763	5554	5347	5142	4940
52	9440	9120	8838	8576	8326	8084	7849	7620	7395	7174	6957	6742	6531	6322	6115	5911	5709	5509	5311	5114
54	9460	9151	8880	8626	8385	8151	7924	7703	7485	7272	7062	6854	6650	6447	6247	6050	5854	5660	5468	5277
56	9479	9181	8918	8673	8440	8214	7994	7780	7570	7363	7159	6959	6761	6565	6371	6179	5989	5801	5615	5430
58	9497	9208	8954	8717	8491	8272	8060	7852	7649	7448	7251	7057	6864	6674	6487	6301	6116	5934	5753	5573
60	9513	9234	8988	8758	8539	8327	8121	7920	7723	7528	7337	7148	6962	6778	6595	6415	6236	6058	5883	5708
62	9528	9258	9019	8797	8584	8379	8179	7984	7792	7604	7418	7235	7054	6874	6697	6522	6348	6176	6005	5835
64	9543	9280	9049	8833	8627	8427	8233	8044	7857	7674	7494	7316	7140	6966	6794	6623	6454	6286	6120	5955
66	9556	9301	9077	8867	8667	8473	8284	8100	7919	7741	7566	7392	7221	7052	6884	6718	6554	6391	6229	6068
68	9569	9321	9103	8899	8704	8516	8333	8153	7977	7804	7633	7465	7298	7133	6970	6808	6648	6489	6332	6175
70	9581	9340	9128	8929	8740	8557	8378	8204	8032	7864	7697	7533	7371	7210	7051	6894	6738	6583	6429	6276
72	9592	9358	9151	8958	8774	8595	8421	8251	8084	7920	7758	7598	7440	7283	7128	6975	6823	6671	6522	6373
74	9603	9375	9174	8985	8806	8632	8462	8297	8134	7974	7816	7660	7505	7353	7202	7052	6903	6756	6609	6464
76	9613	9391	9195	9011	8836	8666	8501	8340	8181	8024	7870	7718	7568	7419	7271	7125	6980	6836	6693	6551
78	9623	9406	9215	9036	8865	8699	8538	8380	8225	8073	7922	7774	7627	7481	7337	7194	7053	6912	6772	6634
80	9632	9421	9234	9059	8892	8731	8573	8419	8268	8119	7972	7827	7683	7541	7400	7261	7122	6985	6848	6713
82	9641	9435	9252	9082	8918	8761	8607	8456	8308	8163	8019	7877	7737	7598	7460	7324	7188	7054	6921	6788
84	9650	9448	9269	9103	8943	8789	8639	8492	8347	8205	8064	7926	7788	7652	7518	7384	7252	7120	6990	6860
86	9658	9460	9286	9123	8967	8816	8669	8525	8384	8245	8107	7972	7837	7704	7573	7442	7312	7184	7056	6929
88	9665	9472	9302	9142	8990	8842	8699	8558	8419	8283	8149	8016	7884	7754	7625	7497	7370	7244	7119	6995
90	9673	9484	9317	9161	9012	8867	8727	8589	8453	8320	8188	8058	7929	7802	7676	7550	7426	7302	7180	7058
92	9680	9495	9331	9179	9033	8891	8753	8618	8486	8355	8226	8099	7972	7848	7724	7601	7479	7358	7238	7119
94	9686	9505	9345	9196	9053	8914	8779	8647	8517	8389	8262	8137	8014	7891	7770	7650	7530	7412	7294	7177
96	9693	9515	9359	9212	9072	8936	8804	8674	8547	8421	8297	8175	8054	7933	7814	7696	7579	7463	7347	7233
98	9699	9525	9371	9228	9090	8957	8827	8700	8575	8452	8331	8211	8092	7974	7857	7741	7626	7512	7399	7286
100	9705	9534	9384	9243	9108	8977	8850	8725	8603	8482	8363	8245	8128	8013	7898	7785	7672	7560	7449	7338
102	9711	9543	9396	9257	9125	8997	8872	8750	8629	8511	8394	8278	8164	8050	7938	7826	7716	7606	7496	7388
104	9716	9552	9407	9271	9141	9016	8893	8773	8655	8538	8424	8310	8198	8086	7976	7866	7758	7650	7542	7436
106	9721	9560	9418	9285	9157	9034	8913	8795	8679	8565	8452	8341	8230	8121	8013	7905	7798	7692	7587	7482
108	9726	9568	9429	9298	9173	9051	8933	8817	8703	8591	8480	8370	8262	8155	8048	7942	7837	7733	7629	7526
110	9731	9576	9439	9310	9187	9068	8952	8838	8726	8616	8507	8399	8292	8187	8082	7978	7875	7772	7671	7569
112	9736	9583	9449	9322	9201	9084	8970	8858	8748	8640	8533	8427	8322	8218	8115	8013	7911	7811	7710	7611
114	9741	9591	9458	9334	9215	9100	8988	8878	8769	8663	8558	8453	8350	8248	8147	8046	7947	7848	7749	7651
116	9745	9598	9467	9345	9228	9115	9005	8896	8790	8685	8582	8479	8378	8277	8178	8079	7981	7883	7786	7690
118	9749	9604	9476	9356	9241	9130	9021	8915	8810	8707	8605	8504	8404	8306	8208	8110	8014	7918	7822	7727
120	9753	9611	9485	9367	9253	9144	9037	8932	8829	8728	8627	8528	8430	8333	8236	8141	8046	7951	7857	7764
122	9757	9617	9493	9377	9265	9158	9052	8949	8848	8748	8649	8552	8455	8359	8264	8170	8076	7983	7891	7799
124	9761	9623	9501	9387	9277	9171	9067	8966	8866	8768	8670	8574	8479	8385	8291	8199	8106	8015	7924	7833
126	9765	9629	9509	9396	9288	9184	9082	8982	8884	8787	8691	8596	8503	8410	8318	8226	8135	8045	7956	7866
128	9769	9635	9516	9405	9299	9196	9096	8997	8901	8805	8711	8618	8525	8434	8343	8253	8164	8075	7986	7898
130	9772	9640	9524	9414	9310	9208	9109	9012	8917	8823	8730	8638	8547	8457	8368	8279	8191	8103	8016	7930
132	9776	9646	9531	9423	9320	9220	9123	9027	8933	8840	8749	8658	8569	8480	8392	8304	8217	8131	8045	7960
134	9779	9651	9538	9432	9330	9231	9135	9041	8949	8857	8767	8678	8589	8502	8415	8329	8243	8158	8073	7989
136	9782	9656	9544	9440	9340	9243	9148	9055	8964	8874	8785	8697	8610	8523	8438	8353	8268	8184	8101	8018
138	9785	9661	9551	9448	9349	9254	9160	9068	8978	8890	8802	8715	8629	8544	8460	8376	8292	8210	8127	8046
140	9788	9666	9557	9456	9358	9264	9172	9081	8993	8905	8819	8733	8648	8564	8481	8398	8316	8234	8153	8073
142	9791	9670	9563	9463	9367	9274	9183	9094	9006	8920	8835	8750	8667	8584	8502	8420	8339	8258	8178	8099
144	9794	9675	9569	9470	9376	9284	9194	9106	9020	8935	8851	8767	8685	8603	8522	8441	8361	8282	8203	8124
146	9797	9679	9575	9478	9384	9293	9205	9118	9033	8949	8866	8784	8702	8622	8542	8462	8383	8305	8227	8149
148	9800	9683	9581	9484	9392	9303	9216	9130	9046	8963	8881	8800	8719	8640	8561	8482	8404	8327	8250	8173
150	9802	9688	9586	9491	9400	9312	9226	9141	9058	8976	8895	8815	8736	8657	8579	8502	8425	8349	8273	8197

All values conform to the international convention (i.e. 0,1 instead of 0.1).

Distribution-Free Tolerance Limits* $\beta_t = 0{,}95$

Top: $l+r = 21$–40, $N = 21(1)50(2)150$; bottom: $l+r = 41$–60, $N = 41(1)50(2)58$. The values in the table are those of β_p

$l+r$	21	22	23	24	25	26	27	28	29	30	31	32	33	34	35	36	37	38	39	40
N	0,	0,	0,	0,	0,	0,	0,	0,	0,	0,	0,	0,	0,	0,	0,	0,	0,	0,	0,	0,
21	0024																			
22	0164	0023																		
23	0365	0157	0022																	
24	0590	0350	0150	0021																
25	0823	0566	0335	0144	0020															
26	1056	0790	0543	0322	0138	0020														
27	1285	1015	0759	0522	0310	0133	0019													
28	1508	1237	0977	0731	0503	0298	0128	0018												
29	1725	1453	1192	0942	0705	0485	0288	0124	0018											
30	1933	1663	1402	1150	0909	0681	0469	0278	0120	0017										
31	2134	1866	1606	1354	1111	0878	0658	0453	0269	0116	0017									
32	2326	2062	1804	1553	1309	1074	0850	0637	0438	0260	0112	0016								
33	2511	2250	1995	1746	1503	1267	1040	0823	0617	0425	0252	0109	0016							
34	2688	2431	2179	1932	1691	1456	1228	1008	0798	0598	0412	0245	0105	0015						
35	2858	2605	2356	2112	1873	1640	1412	1191	0978	0774	0580	0400	0238	0102	0015					
36	3022	2772	2527	2285	2049	1818	1591	1371	1157	0950	0752	0564	0389	0231	0100	0014				
37	3178	2932	2691	2453	2219	1990	1765	1546	1332	1124	0923	0731	0548	0378	0225	0097	0014			
38	3328	3086	2848	2614	2383	2156	1934	1716	1503	1295	1093	0898	0711	0533	0368	0219	0094	0013		
39	3472	3235	3000	2769	2541	2317	2097	1881	1669	1462	1260	1064	0874	0692	0519	0358	0213	0092	0013	
40	3611	3377	3146	2918	2694	2473	2255	2041	1831	1625	1424	1227	1036	0851	0674	0506	0349	0208	0090	0013
41	3744	3514	3287	3062	2841	2623	2408	2196	1988	1784	1583	1387	1196	1010	0830	0657	0493	0340	0202	0087
42	3872	3645	3422	3201	2983	2768	2556	2347	2141	1938	1739	1544	1353	1166	0985	0809	0641	0481	0332	0198
43	3995	3772	3552	3335	3120	2908	2698	2492	2288	2087	1890	1696	1506	1320	1138	0961	0790	0626	0470	0324
44	4113	3894	3678	3464	3252	3043	2836	2632	2431	2233	2037	1845	1655	1470	1288	1111	0938	0771	0611	0459
45	4227	4012	3799	3588	3379	3173	2969	2768	2569	2373	2180	1989	1801	1617	1436	1258	1085	0917	0754	0597
46	4337	4125	3915	3708	3502	3299	3098	2900	2703	2509	2318	2129	1943	1760	1580	1403	1230	1060	0896	0737
47	4443	4234	4028	3824	3621	3421	3223	3027	2833	2642	2452	2265	2081	1899	1720	1544	1372	1202	1037	0876
48	4545	4340	4137	3935	3736	3539	3343	3150	2959	2770	2583	2398	2215	2035	1857	1682	1510	1342	1176	1015
49	4644	4442	4241	4043	3847	3652	3460	3269	3080	2894	2709	2526	2345	2167	1991	1817	1646	1478	1313	1151
50	4739	4540	4343	4148	3954	3762	3573	3384	3198	3014	2831	2651	2472	2295	2121	1949	1782	1612	1447	1286
52	4920	4727	4536	4346	4158	3972	3787	3604	3423	3243	3065	2889	2714	2542	2371	2202	2035	1870	1707	1547
54	5089	4901	4716	4532	4349	4168	3988	3811	3634	3459	3286	3114	2943	2774	2607	2441	2277	2115	1955	1797
56	5247	5065	4885	4706	4529	4353	4178	4005	3833	3663	3493	3326	3159	2994	2830	2668	2508	2349	2191	2035
58	5396	5219	5044	4870	4698	4526	4356	4188	4020	3854	3689	3525	3363	3202	3042	2883	2726	2570	2416	2263
60	5535	5364	5193	5024	4856	4690	4524	4360	4197	4035	3874	3714	3556	3398	3242	3087	2933	2781	2629	2479
62	5667	5500	5334	5170	5006	4844	4683	4523	4364	4206	4049	3893	3738	3585	3432	3280	3130	2980	2832	2685
64	5791	5629	5467	5307	5148	4990	4833	4677	4522	4368	4214	4062	3911	3761	3612	3464	3316	3170	3025	2881
66	5909	5750	5593	5437	5282	5128	4974	4822	4671	4521	4371	4223	4075	3928	3783	3638	3494	3351	3209	3067
68	6020	5865	5712	5560	5409	5258	5109	4960	4813	4666	4520	4375	4231	4087	3945	3803	3662	3522	3383	3245
70	6125	5974	5825	5676	5529	5382	5236	5091	4947	4804	4661	4520	4379	4239	4099	3961	3823	3686	3550	3414
72	6225	6078	5932	5787	5643	5500	5357	5216	5075	4935	4796	4657	4519	4382	4246	4111	3976	3842	3708	3576
74	6320	6176	6034	5892	5752	5612	5473	5334	5196	5060	4924	4788	4653	4519	4386	4253	4121	3990	3860	3730
76	6410	6270	6131	5993	5855	5718	5582	5447	5313	5179	5046	4913	4781	4650	4520	4390	4261	4132	4004	3877
78	6496	6359	6223	6088	5954	5820	5687	5555	5423	5292	5162	5032	4903	4775	4647	4520	4393	4267	4142	4017
80	6578	6444	6311	6179	6048	5917	5787	5657	5529	5400	5273	5146	5020	4894	4769	4644	4520	4397	4274	4152
82	6656	6526	6395	6266	6137	6009	5882	5755	5629	5504	5379	5255	5131	5008	4885	4763	4642	4521	4401	4281
84	6731	6603	6476	6349	6223	6098	5973	5849	5726	5603	5481	5359	5238	5117	4997	4877	4758	4640	4522	4404
86	6803	6677	6553	6429	6305	6183	6061	5939	5818	5698	5578	5459	5340	5222	5104	4987	4870	4754	4638	4522
88	6871	6748	6626	6505	6384	6264	6144	6025	5907	5789	5671	5554	5438	5322	5206	5091	4977	4863	4749	4636
90	6937	6817	6697	6578	6459	6342	6224	6108	5991	5876	5761	5646	5532	5418	5305	5192	5079	4968	4856	4745
92	7000	6882	6765	6648	6532	6416	6301	6187	6073	5959	5846	5734	5622	5510	5399	5288	5178	5068	4959	4850
94	7060	6945	6830	6715	6601	6488	6375	6263	6151	6040	5929	5818	5708	5599	5490	5381	5273	5165	5058	4951
96	7118	7005	6892	6780	6668	6557	6446	6336	6226	6117	6008	5900	5792	5684	5577	5470	5364	5258	5153	5048
98	7174	7063	6952	6842	6732	6623	6514	6406	6298	6191	6084	5978	5872	5766	5661	5556	5452	5348	5244	5141
100	7228	7119	7010	6902	6794	6687	6580	6474	6368	6263	6158	6053	5949	5845	5742	5639	5537	5434	5332	5231
102	7280	7172	7066	6959	6853	6748	6643	6539	6435	6332	6229	6126	6024	5922	5820	5719	5618	5518	5417	5318
104	7330	7224	7119	7015	6911	6807	6704	6602	6500	6398	6297	6196	6095	5995	5895	5796	5697	5598	5500	5401
106	7378	7274	7171	7068	6966	6864	6763	6662	6562	6462	6363	6263	6165	6066	5968	5870	5773	5676	5579	5482
108	7424	7322	7221	7120	7020	6920	6820	6721	6622	6524	6426	6329	6231	6135	6038	5942	5846	5750	5655	5560
110	7469	7369	7269	7170	7071	6973	6875	6777	6680	6584	6487	6392	6296	6201	6106	6011	5917	5823	5729	5636
112	7512	7413	7315	7218	7121	7024	6928	6832	6737	6642	6547	6452	6358	6265	6171	6078	5985	5893	5801	5709
114	7554	7457	7360	7264	7169	7074	6979	6885	6791	6697	6604	6511	6419	6326	6234	6143	6051	5960	5870	5779
116	7594	7499	7404	7309	7216	7122	7029	6936	6843	6751	6660	6568	6477	6386	6296	6206	6116	6026	5937	5847
118	7633	7539	7446	7353	7261	7168	7077	6985	6894	6804	6713	6623	6533	6444	6355	6266	6178	6089	6001	5914
120	7671	7579	7487	7395	7304	7213	7123	7033	6944	6854	6765	6677	6588	6500	6413	6325	6238	6151	6064	5978
122	7708	7617	7526	7436	7346	7257	7168	7080	6991	6903	6816	6728	6641	6555	6468	6382	6296	6210	6125	6040
124	7743	7654	7564	7476	7387	7299	7212	7125	7038	6951	6865	6779	6693	6607	6522	6437	6353	6268	6184	6100
126	7778	7689	7602	7514	7427	7340	7254	7168	7082	6997	6912	6827	6743	6659	6575	6491	6407	6324	6241	6158
128	7811	7724	7638	7551	7466	7380	7295	7210	7126	7042	6958	6874	6791	6708	6625	6543	6461	6379	6297	6215
130	7843	7758	7672	7588	7503	7419	7335	7251	7168	7085	7003	6920	6838	6756	6675	6593	6512	6431	6351	6270
132	7875	7790	7706	7623	7539	7456	7374	7291	7209	7128	7046	6965	6884	6803	6723	6642	6563	6483	6403	6324
134	7906	7822	7739	7657	7575	7493	7411	7330	7249	7169	7088	7008	6928	6849	6769	6690	6611	6533	6454	6376
136	7935	7853	7771	7690	7609	7528	7448	7368	7288	7208	7129	7050	6971	6893	6815	6737	6659	6581	6504	6426
138	7964	7883	7802	7722	7642	7563	7483	7404	7326	7247	7169	7091	7013	6936	6859	6782	6705	6628	6552	6476
140	7992	7912	7833	7754	7675	7596	7518	7440	7362	7285	7208	7131	7054	6978	6901	6825	6750	6674	6599	6524
142	8020	7941	7862	7784	7706	7629	7552	7475	7398	7322	7245	7169	7094	7018	6943	6868	6793	6719	6644	6570
144	8046	7968	7891	7814	7737	7660	7584	7508	7433	7357	7282	7207	7132	7058	6984	6910	6836	6762	6689	6616
146	8072	7995	7919	7843	7767	7691	7616	7541	7466	7392	7318	7244	7170	7097	7023	6950	6877	6805	6732	6660
148	8097	8021	7946	7871	7796	7721	7647	7573	7499	7426	7353	7280	7207	7134	7062	6990	6918	6846	6774	6703
150	8122	8047	7972	7898	7824	7751	7677	7604	7531	7459	7387	7314	7243	7171	7099	7028	6957	6886	6815	6745

$l+r$	41	42	43	44	45	46	47	48	49	50	51	52	53	54	55	56	57	58	59	60
N	0,	0,	0,	0,	0,	0,	0,	0,	0,	0,	0,	0,	0,	0,	0,	0,	0,	0,		
41	0013																			
42	0085	0012																		
43	0193	0083	0012																	
44	0316	0188	0081	0012																
45	0448	0310	0184	0080	0011															
46	0584	0438	0302	0180	0078	0011														
47	0720	0571	0429	0296	0176	0076	0011													
48	0857	0705	0559	0419	0290	0172	0074	0011												
49	0993	0839	0690	0547	0411	0284	0169	0073	0010											
50	1127	0972	0822	0676	0536	0402	0278	0165	0072	0010										
52	1389	1234	1082	0934	0789	0649	0515	0387	0267	0159	0069	0010								
54	1641	1487	1335	1186	1041	0898	0759	0624	0495	0372	0257	0153	0066	0009						
56	1881	1729	1579	1431	1286	1142	1002	0865	0731	0602	0477	0358	0248	0148	0064	0009				
58	2111	1961	1813	1667	1522	1380	1239	1102	0966	0834	0705	0580	0460	0346	0239	0142	0062	0009		

All values conform to the international convention (i.e. 0,1 instead of 0.1).

Distribution-Free Tolerance Limits* $\beta_t = 0,95$

Top: $l+r = 41$–60, $N = 60(2)150$; bottom: $l+r = 61$–80, $N = 62(2)150$. The values in the table are those of β_p

$l+r$	41	42	43	44	45	46	47	48	49	50	51	52	53	54	55	56	57	58	59	60
N	0,	0,	0,	0,	0,	0,	0,	0,	0,	0,	0,	0,	0,	0,	0,	0,	0,	0,	0,	0,
60	2330	2183	2037	1893	1750	1609	1469	1332	1197	1064	0933	0805	0681	0561	0444	0334	0231	0138	0060	0009
62	2539	2394	2251	2109	1968	1828	1691	1554	1420	1287	1157	1028	0902	0779	0658	0542	0430	0323	0223	0133
64	2738	2596	2455	2315	2177	2039	1903	1769	1635	1504	1374	1245	1119	0995	0873	0754	0637	0524	0416	0313
66	2927	2788	2650	2512	2376	2241	2107	1974	1843	1713	1584	1456	1330	1206	1084	0964	0846	0730	0618	0508
68	3108	2971	2835	2701	2567	2434	2302	2172	2042	1913	1786	1660	1535	1412	1290	1170	1051	0934	0820	0708
70	3280	3146	3013	2881	2749	2619	2489	2361	2233	2106	1981	1856	1733	1610	1489	1370	1252	1135	1020	0907
72	3444	3313	3182	3052	2924	2796	2668	2542	2416	2292	2168	2045	1923	1802	1682	1564	1446	1330	1216	1102
74	3600	3472	3344	3217	3090	2965	2840	2715	2592	2469	2347	2226	2106	1987	1869	1751	1635	1520	1406	1293
76	3750	3624	3499	3374	3250	3126	3004	2882	2760	2640	2520	2401	2282	2165	2048	1932	1817	1703	1590	1478
78	3893	3770	3647	3524	3403	3282	3161	3041	2922	2803	2685	2568	2452	2336	2221	2107	1993	1880	1769	1658
80	4030	3909	3788	3668	3549	3430	3312	3194	3077	2960	2844	2729	2615	2500	2387	2275	2163	2051	1941	1831
82	4161	4043	3924	3807	3689	3573	3456	3341	3226	3111	2997	2884	2771	2659	2547	2436	2326	2216	2107	1999
84	4287	4171	4054	3939	3824	3709	3595	3482	3369	3256	3144	3032	2922	2811	2701	2592	2483	2375	2268	2161
86	4408	4293	4179	4066	3953	3840	3728	3617	3506	3395	3285	3176	3066	2958	2850	2742	2635	2529	2423	2317
88	4523	4411	4299	4188	4077	3967	3856	3747	3638	3529	3421	3313	3206	3099	2993	2887	2781	2676	2572	2468
90	4634	4524	4414	4305	4196	4088	3980	3872	3765	3658	3551	3446	3340	3235	3130	3026	2922	2819	2716	2614
92	4741	4633	4525	4418	4311	4204	4098	3992	3887	3782	3677	3573	3469	3366	3263	3160	3058	2956	2855	2754
94	4844	4738	4632	4526	4421	4316	4212	4108	4004	3901	3798	3696	3594	3492	3391	3290	3189	3089	2989	2890
96	4943	4838	4734	4631	4527	4424	4322	4220	4118	4016	3915	3814	3714	3614	3514	3415	3316	3217	3119	3021
98	5038	4935	4833	4731	4630	4529	4428	4327	4227	4127	4028	3928	3830	3731	3633	3535	3438	3341	3244	3148
100	5130	5029	4928	4828	4728	4629	4530	4431	4332	4234	4136	4039	3941	3844	3748	3652	3556	3460	3365	3270
102	5218	5119	5020	4922	4824	4726	4628	4531	4434	4337	4241	4145	4049	3954	3859	3764	3670	3575	3482	3388
104	5304	5206	5109	5012	4915	4819	4723	4628	4532	4437	4342	4248	4154	4060	3966	3873	3780	3687	3595	3502
106	5386	5290	5194	5099	5004	4909	4815	4721	4627	4533	4440	4347	4254	4162	4070	3978	3886	3795	3704	3613
108	5466	5371	5277	5183	5090	4997	4904	4811	4719	4627	4535	4443	4352	4261	4170	4079	3989	3899	3810	3720
110	5542	5450	5357	5265	5173	5081	4990	4898	4807	4717	4626	4536	4446	4356	4267	4178	4089	4000	3912	3824
112	5617	5526	5434	5344	5253	5163	5073	4983	4893	4804	4715	4626	4537	4449	4361	4273	4185	4098	4011	3924
114	5689	5599	5509	5420	5331	5242	5153	5064	4976	4888	4800	4713	4626	4539	4452	4365	4279	4193	4107	4021
116	5759	5670	5582	5493	5406	5318	5231	5144	5057	4970	4884	4797	4711	4626	4540	4455	4370	4285	4200	4116
118	5826	5739	5652	5565	5478	5392	5306	5220	5135	5049	4964	4879	4794	4710	4625	4541	4458	4374	4290	4207
120	5891	5805	5720	5634	5549	5464	5379	5294	5210	5126	5042	4958	4875	4791	4708	4625	4543	4460	4378	4296
122	5955	5870	5786	5701	5617	5534	5450	5367	5283	5200	5118	5035	4953	4871	4789	4707	4625	4544	4463	4382
124	6016	5933	5850	5767	5684	5601	5519	5436	5354	5273	5191	5110	5029	4948	4867	4786	4706	4626	4546	4466
126	6076	5994	5912	5830	5748	5667	5585	5504	5424	5343	5262	5182	5102	5022	4943	4863	4784	4705	4626	4547
128	6134	6053	5972	5891	5811	5730	5650	5570	5491	5411	5332	5252	5174	5095	5016	4938	4859	4781	4704	4626
130	6190	6110	6030	5951	5871	5792	5713	5634	5556	5477	5399	5321	5243	5165	5088	5010	4933	4856	4779	4703
132	6245	6166	6087	6009	5930	5852	5774	5696	5619	5542	5464	5387	5310	5234	5157	5081	5005	4929	4853	4777
134	6298	6220	6142	6065	5988	5911	5834	5757	5680	5604	5528	5452	5376	5300	5225	5149	5074	4999	4924	4850
136	6349	6273	6196	6120	6043	5967	5891	5816	5740	5665	5590	5515	5440	5365	5291	5216	5142	5068	4994	4920
138	6400	6324	6248	6173	6098	6023	5948	5873	5798	5724	5650	5576	5502	5428	5355	5281	5208	5135	5062	4989
140	6449	6374	6299	6225	6150	6076	6002	5929	5855	5782	5708	5635	5562	5490	5417	5344	5272	5200	5128	5056
142	6496	6422	6349	6275	6202	6129	6056	5983	5910	5838	5765	5693	5621	5549	5478	5406	5335	5263	5192	5121
144	6542	6470	6397	6324	6252	6180	6108	6036	5964	5892	5821	5750	5679	5608	5537	5466	5395	5325	5255	5185
146	6588	6516	6444	6372	6301	6229	6158	6087	6016	5946	5875	5805	5734	5664	5594	5524	5455	5385	5316	5246
148	6632	6560	6490	6419	6348	6278	6207	6137	6067	5997	5928	5858	5789	5720	5650	5581	5513	5444	5375	5307
150	6674	6604	6534	6464	6394	6325	6255	6186	6117	6048	5979	5911	5842	5774	5705	5637	5569	5501	5433	5366

$l+r$	61	62	63	64	65	66	67	68	69	70	71	72	73	74	75	76	77	78	79	80
N	0,	0,	0,	0,	0,	0,	0,	0,	0,	0,	0,	0,	0,	0,	0,	0,	0,	0,	0,	0,
62	0058	0008																		
64	0216	0129	0056	0008																
66	0403	0303	0210	0125	0054	0008														
68	0599	0493	0391	0294	0203	0121	0052	0008												
70	0796	0687	0582	0479	0380	0286	0197	0118	0051	0007										
72	0991	0881	0773	0667	0565	0465	0369	0278	0192	0114	0050	0007								
74	1182	1072	0963	0856	0752	0649	0549	0452	0359	0270	0187	0111	0048	0007						
76	1367	1258	1149	1042	0937	0833	0732	0632	0535	0440	0349	0263	0182	0108	0047	0007				
78	1548	1439	1331	1224	1119	1015	0912	0811	0712	0615	0521	0429	0340	0256	0177	0106	0046	0007		
80	1722	1615	1508	1402	1297	1193	1090	0989	0889	0791	0694	0600	0507	0418	0332	0249	0173	0103	0045	0006
82	1891	1785	1679	1574	1469	1366	1264	1163	1063	0964	0867	0771	0677	0585	0495	0407	0323	0243	0168	0100
84	2055	1949	1844	1740	1637	1535	1433	1332	1233	1134	1037	0940	0845	0752	0660	0570	0483	0398	0316	0237
86	2213	2108	2005	1902	1800	1698	1598	1498	1399	1300	1203	1107	1012	0918	0825	0734	0645	0557	0471	0388
88	2365	2262	2160	2058	1957	1857	1757	1658	1560	1462	1366	1270	1175	1081	0988	0896	0806	0717	0630	0544
90	2512	2411	2310	2209	2110	2011	1912	1814	1717	1620	1524	1429	1334	1241	1148	1056	0966	0876	0788	0701
92	2654	2554	2455	2356	2257	2159	2062	1965	1869	1773	1678	1583	1490	1397	1304	1213	1122	1033	0944	0857
94	2791	2693	2595	2497	2400	2303	2207	2111	2016	1921	1827	1734	1641	1549	1457	1366	1276	1186	1098	1010
96	2924	2826	2730	2634	2538	2442	2347	2253	2159	2065	1972	1880	1788	1696	1605	1515	1425	1337	1248	1161
98	3051	2956	2861	2766	2671	2577	2483	2390	2297	2205	2113	2021	1930	1840	1750	1660	1571	1483	1395	1308
100	3175	3081	2987	2894	2800	2708	2615	2523	2431	2340	2249	2159	2069	1979	1890	1802	1713	1626	1539	1452
102	3295	3202	3109	3017	2925	2834	2743	2652	2561	2471	2381	2292	2203	2115	2027	1939	1852	1765	1679	1593
104	3411	3319	3228	3137	3046	2956	2866	2776	2687	2598	2510	2421	2334	2246	2159	2072	1986	1900	1815	1730
106	3523	3432	3342	3253	3163	3074	2986	2897	2809	2721	2634	2547	2460	2374	2288	2202	2117	2032	1947	1863
108	3631	3542	3453	3365	3277	3189	3102	3014	2928	2841	2755	2669	2583	2498	2412	2328	2243	2159	2076	1992
110	3736	3648	3561	3474	3387	3300	3214	3128	3042	2957	2872	2787	2702	2618	2534	2450	2367	2284	2201	2118
112	3838	3751	3665	3579	3493	3408	3323	3238	3154	3069	2985	2901	2818	2734	2651	2569	2486	2404	2323	2241
114	3936	3851	3766	3681	3597	3513	3429	3345	3261	3178	3095	3012	2930	2848	2766	2684	2603	2522	2441	2360
116	4032	3948	3864	3780	3697	3614	3531	3449	3366	3284	3202	3120	3039	2958	2877	2796	2716	2636	2556	2476
118	4124	4041	3959	3876	3794	3712	3631	3549	3468	3387	3306	3225	3145	3065	2985	2905	2826	2747	2668	2589
120	4214	4132	4051	3970	3889	3808	3727	3647	3567	3487	3407	3327	3248	3169	3090	3011	2933	2854	2776	2699
122	4301	4221	4140	4060	3980	3901	3821	3742	3662	3584	3505	3426	3348	3270	3192	3114	3037	2959	2882	2805
124	4386	4307	4227	4148	4069	3991	3912	3834	3756	3678	3600	3522	3445	3368	3291	3214	3138	3061	2985	2909
126	4468	4390	4312	4234	4156	4078	4001	3923	3846	3769	3693	3616	3540	3463	3387	3312	3236	3161	3085	3010
128	4548	4471	4394	4317	4240	4163	4087	4010	3934	3858	3783	3707	3632	3556	3481	3406	3332	3257	3183	3109
130	4626	4550	4473	4397	4322	4246	4170	4095	4020	3945	3870	3795	3721	3647	3573	3499	3425	3351	3278	3204
132	4702	4626	4551	4476	4401	4326	4252	4178	4103	4029	3955	3882	3808	3735	3661	3588	3515	3443	3370	3298
134	4775	4701	4627	4552	4479	4405	4331	4258	4184	4111	4038	3965	3893	3820	3748	3676	3604	3532	3460	3389
136	4847	4773	4700	4627	4554	4481	4408	4336	4263	4191	4119	4047	3975	3904	3832	3761	3690	3619	3548	3477
138	4916	4844	4771	4699	4627	4555	4483	4412	4340	4269	4198	4127	4056	3985	3914	3844	3774	3703	3633	3563
140	4984	4913	4841	4770	4699	4627	4557	4486	4415	4345	4274	4204	4134	4064	3994	3925	3855	3786	3717	3648
142	5050	4979	4909	4838	4768	4698	4628	4558	4488	4419	4349	4280	4210	4141	4072	4004	3935	3866	3798	3730
144	5115	5045	4975	4905	4836	4767	4697	4628	4559	4490	4422	4353	4285	4217	4148	4080	4012	3945	3877	3810
146	5177	5108	5039	4971	4902	4833	4765	4697	4629	4561	4493	4425	4357	4290	4223	4155	4088	4021	3954	3888
148	5238	5170	5102	5034	4966	4899	4831	4764	4696	4629	4562	4495	4428	4361	4295	4228	4162	4096	4030	3964
150	5298	5231	5163	5096	5029	4962	4896	4829	4762	4696	4630	4563	4497	4431	4365	4300	4234	4169	4103	4038

All values conform to the international convention (i.e. 0,1 instead of 0.1).

Top: $l+r = 81$–100, $N = 82(2)150$; middle: $l+r = 101$–120, $N = 102(2)150$; bottom: $l+r = 121$–140, $N = 122(2)150$. The values in the table are those of β_p

$l+r$	81	82	83	84	85	86	87	88	89	90	91	92	93	94	95	96	97	98	99	100
N	0,	0,	0,	0,	0,	0,	0,	0,	0,	0,	0,	0,	0,	0,	0,	0,	0,	0,	0,	0,
82	0043	0006																		
84	0164	0098	0042	0006																
86	0308	0232	0160	0096	0041	0006														
88	0460	0379	0301	0226	0157	0094	0041	0006												
90	0615	0532	0450	0371	0294	0221	0153	0091	0040	0006										
92	0770	0685	0602	0520	0440	0363	0288	0217	0150	0089	0039	0006								
94	0923	0838	0753	0670	0589	0509	0431	0355	0282	0212	0147	0088	0038	0005						
96	1074	0989	0904	0820	0737	0656	0576	0498	0421	0347	0276	0207	0143	0086	0037	0005				
98	1222	1136	1052	0968	0885	0803	0722	0642	0564	0487	0413	0340	0270	0203	0141	0084	0036	0005		
100	1367	1281	1197	1113	1030	0948	0867	0786	0707	0629	0553	0478	0404	0333	0264	0199	0138	0082	0036	0005
102	1508	1423	1339	1256	1173	1091	1009	0929	0849	0771	0693	0617	0542	0468	0396	0326	0259	0195	0135	0081
104	1645	1561	1478	1395	1312	1231	1150	1069	0989	0911	0833	0755	0679	0605	0531	0459	0389	0320	0254	0191
106	1779	1696	1613	1531	1449	1368	1287	1207	1127	1048	0970	0893	0816	0741	0666	0593	0521	0450	0381	0314
108	1910	1827	1745	1663	1582	1501	1421	1342	1262	1184	1106	1028	0952	0876	0801	0727	0654	0582	0511	0442
110	2036	1955	1874	1793	1712	1632	1552	1473	1395	1316	1239	1162	1085	1009	0934	0860	0786	0713	0642	0571
112	2160	2079	1999	1919	1839	1759	1680	1602	1524	1446	1369	1292	1216	1140	1065	0991	0917	0844	0772	0700
114	2280	2200	2120	2041	1962	1884	1805	1727	1650	1573	1496	1420	1344	1269	1194	1120	1046	0973	0901	0829
116	2397	2318	2239	2161	2082	2005	1927	1850	1773	1697	1621	1545	1470	1395	1320	1246	1173	1100	1028	0956
118	2511	2432	2355	2277	2200	2123	2046	1969	1893	1817	1742	1667	1592	1518	1444	1370	1297	1225	1152	1081
120	2621	2544	2467	2390	2314	2237	2161	2086	2010	1935	1861	1786	1712	1638	1565	1492	1419	1347	1275	1204
122	2729	2652	2576	2500	2425	2350	2274	2199	2125	2050	1976	1902	1829	1756	1683	1610	1538	1467	1395	1324
124	2834	2758	2683	2608	2533	2458	2384	2310	2236	2162	2089	2016	1943	1871	1798	1727	1655	1584	1513	1442
126	2935	2861	2787	2712	2638	2564	2491	2418	2345	2272	2199	2127	2055	1983	1911	1840	1769	1698	1628	1558
128	3035	2961	2887	2814	2741	2668	2595	2523	2450	2378	2306	2235	2163	2092	2021	1951	1880	1810	1740	1671
130	3131	3058	2986	2913	2841	2769	2697	2625	2554	2482	2411	2340	2270	2199	2129	2059	1989	1920	1850	1781
132	3226	3153	3082	3010	2938	2867	2796	2725	2654	2584	2513	2443	2373	2303	2234	2164	2095	2027	1958	1890
134	3317	3246	3175	3104	3033	2963	2892	2822	2752	2682	2613	2543	2474	2405	2336	2268	2199	2131	2063	1995
136	3407	3336	3266	3196	3126	3056	2987	2917	2848	2779	2710	2641	2573	2504	2436	2368	2301	2233	2166	2098
138	3494	3424	3355	3285	3216	3147	3078	3010	2941	2873	2805	2737	2669	2601	2534	2467	2400	2333	2266	2199
140	3579	3510	3441	3373	3304	3236	3168	3100	3032	2965	2897	2830	2763	2696	2629	2563	2496	2430	2364	2298
142	3661	3593	3526	3458	3390	3323	3255	3188	3121	3054	2988	2921	2855	2789	2722	2656	2591	2525	2460	2394
144	3742	3675	3608	3541	3474	3407	3341	3274	3208	3142	3076	3010	2944	2879	2813	2748	2683	2618	2553	2489
146	3821	3754	3688	3622	3556	3490	3424	3358	3293	3227	3162	3097	3032	2967	2902	2838	2773	2709	2645	2581
148	3898	3832	3766	3701	3636	3570	3505	3440	3375	3311	3246	3182	3117	3053	2989	2925	2861	2798	2734	2671
150	3973	3908	3843	3778	3714	3649	3585	3520	3456	3392	3328	3264	3201	3137	3074	3010	2947	2884	2821	2759

$l+r$	101	102	103	104	105	106	107	108	109	110	111	112	113	114	115	116	117	118	119	120
N	0,	0,	0,	0,	0,	0,	0,	0,	0,	0,	0,	0,	0,	0,	0,	0,	0,	0,	0,	0,
102	0035	0005																		
104	0132	0079	0034	0005																
106	0249	0188	0130	0078	0034	0005														
108	0374	0308	0245	0184	0127	0076	0033	0005												
110	0502	0433	0367	0302	0240	0181	0125	0075	0032	0005										
112	0630	0561	0492	0426	0360	0297	0236	0178	0123	0073	0032	0005								
114	0758	0688	0619	0551	0484	0418	0354	0292	0232	0174	0121	0072	0031	0004						
116	0885	0814	0745	0676	0608	0541	0475	0411	0348	0287	0228	0171	0119	0071	0031	0004				
118	1010	0939	0869	0800	0732	0664	0597	0532	0467	0404	0342	0282	0224	0168	0117	0070	0030	0004		
120	1133	1062	0992	0923	0855	0787	0719	0653	0587	0523	0459	0397	0336	0277	0220	0166	0115	0068	0030	0004
122	1254	1183	1114	1044	0976	0908	0840	0773	0707	0642	0577	0514	0451	0390	0330	0272	0216	0163	0113	0067
124	1372	1302	1233	1164	1095	1027	0960	0893	0826	0761	0696	0631	0568	0505	0444	0384	0325	0268	0213	0160
126	1488	1419	1350	1281	1213	1145	1077	1011	0944	0878	0813	0748	0684	0621	0559	0497	0437	0378	0320	0264
128	1602	1533	1464	1396	1328	1260	1193	1126	1060	0994	0929	0864	0800	0736	0673	0611	0550	0489	0430	0372
130	1713	1644	1576	1508	1441	1374	1307	1240	1174	1109	1043	0979	0914	0851	0787	0725	0663	0602	0541	0482
132	1821	1753	1686	1619	1552	1485	1418	1352	1287	1221	1156	1091	1027	0964	0900	0837	0775	0714	0653	0592
134	1928	1860	1793	1726	1660	1594	1528	1462	1397	1332	1267	1202	1138	1075	1012	0949	0887	0825	0763	0703
136	2032	1965	1898	1832	1766	1700	1635	1570	1505	1440	1375	1311	1248	1184	1121	1059	0996	0935	0873	0812
138	2133	2067	2001	1935	1870	1805	1740	1675	1610	1546	1482	1418	1355	1292	1229	1167	1105	1043	0982	0921
140	2232	2167	2101	2036	1971	1907	1842	1778	1714	1650	1587	1523	1460	1398	1335	1273	1211	1150	1088	1028
142	2329	2264	2200	2135	2071	2007	1943	1879	1815	1752	1689	1626	1564	1501	1439	1377	1316	1255	1194	1133
144	2424	2360	2296	2232	2168	2104	2041	1978	1915	1852	1789	1727	1665	1603	1541	1480	1419	1358	1297	1237
146	2517	2453	2390	2326	2263	2200	2137	2075	2012	1950	1888	1826	1764	1703	1641	1580	1520	1459	1399	1339
148	2607	2544	2482	2419	2356	2294	2231	2169	2107	2046	1984	1923	1861	1800	1740	1679	1619	1558	1498	1439
150	2696	2634	2571	2509	2447	2385	2324	2262	2201	2139	2078	2017	1957	1896	1836	1776	1716	1656	1596	1537

$l+r$	121	122	123	124	125	126	127	128	129	130	131	132	133	134	135	136	137	138	139	140
N	0,	0,	0,	0,	0,	0,	0,	0,	0,	0,	0,	0,	0,	0,	0,	0,	0,	0,	0,	0,
122	0029	0004																		
124	0111	0066	0029	0004																
126	0209	0158	0109	0065	0028	0004														
128	0315	0259	0206	0155	0107	0064	0028	0004												
130	0423	0366	0310	0255	0203	0153	0106	0063	0027	0004										
132	0533	0474	0417	0360	0305	0252	0200	0150	0104	0062	0027	0004								
134	0643	0583	0525	0467	0410	0355	0301	0248	0197	0148	0103	0061	0027	0004						
136	0752	0692	0633	0575	0517	0460	0404	0350	0296	0244	0194	0146	0101	0060	0026	0004				
138	0860	0800	0741	0682	0624	0566	0509	0453	0398	0344	0292	0240	0191	0144	0100	0060	0026	0004		
140	0967	0907	0848	0789	0730	0672	0615	0558	0502	0447	0393	0339	0287	0237	0188	0142	0098	0059	0025	0004
142	1073	1013	0953	0894	0836	0777	0720	0663	0606	0550	0495	0440	0387	0335	0283	0234	0186	0140	0097	0058
144	1177	1117	1058	0998	0940	0882	0824	0766	0709	0653	0597	0542	0488	0434	0382	0330	0279	0230	0183	0138
146	1279	1219	1160	1101	1043	0984	0927	0869	0812	0756	0700	0644	0589	0535	0481	0428	0376	0325	0276	0227
148	1379	1320	1261	1202	1144	1086	1028	0971	0914	0857	0801	0745	0690	0635	0581	0527	0475	0422	0371	0321
150	1478	1419	1360	1302	1244	1186	1128	1071	1014	0958	0901	0846	0790	0735	0681	0627	0573	0520	0468	0417

All values conform to the international convention (i.e. 0,1 instead of 0.1).

Distribution-Free Tolerance Limits* $\beta_t = 0{,}99$

$l+r = 1\text{–}20$, $N = 2(1)50(2)150$. The values in the table are those of β_p

$l+r$	1	2	3	4	5	6	7	8	9	10	11	12	13	14	15	16	17	18	19	20
N	0,	0,	0,	0,	0,	0,	0,	0,	0,	0,	0,	0,	0,	0,	0,	0,	0,	0,	0,	0,
2	1000	0050																		
3	2154	0589	0033																	
4	3162	1409	0420	0025																
5	3981	2221	1056	0327	0020															
6	4642	2943	1731	0847	0268	0017														
7	5179	3566	2363	1423	0708	0227	0014													
8	5623	4101	2932	1982	1210	0608	0196	0013												
9	5995	4560	3437	2500	1710	1053	0533	0174	0011											
10	6310	4956	3883	2971	2183	1504	0932	0475	0155	0010										
11	6579	5302	4277	3396	2622	1940	1344	0837	0428	0141	0009									
12	6813	5605	4627	3778	3024	2349	1746	1215	0759	0390	0128	0008								
13	7017	5872	4938	4122	3391	2729	2129	1588	1108	0695	0358	0118	0008							
14	7197	6109	5217	4433	3726	3080	2488	1947	1457	1019	0640	0331	0110	0007						
15	7356	6321	5468	4715	4031	3403	2823	2287	1795	1346	0944	0594	0307	0102	0007					
16	7499	6512	5695	4971	4310	3701	3134	2607	2117	1665	1215	0878	0554	0287	0095	0006				
17	7627	6684	5901	5204	4566	3975	3423	2906	2422	1971	1552	1168	0822	0519	0269	0090	0006			
18	7743	6840	6088	5417	4801	4228	3691	3186	2710	2263	1844	1454	1096	0772	0488	0254	0084	0006		
19	7848	6982	6259	5613	5017	4462	3940	3447	2980	2540	2124	1733	1368	1032	0728	0461	0240	0080	0005	
20	7943	7112	6417	5793	5217	4679	4171	3691	3234	2801	2390	2001	1634	1292	0975	0688	0436	0227	0076	0005
21	8031	7232	6561	5959	5402	4880	4387	3918	3472	3047	2642	2257	1891	1547	1223	0925	0653	0414	0216	0072
22	8111	7342	6695	6113	5574	5067	4588	4132	3696	3280	2881	2501	2138	1793	1468	1162	0879	0621	0394	0206
23	8185	7443	6819	6255	5733	5242	4776	4331	3906	3498	3108	2733	2374	2031	1705	1397	1107	0838	0593	0376
24	8254	7538	6934	6388	5882	5405	4952	4519	4104	3705	3322	2953	2599	2260	1935	1625	1332	1056	0800	0566
25	8318	7625	7041	6512	6021	5557	5116	4694	4289	3900	3524	3163	2814	2479	2156	1848	1553	1273	1010	0765
26	8377	7707	7141	6628	6151	5700	5271	4860	4465	4084	3716	3361	3018	2688	2369	2062	1768	1487	1220	0968
27	8432	7783	7234	6736	6273	5834	5416	5016	4630	4258	3898	3550	3213	2887	2572	2268	1976	1695	1426	1170
28	8483	7854	7321	6838	6387	5961	5553	5163	4786	4422	4070	3729	3398	3078	2767	2467	2176	1896	1627	1370
29	8532	7921	7404	6934	6495	6080	5683	5301	4934	4578	4233	3899	3574	3259	2953	2657	2369	2091	1823	1565
30	8577	7984	7481	7024	6597	6192	5805	5433	5073	4726	4388	4061	3742	3433	3132	2840	2555	2280	2013	1755
31	8620	8043	7554	7109	6693	6298	5920	5557	5206	4866	4535	4214	3902	3598	3302	3014	2733	2461	2197	1940
32	8660	8099	7623	7189	6784	6399	6030	5675	5332	4999	4676	4361	4055	3756	3465	3181	2905	2636	2374	2119
33	8697	8152	7688	7265	6870	6494	6134	5787	5451	5126	4809	4501	4200	3907	3621	3342	3069	2803	2545	2293
34	8733	8202	7749	7337	6951	6584	6233	5893	5565	5246	4936	4634	4339	4051	3770	3495	3227	2965	2709	2460
35	8767	8249	7808	7406	7029	6670	6326	5995	5673	5361	5057	4761	4472	4189	3913	3643	3378	3120	2868	2621
36	8799	8294	7863	7470	7102	6752	6416	6091	5777	5471	5173	4883	4599	4321	4050	3784	3524	3269	3020	2777
37	8830	8337	7916	7532	7172	6830	6501	6183	5875	5576	5284	4999	4720	4448	4181	3920	3664	3413	3167	2927
38	8859	8377	7966	7591	7239	6904	6582	6271	5969	5676	5390	5110	4837	4569	4307	4050	3798	3551	3309	3071
39	8886	8416	8014	7647	7303	6975	6660	6355	6059	5772	5491	5217	4948	4685	4428	4175	3927	3684	3445	3211
40	8913	8453	8060	7701	7364	7043	6734	6435	6146	5863	5588	5319	5055	4797	4544	4295	4051	3812	3577	3346
41	8938	8487	8104	7752	7422	7107	6805	6512	6228	5951	5681	5417	5158	4904	4655	4411	4171	3935	3703	3475
42	8962	8521	8145	7801	7478	7169	6873	6586	6307	6036	5770	5511	5256	5007	4762	4522	4286	4053	3825	3601
43	8984	8554	8185	7848	7531	7229	6938	6657	6383	6117	5856	5601	5351	5106	4865	4629	4396	4168	3943	3722
44	9006	8584	8223	7893	7582	7286	7001	6724	6456	6194	5938	5688	5442	5201	4965	4732	4503	4278	4056	3838
45	9027	8614	8260	7936	7631	7341	7061	6790	6526	6269	6018	5772	5530	5293	5060	4831	4606	4384	4166	3951
46	9047	8642	8295	7978	7679	7393	7118	6852	6593	6341	6094	5852	5615	5382	5152	4927	4705	4487	4272	4060
47	9067	8669	8329	8017	7724	7444	7174	6913	6658	6410	6167	5929	5696	5467	5241	5020	4801	4586	4374	4165
48	9085	8695	8362	8056	7768	7492	7227	6971	6721	6477	6238	6004	5775	5549	5327	5109	4894	4682	4473	4267
49	9103	8721	8393	8092	7810	7539	7279	7027	6781	6541	6306	6076	5850	5628	5410	5195	4983	4774	4568	4366
50	9120	8745	8423	8128	7850	7584	7329	7080	6839	6603	6372	6146	5923	5705	5490	5278	5069	4864	4661	4461
52	9152	8790	8480	8195	7927	7670	7423	7183	6949	6721	6497	6278	6062	5851	5642	5436	5234	5034	4837	4642
54	9183	8833	8533	8257	7998	7750	7510	7278	7052	6830	6614	6401	6192	5987	5784	5585	5388	5194	5002	4813
56	9211	8873	8582	8316	8064	7824	7592	7367	7148	6933	6723	6517	6314	6114	5918	5724	5533	5344	5157	4973
58	9237	8910	8628	8370	8127	7894	7669	7451	7238	7030	6826	6625	6428	6234	6043	5855	5669	5485	5303	5124
60	9261	8944	8672	8421	8185	7959	7741	7529	7322	7120	6922	6727	6536	6347	6161	5978	5797	5618	5441	5266
62	9284	8977	8712	8469	8240	8021	7809	7603	7402	7205	7013	6823	6637	6453	6273	6094	5918	5743	5571	5401
64	9306	9007	8751	8515	8292	8078	7872	7672	7477	7286	7098	6914	6733	6554	6378	6204	6032	5862	5694	5528
66	9326	9036	8787	8557	8341	8133	7933	7738	7548	7361	7179	6999	6823	6649	6477	6308	6140	5974	5811	5649
68	9345	9063	8821	8597	8387	8185	7989	7800	7615	7433	7255	7081	6908	6739	6571	6406	6242	6081	5921	5763
70	9363	9089	8853	8636	8430	8233	8043	7858	7678	7501	7328	7157	6989	6824	6660	6499	6340	6182	6026	5871
72	9380	9113	8883	8672	8471	8280	8094	7914	7738	7566	7397	7230	7066	6905	6745	6588	6432	6278	6125	5975
74	9397	9136	8912	8706	8511	8324	8143	7967	7795	7627	7462	7299	7139	6982	6826	6672	6520	6369	6220	6073
76	9412	9158	8940	8738	8548	8365	8189	8017	7850	7685	7524	7365	7209	7055	6903	6752	6604	6456	6311	6166
78	9427	9179	8966	8769	8583	8405	8233	8065	7901	7741	7583	7428	7275	7125	6976	6829	6683	6539	6397	6256
80	9441	9199	8990	8799	8617	8443	8274	8111	7951	7794	7640	7488	7339	7191	7046	6902	6759	6619	6479	6341
82	9454	9218	9014	8827	8649	8479	8314	8154	7998	7844	7693	7545	7399	7255	7112	6972	6832	6694	6558	6422
84	9467	9236	9037	8853	8680	8513	8352	8196	8043	7892	7745	7600	7457	7316	7176	7038	6902	6767	6633	6500
86	9479	9253	9058	8879	8709	8546	8389	8235	8085	7939	7794	7652	7512	7374	7237	7102	6968	6836	6705	6575
88	9490	9269	9079	8903	8737	8578	8424	8273	8127	7983	7841	7702	7565	7429	7296	7163	7032	6903	6774	6647
90	9501	9285	9099	8927	8764	8608	8457	8310	8166	8025	7886	7750	7616	7483	7352	7222	7093	6966	6840	6715
92	9512	9300	9118	8949	8790	8637	8489	8345	8204	8066	7930	7796	7664	7534	7405	7278	7152	7028	6904	6781
94	9522	9315	9136	8971	8815	8665	8520	8378	8240	8105	7971	7840	7711	7583	7457	7332	7209	7086	6965	6845
96	9532	9328	9153	8991	8838	8691	8549	8410	8275	8142	8011	7883	7756	7631	7507	7384	7263	7143	7024	6906
98	9541	9342	9170	9011	8861	8717	8577	8441	8308	8178	8050	7923	7799	7676	7554	7434	7315	7197	7080	6964
100	9550	9355	9186	9030	8883	8741	8604	8471	8341	8213	8087	7963	7840	7720	7600	7482	7365	7250	7135	7021
102	9559	9367	9201	9049	8904	8765	8631	8500	8372	8246	8122	8001	7881	7762	7645	7529	7414	7300	7187	7075
104	9567	9379	9216	9066	8924	8788	8656	8527	8401	8278	8157	8037	7919	7803	7687	7573	7461	7349	7238	7128
106	9575	9390	9231	9083	8944	8810	8680	8554	8430	8309	8190	8072	7956	7842	7729	7616	7506	7396	7287	7178
108	9583	9401	9244	9100	8963	8831	8704	8579	8458	8339	8222	8106	7992	7880	7768	7658	7549	7441	7334	7227
110	9590	9412	9258	9116	8981	8852	8726	8604	8485	8368	8252	8139	8027	7916	7807	7698	7591	7485	7379	7275
112	9597	9422	9271	9131	8999	8871	8748	8628	8511	8395	8282	8170	8060	7951	7844	7737	7632	7527	7423	7320
114	9604	9432	9283	9146	9016	8890	8769	8651	8536	8422	8311	8201	8093	7985	7880	7775	7671	7568	7466	7364
116	9611	9441	9295	9160	9032	8909	8790	8674	8560	8448	8339	8231	8124	8018	7914	7811	7709	7607	7507	7407
118	9617	9451	9307	9174	9048	8927	8809	8695	8583	8474	8366	8259	8154	8050	7948	7846	7746	7646	7547	7449
120	9624	9460	9318	9187	9063	8944	8829	8716	8606	8498	8392	8287	8183	8081	7980	7880	7781	7683	7585	7489
122	9630	9468	9329	9200	9078	8961	8847	8736	8628	8522	8417	8314	8212	8111	8012	7913	7816	7719	7623	7528
124	9635	9477	9339	9213	9092	8977	8865	8756	8649	8544	8441	8340	8239	8140	8042	7945	7849	7754	7659	7565
126	9641	9485	9350	9225	9106	8993	8882	8775	8670	8567	8465	8365	8266	8168	8072	7976	7881	7788	7694	7602
128	9647	9493	9360	9237	9120	9008	8899	8793	8690	8588	8488	8389	8292	8196	8101	8006	7913	7820	7728	7637
130	9652	9500	9369	9248	9133	9023	8916	8811	8709	8609	8510	8413	8317	8222	8128	8036	7943	7852	7762	7672
132	9657	9508	9378	9259	9146	9037	8932	8829	8728	8629	8532	8436	8342	8248	8156	8064	7973	7883	7794	7705
134	9662	9515	9387	9270	9158	9051	8947	8846	8746	8649	8553	8459	8365	8273	8182	8092	8002	7913	7825	7738
136	9667	9522	9396	9280	9170	9065	8962	8862	8764	8668	8574	8480	8388	8297	8207	8118	8030	7942	7856	7769
138	9672	9529	9405	9290	9182	9078	8977	8878	8782	8687	8594	8502	8411	8321	8232	8144	8057	7971	7885	7800
140	9676	9535	9413	9300	9193	9090	8991	8894	8798	8705	8613	8522	8433	8344	8256	8170	8084	7999	7914	7830
142	9681	9542	9421	9310	9204	9103	9005	8909	8815	8722	8632	8542	8454	8366	8280	8194	8110	8025	7942	7859
144	9685	9548	9429	9319	9215	9115	9018	8923	8831	8740	8650	8562	8474	8388	8303	8218	8135	8052	7969	7887
146	9690	9554	9437	9328	9226	9127	9031	8938	8846	8756	8668	8581	8495	8409	8325	8242	8159	8077	7996	7915
148	9694	9560	9444	9337	9236	9138	9044	8951	8861	8772	8685	8599	8514	8430	8347	8265	8183	8102	8022	7942
150	9698	9566	9451	9346	9246	9149	9056	8965	8876	8788	8702	8617	8533	8450	8368	8287	8206	8126	8047	7968

All values conform to the international convention (i.e. 0,1 instead of 0.1).

Distribution-Free Tolerance Limits* $\beta_t = 0{,}99$

Top: $l+r = 21$–40, $N = 21(1)50(2)150$; bottom: $l+r = 41$–60, $N = 41(1)50(2)58$. The values in the table are those of β_p

l+r	21	22	23	24	25	26	27	28	29	30	31	32	33	34	35	36	37	38	39	40
N	0,	0,	0,	0,	0,	0,	0,	0,	0,	0,	0,	0,	0,	0,	0,	0,	0,	0,	0,	0,
21	0005																			
22	0069	0005																		
23	0196	0066	0004																	
24	0360	0188	0063	0004																
25	0542	0345	0180	0060	0004															
26	0734	0520	0331	0173	0058	0004														
27	0929	0705	0500	0318	0166	0056	0004													
28	1125	0894	0678	0481	0306	0160	0054	0004												
29	1318	1083	0860	0653	0465	0295	0155	0052	0003											
30	1508	1270	1044	0830	0630	0447	0285	0149	0050	0003										
31	1693	1454	1225	1007	0801	0609	0432	0275	0144	0049	0003									
32	1873	1634	1404	1184	0973	0773	0588	0418	0267	0140	0047	0003								
33	2047	1810	1580	1358	1145	0942	0749	0570	0405	0258	0135	0046	0003							
34	2217	1980	1751	1529	1315	1109	0912	0726	0552	0392	0250	0131	0044	0003						
35	2380	2146	1918	1696	1481	1274	1075	0884	0704	0535	0381	0243	0127	0043	0003					
36	2539	2306	2079	1859	1644	1436	1236	1043	0858	0683	0520	0370	0236	0124	0042	0003				
37	2691	2461	2236	2017	1803	1595	1394	1199	1012	0833	0664	0505	0359	0229	0120	0041	0003			
38	2839	2611	2389	2171	1958	1751	1550	1354	1165	0984	0810	0645	0491	0349	0223	0117	0040	0003		
39	2981	2756	2536	2320	2109	1903	1702	1506	1317	1133	0957	0788	0628	0478	0340	0217	0114	0039	0003	
40	3119	2897	2679	2465	2255	2051	1851	1655	1466	1281	1103	0931	0767	0611	0466	0331	0212	0111	0038	0003
41	3252	3032	2817	2605	2398	2194	1995	1801	1611	1427	1248	1074	0907	0747	0596	0454	0323	0206	0108	0037
42	3380	3163	2950	2741	2536	2334	2136	1943	1754	1570	1390	1216	1047	0884	0729	0581	0442	0315	0201	0106
43	3504	3290	3080	2873	2669	2470	2274	2082	1894	1710	1530	1355	1185	1021	0863	0711	0567	0432	0307	0196
44	3624	3413	3205	3000	2799	2601	2407	2217	2029	1846	1667	1492	1322	1157	0996	0842	0694	0553	0422	0300
45	3739	3531	3326	3124	2925	2729	2537	2348	2162	1980	1802	1627	1457	1291	1129	0973	0822	0678	0540	0412
46	3851	3646	3443	3243	3047	2853	2663	2475	2291	2110	1933	1759	1589	1423	1260	1103	0950	0803	0662	0528
47	3959	3757	3556	3359	3165	2974	2785	2600	2417	2238	2061	1888	1718	1552	1390	1232	1078	0929	0785	0647
48	4064	3864	3666	3472	3280	3091	2904	2720	2539	2361	2186	2014	1845	1680	1517	1359	1204	1054	0908	0768
49	4165	3968	3773	3581	3391	3204	3019	2838	2658	2482	2308	2137	1969	1804	1642	1484	1329	1178	1031	0889
50	4263	4068	3876	3686	3499	3314	3132	2952	2774	2599	2427	2257	2090	1926	1765	1607	1452	1301	1153	1009
52	4450	4261	4073	3888	3705	3525	3346	3170	2996	2825	2656	2489	2324	2162	2003	1846	1692	1540	1392	1247
54	4626	4441	4258	4078	3900	3723	3549	3377	3207	3039	2873	2709	2547	2387	2230	2075	1922	1772	1624	1479
56	4791	4611	4433	4257	4083	3911	3741	3572	3406	3241	3079	2918	2759	2602	2447	2294	2143	1994	1848	1704
58	4947	4771	4598	4426	4256	4088	3922	3757	3595	3433	3274	3116	2960	2806	2654	2503	2355	2208	2063	1920
60	5094	4923	4753	4586	4420	4256	4094	3933	3773	3616	3460	3305	3152	3001	2851	2703	2557	2412	2269	2128
62	5232	5066	4900	4737	4575	4415	4256	4099	3943	3789	3636	3485	3335	3186	3039	2894	2750	2607	2466	2327
64	5364	5201	5040	4880	4722	4565	4410	4256	4104	3953	3804	3655	3508	3363	3218	3076	2934	2794	2655	2518
66	5488	5329	5172	5016	4862	4709	4557	4406	4257	4110	3963	3818	3674	3531	3389	3249	3110	2973	2836	2701
68	5606	5451	5297	5145	4994	4844	4696	4549	4403	4258	4115	3973	3831	3692	3553	3415	3279	3143	3009	2876
70	5718	5567	5417	5268	5120	4974	4829	4685	4542	4400	4260	4120	3982	3845	3709	3574	3440	3307	3175	3044
72	5825	5677	5530	5384	5240	5097	4955	4814	4674	4535	4398	4261	4126	3991	3857	3725	3593	3463	3333	3205
74	5927	5782	5638	5496	5354	5214	5075	4937	4800	4664	4530	4396	4263	4131	4000	3870	3741	3613	3485	3359
76	6023	5882	5741	5602	5463	5326	5190	5055	4921	4788	4656	4524	4394	4265	4136	4008	3882	3756	3631	3507
78	6116	5977	5839	5703	5568	5433	5300	5168	5036	4906	4776	4647	4520	4393	4266	4141	4017	3893	3771	3649
80	6204	6068	5933	5800	5667	5536	5405	5275	5146	5018	4891	4765	4640	4515	4391	4269	4146	4025	3904	3785
82	6288	6155	6023	5892	5762	5633	5505	5378	5252	5126	5002	4878	4755	4633	4511	4391	4271	4151	4033	3915
84	6369	6239	6109	5981	5854	5727	5602	5477	5353	5230	5108	4986	4865	4746	4626	4508	4390	4273	4157	4041
86	6446	6319	6192	6066	5941	5817	5694	5572	5450	5329	5209	5090	4972	4854	4737	4620	4505	4390	4275	4161
88	6520	6395	6271	6147	6025	5903	5782	5662	5543	5425	5307	5190	5073	4958	4843	4728	4615	4502	4389	4278
90	6592	6469	6347	6226	6105	5986	5868	5750	5633	5516	5401	5286	5171	5058	4945	4832	4721	4610	4499	4389
92	6660	6539	6420	6301	6183	6066	5949	5834	5719	5604	5491	5378	5266	5154	5043	4933	4823	4713	4605	4497
94	6726	6607	6490	6373	6257	6142	6028	5914	5801	5689	5577	5467	5356	5247	5137	5029	4921	4814	4707	4600
96	6789	6672	6557	6443	6329	6216	6103	5992	5881	5771	5661	5552	5444	5336	5228	5122	5016	4910	4805	4700
98	6849	6735	6622	6509	6398	6287	6176	6067	5958	5849	5741	5634	5528	5422	5316	5211	5107	5003	4900	4797
100	6908	6796	6684	6574	6464	6355	6247	6139	6032	5925	5819	5714	5609	5505	5401	5298	5195	5093	4991	4890
102	6964	6854	6745	6636	6528	6421	6314	6208	6103	5998	5894	5790	5687	5585	5483	5381	5280	5179	5079	4980
104	7019	6910	6803	6696	6590	6484	6380	6275	6172	6069	5966	5864	5763	5662	5561	5461	5362	5263	5165	5066
106	7071	6965	6859	6754	6649	6546	6443	6340	6238	6137	6036	5936	5836	5736	5638	5539	5441	5344	5247	5150
108	7122	7017	6913	6810	6707	6605	6504	6403	6302	6203	6103	6005	5906	5809	5711	5614	5518	5422	5327	5232
110	7171	7068	6965	6864	6763	6662	6562	6463	6364	6266	6169	6071	5975	5878	5783	5687	5592	5498	5404	5310
112	7218	7117	7016	6916	6817	6718	6619	6522	6424	6328	6232	6136	6041	5946	5852	5758	5664	5571	5478	5386
114	7264	7164	7065	6966	6869	6771	6675	6578	6483	6387	6293	6198	6105	6011	5918	5826	5734	5642	5551	5460
116	7308	7210	7112	7015	6919	6823	6728	6633	6539	6445	6352	6259	6167	6075	5983	5892	5801	5711	5621	5531
118	7351	7254	7158	7063	6968	6873	6780	6686	6593	6501	6409	6318	6227	6136	6046	5956	5866	5777	5689	5600
120	7393	7297	7203	7109	7015	6922	6830	6738	6646	6555	6465	6374	6285	6195	6107	6018	5930	5842	5755	5668
122	7433	7339	7246	7153	7061	6969	6878	6788	6697	6608	6518	6430	6341	6253	6166	6078	5991	5905	5819	5733
124	7472	7380	7288	7196	7105	7015	6925	6836	6747	6659	6571	6483	6396	6309	6223	6137	6051	5966	5881	5796
126	7510	7419	7328	7238	7149	7060	6971	6883	6795	6708	6621	6535	6449	6364	6278	6193	6109	6025	5941	5857
128	7547	7457	7368	7279	7190	7103	7015	6929	6842	6756	6671	6586	6501	6416	6332	6249	6165	6082	5999	5917
130	7582	7494	7406	7318	7231	7145	7059	6973	6888	6803	6719	6635	6551	6468	6385	6302	6220	6138	6056	5975
132	7617	7530	7443	7357	7271	7185	7100	7016	6932	6848	6765	6682	6600	6517	6436	6354	6273	6192	6112	6031
134	7651	7565	7479	7394	7309	7225	7141	7058	6975	6892	6810	6728	6647	6566	6485	6405	6325	6245	6165	6086
136	7684	7599	7514	7430	7347	7263	7181	7099	7017	6935	6854	6774	6693	6613	6533	6454	6375	6296	6218	6140
138	7716	7632	7548	7465	7383	7301	7219	7138	7057	6977	6897	6817	6738	6659	6580	6502	6424	6346	6269	6192
140	7747	7664	7581	7500	7418	7337	7257	7177	7097	7018	6939	6860	6782	6704	6626	6549	6472	6395	6318	6242
142	7777	7695	7614	7533	7453	7373	7293	7214	7135	7057	6979	6902	6824	6747	6671	6594	6518	6442	6367	6291
144	7806	7725	7645	7565	7486	7407	7329	7251	7173	7096	7019	6942	6866	6790	6714	6638	6563	6488	6414	6339
146	7835	7755	7676	7597	7519	7441	7363	7286	7210	7133	7057	6981	6906	6831	6756	6682	6607	6533	6460	6386
148	7863	7784	7706	7628	7551	7474	7397	7321	7245	7170	7095	7020	6945	6871	6797	6724	6650	6577	6504	6432
150	7890	7812	7735	7658	7582	7506	7430	7355	7280	7205	7131	7057	6984	6910	6837	6765	6692	6620	6548	6476

l+r	41	42	43	44	45	46	47	48	49	50	51	52	53	54	55	56	57	58	59	60
N	0,	0,	0,	0,	0,	0,	0,	0,	0,	0,	0,	0,	0,	0,	0,	0,	0,	0,		
41	0002																			
42	0036	0002																		
43	0103	0035	0002																	
44	0192	0101	0034	0002																
45	0293	0188	0099	0033	0002															
46	0402	0287	0183	0096	0033	0002														
47	0516	0394	0280	0179	0094	0032	0002													
48	0633	0505	0385	0274	0176	0092	0031	0002												
49	0751	0620	0495	0377	0269	0172	0090	0031	0002											
50	0870	0736	0607	0484	0369	0263	0168	0089	0030	0002										
52	1106	0968	0835	0706	0582	0465	0354	0253	0162	0085	0029	0002								
54	1337	1198	1062	0930	0802	0679	0560	0447	0341	0243	0156	0082	0028	0002						
56	1562	1423	1286	1153	1022	0895	0772	0653	0539	0431	0328	0234	0150	0079	0027	0002				
58	1779	1640	1504	1370	1239	1111	0985	0863	0744	0630	0520	0415	0317	0226	0145	0076	0026	0002		

All values conform to the international convention (i.e. 0,1 instead of 0.1).

Distribution-Free Tolerance Limits* $\beta_t = 0{,}99$

Top: $l+r = 41$–60, $N = 60(2)150$; bottom: $l+r = 61$–80, $N = 62(2)150$. The values in the table are those of β_p

$l+r$	41	42	43	44	45	46	47	48	49	50	51	52	53	54	55	56	57	58	59	60
N	0,	0,	0,	0,	0,	0,	0,	0,	0,	0,	0,	0,	0,	0,	0,	0,	0,	0,	0,	0,
60	1988	1851	1715	1582	1451	1322	1195	1072	0951	0833	0718	0608	0502	0401	0306	0218	0140	0074	0025	0002
62	2189	2053	1919	1787	1656	1527	1401	1276	1154	1035	0918	0805	0694	0588	0485	0388	0296	0211	0135	0071
64	2382	2248	2115	1984	1854	1727	1601	1476	1354	1234	1116	1001	0888	0778	0672	0569	0469	0375	0286	0204
66	2567	2435	2304	2174	2046	1919	1794	1671	1549	1429	1311	1195	1081	0969	0860	0754	0650	0551	0455	0363
68	2745	2614	2485	2357	2230	2105	1981	1859	1738	1618	1500	1384	1270	1158	1047	0939	0834	0731	0631	0534
70	2915	2786	2659	2533	2408	2284	2161	2040	1920	1802	1685	1569	1455	1342	1232	1123	1016	0911	0809	0709
72	3078	2951	2826	2702	2578	2456	2335	2215	2097	1979	1863	1748	1635	1523	1412	1303	1196	1090	0986	0885
74	3234	3110	2986	2864	2742	2622	2503	2384	2267	2151	2036	1922	1809	1698	1588	1479	1371	1266	1161	1059
76	3384	3261	3140	3020	2900	2781	2664	2547	2431	2316	2203	2090	1978	1868	1758	1650	1543	1438	1333	1231
78	3528	3407	3288	3169	3052	2935	2819	2704	2589	2476	2364	2252	2142	2032	1924	1817	1710	1605	1501	1399
80	3666	3547	3430	3313	3198	3082	2968	2855	2742	2630	2519	2409	2300	2192	2084	1978	1873	1768	1665	1563
82	3798	3682	3567	3452	3338	3225	3112	3000	2889	2779	2669	2561	2453	2346	2240	2134	2030	1926	1824	1722
84	3926	3812	3698	3585	3473	3361	3250	3140	3031	2922	2814	2707	2601	2495	2390	2286	2182	2080	1978	1877
86	4048	3936	3824	3713	3603	3493	3384	3275	3168	3061	2954	2848	2743	2639	2535	2432	2330	2229	2128	2028
88	4166	4056	3946	3837	3728	3620	3513	3406	3300	3194	3089	2985	2881	2778	2676	2574	2473	2373	2273	2174
90	4280	4171	4063	3956	3849	3742	3636	3531	3427	3323	3219	3116	3014	2913	2812	2711	2612	2512	2414	2316
92	4389	4282	4176	4070	3965	3860	3756	3652	3549	3447	3345	3244	3143	3043	2943	2844	2745	2648	2550	2454
94	4495	4389	4285	4181	4077	3974	3871	3769	3668	3567	3467	3367	3267	3168	3070	2972	2875	2778	2682	2587
96	4596	4493	4390	4287	4185	4084	3983	3882	3782	3683	3584	3485	3387	3290	3193	3097	3001	2905	2810	2716
98	4694	4593	4491	4390	4290	4190	4090	3992	3893	3795	3697	3600	3504	3408	3312	3217	3122	3028	2934	2841
100	4789	4689	4589	4490	4391	4292	4194	4097	4000	3903	3807	3711	3616	3521	3427	3333	3240	3147	3054	2962
102	4880	4782	4684	4586	4488	4391	4295	4199	4103	4008	3913	3819	3725	3632	3539	3446	3354	3262	3171	3080
104	4969	4872	4775	4679	4583	4487	4392	4298	4203	4109	4016	3923	3830	3738	3647	3555	3464	3374	3284	3194
106	5054	4959	4863	4768	4674	4580	4486	4393	4300	4208	4116	4024	3933	3842	3751	3661	3571	3482	3393	3304
108	5137	5043	4949	4855	4762	4670	4577	4485	4394	4303	4212	4121	4031	3942	3853	3764	3675	3587	3499	3412
110	5217	5124	5031	4939	4848	4756	4665	4575	4485	4395	4305	4216	4127	4039	3951	3863	3776	3689	3602	3516
112	5294	5203	5112	5021	4931	4840	4751	4662	4573	4484	4396	4308	4220	4133	4046	3960	3873	3788	3702	3617
114	5369	5279	5189	5100	5011	4922	4834	4746	4658	4570	4483	4397	4310	4224	4139	4053	3968	3883	3799	3715
116	5442	5353	5265	5176	5089	5001	4914	4827	4741	4654	4569	4483	4398	4313	4228	4144	4060	3976	3893	3810
118	5512	5425	5338	5251	5164	5078	4992	4906	4821	4736	4651	4567	4483	4399	4315	4232	4149	4067	3985	3903
120	5581	5494	5408	5323	5237	5152	5067	4983	4899	4815	4731	4648	4565	4482	4400	4318	4236	4155	4073	3993
122	5647	5562	5477	5393	5308	5224	5141	5057	4974	4892	4809	4727	4645	4564	4482	4401	4321	4240	4160	4080
124	5712	5628	5544	5460	5377	5295	5212	5130	5048	4966	4885	4804	4723	4642	4562	4482	4402	4323	4244	4165
126	5774	5691	5609	5526	5444	5363	5281	5200	5119	5039	4958	4878	4799	4719	4640	4561	4482	4404	4326	4248
128	5835	5753	5672	5590	5510	5429	5349	5269	5189	5109	5030	4951	4872	4794	4715	4637	4560	4482	4405	4328
130	5894	5813	5733	5653	5573	5493	5414	5335	5256	5178	5099	5021	4944	4866	4789	4712	4635	4559	4482	4406
132	5951	5872	5792	5713	5635	5556	5478	5400	5322	5244	5167	5090	5013	4937	4860	4784	4709	4633	4558	4482
134	6007	5929	5850	5772	5694	5617	5540	5463	5386	5309	5233	5157	5081	5005	4930	4855	4780	4705	4631	4557
136	6062	5984	5907	5830	5753	5676	5600	5524	5448	5372	5297	5222	5147	5072	4998	4924	4850	4776	4702	4629
138	6115	6038	5962	5886	5810	5734	5659	5584	5509	5434	5359	5285	5211	5138	5064	4991	4918	4845	4772	4699
140	6166	6091	6015	5940	5865	5790	5716	5642	5568	5494	5420	5347	5274	5201	5128	5056	4984	4912	4840	4768
142	6216	6142	6067	5993	5919	5845	5772	5698	5625	5552	5480	5407	5335	5263	5191	5119	5048	4977	4906	4835
144	6265	6191	6118	6045	5971	5899	5826	5753	5681	5609	5537	5466	5394	5323	5252	5182	5111	5041	4970	4900
146	6313	6240	6167	6095	6023	5951	5879	5807	5736	5665	5594	5523	5452	5382	5312	5242	5172	5103	5033	4964
148	6360	6287	6216	6144	6073	6001	5930	5860	5789	5719	5649	5579	5509	5439	5370	5301	5232	5163	5095	5026
150	6405	6334	6263	6192	6121	6051	5981	5911	5841	5772	5702	5633	5564	5496	5427	5359	5290	5222	5155	5087

$l+r$	61	62	63	64	65	66	67	68	69	70	71	72	73	74	75	76	77	78	79	80
N	0,	0,	0,	0,	0,	0,	0,	0,	0,	0,	0,	0,	0,	0,	0,	0,	0,	0,	0,	0,
62	0024	0002																		
64	0131	0069	0023	0002																
66	0277	0198	0127	0067	0023	0002														
68	0441	0352	0269	0192	0123	0065	0022	0001												
70	0612	0518	0428	0342	0261	0186	0119	0063	0021	0001										
72	0785	0688	0594	0503	0416	0332	0254	0181	0116	0061	0021	0001								
74	0958	0860	0763	0669	0578	0489	0404	0323	0247	0176	0113	0060	0020	0001						
76	1129	1030	0932	0836	0742	0651	0562	0476	0393	0314	0240	0171	0110	0058	0020	0001				
78	1297	1197	1099	1002	0907	0814	0722	0633	0547	0463	0383	0306	0234	0167	0107	0056	0019	0001		
80	1462	1362	1263	1166	1070	0976	0883	0793	0704	0617	0533	0451	0373	0298	0228	0163	0104	0055	0019	0001
82	1622	1522	1424	1327	1231	1136	1043	0951	0861	0772	0686	0602	0519	0440	0364	0291	0222	0159	0102	0054
84	1778	1679	1581	1484	1388	1293	1200	1108	1017	0927	0840	0753	0669	0587	0507	0429	0355	0284	0217	0155
86	1929	1831	1734	1637	1542	1447	1354	1262	1171	1081	0992	0905	0819	0735	0653	0573	0495	0419	0346	0277
88	2076	1979	1882	1787	1692	1598	1505	1413	1322	1232	1143	1055	0969	0883	0800	0718	0638	0559	0483	0409
90	2219	2123	2027	1932	1838	1745	1652	1560	1470	1380	1291	1203	1116	1031	0946	0863	0781	0701	0623	0546
92	2358	2262	2168	2073	1980	1887	1796	1704	1614	1525	1436	1348	1261	1176	1091	1007	0925	0844	0764	0686
94	2492	2398	2304	2211	2118	2026	1935	1845	1755	1666	1578	1490	1404	1318	1233	1149	1067	0985	0904	0825
96	2622	2529	2436	2344	2252	2162	2071	1982	1892	1804	1716	1629	1543	1458	1373	1289	1206	1124	1043	0963
98	2748	2656	2565	2473	2383	2293	2203	2115	2026	1939	1851	1765	1679	1594	1510	1426	1344	1262	1181	1100
100	2871	2780	2689	2599	2509	2420	2332	2244	2156	2069	1983	1897	1812	1728	1644	1561	1478	1396	1315	1235
102	2990	2900	2810	2721	2632	2544	2457	2370	2283	2197	2111	2026	1942	1858	1775	1692	1610	1529	1448	1368
104	3105	3016	2927	2839	2752	2665	2578	2492	2406	2321	2236	2152	2068	1985	1902	1820	1739	1658	1577	1498
106	3216	3129	3041	2954	2868	2782	2696	2611	2526	2442	2358	2274	2191	2109	2027	1945	1864	1784	1704	1625
108	3325	3238	3152	3066	2980	2895	2811	2726	2642	2559	2476	2393	2311	2229	2148	2067	1987	1907	1828	1749
110	3430	3344	3259	3174	3090	3006	2922	2839	2756	2673	2591	2509	2428	2347	2266	2186	2107	2027	1949	1870
112	3532	3447	3363	3280	3196	3113	3030	2948	2866	2784	2703	2622	2541	2461	2382	2302	2223	2145	2067	1989
114	3631	3548	3465	3382	3299	3217	3135	3054	2973	2892	2812	2732	2652	2573	2494	2415	2337	2259	2182	2105
116	3727	3645	3563	3481	3400	3319	3238	3157	3077	2997	2918	2839	2760	2681	2603	2525	2448	2371	2294	2218
118	3821	3740	3659	3578	3497	3417	3337	3258	3178	3100	3021	2943	2865	2787	2710	2633	2556	2480	2404	2328
120	3912	3832	3751	3672	3592	3513	3434	3355	3277	3199	3121	3044	2967	2890	2813	2737	2661	2586	2511	2436
122	4000	3921	3842	3763	3684	3606	3528	3451	3373	3296	3219	3143	3066	2990	2915	2839	2764	2689	2615	2541
124	4086	4008	3930	3852	3774	3697	3620	3543	3467	3390	3314	3239	3163	3088	3013	2938	2864	2790	2716	2643
126	4170	4092	4015	3938	3862	3785	3709	3633	3558	3482	3407	3332	3258	3183	3109	3035	2962	2888	2815	2743
128	4251	4175	4099	4023	3947	3871	3796	3721	3646	3572	3497	3423	3350	3276	3203	3130	3057	2984	2912	2840
130	4330	4255	4180	4104	4030	3955	3881	3806	3733	3659	3585	3512	3439	3366	3294	3222	3150	3078	3006	2935
132	4408	4333	4258	4184	4110	4037	3963	3890	3817	3744	3671	3599	3527	3455	3383	3311	3240	3169	3098	3028
134	4483	4409	4335	4262	4189	4116	4043	3971	3899	3827	3754	3683	3612	3541	3470	3399	3329	3258	3188	3118
136	4556	4483	4410	4338	4266	4193	4122	4050	3979	3907	3836	3765	3695	3625	3554	3484	3415	3345	3276	3207
138	4627	4555	4483	4412	4340	4269	4198	4127	4056	3986	3916	3846	3776	3706	3637	3568	3499	3430	3361	3293
140	4697	4625	4554	4484	4413	4343	4272	4202	4132	4063	3993	3924	3855	3786	3718	3649	3581	3513	3445	3377
142	4764	4694	4624	4554	4484	4414	4345	4276	4207	4138	4069	4001	3932	3864	3796	3728	3661	3594	3526	3459
144	4831	4761	4692	4622	4553	4484	4416	4347	4279	4211	4143	4075	4008	3940	3873	3806	3739	3672	3606	3540
146	4895	4826	4758	4689	4621	4553	4485	4417	4350	4282	4215	4148	4081	4014	3948	3882	3816	3750	3684	3618
148	4958	4890	4822	4754	4687	4620	4552	4485	4419	4352	4285	4219	4153	4087	4021	3956	3890	3825	3760	3695
150	5019	4952	4885	4818	4751	4685	4618	4552	4486	4420	4354	4289	4223	4158	4093	4028	3963	3898	3834	3770

All values conform to the international convention (i.e. 0,1 instead of 0.1).

Distribution-Free Tolerance Limits* $\beta_t = 0{,}99$

Top: $l+r = 81$–100, $N = 82(2)150$; middle: $l+r = 101$–120, $N = 102(2)150$; bottom: $l+r = 121$–140, $N = 122(2)150$. The values in the table are those of β_p

$l+r$	81	82	83	84	85	86	87	88	89	90	91	92	93	94	95	96	97	98	99	100
N	0,	0,	0,	0,	0,	0,	0,	0,	0,	0,	0,	0,	0,	0,	0,	0,	0,	0,	0,	0,
82	0018	0001																		
84	0099	0052	0018	0001																
86	0212	0151	0097	0051	0017	0001														
88	0338	0271	0207	0148	0095	0050	0017	0001												
90	0472	0400	0331	0264	0202	0144	0093	0049	0017	0001										
92	0609	0534	0461	0391	0323	0259	0198	0141	0091	0048	0016	0001								
94	0747	0670	0596	0522	0451	0382	0316	0253	0193	0138	0089	0047	0016	0001						
96	0885	0807	0731	0656	0583	0511	0442	0374	0309	0248	0189	0135	0087	0046	0016	0001				
98	1021	0943	0866	0790	0715	0642	0570	0500	0432	0366	0303	0242	0185	0132	0085	0045	0015	0001		
100	1156	1077	1000	0923	0848	0774	0701	0629	0559	0490	0424	0359	0297	0237	0181	0130	0083	0044	0015	0001
102	1288	1210	1132	1055	0980	0905	0831	0758	0686	0616	0547	0480	0415	0352	0291	0233	0178	0127	0082	0043
104	1419	1340	1263	1186	1110	1034	0960	0887	0814	0743	0673	0604	0537	0471	0407	0345	0285	0228	0174	0125
106	1546	1468	1390	1314	1238	1162	1088	1014	0941	0869	0798	0728	0660	0592	0526	0462	0399	0338	0280	0224
108	1671	1593	1516	1439	1363	1288	1214	1140	1067	0994	0923	0853	0783	0714	0647	0581	0516	0453	0391	0332
110	1793	1715	1639	1563	1487	1412	1338	1264	1191	1118	1047	0976	0906	0836	0768	0701	0635	0570	0507	0445
112	1912	1835	1759	1683	1608	1533	1459	1386	1313	1240	1168	1097	1027	0958	0889	0821	0754	0688	0623	0560
114	2028	1952	1876	1801	1726	1652	1578	1505	1432	1360	1289	1217	1147	1077	1008	0940	0873	0806	0740	0676
116	2142	2066	1991	1917	1842	1769	1695	1622	1550	1478	1406	1336	1265	1196	1127	1058	0990	0923	0857	0792
118	2253	2178	2103	2029	1956	1882	1809	1737	1665	1593	1522	1452	1382	1312	1243	1175	1107	1039	0973	0907
120	2361	2287	2213	2140	2066	1994	1921	1849	1778	1707	1636	1565	1496	1426	1357	1289	1221	1154	1088	1021
122	2467	2393	2320	2247	2175	2102	2031	1959	1888	1817	1747	1677	1608	1539	1470	1402	1334	1267	1201	1134
124	2570	2497	2424	2352	2280	2209	2137	2067	1996	1926	1856	1786	1717	1649	1580	1513	1445	1378	1312	1246
126	2670	2598	2526	2455	2384	2313	2242	2172	2102	2032	1963	1894	1825	1757	1689	1621	1554	1487	1421	1355
128	2768	2697	2626	2555	2484	2414	2344	2274	2205	2136	2067	1998	1930	1862	1795	1728	1661	1595	1529	1463
130	2864	2793	2723	2653	2583	2513	2444	2375	2306	2237	2169	2101	2033	1966	1899	1832	1766	1700	1634	1569
132	2958	2888	2818	2748	2679	2610	2541	2473	2404	2336	2269	2201	2134	2067	2001	1935	1869	1803	1738	1673
134	3049	2980	2910	2842	2773	2705	2636	2569	2501	2433	2366	2300	2233	2167	2101	2035	1969	1904	1839	1775
136	3138	3069	3001	2933	2865	2797	2729	2662	2595	2528	2462	2396	2330	2264	2198	2133	2068	2003	1939	1875
138	3225	3157	3089	3022	2954	2887	2820	2754	2687	2621	2555	2489	2424	2359	2294	2229	2165	2100	2036	1973
140	3310	3242	3175	3109	3042	2975	2909	2843	2777	2712	2646	2581	2516	2452	2387	2323	2259	2195	2132	2069
142	3393	3326	3260	3193	3127	3062	2996	2931	2866	2801	2736	2671	2607	2543	2479	2415	2352	2289	2226	2163
144	3474	3408	3342	3276	3211	3146	3081	3016	2952	2887	2823	2759	2695	2632	2568	2505	2442	2380	2317	2255
146	3553	3488	3422	3358	3293	3228	3164	3100	3036	2972	2909	2845	2782	2719	2656	2594	2531	2469	2407	2345
148	3630	3565	3501	3437	3373	3309	3245	3182	3118	3055	2992	2929	2867	2804	2742	2680	2618	2556	2495	2434
150	3706	3642	3578	3514	3451	3388	3325	3262	3199	3136	3074	3012	2950	2888	2826	2764	2703	2642	2581	2520

$l+r$	101	102	103	104	105	106	107	108	109	110	111	112	113	114	115	116	117	118	119	120
N	0,	0,	0,	0,	0,	0,	0,	0,	0,	0,	0,	0,	0,	0,	0,	0,	0,	0,	0,	0,
102	0015	0001																		
104	0080	0042	0014	0001																
106	0171	0122	0078	0041	0014	0001														
108	0274	0220	0168	0120	0077	0041	0014	0001												
110	0384	0326	0269	0215	0165	0118	0076	0040	0014	0001										
112	0497	0436	0377	0320	0264	0212	0162	0116	0074	0039	0013	0001								
114	0612	0550	0488	0429	0370	0314	0260	0208	0159	0114	0073	0039	0013	0001						
116	0727	0664	0601	0540	0480	0421	0364	0308	0255	0204	0156	0112	0072	0038	0013	0001				
118	0842	0778	0715	0652	0591	0530	0471	0413	0358	0303	0251	0201	0153	0110	0070	0037	0013	0001		
120	0956	0892	0828	0764	0702	0641	0581	0521	0463	0407	0351	0298	0246	0197	0151	0108	0069	0037	0012	0001
122	1069	1004	0940	0876	0814	0752	0690	0630	0571	0513	0456	0400	0346	0293	0242	0194	0148	0106	0068	0036
124	1180	1115	1051	0987	0924	0862	0800	0739	0679	0620	0561	0504	0448	0393	0340	0288	0238	0191	0146	0104
126	1290	1225	1161	1097	1034	0971	0909	0848	0787	0727	0668	0610	0552	0496	0441	0387	0334	0283	0234	0188
128	1398	1333	1269	1205	1142	1079	1017	0955	0894	0834	0774	0715	0657	0600	0543	0488	0434	0381	0329	0279
130	1504	1440	1376	1312	1249	1186	1124	1062	1001	0940	0880	0821	0762	0704	0647	0590	0535	0480	0427	0375
132	1608	1544	1480	1417	1354	1291	1229	1167	1106	1045	0985	0925	0866	0808	0750	0693	0637	0581	0526	0473
134	1711	1647	1583	1520	1457	1395	1333	1271	1210	1149	1089	1029	0970	0911	0853	0795	0739	0682	0627	0572
136	1811	1747	1684	1621	1559	1497	1435	1373	1312	1252	1192	1132	1072	1014	0955	0897	0840	0783	0727	0672
138	1909	1846	1783	1721	1659	1597	1535	1474	1413	1353	1293	1233	1174	1115	1056	0998	0941	0884	0827	0772
140	2006	1943	1881	1819	1757	1695	1634	1573	1512	1452	1392	1333	1273	1215	1156	1098	1041	0984	0927	0871
142	2100	2038	1976	1914	1853	1792	1731	1670	1610	1550	1490	1431	1372	1313	1255	1197	1139	1082	1025	0969
144	2193	2131	2070	2008	1947	1886	1826	1766	1706	1646	1587	1527	1469	1410	1352	1294	1237	1180	1123	1067
146	2284	2222	2161	2100	2040	1979	1919	1859	1800	1740	1681	1622	1564	1506	1448	1390	1333	1276	1219	1163
148	2373	2312	2251	2191	2130	2071	2011	1951	1892	1833	1774	1716	1657	1599	1542	1484	1427	1370	1314	1258
150	2460	2399	2339	2279	2219	2160	2101	2041	1983	1924	1866	1807	1749	1692	1634	1577	1520	1464	1407	1351

$l+r$	121	122	123	124	125	126	127	128	129	130	131	132	133	134	135	136	137	138	139	140
N	0,	0,	0,	0,	0,	0,	0,	0,	0,	0,	0,	0,	0,	0,	0,	0,	0,	0,	0,	0,
122	0012	0001																		
124	0067	0035	0012	0001																
126	0144	0103	0066	0035	0012	0001														
128	0231	0185	0141	0101	0065	0034	0012	0001												
130	0324	0275	0227	0182	0139	0099	0064	0034	0011	0001										
132	0420	0369	0319	0270	0224	0179	0137	0098	0063	0033	0011	0001								
134	0518	0466	0414	0363	0314	0266	0220	0176	0135	0096	0062	0033	0011	0001						
136	0617	0564	0511	0459	0408	0358	0309	0262	0217	0174	0133	0095	0061	0032	0011	0001				
138	0717	0662	0608	0555	0503	0452	0402	0353	0305	0258	0214	0171	0131	0094	0060	0032	0011	0001		
140	0815	0760	0706	0652	0599	0547	0496	0445	0396	0347	0300	0255	0211	0169	0129	0092	0059	0031	0011	0001
142	0913	0858	0803	0749	0696	0643	0591	0539	0489	0439	0390	0342	0296	0251	0208	0166	0127	0091	0058	0031
144	1011	0955	0900	0846	0792	0739	0686	0634	0582	0531	0482	0433	0385	0338	0292	0247	0205	0164	0125	0090
146	1107	1051	0996	0942	0888	0834	0781	0728	0676	0625	0574	0524	0475	0427	0379	0333	0288	0244	0202	0162
148	1202	1147	1091	1037	0983	0929	0875	0822	0770	0718	0667	0616	0566	0517	0468	0421	0374	0328	0284	0241
150	1296	1240	1185	1131	1076	1023	0969	0916	0863	0811	0759	0708	0658	0608	0558	0510	0462	0415	0369	0324

All values conform to the international convention (i.e. 0,1 instead of 0.1).

Distribution-Free Tolerance Limits (2 Samples)[◊] $\beta_t = 0{,}80$

N_1: sample size of sample one; N_2: sample size of sample two; N^*: number of observations in the 2nd sample which lies between the tolerance limits of l and r with a probability of at least β_t (assuming that both samples are from the same distribution). For definition of l and r see section 25A. The values in the table are those of N^*

$l+r=1$

N_2 \ N_1	2	3	4	5	6	7	8	9	10	11	12	13	14	15	16	17	18	19	20	22	25	30	35	40	45	50	60	70	80	90	100
2	1	1	1	1	1	1	2	2	2	2	2	2	2	2	2	2	2	2	2	2	2	2	2	2	2	2	2	2	2	2	2
3	1	2	2	2	2	2	2	2	2	2	3	3	3	3	3	3	3	3	3	3	3	3	3	3	3	3	3	3	3	3	3
4	1	2	2	3	3	3	3	3	3	3	3	3	3	3	4	4	4	4	4	4	4	4	4	4	4	4	4	4	4	4	4
5	2	3	3	3	4	4	4	4	4	4	4	4	4	4	4	4	4	4	5	5	5	5	5	5	5	5	5	5	5	5	5
6	2	3	4	4	4	5	5	5	5	5	5	5	5	5	5	5	5	5	5	5	6	6	6	6	6	6	6	6	6	6	6
7	3	4	4	5	5	5	6	6	6	6	6	6	6	6	6	6	6	6	6	6	6	7	7	7	7	7	7	7	7	7	7
8	3	4	5	6	6	6	6	6	7	7	7	7	7	7	7	7	7	7	7	7	7	7	8	8	8	8	8	8	8	8	8
9	4	5	6	6	7	7	7	7	7	8	8	8	8	8	8	8	8	8	8	8	8	8	8	9	9	9	9	9	9	9	9
10	4	6	6	7	7	8	8	8	8	8	9	9	9	9	9	9	9	9	9	9	9	9	9	10	10	10	10	10	10	10	10
11	5	6	7	8	8	8	9	9	9	9	9	10	10	10	10	10	10	10	10	10	10	10	10	10	11	11	11	11	11	11	11
12	5	7	8	8	9	9	10	10	10	10	10	10	10	11	11	11	11	11	11	11	11	11	11	11	11	12	12	12	12	12	12
13	5	7	8	9	10	10	10	11	11	11	11	11	11	11	12	12	12	12	12	12	12	12	12	12	12	12	13	13	13	13	13
14	6	8	9	10	10	11	11	11	12	12	12	12	12	12	12	13	13	13	13	13	13	13	13	13	13	13	14	14	14	14	14
15	6	8	10	11	11	12	12	12	13	13	13	13	13	13	13	13	14	14	14	14	14	14	14	14	14	14	15	15	15	15	15
16	7	9	10	11	12	12	13	13	13	14	14	14	14	14	14	14	14	14	15	15	15	15	15	15	15	15	15	16	16	16	16
17	7	10	11	12	13	13	14	14	14	14	15	15	15	15	15	15	15	15	15	16	16	16	16	16	16	16	16	17	17	17	17
18	8	10	12	13	13	14	14	15	15	15	15	16	16	16	16	16	16	16	16	17	17	17	17	17	17	17	17	17	18	18	18
19	8	11	12	13	14	15	15	16	16	16	16	17	17	17	17	17	17	17	17	17	18	18	18	18	18	18	18	18	19	19	19
20	9	11	13	14	15	16	16	16	17	17	17	17	18	18	18	18	18	18	18	18	19	19	19	19	19	19	19	19	20	20	20
21	9	12	14	15	16	16	17	17	18	18	18	18	18	19	19	19	19	19	19	19	19	20	20	20	20	20	20	20	20	21	21
22	10	13	14	16	17	17	18	18	18	19	19	19	19	20	20	20	20	20	20	20	20	21	21	21	21	21	21	21	21	22	22
23	10	13	15	16	17	18	19	19	19	20	20	20	20	20	21	21	21	21	21	21	21	22	22	22	22	22	22	22	22	22	23
25	11	14	16	18	19	20	20	21	21	21	22	22	22	22	22	22	23	23	23	23	23	23	24	24	24	24	24	24	24	24	25
30	13	17	20	21	23	24	24	25	25	26	26	26	26	27	27	27	27	27	27	28	28	28	28	29	29	29	29	29	29	29	29
35	15	20	23	25	26	28	28	29	30	30	30	31	31	31	31	32	32	32	32	32	33	33	33	33	34	34	34	34	34	34	34
40	18	23	26	29	30	31	32	33	34	34	35	35	35	36	36	36	36	36	37	37	37	38	38	38	38	39	39	39	39	39	39
45	20	26	30	32	34	35	37	37	38	39	39	39	40	40	40	41	41	41	41	42	42	42	43	43	43	43	44	44	44	44	44
50	22	29	33	36	38	39	41	42	42	43	43	44	44	45	45	45	45	46	46	46	47	47	48	48	48	48	48	49	49	49	49

$l+r=2$

N_2 \ N_1	2	3	4	5	6	7	8	9	10	11	12	13	14	15	16	17	18	19	20	22	25	30	35	40	45	50	60	70	80	90	100
2	0	0	1	1	1	1	1	1	1	1	1	1	1	1	1	1	2	2	2	2	2	2	2	2	2	2	2	2	2	2	2
3	0	1	1	1	1	2	2	2	2	2	2	2	2	2	2	2	2	2	2	2	2	3	3	3	3	3	3	3	3	3	3
4	0	1	1	2	2	2	2	2	3	3	3	3	3	3	3	3	3	3	3	3	3	3	4	4	4	4	4	4	4	4	4
5	0	1	2	2	3	3	3	3	3	3	4	4	4	4	4	4	4	4	4	4	4	4	4	4	5	5	5	5	5	5	5
6	0	1	2	3	3	3	4	4	4	4	4	4	4	5	5	5	5	5	5	5	5	5	5	5	5	5	6	6	6	6	6
7	0	2	3	3	4	4	4	5	5	5	5	5	5	5	5	6	6	6	6	6	6	6	6	6	6	6	7	7	7	7	7
8	0	2	3	4	4	5	5	5	5	6	6	6	6	6	6	6	6	6	7	7	7	7	7	7	7	7	7	8	8	8	8
9	1	2	3	4	5	5	6	6	6	6	7	7	7	7	7	7	7	7	7	8	8	8	8	8	8	8	8	8	9	9	9
10	1	2	4	5	5	6	6	7	7	7	7	8	8	8	8	8	8	8	8	8	9	9	9	9	9	9	9	9	9	10	10
11	1	3	4	5	6	7	7	7	8	8	8	8	8	9	9	9	9	9	9	9	9	10	10	10	10	10	10	10	10	10	11
12	1	3	5	6	7	7	8	8	8	9	9	9	9	9	10	10	10	10	10	10	10	11	11	11	11	11	11	11	11	11	11
13	1	3	5	6	7	8	8	9	9	9	10	10	10	10	10	10	11	11	11	11	11	11	12	12	12	12	12	12	12	12	12
14	1	4	5	7	8	8	9	9	10	10	10	11	11	11	11	11	11	12	12	12	12	12	13	13	13	13	13	13	13	13	13
15	1	4	6	7	8	9	10	10	10	10	10	11	12	12	12	12	12	12	13	13	13	13	13	14	14	14	14	14	14	14	14
16	1	4	6	8	9	10	10	11	11	12	12	12	12	13	13	13	13	13	13	14	14	14	14	15	15	15	15	15	15	15	15
17	1	4	7	8	9	10	11	12	12	12	13	13	13	13	14	14	14	14	14	14	15	15	15	15	16	16	16	16	16	16	16
18	2	5	7	9	10	11	12	12	13	13	13	14	14	14	14	15	15	15	15	15	16	16	16	16	17	17	17	17	17	17	17
19	2	5	8	9	11	12	12	13	13	14	14	15	15	15	15	15	16	16	16	16	16	17	17	17	17	18	18	18	18	18	18
20	2	5	8	10	11	12	13	14	14	15	15	15	16	16	16	16	16	17	17	17	17	18	18	18	18	19	19	19	19	19	19
21	2	6	8	10	12	13	14	14	15	15	16	16	16	17	17	17	17	17	18	18	18	19	19	19	19	19	20	20	20	20	20
22	2	6	9	11	12	13	14	15	16	16	17	17	17	17	18	18	18	18	18	19	19	20	20	20	20	20	21	21	21	21	21
23	2	6	9	11	13	14	15	16	16	17	17	18	18	18	19	19	19	19	19	20	20	20	21	21	21	21	22	22	22	22	22
25	2	7	10	12	14	15	16	17	18	18	19	19	20	20	20	20	21	21	21	21	22	22	23	23	23	23	23	24	24	24	24
30	3	8	12	15	17	18	20	21	21	22	23	23	24	24	24	25	25	25	25	26	26	27	27	27	28	28	28	28	29	29	29
35	3	10	14	17	20	22	23	24	25	26	27	27	28	28	28	29	29	29	30	30	31	31	32	32	32	33	33	33	33	34	34
40	4	11	16	20	23	25	26	28	29	30	30	31	32	32	33	33	33	34	34	34	35	36	36	37	37	37	38	38	38	38	39
45	4	13	18	22	26	28	30	31	32	33	34	35	36	36	37	37	37	38	38	39	39	40	41	41	42	42	42	43	43	43	43
50	5	14	20	25	28	31	33	35	36	37	38	39	40	40	41	41	42	42	42	43	44	45	45	46	46	47	47	48	48	48	48

$l+r=3$

N_2 \ N_1	3	4	5	6	7	8	9	10	11	12	13	14	15	16	17	18	19	20	21	22	25	30	35	40	45	50	60	70	80	90	100
2	0	0	0	0	1	1	1	1	1	1	1	1	1	1	1	1	1	1	1	1	1	2	2	2	2	2	2	2	2	2	2
3	0	0	1	1	1	1	1	1	2	2	2	2	2	2	2	2	2	2	2	2	2	2	2	3	3	3	3	3	3	3	3
4	0	0	1	1	2	2	2	2	2	2	2	3	3	3	3	3	3	3	3	3	3	3	3	3	3	3	4	4	4	4	4
5	0	1	1	2	2	2	2	3	3	3	3	3	3	3	3	4	4	4	4	4	4	4	4	4	4	4	4	5	5	5	5
6	0	1	2	2	2	3	3	3	3	4	4	4	4	4	4	4	4	4	4	5	5	5	5	5	5	5	5	5	6	6	6
7	0	1	2	2	3	3	4	4	4	4	4	5	5	5	5	5	5	5	5	5	5	6	6	6	6	6	6	6	6	6	7
8	0	1	2	3	3	4	4	4	4	4	4	5	5	6	6	6	6	6	6	6	6	7	7	7	7	7	7	7	7	7	7
9	0	1	2	3	4	4	5	5	5	6	6	6	6	6	6	7	7	7	7	7	7	7	8	8	8	8	8	8	8	8	8
10	0	2	3	4	4	5	5	6	6	6	7	7	7	7	7	7	7	8	8	8	8	8	8	9	9	9	9	9	9	9	9
11	0	2	3	4	5	5	6	6	7	7	7	7	8	8	8	8	8	8	8	9	9	9	9	10	10	10	10	10	10	10	10
12	0	2	3	4	5	6	6	7	7	8	8	8	8	9	9	9	9	9	9	9	10	10	10	10	11	11	11	11	11	11	11
13	1	2	4	5	6	6	7	8	8	8	9	9	9	9	9	10	10	10	10	10	10	11	11	11	11	12	12	12	12	12	12
14	1	3	4	5	6	7	8	8	9	9	9	10	10	10	10	10	11	11	11	11	11	12	12	12	12	12	13	13	13	13	13
15	1	3	4	6	7	8	8	9	9	10	10	10	11	11	11	11	11	12	12	12	12	13	13	13	13	13	14	14	14	14	14
16	1	3	5	6	7	8	9	9	10	10	11	11	11	12	12	12	12	12	12	13	13	13	14	14	14	14	15	15	15	15	15
17	1	3	5	7	8	9	9	10	11	11	11	12	12	12	13	13	13	13	13	13	14	14	15	15	15	15	15	16	16	16	16
18	1	3	5	7	8	9	10	11	11	12	12	12	13	13	13	13	14	14	14	14	15	15	15	16	16	16	16	17	17	17	17
19	1	4	6	7	9	10	11	11	12	12	13	13	13	14	14	14	14	15	15	15	15	16	16	17	17	17	17	18	18	18	18
20	1	4	6	8	9	10	11	12	12	13	13	14	14	15	15	15	15	15	16	16	16	17	17	17	18	18	18	18	19	19	19
21	1	4	6	8	10	11	12	12	13	14	14	15	15	15	16	16	16	16	16	17	17	18	18	18	19	19	19	19	20	20	20
22	1	4	7	9	10	11	12	13	14	14	15	15	16	16	16	17	17	17	17	17	18	19	19	19	20	20	20	20	20	21	21
23	1	4	7	9	11	12	13	14	14	15	16	16	16	17	17	17	18	18	18	18	19	19	20	20	20	21	21	21	21	22	22
25	1	5	8	10	12	13	14	15	16	16	17	17	18	18	19	19	19	19	20	20	20	21	22	22	22	22	23	23	23	23	24
30	2	6	9	12	14	16	17	18	19	20	20	21	22	22	22	23	23	23	24	24	25	25	26	26	27	27	27	28	28	28	28
35	2	7	11	14	16	18	20	21	22	23	24	25	25	26	26	27	27	27	28	28	28	30	30	31	31	32	32	32	33	33	33
40	3	8	13	16	19	21	23	24	25	26	27	28	29	29	30	31	31	31	32	32	33	34	35	35	36	36	37	37	37	38	38
45	3	9	14	18	21	24	26	27	29	30	31	32	33	33	34	34	35	35	36	36	37	38	39	40	40	41	41	42	42	42	43
50	3	10	16	20	24	26	29	30	32	33	34	35	36	37	38	38	39	39	40	40	41	43	44	44	45	45	46	47	47	47	47

All values conform to the international convention (i.e. 0,1 instead of 0.1).

Distribution-Free Tolerance Limits (2 Samples)[◊] $\beta_t = 0{,}80$

N_1: sample size of sample one; N_2: sample size of sample two; N^*: number of observations in the 2nd sample which lies between the tolerance limits of l and r with a probability of at least β_t (assuming that both samples are from the same distribution). For definition of l and r see section 25A. The values in the table are those of N^*

$l+r=4$

N_2 \ N_1	4	5	6	7	8	9	10	11	12	13	14	15	16	17	18	19	20	21	22	23	25	30	35	40	45	50	60	70	80	90	100
2	0	0	0	0	0	1	1	1	1	1	1	1	1	1	1	1	1	1	1	1	1	1	1	2	2	2	2	2	2	2	2
3	0	0	0	1	1	1	1	1	1	1	2	2	2	2	2	2	2	2	2	2	2	2	2	2	2	2	3	3	3	3	3
4	0	0	1	1	1	1	2	2	2	2	2	2	2	2	2	3	3	3	3	3	3	3	3	3	3	3	3	3	4	4	4
5	0	0	1	1	2	2	2	2	2	3	3	3	3	3	3	3	3	3	3	3	4	4	4	4	4	4	4	4	4	5	5
6	0	1	1	2	2	2	3	3	3	3	3	4	4	4	4	4	4	4	4	4	4	5	5	5	5	5	5	5	5	5	5
7	0	1	1	2	2	3	3	3	4	4	4	4	4	4	5	5	5	5	5	5	5	5	6	6	6	6	6	6	6	6	6
8	0	1	2	2	3	3	4	4	4	4	5	5	5	5	5	5	5	6	6	6	6	6	6	7	7	7	7	7	7	7	7
9	0	1	2	3	3	4	4	4	5	5	5	5	6	6	6	6	6	6	6	6	7	7	7	7	8	8	8	8	8	8	8
10	0	1	2	3	4	4	5	5	5	6	6	6	6	6	7	7	7	7	7	7	7	8	8	8	8	9	9	9	9	9	9
11	0	1	2	3	4	5	5	6	6	6	7	7	7	7	7	7	8	8	8	8	8	9	9	9	9	9	10	10	10	10	10
12	0	2	3	4	4	5	6	6	6	7	7	7	8	8	8	8	8	9	9	9	9	9	10	10	10	10	11	11	11	11	11
13	0	2	3	4	5	6	6	7	7	7	8	8	8	9	9	9	9	9	9	10	10	10	11	11	11	11	11	12	12	12	12
14	0	2	3	4	5	6	7	7	8	8	8	9	9	9	9	10	10	10	10	10	11	11	11	12	12	12	12	13	13	13	13
15	0	2	4	5	6	6	7	8	8	9	9	9	10	10	10	10	11	11	11	11	11	12	12	13	13	13	13	13	14	14	14
16	0	2	4	5	6	7	8	8	9	9	10	10	10	11	11	11	11	11	12	12	12	13	13	13	14	14	14	14	15	15	15
17	1	2	4	5	7	7	8	9	9	10	10	11	11	11	12	12	12	12	12	13	13	13	14	14	14	15	15	15	15	16	16
18	1	3	4	6	7	8	9	9	10	11	11	11	12	12	12	13	13	13	13	13	14	14	15	15	15	16	16	16	16	17	17
19	1	3	5	6	7	8	9	10	11	11	12	12	12	13	13	13	14	14	14	14	14	15	16	16	16	16	17	17	17	17	18
20	1	3	5	6	8	9	10	11	11	12	12	13	13	13	14	14	14	14	15	15	15	16	16	17	17	17	18	18	18	18	19
21	1	3	5	7	8	9	10	11	12	12	13	13	14	14	14	15	15	15	15	16	16	17	17	18	18	18	19	19	19	19	19
22	1	3	5	7	9	10	11	12	12	13	13	14	14	15	15	15	16	16	16	16	17	18	18	19	19	19	20	20	20	20	20
23	1	3	6	7	9	10	11	12	13	14	14	15	15	15	16	16	16	17	17	17	18	18	19	19	20	20	20	21	21	21	21
25	1	4	6	8	10	11	12	13	14	15	15	16	16	17	17	18	18	18	18	19	19	20	21	21	21	22	22	23	23	23	23
30	1	5	8	10	12	14	15	16	17	18	19	19	20	20	21	21	22	22	22	23	23	24	25	25	26	26	27	27	27	28	28
35	2	5	9	12	14	16	17	19	20	21	22	23	23	24	24	25	25	26	26	26	27	28	29	30	30	31	31	32	32	32	33
40	2	6	10	13	16	18	20	22	23	24	25	26	27	27	28	29	29	29	30	30	31	32	33	34	35	35	36	36	37	37	37
45	2	7	12	15	18	21	23	24	26	27	28	29	30	31	32	32	33	33	34	34	35	36	38	38	39	40	40	41	41	42	42
50	2	8	13	17	20	23	25	27	29	30	31	32	33	34	35	36	36	37	38	38	39	41	42	43	43	44	45	46	46	46	47

$l+r=5$

N_2 \ N_1	5	6	7	8	9	10	11	12	13	14	15	16	17	18	19	20	21	22	23	24	25	30	35	40	45	50	60	70	80	90	100
2	0	0	0	0	0	0	1	1	1	1	1	1	1	1	1	1	1	1	1	1	1	1	1	1	1	2	2	2	2	2	2
3	0	0	0	0	1	1	1	1	1	1	1	1	1	2	2	2	2	2	2	2	2	2	2	2	2	2	2	3	3	3	3
4	0	0	0	1	1	1	1	2	2	2	2	2	2	2	2	2	2	2	2	3	3	3	3	3	3	3	3	3	3	4	4
5	0	0	1	1	1	2	2	2	2	2	2	3	3	3	3	3	3	3	3	3	3	4	4	4	4	4	4	4	4	4	4
6	0	0	1	1	2	2	2	2	2	2	3	3	3	3	4	4	4	4	4	4	4	4	4	5	5	5	5	5	5	5	5
7	0	1	1	2	2	2	3	3	3	3	4	4	4	4	4	4	4	4	5	5	5	5	5	5	6	6	6	6	6	6	6
8	0	1	1	2	2	3	3	3	4	4	4	4	5	5	5	5	5	5	5	5	5	6	6	6	6	7	7	7	7	7	7
9	0	1	2	2	3	3	4	4	4	5	5	5	5	5	5	6	6	6	6	6	6	7	7	7	7	7	8	8	8	8	8
10	0	1	2	2	3	4	4	4	5	5	5	6	6	6	6	6	6	7	7	7	7	7	8	8	8	8	8	9	9	9	9
11	0	1	2	3	3	4	5	5	5	6	6	6	6	7	7	7	7	7	7	8	8	8	8	9	9	9	9	10	10	10	10
12	0	1	2	3	4	4	5	5	6	6	7	7	7	7	7	8	8	8	8	8	8	9	9	10	10	10	10	10	11	11	11
13	0	1	2	3	4	5	5	6	6	7	7	7	8	8	8	8	9	9	9	9	9	10	10	10	11	11	11	11	12	12	12
14	0	1	3	4	5	5	6	6	7	7	8	8	8	9	9	9	9	9	10	10	10	10	11	11	11	12	12	12	12	13	13
15	0	2	3	4	5	6	6	7	7	8	8	9	9	9	9	10	10	10	10	10	11	11	12	12	12	13	13	13	13	13	14
16	0	2	3	4	5	6	7	7	8	8	9	9	10	10	10	10	11	11	11	11	11	12	12	13	13	13	14	14	14	14	15
17	0	2	3	5	6	7	7	8	8	9	9	10	10	11	11	11	11	12	12	12	12	13	13	14	14	14	15	15	15	15	15
18	0	2	4	5	6	7	8	8	9	10	10	10	11	11	11	12	12	12	12	13	13	14	14	15	15	15	16	16	16	16	16
19	0	2	4	5	6	7	8	9	10	10	11	11	11	12	12	12	13	13	13	13	14	14	15	15	16	16	16	17	17	17	17
20	0	2	4	5	7	8	9	9	10	11	11	12	12	12	13	13	13	14	14	14	14	15	16	16	17	17	17	18	18	18	18
21	1	2	4	6	7	8	9	10	11	11	12	12	13	13	13	14	14	14	15	15	15	16	17	17	17	18	18	19	19	19	19
22	1	3	4	6	7	9	10	10	11	12	12	13	13	14	14	14	15	15	15	16	16	17	17	18	18	19	19	19	20	20	20
23	1	3	5	6	8	9	10	11	12	12	13	13	14	14	15	15	15	16	16	16	17	17	18	19	19	19	20	20	21	21	21
25	1	3	5	7	9	10	11	12	13	13	14	15	15	16	16	17	17	17	17	18	18	19	20	20	21	21	22	22	22	23	23
30	1	4	6	8	10	12	13	14	15	16	17	18	18	19	19	20	20	21	21	21	22	23	24	24	25	25	26	27	27	27	28
35	1	4	7	10	12	14	16	17	18	19	20	21	22	22	23	23	24	24	25	25	25	27	28	29	29	30	31	31	32	32	32
40	1	5	9	12	14	16	18	19	21	22	23	24	25	25	26	27	27	28	28	29	29	31	32	33	34	34	35	36	36	36	37
45	2	6	10	13	16	18	20	22	23	25	26	27	28	29	30	30	31	31	32	32	33	35	36	37	38	38	39	40	41	41	41
50	2	6	11	15	18	20	23	24	26	28	29	30	31	32	33	34	34	35	36	36	37	39	40	41	42	43	44	45	45	46	46

$l+r=6$

N_2 \ N_1	6	7	8	9	10	11	12	13	14	15	16	17	18	19	20	21	22	23	24	25	26	30	35	40	45	50	60	70	80	90	100
2	0	0	0	0	0	0	0	1	1	1	1	1	1	1	1	1	1	1	1	1	1	1	1	1	1	1	2	2	2	2	2
3	0	0	0	0	1	1	1	1	1	1	1	1	1	1	1	2	2	2	2	2	2	2	2	2	2	2	2	2	2	3	3
4	0	0	0	1	1	1	1	1	1	2	2	2	2	2	2	2	2	2	2	2	2	3	3	3	3	3	3	3	3	3	3
5	0	0	1	1	1	1	2	2	2	2	2	2	2	3	3	3	3	3	3	3	3	3	3	4	4	4	4	4	4	4	4
6	0	0	1	1	1	2	2	2	2	3	3	3	3	3	3	3	3	4	4	4	4	4	4	4	5	5	5	5	5	5	5
7	0	0	1	1	2	2	2	3	3	3	3	3	4	4	4	4	4	4	4	4	4	5	5	5	5	5	6	6	6	6	6
8	0	0	1	2	2	2	3	3	3	4	4	4	4	4	4	5	5	5	5	5	5	5	6	6	6	6	7	7	7	7	7
9	0	1	1	2	2	3	3	4	4	4	4	5	5	5	5	5	5	6	6	6	6	6	7	7	7	7	7	8	8	8	8
10	0	1	1	2	3	3	4	4	4	5	5	5	5	6	6	6	6	6	6	6	7	7	7	8	8	8	8	8	9	9	9
11	0	1	2	2	3	4	4	4	5	5	5	6	6	6	6	7	7	7	7	7	7	8	8	8	9	9	9	9	10	10	10
12	0	1	2	3	3	4	4	5	5	6	6	6	7	7	7	7	7	8	8	8	8	8	9	9	9	10	10	10	10	11	11
13	0	1	2	3	4	4	5	5	6	6	7	7	7	7	8	8	8	8	8	9	9	9	10	10	10	10	11	11	11	11	12
14	0	1	2	3	4	5	5	6	6	7	7	7	8	8	8	8	9	9	9	9	9	10	10	11	11	11	12	12	12	12	12
15	0	1	2	3	4	5	6	6	7	7	8	8	8	9	9	9	9	10	10	10	10	11	11	12	12	12	13	13	13	13	13
16	0	1	3	4	5	5	6	7	7	8	8	9	9	9	9	10	10	10	10	11	11	11	12	12	13	13	13	14	14	14	14
17	0	2	3	4	5	6	7	7	8	8	9	9	9	10	10	10	11	11	11	11	11	12	13	13	14	14	14	15	15	15	15
18	0	2	3	4	5	6	7	8	8	9	9	10	10	10	11	11	11	12	12	12	12	13	13	14	14	15	15	15	16	16	16
19	0	2	3	4	6	7	7	8	9	9	10	10	11	11	11	12	12	12	12	13	13	14	14	15	15	15	16	16	17	17	17
20	0	2	3	5	6	7	8	9	9	10	10	11	11	12	12	12	13	13	13	13	14	14	15	16	16	16	17	17	18	18	18
21	0	2	4	5	6	7	8	9	10	10	11	11	12	12	13	13	13	14	14	14	14	15	16	16	17	17	18	18	18	19	19
22	0	2	4	5	7	8	9	9	10	11	11	12	12	13	13	14	14	14	14	15	15	16	17	17	18	18	19	19	19	20	20
23	0	2	4	6	7	8	9	10	11	11	12	13	13	13	14	14	15	15	15	15	16	17	17	18	18	19	19	20	20	20	21
25	1	2	4	6	8	9	10	11	12	12	13	14	14	15	15	16	16	16	17	17	17	18	19	20	20	21	21	22	22	22	23
30	1	3	5	7	9	11	12	13	14	15	16	17	17	18	18	19	19	20	20	20	21	22	23	24	24	25	25	26	26	27	27
35	1	4	6	9	11	13	14	15	17	18	19	19	20	21	21	22	23	23	23	24	24	25	27	28	28	29	30	30	31	31	32
40	1	4	7	10	12	14	16	18	19	20	21	22	23	24	25	25	26	26	27	27	28	29	31	32	32	33	34	35	35	36	36
45	1	5	8	11	14	16	18	20	22	23	24	25	26	27	28	28	29	30	30	31	31	33	35	36	37	37	39	39	40	40	41
50	1	5	9	13	16	18	20	22	24	25	27	28	29	30	31	32	32	33	34	34	35	37	38	40	41	42	43	44	44	45	45

All values conform to the international convention (i.e. 0,1 instead of 0.1).

Distribution-Free Tolerance Limits (2 Samples)◊ $\beta_t = 0{,}80$

N_1: sample size of sample one; N_2: sample size of sample two; N^*: number of observations in the 2nd sample which lies between the tolerance limits of l and r with a probability of at least β_t (assuming that both samples are from the same distribution). For definition of l and r see section 25A. The values in the table are those of N^*

$l+r=8$

N_2 \ N_1	9	10	11	12	13	14	15	16	17	18	19	20	21	22	23	24	25	26	27	30	35	40	45	50	60	70	80	90	100	120	140
2	0	0	0	0	0	0	0	0	0	1	1	1	1	1	1	1	1	1	1	1	1	1	1	1	1	1	2	2	2	2	2
3	0	0	0	0	0	1	1	1	1	1	1	1	1	1	1	1	1	1	1	2	2	2	2	2	2	2	2	2	2	3	3
4	0	0	0	1	1	1	1	1	1	1	2	2	2	2	2	2	2	2	2	2	2	3	3	3	3	3	3	3	3	3	3
5	0	0	1	1	1	1	1	2	2	2	2	2	2	2	2	2	3	3	3	3	3	3	3	3	4	4	4	4	4	4	4
6	0	0	1	1	1	2	2	2	2	2	2	3	3	3	3	3	3	3	3	4	4	4	4	4	5	5	5	5	5	5	5
7	0	1	1	1	2	2	2	2	3	3	3	3	3	3	3	4	4	4	4	4	4	5	5	5	5	6	6	6	6	6	6
8	0	1	1	2	2	2	3	3	3	3	3	4	4	4	4	4	4	4	5	5	5	5	6	6	6	6	7	7	7	7	7
9	0	1	1	2	2	3	3	3	3	4	4	4	4	4	5	5	5	5	5	5	6	6	6	7	7	7	7	8	8	8	8
10	0	1	2	2	3	3	3	4	4	4	4	5	5	5	5	5	6	6	6	6	7	7	7	7	8	8	8	8	9	9	9
11	1	1	2	2	3	3	4	4	4	5	5	5	5	6	6	6	6	6	6	7	7	8	8	8	9	9	9	9	9	10	10
12	1	1	2	3	3	4	4	4	5	5	5	6	6	6	6	7	7	7	7	7	8	8	9	9	9	10	10	10	10	11	11
13	1	2	2	3	3	4	4	5	5	6	6	6	6	7	7	7	7	8	8	8	9	9	10	10	10	11	11	11	11	11	12
14	1	2	2	3	4	4	5	5	6	6	6	7	7	7	7	8	8	8	8	9	9	10	10	11	11	11	12	12	12	12	13
15	1	2	3	3	4	5	5	6	6	7	7	7	8	8	8	8	9	9	9	9	10	11	11	11	12	12	13	13	13	13	13
16	1	2	3	4	4	5	6	6	7	7	7	8	8	8	9	9	9	9	10	10	11	11	12	12	13	13	13	14	14	14	14
17	1	2	3	4	5	5	6	7	7	7	8	8	9	9	9	10	10	10	10	11	12	12	13	13	14	14	14	15	15	15	15
18	1	2	3	4	5	6	6	7	7	8	8	9	9	10	10	10	10	11	11	11	12	13	13	14	14	15	15	15	16	16	16
19	1	2	3	4	5	6	7	7	8	8	9	9	10	10	10	11	11	11	11	12	13	14	14	15	15	16	16	16	17	17	17
20	1	3	4	5	6	6	7	8	8	9	9	10	10	11	11	11	12	12	12	13	14	14	15	15	16	16	17	17	17	18	18
21	1	3	4	5	6	7	8	8	9	9	10	10	11	11	12	12	12	12	13	13	14	15	16	16	17	17	18	18	18	19	19
22	2	3	4	5	6	7	8	9	9	10	10	11	11	12	12	12	13	13	13	14	15	16	16	17	18	18	19	19	19	20	20
23	2	3	4	6	7	7	8	9	10	10	11	11	12	12	13	13	13	14	14	15	16	17	17	18	18	19	19	20	20	20	21
25	2	3	5	6	7	8	9	10	11	11	12	12	13	13	14	14	15	15	15	16	17	18	19	19	20	21	21	22	22	22	23
30	2	4	6	7	9	10	11	12	13	14	14	15	16	16	17	17	18	18	19	20	21	22	23	23	24	25	26	26	26	27	27
35	3	5	7	9	10	12	13	14	15	16	17	18	18	19	20	20	21	21	22	23	24	26	27	27	28	29	30	30	31	31	32
40	3	6	8	10	12	14	15	16	17	19	20	20	21	22	23	23	24	24	25	26	28	29	30	31	33	34	34	35	35	36	36
45	4	6	9	11	13	15	17	18	20	21	22	23	24	25	26	26	27	28	28	30	32	33	34	35	37	38	39	39	40	40	41
50	4	7	10	13	15	17	19	21	22	23	25	26	27	28	28	29	30	31	31	33	35	37	38	39	41	42	43	44	44	45	46

$l+r=10$

N_2 \ N_1	11	12	13	14	15	16	17	18	19	20	21	22	23	24	25	26	27	28	29	30	35	40	45	50	60	70	80	90	100	120	140
2	0	0	0	0	0	0	0	0	0	0	0	1	1	1	1	1	1	1	1	1	1	1	1	1	1	1	1	1	2	2	2
3	0	0	0	0	0	0	1	1	1	1	1	1	1	1	1	1	1	1	1	1	2	2	2	2	2	2	2	2	2	2	2
4	0	0	0	0	1	1	1	1	1	1	1	1	1	2	2	2	2	2	2	2	2	2	2	3	3	3	3	3	3	3	3
5	0	0	0	1	1	1	1	1	1	2	2	2	2	2	2	2	2	2	2	2	3	3	3	3	4	4	4	4	4	4	4
6	0	0	1	1	1	1	1	2	2	2	2	2	2	2	3	3	3	3	3	3	3	4	4	4	4	4	5	5	5	5	5
7	0	0	1	1	1	2	2	2	2	2	3	3	3	3	3	3	3	3	4	4	4	4	5	5	5	5	5	6	6	6	6
8	0	1	1	1	2	2	2	2	3	3	3	3	3	3	4	4	4	4	4	4	5	5	5	5	6	6	6	6	7	7	7
9	0	1	1	1	2	2	2	3	3	3	3	4	4	4	4	4	4	5	5	5	5	6	6	6	7	7	7	7	7	8	8
10	0	1	1	2	2	2	3	3	3	4	4	4	4	4	5	5	5	5	5	5	6	6	7	7	7	8	8	8	8	8	9
11	0	1	1	2	2	3	3	3	4	4	4	5	5	5	5	5	6	6	6	6	7	7	7	8	8	8	9	9	9	9	10
12	0	1	2	2	3	3	3	4	4	4	5	5	5	5	6	6	6	6	6	7	7	8	8	8	9	9	10	10	10	10	10
13	1	1	2	2	3	3	4	4	5	5	5	5	6	6	6	6	7	7	7	7	8	8	9	9	10	10	10	11	11	11	11
14	1	1	2	3	3	4	4	5	5	5	6	6	6	6	7	7	7	7	8	8	8	9	10	10	10	11	11	11	12	12	12
15	1	1	2	3	3	4	4	5	5	6	6	6	7	7	7	8	8	8	8	8	9	10	10	11	11	12	12	12	13	13	13
16	1	2	2	3	4	4	5	5	6	6	7	7	7	8	8	8	8	9	9	9	10	10	11	11	12	13	13	13	13	14	14
17	1	2	2	3	4	5	5	6	6	7	7	7	8	8	8	9	9	9	9	10	10	11	12	12	13	13	14	14	14	15	15
18	1	2	3	3	4	5	5	6	7	7	7	8	8	9	9	9	9	10	10	10	11	12	12	13	14	14	15	15	15	16	16
19	1	2	3	4	4	5	6	6	7	7	8	8	9	9	9	10	10	10	10	11	12	13	13	14	14	15	15	16	16	16	17
20	1	2	3	4	5	5	6	7	7	8	8	9	9	10	10	10	11	11	11	11	12	13	14	14	15	16	16	17	17	17	18
21	1	2	3	4	5	6	6	7	8	8	9	9	10	10	10	11	11	11	12	12	13	14	15	15	16	17	17	17	18	18	19
22	1	2	3	4	5	6	7	8	8	9	9	10	10	11	11	11	12	12	12	13	14	15	15	16	17	17	18	18	19	19	19
23	1	2	4	5	6	6	7	8	9	9	10	10	11	11	11	12	12	13	13	13	14	15	16	17	18	18	19	19	19	20	20
25	1	3	4	5	6	7	8	9	9	10	11	11	12	12	13	13	13	14	14	14	16	17	17	18	19	20	20	21	21	22	22
30	2	3	5	6	7	9	10	10	11	12	13	13	14	15	15	16	16	17	17	17	19	20	21	22	23	24	25	25	26	26	27
35	2	4	6	7	9	10	11	12	13	14	15	16	17	17	18	18	19	19	20	20	22	24	25	26	27	28	29	29	30	31	31
40	3	5	7	8	10	12	13	14	15	16	17	18	19	20	21	21	22	22	23	23	26	27	28	29	31	32	33	34	34	35	36
45	3	5	8	10	11	13	15	16	17	19	20	21	22	22	23	24	25	25	26	26	29	31	32	33	35	36	37	38	39	40	40
50	3	6	8	11	13	15	16	18	19	21	22	23	24	25	26	27	27	28	29	29	32	34	36	37	39	40	41	42	43	44	45

$l+r=12$

N_2 \ N_1	13	14	15	16	17	18	19	20	21	22	23	24	25	26	27	28	29	30	31	32	35	40	45	50	60	70	80	90	100	120	140
2	0	0	0	0	0	0	0	0	0	0	0	0	0	0	1	1	1	1	1	1	1	1	1	1	1	1	1	1	1	2	2
3	0	0	0	0	0	0	0	0	1	1	1	1	1	1	1	1	1	1	1	1	1	1	2	2	2	2	2	2	2	2	2
4	0	0	0	0	0	1	1	1	1	1	1	1	1	1	1	1	2	2	2	2	2	2	2	2	3	3	3	3	3	3	3
5	0	0	0	0	1	1	1	1	1	1	1	2	2	2	2	2	2	2	2	2	2	3	3	3	3	3	4	4	4	4	4
6	0	0	0	1	1	1	1	1	2	2	2	2	2	2	2	2	3	3	3	3	3	3	4	4	4	4	4	5	5	5	5
7	0	0	1	1	1	1	2	2	2	2	2	2	3	3	3	3	3	3	3	3	4	4	4	4	5	5	5	5	5	6	6
8	0	0	1	1	1	2	2	2	2	2	3	3	3	3	3	3	3	4	4	4	4	5	5	5	5	6	6	6	6	7	7
9	0	0	1	1	2	2	2	2	3	3	3	3	3	4	4	4	4	4	4	4	5	5	5	6	6	7	7	7	7	7	8
10	0	1	1	1	2	2	2	3	3	3	3	4	4	4	4	4	5	5	5	5	5	6	6	6	7	7	8	8	8	8	8
11	0	1	1	2	2	2	3	3	3	4	4	4	4	4	5	5	5	5	5	5	6	6	7	7	8	8	8	9	9	9	9
12	0	1	1	2	2	3	3	3	4	4	4	4	5	5	5	5	6	6	6	6	6	7	7	8	8	9	9	9	10	10	10
13	0	1	1	2	2	3	3	4	4	4	5	5	5	5	6	6	6	6	6	7	7	8	8	9	9	10	10	10	10	11	11
14	0	1	2	2	3	3	4	4	4	5	5	5	6	6	6	6	7	7	7	7	8	8	9	9	10	10	11	11	11	12	12
15	0	1	2	2	3	3	4	4	5	5	5	6	6	6	7	7	7	7	7	8	8	9	9	10	11	11	12	12	12	13	13
16	1	1	2	3	3	4	4	5	5	5	6	6	6	7	7	7	8	8	8	8	9	10	10	11	11	12	12	13	13	13	14
17	1	1	2	3	3	4	4	5	5	6	6	7	7	7	8	8	8	8	9	9	9	10	11	11	12	13	13	14	14	14	15
18	1	1	2	3	4	4	5	5	6	6	7	7	7	8	8	8	9	9	9	10	10	11	12	12	13	14	14	14	15	15	15
19	1	2	2	3	4	4	5	6	6	7	7	7	8	8	9	9	9	9	10	10	11	11	12	13	14	14	15	15	16	16	16
20	1	2	3	3	4	5	5	6	6	7	7	8	8	9	9	9	10	10	10	10	11	12	13	13	14	15	16	16	16	17	17
21	1	2	3	3	4	5	6	6	7	7	8	8	9	9	9	10	10	10	11	11	12	13	14	14	15	16	16	17	17	18	18
22	1	2	3	4	5	5	6	7	7	8	8	9	9	10	10	10	11	11	11	12	12	13	14	15	16	17	17	18	18	19	19
23	1	2	3	4	5	6	6	7	8	8	9	9	10	10	10	11	11	12	12	12	13	14	15	16	17	17	18	19	19	19	20
25	1	2	3	4	5	6	7	8	8	9	9	10	11	11	11	12	12	13	13	13	14	15	16	17	18	19	20	20	21	21	22
30	1	3	4	5	6	7	8	9	10	11	12	12	13	13	14	14	15	15	16	16	17	19	20	21	22	23	24	24	25	26	26
35	2	3	5	6	8	9	10	11	12	13	14	14	15	16	16	17	17	18	18	19	20	22	23	24	26	27	28	28	29	30	31
40	2	4	6	7	9	10	11	13	14	15	16	17	17	18	19	19	20	21	21	22	23	25	26	28	29	31	32	33	33	34	35
45	2	4	6	8	10	12	13	14	16	17	18	19	20	20	21	22	23	23	24	25	26	28	30	31	33	35	36	37	38	39	39
50	3	5	7	9	11	13	14	16	17	19	20	21	22	23	24	24	25	26	27	27	29	31	33	35	37	39	40	41	42	43	44

All values conform to the international convention (i.e. 0,1 instead of 0.1).

Distribution-Free Tolerance Limits (2 Samples)◊ $\beta_t = 0{,}90$

N_1: sample size of sample one; N_2: sample size of sample two; N^*: number of observations in the 2nd sample which lies between the tolerance limits of l and r with a probability of at least β_t (assuming that both samples are from the same distribution). For definition of l and r see section 25A. The values in the table are those of N^*

N_1	2	3	4	5	6	7	8	9	10	11	12	13	14	15	16	17	18	19	20	22	25	30	35	40	45	50	60	70	80	90	100
N_2	$l+r=1$																														
2	0	1	1	1	1	1	1	1	1	1	1	1	1	1	1	1	2	2	2	2	2	2	2	2	2	2	2	2	2	2	2
3	1	1	1	1	2	2	2	2	2	2	2	2	2	2	2	2	2	2	2	2	2	3	3	3	3	3	3	3	3	3	3
4	1	1	2	2	2	2	3	3	3	3	3	3	3	3	3	3	3	3	3	3	3	3	3	4	4	4	4	4	4	4	4
5	1	2	2	3	3	3	3	3	4	4	4	4	4	4	4	4	4	4	4	4	4	4	4	4	5	5	5	5	5	5	5
6	1	2	3	3	4	4	4	4	4	4	5	5	5	5	5	5	5	5	5	5	5	5	5	5	5	5	6	6	6	6	6
7	2	3	3	4	4	5	5	5	5	5	5	5	6	6	6	6	6	6	6	6	6	6	6	6	6	6	6	7	7	7	7
8	2	3	4	5	5	5	5	6	6	6	6	6	6	6	6	7	7	7	7	7	7	7	7	7	7	7	7	7	8	8	8
9	2	4	5	5	6	6	6	6	7	7	7	7	7	7	7	7	7	8	8	8	8	8	8	8	8	8	8	8	8	9	9
10	3	4	5	6	6	7	7	7	7	8	8	8	8	8	8	8	8	8	8	9	9	9	9	9	9	9	9	9	9	10	10
11	3	5	6	6	7	7	8	8	8	8	9	9	9	9	9	9	9	9	9	9	10	10	10	10	10	10	10	10	10	10	11
12	3	5	6	7	8	8	8	9	9	9	10	10	10	10	10	10	10	10	10	10	10	11	11	11	11	11	11	11	11	11	11
13	4	6	7	8	8	9	9	10	10	10	10	10	11	11	11	11	11	11	11	11	11	12	12	12	12	12	12	12	12	12	12
14	4	6	7	8	9	10	10	10	11	11	11	11	11	12	12	12	12	12	12	12	12	13	13	13	13	13	13	13	13	13	13
15	4	6	8	9	10	10	11	11	11	12	12	12	12	12	12	13	13	13	13	13	13	13	14	14	14	14	14	14	14	14	14
16	5	7	8	10	10	11	11	12	12	12	13	13	13	13	13	13	14	14	14	14	14	14	15	15	15	15	15	15	15	15	15
17	5	7	9	10	11	12	12	13	13	13	13	14	14	14	14	14	14	15	15	15	15	15	15	16	16	16	16	16	16	16	16
18	5	8	10	11	12	12	13	13	14	14	14	15	15	15	15	15	15	15	16	16	16	16	16	17	17	17	17	17	17	17	17
19	5	8	10	11	12	13	14	14	15	15	15	15	16	16	16	16	16	16	16	17	17	17	17	18	18	18	18	18	18	18	18
20	6	9	11	12	13	14	14	15	15	16	16	16	16	17	17	17	17	17	17	18	18	18	18	18	19	19	19	19	19	19	19
21	6	9	11	13	14	15	15	16	16	16	17	17	17	17	18	18	18	18	18	18	19	19	19	19	20	20	20	20	20	20	20
22	6	10	12	13	14	15	16	16	17	17	18	18	18	18	19	19	19	19	19	19	20	20	20	20	20	21	21	21	21	21	21
23	7	10	12	14	15	16	17	17	18	18	18	19	19	19	19	20	20	20	20	20	20	21	21	21	21	22	22	22	22	22	22
25	7	11	13	15	16	17	18	19	19	20	20	20	21	21	21	21	21	22	22	22	22	23	23	23	23	23	24	24	24	24	24
30	9	13	16	18	20	21	22	23	23	24	24	25	25	25	25	26	26	26	26	26	27	27	28	28	28	28	28	29	29	29	29
35	11	16	19	22	23	25	26	27	27	28	28	29	29	29	30	30	30	30	31	31	31	32	32	33	33	33	33	33	34	34	34
40	12	18	22	25	27	28	29	30	31	32	32	33	33	34	34	34	35	35	35	35	36	37	37	37	37	38	38	38	38	39	39
45	14	20	25	28	30	32	33	34	35	36	37	37	38	38	38	39	39	39	40	40	40	41	42	42	42	42	43	43	43	43	44
50	15	23	28	31	33	35	37	38	39	40	41	41	42	42	43	43	43	44	44	44	45	46	46	47	47	47	48	48	48	48	48

N_1	2	3	4	5	6	7	8	9	10	11	12	13	14	15	16	17	18	19	20	22	25	30	35	40	45	50	60	70	80	90	100
N_2	$l+r=2$																														
2	0	0	0	0	0	1	1	1	1	1	1	1	1	1	1	1	1	1	1	1	1	1	1	2	2	2	2	2	2	2	2
3	0	0	0	1	1	1	1	1	1	2	2	2	2	2	2	2	2	2	2	2	2	2	2	2	2	2	3	3	3	3	3
4	0	0	1	1	1	2	2	2	2	2	2	2	2	3	3	3	3	3	3	3	3	3	3	3	3	3	3	3	4	4	4
5	0	0	1	1	2	2	2	3	3	3	3	3	3	3	3	3	3	4	4	4	4	4	4	4	4	4	4	4	4	4	5
6	0	1	1	2	2	3	3	3	3	4	4	4	4	4	4	4	4	4	4	4	5	5	5	5	5	5	5	5	5	5	5
7	0	1	2	2	3	3	3	4	4	4	4	4	5	5	5	5	5	5	5	5	5	6	6	6	6	6	6	6	6	6	6
8	0	1	2	3	3	4	4	4	5	5	5	5	5	5	6	6	6	6	6	6	6	6	7	7	7	7	7	7	7	7	7
9	0	1	2	3	4	4	5	5	5	6	6	6	6	6	6	6	7	7	7	7	7	7	7	8	8	8	8	8	8	8	8
10	0	1	3	3	4	5	5	6	6	6	6	7	7	7	7	7	7	7	8	8	8	8	8	9	9	9	9	9	9	9	9
11	0	2	3	4	5	5	6	6	7	7	7	7	8	8	8	8	8	8	8	9	9	9	9	9	10	10	10	10	10	10	10
12	0	2	3	4	5	6	6	7	7	8	8	8	8	8	9	9	9	9	9	9	10	10	10	10	10	11	11	11	11	11	11
13	0	2	4	5	6	6	7	7	8	8	9	9	9	9	9	10	10	10	10	10	10	11	11	11	11	11	12	12	12	12	12
14	0	2	4	5	6	7	8	8	9	9	9	10	10	10	10	10	11	11	11	11	11	12	12	12	12	12	13	13	13	13	13
15	0	2	4	6	7	7	8	9	9	10	10	10	11	11	11	11	11	11	12	12	12	12	13	13	13	13	13	14	14	14	14
16	0	3	4	6	7	8	9	9	10	10	11	11	11	12	12	12	12	12	12	13	13	13	14	14	14	14	14	15	15	15	15
17	0	3	5	6	8	9	9	10	11	11	11	12	12	12	12	13	13	13	13	13	14	14	15	15	15	15	15	16	16	16	16
18	0	3	5	7	8	9	10	11	11	12	12	12	13	13	13	13	14	14	14	14	15	15	15	16	16	16	16	16	17	17	17
19	1	3	5	7	9	10	11	11	12	12	13	13	13	14	14	14	14	15	15	15	16	16	16	17	17	17	17	17	18	18	18
20	1	3	6	8	9	10	11	12	13	13	13	14	14	15	15	15	15	15	16	16	16	17	17	17	18	18	18	18	18	19	19
21	1	4	6	8	10	11	12	13	13	14	14	15	15	16	16	16	16	16	16	17	17	18	18	18	19	19	19	19	19	20	20
22	1	4	6	8	10	11	12	13	14	14	15	15	16	16	16	17	17	17	17	18	18	19	19	19	20	20	20	20	20	21	21
23	1	4	7	9	11	12	13	14	14	15	16	16	16	17	17	17	18	18	18	18	19	19	20	20	20	21	21	21	21	21	22
25	1	4	7	10	12	13	14	15	16	16	17	18	18	18	19	19	19	19	20	20	21	21	22	22	22	22	23	23	23	23	23
30	1	5	9	12	14	16	17	18	19	20	21	21	22	22	23	23	23	24	24	24	25	26	26	26	27	27	27	28	28	28	28
35	1	6	11	14	16	18	20	21	22	23	24	25	25	26	26	27	27	28	28	28	29	30	31	31	31	32	32	32	33	33	33
40	2	7	12	16	19	21	23	24	26	27	28	28	29	30	30	31	31	32	32	33	33	34	35	35	36	36	37	37	37	38	38
45	2	8	14	18	21	24	26	28	29	30	31	32	33	34	34	35	35	36	36	37	38	39	39	40	40	41	41	42	42	42	43
50	2	9	15	20	24	27	29	31	32	34	35	36	37	37	38	39	39	40	40	41	42	43	44	45	45	45	46	47	47	47	47

N_1	3	4	5	6	7	8	9	10	11	12	13	14	15	16	17	18	19	20	21	22	25	30	35	40	45	50	60	70	80	90	100
N_2	$l+r=3$																														
2	0	0	0	0	0	0	0	1	1	1	1	1	1	1	1	1	1	1	1	1	1	1	1	1	1	1	2	2	2	2	2
3	0	0	0	0	1	1	1	1	1	1	1	1	1	2	2	2	2	2	2	2	2	2	2	2	2	2	2	2	2	3	3
4	0	0	0	1	1	1	1	2	2	2	2	2	2	2	2	2	2	2	2	3	3	3	3	3	3	3	3	3	3	3	3
5	0	0	1	1	1	2	2	2	2	2	3	3	3	3	3	3	3	3	3	3	3	4	4	4	4	4	4	4	4	4	4
6	0	0	1	1	2	2	2	3	3	3	3	3	3	3	4	4	4	4	4	4	4	4	5	5	5	5	5	5	5	5	5
7	0	0	1	2	2	2	3	3	3	4	4	4	4	4	4	4	4	5	5	5	5	5	5	6	6	6	6	6	6	6	6
8	0	1	1	2	2	3	3	4	4	4	4	5	5	5	5	5	5	5	5	5	6	6	6	6	6	7	7	7	7	7	7
9	0	1	2	2	3	3	4	4	4	4	4	4	5	6	6	6	6	6	6	6	6	7	7	7	7	7	8	8	8	8	8
10	0	1	2	3	3	4	4	5	5	5	6	6	6	6	6	7	7	7	7	7	7	8	8	8	8	8	9	9	9	9	9
11	0	1	2	3	4	4	5	5	6	6	6	6	7	7	7	7	7	8	8	8	8	8	9	9	9	9	9	10	10	10	10
12	0	1	2	3	4	5	5	6	6	7	7	7	7	8	8	8	8	8	8	9	9	9	10	10	10	10	10	10	11	11	11
13	0	1	3	4	4	5	6	6	7	7	7	8	8	8	8	9	9	9	9	9	10	10	10	11	11	11	11	11	12	12	12
14	0	1	3	4	5	6	6	7	7	8	8	8	9	9	9	9	10	10	10	10	10	11	11	11	12	12	12	12	12	13	13
15	0	2	3	4	5	6	7	7	8	8	9	9	9	10	10	10	10	10	11	11	11	12	12	12	13	13	13	13	13	14	14
16	0	2	3	5	6	7	7	8	9	9	9	10	10	10	11	11	11	11	11	12	12	13	13	13	13	14	14	14	14	14	15
17	0	2	3	5	6	7	8	9	9	10	10	10	11	11	11	12	12	12	12	12	13	13	14	14	15	15	15	15	15	15	15
18	0	2	4	5	6	7	8	9	10	10	11	11	11	12	12	12	13	13	13	13	14	14	15	15	15	15	16	16	16	16	16
19	0	2	4	6	7	8	9	10	10	11	11	12	12	12	13	13	13	13	14	14	14	15	15	16	16	16	17	17	17	17	17
20	0	2	4	6	7	8	9	10	11	11	12	12	13	13	13	14	14	14	14	15	15	16	16	17	17	17	18	18	18	18	18
21	0	2	4	6	8	9	10	11	11	12	13	13	13	14	14	14	15	15	15	15	16	17	17	18	18	18	18	19	19	19	19
22	0	3	5	7	8	9	10	11	12	13	13	14	14	15	15	15	15	16	16	16	17	17	18	18	19	19	19	20	20	20	20
23	0	3	5	7	8	10	11	12	13	13	14	14	15	15	16	16	16	16	17	17	18	18	19	19	20	20	20	21	21	21	21
25	0	3	5	8	9	11	12	13	14	14	15	16	16	17	17	17	18	18	18	18	19	20	21	21	21	22	22	22	23	23	23
30	1	4	7	9	11	13	14	16	17	18	18	19	20	20	21	21	21	22	22	22	23	24	25	25	26	26	27	27	27	28	28
35	1	4	8	11	13	15	17	18	20	21	21	22	23	24	24	25	25	25	26	26	27	28	29	30	30	31	31	32	32	32	32
40	1	5	9	13	15	18	19	21	22	24	25	26	26	27	28	28	29	29	30	30	31	32	33	34	35	35	36	36	37	37	37
45	1	6	10	14	17	20	22	24	25	27	28	29	30	31	31	32	32	33	34	34	35	36	38	38	39	39	40	41	41	42	42
50	1	6	12	16	19	22	25	27	28	30	31	32	33	34	35	36	36	37	37	38	39	41	42	43	43	44	45	45	46	46	47

All values conform to the international convention (i.e. 0,1 instead of 0.1).

Distribution-Free Tolerance Limits (2 Samples)[◊] $\beta_t = 0{,}90$

N_1: sample size of sample one; N_2: sample size of sample two; N^*: number of observations in the 2nd sample which lies between the tolerance limits of l and r with a probability of at least β_t (assuming that both samples are from the same distribution). For definition of l and r see section 25A. The values in the table are those of N^*

$l+r=4$

N_2 \ N_1	5	6	7	8	9	10	11	12	13	14	15	16	17	18	19	20	21	22	23	24	25	30	35	40	45	50	60	70	80	90	100
2	0	0	0	0	0	0	0	0	1	1	1	1	1	1	1	1	1	1	1	1	1	1	1	1	1	1	1	1	2	2	2
3	0	0	0	0	1	1	1	1	1	1	1	1	1	1	1	1	2	2	2	2	2	2	2	2	2	2	2	2	2	2	2
4	0	0	0	1	1	1	1	1	2	2	2	2	2	2	2	2	2	2	2	2	2	3	3	3	3	3	3	3	3	3	3
5	0	0	1	1	1	1	2	2	2	2	2	2	2	3	3	3	3	3	3	3	3	3	3	4	4	4	4	4	4	4	4
6	0	1	1	1	2	2	2	2	3	3	3	3	3	3	3	3	3	4	4	4	4	4	4	4	5	5	5	5	5	5	5
7	0	1	1	2	2	2	3	3	3	3	3	4	4	4	4	4	4	4	4	4	4	5	5	5	5	5	6	6	6	6	6
8	0	1	1	2	2	3	3	3	4	4	4	4	4	4	5	5	5	5	5	5	5	6	6	6	6	6	6	7	7	7	7
9	0	1	2	2	3	3	4	4	4	4	5	5	5	5	5	5	6	6	6	6	6	6	7	7	7	7	7	8	8	8	8
10	1	1	2	3	3	4	4	4	5	5	5	5	6	6	6	6	6	6	6	7	7	7	7	8	8	8	8	8	9	9	9
11	1	2	2	3	4	4	5	5	5	6	6	6	6	6	7	7	7	7	7	7	7	8	8	8	9	9	9	9	9	10	10
12	1	2	3	3	4	5	5	5	6	6	6	7	7	7	7	7	8	8	8	8	8	9	9	9	9	10	10	10	10	10	11
13	1	2	3	4	4	5	5	6	6	7	7	7	8	8	8	8	8	8	9	9	9	9	10	10	10	11	11	11	11	11	11
14	1	2	3	4	5	5	6	6	7	7	8	8	8	8	9	9	9	9	9	9	10	10	11	11	11	11	12	12	12	12	12
15	1	2	3	4	5	6	6	7	7	8	8	8	9	9	9	9	10	10	10	10	10	11	11	12	12	12	13	13	13	13	13
16	1	2	4	5	6	6	7	7	8	8	9	9	9	10	10	10	10	11	11	11	11	12	12	13	13	13	13	14	14	14	14
17	1	3	4	5	6	7	7	8	9	9	9	10	10	10	11	11	11	11	11	12	12	13	13	13	14	14	14	15	15	15	15
18	1	3	4	5	6	7	8	9	9	10	10	10	11	11	11	12	12	12	12	12	13	13	14	14	15	15	15	16	16	16	16
19	2	3	4	6	7	8	8	9	10	10	11	11	11	12	12	12	12	13	13	13	13	14	15	15	15	16	16	16	17	17	17
20	2	3	5	6	7	8	9	10	10	11	11	12	12	12	13	13	13	13	14	14	14	15	15	16	16	17	17	17	18	18	18
21	2	3	5	6	8	8	9	10	11	11	12	12	13	13	13	14	14	14	14	15	15	16	16	17	17	17	18	18	18	19	19
22	2	4	5	7	8	9	10	11	11	12	12	13	13	13	14	14	15	15	15	15	16	16	17	18	18	18	19	19	19	20	20
23	2	4	6	7	8	9	10	11	12	12	13	13	14	14	15	15	15	16	16	16	16	17	18	18	19	19	20	20	20	21	21
25	2	4	6	8	9	10	11	12	13	14	14	15	15	16	16	16	17	17	17	18	18	19	19	20	20	21	21	22	22	22	23
30	3	5	8	9	11	12	14	15	16	16	17	18	18	19	19	20	20	21	21	21	22	23	24	24	25	25	26	26	27	27	27
35	3	6	9	11	13	15	16	17	18	19	20	21	22	22	23	23	24	24	25	25	25	27	28	28	29	29	30	31	31	32	32
40	4	7	10	13	15	17	19	20	21	22	23	24	25	26	26	27	27	28	28	29	29	31	32	33	33	34	35	35	36	36	36
45	4	8	12	15	17	19	21	23	24	25	26	27	28	29	30	30	31	31	32	32	33	34	36	37	38	38	39	40	40	40	41
50	5	9	13	16	19	21	23	25	27	28	29	30	31	32	33	34	34	35	36	36	37	38	40	41	42	43	44	44	45	45	46

$l+r=5$

N_2 \ N_1	6	7	8	9	10	11	12	13	14	15	16	17	18	19	20	21	22	23	24	25	30	35	40	45	50	60	70	80	90	100	120
2	0	0	0	0	0	0	0	0	0	0	1	1	1	1	1	1	1	1	1	1	1	1	1	1	1	1	1	1	1	2	2
3	0	0	0	0	0	1	1	1	1	1	1	1	1	1	1	1	1	1	1	1	2	2	2	2	2	2	2	2	2	2	2
4	0	0	0	1	1	1	1	1	1	1	1	2	2	2	2	2	2	2	2	2	2	2	3	3	3	3	3	3	3	3	3
5	0	0	1	1	1	1	1	2	2	2	2	2	2	2	2	2	3	3	3	3	3	3	3	3	4	4	4	4	4	4	4
6	0	0	1	1	1	2	2	2	2	2	3	3	3	3	3	3	3	3	3	3	4	4	4	4	4	5	5	5	5	5	5
7	0	1	1	1	2	2	2	2	3	3	3	3	3	3	4	4	4	4	4	4	4	5	5	5	5	5	6	6	6	6	6
8	0	1	1	2	2	2	3	3	3	3	4	4	4	4	4	4	4	5	5	5	5	5	6	6	6	6	6	7	7	7	7
9	0	1	1	2	2	3	3	3	4	4	4	4	5	5	5	5	5	5	5	5	6	6	6	7	7	7	7	7	8	8	8
10	0	1	2	2	3	3	4	4	4	4	5	5	5	5	5	6	6	6	6	6	7	7	7	7	8	8	8	8	8	9	9
11	0	1	2	2	3	4	4	4	5	5	5	5	6	6	6	6	6	7	7	7	7	8	8	8	8	9	9	9	9	9	10
12	1	1	2	3	3	4	4	5	5	5	6	6	6	6	7	7	7	7	7	8	8	8	9	9	9	10	10	10	10	10	11
13	1	1	2	3	4	4	5	5	6	6	6	7	7	7	7	8	8	8	8	8	9	9	10	10	10	10	11	11	11	11	11
14	1	2	3	3	4	5	5	6	6	7	7	7	7	8	8	8	8	9	9	9	10	10	10	11	11	11	12	12	12	12	12
15	1	2	3	4	4	5	6	6	7	7	7	8	8	8	9	9	9	9	9	10	10	11	11	12	12	12	12	13	13	13	13
16	1	2	3	4	5	5	6	7	7	8	8	8	9	9	9	9	10	10	10	10	11	12	12	12	13	13	13	14	14	14	14
17	1	2	3	4	5	6	7	7	8	8	9	9	9	10	10	10	10	11	11	11	12	12	13	13	13	14	14	14	15	15	15
18	1	2	3	5	5	6	7	8	8	9	9	9	10	10	10	11	11	11	11	12	12	13	14	14	14	15	15	15	16	16	16
19	1	2	4	5	6	7	7	8	9	9	10	10	10	11	11	11	12	12	12	12	13	14	14	15	15	16	16	16	16	17	17
20	1	3	4	5	6	7	8	9	9	10	10	11	11	11	12	12	12	13	13	13	14	15	15	16	16	16	17	17	17	18	18
21	1	3	4	5	6	7	8	9	10	10	11	11	12	12	12	13	13	13	14	14	15	15	16	16	17	17	18	18	18	19	19
22	1	3	4	6	7	8	9	9	10	11	11	12	12	13	13	13	14	14	14	14	15	16	17	17	18	18	19	19	19	19	20
23	2	3	5	6	7	8	9	10	11	11	12	12	13	13	14	14	14	15	15	15	16	17	18	18	18	19	19	20	20	20	21
25	2	3	5	7	8	9	10	11	12	12	13	14	14	14	15	15	16	16	16	17	18	19	19	20	20	21	21	22	22	22	23
30	2	4	6	8	10	11	12	13	14	15	16	16	17	18	18	19	19	19	20	20	21	22	23	24	24	25	26	26	26	27	27
35	3	5	8	10	11	13	14	16	17	18	19	19	20	21	21	22	22	23	23	24	25	26	27	28	29	29	30	31	31	31	32
40	3	6	9	11	13	15	17	18	19	20	21	22	23	24	24	25	26	26	27	27	29	30	31	32	33	34	34	35	35	36	36
45	4	7	10	13	15	17	19	20	22	23	24	25	26	27	28	28	29	30	30	31	33	34	35	36	37	38	39	40	40	40	41
50	4	8	11	14	17	19	21	23	24	26	27	28	29	30	31	32	32	33	34	34	36	38	39	40	41	42	43	44	45	45	46

$l+r=6$

N_2 \ N_1	7	8	9	10	11	12	13	14	15	16	17	18	19	20	21	22	23	24	25	26	30	35	40	45	50	60	70	80	90	100	120
2	0	0	0	0	0	0	0	0	0	0	0	0	1	1	1	1	1	1	1	1	1	1	1	1	1	1	1	1	1	1	2
3	0	0	0	0	0	0	0	1	1	1	1	1	1	1	1	1	1	1	1	1	1	2	2	2	2	2	2	2	2	2	2
4	0	0	0	0	1	1	1	1	1	1	1	1	1	2	2	2	2	2	2	2	2	2	2	3	3	3	3	3	3	3	3
5	0	0	0	1	1	1	1	1	2	2	2	2	2	2	2	2	2	2	2	3	3	3	3	3	3	4	4	4	4	4	4
6	0	0	1	1	1	1	2	2	2	2	2	2	3	3	3	3	3	3	3	3	3	4	4	4	4	4	5	5	5	5	5
7	0	0	1	1	1	2	2	2	2	3	3	3	3	3	3	3	4	4	4	4	4	4	5	5	5	5	5	6	6	6	6
8	0	0	1	1	2	2	2	3	3	3	3	3	4	4	4	4	4	4	4	4	5	5	5	6	6	6	6	6	7	7	7
9	0	1	1	2	2	2	3	3	3	4	4	4	4	4	4	5	5	5	5	5	5	6	6	6	7	7	7	7	7	7	8
10	0	1	1	2	2	3	3	3	4	4	4	4	5	5	5	5	5	5	6	6	6	7	7	7	7	8	8	8	8	8	9
11	0	1	2	2	3	3	3	4	4	4	5	5	5	5	6	6	6	6	6	6	7	7	8	8	8	8	9	9	9	9	9
12	0	1	2	2	3	3	4	4	5	5	5	6	6	6	6	6	7	7	7	7	8	8	8	9	9	9	10	10	10	10	10
13	0	1	2	3	3	4	4	5	5	5	6	6	6	7	7	7	7	7	8	8	8	9	9	9	10	10	10	11	11	11	11
14	0	1	2	3	4	4	5	5	6	6	6	7	7	7	7	8	8	8	8	8	9	9	10	10	11	11	11	12	12	12	12
15	1	1	2	3	4	4	5	6	6	6	7	7	7	8	8	8	8	9	9	9	10	10	11	11	11	12	12	12	13	13	13
16	1	2	3	3	4	5	5	6	6	7	7	8	8	8	9	9	9	9	9	10	10	11	11	12	12	13	13	13	14	14	14
17	1	2	3	4	4	5	6	6	7	7	8	8	9	9	9	9	10	10	10	10	11	12	12	13	13	13	14	14	14	15	15
18	1	2	3	4	5	6	6	7	7	8	8	9	9	9	10	10	10	11	11	11	12	12	13	13	14	14	15	15	15	15	16
19	1	2	3	4	5	6	7	7	8	8	9	9	10	10	10	11	11	11	11	12	12	13	14	14	15	15	16	16	16	16	17
20	1	2	3	4	5	6	7	8	8	9	9	10	10	11	11	11	12	12	12	12	13	14	15	15	15	16	16	17	17	17	18
21	1	2	4	5	6	7	7	8	9	9	10	10	11	11	12	12	12	12	13	13	14	15	16	16	16	17	17	18	18	18	19
22	1	2	4	5	6	7	8	9	9	10	10	11	11	12	12	12	13	13	13	14	15	15	16	17	17	18	18	19	19	19	19
23	1	3	4	5	6	7	8	9	10	10	11	11	12	12	13	13	13	14	14	14	15	16	17	17	18	19	19	19	20	20	20
25	1	3	4	6	7	8	9	10	11	11	12	12	13	13	14	14	15	15	15	16	17	18	18	19	19	20	21	21	21	22	22
30	2	4	5	7	9	10	11	12	13	14	15	15	16	16	17	17	18	18	19	19	20	21	22	23	24	24	25	26	26	26	27
35	2	4	6	8	10	12	13	14	15	16	17	18	19	19	20	20	21	21	22	22	24	25	26	27	28	29	29	30	30	31	31
40	3	5	8	10	12	13	15	16	18	19	20	21	21	22	23	24	24	25	25	26	27	29	30	31	32	33	34	34	35	35	36
45	3	6	9	11	13	15	17	19	20	21	22	23	24	25	26	27	27	28	28	29	31	33	34	35	36	37	38	39	39	40	40
50	3	7	10	12	15	17	19	21	22	24	25	26	27	28	29	30	30	31	32	32	34	36	38	39	40	41	42	43	44	44	45

All values conform to the international convention (i.e. 0,1 instead of 0.1).

Distribution-Free Tolerance Limits (2 Samples)◊ $\beta_t = 0{,}90$

N_1: sample size of sample one; N_2: sample size of sample two; N^*: number of observations in the 2nd sample which lies between the tolerance limits of l and r with a probability of at least β_t (assuming that both samples are from the same distribution). For definition of l and r see section 25A. The values in the table are those of N^*

$l+r=8$

N_2 \ N_1	9	10	11	12	13	14	15	16	17	18	19	20	21	22	23	24	25	26	27	30	35	40	45	50	60	70	80	90	100	120	140
2	0	0	0	0	0	0	0	0	0	0	0	0	0	0	0	0	0	1	1	1	1	1	1	1	1	1	1	1	1	1	1
3	0	0	0	0	0	0	0	0	0	1	1	1	1	1	1	1	1	1	1	1	1	1	2	2	2	2	2	2	2	2	2
4	0	0	0	0	0	0	1	1	1	1	1	1	1	1	1	1	1	2	2	2	2	2	2	2	3	3	3	3	3	3	3
5	0	0	0	0	1	1	1	1	1	1	1	2	2	2	2	2	2	2	2	2	3	3	3	3	3	3	4	4	4	4	4
6	0	0	0	1	1	1	1	1	2	2	2	2	2	2	2	2	3	3	3	3	3	3	4	4	4	4	4	5	5	5	5
7	0	0	0	1	1	1	1	2	2	2	2	2	3	3	3	3	3	3	3	4	4	4	4	5	5	5	5	5	5	6	6
8	0	0	1	1	1	2	2	2	2	2	3	3	3	3	3	3	4	4	4	4	5	5	5	5	6	6	6	6	6	7	7
9	0	0	1	1	1	2	2	2	3	3	3	3	4	4	4	4	4	4	4	5	5	6	6	6	6	7	7	7	7	7	8
10	0	0	1	1	2	2	2	3	3	3	4	4	4	4	4	5	5	5	5	5	6	6	7	7	7	7	8	8	8	8	8
11	0	1	1	2	2	2	3	3	3	4	4	4	4	5	5	5	5	5	6	6	6	7	7	8	8	8	9	9	9	9	9
12	0	1	1	2	2	3	3	3	4	4	4	5	5	5	5	6	6	6	6	7	7	8	8	8	9	9	9	10	10	10	10
13	0	1	1	2	2	3	3	4	4	5	5	5	5	6	6	6	6	7	7	7	8	8	9	9	10	10	10	10	11	11	11
14	0	1	2	2	3	3	4	4	5	5	5	6	6	6	6	7	7	7	7	8	8	9	9	10	10	11	11	11	11	12	12
15	0	1	2	2	3	4	4	5	5	5	6	6	6	7	7	7	7	8	8	8	9	10	10	11	11	12	12	12	12	13	13
16	0	1	2	3	3	4	4	5	5	6	6	7	7	7	7	8	8	8	8	9	10	10	11	11	12	12	13	13	13	14	14
17	0	1	2	3	4	4	5	5	6	6	7	7	7	8	8	8	9	9	9	10	10	11	12	12	13	13	14	14	14	14	15
18	0	1	2	3	4	4	5	6	6	7	7	8	8	8	9	9	9	9	10	10	11	12	12	13	13	14	14	15	15	15	16
19	1	1	2	3	4	5	5	6	7	7	8	8	8	9	9	9	10	10	10	11	12	13	13	14	14	15	15	16	16	16	16
20	1	2	3	3	4	5	6	6	7	8	8	8	9	9	10	10	10	11	11	12	13	13	14	14	15	16	16	16	17	17	17
21	1	2	3	4	5	5	6	7	7	8	8	9	9	10	10	10	11	11	11	12	13	14	15	15	16	16	17	17	18	18	18
22	1	2	3	4	5	6	6	7	8	8	9	9	10	10	11	11	11	12	12	13	14	15	15	16	17	17	18	18	18	19	19
23	1	2	3	4	5	6	7	7	8	9	9	10	10	11	11	12	12	12	13	13	15	15	16	17	17	18	19	19	19	20	20
25	1	2	3	5	6	7	7	8	9	10	10	11	11	12	12	13	13	13	14	15	16	17	18	18	19	20	20	21	21	22	22
30	1	3	4	6	7	8	9	10	11	12	13	13	14	14	15	15	16	16	17	18	19	20	21	22	23	24	24	25	25	26	26
35	1	3	5	7	8	10	11	12	13	14	15	16	16	17	18	18	19	19	20	21	23	24	25	26	27	28	29	29	30	30	31
40	2	4	6	8	9	11	13	14	15	16	17	18	19	20	20	21	22	22	23	24	26	28	29	30	31	32	33	34	34	35	36
45	2	4	7	9	11	13	14	16	17	18	19	20	21	22	23	24	24	25	26	27	29	31	32	34	35	36	37	38	39	39	40
50	2	5	8	10	12	14	16	18	19	20	22	23	24	25	26	27	27	28	29	31	33	35	36	37	39	40	41	42	43	44	45

$l+r=10$

N_2 \ N_1	11	12	13	14	15	16	17	18	19	20	21	22	23	24	25	26	27	28	29	30	35	40	45	50	60	70	80	90	100	120	140
2	0	0	0	0	0	0	0	0	0	0	0	0	0	0	0	0	0	0	0	0	1	1	1	1	1	1	1	1	1	1	1
3	0	0	0	0	0	0	0	0	0	0	0	1	1	1	1	1	1	1	1	1	1	1	1	1	2	2	2	2	2	2	2
4	0	0	0	0	0	0	0	1	1	1	1	1	1	1	1	1	1	1	1	1	2	2	2	2	2	2	3	3	3	3	3
5	0	0	0	0	0	1	1	1	1	1	1	1	1	1	2	2	2	2	2	2	2	2	3	3	3	3	3	3	4	4	4
6	0	0	0	0	1	1	1	1	1	1	2	2	2	2	2	2	2	2	2	2	3	3	3	3	4	4	4	4	4	5	5
7	0	0	0	1	1	1	1	1	2	2	2	2	2	2	2	3	3	3	3	3	3	4	4	4	4	5	5	5	5	5	6
8	0	0	0	1	1	1	1	2	2	2	2	2	3	3	3	3	3	3	3	3	4	4	5	5	5	5	6	6	6	6	6
9	0	0	1	1	1	1	2	2	2	2	3	3	3	3	3	3	4	4	4	4	5	5	5	6	6	6	7	7	7	7	7
10	0	0	1	1	1	2	2	2	3	3	3	3	3	4	4	4	4	4	4	5	5	6	6	6	7	7	7	8	8	8	8
11	0	0	1	1	2	2	2	3	3	3	3	4	4	4	4	4	5	5	5	5	6	6	7	7	7	8	8	8	9	9	9
12	0	0	1	1	2	2	3	3	3	4	4	4	4	5	5	5	5	5	5	6	6	7	7	8	8	9	9	9	9	10	10
13	0	1	1	2	2	2	3	3	4	4	4	4	5	5	5	5	6	6	6	6	7	7	8	8	9	9	10	10	10	11	11
14	0	1	1	2	2	3	3	4	4	4	5	5	5	5	6	6	6	6	7	7	8	8	9	9	10	10	11	11	11	11	12
15	0	1	1	2	2	3	3	4	4	5	5	5	6	6	6	6	7	7	7	7	8	9	9	10	10	11	11	12	12	12	13
16	0	1	1	2	3	3	4	4	5	5	5	6	6	6	7	7	7	7	8	8	9	9	10	10	11	12	12	12	13	13	13
17	0	1	2	2	3	3	4	4	5	5	6	6	6	7	7	7	8	8	8	8	9	10	11	11	12	12	13	13	14	14	14
18	0	1	2	2	3	4	4	5	5	6	6	7	7	7	8	8	8	8	9	9	10	11	11	12	13	13	14	14	14	15	15
19	0	1	2	3	3	4	5	5	6	6	7	7	7	8	8	8	9	9	9	10	11	11	12	13	13	14	15	15	15	16	16
20	0	1	2	3	3	4	5	5	6	6	7	7	8	8	9	9	9	10	10	10	11	12	13	13	14	15	15	16	16	17	17
21	0	1	2	3	4	4	5	6	6	7	7	8	8	9	9	9	10	10	10	11	12	13	13	14	15	16	16	17	17	17	18
22	0	1	2	3	4	5	5	6	7	7	8	8	9	9	10	10	10	11	11	11	12	13	14	15	16	16	17	17	18	18	19
23	1	1	2	3	4	5	6	6	7	8	8	9	9	10	10	10	11	11	11	12	13	14	15	15	16	17	18	18	19	19	20
25	1	2	3	4	5	5	6	7	8	8	9	10	10	11	11	11	12	12	13	13	14	15	16	17	18	19	19	20	20	21	21
30	1	2	3	5	6	7	8	9	10	10	11	12	12	13	13	14	14	15	15	16	17	19	20	21	22	23	24	24	25	25	26
35	1	3	4	5	7	8	9	10	11	12	13	14	15	15	16	16	17	18	18	18	20	22	23	24	26	27	28	28	29	30	30
40	1	3	5	6	8	9	11	12	13	14	15	16	17	18	18	19	20	20	21	21	24	25	27	28	29	31	32	32	33	34	35
45	2	3	5	7	9	11	12	14	15	16	17	18	19	20	21	21	22	23	23	24	27	29	30	31	33	35	36	37	37	38	39
50	2	4	6	8	10	12	14	15	17	18	19	20	21	22	23	24	25	26	26	27	30	32	34	35	37	39	40	41	42	43	44

$l+r=12$

N_2 \ N_1	13	14	15	16	17	18	19	20	21	22	23	24	25	26	27	28	29	30	31	32	35	40	45	50	60	70	80	90	100	120	140
2	0	0	0	0	0	0	0	0	0	0	0	0	0	0	0	0	0	0	0	0	0	1	1	1	1	1	1	1	1	1	1
3	0	0	0	0	0	0	0	0	0	0	0	0	0	1	1	1	1	1	1	1	1	1	1	1	1	2	2	2	2	2	2
4	0	0	0	0	0	0	0	0	0	1	1	1	1	1	1	1	1	1	1	1	1	2	2	2	2	2	2	3	3	3	3
5	0	0	0	0	0	0	0	1	1	1	1	1	1	1	1	1	1	2	2	2	2	2	2	3	3	3	3	3	3	4	4
6	0	0	0	0	0	1	1	1	1	1	1	1	2	2	2	2	2	2	2	2	2	3	3	3	3	4	4	4	4	4	5
7	0	0	0	0	1	1	1	1	1	1	2	2	2	2	2	2	2	2	3	3	3	3	4	4	4	4	5	5	5	5	5
8	0	0	0	0	1	1	1	1	2	2	2	2	2	2	3	3	3	3	3	3	3	4	4	4	5	5	5	6	6	6	6
9	0	0	0	1	1	1	1	2	2	2	2	2	3	3	3	3	3	3	3	4	4	4	5	5	6	6	6	6	7	7	7
10	0	0	0	1	1	1	2	2	2	2	3	3	3	3	3	4	4	4	4	4	4	5	5	6	6	7	7	7	7	8	8
11	0	0	1	1	1	2	2	2	2	3	3	3	3	4	4	4	4	4	4	5	5	6	6	6	7	7	8	8	8	9	9
12	0	0	1	1	1	2	2	2	3	3	3	4	4	4	4	4	5	5	5	5	6	6	7	7	8	8	8	9	9	9	10
13	0	0	1	1	2	2	2	3	3	3	4	4	4	4	5	5	5	5	5	6	6	7	7	8	8	9	9	10	10	10	10
14	0	0	1	1	2	2	3	3	3	4	4	4	5	5	5	5	6	6	6	6	7	7	8	8	9	10	10	10	11	11	11
15	0	1	1	2	2	2	3	3	4	4	4	5	5	5	6	6	6	6	6	7	7	8	9	9	10	10	11	11	11	12	12
16	0	1	1	2	2	3	3	4	4	4	5	5	5	6	6	6	6	7	7	7	8	9	9	10	10	11	12	12	12	13	13
17	0	1	1	2	2	3	3	4	4	5	5	5	6	6	6	6	7	7	7	7	8	9	10	10	11	12	12	13	13	14	14
18	0	1	1	2	3	3	4	4	5	5	5	6	6	6	7	7	7	8	8	8	9	10	10	11	12	13	13	14	14	14	15
19	0	1	1	2	3	3	4	4	5	5	6	6	7	7	7	8	8	8	8	9	9	10	11	12	13	13	14	14	15	15	16
20	0	1	2	2	3	4	4	5	5	6	6	7	7	7	8	8	8	9	9	9	9	11	12	12	13	14	15	15	16	16	17
21	0	1	2	2	3	4	4	5	6	6	7	7	7	8	8	8	9	9	9	10	10	12	12	13	14	15	15	16	16	17	17
22	0	1	2	3	3	4	5	5	6	6	7	7	8	8	9	9	9	10	10	10	11	12	13	14	15	16	16	17	17	18	18
23	0	1	2	3	3	4	5	6	6	7	7	8	8	9	9	9	10	10	10	11	12	13	14	14	16	16	17	18	18	19	19
25	0	1	2	3	4	5	5	6	7	7	8	8	9	9	10	10	11	11	11	12	13	14	15	16	17	18	19	19	20	20	21
30	1	2	3	4	5	6	7	8	8	9	10	10	11	12	12	13	13	14	14	14	15	17	18	19	21	22	23	23	23	25	25
35	1	2	3	5	6	7	8	9	10	11	12	12	13	14	14	15	15	16	17	17	18	20	21	22	24	26	26	27	28	29	30
40	1	2	4	5	7	8	9	10	12	13	13	14	15	16	17	17	18	18	19	20	21	23	25	26	28	29	30	31	32	33	34
45	1	3	5	6	8	9	11	12	13	14	15	16	17	18	19	20	20	21	22	22	24	26	28	29	32	33	34	35	36	37	38
50	1	3	5	7	9	10	12	13	15	16	17	18	19	20	21	22	23	23	24	25	27	29	31	33	35	37	38	39	40	42	43

All values conform to the international convention (i.e. 0,1 instead of 0.1).

Distribution-Free Tolerance Limits (2 Samples)◊ $\beta_t = 0{,}95$

N_1: sample size of sample one; N_2: sample size of sample two; N^*: number of observations in the 2nd sample which lies between the tolerance limits of l and r with a probability of at least β_t (assuming that both samples are from the same distribution). For definition of l and r see section 25A. The values in the table are those of N^*

N_1	2	3	4	5	6	7	8	9	10	11	12	13	14	15	16	17	18	19	20	22	25	30	35	40	45	50	60	70	80	90	100
N_2	$l+r=1$																														
2	0	0	0	1	1	1	1	1	1	1	1	1	1	1	1	1	1	1	1	1	1	1	1	2	2	2	2	2	2	2	2
3	0	1	1	1	1	1	1	2	2	2	2	2	2	2	2	2	2	2	2	2	2	2	2	2	2	2	3	3	3	3	3
4	0	1	1	2	2	2	2	2	2	2	3	3	3	3	3	3	3	3	3	3	3	3	3	3	3	3	3	3	4	4	4
5	1	1	2	2	2	3	3	3	3	3	3	3	3	3	4	4	4	4	4	4	4	4	4	4	4	4	4	4	4	4	5
6	1	2	2	3	3	3	3	4	4	4	4	4	4	4	4	4	4	5	5	5	5	5	5	5	5	5	5	5	5	5	5
7	1	2	3	3	4	4	4	4	4	5	5	5	5	5	5	5	5	5	5	5	6	6	6	6	6	6	6	6	6	6	7
8	1	2	3	4	4	4	5	5	5	5	6	6	6	6	6	6	6	6	6	6	6	7	7	7	7	7	7	7	7	7	7
9	1	3	4	4	5	5	5	6	6	6	6	6	7	7	7	7	7	7	7	7	7	8	8	8	8	8	8	8	8	8	8
10	2	3	4	5	5	6	6	6	7	7	7	7	7	7	8	8	8	8	8	8	8	8	9	9	9	9	9	9	9	9	9
11	2	3	4	5	6	6	7	7	7	8	8	8	8	8	8	8	9	9	9	9	9	9	9	10	10	10	10	10	10	10	10
12	2	4	5	6	7	7	7	8	8	8	9	9	9	9	9	9	9	10	10	10	10	10	10	10	10	10	10	10	10	11	11
13	2	4	5	6	7	8	8	9	9	9	9	10	10	10	10	10	10	10	10	11	11	11	11	11	12	12	12	12	12	12	12
14	2	4	6	7	8	8	9	9	10	10	10	10	11	11	11	11	11	11	11	11	12	12	12	12	12	13	13	13	13	13	13
15	3	5	6	7	8	9	10	10	10	11	11	11	11	12	12	12	12	12	12	12	13	13	13	13	13	13	14	14	14	14	14
16	3	5	7	8	9	10	10	11	11	11	12	12	12	12	12	13	13	13	13	13	13	14	14	14	14	14	15	15	15	15	15
17	3	6	7	9	10	10	11	11	12	12	12	13	13	13	13	13	14	14	14	14	14	15	15	15	15	15	16	16	16	16	16
18	3	6	8	9	10	11	12	12	13	13	13	13	14	14	14	14	14	15	15	15	15	16	16	16	16	16	16	17	17	17	17
19	4	6	8	10	11	12	12	13	13	14	14	14	15	15	15	15	15	15	16	16	16	16	17	17	17	17	17	18	18	18	18
20	4	7	9	10	11	12	13	14	14	14	15	15	15	16	16	16	16	16	16	17	17	17	18	18	18	18	18	19	19	19	19
21	4	7	9	11	12	13	14	14	15	15	16	16	16	16	17	17	17	17	17	18	18	18	19	19	19	19	19	19	20	20	20
22	4	7	10	11	13	14	14	15	15	16	16	17	17	17	17	18	18	18	18	18	19	19	19	20	20	20	20	20	21	21	21
23	4	8	10	12	13	14	15	16	16	17	17	17	18	18	18	18	18	19	19	19	20	20	20	21	21	21	21	21	22	22	22
25	5	8	11	13	14	15	16	17	18	18	19	19	19	20	20	20	20	21	21	21	21	22	22	22	23	23	23	23	23	24	24
30	6	10	13	16	17	19	20	21	21	22	23	23	23	24	24	24	25	25	25	25	26	26	27	27	27	28	28	28	28	28	28
35	7	12	16	18	20	22	23	24	25	26	26	27	27	28	28	28	29	29	29	30	30	31	31	32	32	32	33	33	33	33	33
40	8	14	18	21	23	25	27	28	29	30	30	31	31	32	32	33	33	33	34	34	35	35	36	36	37	37	37	38	38	38	38
45	9	16	20	24	26	28	30	31	32	33	34	35	35	36	36	37	37	38	38	38	39	40	40	41	41	42	42	42	43	43	43
50	11	18	23	27	30	32	34	35	36	37	38	39	39	40	41	41	41	42	42	43	43	44	45	46	46	46	47	47	47	48	48

N_1	2	3	4	5	6	7	8	9	10	11	12	13	14	15	16	17	18	19	20	22	25	30	35	40	45	50	60	70	80	90	100
N_2	$l+r=2$																														
2	0	0	0	0	0	0	0	0	1	1	1	1	1	1	1	1	1	1	1	1	1	1	1	1	1	1	1	1	2	2	2
3	0	0	0	0	1	1	1	1	1	1	1	1	1	1	1	2	2	2	2	2	2	2	2	2	2	2	2	2	2	2	2
4	0	0	0	1	1	1	1	1	2	2	2	2	2	2	2	2	2	2	2	2	3	3	3	3	3	3	3	3	3	3	3
5	0	0	1	1	1	2	2	2	2	2	2	3	3	3	3	3	3	3	3	3	3	4	4	4	4	4	4	4	4	4	4
6	0	0	1	1	2	2	2	3	3	3	3	3	3	3	4	4	4	4	4	4	4	4	4	5	5	5	5	5	5	5	5
7	0	0	1	2	2	2	3	3	3	4	4	4	4	4	4	4	4	5	5	5	5	5	5	5	6	6	6	6	6	6	6
8	0	0	1	2	2	3	3	4	4	4	4	5	5	5	5	5	5	5	5	6	6	6	6	6	6	7	7	7	7	7	7
9	0	1	1	2	3	3	4	4	5	5	5	5	5	6	6	6	6	6	6	6	7	7	7	7	7	7	8	8	8	8	8
10	0	1	2	3	3	4	4	5	5	5	6	6	6	6	6	7	7	7	7	7	7	8	8	8	8	8	8	9	9	9	9
11	0	1	2	3	4	4	5	5	6	6	6	7	7	7	7	7	7	8	8	8	8	8	9	9	9	9	9	10	10	10	10
12	0	1	2	3	4	5	5	6	6	7	7	7	7	8	8	8	8	8	8	9	9	9	10	10	10	10	10	10	11	11	11
13	0	1	2	4	5	5	6	6	7	7	8	8	8	8	9	9	9	9	9	9	10	10	10	11	11	11	11	11	11	12	12
14	0	1	3	4	5	6	7	7	7	8	8	9	9	9	9	9	10	10	10	10	11	11	11	12	12	12	12	12	12	13	13
15	0	1	3	4	5	6	7	8	8	9	9	9	10	10	10	10	10	11	11	11	11	12	12	12	13	13	13	13	13	13	14
16	0	1	3	5	6	7	7	8	9	9	10	10	10	10	11	11	11	11	12	12	12	13	13	13	13	14	14	14	14	14	15
17	0	2	3	5	6	7	8	9	9	10	10	11	11	11	11	12	12	12	12	13	13	13	14	14	15	15	15	15	15	15	15
18	0	2	4	5	7	8	9	9	10	10	11	11	12	12	12	12	13	13	13	13	14	14	15	15	15	15	16	16	16	16	16
19	0	2	4	6	7	8	9	10	10	11	12	12	12	13	13	13	13	14	14	14	15	15	16	16	16	16	17	17	17	17	17
20	0	2	4	6	7	9	10	10	11	12	12	13	13	13	14	14	14	14	15	15	15	16	16	17	17	17	18	18	18	18	18
21	0	2	4	6	8	9	10	11	12	12	13	13	14	14	14	15	15	15	15	16	16	17	17	18	18	18	18	19	19	19	19
22	0	2	5	7	8	10	11	12	12	13	13	14	14	15	15	15	16	16	16	17	17	18	18	19	19	19	19	20	20	20	20
23	0	2	5	7	9	10	11	12	13	14	14	15	15	15	16	16	16	17	17	17	18	19	19	19	20	20	20	21	21	21	21
25	0	3	5	8	9	11	12	13	14	15	15	16	16	17	17	18	18	18	19	19	20	20	21	21	21	22	22	22	23	23	23
30	0	3	7	9	12	13	15	16	17	18	19	19	20	21	21	21	22	22	22	23	24	24	25	26	26	26	27	27	27	28	28
35	0	4	8	11	14	16	17	19	20	21	22	23	23	24	25	25	26	26	26	27	28	29	29	30	30	31	31	32	32	32	32
40	1	5	9	13	16	18	20	22	23	24	25	26	27	28	28	29	29	30	30	31	32	33	34	34	35	35	36	36	37	37	37
45	1	5	10	14	18	21	23	25	26	27	29	30	31	31	32	33	33	34	34	35	36	37	38	39	39	40	40	41	41	42	42
50	1	6	12	16	20	23	25	27	29	31	32	33	34	35	36	36	37	38	38	39	40	41	42	43	44	44	45	46	46	46	47

N_1	4	5	6	7	8	9	10	11	12	13	14	15	16	17	18	19	20	21	22	23	25	30	35	40	45	50	60	70	80	90	100
N_2	$l+r=3$																														
2	0	0	0	0	0	0	0	0	0	0	1	1	1	1	1	1	1	1	1	1	1	1	1	1	1	1	1	1	1	1	1
3	0	0	0	0	0	1	1	1	1	1	1	1	1	1	1	1	1	1	1	1	2	2	2	2	2	2	2	2	2	2	2
4	0	0	0	1	1	1	1	1	1	1	2	2	2	2	2	2	2	2	2	2	2	2	3	3	3	3	3	3	3	3	3
5	0	0	1	1	1	1	2	2	2	2	2	2	2	2	3	3	3	3	3	3	3	3	3	3	4	4	4	4	4	4	4
6	0	0	1	1	1	2	2	2	2	3	3	3	3	3	3	3	3	3	3	4	4	4	4	4	4	4	5	5	5	5	5
7	0	1	1	1	2	2	2	3	3	3	3	3	4	4	4	4	4	4	4	4	4	4	5	5	5	5	5	6	6	6	6
8	0	1	1	2	2	3	3	3	3	4	4	4	4	4	4	5	5	5	5	5	5	5	6	6	6	6	6	6	7	7	7
9	0	1	2	2	3	3	3	4	4	4	4	5	5	5	5	5	5	6	6	6	6	6	6	7	7	7	7	7	8	8	8
10	0	1	2	2	3	3	4	4	5	5	5	5	5	6	6	6	6	6	6	6	7	7	7	8	8	8	8	8	8	9	9
11	0	1	2	3	3	4	4	5	5	5	6	6	6	6	6	7	7	7	7	7	7	8	8	8	9	9	9	9	9	9	10
12	1	1	2	3	4	4	5	5	6	6	6	7	7	7	7	7	7	8	8	8	8	9	9	9	9	10	10	10	10	10	10
13	1	2	3	3	4	5	5	6	6	7	7	7	7	8	8	8	8	8	8	9	9	9	10	10	10	10	11	11	11	11	11
14	1	2	3	4	5	5	6	6	7	7	7	8	8	8	9	9	9	9	9	9	10	10	11	11	11	11	12	12	12	12	12
15	1	2	3	4	5	6	6	7	7	8	8	8	9	9	9	9	10	10	10	10	10	11	11	12	12	12	12	13	13	13	13
16	1	2	3	4	5	6	7	7	8	8	9	9	9	10	10	10	10	10	11	11	11	12	12	13	13	13	13	14	14	14	14
17	1	2	4	5	6	7	7	8	8	9	9	10	10	10	11	11	11	11	11	12	12	13	13	13	14	14	14	15	15	15	15
18	1	3	4	5	6	7	8	8	9	9	10	10	11	11	11	11	12	12	12	12	13	13	14	14	14	14	14	15	16	16	16
19	1	3	4	5	7	7	8	9	10	10	10	11	11	12	12	12	12	13	13	13	13	14	15	15	15	16	16	16	17	17	17
20	1	3	4	6	7	8	9	9	10	11	11	12	12	12	13	13	13	13	14	14	14	15	15	16	16	16	17	17	17	18	18
21	1	3	5	6	7	8	9	10	11	11	12	12	13	13	13	14	14	14	14	15	15	16	16	17	17	17	18	18	18	19	19
22	1	3	5	6	8	9	10	10	11	12	12	13	13	14	14	14	15	15	15	15	16	16	17	18	18	18	19	19	19	19	20
23	2	3	5	7	8	9	10	11	12	12	13	13	14	14	15	15	15	16	16	16	16	17	18	18	19	19	20	20	20	20	21
25	2	4	6	7	9	10	11	12	13	14	14	14	15	16	16	16	17	17	17	18	18	19	20	20	20	21	21	22	22	22	22
30	2	5	7	9	11	12	14	15	16	16	17	17	18	19	19	20	20	21	21	21	22	23	24	24	25	25	26	26	27	27	27
35	3	6	8	11	13	15	16	17	18	19	20	20	22	22	23	23	24	24	25	25	26	27	28	29	29	30	30	31	31	31	32
40	3	7	10	13	15	17	19	20	21	22	23	24	25	26	26	27	27	28	28	29	29	31	32	33	33	34	35	35	36	36	36
45	4	8	11	14	17	19	21	23	24	25	26	27	28	29	30	30	31	31	32	32	33	35	36	37	38	38	39	40	40	41	41
50	4	9	13	16	19	21	23	25	27	28	29	31	31	32	33	34	35	35	36	36	37	39	40	41	42	43	44	44	45	45	46

◊ Reproduction only by permission of the publishers of the *Geigy Scientific Tables*.

All values conform to the international convention (i.e. 0,1 instead of 0.1).

Distribution-Free Tolerance Limits (2 Samples)◊ $\beta_t = 0{,}95$

N_1: sample size of sample one; N_2: sample size of sample two; N^*: number of observations in the 2nd sample which lies between the tolerance limits of l and r with a probability of at least β_t (assuming that both samples are from the same distribution). For definition of l and r see section 25A. The values in the table are those of N^*

$l+r=4$

N_2 \ N_1	5	6	7	8	9	10	11	12	13	14	15	16	17	18	19	20	21	22	23	24	25	30	35	40	45	50	60	70	80	90	100
2	0	0	0	0	0	0	0	0	0	0	0	0	0	0	1	1	1	1	1	1	1	1	1	1	1	1	1	1	1	1	1
3	0	0	0	0	0	0	0	1	1	1	1	1	1	1	1	1	1	1	1	1	1	1	2	2	2	2	2	2	2	2	2
4	0	0	0	0	1	1	1	1	1	1	1	1	1	2	2	2	2	2	2	2	2	2	2	2	3	3	3	3	3	3	3
5	0	0	0	1	1	1	1	1	2	2	2	2	2	2	2	2	2	2	2	3	3	3	3	3	3	3	4	4	4	4	4
6	0	0	1	1	1	1	2	2	2	2	2	2	3	3	3	3	3	3	3	3	3	4	4	4	4	4	4	5	5	5	5
7	0	0	1	1	1	2	2	2	2	3	3	3	3	3	3	4	4	4	4	4	4	4	5	5	5	5	5	5	6	6	6
8	0	0	1	1	2	2	2	3	3	3	3	4	4	4	4	4	4	4	4	5	5	5	5	6	6	6	6	6	6	6	7
9	0	1	1	2	2	2	3	3	3	4	4	4	4	4	5	5	5	5	5	5	5	6	6	6	6	7	7	7	7	7	7
10	0	1	1	2	2	3	3	4	4	4	4	5	5	5	5	5	6	6	6	6	6	6	7	7	7	7	8	8	8	8	8
11	0	1	2	2	3	3	4	4	4	5	5	5	5	6	6	6	6	6	6	7	7	7	8	8	8	8	9	9	9	9	9
12	0	1	2	2	3	4	4	5	5	5	6	6	6	6	6	7	7	7	7	7	7	8	8	9	9	9	9	10	10	10	10
13	0	1	2	3	3	4	5	5	5	6	6	6	7	7	7	7	7	8	8	8	8	9	9	9	10	10	10	11	11	11	11
14	0	1	2	3	4	4	5	5	6	6	7	7	7	7	8	8	8	8	8	9	9	9	10	10	11	11	11	11	12	12	12
15	0	1	2	3	4	5	5	6	6	7	7	7	8	8	8	9	9	9	9	9	10	10	11	11	11	12	12	12	13	13	13
16	1	2	3	4	4	5	6	6	7	7	8	8	8	9	9	9	9	10	10	10	10	11	11	12	12	12	13	13	13	14	14
17	1	2	3	4	5	6	6	7	7	8	8	9	9	9	10	10	10	10	11	11	11	12	12	13	13	13	14	14	14	15	15
18	1	2	3	4	5	6	7	7	8	8	9	9	10	10	10	11	11	11	11	11	12	12	13	13	14	14	15	15	15	15	16
19	1	2	3	4	5	6	7	8	8	9	9	10	10	11	11	11	11	12	12	12	12	13	14	14	15	15	15	16	16	16	16
20	1	2	4	5	6	7	7	8	9	9	10	10	11	11	11	12	12	12	13	13	13	14	15	15	15	16	16	17	17	17	17
21	1	2	4	5	6	7	8	9	9	10	10	11	11	12	12	12	13	13	13	14	14	15	15	16	16	17	17	18	18	18	18
22	1	2	4	5	6	7	8	9	10	10	11	12	12	12	13	13	13	14	14	14	14	15	16	17	17	17	18	18	19	19	19
23	1	3	4	6	7	8	9	9	10	11	12	12	13	13	13	14	14	14	15	15	15	16	17	17	18	18	19	19	20	20	20
25	1	3	5	6	7	9	10	11	11	12	13	13	14	14	15	15	15	16	16	16	17	18	18	19	20	20	21	21	21	22	22
30	2	4	6	8	9	11	12	13	14	15	15	16	17	17	18	18	19	19	19	20	20	21	22	23	24	24	25	25	26	26	27
35	2	4	7	9	11	13	14	15	16	17	18	19	20	20	21	22	22	23	23	23	24	25	26	27	28	28	29	30	30	31	31
40	2	5	8	10	13	14	16	18	19	20	21	22	23	24	24	25	25	26	26	26	27	29	30	31	32	33	34	34	35	35	36
45	3	6	9	12	14	16	18	20	21	23	24	25	26	27	27	28	29	29	30	30	31	33	34	35	36	37	38	39	39	40	40
50	3	7	10	13	16	18	20	22	24	25	27	28	29	30	31	31	32	33	33	34	34	37	38	39	40	41	42	43	44	44	45

$l+r=5$

N_2 \ N_1	6	7	8	9	10	11	12	13	14	15	16	17	18	19	20	21	22	23	24	25	30	35	40	45	50	60	70	80	90	100	120
2	0	0	0	0	0	0	0	0	0	0	0	0	0	0	0	0	0	1	1	1	1	1	1	1	1	1	1	1	1	1	1
3	0	0	0	0	0	0	0	0	0	1	1	1	1	1	1	1	1	1	1	1	1	1	2	2	2	2	2	2	2	2	2
4	0	0	0	0	0	0	1	1	1	1	1	1	1	1	1	1	2	2	2	2	2	2	2	2	2	3	3	3	3	3	3
5	0	0	0	0	1	1	1	1	1	1	2	2	2	2	2	2	2	2	2	2	3	3	3	3	3	3	4	4	4	4	4
6	0	0	0	1	1	1	1	2	2	2	2	2	2	2	2	3	3	3	3	3	3	3	4	4	4	4	4	4	5	5	5
7	0	0	0	1	1	1	2	2	2	2	3	3	3	3	3	3	3	3	3	4	4	4	4	5	5	5	5	5	5	6	6
8	0	0	1	1	1	2	2	2	3	3	3	3	3	3	4	4	4	4	4	4	5	5	5	5	6	6	6	6	6	6	7
9	0	0	1	1	2	2	2	3	3	3	3	4	4	4	4	4	4	5	5	5	5	6	6	6	6	7	7	7	7	7	7
10	0	0	1	2	2	2	3	3	3	4	4	4	4	5	5	5	5	5	5	5	6	6	7	7	7	7	8	8	8	8	8
11	0	1	1	2	2	3	3	4	4	4	4	5	5	5	5	5	6	6	6	6	7	7	7	8	8	8	9	9	9	9	9
12	0	1	1	2	3	3	4	4	4	5	5	5	5	6	6	6	6	6	7	7	7	8	8	8	9	9	9	10	10	10	10
13	0	1	2	2	3	3	4	4	5	5	5	6	6	6	6	7	7	7	7	7	8	9	9	9	10	10	10	10	11	11	11
14	0	1	2	2	3	4	4	5	5	6	6	6	7	7	7	7	7	8	8	8	9	9	10	10	10	11	11	11	12	12	12
15	0	1	2	3	3	4	5	5	6	6	6	7	7	7	8	8	8	8	9	9	9	10	10	11	11	12	12	12	12	13	13
16	0	1	2	3	4	4	5	6	6	7	7	7	8	8	8	8	9	9	9	9	10	11	11	12	12	12	13	13	13	13	14
17	0	1	2	3	4	5	5	6	7	7	7	8	8	9	9	9	9	10	10	10	11	12	12	12	13	13	14	14	14	14	15
18	0	1	2	3	4	5	6	6	7	7	8	8	9	9	9	10	10	10	10	11	12	12	13	13	14	14	14	15	15	15	16
19	0	2	3	4	5	5	6	7	7	8	8	9	9	10	10	10	11	11	11	11	12	13	14	14	14	15	15	16	16	16	16
20	1	2	3	4	5	6	7	7	8	8	9	9	10	10	11	11	11	11	12	12	13	14	14	15	15	16	16	17	17	17	17
21	1	2	3	4	5	6	7	8	8	9	9	10	10	11	11	11	12	12	12	13	14	14	15	16	16	17	17	17	18	18	18
22	1	2	3	4	5	6	7	8	9	9	10	10	11	11	12	12	12	13	13	13	14	15	16	16	17	17	18	18	19	19	19
23	1	2	3	5	6	7	8	9	9	10	10	11	11	12	12	13	13	13	14	14	15	16	17	17	18	18	19	19	19	20	20
25	1	2	4	5	6	7	8	9	10	11	11	12	13	13	14	14	14	15	15	15	17	17	18	19	19	20	20	21	21	21	22
30	1	3	5	6	8	9	10	11	12	13	14	15	15	16	16	17	17	18	18	19	20	21	22	23	23	24	25	25	26	26	26
35	1	4	6	8	9	11	12	14	15	16	17	17	18	19	19	20	21	21	21	22	24	25	26	27	27	28	29	30	30	30	31
40	2	4	7	9	11	13	14	16	17	18	19	20	21	22	22	23	24	24	25	25	27	29	30	31	31	33	33	34	35	35	36
45	2	5	8	10	12	14	16	18	19	21	22	23	24	25	25	26	27	27	28	29	31	32	34	35	36	37	38	39	39	40	40
50	2	5	9	11	14	16	18	20	22	23	24	25	27	27	28	29	30	31	31	32	34	36	38	39	40	41	42	43	44	44	45

$l+r=6$

N_2 \ N_1	7	8	9	10	11	12	13	14	15	16	17	18	19	20	21	22	23	24	25	26	30	35	40	45	50	60	70	80	90	100	120
2	0	0	0	0	0	0	0	0	0	0	0	0	0	0	0	0	0	0	0	0	1	1	1	1	1	1	1	1	1	1	1
3	0	0	0	0	0	0	0	0	0	0	1	1	1	1	1	1	1	1	1	1	1	1	1	1	2	2	2	2	2	2	2
4	0	0	0	0	0	0	0	1	1	1	1	1	1	1	1	1	1	1	1	2	2	2	2	2	2	2	3	3	3	3	3
5	0	0	0	0	0	1	1	1	1	1	1	1	2	2	2	2	2	2	2	2	2	3	3	3	3	3	3	3	4	4	4
6	0	0	0	0	1	1	1	1	1	2	2	2	2	2	2	2	2	3	3	3	3	3	3	4	4	4	4	4	4	5	5
7	0	0	0	1	1	1	1	2	2	2	2	2	2	3	3	3	3	3	3	3	4	4	4	4	4	5	5	5	5	5	6
8	0	0	0	1	1	1	2	2	2	2	3	3	3	3	3	3	4	4	4	4	4	5	5	5	5	6	6	6	6	6	6
9	0	0	1	1	1	2	2	2	3	3	3	3	3	4	4	4	4	4	4	4	5	5	6	6	6	6	7	7	7	7	7
10	0	0	1	1	2	2	2	3	3	3	4	4	4	4	4	4	5	5	5	5	6	6	6	7	7	7	7	8	8	8	8
11	0	0	1	1	2	2	3	3	3	4	4	4	4	5	5	5	5	5	6	6	6	7	7	7	8	8	8	8	9	9	9
12	0	1	1	2	2	3	3	3	4	4	4	5	5	5	5	6	6	6	6	6	7	7	8	8	8	9	9	9	9	10	10
13	0	1	1	2	2	3	3	4	4	5	5	5	5	6	6	6	6	7	7	7	7	8	8	9	9	10	10	10	10	11	11
14	0	1	1	2	3	3	4	4	5	5	5	6	6	6	6	7	7	7	7	8	8	9	9	10	10	10	11	11	11	11	12
15	0	1	2	2	3	4	4	5	5	5	6	6	6	7	7	7	8	8	8	8	9	9	10	10	11	11	12	12	12	12	13
16	0	1	2	2	3	4	4	5	5	6	6	7	7	7	8	8	8	8	9	9	9	10	11	11	11	12	12	13	13	13	13
17	0	1	2	3	3	4	5	5	6	6	7	7	7	8	8	8	8	9	9	9	10	11	11	12	12	13	13	14	14	14	14
18	0	1	2	3	4	4	5	6	6	7	7	8	8	8	9	9	9	10	10	10	11	12	12	13	13	14	14	14	15	15	15
19	0	1	2	3	4	5	5	6	7	7	8	8	9	9	9	10	10	10	10	11	11	12	13	13	14	14	15	15	16	16	16
20	0	1	2	3	4	5	6	6	7	8	8	9	9	9	10	10	10	11	11	11	12	13	14	14	15	15	16	16	16	17	17
21	0	1	3	4	4	5	6	7	7	8	9	9	10	10	10	11	11	11	12	12	13	14	14	15	15	16	17	17	17	18	18
22	0	2	3	4	5	6	6	7	8	9	9	10	10	10	11	11	12	12	12	12	13	14	15	16	16	17	17	18	18	18	19
23	1	2	3	4	5	6	7	8	8	9	10	10	11	11	11	12	12	13	13	13	14	15	16	16	17	18	18	19	19	19	20
25	1	2	3	4	6	7	8	8	9	10	10	11	12	12	13	13	13	14	14	14	15	17	17	18	18	19	20	20	21	21	22
30	1	2	4	6	7	8	9	10	11	12	13	14	14	15	15	16	16	17	17	18	19	20	21	22	22	23	24	25	25	25	26
35	1	3	5	7	8	10	11	12	13	14	15	16	17	17	18	19	19	20	20	21	22	24	25	26	26	28	28	29	30	30	31
40	1	4	6	8	10	11	13	14	15	17	18	19	19	20	21	22	22	23	23	24	26	27	29	30	30	32	33	33	34	34	35
45	2	4	7	9	11	13	15	16	18	19	20	21	22	23	24	24	25	26	26	27	29	31	32	33	34	36	37	38	38	39	40
50	2	5	7	10	12	14	16	18	20	21	22	24	25	26	27	27	28	29	30	30	32	34	36	37	38	40	41	42	43	43	44

All values conform to the international convention (i.e. 0,1 instead of 0.1).

Distribution-Free Tolerance Limits (2 Samples)◊ $\beta_t = 0{,}95$

N_1: sample size of sample one; N_2: sample size of sample two; N^*: number of observations in the 2nd sample which lies between the tolerance limits of l and r with a probability of at least β_t (assuming that both samples are from the same distribution). For definition of l and r see section 25A. The values in the table are those of N^*

$l+r=8$

N_2 \ N_1	9	10	11	12	13	14	15	16	17	18	19	20	21	22	23	24	25	26	27	30	35	40	45	50	60	70	80	90	100	120	140
2	0	0	0	0	0	0	0	0	0	0	0	0	0	0	0	0	0	0	0	0	0	1	1	1	1	1	1	1	1	1	1
3	0	0	0	0	0	0	0	0	0	0	0	0	0	0	1	1	1	1	1	1	1	1	1	1	1	2	2	2	2	2	2
4	0	0	0	0	0	0	0	0	0	1	1	1	1	1	1	1	1	1	1	1	2	2	2	2	2	2	2	3	3	3	3
5	0	0	0	0	0	0	0	1	1	1	1	1	1	1	1	1	2	2	2	2	2	2	3	3	3	3	3	3	3	4	4
6	0	0	0	0	0	1	1	1	1	1	1	1	2	2	2	2	2	2	2	2	3	3	3	3	4	4	4	4	4	4	5
7	0	0	0	0	1	1	1	1	1	2	2	2	2	2	2	2	2	3	3	3	3	4	4	4	4	5	5	5	5	5	5
8	0	0	0	0	1	1	1	1	2	2	2	2	2	3	3	3	3	3	3	4	4	4	5	5	5	5	6	6	6	6	6
9	0	0	0	1	1	1	2	2	2	2	2	3	3	3	3	3	3	4	4	4	5	5	5	5	6	6	6	7	7	7	7
10	0	0	0	1	1	1	2	2	2	3	3	3	3	3	4	4	4	4	4	5	5	6	6	6	7	7	7	7	8	8	8
11	0	0	1	1	1	2	2	2	3	3	3	3	4	4	4	4	4	5	5	5	6	6	7	7	7	8	8	8	8	9	9
12	0	0	1	1	2	2	2	3	3	3	4	4	4	4	5	5	5	5	5	6	6	7	7	8	8	8	9	9	9	10	10
13	0	0	1	1	2	2	3	3	3	4	4	4	5	5	5	5	6	6	6	6	7	8	8	8	9	9	10	10	10	10	11
14	0	0	1	1	2	2	3	3	4	4	4	5	5	5	6	6	6	6	6	7	8	8	9	9	10	10	10	11	11	11	12
15	0	0	1	2	2	3	3	4	4	4	5	5	5	6	6	6	7	7	7	8	8	9	9	10	10	11	11	12	12	12	12
16	0	1	1	2	2	3	3	4	4	5	5	6	6	6	7	7	7	7	8	8	9	10	10	11	11	12	12	12	13	13	13
17	0	1	1	2	3	3	4	4	5	5	6	6	6	7	7	7	8	8	8	9	10	10	11	11	12	12	13	13	13	14	14
18	0	1	1	2	3	3	4	5	5	6	6	6	7	7	8	8	8	8	9	9	10	11	12	12	13	13	14	14	14	15	15
19	0	1	2	2	3	4	4	5	5	6	6	7	7	8	8	8	9	9	9	10	11	12	12	13	13	14	15	15	15	16	16
20	0	1	2	2	3	4	5	5	6	6	7	7	8	8	8	9	9	9	10	10	11	12	13	13	14	15	15	16	16	16	17
21	0	1	2	3	3	4	5	6	6	7	7	8	8	9	9	9	10	10	10	11	12	13	14	14	15	16	16	17	17	17	18
22	0	1	2	3	4	4	5	6	7	7	8	8	9	9	9	10	10	11	11	12	13	14	14	15	16	16	17	17	18	18	19
23	0	1	2	3	4	5	6	6	7	8	8	9	9	10	10	10	11	11	11	12	13	14	15	16	17	17	18	18	19	19	19
25	0	1	2	3	4	5	6	7	8	8	9	9	10	10	11	11	12	12	13	13	15	16	16	17	18	19	19	20	20	21	21
30	1	2	3	4	5	7	8	9	9	10	11	12	12	13	13	14	14	15	15	16	18	19	20	21	22	23	24	24	25	25	26
35	1	2	4	5	7	8	9	10	11	12	13	14	15	15	16	17	17	18	18	19	21	23	24	25	26	27	28	28	29	30	30
40	1	3	4	6	8	9	11	12	13	14	15	16	17	18	18	19	20	20	21	22	24	26	27	28	30	31	32	33	33	34	35
45	1	3	5	7	9	10	12	13	15	16	17	18	19	20	21	22	22	23	24	25	28	29	31	32	34	35	36	37	37	38	39
50	1	3	6	8	10	12	14	15	17	18	19	20	21	22	23	24	25	26	27	28	31	33	34	36	38	39	40	41	42	43	44

$l+r=10$

N_2 \ N_1	12	13	14	15	16	17	18	19	20	21	22	23	24	25	26	27	28	29	30	35	40	45	50	60	70	80	90	100	120	140	160
2	0	0	0	0	0	0	0	0	0	0	0	0	0	0	0	0	0	0	0	0	0	0	1	1	1	1	1	1	1	1	1
3	0	0	0	0	0	0	0	0	0	0	0	0	0	0	0	0	1	1	1	1	1	1	1	1	1	2	2	2	2	2	2
4	0	0	0	0	0	0	0	0	0	0	1	1	1	1	1	1	1	1	1	1	1	2	2	2	2	2	2	2	3	3	3
5	0	0	0	0	0	0	0	1	1	1	1	1	1	1	1	1	1	1	1	2	2	2	2	3	3	3	3	3	3	4	4
6	0	0	0	0	0	1	1	1	1	1	1	1	1	1	2	2	2	2	2	2	3	3	3	3	4	4	4	4	4	4	4
7	0	0	0	0	1	1	1	1	1	1	2	2	2	2	2	2	2	2	2	3	3	3	4	4	4	4	5	5	5	5	5
8	0	0	0	1	1	1	1	1	2	2	2	2	2	2	2	3	3	3	3	3	4	4	4	5	5	5	5	6	6	6	6
9	0	0	0	1	1	1	1	2	2	2	2	2	3	3	3	3	3	3	3	4	4	5	5	5	6	6	6	6	7	7	7
10	0	0	1	1	1	1	2	2	2	2	3	3	3	3	3	3	4	4	4	4	5	5	6	6	6	7	7	7	7	8	8
11	0	0	1	1	1	2	2	2	2	3	3	3	3	4	4	4	4	4	4	5	6	6	6	7	7	8	8	8	8	9	9
12	0	0	1	1	2	2	2	3	3	3	3	4	4	4	4	4	5	5	5	6	6	7	7	8	8	8	9	9	9	9	10
13	0	1	1	1	2	2	2	3	3	3	4	4	4	4	5	5	5	5	5	6	7	7	8	8	9	9	9	10	10	10	11
14	0	1	1	2	2	2	3	3	3	4	4	4	5	5	5	5	6	6	6	7	7	8	8	8	9	10	10	10	11	11	11
15	0	1	1	2	2	3	3	3	4	4	4	5	5	5	6	6	6	6	6	7	8	9	9	10	10	11	11	11	12	12	12
16	0	1	1	2	2	3	3	4	4	4	5	5	5	6	6	6	6	7	7	8	9	9	10	10	11	11	12	12	13	13	13
17	0	1	1	2	3	3	4	4	4	5	5	6	6	6	6	7	7	7	7	8	9	10	10	11	12	12	13	13	13	14	14
18	0	1	2	2	3	3	4	4	5	5	6	6	6	7	7	7	7	8	8	9	10	10	11	12	13	13	13	14	14	15	15
19	1	1	2	2	3	4	4	5	5	6	6	6	7	7	7	8	8	8	8	10	10	11	12	13	13	14	14	15	15	15	16
20	1	1	2	3	3	4	4	5	5	6	6	7	7	7	8	8	8	9	9	10	11	12	12	13	14	15	15	15	16	16	17
21	1	1	2	3	3	4	5	5	6	6	7	7	8	8	8	9	9	9	10	11	12	12	13	14	15	15	16	16	17	17	18
22	1	1	2	3	4	4	5	6	6	7	7	8	8	8	9	9	9	10	10	11	12	13	14	15	16	16	17	17	18	18	18
23	1	2	2	3	4	5	5	6	6	7	7	8	8	9	9	10	10	10	11	12	13	14	14	16	16	17	17	18	18	19	19
25	1	2	3	4	4	5	6	6	7	8	8	9	9	10	10	11	11	11	12	13	14	15	16	17	18	19	19	20	20	21	21
30	1	2	3	4	5	6	7	8	9	10	10	11	11	12	12	13	13	14	14	16	17	18	19	21	22	23	23	24	24	25	26
35	2	3	4	5	7	8	9	10	11	11	12	13	14	14	15	15	16	16	17	19	20	22	23	24	26	27	27	28	29	29	30
40	2	3	5	6	8	9	10	11	12	13	14	15	16	16	17	18	18	19	20	22	24	25	26	28	29	31	31	32	33	34	34
45	2	4	6	7	9	10	12	13	14	15	16	17	18	19	19	20	21	22	22	25	27	28	30	32	33	35	35	36	37	38	39
50	3	5	6	8	10	11	13	14	16	17	18	19	20	21	22	23	23	24	25	28	30	32	33	36	37	39	40	40	42	43	43

$l+r=12$

N_2 \ N_1	14	15	16	17	18	19	20	21	22	23	24	25	26	27	28	29	30	31	32	35	40	45	50	60	70	80	90	100	120	140	160
2	0	0	0	0	0	0	0	0	0	0	0	0	0	0	0	0	0	0	0	0	0	0	0	1	1	1	1	1	1	1	1
3	0	0	0	0	0	0	0	0	0	0	0	0	0	0	0	0	0	0	0	1	1	1	1	1	1	1	1	2	2	2	2
4	0	0	0	0	0	0	0	0	0	0	0	0	1	1	1	1	1	1	1	1	1	1	2	2	2	2	2	2	2	3	3
5	0	0	0	0	0	0	0	0	0	1	1	1	1	1	1	1	1	1	1	1	2	2	2	2	3	3	3	3	3	3	3
6	0	0	0	0	0	0	0	1	1	1	1	1	1	1	1	1	2	2	2	2	2	2	3	3	3	3	4	4	4	4	4
7	0	0	0	0	0	1	1	1	1	1	1	1	1	2	2	2	2	2	2	2	3	3	3	4	4	4	4	5	5	5	5
8	0	0	0	0	1	1	1	1	1	1	2	2	2	2	2	2	2	2	3	3	3	4	4	4	5	5	5	5	6	6	6
9	0	0	0	0	1	1	1	1	2	2	2	2	2	2	2	3	3	3	3	3	4	4	4	5	5	6	6	6	6	7	7
10	0	0	0	1	1	1	1	2	2	2	2	2	3	3	3	3	3	3	3	4	4	5	5	6	6	7	7	7	7	7	8
11	0	0	0	1	1	1	2	2	2	2	3	3	3	3	3	3	4	4	4	4	5	5	6	6	7	7	7	8	8	8	9
12	0	0	1	1	1	2	2	2	2	3	3	3	3	3	4	4	4	4	4	5	5	6	6	7	7	8	8	8	9	9	9
13	0	0	1	1	1	2	2	2	3	3	3	3	4	4	4	4	4	5	5	5	6	7	7	8	8	9	9	9	10	10	10
14	0	0	1	1	2	2	2	3	3	3	4	4	4	4	4	5	5	5	5	6	7	7	8	8	9	9	10	10	10	11	11
15	0	1	1	1	2	2	3	3	3	4	4	4	4	5	5	5	5	6	6	6	7	8	8	9	10	10	10	11	11	12	12
16	0	1	1	1	2	2	3	3	4	4	4	4	5	5	5	6	6	6	6	7	8	8	9	10	10	11	11	12	12	12	13
17	0	1	1	2	2	3	3	3	4	4	5	5	5	5	6	6	6	6	7	7	8	9	9	10	11	12	12	12	13	13	14
18	0	1	1	2	2	3	3	4	4	4	5	5	6	6	6	6	7	7	7	8	9	10	10	11	12	12	13	13	14	14	15
19	0	1	1	2	2	3	3	4	4	5	5	6	6	6	7	7	7	7	8	8	9	10	11	12	13	13	14	14	15	15	15
20	0	1	2	2	3	3	4	4	5	5	6	6	6	7	7	7	8	8	8	9	10	11	11	12	13	14	14	15	15	16	16
21	0	1	2	2	3	3	4	4	5	5	6	6	7	7	7	8	8	8	9	9	10	11	12	13	14	15	15	16	16	17	17
22	0	1	2	2	3	4	4	5	5	6	6	7	7	7	8	8	9	9	9	10	11	12	13	14	15	15	16	16	17	18	18
23	1	1	2	3	3	4	4	5	6	6	7	7	7	8	8	9	9	9	10	10	12	13	13	15	15	16	17	17	18	18	19
25	1	1	2	3	4	4	5	6	6	7	7	8	8	9	9	9	10	10	11	11	13	14	15	16	17	18	18	19	20	20	21
30	1	2	3	4	5	5	6	7	8	8	9	10	10	11	11	12	12	13	13	14	16	17	18	19	21	22	22	23	24	24	25
35	1	2	3	5	6	7	7	8	9	10	11	11	12	13	13	14	14	15	15	17	18	20	21	23	24	25	26	27	28	29	29
40	2	3	4	5	7	8	9	10	11	12	13	13	14	15	15	16	17	17	18	19	21	23	24	26	28	29	30	31	32	33	34
45	2	3	5	6	8	9	10	11	12	13	14	15	16	17	18	18	19	20	20	22	24	26	28	30	32	33	34	35	36	37	38
50	2	4	5	7	8	10	11	13	14	15	16	17	18	19	20	21	21	22	23	25	27	29	31	34	35	37	38	39	41	42	42

All values conform to the international convention (i.e. 0,1 instead of 0.1).

Distribution-Free Tolerance Limits (2 Samples)◊ $\beta_t = 0{,}99$

N_1: sample size of sample one; N_2: sample size of sample two; N^*: number of observations in the 2nd sample which lies between the tolerance limits of l and r with a probability of at least β_t (assuming that both samples are from the same distribution). For definition of l and r see section 25A. The values in the table are those of N^*

$l+r=1$

N_2 \ N_1	2	3	4	5	6	7	8	9	10	11	12	13	14	15	16	17	18	19	20	22	25	30	35	40	45	50	60	70	80	90	100
2	0	0	0	0	0	0	0	0	0	0	0	1	1	1	1	1	1	1	1	1	1	1	1	1	1	1	1	1	1	1	1
3	0	0	0	0	0	1	1	1	1	1	1	1	1	1	1	1	1	1	1	2	2	2	2	2	2	2	2	2	2	2	2
4	0	0	0	1	1	1	1	1	1	2	2	2	2	2	2	2	2	2	2	2	2	2	3	3	3	3	3	3	3	3	3
5	0	0	1	1	1	1	2	2	2	2	2	2	2	3	3	3	3	3	3	3	3	3	3	3	4	4	4	4	4	4	4
6	0	0	1	1	2	2	2	2	3	3	3	3	3	3	3	3	4	4	4	4	4	4	4	4	4	5	5	5	5	5	5
7	0	1	1	2	2	2	3	3	3	3	4	4	4	4	4	4	4	4	4	5	5	5	5	5	5	5	6	6	6	6	6
8	0	1	1	2	3	3	3	4	4	4	4	4	5	5	5	5	5	5	5	5	5	6	6	6	6	6	6	7	7	7	7
9	0	1	2	2	3	3	4	4	4	5	5	5	5	5	6	6	6	6	6	6	6	7	7	7	7	7	7	7	8	8	8
10	0	1	2	3	3	4	4	5	5	5	6	6	6	6	6	6	6	7	7	7	7	7	8	8	8	8	8	8	8	9	9
11	0	1	2	3	4	4	5	5	6	6	6	6	7	7	7	7	7	7	7	8	8	8	8	9	9	9	9	9	9	9	10
12	0	2	3	4	4	5	5	6	6	7	7	7	7	8	8	8	8	8	8	8	9	9	9	10	10	10	10	10	10	10	10
13	1	2	3	4	5	5	6	6	7	7	8	8	8	8	8	9	9	9	9	9	10	10	10	10	11	11	11	11	11	11	11
14	1	2	3	4	5	6	7	7	8	8	8	8	9	9	9	9	10	10	10	10	10	11	11	11	11	12	12	12	12	12	12
15	1	2	4	5	6	6	7	8	8	9	9	9	9	10	10	10	10	10	11	11	11	12	12	12	12	12	13	13	13	13	13
16	1	2	4	5	6	7	8	8	9	9	10	10	10	10	11	11	11	11	11	12	12	12	13	13	13	13	14	14	14	14	14
17	1	3	4	6	7	8	8	9	9	10	10	11	11	11	11	12	12	12	12	12	13	13	14	14	14	14	15	15	15	15	15
18	1	3	5	6	7	8	9	9	10	10	11	11	12	12	12	12	13	13	13	13	14	14	14	15	15	15	15	16	16	16	16
19	1	3	5	6	8	9	9	10	11	11	12	12	12	13	13	13	13	14	14	14	14	15	15	16	16	16	16	17	17	17	17
20	1	3	5	7	8	9	10	11	11	12	12	13	13	13	14	14	14	14	14	15	15	16	16	17	17	17	17	18	18	18	18
21	1	4	6	7	8	10	10	11	12	12	13	13	14	14	14	15	15	15	15	16	16	17	17	17	18	18	18	18	19	19	19
22	1	4	6	8	9	10	11	12	12	13	14	14	14	14	15	15	16	16	16	16	17	17	18	18	19	19	19	19	20	20	20
23	1	4	6	8	9	11	12	12	13	14	14	15	15	15	16	16	16	17	17	17	18	18	19	19	19	20	20	20	20	21	21
25	2	4	7	9	10	12	13	14	14	15	16	16	17	17	17	18	18	18	18	19	19	20	21	21	21	21	22	22	22	23	23
30	2	5	8	11	13	14	15	17	18	18	19	20	20	21	21	21	22	22	22	23	23	24	25	25	26	26	26	27	27	27	27
35	3	7	10	13	15	17	18	20	21	22	22	23	24	24	25	25	26	26	26	27	28	29	29	30	30	31	31	31	32	32	32
40	3	8	11	15	17	19	21	23	24	25	26	27	27	28	28	29	29	30	30	31	32	33	34	34	35	35	36	36	36	37	37
45	4	9	13	17	20	22	24	26	27	28	29	30	31	32	32	33	33	34	34	35	36	37	38	39	39	40	40	41	41	41	42
50	4	10	15	19	22	25	27	29	30	31	33	34	34	35	36	37	37	38	38	39	40	41	42	43	44	44	45	45	46	46	46

$l+r=2$

N_2 \ N_1	3	4	5	6	7	8	9	10	11	12	13	14	15	16	17	18	19	20	21	22	25	30	35	40	45	50	60	70	80	90	100
2	0	0	0	0	0	0	0	0	0	0	0	0	0	0	0	0	0	0	0	0	1	1	1	1	1	1	1	1	1	1	1
3	0	0	0	0	0	0	0	0	0	1	1	1	1	1	1	1	1	1	1	1	1	1	1	2	2	2	2	2	2	2	2
4	0	0	0	0	0	0	1	1	1	1	1	1	1	1	1	2	2	2	2	2	2	2	2	2	2	2	3	3	3	3	3
5	0	0	0	0	1	1	1	1	1	2	2	2	2	2	2	2	2	2	2	2	3	3	3	3	3	3	3	3	4	4	4
6	0	0	0	1	1	1	1	2	2	2	2	2	2	3	3	3	3	3	3	3	3	3	4	4	4	4	4	4	4	5	5
7	0	0	0	1	1	2	2	2	2	3	3	3	3	3	3	3	3	4	4	4	4	4	4	5	5	5	5	5	5	5	5
8	0	0	1	1	2	2	2	3	3	3	3	3	4	4	4	4	4	4	4	4	5	5	5	5	6	6	6	6	6	6	6
9	0	0	1	1	2	2	3	3	3	3	4	4	4	4	5	5	5	5	5	5	5	6	6	6	6	7	7	7	7	7	7
10	0	0	1	2	2	3	3	4	4	4	4	5	5	5	5	5	5	6	6	6	6	7	7	7	7	7	8	8	8	8	8
11	0	1	1	2	3	3	4	4	4	5	5	5	5	6	6	6	6	6	6	7	7	7	8	8	8	8	8	9	9	9	9
12	0	1	2	2	3	4	4	5	5	5	6	6	6	6	6	7	7	7	7	7	8	8	8	9	9	9	9	10	10	10	10
13	0	1	2	3	3	4	4	5	5	6	6	6	7	7	7	7	7	8	8	8	8	9	9	9	10	10	10	10	11	11	11
14	0	1	2	3	4	4	5	5	6	6	7	7	7	8	8	8	8	8	9	9	9	10	10	10	11	11	11	11	12	12	12
15	0	1	2	3	4	5	5	6	6	7	7	8	8	8	8	9	9	9	9	9	10	10	11	11	11	12	12	12	12	13	13
16	0	1	2	3	4	5	6	6	7	7	8	8	8	9	9	9	10	10	10	10	11	11	12	12	12	12	13	13	13	13	14
17	0	1	3	4	5	6	6	7	7	8	8	9	9	9	10	10	10	10	10	11	11	12	12	13	13	13	14	14	14	14	15
18	0	2	3	4	5	6	7	7	8	8	9	9	10	10	10	11	11	11	11	12	12	13	13	14	14	14	15	15	15	15	15
19	0	2	3	4	5	6	7	8	8	9	10	10	10	11	11	11	12	12	12	12	13	13	14	14	15	15	15	16	16	16	16
20	0	2	3	5	6	7	8	8	9	10	10	11	11	11	12	12	12	13	13	13	14	14	15	15	16	16	16	17	17	17	17
21	0	2	3	5	6	7	8	9	10	10	11	11	12	12	12	13	13	13	13	14	14	15	16	16	16	17	17	18	18	18	18
22	0	2	4	5	6	8	8	9	10	10	11	12	12	13	13	13	14	14	14	14	15	16	16	17	17	18	18	18	19	19	19
23	1	2	4	5	7	8	9	10	11	11	12	12	13	13	14	14	14	15	15	15	16	17	17	18	18	18	19	19	20	20	20
25	1	2	4	6	7	9	10	11	12	12	13	14	14	15	15	15	16	16	16	17	17	18	19	19	20	20	21	21	21	22	22
30	1	3	5	7	9	11	12	13	14	15	16	17	17	18	18	19	19	20	20	20	21	22	23	24	24	25	25	26	26	26	26
35	1	4	7	9	11	13	14	16	17	18	19	20	20	21	22	22	23	23	23	24	25	26	27	28	28	29	30	30	31	31	31
40	2	5	8	10	13	15	17	18	20	21	22	23	23	24	25	26	26	27	27	28	29	30	31	32	33	33	34	35	35	35	36
45	2	5	9	12	15	17	19	21	22	23	25	26	27	27	28	29	30	30	31	31	32	34	35	36	37	38	38	39	40	40	40
50	2	6	10	13	16	19	21	23	25	26	28	29	30	31	32	32	33	34	34	34	36	38	39	40	41	42	43	43	44	45	45

$l+r=3$

N_2 \ N_1	4	5	6	7	8	9	10	11	12	13	14	15	16	17	18	19	20	21	22	23	25	30	35	40	45	50	60	70	80	90	100
2	0	0	0	0	0	0	0	0	0	0	0	0	0	0	0	0	0	0	0	0	0	1	1	1	1	1	1	1	1	1	1
3	0	0	0	0	0	0	0	0	0	0	0	0	0	1	1	1	1	1	1	1	1	1	1	1	2	2	2	2	2	2	2
4	0	0	0	0	0	0	0	0	1	1	1	1	1	1	1	1	1	1	1	2	2	2	2	2	2	2	2	2	3	3	3
5	0	0	0	0	0	0	1	1	1	1	1	1	1	2	2	2	2	2	2	2	2	2	3	3	3	3	3	3	3	3	3
6	0	0	0	0	1	1	1	1	1	2	2	2	2	2	2	2	2	2	3	3	3	3	3	3	4	4	4	4	4	4	4
7	0	0	0	0	1	1	1	2	2	2	2	2	2	3	3	3	3	3	3	3	3	4	4	4	4	4	5	5	5	5	5
8	0	0	0	1	1	1	2	2	2	2	3	3	3	3	3	3	4	4	4	4	4	4	5	5	5	5	6	6	6	6	6
9	0	0	0	1	1	2	2	2	3	3	3	3	4	4	4	4	4	4	4	4	5	5	5	6	6	6	6	7	7	7	7
10	0	0	1	1	2	2	2	3	3	3	4	4	4	4	4	5	5	5	5	5	5	6	6	6	7	7	7	7	8	8	8
11	0	0	1	1	2	2	3	3	3	4	4	4	5	5	5	5	5	6	6	6	6	7	7	7	7	8	8	8	8	9	9
12	0	0	1	2	2	3	3	4	4	4	5	5	5	5	6	6	6	6	6	6	7	7	8	8	8	8	9	9	9	9	10
13	0	0	1	2	2	3	3	4	4	5	5	5	6	6	6	6	7	7	7	7	7	8	8	9	9	9	10	10	10	10	10
14	0	0	1	2	3	3	4	4	5	5	6	6	6	7	7	7	7	7	8	8	8	9	9	10	10	10	10	11	11	11	11
15	0	1	1	2	3	4	4	5	5	6	6	6	7	7	7	8	8	8	8	8	9	9	10	10	11	11	11	12	12	12	12
16	0	1	2	2	3	4	5	5	6	6	7	7	7	8	8	8	8	9	9	9	9	10	11	11	11	12	12	12	13	13	13
17	0	1	2	3	4	4	5	6	6	7	7	8	8	8	9	9	9	9	10	10	10	11	11	12	12	13	13	13	14	14	14
18	0	1	2	3	4	5	5	6	7	7	8	8	8	9	9	9	10	10	10	10	11	12	12	13	13	13	14	14	15	15	15
19	0	1	2	3	4	5	6	6	7	8	8	9	9	9	10	10	10	11	11	11	11	12	13	13	14	14	15	15	15	16	16
20	0	1	2	3	4	5	6	7	8	8	9	9	10	10	10	11	11	11	11	12	12	13	14	14	15	15	16	16	16	17	17
21	0	1	2	4	5	6	7	7	8	9	9	10	10	11	11	11	12	12	12	12	13	14	14	15	15	16	16	17	17	17	18
22	0	1	3	4	5	6	7	8	8	9	10	10	11	11	12	12	12	13	13	13	14	15	15	16	16	17	17	18	18	18	19
23	0	1	3	4	5	6	7	8	9	10	10	11	11	12	12	12	13	13	13	14	14	15	16	17	17	17	18	19	19	19	19
25	0	2	3	4	6	7	8	9	10	11	11	12	12	13	13	14	14	14	15	15	16	17	18	18	19	19	20	20	21	21	21
30	0	2	4	6	7	9	10	11	12	13	14	15	15	16	16	17	17	18	18	18	19	20	21	22	23	23	24	25	25	25	26
35	1	3	5	7	9	10	12	13	14	15	16	17	18	19	19	20	20	21	21	22	23	24	25	26	27	27	28	29	30	30	30
40	1	3	6	8	10	12	14	15	17	18	19	20	21	22	22	23	24	24	25	25	26	28	29	30	31	32	33	33	34	34	35
45	1	4	6	9	12	14	16	17	19	20	22	23	24	25	25	26	27	27	28	29	30	32	33	34	35	36	37	38	38	39	39
50	1	4	7	10	13	15	18	20	21	23	24	25	26	27	28	29	30	31	31	32	33	35	37	38	39	40	41	42	43	43	44

All values conform to the international convention (i.e. 0,1 instead of 0.1).

Distribution-Free Tolerance Limits (2 Samples)◊ $\beta_t = 0{,}99$

N_1: sample size of sample one; N_2: sample size of sample two; N^*: number of observations in the 2nd sample which lies between the tolerance limits of l and r with a probability of at least β_t (assuming that both samples are from the same distribution). For definition of l and r see section 25A. The values in the table are those of N^*

$l+r=4$

N_2 \ N_1	5	6	7	8	9	10	11	12	13	14	15	16	17	18	19	20	21	22	23	24	25	30	35	40	45	50	60	70	80	90	100
2	0	0	0	0	0	0	0	0	0	0	0	0	0	0	0	0	0	0	0	0	0	0	0	0	1	1	1	1	1	1	1
3	0	0	0	0	0	0	0	0	0	0	0	0	0	0	0	0	1	1	1	1	1	1	1	1	1	1	1	1	2	2	2
4	0	0	0	0	0	0	0	0	0	0	1	1	1	1	1	1	1	1	1	1	1	1	2	2	2	2	2	2	2	2	2
5	0	0	0	0	0	0	0	1	1	1	1	1	1	1	1	1	1	2	2	2	2	2	2	2	3	3	3	3	3	3	3
6	0	0	0	0	0	0	1	1	1	1	1	1	2	2	2	2	2	2	2	2	2	3	3	3	3	3	4	4	4	4	4
7	0	0	0	0	0	1	1	1	1	2	2	2	2	2	2	2	3	3	3	3	3	3	4	4	4	4	4	5	5	5	5
8	0	0	0	0	1	1	1	2	2	2	2	2	3	3	3	3	3	3	3	3	4	4	4	4	5	5	5	5	6	6	6
9	0	0	0	1	1	1	2	2	2	2	3	3	3	3	3	3	4	4	4	4	4	5	5	5	5	6	6	6	6	7	7
10	0	0	0	1	1	2	2	2	2	3	3	3	3	4	4	4	4	4	4	5	5	5	6	6	6	6	7	7	7	7	8
11	0	0	0	1	1	2	2	3	3	3	3	4	4	4	4	5	5	5	5	5	5	6	6	7	7	7	8	8	8	8	8
12	0	0	1	1	2	2	2	3	3	4	4	4	4	5	5	5	5	5	5	5	5	6	7	7	8	8	8	9	9	9	9
13	0	0	1	1	2	2	3	3	4	4	4	5	5	5	5	6	6	6	6	6	7	7	8	8	8	9	9	9	10	10	10
14	0	0	1	1	2	3	3	4	4	4	5	5	5	6	6	6	6	7	7	7	7	8	8	9	9	10	10	10	11	11	11
15	0	0	1	2	2	3	3	4	4	5	5	6	6	6	7	7	7	7	7	8	8	9	9	10	10	10	11	11	11	12	12
16	0	0	1	2	3	3	4	4	5	5	6	6	6	7	7	7	8	8	8	8	8	9	10	10	11	11	12	12	12	13	13
17	0	0	1	2	3	3	4	5	5	6	6	7	7	7	8	8	8	8	9	9	9	10	11	11	12	12	12	13	13	13	14
18	0	1	1	2	3	4	4	5	6	6	7	7	7	8	8	8	8	9	9	9	10	11	11	12	12	13	13	14	14	14	14
19	0	1	1	2	3	4	5	5	6	7	7	8	8	8	9	9	9	10	10	10	10	11	12	13	13	13	14	15	15	15	15
20	0	1	2	3	3	4	5	6	6	7	8	8	8	9	9	10	10	10	10	11	11	12	13	13	14	14	15	15	16	16	16
21	0	1	2	3	4	5	5	6	7	7	8	8	9	9	10	10	10	11	11	11	12	13	13	14	15	15	16	16	17	17	17
22	0	1	2	3	4	5	6	7	7	8	8	9	9	10	10	11	11	11	12	12	12	13	14	15	15	16	17	17	17	18	18
23	0	1	2	3	4	5	6	7	8	8	9	9	10	10	11	11	12	12	12	13	13	14	15	16	16	17	17	18	18	19	19
25	0	1	2	4	5	6	7	8	8	9	10	10	11	12	12	12	13	13	14	14	14	15	16	17	18	18	19	20	20	20	21
30	0	1	3	4	6	7	8	9	10	11	12	13	14	14	15	15	16	16	16	17	17	19	20	21	22	22	23	24	24	25	25
35	0	2	4	5	7	9	10	11	13	14	14	15	16	17	18	18	19	19	20	20	21	22	24	25	26	26	27	28	29	29	30
40	0	2	4	6	8	10	12	13	15	16	17	18	19	20	20	21	22	22	23	23	24	26	27	29	29	30	31	32	33	34	34
45	1	3	5	7	10	12	13	15	17	18	19	20	21	22	23	24	25	25	26	26	27	29	31	32	33	34	36	37	37	38	38
50	1	3	6	8	11	13	15	17	19	20	22	23	24	25	26	27	28	28	29	30	30	33	35	36	37	38	40	41	42	42	43

$l+r=5$

N_2 \ N_1	6	7	8	9	10	11	12	13	14	15	16	17	18	19	20	21	22	23	24	25	30	35	40	45	50	60	70	80	90	100	120
2	0	0	0	0	0	0	0	0	0	0	0	0	0	0	0	0	0	0	0	0	0	0	0	0	0	1	1	1	1	1	1
3	0	0	0	0	0	0	0	0	0	0	0	0	0	0	0	0	0	0	0	0	1	1	1	1	1	1	1	1	1	2	2
4	0	0	0	0	0	0	0	0	0	0	0	0	1	1	1	1	1	1	1	1	1	1	2	2	2	2	2	2	2	2	2
5	0	0	0	0	0	0	0	0	0	1	1	1	1	1	1	1	1	1	1	1	2	2	2	2	2	3	3	3	3	3	3
6	0	0	0	0	0	0	0	1	1	1	1	1	1	1	2	2	2	2	2	2	2	3	3	3	3	3	4	4	4	4	4
7	0	0	0	0	0	0	1	1	1	1	1	2	2	2	2	2	2	2	2	2	3	3	3	4	4	4	4	5	5	5	5
8	0	0	0	0	0	1	1	1	1	2	2	2	2	2	2	3	3	3	3	3	3	4	4	4	5	5	5	5	5	6	6
9	0	0	0	0	1	1	1	1	2	2	2	2	2	3	3	3	3	3	3	4	4	4	5	5	5	6	6	6	6	6	7
10	0	0	0	0	1	1	1	2	2	2	3	3	3	3	3	4	4	4	4	4	5	5	5	6	6	6	7	7	7	7	8
11	0	0	0	1	1	1	2	2	2	3	3	3	3	4	4	4	4	4	5	5	5	6	6	7	7	7	7	8	8	8	8
12	0	0	0	1	1	2	2	2	3	3	3	4	4	4	4	5	5	5	5	5	6	6	7	7	8	8	8	9	9	9	9
13	0	0	0	1	1	2	2	3	3	3	4	4	4	5	5	5	5	5	6	6	7	7	8	8	8	9	9	9	10	10	10
14	0	0	1	1	2	2	3	3	3	4	4	5	5	5	5	6	6	6	6	6	7	8	8	9	9	10	10	10	10	11	11
15	0	0	1	1	2	2	3	3	4	4	5	5	5	6	6	6	6	7	7	7	8	8	9	9	10	10	11	11	11	12	12
16	0	0	1	1	2	3	3	4	4	5	5	5	6	6	6	7	7	7	7	8	8	9	10	10	11	11	12	12	12	12	13
17	0	0	1	2	2	3	3	4	5	5	5	6	6	7	7	7	7	8	8	8	9	10	10	11	11	12	12	13	13	13	14
18	0	0	1	2	2	3	4	4	5	5	6	6	7	7	7	8	8	8	8	9	10	11	11	12	12	13	13	14	14	14	14
19	0	0	1	2	3	3	4	5	5	6	6	7	7	7	8	8	8	9	9	9	10	11	12	12	13	13	14	14	15	15	15
20	0	0	1	2	3	4	4	5	6	6	7	7	8	8	8	9	9	9	10	10	11	12	13	13	14	14	15	15	16	16	16
21	0	0	1	2	3	4	5	5	6	7	7	8	8	8	9	9	10	10	10	10	12	13	13	14	14	15	16	16	16	17	17
22	0	1	1	2	3	4	5	6	6	7	7	8	9	9	9	10	10	10	11	11	12	13	14	15	15	16	16	17	17	18	18
23	0	1	2	2	3	4	5	6	7	7	8	8	9	9	10	10	11	11	11	12	13	14	15	15	16	17	17	18	18	18	19
25	0	1	2	3	4	5	6	7	7	8	9	9	10	10	11	11	12	12	12	13	14	15	16	17	17	18	19	19	20	20	21
30	0	1	2	4	5	6	7	8	9	10	11	12	12	13	13	14	14	15	15	16	17	19	20	21	21	22	23	24	24	24	25
35	0	1	3	4	6	7	9	10	11	12	13	14	15	15	16	17	17	18	18	19	21	22	23	24	25	26	27	28	28	29	30
40	0	2	3	5	7	9	10	12	13	14	15	16	17	18	19	19	20	21	21	22	24	26	27	28	29	30	31	32	33	33	34
45	0	2	4	6	8	10	12	13	15	16	17	18	19	20	21	22	23	23	24	25	27	29	31	32	33	34	36	36	37	38	38
50	1	2	5	7	9	11	13	15	17	18	19	21	22	23	24	25	26	26	27	28	31	33	34	36	37	38	40	41	41	42	43

$l+r=6$

N_2 \ N_1	8	9	10	11	12	13	14	15	16	17	18	19	20	21	22	23	24	25	26	27	30	35	40	45	50	60	70	80	90	100	120
2	0	0	0	0	0	0	0	0	0	0	0	0	0	0	0	0	0	0	0	0	0	0	0	0	0	0	1	1	1	1	1
3	0	0	0	0	0	0	0	0	0	0	0	0	0	0	0	0	0	0	0	0	0	1	1	1	1	1	1	1	1	1	2
4	0	0	0	0	0	0	0	0	0	0	0	0	0	1	1	1	1	1	1	1	1	1	1	1	2	2	2	2	2	2	2
5	0	0	0	0	0	0	0	0	0	1	1	1	1	1	1	1	1	1	1	1	1	2	2	2	2	2	3	3	3	3	3
6	0	0	0	0	0	0	0	1	1	1	1	1	1	1	1	1	2	2	2	2	2	2	3	3	3	3	3	4	4	4	4
7	0	0	0	0	0	0	1	1	1	1	1	1	2	2	2	2	2	2	2	2	3	3	3	3	4	4	4	4	4	5	5
8	0	0	0	0	0	1	1	1	1	2	2	2	2	2	2	2	3	3	3	3	3	3	4	4	4	5	5	5	5	5	6
9	0	0	0	0	1	1	1	1	2	2	2	2	2	3	3	3	3	3	3	3	4	4	4	4	4	5	6	6	6	6	6
10	0	0	0	1	1	1	1	2	2	2	2	3	3	3	3	3	3	4	4	4	4	5	5	5	6	6	6	7	7	7	7
11	0	0	0	1	1	1	2	2	2	3	3	3	3	3	4	4	4	4	4	4	5	5	6	6	6	7	7	7	8	8	8
12	0	0	1	1	1	2	2	2	3	3	3	3	4	4	4	4	4	5	5	5	5	6	6	7	7	8	8	8	8	9	9
13	0	0	1	1	2	2	2	3	3	3	4	4	4	4	5	5	5	5	5	6	6	7	7	7	8	8	9	9	9	10	10
14	0	0	1	1	2	2	3	3	3	4	4	4	5	5	5	5	6	6	6	6	7	7	8	8	9	9	10	10	10	10	11
15	0	0	1	1	2	2	3	3	4	4	4	5	5	5	6	6	6	6	6	7	7	8	8	9	9	10	10	11	11	11	12
16	0	1	1	2	2	3	3	4	4	4	5	5	5	6	6	6	7	7	7	7	8	8	9	10	10	11	11	11	12	12	12
17	0	1	1	2	2	3	3	4	4	5	5	6	6	6	7	7	7	7	8	8	8	9	10	10	11	11	12	12	13	13	13
18	0	1	1	2	3	3	4	4	5	5	6	6	6	7	7	7	8	8	8	8	9	10	10	11	11	12	13	13	13	14	14
19	0	1	1	2	3	3	4	5	5	6	6	6	7	7	7	8	8	8	9	9	10	10	11	12	12	13	13	14	14	15	15
20	0	1	2	2	3	4	4	5	5	6	6	7	7	8	8	8	9	9	9	9	10	11	12	12	13	14	14	15	15	15	16
21	0	1	2	3	3	4	5	5	6	6	7	7	8	8	8	9	9	9	10	10	11	12	12	13	14	14	15	16	16	16	17
22	0	1	2	3	3	4	5	6	6	7	7	8	8	9	9	9	10	10	10	11	11	12	13	14	14	15	16	16	17	17	18
23	0	1	2	3	4	4	5	6	7	7	8	8	9	9	9	10	10	11	11	11	12	13	14	15	15	16	17	17	18	18	18
25	0	1	2	3	4	5	6	7	7	8	8	9	10	10	10	11	11	12	12	12	13	14	15	16	17	18	18	19	19	20	20
30	1	2	3	4	5	6	7	8	9	10	11	11	12	12	13	13	14	14	15	15	16	18	19	20	20	21	22	23	23	24	25
35	1	2	4	5	6	8	9	10	11	12	13	13	14	15	15	16	17	17	18	18	19	21	22	23	24	25	26	27	28	28	29
40	1	3	4	6	8	9	10	12	13	14	15	16	16	17	18	19	19	20	20	21	22	24	26	27	28	29	30	31	32	33	33
45	2	3	5	7	9	10	12	13	15	16	17	18	19	20	20	21	22	23	23	24	25	27	29	30	32	33	34	35	36	37	38
50	2	4	6	8	10	12	13	15	16	18	19	20	21	22	23	24	25	25	26	27	28	31	33	34	35	37	39	40	40	41	42

All values conform to the international convention (i.e. 0,1 instead of 0.1).

Distribution-Free Tolerance Limits (2 Samples)◊ $\beta_t = 0{,}99$

N_1: sample size of sample one; N_2: sample size of sample two; N^*: number of observations in the 2nd sample which lies between the tolerance limits of l and r with a probability of at least β_t (assuming that both samples are from the same distribution). For definition of l and r see section 25A. The values in the table are those of N^*

$l+r=8$

N_2 \ N_1	10	11	12	13	14	15	16	17	18	19	20	21	22	23	24	25	26	27	30	35	40	45	50	60	70	80	90	100	120	140	160
2	0	0	0	0	0	0	0	0	0	0	0	0	0	0	0	0	0	0	0	0	0	0	0	0	0	0	1	1	1	1	1
3	0	0	0	0	0	0	0	0	0	0	0	0	0	0	0	0	0	0	0	0	1	1	1	1	1	1	1	1	1	1	2
4	0	0	0	0	0	0	0	0	0	0	0	0	0	0	0	0	0	0	1	1	1	1	1	1	2	2	2	2	2	2	2
5	0	0	0	0	0	0	0	0	0	0	0	0	1	1	1	1	1	1	1	1	2	2	2	2	2	2	3	3	3	3	3
6	0	0	0	0	0	0	0	0	0	1	1	1	1	1	1	1	1	1	1	2	2	2	2	3	3	3	3	3	4	4	4
7	0	0	0	0	0	0	0	1	1	1	1	1	1	1	1	1	2	2	2	2	3	3	3	3	4	4	4	4	4	5	5
8	0	0	0	0	0	0	1	1	1	1	1	1	2	2	2	2	2	2	2	3	3	3	4	4	4	5	5	5	5	5	6
9	0	0	0	0	0	1	1	1	1	1	2	2	2	2	2	2	2	3	3	3	4	4	4	5	5	5	6	6	6	6	6
10	0	0	0	0	1	1	1	1	1	2	2	2	2	2	3	3	3	3	3	4	4	5	5	5	6	6	6	7	7	7	7
11	0	0	0	0	1	1	1	1	2	2	2	2	3	3	3	3	3	3	4	4	5	5	6	6	7	7	7	7	8	8	8
12	0	0	0	1	1	1	1	2	2	2	3	3	3	3	3	4	4	4	4	5	6	6	6	7	7	8	8	8	9	9	9
13	0	0	0	1	1	1	2	2	2	3	3	3	3	4	4	4	4	4	5	6	6	7	7	8	8	8	9	9	9	10	10
14	0	0	0	1	1	2	2	2	3	3	3	3	4	4	4	4	5	5	5	6	7	7	8	8	9	9	10	10	10	11	11
15	0	0	1	1	1	2	2	3	3	3	4	4	4	4	5	5	5	5	6	7	7	8	8	9	10	10	10	11	11	11	12
16	0	0	1	1	2	2	2	3	3	4	4	4	4	5	5	5	6	6	6	7	8	9	9	10	10	11	11	11	12	12	12
17	0	0	1	1	2	2	3	3	3	4	4	5	5	5	5	6	6	6	7	8	9	9	10	10	11	12	12	12	13	13	13
18	0	0	1	1	2	2	3	3	4	4	5	5	5	6	6	6	6	7	7	8	9	10	10	11	12	12	13	13	14	14	14
19	0	0	1	1	2	3	3	4	4	4	5	5	6	6	6	7	7	7	8	9	10	10	11	12	13	13	13	14	14	15	15
20	0	0	1	2	2	3	3	4	4	5	5	6	6	6	7	7	7	8	8	10	10	11	12	13	13	14	14	15	15	16	16
21	0	1	1	2	2	3	4	4	5	5	6	6	6	7	7	8	8	8	9	10	11	12	12	13	14	15	15	15	16	16	17
22	0	1	1	2	3	3	4	4	5	5	6	6	7	7	8	8	8	9	10	11	12	12	13	14	15	15	16	16	17	17	18
23	0	1	1	2	3	3	4	5	5	6	6	7	7	8	8	8	9	9	10	11	12	13	14	15	16	16	17	17	18	18	19
25	0	1	2	2	3	4	5	5	6	6	7	8	8	9	9	9	10	10	11	12	14	14	15	16	17	18	18	19	19	20	20
30	0	1	2	3	4	5	6	7	7	8	9	9	10	11	11	12	12	13	14	15	17	18	19	20	21	22	22	23	24	24	25
35	1	2	3	4	5	6	7	8	9	10	11	11	12	13	13	14	14	15	16	18	20	21	22	24	25	26	26	27	28	29	29
40	1	2	3	5	6	7	8	9	11	12	12	13	14	15	16	16	17	17	19	21	23	24	26	27	29	30	31	31	32	33	34
45	1	2	4	5	7	8	10	11	12	13	14	15	16	17	18	19	19	20	22	24	26	28	29	31	33	34	35	35	37	37	38
50	1	3	5	6	8	9	11	12	14	15	16	17	18	19	20	21	22	22	24	27	29	31	33	35	36	38	39	40	41	42	42

$l+r=10$

N_2 \ N_1	12	13	14	15	16	17	18	19	20	21	22	23	24	25	26	27	28	29	30	35	40	45	50	60	70	80	90	100	120	140	160
2	0	0	0	0	0	0	0	0	0	0	0	0	0	0	0	0	0	0	0	0	0	0	0	0	0	0	0	0	1	1	1
3	0	0	0	0	0	0	0	0	0	0	0	0	0	0	0	0	0	0	0	0	0	0	1	1	1	1	1	1	1	1	1
4	0	0	0	0	0	0	0	0	0	0	0	0	0	0	0	0	0	0	0	1	1	1	1	1	1	2	2	2	2	2	2
5	0	0	0	0	0	0	0	0	0	0	0	0	0	0	0	1	1	1	1	1	1	1	2	2	2	2	2	2	3	3	3
6	0	0	0	0	0	0	0	0	0	0	0	0	1	1	1	1	1	1	1	1	2	2	2	2	3	3	3	3	3	4	4
7	0	0	0	0	0	0	0	0	0	1	1	1	1	1	1	1	1	1	1	2	2	2	3	3	3	4	4	4	4	4	5
8	0	0	0	0	0	0	0	0	1	1	1	1	1	1	1	2	2	2	2	2	3	3	3	4	4	4	4	5	5	5	5
9	0	0	0	0	0	0	0	1	1	1	1	1	1	2	2	2	2	2	2	3	3	4	4	4	5	5	5	5	6	6	6
10	0	0	0	0	0	0	1	1	1	1	1	2	2	2	2	2	2	3	3	3	4	4	4	5	5	6	6	6	7	7	7
11	0	0	0	0	0	1	1	1	1	2	2	2	2	2	2	3	3	3	3	4	4	5	5	6	6	6	7	7	7	8	8
12	0	0	0	0	1	1	1	1	2	2	2	2	2	3	3	3	3	3	3	4	5	5	6	6	7	7	7	8	8	8	9
13	0	0	0	0	1	1	1	2	2	2	2	3	3	3	3	3	4	4	4	5	5	6	6	7	7	8	8	8	9	9	10
14	0	0	0	0	1	1	1	2	2	2	3	3	3	3	4	4	4	4	4	5	6	6	7	8	8	9	9	9	10	10	10
15	0	0	0	1	1	1	2	2	2	3	3	3	3	4	4	4	4	5	5	6	6	7	7	8	9	9	10	10	11	11	11
16	0	0	0	1	1	1	2	2	3	3	3	3	4	4	4	5	5	5	5	6	7	8	8	9	10	10	10	11	11	12	12
17	0	0	0	1	1	2	2	2	3	3	3	4	4	4	5	5	5	5	6	7	7	8	9	10	10	11	11	12	12	13	13
18	0	0	1	1	1	2	2	3	3	3	4	4	4	5	5	5	6	6	6	7	8	9	9	10	11	12	12	12	13	13	14
19	0	0	1	1	2	2	2	3	3	4	4	4	5	5	5	6	6	6	7	8	9	9	10	11	12	12	13	13	14	14	15
20	0	0	1	1	2	2	3	3	4	4	4	5	5	6	6	6	6	7	7	8	9	10	11	12	12	13	14	14	15	15	15
21	0	0	1	1	2	2	3	3	4	4	5	5	6	6	6	7	7	7	7	9	10	11	11	12	13	14	14	15	15	16	16
22	0	0	1	1	2	3	3	4	4	5	5	5	6	6	7	7	7	8	8	9	10	11	12	13	14	15	15	16	16	17	17
23	0	0	1	2	2	3	3	4	4	5	5	6	6	7	7	7	8	8	8	10	11	12	13	14	15	15	16	16	17	18	18
25	0	1	1	2	2	3	4	4	5	5	6	6	7	7	8	8	9	9	9	11	12	13	14	15	16	17	17	18	19	19	20
30	0	1	2	2	3	4	5	6	6	7	8	8	9	9	10	10	11	11	12	13	15	16	17	19	20	21	21	22	23	24	24
35	0	1	2	3	4	5	6	7	8	8	9	10	11	11	12	12	13	13	14	16	18	19	20	22	23	24	25	26	27	28	28
40	1	1	3	4	5	6	7	8	9	10	11	12	12	13	14	14	15	16	16	19	21	22	23	26	27	28	29	30	31	32	33
45	1	2	3	4	6	7	8	9	10	11	12	13	14	15	16	16	17	18	19	21	23	25	27	29	31	32	33	34	35	36	37
50	1	2	4	5	6	8	9	10	12	13	14	15	16	17	18	19	19	20	21	24	26	28	30	33	34	36	37	38	40	41	41

$l+r=12$

N_2 \ N_1	15	16	17	18	19	20	21	22	23	24	25	26	27	28	29	30	31	32	33	35	40	45	50	60	70	80	90	100	120	140	160
2	0	0	0	0	0	0	0	0	0	0	0	0	0	0	0	0	0	0	0	0	0	0	0	0	0	0	0	0	0	1	1
3	0	0	0	0	0	0	0	0	0	0	0	0	0	0	0	0	0	0	0	0	0	0	0	1	1	1	1	1	1	1	1
4	0	0	0	0	0	0	0	0	0	0	0	0	0	0	0	0	0	0	0	0	0	1	1	1	1	1	2	2	2	2	2
5	0	0	0	0	0	0	0	0	0	0	0	0	0	0	0	0	0	0	1	1	1	1	1	2	2	2	2	2	3	3	3
6	0	0	0	0	0	0	0	0	0	0	0	0	0	1	1	1	1	1	1	1	1	2	2	2	2	3	3	3	3	3	4
7	0	0	0	0	0	0	0	0	0	0	1	1	1	1	1	1	1	1	1	1	2	2	2	3	3	3	3	4	4	4	4
8	0	0	0	0	0	0	0	0	1	1	1	1	1	1	1	1	1	2	2	2	2	3	3	3	4	4	4	4	5	5	5
9	0	0	0	0	0	0	0	1	1	1	1	1	1	1	2	2	2	2	2	2	3	3	3	4	4	5	5	5	5	6	6
10	0	0	0	0	0	0	1	1	1	1	1	1	2	2	2	2	2	2	2	3	3	4	4	4	5	5	6	6	6	7	7
11	0	0	0	0	0	1	1	1	1	1	2	2	2	2	2	2	2	3	3	3	4	4	4	5	6	6	6	7	7	7	8
12	0	0	0	0	1	1	1	1	1	2	2	2	2	2	3	3	3	3	3	3	4	5	5	6	6	7	7	7	8	8	8
13	0	0	0	0	1	1	1	1	1	2	2	2	3	3	3	3	3	3	4	4	5	5	6	6	7	7	8	8	9	9	9
14	0	0	0	1	1	1	1	2	2	2	2	3	3	3	3	3	4	4	4	4	5	6	6	7	8	8	8	9	9	10	10
15	0	0	0	1	1	1	2	2	2	2	3	3	3	3	4	4	4	4	4	5	6	6	7	8	8	9	9	10	10	11	11
16	0	0	0	1	1	1	2	2	2	3	3	3	3	4	4	4	4	5	5	5	6	7	7	8	9	9	10	10	11	11	12
17	0	0	1	1	1	2	2	2	3	3	3	4	4	4	4	5	5	5	5	6	7	7	8	9	10	10	11	11	12	12	12
18	0	0	1	1	1	2	2	3	3	3	4	4	4	4	5	5	5	5	6	6	7	8	8	9	10	11	11	12	12	13	13
19	0	0	1	1	2	2	2	3	3	3	4	4	4	5	5	5	6	6	6	7	8	8	9	10	11	12	12	13	13	14	14
20	0	0	1	1	2	2	3	3	3	4	4	4	5	5	5	6	6	6	6	7	8	9	10	11	12	12	13	13	14	15	15
21	0	0	1	1	2	2	3	3	4	4	4	5	5	5	6	6	6	7	7	7	9	9	10	11	12	13	14	14	15	15	16
22	0	1	1	2	2	2	3	3	4	4	5	5	5	6	6	6	7	7	7	8	9	10	11	12	13	14	14	15	16	16	17
23	0	1	1	2	2	3	3	4	4	5	5	5	6	6	7	7	7	7	8	8	10	11	11	13	14	14	15	16	16	17	18
25	0	1	1	2	2	3	4	4	5	5	6	6	6	7	7	8	8	8	9	9	11	12	13	14	15	16	17	17	18	19	19
30	1	1	2	3	3	4	5	5	6	7	7	8	8	9	9	10	10	10	11	12	13	14	16	17	19	20	20	21	22	23	23
35	1	2	2	3	4	5	6	7	7	8	9	9	10	10	11	12	12	13	13	14	16	17	18	20	22	23	24	25	26	27	28
40	1	2	3	4	5	6	7	8	9	9	10	11	12	12	13	14	14	15	15	16	18	20	22	24	25	27	28	29	30	31	32
45	1	2	4	5	6	7	8	9	10	11	12	13	13	14	15	16	16	17	17	19	21	23	25	27	29	31	32	33	34	35	36
50	2	3	4	5	7	8	9	10	11	12	13	14	15	16	17	17	18	19	20	21	24	26	28	30	33	34	36	37	38	39	40

All values conform to the international convention (i.e. 0,1 instead of 0.1).

Distribution-Free Tolerance Limits (2 Samples)[◊]

N_1: sample size of sample one; N_2: sample size of sample two; N_1 is given in the table such that with probability at least β_t the 2nd sample belongs to the same distribution as the 1st sample, provided N^* values lie between the tolerance limits l and r of the 1st sample. $N_2 = 1, 2$ and 3; $N^* = 1, 2$ and 3

β_t	0,50	0,75	0,80	0,90	0,95	0,99	0,50	0,75	0,80	0,90	0,95	0,99	0,50	0,75	0,80	0,90	0,95	0,99
$l+r$	$N_2=1;N^*=1$						$N_2=2;N^*=1$						$N_2=2;N^*=2$					
1	1	3	4	9	19	99	1	2	2	3	5	13	2	6	8	18	38	198
2	3	7	9	19	39	199	2	4	4	7	10	23	6	14	18	38	78	398
3	5	11	14	29	59	299	4	6	7	10	14	34	9	21	27	57	117	597
4	7	15	19	39	79	399	5	8	9	13	19	44	13	29	37	77	157	797
5	9	19	24	49	99	499	7	10	11	16	23	54	16	36	46	96	196	996
6	11	23	29	59	119	599	8	12	13	19	28	64	19	44	56	116	236	1196
7	13	27	34	69	139	699	10	14	16	23	32	74	23	51	65	135	275	1395
8	15	31	39	79	159	799	11	16	18	26	37	84	26	59	75	155	315	1595
9	17	35	44	89	179	899	12	18	20	29	41	94	30	66	84	174	354	1794
10	19	39	49	99	199	999	14	20	22	32	46	104	33	74	94	194	394	1994
11	21	43	54	109	219	1099	15	22	25	35	50	114	37	81	103	213	433	2193
12	23	47	59	119	239	1199	17	24	27	38	55	124	40	89	113	233	473	2393
13	25	51	64	129	259	1299	18	26	29	42	59	134	43	96	122	252	512	2592
14	27	55	69	139	279	1399	19	28	31	45	64	144	47	103	132	272	552	2792
15	29	59	74	149	299	1499	21	30	34	48	68	154	50	111	141	291	591	2991
16	31	63	79	159	319	1599	22	32	36	51	73	164	54	118	151	311	631	3191
17	33	67	84	169	339	1699	24	34	38	54	77	174	57	126	160	330	670	3390
18	35	71	89	179	359	1799	25	36	40	57	82	184	60	133	169	350	710	3590
19	37	75	94	189	379	1899	27	38	43	61	86	194	64	141	179	369	749	3789
20	39	79	99	199	399	1999	28	40	45	64	91	204	67	148	188	389	789	3989
21	41	83	104	209	419	2099	29	42	47	67	95	214	71	156	198	408	828	4188
22	43	87	109	219	439	2199	31	44	49	70	100	224	74	163	207	428	868	4388
23	45	91	114	229	459	2299	32	46	52	73	104	234	78	171	217	447	907	4587
24	47	95	119	239	479	2399	34	48	54	76	109	244	81	178	226	467	947	4787
25	49	99	124	249	499	2499	35	50	56	80	113	254	84	186	236	486	986	4986
26	51	103	129	259	519	2599	36	52	58	83	117	264	88	193	245	506	1026	5186
27	53	107	134	269	539	2699	38	54	60	86	122	274	91	201	255	525	1065	5385
28	55	111	139	279	559	2799	39	56	63	89	126	284	95	208	264	545	1105	5585
29	57	115	144	289	579	2899	41	58	65	92	131	294	98	215	274	564	1144	5784
30	59	119	149	299	599	2999	42	60	67	95	135	304	101	223	283	584	1184	5984
31	61	123	154	309	619	3099	44	62	69	99	140	314	105	230	293	603	1223	6183
32	63	127	159	319	639	3199	45	64	72	102	144	324	108	238	302	623	1263	6383
33	65	131	164	329	659	3299	46	66	74	105	149	334	112	245	312	642	1302	6582
34	67	135	169	339	679	3399	48	68	76	108	153	344	115	253	321	662	1342	6782
35	69	139	174	349	699	3499	49	70	78	111	158	354	118	260	331	681	1381	6981
36	71	143	179	359	719	3599	51	72	81	114	162	364	122	268	340	701	1421	7181
37	73	147	184	369	739	3699	52	74	83	118	167	374	125	275	349	720	1460	7380
38	75	151	189	379	759	3799	53	76	85	121	171	384	129	283	359	739	1500	7580
39	77	155	194	389	779	3899	55	78	87	124	176	394	132	290	368	759	1539	7779
40	79	159	199	399	799	3999	56	80	90	127	180	404	136	298	378	778	1579	7979
41	81	163	204	409	819	4099	58	82	92	130	185	414	139	305	387	798	1618	8178
42	83	167	209	419	839	4199	59	84	94	133	189	424	142	312	397	817	1658	8378
43	85	171	214	429	859	4299	61	86	96	137	194	434	146	320	406	837	1697	8577
44	87	175	219	439	879	4399	62	88	98	140	198	444	149	327	416	856	1737	8777
45	89	179	224	449	899	4499	63	90	101	143	202	454	153	335	425	876	1776	8976
46	91	183	229	459	919	4599	65	92	103	146	207	464	156	342	435	895	1816	9176
47	93	187	234	469	939	4699	66	94	105	149	211	474	159	350	444	915	1855	9375
48	95	191	239	479	959	4799	68	96	107	152	216	484	163	357	454	934	1895	9575
49	97	195	244	489	979	4899	69	98	110	156	220	494	166	365	463	954	1934	9774
50	99	199	249	499	999	4999	70	100	112	159	225	504	170	372	473	973	1974	9974
$l+r$	$N_2=3;N^*=1$						$N_2=3;N^*=2$						$N_2=3;N^*=3$					
1	–	1	2	2	3	7	1	2	3	6	9	22	3	9	12	27	57	297
2	2	2	3	5	6	12	3	6	7	11	17	40	8	20	26	56	116	596
3	3	5	5	7	9	17	6	9	11	16	24	57	13	31	40	85	175	895
4	5	6	7	8	12	21	8	12	14	21	32	74	18	42	54	114	234	1194
5	6	8	9	11	15	26	9	15	18	26	39	91	23	53	68	143	293	1493
6	7	10	10	14	17	31	11	18	21	32	46	109	28	64	82	172	352	1792
7	9	11	12	16	20	35	14	21	25	37	54	126	32	75	96	201	411	2091
8	10	13	14	18	23	40	16	25	28	42	61	143	37	86	110	230	470	2390
9	11	14	16	20	26	45	18	28	32	47	69	160	42	97	124	259	529	2689
10	12	16	17	22	28	49	20	31	35	52	76	177	47	108	138	288	588	2988
11	14	18	19	24	31	54	22	34	39	57	83	194	52	119	152	317	647	3287
12	15	19	21	26	34	59	24	37	42	62	91	211	57	130	166	346	706	3586
13	16	21	22	29	36	63	26	40	45	67	98	228	62	141	180	375	765	3885
14	17	22	24	31	39	68	28	43	49	73	106	245	66	152	194	404	824	4184
15	19	24	26	33	42	73	30	46	52	78	113	262	71	163	208	433	883	4483
16	20	25	28	35	45	77	32	49	56	83	120	278	76	173	222	462	942	4782
17	21	27	29	37	47	82	34	52	59	88	128	295	81	184	236	491	1001	5081
18	22	29	31	39	50	87	36	55	63	93	135	312	86	195	250	520	1060	5380
19	24	30	33	42	53	91	38	58	66	98	143	329	91	206	264	549	1119	5679
20	25	32	34	44	55	96	40	61	70	103	150	346	95	217	278	578	1178	5978
21	26	33	36	46	58	101	42	64	73	108	157	363	100	228	291	607	1237	6277
22	27	35	38	48	61	105	44	67	77	113	165	380	105	239	305	636	1296	6576
23	29	37	40	50	64	110	46	70	80	118	172	397	110	250	319	665	1355	6875
24	30	38	41	52	66	114	48	74	84	124	179	414	115	261	333	694	1414	7174
25	31	40	43	54	69	119	50	77	88	129	187	431	120	272	347	723	1473	7473
26	33	41	45	57	72	124	52	80	91	134	194	448	125	283	361	752	1532	7772
27	34	43	46	59	74	128	54	83	94	139	202	465	129	294	375	781	1591	8071
28	35	45	48	61	77	133	56	86	98	144	209	482	134	305	389	810	1650	8370
29	36	46	50	63	80	138	58	89	101	149	216	499	139	316	403	839	1709	8669
30	38	48	51	65	83	142	60	92	105	154	224	516	144	327	417	868	1768	8968
31	39	49	53	67	85	147	62	95	108	159	231	533	149	338	431	897	1827	9267
32	40	51	55	70	88	152	64	98	112	164	239	550	154	348	445	926	1886	9566
33	41	52	57	72	91	156	66	101	115	170	246	567	158	359	459	955	1945	9865
34	43	54	58	74	93	161	68	104	119	175	253	584	163	370	473	984	2004	10164
35	44	56	60	76	96	166	70	107	122	180	261	601	168	381	487	1013	2063	10463
36	45	57	62	78	99	170	72	110	126	185	268	618	173	392	501	1042	2122	10762
37	46	59	63	80	102	175	74	113	129	190	276	635	178	403	515	1071	2181	11061
38	48	60	65	83	104	179	76	116	133	195	283	652	183	414	529	1100	2240	11360
39	49	62	67	85	107	184	78	120	136	200	290	669	188	425	543	1129	2299	11659
40	50	64	69	87	110	189	80	123	140	205	298	686	192	436	557	1158	2358	11958
41	51	65	70	89	112	193	82	126	143	210	305	703	197	447	570	1187	2417	12257
42	53	67	72	91	115	198	84	129	147	216	312	720	202	458	584	1216	2476	12556
43	54	68	74	93	118	203	86	132	150	221	320	737	207	469	598	1244	2535	12855
44	55	70	75	95	121	207	88	135	153	226	327	754	212	480	612	1273	2594	13154
45	56	72	77	98	123	212	90	138	157	231	335	771	217	491	626	1302	2653	13453
46	58	73	79	100	126	217	92	141	160	236	342	788	221	502	640	1331	2712	13752
47	59	75	81	102	129	221	94	144	164	241	349	805	226	513	654	1360	2771	14051
48	60	76	82	104	131	226	96	147	167	246	357	822	231	523	668	1389	2830	14350
49	61	78	84	106	134	231	98	150	171	251	364	839	236	534	682	1418	2889	14649
50	63	79	86	108	137	235	100	153	174	256	372	856	241	545	696	1447	2948	14948

All values conform to the international convention (i.e. 0,1 instead of 0.1).

Significance Limits for the Fourfold Table Test*

x_1	N_1-x_1	N_1
x_2	N_2-x_2	N_2
X	$N-X$	N

$N=N_1+N_2$
$X=x_1+x_2$
$N_1 \leq N_2$
$x_1 \leq N_1-x_1$

For explanation see page 151

N_1	x_1	2α = 0,20	2α = 0,10	2α = 0,05	2α = 0,02	2α = 0,01	2α = 0,002
		$N=8$					
4	0	•–3	•–4	•–4	•–•	•–•	•–•
	1	•–5	•–•	•–•	•–•	•–•	•–•
	2	•–•	•–•	•–•	•–•	•–•	•–•
		$N=9$					
4	0	•–4	•–4	•–5	•–5	•–•	•–•
	1	•–6	•–6	•–•	•–•	•–•	•–•
	2	•–•	•–•	•–•	•–•	•–•	•–•
		$N=10$					
4	0	•–4	•–5	•–5	•–6	•–6	•–•
	1	•–7	•–7	•–•	•–•	•–•	•–•
	2	•–•	•–•	•–•	•–•	•–•	•–•
5	0	•–3	•–4	•–4	•–5	•–5	•–•
	1	•–6	•–6	•–6	•–•	•–•	•–•
	2	•–7	•–•	•–•	•–•	•–•	•–•
		$N=11$					
4	0	•–5	•–5	•–6	•–7	•–7	•–•
	1	•–7	•–8	•–8	•–•	•–•	•–•
	2	•–•	•–•	•–•	•–•	•–•	•–•
5	0	•–4	•–4	•–5	•–6	•–6	•–•
	1	•–6	•–7	•–7	•–•	•–•	•–•
	2	•–8	•–•	•–•	•–•	•–•	•–•
		$N=12$					
4	0	•–5	•–6	•–7	•–8	•–8	•–•
	1	•–8	•–9	•–9	•–•	•–•	•–•
	2	2–10	•–•	•–•	•–•	•–•	•–•
5	0	•–4	•–5	•–6	•–6	•–7	•–•
	1	•–7	•–7	•–8	•–•	•–•	•–•
	2	•–9	•–9	•–•	•–•	•–•	•–•
6	0	•–3	•–4	•–5	•–5	•–6	•–•
	1	•–6	•–6	•–7	•–7	•–•	•–•
	2	•–8	•–8	•–•	•–•	•–•	•–•
	3	3–9	•–•	•–•	•–•	•–•	•–•
		$N=13$					
4	0	•–5	•–6	•–7	•–8	•–9	•–•
	1	•–9	•–10	•–10	•–•	•–•	•–•
	2	2–11	•–•	•–•	•–•	•–•	•–•
5	0	•–4	•–5	•–6	•–7	•–7	•–8
	1	•–7	•–8	•–9	•–9	•–•	•–•
	2	•–10	•–10	•–•	•–•	•–•	•–•
6	0	•–4	•–4	•–5	•–6	•–6	•–7
	1	•–6	•–7	•–8	•–8	•–8	•–•
	2	•–8	•–9	•–9	•–•	•–•	•–•
	3	3–10	•–•	•–•	•–•	•–•	•–•
		$N=14$					
4	0	•–6	•–7	•–8	•–9	•–9	•–10
	1	•–9	•–10	•–11	•–•	•–•	•–•
	2	2–12	•–•	•–•	•–•	•–•	•–•
5	0	•–5	•–6	•–7	•–8	•–8	•–9
	1	•–8	•–9	•–9	•–10	•–10	•–•
	2	•–10	•–11	•–•	•–•	•–•	•–•
6	0	•–4	•–5	•–6	•–6	•–7	•–8
	1	•–7	•–8	•–8	•–9	•–9	•–•
	2	•–9	•–10	•–10	•–•	•–•	•–•
	3	3–11	•–•	•–•	•–•	•–•	•–•
7	0	•–3	•–4	•–5	•–6	•–6	•–7
	1	•–6	•–7	•–7	•–8	•–8	•–•
	2	•–8	•–9	•–9	•–•	•–•	•–•
	3	3–10	•–10	•–•	•–•	•–•	•–•
		$N=15$					
4	0	•–6	•–8	•–9	•–10	•–10	•–11
	1	•–10	•–11	•–12	•–12	•–•	•–•
	2	2–13	•–•	•–•	•–•	•–•	•–•
5	0	•–5	•–6	•–7	•–8	•–9	•–10
	1	•–9	•–9	•–10	•–11	•–11	•–•
	2	2–11	•–12	•–12	•–•	•–•	•–•
6	0	•–4	•–5	•–6	•–7	•–8	•–9
	1	•–7	•–8	•–9	•–10	•–10	•–•
	2	•–10	•–10	•–11	•–•	•–•	•–•
	3	3–12	3–12	•–•	•–•	•–•	•–•
7	0	•–4	•–5	•–5	•–6	•–7	•–8
	1	•–6	•–7	•–8	•–8	•–9	•–•
	2	•–9	•–9	•–10	•–10	•–•	•–•
	3	3–11	•–11	•–•	•–•	•–•	•–•
		$N=16$					
4	0	•–7	•–8	•–9	•–10	•–11	•–12
	1	•–11	•–12	•–13	•–13	•–•	•–•
	2	2–14	•–•	•–•	•–•	•–•	•–•
5	0	•–6	•–7	•–8	•–9	•–9	•–11
	1	•–9	•–10	•–11	•–12	•–12	•–•
	2	2–12	•–13	•–13	•–•		•–•
		$N=16$ (continued)					
6	0	•–5	•–6	•–7	•–8	•–8	•–9
	1	•–8	•–9	•–9	•–10	•–11	•–•
	2	•–10	•–11	•–12	•–12	•–•	•–•
	3	3–13	3–13	•–•	•–•	•–•	•–•
7	0	•–4	•–5	•–6	•–7	•–7	•–8
	1	•–7	•–8	•–8	•–9	•–10	•–10
	2	•–9	•–10	•–10	•–11	•–11	•–•
	3	3–11	•–12	•–12	•–•	•–•	•–•
8	0	•–3	•–4	•–5	•–6	•–6	•–7
	1	•–6	•–7	•–7	•–8	•–9	•–9
	2	•–8	•–9	•–9	•–10	•–10	•–•
	3	•–10	•–11	•–11	•–•	•–•	•–•
	4	4–12	4–12	•–•	•–•	•–•	•–•
		$N=17$					
4	0	•–7	•–9	•–10	•–11	•–12	•–13
	1	•–11	•–13	•–13	•–14	•–•	•–•
	2	2–15	2–15	•–•	•–•	•–•	•–•
5	0	•–6	•–7	•–8	•–9	•–10	•–11
	1	•–10	•–11	•–12	•–12	•–13	•–•
	2	2–13	•–14	•–14	•–•	•–•	•–•
6	0	•–5	•–6	•–7	•–8	•–9	•–10
	1	•–8	•–9	•–10	•–11	•–12	•–12
	2	•–11	•–12	•–13	•–13	•–•	•–•
	3	4–13	3–14	•–•	•–•	•–•	•–•
7	0	•–4	•–5	•–6	•–7	•–8	•–9
	1	•–7	•–8	•–9	•–10	•–10	•–11
	2	•–10	•–11	•–11	•–12	•–12	•–•
	3	3–12	•–13	•–13	•–•	•–•	•–•
8	0	•–4	•–5	•–5	•–6	•–7	•–8
	1	•–6	•–7	•–8	•–9	•–9	•–10
	2	•–9	•–9	•–10	•–11	•–11	•–•
	3	3–11	•–11	•–12	•–12	•–•	•–•
	4	4–13	4–13	•–•	•–•	•–•	•–•
		$N=18$					
4	0	•–8	•–9	•–10	•–12	•–12	•–14
	1	•–12	•–13	•–14	•–15	•–15	•–•
	2	2–16	2–16	•–•	•–•	•–•	•–•
5	0	•–6	•–8	•–9	•–10	•–11	•–12
	1	•–10	•–11	•–12	•–13	•–14	•–•
	2	2–13	•–14	•–15	•–•	•–•	•–•
6	0	•–5	•–6	•–7	•–9	•–9	•–11
	1	•–9	•–10	•–11	•–12	•–12	•–13
	2	2–12	•–13	•–13	•–14	•–14	•–•
	3	4–14	3–15	3–15	•–•	•–•	•–•
7	0	•–5	•–6	•–6	•–8	•–8	•–10
	1	•–8	•–9	•–9	•–10	•–11	•–12
	2	•–10	•–11	•–12	•–13	•–13	•–•
	3	3–13	3–13	•–14	•–•	•–•	•–•
8	0	•–4	•–5	•–6	•–7	•–7	•–9
	1	•–7	•–8	•–8	•–9	•–10	•–11
	2	•–9	•–10	•–11	•–11	•–12	•–•
	3	3–11	•–12	•–13	•–13	•–•	•–•
	4	5–13	4–14	4–14	•–•	•–•	•–•
9	0	•–4	•–4	•–5	•–6	•–6	•–8
	1	•–6	•–7	•–7	•–8	•–9	•–10
	2	•–8	•–9	•–10	•–10	•–11	•–•
	3	•–10	•–11	•–11	•–12	•–12	•–•
	4	4–12	4–13	•–13	•–•	•–•	•–•
		$N=19$					
4	0	•–8	•–10	•–11	•–12	•–13	•–15
	1	•–13	•–14	•–15	•–16	•–16	•–•
	2	3–16	2–17	•–•	•–•	•–•	•–•
5	0	•–7	•–8	•–9	•–11	•–11	•–13
	1	•–11	•–12	•–13	•–14	•–15	•–•
	2	2–14	•–15	•–16	•–•	•–•	•–•
6	0	•–6	•–7	•–8	•–9	•–10	•–12
	1	•–9	•–10	•–11	•–12	•–13	•–14
	2	2–12	•–13	•–14	•–15	•–15	•–•
	3	4–15	3–16	3–16	•–•	•–•	•–•
7	0	•–5	•–6	•–7	•–8	•–9	•–10
	1	•–8	•–9	•–10	•–11	•–12	•–13
	2	•–11	•–12	•–13	•–13	•–14	•–•
	3	3–13	3–14	•–15	•–15	•–•	•–•
8	0	•–4	•–5	•–6	•–7	•–8	•–9
	1	•–7	•–8	•–9	•–10	•–10	•–12
	2	•–10	•–11	•–11	•–12	•–13	•–•
	3	3–12	•–13	•–13	•–14	•–14	•–•
	4	5–14	4–15	4–15	•–•	•–•	•–•
9	0	•–4	•–5	•–5	•–6	•–7	•–8
	1	•–6	•–7	•–8	•–9	•–9	•–10
	2	•–9	•–10	•–10	•–11	•–11	•–12
	3	3–11	•–12	•–12	•–13	•–13	•–•
	4	4–13	4–13	•–14	•–•	•–•	•–•
		$N=20$					
4	0	•–9	•–10	•–12	•–13	•–14	•–16
	1	•–14	•–15	•–16	•–17	•–17	•–•
	2	3–17	2–18	•–•	•–•	•–•	•–•
		$N=20$ (continued)					
5	0	•–7	•–9	•–10	•–11	•–12	•–14
	1	•–11	•–13	•–14	•–15	•–15	•–•
	2	2–15	•–16	•–17	•–17	•–•	•–•
6	0	•–6	•–7	•–8	•–10	•–11	•–12
	1	•–10	•–11	•–12	•–13	•–14	•–15
	2	2–13	•–14	•–15	•–16	•–16	•–•
	3	4–16	3–17	3–17	•–•	•–•	•–•
7	0	•–5	•–6	•–7	•–9	•–9	•–11
	1	•–9	•–10	•–11	•–12	•–12	•–14
	2	•–12	•–13	•–13	•–14	•–15	•–•
	3	3–14	3–15	•–16	•–16	•–•	•–•
8	0	•–5	•–6	•–6	•–8	•–8	•–10
	1	•–8	•–9	•–9	•–10	•–11	•–12
	2	•–10	•–11	•–12	•–13	•–13	•–14
	3	3–13	3–14	•–14	•–15	•–15	•–•
	4	5–15	4–16	4–16	•–•	•–•	•–•
9	0	•–4	•–5	•–6	•–7	•–7	•–9
	1	•–7	•–8	•–8	•–9	•–10	•–11
	2	•–9	•–10	•–11	•–12	•–12	•–13
	3	3–11	•–12	•–13	•–14	•–14	•–•
	4	5–14	4–14	•–15	•–15	•–•	•–•
10	0	•–4	•–4	•–5	•–6	•–7	•–8
	1	•–6	•–7	•–8	•–8	•–9	•–10
	2	•–8	•–9	•–10	•–11	•–11	•–12
	3	•–10	•–11	•–12	•–12	•–13	•–•
	4	4–12	4–13	•–14	•–14	•–•	•–•
	5	6–14	5–15	5–15	•–•	•–•	•–•
		$N=21$					
4	0	•–9	•–11	•–12	•–14	•–15	•–16
	1	•–14	•–16	•–17	•–18	•–18	•–•
	2	3–18	2–19	•–•	•–•	•–•	•–•
5	0	•–7	•–9	•–10	•–12	•–13	•–15
	1	•–12	•–13	•–15	•–16	•–16	•–17
	2	2–16	2–17	•–18	•–18	•–•	•–•
6	0	•–6	•–8	•–9	•–10	•–11	•–13
	1	•–10	•–12	•–13	•–14	•–15	•–16
	2	2–14	•–15	•–16	•–17	•–17	•–•
	3	4–17	3–18	3–18	•–•	•–•	•–•
7	0	•–5	•–7	•–8	•–9	•–10	•–12
	1	•–9	•–10	•–11	•–12	•–13	•–14
	2	•–12	•–13	•–14	•–15	•–16	•–•
	3	4–15	3–16	•–17	•–17	•–•	•–•
8	0	•–5	•–6	•–7	•–8	•–9	•–10
	1	•–8	•–9	•–10	•–11	•–12	•–13
	2	•–11	•–12	•–13	•–14	•–14	•–15
	3	3–13	3–14	•–15	•–16	•–16	•–•
	4	5–16	5–16	4–17	•–•	•–•	•–•
9	0	•–4	•–5	•–6	•–7	•–8	•–9
	1	•–7	•–8	•–9	•–10	•–11	•–12
	2	•–10	•–11	•–11	•–12	•–13	•–14
	3	3–12	•–13	•–14	•–14	•–15	•–•
	4	5–14	4–15	4–16	•–16	•–•	•–•
10	0	•–4	•–5	•–5	•–6	•–7	•–8
	1	•–6	•–7	•–8	•–9	•–10	•–11
	2	•–9	•–10	•–10	•–11	•–12	•–13
	3	3–11	•–12	•–12	•–13	•–14	•–•
	4	4–13	4–14	•–14	•–15	•–15	•–•
	5	6–15	5–16	5–16	•–•	•–•	•–•
		$N=22$					
4	0	•–9	•–11	•–13	•–14	•–15	•–17
	1	•–15	•–16	•–17	•–18	•–19	•–•
	2	3–19	2–20	•–•	•–•	•–•	•–•
5	0	•–8	•–9	•–11	•–12	•–13	•–15
	1	•–13	•–14	•–15	•–16	•–17	•–18
	2	2–17	2–18	•–18	•–19	•–•	•–•
6	0	•–7	•–8	•–9	•–11	•–12	•–14
	1	•–11	•–12	•–13	•–15	•–15	•–17
	2	2–14	•–16	•–17	•–17	•–18	•–•
	3	4–18	4–18	3–19	•–•	•–•	•–•
7	0	•–6	•–7	•–8	•–10	•–10	•–12
	1	•–10	•–11	•–12	•–13	•–14	•–15
	2	2–13	•–14	•–15	•–16	•–16	•–17
	3	4–16	3–17	3–17	•–18	•–18	•–•
8	0	•–5	•–6	•–7	•–8	•–9	•–11
	1	•–8	•–10	•–11	•–12	•–12	•–14
	2	•–11	•–12	•–13	•–14	•–15	•–16
	3	3–14	3–15	•–16	•–17	•–17	•–•
	4	6–16	5–17	4–18	4–18	•–•	•–•
9	0	•–4	•–5	•–6	•–8	•–8	•–10
	1	•–8	•–9	•–9	•–11	•–11	•–13
	2	•–10	•–11	•–12	•–13	•–14	•–15
	3	3–13	•–14	•–14	•–15	•–16	•–•
	4	5–15	4–16	4–16	•–17	•–17	•–•
10	0	•–4	•–5	•–6	•–7	•–7	•–9
	1	•–7	•–8	•–9	•–10	•–10	•–11
	2	•–9	•–10	•–11	•–12	•–12	•–14
	3	3–11	•–12	•–13	•–14	•–14	•–15
	4	4–14	4–14	•–15	•–16	•–16	•–•
	5	6–16	6–16	5–17	5–17	•–•	•–•
11	0	•–4	•–4	•–5	•–6	•–7	•–8

All values conform to the international convention (i.e. 0,1 instead of 0.1).

Significance Limits for the Fourfold Table Test*

x_1	N_1-x_1	N_1
x_2	N_2-x_2	N_2
X	$N-X$	N

$N=N_1+N_2$, $X=x_1+x_2$, $N_1 \leq N_2$, $x_1 \leq N_1-x_1$

For explanation see page 151

N = 22 (continued)

N_1	x_1	2α = 0,20	2α = 0,10	2α = 0,05	2α = 0,02	2α = 0,01	2α = 0,002
11	1	•– 6	•– 7	•– 8	•– 9	•– 9	•–10
	2	•– 8	•– 9	•–10	•–11	•–11	•–12
	3	•–10	•–11	•–12	•–13	•–13	•–14
	4	4–12	4–13	•–14	•–15	•–15	•–•
	5	6–14	5–15	5–16	•–16	•–•	•–•

N = 23

N_1	x_1	2α = 0,20	2α = 0,10	2α = 0,05	2α = 0,02	2α = 0,01	2α = 0,002
4	0	•–10	•–12	•–13	•–15	•–16	•–18
	1	•–16	•–17	•–18	•–19	•–20	•–•
	2	3–20	2–21	2–21	•–•	•–•	•–•
5	0	•– 8	•–10	•–11	•–13	•–14	•–16
	1	•–13	•–15	•–16	•–17	•–18	•–19
	2	2–17	2–18	•–19	•–20	•–•	•–•
6	0	•– 7	•– 8	•–10	•–11	•–12	•–14
	1	•–11	•–13	•–14	•–15	•–16	•–18
	2	2–15	•–16	•–17	•–18	•–19	•–•
	3	5–18	4–19	3–20	•–•	•–•	•–•
7	0	•– 6	•– 7	•– 9	•–10	•–11	•–13
	1	•–10	•–11	•–12	•–14	•–14	•–16
	2	2–13	•–15	•–16	•–17	•–17	•–18
	3	4–16	3–17	3–18	•–19	•–19	•–•
8	0	•– 5	•– 6	•– 8	•– 9	•–10	•–12
	1	•– 9	•–10	•–11	•–12	•–13	•–15
	2	•–12	•–13	•–14	•–15	•–16	•–17
	3	3–15	3–16	•–17	•–17	•–18	•–•
	4	6–17	5–18	4–19	4–19	•–•	•–•
9	0	•– 5	•– 6	•– 7	•– 8	•– 9	•–10
	1	•– 8	•– 9	•–10	•–11	•–12	•–13
	2	•–11	•–12	•–13	•–14	•–14	•–16
	3	3–13	3–14	•–15	•–16	•–16	•–17
	4	5–16	4–17	4–17	•–18	•–18	•–•
10	0	•– 4	•– 5	•– 6	•– 7	•– 8	•– 9
	1	•– 7	•– 8	•– 9	•–10	•–11	•–12
	2	•–10	•–11	•–12	•–13	•–13	•–14
	3	3–12	•–13	•–14	•–15	•–15	•–16
	4	5–14	4–15	4–16	•–17	•–17	•–•
	5	7–16	6–17	5–18	5–18	•–•	•–•
11	0	•– 4	•– 5	•– 5	•– 6	•– 7	•– 9
	1	•– 6	•– 7	•– 8	•– 9	•–10	•–11
	2	•– 9	•–10	•–11	•–11	•–12	•–13
	3	3–11	•–12	•–13	•–14	•–14	•–15
	4	4–13	4–14	•–15	•–15	•–16	•–•
	5	6–15	5–16	5–16	•–17	•–17	•–•

N = 24

N_1	x_1	2α = 0,20	2α = 0,10	2α = 0,05	2α = 0,02	2α = 0,01	2α = 0,002
4	0	•–10	•–12	•–14	•–16	•–17	•–19
	1	•–16	•–18	•–19	•–20	•–21	•–•
	2	3–21	2–22	2–22	•–•	•–•	•–•
5	0	•– 9	•–10	•–12	•–14	•–15	•–17
	1	•–14	•–15	•–17	•–18	•–19	•–20
	2	3–18	2–19	•–20	•–21	•–21	•–•
6	0	•– 7	•– 9	•–10	•–12	•–13	•–15
	1	•–12	•–13	•–15	•–16	•–17	•–18
	2	2–16	•–17	•–18	•–19	•–20	•–•
	3	5–19	4–20	3–21	3–21	•–•	•–•
7	0	•– 6	•– 8	•– 9	•–10	•–11	•–13
	1	•–10	•–12	•–13	•–14	•–15	•–17
	2	2–14	•–15	•–16	•–17	•–18	•–19
	3	4–17	3–18	3–19	•–20	•–20	•–•
8	0	•– 6	•– 7	•– 8	•– 9	•–10	•–12
	1	•– 9	•–11	•–12	•–13	•–14	•–15
	2	•–12	•–14	•–15	•–16	•–16	•–18
	3	4–15	3–16	•–17	•–18	•–19	•–•
	4	6–18	5–19	4–20	4–20	•–•	•–•
9	0	•– 5	•– 6	•– 7	•– 8	•– 9	•–11
	1	•– 8	•– 9	•–10	•–12	•–12	•–14
	2	•–11	•–12	•–13	•–14	•–15	•–16
	3	3–14	3–15	•–16	•–17	•–17	•–18
	4	5–16	5–17	4–18	•–19	•–19	•–•
10	0	•– 4	•– 5	•– 6	•– 7	•– 8	•–10
	1	•– 7	•– 9	•– 9	•–11	•–11	•–13
	2	•–10	•–11	•–12	•–13	•–14	•–15
	3	3–13	•–14	•–14	•–15	•–16	•–17
	4	5–15	4–16	4–17	•–17	•–18	•–•
	5	7–17	6–18	5–19	5–19	•–•	•–•
11	0	•– 4	•– 5	•– 6	•– 7	•– 7	•– 9
	1	•– 7	•– 8	•– 9	•–10	•–10	•–12
	2	•– 9	•–10	•–11	•–12	•–13	•–14
	3	3–12	•–12	•–13	•–14	•–15	•–16
	4	4–14	4–15	•–15	•–16	•–17	•–17
	5	6–16	6–17	5–17	•–18	•–18	•–•
12	0	•– 4	•– 4	•– 5	•– 6	•– 7	•– 8
	1	•– 6	•– 7	•– 8	•– 9	•– 9	•–11
	2	•– 8	•– 9	•–10	•–11	•–12	•–13
	3	•–11	•–11	•–12	•–13	•–14	•–15
	4	4–13	4–13	•–14	•–15	•–15	•–16
	5	6–15	5–15	5–16	•–17	•–17	•–•
	6	8–16	7–17	6–18	6–18	•–•	•–•

N = 25

N_1	x_1	2α = 0,20	2α = 0,10	2α = 0,05	2α = 0,02	2α = 0,01	2α = 0,002
4	0	•–11	•–13	•–15	•–16	•–18	•–20
	1	•–17	•–19	•–20	•–21	•–22	•–•
	2	3–22	2–23	2–23	•–•	•–•	•–•

N = 25 (continued)

N_1	x_1	2α = 0,20	2α = 0,10	2α = 0,05	2α = 0,02	2α = 0,01	2α = 0,002
5	0	•– 9	•–11	•–12	•–14	•–15	•–18
	1	•–14	•–16	•–17	•–19	•–20	•–21
	2	3–19	2–20	•–21	•–22	•–22	•–•
6	0	•– 8	•– 9	•–11	•–12	•–14	•–16
	1	•–12	•–14	•–15	•–17	•–18	•–19
	2	2–16	•–18	•–19	•–20	•–21	•–•
	3	5–20	4–21	3–22	3–22	•–•	•–•
7	0	•– 7	•– 8	•– 9	•–11	•–12	•–14
	1	•–11	•–12	•–14	•–15	•–16	•–18
	2	2–15	•–16	•–17	•–18	•–19	•–20
	3	4–18	3–19	3–20	•–21	•–21	•–•
8	0	•– 6	•– 7	•– 8	•–10	•–11	•–13
	1	•–10	•–11	•–12	•–13	•–14	•–16
	2	2–13	•–14	•–15	•–16	•–17	•–19
	3	4–16	3–17	3–18	•–19	•–20	•–•
	4	6–19	5–20	5–20	4–21	•–•	•–•
9	0	•– 5	•– 6	•– 7	•– 9	•–10	•–11
	1	•– 9	•–10	•–11	•–12	•–13	•–15
	2	•–12	•–13	•–14	•–15	•–16	•–17
	3	3–14	3–16	•–17	•–17	•–18	•–19
	4	6–17	5–18	4–19	4–20	•–20	•–•
10	0	•– 5	•– 6	•– 7	•– 8	•– 9	•–10
	1	•– 8	•– 9	•–10	•–11	•–12	•–13
	2	•–11	•–12	•–13	•–14	•–14	•–16
	3	3–13	•–14	•–15	•–16	•–17	•–18
	4	5–16	4–17	4–17	•–18	•–19	•–•
	5	7–18	6–19	6–19	5–20	5–20	•–•
11	0	•– 4	•– 5	•– 6	•– 7	•– 8	•– 9
	1	•– 7	•– 8	•– 9	•–10	•–11	•–12
	2	•–10	•–11	•–12	•–13	•–13	•–15
	3	3–12	•–13	•–14	•–15	•–15	•–17
	4	5–14	4–15	•–16	•–17	•–17	•–18
	5	6–16	6–17	5–18	5–19	•–19	•–•
12	0	•– 4	•– 5	•– 5	•– 6	•– 7	•– 9
	1	•– 6	•– 7	•– 8	•– 9	•–10	•–11
	2	•– 9	•–10	•–11	•–12	•–12	•–14
	3	3–11	•–12	•–13	•–14	•–14	•–15
	4	4–13	4–14	•–15	•–16	•–16	•–17
	5	6–15	5–16	5–17	•–17	•–18	•–•
	6	8–17	7–18	6–19	6–19	•–•	•–•

N = 26

N_1	x_1	2α = 0,20	2α = 0,10	2α = 0,05	2α = 0,02	2α = 0,01	2α = 0,002
4	0	•–11	•–13	•–15	•–17	•–18	•–21
	1	•–18	•–19	•–21	•–22	•–23	•–•
	2	4–22	2–24	2–24	•–•	•–•	•–•
5	0	•– 9	•–11	•–13	•–15	•–16	•–18
	1	•–15	•–17	•–18	•–20	•–20	•–22
	2	3–20	2–21	•–22	•–23	•–23	•–•
6	0	•– 8	•–10	•–11	•–13	•–14	•–16
	1	•–13	•–15	•–16	•–17	•–18	•–20
	2	2–17	2–19	•–20	•–21	•–21	•–•
	3	5–21	4–22	3–23	3–23	•–•	•–•
7	0	•– 7	•– 8	•–10	•–11	•–13	•–15
	1	•–11	•–13	•–14	•–16	•–17	•–18
	2	2–15	•–17	•–18	•–19	•–20	•–21
	3	4–19	4–20	3–21	•–22	•–22	•–•
8	0	•– 6	•– 7	•– 9	•–10	•–11	•–13
	1	•–10	•–11	•–13	•–14	•–15	•–17
	2	2–14	•–15	•–16	•–17	•–18	•–19
	3	4–17	3–18	3–19	•–20	•–20	•–21
	4	6–20	5–21	5–21	4–22	4–22	•–•
9	0	•– 5	•– 7	•– 8	•– 9	•–10	•–12
	1	•– 9	•–10	•–11	•–13	•–14	•–15
	2	•–12	•–13	•–15	•–16	•–16	•–18
	3	3–15	3–16	•–17	•–18	•–19	•–20
	4	6–18	5–19	4–20	4–20	•–21	•–•
10	0	•– 5	•– 6	•– 7	•– 8	•– 9	•–11
	1	•– 8	•– 9	•–10	•–12	•–12	•–14
	2	•–11	•–12	•–13	•–14	•–15	•–17
	3	3–14	3–15	•–16	•–17	•–17	•–19
	4	5–16	4–17	4–18	•–19	•–20	•–20
	5	7–19	6–20	6–20	5–21	5–21	•–•
11	0	•– 4	•– 5	•– 6	•– 7	•– 8	•–10
	1	•– 7	•– 8	•– 9	•–11	•–11	•–13
	2	•–10	•–11	•–12	•–13	•–14	•–15
	3	3–13	•–14	•–15	•–16	•–16	•–17
	4	5–15	4–16	4–17	•–18	•–18	•–19
	5	7–17	6–18	5–19	5–20	•–20	•–•
12	0	•– 4	•– 5	•– 6	•– 7	•– 8	•– 9
	1	•– 7	•– 8	•– 9	•–10	•–10	•–12
	2	•– 9	•–10	•–11	•–12	•–13	•–14
	3	3–12	•–13	•–13	•–14	•–15	•–16
	4	4–14	4–15	•–16	•–16	•–17	•–18
	5	6–16	5–17	5–18	•–18	•–19	•–•
	6	8–18	7–19	7–19	6–20	6–20	•–•
13	0	•– 4	•– 4	•– 5	•– 6	•– 7	•– 8
	1	•– 6	•– 7	•– 8	•– 9	•–10	•–11
	2	•– 9	•– 9	•–10	•–11	•–12	•–13
	3	•–11	•–12	•–12	•–13	•–14	•–15
	4	4–13	4–14	•–14	•–15	•–16	•–17
	5	6–15	5–16	5–16	•–17	•–18	•–18
	6	7–17	7–17	6–18	6–19	•–19	•–•

N = 27

N_1	x_1	2α = 0,20	2α = 0,10	2α = 0,05	2α = 0,02	2α = 0,01	2α = 0,002
4	0	•–12	•–14	•–16	•–18	•–19	•–21
	1	•–18	•–20	•–21	•–23	•–24	•–•
	2	4–23	3–24	2–25	•–•	•–•	•–•
5	0	•–10	•–12	•–13	•–15	•–17	•–19
	1	•–16	•–17	•–19	•–20	•–21	•–23
	2	3–20	2–22	•–23	•–24	•–24	•–•
6	0	•– 8	•–10	•–12	•–14	•–15	•–17
	1	•–13	•–15	•–17	•–18	•–19	•–21
	2	2–18	2–19	•–20	•–22	•–22	•–23
	3	5–22	4–23	4–23	3–24	•–•	•–•
7	0	•– 7	•– 9	•–10	•–12	•–13	•–15
	1	•–12	•–13	•–15	•–16	•–17	•–19
	2	2–16	•–17	•–18	•–20	•–20	•–22
	3	5–19	4–20	3–21	•–22	•–23	•–•
8	0	•– 6	•– 8	•– 9	•–11	•–12	•–14
	1	•–10	•–12	•–13	•–15	•–16	•–17
	2	2–14	•–15	•–17	•–18	•–19	•–20
	3	4–17	3–19	3–20	•–21	•–21	•–22
	4	7–20	6–21	5–22	4–23	4–23	•–•
9	0	•– 6	•– 7	•– 8	•–10	•–11	•–13
	1	•– 9	•–11	•–12	•–13	•–14	•–16
	2	•–13	•–14	•–15	•–16	•–17	•–19
	3	4–16	3–17	•–18	•–19	•–20	•–21
	4	6–18	5–20	4–20	4–21	•–22	•–•
10	0	•– 5	•– 6	•– 7	•– 9	•–10	•–11
	1	•– 8	•–10	•–11	•–12	•–13	•–15
	2	•–11	•–13	•–14	•–15	•–16	•–17
	3	3–14	3–15	•–16	•–18	•–18	•–19
	4	5–17	5–18	4–19	•–20	•–20	•–21
	5	8–19	7–20	6–21	5–22	5–22	•–•
11	0	•– 5	•– 6	•– 7	•– 8	•– 9	•–10
	1	•– 8	•– 9	•–10	•–11	•–12	•–14
	2	•–10	•–12	•–13	•–14	•–15	•–16
	3	3–13	•–14	•–15	•–16	•–17	•–18
	4	5–16	4–17	4–17	•–18	•–19	•–20
	5	7–18	6–19	5–20	5–20	•–21	•–•
12	0	•– 4	•– 5	•– 6	•– 7	•– 8	•–10
	1	•– 7	•– 8	•– 9	•–10	•–11	•–12
	2	•–10	•–11	•–12	•–13	•–13	•–15
	3	3–12	•–13	•–14	•–15	•–16	•–17
	4	4–14	4–15	•–16	•–17	•–18	•–19
	5	6–17	6–17	5–18	5–19	•–20	•–20
	6	8–19	8–19	7–20	6–21	6–21	•–•
13	0	•– 4	•– 5	•– 5	•– 7	•– 7	•– 9
	1	•– 6	•– 7	•– 8	•– 9	•–10	•–12
	2	•– 9	•–10	•–11	•–12	•–12	•–14
	3	3–11	•–12	•–13	•–14	•–15	•–16
	4	4–13	4–14	•–15	•–16	•–17	•–18
	5	6–15	5–16	5–17	•–18	•–18	•–19
	6	8–17	7–18	6–19	6–20	•–20	•–•

N = 28

N_1	x_1	2α = 0,20	2α = 0,10	2α = 0,05	2α = 0,02	2α = 0,01	2α = 0,002
4	0	•–12	•–14	•–16	•–19	•–20	•–22
	1	•–19	•–21	•–22	•–24	•–24	•–•
	2	4–24	3–25	2–26	•–•	•–•	•–•
5	0	•–10	•–12	•–14	•–16	•–17	•–20
	1	•–16	•–18	•–20	•–21	•–22	•–24
	2	3–21	2–23	•–24	•–25	•–25	•–•
6	0	•– 9	•–10	•–12	•–14	•–15	•–18
	1	•–14	•–16	•–17	•–19	•–20	•–22
	2	2–18	2–20	•–21	•–22	•–23	•–24
	3	6–22	4–24	4–24	3–25	•–•	•–•
7	0	•– 7	•– 9	•–11	•–12	•–14	•–16
	1	•–12	•–14	•–15	•–17	•–18	•–20
	2	2–16	•–18	•–19	•–20	•–21	•–23
	3	5–20	4–21	3–22	•–23	•–24	•–•
8	0	•– 7	•– 8	•– 9	•–11	•–12	•–14
	1	•–11	•–12	•–14	•–15	•–16	•–18
	2	2–15	•–16	•–17	•–19	•–19	•–21
	3	4–18	3–19	3–20	•–21	•–22	•–23
	4	7–21	6–22	5–23	4–24	4–24	•–•
9	0	•– 6	•– 7	•– 8	•–10	•–11	•–13
	1	•–10	•–11	•–12	•–14	•–15	•–17
	2	2–13	•–15	•–16	•–17	•–18	•–19
	3	4–16	3–18	•–19	•–20	•–20	•–22
	4	6–19	5–20	4–21	4–22	•–23	•–•
10	0	•– 5	•– 6	•– 8	•– 9	•–10	•–12
	1	•– 9	•–10	•–11	•–13	•–14	•–15
	2	•–12	•–13	•–14	•–16	•–16	•–18
	3	3–15	3–16	•–17	•–18	•–19	•–20
	4	6–18	5–19	4–20	•–21	•–21	•–22
	5	8–20	7–21	6–22	5–23	5–23	•–•
11	0	•– 5	•– 6	•– 7	•– 8	•– 9	•–11
	1	•– 8	•– 9	•–10	•–12	•–12	•–14
	2	•–11	•–12	•–13	•–14	•–15	•–17
	3	3–14	•–15	•–16	•–17	•–18	•–19
	4	5–16	4–17	4–18	•–19	•–20	•–21
	5	7–19	6–20	6–20	5–21	5–22	•–•
12	0	•– 4	•– 5	•– 6	•– 7	•– 8	•–10
	1	•– 7	•– 8	•– 9	•–11	•–11	•–13
	2	•–10	•–11	•–12	•–13	•–14	•–16
	3	3–13	•–14	•–15	•–16	•–16	•–18
	4	5–15	4–16	4–17	•–18	•–18	•–20
	5	7–17	6–18	5–19	5–20	•–20	•–21

All values conform to the international convention (i.e. 0,1 instead of 0.1).

Significance Limits for the Fourfold Table Test*

x_1	$N_1 - x_1$	N_1
x_2	$N_2 - x_2$	N_2
X	$N - X$	N

$N = N_1 + N_2$
$X = x_1 + x_2$
$N_1 \leq N_2$
$x_1 \leq N_1 - x_1$

For explanation see page 151

N = 28 (continued)

N_1	x_1	2α = 0,20	2α = 0,10	2α = 0,05	2α = 0,02	2α = 0,01	2α = 0,002
	6	9–19	8–20	7–21	6–22	6–22	•–•
13	0	•– 4	•– 5	•– 6	•– 7	•– 8	•– 9
	1	•– 7	•– 8	•– 9	•–10	•–11	•–12
	2	•– 9	•–10	•–11	•–12	•–13	•–14
	3	3–12	•–13	•–14	•–15	•–15	•–17
	4	4–14	4–15	•–16	•–17	•–17	•–18
	5	6–16	5–17	5–18	•–19	•–19	•–20
	6	8–18	7–19	7–20	6–20	6–21	•–•
14	0	•– 4	•– 4	•– 5	•– 6	•– 7	•– 8
	1	•– 6	•– 7	•– 8	•– 9	•–10	•–11
	2	•– 9	•–10	•–10	•–11	•–12	•–13
	3	•–11	•–12	•–13	•–14	•–14	•–15
	4	4–13	4–14	•–15	•–16	•–16	•–17
	5	6–15	5–16	5–17	•–17	•–18	•–19
	6	7–17	7–18	6–18	6–19	•–20	•–20
	7	9–19	8–20	8–20	7–21	7–21	•–•

N = 29

N_1	x_1	2α = 0,20	2α = 0,10	2α = 0,05	2α = 0,02	2α = 0,01	2α = 0,002
4	0	•–13	•–15	•–17	•–19	•–21	•–23
	1	•–20	•–22	•–23	•–25	•–25	•–•
	2	4–25	3–26	2–27	•–•	•–•	•–•
5	0	•–10	•–13	•–15	•–17	•–18	•–21
	1	•–17	•–19	•–20	•–22	•–23	•–25
	2	3–22	2–23	2–24	•–26	•–26	•–•
6	0	•– 9	•–11	•–13	•–15	•–16	•–18
	1	•–14	•–16	•–18	•–20	•–21	•–22
	2	3–19	2–21	•–22	•–23	•–24	•–25
	3	6–23	5–24	4–25	3–26	•–•	•–•
7	0	•– 8	•– 9	•–11	•–13	•–14	•–17
	1	•–13	•–14	•–16	•–18	•–19	•–21
	2	2–17	•–19	•–20	•–21	•–22	•–23
	3	5–21	4–22	3–23	3–24	•–25	•–•
8	0	•– 7	•– 8	•–10	•–12	•–13	•–15
	1	•–11	•–13	•–14	•–16	•–17	•–19
	2	2–15	•–17	•–18	•–19	•–20	•–22
	3	4–19	3–20	3–21	•–22	•–23	•–24
	4	7–22	6–23	5–24	4–25	4–25	•–•
9	0	•– 6	•– 7	•– 9	•–10	•–11	•–14
	1	•–10	•–12	•–13	•–14	•–15	•–17
	2	2–14	•–15	•–16	•–18	•–19	•–20
	3	4–17	3–18	3–19	•–21	•–21	•–23
	4	6–20	5–21	5–22	4–23	•–24	•–•
10	0	•– 5	•– 7	•– 8	•– 9	•–10	•–12
	1	•– 9	•–11	•–12	•–13	•–14	•–16
	2	•–12	•–14	•–15	•–16	•–17	•–19
	3	3–15	3–17	•–18	•–19	•–20	•–21
	4	6–18	5–19	4–20	4–21	•–22	•–23
	5	8–21	7–22	6–23	5–24	5–24	•–•
11	0	•– 5	•– 6	•– 7	•– 9	•– 9	•–11
	1	•– 8	•–10	•–11	•–12	•–13	•–15
	2	•–11	•–13	•–14	•–15	•–16	•–17
	3	3–14	3–15	•–16	•–18	•–18	•–20
	4	5–17	4–18	4–19	•–20	•–21	•–22
	5	7–19	6–20	6–21	5–22	5–23	•–23
12	0	•– 5	•– 6	•– 7	•– 8	•– 9	•–10
	1	•– 8	•– 9	•–10	•–11	•–12	•–14
	2	•–10	•–12	•–13	•–14	•–15	•–16
	3	3–13	•–14	•–15	•–16	•–17	•–18
	4	5–15	4–17	4–18	•–19	•–19	•–20
	5	7–18	6–19	5–20	5–21	•–21	•–22
	6	9–20	8–21	7–22	6–23	6–23	•–•
13	0	•– 4	•– 5	•– 6	•– 7	•– 8	•–10
	1	•– 7	•– 8	•– 9	•–10	•–11	•–13
	2	•–10	•–11	•–12	•–13	•–14	•–15
	3	3–12	•–13	•–14	•–15	•–16	•–17
	4	4–14	4–15	•–16	•–17	•–18	•–19
	5	6–17	6–18	5–18	•–19	•–20	•–21
	6	8–19	7–20	7–20	6–21	6–22	•–•
14	0	•– 4	•– 5	•– 6	•– 7	•– 7	•– 9
	1	•– 6	•– 7	•– 8	•– 9	•–10	•–12
	2	•– 9	•–10	•–11	•–12	•–13	•–14
	3	3–11	•–12	•–13	•–14	•–15	•–16
	4	4–13	4–14	•–15	•–16	•–17	•–18
	5	6–15	5–16	5–17	•–18	•–19	•–20
	6	8–17	7–18	6–19	6–20	•–20	•–21
	7	10–19	9–20	8–21	7–22	7–22	•–•

N = 30

N_1	x_1	2α = 0,20	2α = 0,10	2α = 0,05	2α = 0,02	2α = 0,01	2α = 0,002
4	0	•–13	•–15	•–18	•–20	•–21	•–24
	1	•–20	•–22	•–24	•–25	•–26	•–27
	2	4–26	3–27	2–28	•–•	•–•	•–•
5	0	•–11	•–13	•–15	•–17	•–19	•–21
	1	•–17	•–19	•–21	•–23	•–24	•–25
	2	3–23	2–24	2–25	•–26	•–27	•–•
6	0	•– 9	•–11	•–13	•–15	•–17	•–19
	1	•–15	•–17	•–19	•–20	•–21	•–23
	2	3–20	2–21	•–23	•–24	•–25	•–26
	3	6–24	5–25	4–26	3–27	3–27	•–•
7	0	•– 8	•–10	•–11	•–13	•–15	•–17
	1	•–13	•–15	•–17	•–18	•–19	•–21
	2	2–18	2–19	•–21	•–22	•–23	•–24
	3	5–21	4–23	3–24	3–25	•–26	•–•
8	0	•– 7	•– 9	•–10	•–12	•–13	•–16
	1	•–12	•–13	•–15	•–16	•–18	•–20

N = 30 (continued)

N_1	x_1	2α = 0,20	2α = 0,10	2α = 0,05	2α = 0,02	2α = 0,01	2α = 0,002
	2	2–16	•–17	•–19	•–20	•–21	•–23
	3	4–19	4–21	3–22	•–23	•–24	•–25
	4	7–23	6–24	5–25	4–26	4–26	•–•
9	0	•– 6	•– 8	•– 9	•–11	•–12	•–14
	1	•–10	•–12	•–13	•–15	•–16	•–18
	2	2–14	•–16	•–17	•–18	•–19	•–21
	3	4–17	3–19	3–20	•–21	•–22	•–23
	4	7–21	6–22	5–23	4–24	4–24	•–25
10	0	•– 6	•– 7	•– 8	•–10	•–11	•–13
	1	•– 9	•–11	•–12	•–14	•–15	•–17
	2	•–13	•–14	•–16	•–17	•–18	•–19
	3	4–16	3–17	•–18	•–20	•–20	•–22
	4	6–19	5–20	4–21	4–22	•–23	•–24
	5	8–22	7–23	6–24	6–24	5–25	•–•
11	0	•– 5	•– 6	•– 7	•– 9	•–10	•–12
	1	•– 9	•–10	•–11	•–13	•–13	•–15
	2	•–12	•–13	•–14	•–16	•–16	•–18
	3	3–15	3–16	•–17	•–18	•–19	•–20
	4	5–17	5–19	4–20	•–21	•–21	•–23
	5	8–20	7–21	6–22	5–23	5–23	•–24
12	0	•– 5	•– 6	•– 7	•– 8	•– 9	•–11
	1	•– 8	•– 9	•–10	•–12	•–12	•–14
	2	•–11	•–12	•–13	•–14	•–15	•–17
	3	3–13	•–15	•–16	•–17	•–18	•–19
	4	5–16	4–17	4–18	•–19	•–20	•–21
	5	7–18	6–20	5–20	5–21	•–22	•–23
	6	9–21	8–22	7–23	7–23	6–24	•–•
13	0	•– 4	•– 5	•– 6	•– 7	•– 8	•–10
	1	•– 7	•– 8	•– 9	•–11	•–11	•–13
	2	•–10	•–11	•–12	•–13	•–14	•–16
	3	3–12	•–14	•–15	•–16	•–17	•–18
	4	5–15	4–16	•–17	•–18	•–19	•–20
	5	6–17	6–18	5–19	5–20	•–21	•–22
	6	9–19	8–20	7–21	6–22	6–23	•–23
14	0	•– 4	•– 5	•– 6	•– 7	•– 8	•– 9
	1	•– 7	•– 8	•– 9	•–10	•–11	•–12
	2	•– 9	•–10	•–11	•–12	•–13	•–15
	3	3–12	•–13	•–14	•–15	•–15	•–17
	4	4–14	4–15	•–16	•–17	•–18	•–19
	5	6–16	5–17	5–18	•–19	•–19	•–21
	6	8–18	7–19	6–20	6–21	•–21	•–22
	7	10–20	9–21	8–22	8–22	7–23	•–•
15	0	•– 4	•– 4	•– 5	•– 6	•– 7	•– 9
	1	•– 6	•– 7	•– 8	•– 9	•–10	•–11
	2	•– 9	•–10	•–11	•–12	•–12	•–14
	3	•–11	•–12	•–13	•–14	•–14	•–16
	4	4–13	4–14	•–15	•–16	•–16	•–18
	5	6–15	5–16	5–17	•–18	•–18	•–19
	6	7–17	7–18	6–19	6–20	•–20	•–21
	7	9–19	8–20	8–21	7–21	7–22	•–•

N = 31

N_1	x_1	2α = 0,20	2α = 0,10	2α = 0,05	2α = 0,02	2α = 0,01	2α = 0,002
4	0	•–13	•–16	•–18	•–21	•–22	•–25
	1	•–21	•–23	•–25	•–26	•–27	•–28
	2	4–27	3–28	2–29	•–•	•–•	•–•
5	0	•–11	•–14	•–16	•–18	•–19	•–22
	1	•–18	•–20	•–22	•–23	•–25	•–26
	2	3–23	2–25	2–26	•–27	•–28	•–•
6	0	•–10	•–12	•–14	•–16	•–17	•–20
	1	•–15	•–18	•–19	•–21	•–22	•–24
	2	3–20	2–22	•–24	•–25	•–26	•–27
	3	6–25	5–26	4–27	3–28	3–28	•–•
7	0	•– 8	•–10	•–12	•–14	•–15	•–18
	1	•–14	•–16	•–17	•–19	•–20	•–22
	2	2–18	2–20	•–21	•–23	•–24	•–25
	3	5–22	4–24	3–25	3–26	•–27	•–•
8	0	•– 7	•– 9	•–11	•–12	•–14	•–16
	1	•–12	•–14	•–15	•–17	•–18	•–20
	2	2–16	•–18	•–19	•–21	•–22	•–23
	3	5–20	4–21	3–23	•–24	•–25	•–26
	4	8–23	6–25	5–26	5–26	4–27	•–•
9	0	•– 7	•– 8	•– 9	•–11	•–12	•–15
	1	•–11	•–12	•–14	•–16	•–17	•–19
	2	2–15	•–16	•–18	•–19	•–20	•–22
	3	4–18	3–20	3–21	•–22	•–23	•–24
	4	7–21	6–23	5–24	4–25	4–25	•–26
10	0	•– 6	•– 7	•– 9	•–10	•–11	•–13
	1	•–10	•–11	•–13	•–14	•–15	•–17
	2	2–13	•–15	•–16	•–17	•–18	•–20
	3	4–17	3–18	•–19	•–20	•–21	•–23
	4	6–20	5–21	4–22	4–23	•–24	•–25
	5	9–22	8–23	7–24	6–25	5–26	•–•
11	0	•– 5	•– 7	•– 8	•– 9	•–10	•–12
	1	•– 9	•–10	•–12	•–13	•–14	•–16
	2	•–12	•–14	•–15	•–16	•–17	•–19
	3	3–15	3–17	•–18	•–19	•–20	•–21
	4	6–18	5–19	4–20	•–21	•–22	•–23
	5	8–21	7–22	6–23	5–24	5–24	•–25
12	0	•– 5	•– 6	•– 7	•– 8	•– 9	•–11
	1	•– 8	•– 9	•–11	•–12	•–13	•–15
	2	•–11	•–12	•–14	•–15	•–16	•–18
	3	3–14	3–15	•–16	•–18	•–18	•–20
	4	5–17	4–18	4–19	•–20	•–21	•–22
	5	7–19	6–20	6–21	5–22	5–23	•–24
	6	9–22	8–23	8–23	7–24	6–25	•–•

N = 31 (continued)

N_1	x_1	2α = 0,20	2α = 0,10	2α = 0,05	2α = 0,02	2α = 0,01	2α = 0,002
13	0	•– 4	•– 6	•– 7	•– 8	•– 9	•–10
	1	•– 8	•– 9	•–10	•–11	•–12	•–14
	2	•–10	•–12	•–13	•–14	•–15	•–16
	3	3–13	•–14	•–15	•–16	•–17	•–19
	4	5–15	4–17	4–18	•–19	•–19	•–21
	5	7–18	6–19	5–20	5–21	•–21	•–23
	6	9–20	8–21	7–22	6–23	6–23	•–24
14	0	•– 4	•– 5	•– 6	•– 7	•– 8	•–10
	1	•– 7	•– 8	•– 9	•–10	•–11	•–13
	2	•–10	•–11	•–12	•–13	•–14	•–15
	3	3–12	•–13	•–14	•–15	•–16	•–17
	4	4–14	4–15	•–16	•–17	•–18	•–20
	5	6–17	5–18	5–19	•–20	•–20	•–21
	6	8–19	7–20	7–21	6–21	6–22	•–23
	7	10–21	9–22	8–23	8–23	7–24	•–•
15	0	•– 4	•– 5	•– 6	•– 7	•– 7	•– 9
	1	•– 6	•– 8	•– 8	•–10	•–10	•–12
	2	•– 9	•–10	•–11	•–12	•–13	•–14
	3	•–11	•–12	•–13	•–14	•–15	•–16
	4	4–13	4–14	•–15	•–16	•–17	•–18
	5	6–16	5–17	5–17	•–18	•–19	•–20
	6	8–18	7–19	6–19	6–20	•–21	•–22
	7	9–20	9–21	8–21	7–22	7–23	•–23

N = 32

N_1	x_1	2α = 0,20	2α = 0,10	2α = 0,05	2α = 0,02	2α = 0,01	2α = 0,002
4	0	•–14	•–17	•–19	•–21	•–23	•–25
	1	•–22	•–24	•–26	•–27	•–28	•–29
	2	4–28	3–29	2–30	•–•	•–•	•–•
5	0	•–12	•–14	•–16	•–18	•–20	•–23
	1	•–18	•–21	•–22	•–24	•–25	•–27
	2	3–24	2–26	2–27	•–28	•–29	•–•
6	0	•–10	•–12	•–14	•–16	•–18	•–21
	1	•–16	•–18	•–20	•–22	•–23	•–25
	2	3–21	2–23	•–24	•–26	•–27	•–28
	3	6–26	5–27	4–28	3–29	3–29	•–•
7	0	•– 9	•–11	•–12	•–14	•–16	•–19
	1	•–14	•–16	•–18	•–20	•–21	•–23
	2	2–19	2–21	•–22	•–24	•–24	•–26
	3	5–23	4–24	3–26	3–27	•–27	•–28
8	0	•– 8	•– 9	•–11	•–13	•–14	•–17
	1	•–13	•–14	•–16	•–18	•–19	•–21
	2	2–17	•–18	•–20	•–21	•–22	•–24
	3	5–21	4–22	3–23	•–25	•–25	•–27
	4	8–24	7–25	6–26	5–27	4–28	•–•
9	0	•– 7	•– 8	•–10	•–12	•–13	•–15
	1	•–11	•–13	•–14	•–16	•–17	•–19
	2	2–15	•–17	•–18	•–20	•–21	•–23
	3	4–19	3–20	3–21	•–23	•–24	•–25
	4	7–22	6–23	5–24	4–26	4–26	•–27
10	0	•– 6	•– 8	•– 9	•–11	•–12	•–14
	1	•–10	•–12	•–13	•–15	•–16	•–18
	2	2–14	•–15	•–17	•–18	•–19	•–21
	3	4–17	3–19	3–20	•–21	•–22	•–24
	4	6–20	5–22	5–23	4–24	•–24	•–26
	5	9–23	8–24	7–25	6–26	5–27	•–•
11	0	•– 6	•– 7	•– 8	•–10	•–11	•–13
	1	•– 9	•–11	•–12	•–13	•–14	•–17
	2	•–13	•–14	•–15	•–17	•–18	•–19
	3	3–16	3–17	•–18	•–20	•–20	•–22
	4	6–19	5–20	4–21	4–22	•–23	•–24
	5	8–21	7–23	6–23	5–24	5–25	•–26
12	0	•– 5	•– 6	•– 7	•– 9	•–10	•–12
	1	•– 9	•–10	•–11	•–12	•–13	•–15
	2	•–12	•–13	•–14	•–15	•–16	•–18
	3	3–14	3–16	•–17	•–18	•–19	•–21
	4	5–17	4–18	4–20	•–21	•–21	•–23
	5	7–20	6–21	6–22	5–23	5–24	•–25
	6	10–22	9–23	8–24	7–25	6–26	•–•
13	0	•– 5	•– 6	•– 7	•– 8	•– 9	•–11
	1	•– 8	•– 9	•–10	•–11	•–12	•–14
	2	•–11	•–12	•–13	•–14	•–15	•–17
	3	3–13	•–15	•–16	•–17	•–18	•–19
	4	5–16	4–17	4–18	•–19	•–20	•–21
	5	7–18	6–20	5–21	5–22	•–22	•–23
	6	9–21	8–22	7–23	6–24	6–24	•–25
14	0	•– 4	•– 5	•– 6	•– 7	•– 8	•–10
	1	•– 7	•– 8	•– 9	•–11	•–11	•–13
	2	•–10	•–11	•–12	•–13	•–14	•–16
	3	3–12	•–14	•–15	•–16	•–17	•–18
	4	5–15	4–16	•–17	•–18	•–19	•–20
	5	6–17	6–18	5–19	5–20	•–21	•–22
	6	8–19	8–20	7–21	6–22	6–23	•–24
	7	10–22	9–23	9–23	8–24	7–25	•–•
15	0	•– 4	•– 5	•– 6	•– 7	•– 8	•– 9
	1	•– 7	•– 8	•– 9	•–10	•–11	•–12
	2	•– 9	•–10	•–11	•–12	•–13	•–15
	3	3–12	•–13	•–14	•–15	•–16	•–17
	4	4–14	4–15	•–16	•–17	•–18	•–19
	5	6–16	5–17	5–18	•–19	•–20	•–21
	6	8–18	7–19	6–20	6–21	•–22	•–23
	7	10–20	9–21	8–22	7–23	7–23	•–24
16	0	•– 4	•– 5	•– 5	•– 6	•– 7	•– 9
	1	•– 6	•– 7	•– 8	•– 9	•–10	•–12
	2	•– 9	•–10	•–11	•–12	•–12	•–14
	3	•–11	•–12	•–13	•–14	•–15	•–16

All values conform to the international convention (i.e. 0,1 instead of 0.1).

Significance Limits for the Fourfold Table Test*

x_1	N_1-x_1	N_1
x_2	N_2-x_2	N_2
X	$N-X$	N

$N=N_1+N_2$, $X=x_1+x_2$, $N_1 \leq N_2$, $x_1 \leq N_1-x_1$

For explanation see page 151

N_1	x_1	2α = 0,20	2α = 0,10	2α = 0,05	2α = 0,02	2α = 0,01	2α = 0,002
		N = 32 (continued)					
16	4	4–13	•–14	•–15	•–16	•–17	•–18
	5	6–15	5–16	5–17	•–18	•–19	•–20
	6	7–17	7–18	6–19	6–20	•–20	•–22
	7	9–19	8–20	8–21	7–22	7–22	•–23
	8	11–21	10–22	9–23	9–23	8–24	•–•
		N = 33					
4	0	•–14	•–17	•–19	•–22	•–24	•–26
	1	•–22	•–25	•–26	•–28	•–29	•–30
	2	5–28	3–30	2–31	•–•	•–•	•–•
5	0	•–12	•–14	•–17	•–19	•–21	•–24
	1	•–19	•–21	•–23	•–25	•–26	•–28
	2	4–25	2–27	2–28	•–29	•–30	•–•
6	0	•–10	•–12	•–14	•–17	•–18	•–21
	1	•–17	•–19	•–20	•–22	•–24	•–26
	2	3–22	2–24	•–25	•–27	•–27	•–29
	3	7–26	5–28	4–29	3–30	3–30	•–•
7	0	•– 9	•–11	•–13	•–15	•–16	•–19
	1	•–15	•–17	•–18	•–20	•–21	•–24
	2	2–19	2–21	•–23	•–24	•–25	•–27
	3	6–24	4–25	4–26	3–28	•–28	•–29
8	0	•– 8	•–10	•–11	•–13	•–15	•–17
	1	•–13	•–15	•–16	•–18	•–19	•–22
	2	2–17	•–19	•–21	•–22	•–23	•–25
	3	5–21	4–23	3–24	•–25	•–26	•–28
	4	8–25	7–26	6–27	5–28	4–29	•–•
9	0	•– 7	•– 9	•–10	•–12	•–13	•–16
	1	•–12	•–13	•–15	•–17	•–18	•–20
	2	2–16	•–17	•–19	•–20	•–21	•–23
	3	4–19	3–21	3–22	•–24	•–24	•–26
	4	7–23	6–24	5–25	4–26	4–27	•–28
10	0	•– 6	•– 8	•– 9	•–11	•–12	•–14
	1	•–11	•–12	•–14	•–15	•–16	•–19
	2	2–14	•–16	•–17	•–19	•–20	•–22
	3	4–18	3–19	3–20	•–22	•–23	•–24
	4	6–21	5–22	5–23	4–25	•–25	•–27
	5	9–24	8–25	7–26	6–27	5–28	•–•
11	0	•– 6	•– 7	•– 8	•–10	•–11	•–13
	1	•–10	•–11	•–12	•–14	•–15	•–17
	2	•–13	•–15	•–16	•–17	•–18	•–20
	3	4–16	3–18	•–19	•–20	•–21	•–23
	4	6–19	5–21	4–22	4–23	•–24	•–25
	5	8–22	7–23	6–24	6–25	5–26	•–27
12	0	•– 5	•– 6	•– 8	•– 9	•–10	•–12
	1	•– 9	•–10	•–11	•–13	•–14	•–16
	2	•–12	•–13	•–15	•–16	•–17	•–19
	3	3–15	3–16	•–18	•–19	•–20	•–21
	4	5–18	5–19	4–20	•–21	•–22	•–24
	5	8–20	7–22	6–23	5–24	5–24	•–26
	6	10–23	9–24	8–25	7–26	7–26	6–27
13	0	•– 5	•– 6	•– 7	•– 8	•– 9	•–11
	1	•– 8	•– 9	•–11	•–12	•–13	•–15
	2	•–11	•–12	•–14	•–15	•–16	•–18
	3	3–14	•–15	•–16	•–18	•–18	•–20
	4	5–16	4–18	4–19	•–20	•–21	•–22
	5	7–19	6–20	6–21	5–22	•–23	•–24
	6	9–21	8–23	7–23	7–24	6–25	•–26
14	0	•– 4	•– 5	•– 6	•– 8	•– 9	•–10
	1	•– 8	•– 9	•–10	•–11	•–12	•–14
	2	•–10	•–12	•–13	•–14	•–15	•–16
	3	3–13	•–14	•–15	•–16	•–17	•–19
	4	5–15	4–17	4–18	•–19	•–20	•–21
	5	7–18	6–19	5–20	5–21	•–22	•–23
	6	9–20	8–21	7–22	6–23	6–24	•–25
	7	11–22	10–23	9–24	8–25	8–25	7–26
15	0	•– 4	•– 5	•– 6	•– 7	•– 8	•–10
	1	•– 7	•– 8	•– 9	•–10	•–11	•–13
	2	•–10	•–11	•–12	•–13	•–14	•–15
	3	3–12	•–13	•–14	•–15	•–16	•–18
	4	4–14	4–16	•–17	•–18	•–18	•–20
	5	6–17	5–18	5–19	•–20	•–20	•–22
	6	8–19	7–20	7–21	6–22	6–22	•–24
	7	10–21	9–22	8–23	8–24	7–24	•–25
16	0	•– 4	•– 5	•– 6	•– 7	•– 7	•– 9
	1	•– 7	•– 8	•– 8	•–10	•–10	•–12
	2	•– 9	•–10	•–11	•–12	•–13	•–14
	3	•–11	•–12	•–13	•–14	•–15	•–17
	4	4–13	4–15	•–16	•–17	•–17	•–19
	5	6–16	5–17	5–18	•–19	•–19	•–21
	6	8–18	7–19	6–20	6–21	•–21	•–22
	7	9–20	9–21	8–22	7–22	7–23	•–24
	8	11–22	10–23	10–23	9–24	8–25	8–25
		N = 34					
4	0	•–15	•–18	•–20	•–23	•–24	•–27
	1	•–23	•–25	•–27	•–29	•–30	•–31
	2	5–29	3–31	2–32	•–•	•–•	•–•
5	0	•–12	•–15	•–17	•–20	•–21	•–24
	1	•–20	•–22	•–24	•–26	•–27	•–29
	2	4–26	2–27	2–29	•–30	•–31	•–•
6	0	•–11	•–13	•–15	•–17	•–19	•–22
	1	•–17	•–19	•–21	•–23	•–24	•–27
	2	3–22	2–24	•–26	•–27	•–28	•–30
	3	7–27	5–29	4–30	3–31	3–31	•–•
		N = 34 (continued)					
7	0	•– 9	•–11	•–13	•–15	•–17	•–20
	1	•–15	•–17	•–19	•–21	•–22	•–24
	2	2–20	2–22	•–23	•–25	•–26	•–28
	3	6–24	5–26	4–27	3–28	•–29	•–30
8	0	•– 8	•–10	•–12	•–14	•–15	•–18
	1	•–13	•–15	•–17	•–19	•–20	•–22
	2	2–18	2–20	•–21	•–23	•–24	•–26
	3	5–22	4–24	3–25	3–26	•–27	•–29
	4	8–26	7–27	6–28	5–29	4–30	•–•
9	0	•– 7	•– 9	•–10	•–12	•–14	•–16
	1	•–12	•–14	•–15	•–17	•–18	•–21
	2	2–16	•–18	•–19	•–21	•–22	•–24
	3	4–20	4–22	3–23	•–24	•–25	•–27
	4	7–23	6–25	5–26	4–27	4–28	•–29
10	0	•– 7	•– 8	•– 9	•–11	•–12	•–15
	1	•–11	•–13	•–14	•–16	•–17	•–19
	2	2–15	•–16	•–18	•–19	•–20	•–22
	3	4–18	3–20	3–21	•–23	•–23	•–25
	4	7–21	6–23	5–24	4–25	4–26	•–27
	5	9–25	8–26	7–27	6–28	6–28	5–29
11	0	•– 6	•– 7	•– 9	•–10	•–11	•–14
	1	•–10	•–11	•–13	•–14	•–16	•–18
	2	2–13	•–15	•–16	•–18	•–19	•–21
	3	4–17	3–18	•–19	•–21	•–22	•–24
	4	6–20	5–21	4–22	4–24	•–24	•–26
	5	9–23	7–24	7–25	6–26	5–27	•–28
12	0	•– 5	•– 7	•– 8	•– 9	•–10	•–13
	1	•– 9	•–11	•–12	•–13	•–14	•–16
	2	•–12	•–14	•–15	•–17	•–18	•–19
	3	3–15	3–17	•–18	•–19	•–20	•–22
	4	6–18	5–20	4–21	•–22	•–23	•–24
	5	8–21	7–22	6–23	5–25	5–25	•–26
	6	10–24	9–25	8–26	7–27	7–27	6–28
13	0	•– 5	•– 6	•– 7	•– 9	•–10	•–12
	1	•– 8	•–10	•–11	•–12	•–13	•–15
	2	•–11	•–13	•–14	•–15	•–16	•–18
	3	3–14	3–16	•–17	•–18	•–19	•–21
	4	5–17	4–18	4–19	•–21	•–22	•–23
	5	7–20	6–21	6–22	5–23	5–24	•–25
	6	10–22	8–23	8–24	7–25	6–26	•–27
14	0	•– 5	•– 6	•– 7	•– 8	•– 9	•–11
	1	•– 8	•– 9	•–10	•–11	•–12	•–14
	2	•–11	•–12	•–13	•–14	•–15	•–17
	3	3–13	•–15	•–16	•–17	•–18	•–20
	4	5–16	4–17	4–18	•–19	•–20	•–22
	5	7–18	6–20	5–21	5–22	•–22	•–24
	6	9–21	8–22	7–23	6–24	6–24	•–26
	7	11–23	10–24	9–25	8–26	8–26	7–27
15	0	•– 4	•– 5	•– 6	•– 7	•– 8	•–10
	1	•– 7	•– 8	•– 9	•–11	•–12	•–13
	2	•–10	•–11	•–12	•–13	•–14	•–16
	3	3–12	•–14	•–15	•–16	•–17	•–18
	4	4–15	4–16	•–17	•–18	•–19	•–21
	5	6–17	6–18	5–19	•–20	•–21	•–22
	6	8–19	7–21	7–21	6–22	6–23	•–24
	7	10–22	9–23	9–23	8–24	7–25	•–26
16	0	•– 4	•– 5	•– 6	•– 7	•– 8	•– 9
	1	•– 7	•– 8	•– 9	•–10	•–11	•–12
	2	•– 9	•–10	•–11	•–13	•–13	•–15
	3	3–12	•–13	•–14	•–15	•–16	•–17
	4	4–14	4–15	•–16	•–17	•–18	•–19
	5	6–16	5–17	5–18	•–19	•–20	•–21
	6	8–18	7–19	6–20	6–21	•–22	•–23
	7	10–20	9–21	8–22	7–23	7–24	•–25
	8	12–22	11–23	10–24	9–25	9–25	8–26
17	0	•– 4	•– 5	•– 5	•– 6	•– 7	•– 9
	1	•– 6	•– 7	•– 8	•– 9	•–10	•–12
	2	•– 9	•–10	•–11	•–12	•–13	•–14
	3	•–11	•–12	•–13	•–14	•–15	•–16
	4	4–13	•–14	•–15	•–16	•–17	•–18
	5	6–15	5–16	5–17	•–18	•–19	•–20
	6	7–17	7–18	6–19	6–20	•–21	•–22
	7	9–19	8–20	8–21	7–22	7–23	•–24
	8	11–21	10–22	9–23	9–24	8–24	•–25
		N = 35					
4	0	•–15	•–18	•–21	•–23	•–25	•–28
	1	•–24	•–26	•–28	•–30	•–31	•–32
	2	5–30	3–32	2–33	•–•	•–•	•–•
5	0	•–13	•–15	•–18	•–20	•–22	•–25
	1	•–20	•–23	•–25	•–27	•–28	•–30
	2	4–26	3–28	2–30	•–31	•–32	•–•
6	0	•–11	•–13	•–15	•–18	•–19	•–23
	1	•–18	•–20	•–22	•–24	•–25	•–27
	2	3–23	2–25	•–27	•–28	•–29	•–31
	3	7–28	6–29	4–31	3–32	3–32	•–•
7	0	•– 9	•–12	•–14	•–16	•–17	•–20
	1	•–15	•–18	•–19	•–21	•–23	•–25
	2	3–21	2–23	•–24	•–26	•–27	•–29
	3	6–25	5–27	4–28	3–29	•–30	•–31
8	0	•– 8	•–10	•–12	•–14	•–16	•–19
	1	•–14	•–16	•–17	•–19	•–21	•–23
	2	2–18	2–20	•–22	•–24	•–25	•–27
	3	5–23	4–24	3–26	3–27	•–28	•–29
	4	9–26	7–28	6–29	5–30	4–31	•–•
		N = 35 (continued)					
9	0	•– 7	•– 9	•–11	•–13	•–14	•–17
	1	•–12	•–14	•–16	•–18	•–19	•–21
	2	2–17	•–18	•–20	•–22	•–23	•–25
	3	5–21	4–22	3–24	•–25	•–26	•–28
	4	8–24	6–26	5–27	4–28	4–29	•–30
10	0	•– 7	•– 8	•–10	•–12	•–13	•–16
	1	•–11	•–13	•–14	•–16	•–17	•–20
	2	2–15	•–17	•–18	•–20	•–21	•–23
	3	4–19	3–20	3–22	•–23	•–24	•–26
	4	7–22	6–24	5–25	4–26	4–27	•–28
	5	10–25	8–27	7–28	6–29	6–29	5–30
11	0	•– 6	•– 8	•– 9	•–11	•–12	•–14
	1	•–10	•–12	•–13	•–15	•–16	•–18
	2	2–14	•–15	•–17	•–18	•–20	•–22
	3	4–17	3–19	•–20	•–22	•–23	•–24
	4	6–20	5–22	4–23	4–24	•–25	•–27
	5	9–23	8–25	7–26	6–27	5–28	•–29
12	0	•– 6	•– 7	•– 8	•–10	•–11	•–13
	1	•– 9	•–11	•–12	•–14	•–15	•–17
	2	•–13	•–14	•–16	•–17	•–18	•–20
	3	3–16	3–17	•–19	•–20	•–21	•–23
	4	6–19	5–20	4–21	4–23	•–24	•–25
	5	8–22	7–23	6–24	5–25	5–26	•–27
	6	11–24	9–26	8–27	7–28	7–28	6–29
13	0	•– 5	•– 6	•– 8	•– 9	•–10	•–12
	1	•– 9	•–10	•–11	•–13	•–14	•–16
	2	•–12	•–13	•–14	•–16	•–17	•–19
	3	3–15	3–16	•–17	•–19	•–20	•–21
	4	5–18	4–19	4–20	•–21	•–22	•–24
	5	7–20	6–22	6–23	5–24	5–25	•–26
	6	10–23	9–24	8–25	7–26	6–27	•–28
14	0	•– 5	•– 6	•– 7	•– 8	•– 9	•–11
	1	•– 8	•– 9	•–10	•–12	•–13	•–15
	2	•–11	•–12	•–13	•–15	•–16	•–18
	3	3–14	•–15	•–16	•–18	•–18	•–20
	4	5–16	4–18	4–19	•–20	•–21	•–22
	5	7–19	6–20	5–21	5–22	•–23	•–25
	6	9–21	8–23	7–23	7–25	6–25	•–26
	7	11–24	10–25	9–26	8–27	8–27	7–28
15	0	•– 4	•– 5	•– 6	•– 8	•– 9	•–11
	1	•– 7	•– 9	•–10	•–11	•–12	•–14
	2	•–10	•–11	•–13	•–14	•–15	•–17
	3	3–13	•–14	•–15	•–16	•–17	•–19
	4	5–15	4–17	•–18	•–19	•–20	•–21
	5	6–18	6–19	5–20	5–21	•–22	•–23
	6	8–20	8–21	7–22	6–23	6–24	•–25
	7	11–22	10–23	9–24	8–25	7–26	7–27
16	0	•– 4	•– 5	•– 6	•– 7	•– 8	•–10
	1	•– 7	•– 8	•– 9	•–10	•–11	•–13
	2	•–10	•–11	•–12	•–13	•–14	•–16
	3	3–12	•–13	•–14	•–15	•–16	•–18
	4	4–14	4–16	•–17	•–18	•–19	•–20
	5	6–17	5–18	5–19	•–20	•–21	•–22
	6	8–19	7–20	7–21	6–22	6–23	•–24
	7	10–21	9–22	8–23	8–24	7–25	•–26
	8	12–23	11–24	10–25	9–26	9–26	8–27
17	0	•– 4	•– 5	•– 6	•– 7	•– 7	•– 9
	1	•– 7	•– 8	•– 8	•–10	•–10	•–12
	2	•– 9	•–10	•–11	•–12	•–13	•–15
	3	•–11	•–12	•–13	•–15	•–15	•–17
	4	4–14	4–15	•–16	•–17	•–17	•–19
	5	6–16	5–17	5–18	•–19	•–20	•–21
	6	8–18	7–19	6–20	6–21	•–21	•–23
	7	9–20	9–21	8–22	7–23	7–23	•–24
	8	11–22	10–23	10–24	9–24	8–25	•–26
		N = 36					
4	0	•–16	•–19	•–21	•–24	•–26	•–29
	1	•–24	•–27	•–29	•–31	•–32	•–33
	2	5–31	3–33	2–34	2–34	•–•	•–•
5	0	•–13	•–16	•–18	•–21	•–23	•–26
	1	•–21	•–23	•–25	•–27	•–29	•–31
	2	4–27	3–29	2–30	•–32	•–33	•–•
6	0	•–11	•–14	•–16	•–18	•–20	•–23
	1	•–18	•–20	•–22	•–25	•–26	•–28
	2	3–24	2–26	2–27	•–29	•–30	•–32
	3	7–29	6–30	5–31	3–33	3–33	•–•
7	0	•–10	•–12	•–14	•–16	•–18	•–21
	1	•–16	•–18	•–20	•–22	•–23	•–26
	2	3–21	2–23	•–25	•–27	•–28	•–30
	3	6–26	5–27	4–29	3–30	3–31	•–32
8	0	•– 9	•–11	•–12	•–15	•–16	•–19
	1	•–14	•–16	•–18	•–20	•–21	•–24
	2	2–19	2–21	•–23	•–24	•–25	•–28
	3	5–23	4–25	3–26	3–28	•–29	•–30
	4	9–27	7–29	6–30	5–31	4–32	•–•
9	0	•– 8	•– 9	•–11	•–13	•–15	•–17
	1	•–13	•–15	•–16	•–18	•–20	•–22
	2	2–17	•–19	•–21	•–22	•–23	•–26
	3	5–21	4–23	3–24	•–26	•–27	•–29
	4	8–25	7–26	6–28	5–29	4–30	•–31
10	0	•– 7	•– 9	•–10	•–12	•–13	•–16
	1	•–12	•–13	•–15	•–17	•–18	•–20
	2	2–16	•–17	•–19	•–21	•–22	•–24
	3	4–19	3–21	3–22	•–24	•–25	•–27

* Reproduction only by permission of the publishers of the *Geigy Scientific Tables.*

All values conform to the international convention (i.e. 0,1 instead of 0.1).

Significance Limits for the Fourfold Table Test*

x_1	N_1-x_1	N_1
x_2	N_2-x_2	N_2
X	$N-X$	N

$N=N_1+N_2$
$X=x_1+x_2$
$N_1\leq N_2$
$x_1\leq N_1-x_1$

For explanation see page 151

N = 36 (continued)

N_1	x_1	2α = 0,20	2α = 0,10	2α = 0,05	2α = 0,02	2α = 0,01	2α = 0,002
	4	7–23	6–24	5–26	4–27	4–28	•–29
	5	10–26	9–27	8–28	6–30	6–30	5–31
11	0	•–6	•–8	•–9	•–11	•–12	•–15
	1	•–11	•–12	•–14	•–15	•–17	•–19
	2	2–14	•–16	•–17	•–19	•–20	•–22
	3	4–18	3–19	3–21	•–22	•–23	•–25
	4	6–21	5–23	5–24	4–25	•–26	•–28
	5	9–24	8–25	7–27	6–28	5–28	•–30
12	0	•–6	•–7	•–8	•–10	•–11	•–14
	1	•–10	•–11	•–13	•–14	•–15	•–18
	2	•–13	•–15	•–16	•–18	•–19	•–21
	3	4–16	3–18	•–19	•–21	•–22	•–24
	4	6–19	5–21	4–22	4–24	•–24	•–26
	5	8–22	7–24	6–25	5–26	5–27	•–28
	6	11–25	10–26	9–27	8–28	7–29	6–30
13	0	•–5	•–7	•–8	•–9	•–10	•–13
	1	•–9	•–10	•–12	•–13	•–14	•–16
	2	•–12	•–14	•–15	•–16	•–17	•–19
	3	3–15	3–17	•–18	•–19	•–20	•–22
	4	5–18	5–19	4–21	•–22	•–23	•–25
	5	8–21	7–22	6–23	5–25	5–25	•–27
	6	10–23	9–25	8–26	7–27	7–27	6–29
14	0	•–5	•–6	•–7	•–9	•–10	•–12
	1	•–8	•–10	•–11	•–12	•–13	•–15
	2	•–11	•–13	•–14	•–15	•–16	•–18
	3	3–14	•–16	•–17	•–18	•–19	•–21
	4	5–17	4–18	4–19	•–21	•–22	•–23
	5	7–19	6–21	6–22	5–23	•–24	•–25
	6	9–22	8–23	7–24	7–25	6–26	•–27
	7	12–24	10–26	10–26	9–27	8–28	7–29
15	0	•–5	•–6	•–7	•–8	•–9	•–11
	1	•–8	•–9	•–10	•–11	•–12	•–14
	2	•–11	•–12	•–13	•–14	•–15	•–17
	3	3–13	•–15	•–16	•–17	•–18	•–20
	4	5–16	4–17	4–18	•–19	•–20	•–22
	5	7–18	6–20	5–21	5–22	•–23	•–24
	6	9–21	8–22	7–23	6–24	6–25	•–26
	7	11–23	10–24	9–25	8–26	8–27	7–28
16	0	•–4	•–5	•–6	•–7	•–8	•–10
	1	•–7	•–8	•–9	•–11	•–12	•–13
	2	•–10	•–11	•–12	•–13	•–14	•–16
	3	3–12	•–14	•–15	•–16	•–17	•–19
	4	4–15	4–16	•–17	•–18	•–19	•–21
	5	6–17	6–18	5–19	•–21	•–21	•–23
	6	8–19	7–21	7–22	6–23	6–23	•–25
	7	10–22	9–23	8–24	8–25	7–25	•–26
	8	12–24	11–25	10–26	9–27	9–27	8–28
17	0	•–4	•–5	•–6	•–7	•–8	•–9
	1	•–7	•–8	•–9	•–10	•–11	•–13
	2	•–9	•–10	•–11	•–13	•–13	•–15
	3	3–12	•–13	•–14	•–15	•–16	•–17
	4	4–14	4–15	•–16	•–17	•–18	•–20
	5	6–16	5–17	5–18	•–19	•–20	•–22
	6	8–18	7–19	6–20	6–21	•–22	•–23
	7	10–20	9–22	8–22	7–23	7–24	•–25
	8	12–22	11–23	10–24	9–25	8–26	8–27
18	0	•–4	•–5	•–5	•–6	•–7	•–9
	1	•–6	•–7	•–8	•–9	•–10	•–12
	2	•–9	•–10	•–11	•–12	•–13	•–14
	3	•–11	•–12	•–13	•–14	•–15	•–17
	4	4–13	•–14	•–15	•–16	•–17	•–19
	5	6–15	5–16	5–17	•–18	•–19	•–21
	6	7–17	7–18	6–19	6–20	•–21	•–22
	7	9–19	8–20	8–21	7–22	7–23	•–24
	8	11–21	10–22	9–23	9–24	8–25	•–26
	9	13–23	12–24	11–25	10–26	10–26	9–27

N = 37 (continued)

N_1	x_1	2α = 0,20	2α = 0,10	2α = 0,05	2α = 0,02	2α = 0,01	2α = 0,002
	3	4–20	3–22	3–23	•–25	•–26	•–28
	4	7–23	6–25	5–26	4–28	4–29	•–30
	5	10–27	9–28	8–29	7–30	6–31	5–32
11	0	•–6	•–8	•–10	•–11	•–13	•–15
	1	•–11	•–13	•–14	•–16	•–17	•–20
	2	2–15	•–16	•–18	•–20	•–21	•–23
	3	4–18	3–20	3–21	•–23	•–24	•–26
	4	7–22	5–23	5–24	4–26	4–27	•–28
	5	9–25	8–26	7–27	6–29	5–29	•–31
12	0	•–6	•–7	•–9	•–10	•–12	•–14
	1	•–10	•–12	•–13	•–15	•–16	•–18
	2	2–14	•–15	•–17	•–18	•–19	•–21
	3	4–17	3–18	•–20	•–21	•–22	•–24
	4	6–20	5–22	4–23	4–24	•–25	•–27
	5	9–23	7–24	6–26	6–27	5–28	•–29
	6	11–26	10–27	9–28	8–29	7–30	6–31
13	0	•–5	•–7	•–8	•–10	•–11	•–13
	1	•–9	•–11	•–12	•–14	•–15	•–17
	2	•–13	•–14	•–15	•–17	•–18	•–20
	3	3–16	3–17	•–18	•–20	•–21	•–23
	4	6–19	5–20	4–21	•–23	•–24	•–25
	5	8–21	7–23	6–24	5–25	5–26	•–28
	6	10–24	9–25	8–26	7–28	7–28	6–30
14	0	•–5	•–6	•–7	•–9	•–10	•–12
	1	•–9	•–10	•–11	•–13	•–14	•–16
	2	•–12	•–13	•–14	•–16	•–17	•–19
	3	3–15	3–16	•–17	•–19	•–20	•–22
	4	5–17	4–19	4–20	•–21	•–22	•–24
	5	7–20	6–21	6–23	5–24	5–25	•–26
	6	10–23	8–24	8–25	7–26	6–27	•–28
	7	12–25	11–26	10–27	9–28	8–29	7–30
15	0	•–5	•–6	•–7	•–8	•–9	•–11
	1	•–8	•–9	•–10	•–12	•–13	•–15
	2	•–11	•–12	•–13	•–15	•–16	•–18
	3	3–14	•–15	•–16	•–18	•–18	•–20
	4	5–16	4–18	4–19	•–20	•–21	•–23
	5	7–19	6–20	5–21	5–22	•–23	•–25
	6	9–21	8–22	7–24	6–25	6–25	•–27
	7	11–24	10–25	9–26	8–27	8–27	7–29
16	0	•–4	•–5	•–6	•–8	•–9	•–11
	1	•–7	•–9	•–10	•–11	•–12	•–14
	2	•–10	•–11	•–13	•–14	•–15	•–17
	3	3–13	•–14	•–15	•–17	•–17	•–19
	4	5–15	4–17	•–18	•–19	•–20	•–21
	5	6–18	6–19	5–20	•–21	•–22	•–24
	6	8–20	7–21	7–22	6–23	6–24	•–25
	7	10–22	9–23	9–24	8–25	7–26	•–27
	8	13–24	11–26	11–26	10–27	9–28	8–29
17	0	•–4	•–5	•–6	•–7	•–8	•–10
	1	•–7	•–8	•–9	•–10	•–11	•–13
	2	•–10	•–11	•–12	•–13	•–14	•–16
	3	3–12	•–13	•–14	•–16	•–16	•–18
	4	4–14	4–16	•–17	•–18	•–19	•–20
	5	6–17	5–18	5–19	•–20	•–21	•–22
	6	8–19	7–20	6–21	6–22	•–23	•–24
	7	10–21	9–22	8–23	7–24	7–25	•–26
	8	12–23	11–24	10–25	9–26	9–27	8–28
18	0	•–4	•–5	•–6	•–7	•–7	•–9
	1	•–7	•–8	•–9	•–10	•–11	•–12
	2	•–9	•–10	•–11	•–12	•–13	•–15
	3	•–11	•–12	•–13	•–15	•–15	•–17
	4	4–14	4–15	•–16	•–17	•–18	•–19
	5	6–16	5–17	5–18	•–19	•–20	•–21
	6	8–18	7–19	6–20	6–21	•–22	•–23
	7	9–20	8–21	8–22	7–23	7–24	•–25
	8	11–22	10–23	10–24	9–25	8–25	•–27
	9	13–24	12–25	11–26	10–27	10–27	9–28

N = 38 (continued)

N_1	x_1	2α = 0,20	2α = 0,10	2α = 0,05	2α = 0,02	2α = 0,01	2α = 0,002
	2	2–16	•–18	•–20	•–22	•–23	•–25
	3	4–20	4–22	3–24	•–25	•–26	•–28
	4	7–24	6–26	5–27	4–28	4–29	•–31
	5	11–27	9–29	8–30	7–31	6–32	5–33
11	0	•–7	•–8	•–10	•–12	•–13	•–16
	1	•–11	•–13	•–14	•–16	•–18	•–20
	2	2–15	•–17	•–18	•–20	•–21	•–24
	3	4–19	3–20	3–22	•–24	•–25	•–27
	4	7–22	6–24	5–25	4–27	4–28	•–29
	5	10–25	8–27	7–28	6–29	6–30	5–32
12	0	•–6	•–8	•–9	•–11	•–12	•–14
	1	•–10	•–12	•–13	•–15	•–16	•–19
	2	2–14	•–16	•–17	•–19	•–20	•–22
	3	4–17	3–19	•–20	•–22	•–23	•–25
	4	6–21	5–22	4–23	4–25	•–26	•–28
	5	9–24	8–25	7–26	6–28	5–28	•–30
	6	11–27	10–28	9–29	8–30	7–31	6–32
13	0	•–6	•–7	•–8	•–10	•–11	•–13
	1	•–9	•–11	•–12	•–14	•–15	•–17
	2	•–13	•–14	•–16	•–17	•–19	•–21
	3	3–16	3–18	•–19	•–21	•–22	•–24
	4	6–19	5–21	4–22	4–23	•–24	•–26
	5	8–22	7–23	6–25	5–26	5–27	•–28
	6	11–25	9–26	8–27	7–28	7–29	6–30
14	0	•–5	•–6	•–8	•–9	•–10	•–12
	1	•–9	•–10	•–11	•–13	•–14	•–16
	2	•–12	•–13	•–15	•–16	•–17	•–19
	3	3–15	3–16	•–18	•–19	•–20	•–22
	4	5–18	4–19	4–21	•–22	•–23	•–25
	5	7–21	7–22	6–23	5–24	5–25	•–27
	6	10–23	9–25	8–26	7–27	6–28	•–29
	7	12–26	11–27	10–28	9–29	8–30	7–31
15	0	•–5	•–6	•–7	•–9	•–10	•–12
	1	•–8	•–10	•–11	•–12	•–13	•–15
	2	•–11	•–13	•–14	•–15	•–16	•–18
	3	3–14	•–15	•–17	•–18	•–19	•–21
	4	5–17	4–18	4–19	•–21	•–22	•–23
	5	7–19	6–21	5–22	5–23	•–24	•–26
	6	9–22	8–23	7–24	7–25	6–26	•–28
	7	11–24	10–25	9–26	8–28	8–28	7–29
16	0	•–4	•–6	•–7	•–8	•–9	•–11
	1	•–8	•–9	•–10	•–11	•–12	•–14
	2	•–10	•–12	•–13	•–14	•–15	•–17
	3	3–13	•–14	•–16	•–17	•–18	•–20
	4	5–16	4–17	4–18	•–20	•–20	•–22
	5	7–18	6–19	5–21	5–22	•–23	•–24
	6	9–21	8–22	7–23	6–24	6–25	•–26
	7	11–23	10–24	9–25	8–26	7–27	7–28
	8	13–25	12–26	11–27	10–28	9–29	8–30
17	0	•–4	•–5	•–6	•–7	•–8	•–10
	1	•–7	•–8	•–9	•–11	•–12	•–13
	2	•–10	•–11	•–12	•–13	•–14	•–16
	3	3–12	•–14	•–15	•–16	•–17	•–19
	4	4–15	4–16	•–17	•–18	•–19	•–21
	5	6–17	5–18	5–19	•–21	•–21	•–23
	6	8–19	7–21	7–22	6–23	6–24	•–25
	7	10–22	9–23	8–24	8–25	7–26	•–27
	8	12–24	11–25	10–26	9–27	9–27	8–29
18	0	•–4	•–5	•–6	•–7	•–8	•–10
	1	•–7	•–8	•–9	•–10	•–11	•–13
	2	•–9	•–10	•–11	•–13	•–14	•–15
	3	3–12	•–13	•–14	•–15	•–16	•–18
	4	4–14	4–15	•–16	•–17	•–18	•–20
	5	6–16	5–17	5–18	•–20	•–20	•–22
	6	8–18	7–20	6–21	6–22	•–22	•–24
	7	10–20	9–22	8–23	7–24	7–24	•–26
	8	11–23	11–24	10–25	9–26	8–26	8–27
	9	13–25	12–26	12–26	11–27	10–28	9–29
19	0	•–4	•–5	•–5	•–6	•–7	•–9
	1	•–6	•–7	•–8	•–9	•–10	•–12
	2	•–9	•–10	•–11	•–12	•–13	•–14
	3	•–11	•–12	•–13	•–14	•–15	•–17
	4	4–13	•–14	•–15	•–17	•–17	•–19
	5	6–15	5–16	5–17	•–19	•–19	•–21
	6	7–17	7–19	6–20	6–21	•–21	•–23
	7	9–19	8–21	8–21	7–23	7–23	•–24
	8	11–21	10–22	9–23	9–24	8–25	•–26
	9	13–23	12–24	11–25	10–26	10–27	9–28

N = 37

N_1	x_1	2α = 0,20	2α = 0,10	2α = 0,05	2α = 0,02	2α = 0,01	2α = 0,002
4	0	•–16	•–19	•–22	•–25	•–26	•–30
	1	•–25	•–28	•–30	•–31	•–32	•–34
	2	5–32	4–33	2–35	2–35	•–	•–
5	0	•–13	•–16	•–19	•–22	•–23	•–27
	1	•–21	•–24	•–26	•–28	•–29	•–32
	2	4–28	3–30	2–31	•–33	•–33	•–
6	0	•–11	•–14	•–16	•–19	•–21	•–24
	1	•–19	•–21	•–23	•–25	•–27	•–29
	2	3–24	2–27	2–28	•–30	•–31	•–33
	3	7–30	6–31	5–32	4–33	3–34	•–
7	0	•–10	•–12	•–14	•–17	•–18	•–22
	1	•–16	•–19	•–21	•–23	•–24	•–27
	2	3–22	2–24	•–26	•–27	•–28	•–30
	3	6–26	5–28	4–30	3–31	3–32	•–33
8	0	•–9	•–11	•–13	•–15	•–17	•–20
	1	•–15	•–17	•–19	•–21	•–22	•–25
	2	2–19	2–22	•–23	•–25	•–26	•–28
	3	5–24	4–26	3–27	3–29	•–30	•–31
	4	9–28	8–29	6–31	5–32	5–32	•–
9	0	•–8	•–10	•–12	•–14	•–15	•–18
	1	•–13	•–15	•–17	•–19	•–20	•–23
	2	2–18	•–20	•–21	•–23	•–24	•–26
	3	5–22	4–24	3–25	•–27	•–28	•–29
	4	8–25	7–27	6–28	5–30	4–30	•–32
10	0	•–7	•–9	•–10	•–12	•–14	•–17
	1	•–12	•–14	•–15	•–17	•–19	•–21
	2	2–16	•–18	•–19	•–21	•–22	•–25

N = 38

N_1	x_1	2α = 0,20	2α = 0,10	2α = 0,05	2α = 0,02	2α = 0,01	2α = 0,002
4	0	•–16	•–20	•–22	•–25	•–27	•–30
	1	•–26	•–28	•–30	•–32	•–33	•–35
	2	5–33	4–34	3–35	2–36	•–	•–
5	0	•–14	•–17	•–19	•–22	•–24	•–27
	1	•–22	•–25	•–27	•–29	•–30	•–32
	2	4–29	3–31	2–32	•–34	•–34	•–
6	0	•–12	•–14	•–17	•–19	•–21	•–25
	1	•–19	•–22	•–24	•–26	•–27	•–30
	2	3–25	2–27	2–29	•–31	•–32	•–33
	3	8–30	6–32	5–33	4–34	3–35	•–
7	0	•–10	•–13	•–15	•–17	•–19	•–22
	1	•–17	•–19	•–21	•–23	•–25	•–28
	2	3–22	2–24	•–26	•–28	•–29	•–31
	3	6–27	5–29	4–30	3–32	3–33	•–34
8	0	•–9	•–11	•–13	•–16	•–17	•–20
	1	•–15	•–17	•–19	•–21	•–23	•–25
	2	2–20	2–22	•–24	•–26	•–27	•–29
	3	6–25	4–26	4–28	3–30	•–30	•–32
	4	9–29	8–30	7–31	5–33	5–33	4–34
9	0	•–8	•–10	•–12	•–14	•–16	•–19
	1	•–13	•–16	•–17	•–19	•–21	•–23
	2	2–18	•–20	•–22	•–24	•–25	•–27
	3	5–22	4–24	3–26	3–27	•–28	•–30
	4	8–26	7–28	6–29	5–31	4–31	•–33
10	0	•–7	•–9	•–11	•–13	•–14	•–17
	1	•–12	•–14	•–16	•–18	•–19	•–22

N = 39

N_1	x_1	2α = 0,20	2α = 0,10	2α = 0,05	2α = 0,02	2α = 0,01	2α = 0,002
4	0	•–17	•–20	•–23	•–26	•–28	•–31
	1	•–26	•–29	•–31	•–33	•–34	•–36
	2	5–34	4–35	3–36	2–37	•–	•–
5	0	•–14	•–17	•–20	•–23	•–25	•–28
	1	•–23	•–25	•–27	•–30	•–31	•–33
	2	4–29	3–31	2–33	•–35	•–35	•–
6	0	•–12	•–15	•–17	•–20	•–22	•–25
	1	•–20	•–22	•–24	•–27	•–28	•–31
	2	3–26	2–28	2–30	•–32	•–33	•–34
	3	8–31	6–33	5–34	4–35	3–36	•–
7	0	•–11	•–13	•–15	•–18	•–20	•–23
	1	•–17	•–20	•–22	•–24	•–26	•–28
	2	3–23	2–25	•–27	•–29	•–30	•–32
	3	7–28	5–30	4–31	3–33	3–34	•–35
8	0	•–9	•–12	•–14	•–16	•–18	•–21
	1	•–15	•–18	•–20	•–22	•–23	•–26

All values conform to the international convention (i.e. 0,1 instead of 0.1).

Significance Limits for the Fourfold Table Test*

x_1	N_1-x_1	N_1
x_2	N_2-x_2	N_2
X	$N-X$	N

$N=N_1+N_2$, $X=x_1+x_2$, $N_1 \leq N_2$, $x_1 \leq N_1-x_1$

For explanation see page 151

N_1	x_1	2α=0,20	2α=0,10	2α=0,05	2α=0,02	2α=0,01	2α=0,002
		N = 39 (continued)					
	2	2–21	2–23	•–25	•–26	•–28	•–30
	3	6–25	5–27	4–29	3–30	•–31	•–33
	4	10–29	8–31	7–32	5–34	5–34	4–35
9	0	•– 8	•–10	•–12	•–14	•–16	•–19
	1	•–14	•–16	•–18	•–20	•–21	•–24
	2	2–19	2–21	•–22	•–24	•–26	•–28
	3	5–23	4–25	3–26	3–28	•–29	•–31
	4	8–27	7–29	6–30	5–31	4–32	•–34
10	0	•– 8	•– 9	•–11	•–13	•–15	•–18
	1	•–13	•–15	•–16	•–18	•–20	•–22
	2	2–17	•–19	•–21	•–22	•–24	•–26
	3	5–21	4–23	3–24	•–26	•–27	•–29
	4	8–25	6–26	5–28	4–29	4–30	•–32
	5	11–28	9–30	8–31	7–32	6–33	5–34
11	0	•– 7	•– 9	•–10	•–12	•–13	•–16
	1	•–11	•–13	•–15	•–17	•–18	•–21
	2	2–16	•–17	•–19	•–21	•–22	•–24
	3	4–19	3–21	3–23	•–24	•–25	•–27
	4	7–23	6–24	5–26	4–27	4–28	•–30
	5	10–26	8–28	7–29	6–30	6–31	5–32
12	0	•– 6	•– 8	•– 9	•–11	•–12	•–15
	1	•–11	•–12	•–14	•–16	•–17	•–19
	2	2–14	•–16	•–18	•–19	•–20	•–23
	3	4–18	3–20	3–21	•–23	•–24	•–26
	4	6–21	5–23	5–24	4–26	•–27	•–28
	5	9–24	8–26	7–27	6–28	5–29	•–31
	6	12–27	10–29	9–30	8–31	7–32	6–33
13	0	•– 6	•– 7	•– 9	•–10	•–11	•–14
	1	•–10	•–11	•–13	•–14	•–16	•–18
	2	•–13	•–15	•–16	•–18	•–19	•–21
	3	4–17	3–18	•–20	•–21	•–22	•–24
	4	6–20	5–21	4–23	4–24	•–25	•–27
	5	8–23	7–24	6–25	5–27	5–28	•–29
	6	11–25	10–27	9–28	8–29	7–30	6–31
14	0	•– 5	•– 7	•– 8	•– 9	•–11	•–13
	1	•– 9	•–11	•–12	•–13	•–15	•–17
	2	•–12	•–14	•–15	•–17	•–18	•–20
	3	3–15	3–17	•–18	•–20	•–21	•–23
	4	5–18	5–20	4–21	•–23	•–24	•–25
	5	8–21	7–23	6–24	5–25	5–26	•–28
	6	10–24	9–25	8–26	7–28	6–28	6–30
	7	13–26	11–28	10–29	9–30	8–31	7–32
15	0	•– 5	•– 6	•– 7	•– 9	•–10	•–12
	1	•– 8	•–10	•–11	•–13	•–14	•–16
	2	•–12	•–13	•–14	•–16	•–17	•–19
	3	3–14	3–16	•–17	•–19	•–20	•–22
	4	5–17	4–19	4–20	•–21	•–22	•–24
	5	7–20	6–21	6–22	5–24	•–25	•–26
	6	9–22	8–24	7–25	7–26	6–27	•–28
	7	12–25	11–26	10–27	9–28	8–29	7–30
16	0	•– 5	•– 6	•– 7	•– 8	•– 9	•–11
	1	•– 8	•– 9	•–10	•–12	•–13	•–15
	2	•–11	•–12	•–13	•–15	•–16	•–18
	3	3–14	•–15	•–16	•–18	•–18	•–20
	4	5–16	4–18	4–19	•–20	•–21	•–23
	5	7–19	6–20	5–21	5–22	•–23	•–25
	6	9–21	8–22	7–24	6–25	6–26	•–27
	7	11–24	10–25	9–26	8–27	8–28	7–29
	8	13–26	12–27	11–28	10–29	9–30	8–31
17	0	•– 4	•– 5	•– 6	•– 8	•– 9	•–11
	1	•– 7	•– 9	•–10	•–11	•–12	•–14
	2	•–10	•–11	•–13	•–14	•–15	•–17
	3	3–13	•–14	•–15	•–17	•–17	•–19
	4	4–15	4–17	•–18	•–19	•–20	•–22
	5	6–18	6–19	5–20	•–21	•–22	•–24
	6	8–20	7–21	7–22	6–23	6–24	•–26
	7	10–22	9–23	9–24	8–26	7–26	•–28
	8	12–24	11–26	10–27	10–28	9–28	8–29
18	0	•– 4	•– 5	•– 6	•– 7	•– 8	•–10
	1	•– 7	•– 8	•– 9	•–10	•–11	•–13
	2	•–10	•–11	•–12	•–13	•–14	•–16
	3	3–12	•–13	•–14	•–16	•–16	•–18
	4	4–14	4–16	•–17	•–18	•–19	•–20
	5	6–17	5–18	5–19	•–20	•–21	•–23
	6	8–19	7–20	6–21	6–22	•–23	•–25
	7	10–21	9–22	8–23	7–24	7–25	•–26
	8	12–23	11–24	10–25	9–26	9–27	8–28
	9	14–25	13–26	12–27	11–28	10–29	9–30
19	0	•– 4	•– 5	•– 6	•– 7	•– 8	•– 9
	1	•– 7	•– 8	•– 9	•–10	•–11	•–12
	2	•– 9	•–10	•–11	•–12	•–13	•–15
	3	•–11	•–13	•–14	•–15	•–16	•–17
	4	4–14	4–15	•–16	•–17	•–18	•–19
	5	6–16	5–17	5–18	•–19	•–20	•–21
	6	7–18	7–19	6–20	6–21	•–22	•–23
	7	9–20	8–21	8–22	7–23	7–24	•–25
	8	11–22	10–23	9–24	9–25	8–26	•–27
	9	13–24	12–25	11–26	10–27	10–27	9–29
		N = 40					
4	0	•–17	•–21	•–24	•–27	•–29	•–32
	1	•–27	•–30	•–32	•–34	•–35	•–37
	2	6–34	4–36	3–37	2–38	•–•	•–•
5	0	•–14	•–18	•–20	•–23	•–25	•–29
	1	•–23	•–26	•–28	•–30	•–32	•–34
	2	4–30	3–32	2–34	•–35	•–36	•–•

N_1	x_1	2α=0,20	2α=0,10	2α=0,05	2α=0,02	2α=0,01	2α=0,002
		N = 40 (continued)					
6	0	•–12	•–15	•–18	•–21	•–22	•–26
	1	•–20	•–23	•–25	•–27	•–29	•–32
	2	4–26	2–29	2–31	•–32	•–33	•–35
	3	8–32	6–34	5–35	4–36	3–37	•–•
7	0	•–11	•–13	•–16	•–18	•–20	•–24
	1	•–18	•–20	•–22	•–25	•–26	•–29
	2	3–24	2–26	•–28	•–30	•–31	•–33
	3	7–29	5–31	4–32	3–34	3–34	•–36
8	0	•–10	•–12	•–14	•–16	•–18	•–21
	1	•–16	•–18	•–20	•–22	•–24	•–27
	2	3–21	2–23	•–25	•–27	•–28	•–31
	3	6–26	5–28	4–29	3–31	•–32	•–34
	4	10–30	8–32	7–33	6–34	5–35	4–36
9	0	•– 9	•–11	•–13	•–15	•–16	•–20
	1	•–14	•–16	•–18	•–20	•–22	•–25
	2	2–19	2–21	•–23	•–25	•–26	•–29
	3	5–24	4–25	3–27	3–29	•–30	•–32
	4	9–28	7–29	6–31	5–32	4–33	•–35
10	0	•– 8	•–10	•–11	•–13	•–15	•–18
	1	•–13	•–15	•–17	•–19	•–20	•–23
	2	2–17	•–19	•–21	•–23	•–24	•–27
	3	5–22	4–23	3–25	•–27	•–28	•–30
	4	8–25	6–27	5–29	5–30	4–31	•–33
	5	11–29	10–30	8–32	7–33	6–34	5–35
11	0	•– 7	•– 9	•–10	•–12	•–14	•–17
	1	•–12	•–14	•–15	•–17	•–19	•–21
	2	2–16	•–18	•–19	•–21	•–23	•–25
	3	4–20	3–22	3–23	•–25	•–26	•–28
	4	7–23	6–25	5–27	4–28	4–29	•–31
	5	10–27	9–28	8–30	6–31	6–32	5–33
12	0	•– 6	•– 8	•–10	•–11	•–13	•–15
	1	•–11	•–13	•–14	•–16	•–17	•–20
	2	2–15	•–16	•–18	•–20	•–21	•–23
	3	4–18	3–20	3–22	•–23	•–24	•–26
	4	6–22	5–23	5–25	4–26	•–27	•–29
	5	9–25	8–26	7–28	6–29	5–30	•–32
	6	12–28	11–29	9–31	8–32	8–32	6–34
13	0	•– 6	•– 7	•– 9	•–10	•–12	•–14
	1	•–10	•–12	•–13	•–15	•–16	•–19
	2	•–14	•–15	•–17	•–18	•–20	•–22
	3	4–17	3–19	•–20	•–22	•–23	•–25
	4	6–20	5–22	4–23	4–25	•–26	•–28
	5	8–23	7–25	6–26	6–27	5–28	•–30
	6	11–26	10–28	9–29	8–30	7–31	6–32
14	0	•– 5	•– 7	•– 8	•–10	•–11	•–13
	1	•– 9	•–11	•–12	•–14	•–15	•–17
	2	•–13	•–14	•–16	•–17	•–18	•–21
	3	3–16	3–17	•–19	•–20	•–21	•–24
	4	6–19	5–20	4–22	•–23	•–24	•–26
	5	8–22	7–23	6–25	5–26	5–27	•–28
	6	10–24	9–26	8–27	7–28	7–29	6–31
	7	13–27	12–28	10–30	9–31	9–31	7–33
15	0	•– 5	•– 6	•– 8	•– 9	•–10	•–12
	1	•– 9	•–10	•–11	•–13	•–14	•–16
	2	•–12	•–13	•–15	•–16	•–17	•–19
	3	3–15	3–16	•–18	•–19	•–20	•–22
	4	5–18	4–19	4–20	•–22	•–23	•–25
	5	7–20	6–22	6–23	5–24	5–25	•–27
	6	10–23	9–24	8–26	7–27	6–28	•–29
	7	12–26	11–27	10–28	9–29	8–30	7–31
16	0	•– 5	•– 6	•– 7	•– 8	•– 9	•–12
	1	•– 8	•– 9	•–11	•–12	•–13	•–15
	2	•–11	•–12	•–14	•–15	•–16	•–18
	3	3–14	•–15	•–17	•–18	•–19	•–21
	4	5–17	4–18	4–19	•–21	•–22	•–23
	5	7–19	6–21	5–22	5–23	•–24	•–26
	6	9–22	8–23	7–24	6–25	6–26	•–28
	7	11–24	10–25	9–27	8–28	8–28	7–30
	8	14–26	12–28	11–29	10–30	10–30	8–32
17	0	•– 4	•– 6	•– 7	•– 8	•– 9	•–11
	1	•– 8	•– 9	•–10	•–11	•–12	•–14
	2	•–10	•–12	•–13	•–14	•–15	•–17
	3	3–13	•–14	•–16	•–17	•–18	•–20
	4	5–16	4–17	•–18	•–20	•–20	•–22
	5	6–18	6–19	5–21	5–22	•–23	•–24
	6	8–21	8–22	7–23	6–24	6–25	•–27
	7	11–23	10–24	9–25	8–26	7–27	•–28
	8	13–25	12–26	11–27	10–28	9–29	8–30
18	0	•– 4	•– 5	•– 6	•– 7	•– 8	•–10
	1	•– 7	•– 8	•– 9	•–11	•–12	•–14
	2	•–10	•–11	•–12	•–13	•–14	•–16
	3	3–12	•–14	•–15	•–16	•–17	•–19
	4	4–15	4–16	•–17	•–18	•–19	•–21
	5	6–17	5–18	5–20	•–21	•–22	•–23
	6	8–19	7–21	7–22	6–23	6–24	•–25
	7	10–22	9–23	8–24	8–25	7–26	•–27
	8	12–24	11–25	10–26	9–27	9–28	8–29
	9	14–26	13–27	12–28	11–29	10–30	9–31
19	0	•– 4	•– 5	•– 6	•– 7	•– 8	•–10
	1	•– 7	•– 8	•– 9	•–10	•–11	•–13
	2	•– 9	•–10	•–11	•–13	•–14	•–15
	3	3–12	•–13	•–14	•–15	•–16	•–18
	4	4–14	4–15	•–16	•–18	•–18	•–20
	5	6–16	5–17	5–19	•–20	•–21	•–22
	6	8–18	7–20	6–21	6–22	•–23	•–24
	7	9–21	9–22	8–23	7–24	7–25	•–26
	8	11–23	10–24	10–25	9–26	8–26	8–28

N_1	x_1	2α=0,20	2α=0,10	2α=0,05	2α=0,02	2α=0,01	2α=0,002
		N = 40 (continued)					
	9	13–25	12–26	11–27	11–28	10–28	9–29
20	0	•– 4	•– 5	•– 5	•– 7	•– 7	•– 9
	1	•– 6	•– 7	•– 8	•– 9	•–10	•–12
	2	•– 9	•–10	•–11	•–12	•–13	•–15
	3	•–11	•–12	•–13	•–14	•–15	•–17
	4	4–13	•–14	•–15	•–17	•–17	•–19
	5	6–15	5–17	5–18	•–19	•–20	•–21
	6	7–18	7–19	6–20	•–21	•–22	•–23
	7	9–20	8–21	8–22	7–23	7–23	•–25
	8	11–22	10–23	9–24	9–25	8–25	•–27
	9	13–24	12–25	11–25	10–26	10–27	9–28
	10	15–25	14–26	13–27	12–28	11–29	10–30
		N = 41					
4	0	•–18	•–21	•–24	•–27	•–29	•–33
	1	1–28	•–31	•–33	•–35	•–36	•–38
	2	6–35	4–37	3–38	2–39	•–•	•–•
5	0	•–15	•–18	•–21	•–24	•–26	•–30
	1	•–24	•–27	•–29	•–31	•–33	•–35
	2	4–31	3–33	2–35	•–36	•–37	•–38
6	0	•–13	•–16	•–18	•–21	•–23	•–27
	1	•–21	•–23	•–26	•–28	•–30	•–32
	2	4–27	2–30	2–31	•–33	•–34	•–36
	3	8–33	6–35	5–36	4–37	3–38	•–•
7	0	•–11	•–14	•–16	•–19	•–21	•–24
	1	•–18	•–21	•–23	•–25	•–27	•–30
	2	3–24	2–26	•–28	•–30	•–32	•–34
	3	7–29	5–31	4–33	3–34	3–35	•–37
8	0	•–10	•–12	•–14	•–17	•–19	•–22
	1	•–16	•–19	•–21	•–23	•–25	•–28
	2	3–22	2–24	•–26	•–28	•–29	•–32
	3	6–27	5–29	4–30	3–32	•–33	•–35
	4	10–31	8–33	7–34	6–35	5–36	4–37
9	0	•– 9	•–11	•–13	•–15	•–17	•–20
	1	•–15	•–17	•–19	•–21	•–23	•–25
	2	2–20	2–22	•–24	•–26	•–27	•–29
	3	5–24	4–26	3–28	3–30	•–31	•–33
	4	9–28	7–30	6–32	5–33	4–34	•–35
10	0	•– 8	•–10	•–12	•–14	•–15	•–19
	1	•–13	•–15	•–17	•–19	•–21	•–24
	2	2–18	•–20	•–22	•–24	•–25	•–27
	3	5–22	4–24	3–26	•–27	•–29	•–31
	4	8–26	7–28	6–29	5–31	4–32	•–34
	5	11–30	10–31	8–33	7–34	6–35	5–36
11	0	•– 7	•– 9	•–11	•–13	•–14	•–17
	1	•–12	•–14	•–16	•–18	•–19	•–22
	2	2–16	•–18	•–20	•–22	•–23	•–26
	3	4–20	3–22	3–24	•–26	•–27	•–29
	4	7–24	6–26	5–27	4–29	4–30	•–32
	5	10–27	9–29	8–30	7–32	6–33	5–34
12	0	•– 7	•– 8	•–10	•–12	•–13	•–16
	1	•–11	•–13	•–15	•–16	•–18	•–20
	2	2–15	•–17	•–19	•–20	•–22	•–24
	3	4–19	3–21	3–22	•–24	•–25	•–27
	4	7–22	5–24	5–25	4–27	4–28	•–30
	5	9–26	8–27	7–28	6–30	5–31	•–32
	6	12–29	11–30	10–31	8–33	8–33	6–35
13	0	•– 6	•– 8	•– 9	•–11	•–12	•–15
	1	•–10	•–12	•–13	•–15	•–17	•–19
	2	2–14	•–16	•–17	•–19	•–20	•–23
	3	4–17	3–19	•–21	•–22	•–23	•–26
	4	6–21	5–22	4–24	4–25	•–26	•–28
	5	9–24	7–25	7–27	6–28	5–29	•–31
	6	11–27	10–28	9–29	8–31	7–32	6–33
14	0	•– 6	•– 7	•– 8	•–10	•–11	•–14
	1	•–10	•–11	•–13	•–14	•–15	•–18
	2	•–13	•–15	•–16	•–18	•–19	•–21
	3	3–16	3–18	•–19	•–21	•–22	•–24
	4	6–19	5–21	4–22	4–24	•–25	•–27
	5	8–22	7–24	6–25	5–27	5–28	•–29
	6	11–25	9–27	8–28	7–29	7–30	6–31
	7	13–28	12–29	11–30	10–31	9–32	7–34
15	0	•– 5	•– 7	•– 8	•– 9	•–10	•–13
	1	•– 9	•–10	•–12	•–13	•–14	•–17
	2	•–12	•–14	•–15	•–17	•–18	•–20
	3	3–15	3–17	•–18	•–20	•–21	•–23
	4	5–18	4–20	4–21	•–23	•–23	•–25
	5	7–21	7–22	6–24	5–25	5–26	•–28
	6	10–24	9–25	8–26	7–28	6–28	•–30
	7	12–26	11–28	10–29	9–30	8–31	7–32
16	0	•– 5	•– 6	•– 7	•– 9	•–10	•–12
	1	•– 8	•–10	•–11	•–12	•–14	•–16
	2	•–11	•–13	•–14	•–16	•–17	•–19
	3	3–14	•–16	•–17	•–19	•–20	•–22
	4	5–17	4–19	4–20	•–21	•–22	•–24
	5	7–20	6–21	5–22	5–24	•–25	•–26
	6	9–22	8–24	7–25	7–26	6–27	•–29
	7	11–25	10–26	9–27	8–28	8–29	7–31
	8	14–27	13–28	12–29	10–31	10–31	9–32
17	0	•– 5	•– 6	•– 7	•– 8	•– 9	•–11
	1	•– 8	•– 9	•–10	•–12	•–13	•–15
	2	•–11	•–12	•–13	•–15	•–16	•–18
	3	3–13	•–15	•–16	•–18	•–18	•–20
	4	5–16	4–17	4–19	•–20	•–21	•–23
	5	7–19	6–20	5–21	5–23	•–23	•–25
	6	9–21	8–22	7–24	6–25	6–26	•–27

All values conform to the international convention (i.e. 0,1 instead of 0.1).

Significance Limits for the Fourfold Table Test*

x_1	$N_1 - x_1$	N_1
x_2	$N_2 - x_2$	N_2
X	$N - X$	N

$N = N_1 + N_2$, $X = x_1 + x_2$, $N_1 \le N_2$, $x_1 \le N_1 - x_1$

For explanation see page 151

N_1	x_1	2α = 0,20	2α = 0,10	2α = 0,05	2α = 0,02	2α = 0,01	2α = 0,002
		N = 41 (continued)					
	7	11-23	10-25	9-26	8-27	7-28	7-29
	8	13-26	12-27	11-28	10-29	9-30	8-31
18	0	•-4	•-5	•-6	•-8	•-9	•-11
	1	•-7	•-9	•-10	•-11	•-12	•-14
	2	•-10	•-11	•-13	•-14	•-15	•-17
	3	3-13	•-14	•-15	•-17	•-17	•-19
	4	4-15	4-17	•-18	•-19	•-20	•-22
	5	6-18	6-19	5-20	•-21	•-22	•-24
	6	8-20	7-21	7-22	6-24	6-24	•-26
	7	10-22	9-23	8-25	8-26	7-26	•-28
	8	12-24	11-26	10-27	9-28	9-28	8-30
	9	14-27	13-28	12-29	11-30	11-30	9-32
19	0	•-4	•-5	•-6	•-7	•-8	•-10
	1	•-7	•-8	•-9	•-10	•-11	•-13
	2	•-10	•-11	•-12	•-13	•-14	•-16
	3	3-12	•-13	•-14	•-16	•-17	•-18
	4	4-14	4-16	•-17	•-18	•-19	•-21
	5	6-17	5-18	5-19	•-20	•-21	•-23
	6	8-19	7-20	6-21	6-22	•-23	•-25
	7	10-21	9-22	8-23	7-25	7-25	•-27
	8	12-23	11-24	10-25	9-27	8-27	8-29
	9	14-25	13-26	12-27	11-28	10-29	9-30
20	0	•-4	•-5	•-6	•-7	•-8	•-9
	1	•-7	•-8	•-9	•-10	•-11	•-12
	2	•-9	•-10	•-11	•-12	•-13	•-15
	3	•-11	•-13	•-14	•-15	•-16	•-17
	4	4-14	4-15	•-16	•-17	•-18	•-20
	5	6-16	5-17	5-18	•-19	•-20	•-22
	6	7-18	7-19	6-20	6-21	•-22	•-24
	7	9-20	8-21	8-22	7-23	7-24	•-26
	8	11-22	10-23	9-24	9-25	8-26	•-27
	9	13-24	12-25	11-26	10-27	10-28	9-29
	10	15-26	14-27	13-28	12-29	11-30	10-31
		N = 42					
4	0	•-18	•-22	•-25	•-28	•-30	•-34
	1	1-28	•-31	•-34	•-36	•-37	•-39
	2	6-36	4-38	3-39	2-40	•-•	•-•
5	0	•-15	•-18	•-21	•-25	•-27	•-30
	1	•-24	•-27	•-30	•-32	•-34	•-36
	2	5-32	3-34	2-36	•-37	•-38	•-39
6	0	•-13	•-16	•-19	•-22	•-24	•-27
	1	•-21	•-24	•-26	•-29	•-30	•-33
	2	4-28	3-30	2-32	•-34	•-35	•-37
	3	8-34	7-35	5-37	4-38	3-39	•-•
7	0	•-11	•-14	•-16	•-19	•-21	•-25
	1	•-19	•-21	•-23	•-26	•-28	•-31
	2	3-25	2-27	2-29	•-31	•-32	•-35
	3	7-30	6-32	4-34	3-35	3-36	•-38
8	0	•-10	•-12	•-15	•-17	•-19	•-23
	1	•-17	•-19	•-21	•-24	•-25	•-28
	2	3-22	2-25	•-26	•-29	•-30	•-32
	3	6-27	5-29	4-31	3-33	3-34	•-36
	4	10-32	9-33	7-35	6-36	5-37	4-38
9	0	•-9	•-11	•-13	•-16	•-17	•-21
	1	•-15	•-17	•-19	•-22	•-23	•-26
	2	2-20	2-22	•-24	•-26	•-28	•-30
	3	5-25	4-27	3-29	3-30	•-32	•-34
	4	9-29	8-31	6-32	5-34	4-35	•-36
10	0	•-8	•-10	•-12	•-14	•-16	•-19
	1	•-14	•-16	•-18	•-20	•-21	•-24
	2	2-18	•-20	•-22	•-24	•-26	•-28
	3	5-23	4-25	3-26	•-28	•-29	•-32
	4	8-27	7-29	6-30	5-32	4-33	•-34
	5	12-30	10-32	9-33	7-35	7-35	5-37
11	0	•-7	•-9	•-11	•-13	•-15	•-18
	1	•-12	•-14	•-16	•-18	•-20	•-22
	2	2-17	•-19	•-21	•-23	•-24	•-26
	3	4-21	4-23	3-24	•-26	•-27	•-30
	4	7-25	6-26	5-28	4-30	4-31	•-33
	5	10-28	9-30	8-31	7-33	6-34	5-35
12	0	•-7	•-8	•-10	•-12	•-13	•-16
	1	•-11	•-13	•-15	•-17	•-18	•-21
	2	2-15	•-17	•-19	•-21	•-22	•-25
	3	4-19	3-21	3-23	•-25	•-26	•-28
	4	7-23	6-25	5-26	4-28	4-29	•-31
	5	10-26	8-28	7-29	6-31	6-32	5-33
	6	13-29	11-31	10-32	9-33	8-34	6-36
13	0	•-6	•-8	•-9	•-11	•-12	•-15
	1	•-11	•-12	•-14	•-16	•-17	•-20
	2	2-14	•-16	•-18	•-20	•-21	•-23
	3	4-18	3-20	3-21	•-23	•-24	•-26
	4	6-21	5-23	4-24	4-26	•-27	•-29
	5	9-24	8-26	7-27	6-29	5-30	•-32
	6	12-27	10-29	9-30	8-32	7-32	6-34
14	0	•-6	•-7	•-9	•-10	•-12	•-14
	1	•-10	•-11	•-13	•-15	•-16	•-18
	2	•-13	•-15	•-17	•-18	•-19	•-22
	3	4-17	3-18	•-20	•-22	•-23	•-25
	4	6-20	5-22	4-23	4-25	•-26	•-28
	5	8-23	7-24	6-26	5-27	5-28	•-30
	6	11-26	9-27	8-29	7-30	7-31	6-32
	7	13-29	12-30	11-31	10-32	9-33	8-34
15	0	•-5	•-7	•-8	•-10	•-11	•-13
	1	•-9	•-11	•-12	•-14	•-15	•-17

N_1	x_1	2α = 0,20	2α = 0,10	2α = 0,05	2α = 0,02	2α = 0,01	2α = 0,002
		N = 42 (continued)					
	2	•-12	•-14	•-15	•-17	•-18	•-21
	3	3-16	3-17	•-19	•-20	•-21	•-23
	4	5-19	5-20	4-22	•-23	•-24	•-26
	5	8-21	7-23	6-24	5-26	5-27	•-29
	6	10-24	9-26	8-27	7-28	6-29	6-31
	7	13-27	11-28	10-29	9-31	8-31	7-33
16	0	•-5	•-6	•-7	•-9	•-10	•-12
	1	•-9	•-10	•-11	•-13	•-14	•-16
	2	•-12	•-13	•-15	•-16	•-17	•-19
	3	3-15	3-16	•-18	•-19	•-20	•-22
	4	5-17	4-19	4-20	•-22	•-23	•-25
	5	7-20	6-22	6-23	5-24	•-25	•-27
	6	9-23	8-24	8-26	7-27	6-28	•-29
	7	12-25	11-27	10-28	9-29	8-30	7-31
	8	14-28	13-29	12-30	11-31	10-32	9-33
17	0	•-5	•-6	•-7	•-8	•-9	•-12
	1	•-8	•-9	•-11	•-12	•-13	•-15
	2	•-11	•-12	•-14	•-15	•-16	•-18
	3	3-14	•-15	•-17	•-18	•-19	•-21
	4	5-16	4-18	4-19	•-21	•-22	•-24
	5	7-19	6-21	5-22	5-23	•-24	•-26
	6	9-22	8-23	7-24	6-26	6-26	•-28
	7	11-24	10-25	9-27	8-28	8-29	7-30
	8	13-26	12-28	11-29	10-30	9-31	8-32
18	0	•-4	•-5	•-7	•-8	•-9	•-11
	1	•-8	•-9	•-10	•-11	•-12	•-14
	2	•-10	•-12	•-13	•-14	•-15	•-17
	3	3-13	•-14	•-16	•-17	•-18	•-20
	4	5-16	4-17	•-18	•-20	•-20	•-22
	5	6-18	6-19	5-21	•-22	•-23	•-25
	6	8-20	7-22	7-23	6-24	6-25	•-27
	7	10-23	9-24	9-25	8-26	7-27	•-29
	8	13-25	11-26	11-27	10-29	9-29	8-31
	9	15-27	14-28	13-29	11-31	11-31	10-32
19	0	•-4	•-5	•-6	•-7	•-8	•-10
	1	•-7	•-8	•-9	•-11	•-12	•-14
	2	•-10	•-11	•-12	•-14	•-14	•-16
	3	3-12	•-14	•-15	•-16	•-17	•-19
	4	4-15	4-16	•-17	•-19	•-19	•-21
	5	6-17	5-18	5-20	•-21	•-22	•-23
	6	8-19	7-21	7-22	6-23	•-24	•-26
	7	10-22	9-23	8-24	7-25	7-26	•-27
	8	12-24	11-25	10-26	9-27	9-28	8-29
	9	14-26	13-27	12-28	11-29	10-30	9-31
20	0	•-4	•-5	•-6	•-7	•-8	•-10
	1	•-7	•-8	•-9	•-10	•-11	•-13
	2	•-9	•-10	•-12	•-13	•-14	•-16
	3	3-12	•-13	•-14	•-15	•-16	•-18
	4	4-14	4-15	•-16	•-18	•-18	•-20
	5	6-16	5-18	5-19	•-20	•-21	•-22
	6	8-18	7-20	6-21	6-22	•-23	•-24
	7	9-21	9-22	8-23	7-24	7-25	•-26
	8	11-23	10-24	10-25	9-26	8-27	•-28
	9	13-25	12-26	11-27	10-28	10-29	9-30
	10	15-27	14-28	13-29	12-30	12-30	11-31
21	0	•-4	•-5	•-5	•-7	•-7	•-9
	1	•-6	•-7	•-8	•-10	•-10	•-12
	2	•-9	•-10	•-11	•-12	•-13	•-15
	3	•-11	•-12	•-13	•-15	•-15	•-17
	4	4-13	•-15	•-16	•-17	•-18	•-19
	5	6-15	5-17	5-18	•-19	•-20	•-21
	6	7-18	7-19	6-20	•-21	•-22	•-23
	7	9-20	8-21	8-22	7-23	7-24	•-25
	8	11-22	10-23	9-24	8-25	8-26	•-27
	9	13-24	12-25	11-26	10-27	10-27	9-29
	10	15-26	13-27	13-28	12-29	11-29	10-30
		N = 43					
4	0	•-19	•-22	•-25	•-29	•-31	•-35
	1	1-29	•-32	•-34	•-37	•-38	•-40
	2	6-37	4-39	3-40	2-41	•-•	•-•
5	0	•-16	•-19	•-22	•-25	•-27	•-31
	1	•-25	•-28	•-30	•-33	•-34	•-37
	2	5-32	3-35	2-36	•-38	•-39	•-40
6	0	•-13	•-16	•-19	•-22	•-24	•-28
	1	•-22	•-25	•-27	•-30	•-31	•-34
	2	4-28	3-31	2-33	•-35	•-36	•-38
	3	9-34	7-36	5-38	4-39	3-40	•-•
7	0	•-12	•-14	•-17	•-20	•-22	•-25
	1	•-19	•-22	•-24	•-27	•-28	•-31
	2	3-25	2-28	2-30	•-32	•-33	•-36
	3	7-31	6-33	5-35	3-36	3-37	•-39
8	0	•-10	•-13	•-15	•-18	•-20	•-23
	1	•-17	•-20	•-22	•-24	•-26	•-29
	2	3-23	2-25	•-27	•-29	•-31	•-33
	3	6-28	5-30	4-32	3-34	3-35	•-37
	4	11-32	9-34	7-36	6-37	5-38	4-39
9	0	•-9	•-11	•-14	•-16	•-18	•-21
	1	•-15	•-18	•-20	•-22	•-24	•-27
	2	2-21	2-23	•-25	•-27	•-28	•-31
	3	6-25	4-27	4-29	3-31	•-32	•-34
	4	9-30	8-32	6-33	5-35	5-36	•-37
10	0	•-8	•-10	•-12	•-15	•-16	•-20
	1	•-14	•-16	•-18	•-20	•-22	•-25
	2	2-19	2-21	•-23	•-25	•-26	•-29
	3	5-23	4-25	3-27	3-29	•-30	•-32

N_1	x_1	2α = 0,20	2α = 0,10	2α = 0,05	2α = 0,02	2α = 0,01	2α = 0,002
		N = 43 (continued)					
	4	8-27	7-29	6-31	5-32	4-33	•-35
	5	12-31	10-33	9-34	7-36	7-36	5-38
11	0	•-8	•-9	•-11	•-13	•-15	•-18
	1	•-13	•-15	•-17	•-19	•-20	•-23
	2	2-17	•-19	•-21	•-23	•-24	•-27
	3	5-21	4-23	3-25	•-27	•-28	•-30
	4	8-25	6-27	5-29	4-30	4-31	•-33
	5	11-29	9-31	8-32	7-33	6-34	5-36
12	0	•-7	•-9	•-10	•-12	•-14	•-17
	1	•-12	•-14	•-15	•-17	•-19	•-22
	2	2-16	•-18	•-20	•-21	•-23	•-25
	3	4-20	3-22	3-23	•-25	•-26	•-29
	4	7-23	6-25	5-27	4-28	4-30	•-32
	5	10-27	8-29	7-30	6-31	6-32	5-34
	6	13-30	11-32	10-33	9-34	8-35	7-36
13	0	•-6	•-8	•-10	•-11	•-13	•-16
	1	•-11	•-13	•-14	•-16	•-17	•-20
	2	2-15	•-17	•-18	•-20	•-21	•-24
	3	4-18	3-20	3-22	•-24	•-25	•-27
	4	6-22	5-24	5-25	4-27	•-28	•-30
	5	9-25	8-27	7-28	6-30	5-31	•-32
	6	12-28	10-30	9-31	8-32	7-33	6-35
14	0	•-6	•-7	•-9	•-11	•-12	•-14
	1	•-10	•-12	•-13	•-15	•-16	•-19
	2	•-14	•-15	•-17	•-19	•-20	•-22
	3	4-17	3-19	•-20	•-22	•-23	•-26
	4	6-20	5-22	4-24	4-25	•-26	•-28
	5	8-23	7-25	6-26	5-28	5-29	•-31
	6	11-26	10-28	9-29	8-31	7-32	6-33
	7	14-29	12-31	11-32	10-33	9-34	8-35
15	0	•-6	•-7	•-8	•-10	•-11	•-14
	1	•-9	•-11	•-12	•-14	•-15	•-18
	2	•-13	•-14	•-16	•-18	•-19	•-21
	3	3-16	3-18	•-19	•-21	•-22	•-24
	4	6-19	5-21	4-22	•-24	•-25	•-27
	5	8-22	7-24	6-25	5-26	5-27	•-29
	6	10-25	9-26	8-28	7-29	7-30	6-32
	7	13-28	11-29	10-30	9-31	9-32	7-34
16	0	•-5	•-6	•-8	•-9	•-10	•-13
	1	•-9	•-10	•-12	•-13	•-14	•-17
	2	•-12	•-14	•-15	•-17	•-18	•-20
	3	3-15	3-17	•-18	•-20	•-21	•-23
	4	5-18	4-20	4-21	•-22	•-23	•-25
	5	7-21	6-22	6-24	5-25	5-26	•-28
	6	10-23	9-25	8-26	7-28	6-28	•-30
	7	12-26	11-27	10-29	9-30	8-31	7-32
	8	14-29	13-30	12-31	11-32	10-33	9-34
17	0	•-5	•-6	•-7	•-9	•-10	•-12
	1	•-8	•-10	•-11	•-12	•-13	•-16
	2	•-11	•-13	•-14	•-16	•-17	•-19
	3	3-14	•-14	•-17	•-18	•-20	•-22
	4	5-17	4-18	4-20	•-21	•-22	•-24
	5	7-20	6-21	5-22	5-24	•-25	•-27
	6	9-22	8-24	7-25	6-26	6-27	•-29
	7	11-25	10-26	9-27	8-28	8-29	7-31
	8	14-27	12-28	11-29	10-31	10-31	8-33
18	0	•-5	•-6	•-7	•-8	•-9	•-11
	1	•-8	•-9	•-10	•-12	•-13	•-15
	2	•-11	•-12	•-13	•-15	•-16	•-18
	3	3-13	•-15	•-16	•-17	•-18	•-20
	4	5-16	4-17	4-19	•-20	•-21	•-23
	5	7-19	6-20	5-21	5-23	•-23	•-25
	6	9-21	8-22	7-24	6-25	6-26	•-27
	7	11-23	10-25	9-26	8-27	7-28	7-30
	8	13-26	12-27	11-28	10-29	9-30	8-31
	9	15-28	14-29	13-30	12-31	11-32	10-33
19	0	•-4	•-5	•-6	•-8	•-9	•-11
	1	•-7	•-9	•-10	•-11	•-12	•-14
	2	•-10	•-11	•-13	•-14	•-15	•-17
	3	3-13	•-14	•-15	•-17	•-18	•-19
	4	4-15	4-17	•-18	•-19	•-20	•-22
	5	6-18	5-19	5-20	•-21	•-22	•-24
	6	8-20	7-21	7-22	6-24	6-25	•-26
	7	10-22	9-24	8-25	8-26	7-27	•-28
	8	12-24	11-26	10-27	9-28	9-29	8-30
	9	14-27	13-28	12-29	11-30	11-31	9-32
20	0	•-4	•-5	•-6	•-7	•-8	•-10
	1	•-7	•-8	•-9	•-10	•-11	•-13
	2	•-10	•-11	•-12	•-13	•-14	•-16
	3	3-12	•-13	•-14	•-16	•-17	•-18
	4	4-14	4-16	•-17	•-18	•-19	•-21
	5	6-17	5-18	5-19	•-20	•-21	•-23
	6	8-19	7-20	6-21	6-23	•-23	•-25
	7	10-21	9-22	8-23	7-25	7-25	•-27
	8	12-23	11-25	10-26	9-27	8-27	8-29
	9	14-25	12-27	12-28	11-29	10-29	9-31
	10	16-27	14-29	13-30	12-31	12-31	11-32
21	0	•-4	•-5	•-6	•-7	•-8	•-9
	1	•-7	•-8	•-9	•-10	•-11	•-13
	2	•-9	•-10	•-11	•-12	•-13	•-15
	3	•-11	•-13	•-14	•-15	•-16	•-18
	4	4-14	4-15	•-16	•-17	•-18	•-20
	5	6-16	5-17	5-18	•-19	•-20	•-22
	6	7-18	7-19	6-20	6-22	•-22	•-24
	7	9-20	8-21	8-22	7-24	7-24	•-26
	8	11-22	10-23	9-24	9-26	8-26	•-28
	9	13-24	12-25	11-26	10-27	10-28	9-29
	10	15-26	14-27	13-28	12-29	11-30	10-31

All values conform to the international convention (i.e. 0,1 instead of 0.1).

Significance Limits for the Fourfold Table Test*

x_1	N_1-x_1	N_1
x_2	N_2-x_2	N_2
X	$N-X$	N

$N = N_1 + N_2$
$X = x_1 + x_2$
$N_1 \leq N_2$
$x_1 \leq N_1 - x_1$

For explanation see page 151

$N = 44$

N_1	x_1	2α = 0,20	2α = 0,10	2α = 0,05	2α = 0,02	2α = 0,01	2α = 0,002
4	0	•–19	•–23	•–26	•–30	•–32	•–35
	1	1–30	•–33	•–35	•–37	•–39	•–41
	2	6–38	4–40	3–41	2–42	•–•	•–•
5	0	•–16	–19	•–22	•–26	•–28	•–32
	1	•–25	•–29	•–31	•–34	•–35	•–38
	2	5–33	3–36	2–37	•–39	•–40	•–41
6	0	•–14	•–17	•–20	•–23	•–25	•–29
	1	•–22	•–25	•–28	•–30	•–32	•–35
	2	4–29	3–32	2–34	•–36	•–37	•–39
	3	9–35	7–37	5–39	4–40	3–41	•–•
7	0	•–12	•–15	•–17	•–20	•–22	•–26
	1	•–20	•–22	•–25	•–27	•–29	•–32
	2	3–26	2–28	2–31	•–33	•–34	•–36
	3	7–32	6–34	5–35	4–37	3–38	•–40
8	0	•–11	•–13	•–15	•–18	•–20	•–24
	1	•–17	•–20	•–22	•–25	•–26	•–30
	2	3–23	2–26	•–28	•–30	•–31	•–34
	3	6–28	5–31	4–32	3–34	3–35	•–37
	4	11–33	9–35	7–37	6–38	5–39	4–40
9	0	•– 9	•–12	•–14	•–16	•–18	•–22
	1	•–16	•–18	•–20	•–23	•–24	•–27
	2	2–21	2–23	•–25	•–28	•–29	•–32
	3	6–26	4–28	4–30	3–32	•–33	•–35
	4	9–30	8–32	7–34	5–36	5–36	4–38
10	0	•– 9	•–11	•–13	•–15	•–17	•–20
	1	•–14	•–16	•–18	•–21	•–22	•–25
	2	2–19	2–21	•–23	•–26	•–27	•–30
	3	5–24	4–26	3–28	3–30	•–31	•–33
	4	8–28	7–30	6–32	5–33	4–34	•–36
	5	12–32	10–34	9–35	8–36	7–37	5–39
11	0	•– 8	•–10	•–12	•–14	•–15	•–19
	1	•–13	•–15	•–17	•–19	•–21	•–24
	2	2–18	•–20	•–22	•–24	•–25	•–28
	3	5–22	4–24	3–26	•–28	•–29	•–31
	4	8–26	6–28	5–29	4–31	4–32	•–34
	5	11–30	9–31	8–33	7–34	6–35	5–37
12	0	•– 7	•– 9	•–11	•–13	•–14	•–17
	1	•–12	•–14	•–16	•–18	•–19	•–22
	2	2–16	•–18	•–20	•–22	•–23	•–26
	3	4–20	3–22	3–24	•–26	•–27	•–29
	4	7–24	6–26	5–27	4–29	4–30	•–32
	5	10–27	9–29	8–31	6–32	6–33	5–35
	6	13–31	12–32	10–34	9–35	8–36	7–37
13	0	•– 7	•– 8	•–10	•–12	•–13	•–16
	1	•–11	•–13	•–15	•–17	•–18	•–21
	2	2–15	•–17	•–19	•–21	•–22	•–24
	3	4–19	3–21	3–22	•–24	•–25	•–28
	4	6–22	5–24	5–26	4–27	•–29	•–31
	5	9–26	8–27	7–29	6–30	5–31	•–33
	6	12–29	11–30	9–32	8–33	8–34	6–36
14	0	•– 6	•– 8	•– 9	•–11	•–12	•–15
	1	•–10	•–12	•–14	•–15	•–17	•–19
	2	2–14	•–16	•–17	•–19	•–20	•–23
	3	4–18	3–19	•–21	•–23	•–24	•–26
	4	6–21	5–23	4–24	4–26	•–27	•–29
	5	9–24	7–26	6–27	6–29	5–30	•–32
	6	11–27	10–29	9–30	8–31	7–32	6–34
	7	14–30	13–31	11–33	10–34	9–35	8–36
15	0	•– 6	•– 7	•– 8	•–10	•–11	•–14
	1	•–10	•–11	•–13	•–14	•–16	•–18
	2	•–13	•–15	•–16	•–18	•–19	•–22
	3	3–16	3–18	•–20	•–21	•–22	•–25
	4	6–20	5–21	4–23	•–24	•–25	•–28
	5	8–23	7–24	6–26	5–27	5–28	•–30
	6	10–25	9–27	8–28	7–30	7–31	6–32
	7	13–28	12–30	11–31	9–32	9–33	7–35
16	0	•– 5	•– 7	•– 8	•– 9	•–11	•–13
	1	•– 9	•–10	•–12	•–14	•–15	•–17
	2	•–12	•–14	•–15	•–17	•–18	•–20
	3	3–15	3–17	•–18	•–20	•–21	•–23
	4	5–18	4–20	4–21	•–23	•–24	•–26
	5	8–21	7–23	6–24	5–26	5–27	•–29
	6	10–24	9–26	8–27	7–28	6–29	•–31
	7	12–27	11–28	10–29	9–31	8–32	7–33
	8	15–29	13–31	12–32	11–33	10–34	9–35
17	0	•– 5	•– 6	•– 7	•– 9	•–10	•–12
	1	•– 8	•–10	•–11	•–13	•–14	•–16
	2	•–12	•–13	•–14	•–16	•–17	•–19
	3	3–15	•–16	•–17	•–19	•–20	•–22
	4	5–17	4–19	4–20	•–22	•–23	•–25
	5	7–20	6–22	5–23	5–24	•–25	•–27
	6	9–23	8–24	7–25	7–27	6–28	•–30
	7	12–25	10–27	9–28	8–29	8–30	7–32
	8	14–28	13–29	12–30	10–31	10–32	9–34
18	0	•– 5	•– 6	•– 7	•– 8	•– 9	•–12
	1	•– 8	•– 9	•–10	•–12	•–13	•–15
	2	•–11	•–12	•–14	•–15	•–16	•–18
	3	3–14	•–15	•–16	•–18	•–19	•–21
	4	5–16	4–18	4–19	•–21	•–22	•–24
	5	7–19	6–20	5–22	5–23	•–24	•–26
	6	9–21	8–23	7–24	6–26	6–26	•–28
	7	11–24	10–25	9–27	8–28	8–29	7–30
	8	13–26	12–28	11–29	10–30	9–31	8–32
	9	15–29	14–30	13–31	12–32	11–33	10–34
19	0	•– 4	•– 5	•– 7	•– 8	•– 9	•–11
	1	•– 8	•– 9	•–10	•–11	•–12	•–14

$N = 44$ (continued)

N_1	x_1	2α = 0,20	2α = 0,10	2α = 0,05	2α = 0,02	2α = 0,01	2α = 0,002
	2	•–10	•–12	•–13	•–14	•–15	•–17
	3	3–13	•–14	•–16	•–17	•–18	•–20
	4	5–16	4–17	•–18	•–20	•–21	•–22
	5	6–18	6–19	5–21	•–22	•–23	•–25
	6	8–20	7–22	7–23	6–24	6–25	•–27
	7	10–23	9–24	9–25	8–27	7–27	•–29
	8	12–25	11–26	10–27	9–29	9–29	8–31
	9	15–27	13–29	12–30	11–31	11–31	10–33
20	0	•– 4	•– 5	•– 6	•– 7	•– 8	•–10
	1	•– 7	•– 8	•– 9	•–11	•–12	•–14
	2	•–10	•–11	•–12	•–14	•–14	•–16
	3	3–12	•–14	•–15	•–16	•–17	•–19
	4	4–15	4–16	•–17	•–19	•–20	•–21
	5	6–17	5–18	5–20	•–21	•–22	•–24
	6	8–19	7–21	6–22	6–23	•–24	•–26
	7	10–22	9–23	8–24	7–25	7–26	•–28
	8	12–24	11–25	10–26	9–27	9–28	8–30
	9	14–26	13–27	12–28	11–29	10–30	9–31
	10	16–28	15–29	14–30	13–31	12–32	11–33
21	0	•– 4	•– 5	•– 6	•– 7	•– 8	•–10
	1	•– 7	•– 8	•– 9	•–10	•–11	•–13
	2	•– 9	•–10	•–12	•–13	•–14	•–16
	3	•–12	•–13	•–14	•–15	•–16	•–18
	4	4–14	4–15	•–16	•–18	•–19	•–20
	5	6–16	5–18	5–19	•–20	•–21	•–23
	6	8–18	7–20	6–21	6–22	•–23	•–25
	7	9–21	9–22	8–23	7–24	7–25	•–27
	8	11–23	10–24	10–25	9–26	8–27	•–28
	9	13–25	12–26	11–27	10–28	10–29	9–30
	10	15–27	14–28	13–29	12–30	12–31	10–32
22	0	•– 4	•– 5	•– 5	•– 7	•– 7	•– 9
	1	•– 6	•– 7	•– 8	•–10	•–10	•–12
	2	•– 9	•–10	•–11	•–12	•–13	•–15
	3	•–11	•–12	•–13	•–15	•–15	•–17
	4	4–13	•–15	•–16	•–17	•–18	•–19
	5	6–16	5–17	5–18	•–19	•–20	•–22
	6	7–18	7–19	6–20	•–21	•–22	•–24
	7	9–20	8–21	8–22	7–23	7–24	•–25
	8	11–22	10–23	9–24	8–25	8–26	•–27
	9	13–24	12–25	11–26	10–27	10–28	9–29
	10	14–26	13–27	13–28	12–29	11–29	10–31
	11	16–28	15–29	14–30	13–31	13–31	12–32

$N = 45$

N_1	x_1	2α = 0,20	2α = 0,10	2α = 0,05	2α = 0,02	2α = 0,01	2α = 0,002
4	0	•–20	•–23	•–27	•–30	•–32	•–36
	1	1–31	•–34	•–36	•–38	•–40	•–42
	2	6–39	4–41	3–42	2–43	•–•	•–•
5	0	•–16	•–20	•–23	•–26	•–29	•–33
	1	•–26	•–29	•–32	•–34	•–36	•–39
	2	5–34	3–36	2–38	•–40	•–41	•–42
6	0	•–14	•–17	•–20	•–23	•–25	•–29
	1	•–23	•–26	•–28	•–31	•–33	•–36
	2	4–30	3–32	2–34	•–37	•–38	•–40
	3	9–36	7–38	6–39	4–41	3–42	•–•
7	0	•–12	•–15	•–18	•–21	•–23	•–27
	1	•–20	•–23	•–25	•–28	•–30	•–33
	2	3–26	2–29	2–31	•–33	•–35	•–37
	3	8–32	6–34	5–36	4–38	3–39	•–41
8	0	•–11	•–13	•–16	•–19	•–21	•–24
	1	•–18	•–20	•–23	•–25	•–27	•–30
	2	3–24	2–26	•–28	•–31	•–32	•–35
	3	7–29	5–31	4–33	3–35	3–36	•–38
	4	11–34	9–36	8–37	6–39	5–40	4–41
9	0	•–10	•–12	•–14	•–17	•–19	•–22
	1	•–16	•–19	•–21	•–23	•–25	•–28
	2	3–22	2–24	•–26	•–28	•–30	•–33
	3	6–27	5–29	4–31	3–33	•–34	•–36
	4	10–31	8–33	7–35	5–36	5–37	4–39
10	0	•– 9	•–11	•–13	•–15	•–17	•–21
	1	•–15	•–17	•–19	•–21	•–23	•–26
	2	2–20	2–22	•–24	•–26	•–28	•–30
	3	5–24	4–26	3–28	3–30	•–32	•–34
	4	9–29	7–31	6–32	5–34	4–35	•–37
	5	12–33	11–34	9–36	8–37	7–38	5–40
11	0	•– 8	•–10	•–12	•–14	•–16	•–19
	1	•–13	•–15	•–17	•–20	•–21	•–24
	2	2–18	•–20	•–22	•–24	•–26	•–28
	3	5–22	4–24	3–26	•–28	•–30	•–32
	4	8–26	7–28	6–30	5–32	4–33	•–35
	5	11–30	10–32	8–34	7–35	6–36	5–38
12	0	•– 7	•– 9	•–11	•–13	•–14	•–18
	1	•–12	•–14	•–16	•–18	•–20	•–23
	2	2–17	•–19	•–20	•–23	•–24	•–27
	3	4–21	3–23	3–24	•–26	•–28	•–30
	4	7–24	6–26	5–28	4–30	4–31	•–33
	5	10–28	9–30	8–31	7–33	6–34	5–36
	6	13–32	12–33	10–35	9–36	8–37	7–38
13	0	•– 7	•– 8	•–10	•–12	•–13	•–16
	1	•–11	•–13	•–15	•–17	•–18	•–21
	2	2–15	•–17	•–19	•–21	•–22	•–25
	3	4–19	3–21	3–23	•–25	•–26	•–28
	4	7–23	6–25	5–26	4–28	4–29	•–31
	5	9–26	8–28	7–30	6–31	5–32	•–34
	6	12–29	11–31	10–33	8–34	8–35	6–37
14	0	•– 6	•– 8	•– 9	•–11	•–12	•–15
	1	•–11	•–12	•–14	•–16	•–17	•–20

$N = 45$ (continued)

N_1	x_1	2α = 0,20	2α = 0,10	2α = 0,05	2α = 0,02	2α = 0,01	2α = 0,002
	2	2–14	•–16	•–18	•–20	•–21	•–24
	3	4–18	3–20	•–21	•–23	•–24	•–27
	4	6–21	5–23	4–25	4–26	•–28	•–30
	5	9–25	8–26	7–28	6–29	5–30	•–32
	6	11–28	10–29	9–31	8–32	7–33	6–35
	7	14–31	13–32	12–33	10–35	9–36	8–37
15	0	•– 6	•– 7	•– 9	•–10	•–12	•–14
	1	•–10	•–11	•–13	•–15	•–16	•–19
	2	•–13	•–15	•–17	•–18	•–20	•–22
	3	3–17	3–19	•–20	•–22	•–23	•–25
	4	6–20	5–22	4–23	4–25	•–26	•–28
	5	8–23	7–25	6–26	5–28	5–29	•–31
	6	11–26	9–28	8–29	7–30	7–31	6–33
	7	13–29	12–30	11–32	10–33	9–34	8–35
16	0	•– 5	•– 7	•– 8	•–10	•–11	•–13
	1	•– 9	•–11	•–12	•–14	•–15	•–18
	2	•–13	•–14	•–16	•–17	•–19	•–21
	3	3–16	3–17	•–19	•–21	•–22	•–24
	4	5–19	5–20	4–22	•–24	•–25	•–27
	5	8–22	7–23	6–25	5–26	5–27	•–29
	6	10–25	9–26	8–27	7–29	6–30	6–32
	7	13–27	11–29	10–30	9–31	8–32	7–34
	8	15–30	14–31	12–33	11–34	10–35	9–36
17	0	•– 5	•– 6	•– 8	•– 9	•–10	•–13
	1	•– 9	•–10	•–11	•–13	•–14	•–17
	2	•–12	•–13	•–15	•–16	•–18	•–20
	3	3–15	3–16	•–18	•–19	•–21	•–23
	4	5–18	4–19	4–21	•–22	•–23	•–25
	5	7–21	6–22	6–23	5–25	•–26	•–28
	6	9–23	8–25	8–26	7–28	6–28	•–30
	7	12–26	11–27	10–29	9–30	8–31	7–32
	8	14–28	13–30	12–31	11–32	10–33	9–34
18	0	•– 5	•– 6	•– 7	•– 9	•–10	•–12
	1	•– 8	•–10	•–11	•–12	•–13	•–16
	2	•–11	•–13	•–14	•–15	•–17	•–19
	3	3–14	•–16	•–17	•–18	•–19	•–22
	4	5–17	4–18	4–20	•–21	•–22	•–24
	5	7–19	6–21	5–22	5–24	•–25	•–27
	6	9–22	8–23	7–25	6–26	6–27	•–29
	7	11–25	10–26	9–27	8–29	8–29	7–31
	8	13–27	12–28	11–29	10–31	9–32	8–33
	9	16–29	14–31	13–32	12–33	11–34	10–35
19	0	•– 5	•– 6	•– 7	•– 8	•– 9	•–11
	1	•– 8	•– 9	•–10	•–12	•–13	•–15
	2	•–11	•–12	•–13	•–15	•–16	•–18
	3	3–13	•–15	•–16	•–17	•–18	•–21
	4	5–16	4–17	•–19	•–20	•–21	•–23
	5	7–18	6–20	5–21	5–23	•–24	•–25
	6	8–21	8–22	7–24	6–25	6–26	•–28
	7	11–23	10–25	9–26	8–27	7–28	•–30
	8	13–26	12–27	11–28	10–29	9–30	8–32
	9	15–28	14–29	13–30	12–31	11–32	10–34
20	0	•– 4	•– 5	•– 6	•– 8	•– 9	•–11
	1	•– 7	•– 8	•–10	•–11	•–12	•–14
	2	•–10	•–11	•–12	•–14	•–15	•–17
	3	3–13	•–14	•–15	•–17	•–18	•–20
	4	4–15	4–16	•–18	•–19	•–20	•–22
	5	6–18	5–19	5–20	•–21	•–22	•–24
	6	8–20	7–21	7–22	6–24	6–25	•–26
	7	10–22	9–24	8–25	8–26	7–27	•–28
	8	12–24	11–26	10–27	9–28	9–29	8–30
	9	14–27	13–28	12–29	11–30	10–31	9–32
	10	16–29	15–30	14–31	13–32	12–33	11–34
21	0	•– 4	•– 5	•– 6	•– 7	•– 8	•–10
	1	•– 7	•– 8	•– 9	•–10	•–11	•–13
	2	•–10	•–11	•–12	•–13	•–14	•–16
	3	3–12	•–13	•–14	•–16	•–17	•–19
	4	4–14	4–16	•–17	•–18	•–19	•–21
	5	6–17	5–18	5–19	•–20	•–21	•–23
	6	8–19	7–20	6–21	6–23	•–24	•–25
	7	10–21	9–22	8–24	7–25	7–26	•–27
	8	12–23	11–25	10–26	9–27	8–28	8–29
	9	13–25	12–27	12–28	11–29	10–30	9–31
	10	15–28	14–29	13–30	12–31	12–31	11–33
22	0	•– 4	•– 5	•– 6	•– 7	•– 8	•– 9
	1	•– 7	•– 8	•– 9	•–10	•–11	•–13
	2	•– 9	•–10	•–11	•–13	•–13	•–15
	3	•–11	•–13	•–14	•–15	•–16	•–18
	4	4–14	4–15	•–16	•–17	•–18	•–20
	5	6–16	5–17	5–18	•–20	•–20	•–22
	6	7–18	7–19	6–20	6–22	•–23	•–24
	7	9–20	8–21	8–23	7–24	7–25	•–26
	8	11–22	10–24	9–25	9–26	8–27	•–28
	9	13–24	12–26	11–27	10–28	10–28	9–30
	10	15–26	14–27	13–28	12–30	11–30	10–32
	11	17–28	16–29	15–30	14–31	13–32	12–33

$N = 46$

N_1	x_1	2α = 0,20	2α = 0,10	2α = 0,05	2α = 0,02	2α = 0,01	2α = 0,002
4	0	•–20	•–24	•–27	•–31	•–33	•–37
	1	1–31	•–34	•–37	•–39	•–40	•–43
	2	6–40	4–42	3–43	2–44	•–•	•–•
5	0	•–17	•–20	•–23	•–27	•–29	•–33
	1	•–27	•–30	•–32	•–35	•–37	•–40
	2	5–35	3–37	2–39	2–41	•–42	•–43
6	0	•–14	•–18	•–20	•–24	•–26	•–30
	1	•–23	•–26	•–29	•–32	•–33	•–36
	2	4–30	3–33	2–35	•–37	•–39	•–41

All values conform to the international convention (i.e. 0,1 instead of 0.1).

x_1	N_1-x_1	N_1
x_2	N_2-x_2	N_2
X	$N-X$	N

$N=N_1+N_2$
$X=x_1+x_2$
$N_1 \leq N_2$
$x_1 \leq N_1-x_1$

For explanation see page 151

N_1	x_1	2α = 0,20	2α = 0,10	2α = 0,05	2α = 0,02	2α = 0,01	2α = 0,002
		N = 46 (continued)					
	3	9–37	7–39	6–40	4–42	4–42	•–•
7	0	•–13	•–15	•–18	•–21	•–23	•–27
	1	•–20	•–23	•–26	•–29	•–30	•–34
	2	3–27	2–30	2–32	•–34	•–36	•–38
	3	8–33	6–35	5–37	4–39	3–40	•–42
8	0	•–11	•–14	•–16	•–19	•–21	•–25
	1	•–18	•–21	•–23	•–26	•–28	•–31
	2	3–24	2–27	•–29	•–31	•–33	•–36
	3	7–30	5–32	4–34	3–36	3–37	•–39
	4	11–35	9–37	8–38	6–40	5–41	4–42
9	0	•–10	•–12	•–15	•–17	•–19	•–23
	1	•–16	•–19	•–21	•–24	•–25	•–29
	2	3–22	2–25	•–27	•–29	•–30	•–33
	3	6–27	5–29	4–31	3–33	•–35	•–37
	4	10–32	8–34	7–35	6–37	5–38	4–40
10	0	•– 9	•–11	•–13	•–16	•–17	•–21
	1	•–15	•–17	•–19	•–22	•–23	•–27
	2	2–20	2–22	•–24	•–27	•–28	•–31
	3	5–25	4–27	3–29	3–31	•–32	•–35
	4	9–29	7–31	6–33	5–35	4–36	•–38
	5	13–33	11–35	9–37	8–38	7–39	6–40
11	0	•– 8	•–10	•–12	•–14	•–16	•–19
	1	•–14	•–16	•–18	•–20	•–22	•–25
	2	2–18	•–21	•–23	•–25	•–26	•–29
	3	5–23	4–25	3–27	•–29	•–30	•–33
	4	8–27	7–29	6–31	5–33	4–34	•–36
	5	11–31	10–33	9–34	7–36	6–37	5–39
12	0	•– 8	•– 9	•–11	•–13	•–15	•–18
	1	•–13	•–15	•–16	•–19	•–20	•–23
	2	2–17	•–19	•–21	•–23	•–25	•–27
	3	4–21	4–23	3–25	•–27	•–28	•–31
	4	7–25	6–27	5–29	4–31	4–32	•–34
	5	10–29	9–31	8–32	7–34	6–35	5–37
	6	14–32	12–34	11–35	9–37	8–38	7–39
13	0	•– 7	•– 9	•–10	•–12	•–14	•–17
	1	•–12	•–14	•–15	•–17	•–19	•–22
	2	2–16	•–18	•–20	•–22	•–23	•–26
	3	4–20	3–22	3–23	•–25	•–27	•–29
	4	7–23	6–25	5–27	4–29	4–30	•–32
	5	10–27	8–29	7–30	6–32	6–33	5–35
	6	13–30	11–32	10–33	9–35	8–36	6–37
14	0	•– 6	•– 8	•–10	•–11	•–13	•–16
	1	•–11	•–13	•–14	•–16	•–18	•–20
	2	2–15	•–17	•–18	•–20	•–22	•–24
	3	4–18	3–20	3–22	•–24	•–25	•–27
	4	6–22	5–24	5–25	4–27	•–28	•–30
	5	9–25	8–27	7–28	6–30	5–31	•–33
	6	12–28	10–30	9–31	8–33	7–34	6–36
	7	15–31	13–33	12–34	10–36	10–36	8–38
15	0	•– 6	•– 7	•– 9	•–11	•–12	•–15
	1	•–10	•–12	•–13	•–15	•–16	•–19
	2	•–14	•–16	•–17	•–19	•–20	•–23
	3	4–17	3–19	•–21	•–22	•–24	•–26
	4	6–20	5–22	4–24	4–26	•–27	•–29
	5	8–24	7–25	6–27	5–28	5–30	•–32
	6	11–27	10–28	9–30	8–31	7–32	6–34
	7	14–30	12–31	11–32	10–34	9–35	8–36
16	0	•– 6	•– 7	•– 8	•–10	•–11	•–14
	1	•– 9	•–11	•–12	•–14	•–15	•–18
	2	•–13	•–15	•–16	•–18	•–19	•–22
	3	3–16	3–18	•–19	•–21	•–22	•–25
	4	6–19	5–21	4–22	•–24	•–25	•–27
	5	8–22	7–24	6–25	5–27	5–28	•–30
	6	10–25	9–27	8–28	7–30	7–31	6–32
	7	13–28	11–29	10–31	9–32	9–33	7–35
	8	15–31	14–32	13–33	11–35	11–35	9–37
17	0	•– 5	•– 7	•– 8	•– 9	•–10	•–13
	1	•– 9	•–10	•–12	•–13	•–15	•–17
	2	•–12	•–14	•–15	•–17	•–18	•–20
	3	3–15	3–17	•–18	•–20	•–21	•–23
	4	5–18	4–20	4–21	•–23	•–24	•–26
	5	7–21	6–23	6–24	5–26	5–27	•–29
	6	10–24	9–25	8–27	7–28	6–29	•–31
	7	12–26	11–28	10–29	9–31	8–32	7–33
	8	14–29	13–30	12–32	11–33	10–34	9–35
18	0	•– 5	•– 6	•– 7	•– 9	•–10	•–12
	1	•– 8	•–10	•–11	•–13	•–14	•–16
	2	•–11	•–13	•–14	•–16	•–17	•–19
	3	3–14	•–16	•–17	•–19	•–20	•–22
	4	5–17	4–19	4–20	•–22	•–23	•–25
	5	7–20	6–21	5–23	5–24	•–25	•–27
	6	9–23	8–24	7–25	6–27	6–28	•–30
	7	11–25	10–27	9–28	8–29	8–30	7–32
	8	14–28	12–29	11–30	10–31	10–32	8–34
	9	16–30	15–31	14–32	12–34	12–34	10–36
19	0	•– 5	•– 6	•– 7	•– 8	•– 9	•–11
	1	•– 8	•– 9	•–10	•–12	•–13	•–15
	2	•–11	•–12	•–14	•–15	•–16	•–18
	3	3–14	•–15	•–16	•–18	•–19	•–21
	4	5–16	4–18	4–19	•–21	•–22	•–24
	5	7–19	6–20	5–22	5–23	•–24	•–26
	6	9–21	8–23	7–24	6–26	6–26	•–28
	7	11–24	10–25	9–26	8–28	7–29	7–30
	8	13–26	12–28	11–29	10–30	9–31	8–32
	9	15–29	14–30	13–31	12–32	11–33	10–34
20	0	•– 4	•– 5	•– 6	•– 8	•– 9	•–11

N_1	x_1	2α = 0,20	2α = 0,10	2α = 0,05	2α = 0,02	2α = 0,01	2α = 0,002
		N = 46 (continued)					
	1	•– 7	•– 9	•–10	•–11	•–12	•–14
	2	•–10	•–12	•–13	•–14	•–15	•–17
	3	3–13	3–14	•–16	•–17	•–18	•–20
	4	4–15	4–17	•–18	•–20	•–21	•–23
	5	6–18	6–19	5–21	•–22	•–23	•–25
	6	8–20	7–22	7–23	6–24	6–25	•–27
	7	10–23	9–24	8–25	8–27	7–27	•–29
	8	12–25	11–26	10–27	9–29	9–30	8–31
	9	14–27	13–29	12–30	11–31	11–32	9–33
	10	17–29	15–31	14–32	13–33	12–34	11–35
21	0	•– 4	•– 5	•– 6	•– 7	•– 8	•–10
	1	•– 7	•– 8	•– 9	•–11	•–12	•–14
	2	•–10	•–11	•–12	•–14	•–15	•–17
	3	3–12	•–14	•–15	•–16	•–17	•–19
	4	4–15	4–16	•–17	•–19	•–20	•–22
	5	6–17	5–18	5–20	•–21	•–22	•–24
	6	8–19	7–21	6–22	6–23	•–24	•–26
	7	10–22	9–23	8–24	7–25	7–26	•–28
	8	12–24	11–25	10–26	9–28	9–28	8–30
	9	14–26	13–27	12–28	11–30	10–30	9–32
	10	16–28	15–29	14–30	13–32	12–32	11–34
22	0	•– 4	•– 5	•– 6	•– 7	•– 8	•–10
	1	•– 7	•– 8	•– 9	•–10	•–11	•–13
	2	•– 9	•–10	•–12	•–13	•–14	•–16
	3	•–12	•–13	•–14	•–15	•–16	•–18
	4	4–14	4–15	•–16	•–18	•–19	•–21
	5	6–16	5–18	5–19	•–20	•–21	•–23
	6	8–19	7–20	6–21	6–22	•–23	•–25
	7	9–21	8–22	8–23	7–24	7–25	•–27
	8	11–23	10–24	10–25	9–26	8–27	•–29
	9	13–25	12–26	11–27	10–28	10–29	9–31
	10	15–27	14–28	13–29	12–30	11–31	10–32
	11	17–29	16–30	15–31	14–32	13–33	12–34
23	0	•– 4	•– 5	•– 5	•– 7	•– 7	•– 9
	1	•– 6	•– 7	•– 8	•–10	•–10	•–12
	2	•– 9	•–10	•–11	•–12	•–13	•–15
	3	•–11	•–12	•–13	•–15	•–16	•–17
	4	4–13	•–15	•–16	•–17	•–18	•–20
	5	6–16	5–17	5–18	•–19	•–20	•–22
	6	7–18	7–19	6–20	•–21	•–22	•–24
	7	9–20	8–21	8–22	7–23	7–24	•–26
	8	11–22	10–23	9–24	8–25	8–26	•–28
	9	13–24	12–25	11–26	10–27	10–28	9–29
	10	14–26	13–27	13–28	12–29	11–30	10–31
	11	16–28	15–29	14–30	13–31	13–32	12–33
		N = 47					
4	0	•–20	•–24	•–28	•–32	•–34	•–38
	1	1–32	•–35	•–38	•–40	•–41	•–43
	2	7–40	4–43	3–44	2–45	•–•	•–•
5	0	•–17	•–21	•–24	•–28	•–30	•–34
	1	•–27	•–31	•–33	•–36	•–38	•–40
	2	5–35	3–38	2–40	2–42	•–43	•–44
6	0	•–15	•–18	•–21	•–24	•–27	•–31
	1	•–24	•–27	•–29	•–32	•–34	•–37
	2	4–31	3–34	2–36	•–38	•–40	•–42
	3	9–38	7–40	6–41	4–43	4–43	•–•
7	0	•–13	•–16	•–18	•–22	•–24	•–28
	1	•–21	•–24	•–26	•–29	•–31	•–34
	2	4–28	2–30	2–33	•–35	•–36	•–39
	3	8–34	6–36	5–38	4–40	3–41	•–42
8	0	•–11	•–14	•–17	•–19	•–21	•–26
	1	•–19	•–21	•–24	•–27	•–28	•–32
	2	3–25	2–28	•–30	•–32	•–34	•–36
	3	7–30	5–33	4–35	3–37	3–38	•–40
	4	11–36	9–38	8–39	6–41	5–42	4–43
9	0	•–10	•–13	•–15	•–18	•–20	•–23
	1	•–17	•–19	•–22	•–24	•–26	•–29
	2	3–23	2–25	•–27	•–30	•–31	•–34
	3	6–28	5–30	4–32	3–34	•–35	•–38
	4	10–32	8–35	7–36	6–38	5–39	4–41
10	0	•– 9	•–11	•–14	•–16	•–18	•–22
	1	•–15	•–18	•–20	•–22	•–24	•–27
	2	2–21	2–23	•–25	•–27	•–29	•–32
	3	5–25	4–28	3–30	3–32	•–33	•–36
	4	9–30	7–32	6–34	5–36	4–37	•–39
	5	13–34	11–36	10–37	8–39	7–40	6–41
11	0	•– 8	•–10	•–12	•–15	•–16	•–20
	1	•–14	•–16	•–18	•–21	•–22	•–25
	2	2–19	•–21	•–23	•–25	•–27	•–30
	3	5–23	4–26	3–27	•–30	•–31	•–34
	4	8–28	7–30	6–31	5–33	4–35	•–37
	5	12–32	10–33	9–35	7–37	7–38	5–39
12	0	•– 8	•–10	•–11	•–14	•–15	•–18
	1	•–13	•–15	•–17	•–19	•–21	•–24
	2	2–17	•–20	•–21	•–24	•–25	•–28
	3	5–22	4–24	3–26	•–28	•–29	•–32
	4	7–26	6–28	5–29	4–31	4–32	•–35
	5	11–29	9–31	8–33	7–35	6–36	5–38
	6	14–33	12–35	11–36	9–38	9–38	7–40
13	0	•– 7	•– 9	•–11	•–13	•–14	•–17
	1	•–12	•–14	•–16	•–18	•–19	•–22
	2	2–16	•–18	•–20	•–22	•–23	•–26
	3	4–20	3–22	3–24	•–26	•–27	•–30
	4	7–24	6–26	5–28	4–29	4–31	•–33
	5	10–27	8–29	7–31	6–33	6–34	5–36

N_1	x_1	2α = 0,20	2α = 0,10	2α = 0,05	2α = 0,02	2α = 0,01	2α = 0,002
		N = 47 (continued)					
	6	13–31	11–33	10–34	9–36	8–37	7–38
14	0	•– 7	•– 8	•–10	•–12	•–13	•–16
	1	•–11	•–13	•–15	•–17	•–18	•–21
	2	2–15	•–17	•–19	•–21	•–22	•–25
	3	4–19	3–21	3–22	•–24	•–26	•–28
	4	6–22	5–24	5–26	4–28	•–29	•–31
	5	9–26	8–28	7–29	6–31	5–32	•–34
	6	12–29	11–31	9–32	8–34	7–35	6–37
	7	15–32	13–34	12–35	11–36	10–37	8–39
15	0	•– 6	•– 8	•– 9	•–11	•–12	•–15
	1	•–10	•–12	•–14	•–16	•–17	•–20
	2	2–14	•–16	•–18	•–19	•–21	•–23
	3	4–18	3–19	•–21	•–23	•–24	•–27
	4	6–21	5–23	4–24	4–26	•–27	•–30
	5	9–24	7–26	6–27	6–29	5–30	•–32
	6	11–27	10–29	9–30	8–32	7–33	6–35
	7	14–30	12–32	11–33	10–35	9–35	8–37
16	0	•– 6	•– 7	•– 9	•–10	•–11	•–14
	1	•–10	•–11	•–13	•–15	•–16	•–18
	2	•–13	•–15	•–16	•–18	•–20	•–22
	3	3–17	3–18	•–20	•–22	•–23	•–25
	4	6–20	5–21	4–23	•–25	•–26	•–28
	5	8–23	7–24	6–26	5–28	5–29	•–31
	6	10–26	9–27	8–29	7–30	7–31	6–33
	7	13–29	12–30	11–31	9–33	9–34	7–36
	8	16–31	14–33	13–34	12–35	11–36	9–38
17	0	•– 5	•– 7	•– 8	•–10	•–11	•–13
	1	•– 9	•–11	•–12	•–14	•–15	•–17
	2	•–12	•–14	•–16	•–17	•–18	•–21
	3	3–16	3–17	•–19	•–20	•–22	•–24
	4	5–19	4–20	4–22	•–23	•–25	•–27
	5	8–21	7–23	6–25	5–26	5–27	•–29
	6	10–24	9–26	8–27	7–29	6–30	•–32
	7	12–27	11–29	10–30	9–31	8–32	7–34
	8	15–30	13–31	12–32	11–34	10–35	9–36
18	0	•– 5	•– 6	•– 7	•– 9	•–10	•–12
	1	•– 9	•–10	•–11	•–13	•–14	•–16
	2	•–12	•–13	•–15	•–16	•–17	•–20
	3	3–15	•–16	•–18	•–19	•–20	•–23
	4	5–18	4–19	4–21	•–22	•–23	•–25
	5	7–20	6–22	6–23	5–25	•–26	•–28
	6	9–23	8–25	7–26	7–27	6–28	•–30
	7	12–26	10–27	9–28	8–30	8–31	7–33
	8	14–28	13–30	12–31	10–32	10–33	9–35
	9	16–31	15–32	14–33	13–34	12–35	10–37
19	0	•– 5	•– 6	•– 7	•– 8	•–10	•–12
	1	•– 8	•– 9	•–11	•–12	•–13	•–16
	2	•–11	•–13	•–14	•–15	•–17	•–19
	3	3–14	•–15	•–17	•–18	•–19	•–22
	4	5–17	4–18	4–20	•–21	•–22	•–24
	5	7–19	6–21	5–22	5–24	•–25	•–27
	6	9–22	8–23	7–25	6–26	6–27	•–29
	7	11–24	10–26	9–27	8–29	8–29	7–31
	8	13–27	12–28	11–29	10–31	9–32	8–33
	9	15–29	14–31	13–32	12–33	11–34	10–35
20	0	•– 4	•– 6	•– 7	•– 8	•– 9	•–11
	1	•– 8	•– 9	•–10	•–12	•–13	•–15
	2	•–11	•–12	•–13	•–15	•–16	•–18
	3	3–13	•–15	•–16	•–17	•–18	•–21
	4	5–16	4–17	•–19	•–20	•–21	•–23
	5	6–18	6–20	5–21	•–23	•–24	•–26
	6	8–21	7–22	7–24	6–25	6–26	•–28
	7	10–23	9–25	9–26	8–27	7–28	•–30
	8	13–26	11–27	11–28	10–29	9–30	8–32
	9	15–28	13–29	12–30	11–32	11–32	10–34
	10	17–30	16–31	15–32	13–34	13–34	11–36
21	0	•– 4	•– 5	•– 6	•– 8	•– 8	•–11
	1	•– 7	•– 8	•–10	•–11	•–12	•–14
	2	•–10	•–11	•–12	•–14	•–15	•–17
	3	3–13	•–14	•–15	•–17	•–18	•–20
	4	4–15	4–16	•–18	•–19	•–20	•–22
	5	6–17	5–19	5–20	•–22	•–22	•–24
	6	8–20	7–21	7–22	6–24	•–25	•–27
	7	10–22	9–24	8–25	7–26	7–27	•–29
	8	12–24	11–26	10–27	9–28	9–29	8–31
	9	14–27	13–28	12–29	11–30	10–31	9–33
	10	16–29	15–30	14–31	13–32	12–33	11–34
22	0	•– 4	•– 5	•– 6	•– 7	•– 8	•–10
	1	•– 7	•– 8	•– 9	•–10	•–11	•–13
	2	•–10	•–11	•–12	•–13	•–14	•–16
	3	3–12	•–13	•–14	•–16	•–17	•–19
	4	4–14	4–16	•–17	•–18	•–19	•–21
	5	6–17	5–18	5–19	•–21	•–21	•–23
	6	8–19	7–20	6–21	6–23	•–24	•–25
	7	10–21	9–23	8–24	7–25	7–26	•–28
	8	11–23	10–25	10–26	9–27	8–28	•–29
	9	13–25	12–27	11–28	11–29	10–30	9–31
	10	15–28	14–29	13–30	12–31	12–32	11–33
	11	17–30	16–31	15–32	14–33	13–34	12–35
23	0	•– 4	•– 5	•– 6	•– 7	•– 8	•– 9
	1	•– 7	•– 8	•– 9	•–10	•–11	•–13
	2	•– 9	•–10	•–11	•–13	•–13	•–15
	3	•–11	•–13	•–14	•–15	•–16	•–18
	4	4–14	4–15	•–16	•–17	•–18	•–20
	5	6–16	5–17	5–18	•–20	•–21	•–22
	6	7–18	7–19	6–21	6–22	•–23	•–24
	7	9–20	8–22	8–23	7–24	7–25	•–26
	8	11–22	10–24	9–25	9–26	8–27	•–28

All values conform to the international convention (i.e. 0,1 instead of 0.1).

Significance Limits for the Fourfold Table Test*

x_1	N_1-x_1	N_1
x_2	N_2-x_2	N_2
X	$N-X$	N

$N = N_1+N_2$, $X = x_1+x_2$, $N_1 \leq N_2$, $x_1 \leq N_1-x_1$

For explanation see page 151

N_1	x_1	2α = 0,20	2α = 0,10	2α = 0,05	2α = 0,02	2α = 0,01	2α = 0,002
		$N = 47$ (continued)					
	9	13–24	12–26	11–27	10–28	10–29	9–30
	10	15–26	14–28	13–29	12–30	11–31	10–32
	11	17–28	16–30	15–31	14–32	13–32	12–34
		$N = 48$					
4	0	•–21	•–25	•–28	•–32	•–35	•–39
	1	1–33	•–36	•–38	•–41	•–42	•–44
	2	7–41	5–43	3–45	2–46	•–•	•–•
5	0	•–17	•–21	•–24	•–28	•–31	•–35
	1	•–28	•–31	•–34	•–37	•–38	•–41
	2	5–36	4–39	2–41	2–43	•–44	•–45
6	0	•–15	•–18	•–21	•–25	•–27	•–32
	1	•–24	•–27	•–30	•–33	•–35	•–38
	2	4–32	3–35	2–37	•–39	•–40	•–43
	3	10–38	8–40	6–42	4–44	4–44	•–•
7	0	•–13	•–16	•–19	•–22	•–24	•–29
	1	•–21	•–24	•–27	•–30	•–32	•–35
	2	4–28	2–31	2–33	•–36	•–37	•–40
	3	8–34	6–37	5–39	4–41	3–42	•–43
8	0	•–12	•–14	•–17	•–20	•–22	•–26
	1	•–19	•–22	•–24	•–27	•–29	•–33
	2	3–25	2–28	2–30	•–33	•–34	•–37
	3	7–31	6–34	4–36	3–38	3–39	•–41
	4	12–36	10–38	8–40	6–42	6–42	4–44
9	0	•–10	•–13	•–15	•–18	•–20	•–24
	1	•–17	•–20	•–22	•–25	•–27	•–30
	2	3–23	2–26	•–28	•–30	•–32	•–35
	3	6–28	5–31	4–33	3–35	3–36	•–39
	4	10–33	9–35	7–37	6–39	5–40	4–42
10	0	•– 9	•–12	•–14	•–16	•–18	•–22
	1	•–16	•–18	•–20	•–23	•–25	•–28
	2	2–21	2–23	•–26	•–28	•–30	•–33
	3	6–26	4–28	4–30	3–32	•–34	•–36
	4	9–31	8–33	6–34	5–36	5–38	•–40
	5	13–35	11–37	10–38	8–40	7–41	6–42
11	0	•– 9	•–11	•–13	•–15	•–17	•–20
	1	•–14	•–17	•–19	•–21	•–23	•–26
	2	2–19	2–22	•–24	•–26	•–28	•–30
	3	5–24	4–26	3–28	3–30	•–32	•–34
	4	8–28	7–30	6–32	5–34	4–35	•–38
	5	12–32	10–34	9–36	7–37	7–39	5–40
12	0	•– 8	•–10	•–12	•–14	•–16	•–19
	1	•–13	•–15	•–17	•–20	•–21	•–24
	2	2–18	•–20	•–22	•–24	•–26	•–29
	3	5–22	4–24	3–26	•–28	•–30	•–32
	4	8–26	6–28	5–30	4–32	4–33	•–36
	5	11–30	9–32	8–34	7–35	6–36	5–38
	6	14–34	13–35	11–37	10–38	9–39	7–41
13	0	•– 7	•– 9	•–11	•–13	•–14	•–18
	1	•–12	•–14	•–16	•–18	•–20	•–23
	2	2–17	•–19	•–20	•–23	•–24	•–27
	3	4–21	3–23	3–24	•–26	•–28	•–30
	4	7–24	6–26	5–28	4–30	4–31	•–34
	5	10–28	9–30	7–32	6–33	6–34	5–37
	6	13–32	12–33	10–35	9–36	8–37	7–39
14	0	•– 7	•– 8	•–10	•–12	•–13	•–16
	1	•–11	•–13	•–15	•–17	•–18	•–21
	2	2–15	•–17	•–19	•–21	•–23	•–25
	3	4–19	3–21	3–23	•–25	•–26	•–29
	4	7–23	5–25	5–26	4–28	•–30	•–32
	5	9–26	8–28	7–30	6–31	5–33	•–35
	6	12–30	11–31	10–33	8–34	8–35	6–37
	7	15–33	14–34	12–36	11–37	10–38	8–40
15	0	•– 6	•– 8	•– 9	•–11	•–13	•–15
	1	•–11	•–12	•–14	•–16	•–17	•–20
	2	2–14	•–16	•–18	•–20	•–21	•–24
	3	4–18	3–20	•–22	•–23	•–25	•–27
	4	6–21	5–23	4–25	4–27	•–28	•–30
	5	9–25	7–27	7–28	6–30	5–31	•–33
	6	11–28	10–30	9–31	8–33	7–34	6–36
	7	14–31	13–33	11–34	10–35	9–36	8–38
16	0	•– 6	•– 7	•– 9	•–10	•–12	•–14
	1	•–10	•–12	•–13	•–15	•–16	•–19
	2	•–14	•–15	•–17	•–19	•–20	•–23
	3	3–17	3–19	•–20	•–22	•–23	•–26
	4	6–20	5–22	4–24	4–25	•–26	•–29
	5	8–23	7–25	6–27	5–28	5–29	•–32
	6	11–26	9–28	8–29	7–31	7–32	6–34
	7	13–29	12–31	11–32	10–34	9–35	7–36
	8	16–32	14–34	13–35	12–36	11–37	9–39
17	0	•– 5	•– 7	•– 8	•–10	•–11	•–14
	1	•– 9	•–11	•–12	•–14	•–15	•–18
	2	•–13	•–14	•–16	•–18	•–19	•–21
	3	3–16	3–18	•–19	•–21	•–22	•–25
	4	5–19	5–21	4–22	•–24	•–25	•–27
	5	8–22	7–24	6–25	5–27	5–28	•–30
	6	10–25	9–27	8–28	7–30	6–31	•–33
	7	12–28	11–29	10–31	9–32	8–33	7–35
	8	15–30	14–32	12–33	11–34	10–35	9–37
18	0	•– 5	•– 6	•– 8	•– 9	•–10	•–13
	1	•– 9	•–10	•–12	•–13	•–14	•–17
	2	•–12	•–14	•–15	•–17	•–18	•–20
	3	3–15	3–17	•–18	•–20	•–21	•–23
	4	5–18	4–20	4–21	•–23	•–24	•–26
	5	7–21	6–22	6–24	5–25	•–27	•–29

N_1	x_1	2α = 0,20	2α = 0,10	2α = 0,05	2α = 0,02	2α = 0,01	2α = 0,002
		$N = 48$ (continued)					
	6	9–24	8–25	8–27	7–28	6–29	•–31
	7	12–26	11–28	10–29	9–31	8–32	7–33
	8	14–29	13–30	12–32	11–33	10–34	9–35
	9	17–31	15–33	14–34	13–35	12–36	11–37
19	0	•– 5	•– 6	•– 7	•– 9	•–10	•–12
	1	•– 8	•–10	•–11	•–13	•–14	•–16
	2	•–11	•–13	•–14	•–16	•–17	•–19
	3	3–14	•–16	•–17	•–19	•–20	•–22
	4	5–17	4–19	4–20	•–22	•–23	•–25
	5	7–20	6–21	5–23	5–24	•–25	•–27
	6	9–22	8–24	7–25	6–27	6–28	•–30
	7	11–25	10–26	9–28	8–29	8–30	7–32
	8	13–27	12–29	11–30	10–32	9–32	8–34
	9	16–30	14–31	13–32	12–34	11–35	10–36
20	0	•– 5	•– 6	•– 7	•– 8	•– 9	•–11
	1	•– 8	•– 9	•–10	•–12	•–13	•–15
	2	•–11	•–12	•–13	•–15	•–16	•–18
	3	3–14	•–15	•–16	•–18	•–19	•–21
	4	5–16	4–18	4–19	•–21	•–22	•–24
	5	7–19	6–20	5–22	5–23	•–24	•–26
	6	9–21	8–23	7–24	6–26	6–27	•–28
	7	11–24	10–25	9–26	8–28	7–29	•–31
	8	13–26	12–28	11–29	10–30	9–31	8–33
	9	15–28	14–30	13–31	12–32	11–33	10–35
	10	17–31	16–32	15–33	14–34	13–35	11–37
21	0	•– 4	•– 5	•– 6	•– 8	•– 9	•–11
	1	•– 7	•– 9	•–10	•–11	•–12	•–14
	2	•–10	•–12	•–13	•–14	•–15	•–17
	3	3–13	•–14	•–16	•–17	•–18	•–20
	4	4–15	4–17	•–18	•–20	•–21	•–23
	5	6–18	6–19	5–21	•–22	•–23	•–25
	6	8–20	7–22	7–23	6–24	6–25	•–27
	7	10–23	9–24	8–25	8–27	7–28	•–29
	8	12–25	11–26	10–28	9–29	9–30	8–31
	9	14–27	13–29	12–30	11–31	10–32	9–33
	10	16–29	15–31	14–32	13–33	12–34	11–35
22	0	•– 4	•– 5	•– 6	•– 7	•– 8	•–10
	1	•– 7	•– 8	•– 9	•–11	•–12	•–14
	2	•–10	•–11	•–12	•–14	•–15	•–17
	3	3–12	•–14	•–15	•–16	•–17	•–19
	4	4–15	4–16	•–17	•–19	•–20	•–22
	5	6–17	5–18	5–20	•–21	•–22	•–24
	6	8–19	7–21	6–22	6–23	•–24	•–26
	7	10–22	9–23	8–24	7–26	7–26	•–28
	8	12–24	11–25	10–26	9–28	8–29	8–30
	9	14–26	13–27	12–28	11–30	10–31	9–32
	10	16–28	14–29	14–31	13–32	12–32	11–34
	11	18–30	16–32	15–33	14–34	14–34	12–36
23	0	•– 4	•– 5	•– 6	•– 7	•– 8	•–10
	1	•– 7	•– 8	•– 9	•–10	•–11	•–13
	2	•– 9	•–10	•–12	•–13	•–14	•–16
	3	•–12	•–13	•–14	•–15	•–16	•–18
	4	4–14	4–15	•–17	•–18	•–19	•–21
	5	6–16	5–18	5–19	•–20	•–21	•–23
	6	8–19	7–20	6–21	6–22	•–23	•–25
	7	9–21	8–22	8–23	7–24	7–25	•–27
	8	11–23	10–24	9–25	9–27	8–27	•–29
	9	13–25	12–26	11–27	10–29	10–29	9–31
	10	15–27	14–28	13–29	12–30	11–31	10–33
	11	17–29	16–30	15–31	14–32	13–33	12–34
24	0	•– 4	•– 5	•– 5	•– 7	•– 7	•– 9
	1	•– 6	•– 7	•– 8	•–10	•–11	•–12
	2	•– 9	•–10	•–11	•–12	•–13	•–15
	3	•–11	•–12	•–13	•–15	•–16	•–18
	4	4–13	•–15	•–16	•–17	•–18	•–20
	5	6–16	5–17	5–18	•–19	•–20	•–22
	6	7–18	7–19	6–20	•–21	•–22	•–24
	7	9–20	8–21	8–22	7–23	7–24	•–26
	8	11–22	10–23	9–24	8–25	8–26	•–28
	9	13–24	12–25	11–26	10–27	9–28	9–30
	10	14–26	13–27	13–28	12–29	11–30	10–32
	11	16–28	15–29	14–30	13–31	13–32	12–33
	12	18–30	17–31	16–32	15–33	14–34	13–35
		$N = 49$					
4	0	•–21	•–26	•–29	•–33	•–35	•–39
	1	1–33	•–37	•–39	•–42	•–43	•–45
	2	7–42	5–44	3–46	2–47	•–•	•–•
5	0	•–18	•–22	•–25	•–29	•–31	•–36
	1	•–28	•–32	•–35	•–38	•–39	•–42
	2	5–37	4–40	3–42	2–43	•–45	•–46
6	0	•–15	•–19	•–22	•–25	•–28	•–32
	1	•–25	•–28	•–31	•–34	•–36	•–39
	2	4–32	3–35	2–38	•–40	•–41	•–43
	3	10–39	8–41	6–43	5–44	4–45	•–•
7	0	•–13	•–16	•–19	•–23	•–25	•–29
	1	•–22	•–25	•–28	•–31	•–32	•–36
	2	4–29	3–32	2–34	•–37	•–38	•–41
	3	8–35	6–38	5–39	4–41	3–42	•–44
8	0	•–12	•–15	•–17	•–20	•–22	•–27
	1	•–19	•–22	•–25	•–28	•–30	•–33
	2	3–26	2–29	2–31	•–34	•–35	•–38
	3	7–32	6–34	4–36	3–38	3–40	•–42
	4	12–37	10–39	8–41	7–42	6–43	4–45
9	0	•–11	•–13	•–16	•–18	•–20	•–24
	1	•–18	•–20	•–23	•–25	•–27	•–31

N_1	x_1	2α = 0,20	2α = 0,10	2α = 0,05	2α = 0,02	2α = 0,01	2α = 0,002
		$N = 49$ (continued)					
	2	3–24	2–26	•–28	•–31	•–33	•–36
	3	6–29	5–31	4–33	3–36	3–37	•–39
	4	11–34	9–36	7–38	6–40	5–41	4–43
10	0	•–10	•–12	•–14	•–17	•–19	•–23
	1	•–16	•–18	•–21	•–23	•–25	•–29
	2	2–21	2–24	•–26	•–29	•–30	•–33
	3	6–26	4–29	4–31	3–33	•–35	•–37
	4	9–31	8–33	7–35	5–37	5–38	4–40
	5	13–36	11–38	10–39	8–41	7–42	6–43
11	0	•– 9	•–11	•–13	•–15	•–17	•–21
	1	•–15	•–17	•–19	•–22	•–23	•–27
	2	2–20	2–22	•–24	•–27	•–28	•–31
	3	5–24	4–27	3–29	3–31	•–32	•–35
	4	9–29	7–31	6–33	5–35	4–36	•–38
	5	12–33	10–35	9–37	8–38	7–39	5–41
12	0	•– 8	•–10	•–12	•–14	•–16	•–19
	1	•–13	•–16	•–18	•–20	•–22	•–25
	2	2–18	•–20	•–22	•–25	•–26	•–29
	3	5–23	4–25	3–27	•–29	•–30	•–33
	4	8–27	6–29	5–31	4–33	4–34	•–36
	5	11–31	9–33	8–34	7–36	6–37	5–39
	6	15–34	13–36	11–38	10–39	9–40	7–42
13	0	•– 7	•– 9	•–11	•–13	•–15	•–18
	1	•–12	•–15	•–16	•–19	•–20	•–23
	2	2–17	•–19	•–21	•–23	•–25	•–28
	3	4–21	3–23	3–25	•–27	•–28	•–31
	4	7–25	6–27	5–29	4–31	4–32	•–34
	5	10–29	9–31	8–32	6–34	6–35	5–37
	6	13–32	12–34	10–36	9–37	8–38	7–40
14	0	•– 7	•– 9	•–10	•–12	•–14	•–17
	1	•–12	•–14	•–15	•–17	•–19	•–22
	2	2–16	•–18	•–20	•–22	•–23	•–26
	3	4–20	3–22	3–23	•–25	•–27	•–29
	4	7–23	6–25	5–27	4–29	4–30	•–33
	5	9–27	8–29	7–30	6–32	5–33	•–36
	6	12–30	11–32	10–34	8–35	8–36	6–38
	7	16–33	14–35	12–37	11–38	10–39	8–41
15	0	•– 6	•– 8	•–10	•–11	•–13	•–16
	1	•–11	•–13	•–14	•–16	•–18	•–21
	2	2–15	•–17	•–18	•–20	•–22	•–24
	3	4–18	3–20	3–22	•–24	•–25	•–28
	4	6–22	5–24	4–25	4–27	•–29	•–31
	5	9–25	8–27	7–29	6–30	5–32	•–34
	6	12–28	10–30	9–32	8–33	7–34	6–36
	7	14–32	13–33	12–35	10–36	9–37	8–39
16	0	•– 6	•– 7	•– 9	•–11	•–12	•–15
	1	•–10	•–12	•–13	•–15	•–17	•–19
	2	•–14	•–16	•–17	•–19	•–20	•–23
	3	4–17	3–19	•–21	•–23	•–24	•–26
	4	6–21	5–22	4–24	4–26	•–27	•–29
	5	8–24	7–26	6–27	5–29	5–30	•–32
	6	11–27	10–29	9–30	7–32	7–33	6–35
	7	14–30	12–31	11–33	10–34	9–35	8–37
	8	16–33	15–34	13–36	12–37	11–38	10–39
17	0	•– 6	•– 7	•– 8	•–10	•–11	•–14
	1	•–10	•–11	•–13	•–14	•–16	•–18
	2	•–13	•–15	•–16	•–18	•–19	•–22
	3	3–16	3–18	•–20	•–21	•–23	•–25
	4	6–19	5–21	4–23	•–25	•–26	•–28
	5	8–22	7–24	6–26	5–27	5–29	•–31
	6	10–25	9–27	8–29	7–30	7–31	6–33
	7	13–28	11–30	10–31	9–33	8–34	7–36
	8	15–31	14–33	13–34	11–35	11–36	9–38
18	0	•– 5	•– 7	•– 8	•– 9	•–11	•–13
	1	•– 9	•–10	•–12	•–14	•–15	•–17
	2	•–12	•–14	•–15	•–17	•–18	•–21
	3	3–15	3–17	•–19	•–20	•–21	•–24
	4	5–18	4–20	4–22	•–23	•–24	•–27
	5	7–21	6–23	6–24	5–26	5–27	•–29
	6	10–24	9–26	8–27	7–29	6–30	•–32
	7	12–27	11–28	10–30	9–31	8–32	7–34
	8	14–29	13–31	12–32	11–34	10–35	9–36
	9	17–32	16–33	14–35	13–36	12–37	11–38
19	0	•– 5	•– 6	•– 7	•– 9	•–10	•–12
	1	•– 8	•–10	•–11	•–13	•–14	•–16
	2	•–12	•–13	•–15	•–16	•–17	•–20
	3	3–15	•–16	•–18	•–19	•–20	•–23
	4	5–17	4–19	4–20	•–22	•–23	•–25
	5	7–20	6–22	5–23	5–25	•–26	•–28
	6	9–23	8–24	7–26	6–27	6–28	•–30
	7	11–25	10–27	9–28	8–30	8–31	7–33
	8	14–28	12–30	11–31	10–32	10–33	8–35
	9	16–30	15–32	14–33	12–34	12–35	10–37
20	0	•– 5	•– 6	•– 7	•– 8	•– 9	•–12
	1	•– 8	•– 9	•–11	•–12	•–13	•–16
	2	•–11	•–12	•–14	•–15	•–16	•–19
	3	3–14	•–15	•–17	•–18	•–19	•–22
	4	5–17	4–18	4–19	•–21	•–22	•–24
	5	7–19	6–21	5–22	5–24	•–25	•–27
	6	9–22	8–23	7–25	6–26	6–27	•–29
	7	11–24	10–26	9–27	8–29	7–29	7–31
	8	13–27	12–28	11–29	10–31	9–32	8–33
	9	15–29	14–31	13–32	12–33	11–34	10–35
	10	18–31	16–33	15–34	14–35	13–36	12–37
21	0	•– 4	•– 6	•– 7	•– 8	•– 9	•–11
	1	•– 8	•– 9	•–10	•–12	•–13	•–15
	2	•–10	•–12	•–13	•–15	•–16	•–18

All values conform to the international convention (i.e. 0,1 instead of 0.1).

Significance Limits for the Fourfold Table Test*

x_1	$N_1 - x_1$	N_1
x_2	$N_2 - x_2$	N_2
X	$N - X$	N

$N = N_1 + N_2$
$X = x_1 + x_2$
$N_1 \leq N_2$
$x_1 \leq N_1 - x_1$

For explanation see page 151

N_1	x_1	2α = 0,20	2α = 0,10	2α = 0,05	2α = 0,02	2α = 0,01	2α = 0,002
N = 49 (continued)							
	3	3–13	•–15	•–16	•–17	•–18	•–21
	4	5–16	4–17	•–19	•–20	•–21	•–23
	5	6–18	6–20	5–21	•–23	•–24	•–26
	6	8–21	7–22	7–24	6–25	6–26	•–28
	7	10–23	9–25	9–26	8–27	7–28	•–30
	8	12–26	11–27	10–28	9–30	9–30	8–32
	9	15–28	13–29	12–30	11–32	11–33	9–34
	10	17–30	15–31	14–33	13–34	13–35	11–36
22	0	•– 4	•– 5	•– 6	•– 8	•– 8	•–11
	1	•– 7	•– 8	•–10	•–11	•–12	•–14
	2	•–10	•–11	•–12	•–14	•–15	•–17
	3	3–13	•–14	•–15	•–17	•–18	•–20
	4	4–15	4–16	•–18	•–19	•–20	•–22
	5	6–17	5–19	5–20	•–22	•–23	•–25
	6	8–20	7–21	6–22	6–24	•–25	•–27
	7	10–22	9–24	8–25	7–26	7–27	•–29
	8	12–24	11–26	10–27	9–28	9–29	8–31
	9	14–27	13–28	12–29	11–30	10–31	9–33
	10	16–29	15–30	14–31	13–32	12–33	11–35
	11	18–31	17–32	16–33	15–34	14–35	12–37
23	0	•– 4	•– 5	•– 6	•– 7	•– 8	•–10
	1	•– 7	•– 8	•– 9	•–10	•–11	•–13
	2	•–10	•–11	•–12	•–13	•–14	•–16
	3	3–12	•–13	•–14	•–16	•–17	•–19
	4	4–14	4–16	•–17	•–18	•–19	•–21
	5	6–17	5–18	5–19	•–21	•–22	•–24
	6	8–19	7–20	6–22	6–23	•–24	•–26
	7	10–21	9–23	8–24	7–25	7–26	•–28
	8	11–23	10–25	10–26	9–27	8–28	•–30
	9	13–26	12–27	11–28	10–29	10–30	9–32
	10	15–28	14–29	13–30	12–31	12–32	10–33
	11	17–30	16–31	15–32	14–33	13–34	12–35
24	0	•– 4	•– 5	•– 6	•– 7	•– 8	•– 9
	1	•– 7	•– 8	•– 9	•–10	•–11	•–13
	2	•– 9	•–10	•–11	•–13	•–14	•–15
	3	•–11	•–13	•–14	•–15	•–16	•–18
	4	4–14	•–15	•–16	•–18	•–18	•–20
	5	6–16	5–17	5–18	•–20	•–21	•–23
	6	7–18	7–19	6–21	6–22	•–23	•–25
	7	9–20	8–22	8–23	7–24	7–25	•–27
	8	11–22	10–24	9–25	9–26	8–27	•–29
	9	13–24	12–26	11–27	10–28	10–29	9–30
	10	15–27	14–28	13–29	12–30	11–31	10–32
	11	17–29	15–30	15–31	14–32	13–33	12–34
	12	19–30	17–32	16–33	15–34	15–34	13–36
N = 50							
4	0	•–22	•–26	•–30	•–34	•–36	•–40
	1	1–34	•–37	•–40	•–43	•–44	•–46
	2	7–43	5–45	3–47	2–48	2–48	•–•
5	0	•–18	•–22	•–26	•–29	•–32	•–36
	1	•–29	•–33	•–35	•–38	•–40	•–43
	2	5–38	4–40	3–42	2–44	•–45	•–47
6	0	•–16	•–19	•–22	•–26	•–28	•–33
	1	•–25	•–29	•–31	•–34	•–36	•–40
	2	4–33	3–36	2–38	•–41	•–42	•–44
	3	10–40	8–42	6–44	5–45	4–46	•–•
7	0	•–14	•–17	•–20	•–23	•–25	•–30
	1	•–22	•–25	•–28	•–31	•–33	•–37
	2	4–29	3–32	2–35	•–37	•–39	•–42
	3	9–36	7–38	5–40	4–42	3–43	•–45
8	0	•–12	•–15	•–18	•–21	•–23	•–27
	1	•–20	•–23	•–25	•–28	•–30	•–34
	2	3–26	2–29	2–32	•–34	•–36	•–39
	3	7–32	6–35	5–37	3–39	3–40	•–43
	4	12–38	10–40	8–42	7–43	6–44	4–46
9	0	•–11	•–13	•–16	•–19	•–21	•–25
	1	•–18	•–21	•–23	•–26	•–28	•–31
	2	3–24	2–27	•–29	•–32	•–33	•–36
	3	7–30	5–32	4–34	3–36	3–38	•–40
	4	11–35	9–37	7–39	6–41	5–42	4–44
10	0	•–10	•–12	•–14	•–17	•–19	•–23
	1	•–16	•–19	•–21	•–24	•–26	•–29
	2	3–22	2–24	•–27	•–29	•–31	•–34
	3	6–27	5–30	4–32	3–34	•–35	•–38
	4	10–32	8–34	7–36	5–38	5–39	4–41
	5	14–36	12–38	10–40	8–42	8–42	6–44
11	0	•– 9	•–11	•–13	•–16	•–18	•–21
	1	•–15	•–17	•–19	•–22	•–24	•–27
	2	2–20	2–23	•–25	•–27	•–29	•–32
	3	5–25	4–27	3–29	3–32	•–33	•–36
	4	9–29	7–32	6–34	5–36	4–37	•–39
	5	12–34	11–36	9–37	8–39	7–40	5–42
12	0	•– 8	•–10	•–12	•–15	•–16	•–20
	1	•–14	•–16	•–18	•–20	•–22	•–25
	2	2–19	•–21	•–23	•–25	•–27	•–30
	3	5–23	4–25	3–27	•–30	•–31	•–34
	4	8–27	7–29	6–31	5–33	4–35	•–37
	5	11–31	10–33	8–35	7–37	6–38	5–40
	6	15–35	13–37	12–38	10–40	9–41	7–43
13	0	•– 8	•– 9	•–11	•–14	•–15	•–18
	1	•–13	•–15	•–17	•–19	•–21	•–24
	2	2–17	•–19	•–21	•–24	•–25	•–28
	3	4–21	4–24	3–26	•–28	•–29	•–32
	4	7–25	6–28	5–29	4–31	4–33	•–35
	5	10–29	9–31	8–33	7–35	6–36	5–38

N_1	x_1	2α = 0,20	2α = 0,10	2α = 0,05	2α = 0,02	2α = 0,01	2α = 0,002
N = 50 (continued)							
	6	14–33	12–35	11–36	9–38	8–39	7–41
14	0	•– 7	•– 9	•–10	•–13	•–14	•–17
	1	•–12	•–14	•–16	•–18	•–19	•–22
	2	2–16	•–18	•–20	•–22	•–24	•–27
	3	4–20	3–22	3–24	•–26	•–27	•–30
	4	7–24	6–26	5–28	4–30	4–31	•–33
	5	10–27	8–29	7–31	6–33	6–34	5–36
	6	13–31	11–33	10–34	9–36	8–37	6–39
	7	16–34	14–36	13–37	11–39	10–40	9–41
15	0	•– 7	•– 8	•–10	•–12	•–13	•–16
	1	•–11	•–13	•–15	•–17	•–18	•–21
	2	2–15	•–17	•–19	•–21	•–22	•–25
	3	4–19	3–21	3–23	•–25	•–26	•–29
	4	6–22	5–24	5–26	4–28	•–29	•–32
	5	9–26	8–28	7–29	6–31	5–32	•–35
	6	12–29	10–31	9–32	8–34	7–35	6–37
	7	15–32	13–34	12–35	10–37	10–38	8–40
16	0	•– 6	•– 8	•– 9	•–11	•–12	•–15
	1	•–10	•–12	•–14	•–16	•–17	•–20
	2	2–14	•–16	•–18	•–20	•–21	•–24
	3	4–18	3–20	•–21	•–23	•–24	•–27
	4	6–21	5–23	4–25	4–26	•–28	•–30
	5	8–24	7–26	6–28	6–30	5–31	•–33
	6	11–27	10–29	9–31	8–32	7–34	6–36
	7	14–30	12–32	11–34	10–35	9–36	8–38
	8	17–33	15–35	14–36	12–38	11–39	10–40
17	0	•– 6	•– 7	•– 9	•–10	•–12	•–14
	1	•–10	•–11	•–13	•–15	•–16	•–19
	2	•–13	•–15	•–17	•–18	•–20	•–22
	3	3–17	3–18	•–20	•–22	•–23	•–26
	4	6–20	5–22	4–23	•–25	•–26	•–29
	5	8–23	7–25	6–26	5–28	5–29	•–31
	6	10–26	9–28	8–29	7–31	7–32	6–34
	7	13–29	12–31	10–32	9–33	9–35	7–36
	8	16–32	14–33	13–35	12–36	11–37	9–39
18	0	•– 5	•– 7	•– 8	•–10	•–11	•–13
	1	•– 9	•–11	•–12	•–14	•–15	•–18
	2	•–13	•–14	•–16	•–17	•–19	•–21
	3	3–16	3–17	•–19	•–21	•–22	•–24
	4	5–19	4–21	4–22	•–24	•–25	•–27
	5	8–22	7–23	6–25	5–27	5–28	•–30
	6	10–25	9–26	8–28	7–29	6–30	•–33
	7	12–27	11–29	10–30	9–32	8–33	7–35
	8	15–30	13–32	12–33	11–34	10–35	9–37
	9	17–33	16–34	15–35	13–37	12–38	11–39
19	0	•– 5	•– 6	•– 8	•– 9	•–10	•–13
	1	•– 9	•–10	•–11	•–13	•–14	•–17
	2	•–12	•–13	•–15	•–17	•–18	•–20
	3	3–15	3–17	•–18	•–20	•–21	•–23
	4	5–18	4–19	4–21	•–23	•–24	•–26
	5	7–21	6–22	6–24	5–25	•–26	•–29
	6	9–23	8–25	7–26	7–28	6–29	•–31
	7	12–26	10–28	9–29	8–31	8–32	7–33
	8	14–29	13–30	12–31	10–33	10–34	9–36
	9	16–31	15–33	14–34	13–35	12–36	10–38
20	0	•– 5	•– 6	•– 7	•– 9	•–10	•–12
	1	•– 8	•–10	•–11	•–12	•–14	•–16
	2	•–11	•–13	•–14	•–16	•–17	•–19
	3	3–14	•–16	•–17	•–19	•–20	•–22
	4	5–17	4–19	4–20	•–22	•–23	•–25
	5	7–20	6–21	5–23	5–24	•–25	•–27
	6	9–22	8–24	7–25	6–27	6–28	•–30
	7	11–25	10–26	9–28	8–29	8–30	7–32
	8	13–27	12–29	11–30	10–32	9–32	8–34
	9	16–30	14–31	13–32	12–34	11–35	10–36
	10	18–32	16–34	15–35	14–36	13–37	12–38
21	0	•– 5	•– 6	•– 7	•– 8	•– 9	•–11
	1	•– 8	•– 9	•–10	•–12	•–13	•–15
	2	•–11	•–12	•–13	•–15	•–16	•–18
	3	3–13	•–15	•–16	•–18	•–19	•–21
	4	5–16	4–18	•–19	•–21	•–22	•–24
	5	7–19	6–20	5–22	5–23	•–24	•–26
	6	8–21	8–23	7–24	6–26	6–27	•–29
	7	11–24	9–25	9–26	8–28	7–29	•–31
	8	13–26	12–28	11–29	10–30	9–31	8–33
	9	15–28	14–30	13–31	11–32	11–33	10–35
	10	17–31	16–32	15–33	13–35	13–35	11–37
22	0	•– 4	•– 5	•– 6	•– 8	•– 9	•–11
	1	•– 7	•– 9	•–10	•–11	•–12	•–14
	2	•–10	•–12	•–13	•–14	•–15	•–17
	3	3–13	•–14	•–16	•–17	•–18	•–20
	4	4–15	4–17	•–18	•–20	•–21	•–23
	5	6–18	5–19	5–21	•–22	•–23	•–25
	6	8–20	7–22	7–23	6–24	6–25	•–27
	7	10–23	9–24	8–25	8–27	7–28	•–30
	8	12–25	11–26	10–28	9–29	9–30	8–32
	9	14–27	13–29	12–30	11–31	10–32	9–34
	10	16–29	15–31	14–32	13–33	12–34	11–36
	11	18–32	17–33	16–34	15–35	14–36	13–37
23	0	•– 4	•– 5	•– 6	•– 7	•– 8	•–10
	1	•– 7	•– 8	•– 9	•–11	•–12	•–14
	2	•–10	•–11	•–12	•–14	•–15	•–17
	3	3–12	•–14	•–15	•–16	•–17	•–19
	4	4–15	4–16	•–17	•–19	•–20	•–22
	5	6–17	5–18	5–20	•–21	•–22	•–24
	6	8–19	7–21	6–22	6–23	•–24	•–26
	7	10–22	9–23	8–24	7–26	7–27	•–28
	8	12–24	11–25	10–26	9–28	8–29	8–30

N_1	x_1	2α = 0,20	2α = 0,10	2α = 0,05	2α = 0,02	2α = 0,01	2α = 0,002
N = 50 (continued)							
	9	14–26	12–27	12–29	11–30	10–31	9–32
	10	16–28	14–30	13–31	12–32	12–33	11–34
	11	18–30	16–32	15–33	14–34	14–35	12–36
24	0	•– 4	•– 5	•– 6	•– 7	•– 8	•–10
	1	•– 7	•– 8	•– 9	•–10	•–11	•–13
	2	•– 9	•–10	•–12	•–13	•–14	•–16
	3	•–12	•–13	•–14	•–16	•–16	•–18
	4	4–14	4–15	•–17	•–18	•–19	•–21
	5	6–16	5–18	5–19	•–20	•–21	•–23
	6	8–19	7–20	6–21	6–22	•–23	•–25
	7	9–21	8–22	8–23	7–25	7–26	•–27
	8	11–23	10–24	9–25	9–27	8–28	•–29
	9	13–25	12–26	11–27	10–29	10–30	9–31
	10	15–27	14–28	13–29	12–31	11–31	10–33
	11	17–29	16–30	15–31	14–33	13–33	12–35
	12	19–31	18–32	17–33	16–34	15–35	13–37
25	0	•– 4	•– 5	•– 6	•– 7	•– 7	•– 9
	1	•– 6	•– 7	•– 8	•–10	•–11	•–12
	2	•– 9	•–10	•–11	•–12	•–13	•–15
	3	•–11	•–12	•–14	•–15	•–16	•–18
	4	4–13	•–15	•–16	•–17	•–18	•–20
	5	6–16	5–17	•–18	•–19	•–20	•–22
	6	7–18	7–19	6–20	•–22	•–22	•–24
	7	9–20	8–21	8–22	7–24	7–25	•–26
	8	11–22	10–23	9–24	8–26	8–27	•–28
	9	13–24	12–25	11–26	10–28	9–28	9–30
	10	14–26	13–27	12–28	12–30	11–30	10–32
	11	16–28	15–29	14–30	13–31	13–32	12–34
	12	18–30	17–31	16–32	15–33	14–34	13–35
N = 52							
	0	•–23	•–27	•–31	•–35	•–38	•–42
	1	1–35	•–39	•–42	•–44	•–46	•–48
	2	7–45	5–47	3–49	2–50	2–50	•–•
5	0	•–19	•–23	•–27	•–31	•–33	•–38
	1	1–30	•–34	•–37	•–40	•–42	•–45
	2	6–39	4–42	3–44	2–46	•–47	•–49
6	0	•–16	•–20	•–23	•–27	•–29	•–34
	1	•–26	•–30	•–33	•–36	•–38	•–41
	2	5–34	3–38	2–40	•–42	•–44	•–46
	3	10–42	8–44	6–46	5–47	4–48	3–49
7	0	•–14	•–18	•–21	•–24	•–26	•–31
	1	•–23	•–26	•–29	•–32	•–34	•–38
	2	4–31	3–34	2–36	•–39	•–40	•–43
	3	9–37	7–40	5–42	4–44	3–45	•–47
8	0	•–13	•–16	•–18	•–22	•–24	•–28
	1	•–21	•–24	•–26	•–30	•–32	•–35
	2	3–28	2–31	2–33	•–36	•–37	•–41
	3	8–34	6–36	5–39	4–41	3–42	•–45
	4	13–39	10–42	9–43	7–45	6–46	4–48
9	0	•–11	•–14	•–17	•–20	•–22	•–26
	1	•–19	•–22	•–24	•–27	•–29	•–33
	2	3–25	2–28	•–30	•–33	•–35	•–38
	3	7–31	5–33	4–36	3–38	3–39	•–42
	4	11–36	9–38	8–40	6–42	5–43	4–45
10	0	•–10	•–13	•–15	•–18	•–20	•–24
	1	•–17	•–20	•–22	•–25	•–27	•–30
	2	3–23	2–26	•–28	•–30	•–32	•–35
	3	6–28	5–31	4–33	3–35	•–37	•–40
	4	10–33	8–35	7–37	6–39	5–41	4–43
	5	14–38	12–40	10–42	9–43	8–44	6–46
11	0	•– 9	•–12	•–14	•–16	•–18	•–22
	1	•–16	•–18	•–20	•–23	•–25	•–28
	2	2–21	2–24	•–26	•–28	•–30	•–33
	3	5–26	4–28	3–31	3–33	•–34	•–37
	4	9–31	7–33	6–35	5–37	4–38	•–41
	5	13–35	11–37	9–39	8–41	7–42	6–44
12	0	•– 9	•–11	•–13	•–15	•–17	•–21
	1	•–14	•–17	•–19	•–21	•–23	•–27
	2	2–19	2–22	•–24	•–26	•–28	•–31
	3	5–24	4–26	3–28	3–31	•–32	•–35
	4	8–28	7–31	6–33	5–35	4–36	•–39
	5	12–33	10–35	9–36	7–38	7–40	5–42
	6	15–37	14–38	12–40	10–42	9–43	7–45
13	0	•– 8	•–10	•–12	•–14	•–16	•–19
	1	•–13	•–15	•–17	•–20	•–21	•–25
	2	2–18	•–20	•–22	•–25	•–26	•–29
	3	5–22	4–25	3–27	•–29	•–30	•–33
	4	8–26	6–29	5–31	4–33	4–34	•–37
	5	11–30	9–33	8–34	7–36	6–37	5–40
	6	14–34	12–36	11–38	10–40	9–41	7–43
14	0	•– 7	•– 9	•–11	•–13	•–15	•–18
	1	•–12	•–14	•–16	•–19	•–20	•–23
	2	2–17	•–19	•–21	•–23	•–25	•–28
	3	4–21	3–23	3–25	•–27	•–29	•–31
	4	7–25	6–27	5–29	4–31	4–32	•–35
	5	10–29	9–31	7–32	6–34	6–36	5–38
	6	13–32	12–34	10–36	9–37	8–39	7–41
	7	16–36	15–37	13–39	12–40	11–41	9–43
15	0	•– 7	•– 9	•–10	•–12	•–14	•–17
	1	•–12	•–13	•–15	•–17	•–19	•–22
	2	2–16	•–18	•–20	•–22	•–23	•–26
	3	4–20	3–22	3–23	•–26	•–27	•–30
	4	7–23	5–25	5–27	4–29	•–30	•–33
	5	9–27	8–29	7–31	6–32	5–34	•–36
	6	12–30	11–32	10–34	8–36	8–37	6–39

All values conform to the international convention (i.e. 0,1 instead of 0.1).

Significance Limits for the Fourfold Table Test*

x_1	N_1-x_1	N_1
x_2	N_2-x_2	N_2
X	$N-X$	N

$N=N_1+N_2$
$X=x_1+x_2$
$N_1 \leq N_2$
$x_1 \leq N_1-x_1$

For explanation see page 151

N_1	x_1	2α= 0,20	2α= 0,10	2α= 0,05	2α= 0,02	2α= 0,01	2α= 0,002
		$N=52$ (continued)					
	7	15–34	14–35	12–37	11–38	10–39	8–41
16	0	•– 6	•– 8	•–10	•–11	•–13	•–16
	1	•–11	•–13	•–14	•–16	•–18	•–21
	2	2–15	•–17	•–18	•–20	•–22	•–25
	3	4–18	3–20	•–22	•–24	•–26	•–28
	4	6–22	5–24	4–26	4–28	•–29	•–31
	5	9–25	8–27	7–29	6–31	5–32	•–34
	6	11–29	10–30	9–32	8–34	7–35	6–37
	7	14–32	13–33	12–35	10–37	9–38	8–40
	8	17–35	16–36	14–38	13–39	12–40	10–42
17	0	•– 6	•– 8	•– 9	•–11	•–12	•–15
	1	•–10	•–12	•–13	•–15	•–17	•–20
	2	•–14	•–16	•–17	•–19	•–21	•–23
	3	4–17	3–19	•–21	•–23	•–24	•–27
	4	6–21	5–23	4–24	4–26	•–27	•–30
	5	8–24	7–26	6–27	5–29	5–30	•–33
	6	11–27	10–29	8–30	7–32	7–33	6–36
	7	13–30	12–32	11–33	10–35	9–36	8–38
	8	16–33	15–35	13–36	12–38	11–39	10–40
18	0	•– 6	•– 7	•– 8	•–10	•–11	•–14
	1	•–10	•–11	•–13	•–15	•–16	•–19
	2	•–13	•–15	•–16	•–18	•–20	•–22
	3	3–16	3–18	•–20	•–22	•–23	•–26
	4	6–20	5–21	4–23	•–25	•–26	•–29
	5	8–23	7–24	6–26	5–28	5–29	•–31
	6	10–26	9–27	8–29	7–31	7–32	6–34
	7	13–28	11–30	10–32	9–33	8–34	7–36
	8	15–31	14–33	13–34	11–36	11–37	9–39
	9	18–34	16–36	15–37	14–38	13–39	11–41
19	0	•– 5	•– 7	•– 8	•–10	•–11	•–13
	1	•– 9	•–11	•–12	•–14	•–15	•–18
	2	•–12	•–14	•–16	•–17	•–19	•–21
	3	3–16	3–17	•–19	•–21	•–22	•–24
	4	5–19	4–20	4–22	•–24	•–25	•–27
	5	7–22	6–23	6–25	5–27	5–28	•–30
	6	10–24	9–26	8–28	7–29	6–30	•–33
	7	12–27	11–29	10–30	9–32	8–33	7–35
	8	14–30	13–31	12–33	11–34	10–35	9–37
	9	17–32	16–34	14–35	13–37	12–38	11–39
20	0	•– 5	•– 6	•– 8	•– 9	•–10	•–13
	1	•– 9	•–10	•–11	•–13	•–14	•–17
	2	•–12	•–13	•–15	•–16	•–18	•–20
	3	3–15	•–16	•–18	•–20	•–21	•–23
	4	5–18	4–19	4–21	•–23	•–24	•–26
	5	7–20	6–22	5–24	5–25	•–26	•–29
	6	9–23	8–25	7–26	7–28	6–29	•–31
	7	11–26	10–27	9–29	8–30	8–32	7–34
	8	14–28	12–30	11–31	10–33	10–34	8–36
	9	16–31	15–33	14–34	12–35	12–36	10–38
	10	19–33	17–35	16–36	15–37	14–38	12–40
21	0	•– 5	•– 6	•– 7	•– 9	•–10	•–12
	1	•– 8	•–10	•–11	•–12	•–13	•–16
	2	•–11	•–13	•–14	•–16	•–17	•–19
	3	3–14	•–16	•–17	•–19	•–20	•–22
	4	5–17	4–18	4–20	•–21	•–23	•–25
	5	7–20	6–21	5–23	5–24	•–25	•–27
	6	9–22	8–24	7–25	6–27	6–28	•–30
	7	11–25	10–26	9–28	8–29	7–30	7–32
	8	13–27	12–29	11–30	10–32	9–33	8–34
	9	15–30	14–31	13–32	12–34	11–35	10–36
	10	18–32	16–33	15–35	14–36	13–37	12–38
22	0	•– 5	•– 6	•– 7	•– 8	•– 9	•–11
	1	•– 8	•– 9	•–10	•–12	•–13	•–15
	2	•–11	•–12	•–13	•–15	•–16	•–18
	3	3–13	•–15	•–16	•–18	•–19	•–21
	4	5–16	4–18	•–19	•–21	•–22	•–24
	5	6–19	6–20	5–22	•–23	•–24	•–26
	6	8–21	7–23	7–24	6–26	6–27	•–29
	7	10–24	9–25	9–26	8–28	7–29	•–31
	8	13–26	11–27	10–29	10–30	9–31	8–33
	9	15–28	13–30	12–31	11–32	11–33	10–35
	10	17–31	16–32	14–33	13–35	13–35	11–37
	11	19–33	18–34	17–35	15–37	15–37	13–39
23	0	•– 4	•– 5	•– 6	•– 8	•– 9	•–11
	1	•– 7	•– 9	•–10	•–11	•–12	•–14
	2	•–10	•–12	•–13	•–14	•–15	•–17
	3	3–13	•–14	•–15	•–17	•–18	•–20
	4	4–15	4–17	•–18	•–20	•–21	•–23
	5	6–18	5–19	5–21	•–22	•–23	•–25
	6	8–20	7–22	7–23	6–24	6–26	•–28
	7	10–23	9–24	8–25	7–27	7–27	•–30
	8	12–25	11–26	10–28	9–29	9–30	8–32
	9	14–27	13–29	12–30	11–31	10–32	9–34
	10	16–29	15–31	14–32	13–33	12–34	11–36
	11	18–32	17–33	16–34	15–35	14–36	13–38
24	0	•– 4	•– 5	•– 6	•– 7	•– 8	•–10
	1	•– 7	•– 8	•– 9	•–11	•–12	•–14
	2	•–10	•–11	•–12	•–14	•–15	•–17
	3	3–12	•–14	•–15	•–16	•–17	•–19
	4	4–15	4–16	•–17	•–19	•–20	•–22
	5	6–17	5–18	5–20	•–21	•–22	•–24
	6	8–19	7–21	6–22	6–23	•–24	•–26
	7	10–22	9–23	8–24	7–26	7–27	•–29
	8	12–24	11–25	10–27	9–28	8–29	8–31
	9	13–26	12–27	12–29	11–30	10–31	9–33
	10	15–28	14–30	13–31	12–32	12–33	11–35
	11	18–30	16–32	15–33	14–34	13–35	12–36
	12	20–32	18–34	17–35	16–36	15–37	14–38

N_1	x_1	2α= 0,20	2α= 0,10	2α= 0,05	2α= 0,02	2α= 0,01	2α= 0,002
		$N=52$ (continued)					
25	0	•– 4	•– 5	•– 6	•– 7	•– 8	•–10
	1	•– 7	•– 8	•– 9	•–10	•–11	•–13
	2	•– 9	•–11	•–12	•–13	•–14	•–16
	3	•–12	•–13	•–14	•–16	•–17	•–19
	4	4–14	4–15	•–17	•–18	•–19	•–21
	5	6–16	5–18	5–19	•–20	•–21	•–23
	6	7–19	7–20	6–21	6–23	•–24	•–25
	7	9–21	8–22	8–23	7–25	7–26	•–28
	8	11–23	10–24	9–25	9–27	8–28	•–30
	9	13–25	12–26	11–28	10–29	10–30	9–31
	10	15–27	14–28	13–30	12–31	11–32	10–33
	11	17–29	16–30	15–32	14–33	13–34	12–35
	12	19–31	18–32	17–34	15–35	15–35	13–37
26	0	•– 4	•– 5	•– 6	•– 7	•– 7	•– 9
	1	•– 6	•– 7	•– 8	•–10	•–11	•–13
	2	•– 9	•–10	•–11	•–12	•–13	•–15
	3	•–11	•–12	•–14	•–15	•–16	•–18
	4	4–13	•–15	•–16	•–17	•–18	•–20
	5	6–16	5–17	•–18	•–20	•–20	•–22
	6	7–18	7–19	6–20	•–22	•–23	•–24
	7	9–20	8–21	8–22	7–24	7–25	•–26
	8	11–22	10–23	9–25	8–26	8–27	•–28
	9	13–24	12–25	11–27	10–28	9–29	9–30
	10	14–26	13–27	12–29	12–30	11–31	10–32
	11	16–28	15–29	14–30	13–32	13–32	11–34
	12	18–30	17–31	16–32	15–34	14–34	13–36
	13	20–32	19–33	18–34	17–35	16–36	15–37
		$N=54$					
4	0	•–23	•–28	•–32	•–36	•–39	•–44
	1	1–37	•–40	•–43	•–46	•–48	•–50
	2	7–47	5–49	4–50	2–52	2–52	•–•
5	0	•–20	•–24	•–28	•–32	•–34	•–39
	1	1–31	•–35	•–38	•–41	•–43	•–47
	2	6–41	4–44	3–46	2–48	•–49	•–51
6	0	•–17	•–21	•–24	•–28	•–31	•–36
	1	•–27	•–31	•–34	•–37	•–39	•–43
	2	5–36	3–39	2–41	•–44	•–46	•–48
	3	11–43	8–46	7–47	5–49	4–50	3–51
7	0	•–15	•–18	•–21	•–25	•–28	•–32
	1	•–24	•–28	•–30	•–34	•–36	•–40
	2	4–32	3–35	2–38	•–40	•–42	•–45
	3	9–39	7–41	6–44	4–46	3–47	•–49
8	0	•–13	•–16	•–19	•–23	•–25	•–30
	1	•–21	•–25	•–28	•–31	•–33	•–37
	2	3–29	2–32	2–34	•–37	•–39	•–42
	3	8–35	6–38	5–40	4–42	3–44	•–46
	4	13–41	11–43	9–45	7–47	6–48	4–50
9	0	•–12	•–15	•–17	•–20	•–23	•–27
	1	•–19	•–22	•–25	•–28	•–30	•–34
	2	3–26	2–29	•–31	•–34	•–36	•–39
	3	7–32	5–35	4–37	3–39	3–41	•–44
	4	12–37	10–40	8–42	6–44	5–45	4–47
10	0	•–11	•–13	•–16	•–19	•–21	•–25
	1	•–18	•–20	•–23	•–26	•–28	•–32
	2	3–24	2–27	•–29	•–32	•–33	•–37
	3	6–29	5–32	4–34	3–37	3–38	•–41
	4	10–34	9–37	7–39	6–41	5–42	4–45
	5	15–39	13–41	11–43	9–45	8–46	6–48
11	0	•–10	•–12	•–14	•–17	•–19	•–23
	1	•–16	•–19	•–21	•–24	•–26	•–30
	2	2–22	2–24	•–27	•–29	•–31	•–35
	3	6–27	4–30	4–32	3–34	•–36	•–39
	4	9–32	8–34	6–36	5–39	5–40	•–42
	5	13–36	11–39	10–40	8–42	7–44	6–46
12	0	•– 9	•–11	•–13	•–16	•–18	•–22
	1	•–15	•–17	•–20	•–22	•–24	•–28
	2	2–20	2–23	•–25	•–27	•–29	•–33
	3	5–25	4–27	3–30	3–32	•–34	•–37
	4	9–30	7–32	6–34	5–36	4–38	•–40
	5	12–34	10–36	9–38	8–40	7–41	5–43
	6	16–38	14–40	12–42	11–43	10–44	8–46
13	0	•– 8	•–10	•–12	•–15	•–16	•–20
	1	•–14	•–16	•–18	•–21	•–22	•–26
	2	2–19	•–21	•–23	•–26	•–27	•–31
	3	5–23	4–26	3–28	•–30	•–32	•–35
	4	8–28	7–30	6–32	5–34	4–35	•–38
	5	11–32	10–34	8–36	7–38	6–39	5–41
	6	15–36	13–38	11–39	10–41	9–42	7–44
14	0	•– 8	•–10	•–11	•–14	•–15	•–19
	1	•–13	•–15	•–17	•–19	•–21	•–24
	2	2–17	•–20	•–22	•–24	•–26	•–29
	3	4–22	4–24	3–26	•–28	•–30	•–33
	4	7–26	6–28	5–30	4–32	4–34	•–36
	5	10–30	9–32	8–34	7–36	6–37	5–39
	6	14–33	12–35	11–37	9–39	8–40	7–42
	7	17–37	15–39	14–40	12–42	11–43	9–45
15	0	•– 7	•– 9	•–11	•–13	•–14	•–18
	1	•–12	•–14	•–16	•–18	•–20	•–23
	2	2–16	•–18	•–20	•–23	•–24	•–27
	3	4–20	3–23	3–24	•–27	•–28	•–31
	4	7–24	6–26	5–28	4–30	4–32	•–34
	5	10–28	8–30	7–32	6–34	6–35	5–38
	6	13–31	11–33	10–35	9–37	8–38	6–40
	7	16–35	14–37	13–38	11–40	10–41	9–43
16	0	•– 7	•– 8	•–10	•–12	•–13	•–17

N_1	x_1	2α= 0,20	2α= 0,10	2α= 0,05	2α= 0,02	2α= 0,01	2α= 0,002
		$N=54$ (continued)					
	1	•–11	•–13	•–15	•–17	•–19	•–22
	2	2–15	•–17	•–19	•–21	•–23	•–26
	3	4–19	3–21	3–23	•–25	•–27	•–29
	4	6–23	5–25	5–27	4–29	•–30	•–33
	5	9–26	8–28	7–30	6–32	5–33	•–36
	6	12–30	10–32	9–33	8–35	7–36	6–39
	7	15–33	13–35	12–36	10–38	10–39	8–41
	8	18–36	16–38	15–39	13–41	12–42	10–44
17	0	•– 6	•– 8	•– 9	•–11	•–13	•–16
	1	•–11	•–12	•–14	•–16	•–17	•–20
	2	2–14	•–16	•–18	•–20	•–22	•–24
	3	4–18	3–20	•–22	•–24	•–25	•–28
	4	6–22	5–24	4–25	4–27	•–29	•–31
	5	9–25	7–27	6–29	6–30	5–32	•–34
	6	11–28	10–30	9–32	8–33	7–35	6–37
	7	14–31	12–33	11–35	10–36	9–37	8–40
	8	17–34	15–36	14–37	12–39	11–40	10–42
18	0	•– 6	•– 7	•– 9	•–11	•–12	•–15
	1	•–10	•–12	•–13	•–15	•–17	•–19
	2	•–14	•–15	•–17	•–19	•–20	•–23
	3	3–17	3–19	•–21	•–23	•–24	•–27
	4	6–20	5–22	4–24	4–26	•–27	•–30
	5	8–24	7–25	6–27	5–29	5–30	•–33
	6	11–27	9–29	8–30	7–32	7–33	6–35
	7	13–30	12–31	11–33	9–35	9–36	7–38
	8	16–33	14–34	13–36	12–37	11–38	9–40
	9	19–35	17–37	16–38	14–40	13–41	11–43
19	0	•– 6	•– 7	•– 8	•–10	•–11	•–14
	1	•– 9	•–11	•–13	•–14	•–16	•–18
	2	•–13	•–15	•–16	•–18	•–19	•–22
	3	3–16	3–18	•–20	•–21	•–23	•–25
	4	5–19	5–21	4–23	•–25	•–26	•–28
	5	8–22	7–24	6–26	5–28	5–29	•–31
	6	10–25	9–27	8–29	7–30	6–32	•–34
	7	12–28	11–30	10–31	9–33	8–34	7–36
	8	15–31	14–33	12–34	11–36	10–37	9–39
	9	18–34	16–35	15–37	13–38	13–39	11–41
20	0	•– 5	•– 7	•– 8	•– 9	•–11	•–13
	1	•– 9	•–10	•–12	•–14	•–15	•–17
	2	•–12	•–14	•–15	•–17	•–18	•–21
	3	3–15	3–17	•–19	•–20	•–22	•–24
	4	5–18	4–20	4–22	•–23	•–25	•–27
	5	7–21	6–23	6–25	5–26	5–28	•–30
	6	10–24	8–26	8–27	7–29	6–30	•–33
	7	12–27	11–29	10–30	9–32	8–33	7–35
	8	14–30	13–31	12–33	11–34	10–35	9–37
	9	17–32	15–34	14–35	13–37	12–38	10–39
	10	19–35	18–36	16–38	15–39	14–40	12–42
21	0	•– 5	•– 6	•– 7	•– 9	•–10	•–13
	1	•– 8	•–10	•–11	•–13	•–14	•–17
	2	•–12	•–13	•–15	•–16	•–18	•–20
	3	3–15	•–16	•–18	•–19	•–21	•–23
	4	5–18	4–19	4–21	•–22	•–24	•–26
	5	7–20	6–22	5–23	5–25	•–26	•–29
	6	9–23	8–25	7–26	6–28	6–29	•–31
	7	11–26	10–27	9–29	8–30	8–31	7–34
	8	14–28	12–30	11–31	10–33	10–34	8–36
	9	16–31	15–32	13–34	12–35	11–36	10–38
	10	18–33	17–35	16–36	14–37	13–38	12–40
22	0	•– 5	•– 6	•– 7	•– 9	•–10	•–12
	1	•– 8	•– 9	•–11	•–12	•–13	•–16
	2	•–11	•–13	•–14	•–16	•–17	•–19
	3	3–14	•–16	•–17	•–19	•–20	•–22
	4	5–17	4–18	4–20	•–21	•–23	•–25
	5	7–19	6–21	5–22	5–24	•–25	•–27
	6	9–22	8–24	7–25	6–27	6–28	•–30
	7	11–25	10–26	9–28	8–29	7–30	7–32
	8	13–27	12–29	11–30	10–32	9–33	8–35
	9	15–29	14–31	13–32	12–34	11–35	10–37
	10	17–32	16–33	15–35	14–36	13–37	11–39
	11	20–34	18–36	17–37	16–38	15–39	13–41
23	0	•– 4	•– 6	•– 7	•– 8	•– 9	•–11
	1	•– 8	•– 9	•–10	•–12	•–13	•–15
	2	•–11	•–12	•–13	•–15	•–16	•–18
	3	3–13	•–15	•–16	•–18	•–19	•–21
	4	5–16	4–18	•–19	•–20	•–22	•–24
	5	6–19	6–20	5–21	•–23	•–24	•–26
	6	8–21	7–23	7–24	6–26	6–27	•–29
	7	10–24	9–25	9–26	8–28	7–29	•–31
	8	12–26	11–27	10–29	9–30	9–31	8–33
	9	15–28	13–30	12–31	11–33	11–33	9–35
	10	17–31	15–32	14–33	13–35	12–36	11–37
	11	19–33	18–34	16–35	15–37	14–38	13–39
24	0	•– 4	•– 5	•– 6	•– 8	•– 9	•–11
	1	•– 7	•– 9	•–10	•–11	•–12	•–14
	2	•–10	•–11	•–13	•–14	•–15	•–17
	3	3–13	•–14	•–15	•–17	•–18	•–20
	4	4–15	4–17	•–18	•–20	•–21	•–23
	5	6–18	5–19	5–21	•–22	•–23	•–25
	6	8–20	7–22	7–23	6–25	•–26	•–28
	7	10–23	9–24	8–25	7–27	7–28	•–30
	8	12–25	11–26	10–28	9–29	9–30	8–32
	9	14–27	13–29	12–30	11–31	10–32	9–34
	10	16–29	15–31	14–32	13–33	12–34	11–36
	11	18–32	17–33	16–34	15–35	14–36	12–38
	12	20–34	19–35	18–36	17–37	16–38	14–40
25	0	•– 4	•– 5	•– 6	•– 7	•– 8	•–10
	1	•– 7	•– 8	•– 9	•–11	•–12	•–14

All values conform to the international convention (i.e. 0,1 instead of 0.1).

Significance Limits for the Fourfold Table Test*

x_1	$N_1 - x_1$	N_1
x_2	$N_2 - x_2$	N_2
X	$N - X$	N

$N = N_1 + N_2$
$X = x_1 + x_2$
$N_1 \leq N_2$
$x_1 \leq N_1 - x_1$

For explanation see page 151

$N = 54$ (continued)

N_1	x_1	2α = 0,20	2α = 0,10	2α = 0,05	2α = 0,02	2α = 0,01	2α = 0,002
	2	•–10	•–11	•–12	•–14	•–15	•–17
	3	3–12	•–14	•–15	•–16	•–17	•–19
	4	4–15	4–16	•–17	•–19	•–20	•–22
	5	6–17	5–18	5–20	•–21	•–22	•–24
	6	8–19	7–21	6–22	6–24	•–25	•–27
	7	10–22	9–23	8–24	7–26	7–27	•–29
	8	11–24	10–25	10–27	9–28	8–29	•–31
	9	13–26	12–28	11–29	11–30	10–31	9–33
	10	15–28	14–30	13–31	12–32	12–33	10–35
	11	17–30	16–32	15–33	14–34	13–35	12–37
	12	19–32	18–34	17–35	16–36	15–37	14–38
26	0	•– 4	•– 5	•– 6	•– 7	•– 8	•–10
	1	•– 7	•– 8	•– 9	•–10	•–11	•–13
	2	•– 9	•–11	•–12	•–13	•–14	•–16
	3	•–12	•–13	•–14	•–16	•–17	•–19
	4	4–14	4–15	•–17	•–18	•–19	•–21
	5	6–16	5–18	5–19	•–20	•–21	•–23
	6	7–19	7–20	6–21	6–23	•–24	•–26
	7	9–21	8–22	8–23	7–25	7–26	•–28
	8	11–23	10–24	9–26	9–27	8–28	•–30
	9	13–25	12–26	11–28	10–29	10–30	9–32
	10	15–27	14–29	13–30	12–31	11–32	10–34
	11	17–29	16–31	15–32	14–33	13–34	12–35
	12	19–31	17–33	16–34	15–35	15–36	13–37
	13	21–33	19–35	18–36	17–37	16–38	15–39
27	0	•– 4	•– 5	•– 6	•– 7	•– 8	•– 9
	1	•– 6	•– 8	•– 9	•–10	•–11	•–13
	2	•– 9	•–10	•–11	•–12	•–13	•–15
	3	•–11	•–12	•–14	•–15	•–16	•–18
	4	4–14	•–15	•–16	•–17	•–18	•–20
	5	6–16	5–17	•–18	•–20	•–21	•–22
	6	7–18	6–19	6–20	•–22	•–23	•–25
	7	9–20	8–21	7–23	7–24	•–25	•–27
	8	11–22	10–23	9–25	8–26	8–27	•–29
	9	12–24	12–26	11–27	10–28	9–29	9–31
	10	14–26	13–28	12–29	12–30	11–31	10–32
	11	16–28	15–30	14–31	13–32	13–33	11–34
	12	18–30	17–31	16–33	15–34	14–35	13–36
	13	20–32	19–33	18–34	17–36	16–36	15–38

$N = 56$

N_1	x_1	2α = 0,20	2α = 0,10	2α = 0,05	2α = 0,02	2α = 0,01	2α = 0,002
4	0	•–24	•–29	•–33	•–38	•–40	•–45
	1	1–38	•–42	•–45	•–48	•–49	•–52
	2	8–48	5–51	4–52	2–54	2–54	•–•
5	0	•–20	•–25	•–29	•–33	•–36	•–41
	1	1–33	•–36	•–40	•–43	•–45	•–48
	2	6–42	4–45	3–48	2–50	•–51	•–53
6	0	•–18	•–21	•–25	•–29	•–32	•–37
	1	•–28	•–32	•–35	•–39	•–41	•–45
	2	5–37	3–40	2–43	2–46	•–47	•–50
	3	11–45	9–47	7–49	5–51	4–52	3–53
7	0	•–15	•–19	•–22	•–26	•–29	•–34
	1	•–25	•–29	•–32	•–35	•–37	•–41
	2	4–33	3–36	2–39	•–42	•–44	•–47
	3	10–40	7–43	6–45	4–47	4–49	•–51
8	0	•–14	•–17	•–20	•–23	•–26	•–31
	1	•–22	•–26	•–29	•–32	•–34	•–38
	2	4–30	2–33	2–36	•–39	•–40	•–44
	3	8–36	6–39	5–42	4–44	3–45	•–48
	4	14–42	11–45	9–47	7–49	6–50	5–51
9	0	•–12	•–15	•–18	•–21	•–24	•–28
	1	•–20	•–23	•–26	•–29	•–31	•–35
	2	3–27	2–30	2–33	•–36	•–37	•–41
	3	7–33	6–36	4–38	3–41	3–42	•–45
	4	12–39	10–41	8–43	7–45	6–47	4–49
10	0	•–11	•–14	•–16	•–19	•–22	•–26
	1	•–18	•–21	•–24	•–27	•–29	•–33
	2	3–25	2–28	•–30	•–33	•–35	•–38
	3	7–30	5–33	4–36	3–38	3–40	•–43
	4	11–36	9–38	7–40	6–43	5–44	4–47
	5	15–41	13–43	11–45	9–47	8–48	6–50
11	0	•–10	•–13	•–15	•–18	•–20	•–24
	1	•–17	•–20	•–22	•–25	•–27	•–31
	2	3–23	2–25	•–28	•–31	•–32	•–36
	3	6–28	5–31	4–33	3–36	•–37	•–40
	4	10–33	8–36	7–38	5–40	5–41	4–44
	5	14–38	12–40	10–42	9–44	8–45	6–47
12	0	•– 9	•–12	•–14	•–17	•–18	•–22
	1	•–15	•–18	•–20	•–23	•–25	•–29
	2	2–21	2–24	•–26	•–29	•–30	•–34
	3	5–26	4–29	3–31	3–33	•–35	•–38
	4	9–31	7–33	6–35	5–38	4–39	•–42
	5	13–35	11–37	9–39	8–41	7–43	5–45
	6	17–39	14–42	13–43	11–45	10–46	8–48
13	0	•– 9	•–11	•–13	•–15	•–17	•–21
	1	•–14	•–17	•–19	•–22	•–23	•–27
	2	2–19	•–22	•–24	•–27	•–28	•–32
	3	5–24	4–27	3–29	•–31	•–33	•–36
	4	8–29	7–31	6–33	5–35	4–37	•–40
	5	12–33	10–35	9–37	7–39	6–41	5–43
	6	15–37	13–39	12–41	10–43	9–44	7–46
14	0	•– 8	•–10	•–12	•–14	•–16	•–20
	1	•–13	•–16	•–18	•–20	•–22	•–25
	2	2–18	•–20	•–23	•–25	•–27	•–30
	3	5–23	4–25	3–27	•–29	•–31	•–34
	4	8–27	6–29	5–31	4–33	4–35	•–38

$N = 56$ (continued)

N_1	x_1	2α = 0,20	2α = 0,10	2α = 0,05	2α = 0,02	2α = 0,01	2α = 0,002
	5	11–31	9–33	8–35	7–37	6–38	5–41
	6	14–35	12–37	11–39	9–40	9–42	7–44
	7	18–38	16–40	14–42	12–44	11–45	9–47
15	0	•– 7	•– 9	•–11	•–13	•–15	•–18
	1	•–12	•–15	•–17	•–19	•–21	•–24
	2	2–17	•–19	•–21	•–24	•–25	•–28
	3	4–21	3–23	3–25	•–28	•–29	•–32
	4	7–25	6–27	5–29	4–32	4–33	•–36
	5	10–29	9–31	7–33	6–35	6–36	5–39
	6	13–33	11–35	10–37	9–38	8–40	7–42
	7	16–36	15–38	13–40	12–42	11–43	9–45
16	0	•– 7	•– 9	•–10	•–13	•–14	•–17
	1	•–12	•–14	•–16	•–18	•–19	•–23
	2	2–16	•–18	•–20	•–22	•–24	•–27
	3	4–20	3–22	3–24	•–26	•–28	•–31
	4	7–24	6–26	5–28	4–30	4–31	•–34
	5	9–27	8–29	7–31	6–33	5–35	•–37
	6	12–31	11–33	10–35	8–37	8–38	6–40
	7	15–34	14–36	12–38	11–40	10–41	8–43
	8	19–37	17–39	15–41	14–42	12–44	11–45
17	0	•– 7	•– 8	•–10	•–12	•–13	•–16
	1	•–11	•–13	•–15	•–17	•–18	•–21
	2	2–15	•–17	•–19	•–21	•–22	•–25
	3	4–19	3–21	3–23	•–25	•–26	•–29
	4	6–22	5–24	4–26	4–28	•–30	•–33
	5	9–26	8–28	7–30	6–32	5–33	•–36
	6	12–29	10–31	9–33	8–35	7–36	6–38
	7	14–32	13–34	12–36	10–38	9–39	8–41
	8	17–36	16–37	14–39	13–41	12–42	10–44
18	0	•– 6	•– 8	•– 9	•–11	•–12	•–15
	1	•–10	•–12	•–14	•–16	•–17	•–20
	2	2–14	•–16	•–18	•–20	•–21	•–24
	3	4–18	3–20	•–21	•–24	•–25	•–28
	4	6–21	5–23	4–25	4–27	•–28	•–31
	5	8–24	7–26	6–28	5–30	5–31	•–34
	6	11–28	10–30	9–31	7–33	7–34	6–37
	7	14–31	12–33	11–34	10–36	9–37	8–39
	8	16–34	15–36	13–37	12–39	11–40	10–42
	9	19–37	18–38	16–40	15–41	14–42	12–44
19	0	•– 6	•– 7	•– 9	•–10	•–12	•–15
	1	•–10	•–12	•–13	•–15	•–16	•–19
	2	•–13	•–15	•–17	•–19	•–20	•–23
	3	3–17	3–19	•–20	•–22	•–24	•–26
	4	6–20	5–22	4–24	•–26	•–27	•–30
	5	8–23	7–25	6–27	5–29	5–30	•–33
	6	10–26	9–28	8–30	7–32	7–33	6–35
	7	13–29	12–31	10–33	9–34	9–36	7–38
	8	16–32	14–34	13–36	11–37	11–38	9–40
	9	18–35	17–37	15–38	14–40	13–41	11–43
20	0	•– 5	•– 7	•– 8	•–10	•–11	•–14
	1	•– 9	•–11	•–12	•–14	•–16	•–18
	2	•–13	•–14	•–16	•–18	•–19	•–22
	3	3–16	3–18	•–19	•–21	•–23	•–25
	4	5–19	5–21	4–23	•–24	•–26	•–28
	5	8–22	7–24	6–26	5–27	5–29	•–31
	6	10–25	9–27	8–28	7–30	6–31	•–34
	7	12–28	11–30	10–31	9–33	8–34	7–36
	8	15–31	13–32	12–34	11–36	10–37	9–39
	9	17–33	16–35	14–37	13–38	12–39	11–41
	10	20–36	18–38	17–39	15–41	15–41	13–43
21	0	•– 5	•– 6	•– 8	•– 9	•–11	•–13
	1	•– 9	•–10	•–12	•–14	•–15	•–17
	2	•–12	•–14	•–15	•–17	•–18	•–21
	3	3–15	3–17	•–18	•–20	•–22	•–24
	4	5–18	4–20	4–22	•–23	•–25	•–27
	5	7–21	6–23	6–24	5–26	•–27	•–30
	6	9–24	8–26	7–27	7–29	6–30	•–32
	7	12–27	10–28	9–30	8–32	8–33	7–35
	8	14–29	13–31	12–33	10–34	10–35	9–37
	9	16–32	15–34	14–35	13–37	12–38	10–40
	10	19–35	17–36	16–38	15–39	14–40	12–42
22	0	•– 5	•– 6	•– 7	•– 9	•–10	•–12
	1	•– 8	•–10	•–11	•–13	•–14	•–17
	2	•–12	•–13	•–15	•–16	•–17	•–20
	3	3–15	•–16	•–18	•–19	•–21	•–23
	4	5–17	4–19	4–21	•–22	•–24	•–26
	5	7–20	6–22	5–23	5–25	•–26	•–29
	6	9–23	8–25	7–26	6–28	6–29	•–31
	7	11–26	10–27	9–29	8–30	8–31	7–34
	8	13–28	12–30	11–31	10–33	9–34	8–36
	9	16–31	14–32	13–34	12–35	11–36	10–38
	10	18–33	17–35	15–36	14–37	13–38	12–40
	11	20–36	19–37	18–38	16–40	15–41	14–42
23	0	•– 5	•– 6	•– 7	•– 8	•–10	•–12
	1	•– 8	•– 9	•–11	•–12	•–13	•–16
	2	•–11	•–13	•–14	•–16	•–17	•–19
	3	3–14	•–15	•–17	•–19	•–20	•–22
	4	5–17	4–18	4–20	•–21	•–23	•–25
	5	7–19	6–21	5–22	5–24	•–25	•–28
	6	9–22	8–24	7–25	6–27	6–28	•–30
	7	11–24	10–26	9–27	8–29	7–30	•–32
	8	13–27	12–29	11–30	10–32	9–33	8–35
	9	15–29	14–31	13–32	12–34	11–35	10–37
	10	17–32	16–33	15–35	14–36	13–37	11–39
	11	20–34	18–36	17–37	16–38	15–39	13–41
24	0	•– 4	•– 6	•– 7	•– 8	•– 9	•–11
	1	•– 8	•– 9	•–10	•–12	•–13	•–15
	2	•–11	•–12	•–13	•–15	•–16	•–18

$N = 56$ (continued)

N_1	x_1	2α = 0,20	2α = 0,10	2α = 0,05	2α = 0,02	2α = 0,01	2α = 0,002
	3	3–13	•–15	•–16	•–18	•–19	•–21
	4	4–16	4–17	•–19	•–20	•–22	•–24
	5	6–18	6–20	5–21	•–23	•–24	•–26
	6	8–21	7–23	7–24	6–26	6–27	•–29
	7	10–23	9–25	8–26	8–28	7–29	•–31
	8	12–26	11–27	10–29	9–30	9–31	8–33
	9	14–28	13–30	12–31	11–33	11–34	9–35
	10	17–31	15–32	14–33	13–35	12–36	11–38
	11	19–33	17–34	16–36	15–37	14–38	13–40
	12	21–35	20–36	18–38	17–39	16–40	15–41
25	0	•– 4	•– 5	•– 6	•– 8	•– 9	•–11
	1	•– 7	•– 9	•–10	•–11	•–12	•–14
	2	•–10	•–11	•–13	•–14	•–15	•–17
	3	3–13	•–14	•–15	•–17	•–18	•–20
	4	4–15	4–17	•–18	•–20	•–21	•–23
	5	6–18	5–19	5–21	•–22	•–23	•–25
	6	8–20	7–22	6–23	6–25	•–26	•–28
	7	10–23	9–24	8–25	7–27	7–28	•–30
	8	12–25	11–26	10–28	9–29	9–30	8–32
	9	14–27	13–29	12–30	11–31	10–32	9–34
	10	16–29	15–31	14–32	13–34	12–34	11–36
	11	18–32	17–33	16–34	14–36	14–36	12–38
	12	20–34	19–35	18–36	16–38	16–38	14–40
26	0	•– 4	•– 5	•– 6	•– 7	•– 8	•–10
	1	•– 7	•– 8	•– 9	•–11	•–12	•–14
	2	•–10	•–11	•–12	•–14	•–15	•–17
	3	3–12	•–14	•–15	•–16	•–17	•–19
	4	4–15	4–16	•–17	•–19	•–20	•–22
	5	6–17	5–18	5–20	•–21	•–22	•–24
	6	8–19	7–21	6–22	6–24	•–25	•–27
	7	10–22	9–23	8–24	7–26	7–27	•–29
	8	11–24	10–25	10–27	9–28	8–29	•–31
	9	13–26	12–28	11–29	10–30	10–31	9–33
	10	15–28	14–30	13–31	12–32	12–33	10–35
	11	17–30	16–32	15–33	14–34	13–35	12–37
	12	19–33	18–34	17–35	16–36	15–37	14–39
	13	21–35	20–36	19–37	18–38	17–39	15–41
27	0	•– 4	•– 5	•– 6	•– 7	•– 8	•–10
	1	•– 7	•– 8	•– 9	•–10	•–11	•–13
	2	•– 9	•–11	•–12	•–13	•–14	•–16
	3	•–12	•–13	•–14	•–16	•–17	•–19
	4	4–14	4–15	•–17	•–18	•–19	•–21
	5	6–16	5–18	5–19	•–20	•–21	•–24
	6	7–19	7–20	6–21	6–23	•–24	•–26
	7	9–21	8–22	8–23	7–25	7–26	•–28
	8	11–23	10–24	9–26	9–27	8–28	•–30
	9	13–25	12–27	11–28	10–29	10–30	9–32
	10	15–27	14–29	13–30	12–31	11–32	10–34
	11	17–29	16–31	15–32	14–33	13–34	12–36
	12	19–31	17–33	16–34	15–35	15–36	13–38
	13	21–33	19–35	18–36	17–37	16–38	15–39
28	0	•– 4	•– 5	•– 6	•– 7	•– 8	•– 9
	1	•– 6	•– 8	•– 9	•–10	•–11	•–13
	2	•– 9	•–10	•–11	•–13	•–13	•–15
	3	•–11	•–13	•–14	•–15	•–16	•–18
	4	4–14	•–15	•–16	•–17	•–18	•–20
	5	6–16	5–17	•–18	•–20	•–21	•–23
	6	7–18	6–19	6–20	•–22	•–23	•–25
	7	9–20	8–21	7–23	7–24	•–25	•–27
	8	11–22	10–24	9–25	8–26	8–27	•–29
	9	12–24	11–26	11–27	10–28	9–29	9–31
	10	14–26	13–28	12–29	11–30	11–31	10–33
	11	16–28	15–30	14–31	13–32	13–33	11–35
	12	18–30	17–32	16–33	15–34	14–35	13–36
	13	20–32	19–34	18–35	17–36	16–37	15–38
	14	22–34	21–35	20–36	18–38	18–38	16–40

$N = 58$

N_1	x_1	2α = 0,20	2α = 0,10	2α = 0,05	2α = 0,02	2α = 0,01	2α = 0,002
4	0	•–25	•–30	•–35	•–39	•–42	•–47
	1	1–39	•–43	•–47	•–49	•–51	•–54
	2	8–50	6–52	4–54	2–56	2–56	•–•
5	0	•–21	•–26	•–30	•–34	•–37	•–42
	1	1–34	•–38	•–41	•–45	•–47	•–50
	2	6–44	4–47	3–49	2–52	•–53	•–55
6	0	•–18	•–22	•–26	•–30	•–33	•–38
	1	•–29	•–33	•–37	•–40	•–42	•–46
	2	5–38	4–42	2–45	2–47	•–49	•–52
	3	12–46	9–49	7–51	5–53	4–54	3–55
7	0	•–16	•–20	•–23	•–27	•–30	•–35
	1	•–26	•–30	•–33	•–36	•–39	•–43
	2	4–34	3–38	2–40	•–43	•–45	•–48
	3	10–42	8–45	6–47	4–49	4–50	•–53
8	0	•–14	•–17	•–21	•–24	•–27	•–32
	1	•–23	•–27	•–30	•–33	•–35	•–40
	2	4–31	3–34	2–37	•–40	•–42	•–45
	3	9–38	7–41	5–43	4–46	3–47	•–50
	4	14–44	12–46	10–48	8–50	7–51	5–53
9	0	•–13	•–16	•–19	•–22	•–24	•–29
	1	•–21	•–24	•–27	•–30	•–32	•–37
	2	3–28	2–31	2–34	•–37	•–39	•–42
	3	8–34	6–37	5–40	4–42	3–44	•–47
	4	12–40	10–43	8–45	7–47	6–48	4–51
10	0	•–11	•–14	•–17	•–20	•–22	•–27
	1	•–19	•–22	•–25	•–28	•–30	•–34
	2	3–26	2–29	•–31	•–34	•–36	•–40
	3	7–31	5–34	4–37	3–39	3–41	•–44
	4	11–37	9–40	8–42	6–44	5–46	4–48

All values conform to the international convention (i.e. 0,1 instead of 0.1).

Significance Limits for the Fourfold Table Test*

x_1	N_1-x_1	N_1
x_2	N_2-x_2	N_2
X	$N-X$	N

$N = N_1+N_2$, $X = x_1+x_2$, $N_1 \le N_2$, $x_1 \le N_1-x_1$

For explanation see next page

N_1	x_1	2α = 0,20	2α = 0,10	2α = 0,05	2α = 0,02	2α = 0,01	2α = 0,002
		$N=58$ (continued)					
	5	16–42	13–45	12–46	10–48	9–49	7–51
11	0	•–10	•–13	•–16	•–19	•–21	•–25
	1	•–17	•–20	•–23	•–26	•–28	•–32
	2	3–23	2–26	•–29	•–32	•–34	•–37
	3	6–29	5–32	4–34	3–37	•–39	•–42
	4	10–34	8–37	7–39	6–41	5–43	4–46
	5	14–39	12–42	10–44	9–46	8–47	6–49
12	0	•–10	•–12	•–14	•–17	•–19	•–23
	1	•–16	•–19	•–21	•–24	•–26	•–30
	2	2–22	2–24	•–27	•–30	•–31	•–35
	3	6–27	4–30	3–32	3–35	•–36	•–40
	4	9–32	8–34	6–37	5–39	4–41	•–43
	5	13–36	11–39	10–41	8–43	7–44	6–47
	6	17–41	15–43	13–45	11–47	10–48	8–50
13	0	•– 9	•–11	•–13	•–16	•–18	•–22
	1	•–15	•–17	•–20	•–22	•–24	•–28
	2	2–20	2–23	•–25	•–28	•–29	•–33
	3	5–25	4–28	3–30	3–32	•–34	•–37
	4	8–30	7–32	6–34	5–37	4–38	•–41
	5	12–34	10–36	9–38	7–41	7–42	5–45
	6	16–38	14–40	12–42	10–44	9–45	8–48
14	0	•– 8	•–10	•–12	•–15	•–17	•–20
	1	•–14	•–16	•–18	•–21	•–23	•–26
	2	2–19	•–21	•–23	•–26	•–28	•–31
	3	5–23	4–26	3–28	•–31	•–32	•–35
	4	8–28	6–30	5–32	4–35	4–36	•–39
	5	11–32	9–34	8–36	7–38	6–40	5–43
	6	15–36	13–38	11–40	10–42	9–43	7–46
	7	18–40	16–42	15–43	13–45	12–46	10–48
15	0	•– 8	•–10	•–12	•–14	•–16	•–19
	1	•–13	•–15	•–17	•–20	•–21	•–25
	2	2–18	•–20	•–22	•–24	•–26	•–30
	3	4–22	4–24	3–26	•–29	•–30	•–34
	4	7–26	6–28	5–30	4–33	4–34	•–37
	5	10–30	9–32	8–34	7–36	6–38	5–41
	6	14–34	12–36	10–38	9–40	8–41	7–44
	7	17–37	15–40	14–41	12–43	11–44	9–46
16	0	•– 7	•– 9	•–11	•–13	•–15	•–18
	1	•–12	•–14	•–16	•–18	•–20	•–23
	2	2–17	•–19	•–21	•–23	•–25	•–28
	3	4–21	3–23	3–25	•–27	•–29	•–32
	4	7–25	6–27	5–29	4–31	4–33	•–35
	5	10–28	8–31	7–32	6–35	6–36	5–39
	6	13–32	11–34	10–36	9–38	8–39	6–42
	7	16–35	14–38	13–39	11–41	10–42	9–45
	8	19–39	17–41	16–42	14–44	13–45	11–47
17	0	•– 7	•– 8	•–10	•–12	•–14	•–17
	1	•–11	•–13	•–15	•–17	•–19	•–22
	2	2–16	•–18	•–20	•–22	•–23	•–27
	3	4–19	3–22	3–24	•–26	•–27	•–30
	4	6–23	5–25	5–27	4–29	•–31	•–34
	5	9–27	8–29	7–31	6–33	5–34	•–37
	6	12–30	10–32	9–34	8–36	7–37	6–40
	7	15–34	13–36	12–37	11–39	10–40	8–43
	8	18–37	16–39	15–40	13–42	12–43	10–45
18	0	•– 6	•– 8	•–10	•–12	•–13	•–16
	1	•–11	•–13	•–14	•–16	•–18	•–21
	2	2–15	•–17	•–19	•–21	•–22	•–25
	3	4–18	3–20	•–22	•–24	•–26	•–29
	4	6–22	5–24	4–26	4–28	•–29	•–32
	5	9–25	7–27	7–29	6–31	5–33	•–35
	6	11–29	10–31	9–32	8–34	7–36	6–38
	7	14–32	13–34	11–36	10–37	9–39	8–41
	8	17–35	15–37	14–39	12–40	11–41	10–44
	9	20–38	18–40	17–41	15–43	14–44	12–46
19	0	•– 6	•– 8	•– 9	•–11	•–12	•–15
	1	•–10	•–12	•–14	•–16	•–17	•–20
	2	•–14	•–16	•–18	•–20	•–21	•–24
	3	4–17	3–19	•–21	•–23	•–25	•–28
	4	6–21	5–23	4–25	4–27	•–28	•–31
	5	8–24	7–26	6–28	5–30	5–31	•–34
	6	11–27	9–29	8–31	7–33	7–34	6–37
	7	13–30	12–32	11–34	10–36	9–37	7–39
	8	16–33	14–35	13–37	12–39	11–40	9–42
	9	19–36	17–38	16–40	14–41	13–42	11–44
20	0	•– 6	•– 7	•– 9	•–10	•–12	•–14
	1	•–10	•–11	•–13	•–15	•–16	•–19
	2	•–13	•–15	•–17	•–19	•–20	•–23
	3	3–17	3–18	•–20	•–22	•–24	•–26
	4	6–20	5–22	4–23	•–25	•–27	•–29
	5	8–23	7–25	6–27	5–29	5–30	•–32
	6	10–26	9–28	8–30	7–31	6–33	6–35
	7	13–29	11–31	10–32	9–34	8–35	7–38
	8	15–32	14–34	13–35	11–37	10–38	9–40
	9	18–35	16–36	15–38	14–40	13–41	11–43
	10	21–37	19–39	17–41	16–42	15–43	13–45
21	0	•– 5	•– 7	•– 8	•–10	•–11	•–14
	1	•– 9	•–11	•–12	•–14	•–15	•–18
	2	•–13	•–14	•–16	•–18	•–19	•–22
	3	3–16	3–18	•–19	•–21	•–22	•–25
	4	5–19	4–21	4–22	•–24	•–26	•–28
	5	7–22	6–24	6–25	5–27	5–29	•–31
	6	10–25	9–27	8–28	7–30	6–31	•–34
	7	12–28	11–30	10–31	9–33	8–34	7–36
	8	15–30	13–32	12–34	11–35	10–37	9–39
	9	17–33	15–35	14–36	13–38	12–39	11–41
	10	20–36	18–38	17–39	15–40	14–41	13–43

N_1	x_1	2α = 0,20	2α = 0,10	2α = 0,05	2α = 0,02	2α = 0,01	2α = 0,002
		$N=58$ (continued)					
22	0	•– 5	•– 6	•– 8	•– 9	•–10	•–13
	1	•– 9	•–10	•–12	•–13	•–15	•–17
	2	•–12	•–14	•–15	•–17	•–18	•–21
	3	3–15	3–17	•–18	•–20	•–21	•–24
	4	5–18	4–20	4–21	•–23	•–24	•–27
	5	7–21	6–23	5–24	5–26	•–27	•–30
	6	9–24	8–26	7–27	7–29	6–30	•–32
	7	12–26	10–28	9–30	8–32	8–33	7–35
	8	14–29	13–31	11–32	10–34	10–35	8–37
	9	16–32	15–33	14–35	12–37	12–38	10–40
	10	19–34	17–36	16–37	15–39	14–40	12–42
	11	21–37	20–38	18–40	17–41	16–42	14–44
23	0	•– 5	•– 6	•– 7	•– 9	•–10	•–12
	1	•– 8	•–10	•–11	•–13	•–14	•–16
	2	•–11	•–13	•–14	•–16	•–17	•–20
	3	3–14	•–16	•–18	•–19	•–21	•–23
	4	5–17	4–19	4–20	•–22	•–23	•–26
	5	7–20	6–22	5–23	5–25	•–26	•–29
	6	9–23	8–24	7–26	6–28	6–29	•–31
	7	11–25	10–27	9–29	8–30	8–31	7–34
	8	13–28	12–30	11–31	10–33	9–34	8–36
	9	16–30	14–32	13–34	12–35	11–36	10–38
	10	18–33	16–35	15–36	14–37	13–38	12–40
	11	20–35	19–37	17–38	16–40	15–41	14–42
24	0	•– 5	•– 6	•– 7	•– 8	•– 9	•–12
	1	•– 8	•– 9	•–11	•–12	•–13	•–16
	2	•–11	•–12	•–14	•–15	•–17	•–19
	3	3–14	•–15	•–17	•–18	•–20	•–22
	4	5–17	4–18	•–20	•–21	•–22	•–25
	5	7–19	6–21	5–22	5–24	•–25	•–28
	6	9–22	8–23	7–25	6–27	6–28	•–30
	7	11–24	10–26	9–27	8–29	7–30	•–32
	8	13–27	12–28	11–30	10–32	9–33	8–35
	9	15–29	14–31	13–32	11–34	11–35	10–37
	10	17–32	16–33	15–35	13–36	13–37	11–39
	11	19–34	18–36	17–37	15–38	15–39	13–41
	12	22–36	20–38	19–39	18–40	17–41	15–43
25	0	•– 4	•– 6	•– 7	•– 8	•– 9	•–11
	1	•– 8	•– 9	•–10	•–12	•–13	•–15
	2	•–11	•–12	•–13	•–15	•–16	•–18
	3	3–13	•–15	•–16	•–18	•–19	•–21
	4	4–16	4–17	•–19	•–20	•–22	•–24
	5	6–18	6–20	5–21	•–23	•–24	•–26
	6	8–21	7–23	7–24	6–26	6–27	•–29
	7	10–23	9–25	8–26	8–28	7–29	•–31
	8	12–26	11–27	10–29	9–30	9–31	8–33
	9	14–28	13–30	12–31	11–33	10–34	9–36
	10	16–30	15–32	14–33	13–35	12–36	11–38
	11	19–33	17–34	16–36	15–37	14–38	13–40
	12	21–35	19–36	18–38	17–39	16–40	14–42
26	0	•– 4	•– 5	•– 6	•– 8	•– 9	•–11
	1	•– 7	•– 9	•–10	•–11	•–12	•–14
	2	•–10	•–11	•–13	•–14	•–15	•–18
	3	3–13	•–14	•–15	•–17	•–18	•–20
	4	4–15	4–17	•–18	•–20	•–21	•–23
	5	6–18	5–19	5–21	•–22	•–23	•–25
	6	8–20	7–22	6–23	6–25	•–26	•–28
	7	10–22	9–24	8–25	7–27	7–28	•–30
	8	12–25	11–26	10–28	9–29	9–30	8–32
	9	14–27	13–29	12–30	11–31	10–32	9–34
	10	16–29	15–31	14–32	13–34	12–35	11–36
	11	18–32	17–33	16–34	14–36	14–37	12–38
	12	20–34	19–35	18–36	16–38	15–39	14–40
	13	22–36	21–37	20–38	18–40	17–41	16–42
27	0	•– 4	•– 5	•– 6	•– 7	•– 8	•–10
	1	•– 7	•– 8	•– 9	•–11	•–12	•–14
	2	•–10	•–11	•–12	•–14	•–15	•–17
	3	3–12	•–14	•–15	•–16	•–17	•–20
	4	4–15	4–16	•–17	•–19	•–20	•–22
	5	6–17	5–18	5–20	•–21	•–22	•–25
	6	8–19	7–21	6–22	6–24	•–25	•–27
	7	10–22	9–23	8–24	7–26	7–27	•–29
	8	11–24	10–25	10–27	9–28	8–29	•–31
	9	13–26	12–28	11–29	10–30	10–31	9–33
	10	15–28	14–30	13–31	12–32	12–33	10–35
	11	17–30	16–32	15–33	14–35	13–35	12–37
	12	19–33	18–34	17–35	16–37	15–37	14–39
	13	21–35	20–36	19–37	18–38	17–39	15–41
28	0	•– 4	•– 5	•– 6	•– 7	•– 8	•–10
	1	•– 7	•– 8	•– 9	•–10	•–11	•–13
	2	•– 9	•–11	•–12	•–13	•–14	•–16
	3	•–12	•–13	•–14	•–16	•–17	•–19
	4	4–14	4–15	•–17	•–18	•–19	•–21
	5	6–16	5–18	5–19	•–21	•–22	•–24
	6	7–19	7–20	6–21	6–23	•–24	•–26
	7	9–21	8–22	8–24	7–25	7–26	•–28
	8	11–23	10–24	9–26	9–27	8–28	•–30
	9	13–25	12–27	11–28	10–29	10–30	9–32
	10	15–27	14–29	13–30	12–31	11–32	10–34
	11	17–29	15–31	15–32	13–33	13–34	12–36
	12	19–31	17–33	16–34	15–35	15–36	13–38
	13	21–33	19–35	18–36	17–37	16–38	15–40
	14	23–35	21–37	20–38	19–39	18–40	17–41
29	0	•– 4	•– 5	•– 6	•– 7	•– 8	•– 9
	1	•– 6	•– 8	•– 9	•–10	•–11	•–13
	2	•– 9	•–10	•–11	•–13	•–13	•–16
	3	•–11	•–13	•–14	•–15	•–16	•–18
	4	4–14	•–15	•–16	•–17	•–18	•–20
	5	6–16	5–17	•–18	•–20	•–21	•–23

N_1	x_1	2α = 0,20	2α = 0,10	2α = 0,05	2α = 0,02	2α = 0,01	2α = 0,002
		$N=58$ (continued)					
	6	7–18	6–19	6–21	•–22	•–23	•–25
	7	9–20	8–22	7–23	7–24	•–25	•–27
	8	11–22	10–24	9–25	8–26	8–27	•–29
	9	12–24	11–26	11–27	10–28	9–29	9–31
	10	14–26	13–28	12–29	11–30	11–31	10–33
	11	16–28	15–30	14–31	13–32	13–33	11–35
	12	18–30	17–32	16–33	15–34	14–35	13–37
	13	20–32	19–34	18–35	17–36	16–37	14–38
	14	22–34	20–36	19–37	18–38	18–39	16–40
		$N=60$					
4	0	•–26	•–31	•–36	•–40	•–43	•–49
	1	1–41	•–45	•–48	•–51	•–53	•–56
	2	8–52	6–54	4–56	3–57	2–58	•–•
5	0	•–22	•–27	•–31	•–35	•–38	•–44
	1	1–35	•–39	•–43	•–46	•–48	•–52
	2	7–45	4–48	3–51	2–53	•–55	•–57
6	0	•–19	•–23	•–27	•–31	•–34	•–40
	1	•–30	•–34	•–38	•–42	•–44	•–48
	2	5–40	4–43	3–46	2–49	•–51	•–53
	3	12–48	9–51	7–53	5–55	4–56	3–57
7	0	•–16	•–20	•–24	•–28	•–31	•–36
	1	•–27	•–31	•–34	•–38	•–40	•–44
	2	5–35	3–39	2–42	•–45	•–47	•–50
	3	10–43	8–46	6–48	5–51	4–52	•–54
8	0	•–15	•–18	•–21	•–25	•–28	•–33
	1	•–24	•–28	•–31	•–34	•–37	•–41
	2	4–32	3–35	2–38	•–41	•–43	•–47
	3	9–39	7–42	5–45	4–47	3–49	•–52
	4	15–45	12–48	10–50	8–52	7–53	5–55
9	0	•–13	•–16	•–19	•–23	•–25	•–30
	1	•–22	•–25	•–28	•–31	•–34	•–38
	2	3–29	2–32	2–35	•–38	•–40	•–44
	3	8–36	6–39	5–41	4–44	3–46	•–49
	4	13–42	11–44	9–47	7–49	6–50	4–53
10	0	•–12	•–15	•–18	•–21	•–23	•–28
	1	•–20	•–23	•–26	•–29	•–31	•–35
	2	3–26	2–30	•–32	•–35	•–37	•–41
	3	7–33	5–36	4–38	3–41	3–43	•–46
	4	11–38	9–41	8–43	6–46	5–47	4–50
	5	16–44	14–46	12–48	10–50	9–51	7–53
11	0	•–11	•–14	•–16	•–19	•–21	•–26
	1	•–18	•–21	•–24	•–27	•–29	•–33
	2	3–24	2–27	•–30	•–33	•–35	•–39
	3	6–30	5–33	4–35	3–38	3–40	•–43
	4	10–35	9–38	7–40	6–43	5–45	4–47
	5	15–40	13–43	11–45	9–47	8–49	6–51
12	0	•–10	•–12	•–15	•–18	•–20	•–24
	1	•–17	•–19	•–22	•–25	•–27	•–31
	2	3–22	2–25	•–28	•–31	•–33	•–36
	3	6–28	5–31	4–33	3–36	•–38	•–41
	4	9–33	8–36	7–38	5–40	5–42	•–45
	5	13–38	11–40	10–42	8–45	7–46	6–49
	6	18–42	15–45	14–46	12–48	10–50	8–52
13	0	•– 9	•–12	•–14	•–17	•–18	•–23
	1	•–15	•–18	•–20	•–23	•–25	•–29
	2	2–21	2–24	•–26	•–29	•–31	•–34
	3	5–26	4–29	3–31	3–34	•–35	•–39
	4	9–31	7–33	6–36	5–38	4–40	•–43
	5	12–35	11–38	9–40	8–42	7–44	5–46
	6	16–40	14–42	13–44	11–46	10–47	8–49
14	0	•– 9	•–11	•–13	•–15	•–17	•–21
	1	•–14	•–17	•–19	•–22	•–24	•–27
	2	2–19	•–22	•–24	•–27	•–29	•–32
	3	5–24	4–27	3–29	•–32	•–33	•–37
	4	8–29	7–31	6–33	5–36	4–38	•–41
	5	11–33	10–35	8–38	7–40	6–41	5–44
	6	15–37	13–39	12–41	10–44	9–45	7–47
	7	19–41	17–43	15–45	13–47	12–48	10–50
15	0	•– 8	•–10	•–12	•–14	•–16	•–20
	1	•–13	•–16	•–18	•–20	•–22	•–26
	2	2–18	•–21	•–23	•–25	•–27	•–31
	3	5–23	4–25	3–27	•–30	•–32	•–35
	4	8–27	6–29	5–32	4–34	4–36	•–39
	5	11–31	9–33	8–36	7–38	6–39	5–42
	6	14–35	12–37	11–39	9–41	8–43	7–45
	7	18–39	16–41	14–43	12–45	11–46	9–48
16	0	•– 7	•– 9	•–11	•–14	•–15	•–19
	1	•–13	•–15	•–17	•–19	•–21	•–24
	2	2–17	•–19	•–21	•–24	•–26	•–29
	3	4–21	3–24	3–26	•–28	•–30	•–33
	4	7–25	6–28	5–30	4–32	4–34	•–37
	5	10–29	9–32	7–34	6–36	6–37	5–40
	6	13–33	11–35	10–37	9–39	8–41	7–43
	7	16–37	15–39	13–41	11–43	10–44	9–46
	8	20–40	18–42	16–44	14–46	13–47	11–49
17	0	•– 7	•– 9	•–11	•–13	•–14	•–18
	1	•–12	•–14	•–16	•–18	•–20	•–23
	2	2–16	•–18	•–20	•–23	•–24	•–28
	3	4–20	3–22	3–24	•–27	•–28	•–31
	4	7–24	6–26	5–28	4–31	4–32	•–35
	5	9–28	8–30	7–32	6–34	5–36	•–38
	6	12–31	11–34	10–35	8–37	8–39	6–41
	7	15–35	14–37	12–39	11–41	10–42	8–44
	8	19–38	17–40	15–42	13–44	12–45	11–47

All values conform to the international convention (i.e. 0,1 instead of 0.1).

Significance Limits for the Fourfold Table Test*

x_1	N_1-x_1	N_1
x_2	N_2-x_2	N_2
X	$N-X$	N

$N=N_1+N_2$
$X=x_1+x_2$
$N_1 \leq N_2$
$x_1 \leq N_1-x_1$

For explanation see below

N_1	x_1	$2\alpha=$ 0,20	$2\alpha=$ 0,10	$2\alpha=$ 0,05	$2\alpha=$ 0,02	$2\alpha=$ 0,01	$2\alpha=$ 0,002
		$N=60$ (continued)					
18	0	•– 7	•– 8	•–10	•–12	•–13	•–17
	1	•–11	•–13	•–15	•–17	•–19	•–22
	2	2–15	•–17	•–19	•–21	•–23	•–26
	3	4–19	3–21	3–23	•–25	•–27	•–30
	4	6–23	5–25	4–27	4–29	•–31	•–33
	5	9–26	8–28	7–30	6–32	5–34	•–37
	6	12–30	10–32	9–34	8–36	7–37	6–40
	7	15–33	13–35	12–37	10–39	9–40	8–43
	8	18–36	16–38	14–40	13–42	12–43	10–45
	9	21–39	19–41	17–43	15–45	14–46	12–48
19	0	•– 6	•– 8	•– 9	•–11	•–13	•–16
	1	•–11	•–12	•–14	•–16	•–18	•–21
	2	2–14	•–16	•–18	•–20	•–22	•–25
	3	4–18	3–20	•–22	•–24	•–26	•–29
	4	6–22	5–24	4–26	4–28	•–29	•–32
	5	8–25	7–27	6–29	5–31	5–32	•–35
	6	11–28	10–30	9–32	8–34	7–35	6–38
	7	14–31	12–33	11–35	10–37	9–38	8–41
	8	17–35	15–37	14–38	12–40	11–41	10–43
	9	19–38	18–39	16–41	15–43	14–44	12–46
20	0	•– 6	•– 7	•– 9	•–11	•–12	•–15
	1	•–10	•–12	•–13	•–15	•–17	•–20
	2	•–14	•–16	•–17	•–19	•–21	•–24
	3	3–17	3–19	•–21	•–23	•–24	•–27
	4	6–21	5–23	4–24	4–26	•–28	•–31
	5	8–24	7–26	6–28	5–30	5–31	•–34
	6	11–27	9–29	8–31	7–33	7–34	6–37
	7	13–30	12–32	11–34	9–36	9–37	7–39
	8	16–33	14–35	13–37	12–38	11–40	9–42
	9	18–36	17–38	15–39	14–41	13–42	11–44
	10	21–39	19–41	18–42	16–44	15–45	13–47
21	0	•– 6	•– 7	•– 8	•–10	•–11	•–14
	1	•–10	•–11	•–13	•–15	•–16	•–19
	2	•–13	•–15	•–16	•–18	•–20	•–23
	3	3–16	3–18	•–20	•–22	•–23	•–26
	4	5–20	5–22	4–23	•–25	•–27	•–29
	5	8–23	7–25	6–26	5–28	5–30	•–32
	6	10–26	9–28	8–29	7–31	6–33	•–35
	7	12–29	11–31	10–32	9–34	8–35	7–38
	8	15–32	14–33	12–35	11–37	10–38	9–40
	9	18–34	16–36	15–38	13–39	12–41	11–43
	10	20–37	19–39	17–40	16–42	15–43	13–45
22	0	•– 5	•– 7	•– 8	•–10	•–11	•–14
	1	•– 9	•–11	•–12	•–14	•–15	•–18
	2	•–12	•–14	•–16	•–18	•–19	•–22
	3	3–16	3–17	•–19	•–21	•–22	•–25
	4	5–19	4–21	4–22	•–24	•–25	•–28
	5	7–22	6–24	6–25	5–27	5–28	•–31
	6	10–25	8–26	8–28	7–30	6–31	•–34
	7	12–27	11–29	10–31	9–33	8–34	7–36
	8	14–30	13–32	12–34	11–35	10–37	9–39
	9	17–33	15–35	14–36	13–38	12–39	10–41
	10	19–36	18–37	16–39	15–40	14–41	12–43
	11	22–38	20–40	19–41	17–43	16–44	14–46
23	0	•– 5	•– 6	•– 8	•– 9	•–10	•–13

N_1	x_1	$2\alpha=$ 0,20	$2\alpha=$ 0,10	$2\alpha=$ 0,05	$2\alpha=$ 0,02	$2\alpha=$ 0,01	$2\alpha=$ 0,002
		$N=60$ (continued)					
	1	•– 9	•–10	•–12	•–13	•–15	•–17
	2	•–12	•–14	•–15	•–17	•–18	•–21
	3	3–15	•–17	•–18	•–20	•–21	•–24
	4	5–18	4–20	4–21	•–23	•–24	•–27
	5	7–21	6–23	5–24	5–26	•–27	•–30
	6	9–24	8–25	7–27	6–29	6–30	•–32
	7	11–26	10–28	9–30	8–31	8–33	7–35
	8	14–29	12–31	11–32	10–34	10–35	8–37
	9	16–32	15–33	13–35	12–36	11–38	10–40
	10	18–34	17–36	16–37	14–39	13–40	12–42
	11	21–37	19–38	18–40	17–41	16–42	14–44
24	0	•– 5	•– 6	•– 7	•– 9	•–10	•–12
	1	•– 8	•–10	•–11	•–13	•–14	•–16
	2	•–11	•–13	•–14	•–16	•–17	•–20
	3	3–14	•–16	•–17	•–19	•–20	•–23
	4	5–17	4–19	4–20	•–22	•–23	•–26
	5	7–20	6–22	5–23	5–25	•–26	•–29
	6	9–23	8–24	7–26	6–28	6–29	•–31
	7	11–25	10–27	9–28	8–30	7–31	7–34
	8	13–28	12–30	11–31	10–33	9–34	8–36
	9	15–30	14–32	13–33	12–35	11–36	10–38
	10	18–33	16–34	15–36	14–37	13–39	12–41
	11	20–35	18–37	17–38	16–40	15–41	13–43
	12	22–38	21–39	19–41	18–42	17–43	15–45
25	0	•– 5	•– 6	•– 7	•– 8	•– 9	•–12
	1	•– 8	•– 9	•–11	•–12	•–13	•–16
	2	•–11	•–12	•–14	•–15	•–17	•–19
	3	3–14	•–15	•–17	•–18	•–20	•–22
	4	5–16	4–18	•–20	•–21	•–22	•–25
	5	7–19	6–21	5–22	5–24	•–25	•–28
	6	8–22	8–23	7–25	6–27	6–28	•–30
	7	11–24	9–26	9–27	8–29	7–30	•–32
	8	13–27	11–28	11–30	10–31	9–33	8–35
	9	15–29	14–31	12–32	11–34	11–35	10–37
	10	17–32	16–33	14–35	13–36	13–37	11–39
	11	19–34	18–36	17–37	15–38	14–39	13–41
	12	21–36	20–38	19–39	17–41	16–41	15–43
26	0	•– 4	•– 6	•– 7	•– 8	•– 9	•–11
	1	•– 8	•– 9	•–10	•–12	•–13	•–15
	2	•–10	•–12	•–13	•–15	•–16	•–18
	3	3–13	•–15	•–16	•–18	•–19	•–21
	4	4–16	4–17	•–19	•–20	•–22	•–24
	5	6–18	6–20	5–21	•–23	•–24	•–27
	6	8–21	7–22	7–24	6–26	6–27	•–29
	7	10–23	9–25	8–26	8–28	7–29	•–31
	8	12–26	11–27	10–29	9–30	9–31	8–34
	9	14–28	13–30	12–31	11–33	10–34	9–36
	10	16–30	15–32	14–33	13–35	12–36	11–38
	11	18–33	17–34	16–36	15–37	14–38	13–40
	12	21–35	19–36	18–38	17–39	16–40	14–42
	13	23–37	21–39	20–40	19–41	18–42	16–44
27	0	•– 4	•– 5	•– 6	•– 8	•– 9	•–11
	1	•– 7	•– 9	•–10	•–11	•–12	•–14
	2	•–10	•–11	•–13	•–14	•–15	•–18
	3	3–13	•–14	•–15	•–17	•–18	•–20

N_1	x_1	$2\alpha=$ 0,20	$2\alpha=$ 0,10	$2\alpha=$ 0,05	$2\alpha=$ 0,02	$2\alpha=$ 0,01	$2\alpha=$ 0,002
		$N=60$ (continued)					
	4	4–15	4–17	•–18	•–20	•–21	•–23
	5	6–18	5–19	5–21	•–22	•–23	•–26
	6	8–20	7–22	6–23	6–25	•–26	•–28
	7	10–22	9–24	8–25	7–27	7–28	•–30
	8	12–25	11–26	10–28	9–29	8–30	8–32
	9	14–27	13–29	12–30	11–32	10–33	9–35
	10	16–29	15–31	14–32	12–34	12–35	11–37
	11	18–32	16–33	15–34	14–36	14–37	12–39
	12	20–34	19–35	17–36	16–38	15–39	14–41
	13	22–36	21–37	19–39	18–40	17–41	16–42
28	0	•– 4	•– 5	•– 6	•– 7	•– 8	•–10
	1	•– 7	•– 8	•– 9	•–11	•–12	•–14
	2	•–10	•–11	•–12	•–14	•–15	•–17
	3	3–12	•–14	•–15	•–16	•–17	•–20
	4	4–15	4–16	•–17	•–19	•–20	•–22
	5	6–17	5–18	5–20	•–21	•–22	•–25
	6	8–19	7–21	6–22	6–24	•–25	•–27
	7	9–22	9–23	8–24	7–26	7–27	•–29
	8	11–24	10–25	10–27	9–28	8–29	•–31
	9	13–26	12–28	11–29	10–30	10–31	9–33
	10	15–28	14–30	13–31	12–33	11–34	10–35
	11	17–30	16–32	15–33	14–35	13–36	12–37
	12	19–33	18–34	17–35	16–37	15–38	14–39
	13	21–35	20–36	19–37	18–39	17–40	15–41
	14	23–37	22–38	21–39	19–41	19–41	17–43
29	0	•– 4	•– 5	•– 6	•– 7	•– 8	•–10
	1	•– 7	•– 8	•– 9	•–10	•–11	•–13
	2	•– 9	•–11	•–12	•–13	•–14	•–16
	3	•–12	•–13	•–14	•–16	•–17	•–19
	4	4–14	4–15	•–17	•–18	•–19	•–21
	5	6–16	5–18	5–19	•–21	•–22	•–24
	6	7–19	7–20	6–21	6–23	•–24	•–26
	7	9–21	8–22	8–24	7–25	7–26	•–28
	8	11–23	10–25	9–26	9–27	8–28	•–30
	9	13–25	12–27	11–28	10–29	10–30	9–32
	10	15–27	14–29	13–30	12–31	11–32	10–34
	11	17–29	15–31	14–32	13–34	13–34	12–36
	12	19–31	17–33	16–34	15–35	14–36	13–38
	13	20–34	19–35	18–36	17–37	16–38	15–40
	14	22–36	21–37	20–38	19–39	18–40	17–42
30	0	•– 4	•– 5	•– 6	•– 7	•– 8	•– 9
	1	•– 6	•– 8	•– 9	•–10	•–11	•–13
	2	•– 9	•–10	•–11	•–13	•–14	•–16
	3	•–11	•–13	•–14	•–15	•–16	•–18
	4	4–14	•–15	•–16	•–18	•–19	•–21
	5	6–16	5–17	•–18	•–20	•–21	•–23
	6	7–18	6–19	6–21	•–22	•–23	•–25
	7	9–20	8–22	7–23	7–24	•–25	•–27
	8	11–22	10–24	9–25	8–26	8–27	•–29
	9	12–24	11–26	11–27	10–28	9–29	9–31
	10	14–26	13–28	12–29	11–30	11–31	10–33
	11	16–28	15–30	14–31	13–32	12–33	11–35
	12	18–30	17–32	16–33	15–34	14–35	13–37
	13	20–32	19–34	18–35	16–36	16–37	14–39
	14	22–34	20–36	19–37	18–38	17–39	16–41
	15	24–36	22–38	21–39	20–40	19–41	18–42

Explanation of the tables on pages 137–151

If the data of an experiment can be arranged in a fourfold table

x_1	N_1-x_1	N_1
x_2	N_2-x_2	N_2
X	$N-X$	N

they can always be arranged such that $N_1 \leq N_2$ and $x_1 \leq N_1-x_1$. Let $N=N_1+N_2$ and $X=x_1+x_2$. To use the tables on pages 137–151 first look up N and then N_1. For a given x_1 the table then gives the limits X_l and X_r for X for a given level of significance α with $2\alpha=$ 0,20, 0,10, 0,05, 0,02, 0,01 and 0,002.

Let $p_1 = x_1/N_1$ and $p_2 = x_2/N_2$.

If $X \leq X_l$, then $\begin{cases} \text{Prob}(p_1 > p_2) \leq \alpha \\ \text{Prob}(p_1 \neq p_2) \leq 2\alpha \end{cases}$

If $X \geq X_r$, then $\begin{cases} \text{Prob}(p_1 < p_2) \leq \alpha \\ \text{Prob}(p_1 \neq p_2) \leq 2\alpha \end{cases}$

If $X_l < X < X_r$, then the null hypothesis $\boldsymbol{p}_1 = \boldsymbol{p}_2$ cannot be rejected.

All values conform to the international convention (i.e. 0,1 instead of 0.1).

For $x = 0$–199 the limits are exact, but for $x \geq 200$ they are only approximate (see page 224)

x	0	1 10 100	2 20 200	3 30 300	4 40 400	5 50 500	6 60 600	7 70 700	8 80 800	9 90 900
	λ_l λ_r	λ_l λ_r	λ_l λ_r	λ_l λ_r	λ_l λ_r	λ_l λ_r	λ_l λ_r	λ_l λ_r	λ_l λ_r	λ_l λ_r
0	0 –3,6889	0,0253–5,5716	0,2422–7,2247	0,6187–8,7673	1,0899–10,242	1,6234–11,668	2,2019–13,059	2,8144–14,423	3,4538–15,763	4,1154–17,085
10	4,7954–18,390	5,4912–19,682	6,2006–20,962	6,9220–22,230	7,6539–23,490	8,3954–24,740	9,1454–25,983	9,9031–27,219	10,668–28,448	11,439–29,671
20	12,217–30,888	12,999–32,101	13,787–33,308	14,580–34,511	15,377–35,710	16,179–36,905	16,984–38,096	17,793–39,284	18,606–40,468	19,422–41,649
30	20,241–42,827	21,063–44,002	21,888–45,174	22,716–46,344	23,546–47,512	24,379–48,677	25,214–49,939	26,051–51,000	26,891–52,158	27,733–53,314
40	28,577–54,469	29,422–55,621	30,270–56,772	31,119–57,921	31,970–59,068	32,823–60,214	33,678–61,358	34,534–62,500	35,391–63,641	36,250–64,781
50	37,111–65,919	37,973–67,056	38,836–68,191	39,701–69,325	40,566–70,458	41,434–71,590	42,302–72,721	43,171–73,850	44,042–74,978	44,914–76,106
60	45,786–77,232	46,660–78,357	47,535–79,481	48,411–80,604	49,288–81,727	50,166–82,848	51,044–83,968	51,924–85,088	52,805–86,206	53,686–87,324
70	54,568–88,441	55,452–89,557	56,336–90,672	57,220–91,787	58,106–92,900	58,992–94,013	59,879–95,125	60,767–96,237	61,656–97,348	62,545–98,458
80	63,435–99,567	64,326–100,68	65,217–101,78	66,109–102,89	67,002–104,00	67,895–105,10	68,789–106,21	69,683–107,31	70,577–108,42	71,474–109,52
90	72,371–110,63	73,268–111,73	74,165–112,83	75,063–113,93	75,962–115,03	76,861–116,13	77,760–117,23	78,660–118,33	79,561–119,43	80,462–120,53
100	81,364–121,63	82,266–122,72	83,169–123,82	84,072–124,92	84,976–126,01	85,880–127,11	86,784–128,20	87,689–129,30	88,594–130,39	89,500–131,49
110	90,407–132,58	91,313–133,67	92,220–134,77	93,128–135,86	94,036–136,95	94,944–138,04	95,853–139,13	96,762–140,22	97,672–141,31	98,582–142,40
120	99,492–143,49	100,40–144,58	101,31–145,67	102,23–146,76	103,14–147,84	104,05–148,93	104,96–150,02	105,87–151,11	106,79–152,19	107,70–153,28
130	108,61–154,36	109,53–155,45	110,44–156,54	111,36–157,62	112,27–158,70	113,19–159,79	114,10–160,87	115,02–161,96	115,94–163,04	116,85–164,12
140	117,77–165,21	118,69–166,29	119,61–167,37	120,52–168,45	121,44–169,53	122,36–170,61	123,28–171,70	124,20–172,78	125,12–173,86	126,04–174,94
150	126,96–176,02	127,88–177,10	128,80–178,18	129,72–179,26	130,64–180,33	131,56–181,41	132,48–182,49	133,40–183,57	134,32–184,65	135,25–185,74
160	136,17–186,80	137,09–187,88	138,01–188,96	138,94–190,03	139,86–191,11	140,78–192,19	141,71–193,26	142,63–194,34	143,56–195,41	144,48–196,49
170	145,41–197,56	146,33–198,64	147,26–199,71	148,18–200,79	149,11–201,86	150,03–202,94	150,96–204,01	151,88–205,08	152,81–206,16	153,74–207,23
180	154,66–208,30	155,59–209,38	156,52–210,45	157,45–211,52	158,38–212,59	159,30–213,66	160,23–214,74	161,16–215,81	162,09–216,88	163,01–217,95
190	163,94–219,02	164,87–220,09	165,80–221,16	166,73–222,23	167,66–223,30	168,59–224,37	169,52–225,44	170,45–226,51	171,38–227,58	172,31–228,65
200	173,24–229,72	182,56–240,41	191,89–251,07	201,23–261,72	210,59–272,36	219,97–282,99	229,35–293,60	238,75–304,20	248,16–314,79	257,58–325,37
300	267,01–335,94	276,45–346,50	285,90–357,05	295,35–367,60	304,82–378,13	314,29–388,66	323,77–399,18	333,26–409,69	342,75–420,20	352,25–430,69
400	361,76–441,19	371,27–451,67	380,79–462,15	390,31–472,63	399,84–483,10	409,38–493,56	418,92–504,02	428,46–514,48	438,01–524,92	447,57–535,37
500	457,13–545,81	466,69–556,25	476,26–566,68	485,83–577,10	495,41–587,53	504,99–597,95	514,57–608,36	524,16–618,77	533,75–629,18	543,35–639,59
600	552,95–649,99	562,55–660,39	572,15–670,78	581,76–681,17	591,37–691,56	600,98–701,95	610,60–712,33	620,22–722,71	629,84–733,09	639,47–743,46
700	649,10–753,83	658,73–764,20	668,36–774,57	678,00–784,93	687,64–795,29	697,28–805,65	706,92–816,01	716,57–826,36	726,21–836,71	735,86–847,06
800	745,52–857,41	755,17–867,76	764,83–878,10	774,49–888,44	784,15–898,78	793,81–909,12	803,48–919,45	813,14–929,79	822,81–940,12	832,48–950,45
900	842,15–960,77	851,83–971,10	861,50–981,42	871,18–991,74	880,86–1002,1	890,54–1012,4	900,23–1022,7	909,91–1033,0	919,60–1043,3	929,28–1053,6
1000	938,97–1064,0	948,66–1074,3	958,36–1084,6	968,05–1094,9	977,75–1105,2	987,44–1115,5	997,14–1125,8	1006,9–1136,1	1016,5–1146,4	1026,2–1156,7
1100	1035,9–1167,0	1045,7–1177,3	1055,4–1187,6	1065,1–1197,9	1074,8–1208,1	1084,5–1218,4	1094,2–1228,7	1103,9–1239,0	1113,6–1249,3	1123,3–1259,6
1200	1133,1–1269,9	1142,8–1280,1	1152,5–1290,4	1162,2–1300,7	1171,9–1311,0	1181,7–1321,3	1191,4–1331,5	1201,1–1341,8	1210,8–1352,1	1220,6–1362,4
1300	1230,3–1372,6	1240,0–1382,9	1249,7–1393,2	1259,5–1403,4	1269,2–1413,7	1278,9–1424,0	1288,7–1434,2	1298,4–1444,5	1308,1–1454,8	1317,9–1465,0
1400	1327,6–1475,3	1337,4–1485,6	1347,1–1495,8	1356,8–1506,1	1366,6–1516,3	1376,3–1526,6	1386,1–1536,9	1395,8–1547,1	1405,6–1557,4	1415,3–1567,6
1500	1425,0–1577,9	1434,8–1588,1	1444,5–1598,4	1454,3–1608,6	1464,0–1618,9	1473,8–1629,1	1483,5–1639,4	1493,3–1649,6	1503,0–1659,9	1512,8–1670,1
1600	1522,6–1680,4	1532,3–1690,6	1542,1–1700,9	1551,8–1711,1	1561,6–1721,3	1571,3–1731,6	1581,1–1741,8	1590,9–1752,1	1600,6–1762,3	1610,4–1772,5
1700	1620,1–1782,8	1629,9–1793,0	1639,7–1803,3	1649,4–1813,5	1659,2–1823,7	1669,0–1834,0	1678,7–1844,2	1688,5–1854,4	1698,3–1864,7	1708,0–1874,9
1800	1717,8–1885,1	1727,6–1895,4	1737,3–1905,6	1747,1–1915,8	1756,9–1926,0	1766,6–1936,3	1776,4–1946,5	1786,2–1956,7	1796,0–1966,9	1805,7–1977,2
1900	1815,5–1987,4	1825,3–1997,6	1835,1–2007,8	1844,8–2018,1	1854,6–2028,3	1864,4–2038,5	1874,2–2048,7	1884,0–2059,0	1893,7–2069,2	1903,5–2079,4
2000	1913,3–2089,6	1923,1–2099,8	1932,9–2110,1	1942,6–2120,3	1952,4–2130,5	1962,2–2140,7	1972,0–2150,9	1981,8–2161,1	1991,6–2171,4	2001,3–2181,6
2100	2011,1–2191,8	2020,9–2202,0	2030,7–2212,2	2040,5–2222,4	2050,3–2232,6	2060,1–2242,8	2069,9–2253,1	2079,6–2263,3	2089,4–2273,5	2099,2–2283,7
2200	2109,0–2293,9	2118,8–2304,1	2128,6–2314,3	2138,4–2324,5	2148,2–2334,7	2158,0–2344,9	2167,8–2355,1	2177,6–2365,3	2187,4–2375,6	2197,2–2385,8
2300	2207,0–2396,0	2216,8–2406,2	2226,5–2416,4	2236,3–2426,6	2246,1–2436,8	2255,9–2447,0	2265,7–2457,2	2275,5–2467,4	2285,3–2477,6	2295,1–2487,8
2400	2304,9–2498,0	2314,7–2508,2	2324,5–2518,4	2334,3–2528,6	2344,1–2538,8	2353,9–2549,0	2363,7–2559,2	2373,5–2569,4	2383,3–2579,6	2393,1–2589,8
2500	2403,0–2600,0	2412,8–2610,2	2422,6–2620,4	2432,4–2630,5	2442,2–2640,7	2452,0–2650,9	2461,8–2661,1	2471,6–2671,3	2481,4–2681,5	2491,2–2691,7
2600	2501,0–2701,9	2510,8–2712,1	2520,6–2722,3	2530,4–2732,5	2540,2–2742,7	2550,1–2752,9	2559,9–2763,0	2569,7–2773,2	2579,5–2783,4	2589,3–2793,6
2700	2599,1–2803,8	2608,9–2814,0	2618,7–2824,2	2628,5–2834,4	2638,4–2844,6	2648,2–2854,7	2658,0–2864,9	2667,8–2875,1	2677,6–2885,3	2687,4–2895,5
2800	2697,2–2905,7	2707,1–2915,9	2716,9–2926,0	2726,7–2936,2	2736,5–2946,4	2746,3–2956,6	2756,1–2966,8	2766,0–2977,0	2775,8–2987,1	2785,6–2997,3
2900	2795,4–3007,5	2805,2–3017,7	2815,0–3027,9	2824,9–3038,1	2834,7–3048,2	2844,5–3058,4	2854,3–3068,6	2864,1–3078,8	2874,0–3089,0	2883,8–3099,1
3000	2893,6–3109,3	2903,4–3119,5	2913,2–3129,7	2923,1–3139,8	2932,9–3150,0	2942,7–3160,2	2952,5–3170,4	2962,4–3180,6	2972,2–3190,7	2982,0–3200,9
3100	2991,8–3211,1	3001,6–3221,3	3011,5–3231,4	3021,3–3241,6	3031,1–3251,8	3040,9–3262,0	3050,8–3272,1	3060,6–3282,3	3070,4–3292,5	3080,3–3302,7
3200	3090,1–3312,8	3099,9–3323,0	3109,7–3333,2	3119,6–3343,4	3129,4–3353,5	3139,2–3363,7	3149,0–3373,9	3158,9–3384,0	3168,7–3394,2	3178,5–3404,4
3300	3188,4–3414,6	3198,2–3424,7	3208,0–3434,9	3217,8–3445,1	3227,7–3455,2	3237,5–3465,4	3247,3–3475,6	3257,2–3485,7	3267,0–3495,9	3276,8–3506,1
3400	3286,7–3516,2	3296,5–3526,4	3306,3–3536,6	3316,2–3546,7	3326,0–3556,9	3335,8–3567,1	3345,7–3577,2	3355,5–3587,4	3365,3–3597,6	3375,2–3607,7
3500	3385,0–3617,9	3394,8–3628,1	3404,7–3638,2	3414,5–3648,4	3424,3–3658,6	3434,2–3668,7	3444,0–3678,9	3453,8–3689,1	3463,7–3699,2	3473,5–3709,4
3600	3483,4–3719,6	3493,2–3729,7	3503,0–3739,9	3512,9–3750,0	3522,7–3760,2	3532,5–3770,4	3542,4–3780,5	3552,2–3790,7	3562,1–3800,9	3571,9–3811,0
3700	3581,7–3821,2	3591,6–3831,3	3601,4–3841,5	3611,2–3851,7	3621,1–3861,8	3630,9–3872,0	3640,8–3882,1	3650,6–3892,3	3660,4–3902,5	3670,3–3912,6
3800	3680,1–3922,8	3690,0–3932,9	3699,8–3943,1	3709,7–3953,3	3719,5–3963,4	3729,3–3973,6	3739,2–3983,7	3749,0–3993,9	3758,9–4004,0	3768,7–4014,2
3900	3778,6–4024,4	3788,4–4034,5	3798,2–4044,7	3808,1–4054,8	3817,9–4065,0	3827,8–4075,1	3837,6–4085,3	3847,5–4095,5	3857,3–4105,6	3867,1–4115,8
4000	3877,0–4125,9	3886,8–4136,1	3896,7–4146,2	3906,5–4156,4	3916,4–4166,5	3926,2–4176,7	3936,1–4186,8	3945,9–4197,0	3955,8–4207,2	3965,6–4217,3
4100	3975,5–4227,5	3985,3–4237,6	3995,1–4247,8	4005,0–4257,9	4014,8–4268,1	4024,7–4278,2	4034,5–4288,4	4044,4–4298,5	4054,2–4308,7	4064,1–4318,8
4200	4073,9–4329,0	4083,8–4339,1	4093,6–4349,3	4103,5–4359,4	4113,3–4369,6	4123,2–4379,7	4133,0–4389,9	4142,9–4400,0	4152,7–4410,2	4162,6–4420,3
4300	4172,4–4430,5	4182,3–4440,6	4192,1–4450,8	4202,0–4460,9	4211,8–4471,1	4221,7–4481,2	4231,5–4491,4	4241,4–4501,5	4251,2–4511,7	4261,1–4521,8
4400	4270,9–4532,0	4280,8–4542,1	4290,6–4552,3	4300,5–4562,4	4310,4–4572,6	4320,2–4582,7	4330,1–4592,9	4339,9–4603,0	4349,8–4613,1	4359,6–4623,3
4500	4369,5–4633,4	4379,3–4643,6	4389,2–4653,7	4399,0–4663,9	4408,9–4674,0	4418,7–4684,2	4428,6–4694,3	4438,5–4704,5	4448,3–4714,6	4458,2–4724,7
4600	4468,0–4734,9	4477,9–4745,0	4487,7–4755,2	4497,6–4765,3	4507,4–4775,5	4517,3–4785,6	4527,2–4795,8	4537,0–4805,9	4546,9–4816,0	4556,7–4826,2
4700	4566,6–4836,3	4576,4–4846,5	4586,3–4856,6	4596,2–4866,8	4606,0–4876,9	4615,9–4887,0	4625,7–4897,2	4635,6–4907,3	4645,4–4917,5	4655,3–4927,6
4800	4665,2–4937,7	4675,0–4947,9	4684,9–4958,0	4694,7–4968,2	4704,6–4978,3	4714,5–4988,5	4724,3–4998,6	4734,2–5008,7	4744,0–5018,9	4753,9–5029,0
4900	4763,8–5039,2	4773,6–5049,3	4783,5–5059,4	4793,3–5069,6	4803,2–5079,7	4813,1–5089,9	4822,9–5100,0	4832,8–5110,1	4842,6–5120,3	4852,5–5130,4
5000	4862,4–5140,5	4961,0–5241,9	5059,6–5343,3	5158,3–5444,6	5256,9–5546,0	5355,6–5647,3	5454,3–5748,6	5553,0–5849,9	5651,7–5951,2	5750,4–6052,5
6000	5849,1–6153,8	5947,9–6255,0	6046,6–6356,3	6145,4–6457,5	6244,2–6558,8	6342,9–6660,0	6441,7–6761,2	6540,5–6862,4	6639,3–6963,6	6738,1–7064,8
7000	6837,0–7165,9	6935,8–7267,1	7034,6–7368,3	7133,5–7469,4	7232,3–7570,6	7331,2–7671,7	7430,1–7772,8	7529,0–7873,9	7627,8–7975,1	7726,7–8076,2
8000	7825,6–8177,3	7924,6–8278,4	8023,5–8379,4	8122,4–8480,5	8221,3–8581,6	8320,2–8682,7	8419,2–8783,7	8518,1–8884,8	8617,1–8985,8	8716,0–9086,9
9000	8815,0–9187,9	8914,0–9288,9	9013,0–9389,9	9111,9–9491,0	9210,9–9592,0	9309,9–9693,0	9408,9–9794,0	9507,9–9895,0	9606,9–9996,0	9705,9–10097
10000	9805,0–10198	9904,0–10298	10003–10400	10102–10501	10201–10602	10300–10703	10399–10804	10498–10905	10597–11006	10696–11107
11000	10795–11208	10894–11308	10994–11409	11093–11510	11192–11611	11291–11712	11390–11813	11489–11914	11588–12015	11687–12116
12000	11786–12217	11885–12318	11984–12418	12084–12519	12183–12620	12282–12721	12381–12822	12480–12923	12579–13024	12678–13125
13000	12777–13225	12877–13326	12976–13427	13075–13528	13174–13629	13273–13730	13372–13831	13472–13931	13571–14032	13670–14133
14000	13769–14234	13868–14335	13967–14436	14067–14536	14166–14637	14265–14738	14364–14839	14463–14940	14563–15040	14662–15141
15000	14761–15242	14860–15343	14959–15444	15059–15544	15158–15645	15257–15746	15356–15847	15455–15948	15555–16048	15654–16149
16000	15753–16250	15852–16351	15951–16451	16051–16552	16150–16653	16249–16754	16348–16854	16448–16955	16547–17056	16646–17157
17000	16745–17258	16845–17358	16944–17459	17043–17560	17142–17660	17242–17761	17341–17862	17440–17963	17539–18063	17639–18164
18000	17738–18265	17837–18366	17937–18466	18036–18567	18135–18668	18234–18769	18334–18869	18433–18970	18532–19071	18631–19171
19000	18731–19272	18830–19373	18929–19474	19029–19574	19128–19675	19227–19776	19327–19876	19426–19977	19525–20078	19624–20178
20000	19724–20279	19823–20380	19922–20481	20022–20581	20121–20682	20220–20783	20320–20883	20419–20984	20518–21085	20618–21185
21000	20717–21286	20816–21387	20916–21487	21015–21588	21114–21689	21214–21789	21313–21890	21412–21991	21512–22091	21611–22192
22000	21710–22293	21810–22393	21909–22494	22008–22595	22108–22695	22207–22796	22306–22897	22406–22997	22505–23098	22604–23199
23000	22704–23299	22803–23400	22902–23500	23002–23601	23101–23702	23200–23802	23300–23903	23399–24004	23499–24104	23598–24205
24000	23697–24306	23797–24406	23896–24507	23995–24607	24095–24708	24194–24809	24294–24909	24393–25010	24492–25111	24592–25211
25000	24691–25312	24790–25412	24890–25513	24989–25614	25089–25714	25188–25815	25287–25916	25387–26016	25486–26117	25586–26217
26000	25685–26318	25784–26419	25884–26519	25983–26620	26082–26720	26182–26821	26281–26922	26381–27022	26480–27123	26579–27223
27000	26679–27324	26778–27425	26878–27525	26977–27626	27077–27726	27176–27827	27275–27928	27375–28028	27474–28129	27574–28229
28000	27673–28330	27772–28431	27872–28531	27971–28632	28071–28732	28170–28833	28269–28933	28369–29034	28468–29135	28568–29235
29000	28667–29336	28767–29436	28866–29537	28965–29637	29065–29738	29164–29839	29264–29939	29363–30040	29463–30140	29562–30241
30000	29661–30341	29761–30442	29860–30543	29960–30643	30059–30744	30159–30844	30258–30945	30358–31045	30457–31146	30556–31246
31000	30656–31347	30755–31448	30855–31548	30954–31649	31054–31749	31153–31850	31253–31950	31352–32051	31451–32151	31551–32252
32000	31650–32353	31750–32453	31849–32554	31949–32654	32048–32755	32148–32855	32247–32956	32347–33056	32446–33157	32545–33257
33000	32645–33358	32744–33459	32844–33559	32943–33660	33043–33760	33142–33861	33242–33961	33341–34062	33441–34162	33540–34263
34000	33640–34363	33739–34464	33838–34564	33938–34665	34037–34765	34137–34866	34236–34967	34336–35067	34435–35168	34535–35268

All values conform to the international convention (i.e. 0,1 instead of 0.1).

Significance Limits* for x for given λ $2\alpha = 0{,}05$

For λ = 0–100 the limits are exact, but for $\lambda > 100$ they are only approximate (see page 224)

λ	0,0	0,1 1 10	0,2 2 20	0,3 3 30	0,4 4 40	0,5 5 50	0,6 6 60	0,7 7 70	0,8 8 80	0,9 9 90
0		•– 2	•– 2	•– 3	•– 3	•– 3	•– 3	•– 4	•– 4	•– 4
1	•– 4	•– 5	•– 5	•– 5	•– 5	•– 5	•– 5	•– 6	•– 6	•– 6
2	•– 6	•– 6	•– 7	•– 7	•– 7	•– 7	•– 7	•– 7	•– 7	•– 8
3	•– 8	•– 8	•– 8	•– 8	•– 8	•– 9	•– 9	0– 9	0– 9	0– 9
4	0– 9	0– 9	0– 10	0– 10	0– 10	0– 10	0– 10	0– 10	0– 11	0– 11
5	0– 11	0– 11	0– 11	0– 11	0– 11	0– 12	1– 12	1– 12	1– 12	1– 12
6	1– 12	1– 12	1– 12	1– 13	1– 13	1– 13	1– 13	1– 13	1– 13	1– 13
7	1– 14	1– 14	1– 14	2– 14	2– 14	2– 14	2– 14	2– 15	2– 15	2– 15
8	2– 15	2– 15	2– 15	2– 15	2– 16	2– 16	2– 16	2– 16	3– 16	3– 16
9	3– 16	3– 16	3– 17	3– 17	3– 17	3– 17	3– 17	3– 17	3– 17	3– 17
10	3– 18	4– 19	5– 20	5– 22	6– 23	7– 24	8– 25	8– 27	9– 28	10– 29
20	11– 30	12– 31	12– 33	13– 34	14– 35	15– 36	16– 37	16– 39	17– 40	18– 41
30	19– 42	20– 43	20– 45	21– 46	22– 47	23– 48	24– 49	25– 50	25– 52	26– 53
40	27– 54	28– 55	29– 56	30– 57	30– 58	31– 60	32– 61	33– 62	34– 63	35– 64
50	36– 65	37– 66	37– 68	38– 69	39– 70	40– 71	41– 72	42– 73	43– 74	43– 76
60	44– 77	45– 78	46– 79	47– 80	48– 81	49– 82	50– 83	50– 84	51– 86	52– 87
70	53– 88	54– 89	55– 90	56– 91	57– 92	58– 93	58– 95	59– 96	60– 97	61– 98
80	62– 99	63– 100	64– 101	65– 102	66– 103	66– 105	67– 106	68– 107	69– 108	70– 109
90	71– 110	72– 111	73– 112	74– 113	74– 114	75– 116	76– 117	77– 118	78– 119	79– 120
100	80– 121	81– 122	82– 123	83– 124	84– 125	84– 127	85– 128	86– 129	87– 130	88– 131
110	89– 132	90– 133	91– 134	92– 135	93– 136	93– 137	94– 139	95– 140	96– 141	97– 142
120	98– 143	99– 144	100– 145	101– 146	102– 147	103– 148	103– 149	104– 151	105– 152	106– 153
130	107– 154	108– 155	109– 156	110– 157	111– 158	112– 159	113– 160	114– 161	114– 162	115– 164
140	116– 165	117– 166	118– 167	119– 168	120– 169	121– 170	122– 171	123– 172	124– 173	125– 174
150	125– 175	126– 177	127– 178	128– 179	129– 180	130– 181	131– 182	132– 183	133– 184	134– 185
160	135– 186	136– 187	137– 188	137– 189	138– 191	139– 192	140– 193	141– 194	142– 195	143– 196
170	144– 197	145– 198	146– 199	147– 200	148– 201	149– 202	149– 203	150– 205	151– 206	152– 207
180	153– 208	154– 209	155– 210	156– 211	157– 212	158– 213	159– 214	160– 215	161– 216	162– 217
190	162– 218	163– 220	164– 221	165– 222	166– 223	167– 224	168– 225	169– 226	170– 227	171– 228
200	172– 229	181– 240	190– 251	200– 261	209– 272	218– 282	228– 293	237– 304	247– 314	256– 325
300	266– 335	275– 346	284– 357	294– 367	303– 378	313– 388	322– 399	332– 409	341– 420	351– 430
400	360– 441	370– 451	379– 462	389– 472	398– 483	408– 493	417– 504	427– 514	437– 524	446– 535
500	456– 545	465– 556	475– 566	484– 577	494– 587	504– 597	513– 608	523– 618	532– 629	542– 639
600	551– 649	561– 660	571– 670	580– 681	590– 691	600– 701	609– 712	619– 722	628– 733	638– 743
700	648– 753	657– 764	667– 774	677– 784	686– 795	696– 805	705– 816	715– 826	725– 836	734– 847
800	744– 857	754– 867	763– 878	773– 888	783– 898	792– 909	802– 919	812– 929	821– 940	831– 950
900	841– 960	850– 971	860– 981	870– 991	879– 1002	889– 1012	899– 1022	908– 1033	918– 1043	928– 1053
1000	937– 1063	947– 1074	957– 1084	967– 1094	976– 1105	986– 1115	996– 1125	1005– 1136	1015– 1146	1025– 1156
1100	1034– 1166	1044– 1177	1054– 1187	1064– 1197	1073– 1208	1083– 1218	1093– 1228	1102– 1239	1112– 1249	1122– 1259
1200	1132– 1269	1141– 1280	1151– 1290	1161– 1300	1170– 1310	1180– 1321	1190– 1331	1200– 1341	1209– 1352	1219– 1362
1300	1229– 1372	1239– 1382	1248– 1393	1258– 1403	1268– 1413	1277– 1423	1287– 1434	1297– 1444	1307– 1454	1316– 1465
1400	1326– 1475	1336– 1485	1346– 1495	1355– 1506	1365– 1516	1375– 1526	1385– 1536	1394– 1547	1404– 1557	1414– 1567
1500	1424– 1577	1433– 1588	1443– 1598	1453– 1608	1463– 1618	1472– 1629	1482– 1639	1492– 1649	1502– 1659	1511– 1670
1600	1521– 1680	1531– 1690	1541– 1700	1550– 1711	1560– 1721	1570– 1731	1580– 1741	1589– 1752	1599– 1762	1609– 1772
1700	1619– 1782	1628– 1793	1638– 1803	1648– 1813	1658– 1823	1667– 1833	1677– 1844	1687– 1854	1697– 1864	1707– 1874
1800	1716– 1885	1726– 1895	1736– 1905	1746– 1915	1755– 1926	1765– 1936	1775– 1946	1785– 1956	1794– 1966	1804– 1977
1900	1814– 1987	1824– 1997	1834– 2007	1843– 2018	1853– 2028	1863– 2038	1873– 2048	1882– 2058	1892– 2069	1902– 2079
2000	1912– 2089	1922– 2099	1931– 2110	1941– 2120	1951– 2130	1961– 2140	1971– 2150	1980– 2161	1990– 2171	2000– 2181
2100	2010– 2191	2019– 2202	2029– 2212	2039– 2222	2049– 2232	2059– 2242	2068– 2253	2078– 2263	2088– 2273	2098– 2283
2200	2108– 2293	2117– 2304	2127– 2314	2137– 2324	2147– 2334	2157– 2344	2166– 2355	2176– 2365	2186– 2375	2196– 2385
2300	2205– 2395	2215– 2406	2225– 2416	2235– 2426	2245– 2436	2254– 2446	2264– 2457	2274– 2467	2284– 2477	2294– 2487
2400	2303– 2497	2313– 2508	2323– 2518	2333– 2528	2343– 2538	2352– 2548	2362– 2559	2372– 2569	2382– 2579	2392– 2589
2500	2401– 2599	2411– 2610	2421– 2620	2431– 2630	2441– 2640	2451– 2650	2460– 2661	2470– 2671	2480– 2681	2490– 2691
2600	2500– 2701	2509– 2712	2519– 2722	2529– 2732	2539– 2742	2549– 2752	2558– 2763	2568– 2773	2578– 2783	2588– 2793
2700	2598– 2803	2607– 2814	2617– 2824	2627– 2834	2637– 2844	2647– 2854	2657– 2864	2666– 2875	2676– 2885	2686– 2895
2800	2696– 2905	2706– 2915	2715– 2926	2725– 2936	2735– 2946	2745– 2956	2755– 2966	2764– 2976	2774– 2987	2784– 2997
2900	2794– 3007	2804– 3017	2814– 3027	2823– 3038	2833– 3048	2843– 3058	2853– 3068	2863– 3078	2872– 3088	2882– 3099
3000	2892– 3109	2902– 3119	2912– 3129	2922– 3139	2931– 3150	2941– 3160	2951– 3170	2961– 3180	2971– 3190	2981– 3200
3100	2990– 3211	3000– 3221	3010– 3231	3020– 3241	3030– 3251	3039– 3261	3049– 3272	3059– 3282	3069– 3292	3079– 3302
3200	3089– 3312	3098– 3323	3108– 3333	3118– 3343	3128– 3353	3138– 3363	3148– 3373	3157– 3384	3167– 3394	3177– 3404
3300	3187– 3414	3197– 3424	3207– 3434	3216– 3445	3226– 3455	3236– 3465	3246– 3475	3256– 3485	3266– 3495	3275– 3506
3400	3285– 3516	3295– 3526	3305– 3536	3315– 3546	3325– 3556	3334– 3567	3344– 3577	3354– 3587	3364– 3597	3374– 3607
3500	3384– 3617	3393– 3628	3403– 3638	3413– 3648	3423– 3658	3433– 3668	3443– 3678	3452– 3689	3462– 3699	3472– 3709
3600	3482– 3719	3492– 3729	3502– 3739	3511– 3750	3521– 3760	3531– 3770	3541– 3780	3551– 3790	3561– 3800	3570– 3811
3700	3580– 3821	3590– 3831	3600– 3841	3610– 3851	3620– 3861	3629– 3871	3639– 3882	3649– 3892	3659– 3902	3669– 3912
3800	3679– 3922	3688– 3932	3698– 3943	3708– 3953	3718– 3963	3728– 3973	3738– 3983	3748– 3993	3757– 4004	3767– 4014
3900	3777– 4024	3787– 4034	3797– 4044	3807– 4054	3816– 4064	3826– 4075	3836– 4085	3846– 4095	3856– 4105	3866– 4115
4000	3876– 4125	3885– 4136	3895– 4146	3905– 4156	3915– 4166	3925– 4176	3935– 4186	3944– 4197	3954– 4207	3964– 4217
4100	3974– 4227	3984– 4237	3994– 4247	4004– 4257	4013– 4268	4023– 4278	4033– 4288	4043– 4298	4053– 4308	4063– 4318
4200	4072– 4328	4082– 4339	4092– 4349	4102– 4359	4112– 4369	4122– 4379	4132– 4389	4141– 4400	4151– 4410	4161– 4420
4300	4171– 4430	4181– 4440	4191– 4450	4201– 4460	4210– 4471	4220– 4481	4230– 4491	4240– 4501	4250– 4511	4260– 4521
4400	4269– 4531	4279– 4542	4289– 4552	4299– 4562	4309– 4572	4319– 4582	4329– 4592	4338– 4603	4348– 4613	4358– 4623
4500	4368– 4633	4378– 4643	4388– 4653	4398– 4663	4407– 4674	4417– 4684	4427– 4694	4437– 4704	4447– 4714	4457– 4724
4600	4467– 4734	4476– 4745	4486– 4755	4496– 4765	4506– 4775	4516– 4785	4526– 4795	4536– 4805	4545– 4816	4555– 4826
4700	4565– 4836	4575– 4846	4585– 4856	4595– 4866	4605– 4876	4614– 4887	4624– 4897	4634– 4907	4644– 4917	4654– 4927
4800	4664– 4937	4674– 4947	4683– 4958	4693– 4968	4703– 4978	4713– 4988	4723– 4998	4733– 5008	4743– 5018	4752– 5029
4900	4762– 5039	4772– 5049	4782– 5059	4792– 5069	4802– 5079	4812– 5089	4821– 5100	4831– 5110	4841– 5120	4851– 5130

λ	0	100	200	300	400	500	600	700	800	900
5000	4861– 5140	4960– 5241	5058– 5343	5157– 5444	5255– 5545	5354– 5647	5453– 5748	5552– 5849	5650– 5951	5749– 6052
6000	5848– 6153	5946– 6255	6045– 6356	6144– 6457	6243– 6558	6341– 6659	6440– 6761	6539– 6862	6638– 6963	6737– 7064
7000	6835– 7165	6934– 7267	7033– 7368	7132– 7469	7231– 7570	7330– 7671	7429– 7772	7527– 7873	7626– 7975	7725– 8076
8000	7824– 8177	7923– 8278	8022– 8379	8121– 8480	8220– 8581	8319– 8682	8418– 8783	8517– 8884	8616– 8985	8715– 9086
9000	8814– 9187	8913– 9288	9011– 9389	9110– 9490	9209– 9591	9308– 9693	9407– 9794	9506– 9895	9605– 9995	9704–10096
10000	9803–10197	9903–10298	10002–10399	10101–10500	10200–10601	10299–10702	10398–10803	10497–10904	10596–11005	10695–11106
11000	10794–11207	10893–11308	10992–11409	11091–11510	11190–11611	11289–11712	11388–11813	11487–11913	11587–12014	11686–12115
12000	11785–12216	11884–12317	11983–12418	12082–12519	12181–12620	12280–12721	12379–12821	12479–12922	12578–13023	12677–13124
13000	12776–13225	12875–13326	12974–13427	13073–13528	13173–13628	13272–13729	13371–13830	13470–13931	13569–14032	13668–14133
14000	13768–14233	13867–14334	13966–14435	14065–14536	14164–14637	14263–14737	14363–14838	14462–14939	14561–15040	14660–15141
15000	14759–15242	14859–15342	14958–15443	15057–15544	15156–15645	15255–15745	15355–15846	15454–15947	15553–16048	15652–16149
16000	15752–16249	15851–16350	15950–16451	16049–16552	16148–16652	16248–16753	16347–16854	16446–16955	16545–17056	16645–17156
17000	16744–17257	16843–17358	16942–17459	17042–17559	17141–17660	17240–17761	17339–17861	17439–17962	17538–18063	17637–18164
18000	17737–18264	17836–18365	17935–18466	18034–18567	18134–18667	18233–18768	18332–18869	18431–18969	18531–19070	18630–19171
19000	18729–19272	18829–19372	18928–19473	19027–19574	19126–19674	19226–19775	19325–19876	19424–19977	19524–20077	19623–20178
20000	19722–20279	19822–20379	19921–20480	20020–20581	20120–20681	20219–20782	20318–20883	20417–20983	20517–21084	20616–21185
21000	20715–21285	20815–21386	20914–21487	21013–21588	21113–21688	21212–21789	21311–21890	21411–21990	21510–22091	21609–22192
22000	21709–22292	21808–22393	21907–22494	22007–22594	22106–22695	22205–22795	22305–22896	22404–22997	22504–23097	22603–23198
23000	22702–23299	22802–23399	22901–23500	23000–23601	23100–23701	23199–23802	23298–23903	23398–24003	23497–24104	23596–24204
24000	23696–24305	23795–24406	23895–24506	23994–24607	24093–24708	24193–24808	24292–24909	24391–25010	24491–25110	24590–25211

All values conform to the international convention (i.e. 0,1 instead of 0.1).

For x = 0–199 the limits are exact, but for x > 200 they are only approximate (see page 224)

x	0	1 10 100	2 20 200	3 30 300	4 40 400	5 50 500	6 60 600	7 70 700	8 80 800	9 90 900
	λ_l λ_r	λ_l λ_r	λ_l λ_r	λ_l λ_r	λ_l λ_r	λ_l λ_r	λ_l λ_r	λ_l λ_r	λ_l λ_r	λ_l λ_r
0	0 –5,2983	0,0050–7,4301	0,1035–9,2738	0,3379–10,977	0,6722–12,594	1,0779–14,150	1,5369–15,660	2,0373–17,134	2,5711–18,578	3,1324–19,998
10	3,7169–21,398	4,3213–22,779	4,9431–24,145	5,5801–25,497	6,2307–26,836	6,8934–28,164	7,5670–29,482	8,2506–30,791	8,9434–32,091	9,6445–33,383
20	10,353–34,668	11,069–35,946	11,792–37,218	12,521–38,484	13,255–39,745	13,995–41,000	14,741–42,251	15,491–43,497	16,245–44,738	17,004–45,976
30	17,767–47,209	18,534–48,439	19,305–49,665	20,079–50,888	20,857–52,107	21,638–53,324	22,422–54,537	23,208–55,742	23,998–56,955	24,791–58,161
40	25,586–59,363	26,384–60,563	27,184–61,761	27,986–62,956	28,791–64,149	29,598–65,341	30,407–66,530	31,218–67,717	32,032–68,902	32,847–70,085
50	33,664–71,266	34,483–72,446	35,303–73,624	36,125–74,800	36,949–75,974	37,775–77,147	38,602–78,319	39,431–79,489	40,261–80,657	41,093–81,824
60	41,926–82,990	42,760–84,154	43,596–85,317	44,433–86,479	45,272–87,639	46,111–88,798	46,952–89,956	47,794–91,113	48,637–92,269	49,482–93,423
70	50,327–94,577	51,174–95,729	52,022–96,881	52,871–98,031	53,720–99,180	54,571–100,33	55,423–101,48	56,276–102,62	57,129–103,77	57,984–104,91
80	58,840–106,06	59,696–107,20	60,553–108,34	61,412–109,48	62,271–110,62	63,131–111,76	63,991–112,90	64,853–114,04	65,715–115,17	66,578–116,31
90	67,442–117,45	68,307–118,58	69,172–119,71	70,038–120,85	70,905–121,98	71,773–123,11	72,641–124,24	73,510–125,37	74,379–126,50	75,250–127,63
100	76,120–128,76	76,992–129,89	77,864–131,02	78,737–132,14	79,610–133,27	80,484–134,39	81,359–135,52	82,234–136,64	83,110–137,77	83,986–138,89
110	84,863–140,01	85,741–141,13	86,619–142,26	87,497–143,38	88,377–144,50	89,256–145,62	90,136–146,74	91,017–147,86	91,898–148,97	92,780–150,09
120	93,662–151,21	94,545–152,33	95,428–153,44	96,312–154,56	97,196–155,67	98,080–156,79	98,965–157,90	99,851–159,02	100,74–160,13	101,62–161,24
130	102,51–162,36	103,40–163,47	104,28–164,58	105,17–165,59	106,06–166,80	106,95–167,91	107,84–169,02	108,73–170,13	109,62–171,24	110,51–172,35
140	111,40–173,46	112,29–174,57	113,18–175,68	114,08–176,78	114,97–177,89	115,86–179,00	116,76–180,11	117,65–181,21	118,54–182,32	119,44–183,42
150	120,33–184,53	121,23–185,63	122,12–186,74	123,02–187,84	123,91–188,94	124,81–190,05	125,71–191,15	126,60–192,25	127,50–193,36	128,40–194,46
160	129,30–195,56	130,20–196,66	131,09–197,76	131,99–198,86	132,89–199,96	133,79–201,06	134,69–202,16	135,59–203,26	136,49–204,36	137,39–205,46
170	138,29–206,56	139,20–207,66	140,10–208,75	141,00–209,85	141,90–210,95	142,80–212,05	143,71–213,14	144,61–214,24	145,51–215,34	146,42–216,43
180	147,32–217,53	148,22–218,63	149,13–219,72	150,03–220,82	150,94–221,91	151,84–223,01	152,75–224,10	153,66–225,19	154,56–226,29	155,47–227,38
190	156,37–228,47	157,28–229,57	158,19–230,66	159,09–231,75	160,00–232,84	160,91–233,94	161,82–235,03	162,73–236,12	163,63–237,21	164,54–238,30
200	165,45–239,40	174,55–250,29	183,67–261,17	192,82–272,03	201,98–282,86	211,15–293,69	220,35–304,49	229,55–315,28	238,78–326,06	248,02–336,82
300	257,27–347,57	266,53–358,30	275,80–369,03	285,09–379,74	294,38–390,44	303,69–401,14	313,01–411,82	322,33–422,49	331,67–433,16	341,01–443,81
400	350,36–454,46	359,72–465,10	369,09–475,73	378,47–486,35	387,85–496,97	397,24–507,58	406,63–518,18	416,04–528,78	425,45–539,37	434,86–549,95
500	444,28–560,53	453,71–571,10	463,14–581,67	472,58–592,23	482,02–602,79	491,47–613,34	500,92–623,89	510,38–634,43	519,85–644,96	529,31–655,50
600	538,78–666,02	548,26–676,55	557,74–687,07	567,23–697,58	576,72–708,09	586,21–718,60	595,71–729,10	605,21–739,60	614,71–750,10	624,22–760,59
700	633,73–771,08	643,24–781,56	652,76–792,04	662,28–802,52	671,81–812,99	681,34–823,47	690,87–833,93	700,40–844,40	709,94–854,86	719,48–865,32
800	729,02–875,78	738,57–886,23	748,12–896,68	757,67–907,13	767,22–917,58	776,78–928,02	786,34–938,46	795,90–948,90	805,47–959,33	815,03–969,76
900	824,60–980,20	834,18–990,62	843,75–1001,1	853,33–1011,5	862,91–1021,9	872,49–1032,3	882,07–1042,7	891,66–1053,1	901,24–1063,6	910,83–1074,0
1000	920,42–1084,4	930,02–1094,8	939,61–1105,2	949,21–1115,6	958,81–1126,0	968,41–1136,4	978,02–1146,8	987,62–1157,2	997,23–1167,6	1006,8–1178,0
1100	1016,4–1188,3	1026,1–1198,7	1035,7–1209,1	1045,3–1219,5	1054,9–1229,9	1064,5–1240,3	1074,1–1250,6	1083,8–1261,0	1093,4–1271,4	1103,0–1281,8
1200	1112,6–1292,1	1122,3–1302,5	1131,9–1312,9	1141,5–1323,3	1151,2–1333,6	1160,8–1344,0	1170,4–1354,3	1180,1–1364,7	1189,7–1375,1	1199,4–1385,4
1300	1209,0–1395,8	1218,6–1406,1	1228,3–1416,5	1237,9–1426,9	1247,6–1437,2	1257,2–1447,6	1266,9–1457,9	1276,5–1468,3	1286,2–1478,6	1295,8–1488,9
1400	1305,5–1499,3	1315,2–1509,6	1324,8–1520,0	1334,5–1530,3	1344,1–1540,7	1353,8–1551,0	1363,5–1561,3	1373,1–1571,7	1382,8–1582,0	1392,5–1592,3
1500	1402,1–1602,7	1411,8–1613,0	1421,5–1623,3	1431,1–1633,7	1440,8–1644,0	1450,5–1654,3	1460,1–1664,6	1469,8–1675,0	1479,5–1685,3	1489,2–1695,6
1600	1498,8–1705,9	1508,5–1716,3	1518,2–1726,6	1527,9–1736,9	1537,6–1747,2	1547,2–1757,5	1556,9–1767,9	1566,6–1778,2	1576,3–1788,5	1586,0–1798,8
1700	1595,7–1809,1	1605,4–1819,4	1615,1–1829,7	1624,7–1840,0	1634,4–1850,4	1644,1–1860,7	1653,8–1871,0	1663,5–1881,3	1673,2–1891,6	1682,9–1901,9
1800	1692,6–1912,2	1702,3–1922,5	1712,0–1932,8	1721,7–1943,1	1731,4–1953,4	1741,1–1963,7	1750,8–1974,0	1760,5–1984,3	1770,2–1994,6	1779,9–2004,9
1900	1789,6–2015,2	1799,3–2025,5	1809,0–2035,8	1818,7–2046,1	1828,4–2056,4	1838,1–2066,7	1847,8–2076,9	1857,6–2087,2	1867,3–2097,5	1877,0–2107,8
2000	1886,7–2118,1	1896,4–2128,4	1906,1–2138,7	1915,8–2149,0	1925,5–2159,2	1935,3–2169,5	1945,0–2179,8	1954,7–2190,1	1964,4–2200,4	1974,1–2210,7
2100	1983,8–2220,9	1993,6–2231,2	2003,3–2241,5	2013,0–2251,8	2022,7–2262,1	2032,4–2272,3	2042,2–2282,6	2051,9–2292,9	2061,6–2303,2	2071,3–2313,4
2200	2081,1–2323,7	2090,8–2334,0	2100,5–2344,3	2110,2–2354,5	2120,0–2364,8	2129,7–2375,1	2139,4–2385,4	2149,2–2395,6	2158,9–2405,9	2168,6–2416,2
2300	2178,3–2426,4	2188,1–2436,7	2197,8–2447,0	2207,5–2457,2	2217,3–2467,5	2227,0–2477,8	2236,7–2488,0	2246,5–2498,3	2256,2–2508,6	2266,0–2518,8
2400	2275,7–2529,1	2285,4–2539,4	2295,2–2549,6	2304,9–2559,9	2314,6–2570,1	2324,4–2580,4	2334,1–2590,7	2343,9–2600,9	2353,6–2611,2	2363,3–2621,4
2500	2373,1–2631,7	2382,8–2642,0	2392,6–2652,2	2402,3–2662,5	2412,1–2672,7	2421,8–2683,0	2431,6–2693,2	2441,3–2703,5	2451,0–2713,7	2460,8–2724,0
2600	2470,5–2734,2	2480,3–2744,5	2490,0–2754,7	2499,8–2765,0	2509,5–2775,3	2519,3–2785,5	2529,0–2795,8	2538,8–2806,0	2548,5–2816,3	2558,3–2826,5
2700	2568,0–2836,7	2577,8–2847,0	2587,5–2857,2	2597,3–2867,5	2607,0–2877,7	2616,8–2888,0	2626,6–2898,2	2636,3–2908,5	2646,1–2918,7	2655,8–2929,0
2800	2665,6–2939,2	2675,3–2949,4	2685,1–2959,7	2694,9–2969,9	2704,6–2980,2	2714,4–2990,4	2724,1–3000,7	2733,9–3010,9	2743,6–3021,1	2753,4–3031,4
2900	2763,2–3041,6	2772,9–3051,9	2782,7–3062,1	2792,5–3072,3	2802,2–3082,6	2812,0–3092,8	2821,7–3103,0	2831,5–3113,3	2841,3–3123,5	2851,0–3133,8
3000	2860,8–3144,0	2870,6–3154,2	2880,3–3164,5	2890,1–3174,7	2899,9–3184,9	2909,6–3195,2	2919,4–3205,4	2929,2–3215,6	2938,9–3225,9	2948,7–3236,1
3100	2958,5–3246,3	2968,2–3256,5	2978,0–3266,8	2987,8–3277,0	2997,5–3287,2	3007,3–3297,5	3017,1–3307,7	3026,9–3317,9	3036,6–3328,2	3046,4–3338,4
3200	3056,2–3348,6	3065,9–3358,8	3075,7–3369,1	3085,5–3379,3	3095,3–3389,5	3105,0–3399,7	3114,8–3410,0	3124,6–3420,2	3134,4–3430,4	3144,1–3440,6
3300	3153,9–3450,9	3163,7–3461,1	3173,5–3471,3	3183,2–3481,5	3193,0–3491,8	3202,8–3502,0	3212,6–3512,2	3222,3–3522,4	3232,1–3532,7	3241,9–3542,9
3400	3251,7–3553,1	3261,5–3563,3	3271,2–3573,5	3281,0–3583,8	3290,8–3594,0	3300,6–3604,2	3310,4–3614,4	3320,1–3624,6	3329,9–3634,9	3339,7–3645,1
3500	3349,5–3655,3	3359,3–3665,5	3369,1–3675,7	3378,8–3685,9	3388,6–3696,2	3398,4–3706,4	3408,2–3716,6	3418,0–3726,8	3427,8–3737,0	3437,5–3747,2
3600	3447,3–3757,4	3457,1–3767,7	3466,9–3777,9	3476,7–3788,1	3486,5–3798,3	3496,3–3808,5	3506,0–3818,7	3515,8–3828,9	3525,6–3839,2	3535,4–3849,4
3700	3545,2–3859,6	3555,0–3869,8	3564,8–3880,0	3574,6–3890,2	3584,4–3900,4	3594,1–3910,6	3603,9–3920,8	3613,7–3931,1	3623,5–3941,3	3633,3–3951,5
3800	3643,1–3961,7	3652,9–3971,9	3662,7–3982,1	3672,5–3992,3	3682,3–4002,5	3692,1–4012,7	3701,8–4022,9	3711,6–4033,1	3721,4–4043,3	3731,2–4053,6
3900	3741,0–4063,8	3750,8–4074,0	3760,6–4084,2	3770,4–4094,4	3780,2–4104,6	3790,0–4114,8	3799,8–4125,0	3809,6–4135,2	3819,4–4145,4	3829,2–4155,6
4000	3839,0–4165,8	3848,8–4176,0	3858,6–4186,2	3868,4–4196,4	3878,2–4206,6	3888,0–4216,8	3897,8–4227,0	3907,5–4237,2	3917,3–4247,4	3927,1–4257,6
4100	3936,9–4267,8	3946,7–4278,0	3956,5–4288,2	3966,3–4298,4	3976,1–4308,6	3985,9–4318,8	3995,7–4329,0	4005,5–4339,2	4015,3–4349,4	4025,1–4359,6
4200	4034,9–4369,8	4044,7–4380,0	4054,5–4390,2	4064,4–4400,4	4074,2–4410,6	4084,0–4420,8	4093,8–4431,0	4103,6–4441,2	4113,4–4451,4	4123,2–4461,6
4300	4133,0–4471,8	4142,8–4482,0	4152,6–4492,2	4162,4–4502,4	4172,2–4512,6	4182,0–4522,8	4191,8–4533,0	4201,6–4543,2	4211,4–4553,4	4221,2–4563,6
4400	4231,0–4573,8	4240,8–4584,0	4250,6–4594,1	4260,4–4604,3	4270,2–4614,5	4280,0–4624,7	4289,9–4634,9	4299,7–4645,1	4309,5–4655,3	4319,3–4665,5
4500	4329,1–4675,7	4338,9–4685,9	4348,7–4696,1	4358,5–4706,3	4368,3–4716,5	4378,1–4726,6	4387,9–4736,8	4397,7–4747,0	4407,6–4757,2	4417,4–4767,4
4600	4427,2–4777,6	4437,0–4787,8	4446,8–4798,0	4456,6–4808,2	4466,4–4818,4	4476,2–4828,5	4486,0–4838,7	4495,9–4848,9	4505,7–4859,1	4515,5–4869,3
4700	4525,3–4879,5	4535,1–4889,7	4544,9–4899,9	4554,7–4910,0	4564,5–4920,2	4574,4–4930,4	4584,2–4940,6	4594,0–4950,8	4603,8–4961,0	4613,6–4971,2
4800	4623,4–4981,4	4633,2–4991,5	4643,0–5001,7	4652,9–5011,9	4662,7–5022,1	4672,5–5032,3	4682,3–5042,5	4692,1–5052,7	4701,9–5062,8	4711,8–5073,0
4900	4721,6–5083,2	4731,4–5093,4	4741,2–5103,6	4751,0–5113,8	4760,8–5123,9	4770,7–5134,1	4780,5–5144,3	4790,3–5154,5	4800,1–5164,7	4809,9–5174,9
5000	4819,7–5185,0	4917,9–5286,8	5016,1–5388,6	5114,4–5490,4	5212,6–5592,2	5310,9–5693,9	5409,1–5795,7	5507,4–5897,4	5605,7–5999,1	5704,0–6100,7
6000	5802,4–6202,4	5900,7–6304,1	5999,1–6405,7	6097,4–6507,3	6195,8–6609,0	6294,2–6710,6	6392,6–6812,2	6491,0–6913,7	6589,5–7015,3	6687,9–7116,9
7000	6786,4–7218,4	6884,8–7319,9	6983,3–7421,5	7081,8–7523,0	7180,3–7624,5	7278,8–7726,0	7377,3–7827,4	7475,9–7928,9	7574,4–8030,4	7672,9–8131,8
8000	7771,5–8233,3	7870,1–8334,7	7968,6–8436,1	8067,2–8537,6	8165,8–8639,0	8264,4–8740,4	8363,0–8841,8	8461,6–8943,1	8560,2–9044,5	8658,9–9145,9
9000	8757,5–9247,3	8856,2–9348,6	8954,8–9450,0	9053,5–9551,3	9152,1–9652,6	9250,8–9754,0	9349,5–9855,3	9448,2–9956,6	9546,9–10058	9645,6–10159
10000	9744,3–10260	9843,0–10361	9941,7–10463	10040–10564	10139–10666	10238–10767	10337–10868	10435–10969	10534–11071	10633–11172
11000	10732–11273	10830–11374	10929–11475	11028–11577	11127–11678	11226–11779	11324–11880	11423–11982	11522–12083	11621–12184
12000	11720–12285	11819–12386	11917–12487	12016–12589	12115–12690	12214–12791	12313–12892	12412–12993	12510–13094	12609–13195
13000	12708–13297	12807–13398	12906–13499	13005–13600	13104–13701	13203–13802	13301–13903	13400–14004	13499–14105	13598–14207
14000	13697–14308	13796–14409	13895–14510	13994–14611	14093–14712	14192–14813	14291–14914	14390–15015	14489–15116	14587–15217
15000	14686–15318	14785–15419	14884–15520	14983–15622	15082–15723	15181–15824	15280–15925	15379–16026	15478–16127	15577–16228
16000	15676–16329	15775–16430	15874–16531	15973–16632	16072–16733	16171–16834	16270–16935	16369–17036	16468–17137	16567–17238
17000	16666–17339	16765–17440	16864–17541	16963–17642	17062–17743	17161–17844	17260–17945	17359–18046	17458–18147	17557–18248
18000	17656–18348	17755–18449	17854–18550	17953–18651	18052–18752	18152–18853	18251–18954	18350–19055	18449–19156	18548–19257
19000	18647–19358	18746–19459	18845–19560	18944–19661	19043–19762	19142–19863	19241–19964	19340–20064	19439–20165	19539–20266
20000	19638–20367	19737–20468	19836–20569	19935–20670	20034–20771	20133–20872	20232–20973	20331–21073	20430–21174	20529–21275
21000	20629–21376	20728–21477	20827–21578	20926–21679	21025–21780	21124–21881	21223–21981	21322–22082	21422–22183	21521–22284
22000	21620–22385	21719–22486	21818–22587	21917–22688	22016–22788	22116–22889	22215–22990	22314–23091	22413–23192	22512–23293
23000	22611–23394	22710–23494	22810–23595	22909–23696	23008–23797	23107–23898	23206–23999	23305–24099	23404–24200	23504–24301
24000	23603–24402	23702–24503	23801–24604	23900–24704	24000–24805	24099–24906	24198–25007	24297–25108	24396–25209	24495–25309
25000	24595–25410	24694–25511	24793–25612	24892–25713	24991–25813	25091–25914	25190–26015	25289–26116	25388–26217	25487–26317
26000	25587–26418	25686–26519	25785–26620	25884–26721	25983–26821	26083–26922	26182–27023	26281–27124	26380–27225	26479–27325
27000	26579–27426	26678–27527	26777–27628	26876–27728	26976–27829	27075–27930	27174–28031	27273–28132	27372–28232	27472–28333
28000	27571–28434	27670–28535	27769–28635	27869–28736	27968–28837	28067–28938	28166–29038	28266–29139	28365–29240	28464–29341
29000	28563–29442	28662–29542	28762–29643	28861–29744	28960–29845	29059–29945	29159–30046	29258–30147	29357–30248	29456–30348
30000	29556–30449	29655–30550	29754–30651	29854–30751	29953–30852	30052–30953	30151–31053	30251–31154	30350–31255	30449–31356
31000	30548–31456	30648–31557	30747–31658	30846–31759	30945–31859	31045–31960	31144–32061	31243–32161	31343–32262	31442–32363
32000	31541–32464	31640–32564	31740–32665	31839–32766	31938–32867	32038–32967	32137–33068	32236–33169	32335–33269	32435–33370
33000	32534–33471	32633–33572	32733–33672	32832–33773	32931–33874	33030–33974	33130–34075	33229–34176	33328–34276	33428–34377
34000	33527–34478	33626–34579	33726–34679	33825–34780	33924–34881	34023–34981	34123–35082	34222–35183	34321–35283	34421–35384

All values conform to the international convention (i.e. 0,1 instead of 0.1).

Significance Limits* for x for given λ $2\alpha = 0{,}01$

For $\lambda = 0$–100 the limits are exact, but for $\lambda > 100$ they are only approximate (see page 224)

λ	0,0	0,1 1 10	0,2 2 20	0,3 3 30	0,4 4 40	0,5 5 50	0,6 6 60	0,7 7 70	0,8 8 80	0,9 9 90
0		•– 2	•– 3	•– 3	•– 4	•– 4	•– 4	•– 5	•– 5	•– 5
1	•– 5	•– 6	•– 6	•– 6	•– 6	•– 6	•– 7	•– 7	•– 7	•– 7
2	•– 7	•– 8	•– 8	•– 8	•– 8	•– 8	•– 9	•– 9	•– 9	•– 9
3	•– 9	•– 9	•– 10	•– 10	•– 10	•– 10	•– 10	•– 10	•– 11	•– 11
4	•– 11	•– 11	•– 11	•– 11	•– 12	•– 12	•– 12	•– 12	•– 12	•– 12
5	•– 13	•– 13	•– 13	0– 13	0– 13	0– 13	0– 14	0– 14	0– 14	0– 14
6	0– 14	0– 14	0– 14	0– 15	0– 15	0– 15	0– 15	0– 15	0– 15	0– 16
7	0– 16	0– 16	0– 16	0– 16	0– 16	1– 16	1– 17	1– 17	1– 17	1– 17
8	1– 17	1– 17	1– 17	1– 18	1– 18	1– 18	1– 18	1– 18	1– 18	1– 18
9	1– 19	1– 19	1– 19	2– 19	2– 19	2– 19	2– 19	2– 20	2– 20	2– 20
10	2– 20	2– 21	3– 23	4– 24	4– 26	5– 27	6– 28	6– 29	7– 31	8– 32
20	8– 33	9– 35	10– 36	11– 37	11– 39	12– 40	13– 41	14– 42	14– 44	15– 45
30	16– 46	17– 47	17– 48	18– 50	19– 51	20– 52	21– 53	21– 55	22– 56	23– 57
40	24– 58	24– 59	25– 61	26– 62	27– 63	28– 64	29– 65	29– 67	30– 68	31– 69
50	32– 70	33– 71	33– 72	34– 74	35– 75	36– 76	37– 77	38– 78	38– 80	39– 81
60	40– 82	41– 83	42– 84	43– 85	43– 87	44– 88	45– 89	46– 90	47– 91	48– 92
70	48– 93	49– 95	50– 96	51– 97	52– 98	53– 99	54– 100	54– 102	55– 103	56– 104
80	57– 105	58– 106	59– 107	60– 108	60– 110	61– 111	62– 112	63– 113	64– 114	65– 115
90	66– 116	66– 117	67– 119	68– 120	69– 121	70– 122	71– 123	72– 124	72– 125	73– 127
100	74– 128	75– 129	76– 130	77– 131	78– 132	79– 133	79– 134	80– 136	81– 137	82– 138
110	83– 139	84– 140	85– 141	86– 142	86– 143	87– 145	88– 146	89– 147	90– 148	91– 149
120	92– 150	93– 151	94– 152	94– 153	95– 155	96– 156	97– 157	98– 158	99– 159	100– 160
130	101– 161	101– 162	102– 164	103– 165	104– 166	105– 167	106– 168	107– 169	108– 170	109– 171
140	109– 172	110– 173	111– 175	112– 176	113– 177	114– 178	115– 179	116– 180	117– 181	118– 182
150	118– 183	119– 185	120– 186	121– 187	122– 188	123– 189	124– 190	125– 191	126– 192	126– 193
160	127– 194	128– 196	129– 197	130– 198	131– 199	132– 200	133– 201	134– 202	135– 203	135– 204
170	136– 206	137– 207	138– 208	139– 209	140– 210	141– 211	142– 212	143– 213	144– 214	145– 215
180	145– 216	146– 218	147– 219	148– 220	149– 221	150– 222	151– 223	152– 224	153– 225	154– 226
190	154– 227	155– 229	156– 230	157– 231	158– 232	159– 233	160– 234	161– 235	162– 236	163– 237
200	164– 238	173– 249	182– 260	191– 271	200– 282	209– 293	218– 303	228– 314	237– 325	246– 336
300	255– 347	265– 357	274– 368	283– 379	292– 389	302– 400	311– 411	320– 421	330– 432	339– 443
400	348– 453	358– 464	367– 475	377– 485	386– 496	395– 507	405– 517	414– 528	424– 538	433– 549
500	442– 560	452– 570	461– 581	471– 591	480– 602	490– 612	499– 623	508– 633	518– 644	527– 654
600	537– 665	546– 676	556– 686	565– 697	575– 707	584– 718	594– 728	603– 739	613– 749	622– 760
700	632– 770	641– 781	651– 791	660– 802	670– 812	679– 822	689– 833	698– 843	708– 854	718– 864
800	727– 875	737– 885	746– 896	756– 906	765– 917	775– 927	784– 937	794– 948	804– 958	813– 969
900	823– 979	832– 990	842– 1000	851– 1010	861– 1021	871– 1031	880– 1042	890– 1052	899– 1063	909– 1073
1000	918– 1083	928– 1094	938– 1104	947– 1115	957– 1125	966– 1135	976– 1146	986– 1156	995– 1167	1005– 1177
1100	1015– 1187	1024– 1198	1034– 1208	1043– 1219	1053– 1229	1063– 1239	1072– 1250	1082– 1260	1091– 1270	1101– 1281
1200	1111– 1291	1120– 1302	1130– 1312	1140– 1322	1149– 1333	1159– 1343	1169– 1353	1178– 1364	1188– 1374	1197– 1384
1300	1207– 1395	1217– 1405	1226– 1416	1236– 1426	1246– 1436	1255– 1447	1265– 1457	1275– 1467	1284– 1478	1294– 1488
1400	1304– 1498	1313– 1509	1323– 1519	1333– 1529	1342– 1540	1352– 1550	1362– 1560	1371– 1571	1381– 1581	1391– 1591
1500	1400– 1602	1410– 1612	1420– 1622	1429– 1633	1439– 1643	1449– 1653	1458– 1664	1468– 1674	1478– 1684	1487– 1695
1600	1497– 1705	1507– 1715	1516– 1726	1526– 1736	1536– 1746	1545– 1757	1555– 1767	1565– 1777	1574– 1788	1584– 1798
1700	1594– 1808	1603– 1818	1613– 1829	1623– 1839	1633– 1849	1642– 1860	1652– 1870	1662– 1880	1671– 1891	1681– 1901
1800	1691– 1911	1700– 1922	1710– 1932	1720– 1942	1729– 1952	1739– 1963	1749– 1973	1759– 1983	1768– 1994	1778– 2004
1900	1788– 2014	1797– 2025	1807– 2035	1817– 2045	1826– 2055	1836– 2066	1846– 2076	1856– 2086	1865– 2097	1875– 2107
2000	1885– 2117	1894– 2127	1904– 2138	1914– 2148	1924– 2158	1933– 2169	1943– 2179	1953– 2189	1962– 2199	1972– 2210
2100	1982– 2220	1992– 2230	2001– 2241	2011– 2251	2021– 2261	2031– 2271	2040– 2282	2050– 2292	2060– 2302	2069– 2312
2200	2079– 2323	2089– 2333	2099– 2343	2108– 2354	2118– 2364	2128– 2374	2137– 2384	2147– 2395	2157– 2405	2167– 2415
2300	2176– 2425	2186– 2436	2196– 2446	2206– 2456	2215– 2467	2225– 2477	2235– 2487	2245– 2497	2254– 2508	2264– 2518
2400	2274– 2528	2283– 2538	2293– 2549	2303– 2559	2313– 2569	2322– 2579	2332– 2590	2342– 2600	2352– 2610	2361– 2620
2500	2371– 2631	2381– 2641	2391– 2651	2400– 2661	2410– 2672	2420– 2682	2430– 2692	2439– 2703	2449– 2713	2459– 2723
2600	2469– 2733	2478– 2744	2488– 2754	2498– 2764	2508– 2774	2517– 2785	2527– 2795	2537– 2805	2547– 2815	2556– 2826
2700	2566– 2836	2576– 2846	2586– 2856	2595– 2867	2605– 2877	2615– 2887	2625– 2897	2634– 2908	2644– 2918	2654– 2928
2800	2664– 2938	2673– 2948	2683– 2959	2693– 2969	2703– 2979	2712– 2989	2722– 3000	2732– 3010	2742– 3020	2751– 3030
2900	2761– 3041	2771– 3051	2781– 3061	2791– 3071	2800– 3082	2810– 3092	2820– 3102	2830– 3112	2839– 3123	2849– 3133
3000	2859– 3143	2869– 3153	2878– 3163	2888– 3174	2898– 3184	2908– 3194	2917– 3204	2927– 3215	2937– 3225	2947– 3235
3100	2957– 3245	2966– 3256	2976– 3266	2986– 3276	2996– 3286	3005– 3297	3015– 3307	3025– 3317	3035– 3327	3044– 3337
3200	3054– 3348	3064– 3358	3074– 3368	3084– 3378	3093– 3389	3103– 3399	3113– 3409	3123– 3419	3132– 3429	3142– 3440
3300	3152– 3450	3162– 3460	3172– 3470	3181– 3481	3191– 3491	3201– 3501	3211– 3511	3220– 3521	3230– 3532	3240– 3542
3400	3250– 3552	3260– 3562	3269– 3573	3279– 3583	3289– 3593	3299– 3603	3308– 3613	3318– 3624	3328– 3634	3338– 3644
3500	3348– 3654	3357– 3665	3367– 3675	3377– 3685	3387– 3695	3396– 3705	3406– 3716	3416– 3726	3426– 3736	3436– 3746
3600	3445– 3756	3455– 3767	3465– 3777	3475– 3787	3485– 3797	3494– 3808	3504– 3818	3514– 3828	3524– 3838	3533– 3848
3700	3543– 3859	3553– 3869	3563– 3879	3573– 3889	3582– 3899	3592– 3910	3602– 3920	3612– 3930	3622– 3940	3631– 3951
3800	3641– 3961	3651– 3971	3661– 3981	3671– 3991	3680– 4002	3690– 4012	3700– 4022	3710– 4032	3719– 4042	3729– 4053
3900	3739– 4063	3749– 4073	3759– 4083	3768– 4093	3778– 4104	3788– 4114	3798– 4124	3808– 4134	3817– 4144	3827– 4155
4000	3837– 4165	3847– 4175	3857– 4185	3866– 4195	3876– 4206	3886– 4216	3896– 4226	3906– 4236	3915– 4246	3925– 4257
4100	3935– 4267	3945– 4277	3955– 4287	3964– 4297	3974– 4308	3984– 4318	3994– 4328	4004– 4338	4013– 4348	4023– 4359
4200	4033– 4369	4043– 4379	4053– 4389	4062– 4399	4072– 4410	4082– 4420	4092– 4430	4102– 4440	4111– 4450	4121– 4461
4300	4131– 4471	4141– 4481	4151– 4491	4160– 4501	4170– 4512	4180– 4522	4190– 4532	4200– 4542	4209– 4552	4219– 4563
4400	4229– 4573	4239– 4583	4249– 4593	4259– 4603	4268– 4614	4278– 4624	4288– 4634	4298– 4644	4308– 4654	4317– 4665
4500	4327– 4675	4337– 4685	4347– 3695	4357– 4705	4366– 4715	4376– 4726	4386– 4736	4396– 4746	4406– 4756	4415– 4766
4600	4425– 4777	4435– 4787	4445– 4797	4455– 4807	4464– 4817	4474– 4828	4484– 4838	4494– 4848	4504– 4858	4514– 4868
4700	4523– 4879	4533– 4889	4543– 4899	4553– 4909	4563– 4919	4572– 4929	4582– 4940	4592– 4950	4602– 4960	4612– 4970
4800	4621– 4980	4631– 4991	4641– 5001	4651– 5011	4661– 5021	4671– 5031	4680– 5042	4690– 5052	4700– 5062	4710– 5072
4900	4720– 5082	4729– 5092	4739– 5103	4749– 5113	4759– 5123	4769– 5133	4779– 5143	4788– 5154	4798– 5164	4808– 5174

λ	0	100	200	300	400	500	600	700	800	900
5000	4818– 5184	4916– 5286	5014– 5388	5112– 5489	5211– 5591	5309– 5693	5407– 5795	5505– 5896	5604– 5998	5702– 6100
6000	5800– 6201	5899– 6303	5997– 6405	6095– 6506	6194– 6608	6292– 6710	6391– 6811	6489– 6913	6588– 7014	6686– 7116
7000	6784– 7217	6883– 7319	6981– 7421	7080– 7522	7178– 7624	7277– 7725	7375– 7826	7474– 7928	7572– 8029	7671– 8131
8000	7770– 8232	7868– 8334	7967– 8435	8065– 8537	8164– 8638	8262– 8739	8361– 8841	8460– 8942	8558– 9044	8657– 9145
9000	8756– 9246	8854– 9348	8953– 9449	9052– 9550	9150– 9652	9249– 9753	9348– 9854	9446– 9956	9545–10057	9644–10158
10000	9742–10260	9841–10361	9940–10462	10039–10563	10137–10665	10236–10766	10335–10867	10433–10968	10532–11070	10631–11171
11000	10730–11272	10829–11373	10927–11475	11026–11576	11125–11677	11224–11778	11323–11879	11421–11981	11520–12082	11619–12183
12000	11718–12284	11817–12385	11915–12486	12014–12588	12113–12689	12212–12790	12311–12891	12410–12992	12509–13093	12607–13194
13000	12706–13296	12805–13397	12904–13498	13003–13599	13102–13700	13201–13801	13300–13902	13398–14003	13497–14105	13596–14206
14000	13695–14307	13794–14408	13893–14509	13992–14610	14091–14711	14190–14812	14289–14913	14388–15014	14487–15115	14586–15216
15000	14684–15317	14783–15418	14882–15520	14981–15621	15080–15722	15179–15823	15278–15924	15377–16025	15476–16126	15575–16227
16000	15674–16328	15773–16429	15872–16530	15971–16631	16070–16732	16169–16833	16268–16934	16367–17035	16466–17136	16565–17237
17000	16664–17338	16763–17439	16862–17540	16961–17641	17060–17742	17159–17843	17258–17944	17357–18045	17456–18146	17555–18247
18000	17654–18348	17753–18448	17852–18549	17951–18650	18051–18751	18150–18852	18249–18953	18348–19054	18447–19155	18546–19256
19000	18645–19357	18744–19458	18843–19559	18942–19660	19041–19761	19140–19862	19239–19963	19338–20063	19437–20164	19537–20265
20000	19636–20366	19735–20467	19834–20568	19933–20669	20032–20770	20131–20871	20230–20972	20329–21073	20428–21173	20528–21274
21000	20627–21375	20726–21476	20825–21577	20924–21678	21023–21779	21122–21880	21221–21981	21320–22081	21420–22182	21519–22283
22000	21618–22384	21717–22485	21816–22586	21915–22687	22014–22787	22114–22888	22213–22989	22312–23090	22411–23191	22510–23292
23000	22609–23393	22708–23493	22808–23594	22907–23695	23006–23796	23105–23897	23204–23998	23303–24098	23403–24199	23502–24300
24000	23601–24401	23700–24502	23799–24603	23898–24703	23998–24804	24097–24905	24196–25006	24295–25107	24394–25208	24493–25308

All values conform to the international convention (i.e. 0,1 instead of 0.1).

Acceptance Region[1] for the Rank Sum T $2\alpha = 0{,}1$ (Wilcoxon 2-Sample Test)

$\text{Prob}(T_l < \boldsymbol{T} < T_r) \geq 1 - 2\alpha$. For explanation see page 228

$2\alpha = 0{,}100$

Each cell gives T_l–T_r.

N_2 \ N_1	1	2	3	4	5	6	7	8	9	10	11	12	13	14	15	16	17	18	19	20	21	22	23	24	25
1	–	–	–	–	–	–	–	–	–	–	–	–	–	–	–	–	–	–	190–209	210–230	231–252	253–275	276–299	300–324	325–350
2	–	–	–	–	15–25	21–33	28–42	37–51	46–62	56–74	67–87	80–100	93–115	108–130	123–147	139–165	156–184	175–203	194–224	214–246	236–268	258–292	281–317	306–342	331–369
3	–	–	6–15	10–22	16–29	23–37	30–47	39–57	49–68	59–81	71–94	83–109	97–124	112–140	127–158	144–176	162–195	180–216	200–237	221–259	242–283	265–307	289–332	313–359	339–386
4	–	–	6–18	11–25	17–33	24–42	32–52	41–63	51–75	62–88	74–102	87–117	101–133	116–150	132–168	150–186	168–206	187–227	207–249	228–272	250–296	273–321	297–347	322–374	348–402
5	–	3–13	7–20	12–28	19–36	26–46	34–57	44–68	54–81	66–94	78–109	91–125	106–141	121–159	138–177	155–197	173–218	193–239	213–262	235–285	257–310	281–335	305–362	330–390	357–418
6	–	3–15	8–22	13–31	20–40	28–50	36–62	46–74	57–87	69–101	82–116	95–133	110–150	126–168	143–187	161–207	179–229	199–251	220–274	242–298	265–323	289–349	313–377	339–405	366–434
7	–	3–17	8–25	14–34	21–44	29–55	39–66	49–79	60–93	72–108	85–124	99–141	115–158	131–177	148–197	166–218	186–239	206–262	227–286	249–311	272–337	297–363	322–391	348–420	375–450
8	–	4–18	9–27	15–37	23–47	31–59	41–71	51–85	63–99	75–115	89–131	104–148	119–167	136–186	153–207	172–228	192–250	212–274	234–298	257–323	280–350	305–377	330–406	357–435	385–465
9	–	4–20	10–29	16–40	24–51	33–63	43–76	54–90	66–105	79–121	93–138	108–156	124–175	141–195	159–216	178–238	198–261	219–285	241–310	264–336	288–363	313–391	339–420	366–450	394–481
10	–	4–22	10–32	17–43	26–54	35–67	45–81	56–96	69–111	82–128	97–145	112–164	128–184	146–204	164–226	184–248	204–272	226–296	248–322	272–348	296–376	321–405	348–434	375–465	404–496
11	–	4–24	11–34	18–46	27–58	37–71	47–86	59–101	72–117	86–134	100–153	116–172	133–192	151–213	170–235	190–258	210–283	232–308	255–334	279–361	304–389	330–418	357–448	385–479	414–511
12	–	5–25	11–37	19–49	28–62	38–76	49–91	62–106	75–123	89–141	104–160	120–180	138–200	156–222	175–245	196–268	217–293	239–319	262–346	287–373	312–402	338–432	366–462	394–494	423–527
13	–	5–27	12–39	20–52	30–65	40–80	52–95	64–112	78–129	92–148	108–167	125–187	142–209	161–231	181–254	201–279	223–304	246–330	270–357	294–386	320–415	347–445	374–477	403–509	433–542
14	–	6–28	13–41	21–55	31–69	42–84	54–100	67–117	81–135	96–154	112–174	129–195	147–217	166–240	186–264	207–289	230–314	253–341	277–369	302–398	328–428	355–459	383–491	413–523	443–557
15	–	6–30	13–44	22–58	33–72	44–88	56–105	69–123	84–141	99–161	116–181	133–203	152–225	171–249	192–273	213–299	236–325	259–353	284–381	310–410	336–441	364–472	392–505	422–538	453–572
16	–	6–32	14–46	24–60	34–76	46–92	58–110	72–128	87–147	103–167	120–188	138–210	156–234	176–258	197–283	219–309	242–336	266–364	291–393	317–423	344–454	372–486	401–519	431–553	462–588
17	–	6–34	15–48	25–63	35–80	47–97	61–114	75–133	90–153	106–174	123–196	142–218	161–242	182–266	203–292	225–319	249–346	273–375	299–404	325–435	352–467	381–499	410–533	441–567	472–603
18	–	7–35	15–51	26–66	37–83	49–101	63–119	77–139	93–159	110–180	127–203	146–226	166–250	187–275	208–302	231–329	255–357	280–386	306–416	333–447	361–479	389–513	419–547	450–582	482–618
19	1–20	7–37	16–53	27–69	38–87	51–105	65–124	80–144	96–165	113–187	131–210	150–234	171–258	192–284	214–311	237–339	262–367	287–397	313–428	340–460	369–492	398–526	428–561	460–596	492–633
20	1–21	7–39	17–55	28–72	40–90	53–109	67–129	83–149	99–171	117–193	135–217	155–241	175–267	197–293	220–320	243–349	268–378	294–408	320–440	348–472	377–505	407–539	437–575	469–611	502–648
21	1–22	8–40	17–58	29–75	41–94	55–113	69–134	85–155	102–177	120–200	139–224	159–249	180–275	202–302	225–330	249–359	274–389	301–419	328–451	356–484	385–518	415–553	446–589	479–625	512–663
22	1–23	8–42	18–60	30–78	43–97	57–117	72–138	88–160	105–183	123–207	143–231	163–257	185–283	207–311	231–339	255–369	281–399	307–431	335–463	364–496	393–531	424–566	455–603	488–640	522–678
23	1–24	8–44	19–62	31–81	44–101	58–122	74–143	90–166	108–189	127–213	147–238	168–264	189–292	212–320	236–349	261–379	287–410	314–442	342–475	371–509	401–544	432–580	465–616	498–654	532–693
24	1–25	9–45	19–65	32–84	45–105	60–126	76–148	93–171	111–195	130–220	151–245	172–272	194–300	218–328	242–358	267–389	294–420	321–453	350–486	379–521	410–556	441–593	474–630	507–669	542–708
25	1–26	9–47	20–67	33–87	47–108	62–130	78–153	96–176	114–201	134–226	155–252	176–280	199–308	223–337	248–367	273–399	300–431	328–464	357–498	387–533	418–569	450–606	483–644	517–683	552–723
26	1–27	9–49	21–69	34–90	48–112	64–134	81–157	98–182	117–207	137–233	158–260	181–287	204–316	228–346	253–377	279–409	307–441	335–475	364–510	395–545	426–582	458–620	492–658	526–698	562–738
27	1–28	10–50	21–72	35–93	50–115	66–138	83–162	101–187	120–213	141–239	162–267	185–295	208–325	233–355	259–386	285–419	313–452	342–486	372–521	402–558	434–595	467–633	501–672	536–712	572–753
28	1–29	10–52	22–74	36–96	51–119	67–143	85–167	104–192	123–219	144–246	166–274	189–303	213–333	238–364	264–396	292–428	320–462	349–497	379–533	410–570	443–607	476–646	510–686	545–727	582–768
29	1–30	10–54	23–76	37–99	53–122	69–147	87–172	106–198	127–224	148–252	170–281	194–310	218–341	243–373	270–405	298–438	326–473	356–508	386–545	418–582	451–620	484–660	519–700	555–741	592–783
30	1–31	10–56	23–79	38–102	54–126	71–151	89–177	109–203	130–230	151–259	174–288	198–318	223–349	249–381	276–414	304–448	333–483	363–519	394–556	426–594	459–633	493–673	528–714	564–756	602–798
31	1–32	11–57	24–81	39–105	55–130	73–155	92–181	112–208	133–236	155–265	178–295	202–326	227–358	254–390	281–424	310–458	339–494	370–530	401–568	434–606	467–646	502–686	537–728	574–770	612–813
32	1–33	11–59	25–83	40–108	57–133	75–159	94–186	114–214	136–242	158–272	182–302	206–334	232–366	259–399	287–433	316–468	346–504	377–541	408–580	441–619	475–659	510–700	547–741	584–784	622–828
33	1–34	11–61	25–86	41–111	58–137	77–163	96–191	117–219	139–248	162–278	186–309	211–341	237–374	264–408	292–443	322–478	352–515	383–553	416–591	449–631	484–671	519–713	556–755	593–799	632–843
34	1–35	12–62	26–88	42–114	60–140	78–168	98–196	120–224	142–254	165–285	190–316	215–349	242–382	269–417	298–452	328–488	359–525	390–564	423–603	457–643	492–684	528–726	565–769	603–813	642–858
35	1–36	12–64	27–90	43–117	61–144	80–172	101–200	122–230	145–260	169–291	194–323	219–357	247–390	275–425	304–461	334–498	365–536	397–575	431–614	465–655	500–697	537–739	574–783	612–828	652–873
36	1–37	12–66	27–93	44–120	63–147	82–176	103–205	125–235	148–266	172–298	197–331	224–364	251–399	280–434	309–471	340–508	372–546	404–586	438–626	473–667	508–710	545–753	583–797	622–842	662–888
37	1–38	13–67	28–95	45–123	64–151	84–180	105–210	127–241	151–272	176–304	201–338	228–372	256–407	285–443	315–480	346–518	378–557	411–597	445–638	481–679	517–722	554–766	592–811	631–857	672–903
38	1–39	13–69	29–97	46–126	65–155	86–184	107–215	130–246	154–278	179–311	205–345	232–380	261–415	290–452	321–489	352–528	385–567	418–608	453–649	488–692	525–735	563–779	601–825	641–871	682–918
39	2–39	13–71	29–100	48–128	67–158	88–188	110–219	133–251	157–284	183–317	209–352	237–387	266–423	295–461	326–499	358–538	391–578	425–619	460–661	496–704	533–748	571–793	611–838	651–885	692–933
40	2–40	14–72	30–102	49–131	68–162	89–193	112–224	135–257	160–290	186–324	213–359	241–395	270–432	301–469	332–508	364–548	398–588	432–630	468–672	504–716	542–760	580–806	620–852	660–900	702–948
41	2–41	14–74	31–104	50–134	70–165	91–197	114–229	138–262	163–296	190–330	217–366	245–403	275–440	306–478	337–518	370–558	404–599	439–641	475–684	512–728	550–773	589–819	629–866	670–914	712–963
42	2–42	14–76	31–107	51–137	71–169	93–201	116–234	141–267	166–302	193–337	221–373	250–410	280–448	311–487	343–527	376–568	411–609	446–652	482–696	520–740	558–786	598–832	638–880	680–928	722–978
43	2–43	15–77	32–109	52–140	73–172	95–205	119–238	143–273	169–308	197–343	225–380	254–418	285–456	316–496	349–536	382–578	417–620	453–663	490–707	528–752	566–799	606–846	647–894	689–943	732–993
44	2–44	15–79	33–111	53–143	74–176	97–209	121–243	146–278	172–314	200–350	229–387	259–425	289–465	321–505	354–546	388–588	424–630	460–674	497–719	535–765	575–811	615–859	656–908	699–957	742–1008
45	2–45	15–81	33–114	54–146	75–180	99–213	123–248	149–283	176–319	204–356	233–394	263–433	294–473	327–513	360–555	395–597	430–641	467–685	504–731	543–777	583–824	624–872	666–921	708–972	752–1023
46	2–46	16–82	34–116	55–149	77–183	100–218	125–253	151–289	179–325	207–363	237–401	267–441	299–481	332–522	366–564	401–607	437–651	474–696	512–742	551–789	591–837	632–886	675–935	718–986	762–1038
47	2–47	16–84	35–118	56–152	78–187	102–222	127–258	154–294	182–331	210–370	240–409	272–448	304–489	337–531	371–574	407–617	443–662	481–707	519–754	559–801	599–850	641–899	684–949	728–1000	772–1053
48	2–48	16–86	36–120	57–155	80–190	104–226	130–262	157–299	185–337	214–376	244–416	276–456	308–498	342–540	377–583	413–627	450–672	488–718	527–765	567–813	608–862	650–912	693–963	737–1015	782–1068
49	2–49	16–88	36–123	58–158	81–194	106–230	132–267	159–305	188–343	217–383	248–423	280–464	313–506	347–549	383–592	419–637	456–683	495–729	534–777	575–825	616–875	659–925	702–977	747–1029	792–1083
50	2–50	17–89	37–125	59–161	83–197	108–234	134–272	162–310	191–349	221–389	252–430	285–471	318–514	353–557	388–602	425–647	463–693	502–740	541–789	582–838	624–888	667–939	711–991	756–1044	803–1097

[1] W. SEEWALD, Swiss Federal Institute of Technology, Zurich, 1977.

All values conform to the international convention (i.e. 0,1 instead of 0.1).

Acceptance Region[1] for the Rank Sum T $2\alpha = 0{,}05$

$\mathrm{Prob}(T_l < \boldsymbol{T} < T_r) \geq 1 - 2\alpha$. For explanation see page 228

$2\alpha = 0{,}050$

Each cell gives T_l–T_r.

N_2 \ N_1	1	2	3	4	5	6	7	8	9	10	11	12	13	14	15	16	17	18	19	20	21	22	23	24	25
1	–	–	–	–	–	–	–	–	–	–	–	–	–	–	–	–	–	–	–	–	–	–	–	–	–
2	–	–	–	–	–	–	–	36–52	45–63	55–75	66–88	79–101	92–116	106–132	121–149	137–167	155–185	173–205	192–226	212–248	234–270	256–294	279–319	303–345	328–372
3	–	–	–	–	15–30	22–38	29–48	38–58	47–70	58–82	69–96	82–110	95–126	110–142	125–160	142–178	159–198	178–218	197–240	218–262	239–286	262–310	285–336	310–362	335–390
4	–	–	–	10–26	16–34	23–43	31–53	40–64	49–77	60–90	72–104	85–119	99–135	114–152	130–170	147–189	164–210	183–231	203–253	224–276	246–300	269–325	293–351	317–379	343–407
5	–	–	6–21	11–29	17–38	24–48	33–58	42–70	52–83	63–97	75–112	89–127	103–144	118–162	134–181	151–201	170–221	189–243	209–266	230–290	253–314	276–340	300–367	325–395	352–423
6	–	–	7–23	12–32	18–42	26–52	34–64	44–76	55–89	66–104	79–119	92–136	107–153	122–172	139–191	157–211	175–233	195–255	215–279	237–303	260–328	283–355	308–382	333–411	360–440
7	–	–	7–26	13–35	20–45	27–57	36–69	46–82	57–96	69–111	82–127	96–144	111–162	127–181	144–201	162–222	181–244	201–267	222–291	244–316	267–342	291–369	316–397	342–426	369–456
8	–	3–19	8–28	14–38	21–49	29–61	38–74	49–87	60–102	72–118	85–135	100–152	115–171	131–191	149–211	167–233	187–255	207–279	228–304	251–329	274–356	298–384	324–412	350–442	378–472
9	–	3–21	8–31	14–42	22–53	31–65	40–79	51–93	62–109	75–125	89–142	104–160	119–180	136–200	154–221	173–243	192–267	213–291	235–316	258–342	281–370	306–398	332–427	359–457	387–488
10	–	3–23	9–33	15–45	23–57	32–70	42–84	53–99	65–115	78–132	92–150	107–169	124–188	141–209	159–231	178–254	198–278	219–303	242–328	265–355	289–383	314–412	340–442	367–473	396–504
11	–	3–25	9–36	16–48	24–61	34–74	44–89	55–105	68–121	81–139	96–157	111–177	128–197	145–219	164–241	183–265	204–289	226–314	248–341	272–368	296–397	322–426	349–456	376–488	405–520
12	–	4–26	10–38	17–51	26–64	35–79	46–94	58–110	71–127	84–146	99–165	115–185	132–206	150–228	169–251	189–275	210–300	232–326	255–353	279–381	304–410	330–440	357–471	385–503	414–536
13	–	4–28	10–41	18–54	27–68	37–83	48–99	60–116	73–134	88–152	103–172	119–193	136–215	155–237	174–261	195–285	216–311	238–338	262–365	286–394	311–424	338–454	365–486	394–518	423–552
14	–	4–30	11–43	19–57	28–72	38–88	50–104	62–122	76–140	91–159	106–180	123–201	141–223	160–246	179–271	200–296	222–322	245–349	268–378	293–407	319–437	346–468	374–500	402–534	432–568
15	–	4–32	11–46	20–60	29–76	40–92	52–109	65–127	79–146	94–166	110–187	127–209	145–232	164–256	184–281	206–306	228–333	251–361	275–390	300–420	327–450	354–482	382–515	411–549	442–583
16	–	4–34	12–48	21–63	30–80	42–96	54–114	67–133	82–152	97–173	113–195	131–217	150–240	169–265	190–290	211–317	234–344	257–373	282–402	308–432	334–464	362–496	391–529	420–564	451–599
17	–	5–35	12–51	21–67	32–83	43–101	56–119	70–138	84–159	100–180	117–202	135–225	154–249	174–274	195–300	217–327	240–355	264–384	289–414	315–445	342–477	370–510	399–544	429–579	460–615
18	–	5–37	13–53	22–70	33–87	45–105	58–124	72–144	87–165	103–187	121–209	139–233	158–258	179–283	200–310	222–338	246–366	270–396	296–426	322–458	350–490	378–524	408–558	438–594	470–630
19	–	5–39	13–56	23–73	34–91	46–110	60–129	74–150	90–171	107–193	124–217	143–241	163–266	183–293	205–320	228–348	252–377	277–407	303–438	329–471	357–504	386–538	416–573	447–609	479–646
20	–	5–41	14–58	24–76	35–95	48–114	62–134	77–155	93–177	110–200	128–224	147–249	167–275	188–302	210–330	234–358	258–388	283–419	309–451	337–483	365–517	394–552	425–587	456–624	488–662
21	–	6–42	14–61	25–79	37–98	50–118	64–139	79–161	95–184	113–207	131–232	151–257	171–284	193–311	216–339	239–369	264–399	290–430	316–463	344–496	373–530	403–565	433–602	465–639	498–677
22	–	6–44	15–63	26–82	38–102	51–123	66–144	81–167	98–190	116–214	135–239	155–265	176–292	198–320	221–349	245–379	270–410	296–442	323–475	351–509	381–543	411–579	442–616	474–654	507–693
23	–	6–46	15–66	27–85	39–106	53–127	68–149	84–172	101–196	119–221	139–246	159–273	180–301	203–329	226–359	251–389	276–421	303–453	330–487	359–521	388–557	419–593	451–630	483–669	517–708
24	–	6–48	16–68	27–89	40–110	54–132	70–154	86–178	104–202	122–228	142–254	163–281	185–309	207–339	231–369	256–400	282–432	309–465	337–499	366–534	396–570	427–607	459–645	492–684	526–724
25	–	6–50	16–71	28–92	42–113	56–136	72–159	89–183	107–208	126–234	146–261	167–289	189–318	212–348	237–378	262–410	288–443	316–476	344–511	373–547	404–583	435–621	468–659	501–699	536–739
26	–	7–51	17–73	29–95	43–117	58–140	74–164	91–189	109–215	129–241	149–269	171–297	193–327	217–357	242–388	268–420	294–454	322–488	351–523	381–559	412–596	444–634	476–674	510–714	545–755
27	–	7–53	17–76	30–98	44–121	59–145	76–169	93–195	112–221	132–248	153–276	175–305	198–335	222–366	247–398	273–431	300–465	329–499	358–535	388–572	419–610	452–648	485–688	519–729	555–770
28	–	7–55	18–78	31–101	45–125	61–149	78–174	96–200	115–227	135–255	156–284	179–313	202–344	227–375	252–408	279–441	307–475	335–511	365–547	396–584	427–623	460–662	494–702	528–744	564–786
29	–	7–57	19–80	32–104	47–128	63–153	80–179	98–206	118–233	138–262	160–291	183–321	207–352	232–384	258–417	285–451	313–486	342–522	372–559	403–597	435–636	468–676	502–717	538–758	574–801
30	–	8–58	19–83	33–107	48–132	64–158	82–184	101–211	121–239	142–268	164–298	187–329	211–361	236–394	263–427	290–462	319–497	348–534	379–571	410–610	443–649	476–690	511–731	547–773	583–817
31	–	8–60	20–85	34–110	49–136	66–162	84–189	103–217	123–246	145–275	167–306	191–337	216–369	241–403	268–437	296–472	325–508	355–545	386–583	418–622	451–662	485–703	520–745	556–788	593–832
32	–	8–62	20–88	34–114	50–140	67–167	86–194	105–223	126–252	148–282	171–313	195–345	220–378	246–412	273–447	302–482	331–519	361–557	393–595	425–635	458–676	493–717	528–760	565–803	602–848
33	–	8–64	21–90	35–117	52–143	69–171	88–199	108–228	129–258	151–289	174–321	199–353	224–387	251–421	279–456	307–493	337–530	368–568	400–607	432–648	466–689	501–731	537–774	574–818	612–863
34	–	8–66	21–93	36–120	53–147	71–175	90–204	110–234	132–264	154–296	178–328	203–361	229–395	256–430	284–466	313–503	343–541	374–580	407–619	440–660	474–702	509–745	546–788	583–833	622–878
35	–	9–67	22–95	37–123	54–151	72–180	92–209	113–239	134–271	158–302	182–335	207–369	233–404	261–439	289–476	319–513	349–552	381–591	414–631	447–673	482–715	518–758	554–803	592–848	631–894
36	–	9–69	22–98	38–126	55–155	74–184	94–214	115–245	137–277	161–309	185–343	211–377	238–412	266–448	294–486	324–524	355–563	387–603	421–643	455–685	490–728	526–772	563–817	601–863	641–909
37	–	9–71	23–100	39–129	56–159	76–188	96–219	117–251	140–283	164–316	189–350	215–385	242–421	270–458	300–495	330–534	362–573	394–614	428–655	462–698	498–741	534–786	572–831	611–877	650–925
38	–	9–73	23–103	40–132	58–162	77–193	98–224	120–256	143–289	167–323	193–357	219–393	247–429	275–467	305–505	336–544	368–584	401–625	435–667	469–711	506–754	543–799	581–845	620–892	660–940
39	1–40	10–74	24–105	41–135	59–166	79–197	100–229	122–262	146–295	170–330	196–365	223–401	251–438	280–476	310–515	342–554	374–595	407–637	442–679	477–723	513–768	551–813	589–860	629–907	669–956
40	1–41	10–76	24–108	41–139	60–170	80–202	102–234	125–267	148–302	174–336	200–372	227–409	256–446	285–485	316–524	347–565	380–606	414–648	448–692	484–736	521–781	559–827	598–874	638–922	679–971
41	1–42	10–78	25–110	42–142	61–174	82–206	104–239	127–273	151–308	177–343	203–380	231–417	260–455	290–494	321–534	353–575	386–617	420–660	455–704	492–748	529–794	567–841	607–888	647–937	689–986
42	1–43	10–80	25–113	43–145	63–177	84–210	106–244	129–279	154–314	180–350	207–387	235–425	264–464	295–503	326–544	359–585	392–628	427–671	462–716	499–761	537–807	576–854	615–903	656–952	698–1002
43	1–44	10–82	26–115	44–148	64–181	85–215	108–249	132–284	157–320	183–357	211–394	239–433	269–472	300–512	331–554	364–596	398–639	433–683	469–728	507–773	545–820	584–868	624–917	665–967	708–1017
44	1–45	11–83	26–118	45–151	65–185	87–219	110–254	134–290	160–326	186–364	214–402	243–441	273–481	304–522	337–563	370–606	404–650	440–694	476–740	514–786	553–833	592–882	633–931	675–981	717–1033
45	1–46	11–85	27–120	46–154	66–189	88–224	112–259	137–295	162–333	190–370	218–409	247–449	278–489	309–531	342–573	376–616	411–660	447–705	483–752	521–799	560–847	601–895	642–945	684–996	727–1048
46	1–47	11–87	28–122	47–157	68–192	90–228	114–264	139–301	165–339	193–377	221–417	251–457	282–498	314–540	347–583	382–626	417–671	453–717	490–764	529–811	568–860	609–909	650–960	693–1011	737–1063
47	1–48	11–89	28–125	48–160	69–196	92–232	116–269	141–307	168–345	196–384	225–424	255–465	287–506	319–549	353–592	387–637	423–682	460–728	497–776	536–824	576–873	617–923	659–974	702–1026	746–1079
48	1–49	12–90	29–127	49–163	70–200	93–237	118–274	144–312	171–351	199–391	229–431	259–473	291–515	324–558	358–602	393–647	429–693	466–740	504–788	544–836	584–886	625–937	668–988	711–1041	756–1094
49	1–50	12–92	29–130	49–167	71–204	95–241	120–279	146–318	174–357	202–398	232–439	263–481	296–523	329–567	363–612	399–657	435–704	473–751	511–800	551–849	592–899	634–950	677–1002	720–1056	765–1110
50	1–51	12–94	30–132	50–170	73–207	97–245	122–284	149–323	176–364	206–404	236–446	267–489	300–532	334–576	369–621	404–668	441–715	479–763	518–812	559–861	600–912	642–964	685–1017	730–1070	775–1125

[1] W. SEEWALD, Swiss Federal Institute of Technology, Zurich, 1977.

All values conform to the international convention (i.e. 0,1 instead of 0.1).

Acceptance Region[1] for the Rank Sum T $2\alpha = 0{,}02$ (Wilcoxon 2-Sample Test)

$\text{Prob}(T_l < \boldsymbol{T} < T_r) \geq 1 - 2\alpha$. For explanation see page 228

$2\alpha = 0{,}020$

N_1	1	2	3	4	5	6	7	8	9	10	11	12	13	14	15	16	17	18	19	20	21	22	23	24	25
N_2	T_l T_r	T_l T_r	T_l T_r	T_l T_r	T_l T_r	T_l T_r	T_l T_r	T_l T_r	T_l T_r	T_l T_r	T_l T_r	T_l T_r	T_l T_r	T_l T_r	T_l T_r	T_l T_r	T_l T_r	T_l T_r	T_l T_r	T_l T_r	T_l T_r	T_l T_r	T_l T_r	T_l T_r	T_l T_r
1	–	–	–	–	–	–	–	–	–	–	–	–	–	–	–	–	–	–	–	–	–	–	–	–	–
2	–	–	–	–	–	–	–	–	–	–	–	–	91–117	105–133	120–150	136–168	153–187	171–207	191–227	211–249	232–272	254–296	277–321	301–347	326–374
3	–	–	–	–	–	–	28–49	36–60	46–71	56–84	67–98	80–112	93–128	107–145	123–162	139–181	157–200	175–221	194–243	215–265	236–289	259–313	282–339	306–366	332–393
4	–	–	–	–	15–35	22–44	29–55	38–66	48–78	58–92	70–106	83–121	96–138	111–155	127–173	143–193	161–213	180–234	199–257	220–280	242–304	264–330	288–356	313–383	338–412
5	–	–	–	10–30	16–39	23–49	31–60	40–72	50–85	61–99	73–114	86–130	100–147	115–165	131–184	148–204	166–225	185–247	205–270	226–294	248–319	271–345	295–372	320–400	346–429
6	–	–	–	11–33	17–43	24–54	32–66	42–78	52–92	63–107	75–123	89–139	103–157	118–176	135–195	152–216	171–237	190–260	210–284	232–308	254–334	277–361	302–388	327–417	354–446
7	–	–	6–27	11–37	18–47	25–59	34–71	43–85	54–99	66–114	78–131	92–148	107–166	122–186	139–206	157–227	176–249	195–273	216–297	238–322	261–348	284–376	309–404	335–433	361–464
8	–	–	6–30	12–40	19–51	27–63	35–77	45–91	56–106	68–122	81–139	95–157	111–175	127–195	144–216	162–238	181–261	201–285	222–310	244–336	267–363	291–391	316–420	342–450	370–480
9	–	–	7–32	13–43	20–55	28–68	37–82	47–97	59–112	71–129	84–147	99–165	114–185	131–205	148–227	167–249	186–273	207–297	228–323	250–350	274–377	298–406	324–435	350–466	378–497
10	–	–	7–35	13–47	21–59	29–73	39–87	49–103	61–119	74–136	88–154	102–174	118–194	135–215	153–237	172–260	191–285	212–310	234–336	257–363	281–391	306–420	331–451	358–482	386–514
11	–	–	7–38	14–50	22–63	30–78	40–93	51–109	63–126	77–143	91–162	106–182	122–203	139–225	157–248	177–271	197–296	218–322	240–349	263–377	288–405	313–435	339–466	366–498	395–530
12	–	–	8–40	15–53	23–67	32–82	42–98	53–115	66–132	79–151	94–170	109–191	126–212	143–235	162–258	182–282	202–308	224–334	246–362	270–390	295–419	320–450	347–481	375–513	403–547
13	–	3–29	8–43	15–57	24–71	33–87	44–103	56–120	68–139	82–158	97–178	113–199	130–221	148–244	167–268	187–293	208–319	230–346	253–374	277–403	302–433	328–464	355–496	383–529	412–563
14	–	3–31	8–46	16–60	25–75	34–92	45–109	58–126	71–145	85–165	100–186	116–208	134–230	152–254	171–279	192–304	213–331	236–358	259–387	283–417	309–447	335–479	363–511	391–545	420–580
15	–	3–33	9–48	17–63	26–79	36–96	47–114	60–132	73–152	88–172	103–194	120–216	138–239	156–264	176–289	197–315	219–342	241–371	265–400	290–430	316–461	343–493	370–527	399–561	429–596
16	–	3–35	9–51	17–67	27–83	37–101	49–119	62–138	76–158	91–179	107–201	124–224	142–248	161–273	181–299	202–326	224–354	247–383	272–412	297–443	323–475	350–508	378–542	408–576	438–612
17	–	3–37	10–53	18–70	28–87	39–105	51–124	64–144	78–165	93–187	110–209	127–233	146–257	165–283	186–309	207–337	230–365	253–395	278–425	303–457	330–489	358–522	386–557	416–592	447–628
18	–	3–39	10–56	19–73	29–91	40–110	52–130	66–150	81–171	96–194	113–217	131–241	150–266	170–292	190–320	212–348	235–377	259–407	284–438	310–470	337–503	365–537	394–572	424–608	455–645
19	–	4–40	10–59	19–77	30–95	41–115	54–135	68–156	83–178	99–201	116–225	134–250	154–275	174–302	195–330	218–358	241–388	265–419	291–450	317–483	344–517	373–551	402–587	433–623	464–661
20	–	4–42	11–61	20–80	31–99	43–119	56–140	70–162	85–185	102–208	119–233	138–258	158–284	178–312	200–340	223–369	246–400	271–431	297–463	324–496	352–530	380–566	410–602	441–639	473–677
21	–	4–44	11–64	21–83	32–103	44–124	58–145	72–168	88–191	105–215	123–240	142–266	162–293	183–321	205–350	228–380	252–411	277–443	303–476	331–509	359–544	388–580	418–617	450–654	482–693
22	–	4–46	12–66	21–87	33–107	45–129	59–151	74–174	90–198	108–222	126–248	145–275	166–302	187–331	210–360	233–391	258–422	283–455	310–488	337–523	366–558	396–594	426–632	458–670	491–709
23	–	4–48	12–69	22–90	34–111	47–133	61–156	76–180	93–204	110–230	129–256	149–283	170–311	192–340	214–371	238–402	263–434	289–467	316–501	344–536	373–572	403–609	434–647	467–685	500–725
24	–	4–50	12–72	23–93	35–115	48–138	63–161	78–186	95–211	113–237	132–264	153–291	174–320	196–350	219–381	244–412	269–445	295–479	323–513	351–549	381–585	411–623	443–661	475–701	509–741
25	–	4–52	13–74	23–97	36–119	50–142	64–167	81–191	98–217	116–244	136–271	156–300	178–329	200–360	224–391	249–423	275–456	301–491	329–526	358–562	388–599	419–637	451–676	484–716	517–758
26	–	4–54	13–77	24–100	37–123	51–147	66–172	83–197	100–224	119–251	139–279	160–308	182–338	205–369	229–401	254–434	280–468	307–503	336–538	365–575	395–613	426–652	459–691	492–732	526–774
27	–	5–55	13–80	25–103	38–127	52–152	68–177	85–203	103–230	122–258	142–287	163–317	186–347	209–379	234–411	259–445	286–479	313–515	342–551	372–588	402–627	434–666	467–706	501–747	535–790
28	–	5–57	14–82	26–106	39–131	54–156	70–182	87–209	105–237	125–265	145–295	167–325	190–356	214–388	239–421	265–455	292–490	320–526	349–563	379–601	410–640	442–680	475–721	509–763	544–806
29	–	5–59	14–85	26–110	40–135	55–161	71–188	89–215	108–243	128–272	149–302	171–333	194–365	218–398	243–432	270–466	297–502	326–538	355–576	386–614	417–654	450–694	483–736	518–778	553–822
30	–	5–61	15–87	27–113	41–139	56–166	73–193	91–221	110–250	131–279	152–310	174–342	198–374	223–407	248–442	275–477	303–513	332–550	362–588	392–628	424–668	457–709	491–751	526–794	562–838
31	–	5–63	15–90	28–116	42–143	58–170	75–198	93–227	113–256	133–287	155–318	178–350	202–383	227–417	253–452	280–488	309–524	338–562	368–601	399–641	432–681	465–723	499–766	535–809	571–854
32	–	5–65	15–93	28–120	43–147	59–175	77–203	95–233	115–263	136–294	158–326	182–358	206–392	232–426	258–462	286–498	314–536	344–574	375–613	406–654	439–695	473–737	508–780	543–825	580–870
33	–	5–67	16–95	29–123	44–151	61–179	78–209	97–239	118–269	139–301	162–333	185–367	210–401	236–436	263–472	291–509	320–547	350–586	381–626	413–667	446–709	481–751	516–795	552–840	589–886
34	–	6–68	16–98	30–126	45–155	62–184	80–214	100–244	120–276	142–308	165–341	189–375	214–410	240–446	268–482	296–520	326–558	356–598	388–638	420–680	454–722	488–766	524–810	561–855	598–902
35	–	6–70	17–100	30–130	46–159	63–189	82–219	102–250	123–282	145–315	168–349	193–383	218–419	245–455	273–492	301–531	331–570	362–610	394–651	427–693	461–736	496–780	532–825	569–871	607–918
36	–	6–72	17–103	31–133	47–163	65–193	84–224	104–256	125–289	148–322	172–356	196–392	222–428	249–465	278–502	307–541	337–581	368–622	401–663	434–706	468–750	504–794	540–840	578–886	616–934
37	–	6–74	17–106	32–136	48–167	66–198	85–230	106–262	128–295	151–329	175–364	200–400	226–437	254–474	282–513	312–552	343–592	374–634	407–676	441–719	476–763	512–808	549–854	586–902	625–950
38	–	6–76	18–108	32–140	49–171	67–203	87–235	108–268	130–302	154–336	178–372	204–408	230–446	258–484	287–523	317–563	348–604	380–646	414–688	448–732	483–777	519–823	557–869	595–917	634–966
39	–	6–78	18–111	33–143	50–175	69–207	89–240	110–274	133–308	156–344	181–380	207–417	235–454	263–493	292–533	323–573	354–615	387–657	420–701	455–745	490–791	527–837	565–884	604–932	643–982
40	–	6–80	19–113	34–146	51–179	70–212	91–245	112–280	135–315	159–351	185–387	211–425	239–463	267–503	297–543	328–584	360–626	393–669	427–713	462–758	498–804	535–851	573–899	612–948	653–997
41	–	7–81	19–116	35–149	52–183	72–216	92–251	114–286	138–321	162–358	188–395	215–433	243–472	272–512	302–553	333–595	365–638	399–681	433–726	469–771	505–818	543–865	581–914	621–963	662–1013
42	–	7–83	19–119	35–153	53–187	73–221	94–256	117–291	140–328	165–365	191–403	218–442	247–481	276–522	307–563	338–606	371–649	405–693	440–738	476–784	513–831	551–879	590–928	630–978	671–1029
43	–	7–85	20–121	36–156	54–191	74–226	96–261	119–297	143–334	168–372	194–411	222–450	251–490	281–531	312–573	344–616	377–660	411–705	446–751	483–797	520–845	558–894	598–943	638–994	680–1045
44	–	7–87	20–124	37–159	55–195	76–230	98–266	121–303	145–341	171–379	198–418	226–458	255–499	285–541	317–583	349–627	383–671	417–717	453–763	490–810	527–859	566–908	606–958	647–1009	689–1061
45	–	7–89	20–127	37–163	56–199	77–235	99–272	123–309	148–347	174–386	201–426	229–467	259–508	290–550	321–594	354–638	388–683	423–729	459–776	496–824	535–872	574–922	614–973	655–1025	698–1077
46	–	7–91	21–129	38–166	57–203	79–239	101–277	125–315	150–354	177–393	204–434	233–475	263–517	294–560	326–604	360–648	394–694	429–741	466–788	503–837	542–886	582–936	622–988	664–1040	707–1093
47	–	7–93	21–132	39–169	59–206	80–244	103–282	127–321	153–360	180–400	208–441	237–483	267–526	299–569	331–614	365–659	400–705	436–752	472–801	510–850	549–900	589–951	631–1002	673–1055	716–1109
48	–	8–94	22–134	39–173	60–210	81–249	105–287	129–327	155–367	182–408	211–449	240–492	271–535	303–579	336–624	370–670	405–717	442–764	479–813	517–863	557–913	597–965	639–1017	681–1071	725–1125
49	–	8–96	22–137	40–176	61–214	83–253	106–293	131–333	158–373	185–415	214–457	244–500	275–544	308–588	341–634	376–680	411–728	448–776	486–825	524–876	564–927	605–979	647–1032	690–1086	734–1141
50	–	8–98	22–140	41–179	62–218	84–258	108–298	134–338	160–380	188–422	217–465	248–508	279–553	312–598	346–644	381–691	417–739	454–788	492–838	531–889	572–940	613–993	655–1047	699–1101	743–1157

[1] W. Seewald, Swiss Federal Institute of Technology, Zurich, 1977.

All values conform to the international convention (i.e. 0,1 instead of 0.1).

Charts for Sequential Analysis Based on Paired Differences

For method of use, see *Geigy Scientific Tables*, 8th ed., Volume 2, 'Introduction to Statistics' (1982), page 235; from Bross, I., *Biometrics*, **8**, 188 (1952), reproduced by kind permission of the author and publishers

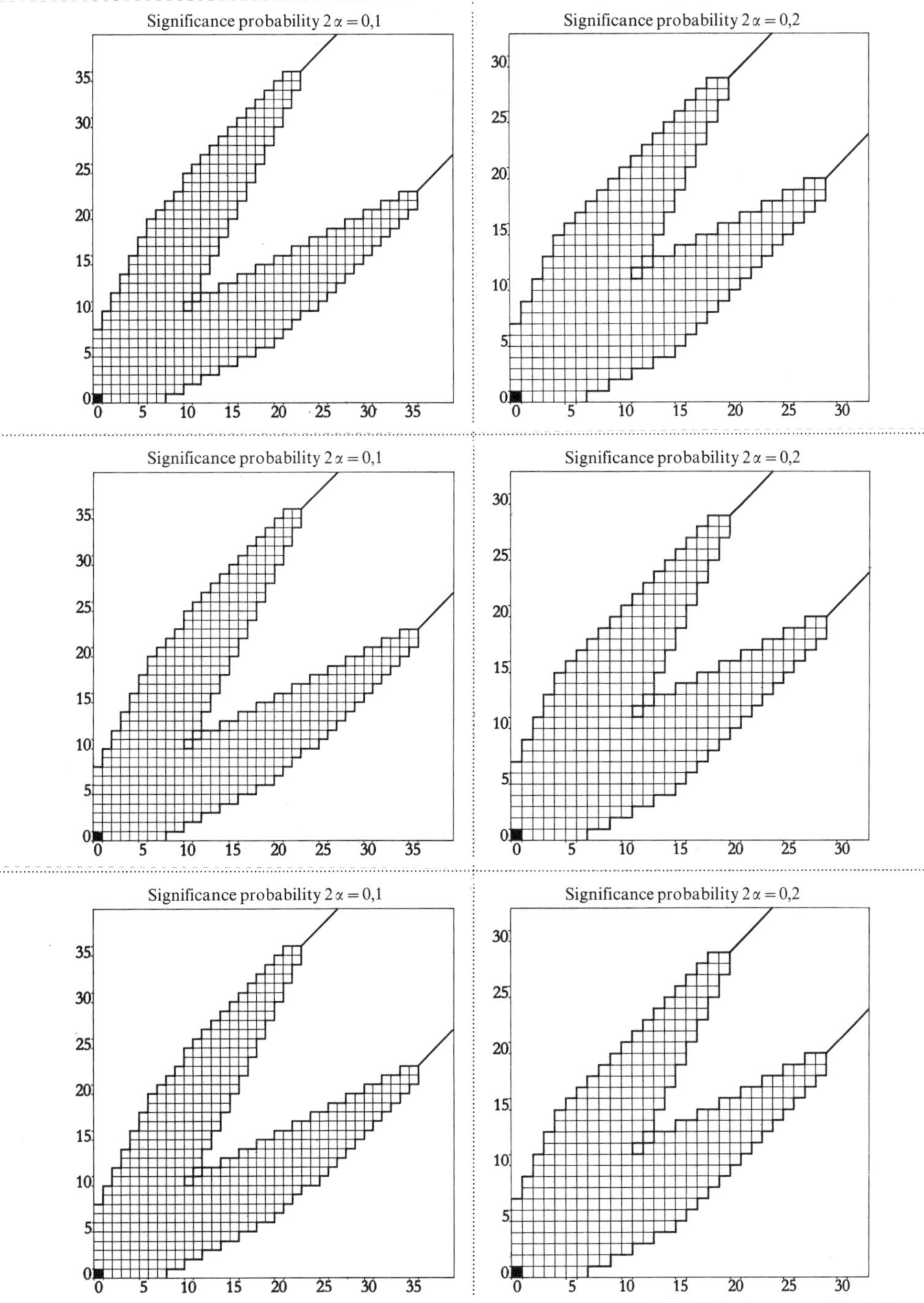

Acceptance Region[7] for the Rank Sum T $2\alpha = 0{,}01$

$\mathrm{Prob}(T_l < \boldsymbol{T} < T_r) \geq 1 - 2\alpha$. For explanation see page 228

$2\alpha = 0{,}010$

N_2 \ N_1	1	2	3	4	5	6	7	8	9	10	11	12	13	14	15	16	17	18	19	20	21	22	23	24	25
	T_l T_r	T_l T_r	T_l T_r	T_l T_r	T_l T_r	T_l T_r	T_l T_r	T_l T_r	T_l T_r	T_l T_r	T_l T_r	T_l T_r	T_l T_r	T_l T_r	T_l T_r	T_l T_r	T_l T_r	T_l T_r	T_l T_r	T_l T_r	T_l T_r	T_l T_r	T_l T_r	T_l T_r	T_l T_r
1	–	–	–	–	–	–	–	–	–	–	–	–	–	–	–	–	–	–	–	–	–	–	–	–	–
2	–	–	–	–	–	–	–	–	–	–	–	–	–	–	–	–	–	–	190–228	210–250	231–273	253–297	276–322	300–348	325–375
3	–	–	–	–	–	–	–	–	45–72	55–85	66–99	79–113	92–129	106–146	122–163	138–182	155–202	173–223	193–244	213–267	234–291	257–315	280–341	304–368	330–395
4	–	–	–	–	–	21–45	28–56	37–67	46–80	57–93	68–108	81–123	94–140	109–157	125–175	141–195	159–215	177–237	197–259	218–282	239–307	262–332	285–359	310–386	335–415
5	–	–	–	–	15–40	22–50	29–62	38–74	48–87	59–101	71–116	84–132	98–149	112–168	128–187	145–207	163–228	182–250	202–273	223–297	245–322	267–349	291–376	316–404	342–433
6	–	–	–	10–34	16–44	23–55	31–67	40–80	50–94	61–109	73–125	87–141	101–159	116–178	132–198	149–219	168–240	187–263	207–287	228–312	250–338	274–364	298–392	323–421	349–451
7	–	–	–	10–38	16–49	24–60	32–73	42–86	52–101	64–116	76–133	90–150	104–169	120–188	136–209	154–230	172–253	192–276	212–301	234–326	256–353	280–380	305–408	330–438	357–468
8	–	–	–	11–41	17–53	25–65	34–78	43–93	54–108	66–124	79–141	93–159	108–178	123–199	140–220	158–242	177–265	197–289	218–314	240–340	263–367	287–395	311–425	337–455	364–486
9	–	–	6–33	11–45	18–57	26–70	35–84	45–99	56–115	68–132	82–149	96–168	111–188	127–209	144–231	163–253	182–277	202–302	223–328	246–354	269–382	293–411	319–440	345–471	372–503
10	–	–	6–36	12–48	19–61	27–75	37–89	47–105	58–122	71–139	84–158	99–177	115–197	131–219	149–241	167–265	187–289	208–314	229–341	252–368	275–397	300–426	326–456	352–488	380–520
11	–	–	6–39	12–52	20–65	28–80	38–95	49–111	61–128	73–147	87–166	102–186	118–207	135–229	153–252	172–276	192–301	213–327	235–354	258–382	282–411	307–441	333–472	360–504	388–537
12	–	–	7–41	13–55	21–69	30–84	40–100	51–117	63–135	76–154	90–174	105–195	122–216	139–239	157–263	177–287	197–313	218–340	241–367	264–396	289–425	314–456	340–488	368–520	396–554
13	–	–	7–44	13–59	22–73	31–89	41–106	53–123	65–142	79–161	93–182	109–203	125–226	143–249	162–273	181–299	202–325	224–352	247–380	270–410	295–440	321–471	348–503	375–537	404–571
14	–	–	7–47	14–62	22–78	32–94	43–111	54–130	67–149	81–169	96–190	112–212	129–235	147–259	166–284	186–310	207–337	229–365	253–393	277–423	302–454	328–486	355–519	383–553	412–588
15	–	–	8–49	15–65	23–82	33–99	44–117	56–136	69–156	84–176	99–198	115–221	133–244	151–269	171–294	191–321	213–348	235–377	259–406	283–437	309–468	335–501	363–534	391–569	421–604
16	–	–	8–52	15–69	24–86	34–104	46–122	58–142	72–162	86–184	102–206	119–229	136–254	155–279	175–305	196–332	218–360	241–389	264–420	289–451	315–483	342–516	370–550	399–585	429–621
17	–	–	8–55	16–72	25–90	36–108	47–128	60–148	74–169	89–191	105–214	122–238	140–263	159–289	180–315	201–343	223–372	246–402	271–432	296–464	322–497	349–531	378–565	407–601	437–638
18	–	–	8–58	16–76	26–94	37–113	49–133	62–154	76–176	92–198	108–222	125–247	144–272	163–299	184–326	206–354	228–384	252–414	277–445	302–478	329–511	357–545	385–581	415–617	446–654
19	–	3–41	9–60	17–79	27–98	38–118	50–139	64–160	78–183	94–206	111–230	129–255	148–281	168–308	189–336	210–366	234–395	258–426	283–458	309–491	336–525	364–560	393–596	423–633	454–671
20	–	3–43	9–63	18–82	28–102	39–123	52–144	66–166	81–189	97–213	114–238	132–264	151–291	172–318	193–347	215–377	239–407	263–439	289–471	315–505	343–539	371–575	401–611	431–649	463–687
21	–	3–45	9–66	18–86	29–106	40–128	53–150	68–172	83–196	99–221	117–246	136–272	155–300	176–328	198–357	220–388	244–419	269–451	295–484	322–518	349–554	378–590	408–627	439–665	471–704
22	–	3–47	10–68	19–89	29–111	42–132	55–155	70–178	85–203	102–228	120–254	139–281	159–309	180–338	202–368	225–399	249–431	275–463	301–497	328–532	356–568	386–604	416–642	447–681	480–720
23	–	3–49	10–71	19–93	30–115	43–137	57–160	71–185	88–209	105–235	123–262	142–290	163–318	184–348	207–378	230–410	255–442	280–476	307–510	335–545	363–582	393–619	424–657	455–697	488–737
24	–	3–51	10–74	20–96	31–119	44–142	58–166	73–191	90–216	107–243	126–270	146–298	166–328	188–358	211–389	235–421	260–454	286–488	313–523	341–559	370–596	400–634	431–673	464–712	497–753
25	–	3–53	11–76	20–100	32–123	45–147	60–171	75–197	92–223	110–250	129–278	149–307	170–337	192–368	216–399	240–432	265–466	292–500	319–536	348–572	377–610	408–648	439–688	472–728	505–770
26	–	3–55	11–79	21–103	33–127	46–152	61–177	77–203	94–230	113–257	132–286	152–316	174–346	197–377	220–410	245–443	271–477	298–512	325–549	354–586	384–624	415–663	447–703	480–744	514–786
27	–	4–56	11–82	22–106	34–131	48–156	63–182	79–209	97–236	115–265	135–294	156–324	178–355	201–387	225–420	250–454	276–489	303–525	332–561	361–599	391–638	422–678	455–718	488–760	522–803
28	–	4–58	11–85	22–110	35–135	49–161	64–188	81–215	99–243	118–272	138–302	159–333	182–364	205–397	229–431	255–465	281–501	309–537	338–574	367–613	398–652	430–692	462–734	496–776	531–819
29	–	4–60	12–87	23–113	36–139	50–166	66–193	83–221	101–250	121–279	141–310	163–341	185–374	209–407	234–441	260–476	287–512	315–549	344–587	374–626	405–666	437–707	470–749	504–792	540–835
30	–	4–62	12–90	23–117	37–143	51–171	68–198	85–227	103–257	123–287	144–318	166–350	189–383	213–417	239–451	265–487	292–524	321–561	350–600	380–640	412–680	444–722	478–764	513–807	548–852
31	–	4–64	12–93	24–120	37–148	53–175	69–204	87–233	106–263	126–294	147–326	170–358	193–392	218–426	243–462	270–498	298–535	326–574	356–613	387–653	419–694	452–736	486–779	521–823	557–868
32	–	4–66	13–95	24–124	38–152	54–180	71–209	89–239	108–270	129–301	150–334	173–367	197–401	222–436	248–472	275–509	303–547	332–586	362–626	394–666	426–708	459–751	494–794	529–839	565–885
33	–	4–68	13–98	25–127	39–156	55–185	72–215	91–245	110–277	131–309	153–342	176–376	201–410	226–446	252–483	280–520	308–559	338–598	369–638	400–680	433–722	467–765	501–810	537–855	574–901
34	–	4–70	13–101	26–130	40–160	56–190	74–220	93–251	113–283	134–316	156–350	180–384	204–420	230–456	257–493	285–531	314–570	344–610	375–651	407–693	440–736	474–780	509–825	545–871	583–917
35	–	4–72	14–103	26–134	41–164	58–194	75–226	95–257	115–290	137–323	159–358	183–393	208–429	234–466	262–503	290–542	319–582	350–622	381–664	413–707	447–750	482–794	517–840	554–886	591–934
36	–	4–74	14–106	27–137	42–168	59–199	77–231	96–264	117–297	139–331	162–366	187–401	212–438	239–475	266–514	295–553	325–593	355–635	387–677	420–720	454–764	489–809	525–855	562–902	600–950
37	–	4–76	14–109	27–141	43–172	60–204	79–236	98–270	120–303	142–338	165–374	190–410	216–447	243–485	271–524	300–564	330–605	361–647	393–690	427–733	461–778	496–824	533–870	570–918	609–966
38	–	4–78	15–111	28–144	44–176	61–209	80–242	100–276	122–310	145–345	168–382	194–418	220–456	247–495	275–535	305–575	335–617	367–659	400–702	433–747	468–792	504–838	541–885	578–934	617–983
39	–	5–79	15–114	29–147	45–180	62–214	82–247	102–282	124–317	147–353	172–389	197–427	224–465	251–505	280–545	310–586	341–628	373–671	406–715	440–760	475–806	511–853	548–901	587–949	626–999
40	–	5–81	15–117	29–151	46–184	64–218	83–253	104–288	126–324	150–360	175–397	200–436	227–475	255–515	285–555	315–597	346–640	379–683	412–728	447–773	482–820	519–867	556–916	595–965	635–1015
41	–	5–83	15–120	30–154	46–189	65–223	85–258	106–294	129–330	153–367	178–405	204–444	231–484	260–524	289–566	320–608	352–651	384–696	418–741	453–787	489–834	526–882	564–931	603–981	643–1032
42	–	5–85	16–122	30–158	47–193	66–228	86–264	108–300	131–337	155–375	181–413	207–453	235–493	264–534	294–576	325–619	357–663	390–708	424–754	460–800	496–848	534–896	572–946	612–996	652–1048
43	–	5–87	16–125	31–161	48–197	67–233	88–269	110–306	133–344	158–382	184–421	211–461	239–502	268–544	298–587	330–630	362–675	396–720	431–766	466–814	503–862	541–911	580–961	620–1012	661–1064
44	–	5–89	16–128	31–165	49–201	69–237	90–274	112–312	136–350	161–389	187–429	214–470	243–511	272–554	303–597	335–641	368–686	402–732	437–779	473–827	510–876	549–925	588–976	628–1028	670–1080
45	–	5–91	17–130	32–168	50–205	70–242	91–280	114–318	138–357	163–397	190–437	218–478	246–521	277–563	308–607	340–652	373–698	408–744	443–792	480–840	517–890	556–940	596–991	636–1044	678–1097
46	–	5–93	17–133	33–171	51–209	71–247	93–285	116–324	140–364	166–404	193–445	221–487	250–530	281–573	312–618	345–663	379–709	413–757	449–805	486–854	524–904	563–955	604–1006	645–1059	687–1113
47	–	5–95	17–136	33–175	52–213	72–252	94–291	118–330	143–370	169–411	196–453	224–496	254–539	285–583	317–628	350–674	384–721	419–769	456–817	493–867	531–918	571–969	611–1022	653–1075	696–1129
48	–	6–96	18–138	34–178	53–217	74–256	96–296	120–336	145–377	171–419	199–461	228–504	258–548	289–593	322–638	355–685	390–732	425–781	462–830	500–880	538–932	578–984	619–1037	661–1091	704–1146
49	–	6–98	18–141	34–182	54–221	75–261	97–302	122–342	147–384	174–426	202–469	231–513	262–557	293–603	326–649	360–696	395–744	431–793	468–843	506–894	546–945	586–998	627–1052	670–1106	713–1162
50	–	6–100	18–144	35–185	55–225	76–266	99–307	124–348	149–391	177–433	205–477	235–521	266–566	298–612	331–659	365–707	400–756	437–805	474–856	513–907	553–959	593–1013	635–1067	678–1122	722–1178

[7] W. SEEWALD, Swiss Federal Institute of Technology, Zurich, 1977.

All values conform to the international convention (i.e. 0,1 instead of 0.1).

Acceptance Region[1] for the Rank Sum T $2\alpha = 0{,}005$ (Wilcoxon 2-Sample Test)

$\mathrm{Prob}(T_l < \boldsymbol{T} < T_r) \geq 1 - 2\alpha$. For explanation see page 228

$2\alpha = 0{,}005$

N_2 \ N_1 (T_l–T_r)	1	2	3	4	5	6	7	8	9	10	11	12	13	14	15	16	17	18	19	20	21	22	23	24	25
1	–	–	–	–	–	–	–	–	–	–	–	–	–	–	–	–	–	–	–	–	–	–	–	–	–
2	–	–	–	–	–	–	–	–	–	–	–	–	–	–	–	–	–	–	–	–	–	–	–	–	–
3	–	–	–	–	–	–	–	–	–	–	–	78–114	91–130	105–147	121–164	137–183	154–203	172–224	191–246	212–268	233–292	255–317	278–343	303–369	328–397
4	–	–	–	–	–	–	–	36–68	45–81	56–94	67–109	80–124	93–141	108–158	123–177	140–196	157–217	176–238	195–261	215–285	237–309	259–335	283–361	307–389	333–417
5	–	–	–	–	–	21–51	28–63	37–75	47–88	58–102	69–118	82–134	96–151	111–169	126–189	143–209	161–230	180–252	199–276	220–300	242–325	265–351	288–379	313–407	339–436
6	–	–	–	–	15–45	22–56	30–68	39–81	49–95	60–110	72–126	85–143	99–161	114–180	130–200	147–221	165–243	184–266	204–290	225–315	247–341	270–368	294–396	319–425	345–455
7	–	–	–	–	15–50	23–61	31–74	40–88	50–103	62–118	74–135	87–153	102–171	117–191	133–212	151–233	169–256	189–279	209–304	230–330	253–356	276–384	301–412	326–442	352–473
8	–	–	–	10–42	16–54	24–66	32–80	42–94	52–110	64–126	77–143	90–162	105–181	121–201	137–223	155–245	174–268	193–293	214–318	236–344	259–371	282–400	307–429	333–459	360–490
9	–	–	–	10–46	17–58	25–71	33–86	43–101	54–117	66–134	79–152	93–171	108–191	124–212	141–234	159–257	178–281	198–306	219–332	241–359	265–386	289–415	314–445	340–476	367–508
10	–	–	–	11–49	18–62	26–76	35–91	45–107	56–124	68–142	82–160	96–180	111–201	128–222	145–245	163–269	183–293	203–319	225–345	247–373	271–401	295–431	320–462	347–493	374–526
11	–	–	–	11–53	18–67	27–81	36–97	47–113	58–131	71–149	84–169	99–189	115–210	131–233	149–256	168–280	188–305	208–332	230–359	253–387	277–416	302–446	327–478	354–510	382–543
12	–	–	6–42	12–56	19–71	28–86	37–103	48–120	60–138	73–157	87–177	102–198	118–220	135–243	153–267	172–292	192–318	214–344	236–372	259–401	283–431	308–462	334–494	361–527	390–560
13	–	–	6–45	12–60	20–75	29–91	39–108	50–126	62–145	75–165	90–185	105–207	121–230	139–253	157–278	177–303	197–330	219–357	241–386	265–415	289–446	315–477	341–510	369–543	397–578
14	–	–	6–48	13–63	21–79	30–96	40–114	52–132	64–152	78–172	92–194	108–216	125–239	143–263	161–289	181–315	202–342	224–370	247–399	271–429	296–460	321–493	348–526	376–560	405–595
15	–	–	7–50	13–67	21–84	31–101	41–120	53–139	66–159	80–180	95–202	111–225	128–249	146–274	166–299	186–326	207–354	229–383	252–413	277–443	302–475	328–508	356–541	384–576	413–612
16	–	–	7–53	14–70	22–88	32–106	43–125	55–145	68–166	82–188	98–210	114–234	132–258	150–284	170–310	190–338	212–366	235–395	258–426	283–457	308–490	335–523	363–557	391–593	421–629
17	–	–	7–56	14–74	23–92	33–111	44–131	57–151	70–173	85–195	101–218	117–243	135–268	154–294	174–321	195–349	217–378	240–408	264–439	289–471	315–504	342–538	370–573	399–609	429–646
18	–	–	7–59	15–77	24–96	34–116	46–136	58–158	72–180	87–203	103–227	121–251	139–277	158–304	178–332	200–360	222–390	245–421	270–452	295–485	321–519	349–553	377–589	407–625	437–663
19	–	–	7–62	15–81	24–101	35–121	47–142	60–164	74–187	90–210	106–235	124–260	142–287	162–314	182–343	204–372	227–402	251–433	275–466	301–499	328–533	356–568	384–605	414–642	445–680
20	–	–	8–64	15–85	25–105	36–126	48–148	62–170	76–194	92–218	109–243	127–269	146–296	166–324	187–353	209–383	232–414	256–446	281–479	307–513	334–548	363–583	392–620	422–658	453–697
21	–	–	8–67	16–88	26–109	37–131	50–153	64–176	79–200	95–225	112–251	130–278	149–306	170–334	191–364	213–395	237–426	261–459	287–492	313–527	341–562	370–598	399–636	430–674	461–714
22	–	–	8–70	16–92	27–113	38–136	51–159	65–183	81–207	97–233	115–259	133–287	153–315	173–345	195–375	218–406	242–438	267–471	293–505	320–540	348–576	376–614	406–652	437–691	469–731
23	–	–	8–73	17–95	27–118	39–141	53–164	67–189	83–214	99–241	117–268	136–296	156–325	177–355	200–385	223–417	247–450	272–484	298–519	326–554	354–591	383–629	414–667	445–707	478–747
24	–	–	9–75	17–99	28–122	40–146	54–170	69–195	85–221	102–248	120–276	139–305	160–334	181–365	204–396	227–429	252–462	278–496	304–532	332–568	361–605	390–644	421–683	453–723	486–764
25	–	–	9–78	18–102	29–126	41–151	55–176	71–201	87–228	104–256	123–284	143–313	163–344	185–375	208–407	232–440	257–474	283–509	310–545	338–582	367–620	397–659	429–698	461–739	494–781
26	–	–	9–81	18–106	30–130	43–155	57–181	72–208	89–235	107–263	126–292	146–322	167–353	189–385	212–418	237–451	262–486	289–521	316–558	344–596	374–634	405–673	436–714	469–755	502–798
27	–	3–57	9–84	19–109	30–135	44–160	58–187	74–214	91–242	109–271	129–300	149–331	171–362	193–395	217–428	241–463	267–498	294–534	322–571	351–609	381–648	412–688	444–729	476–772	510–815
28	–	3–59	10–86	19–113	31–139	45–165	60–192	76–220	93–249	112–278	131–309	152–340	174–372	197–405	221–439	246–474	272–510	299–547	328–584	357–623	387–663	419–703	451–745	484–788	519–831
29	–	3–61	10–89	20–116	32–143	46–170	61–198	78–226	95–256	114–286	134–317	155–349	178–381	201–415	225–450	251–485	277–522	305–559	334–597	363–637	394–677	426–718	458–761	492–804	527–848
30	–	3–63	10–92	20–120	33–147	47–175	62–204	79–233	97–263	117–293	137–325	159–357	181–391	205–425	230–460	256–496	283–533	310–572	339–611	370–650	401–691	433–733	466–776	500–820	535–865
31	–	3–65	10–95	21–123	34–151	48–180	64–209	81–239	100–269	119–301	140–333	162–366	185–400	209–435	234–471	260–508	288–545	316–584	345–624	376–664	407–706	440–748	473–792	508–836	544–881
32	–	3–67	11–97	21–127	34–156	49–185	65–215	83–245	102–276	122–308	143–341	165–375	188–410	213–445	238–482	265–519	293–557	321–597	351–637	382–678	414–720	447–763	481–807	516–852	552–898
33	–	3–69	11–100	22–130	35–160	50–190	67–220	85–251	104–283	124–316	146–349	168–384	192–419	217–455	243–492	270–530	298–569	327–609	357–650	388–692	421–734	454–778	488–823	524–868	560–915
34	–	3–71	11–103	22–134	36–164	51–195	68–226	86–258	106–290	127–323	148–358	171–393	196–428	221–465	247–503	274–542	303–581	332–622	363–663	395–705	427–749	461–793	496–838	532–884	568–932
35	–	3–73	11–106	23–137	37–168	52–200	70–231	88–264	108–297	129–331	151–366	175–401	199–438	225–475	251–514	279–553	308–593	338–634	369–676	401–719	434–763	468–808	503–854	540–900	577–948
36	–	3–75	11–109	23–141	37–173	53–205	71–237	90–270	110–304	131–339	154–374	178–410	203–447	229–485	256–524	284–564	313–605	344–646	375–689	407–733	441–777	475–823	511–869	547–917	585–965
37	–	3–77	12–111	24–144	38–177	55–209	72–243	92–276	112–311	134–346	157–382	181–419	206–457	233–495	260–535	289–575	318–617	349–659	381–702	414–746	448–791	482–838	518–885	555–933	593–982
38	–	3–79	12–114	24–148	39–181	56–214	74–248	93–283	114–318	136–354	160–390	184–428	210–466	237–505	265–545	293–587	323–629	355–671	387–715	420–760	454–806	490–852	526–900	563–949	602–998
39	–	4–80	12–117	25–151	40–185	57–219	75–254	95–289	116–325	139–361	163–398	187–437	213–476	241–515	269–556	298–598	329–640	360–684	393–728	426–774	461–820	497–867	533–916	571–965	610–1015
40	–	4–82	12–120	25–155	41–189	58–224	77–259	97–295	119–331	141–369	165–407	191–445	217–485	245–525	273–567	303–609	334–652	366–696	399–741	433–787	468–834	504–882	541–931	579–981	618–1032
41	–	4–84	13–122	26–158	41–194	59–229	78–265	99–301	121–338	144–376	168–415	194–454	221–494	249–535	278–577	308–620	339–664	371–709	405–754	439–801	474–849	511–897	549–946	587–997	627–1048
42	–	4–86	13–125	26–162	42–198	60–234	80–270	100–308	123–345	146–384	171–423	197–463	224–504	253–545	282–588	312–632	344–676	377–721	410–768	445–815	481–863	518–912	556–962	595–1013	635–1065
43	–	4–88	13–128	27–165	43–202	61–239	81–276	102–314	125–352	149–391	174–431	200–472	228–513	257–555	286–599	317–643	349–688	382–734	416–781	452–828	488–877	525–927	564–977	603–1029	643–1082
44	–	4–90	13–131	27–169	44–206	62–244	82–282	104–320	127–359	151–399	177–439	204–480	231–523	261–565	291–609	322–654	354–700	388–746	422–794	458–842	495–891	532–942	571–993	611–1045	652–1098
45	–	4–92	14–133	28–172	44–211	63–249	84–287	106–326	129–366	154–406	180–447	207–489	235–532	265–575	295–620	327–665	360–711	393–759	428–807	464–856	501–906	540–956	579–1008	619–1061	660–1115
46	–	4–94	14–136	28–176	45–215	64–254	85–293	108–332	131–373	156–414	183–455	210–498	239–541	269–585	299–631	332–676	365–723	399–771	434–820	471–869	508–920	547–971	586–1024	627–1077	669–1131
47	–	4–96	14–139	29–179	46–219	66–258	87–298	109–339	133–380	159–421	185–464	213–507	242–551	273–595	304–641	336–688	370–735	404–784	440–833	477–883	515–934	554–986	594–1039	635–1093	677–1148
48	–	4–98	14–142	29–183	47–223	67–263	88–304	111–345	136–386	161–429	188–472	217–515	246–560	276–606	308–652	341–699	375–747	410–796	446–846	483–897	522–948	561–1001	601–1055	643–1109	685–1165
49	–	4–100	15–144	30–186	48–227	68–268	90–309	113–351	138–393	164–436	191–480	220–524	250–569	280–616	313–662	346–710	380–759	416–808	452–859	490–910	528–963	568–1016	609–1070	651–1125	694–1181
50	–	4–102	15–147	30–190	48–232	69–273	91–315	115–357	140–400	166–444	194–488	223–533	253–579	284–626	317–673	351–721	385–771	421–821	458–872	496–924	535–977	575–1031	617–1085	659–1141	702–1198

[1] W. Seewald, Swiss Federal Institute of Technology, Zurich, 1977.

All values conform to the international convention (i.e. 0,1 instead of 0.1).

Acceptance Region[1] for the Rank Sum T $2\alpha = 0{,}002$

$\mathrm{Prob}(T_l < \boldsymbol{T} < T_r) \geq 1 - 2\alpha$. For explanation see page 228

$2\alpha = 0{,}002$ (each cell gives T_l–T_r)

N_2 \ N_1	1	2	3	4	5	6	7	8	9	10	11	12	13	14	15	16	17	18	19	20	21	22	23	24	25
1	–	–	–	–	–	–	–	–	–	–	–	–	–	–	–	–	–	–	–	–	–	–	–	–	–
2	–	–	–	–	–	–	–	–	–	–	–	–	–	–	–	–	–	–	–	–	–	–	–	–	–
3	–	–	–	–	–	–	–	–	–	–	–	–	–	–	–	–	153–204	171–225	190–247	210–270	232–293	254–318	277–344	301–371	326–399
4	–	–	–	–	–	–	–	–	–	55–95	66–110	78–126	92–142	106–160	121–179	138–198	155–219	174–240	193–263	213–287	235–311	257–337	280–364	305–391	330–420
5	–	–	–	–	–	–	–	36–76	46–89	56–104	68–119	80–136	94–153	108–172	124–191	141–211	158–233	177–255	197–278	217–303	239–328	261–355	285–382	310–410	335–440
6	–	–	–	–	–	–	28–70	37–83	47–97	58–112	70–128	82–146	96–164	111–183	127–203	144–224	162–246	181–269	201–293	222–318	243–345	266–372	290–400	315–429	341–459
7	–	–	–	–	–	21–63	29–76	38–90	48–105	60–120	72–137	85–155	99–174	114–194	130–215	147–237	166–259	185–283	205–308	226–334	249–360	272–388	296–417	321–447	347–478
8	–	–	–	–	15–55	22–68	30–82	40–96	50–112	61–129	74–146	87–165	102–184	117–205	134–226	151–249	170–272	189–297	210–322	231–349	254–376	277–405	302–434	327–465	354–496
9	–	–	–	–	16–59	23–73	31–88	41–103	52–119	63–137	76–155	90–174	105–194	120–216	137–238	155–261	174–285	194–310	215–336	236–364	259–392	283–421	308–451	334–482	361–514
10	–	–	–	10–50	16–64	24–78	33–93	42–110	53–127	65–145	78–164	92–184	108–204	124–226	141–249	159–273	178–298	198–324	219–351	242–378	265–407	289–437	314–468	340–500	368–532
11	–	–	–	10–54	17–68	25–83	34–99	44–116	55–134	67–153	81–172	95–193	111–214	127–237	144–261	163–285	182–311	203–337	224–365	247–393	271–422	295–453	321–484	347–517	375–550
12	–	–	–	10–58	17–73	25–89	35–105	45–123	57–141	69–161	83–181	98–202	114–224	130–248	148–272	167–297	187–323	208–350	230–378	252–408	276–438	301–469	327–501	354–534	382–568
13	–	–	–	11–61	18–77	26–94	36–111	47–129	59–148	72–168	86–189	101–211	117–234	134–258	152–283	171–309	191–336	213–363	235–392	258–422	282–453	307–485	334–517	361–551	389–586
14	–	–	–	11–65	18–82	27–99	37–117	48–136	60–156	74–176	88–198	103–221	120–244	137–269	156–294	175–321	196–348	217–377	240–406	264–436	288–468	314–500	340–534	368–568	397–603
15	–	–	–	11–69	19–86	28–104	38–123	50–142	62–163	76–184	90–207	106–230	123–254	141–279	160–305	179–333	200–361	222–390	245–420	269–451	294–483	320–516	347–550	375–585	404–621
16	–	–	–	12–72	20–90	29–109	39–129	51–149	64–170	78–192	93–215	109–239	126–264	144–290	163–317	184–344	205–373	227–403	250–434	275–465	300–498	326–532	354–566	382–602	411–639
17	–	–	6–57	12–76	20–95	30–114	41–134	53–155	66–177	80–200	95–224	112–248	129–274	148–300	167–328	188–356	210–385	232–416	256–447	280–480	306–513	333–547	361–582	389–619	419–656
18	–	–	6–60	13–79	21–99	31–119	42–140	54–162	68–184	82–208	98–232	115–257	133–283	151–311	171–339	192–368	214–398	237–429	261–461	286–494	312–528	339–563	367–599	396–636	427–673
19	–	–	6–63	13–83	22–103	32–124	43–146	56–168	70–191	84–216	100–241	118–266	136–293	155–321	175–350	196–380	219–410	242–442	267–474	292–508	318–543	346–578	374–615	404–652	434–691
20	–	–	6–66	13–87	22–108	33–129	44–152	57–175	71–199	87–223	103–249	120–276	139–303	159–331	179–361	201–391	223–423	247–455	272–488	298–522	325–557	352–594	381–631	411–669	442–708
21	–	–	7–68	14–90	23–112	33–135	46–157	59–181	73–206	89–231	106–257	123–285	142–313	162–342	183–372	205–403	228–435	252–468	277–502	304–536	331–572	359–609	388–647	418–686	450–725
22	–	–	7–71	14–94	23–117	34–140	47–163	60–188	75–213	91–239	108–266	126–294	145–323	166–352	187–383	209–415	233–447	257–481	283–515	309–551	337–587	365–625	395–663	426–702	457–743
23	–	–	7–74	14–98	24–121	35–145	48–169	62–194	77–220	93–247	111–274	129–303	149–332	169–363	191–394	214–426	238–459	262–494	288–529	315–565	343–602	372–640	402–679	433–719	465–760
24	–	–	7–77	15–101	25–125	36–150	49–175	63–201	79–227	95–255	113–283	132–312	152–342	173–373	195–405	218–438	242–472	267–507	294–542	321–579	349–617	379–655	409–695	440–736	473–777
25	–	–	7–80	15–105	25–130	37–155	50–181	65–207	81–234	98–262	116–291	135–321	155–352	177–383	199–416	222–450	247–484	273–519	299–556	327–593	356–631	385–671	416–711	448–752	480–795
26	–	–	7–83	16–108	26–134	38–160	52–186	67–213	83–241	100–270	118–300	138–330	159–361	180–394	203–427	227–461	252–496	278–532	305–569	333–607	362–646	392–686	423–727	455–769	488–812
27	–	–	8–85	16–112	27–138	39–165	53–192	68–220	85–248	102–278	121–308	141–339	162–371	184–404	207–438	231–473	257–508	283–545	310–583	339–621	368–661	399–701	430–743	463–785	496–829
28	–	–	8–88	16–116	27–143	40–170	54–198	70–226	86–256	104–286	123–317	144–348	165–381	188–414	211–449	236–484	261–521	288–558	316–596	345–635	374–676	405–717	437–759	470–802	504–846
29	–	–	8–91	17–119	28–147	41–175	55–204	71–233	88–263	107–293	126–325	147–357	168–391	191–425	215–460	240–496	266–533	293–571	321–610	350–650	381–690	412–732	444–775	477–819	512–863
30	–	–	8–94	17–123	29–151	42–180	57–209	73–239	90–270	109–301	129–333	150–366	172–400	195–435	219–471	244–508	271–545	298–584	327–623	356–664	387–705	419–747	451–791	485–835	520–880
31	–	–	8–97	17–127	29–156	43–185	58–215	74–246	92–277	111–309	131–342	153–375	175–410	199–445	223–482	249–519	276–557	303–597	332–637	362–678	393–720	425–763	458–807	492–852	527–898
32	–	–	8–100	18–130	30–160	44–190	59–221	76–252	94–284	113–317	134–350	155–385	178–420	202–456	227–493	253–531	280–570	309–609	338–650	368–692	400–734	432–778	465–823	500–868	535–915
33	–	–	9–102	18–134	30–165	45–195	60–227	77–259	96–291	116–324	136–359	158–394	182–429	206–466	231–504	258–542	285–582	314–622	343–664	374–706	406–749	439–793	472–839	507–885	543–932
34	–	–	9–105	19–137	31–169	46–200	62–232	79–265	98–298	118–332	139–367	161–403	185–439	210–476	235–515	262–554	290–594	319–635	349–677	380–720	412–764	445–809	480–854	515–901	551–949
35	–	–	9–108	19–141	32–173	46–206	63–238	81–271	100–305	120–340	142–375	164–412	188–449	213–487	239–526	267–565	295–606	324–648	355–690	386–734	419–778	452–824	487–870	522–918	559–966
36	–	–	9–111	19–145	32–178	47–211	64–244	82–278	102–312	122–348	144–384	167–421	192–458	217–497	243–537	271–577	300–618	329–661	360–704	392–748	425–793	459–839	494–886	530–934	567–983
37	–	–	9–114	20–148	33–182	48–216	65–250	84–284	103–320	125–355	147–392	170–430	195–468	221–507	247–548	275–589	304–631	335–673	366–717	398–762	431–808	466–854	501–902	537–951	575–1000
38	–	–	9–117	20–152	34–186	49–221	67–255	85–291	105–327	127–363	149–401	173–439	198–478	224–518	251–559	280–600	309–643	340–686	371–731	404–776	438–822	472–870	508–918	545–967	583–1017
39	–	–	10–119	21–155	34–191	50–226	68–261	87–297	107–334	129–371	152–409	176–448	201–488	228–528	256–569	284–612	314–655	345–699	377–744	410–790	444–837	479–885	515–934	552–984	591–1034
40	–	–	10–122	21–159	35–195	51–231	69–267	88–304	109–341	131–379	155–417	179–457	205–497	232–538	260–580	289–623	319–667	350–712	382–758	416–804	450–852	486–900	522–950	560–1000	599–1051
41	–	–	10–125	21–163	36–199	52–236	70–273	90–310	111–348	134–386	157–426	182–466	208–507	235–549	264–591	293–635	324–679	355–725	388–771	422–818	457–866	493–915	530–965	568–1016	607–1068
42	–	–	10–128	22–166	36–204	53–241	72–278	92–316	113–355	136–394	160–434	185–475	211–517	239–559	268–602	298–646	329–691	361–737	394–784	428–832	463–881	499–931	537–981	575–1033	615–1085
43	–	–	10–131	22–170	37–208	54–246	73–284	93–323	115–362	138–402	162–443	188–484	215–526	243–569	272–613	302–658	333–704	366–750	399–798	434–846	469–896	506–946	544–997	583–1049	623–1102
44	–	3–91	11–133	23–173	38–212	55–251	74–290	95–329	117–369	140–410	165–451	191–493	218–536	246–580	276–624	306–670	338–716	371–763	405–811	440–860	476–910	513–961	551–1013	590–1066	630–1120
45	–	3–93	11–136	23–177	38–217	56–256	75–296	96–336	119–376	143–417	168–459	194–502	221–546	250–590	280–635	311–681	343–728	376–776	410–825	446–874	482–925	520–976	558–1029	598–1082	638–1137
46	–	3–95	11–139	23–181	39–221	57–261	77–301	98–342	121–383	145–425	170–468	197–511	225–555	254–600	284–646	315–693	348–740	381–789	416–838	452–888	489–939	526–992	565–1045	605–1099	646–1154
47	–	3–97	11–142	24–184	39–226	58–266	78–307	99–349	123–390	147–433	173–476	200–520	228–565	258–610	288–657	320–704	353–752	387–801	422–851	458–902	495–954	533–1007	573–1060	613–1115	654–1171
48	–	3–99	11–145	24–188	40–230	59–271	79–313	101–355	124–398	149–441	175–485	203–529	231–575	261–621	292–668	324–716	358–764	392–814	427–865	464–916	501–969	540–1022	580–1076	621–1131	662–1188
49	–	3–101	11–148	24–192	41–234	60–276	80–319	103–361	126–405	152–448	178–493	206–538	235–584	265–631	296–679	329–727	362–777	397–827	433–878	470–930	508–983	547–1037	587–1092	628–1148	670–1205
50	–	3–103	12–150	25–195	41–239	61–281	82–324	104–368	128–412	154–456	181–501	209–547	238–594	269–641	300–690	333–739	367–789	402–840	438–892	476–944	514–998	554–1052	594–1108	636–1164	678–1222

[1] W. SEEWALD, Swiss Federal Institute of Technology, Zurich, 1977.

All values conform to the international convention (i.e. 0,1 instead of 0.1).

Acceptance Region[1] for the Rank Sum T $2\alpha = 0{,}001$ (Wilcoxon 2-Sample Test)

$\mathrm{Prob}(T_l < \boldsymbol{T} < T_r) \geq 1 - 2\alpha$. For explanation see page 228

$2\alpha = 0{,}001$

N_1	1	2	3	4	5	6	7	8	9	10	11	12	13	14	15	16	17	18	19	20	21	22	23	24	25
N_2	T_l T_r	T_l T_r	T_l T_r	T_l T_r	T_l T_r	T_l T_r	T_l T_r	T_l T_r	T_l T_r	T_l T_r	T_l T_r	T_l T_r	T_l T_r	T_l T_r	T_l T_r	T_l T_r	T_l T_r	T_l T_r	T_l T_r	T_l T_r	T_l T_r	T_l T_r	T_l T_r	T_l T_r	T_l T_r
1	–	–	–	–	–	–	–	–	–	–	–	–	–	–	–	–	–	–	–	–	–	–	–	–	–
2	–	–	–	–	–	–	–	–	–	–	–	–	–	–	–	–	–	–	–	–	–	–	–	–	–
3	–	–	–	–	–	–	–	–	–	–	–	–	–	–	–	–	–	–	–	–	231–294	253–319	276–345	300–372	325–400
4	–	–	–	–	–	–	–	–	–	–	–	–	91–143	105–161	120–180	137–199	154–220	172–242	192–264	212–288	233–313	256–338	279–365	303–393	328–422
5	–	–	–	–	–	–	–	–	45–90	55–105	67–120	79–137	93–154	107–173	123–192	139–213	157–234	175–257	195–280	215–305	237–330	259–357	283–384	307–413	333–442
6	–	–	–	–	–	–	–	36–84	46–98	57–113	68–130	81–147	95–165	110–184	125–205	142–226	160–248	179–271	198–296	219–321	241–347	264–374	288–402	312–432	338–462
7	–	–	–	–	–	–	28–77	37–91	47–106	58–122	70–139	83–157	97–176	112–196	128–217	145–239	163–262	182–286	203–310	224–336	246–363	269–391	293–420	318–450	344–481
8	–	–	–	–	–	21–69	29–83	38–98	49–113	60–130	72–148	85–167	100–186	115–207	131–229	149–251	167–275	186–300	207–325	228–352	251–379	274–408	298–438	324–468	350–500
9	–	–	–	–	15–60	22–74	30–89	40–104	50–121	62–138	74–157	88–176	102–197	118–218	135–240	152–264	171–288	191–313	211–340	233–367	256–395	279–425	304–455	330–486	357–518
10	–	–	–	–	15–65	23–79	31–95	41–111	52–128	63–147	76–166	90–186	105–207	121–229	138–252	156–276	175–301	195–327	216–354	238–382	261–411	285–441	310–472	336–504	363–537
11	–	–	–	–	16–69	23–85	32–101	42–118	53–136	65–155	78–175	93–195	108–217	124–240	141–264	160–288	179–314	199–341	221–368	243–397	266–427	291–457	316–489	342–522	370–555
12	–	–	–	–	16–74	24–90	33–107	43–125	55–143	67–163	81–183	95–205	111–227	127–251	145–275	163–301	183–327	204–354	225–383	248–412	272–442	297–473	322–506	349–539	377–573
13	–	–	–	10–62	17–78	25–95	34–113	45–131	56–151	69–171	83–192	98–214	114–237	130–262	148–287	167–313	187–340	208–368	230–397	253–427	277–458	302–490	328–523	356–556	384–591
14	–	–	–	10–66	17–83	26–100	35–119	46–138	58–158	71–179	85–201	100–224	116–248	134–272	152–298	171–325	192–352	213–381	235–411	259–441	283–473	308–506	335–539	362–574	391–609
15	–	–	–	10–70	18–87	26–106	36–125	47–145	60–165	73–187	87–210	103–233	119–258	137–283	156–309	175–337	196–365	217–395	240–425	264–456	289–488	314–522	341–556	369–591	398–627
16	–	–	–	11–73	18–92	27–111	37–131	49–151	61–173	75–195	90–218	105–243	122–268	140–294	159–321	179–349	200–378	222–408	245–439	269–471	294–504	320–538	348–572	376–608	405–645
17	–	–	–	11–77	19–96	28–116	38–137	50–158	63–180	77–203	92–227	108–252	125–278	144–304	163–332	183–361	204–391	227–421	250–453	275–485	300–519	327–553	354–589	383–625	412–663
18	–	–	–	11–81	19–101	29–121	39–143	51–165	65–187	79–211	94–236	111–261	128–288	147–315	166–344	187–373	209–403	232–434	255–467	280–500	306–534	333–569	361–605	389–643	419–681
19	–	–	–	12–84	20–105	29–127	41–148	53–171	66–195	81–219	97–244	113–271	131–298	150–326	170–355	191–385	213–416	236–448	260–481	286–514	312–549	339–585	367–622	396–660	427–698
20	–	–	–	12–88	20–110	30–132	42–154	54–178	68–202	83–227	99–253	116–280	134–308	154–336	174–366	195–397	218–428	241–461	266–494	291–529	318–564	345–601	374–638	403–677	434–716
21	–	–	6–69	12–92	21–114	31–137	43–160	56–184	70–209	85–235	101–262	119–289	137–318	157–347	178–377	199–409	222–441	246–474	271–508	297–543	324–579	351–617	380–655	410–694	441–734
22	–	–	6–72	13–95	21–119	32–142	44–166	57–191	71–217	87–243	104–270	122–298	140–328	160–358	181–389	203–421	227–453	251–487	276–522	302–558	329–595	358–632	387–671	417–711	449–751
23	–	–	6–75	13–99	22–123	33–147	45–172	58–198	73–224	89–251	106–279	124–308	143–338	164–368	185–400	208–432	231–466	256–500	281–536	308–572	335–610	364–648	394–687	424–728	456–769
24	–	–	6–78	13–103	22–128	33–153	46–178	60–204	75–231	91–259	108–288	127–317	147–347	167–379	189–411	212–444	236–478	260–514	286–550	313–587	341–625	370–664	400–704	432–744	464–786
25	–	–	6–81	13–107	23–132	34–158	47–184	61–211	77–238	93–267	111–296	130–326	150–357	171–389	193–422	216–456	240–491	265–527	292–563	319–601	347–640	377–679	407–720	439–761	471–804
26	–	–	6–84	14–110	24–136	35–163	48–190	63–217	78–246	95–275	113–305	132–336	153–367	174–400	197–433	220–468	245–503	270–540	297–577	325–615	353–655	383–695	414–736	446–778	479–821
27	–	–	7–86	14–114	24–141	36–168	49–196	64–224	80–253	97–283	116–313	135–345	156–377	177–411	200–445	224–480	249–516	275–553	302–591	330–630	359–670	389–711	421–752	453–795	486–839
28	–	–	7–89	14–118	25–145	37–173	50–202	65–231	82–260	99–291	118–322	138–354	159–387	181–421	204–456	228–492	254–528	280–566	307–605	336–644	365–685	396–726	427–769	460–812	494–856
29	–	–	7–92	15–121	25–150	38–178	52–207	67–237	84–267	101–299	120–331	141–363	162–397	184–432	208–467	233–503	258–541	285–579	313–618	341–659	371–700	402–742	434–785	467–829	501–874
30	–	–	7–95	15–125	26–154	38–184	53–213	68–244	85–275	103–307	123–339	143–373	165–407	188–442	212–478	237–515	263–553	290–592	318–632	347–673	377–715	409–757	441–801	474–846	509–891
31	–	–	7–98	15–129	26–159	39–189	54–219	70–250	87–282	106–314	125–348	146–382	168–417	191–453	216–489	241–527	267–566	295–605	323–646	353–687	383–730	415–773	448–817	482–862	516–909
32	–	–	7–101	16–132	27–163	40–194	55–225	71–257	89–289	108–322	128–356	149–391	171–427	195–463	219–501	245–539	272–578	300–618	329–659	358–702	389–745	422–788	455–833	489–879	524–926
33	–	–	7–104	16–136	27–168	41–199	56–231	73–263	91–296	110–330	130–365	152–400	174–437	198–474	223–512	249–551	276–591	305–631	334–673	364–716	396–759	428–804	461–850	496–896	531–944
34	–	–	7–107	16–140	28–172	42–204	57–237	74–270	92–304	112–338	133–373	154–410	178–446	202–484	227–523	253–563	281–603	310–644	339–687	370–730	402–774	434–820	468–866	503–913	539–961
35	–	–	8–109	17–143	29–176	43–209	58–243	75–277	94–311	114–346	135–382	157–419	181–456	205–495	231–534	258–574	286–615	314–658	344–701	376–744	408–789	441–835	475–882	510–930	547–978
36	–	–	8–112	17–147	29–181	43–215	59–249	77–283	96–318	116–354	137–391	160–428	184–466	209–505	235–545	262–586	290–628	319–671	350–714	381–759	414–804	447–851	482–898	518–946	554–996
37	–	–	8–115	17–151	30–185	44–220	60–255	78–290	98–325	118–362	140–399	163–437	187–476	212–516	239–556	266–598	295–640	324–684	355–728	387–773	420–819	454–866	489–914	525–963	562–1013
38	–	–	8–118	18–154	30–190	45–225	62–260	80–296	99–333	120–370	142–408	166–446	190–486	216–526	242–568	270–610	299–653	329–697	360–742	393–787	426–834	460–882	496–930	532–980	570–1030
39	–	–	8–121	18–158	31–194	46–230	63–266	81–303	101–340	122–378	145–416	168–456	193–496	219–537	246–579	275–621	304–665	334–710	366–755	398–802	432–849	467–897	503–946	539–997	577–1048
40	–	–	8–124	18–162	31–199	47–235	64–272	83–309	103–347	124–386	147–425	171–465	196–506	223–547	250–590	279–633	308–678	339–723	371–769	404–816	438–864	473–913	509–963	547–1013	585–1065
41	–	–	8–127	19–165	32–203	48–240	65–278	84–316	105–354	126–394	150–433	174–474	199–516	226–558	254–601	283–645	313–690	344–736	377–782	410–830	444–879	480–928	516–979	554–1030	593–1082
42	–	–	9–129	19–169	32–208	48–246	66–284	85–323	106–362	129–401	152–442	177–483	203–525	230–568	258–612	287–657	318–702	349–749	382–796	416–844	450–894	486–944	523–995	561–1047	600–1100
43	–	–	9–132	19–173	33–212	49–251	67–290	87–329	108–369	131–409	154–451	179–493	206–535	233–579	262–623	291–669	322–715	354–762	387–810	421–859	457–908	493–959	530–1011	568–1064	608–1117
44	–	–	9–135	20–176	34–216	50–256	68–296	88–336	110–376	133–417	157–459	182–502	209–545	237–589	266–634	296–680	327–727	359–775	393–823	427–873	463–923	499–975	537–1027	576–1080	616–1134
45	–	–	9–138	20–180	34–221	51–261	70–301	90–342	112–383	135–425	159–468	185–511	212–555	240–600	269–646	300–692	332–739	364–788	398–837	433–887	469–938	506–990	544–1043	583–1097	623–1152
46	–	–	9–141	20–184	35–225	52–266	71–307	91–349	113–391	137–433	162–476	188–520	215–565	244–610	273–657	304–704	336–752	369–801	403–851	439–901	475–953	512–1006	551–1059	590–1114	631–1169
47	–	–	9–144	21–187	35–230	53–271	72–313	93–355	115–398	139–441	164–485	191–529	218–575	247–621	277–668	308–716	341–764	374–814	409–864	444–916	481–968	519–1021	558–1075	598–1130	639–1186
48	–	–	9–147	21–191	36–234	53–277	73–319	94–362	117–405	141–449	167–493	193–539	221–585	251–631	281–679	313–727	345–777	379–827	414–878	450–930	487–983	525–1037	565–1091	605–1147	646–1204
49	–	–	10–149	21–195	36–239	54–282	74–325	96–368	119–412	143–457	169–502	196–548	225–594	254–642	285–690	317–739	350–789	384–840	419–892	456–944	493–998	532–1052	572–1107	612–1164	654–1221
50	–	–	10–152	22–198	37–243	55–287	75–331	97–375	120–420	145–465	171–511	199–557	228–604	258–652	289–701	321–751	355–801	389–853	425–905	462–958	499–1013	538–1068	578–1124	620–1180	662–1238

[1] W. SEEWALD, Swiss Federal Institute of Technology, Zurich, 1977.

All values conform to the international convention (i.e. 0,1 instead of 0.1).

Wilcoxon matched-pairs test* n: number of pairs (for explanation see page 228)

$2\alpha \leq$	0,4	0,2	0,1	0,05	0,02	0,01	0,002	0,001	0,0002	0,0001
n										
4	2– 8	0– 10	–	–	–	–	–	–	–	–
5	3– 12	2– 13	0– 15	–	–	–	–	–	–	–
6	5– 16	3– 18	2– 19	0– 21	–	–	–	–	–	–
7	8– 20	5– 23	3– 25	2– 26	0– 28	–	–	–	–	–
8	11– 25	8– 28	5– 31	3– 33	1– 35	0– 36	–	–	–	–
9	14– 31	10– 35	8– 37	5– 40	3– 42	1– 44	–	–	–	–
10	18– 37	14– 41	10– 45	8– 47	5– 50	3– 52	0– 55	–	–	–
11	22– 44	17– 49	13– 53	10– 56	7– 59	5– 61	1– 65	0– 66	–	–
12	27– 51	21– 57	17– 61	13– 65	9– 69	7– 71	2– 76	1– 77	–	–
13	32– 59	26– 65	21– 70	17– 74	12– 79	9– 82	4– 87	2– 89	–	–
14	38– 67	31– 74	25– 80	21– 84	15– 90	12– 93	6– 99	4–101	0–105	–
15	44– 76	36– 84	30– 90	25– 95	19–101	15–105	8–112	6–114	2–118	0–120
16	50– 86	42– 94	35–101	29–107	23–113	19–117	11–125	9–127	3–133	2–134
17	57– 96	48–105	41–112	34–119	28–125	23–130	14–139	11–142	5–148	3–150
18	65–106	55–116	47–124	40–131	32–139	27–144	18–153	14–157	8–163	5–166
19	73–117	62–128	53–137	46–144	37–153	32–158	21–169	18–172	10–180	8–182
20	81–129	69–141	60–150	52–158	43–167	37–173	26–184	21–189	13–190	10–200
21	90–141	77–154	67–164	58–173	49–182	42–189	30–201	26–205	17–214	13–218
22	99–154	86–167	75–178	66–187	55–198	48–205	35–218	30–223	20–233	17–236
23	109–167	95–181	83–193	73–203	62–214	54–222	40–236	35–241	24–252	20–256
24	119–181	104–196	91–209	81–219	69–231	61–239	46–254	40–260	28–272	24–276
25	130–195	114–211	100–225	89–236	76–249	68–257	51–274	45–280	33–292	28–297

Spearman's rank correlation coefficient r_S[1]: significance levels for testing $r_S = 0$

ΣD_i^2: the sum of the squared paired differences from n paired observations

2α	0,2		0,1		0,05		0,02		0,01		0,002	
n	ΣD_i^2	$r_S(\pm)$	ΣD_i^2	$r_S(\pm)$	ΣD_i^2	$r_S(\pm)$	ΣD_i^2	$r_S(\pm)$	ΣD_i^2	$r_S(\pm)$	ΣD_i^2	$r_S(\pm)$
4	0– 20	0,9999	0– 20	0,9999	–	–	–	–	–	–	–	–
5	4– 36	0,8000	2– 38	0,9000	0– 40	0,9999	0– 40	0,9999	–	–	–	–
6	12– 58	0,6571	6– 64	0,8286	4– 66	0,8857	2– 68	0,9429	0– 70	0,9999	–	–
7	24– 88	0,5714	16– 96	0,7143	12– 100	0,7857	6– 106	0,8929	4– 108	0,9286	0– 112	0,9999
8	40– 128	0,5238	30– 138	0,6429	22– 146	0,7381	14– 154	0,8333	10– 158	0,8810	4– 164	0,9524
9	62– 178	0,4833	48– 192	0,6000	38– 202	0,6833	26– 214	0,7833	20– 220	0,8333	12– 228	0,9000
10	90– 240	0,4545	72– 258	0,5636	58– 272	0,6485	44– 286	0,7333	34– 296	0,7939	20– 310	0,8788
11	126– 314	0,4273	102– 338	0,5364	84– 356	0,6182	66– 374	0,7000	54– 386	0,7545	34– 406	0,8455
12	170– 402	0,4056	142– 430	0,5035	118– 454	0,5874	92– 480	0,6783	76– 496	0,7343	50– 522	0,8552
13	224– 504	0,3846	188– 540	0,4835	160– 568	0,5604	128– 600	0,6484	108– 620	0,7033	74– 654	0,7967
14	288– 622	0,3670	244– 666	0,4637	210– 700	0,5385	170– 740	0,6264	146– 764	0,6791	104– 806	0,7714
15	362– 758	0,3536	310– 810	0,4464	268– 852	0,5214	222– 898	0,6036	192– 928	0,6571	140– 980	0,7500
16	448– 912	0,3412	388– 972	0,4294	338–1022	0,5029	282–1078	0,5853	248–1112	0,6353	184–1176	0,7294
17	548–1084	0,3284	478–1154	0,4142	418–1214	0,4877	354–1278	0,5662	312–1320	0,6176	236–1396	0,7108
18	662–1276	0,3168	580–1358	0,4014	510–1428	0,4737	436–1502	0,5501	388–1550	0,5996	298–1640	0,6925
19	788–1492	0,3088	694–1586	0,3912	616–1664	0,4596	530–1750	0,5351	474–1806	0,5842	370–1910	0,6754
20	932–1728	0,2992	824–1836	0,3805	736–1924	0,4466	636–2024	0,5218	572–2088	0,5699	452–2208	0,6602
21	1090–1990	0,2922	970–2110	0,3701	868–2212	0,4364	756–2324	0,5091	684–2396	0,5558	544–2536	0,6468
22	1268–2274	0,2840	1132–2410	0,3608	1018–2524	0,4252	890–2652	0,4975	808–2734	0,5438	650–2892	0,6330
23	1462–2586	0,2777	1310–2738	0,3528	1182–2866	0,4160	1040–3008	0,4862	948–3100	0,5316	770–3278	0,6196
24	1676–2924	0,2713	1508–3092	0,3443	1364–3236	0,4070	1206–3394	0,4757	1102–3498	0,5209	902–3698	0,6078
25	1910–3290	0,2654	1724–3476	0,3369	1564–3636	0,3985	1388–3812	0,4662	1272–3928	0,5108	1048–4152	0,5969
26	2166–3684	0,2595	1958–3892	0,3306	1784–4066	0,3901	1588–4262	0,4571	1460–4390	0,5009	1210–4640	0,5863
27	2442–4110	0,2546	2214–4338	0,3242	2022–4530	0,3828	1806–4746	0,4487	1664–4888	0,4921	1388–5164	0,5763
28	2742–4566	0,2496	2492–4816	0,3180	2282–5026	0,3755	2044–5264	0,4406	1888–5420	0,4833	1584–5724	0,5665
29	3066–5054	0,2448	2794–5326	0,3118	2562–5558	0,3690	2304–5816	0,4325	2132–5988	0,4749	1798–6322	0,5571
30	3414–5576	0,2405	3118–5872	0,3063	2866–6124	0,3624	2582–6408	0,4256	2396–6594	0,4670	2030–6960	0,5484

For $n > 30$ the following approximation may be used:

Let $\pm c_\alpha = \pm r_S\sqrt{n-1}$, then $\sum D_i^2 = \frac{n^3-n}{6}\left(1 \pm \frac{|c_\alpha|}{\sqrt{n-1}}\right)$

and $\pm t_{\alpha;\, \nu=n-2} = \pm r_S\sqrt{\frac{n-2}{1-r_S^2}}$, then $\sum D_i^2 = \frac{n^3-n}{6}\left(1 \pm \frac{|t_\alpha|}{\sqrt{n-2+t_\alpha^2}}\right)$

* Reproduction only by permission of the publishers of the *Geigy Scientific Tables*.

[1] Exact values ($n = 4$–10) from Kendall, M.G., *Rank Correlation Methods*, 4th ed., Griffin, London and High Wycombe (Buckinghamshire), 1975. Approximate values ($n = 11$–30) from Glasser and Winter, *Biometrika*, **48**, 444 (1961). Certain corrections to the exact values from Owen, D.B., *Handbook of Statistical Tables*, Addison-Wesley, Reading (Mass.), 1962.

All values conform to the international convention (i.e. 0,1 instead of 0.1).

Values* of $6/(n^3-n)$ for calculating Spearman's rank correlation coefficient r_S

n	0	1	2	3	4	5	6	7	8	9
0			1,00000	$10^{-1}\times$2,50000	$10^{-1}\times$1,00000	$10^{-2}\times$5,00000	$10^{-2}\times$2,85714	$10^{-2}\times$1,78571	$10^{-2}\times$1,19048	$10^{-3}\times$8,33333
10	$10^{-3}\times$6,06061	$10^{-3}\times$4,54545	$10^{-3}\times$3,49650	$10^{-3}\times$2,74725	$10^{-3}\times$2,19780	$10^{-3}\times$1,78571	$10^{-3}\times$1,47059	$10^{-3}\times$1,22549	$10^{-3}\times$1,03199	$10^{-4}\times$8,77193
20	$10^{-4}\times$7,51880	$10^{-4}\times$6,49351	$10^{-4}\times$5,64653	$10^{-4}\times$4,94071	$10^{-4}\times$4,34783	$10^{-4}\times$3,84615	$10^{-4}\times$3,41880	$10^{-4}\times$3,05250	$10^{-4}\times$2,73673	2,46305
30	2,22469	2,01613	1,83284	1,67112	1,52788	1,40056	1,28700	1,18540	1,09421	1,01215
40	$10^{-5}\times$9,38086	$10^{-5}\times$8,71080	$10^{-5}\times$8,10307	$10^{-5}\times$7,55059	$10^{-5}\times$7,04722	$10^{-5}\times$6,58762	$10^{-5}\times$6,16713	$10^{-5}\times$5,78168	$10^{-5}\times$5,42770	$10^{-5}\times$5,10204
50	4,80192	4,52489	4,26876	4,03161	3,81170	3,60750	3,41763	3,24086	3,07607	2,92227
60	2,77855	2,64410	2,51819	2,40015	2,28938	2,18531	2,08746	1,99537	1,90862	1,82682
70	1,74963	1,67673	1,60782	1,54264	1,48093	1,42248	1,36705	1,31447	1,26456	1,21714
80	1,17206	1,12918	1,08836	1,04949	1,01245	$10^{-6}\times$9,77135	$10^{-6}\times$9,43441	$10^{-6}\times$9,11278	$10^{-6}\times$8,80561	$10^{-6}\times$8,51209
90	$10^{-6}\times$8,23147	$10^{-6}\times$7,96305	$10^{-6}\times$7,70618	$10^{-6}\times$7,46024	$10^{-6}\times$7,22465	6,99888	6,78242	6,57479	6,37556	6,18429
100	$10^{-6}\times$6,00060	$10^{-6}\times$5,82411	$10^{-6}\times$5,65448	$10^{-6}\times$5,49137	$10^{-6}\times$5,33447	$10^{-6}\times$5,18350	$10^{-6}\times$5,03816	$10^{-6}\times$4,89822	$10^{-6}\times$4,76340	$10^{-6}\times$4,63349
110	4,50826	4,38750	4,27102	4,15863	4,05014	3,94540	3,84423	3,74650	3,65205	3,56075
120	3,47246	3,38707	3,30446	3,22452	3,14713	3,07220	2,99963	2,92932	2,86120	2,79517
130	2,73116	2,66909	2,60888	2,55047	2,49380	2,43879	2,38538	2,33353	2,28316	2,23424
140	2,18670	2,14050	2,09560	2,05194	2,00948	1,96819	1,92803	1,88895	1,85091	1,81389
150	1,77786	1,74277	1,70860	1,67531	1,64289	1,61129	1,58050	1,55049	1,52124	1,49272
160	1,46490	1,43777	1,41131	1,38549	1,36030	1,33572	1,31172	1,28830	1,26543	1,24310
170	1,22129	1,19999	1,17918	1,15885	1,13898	1,11957	1,10059	1,08204	1,06391	1,04618
180	1,02884	1,01188	$10^{-7}\times$9,95291	$10^{-7}\times$9,79064	$10^{-7}\times$9,63187	$10^{-7}\times$9,47652	$10^{-7}\times$9,32449	$10^{-7}\times$9,17569	$10^{-7}\times$9,03005	$10^{-7}\times$8,88747
190	$10^{-7}\times$8,74787	$10^{-7}\times$8,61119	8,47733	8,34624	8,21784	8,09206	7,96883	7,84809	7,72977	7,61383
200	$10^{-7}\times$7,50019	$10^{-7}\times$7,38880	$10^{-7}\times$7,27960	$10^{-7}\times$7,17255	$10^{-7}\times$7,06759	$10^{-7}\times$6,96466	$10^{-7}\times$6,86372	$10^{-7}\times$6,76473	$10^{-7}\times$6,66763	$10^{-7}\times$6,57237
210	6,47893	6,38725	6,29728	6,20901	6,12237	6,03733	5,95387	5,87194	5,79150	5,71252
220	5,63498	5,55883	5,48405	5,41060	5,33846	5,26759	5,19798	5,12958	5,06238	4,99635
230	4,93146	4,86770	4,80502	4,74342	4,68286	4,62334	4,56481	4,50727	4,45070	4,39506
240	4,34035	4,28655	4,23363	4,18157	4,13037	4,08000	4,03045	3,98169	3,93372	3,88651
250	3,84006	3,79435	3,74935	3,70507	3,66148	3,61857	3,57633	3,53475	3,49380	3,45349
260	3,41380	3,37471	3,33621	3,29830	3,26096	3,22418	3,18796	3,15227	3,11712	3,08248
270	3,04836	3,01474	2,98161	2,94896	2,91679	2,88509	2,85384	2,82304	2,79269	2,76277
280	2,73327	2,70419	2,67553	2,64726	2,61940	2,59192	2,56483	2,53811	2,51177	2,48578
290	2,46015	2,43488	2,40995	2,38536	2,36110	2,33717	2,31356	2,29027	2,26729	2,24462
300	$10^{-7}\times$2,22225	$10^{-7}\times$2,20017	$10^{-7}\times$2,17839	$10^{-7}\times$2,15689	$10^{-7}\times$2,13568	$10^{-7}\times$2,11474	$10^{-7}\times$2,09407	$10^{-7}\times$2,07368	$10^{-7}\times$2,05354	$10^{-7}\times$2,03367
310	2,01405	1,99469	1,97557	1,95669	1,93806	1,91966	1,90149	1,88355	1,86584	1,84835
320	1,83107	1,81401	1,79716	1,78052	1,76409	1,74785	1,73182	1,71598	1,70033	1,68487
330	1,66960	1,65452	1,63961	1,62488	1,61033	1,59596	1,58175	1,56771	1,55384	1,54012
340	1,52658	1,51318	1,49995	1,48687	1,47394	1,46116	1,44853	1,43604	1,42370	1,41149
350	1,39943	1,38750	1,37571	1,36405	1,35252	1,34113	1,32986	1,31871	1,30769	1,29679
360	1,28602	1,27536	1,26482	1,25440	1,24409	1,23389	1,22380	1,21383	1,20396	1,19420
370	1,18454	1,17499	1,16554	1,15619	1,14694	1,13779	1,12873	1,11977	1,11091	1,10214
380	1,09346	1,08487	1,07638	1,06797	1,05965	1,05141	1,04326	1,03519	1,02721	1,01931
390	1,01149	1,00375	$10^{-8}\times$9,96084	$10^{-8}\times$9,88499	$10^{-8}\times$9,80992	$10^{-8}\times$9,73560	$10^{-8}\times$9,66203	$10^{-8}\times$9,58920	$10^{-8}\times$9,51710	$10^{-8}\times$9,44572
400	$10^{-8}\times$9,37506	$10^{-8}\times$9,30510	$10^{-8}\times$9,23583	$10^{-8}\times$9,16724	$10^{-8}\times$9,09934	$10^{-8}\times$9,03210	$10^{-8}\times$8,96553	$10^{-8}\times$8,89960	$10^{-8}\times$8,83432	$10^{-8}\times$8,76968
410	8,70567	8,64228	8,57950	8,51733	8,45576	8,39478	8,33439	8,27457	8,21533	8,15665
420	8,09852	8,04095	7,98392	7,92743	7,87147	7,81604	7,76113	7,70673	7,65283	7,59944
430	7,54655	7,49414	7,44222	7,39077	7,33980	7,28930	7,23926	7,18967	7,14054	7,09186
440	7,04361	6,99581	6,94843	6,90148	6,85495	6,80884	6,76315	6,71786	6,67297	6,62849
450	6,58439	6,54069	6,49738	6,45444	6,41189	6,36970	6,32789	6,28644	6,24535	6,20462
460	6,16424	6,12422	6,08453	6,04519	6,00619	5,96753	5,92919	5,89118	5,85350	5,81614
470	5,77909	5,74236	5,70594	5,66983	5,63402	5,59851	5,56330	5,52838	5,49376	5,45942
480	5,42537	5,39160	5,35811	5,32490	5,29197	5,25930	5,22690	5,19477	5,16290	5,13129
490	5,09994	5,06884	5,03800	5,00740	4,97705	4,94695	4,91709	4,88747	4,85808	4,82893

Relationship between r_S and r $r \approx 2\sin(\pi/6)r_S$

r_S	0,000	0,001	0,002	0,003	0,004	0,005	0,006	0,007	0,008	0,009
0,00	0,000	0,001	0,002	0,003	0,004	0,005	0,006	0,007	0,008	0,009
01	010	012	013	014	015	016	017	018	019	020
02	021	022	023	024	025	026	027	028	029	030
03	031	032	034	035	036	037	038	039	040	041
04	042	043	044	045	046	047	048	049	050	051
0,05	0,052	0,053	0,054	0,055	0,057	0,058	0,059	0,060	0,061	0,062
06	063	064	065	066	067	068	069	070	071	072
07	073	074	075	076	077	079	080	081	082	083
08	084	085	086	087	088	089	090	091	092	093
09	094	095	096	097	098	099	100	102	103	104
0,10	0,105	0,106	0,107	0,108	0,109	0,110	0,111	0,112	0,113	0,114
11	115	116	117	118	119	120	121	122	123	125
12	126	127	128	129	130	131	132	133	134	135
13	136	137	138	139	140	141	142	143	144	145
14	146	148	149	150	151	152	153	154	155	156
0,15	0,157	0,158	0,159	0,160	0,161	0,162	0,163	0,164	0,165	0,166
16	167	168	169	170	172	173	174	175	176	177
17	178	179	180	181	182	183	184	185	186	187
18	188	189	190	191	192	193	194	196	197	198
19	199	200	201	202	203	204	205	206	207	208
0,20	0,209	0,210	0,211	0,212	0,213	0,214	0,215	0,216	0,217	0,218
21	219	221	222	223	224	225	226	227	228	229
22	230	231	232	233	234	235	236	237	238	239
23	240	241	242	243	244	245	247	248	249	250
24	251	252	253	254	255	256	257	258	259	260
0,25	0,261	0,262	0,263	0,264	0,265	0,266	0,267	0,268	0,269	0,270
26	271	272	274	275	276	277	278	279	280	281
27	282	283	284	285	286	287	288	289	290	291
28	292	293	294	295	296	297	298	299	300	301
29	303	304	305	306	307	308	309	310	311	312
0,30	0,313	0,314	0,315	0,316	0,317	0,318	0,319	0,320	0,321	0,322
31	323	324	325	326	327	328	329	330	331	333
32	334	335	336	337	338	339	340	341	342	343
33	344	345	346	347	348	349	350	351	352	353
34	354	355	356	357	358	359	360	361	362	363
0,35	0,364	0,366	0,367	0,368	0,369	0,370	0,371	0,372	0,373	0,374
36	375	376	377	378	379	380	381	382	383	384
37	385	386	387	388	389	390	391	392	393	394
38	395	396	397	398	399	400	401	402	404	405
39	406	407	408	409	410	411	412	413	414	415
0,40	0,416	0,417	0,418	0,419	0,420	0,421	0,422	0,423	0,424	0,425
41	426	427	428	429	430	431	432	433	434	435
42	436	437	438	439	440	441	442	443	444	445
43	447	448	449	450	451	452	453	454	455	456
44	457	458	459	460	461	462	463	464	465	466
0,45	0,467	0,468	0,469	0,470	0,471	0,472	0,473	0,474	0,475	0,476
46	477	478	479	480	481	482	483	484	485	486
47	487	488	489	490	491	492	493	494	495	496
48	497	498	499	500	501	502	503	504	505	507
49	508	509	510	511	512	513	514	515	516	517

r_S	0,000	0,001	0,002	0,003	0,004	0,005	0,006	0,007	0,008	0,009
0,50	0,518	0,519	0,520	0,521	0,522	0,523	0,524	0,525	0,526	0,527
51	528	529	530	531	532	533	534	535	536	537
52	538	539	540	541	542	543	544	545	546	547
53	548	549	550	551	552	553	554	555	556	557
54	558	559	560	561	562	563	564	565	566	567
0,55	0,568	0,569	0,570	0,571	0,572	0,573	0,574	0,575	0,576	0,577
56	578	579	580	581	582	583	584	585	586	587
57	588	589	590	591	592	593	594	595	596	597
58	598	599	600	601	602	603	604	605	606	607
59	608	609	610	611	612	613	614	615	616	617
0,60	0,618	0,619	0,620	0,621	0,622	0,623	0,624	0,625	0,626	0,627
61	628	629	630	631	632	633	634	635	636	637
62	638	639	640	641	642	643	644	645	646	647
63	648	649	650	651	652	653	654	655	656	657
64	658	659	660	661	662	663	664	665	666	667
0,65	0,668	0,669	0,670	0,671	0,672	0,673	0,674	0,675	0,676	0,676
66	677	678	679	680	681	682	683	684	685	686
67	687	688	689	690	691	692	693	694	695	696
68	697	698	699	700	701	702	703	704	705	706
69	707	708	709	710	711	712	713	714	715	716
0,70	0,717	0,718	0,719	0,720	0,721	0,722	0,723	0,724	0,725	0,726
71	727	727	728	729	730	731	732	733	734	735
72	736	737	738	739	740	741	742	743	744	745
73	746	747	748	749	750	751	752	753	754	755
74	756	757	758	759	760	761	761	762	763	764
0,75	0,765	0,766	0,767	0,768	0,769	0,770	0,771	0,772	0,773	0,774
76	775	776	777	778	779	780	781	782	783	784
77	785	786	787	788	789	789	790	791	792	793
78	794	795	796	797	798	799	800	801	802	803
79	804	805	806	807	808	809	810	811	812	813
0,80	0,813	0,814	0,815	0,816	0,817	0,818	0,819	0,820	0,821	0,822
81	823	824	825	826	827	828	829	830	831	832
82	833	834	834	835	836	837	838	839	840	841
83	842	843	844	845	846	847	848	849	850	851
84	852	853	853	854	855	856	857	858	859	860
0,85	0,861	0,862	0,863	0,864	0,865	0,866	0,867	0,868	0,869	0,870
86	870	871	872	873	874	875	876	877	878	879
87	880	881	882	883	884	885	886	886	887	888
88	889	890	891	892	893	894	895	896	897	898
89	899	900	901	901	902	903	904	905	906	907
0,90	0,908	0,909	0,910	0,911	0,912	0,913	0,914	0,915	0,915	0,916
91	917	918	919	920	921	922	923	924	925	926
92	927	928	928	929	930	931	932	933	934	935
93	936	937	938	939	940	940	941	942	943	944
94	945	946	947	948	949	950	951	952	952	953
0,95	0,954	0,955	0,956	0,957	0,958	0,959	0,960	0,961	0,962	0,963
96	964	964	965	966	967	968	969	970	971	972
97	973	974	975	975	976	977	978	979	980	981
98	982	983	984	985	985	986	987	988	989	990
99	991	992	993	994	995	995	996	997	998	999

All values conform to the international convention (i.e. 0,1 instead of 0.1).

Runs: Confidence Limits[7] for the Total Number of Runs I

A point (.) indicates the absence of a limit

$N_1 = N_2 = ½ N$; $½ N \leq 100$

½ N	2α = 0,10	2α = 0,05	2α = 0,02	2α = 0,01
4	2–8	•–•	•–•	•–•
5	3–9	2–10	2–10	•–•
6	3–11	3–11	2–12	2–12
7	4–12	3–13	3–13	3–13
8	5–13	4–14	4–14	3–15
9	6–14	5–15	4–16	4–16
10	6–16	6–16	5–17	5–17
11	7–17	7–17	6–18	5–19
12	8–18	7–19	7–19	6–20
13	9–19	8–20	7–21	7–21
14	10–20	9–21	8–22	7–23
15	11–21	10–22	9–23	8–24
16	11–23	11–23	10–24	9–25
17	12–24	11–25	10–26	10–26
18	13–25	12–26	11–27	11–27
19	14–26	13–27	12–28	11–29
20	15–27	14–28	13–29	12–30
21	16–28	15–29	14–30	13–31
22	17–29	16–30	14–32	14–32
23	17–31	16–32	15–33	14–34
24	18–32	17–33	16–34	15–35
25	19–33	18–34	17–35	16–36
26	20–34	19–35	18–36	17–37
27	21–35	20–36	19–37	18–38
28	22–36	21–37	19–39	18–40
29	23–37	22–38	20–40	19–41
30	24–38	22–40	21–41	20–42
31	25–39	23–41	22–42	21–43
32	25–41	24–42	23–43	22–44
33	26–42	25–43	24–44	23–45
34	27–43	26–44	24–46	23–47
35	28–44	27–45	25–47	24–48
36	29–45	28–46	26–48	25–49
37	30–46	29–47	27–49	26–50
38	31–47	30–48	28–50	27–51
39	32–48	30–50	29–51	28–52
40	33–49	31–51	30–52	29–53
41	34–50	32–52	31–53	29–55
42	35–51	33–53	31–54	30–56
43	35–53	34–54	32–56	31–57
44	36–54	35–55	33–57	32–58
45	37–55	36–56	34–58	33–59
46	38–56	37–57	35–59	34–60
47	39–57	38–58	36–60	35–61
48	40–58	38–60	37–61	36–63
49	41–59	39–61	38–62	36–64
50	42–60	40–62	38–64	37–65
51	43–61	41–63	39–65	38–66
52	44–62	42–64	40–66	39–67
53	45–63	43–65	41–67	40–68
54	45–65	44–66	42–68	41–69
55	46–66	45–67	43–69	42–70
56	47–67	46–68	44–70	42–72
57	48–68	47–69	45–71	43–73
58	49–69	47–71	46–72	44–74
59	50–70	48–72	46–74	45–75
60	51–71	49–73	47–75	46–76
61	52–72	50–74	48–76	47–77
62	53–73	51–75	49–77	48–78
63	54–74	52–76	50–78	49–79
64	55–75	53–77	51–79	49–81
65	56–76	54–78	52–80	50–82
66	57–77	55–79	53–81	51–83
67	58–78	56–80	54–82	52–84
68	58–80	57–81	54–84	53–85
69	59–81	58–82	55–85	54–86
70	60–82	58–84	56–86	55–87
71	61–83	59–85	57–87	56–88
72	62–84	60–86	58–88	57–89
73	63–85	61–87	59–89	57–91
74	64–86	62–88	60–90	58–92
75	65–87	63–89	61–91	59–93
76	66–88	64–90	62–92	60–94
77	67–89	65–91	63–93	61–95
78	68–90	66–92	64–94	62–96
79	69–91	67–93	64–96	63–97
80	70–92	68–94	65–97	64–98
81	71–93	69–95	66–98	65–99
82	71–95	69–97	67–99	66–100
83	72–96	70–98	68–100	66–102
84	73–97	71–99	69–101	67–103
85	74–98	72–100	70–102	68–104
86	75–99	73–101	71–103	69–105
87	76–100	74–102	72–104	70–106
88	77–101	75–103	73–105	71–107
89	78–102	76–104	74–106	72–108
90	79–103	77–105	74–108	73–109
91	80–104	78–106	75–109	74–110
92	81–105	79–107	76–110	75–111
93	82–106	80–108	77–111	75–113
94	83–107	81–109	78–112	76–114
95	84–108	82–110	79–113	77–115
96	85–109	82–112	80–114	78–116
97	86–110	83–113	81–115	79–117
98	87–111	84–114	82–116	80–118
99	87–113	85–115	83–117	81–119
100	88–114	86–116	84–118	82–120

$N_1 < N_2$; $N_2 \leq 20$

N_2	2α = 0,10	2α = 0,05	2α = 0,02	2α = 0,01
$N_1 = 2$				
2	•–•	•–•	•–•	•–•
3	•–•	•–•	•–•	•–•
4	•–•	•–•	•–•	•–•
5	•–•	•–•	•–•	•–•
6	•–•	•–•	•–•	•–•
7	•–•	•–•	•–•	•–•
8	2–•	•–•	•–•	•–•
9	2–•	•–•	•–•	•–•
10	2–•	•–•	•–•	•–•
11	2–•	•–•	•–•	•–•
12	2–•	2–•	•–•	•–•
13	2–•	2–•	•–•	•–•
14	2–•	2–•	•–•	•–•
15	2–•	2–•	•–•	•–•
16	2–•	2–•	•–•	•–•
17	2–•	2–•	•–•	•–•
18	2–•	2–•	•–•	•–•
19	2–•	2–•	2–•	•–•
20	2–•	2–•	2–•	•–•
$N_1 = 3$				
3	•–•	•–•	•–•	•–•
4	•–7	•–•	•–•	•–•
5	2–•	•–•	•–•	•–•
6	2–•	2–•	•–•	•–•
7	2–•	2–•	•–•	•–•
8	2–•	2–•	•–•	•–•
9	2–•	2–•	2–•	•–•
10	3–•	2–•	2–•	•–•
11	3–•	2–•	2–•	•–•
12	3–•	2–•	2–•	2–•
13	3–•	2–•	2–•	2–•
14	3–•	2–•	2–•	2–•
15	3–•	3–•	2–•	2–•
16	3–•	3–•	2–•	2–•
17	3–•	3–•	2–•	2–•
18	3–•	3–•	2–•	2–•
19	3–•	3–•	2–•	2–•
20	3–•	3–•	2–•	2–•
$N_1 = 4$				
4	2–8	•–•	•–•	•–•
5	2–9	2–9	•–9	•–•
6	3–9	2–9	2–•	•–•
7	3–9	2–•	2–•	•–•
8	3–•	3–•	2–•	2–•
9	3–•	3–•	2–•	2–•
10	3–•	3–•	2–•	2–•
11	3–•	3–•	2–•	2–•
12	4–•	3–•	3–•	2–•
13	4–•	3–•	3–•	2–•
14	4–•	3–•	3–•	2–•
15	4–•	3–•	3–•	3–•
16	4–•	4–•	3–•	3–•
17	4–•	4–•	3–•	3–•
18	4–•	4–•	3–•	3–•
19	4–•	4–•	3–•	3–•
20	4–•	4–•	3–•	3–•
$N_1 = 5$				
5	3–9	2–10	2–10	•–•
6	3–10	3–10	2–11	2–•
7	3–10	3–11	2–11	2–11
8	3–11	3–11	2–•	2–•
9	4–11	3–•	3–•	2–•
10	4–11	3–•	3–•	3–•
11	4–•	4–•	3–•	3–•
12	4–•	4–•	3–•	3–•
13	4–•	4–•	3–•	3–•
14	5–•	4–•	3–•	3–•
15	5–•	4–•	4–•	3–•
16	5–•	4–•	4–•	3–•
17	5–•	4–•	4–•	3–•
18	5–•	5–•	4–•	4–•
19	5–•	5–•	4–•	4–•
20	5–•	5–•	4–•	4–•
$N_1 = 6$				
6	3–11	3–11	2–12	2–12
7	4–11	3–12	3–12	2–13
8	4–12	3–12	3–13	3–13
9	4–12	4–13	3–13	3–•
10	5–12	4–13	3–•	3–•
11	5–13	4–13	4–•	3–•
12	5–13	4–13	4–•	3–•
13	5–13	5–•	4–•	3–•
14	5–13	5–•	4–•	4–•
15	6–•	5–•	4–•	4–•
16	6–•	5–•	4–•	4–•
17	6–•	5–•	5–•	4–•
18	6–•	5–•	5–•	4–•
19	6–•	6–•	5–•	4–•
20	6–•	6–•	5–•	4–•
$N_1 = 7$				
7	4–12	3–13	3–13	3–13
8	4–13	4–13	3–14	3–14
9	5–13	4–14	4–14	3–15
10	5–13	5–14	4–15	3–15
11	5–14	5–14	4–15	4–15
12	6–14	5–14	4–15	4–•
13	6–14	5–15	5–•	4–•
14	6–14	5–15	5–•	4–•
15	6–15	6–15	5–•	4–•
16	6–15	6–•	5–•	5–•
17	7–15	6–•	5–•	5–•
18	7–15	6–•	5–•	5–•
19	7–15	6–•	6–•	5–•
20	7–15	6–•	6–•	5–•
$N_1 = 8$				
8	5–13	4–14	4–14	3–15
9	5–14	5–14	4–15	3–15
10	6–14	5–15	4–15	4–16
11	6–15	5–15	5–16	4–16
12	6–15	6–16	5–16	4–17
13	6–15	6–16	5–17	5–17
14	7–16	6–16	5–17	5–17
15	7–16	6–16	5–17	5–•
16	7–16	6–17	6–17	5–•
17	7–16	7–17	6–•	5–•
18	8–16	7–17	6–•	6–•
19	8–16	7–17	6–•	6–•
20	8–17	7–17	6–•	6–•
$N_1 = 9$				
9	6–14	5–15	4–16	4–16
10	6–15	5–16	5–16	4–17
11	6–15	6–16	5–17	5–17
12	7–16	6–16	5–17	5–18
13	7–16	6–17	6–18	5–18
14	7–17	7–17	6–18	5–18
15	8–17	7–18	6–18	6–19
16	8–17	7–18	6–18	6–19
17	8–17	7–18	7–19	6–19
18	8–18	8–18	7–19	6–•
19	8–18	8–18	7–19	6–•
20	9–18	8–18	7–19	7–•
$N_1 = 10$				
10	6–16	6–16	5–17	5–17
11	7–16	6–17	5–18	5–18
12	7–17	7–17	6–18	5–19
13	8–17	7–18	6–19	5–19
14	8–17	7–18	6–19	6–19
15	8–18	7–18	7–19	6–20
16	8–18	8–19	7–20	6–20
17	9–18	8–19	7–20	7–20
18	9–19	8–19	7–20	7–21
19	9–19	8–20	8–20	7–21
20	9–19	9–20	8–20	7–21
$N_1 = 11$				
11	7–17	7–17	6–18	5–19
12	8–17	7–18	6–19	6–19
13	8–18	7–19	6–19	6–20
14	8–18	8–19	7–20	6–20
15	9–19	8–19	7–20	7–21
16	9–19	8–20	7–21	7–21
17	9–19	9–20	8–21	7–22
18	10–20	9–20	8–21	7–22
19	10–20	9–21	8–22	8–22
20	10–20	9–21	8–22	8–22
$N_1 = 12$				
12	8–18	7–19	7–19	6–20
13	9–18	8–19	7–20	6–21
14	9–19	8–20	7–21	7–21
15	9–19	8–20	8–21	7–22
16	10–20	9–21	8–22	7–22
17	10–20	9–21	8–22	8–22
18	10–21	9–21	8–22	8–23
19	10–21	10–22	9–23	8–23
20	11–21	10–22	9–23	8–23
$N_1 = 13$				
13	9–19	8–20	7–21	7–21
14	9–20	9–20	8–21	7–22
15	10–20	9–21	8–22	7–22
16	10–21	9–21	8–22	8–23
17	10–21	10–22	9–23	8–23
18	11–21	10–22	9–23	8–24
19	11–22	10–23	9–24	9–24
20	11–22	10–23	10–24	9–24
$N_1 = 14$				
14	10–20	9–21	8–22	7–23
15	10–21	9–22	8–23	8–23
16	11–21	10–22	9–23	8–24
17	11–22	10–23	9–24	8–24
18	11–22	10–23	9–24	9–25
19	12–23	11–23	10–24	9–25
20	12–23	11–24	10–25	9–25
$N_1 = 15$				
15	11–21	10–22	9–23	8–24
16	11–22	10–23	9–24	9–24
17	11–22	11–23	10–24	9–25
18	12–23	11–24	10–25	9–25
19	12–23	11–24	10–25	10–26
20	12–24	12–25	11–26	10–26
$N_1 = 16$				
16	11–23	11–23	10–24	9–25
17	12–23	11–24	10–25	9–26
18	12–24	11–25	10–26	10–26
19	13–24	12–25	11–26	10–27
20	13–25	12–25	11–26	10–27
$N_1 = 17$				
17	12–24	11–25	10–26	10–26
18	13–24	12–25	11–26	10–27
19	13–25	12–26	11–27	10–27
20	13–25	13–26	11–27	11–28
$N_1 = 18$				
18	13–25	12–26	11–27	11–27
19	14–25	13–26	12–27	11–28
20	14–26	13–27	12–28	11–29
$N_1 = 19$				
19	14–26	13–27	12–28	11–29
20	14–27	13–27	12–29	12–29

Explanation:

(Time)	1	2	3	4	5	6	7	8	9	10
Series (I)	A	B	A	A	A	B	B	A	B	A
Series (II)	A	B	A	B	A	A	B	A	B	A
Series (III)	A	A	A	A	A	A	B	B	B	B

Each of the series (I), (II), (III) has a size $N = 10$ and contains $N_1 = 4$ B's and $N_2 = 6$ A's. (For $N = N_1 + N_2 < 40$ the smaller number is denoted by N_1.) In these series the underscored letters in each case form a run. The total number of runs I is 7 in series (I), 9 in series (II), 2 in series (III).

The table gives the confidence limits of the expectation $\mathbf{I}_{(total)}$ of total number of runs:

(a) If I is *less* than or *equal* to the left-hand limit
$I < \mathbf{I}$ with probability α or
$I \neq \mathbf{I}$ with probability 2α.
Wald-Wolfowitz test: significance level 2α.

(b) If I is greater than or equal to the right-hand limit
$I > \mathbf{I}$ with probability α or
$I \neq \mathbf{I}$ with probability 2α.

(c) If I lies between the limits and *attains neither*, then the null hypothesis cannot be rejected.

[7] SWED and EISENHART, *Ann. math. Statist.*, **14**, 66 (1943). Reprinted by kind permission of the authors and publishers.

All values conform to the international convention (i.e. 0,1 instead of 0.1).

l	$\alpha \leq 0{,}01$	$\alpha \leq 0{,}10$	$\alpha \leq 0{,}50$	$\alpha \leq 0{,}90$	$\alpha \leq 0{,}99$
1	2	2	2	2	2
2	4	4	6	8	12
3	6	6	12	22	38
4	8	10	22	54	100
5	10	16	46	116	230
6	14	26	92	260	490
7	18	44	182	530	1044
8	26	78	360	1104	2140
9	38	142	714	2240	4370
10	56	256	1424	4530	8980
11	86	480	2850	9190	18240
12	140	930	5680	18540	37200
13	234	1838	11330	37600	75500
14	410	3630	22700	75700	151700
15	748	7160	45300	151700	303000
16	1446	14190	90600	303000	607000
17	2830	28100	181200	607000	1214000
18	5530	56100	362000	1214000	2430000
19	10860	117300	725000	2430000	4850000
20	21500	235000	1450000	4850000	9710000

The table[1] gives the sample size for which the longest run above or below the median will attain or exceed the length l with probability α. The choice of which side of the median is to be tested must be made beforehand.

Example: Size of sample = 28. Longest run above = 4. Result: $0{,}50 < \alpha < 0{,}90$.

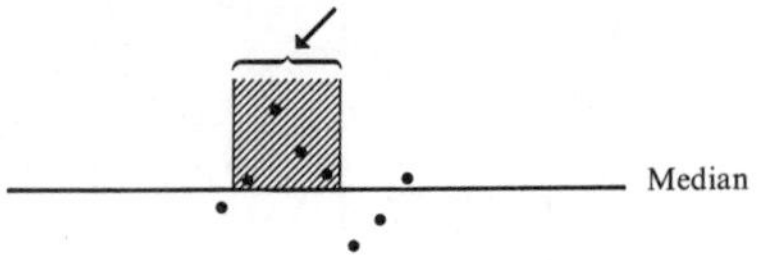

l	$\alpha \leq 0{,}01$	$\alpha \leq 0{,}10$	$\alpha \leq 0{,}50$	$\alpha \leq 0{,}90$	$\alpha \leq 0{,}99$
1	2	2	2	2	2
2	4	4	6	10	14
3	6	8	14	26	44
4	8	14	30	68	116
5	12	26	68	152	252
6	20	50	140	322	552
7	34	98	290	676	1164
8	62	194	596	1390	2390
9	116	390	1208	2830	4930
10	216	782	2440	5650	10140
11	446	1182	4910	11750	20700
12	884	2360	9840	23800	42500
13	1762	4720	19890	48600	86700
14	3510	9450	39900	98600	174200
15	6990	18900	80500	197300	348000
16	13930	37800	161300	395000	697000
17	27900	75600	323000	789000	1394000
18	55500	151200	645000	1578000	2790000
19	111000	302000	1290000	3160000	5570000
20	222000	605000	2580000	6310000	11150000

The table[1] gives the probability α that for the size of sample given in the table the *shorter* of the two runs that are respectively the longest above and the longest below the median will attain or exceed the length l.

Example: Size of sample = 28. Longest run above = 4, below = 9. Result: $0{,}10 < \alpha < 0{,}50$.

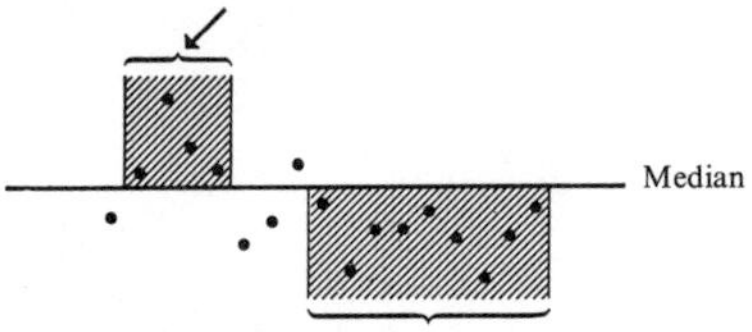

l	$\alpha \leq 0{,}01$	$\alpha \leq 0{,}10$	$\alpha \leq 0{,}50$	$\alpha \leq 0{,}90$	$\alpha \leq 0{,}99$
1	2	2	2	2	2
2	4	4	4	8	10
3	6	6	8	16	28
4	8	8	16	36	64
5	10	14	30	76	136
6	12	20	58	152	282
7	16	32	106	296	568
8	22	52	200	580	1150
9	32	86	388	1174	2310
10	42	150	758	2350	4640
11	62	262	1488	4720	9330
12	94	500	2920	9460	18730
13	156	962	5860	10660	37700
14	256	1876	11250	21300	75700
15	418	3670	22600	42600	151600
16	766	7330	45200	85300	303000
17	1472	14090	90100	170500	606000
18	2860	27900	180300	341000	1213000
19	5570	55500	361000	682000	2430000
20	10860	111100	721000	1364000	4850000

The table[1] gives the probability α that for the size of sample given in the table the *longer* of the two runs that are respectively the longest above and the longest below the median will attain or exceed the length l.

Example: Size of sample = 28. Longest run above = 4, below = 9. Result: $\alpha < 0{,}01$.

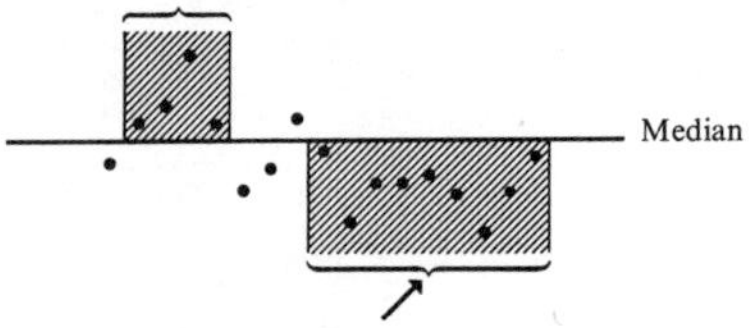

l	$\alpha \leq 0{,}01$	$\alpha \leq 0{,}10$	$\alpha \leq 0{,}50$	$\alpha \leq 0{,}90$	$\alpha \leq 0{,}99$
1	2	2	2	2	2
2	4	4	6	8	12
3	6	8	12	22	34
4	8	12	22	48	76
5	12	18	46	96	162
6	16	34	86	192	380
7	24	58	166	382	668
8	38	108	324	760	1342
9	66	204	638	1518	2690
10	118	400	1266	3030	5410
11	228	790	2530	6070	10870
12	444	1568	5050	12130	21500
13	878	3130	10070	24300	43100
14	1750	6220	20100	48500	86200
15	3480	12490	40300	97000	172300
16	6790	25000	80600	194100	345000
17	13860	49900	161100	388000	689000
18	27700	99900	322000	776000	1379000
19	55400	199800	644000	1553000	2760000
20	110800	400000	1289000	3110000	5510000

The table[1] gives the probability α that for the size of sample given in the table the *shorter* of the two runs that are respectively the longest run above and the longest run below a maximal cut will attain or exceed the length l. The maximal cut is so made that this particular run is maximalized.

Example: Size of sample = 28. Longest run above the maximal cut = 8, below = 9. Result: $\alpha < 0{,}01$.

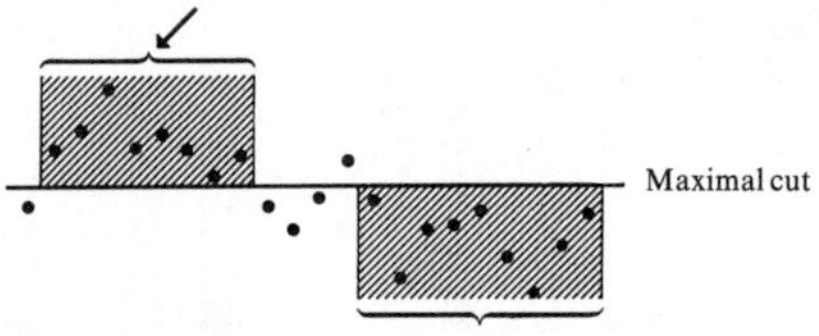

l	$\alpha \leq 0{,}01$	$\alpha \leq 0{,}05$	$\alpha \leq 0{,}10$	$\alpha \leq 0{,}90$	$\alpha \leq 0{,}95$	$\alpha \leq 0{,}99$
2	–	–	–	7	8	12
3	–	–	4	32	40	61
4	–	7	11	162	210	321
5	9	26	48	964	1253	1923
6	34	153	309	6637	8633	13268
7	234	1170	2396	52229	67950	104452
8	2034	10348	21248	464209	603947	928410
9	20067	102382	210291	4595600	5979012	9191191
10	218833	1116808	2294003	50133734	65225489	100267459

The table[2] gives the probability α that for the size of sample given in the table at least one run up or down of length l or longer will occur.

Example: Size of sample = 28. Up-run to be tested = 5. Result: $0{,}05 < \alpha < 0{,}10$.

Illustration of up- and down-runs:

Time sequence:	1	2	3	4	5	6
Values:	1,14	1,17	1,20	1,19	1,21	1,16
	up			down	up	down
Length l:	3			1	1	1

[1] Olmstead, P. S., *Runs Determined in a Sample by an Arbitrary Cut*, Bell Telephone System, Technical Publications, Monograph 2937, New York, 1958.

[2] Values of $l = 2$–5 from Olmstead, P. S., *Distribution of Sample Arrangements for Runs Up and Down*, Bell Telephone System, Technical Publications, Monograph 2289, New York, 1946, and *Ann. math. Statist.*, **17**, 24 (1946). Values of $l = 6$–10 calculated by K. Diem using the Poisson approximation.

All values conform to the international convention (i.e. 0,1 instead of 0.1).

72137	73850	32733	35321	80647	39713	61060	57865	88049	20557	43375	50914	83628	73935	72502	48174	62551	96122	22375	96488
04254	60099	50584	10961	57642	19101	30613	01549	96531	83936	45842	78222	88481	44933	12839	20750	47116	58973	99018	22769
48083	50731	81250	57995	41467	29834	08059	22945	72193	36077	82577	16210	76092	87730	90049	02115	37096	20505	91937	69776
16602	26772	89693	92558	38394	84119	68486	17622	30953	78267	31568	58297	88922	50436	86135	42726	54307	29170	13045	65527
29910	55480	47184	79775	09779	08718	45822	17643	63252	00232	98059	07255	90786	95246	15280	61692	45137	17539	31799	64780
77708	83761	89238	86521	82711	79266	47763	26173	36183	65869	64355	91271	49295	98354	28005	69792	01480	51557	70726	35862
90715	65115	12870	89922	24926	44062	94896	97561	96490	35454	51623	98381	11055	32951	28363	16451	67912	66404	76254	75495
79666	48119	38525	82189	34921	49838	47558	92343	47408	99542	44247	12762	54488	74321	36224	95619	16238	25374	13653	25345
53294	49761	76235	55814	29900	03796	73326	94291	10739	36087	32326	52225	72447	77804	57045	27552	72387	34001	83792	66764
44422	78305	76369	20601	39701	80769	17322	78280	42376	64899	62390	68375	42921	28545	33167	85710	11035	40171	04840	69848
12601	54432	65017	91131	50515	97477	80691	31834	32401	11994	97820	06653	27477	61364	22681	02280	53815	47479	44017	37563
65664	73669	24910	25458	23699	86413	19985	49355	24358	02915	81553	92012	50435	73814	96290	86827	81430	45597	82296	28947
18363	66515	23098	22384	87756	66396	63646	50963	99099	62895	09202	48494	95974	33534	94657	71126	71770	16092	03942	90111
00491	53688	72033	68063	86104	90576	04119	65531	30304	39202	82110	82254	03669	03281	11613	36336	98297	48100	71594	52667
02878	83197	94318	47901	85252	91124	32939	75043	40325	53252	18175	09457	83810	46392	02705	85591	33192	65127	80852	42030
79920	22780	43100	83886	26378	66010	00020	80666	66861	17820	50756	80608	35695	72641	26306	76298	32532	22644	96853	18610
97556	54260	42361	12741	56996	48177	85725	36668	45531	85245	12710	60264	74650	92126	08152	32147	17457	56298	48964	64733
79435	52143	12322	12254	04314	98550	58315	78036	24355	85822	44424	88508	66190	74060	93206	92840	44833	81146	64060	62975
93903	78220	09178	33676	58996	78675	11648	96220	54127	24804	24720	66501	74157	42246	41688	72835	87258	89384	11251	34329
04758	50961	90230	72006	24268	77817	10524	60304	79352	31942	85419	93017	28087	78323	77109	56832	78400	24190	37978	85863
53841	28758	93442	42983	25254	96336	16570	89358	36619	72838	10933	99964	13468	17211	48046	51122	92668	96750	11139	06275
07626	78473	17708	59059	33584	52451	11575	55992	83228	38546	49559	71671	53603	24491	57570	90789	32932	67449	05115	45941
40645	27008	16341	05870	42604	79286	08720	13175	89573	38051	39391	92039	71664	40219	97707	93975	66981	19556	24605	52169
82666	14127	94390	07069	39152	10357	94612	56748	75428	28101	38543	54214	48928	32818	51963	87353	15094	29529	87305	01361
60147	99378	58310	34655	48242	58656	30544	01860	08322	70476	44242	54227	28598	64422	29361	20359	48577	05971	92373	22765
61557	43927	11643	65522	76713	95782	34956	67384	47654	64999	11468	74149	81386	94127	67342	38010	92522	57728	39432	27914
71522	16545	68464	62540	76143	06328	94718	58404	84099	73641	52165	54336	89196	40042	37889	06003	58033	59082	94988	62152
05366	66273	49518	25413	20346	22719	18255	47685	78475	67421	83093	77038	55399	67893	89597	85630	08059	35757	49479	63531
72668	62720	08971	97908	15905	86615	97559	68107	10649	30976	66455	90708	08450	50120	17795	55604	51222	17900	55553	02980
51497	78491	83680	08319	51223	19735	72708	82599	28127	29660	30790	65154	19582	20942	81439	83917	90452	64753	99645	19799
66170	68781	91423	86645	02925	51327	41022	76893	29200	82747	97297	74420	18783	93471	89055	56413	77817	10655	52915	68198
23361	60672	52451	03774	06365	94880	70978	57385	70532	46978	87390	53319	90155	03154	20301	47831	86786	11284	49160	79852
53608	59661	70966	24937	56559	98856	19207	41684	20288	19783	82215	35810	39852	43795	21530	96315	55657	76473	08217	46810
24079	01177	02666	35515	24819	73382	50172	23114	28745	12249	35844	63265	26451	06986	08707	99251	06260	74779	96285	31998
50495	87947	20592	91917	59595	55083	43112	94833	72864	58785	53473	06308	56778	30474	57277	23425	27092	47759	18422	56074
93550	48308	20282	92711	74402	51335	64031	41740	69680	69373	73674	97914	77989	47280	71804	74587	70563	77813	50242	60398
16269	03381	09798	89487	33632	47073	92357	38870	73784	95662	83923	90790	49474	11901	30322	80254	99608	17019	17892	76813
32868	72831	55156	90166	91599	09471	79945	42580	86605	97758	08206	54199	41327	01170	21745	71318	07978	35440	26128	10545
80722	21328	19977	82161	29385	62151	48030	05125	70866	72154	86385	39490	57482	32921	33795	43155	30432	48384	85430	51828
67362	87389	09559	98456	70498	40173	80016	81500	48061	25583	74101	87573	01556	89183	64830	16779	35724	82103	61658	20296
83452	92994	85019	57720	36951	03383	34265	65728	89776	04006	06089	84076	12445	47416	83620	59151	97420	23689	74515	55211
51168	41624	94768	53124	95920	04777	82534	76335	21108	42302	79496	21054	80132	67719	72662	58360	57384	65406	63918	17046
83805	28803	63272	65480	08764	16379	72055	61146	82780	89411	53131	57879	39099	42715	24830	60045	23250	39847	46616	17817
59782	50488	77081	10186	86577	28581	26999	96294	20431	30114	23035	30380	76272	60343	57573	42492	47962	21439	54664	97968
09627	26695	79373	09119	79765	99918	01628	47335	17893	53176	07436	14799	78197	48601	97557	83918	20530	61565	69344	71964
20160	50603	71684	34875	60617	77991	66322	27390	73834	73494	21527	93579	20949	85666	25102	64733	93872	72698	87520	43340
04375	15463	49139	17369	71179	77472	96239	18521	67354	41883	58939	36222	43935	36272	47817	90287	91434	86453	84477	03559
67163	48629	25607	27003	09721	70206	10497	83617	39176	45062	63903	33862	14903	38996	60027	41702	78189	28598	12707	91191
49380	42273	93835	32621	60848	67721	69712	33438	85908	58620	50646	47857	96024	58568	67614	44370	40276	85964	71604	05691
56013	02278	53110	33235	62949	53799	51375	42451	76889	68096	80657	91046	95340	70209	23825	46031	45306	64476	31460	61553
46596	51960	02957	56574	18672	02994	39960	02489	53079	72789	22562	39359	38220	13972	86115	17196	24569	26820	66299	50962
52928	66296	15570	31407	54988	78749	16135	82797	31296	93268	10104	95616	82618	85756	51156	74037	12501	94162	42006	99213
09403	50848	71088	31308	35677	49046	10870	72107	11550	61175	33345	56717	07896	74085	59886	03051	78702	13402	74318	20992
30328	72163	66728	81091	52307	78952	60261	11207	73065	48286	57057	49472	95241	84360	13960	95736	43637	60399	19080	72417
78707	57821	28410	64908	30432	78760	36880	02564	96978	62332	77321	92228	53849	26578	39954	86726	91039	13884	25376	60187
73597	94657	72927	46459	61325	50908	25601	30038	78786	65197	65283	18169	72967	53031	47906	99501	27753	69946	66875	31598
07446	66408	19958	65159	11338	39231	72802	70630	87336	16385	32784	38073	87910	89260	66444	15979	83469	76952	50065	89540
47870	55448	14158	83451	58729	42430	42234	04905	83274	22459	75032	93544	10482	34277	40177	01081	57788	08612	39886	33050
84269	35324	35508	49481	56478	30246	41771	61398	98154	61644	12405	45037	68034	98561	46747	30655	41878	93610	51745	97527
52704	71441	50581	65679	37597	17182	60733	11765	09293	70076	40751	95846	80277	92450	60888	18689	45966	25837	70906	62841
19020	09999	08316	32781	89731	52148	09111	64205	77930	32391	69076	13459	59896	78185	60268	03650	36814	88460	34049	19544
19442	94873	36976	30366	65815	66895	27222	17378	59359	00055	66780	54939	78369	04163	77673	73342	78915	20537	06126	92480
39523	74227	51895	39733	29426	76685	93548	87546	07687	47338	12240	32277	23015	54261	95020	77705	81682	96907	37411	90717
01201	85057	93409	81200	21176	78459	18960	85182	02245	11566	52527	62992	55171	85448	12545	75992	08790	88992	69756	46722
51725	60273	84903	84374	31438	36959	83719	40702	79038	68639	63329	93821	58095	62204	69319	00672	96037	78680	98734	92743
91045	72642	42684	32419	12825	58785	84563	62071	17799	96994	41635	52830	19700	98193	37600	70617	58959	45486	58338	12464
54896	95603	17290	91508	95605	82514	32257	15699	02654	83110	44278	95523	12666	87597	23190	26243	36690	75829	71060	91605
92324	88115	77848	38006	45600	02181	79261	49705	31491	25318	52586	72494	66685	05344	71633	68536	18786	28575	08455	93825
88397	78035	06366	37342	62070	74459	62026	13032	14048	16304	11959	78684	72590	47283	45445	35611	98354	53680	45747	87442
52118	65337	13461	18438	16099	57330	05018	92605	10316	07351	78020	86361	30286	06434	50229	09070	44848	09996	77753	49227
37202	05623	23595	79677	59772	37141	63390	48093	02366	05407	08325	52046	87494	95585	25547	53500	45047	08406	66984	71128
71637	80269	83299	89743	94628	26784	17792	09214	53781	90102	25774	92525	32301	25923	76556	13274	39776	97027	56919	88547
35790	19603	31212	34419	34728	47391	93272	09887	34196	98251	62453	37703	70711	37921	54989	17828	60976	57662	61757	71249
99087	72525	34402	50115	09825	54728	37514	24437	01316	04770	06534	17768	36086	05468	41631	95632	78154	38634	47463	99728
89768	36608	49108	92337	79809	81934	06370	18703	90858	55130	40869	88243	37403	42231	17073	49097	54147	03654	14735	78351
83816	00718	94663	39629	27812	28250	44983	33834	54280	67850	96025	96117	00768	14821	69029	25453	48798	15486	73835	51776
00806	20667	81224	24296	39967	60239	89494	34431	44890	59892	79682	20308	82510	53609	13258	89631	80497	49167	81559	47202
65733	03902	29140	05414	62087	65727	54430	52632	94126	95597	48338	67645	44676	14730	22642	21919	21050	87791	76192	56686
60671	23190	47433	86979	45281	69750	96999	42104	34377	63309	82181	00278	28209	95629	75818	09043	48564	87355	27209	09827
45326	86280	74876	51858	03263	10215	87947	09427	32380	43636	58578	07761	28456	46570	11623	50417	37763	30136	58254	71090
54419	65493	88741	89069	10789	00973	30238	46126	85306	37114	22718	50584	92291	56575	24075	43889	40909	18741	86154	20843
72845	68939	06483	40835	16564	75047	22938	13073	32066	43098	75738	94910	15403	89151	73322	18370	90586	46115	87375	79147
01828	48113	60005	87083	90000	22346	89182	27750	63314	87302	49472	24885	79506	60638	07132	00908	92035	75518	30878	14979
89871	81320	05251	25930	37320	11895	16187	03303	40287	52435	23926	92544	54099	31497	03863	22864	72620	74169	25311	80669
74883	93005	77888	64673	19302	54669	21526	07401	30925	46148	20138	33874	56715	38424	38273	11361	15203	64912	62494	31231
25493	56247	46907	25634	84761	76421	42907	95158	27146	37012	43361	03173	97911	71313	44256	66609	42504	76799	46790	28464
28278	93841	13134	25129	65536	19838	21479	48265	01674	47274	56350	37512	14883	99673	62298	33948	32456	28675	04242	20735
44834	89816	52509	85192	32114	83770	90076	70233	76730	25043	16686	54737	57431	01786	20803	69465	37970	05673	49516	98035
23329	74767	85661	54449	76606	02131	93202	25355	93941	84434	22384	13240	93617	51549	28532	57150	77261	62643	74966	08777
33176	16108	98145	27652	76918	41000	46059	72208	90475	10341	39703	83224	37858	61657	04184	15597	29448	01922	05709	77900
44597	28074	92908	22392	38034	83739	32876	98604	75652	95680	51386	48724	76069	94867	93570	20306	31712	96238	57864	86267
81456	81110	94771	13664	07478	80992	58485	18882	13238	59865	55644	05528	94935	58972	43340	94718	97397	92197	57257	73187
91503	59589	22803	18122	17790	00236	93750	20468	92189	66781	06210	18208	13973	57905	66878	55721	67437	61709	88182	92769
63651	64109	13207	68346	42140	00052	04099	48767	23355	42505	34539	51129	48580	59386	62209	29754	77409	48146	50411	50511
30709	25869	68851	65221	69392	35106	36393	27129	17326	86452	69952	68433	72332	62502	76323	38379	07293	76788	84281	58581
50664	89487	41973	98456	51147	51327	26590	94684	58103	96936	71276	30275	22753	46046	67196	65135	54879	71903	23541	92400
80089	83750	36605	85343	26090	28447	33179	69730	09683	08770	50381	43130	88108	64709	15191	68718	38375	46747	19860	76129
19293	91304	37043	82077	42231	31534	54358	52939	26655	72687	26616	09608	59223	74533	64986	49667	78039	61030	46122	54941
97754	28401	62553	98641	48553	35996	08033	91811	70471	81538	20017	19613	81103	37642	41866	96777	08667	74544	92903	58427
47923	38366	81939	61526	27691	13988	21630	00957	50599	91260	72832	89364	14158	71740	91289	61204	91185	23485	18424	65084

[1] LINDER, A., *Planen und Auswerten von Versuchen*, 3rd ed., Birkhäuser, Basle, 1969, page 329. Reprinted by kind permission of the author and publishers.

All values conform to the international convention (i.e. 0,1 instead of 0.1).

I. Symbols

$a \to b$	a tending toward b
∞	Infinity
lim	Limiting value
$a \sim b$	a approximately equal to b
$a \approx b$	a very nearly equal to b
$a = b$	a equal to b [cf. (**1**) below]
$a \equiv b$	a identical with b (for formulae only)
$a > b$	a greater than b [cf. (**2**) and (**3**) below]
$a < b$	a smaller than b [cf. (**2**) and (**3**) below]
$a \gg b$	a much greater than b
$a \ll b$	a much smaller than b
$a \neq b$, $a \lessgtr b$	a not equal to b
$b < a < c$	a greater than b and smaller than c
$a \geq b$, $a \geqq b$	a equal to or greater than b, i.e., a at least as great as b
$a \leq b$, $a \leqq b$	a equal to or smaller than b, i.e., a at most as great as b
$b \leq a \leq c$	a lying between b and c
$\|a\|$	Absolute value of a; this is always positive, for example $\|-5\| = 5$
$+$	Addition sign, plus, positive
$-$	Subtraction sign, minus, negative
$\times$	Multiplication sign, times
: or /	Division sign, divided by
$a + b = c$	$a + b$, read as 'a plus b', denotes the sum of a and b. The result of the addition, c, is also known as the sum
$\sum_1^k x_i$	Sum of all values $x_1, x_2, x_3, \ldots$, i.e., of all values x_i, from $i = 1$ to $i = k$ inclusive, or $\sum_1^k x_i = x_1 + x_2 + x_3 + \cdots + x_k$ (the limits of the summation above and below the sign Σ are usually omitted if there is no possibility of confusion)
$\int$	Indefinite integral
$\int_a^b$	Definite integral, or integral between a and b
$a - b = c$	$a - b$, read as 'a minus b', denotes subtraction of b from a. a is the minuend, b the subtrahend; $a - b$, or c, is the difference. Subtraction is the opposite of addition
$a \times b = c$, $a\,b = c$	$a \times b$, read as 'a times b', denotes multiplication of a by b. a and b are the multiplicands or factors; $a \times b$, or c, is the product
$a/b = c$, $\frac{a}{b} = c$, $a : b = c$	a/b, read as 'a divided by b', denotes division. a is the dividend, b the divisor; a/b, or c, is the quotient $\frac{a}{b}$ or a/b. In fractions, a is the numerator (= dividend), b the denominator (= divisor). Division is the opposite of multiplication
$a^b = c$	a^b, read as 'a to the power b', is known as involution. a is the base, b the exponent; a^b, or c, is the bth power of a. In the special case of $a^2 = c$, a^2 or c is the square of a; in that of $a^3 = c$, a^3 or c is the cube of a
$\sqrt[b]{a} = c$	$\sqrt[b]{a}$, is the bth root of a, b being known as the root exponent. In the special case of $\sqrt[2]{a} = c$, $\sqrt[2]{a}$ or c is known as the square root of a, and the root exponent is usually omitted, i.e., $\sqrt[2]{a} = \sqrt{a}$. In the special case of $\sqrt[3]{a} = c$, $\sqrt[3]{a}$ or c is known as the cube root of a. Extraction of a root is the opposite of involution. See also 'Logarithms', page 170
log, ln	See 'Logarithms', page 170
e	Base of natural (napierian) logarithms = 2,718 281 828 4...
π	Ratio of the circumference of a circle to its diameter = 3,141 592 653 5...
sin, cos, tan, tg	See pages 174 and 175
arc sin	See page 175

All values conform to the international convention (i.e. 0,1 instead of 0.1).

II. Numbers

The *natural numbers* consist of all positive whole numbers (positive integers). Zero* and negative numbers are not natural numbers.
The *rational numbers* consist of all positive and negative integers, the fractions formed from them, and zero.
The *irrational numbers* are incommensurable quantities that cannot be expressed as quotients either of integers or of rational fractions. Examples are $\sqrt{2}$ and $\sqrt{5}$. π and e are also irrational numbers.
The *real numbers* consist of all rational and irrational numbers. The fundamental laws of real numbers are the following:

1. The 4 fundamental operations

Addition, subtraction, multiplication and division (except division by 0) can always and without ambiguity be carried out with real numbers.

2. The order of numbers

Between any two real numbers a and b there can exist *only one* of the three relationships

$$a = b \text{ or } a > b \text{ or } a < b$$

where

$$a = b \text{ when } a - b = 0 \quad (1)$$

$$a > b \text{ when } a - b > 0 \quad (2)$$

$$a < b \text{ when } a - b < 0 \quad (3)$$

Examples of inequalities (**2**) and (**3**) are

$$\cdots > 10 > 9 > \cdots > 1 > 0 > -1 > \cdots > -10 > \cdots$$

$$\cdots < -10 < -9 < \cdots < -1 < 0 < 1 < \cdots < 10 < \cdots$$

3. The commutative law

$$a + b = b + a \quad (4)$$

$$a\,b = b\,a \quad (5)$$

4. The associative law

$$(a + b) + c = a + (b + c) \quad (6)$$

$$(a\,b)\,c = a\,(b\,c) \quad (7)$$

5. The distributive law

$$a\,(b + c) = a\,b + a\,c \quad (8)$$

III. Calculations with 0 and ∞

$$a - a = 0 \quad (9)$$

$$|0| = 0 \quad (10)$$

$$0 \times a = 0 \quad (11)$$

* Some mathematicians regard zero also as a natural number.

$\frac{a}{\infty} = 0 \quad [a \neq \infty]$ (12)

$\frac{0}{a} = 0 \quad [a \neq 0]$ (13)

$\frac{a}{0}$ not defined (14)

$0^a = 0 \quad [a > 0]$ (15)

$a^0 = 1 \quad [a \neq 0]$ (16)

$$\lim_{(n \to \infty)} a^n = \begin{cases} \infty \text{ for } a > 1 \\ 1 \text{ for } a = 1 \\ 0 \text{ for } -1 < a < 1 \text{ and } a \neq 0 \\ \text{nonconvergent for } a \leq -1 \end{cases} \quad (17)$$

$\log_c 0 = -\infty \quad [c > 1]$ (18)

$\log_c \infty = +\infty \quad [c > 1]$ (19)

$\log_c 1 = 0$ (20)

$0! = 1$ (21)

$\binom{n}{0} = 1$ (22)

IV. Addition, subtraction, multiplication, division

1. Algebraic signs

If a, b, c are positive numbers, then

$a \pm b = a \mp (-b)$ (23)

$a(-b) = (-a)b = -(ab) = -c$ (24)

$(-a)(-b) = +ab = +c$ (25)

$\frac{-b}{a} = \frac{b}{-a} = -\frac{b}{a} = -c$ (26)

$\frac{-b}{-a} = +\frac{b}{a} = +c$ (27)

2. Brackets

$a - b - c - d - \cdots = a - (b + c + d + \cdots)$ (28)

$\pm ab \pm ac \pm ad \pm \cdots = a(\pm b \pm c \pm d \pm \cdots) = \pm a(b + c + d + \cdots)$ (29)

3. Conversion of divisions into multiplications

$\frac{b}{a} = \frac{1}{a} \times b$ (30)

For values of $1/a$ for $a = 1$–999 see page 18. Equation (**30**) is particularly useful in calculations with a constant divisor.

4. Conversion of multiplications and divisions into additions

If b is an integer (or can be converted into an integer), then

$$\left.\begin{aligned} ab &= a + a + a + \cdots \quad [b \text{ components}] \\ \frac{b}{a} &= \frac{1}{a} + \frac{1}{a} + \frac{1}{a} + \cdots \quad [b \text{ components}] \end{aligned}\right\} \quad (31)$$

Equation (**31**) is particularly useful in the tabulation of linear functions.

5. Fractions

$\frac{a}{a} = 1 \quad [a \neq 0]$ (32)

$\frac{ma}{mb} = \frac{a}{b} \quad [m \neq 0]$ (33)

$\frac{a}{b} + \frac{c}{b} = \frac{a+c}{b}$ [can also be used from right to left] (34)

$\frac{a}{b} + \frac{c}{d} = \frac{ad+bc}{bd}$ [can also be used from right to left] (35)

$\frac{a}{b} \times \frac{c}{d} = \frac{a}{d} \times \frac{c}{b} = \frac{ac}{bd}$ (36)

$\frac{a}{b} : \frac{c}{d} = \frac{a}{b} \times \frac{d}{c} = \frac{a}{c} \times \frac{d}{b} = \frac{a}{c} : \frac{b}{d}$ (37)

6. Proportions

The equation

$a : b = c : d$ (38)

read as 'a is to b as c is to d', is known as a proportion. a and d are the extremes, b and c the means of the proportion. The product of the extremes equals the product of the means:

$ad = bc$ (39)

If a proportion is of the type expressed by

$a : b = b : c$ (40)

then in accordance with equation (**39**)

$ac = b^2$, that is, $b = \sqrt{ac}$ (41)

b is known as the mean proportional between a and c, or the geometric mean of a and c. c is known as the third proportional to a and b.

A special case of proportions of type (**40**) is the so-called 'golden section' (extreme and mean ratio)

$$\left.\begin{aligned} &\frac{a}{b} = \frac{b}{a-b} \quad \text{that is} \\ &b = \frac{a(\sqrt{5}-1)}{2} = 0{,}618034\,a \quad \text{or} \quad \frac{a}{b} = 1{,}618034 \end{aligned}\right\} \quad (42)$$

Another special case is that of the so-called 'normal' format, expressed by

$$\left.\begin{aligned} &\frac{a}{b} = \frac{b}{a/2} \quad \text{that is} \\ &b = a/\sqrt{2} = 0{,}707107\,a \quad \text{or} \quad \frac{a}{b} = 1{,}414214 \end{aligned}\right\} \quad (43)$$

If the individual values of two related variables x, y are such that

$\frac{y_1}{x_1} = \frac{y_2}{x_2} = \frac{y_3}{x_3} = \cdots = k$ (44)

then

$y = kx$ (45)

read as 'y is proportional to x in the ratio k' (k is known as the proportionality constant). As x increases, y increases in proportion when k is positive, decreases when k is negative. The graphical representation of a proportional relationship on rectangular coordinates results in a straight line, whence the expression linear relationship. On the other hand, a linear relationship between x and y does not necessarily mean that they are proportional to one another since there are many straight lines that do not correspond to equation (**45**). For example, $y = a + kx$ is *not* a proportional relationship between x and y. In this case $(y - a)$ is proportional to x.

If the individual values of two related variables x, y are such that

$$\left.\begin{aligned} &\frac{y_1}{1/x_1} = \frac{y_2}{1/x_2} = \frac{y_3}{1/x_3} = \cdots = k \\ &\text{that is} \\ &y_1 x_1 = y_2 x_2 = y_3 x_3 = \cdots = k \end{aligned}\right\} \quad (46)$$

then

$y = \frac{k}{x}$ (47)

read as 'y is inversely proportional to x in the ratio k'. The graphical representation of an inversely proportional relationship on rectangular coordinates results in a hyperbola. Such a relationship is therefore a nonlinear one.

All values conform to the international convention (i.e. 0,1 instead of 0.1).

V. Powers and roots

1. Powers with integer exponents

If a and b are any real numbers, m and r positive integers, then

$$0^m = 0 \quad (15)$$

$$a^0 = 1 \quad [a \neq 0] \quad (16)$$

$$\lim_{(m\to\infty)} a^m = \begin{cases} \infty \text{ for } a>1 \\ 1 \text{ for } a=1 \\ 0 \text{ for } -1<a<1 \text{ and } a\neq 0 \\ \text{nonconvergent for } a\leq -1 \end{cases} \quad (17)$$

$$a \times a \times a \times \cdots (m \text{ factors}) = a^m \quad (48)$$

$$\frac{1}{a} \times \frac{1}{a} \times \frac{1}{a} \times \cdots (m \text{ factors}) = \frac{1}{a^m} = a^{-m} \quad [a \neq 0] \quad (49)$$

$$a^m \times b^m = (a\,b)^m \quad (50)$$

$$\frac{a^m}{b^m} = \left(\frac{a}{b}\right)^m = a^m\,b^{-m} \quad [b \neq 0] \quad (51)$$

$$a^m \times a^r = a^{m+r} \quad (52)$$

$$\frac{a^m}{a^r} = a^m\,a^{-r} = a^{m-r} \quad [a \neq 0] \quad (53)$$

$$(a^m)^r = (a^r)^m = a^{m\,r} \quad (54)$$

Algebraic signs: If in equations **(48)** to **(54)** R is the resulting *absolute value* of the base, c the absolute value of the power, $2\,m$ or $2\,m-1$ the resulting even or odd exponent, then

$$(\pm R)^{2m} = +c \quad (55)$$

$$(\pm R)^{2m-1} = \pm c \quad (56)$$

2. Extraction of roots with integer exponents

If a and b are any real numbers, n and s positive integers but not 0, then

$$\sqrt[n]{a} = a^{\frac{1}{n}} \quad (57)$$

$$\frac{1}{\sqrt[n]{a}} = a^{-\frac{1}{n}} \quad [a \neq 0] \quad (58)$$

$$\sqrt[n]{a\,b} = \sqrt[n]{a}\,\sqrt[n]{b} = (a\,b)^{\frac{1}{n}} \quad (59)$$

$$\sqrt[n]{\frac{a}{b}} = \frac{\sqrt[n]{a}}{\sqrt[n]{b}} = \left(\frac{a}{b}\right)^{\frac{1}{n}} \quad [b \neq 0] \quad (60)$$

$$\sqrt[s]{\sqrt[n]{a}} = \sqrt[n]{\sqrt[s]{a}} = a^{\frac{1}{n\,s}} \quad (61)$$

Algebraic signs: If in equations **(57)** to **(61)** R is the resulting *absolute value* of the base, c the absolute value of the power, $2n$ or $2n-1$ the resulting even or odd exponent, then

$$\sqrt[2n]{(+R)} = (+R)^{\frac{1}{2n}} = +c \quad (62)$$

$$\sqrt[2n]{(-R)} = (-R)^{\frac{1}{2n}} \text{ has no real solution} \quad (63)$$

$$\sqrt[2n-1]{(\pm R)} = (\pm R)^{\frac{1}{2n-1}} = \pm c \quad (64)$$

3. Mixed powers and roots

If a and b are any real numbers, m and r positive integers, k, n and s likewise positive integers but not 0, then

$$\sqrt[n]{a^m} = a^{\frac{m}{n}} \quad (65)$$

$$\frac{1}{\sqrt[n]{a^m}} = a^{-\frac{m}{n}} \quad [a \neq 0] \quad (66)$$

$$\sqrt[k\,n]{a^{k\,m}} = \sqrt[n]{a^m} = a^{\frac{m}{n}} \quad (67)$$

If in equation **(67)** a is negative it is important that all other necessary conversion operations on the exponent should be performed *before* reduction is carried out. If the resulting numerator in the exponent is even, then a negative a is made positive and reduction carried out.

$$\sqrt[n]{(a\,b)^m} = \sqrt[n]{a^m} \times \sqrt[n]{b^m} = (a\,b)^{\frac{m}{n}} \quad (68)$$

$$\frac{\sqrt[n]{a^m}}{\sqrt[n]{b^m}} = \sqrt[n]{\left(\frac{a}{b}\right)^m} = \left(\frac{a}{b}\right)^{\frac{m}{n}} \quad [b \neq 0] \quad (69)$$

$$\sqrt[n]{a} \times \sqrt[s]{a} = a^{\frac{1}{n}+\frac{1}{s}} = a^{\frac{n+s}{n\,s}} = \sqrt[n\,s]{a^{n+s}} \quad (70)$$

$$\sqrt[n]{a^m} \times \sqrt[s]{a^r} = a^{\frac{m}{n}+\frac{r}{s}} = a^{\frac{m\,s+n\,r}{n\,s}} = \sqrt[n\,s]{a^{m\,s+n\,r}} \quad (71)$$

$$\left(a^{\frac{m}{n}}\right)^{\frac{r}{s}} = \left(a^{\frac{r}{s}}\right)^{\frac{m}{n}} = a^{\frac{m\,r}{n\,s}} \quad (72)$$

Algebraic signs: If in equations **(65)** to **(72)** R is the resulting *absolute value* of the base, c the absolute value of the power, $2\,m$, $2\,n$, or $2\,m-1$, $2\,n-1$ respectively the resulting even or odd numerator and denominator of the exponent, then

$$\sqrt[2n]{(\pm R)^{2m}} = (\pm R)^{\frac{2m}{2n}} = (+R)^{\frac{2m}{2n}} = +c \quad (73)$$

[always to be used in any reduction of an exponent]

$$\sqrt[2n]{(+R)^{2m-1}} = (+R)^{\frac{2m-1}{2n}} = +c \quad (74)$$

$$\sqrt[2n]{(-R)^{2m-1}} = (-R)^{\frac{2m-1}{2n}} \text{ has no real solution} \quad (75)$$

$$\sqrt[2n-1]{(\pm R)^{2m}} = (\pm R)^{\frac{2m}{2n-1}} = +c \quad (76)$$

$$\sqrt[2n-1]{(\pm R)^{2m-1}} = (\pm R)^{\frac{2m-1}{2n-1}} = \pm c \quad (77)$$

VI. Logarithms

In accordance with the equation

$$a = c^{\log_c a} \quad (78)$$

[a: number or antilogarithm; c: base; $\log_c a$: logarithm of a to the base c]

the logarithm of a to the base c is defined as the exponent of the power of the base c which equals the number a. The usual bases are 10 (common or briggsian logarithms) and e = 2,718 281 828 5 (natural, napierian or hyperbolic logarithms). In this volume the symbol log is used for common logarithms and the symbol ln for natural logarithms. The relation between the two is given by

$$\ln a = \frac{\log a}{\log e} = 2{,}302\,585\,093\,0 \log a = \ln 10 \times \log a \quad (79)$$

$$\log a = \frac{\ln a}{\ln 10} = 0{,}434\,294\,481\,9 \ln a = \log e \times \ln a \quad (80)$$

In general the relation is expressed by

$$\log_c a = \frac{\log_{10} a}{\log_{10} c} \quad (81)$$

Example. It is required to find the logarithm of 20 to the base 2.

$$\log_2 20 = \frac{\log_{10} 20}{\log_{10} 2} = \frac{1{,}301\,0300}{0{,}301\,0300} = 4{,}321\,928$$

The use of logarithms reduces multiplication, division, raising to powers and the extraction of roots to addition, subtraction, multiplication and division respectively.
For common logarithms equation **(78)** gives

$$a = 10^{\log a} \quad \text{and} \quad b = 10^{\log b}$$

so that according to equation **(52)**

$$a \times b = 10^{\log a} \times 10^{\log b} = 10^{\log a + \log b}$$

that is

$$\log(a \times b) = \log a + \log b$$

whence

$$(a \times b) = \text{antilog}(\log a + \log b)$$

All values conform to the international convention (i.e. 0,1 instead of 0.1).

All the principles of logarithmic calculation can be deduced from section V in an analogous manner. The most important are:

$$\log(a\times b)=\log a+\log b \qquad \textbf{(82)}$$

$$\log\left(\frac{a}{b}\right)=\log a-\log b \qquad \textbf{(83)}$$

$$\log a^{b}=b\log a \qquad \textbf{(84)}$$

$$\log\sqrt[b]{a}=\frac{\log a}{b} \qquad \textbf{(85)}$$

Since logarithms are only defined for positive numbers, logarithmic calculation is made without regard to the algebraic sign of $a, b, \ldots$ and the result assigned the appropriate sign according to the rules already given.
A logarithmic calculation falls into three parts:

1. Finding the logarithms
2. Operating with them according to the above rules
3. Finding the antilogarithms.

1. Finding the logarithm

The number of which the logarithm is required is first converted into a product as follows:

$$a=10^{x}\times\frac{a}{10^{x}}=K'\times M' \qquad \textbf{(86)}$$

x is determined for $|a|\geq 1$ by counting the number b of places to the left of the comma, for $|a|<1$ by counting the number b of digits to the right of the comma, so that

$$x=b-1 \text{ when } |a|\geq 1 \qquad \textbf{(87)}$$

and

$$x=-b-1 \text{ when } |a|<1 \qquad \textbf{(88)}$$

Examples

a	b	x	K'	$K'\times M'$
1566,3	4	3	10^{3}	$10^{3}\times 1{,}5663$
1,2	1	0	10^{0}	$10^{0}\times 1{,}2$
0,12	0	-1	10^{-1}	$10^{-1}\times 1{,}2$
0,00034	-3	-4	10^{-4}	$10^{-4}\times 3{,}4$

In accordance with equation **(82)**

$$\log a=\log(K'\times M')=\log K'+\log M'=K+M \qquad \textbf{(89)}$$

[K is known as the characteristic, M as the mantissa of the logarithm of a]

The characteristic K is the positive or negative exponent x of K' in equation **(86)**. The mantissa M must be determined from a table of logarithms. For this purpose M' is first rounded off so that it contains the same number of figures as the logarithms in the table used. In the following examples four-figure logarithms are used:

For $M'<1{,}1$, round off M' to 5 significant places

For $M'\geq 1{,}1$, round off M' to 4 significant places

Examples

$\log 1{,}0993=?$
$\log 1{,}5663\approx\log 1{,}566=?$

From the table on page 10:

x	$\log_{10}x$		Proportional parts	
	6	9	3	6
109		0410	1	
15	1931			17

$\log 1{,}0993=0{,}0410+0{,}0001=0{,}0411$
$\log 1{,}566\ \ =0{,}1931+0{,}0017=0{,}1948$

All values conform to the international convention (i.e. 0,1 instead of 0.1).

Further examples

(a) $\log 3048 =\log(10^{3}\times 3{,}048) =3+0{,}4829+0{,}0011=3{,}4840$

(b) $\log 0{,}2130 =\log(10^{-1}\times 2{,}130) =-1+0{,}3284+0=0{,}3284-1$

(c) $\log 1/3048 =\log(10^{-3}\times 3{,}048^{-1}) =-3-(0{,}4829+0{,}0011)=-0{,}4840-3$

(d) $\log 1/0{,}2130=\log(10^{1}\times 2{,}13^{-1}) =1-0{,}3284=0{,}6716$

In example (c) the mantissa as well as the characteristic is negative. A negative mantissa must be converted into a positive one by adding 1 to the mantissa and subtracting 1 from the characteristic. For example:

$$-0{,}4840-3=\underbrace{-0{,}4840+1}_{=0{,}5160}\underbrace{-3-1}_{-4}$$

2. Operating with logarithms

This is done in accordance with equations **(82)** to **(85)** and the following rules:

1. Calculations are so made that no negative mantissa arises.
2. In extracting the roots of fractions, the difference between the root exponent and the characteristic is subtracted from the characteristic and added to the mantissa [examples (e) and (f)].
3. When the logarithmic calculation is complete, positive and negative characteristics are added together. The resulting characteristic x gives the number b of places to the left of the comma (when $x\geq 0$) or the number b of digits to the right of the comma (when $x<0$), as follows:

$$b=x+1 \text{ when } x\geq 0 \qquad \textbf{(90)}$$

$$b=-(x+1) \text{ when } x<0 \qquad \textbf{(91)}$$

Examples

(a) $\log(3048\times 0{,}2130) = \begin{array}{r} 3{,}4840 \\ +0{,}3284-1 \\ \hline 3{,}8124-1 \end{array} =2{,}8124$

(b) $\log(0{,}2130:3048) = \begin{array}{r} 0{,}3284-1 \\ +0{,}5160-4 \\ \hline 0{,}8444-5 \end{array} =0{,}8444-5$

(c) $\log(0{,}2130:0{,}0003281) = \begin{array}{r} 0{,}3284-1 \\ -(0{,}5160-4) \end{array}$
$= \begin{array}{r} 1{,}3284-2 \\ -0{,}5160+4 \\ \hline 0{,}8124+2 \end{array} =2{,}8124$

(d) $\log(0{,}2130^{5})=5\log 0{,}2130=5\times(0{,}3284-1) =1{,}6420-5 \ =0{,}6420-4$

(e) $\log\left(\sqrt[6]{0{,}2130}\right)=\frac{\log 0{,}2130}{6}=\frac{0{,}3284-1}{6}=\frac{5{,}3284-6}{6} =0{,}8881-1$

(f) $\log\left(\sqrt[1{,}5]{0{,}2130}\right)=\frac{\log 0{,}2130}{1{,}5}=\frac{0{,}3284-1}{1{,}5}=\frac{0{,}8284-1{,}5}{1{,}5} =0{,}5523-1$

3. Finding the antilogarithm

The antilogarithm corresponding to a mantissa is found in a table of antilogarithms (see page 11) in the same way as a logarithm is found in a table of logarithms. (Care should be taken not to confuse the two tables.) The position of the comma is determined by means of equations **(90)** and **(91)**.

Examples

antilog $2{,}8124 \quad =649{,}2$
antilog $(0{,}8881-1)=0{,}7729$
antilog $(0{,}6420-4)=0{,}0004385$

VII. Factorials and binomial coefficients

1. $n^{(r)}$

For a positive integer r and any real number n the symbol $n^{(r)}$ represents the product

$$n^{(r)} = n(n-1)(n-2)\cdots(n-r+1) \qquad \textbf{(92)}$$

where

$$n^{(0)} = 1 \qquad \textbf{(93)}$$

by definition.

Examples

(a) $10^{(4)} = ?$

In this case

$(n-r+1) = 10-4+1 = 7$

so that

$10^{(4)} = 10 \times 9 \times 8 \times 7 = 5040$

(b) $4^{(5)} = ?$

In this case

$(n-r+1) = 4-5+1 = 0$

so that

$4^{(5)} = 4 \times 3 \times 2 \times 1 \times 0 = 0$

From example (b) it can be seen that

$$n^{(r)} = 0 \qquad \textbf{(94)}$$

when $r > n$ and n is a positive integer.

2. Factorials

The factorial of a positive integer n, symbol $n!$, is defined as

$$n! = n(n-1)(n-2)\cdots 3 \times 2 \times 1 \qquad \textbf{(95)}$$

where

$$0! = 1 \qquad \textbf{(96)}$$

by definition. For positive integers n, the factorial $n!$ can be expressed as $n^{(n)}$, in which case equation **(92)** can be written

$$n^{(r)} = \frac{n!}{(n-r)!} \qquad \textbf{(97)}$$

Equations **(93)** and **(94)** remain valid.

Common logarithms of the factorials of numbers n from 1 to 999 and of their reciprocals are given on pages 24 and 25. For the factorials of numbers $n \geq 1000$ the Stirling approximation is used:

$$\underset{(n\to\infty)}{n!} \to n^n\, e^{-n} \sqrt{2\pi n} \qquad \textbf{(98)}$$

or

$$\log n! \to 0{,}5 \times [2n\,(\log n - 0{,}4342944819) + \log n + 0{,}798178] \qquad \textbf{(99)}$$

3. Binomial coefficients

In its general form the binomial coefficient $\binom{n}{r}$ or $C(n,r)$ is defined as

$$\binom{n}{r} = \frac{n^{(r)}}{r!} \qquad \textbf{(100)}$$

For $n^{(r)}$ and $r!$ see subsections 1 and 2 above.

When n is a positive integer equations **(97)** and **(100)** give

$$\binom{n}{r} = \frac{n!}{r!(n-r)!} \qquad \textbf{(101)}$$

From equations **(93)**, **(94)** and **(96)** it follows that

$$\binom{n}{0} = 1 \qquad \textbf{(102)}$$

$$\binom{0}{0} = 1 \qquad \textbf{(103)}$$

All values conform to the international convention (i.e. 0,1 instead of 0.1).

$$\binom{n}{r} = 0 \text{ when } r > n \text{ and } n \text{ is a positive integer.} \qquad \textbf{(104)}$$

It is also clear that

$$\binom{n}{n} = 1 \qquad \textbf{(105)}$$

Example. For $n=9$ and $n=10$ all the coefficients for values of r between 0 and n are tabulated:

r	0	1	2	3	4	5	6	7	8	9	
$n=9$	1	9	36	84	126	126	84	36	9	1	
$n=10$	1	10	45	120	210	252	210	120	45	10	1
r	0	1	2	3	4	5	6	7	8	9	10

($n/2$ marked between $r=4$ and $r=5$ for $n=9$, and at $r=5$ for $n=10$.)

It will be seen that as r increases, the values of $\binom{n}{r}$ increase up to $n/2$ and then decrease again symmetrically:

$$\binom{n}{r} = \binom{n}{n-r} \qquad \textbf{(106)}$$

For odd numbers n, the median falls between the two highest values of the series; for even numbers n it is the highest value.

Common logarithms of the binomial coefficients for n from 2 to 100 and for r from 0 to $n/2$ are given on pages 74–81. For $101 \leq n \leq 999$ the binomial coefficients are calculated from equation **(101)** using the common logarithms of factorials and their reciprocals given on pages 24 and 25.

VIII. Series

The sum $a_1 + a_2 + a_3 + \cdots + a_n$ of a sequence of numbers $a_1, a_2, a_3, \cdots a_n$ formed according to some fixed rule or law is known as a series.

1. Arithmetic series of the 1st order

An arithmetic series of the 1st order is one in which the difference d between successive terms is constant:

$$\left.\begin{matrix} a_1 & a_2 & a_3 & \dots & a_n \\ a_1 & (a_1+d) & (a_1+2d) & \dots & a_1+(n-1)d \end{matrix}\right\} \qquad \textbf{(107)}$$

The sum of the first n terms is

$$S = \frac{n(a_1+a_n)}{2} \qquad \textbf{(108)}$$

A special case of **(108)** is the sum of the natural sequence of numbers $1, 2, 3, \ldots, n$

$$1+2+3+\cdots+n = \frac{n(n+1)}{2} \qquad \textbf{(109)}$$

Example. The sum of all numbers from 1 to 81 is

$(81 \times 82)/2 = 3321$

2. Geometric series

A geometric series is one in which there is a constant ratio q between successive terms

$$\left.\begin{matrix} a_1 & a_2 & a_3 & \dots & a_n \\ a_1 & a_1 q & a_1 q^2 & \dots & a_1 q^{n-1} \end{matrix}\right\} \qquad \textbf{(110)}$$

The sum of the first n terms is

$$S = a_1 \frac{1-q^n}{1-q} = a_1 \frac{q^n-1}{q-1} \quad [q \neq 1] \qquad \textbf{(111)}$$

When $-1 < q < 1$, $q^\infty = 0$ in accordance with **(17)**, and **(111)** becomes

$$S_\infty = \frac{a_1}{1-q} \quad [-1 < q < 1] \qquad \textbf{(112)}$$

With the aid of equation **(112)** infinite periodic decimal fractions, for example, can be converted into true fractions.

Examples

(a) $0{,}333\,3\dot{3} = \frac{3}{10} + \frac{3}{100} + \frac{3}{1000} + \cdots$

$q = \frac{1}{10} \quad a_1 = \frac{3}{10}$

$0{,}333\,3\dot{3} = \frac{3}{10} \Big/ \frac{9}{10} = \frac{3}{9} = \frac{1}{3}$

(b) $0{,}033\,3\dot{3} = \frac{3}{100} + \frac{3}{1000} + \cdots$

$q = \frac{1}{10} \quad a_1 = \frac{3}{100}$

$0{,}033\,3\dot{3} = \frac{3}{100} \Big/ \frac{9}{10} = \frac{3}{90} = \frac{1}{30}$

(c) $0{,}233\,3\dot{3} = \frac{2}{10} + \frac{3}{100} + \frac{3}{1000} + \cdots$

The infinite series begins with 3/100, whence $q = 1/10$, $a_1 = 3/100$, etc., as in the previous example. A further 2/10 has to be added to it.

$0{,}233\,3\dot{3} = \frac{2}{10} + \frac{1}{30} = \frac{60+10}{300} = \frac{7}{30}$

(d) $0{,}123\,123\,\dot{1}\dot{2}\dot{3} = \frac{123}{1000} + \frac{123}{1\,000\,000} + \cdots$

$q = \frac{1}{1000} \quad a_1 = \frac{123}{1000}$

$0{,}123\,\dot{1}\dot{2}\dot{3} = \frac{123}{1000} \Big/ \frac{999}{1000} = \frac{123}{999} = \frac{41}{333}$

3. Binomial series for positive integers n

$$(a+b)^n = \binom{n}{0} a^n b^0 + \binom{n}{1} a^{n-1} b^1 + \binom{n}{2} a^{n-2} b^2 + + \binom{n}{3} a^{n-3} b^3 + \cdots + \binom{n}{n} a^0 b^n \quad \textbf{(113)}$$

Algebraic signs: When b is negative, all terms in which the exponent of b is odd are negative.

Examples

$(a+b)^2 = a^2 + 2ab + b^2$

$(a+b)^3 = a^3 + 3a^2b + 3ab^2 + b^3$

$(a-b)^2 = a^2 - 2ab + b^2$

$(a-b)^3 = a^3 - 3a^2b + 3ab^2 - b^3$ etc.

IX. Means

For n positive variables $x_1, x_2, \ldots, x_n$

(a) the arithmetic mean $m_a = \frac{x_1 + x_2 + \cdots + x_n}{n} = \frac{\sum_1^n x_i}{n}$ **(114)**

(b) the geometric mean $m_g = \sqrt[n]{x_1 \times x_2 \times \cdots \times x_n}$ **(115)**

(c) the harmonic mean $m_h = 1 : \frac{1}{n}\left(\frac{1}{x_1} + \frac{1}{x_2} + \cdots + \frac{1}{x_n}\right)$ **(116)**

When $n = 2$, then

$m_a = \frac{x_1 + x_2}{2}$ **(117)**

$m_g = \sqrt{x_1 x_2}$ **(118)**

$m_h = \frac{2 x_1 x_2}{x_1 + x_2}$ **(119)**

Cauchy's principle:
$m_a \geq m_g \geq m_h$
[where the equality signs are valid only when $x_1 = x_2 = \cdots = x_n$] **(120)**

All values conform to the international convention (i.e. 0,1 instead of 0.1).

X. Solutions of equations

Solutions of equations exist only when all the denominators differ from 0. Solve for x.

$a x \pm b = 0 \quad x = \mp \frac{b}{a}$ **(121)**

$\frac{a}{x} \pm b = 0 \quad x = \mp \frac{a}{b}$ **(122)**

1. Simplification of equations of higher degree

$(ax \pm b)^m \pm c = 0 \quad x = \frac{\sqrt[m]{\mp c} \mp b}{a}$ **(123)**

$\sqrt[n]{ax \pm b} \pm c = 0 \quad x = \frac{(\mp c)^n \mp b}{a}$ **(124)**

2. Equations of the first degree with two unknowns

Solve for x and y.

$a_1 x + b_1 y + c_1 = 0$

$a_2 x + b_2 y + c_2 = 0$

$$x = \frac{b_1 c_2 - b_2 c_1}{a_1 b_2 - a_2 b_1}, \quad y = -\frac{a_1 x + c_1}{b_1} = -\frac{a_2 x + c_2}{b_2} \quad \textbf{(125)}$$

3. Equations of the first degree with three unknowns

Solve for x, y and z.

$a_1 x + b_1 y + c_1 z + d_1 = 0$

$a_2 x + b_2 y + c_2 z + d_2 = 0$

$a_3 x + b_3 y + c_3 z + d_3 = 0$

Let

$$A = c_2 a_1 - c_1 a_2, \quad B = c_2 b_1 - c_1 b_2, \quad C = c_2 d_1 - c_1 d_2, \quad D = c_2 a_3 - c_3 a_2, \quad E = c_2 b_3 - c_3 b_2, \quad F = c_2 d_3 - c_3 d_2 \quad \textbf{(126)}$$

then

$x = \frac{BF - CE}{AE - BD}$

$y = -\frac{C + Ax}{B} = -\frac{F + Dx}{E}$

$z = -\frac{a_1 x + b_1 y + d_1}{c_1} = -\frac{a_2 x + b_2 y + d_2}{c_2} = -\frac{a_3 x + b_3 y + d_3}{c_3}$

4. Quadratic equations with one unknown

$a x^2 + b x + c = 0$

$x_{(1,2)} = \frac{-b \pm \sqrt{b^2 - 4ac}}{2a} = \frac{-b}{2a} \pm \sqrt{\left(\frac{b}{2a}\right)^2 - \frac{c}{a}}$ **(127)**

The magnitude $D = b^2 - 4ac$ is known as the discriminant of the equation. When

$D > 0$ there are two real solutions
$D = 0$ there is only one real solution
$D < 0$ there is no real solution

5. Exponential equations in common use

$x = 1 - e^{-\lambda}; \quad x = 1 - \text{antilog}(-0{,}4342944819\,\lambda)$ **(128)**

$a = 1 - e^{-z}; \quad z = -2{,}3025850930 \log(1-a) \quad [0 \leq a \leq 1]$ **(129)**

If in equation (129)
$z = \frac{ax^b \pm c}{d}$, then $\log x = \frac{\log\left(\frac{dz \mp c}{a}\right)}{b}$
[when $b = 1$ the log sign disappears on both sides] **(130)**

$$z=\frac{a\,b^{x}\pm c}{d},\ \text{then}\qquad x=\frac{\log\left(\frac{d\,z\mp c}{a}\right)}{\log b}\qquad [b\neq 1] \tag{131}$$

$$\left.\begin{array}{l} z=\dfrac{d}{a\,x^{b}\pm c},\ \text{then}\log x=\dfrac{\log\left(\frac{d/z\mp c}{a}\right)}{b} \\ \text{[when } b=1 \text{ the log sign disappears on both sides]}\end{array}\right\} \tag{132}$$

$$z=\frac{d}{a\,b^{x}\pm c},\ \text{then}\ x=\frac{\log\left(\frac{d/z\mp c}{a}\right)}{\log b}\qquad [b\neq 1] \tag{133}$$

Equations (**130**) to (**133**) have no solution when

$(d\,z\mp c)<0$ or $(d/z\mp c)<0$

(This is true for equations (**130**) and (**132**), however, only when $b\neq 1$.)

The following table gives z values [solutions of equation (**129**)] for various numbers a in common use:

a	$1-a$	$\log(1-a)$	$z=-\ln 10\times\log(1-a)$ $=-\ln(1-a)$
0,999	0,001	−3	6,907 755 279
0,995	0,005	0,698 970 004 3 − 3	5,298 317 367
0,99	0,01	−2	4,605 170 186
0,975	0,025	0,397 940 008 7 − 2	3,688 879 454
0,95	0,05	0,698 970 004 3 − 2	2,995 732 274
0,90	0,10	−1	2,302 585 093
0,85	0,15	0,176 091 259 1 − 1	1,897 119 985
0,80	0,20	0,301 029 995 7 − 1	1,609 437 912
0,75	0,25	0,397 940 008 7 − 1	1,386 294 361
0,70	0,30	0,477 121 254 7 − 1	1,203 972 804
0,65	0,35	0,544 068 044 3 − 1	1,049 822 124
0,60	0,40	0,602 059 991 3 − 1	0,916 290 731 9
0,55	0,45	0,653 212 513 8 − 1	0,798 507 696 2
0,50	0,50	0,698 970 004 3 − 1	0,693 147 180 5
0,45	0,55	0,740 362 689 5 − 1	0,597 837 000 7
0,40	0,60	0,778 151 250 4 − 1	0,510 825 623 7
0,35	0,65	0,812 913 356 6 − 1	0,430 782 916 1
0,30	0,70	0,845 098 040 0 − 1	0,356 674 944 0
0,25	0,75	0,875 061 263 4 − 1	0,287 682 072 4
0,20	0,80	0,903 089 987 0 − 1	0,223 143 551 5
0,15	0,85	0,929 418 925 7 − 1	0,162 518 929 5
0,10	0,90	0,954 242 509 4 − 1	0,105 360 515 7
0,05	0,95	0,977 723 605 3 − 1	0,051 293 294 42
0,025	0,975	0,989 004 615 7 − 1	0,025 317 807 99
0,01	0,99	0,995 635 194 6 − 1	0,010 050 335 86
0,005	0,995	0,997 823 080 7 − 1	0,005 012 541 823
0,001	0,999	0,999 565 488 2 − 1	0,001 000 500 333

XI. Rectangular coordinate system

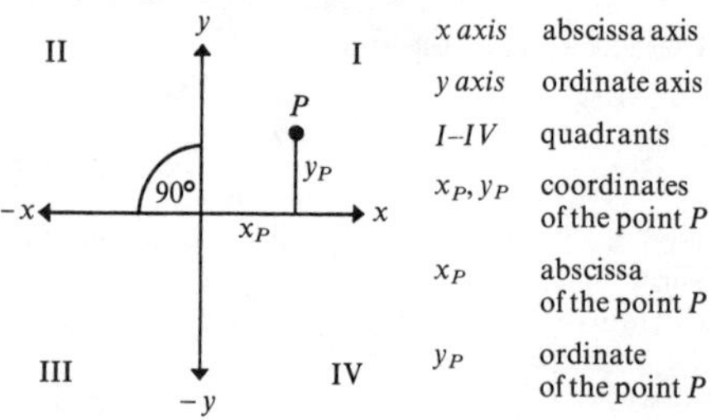

Signs of the coordinates of points in each of the 4 quadrants

Quadrant	x	y
I	+	+
II	−	+
III	−	−
IV	+	−

All values conform to the international convention (i.e. 0,1 instead of 0.1).

XII. Angles, trigonometric functions, inverse trigonometric functions

1. Positive and negative angles

Rotation in an *anti*clockwise direction is defined as positive rotation, rotation in a clockwise direction as negative rotation. Similarly an angle measured by positive rotation is a positive angle, one measured by negative rotation a negative angle.

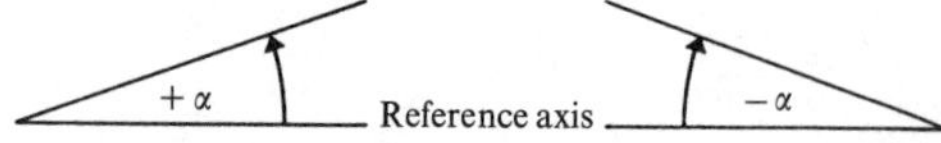

By angle of inclination of a straight line a is usually meant the *acute* angle between the straight line and the x axis.

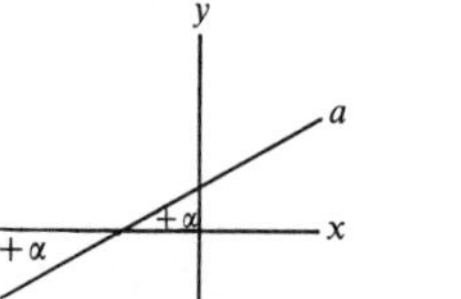

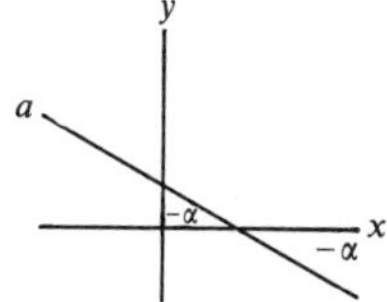

2. Angle units

The basis of all angle units is the circumference of a circle drawn with its center at the point of intersection of the lines forming the angle. This is divided into 360 equal parts (degrees, the unit normally used) or into 400 equal parts (grades), or measured in terms of its own radius (arc, circular or radian measure). Since the circumference of a circle is 2π times its radius, angles are often expressed as fractions or multiples of π. The arc measure of the angle α is designated arcus α (arc α).

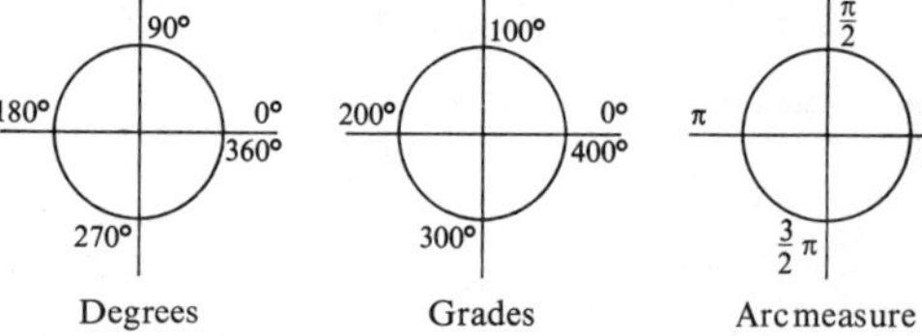

Degrees	0°	1°	30°	57°17′45″	60°	90°	180°	270°	360°
Arc measure	0	0,01745	$\frac{\pi}{6}$	1	$\frac{\pi}{3}$	$\frac{\pi}{2}$	π	$\frac{3}{2}\pi$	2π

3. Trigonometric functions

(other than secant and cosecant)

Definitions based on the right triangle
(valid only for acute angles between 0 and 90°)

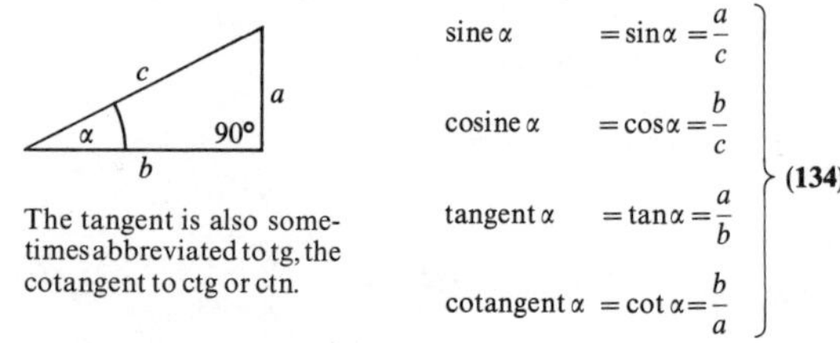

$$\left.\begin{array}{lll} \text{sine}\ \alpha & =\sin\alpha & =\dfrac{a}{c} \\ \text{cosine}\ \alpha & =\cos\alpha & =\dfrac{b}{c} \\ \text{tangent}\ \alpha & =\tan\alpha & =\dfrac{a}{b} \\ \text{cotangent}\ \alpha & =\cot\alpha & =\dfrac{b}{a} \end{array}\right\} \tag{134}$$

The tangent is also sometimes abbreviated to tg, the cotangent to ctg or ctn.

Representation of trigonometric functions on the unit circle (circle with radius = 1)

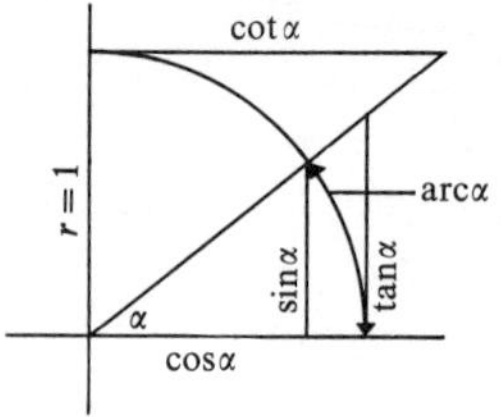

Algebraic signs of trigonometric functions in the 4 quadrants

Function	Quadrant			
	I	II	III	IV
sin	+	+	−	−
cos	+	−	−	+
tan	+	−	+	−
cot	+	−	+	−

(135)

Ranges of trigonometric functions in the 4 quadrants

Function	Quadrant			
	I	II	III	IV
sin	0 to 1	1 to 0	0 to −1	−1 to 0
cos	1 to 0	0 to −1	−1 to 0	0 to 1
tan	0 to ∞	−∞ to 0	0 to ∞	−∞ to 0
cot	∞ to 0	0 to −∞	∞ to 0	0 to −∞

(136)

Graphs of trigonometric functions

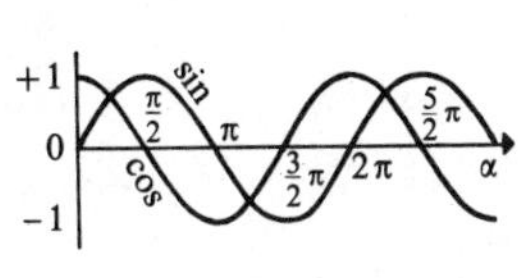

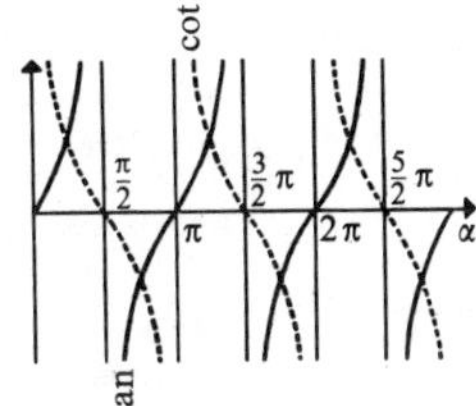

Functions of negative angles

$$\left.\begin{aligned}\sin(-\alpha) &= -\sin\alpha\\ \cos(-\alpha) &= +\cos\alpha\\ \tan(-\alpha) &= -\tan\alpha\\ \cot(-\alpha) &= -\cot\alpha\end{aligned}\right\}\quad(137)$$

Conversion of the functions of obtuse angles into those of acute angles

Function	$90°\pm\alpha$	$180°\pm\alpha$	$270°\pm\alpha$	$n(360°)\pm\alpha$
sin	$+\cos\alpha$	$\mp\sin\alpha$	$-\cos\alpha$	$\pm\sin\alpha$
cos	$\mp\sin\alpha$	$-\cos\alpha$	$\pm\sin\alpha$	$+\cos\alpha$
tan	$\mp\cot\alpha$	$\pm\tan\alpha$	$\mp\cot\alpha$	$\pm\tan\alpha$
cot	$\mp\tan\alpha$	$\pm\cot\alpha$	$\mp\tan\alpha$	$\pm\cot\alpha$
n: positive integer.				

(138)

Example

$\sin 125° = \cos 35°$

Relationships between trigonometric functions

Function	$\sin\alpha$	$\cos\alpha$	$\tan\alpha$	$\cot\alpha$
$\sin\alpha$	$\sin\alpha$	$\pm\sqrt{1-\cos^2\alpha}$	$\frac{\tan\alpha}{\pm\sqrt{1+\tan^2\alpha}}$	$\frac{1}{\pm\sqrt{1+\cot^2\alpha}}$
$\cos\alpha$	$\pm\sqrt{1-\sin^2\alpha}$	$\cos\alpha$	$\frac{1}{\pm\sqrt{1+\tan^2\alpha}}$	$\frac{\cot\alpha}{\pm\sqrt{1+\cot^2\alpha}}$
$\tan\alpha$	$\frac{\sin\alpha}{\pm\sqrt{1-\sin^2\alpha}}$	$\frac{\pm\sqrt{1-\cos^2\alpha}}{\cos\alpha}$	$\tan\alpha$	$\frac{1}{\cot\alpha}$
$\cot\alpha$	$\frac{\pm\sqrt{1-\sin^2\alpha}}{\sin\alpha}$	$\frac{\cos\alpha}{\pm\sqrt{1-\cos^2\alpha}}$	$\frac{1}{\tan\alpha}$	$\cot\alpha$

(139)

Algebraic sign of the square root: This is determined by the quadrant into which the angle falls. For algebraic signs in the quadrants see **(135)**.

Functions of half the angle and of twice the angle

$$\sin\frac{\alpha}{2} = \pm\tfrac{1}{2}\left(\sqrt{1+\sin\alpha}-\sqrt{1-\sin\alpha}\right) = \pm\sqrt{\frac{1-\cos\alpha}{2}} \quad (140)$$

$$\cos\frac{\alpha}{2} = \pm\sqrt{\frac{1+\cos\alpha}{2}} \quad (141)$$

$$\left.\begin{aligned}\tan\frac{\alpha}{2} &= \frac{-1\pm\sqrt{1+\tan^2\alpha}}{\tan\alpha} = \frac{1-\cos\alpha}{\sin\alpha} = \frac{\sin\alpha}{1+\cos\alpha}\\ &= \pm\sqrt{\frac{1-\cos\alpha}{1+\sin\alpha}}\end{aligned}\right\} \quad (142)$$

$$\sin 2\alpha = 2\sin\alpha\cos\alpha \quad (143)$$

$$\cos 2\alpha = 2\cos^2\alpha - 1 = 1 - 2\sin^2\alpha = \cos^2\alpha - \sin^2\alpha \quad (144)$$

$$\tan 2\alpha = \frac{2\tan\alpha}{1-\tan^2\alpha} \quad (145)$$

Algebraic signs: $\pm$ indicates that the algebraic sign is determined by the quadrant into which the *required* angle falls. For algebraic signs in the quadrants see **(135)**.

Relationships between the functions of two angles

$$\sin(\alpha\pm\beta) = \sin\alpha\cos\beta \pm \cos\alpha\sin\beta \quad (146)$$

$$\cos(\alpha\pm\beta) = \cos\alpha\cos\beta \mp \sin\alpha\sin\beta \quad (147)$$

$$\tan(\alpha\pm\beta) = \frac{\tan\alpha\pm\tan\beta}{1\mp\tan\alpha\tan\beta} = \frac{\sin(\alpha\pm\beta)}{\cos(\alpha\pm\beta)} \quad (148)$$

$$\sin\alpha+\sin\beta = 2\sin\left(\frac{\alpha+\beta}{2}\right)\cos\left(\frac{\alpha-\beta}{2}\right) \quad (149)$$

$$\sin\alpha-\sin\beta = 2\cos\left(\frac{\alpha+\beta}{2}\right)\sin\left(\frac{\alpha-\beta}{2}\right) \quad (150)$$

$$\cos\alpha+\cos\beta = 2\cos\left(\frac{\alpha+\beta}{2}\right)\cos\left(\frac{\alpha-\beta}{2}\right) \quad (151)$$

$$\cos\alpha-\cos\beta = -2\sin\left(\frac{\alpha+\beta}{2}\right)\sin\left(\frac{\alpha-\beta}{2}\right) \quad (152)$$

$$\tan\alpha\pm\tan\beta = \frac{\sin(\alpha\pm\beta)}{\cos\alpha\cos\beta} \quad (153)$$

$$\sin\alpha\sin\beta = \tfrac{1}{2}\cos(\alpha-\beta) - \tfrac{1}{2}\cos(\alpha+\beta) \quad (154)$$

$$\cos\alpha\cos\beta = \tfrac{1}{2}\cos(\alpha-\beta) + \tfrac{1}{2}\cos(\alpha+\beta) \quad (155)$$

$$\sin\alpha\cos\beta = \tfrac{1}{2}\sin(\alpha+\beta) + \tfrac{1}{2}\sin(\alpha-\beta) \quad (156)$$

4. Inverse trigonometric functions

These are also known as arc or cyclometric functions. Only the inverse sine (arc-sine) function will be described here, since this is used for the stabilization of the variance of binomial distributions (see page 222).

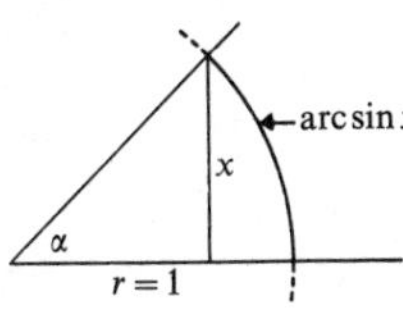

Arc sine x, abbreviated to $\sin^{-1} x$ or arc sin x, is the arc or degree measure of the angle with sine $= x$. An arc-sine table in arc measure for the range $0 \le x \le 1$ is given on page 73. If the value of an arc sine in degrees is required, the value given in this table must be multiplied by $180/\pi$ = 57,295 779 513.

Graph of the function arc sin x in the range $0 \le x \le 1$

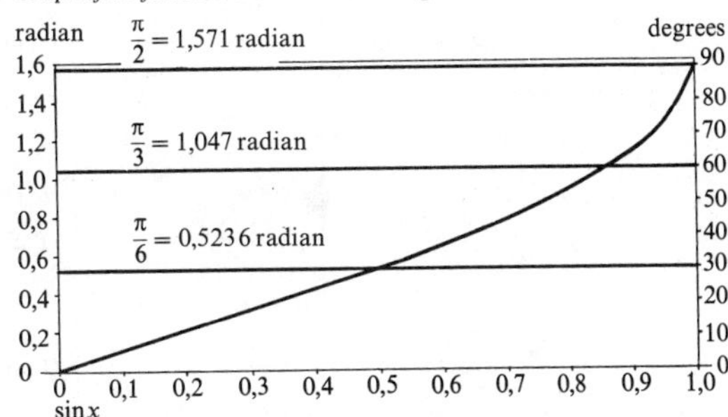

All values conform to the international convention (i.e. 0,1 instead of 0.1).

XIII. Hyperbolic functions

These derive their name from their geometric representation in relation to a rectangular hyperbola in a manner similar to that in which the trigonometric functions are related to a circle. Here only the hyperbolic tangent ($\tanh z$) and the corresponding inverse function ($\tanh^{-1} r$) will be dealt with, since these functions are required for the transformation of the correlation coefficient r (see page 215). They are defined as follows:

$$\tanh z = r = \frac{e^{2z}-1}{e^{2z}+1} \qquad \textbf{(157)}$$

$$\tanh^{-1} r = z = ½ \ln \frac{1+r}{1-r} = 1{,}151\,29255 \log_{10} \frac{1+r}{1-r} \qquad \textbf{(158)}$$

Only the following two relationships are required:

$$\tanh(-z) = -\tanh z \qquad \textbf{(159)}$$

$$\tanh^{-1}(-r) = -\tanh^{-1} r \qquad \textbf{(160)}$$

The range of variation of $\tanh z$ is -1 to $+1$ for values of z from $-\infty$ to $+\infty$.

Graph of the function $\tanh z$ in the range $-3{,}2 \leq z \leq +3{,}2$

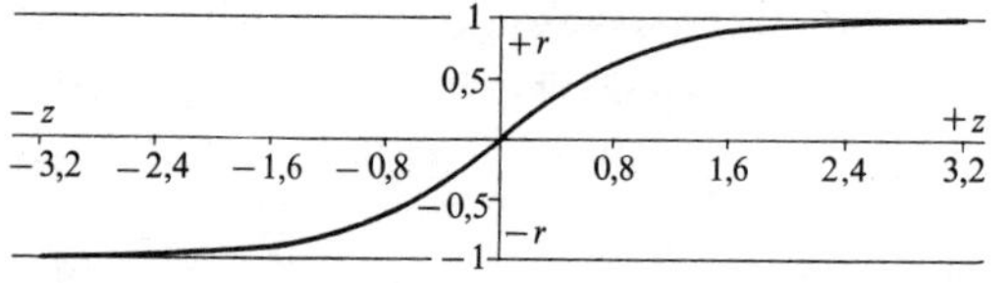

Tables of $\tanh z$ are given on pages 66 and 67, of $\tanh^{-1} r$ on page 64.

XIV. Geometric calculations

1. Right triangle *ABC*

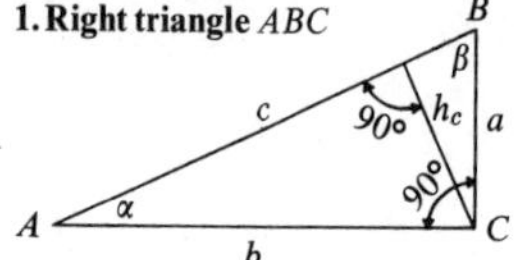

a = perpendicular } sides
b = base } sides
c = hypotenuse
h_c = height above hypotenuse

Given	Required	Solutions	
β	α	$90° - \beta$	**(161)**
a, b	α	$\tan\alpha = \frac{a}{b}$	**(162)**
	c	$\frac{a}{\sin\alpha}$	**(163)**
		$\frac{b}{\cos\alpha}$	**(164)**
		$+\sqrt{a^2+b^2}$	**(165)**
	h_c	$a\cos\alpha$	**(166)**
		$b\sin\alpha$	**(167)**
		$\frac{ab}{c}$	**(168)**
	Area A	$\frac{ab}{2}$	**(169)**
a, c	α	$\sin\alpha = \frac{a}{c}$	**(170)**
	b	$c\cos\alpha$	**(171)**
		$+\sqrt{c^2-a^2}$	**(172)**
	h_c	$a\cos\alpha$	**(173)**
	Area A	$\frac{ac\cos\alpha}{2}$	**(174)**
b, c	α	$\cos\alpha = \frac{b}{c}$	**(175)**
	a	$c\sin\alpha$	**(176)**
		$+\sqrt{c^2-b^2}$	**(177)**
	h_c	$b\sin\alpha$	**(178)**
	Area A	$\frac{bc\sin\alpha}{2}$	**(179)**
a, α	b	$\frac{a}{\tan\alpha}$	**(180)**
	c	$\frac{a}{\sin\alpha}$	**(181)**
	h_c	$a\cos\alpha$	**(182)**
	Area A	$\frac{a^2}{2\tan\alpha}$	**(183)**
c, α	a	$c\sin\alpha$	**(184)**
	b	$c\cos\alpha$	**(185)**
	h_c	$\frac{c\sin 2\alpha}{2}$	**(186)**
	Area A	$\frac{c^2\sin 2\alpha}{4}$	**(187)**
c, h_c	α	$\sin 2\alpha = \frac{2h_c}{c}$	**(188)**
	a	$\frac{h_c}{\cos\alpha}$	**(189)**
	b	$\frac{h_c}{\sin\alpha}$	**(190)**
	Area A	$\frac{c\,h_c}{2}$	**(191)**

2. Obtuse triangle

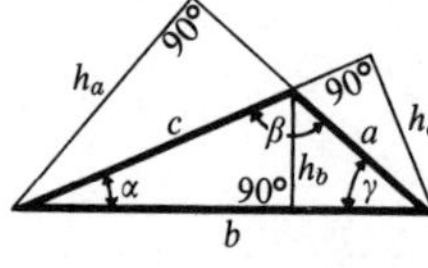

All the sides are of equal value in the obtuse triangle, and permutation of a, b, c, etc. in a cyclic fashion results in different formulae which are equally valid. When one of the symbols in any formula in a group is permuted, the symbols in all the other formulae of the group must be permuted in accordance with the following scheme:

Permutation by one step	Permutation by two steps	
$a \to b$	$a \to c$	
$b \to c$	$b \to a$	
$c \to a$	$c \to b$	**(192)**
$\alpha \to \beta$	$\alpha \to \gamma$	
$\beta \to \gamma$	$\beta \to \alpha$	
$\gamma \to \alpha$	$\gamma \to \beta$	
$h_a \to h_b$	$h_a \to h_c$	

All values conform to the international convention (i.e. 0,1 instead of 0.1).

Heights and areas

$$h_a = b \sin\gamma \qquad (193)$$

$$= c \sin\beta \qquad (194)$$

$$= a \frac{\sin\beta \sin\gamma}{\sin\alpha} \qquad (195)$$

$$\text{Area } A = \frac{a\,h_a}{2} \qquad (196)$$

Given	Required	Solutions	
$\beta+\gamma$	α	$180° - (\beta+\gamma)$	**(197)**
$\sin\alpha$	$\sin(\beta+\gamma)$	$\sin\alpha$	**(198)**
$\cos\alpha$	$\cos(\beta+\gamma)$	$-\cos\alpha$	
$\tan\alpha$	$\tan(\beta+\gamma)$	$-\tan\alpha$	
a, b, c	α	$\cos\alpha = \frac{b^2+c^2-a^2}{2\,b\,c}$	**(199)**
	h_a	$b \sin\gamma$	**(200)**
		$\frac{2\,A}{a}$	**(201)**
	Area A	$\frac{b\,c \sin\alpha}{2}$	**(202)**
		$\sqrt{s\,(s-a)\,(s-b)\,(s-c)}$ $[s=(a+b+c)/2]$	**(203)**
a, b, γ	α	$\tan\alpha = \frac{a \sin\gamma}{b - a\cos\gamma}$	**(204)**
	c	$\frac{a \sin\gamma}{\sin\alpha}$	**(205)**
		$\sqrt{a^2+b^2-2\,a\,b\cos\gamma}$	**(206)**
	h_a	$b \sin\gamma$	**(207)**
	h_b	$a \sin\gamma$	**(208)**
	Area A	$\frac{a\,b \sin\gamma}{2}$	**(209)**
a, b, α	β	$\sin\beta = \frac{b \sin\alpha}{a}$	**(210)**
	c	$\frac{a \sin\gamma}{\sin\alpha}$	**(211)**
		$b\cos\alpha \pm \sqrt{a^2 - b^2 \sin^2\alpha}$	**(212)**
	h_a	$b \sin\gamma$	**(213)**
	h_b	$a \sin\gamma$	**(214)**
	h_c	$b \sin\alpha$	**(215)**
	Area A	$\frac{b}{2}\sin\alpha \times$ $\times\left(b\cos\alpha \pm \sqrt{a^2-b^2\sin^2\alpha}\right)$	**(216)**
a, b, β	α	$\sin\alpha = \frac{a \sin\beta}{b}$	**(217)**
	c	$\frac{b \sin\gamma}{\sin\beta}$	**(218)**
	h_a	$b \sin\gamma$	**(219)**
	h_b	$a \sin\gamma$	**(220)**
	h_c	$a \sin\beta$	**(221)**
	Area A	$\frac{a}{2}\sin\beta \times$ $\times\left(a\cos\beta \pm \sqrt{b^2-a^2\sin^2\beta}\right)$	**(222)**

All values conform to the international convention (i.e. 0,1 instead of 0.1).

Note that in the left-hand group of equations (given two sides and the angle they enclose), the following conditions hold:

	(210) to **(216)**	**(217)** to **(222)**
Solution is only possible when	$b \sin\alpha \le a$	$a \sin\beta \le b$
If	$b \sin\alpha = a$	$a \sin\beta = b$
then	$\beta = 90°$	$\alpha = 90°$
If	$b \sin\alpha < a$ and $a < b$	$a \sin\beta < b$ and $b < a$
two solutions are possible	β_1 and $\beta_2 = 180° - \beta_1$	α_1 and $\alpha_2 = 180° - \alpha_1$
No solution is possible when	$b \sin\alpha < a$ and $a \ge b$	$a \sin\beta < a$ and $b \ge a$

Given	Required	Solutions	
a, β, γ	b	$\frac{a \sin\beta}{\sin(\beta+\gamma)}$	**(223)**
	c	$\frac{a \sin\gamma}{\sin(\beta+\gamma)}$	**(224)**
	h_a	$\frac{a \sin\beta \sin\gamma}{\sin(\beta+\gamma)}$	**(225)**
	h_b	$a \sin\gamma$	**(226)**
	h_c	$a \sin\beta$	**(227)**
	Area A	$\frac{a^2}{2} \times \frac{\sin\beta \sin\gamma}{\sin(\beta+\gamma)}$	**(228)**

Note that if two angles are given, the third is known:

$$\alpha = 180° - (\beta+\gamma) \quad \beta = 180° - (\alpha+\gamma) \quad \gamma = 180° - (\alpha+\beta)$$

3. Quadrilateral

In general the area of any quadrilateral can be calculated from the diagonals and the angle ϑ or $\vartheta' = 180° - \vartheta$ enclosed by them.

Any quadrilateral

Any triangle can be chosen, but the sides indicated by b, c must *enclose* the angle ϑ or ϑ'.

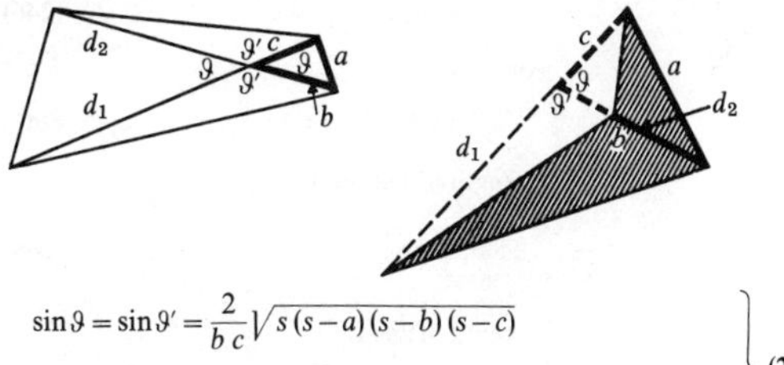

$$\sin\vartheta = \sin\vartheta' = \frac{2}{b\,c}\sqrt{s\,(s-a)\,(s-b)\,(s-c)} \qquad (229)$$

where $s = ½\,(a+b+c)$ is half the circumference of the triangle bounded by the two diagonals and the side a

$$\text{Area of shaded part } A = \frac{d_1 d_2 \sin\vartheta}{2} \qquad (230)$$

Square

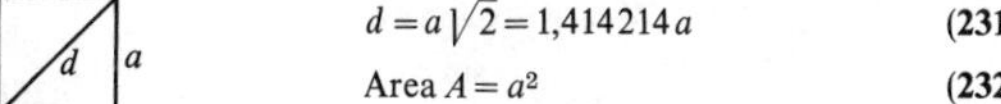

$$d = a\sqrt{2} = 1{,}414214\,a \qquad (231)$$

$$\text{Area } A = a^2 \qquad (232)$$

Rectangle

$$d = \sqrt{a^2+b^2} \qquad (233)$$

$$\text{Area } A = a\,b \qquad (234)$$

Parallelogram

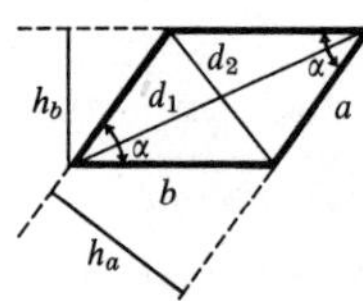

$$d_1, d_2 = \sqrt{a^2+b^2 \pm 2\,a\,b\cos\alpha} \quad (235)$$

$$= \sqrt{a^2+b^2 \pm 2\,a\sqrt{b^2-h_a^2}} \quad (236)$$

$$h_a = b\sin\alpha \quad (237)$$

$$h_b = a\sin\alpha \quad (238)$$

$$\text{Area } A = a\,h_a = b\,h_b = a\,b\sin\alpha \quad (239)$$

Trapezoid

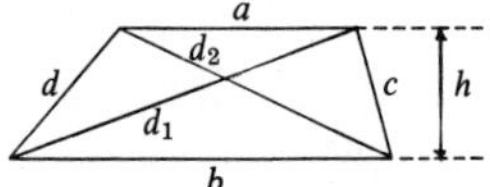

a, b are parallel, c, d nonparallel sides; d_1 = diagonal drawn between the points of intersection of d with b and a with c.

$$d_1 = \sqrt{a\,b + \frac{a\,c^2 - b\,d^2}{a-b}} \quad (240)$$

$$d_2 = \sqrt{a\,b + \frac{a\,d^2 - b\,c^2}{a-b}} \quad (241)$$

$$\left.\begin{aligned} h &= \frac{2}{a-b}\times \\ &\times\sqrt{s\,(s-a+b)\,(s-c)\,(s-d)} \\ [s &= \tfrac{1}{2}(a-b+c+d)] \end{aligned}\right\} \quad (242)$$

$$\text{Area } A = \frac{(a+b)\,h}{2} \quad (243)$$

4. Circle

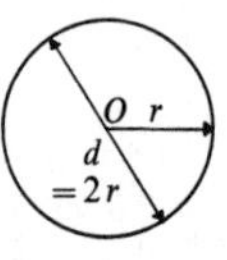

$$\left.\begin{aligned} &\text{Circumference } c \\ &\quad = 2\,r\,\pi = 6{,}283\,1853\,r \\ &\quad = 3{,}141\,592\,65\,d \end{aligned}\right\} \quad (244)$$

$$\left.\begin{aligned} \text{Area } A &= r^2\,\pi = 3{,}141\,592\,65\,r^2 \\ &= 0{,}785\,398\,16\,d^2 \end{aligned}\right\} \quad (245)$$

Sector

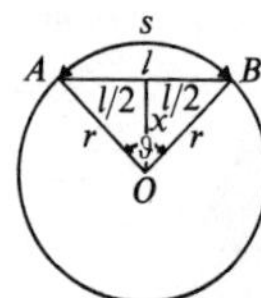

Angle ϑ between two radii r:

$$\cos\vartheta = 1 - \frac{l^2}{2\,r^2} \quad (246)$$

or

$$\vartheta = 180^\circ - 2\arcsin(x/r) \quad (247)$$

Length of a chord l:

$$l = 2\,r\sin\frac{\vartheta}{2} \quad (248)$$

Length of an arc s:

$$s = \frac{r\,\pi\,\vartheta}{180} = 0{,}017\,453\,293\,r\,\vartheta \quad (249)$$

Area A_{Se} of a sector:

$$A_{Se} = \frac{r^2\,\pi\,\vartheta}{360} = 0{,}008\,726\,646\,3\,r^2\,\vartheta \quad (250)$$

Area of a triangle OAB:

$$A_\triangle = \frac{r^2\sin\vartheta}{2} \quad (251)$$

Area of a segment AsB:

$$\left.\begin{aligned} A_{Sg} &= \frac{r^2\,\pi\,\vartheta}{360} - \frac{r^2\sin\vartheta}{2} \\ &= 0{,}008\,726\,646\,3\,r^2\times \\ &\quad\times(\vartheta - 57{,}295\,779\,5\sin\vartheta) \end{aligned}\right\} \quad (252)$$

Annulus

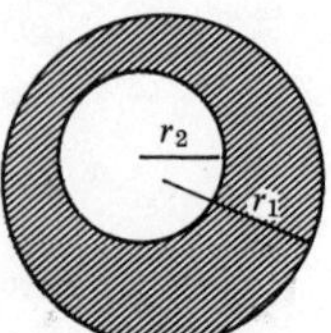

(The two circles bounding an annulus need not be concentric.)

Area of shaded part:

$$\left.\begin{aligned} A &= \pi\,(r_1+r_2)\,(r_1-r_2) \quad [r_1 \geq r_2] \\ &= 3{,}141\,592\,65\,(r_1+r_2)\,(r_1-r_2) \end{aligned}\right\} \quad (253)$$

Annular segment (concentric)

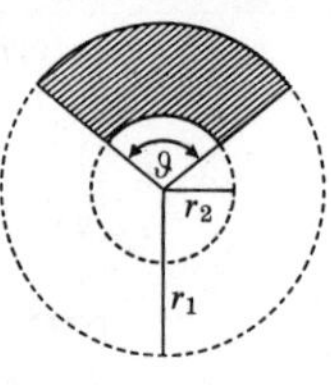

Area of shaded part:

$$A = \frac{\pi\,\vartheta}{360}\,(r_1+r_2)\,(r_1-r_2) \quad (254)$$

[$\pi/360 = 0{,}008\,726\,646\,26$; for the angle ϑ see equations **(246)** and **(247)**; $r_1 \geq r_2$]

5. Ellipse

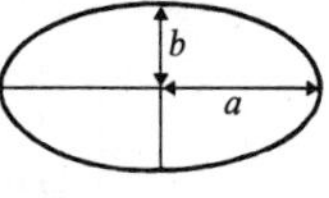

$$\left.\begin{aligned} \text{Circumference} &\sim 2\,\pi\sqrt{\frac{a^2+b^2}{2}} \\ &\sim 4{,}443\sqrt{a^2+b^2} \end{aligned}\right\} \quad (255)$$

$$\text{Area } A = \pi\,a\,b = 3{,}141\,592\,65\,a\,b \quad (256)$$

XV. Solid geometry

1. Rectangular parallelepiped (all edges at right angles to the adjacent ones)

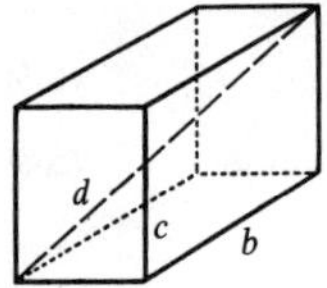

Surface area:

$$A = 2\,(a\,b + b\,c + c\,a) \quad (257)$$

Internal diagonal:

$$d = \sqrt{a^2+b^2+c^2} \quad (258)$$

Volume:

$$V = a\,b\,c \quad (259)$$

In the case of the cube, equations **(257)** to **(259)** become

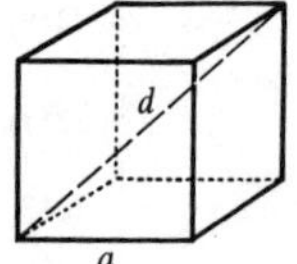

$$A = 6\,a^2 \quad (260)$$

$$d = a\sqrt{3} = 1{,}732\,050\,8\,a \quad (261)$$

$$V = a^3 \quad (262)$$

2. Pyramid (any base)

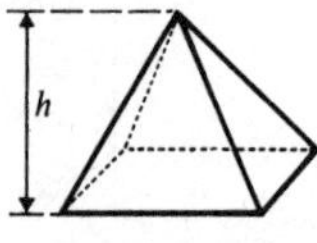

Volume:

$$V = \frac{h}{3}\,A_B \quad [A_B\text{: area of base}] \quad (263)$$

3. Right circular cylinder

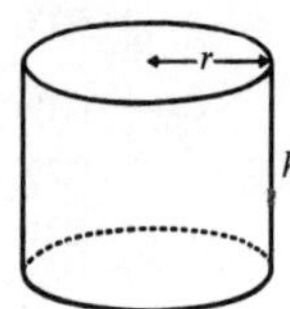

Area of convex surface:

$$A_C = 2\,r\,\pi\,h = 6{,}283\,185\,3\,r\,h \quad (264)$$

Total surface area:

$$\left.\begin{aligned} A &= 2\,r\,\pi\,(r+h) \\ &= 6{,}283\,185\,3\,r\,(r+h) \end{aligned}\right\} \quad (265)$$

Volume:

$$V = r^2\,\pi\,h = 3{,}141\,592\,65\,r^2\,h \quad (266)$$

All values conform to the international convention (i.e. 0,1 instead of 0.1).

Hollow cylinder

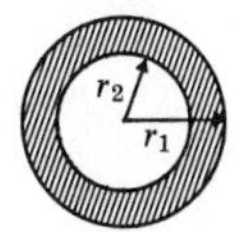

Internal volume:

$$V_I = \pi(r_1^2 - r_2^2)h \quad [r_1 \geq r_2] = 3{,}141\,592\,65\,(r_1^2 - r_2^2)\,h \qquad (267)$$

4. Right circular cone

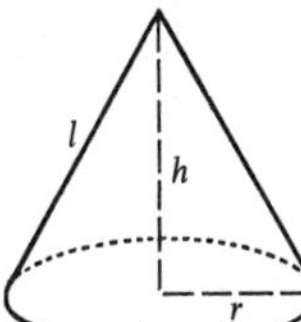

Area of convex surface:

$$A_C = r\pi l = 3{,}141\,592\,65\,r\,l \quad [l\text{: slant height} = \sqrt{r^2 + h^2}] \qquad (268)$$

Total surface area:

$$A = r\,\pi\,(r + l) = 3{,}141\,592\,65\,r\,(r + l) \qquad (269)$$

Volume:

$$V = \frac{1}{3} r^2\,\pi\,h = 1{,}047\,197\,55\,r^2\,h \qquad (270)$$

Truncated cone (right circular, plane surfaces parallel)

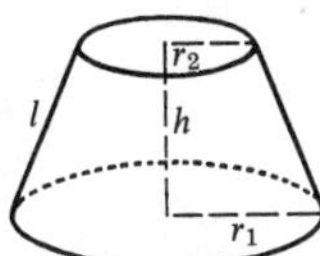

Area of convex surface:

$$A_C = \pi\,l(r_1 + r_2) \qquad (271)$$

Total surface area:

$$A = \pi\,[r_1(r_1 + l) + r_2\,(r_2 + l)] \qquad (272)$$

Volume:

$$V = \frac{\pi\,h}{3}(r_1^2 + r_1\,r_2 + r_2^2) = 1{,}047\,197\,55\,h\,(r_1^2 + r_1\,r_2 + r_2^2) \qquad (273)$$

5. Sphere

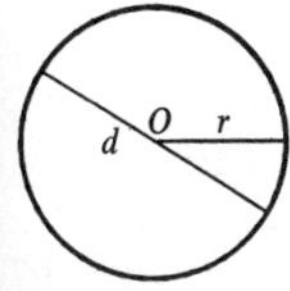

Surface area:

$$A = 4\,r^2\,\pi = \pi\,d^2 = 12{,}566\,370\,6\,r^2 = 3{,}141\,592\,65\,d^2 \qquad (274)$$

Volume:

$$V = \frac{4\,r^3\,\pi}{3} = \frac{\pi\,d^3}{6} = 4{,}188\,790\,20\,r^3 = 0{,}523\,598\,78\,d^3 \qquad (275)$$

Segment of a sphere (cut by a single plane)

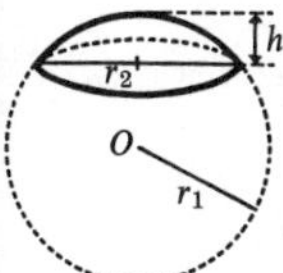

Area of convex surface:

$$A_C = \pi(r_2^2 + h^2) = 2\,r_1\,\pi\,h \qquad (276)$$

Total surface area:

$$A = \pi\,(2\,r_2^2 + h^2) \qquad (277)$$

Volume:

$$V = \frac{\pi\,h}{6}\,(3\,r_2^2 + h^2) = \frac{\pi\,h^2}{3}\,(3\,r_1 - h) \qquad (278)$$

$[\pi/6 = 0{,}523\,598\,78;\ \pi/3 = 1{,}047\,197\,55]$

Segment of a sphere (between two parallel planes)

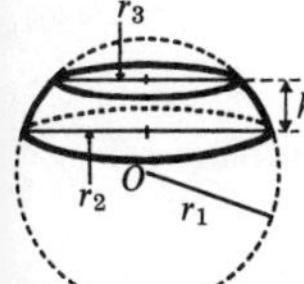

Area of convex surface:

$$A_C = 2\,r_1\,\pi\,h = 6{,}283\,185\,3\,r_1\,h \qquad (279)$$

Total surface area:

$$A = \pi\,(r_2^2 + 2\,r_1\,h + r_3^2) \qquad (280)$$

Volume:

$$V = \frac{\pi\,h}{6}\,(3\,r_2^2 + 3\,r_3^2 + h^2) = 0{,}523\,598\,78\,h\,(3\,r_2^2 + 3\,r_3^2 + h^2) \qquad (281)$$

All values conform to the international convention (i.e. 0,1 instead of 0.1).

Wedge segment of a sphere

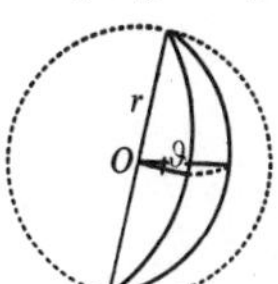

Volume:

$$V = \frac{\pi\,r^3\,\vartheta}{270} = 0{,}011\,635\,528\,r^3\,\vartheta \qquad (282)$$

[for ϑ: angle between the two planes passing through the center of the sphere; see (**246**) and (**247**)]

6. Bodies of the same shape

Bodies of the same shape, i.e., those in which *all corresponding linear measurements are in the same ratio* $a:b$*, have surface areas in the ratio $a^2:b^2$ and weights and volumes in the ratio $a^3:b^3$. **(283)**

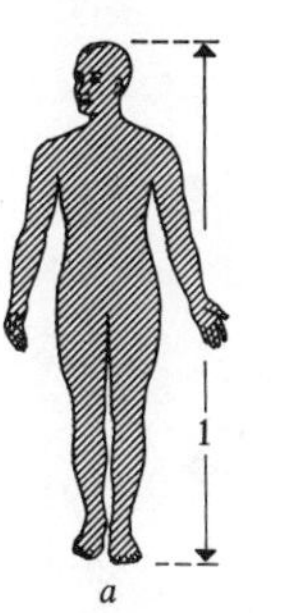

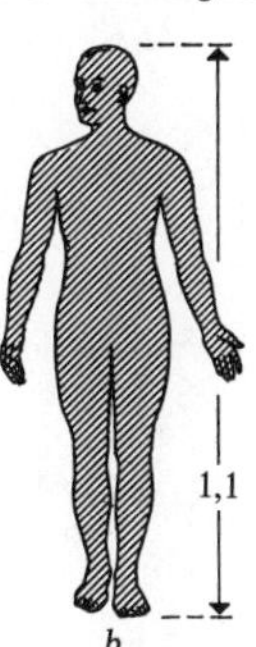

All linear dimensions of body *b* are 10% greater than those of body *a*; *b* has 21% more surface area and 33% more weight.

XVI. Formulae of analytical geometry

1. Transformation of rectangular coordinates

The new coordinates are indicated by *C*, the transformed variables by *X*, *Y*, the old coordinates and variables by *c*, *x*, *y*. For the sake of simplicity the transformation is illustrated in the first quadrant (see section XI, page 174) but the equations are valid for all quadrants.

(a) Translation of coordinate axes

The origin is translated from *O* to *O′*, i.e., a distance *a* in the direction *x* and a distance *b* in the direction *y*.

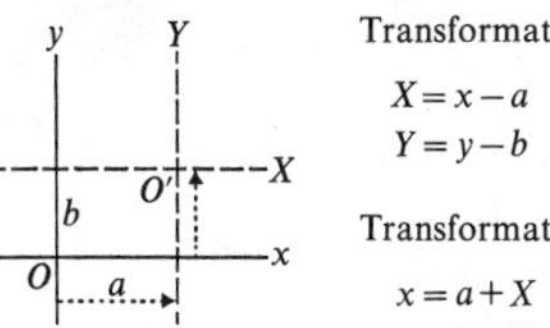

Transformation $c \rightarrow C$:

$$X = x - a, \quad Y = y - b \qquad (284)$$

Transformation $C \rightarrow c$:

$$x = a + X, \quad y = b + Y \qquad (285)$$

(b) Alteration of linear scale

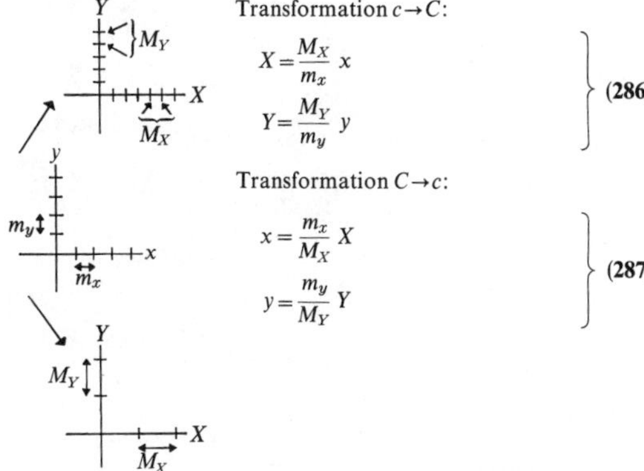

Transformation $c \rightarrow C$:

$$X = \frac{M_X}{m_x}\,x, \quad Y = \frac{M_Y}{m_y}\,y \qquad (286)$$

Transformation $C \rightarrow c$:

$$x = \frac{m_x}{M_X}\,X, \quad y = \frac{m_y}{M_Y}\,Y \qquad (287)$$

* Note that this is usually not true of human bodies of different *heights*.

(c) Translation of axes and alteration of linear scale

Transformation $c \rightarrow C$:

$$X = \frac{M_X}{m_x}(x-a) \quad Y = \frac{M_Y}{m_y}(y-b) \tag{288}$$

Transformation $C \rightarrow c$:

$$x = a + \frac{m_x}{M_X} X \quad y = b + \frac{m_y}{M_Y} Y \tag{289}$$

(d) Rotation of coordinate axes

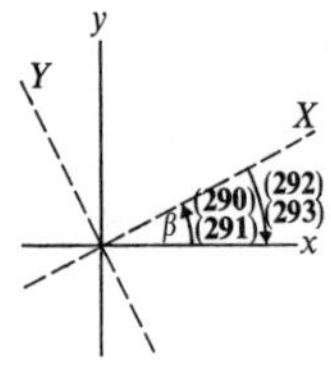

Transformation $c \rightarrow C$:

$$X = x\cos\beta + y\sin\beta \quad Y = y\cos\beta - x\sin\beta \tag{290}$$

or

$$X = \frac{1}{\sqrt{1+\tan^2\beta}}(x + y\tan\beta) \quad Y = \frac{1}{\sqrt{1+\tan^2\beta}}(y - x\tan\beta) \tag{291}$$

Transformation $C \rightarrow c$:

$$x = X\cos\beta - Y\sin\beta \quad y = X\sin\beta + Y\cos\beta \tag{292}$$

or

$$x = \frac{1}{\sqrt{1+\tan^2\beta}}(X - Y\tan\beta) \quad y = \frac{1}{\sqrt{1+\tan^2\beta}}(Y + X\tan\beta) \tag{293}$$

(e) Rotation and translation of the coordinate axes

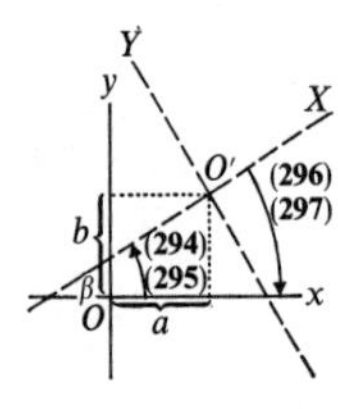

Transformation $c \rightarrow C$:

$$X = (x-a)\cos\beta + (y-b)\sin\beta \quad Y = (y-b)\cos\beta - (x-a)\sin\beta \tag{294}$$

or

$$X = \frac{1}{\sqrt{1+\tan^2\beta}} \times [x - a + (y-b)\tan\beta] \quad Y = \frac{1}{\sqrt{1+\tan^2\beta}} \times [y - b - (x-a)\tan\beta] \tag{295}$$

Transformation $C \rightarrow c$:

$$x = a + X\cos\beta - Y\sin\beta \quad y = b + Y\cos\beta + X\sin\beta \tag{296}$$

or

$$x = a + \frac{1}{\sqrt{1+\tan^2\beta}}(X - Y\tan\beta) \quad y = b + \frac{1}{\sqrt{1+\tan^2\beta}}(Y + X\tan\beta) \tag{297}$$

2. Straight line

General equation:

$$Ax + By + C = 0 \tag{298}$$

All values conform to the international convention (i.e. 0,1 instead of 0.1).

Equation of slope:

$y = a + bx$ or $x = \frac{y-a}{b}$

[a: Intercept with y axis; b: tangent of the angle β. Note that $b = \tan\beta$ is valid only when the same unit is used for both coordinate axes.] **(299)**

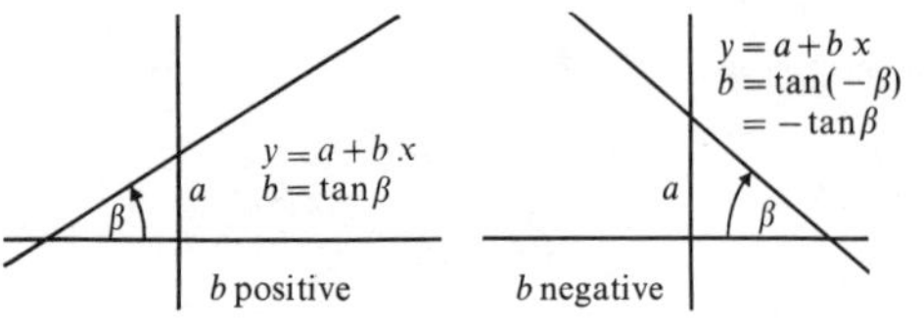

Special cases

$x = a$ is the equation of a line parallel to the y axis **(300)**

$y = c$ is the equation of a line parallel to the x axis **(301)**

A straight line is at right angles to another straight line with slope b when its slope is $-1/b$. **(302)**

Straight line through two points with coordinates $x_1, y_1; x_2, y_2$:

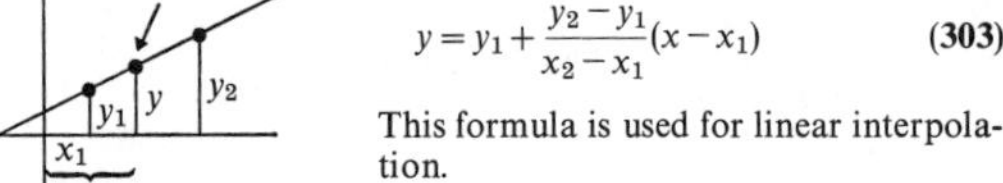

$$y = y_1 + \frac{y_2 - y_1}{x_2 - x_1}(x - x_1) \tag{303}$$

This formula is used for linear interpolation.

Example

Given: $x_1 = 110$ $y_1 = 83{,}83$
$x_2 = 120$ $y_2 = 95{,}66$

Required: y value for $x = 116$

Solution: $y = 83{,}83 + \frac{95{,}66 - 83{,}83}{120 - 110}(116 - 110) = 90{,}93$

Straight line with slope b through a point x_1, y_1:

$$y = y_1 + b(x - x_1) \tag{304}$$

Straight line through the origin and a point x_1, y_1:

$$y = \frac{y_1}{x_1} x \tag{305}$$

Length p of the straight line parallel to the y axis between a point x_1, y_1 and the straight line $y = a + bx$:

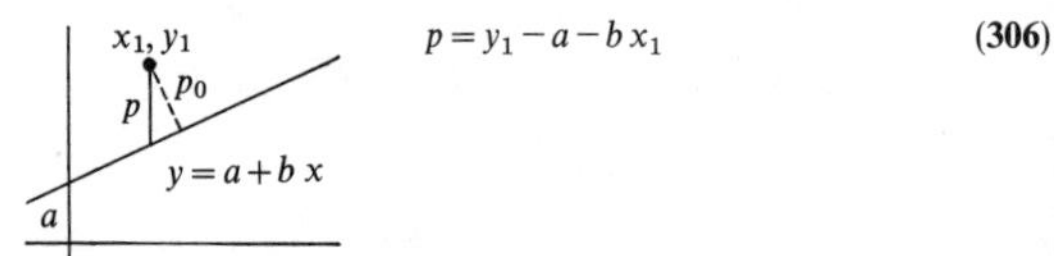

$$p = y_1 - a - bx_1 \tag{306}$$

Shortest (orthogonal) distance p_0 between a point and the straight line $y = a + bx$:

$$p_0 = \frac{y_1 - a - bx_1}{\sqrt{1+b^2}} \tag{307}$$

Distance p_x parallel to the x axis at a height y_p between two straight lines $y = a_1 + b_1 x$ and $y = a_2 + b_2 x$:

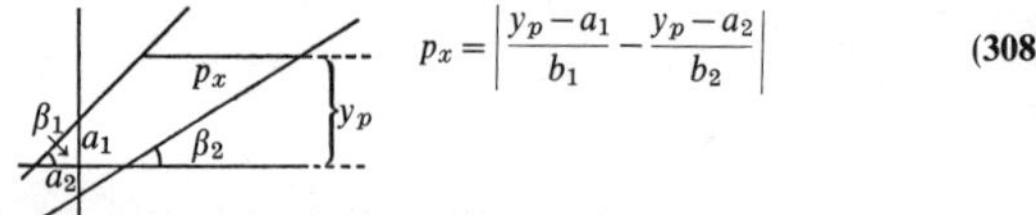

$$p_x = \left| \frac{y_p - a_1}{b_1} - \frac{y_p - a_2}{b_2} \right| \tag{308}$$

Distance p_x parallel to the x axis between two parallel lines $y = a_1 + b\,x$ and $y = a_2 + b\,x$ [special case of (**308**) with $b_1 = b_2$]:

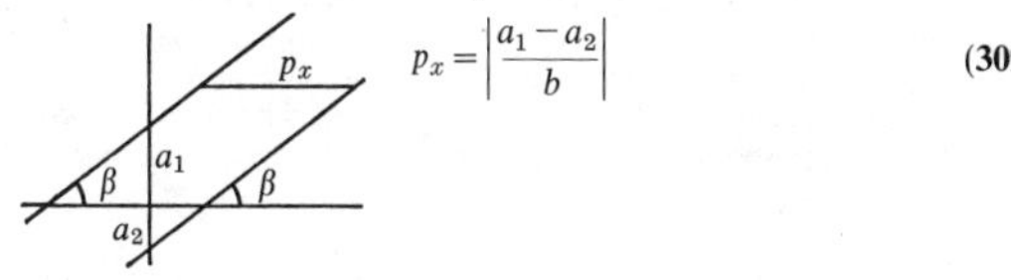

$$p_x = \left|\frac{a_1 - a_2}{b}\right| \qquad \textbf{(309)}$$

Coordinates of the intersection of two straight lines $y = a_1 + b_1\,x$ and $y = a_2 + b_2\,x$:

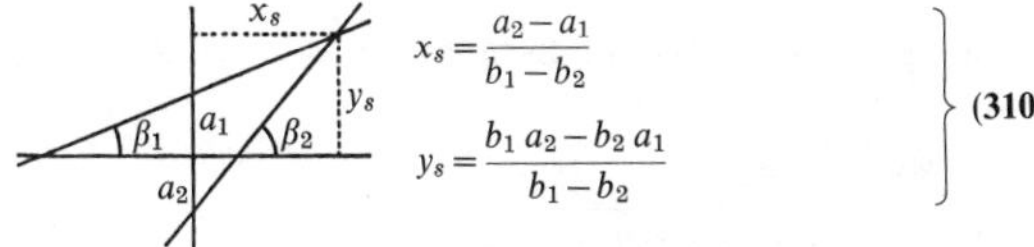

$$\left.\begin{aligned} x_s &= \frac{a_2 - a_1}{b_1 - b_2} \\ y_s &= \frac{b_1\,a_2 - b_2\,a_1}{b_1 - b_2} \end{aligned}\right\} \qquad \textbf{(310)}$$

Angle ϑ between two straight lines with slopes b_1 and b_2:

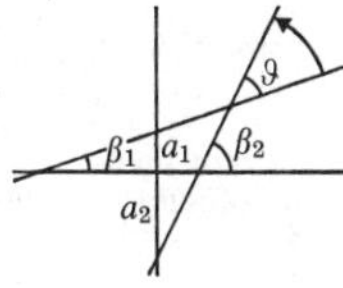

$$\tan\vartheta = \frac{b_1 - b_2}{b_1\,b_2 + 1} \qquad \textbf{(311)}$$

The angle ϑ is the positive angle through which the first straight line must be rotated in order that it shall coincide with the second straight line. Note that equation (**311**) is valid only when the same units are used for both coordinate axes.

3. Ellipse

Standard equation in rectangular coordinates (the principal axes):

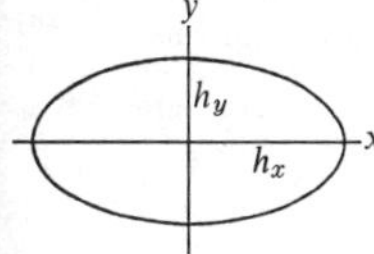

$$\frac{x^2}{a^2} + \frac{y^2}{b^2} = c^2 \qquad \textbf{(312)}$$

a and b determine the relation between the two semi-axes and thus the shape of the ellipse.

If h_x is the semi-major, h_y the semi-minor axis, equation (**312**) becomes

$$\left.\begin{aligned} &\frac{x^2}{h_x^2} + \frac{y^2}{h_y^2} = 1 \\ &[h_x^2 = c^2\,a^2;\, h_y^2 = c^2\,b^2] \end{aligned}\right\} \qquad \textbf{(313)}$$

The focal width F_1F_2 is given by

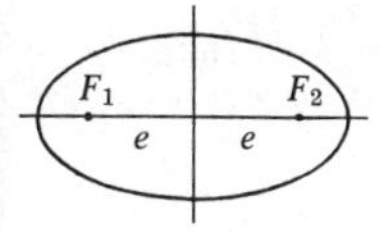

$$\left.\begin{aligned} &2\,e = 2\sqrt{h_x^2 - h_y^2} \\ &[e\text{: linear eccentricity}] \end{aligned}\right\} \qquad \textbf{(314)}$$

If s is the sum of the distances from a point P on the curve to the foci F_1 and F_2, then

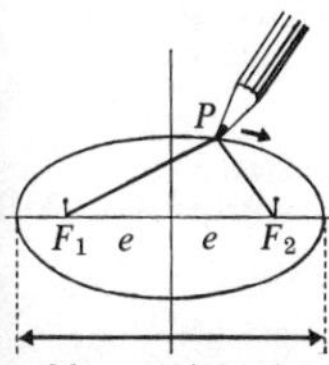

$2\,h_x$ = major axis

$$s = 2\,h_x = \text{major axis} \qquad \textbf{(315)}$$

Any desired ellipse may therefore be drawn by means of a thread of length $2\,h_x$ attached to the foci, e being determined from equation (**314**).

For area and circumference of the ellipse see equations (**255**) and (**256**) on page 178.

In the limited space available it is impossible to give more than a brief explanation of the mathematical and statistical tables on pages 10–167. The following description is therefore limited to those fundamentals the non-mathematician requires to enable him to solve simple statistical problems.

The calculation of probabilities by statistical methods is an essential step in the proper interpretation of experimental results that comply with certain basic laws but are at the same time subject to modification by unknown factors, in other words, to so-called 'chance' variation. This holds not only for the empirical sciences, the exact as well as the biological, but in a wider sense also for the abstract sciences:

On peut même dire, à parler en rigueur, que presque toutes nos connaissances ne sont que probables; et dans le petit nombre des choses que nous pouvons savoir avec certitude, dans les sciences mathématiques elles-mêmes, les principaux moyens de parvenir à la vérité, l'induction et l'analogie, se fondent sur les probabilités ... (LAPLACE, 1820)[7].

One reason for the physician's frequent mistrust of statistical methods is epitomized in the well-known allegation that 'you can prove anything with statistics'. Some prejudice against mathematics is also understandable in a profession in which intuitive reasoning is generally preferred. These are sentiments without any logical basis. Statistics is one of the most vigorous branches of mathematics, and its techniques for the disciplined assessment of observational data can be readily mastered. Furthermore, it should not be forgotten that every medical diagnosis represents the result of an intentional or unintentional calculation of probabilities.

This critical attitude towards statistics has its origin in their improper use as well as in their false interpretation. The statistical method is no more than another scientific method and cannot by its nature provide proof or disproof. On the other hand it constitutes the only method of subjecting values liable to chance variation (stochastic variables) to fixed and reproducible criteria based on logical mathematical considerations. The converse of the saying quoted is therefore much nearer the truth, namely that *no scientific investigation is capable of proving anything without the aid of statistics.* Human judgement is influenced to a very large extent by the subconscious wish and by the deep-rooted tendency – even in the worst of pessimists – to overrate one's own chances. The most careful investigator can be led astray by these psychological factors if he fails to arm himself against them with an adequate measure of self-control:

Le sentiment par lequel l'homme s'est placé longtemps au centre de l'univers, en se considérant comme l'objet spécial des soins de la nature, porte chaque individu à se faire le centre d'une sphère plus ou moins étendue, et à croire que le hasard a pour lui des préférences. Soutenus par cette opinion, les joueurs exposent souvent des sommes considérables à des jeux dont ils savent que les chances leur sont contraires. Dans la conduite de la vie, une semblable opinion peut quelquefois avoir des avantages; mais le plus souvent elle conduit à des entreprises funestes. Ici, comme en tout, les illusions sont dangereuses et la vérité seule est généralement utile.

Un des grands avantages du Calcul des Probabilités est d'apprendre à se défier des premiers aperçus. Comme on reconnaît qu'ils trompent souvent lorsqu'on peut les soumettre au calcul, on doit en conclure que sur d'autres objets il ne faut s'y livrer qu'avec une circonspection extrême (LAPLACE, 1820)[7].

'The wish' as 'father to the thought' may be an indispensable stimulus to research, but it has also been responsible – in the guise of 'our experience' or 'our opinion' backed by a few percentages – for much misunderstanding. One need only reflect on the wealth of new treatments and new drugs which after an enthusiastic reception have been allowed to fall quietly into oblivion.

Many a research worker in the past could have saved himself much time and effort had he submitted his observations and hypotheses to statistical testing before publication, but generally much closer links now exist between medicine and statistics. Such recognition is encouraging.

The growing use of statistical methods, however, is not without its own dangers. The general tendency is to overrate any new research tool, particularly when it is unfamiliar and complicated in operation. Too much uncritical dependence is placed on the results obtained; the limitations of the method may not be clearly recognized and the experimental data may be inadequately checked. Statistical methods obviously allow no such dispensation. On the other hand, the beginner will find that with increasing experience statistical ways of thinking will not only render him more circumspect but give him a deeper insight.

All values conform to the international convention (i.e. 0,1 instead of 0.1).

1. Introductory definitions*

An experiment subject to the influence of chance may be compared to an operation such as the drawing of numbers in a lottery. Imagine a box containing balls bearing the numbers 0, 1, 2, ..., 9. These are thoroughly mixed before the draw is commenced. The player drawing the balls is supposed to have no influence on the selection. Using this analogy, we designate

- the mixing of the balls as the *randomization* of the experimental material (316)
- the numbers 0, 1, 2, ..., 9 distinguishing the balls as *variables* or *attributes* (317)
- the aggregate number of balls in the box as the *parent population* (318)
- a draw as a *trial* (319)
- N trials as *random sampling* (320)
- the result of a trial represented by the drawing of the number 5 as the *random event* 5 (321)
- the result of N trials as a *random sample* of size N, or briefly as a sample N (322)
- the succession of events as a *random sequence* (in the numbered balls analogy it is the random series of numbers, or *random numbers*) (323)
- the relative frequency of the variate values in the population as the *probabilities* with which these values will be drawn (324)
- the relative frequency of the variate values in the sample as *estimate* of their probability (325)
- the distribution of the probabilities of the different variate values as probability distribution, or briefly as *distribution* (326)

Some of these definitions will be discussed in more detail later in this volume.

2. Population and sample

A population is finite or infinite when the trials (draws) can be repeated a finite or infinite number of times. (327)

A finite population, such as a finite number of balls in a box, can be converted into an effectively infinite one by putting the balls back into the box after each draw. Such an operation is known as *sampling with replacement.* (328)

From an infinite population an infinite number of samples can be taken, for example all of the same size N. The totality of such samples of size N is known as the *sampling population N* and their probability distribution as the *sampling distribution N.* (329)

An infinite sampling population can also be taken from a finite population in a manner similar to that in **(328)**, i.e., by returning the whole of the first sample to the box, drawing a second sample of the same size, returning this sample also to the box, and so on. *All sampling populations can therefore be regarded as infinite.* This is one of the fundamental concepts of mathematical statistics. (330)

Quantities such as mean value and variance which relate to the population are known as *parameters*, their counterparts in the sample as *statistics.* (331)

Symbols relating to the population are here printed in bold type whenever it is necessary to distinguish them from symbols relating to samples. Exceptions are the symbols for mean value and variance: these are respectively μ and σ^2 for the population and $\bar{x}$ and s^2 for the sample. (332)

*The mathematician will appreciate that this presentation is more readily understandable to non-mathematicians than a strictly mathematical one would be. Note that decimal commas are used instead of decimal points.

3. Variable and event

Variables are accumulated (possible) events in the box, events variables which have been drawn from the box. Where no possibility of confusion exists, the word 'event' is therefore here also used for 'variable', for example in the expression 'population of red and black events'. **(333)**

If A is an event, then the non-occurrence of A is its *complementary event*, designated here as non-A. Examples are success or failure, alive or dead, 6 or non-6 in die throwing, etc. **(334)**

The complementary event non-A is often an event B. For example, a girl can be born instead of a boy. Such events are known as *mutually exclusive events*, denoted by A or B, or by A, B. A and non-A in **(334)** are therefore by definition mutually exclusive events. **(335)**

Simultaneously occurring events can be treated as *successive* events. Whether the events $A, B, C, \dots$ occur simultaneously or successively, they are denoted by A and B and C and ..., or by ABC... **(336)**

Simultaneous or successive events can together form *an* event. For example, if two sixes are obtained by throwing two dice simultaneously or a single die twice, then the sum 12 is a *combined event.* **(337)**

If the occurrence (or non-occurrence) of an event A is restricted by the condition that an event B has occurred [or occurs simultaneously, cf. **(336)**], then event A is known as a *conditioned event*, denoted by $A|B$ and read as event A under the condition B. B can represent several conditions. **(338)**

Qualitative variables can be denoted by numbers, for example 1 for success, 0 for failure. **(339)**

If the events are already numbers they are here denoted by x provided that other symbols are not in general use, as in the case of some sampling distributions. **(340)**

If x (within a finite interval) takes only a finite number of values it is known as a *discrete random variable* or *variate.* In this case x changes by *discrete* amounts. Examples are 0, 1, 2, 3, ... successes, 25, 26, 27, ... respirations, etc. **(341)**

If the numbers 1, 2, 3, ... denote the smallest, second smallest, third smallest value, etc., the series is known as an ordered (by magnitude) or *ranked* series. In such a series the *exact* magnitudes determining the ranks of the smallest, second smallest, etc., may be unknown. **(342)**

Example 1. A group of people can be arranged in order of height without their exact heights being known.

If x can take all possible values in some interval it is known as a *continuous random variable* or *variate.* In this case x changes *continuously*. Examples of continuous variates are length, area, volume, weight, temperature, time and concentration, i.e., variables that can be *measured.* **(343)**

In practice, continuous variates do not exist since all measured values are rounded values. For example, when the smallest interval a balance can measure is a milligram, any weight measured will be rounded off to the nearest milligram. In this case x changes by discrete intervals of one milligram. Such a variable is often called a *'granulated'* (or *'atomic'*) *variable.* 'Granulated' variables are actually continuous variables that have been converted into discrete variables by rounding off. **(344)**

In the case of discrete variables the same value may occur two or more times in a sample from two or more tests. This is an almost impossible event in the case of continuous variables [cf. **(352)**], but occurs all the more often the more 'coarsely granulated' they are. Cf. **(344)**. **(345)**

If two or more identical values occur in a sample of a 'granulated' variable they are known as *ties* or tied values. Cf. **(344)** and **(345)**. **(346)**

All values conform to the international convention (i.e. 0,1 instead of 0.1).

4. Frequency, probability, compound events

If in a group of N individuals there are x females and $N-x$ males, then x and $N-x$ are the *absolute* and x/N and $(N-x)/N$ the *relative frequencies* of females and males in the group. Here the expression frequency will be used to mean the relative frequency. **(347)**

The relative frequency multiplied by 100 is known as the *percentage frequency.* **(348)**

Example 2. In 81 operations there are 3 fatalities. The percentage frequency is then $(3/81) \times 100 = 3{,}7\%$.

The percentage frequencies for values of N between 2 and 100 and for any values of $x \leq N$ are given in the column 100 p_x of the tables on pages 89–102. For the example 2 see page 97, $N = 81$, $x = 3$.

The following symbols are used here for probability: **(349)**

- 'Probability' in general .... Prob
- Probabilities of mutually exclusive events .... $\dot{\boldsymbol{p}}$
- Probabilities of two complementary events ... $\boldsymbol{p}$ and $\boldsymbol{q}$

In a later section the symbols α and $\boldsymbol{P}$ will also be used [cf. **(378)** and **(379)**].

In **(324)** *probability* was defined as the *relative frequency of a variable* [or of an event, cf. **(333)**] *in the population.* Propositions **(350)** to **(355)** follow directly from this definition:

Every probability is a number between 0 and 1: **(350)**

$0 \leq \text{Prob} \leq 1$

An impossible event has a probability of 0, a certain event a probability of 1. **(351)**

The converse of **(351)** *is not valid:*

An event with a probability of 0 is an *almost* impossible event, an event with a probability of 1 an *almost* certain event. **(352)**

Example 3. A box contains all the positive integers 1, 2, 3, ..., ∞. The probability of drawing, say, the number 1980 is $1/\infty = 0$. Nevertheless the possibility exists of drawing this number since it is present in the population.

The sum of the probabilities of *all* mutually exclusive events $E_0, E_1, \dots, E_N$ in a single population is equal to 1: **(353)**

$$\text{Prob}(E_0 \text{ or } E_1 \text{ or} \dots E_N) = \dot{\boldsymbol{p}}_0 + \dot{\boldsymbol{p}}_1 + \dots + \dot{\boldsymbol{p}}_N = 1$$

where the total of all mutually exclusive events is $N+1$, and

$$\text{Prob}(E \text{ or non-}E) = \boldsymbol{p} + \boldsymbol{q} = 1$$

It follows from **(353)** that a population with many mutually exclusive events can be converted in various ways into one with two complementary events. **(354)**

For example:

$$\text{Prob}[\underbrace{(E_0 \text{ or } E_1)}_{=E} \text{ or } \underbrace{(E_2 \text{ or} \dots E_N)}_{=\text{non-}E}]$$

$$= \underbrace{(\dot{\boldsymbol{p}}_0 + \dot{\boldsymbol{p}}_1)}_{=\boldsymbol{p}} + \underbrace{(\dot{\boldsymbol{p}}_2 + \dots + \dot{\boldsymbol{p}}_N)}_{=\boldsymbol{q}}$$

where the total number of mutually exclusive events is $N+1$.

Example 4 [of **(354)**]. With a true die the probability of throwing any one number is 1/6. The probability of throwing a 6 is 1/6, of throwing a non-6 (1 or 2 or ... 5) 5/6. The probability of throwing an even number (2 or 4 or 6) is $1/6 + 1/6 + 1/6 = 1/2$, of throwing an odd number likewise 1/2.

From **(353)** it follows that:

Of the mutually exclusive events $A, B, \dots$, the probability that either the event A or the event B will occur is equal to the sum of their probabilities, *provided that the events are from one and the same population:* **(355)**

$$\text{Prob}(A \text{ or } B \text{ or} \dots) = \dot{\boldsymbol{p}}_A + \dot{\boldsymbol{p}}_B + \cdots$$

Example 5 [of (**355**)]. *Correct application.* Assuming that the probability of an 85-year-old person dying of pneumonia is 0,2 and of dying of cancer also 0,2, then the probability that he will die either of pneumonia or cancer is 0,2 + 0,2 = 0,4.

Example 6 [of (**355**)]. *Incorrect application.* Assuming that the mortality of 85-year-olds is 0,5 and that of 86-year-olds 0,6, then the statement that there is a 1,1 probability of an 85-year-old dying either at 85 or at 86 is false. Here the error is already indicated by the probability figure of 1,1, which according to (**350**) is an impossibility, but it might well have been overlooked had the figure been 0,4, as in example 5. The error arises from the fact that mutually exclusive events from *different* populations, that of the 85-year-olds and that of the 86-year-olds, have been added together.

The probability of two simultaneous or successive events A and B is equal to the probability of the event A multiplied by the probability of the event B given the condition A, or to the probability of the event B multiplied by the probability of the event A given the condition B. On conditioned events see (**338**):

$$\text{Prob}(A \text{ and } B) = \text{Prob}(A) \times \text{Prob}(B|A) = \text{Prob}(B) \times \text{Prob}(A|B)$$ **(356)**

Example 7 [of (**356**)]. A box contains N balls, x red and $N-x$ white. A sample consisting of two balls is drawn *without replacement.* What is the probability of drawing (a) two red balls, (b) a red and then a white ball, (c) a red and a white ball in any order?

(a) The probability of a red ball at the first draw is x/N. The conditional probability of a red ball at the second draw (when there is one red ball less in the box) is $(x-1)/(N-1)$. The probability of drawing two red balls is therefore

$$\text{Prob(red, red)} = \frac{x}{N} \times \frac{x-1}{N-1}$$

(b) $$\text{Prob(red, white)} = \frac{x}{N} \times \frac{N-x}{N-1} = \frac{N-x}{N} \times \frac{x}{N-1} = \text{Prob(white, red)}$$

(c) Prob(red and white) or Prob(white and red) = Prob(red, white) + Prob(white, red)

$$= \frac{2x(N-x)}{N(N-1)}$$

Example 8 [of (**356**)]. From the same box as in example 7 a sample of the same size is taken, but *with replacement.* In this case the probabilities are as follows:

(a) The probability of a red ball at the first draw remains x/N. Since this ball is replaced in the box, the probability of a red ball at the second draw is the same:

$$\text{Prob(red, red)} = \frac{x}{N} \times \frac{x}{N}$$

(b) $$\text{Prob(red, white)} = \frac{x}{N} \times \frac{N-x}{N} = \frac{N-x}{N} \times \frac{x}{N} = \text{Prob(white, red)}$$

(c) Prob(red and white) or Prob(white and red) = Prob(red, white) + Prob(white, red)

$$= \frac{2x(N-x)}{N^2}$$

From example 7 it will be seen that the probabilities change with each draw, i.e., each successive draw is *dependent* on the previous one. The corresponding statistical expressions are *dependent trials* and *dependent events.* In example 8 the second draw is unaffected by the previous one, in which case the trials as well as the events are *independent.*

In other words, in the collection of samples from *finite* populations (no replacement), the trials and events are *dependent* on one another; in the collection of samples from *infinite* populations (replacement), they are *independent* of one another. **(357)**

Two simultaneous or successive events are known as stochastically *dependent* events when in (**356**) the conditional and the absolute probability of an event are *not the same,* i.e., when

$\text{Prob}(A|B) \neq \text{Prob}(A)$ or $\text{Prob}(B|A) \neq \text{Prob}(B)$ **(358)**

Two simultaneous or successive events are known as stochastically *independent* events when in (**356**) the conditional and the absolute probability of an event are *the same,* i.e., when

$\text{Prob}(A|B) = \text{Prob}(A)$ or $\text{Prob}(B|A) = \text{Prob}(B)$ **(359)**

From (**356**) and (**359**) it follows that the two events A and B are stochastically independent of one another when the probability of their simultaneous or successive occurrence is equal to the product of their probabilities:

If $\text{Prob}(A \text{ and } B) = \text{Prob}(A) \times \text{Prob}(B)$, *then* A and B are stochastically independent of one another. **(360)**

In (**358**) to (**360**) the expressions 'dependent' and 'independent' are coupled with the qualification 'stochastic'. This is a precautionary measure of the statistician. *In* (**358**) *to* (**360**) *a factual conclusion is reached on the basis of a mathematical result.* If such conclusions lie wholly within the domain of the probability calculation the expressions 'dependent' and 'independent' are completely valid, as in examples 7 and 8 under (**356**). However, if they are extended beyond the mathematical domain into those of physics, chemistry, physiology, etc., then the qualification 'stochastic' is necessary since the conceptions 'dependent' and 'independent' do not necessarily imply a *causal* connection. Stochastically independent events can very well be dependent on one another in reality. *The conclusion 'independent' implies only actual independence of the events.* It can be accepted if it is not incompatible with the physical circumstances. *On the other hand it can be regarded as proof* if independence were *presumable* from the physical circumstances and the mathematical treatment led to the *same* result. For this reason the converse of (**360**) should also be noted: **(361)**

If A and B are events independent of one another, then the probability of their simultaneous or successive occurrence is equal to the product of their probabilities:

$\text{Prob}(A \text{ and } B) = \text{Prob}(A) \times \text{Prob}(B)$, *when* A and B are independent of one another. **(362)**

Example 9 [of (**362**)]. A box contains the events '+' and '−' in equal numbers, so that the probabilities are 1/2. Samples are collected with replacement, so that in accordance with (**357**) the events are independent of one another. What is the probability of drawing a '+' 5, 6 or 7 times in succession? The respective probabilities are $(1/2)^5$, $(1/2)^6$, $(1/2)^7$, or 0,031 25, 0,015 625, 0,007 812 5.

Example 10 [of (**362**)]. An infinite population contains the events A and B with the probabilities $\boldsymbol{p}$ and $\boldsymbol{q}$ respectively. What are the probabilities of the events AA, AB, BA, BB in two draws?

Event	Probability	
AA	$\boldsymbol{p} \times \boldsymbol{p} = \boldsymbol{p}^2$	$= \boldsymbol{p}^2 + 2\boldsymbol{pq} + \boldsymbol{q}^2 = (\boldsymbol{p}+\boldsymbol{q})^2$
AB	$\boldsymbol{p} \times \boldsymbol{q}$ } $= 2\boldsymbol{pq}$	$= 1^2 = 1$, as it should be according
BA	$\boldsymbol{q} \times \boldsymbol{p}$	to (**353**)
BB	$\boldsymbol{q} \times \boldsymbol{q} = \boldsymbol{q}^2$	

In the expression $\boldsymbol{p}^2 + 2\boldsymbol{pq} + \boldsymbol{q}^2$ the individual terms represent the *probability distribution* for the events two A's, one A, and no A's (provided that no importance is attached to the order in the event one A). A *sampling distribution* [cf. (**329**)] is thus obtained for samples of size 2 from an infinite population, the complementary variables A or B, and the probabilities $\boldsymbol{p}$ and $\boldsymbol{q}$. From this example it will be seen intuitively how samples with 3, 4, ... draws can be dealt with: the sampling distributions can be written in accordance with (**113**) as developments of $(\boldsymbol{p}+\boldsymbol{q})^3$, $(\boldsymbol{p}+\boldsymbol{q})^4$, ... Cf. Binomial distribution (page 219).

5. Discrete probability distribution

Example 10 under (**362**) demonstrated a simple sampling distribution of practical importance that will be further discussed later in this chapter. At this point, discussion will be limited to a few conceptions related to such a distribution.

All values conform to the international convention (i.e. 0,1 instead of 0.1).

Given an infinite population with the events $x = 0, 1, 2, ..., 10$ and the probabilities P_x, then:

x	$P_x = f(x)$	$\sum_{k=0}^{k=x} P_k = F(x)$
0	0,0010	$0,0010 = P_0$
1	0,0098	$0,0108 = P_0 + P_1$
2	0,0439	$0,0547 = P_0 + P_1 + P_2$
3	0,1172	$0,1719 = P_0 + P_1 + P_2 + P_3$
4	0,2051	$0,3770 = P_0 + P_1 + P_2 + P_3 + P_4$
5	0,2460	$0,6230 = P_0 + P_1 + P_2 + P_3 + P_4 + P_5$
6	0,2051	$0,8281 = P_0 + P_1 + P_2 + P_3 + P_4 + P_5 + P_6$
7	0,1172	0,9453 etc.
8	0,0439	0,9892
9	0,0098	0,9990
10	0,0010	1,0000

The column $P_x = f(x)$ gives the probabilities for the events $x = 0$, $x = 1, x = 2$, etc.:

According to (**326**) this is the *probability distribution* for the events $x = 0, x = 1, x = 2$, etc., denoted by $f(x)$. **(363)**

In column $\sum_{k=0}^{k=x} P_k = F(x)$ the probabilities P_x are summed, thus giving the probabilities for $x = 0$, $x = 0$ or 1, $x = 0$ or 1 or 2, etc. This is the *cumulative probability distribution* of x, denoted by $F(x)$. **(364)**

These data may be represented graphically:

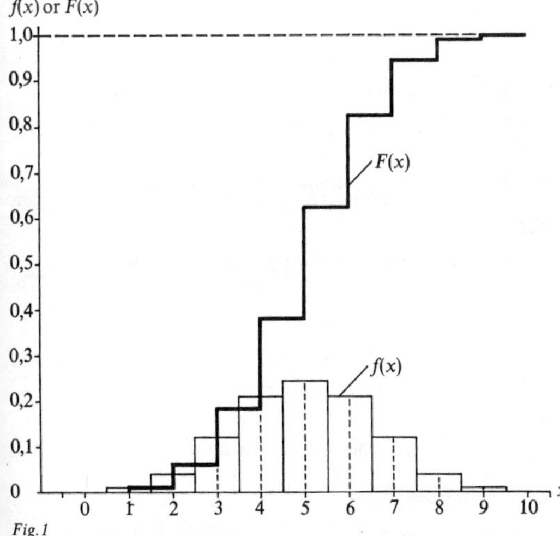

Fig. 1

Since x is a discrete variable [cf. (**341**)] the distributions $f(x)$ and $F(x)$ give stepped curves (Fig. 1). It follows that:

A discrete random variable has a discrete probability distribution. **(365)**

The probabilities are dependent on x, i.e., *for every value of x there is a definite probability*: $f(x)$ and $F(x)$ are *functions* of x, whence the use of the symbols f and F (the Greek letters φ and Φ are also frequently used). The pattern of probabilities can be expressed by a mathematical formula or in some other appropriate manner. **(366)**

In Figure 1 the probabilities $f(x)$ and $F(x)$ are shown as stepped lines in order to emphasize the similarity between discrete and continuous distributions (cf. Fig. 8). In fact, such a stepped curve could represent a *'granulated'* distribution [cf. (**344**)] in which the values of x have been rounded off to whole numbers. In this case all events between 4,5 and 5,5, for example, would be assigned to event 5. For this reason, another method is preferred here for representing discrete distributions which shows clearly that the events x are *discrete:*

All values conform to the international convention (i.e. 0,1 instead of 0.1).

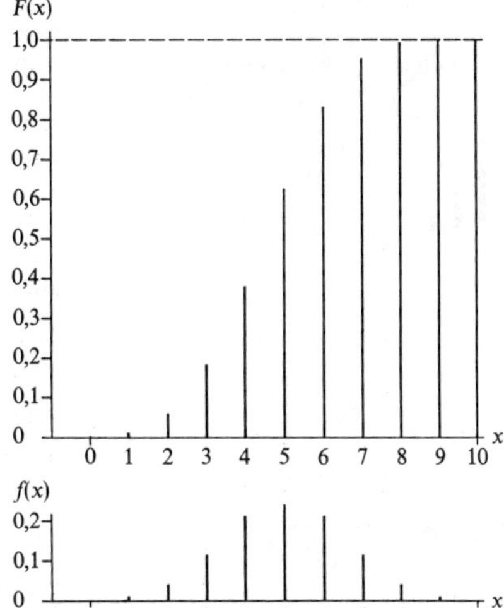

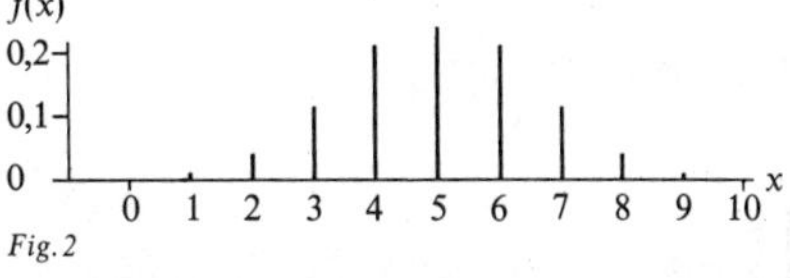

Fig. 2

In the cumulative distribution $F(x)$ representing the probabilities of the events $x = 0$, $x = 0$ or 1, $x = 0$ or 1 or 2, etc., the expression $x = 0, 1$ will in future be used in place of $x = 0$ or 1. Prob($x = 0, 1$) can also be written as Prob($x \leq 1$). From (**364**) another notation is Prob($x < 2, 3, ..., N$), equivalent to Prob($x < 2$).

In general, the following expressions are valid for such discrete distributions: **(367)**

$$\text{Prob}(x < k+1) = \text{Prob}(x \leq k)$$

or

$$\text{Prob}(x < k) = \text{Prob}(x \leq k-1)$$

and

$$\text{Prob}(x > k-1) = \text{Prob}(x \geq k)$$

or

$$\text{Prob}(x > k) = \text{Prob}(x \geq k+1)$$

With increasing values of k, the distribution $F(x)$ thus produces the probabilities for $x \leq k$ or $x < k+1$. **(368)**

Conversely, with decreasing values of k the cumulative distribution $\sum_{x=k}^{N} P_x$ from N in the direction of zero produces the probabilities for $x \geq k$ or $x > k-1$. **(369)**

For discrete distributions in general the following should be noted:

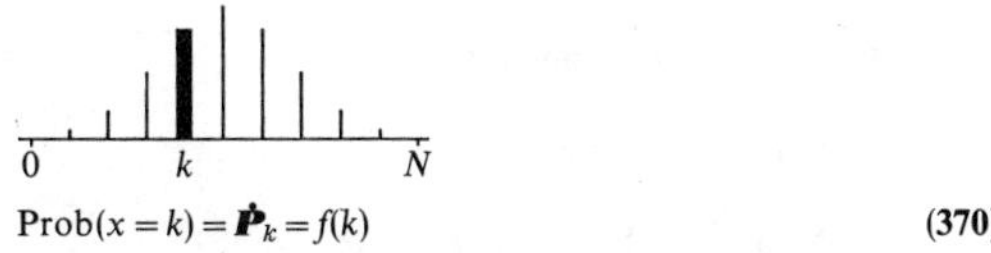

$$\text{Prob}(x = k) = P_k = f(k) \quad \textbf{(370)}$$

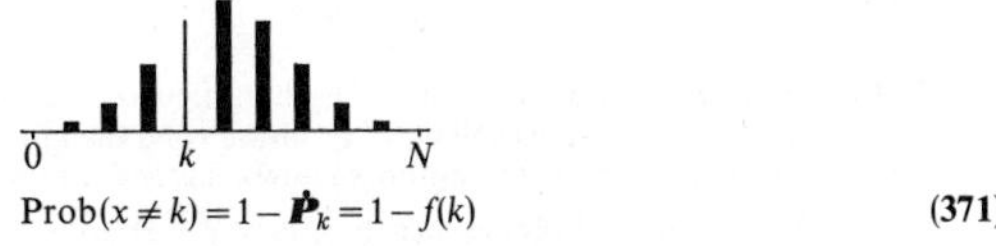

$$\text{Prob}(x \neq k) = 1 - P_k = 1 - f(k) \quad \textbf{(371)}$$

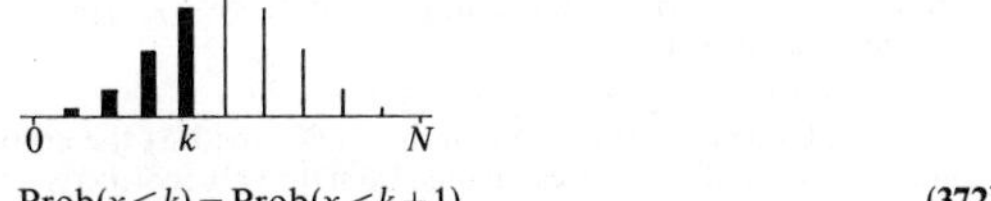

$$\text{Prob}(x \leq k) = \text{Prob}(x < k+1) \quad \textbf{(372)}$$

$$= \sum_{0}^{k} P_x \quad \text{[best formula if } k \leq N/2] \quad \text{(a)}$$

$$= 1 - \sum_{k+1}^{N} P_x \quad \text{[best formula if } k \geq N/2] \quad \text{(b)}$$

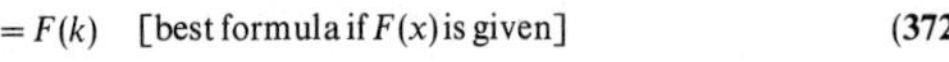

$= F(k)$ [best formula if $F(x)$ is given] **(372c)**

$= 1 - \sum\limits_{k+1}^{N} \dot{\boldsymbol{P}}_x$ [best formula if $\sum\limits_{k}^{N} \dot{\boldsymbol{P}}_x$ is given] (d)

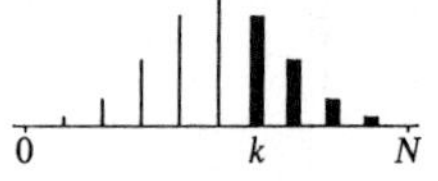

$\text{Prob}(x \geq k) = \text{Prob}(x > k-1)$ **(373)**

$= 1 - \sum\limits_{0}^{k-1} \dot{\boldsymbol{P}}_x$ [best formula if $k \leq N/2$] (a)

$= \sum\limits_{k}^{N} \dot{\boldsymbol{P}}_x$ [best formula if $k \geq N/2$] (b)

$= 1 - F(k-1)$ [best formula if $F(x)$ is given] (c)

$= \sum\limits_{k}^{N} \dot{\boldsymbol{P}}_x$ [best formula if $\sum\limits_{k}^{N} \dot{\boldsymbol{P}}_x$ is given] (d)

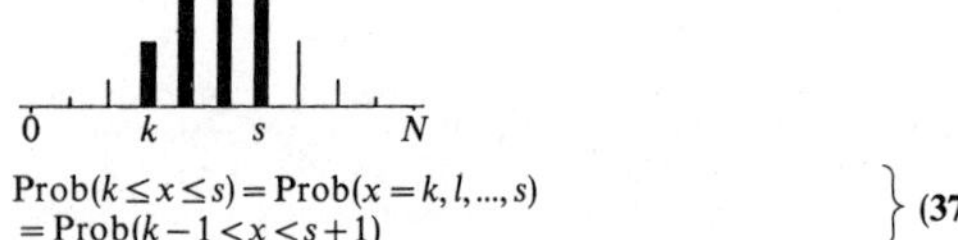

$\text{Prob}(k \leq x \leq s) = \text{Prob}(x = k, l, ..., s)$
$= \text{Prob}(k-1 < x < s+1)$ **(374)**

$= \sum\limits_{k}^{s} \dot{\boldsymbol{P}}_x$ [best formula if $s - k \leq N/2$] (a)

$= 1 - \sum\limits_{0}^{k-1} \dot{\boldsymbol{P}}_x - \sum\limits_{s+1}^{N} \dot{\boldsymbol{P}}_x$ [best formula if $s - k \geq N/2$] (b)

$= F(s) - F(k-1)$ [best formula if $F(x)$ is given] (c)

$= \sum\limits_{k}^{N} \dot{\boldsymbol{P}}_x - \sum\limits_{s+1}^{N} \dot{\boldsymbol{P}}_x$ [best formula if $\sum\limits_{k}^{N} \dot{\boldsymbol{P}}_x$ is given] (d)

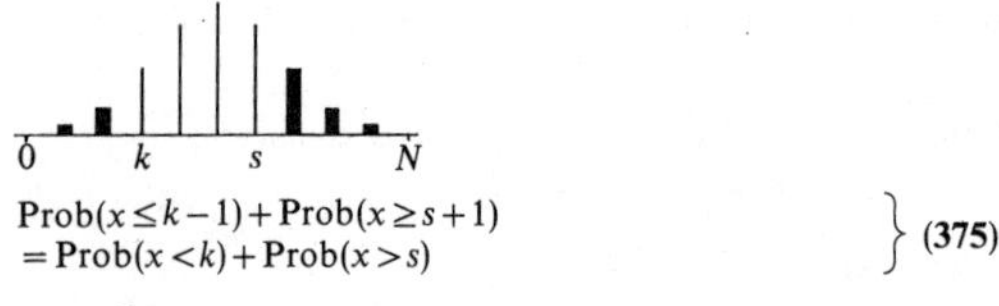

$\text{Prob}(x \leq k-1) + \text{Prob}(x \geq s+1)$
$= \text{Prob}(x < k) + \text{Prob}(x > s)$ **(375)**

$= 1 - \sum\limits_{k}^{s} \dot{\boldsymbol{P}}_x$ [best formula if $s - k \leq N/2$] (a)

$= \sum\limits_{0}^{k-1} \dot{\boldsymbol{P}}_x + \sum\limits_{s+1}^{N} \dot{\boldsymbol{P}}_x$ [best formula if $s - k \geq N/2$] (b)

$= 1 - F(s) + F(k-1)$ [best formula if $F(x)$ is given] (c)

$= 1 - \sum\limits_{k}^{N} \dot{\boldsymbol{P}}_x + \sum\limits_{s+1}^{N} \dot{\boldsymbol{P}}_x$ [best formula if $\sum\limits_{k}^{N} \dot{\boldsymbol{P}}_x$ is given] (d)

In **(370)** to **(375)** the best formulae for use in each particular case are indicated. As a rule, the user must calculate $\dot{\boldsymbol{P}}_x$ himself and then proceed with the formulae (a) or (b). The authors know of extensive tabulations of $\sum\limits_{k}^{\infty} \dot{\boldsymbol{P}}_x$ only for the Poisson distribution[2], of $\sum\limits_{k}^{N} \dot{\boldsymbol{P}}_x$ only for the binomial distribution[3, 4], of $\sum\limits_{0}^{k} \dot{\boldsymbol{P}}_x \mid N, n, k$ only for the hypergeometric probability distribution[5]. Some publications[2, 3, 5] also include tabulated values of $f(x)$.

Example 11. Using the formulae (a) or (b) in **(370)** to **(375)**, the probabilities for $k = 2$ and $s = 8$ are calculated from the values of $f(x)$ given in the table on page 185.

(370) $\text{Prob}(x = 2) = \dot{\boldsymbol{P}}_2 = 0{,}0439$

(371) $\text{Prob}(x \neq 2) = 1 - \dot{\boldsymbol{P}}_2 = 0{,}9561$

(372) $\text{Prob}(x \leq 2) = \dot{\boldsymbol{P}}_0 + \dot{\boldsymbol{P}}_1 + \dot{\boldsymbol{P}}_2 = 0{,}0547$
[by formula (a), since $k \leq N/2$]

(373) $\text{Prob}(x \geq 2) = 1 - (\dot{\boldsymbol{P}}_0 + \dot{\boldsymbol{P}}_1) = 0{,}9892$
[by formula (a), since $k \leq N/2$]

(374) $\text{Prob}(2 \leq x \leq 8) = \text{Prob}(x = 2, 3, ..., 8)$
$= 1 - (\dot{\boldsymbol{P}}_0 + \dot{\boldsymbol{P}}_1) - (\dot{\boldsymbol{P}}_9 + \dot{\boldsymbol{P}}_{10}) = 0{,}9784$
[by formula (b), since $s - k \geq N/2$]

(375) $\text{Prob}(x \neq 2, 3, ..., 8) = (\dot{\boldsymbol{P}}_0 + \dot{\boldsymbol{P}}_1) + (\dot{\boldsymbol{P}}_9 + \dot{\boldsymbol{P}}_{10}) = 0{,}0216$
[by formula (b), since $s - k \geq N/2$]

Example 12. What is the probability of the event 'x at least equal to 1'? This is the same as saying 'x equal to 1 or more' (cf. page 168), and calculation using **(373a)** gives

$\text{Prob}(x \geq 1) = 1 - \dot{\boldsymbol{P}}_0 = 0{,}9990$

Confidence intervals* and significance limits
(cf. also sections 8 and 9, pages 190–195)

A. One-sided significance limits

Example 13. Calculate the distribution $f(x)$ from the values given at the beginning of this section. Given α, where $0 < \alpha \leq 0{,}5$, determine x_l and x_r in such a way that

$$\left.\begin{aligned} &\text{Prob}(x \leq x_l) = \boldsymbol{P}_l = \sum_{0}^{x_l} \dot{\boldsymbol{P}}_x \leq \alpha \\ &\text{and} \\ &\text{Prob}(x \leq x_l + 1) = \sum_{0}^{x_l+1} \dot{\boldsymbol{P}}_x > \alpha \end{aligned}\right\} \quad \textbf{(376)}$$

$$\left.\begin{aligned} &\text{Prob}(x \geq x_r) = \boldsymbol{P}_r = \sum_{x_r}^{N} \dot{\boldsymbol{P}}_x \leq \alpha \\ &\text{and} \\ &\text{Prob}(x \geq x_r - 1) = \sum_{x_r-1}^{N} \dot{\boldsymbol{P}}_x > \alpha \end{aligned}\right\} \quad \textbf{(377)}$$

For $\alpha = 0{,}10$, $x_l = 2$ and $x_r = 8$; for $\alpha = 0{,}025$, $x_l = 1$ and $x_r = 9$

The following definitions follow from the above example:

- α is the *postulated* or *nominal one-sided significance probability* **(378)**
- $\boldsymbol{P}$ is the *actual one-sided significance probability*, $\boldsymbol{P}_l$ being the *left* (lower) and $\boldsymbol{P}_r$ the *right* (upper) level, with $\boldsymbol{P}_l$ and $\boldsymbol{P}_r \leq \alpha$ **(379)**
- x_l is the *left* (lower) and x_r the *right* (upper) *significance limit* **(380)**

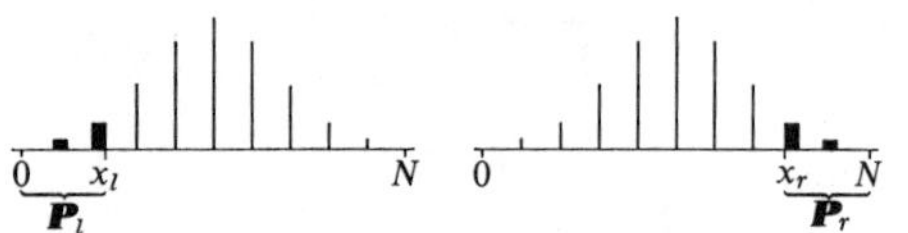

Fig. 3. One-sided significance limits of discrete distributions.

It should be noted that

- if x *attains or exceeds* (to the left) the *left* (lower) significance limit x_l, then in a *one-tailed* test
  $\text{Prob}(x \leq x_l) \leq \alpha = \text{Prob}(x < x_l + 1)$ **(381)**
- if x *attains or exceeds* (to the right) the *right* (upper) significance limit x_r, then in a *one-tailed* test
  $\text{Prob}(x \geq x_r) \geq \alpha = \text{Prob}(x > x_r - 1)$ **(382)**
- rules **(381)** and **(382)** are valid for *all* significance limits of *discrete* distributions tabulated in this volume. Elsewhere, significance limits of discrete distributions may be found which must be exceeded in an *outward* direction if, for example, they are to satisfy the rule $\boldsymbol{P}_l \leq \alpha$ **(383)**
- as a rule the *actual* significance probability $\boldsymbol{P}$ in *discrete* distributions is *smaller* than the *nominal* α, for small values of N often considerably smaller. With increasing values of N this difference decreases rapidly. (In example 13 with $\alpha = 0{,}10$ or $0{,}025$, the corresponding values of $\boldsymbol{P}$ are $0{,}0547$ or $0{,}0108$. In this case the actual significance probability amounts to only about 50% of the nominal.) **(384)**

* Also known as 'tolerance intervals'.

All values conform to the international convention (i.e. 0,1 instead of 0.1).

The following definitions should also be noted:

– The range between x_l+1 and N or between 0 and x_r-1 is the *one-sided confidence interval* **(385)**

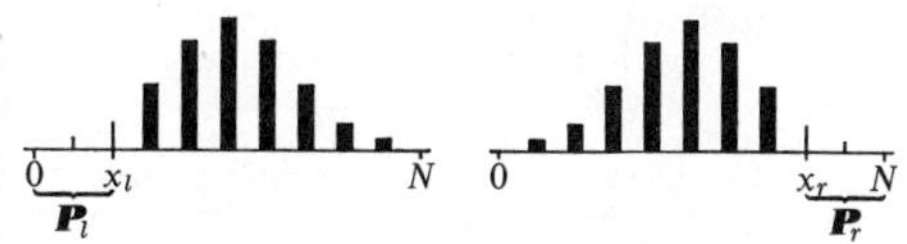

Fig. 4. One-sided confidence intervals for discrete distributions.

– x_l or x_r is the *one-sided confidence limit* when the other limit lies at N or 0 **(386)**

– The probabilities $1-\boldsymbol{P}_l \geq 1-\alpha$ and $1-\boldsymbol{P}_r \geq 1-\alpha$ are the *one-sided confidence probabilities:*

$$\text{Prob}(x_l < x \leq N) = 1-\boldsymbol{P}_l = 1-\sum_{0}^{x_l} \dot{\boldsymbol{P}}_x \geq 1-\alpha \quad \textbf{(387)}$$

$$\text{Prob}(0 \leq x < x_r) = 1-\boldsymbol{P}_r = 1-\sum_{x_r}^{N} \dot{\boldsymbol{P}}_x \geq 1-\alpha \quad \textbf{(388)}$$

From **(380)** and **(386)** it will be seen that significance limits and confidence intervals are determined mathematically according to the same principles. **(389)**

B. Two-sided significance limits

If a left and a right significance limit are determined jointly for a discrete distribution according to rules **(376)** and **(377)**, then for the two together $\boldsymbol{P}_l+\boldsymbol{P}_r \leq 2\alpha$. **(390)**

In this case the following definitions apply:

– 2α is the *postulated* or *nominal two-sided significance probability* **(391)**

– $\boldsymbol{P}_l+\boldsymbol{P}_r$ is the *actual two-sided significance probability* [note also **(384)**], where $\boldsymbol{P}_l=\boldsymbol{P}_r$ in symmetrical distributions and $\boldsymbol{P}_l \neq \boldsymbol{P}_r$ in non-symmetrical distributions, although both satisfy rules **(376)** and **(377)** (cf. Fig. 5) **(392)**

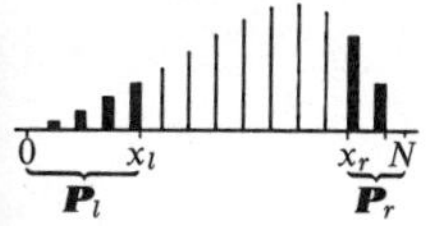

Fig. 5. Two-sided significance limits for discrete (non-symmetrical) distributions.

– x_l and x_r together are the *two-sided* significance limits (with symmetrical probability), or briefly *significance limits* **(393)**

It should be noted that

when x *attains or exceeds* (outwards) *one of the two* significance limits x_l or x_r, then in a *two-tailed* test **(394)**

$$\text{Prob}(x \leq x_l) + \text{Prob}(x \geq x_r) \leq 2\alpha$$
$$= \text{Prob}(x < x_l+1) + \text{Prob}(x > x_r-1)$$

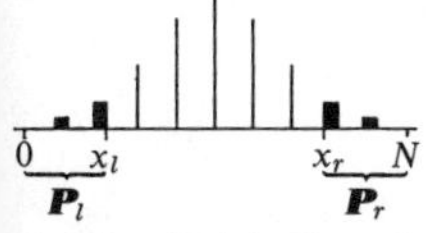

Fig. 6. Two-sided significance limits for discrete (symmetrical) distributions.

The following definitions should also be noted:

– The range between x_l+1 and x_r-1 is the two-sided confidence interval, or briefly *confidence interval* **(395)**

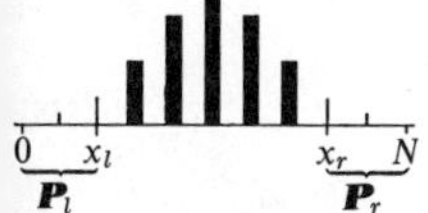

Fig. 7. Two-sided confidence interval for discrete distributions.

All values conform to the international convention (i.e. 0,1 instead of 0.1).

– x_l and x_r are the two-sided confidence limits, or briefly *confidence limits*, and it should again be noted that significance limits and confidence intervals are determined mathematically according to the same principles **(396)**

– the probability $1-\boldsymbol{P}_l-\boldsymbol{P}_r \geq 1-2\alpha$ is the actual two-sided confidence probability, or briefly *confidence probability:* **(397)**

$$\text{Prob}(x_l < x < x_r) = 1-\boldsymbol{P}_l-\boldsymbol{P}_r = 1-\sum_{0}^{x_l} \dot{\boldsymbol{P}}_x - \sum_{x_r}^{N} \dot{\boldsymbol{P}}_x \geq 1-2\alpha$$

6. Continuous probability distribution

A comparison of Figures 1 and 8 reveals the similarity between discrete and continuous distributions. When the distribution shown at the beginning of the previous section (page 185) is worked out for increasing values of N, the steps in the $f(x)$ and $F(x)$ curves will become smaller and smaller until finally, with infinite N, a continuous curve such as that shown in Figure 8 is obtained. This will be further discussed later.

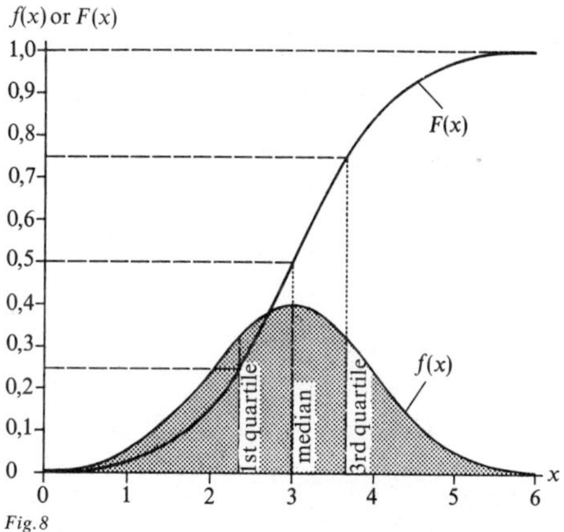

Fig. 8

In probability distributions such as those of Figure 8, x is a *continuous random variable* [cf. **(343)**]; there is an infinite number of events x, so that

$$\text{Prob}(x=k) = 1/\infty = 0 \quad \textbf{(398)}$$

and

$$\text{Prob}(x \leq k) = \text{Prob}(x<k) + \text{Prob}(x=k) = \text{Prob}(x<k)+0$$

In practice therefore the following should be noted:

For *continuous* distributions **(399)**

$\text{Prob}(x \leq k)$ can be written as $\text{Prob}(x<k)$
$\text{Prob}(x \geq k)$ can be written as $\text{Prob}(x>k)$
since $\text{Prob}(x=k)=0$.

In discrete distributions the individual probability $\text{Prob}(x=k)$ can be read from $f(x)$ but this no longer applies in continuous distributions:

In a continuous distribution, $f(x)$ is the *probability density function* at the point x. **(400)**

The *cumulative probability distribution* $F(x)$ has the same significance in continuous distributions, however, as in discrete distributions: it represents the probabilities of the events $x \leq k$. This is equivalent to the events $x<k$ [cf. **(399)**] in contrast to the case with discrete distributions. **(401)**

In discrete distributions, $F(x)$ is the *sum* of the individual probabilities [cf. **(372)**]. In continuous distributions, $F(x)$ is an *integral:* **(402)**

$$F(x) = \int_{-\infty}^{x} f(x)\,dx$$

i.e., $F(x)$ corresponds to the area between the abscissa and the curve $f(x)$ from $-\infty$ to x (cf. Fig. 9).

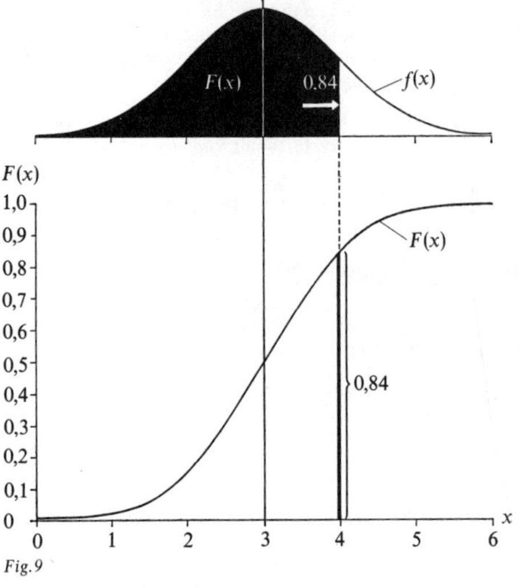

Fig. 9

The total area between the abscissa and the curve $f(x)$ from $-\infty$ to $+\infty$ is equal to 1 [cf. **(353)**]: **(403)**

$$F(\infty)=1;\ F(-\infty)=0$$

Fig. 10

For continuous distributions the equations analogous to **(370)** to **(375)** are the following:

$\mathrm{Prob}(x=k)=0$ [cf. **(352)** and **(398)**]
$\mathrm{Prob}(x\neq k)=1$ [cf. **(352)**] **(404)**

$$\mathrm{Prob}(x\le k)=\mathrm{Prob}(x<k) \quad \textbf{(405)}$$

$$=\int_{-\infty}^{k} f(x)\,\mathrm{d}x=F(k) \quad \text{(a)}$$

$$=1-\int_{k}^{\infty} f(x)\,\mathrm{d}x \quad \text{(b)}$$

$$\mathrm{Prob}(x\ge k)=\mathrm{Prob}(x>k) \quad \textbf{(406)}$$

$$=1-\int_{-\infty}^{k} f(x)\,\mathrm{d}x=1-F(k) \quad \text{(a)}$$

$$=\int_{k}^{\infty} f(x)\,\mathrm{d}x \quad \text{(b)}$$

$$\mathrm{Prob}(k\le x\le s)=\int_{-\infty}^{s} f(x)\,\mathrm{d}x-\int_{-\infty}^{k} f(x)\,\mathrm{d}x = F(s)-F(k) \quad \textbf{(407a)}$$

$$=1-\int_{-\infty}^{k} f(x)\,\mathrm{d}x-\int_{s}^{\infty} f(x)\,\mathrm{d}x \quad \text{(b)}$$

$$=\int_{k}^{s} f(x)\,\mathrm{d}x \quad \text{(c)}$$

$$\mathrm{Prob}(x<k)+\mathrm{Prob}(x>s)=1-\int_{-\infty}^{s} f(x)\,\mathrm{d}x+\int_{-\infty}^{k} f(x)\,\mathrm{d}x = 1-F(s)+F(k) \quad \textbf{(408a)}$$

$$=\int_{-\infty}^{k} f(x)\,\mathrm{d}x+\int_{s}^{\infty} f(x)\,\mathrm{d}x \quad \text{(b)}$$

$$=1-\int_{k}^{s} f(x)\,\mathrm{d}x \quad \text{(c)}$$

All values conform to the international convention (i.e. 0,1 instead of 0.1).

In equations **(405)** to **(408)**, comparison with **(399)** shows for example that $\mathrm{Prob}(k\le x\le s)$ is the same as $\mathrm{Prob}(k<x\le s)$, $\mathrm{Prob}(k\le x<s)$ and $\mathrm{Prob}(k<x<s)$.

The numerical values of the various integrals in **(405)** to **(408)** for the most important distributions will be found in the statistical tables on pages 26 onward. They will be discussed further under the headings of the individual distributions. In the examples below in which probabilities associated with the normal distribution are calculated, the abscissae x are designated deviations c. In the table on page 26, $F(c)$ values are tabulated on the right (deviation → integral), i.e., *the probabilities F(c) for given deviations c.* On the left (integral → deviation) are deviations c for given probabilities, so that here the deviation c is a function of $F(c)$, known as the quantile c (cf. section 10E, page 196). Such a function is known as an *inverse function.* Tables of inverse functions are useful but not absolutely necessary. The values required can also be obtained from tables of basic functions by interpolation.

Example 14. The probabilities for $k=-1{,}65$ and $s=1{,}96$ are calculated for the normal distribution using the form (a) of equations **(405)** to **(408)**.
The right-hand side of the table on page 26 gives $F(-1{,}65)=0{,}04947$ and $F(1{,}96)=0{,}97500$, so that

(405) $\mathrm{Prob}(x\le -1{,}65)=0{,}04947$
(406) $\mathrm{Prob}(x\ge -1{,}65)=1-0{,}04947=0{,}95053$
(407) $\mathrm{Prob}(-1{,}65\le x\le 1{,}96)=0{,}97500-0{,}04947=0{,}92553$
(408) $\mathrm{Prob}(x\neq -1{,}65 \text{ to } +1{,}96)=1-0{,}97500+0{,}04947=0{,}07447$

Example 15. Given the probabilities $F(c)=0{,}001$ and $0{,}995$ it is required to find the corresponding deviations c. The left-hand side of the table on page 26 gives $c=-3{,}0902$ and $2{,}5758$. The corresponding values taken from the right-hand side without interpolation are 3,09 and 2,58.

Confidence intervals* and significance limits
(cf. also sections 8 and 9, pages 190–195)

A. One-sided significance limits

Example 16. Given α, where $0<\alpha\le 0{,}5$, determine x_l and x_r such that

$$\mathrm{Prob}(x<x_l)=\boldsymbol{P}_l=\int_{-\infty}^{x_l} f(x)\,\mathrm{d}x=F(x_l)=\alpha \quad \textbf{(409)}$$

$$\mathrm{Prob}(x>x_r)=\boldsymbol{P}_r=\int_{x_r}^{\infty} f(x)\,\mathrm{d}x=1-\int_{-\infty}^{x_r} f(x)\,\mathrm{d}x = 1-F(x_r)=\alpha \quad \textbf{(410)}$$

From **(410)** it follows that
$F(x_r)=1-\alpha$ **(411)**

For the normal distribution, the table on page 26, left-hand side, gives for $\alpha=0{,}025$, $x_l=-1{,}96$ and $x_r=1{,}96$.
The definitions of the symbols α, $\boldsymbol{P}_l$, $\boldsymbol{P}_r$, x_l and x_r in **(409)** and **(410)** are the same as in **(378)**, **(379)** and **(380)**.

It will be noted, however, that in contrast to discrete distributions [cf. **(384)**], the actual and nominal significance probabilities in continuous distributions are of the same magnitude. In continuous distributions therefore, the simple expression 'significance probability' is used, the symbols $\boldsymbol{P}$ and α becoming synonymous. **(412)**

As in the case of discrete distributions it follows that:

– If x *attains or exceeds* (to the left) the *left* (lower) significance limit x_l, then in a *one-tailed* test
$\mathrm{Prob}(x\le x_l)\le\alpha=\mathrm{Prob}(x<x_l)$ **(413)**

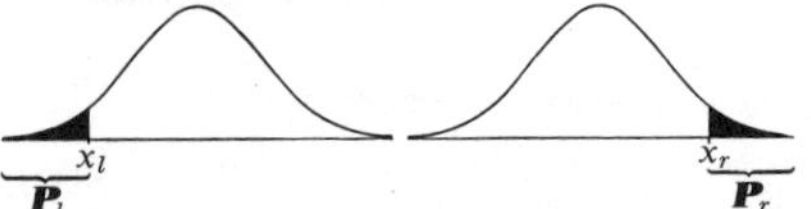

Fig. 11. One-sided significance limits for continuous distributions.

– if x *attains or exceeds* (to the right) the *right* (upper) significance limit x_r, then in a *one-tailed* test
$\mathrm{Prob}(x\ge x_r)\le\alpha=\mathrm{Prob}(x>x_r)$ **(414)**

* Also known as 'tolerance intervals'.

The following definitions should also be noted:

- The range between x_l and ∞ or between $-\infty$ and x_r is the *one-sided confidence interval* **(415)**

Fig. 12. One-sided confidence intervals for continuous distributions.

- x_l and x_r are the *one-sided confidence limits* when the other limit lies at ∞ and $-\infty$ respectively. Again, significance limits and confidence intervals for continuous distributions are determined according to the same mathematical principles. **(416)**

B. Two-sided significance limits

When a left and a right significance limit are jointly determined for a continuous distribution according to rules **(409)** and **(410)**, then for the two together $\boldsymbol{P}_l + \boldsymbol{P}_r = 2\,\boldsymbol{P} = 2\alpha$. **(417)**

In this case

- $2\,\boldsymbol{P} = 2\alpha$ is the *two-sided significance probability* **(418)**
- x_l and x_r together are the *two-sided* significance limits, or briefly the *significance limits* **(419)**

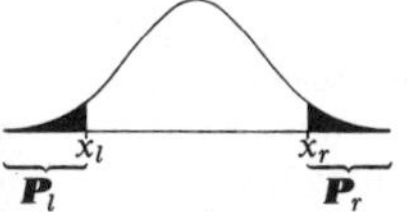

Fig. 13. Two-sided significance limits for continuous distributions.

It should be noted:

If x *attains or exceeds* (outwards) *one of the two* significance limits x_l or x_r, then in a *two-tailed* test **(420)**

$$\text{Prob}(x \le x_l) + \text{Prob}(x \ge x_r) \le 2\alpha$$
$$= \text{Prob}(x < x_l) + \text{Prob}(x > x_r)$$

The following definitions should also be noted:

- The range between x_l and x_r is the *two-sided* confidence interval, or briefly the *confidence interval* **(421)**

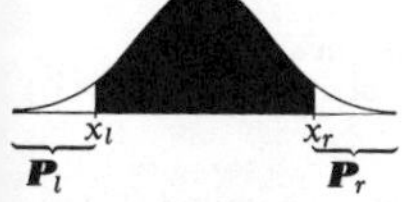

Fig. 14. Two-sided confidence interval for continuous distributions.

- x_l and x_r are the *two-sided* confidence limits (with symmetrical probability density function), or briefly the *confidence limits* **(422)**
- the probability $1 - 2\,\boldsymbol{P} = 1 - 2\,\alpha$ is the two-sided confidence probability, or briefly the *confidence probability:* **(423)**

$$\text{Prob}(x_l \le x \le x_r) = 1 - 2\,\boldsymbol{P}$$
$$= 1 - \int_{-\infty}^{x_l} f(x)\,dx - \int_{x_r}^{\infty} f(x)\,dx = \int_{x_l}^{x_r} f(x)\,dx$$
$$= \int_{-\infty}^{x_r} f(x)\,dx - \int_{-\infty}^{x_l} f(x)\,dx = F(x_r) - F(x_l) = 1 - 2\alpha$$

7. Estimates

The variables of a population are usually known but not always the type of distribution and rarely the parameters, so that the distribution or its parameters must be estimated on the basis of samples. Estimates can be calculated from a sample using the same rules as for calculating the corresponding parameter of the population. This method of estimating is frequently used but it is not the only one and does not always give the best estimates. A general discussion of methods of estimation, such as the *maximum-likelihood method* of R. A. Fisher, would not be appropriate here since their understanding requires a knowledge of higher mathematics*.

7A. Expectation and bias

It is assumed that an estimate of some parameter P from a sample of size N is required.

Experience has shown that when a number of similar estimates are made from samples of the *same* size the mean of these estimates approaches closer and closer to a definite value – the *expected value* or *expectation* of the estimate – when the number of samples is increased toward infinity (cf. Fig. 15). This is known as the central limit theorem. **(424)**

This convergence, however, is not a convergence in the usual mathematical sense but *a convergence in probability* or *stochastic convergence*, i.e., *'the probability that …' converges toward one or zero* [cf. **(427)**].

When the expectation of an estimate is equal to the parameter, the estimate is said to be *unbiased*. When this is not the case, the estimate has *bias* (Fig. 15). **(425)**

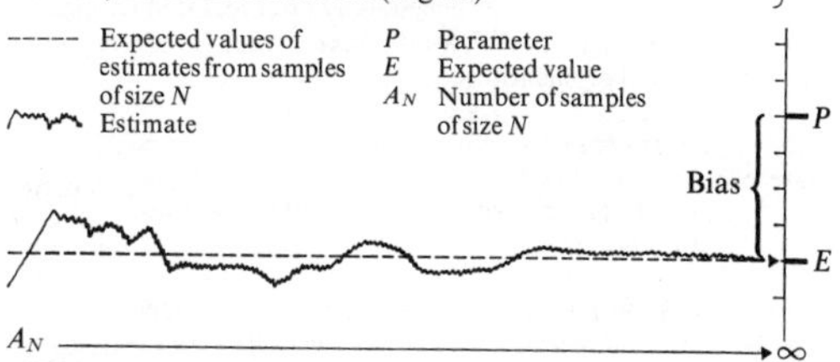

Fig. 15. Estimation with bias.

The bias can be dependent on the size of the sample. As a rule it is larger with small samples and tends toward zero when the sample size N approaches infinity. Such estimates are known as *asymptotically unbiased* estimates (cf. Fig. 16). **(426)**

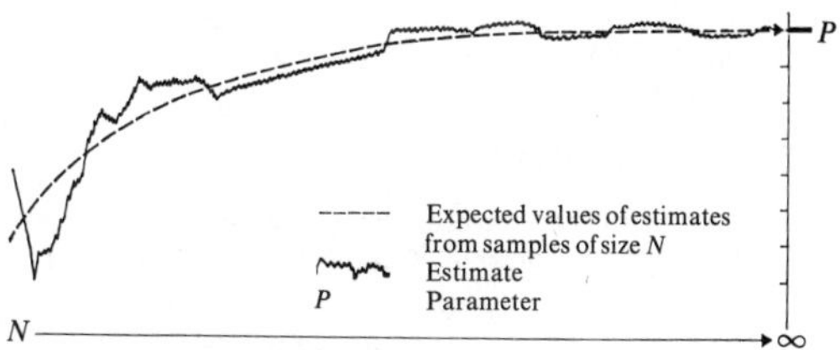

Fig. 16. Asymptotically unbiased estimation.

The bias described above is a mathematical one, that is, one inherent in the estimation. If the magnitude of this 'internal' bias is known, it can be eliminated by appropriate corrections◊. An estimate can also have a non-mathematical, 'external' bias, however, due to errors of measurement or judgment, to non-random collection of samples, or to both these causes. Such a bias is more dangerous than a mathematical one since only in rare cases can it be eliminated by recognition of its extent and direction. External bias can be avoided only by careful experimental design.

When estimates are made in order to determine the *difference between samples*, the results will *not* be subject to a bias in those cases in which the samples being compared are subject to *the same* bias, e.g., when the samples are collected under identical conditions. To this must be added the obvious mathematical condition that *all estimates to be compared are calculated according to the same rule.*

7B. Consistency

As in **(424)**, experience has shown that with increasing sample size, estimates also usually tend toward a definite value, the expected value in *infinitely large* samples:

(427)

(a) If with increasing sample size N a parameter remains *constant*, then

$$\text{Prob}(|\text{estimate minus expectation}| < \varepsilon) \to 1$$
$[\varepsilon > 0]$, as the sample size $N \to \infty$

(b) (a) is also valid for parameters that with increasing sample size N increase in proportion to N, N^2, etc. when the absolute value of the difference between estimate and expected value is divided by N, N^2, etc.

* 'Higher' from the standpoint of the non-mathematician.

All values conform to the international convention (i.e. 0,1 instead of 0.1).

◊ Corrections are not always possible when N is finite.

(**427**) is interpreted as follows: The probability that the absolute difference between estimate and expectation will not exceed any chosen small number ε tends toward one as the sample size N tends toward infinity. This is the so-called (weak) *law of large numbers*.
Estimates that satisfy (**427**), i.e., follow the law of large numbers, are known as *consistent estimates*.

7C. Efficiency

Estimates are the result of calculations based on random events and are therefore themselves *random variables* that fluctuate from sample to sample around their expected value within a range dependent on the sample size; in other words, they exhibit *variance*. It is apparent that the accuracy of the estimate will increase or decrease with the range of this fluctuation, i.e., with the magnitude of the standard deviation or of its square, the variance.
The estimate with the *lowest* variance is known as the *most efficient estimate*. The variance of the most efficient estimate, provided that one exists for the parameter concerned, may be calculated by means of the Rao-Cramér inequality[6, 7], for details of which the reader is referred to the original publications.

Here the *most efficient estimate* is defined as that unbiased estimate of a parameter with variance equal to the lower bound of the Rao-Cramér inequality. This will be assigned an efficiency of 100%. (**428**)

Estimates fulfilling condition (**428**) for every size of sample are rare. However, there are estimates that meet this condition when the sample size tends toward infinity. Such estimates are known as *asymptotically most efficient estimates* (with an asymptotic efficiency of 100%). (**429**)

Asymptotically most efficient estimates of (**429**) are suitable for χ^2-tests, others not. (**430**)

(**430**) must be qualified to the extent that such estimates do not always exist. In this case, the asymptotically most efficient estimate should be selected from those known, and this one used for χ^2-tests even though its asymptotic efficiency according to (**429**) does not amount to 100%. (**431**)

As a rule, the standard deviation of an estimate decreases either absolutely or relatively (to the magnitude of the estimate) as the sample size increases (cf. Fig. 17):

(**432**)

(a) If a parameter remains *constant* with increasing sample size, the standard deviation of its estimate shows stochastic convergence toward zero of the order of $1/\sqrt{N}$ with increasing sample size N.

(b) (a) is also valid for parameters that with increasing sample size N *increase* in proportion to N, N^2, etc. when the parameter, the estimate and its standard deviation are divided by N, N^2, etc.

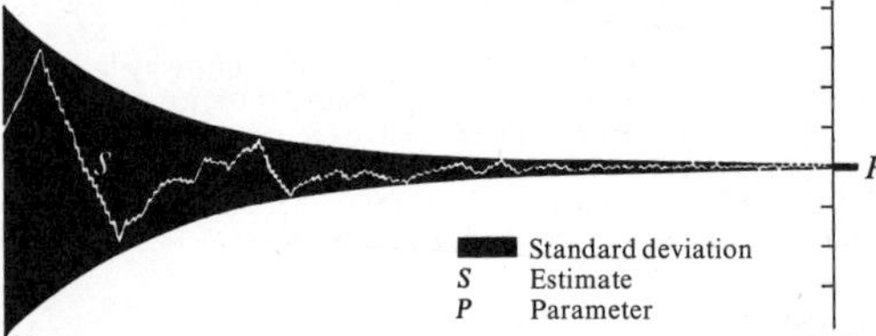

Fig. 17

If the efficiency of the estimate A is 100%, that of the estimate B for the same parameter 75%, then the sample size when using method B must be $100/75 = 1\frac{1}{3}$ times larger than when using method A if the same degree of precision is to be obtained [provided that (**432**) applies]. (**433**)

Thus by increasing the size of the sample a less efficient estimate can be given the same precision as a more efficient one, or conversely, for a given degree of precision the sample size can be smaller when a more efficient method of estimation is used (cf. Fig. 18). (**434**)

All values conform to the international convention (i.e. 0,1 instead of 0.1).

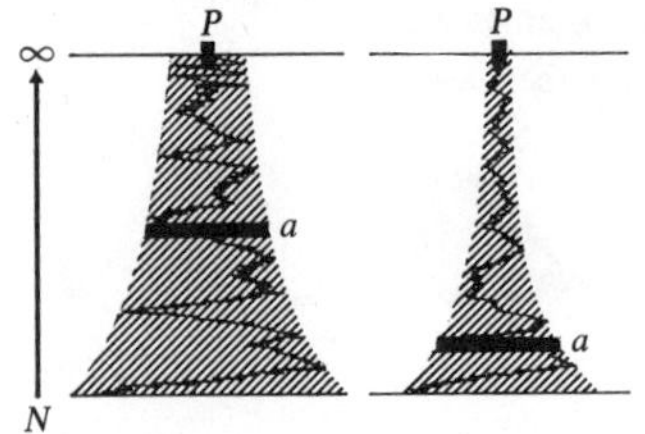

Fig. 18. Precision of the estimate (a).

The question arises of which method to use in estimating a parameter when several formulae are available: that which yields the most efficient estimate but is more complicated, or a simpler but less efficient method? Theoretically, only the most efficient method should be used; in practice, however, the niceties of mathematical usage must be tempered by other considerations.

The most efficient of the known estimates of a parameter should be used (**435**)
- when tests are expensive in comparison with simple counting [cf. (**434**)]
- when the tests cannot be repeated
- when χ^2-tests are planned
- when the result must be as exact and informative as possible
- when the most efficient estimate has been used in similar studies by other investigators (thus offering the possibility of comparisons and significance tests)

Where none of the reasons given in (**435**) apply, a less efficient but rapid method of estimating should be used (**436**)
- when simple counting is more costly than the tests [cf. (**434**)]
- when the precision of the method suffices for the purpose in mind
- when the object is simply a rapid preliminary check of the results
- when the investigations are of a routine nature
- when it is necessary to check more efficient estimates in the calculation of which there is a high possibility of error

7D. Sufficiency

An estimate or combination of estimates that in any given case yields *all the information* it is possible to obtain is known as a *sufficient estimate*. (**437**)

Information may be imagined (more or less) as the reciprocal of the variance. (**438**)

In conclusion it should be noted that as in the case of bias, the variance of an estimate is dependent on the experimental conditions and can be reduced by suitable planning of the investigation.
The terms 'consistent', 'efficient' and 'sufficient' are due to R. A. Fisher. However, Fisher reserves the term 'efficient' for those estimates described here as suitable for χ^2-tests [cf. (**430**) and (**431**)].

8. Confidence limits and tolerance limits

8A. Confidence limits for continuous and discrete distributions

In this subsection it is assumed that the reader is familiar with examples 13 and 16, pages 186 and 188.
The estimation of a parameter alone does not yield a great deal of information. In a continuous distribution, for example, as (**398**) shows, the probability that the estimate [x in (**398**)] and parameter [k in (**398**)] agree is equal to zero. More information is provided by calculating from the sample the two values x_l and x_r that with a *high probability* enclose the parameter. Such limits are known as *confidence limits*. The associated terminology and mathematical definitions are given in examples 13 and 16 (pages 186 and 188). The confidence limits used here are characterized as follows:

They are identical with the confidence limits of J. Neyman[8]. (**439**)

The parameter to which they relate is a *constant*. (**440**)

They are *estimates* and therefore *random variables.* Moreover, the *position of the limits* as well as the *width of the confidence interval* is a random variable (cf. Fig. 19). (441)

Fig. 19. 95% confidence intervals for the parameter $\boldsymbol{p}$ of a binomially distributed population, calculated from 20 samples of size 40.

For a given sample size, *more efficient* estimates result in a *narrower* confidence interval than less efficient ones. (442)

In analogy with (**432**), the confidence interval becomes absolutely or relatively (to the magnitude of the estimate) narrower with increasing sample size.

When a parameter remains *constant* with increasing sample size N, the confidence limits show stochastic convergence of the order of $1/\sqrt{N}$ toward the parameter and the width of the confidence interval shows stochastic convergence toward zero (cf. Fig. 20). (a)

When the parameter is divided by N, N^2, etc. and its confidence limits by N, N^2, etc., (a) is also valid for parameters that with increasing sample size N *increase* in proportion to N, N^2, etc. (b) (443)

Confidence limits are to be interpreted as follows [see also (**456**)]:
When very many (infinitely many) samples *of the same size* are taken *from the same stable population* and the confidence limits calculated for each, then these limits

(*one-sided confidence intervals*)

- will enclose the true value of the parameter on the average in $\geq 100(1-\alpha)\%$ of cases* (a)

  or (an equally valid interpretation)

- will *not* enclose the true value of the parameter on the average in $\leq 100\alpha\%$ of cases* (b) (444)

(*two-sided confidence intervals*)

- will enclose the true value of the parameter on the average in $\geq 100(1-2\alpha)\%$ of cases* (c)

  or (an equally valid interpretation)

- will *not* enclose the true value of the parameter on the average in $\leq 100\,(2\alpha)\%$ of cases*. Further, in an average of $\leq 100\,\alpha\%$ of cases*, x_l the lower limit) will lie *above* the parameter; and in an average of $\leq 100\,\alpha\%$ of cases*, x_r (the upper limit) will lie *below* the parameter. (d)

As a rule, the confidence probability 0,95 (more rarely 0,99) is used in medical and biological studies, i.e., α (one-sided intervals) or 2α (two-sided intervals) is equal to 0,05 (more rarely 0,01). (445)

Formulae for the calculation of confidence intervals for various parameters will be given later for individual cases.
When the object is the estimation of a parameter, the corresponding confidence limits should always be determined as well. When these limits are known, an estimate (the result of a series of investigations) gives trustworthy information; without confidence limits it gives no such information. The statistical tables provided in this volume permit the calculation of confidence limits with *little* or *no* additional calculation. *Fiducial limits.* This concept, introduced by R.A. Fisher, strictly speaking has a meaning different to that of the *confidence limits* of J. Neyman. *Fiducial limits* can be precisely determined only for certain continuous distributions. For discrete distributions they can be determined approximately, but then only when the sample size is large. *Confidence limits* are not subject to these limitations and their use is therefore preferred here.

*The 'greater than' and 'smaller than' signs apply to discrete distributions, the 'equals' sign to continuous distributions.

All values conform to the international convention (i.e. 0,1 instead of 0.1).

8B. Tolerance limits for continuous distributions

Limits for a percentage of a population are known as tolerance limits. (446)

The percentage of the population is expressed as $100\,\beta_p\%$, the confidence probabilities associated with tolerance limits as β_t. (447)

(**441**) and (**442**) are also valid for tolerance limits. (448)

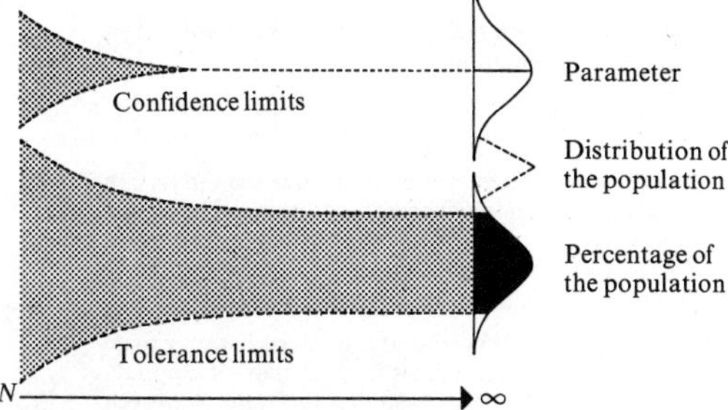

Fig. 20. Convergence of confidence and tolerance limits.

In analogy with (**443**), tolerance limits also converge stochastically with increasing sample size, *but not toward one but toward two* limiting parameters, namely those corresponding to the quantiles of the population between which lies the percentage of the population to which the tolerance limits relate. The tolerance interval between these limits thus tends *not toward zero* but toward a *positive whole number* (cf. Fig. 20). (449)

Like confidence limits, tolerance limits can be one- or two-sided. The following statements refer to two-sided tolerance limits in which

$$\beta_p = 1 - 2\alpha$$

and

$$\alpha\,(\text{left}) = \alpha\,(\text{right}) = \int_{-\infty}^{x_l} f(x)\,dx = \int_{x_r}^{\infty} f(x)\,dx$$

Tolerance limits with confidence probability β_t must be distinguished from those without. They are interpreted as follows [note also (**456**)]:

Sample tolerance limits without confidence probability. When very many (infinitely many) samples of the *same size* are taken from the *same stable population* and the tolerance limits calculated each time, then these limits

- will enclose *on the average* $100\,\beta_p\%$ of the population (a) (450)

  or (an equally valid interpretation)

- will *not* enclose on the average $100\,(1-\beta_p)\%$ of the population, whereby on the average $100\,\alpha\%$ of the population will lie *below* the left (lower) limit and $100\,\alpha\%$ *above* the right (upper) limit. (b)

Sample tolerance limits with confidence probability β_t. When very many (infinitely many) samples of the *same size* are taken from the *same stable population* and the tolerance limits calculated each time, then these limits will include *at least* $100\,\beta_p\%$ of the population in an average of $100\,\beta_t\%$ of cases. (451)

The tolerance factors for tolerance intervals without confidence probability [interpretation (**450**)] given in the left-hand table on page 51 are valid for *normally distributed* populations. These tolerance intervals are identical with the confidence limits for the difference between the mean of a sample and a later single observation[9]. (452)

Tolerance intervals *with* confidence probability [interpretation (**451**)] are wider than those *without*, as would be expected. With increasing sample size, however, both intervals converge toward the limiting interval of (**449**). (453)

Formulae for the calculation of tolerance intervals for normally distributed populations are given in section 13B, page 205.
Of particular importance in medical and biological studies are tolerance limits for the determination of *normal ranges.* Up to the present

these have rarely been calculated precisely according to the rules for tolerance limits*. However, with the aid of the tables given in this volume, their exact calculation will involve additional calculation only in a minimum number of cases.

Normal ranges should therefore be determined in accordance with the rules for tolerance limits, thus
- either, as tolerance intervals *without* confidence probability [interpretation (**450**)] for 100 β_p% = 95% of the population [cf. (**452**)] (a)
- or as tolerance intervals *with* confidence probability β_t [interpretation (**451**)] (b)

(454)

In the above text the word 'normal' has been used – in 'normally distributed' and 'normal range' – in two different senses:

In 'normally distributed', the expression is used in its conventional sense and has no deeper significance. The normal distribution is so named because it is frequently encountered and important, although it is not the only distribution that has these attributes.

In 'normal range', the expression is used deliberately to denote that range which embraces the 'normals' of a population. In medical and biological studies this range is conventionally the 95% tolerance interval without confidence probability [cf. (**450**)]. **(455)**

8C. Distribution-free confidence and tolerance limits

(cf. also section 10F, page 197, and 24F to 24H, pages 229 and 230)

The formulae for calculating the limits referred to in (**444**), (**450**) and (**451**) are specific for the individual types of population. **(456)**

If the type of distribution of a population is unknown, as is often the case, it is pointless – particularly with *small* samples – to calculate confidence and tolerance limits on the basis of *assumptions* concerning the distribution that are not justified by experience, the experimental conditions, and so on.

In such cases the so-called *distribution-free* confidence and tolerance limits are used, provided that these are available for the case concerned. Statements (**444**), (**450**) and (**451**) are then valid *without any stipulation as to the distribution* of the population◊, i.e., they are valid for *all* populations with the sole provision that these are *continuous*. **(457)**

Distribution-free confidence and tolerance limits are *wider* than those calculated for populations of a specific type. This is understandable in view of the fact that they must satisfy (**444**), (**450**) and (**451**) for populations of widely differing kinds.
Distribution-free confidence limits for quantiles (median, quartile, percentile, etc.) of small samples (up to $N = 100$) from continuous populations can be read off the table on page 103. The use of this table is explained in section 10F, page 197.
Tables for distribution-free tolerance limits with confidence probability β_t may be found on pages 108–136 for both the one and two sample problem. The corresponding text is found on pages 231–232.

9. Statistical significance tests

9A. Introduction

With a 'true' die the probability of throwing the number 1, 2, ..., 6 is by definition exactly 1/6, and the probability of throwing an even number is exactly 0,5. In accordance with (**331**), the probability 0,5 is a parameter of the population of events 'even number' and 'uneven number' produced by throwing the die.
Such a die can be used to check statement (**444d**). 20 samples of 40 throws each are made and in each sample the uneven numbers thrown used to determine the 95% confidence limits given in Figure 21a for the parameter 0,5. In accordance with (**444d**), one of the 20 confidence intervals does not include the parameter (note arrow).
Supposing now that these confidence limits had been obtained not with samples consisting of *twenty throws of a known die* but with separate samples from *each of twenty unknown dice*. The suspicion would immediately arise that 'something was wrong' with that die for which the confidence interval did not include the parameter 0,5. Only one sample has been thrown with this die, and in this first single sample a rare event occurs that according to (**444d**) should only occur in the long run in 5% of cases†. The suspected die is therefore declared to be loaded, but with the reservation that this assertion may err with a significance probability of 0,05.
This is the principle on which, mutatis mutandis, all statistical tests are based.

* With large samples this is in any case pointless.
◊ Hence the expression 'distribution-free'.

All values conform to the international convention (i.e. 0,1 instead of 0.1).

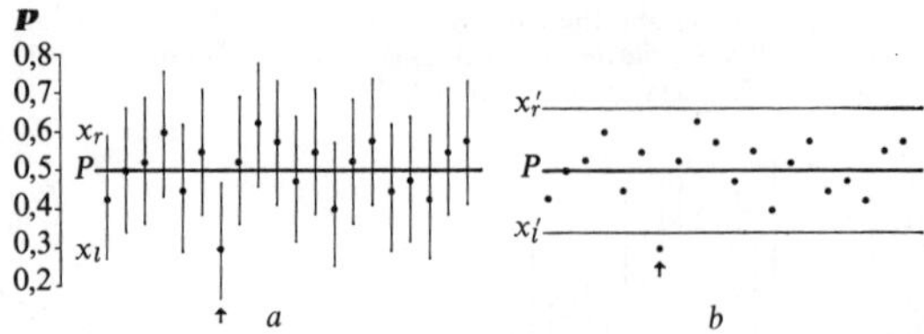

Fig. 21. 95% confidence limits (*a*) and corresponding 5% significance limits (*b*) for a given sample size (cf. legend of Fig. 19). The points are estimates p of the probability $\boldsymbol{p} = 0{,}5$ (shown here as the parameter P).

9B. Significance limits

The example given above demonstrates that significance tests can be performed with the aid of confidence limits:

In a significance test based on *confidence or tolerance limits*, 1 or 2 *randomly variable limiting values* are compared with a known or hypothetical *fixed parameter value* (cf. Fig. 21a). **(458)**

Many significance tests are based on significance limits:

In a significance test based on *significance limits* in the usual sense, 1 or 2 *constant limiting values* are compared with a *randomly variable test statistic* (cf. Fig. 21b). **(459)**

It is *immaterial* whether significance tests are made on the basis of confidence and tolerance limits or on the basis of significance limits in the usual sense: the result is the same (cf. Fig. 21a and b). With both methods it is valid to deduce a significant difference [cf. (**381**), (**382**), (**394**), (**413**), (**414**) and (**420**)] *when the test statistic lies at or outside the limits.* **(460)**

Confidence limits, tolerance limits and significance limits are intimately bound up with one another:
- either they differ from one another merely symbolically and are numerically identical (a)
- or they differ in respect of formula and numerical value, with the formulae mutually interconvertible (b)

(461)

Example 17 [of (**461a**)]. In the binomial distribution

$\boldsymbol{p}_l < p < \boldsymbol{p}_r$ are significance limits for p
$p_l < \boldsymbol{p} < p_r$ are confidence limits for $\boldsymbol{p}$

where $\boldsymbol{p}$ are constants and p random variables. When $p = \boldsymbol{p}$, then $\boldsymbol{p}_l = p_l$ and $\boldsymbol{p}_r = p_r$ (for the same sample size).

Example 18 [of (**461b**)]. $\bar{x}$ is the mean, $s_{\bar{x}}$ the estimated standard deviation of the mean of a sample from a normally distributed population. μ_1 is the population mean, t the significance limit (corresponding to the sample size and desired significance probability) of the Student distribution (see section 12A, page 202). Then

$\bar{x} - t\,s_{\bar{x}} < \mu_1 < \bar{x} + t\,s_{\bar{x}}$	are confidence limits for μ_1
$-t\,s_{\bar{x}} < \bar{x} - \mu_1 < +t\,s_{\bar{x}}$	are neither confidence limits nor significance limits in the usual sense (like the test statistic, the limits are random variables)
$-t < \dfrac{\bar{x} - \mu_1}{s_{\bar{x}}} < +t$	are significance limits for $\dfrac{\bar{x} - \mu_1}{s_{\bar{x}}}$

All three formulae are suitable for testing the null hypothesis $\mu_1 = \mu_0$ [see (**466**)]. This is done by replacing μ_1 by the hypothetical comparison parameter μ_0 and noting the position of the latter with regard to the limits. The simplest formula is the first, the second allows the quickest calculation, while the third is that most commonly used.

---

† Further consideration will show that such an occurrence is possible, although with a much lower probability, since (**444d**) gives no indication *when* a rare event has to occur in a series of tests. *With random events no such forecast can be made when the tests are independent.*

The 'limits' used here in connection with significance tests [cf. (**460**) and (**461**) and their examples] are those limits which conform with rules (**376**) and (**377**) or (**409**) and (**410**), depending on the population under consideration.

All limits suitable for significance tests converge absolutely or relatively with increasing sample size or with increasing numbers of samples of the same size [when (**432**) holds]. The statements in (**443**) and (**449**) concerning confidence and tolerance limits are valid for all such limits. (**462**)

It follows from (**462**) that: (**463**)

With increasing sample size, any real difference can be demonstrated more and more significantly. (a)

With increasing sample size, smaller and smaller differences can be demonstrated for any given significance probability. (b)

When there is a real difference – shown by small samples to be significant – between a real and a hypothetical population, then with increasing sample size the assumption that the real population *differs* from the hypothetical will be *confirmed* (usually) with increasing significance (cf. Fig. 22a). (c)

When there is a real difference that *cannot* be shown with small samples to be significant between a real and a hypothetical population, then with increasing sample size the assumption that the real population is *the same* as the hypothetical will be *rejected* (as a rule) (cf. Fig. 22b). (d)

When there is in fact *no* difference between a real and a hypothetical population, then it *may* be possible to demonstrate this with some certainty with very large samples (with complete certainty only with infinitely large samples). (e)

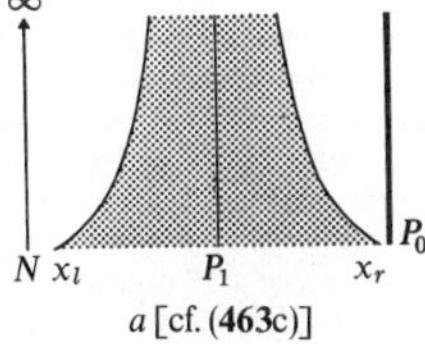

a [cf. (**463**c)]

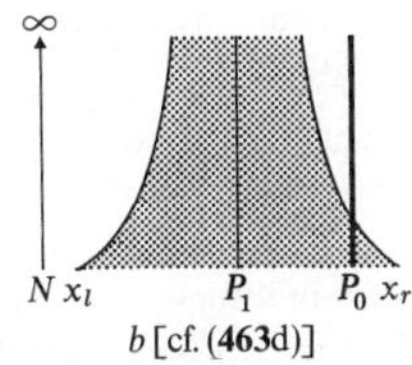

b [cf. (**463**d)]

Fig. 22. P_0 is the hypothetical parameter, P_1 that to be tested; x_l and x_r are the confidence limits of P_1 converging with increasing sample size.

9C. Significance tests

General

All statistical tests are based on the fundamental principle of comparing an *unknown population* from which the sample originates with a *known or hypothetical population.* (**464**)

All statistical tests confirm with precise probability only differences between the populations compared, *not* their identity [cf. also (**463**)]. (**465**)

The hypothesis H_0 that 2 populations are identical is known as the *null hypothesis.* As implied in (**465**), it is usually postulated in order to be *disproved.* (**466**)

The expression null hypothesis is derived from the postulated identity of the population P_1 from which the sample originates with the hypothetical population P_0, whence $P_1 = P_0$, so that $P_1 - P_0 = 0$ (null).

When a statistical test* 'demonstrates' a difference between two populations with a probability α or 2α [cf. (**460**)], then if α is sufficiently small, the null hypothesis may be regarded as provisionally disproved, and the alternative hypothesis – that the populations are different – is provisionally accepted. The probability of making an *error of the first kind* in this decision, i.e., of rejecting the null hypothesis when it is true, in other words of determining a difference where none exists, is α or 2α. (**467**)

The probability of making an *error of the second kind*, i.e., of accepting the null hypothesis when it is untrue, in other words of not determining a difference where one exists, is β. The probabilities α and β are closely related: as α decreases β increases, and vice versa (note, however, that β is *not* $1-\alpha$ or $1-2\alpha$; the reader is referred to more advanced statistical texts for a detailed discussion of this relationship). (**468**)

The probability of making an error of the first or the second kind decreases with increasing sample size. (**469**)

Remarks on (**467**) *and* (**468**): When it is important to avoid making an error of the first kind, i.e., when it is necessary to be quite certain that a difference exists before accepting it, then a small value of α or 2α is chosen, say between 10^{-2} and 10^{-6} or less, according to the risk it is permissible to take.

On the other hand, in a series of experiments designed to *uncover* a difference, larger values of α or 2α are chosen, say between 0,2 and 0,05. In any later and more elaborate experiments the significance probability can always be reduced in order to increase the certainty of a difference already disclosed. However, even though a difference has a probability in large samples of only 0,1 it is permissible in some circumstances (for example, with drugs that are life-saving) to reject the null hypothesis. The physician would willingly take the risk that in one case out of ten he has failed to administer a better drug. The tendency in medical and biological investigations is to use *too small* a significance probability.

Power of a test

The probability $1-\beta$, i.e., the probability of disclosing a difference when one actually exists, is known as the *power* of a test. (**470**)

From (**469**) it follows that the power of a test can be increased (usually) by increasing the sample size. (**471**)

The *more* that is *known* about the populations being compared, the *more powerful* are the tests which can (but need not) be carried out on the basis of this knowledge. (Less powerful tests can be used in such cases if they are adequate to meet the purpose in hand.) (**472**)

Remarks on (**472**): A useful analogy is that of the police searching for a criminal: the more that is known about him, the more effective (more powerful) will the search (the test) be.

The *relative* power of different tests having the same objective can *only* be decided by their use on *known* populations. (**473**)

Remarks on (**473**): The relative power of a test (previously calculated on the basis of some specific situation) is thus useless as a criterion in any situation in which the populations to be compared are unknown. In such cases care should be taken not to confuse known facts with *assumptions.* The results of statistical tests based on assumptions may not be reliable.

Interpretations [cf. also (**476**)]

When the purpose of a series of experiments is to demonstrate the *identity* of two populations, then the *failure* of an appropriate test to establish a significant difference justifies acceptance of the null hypothesis as long as it is not controverted by further experimentation. (**474**)

Remarks on (**474**): It is a common mistake to consider the identity of two populations as proven when no significant difference can be shown [cf. also (**463**d) and (**463**e) and Fig. 22b].

When the purpose of a series of experiments is to demonstrate a *difference* between two populations, then the *failure* of an appropriate test to establish a significant difference justifies the interpretation: 'On the basis of the present sample a difference cannot (with the significance probability used) be statistically guaranteed.' (**475**)

Remarks on (**475**): The interpretation: 'There is *no* difference' would be incorrect [cf. also (**463**d) and (**463**e) and Fig. 22b].

One-tailed and two-tailed tests

When from previous experience or on theoretical grounds the nature of an assumed difference between two parameters is known or thought to be known, then a *one-tailed* test should be made after de-

*In the subsequent text the word 'test' is used to mean 'statistical test'.

All values conform to the international convention (i.e. 0,1 instead of 0.1).

ciding on the assumed nature of the difference ($A<B$ or $A>B$) and on the significance probability α, conventionally 0,05 or 0,01* [cf. remarks on **(468)**]. The one-tailed test checks only one of the limits, either the left or the right, in accordance with the prearranged direction of the test, whence its name. One-tailed tests are more sensitive (more powerful) than two-tailed tests as far as the disclosure of a difference is concerned. However, they are justified only when the nature of the assumed difference is *a priori* fairly certain for reasons other than those connected with the sample. For the interpretation of one-tailed tests see **(476)**.

Required significance	Test statistic		Interpretation and [in brackets] significance	
	Hypothetical	Test	One-tailed	Two-tailed
Interpretation of one-tailed tests◊				
α	$x<x_l$	$\begin{cases}x\leq x_l\\ x>x_l\end{cases}$	$x<x_l$ [$\leq\alpha$] **(475)**	None
α	$x>x_r$	$\begin{cases}x\geq x_r\\ x<x_r\end{cases}$	$x>x_r$ [$\leq\alpha$] **(475)**	None
Interpretation of two-tailed tests◊				
2α	Uncertain	$\begin{cases}x\leq x_l\\ x\geq x_r\\ x_l<x<x_r\end{cases}$	$x<x_l$ [$\leq 2\alpha$] $x>x_r$ [$\leq 2\alpha$] **(475)** or **(474)**	Not equal [2α]

◊ For discrete distributions $x<x_l+1$ and $x>x_r-1$ are used. **(476)**

In general, however, particularly at the start of an investigation, there will be considerable doubt as to which of the populations is the smaller and which the larger, even if they can be distinguished at all. In this case a *two-tailed test* should be made. If no definite choice between a one- or a two-tailed test was made before sampling then no alternative to the latter test remains. The significance probability is 2α, conventionally 0 05 or 0,01*, i.e., $\alpha=0{,}025$ or 0.005 [cf. remarks on **(467)** and **(468)**]. Note that even when the two-tailed test is interpreted as a one-tailed test, the significance probability of this interpretation is still 2α.
It should also be noted that the interpretation referred to here relates to the *test statistic*. The *real* interpretation based on this may be different. **(476)** is merely a summarized form of **(381)**, **(382)**, **(392)**, **(413)**, **(414)**, **(420)**, **(474)** and **(475)**.

Conditions requiring fulfilment

It follows from **(472)** that in a situation in which several tests are available the one chosen will usually be that with the greatest power. According to **(473)**, however, the choice is only possible when the form of the populations to be compared is known. The form may be known from *previous experience* or from *theoretical considerations* (game of chance, central limit theorem), or may be deduced from the sample itself when this is very large. When the sample is small, however, particularly in complex biological, medical or psychological studies, the form of the population is often unknown. In such cases, *assumptions* concerning the form are only too often made simply for the purpose of being able to apply a 'more powerful' test [which in actual fact it may not be; cf. **(473)**]. For the following reasons this should be avoided as far as possible:

In regard to the *reliability* of a statistical test result, it is wiser to risk losing a little of the information contained in the sample and to use a test contingent on fewer conditions and involving fewer assumptions or even none at all. A possibly more powerful test would require assumptions to be made that may result in illusory information not contained in the sample. **(477)**

When the conditions on which a test is based are not, or only partly, fulfilled, then the probabilities of making an error of the first or second kind are modified in a manner difficult to estimate. The one certainty is that the probabilities are *no longer precise* although *valid* when the conditions are *fulfilled* and may be misleading when the conditions are not, or only partly, fulfilled. **(478)**

*When α or 2α serves as a criterion for *decision* it should be fixed in *advance* of the experiment.

All values conform to the international convention (i.e. 0,1 instead of 0.1).

First of all therefore, in situations where several tests are available, care should be taken to choose a test in which (if possible) all the conditions it involves are *actually* fulfilled in the case under consideration. **(479)**

Situations are often encountered in which a choice according to **(479)** is impossible because in none of the available tests (sometimes there is only one) can all the conditions be fulfilled. In such a case the test result should be interpreted with a degree of *caution* depending on the effects the non-fulfillment of the conditions could have in the case concerned. It is advisable to *specify the conditions which cannot be fulfilled*, for example as follows: 'On condition that both samples originate from the same normally distributed population, there exists ...' **(480)**

It has already been stressed that the form of the population has an important bearing on the validity of many tests. In **(477)** to **(480)**, however, conditions for tests are mentioned in a quite general sense. The number of conditions and their 'severity' varies from test to test; obviously as many as possible should be fulfilled and not only those concerned with the form of the population. One condition which is fundamental to *all* tests is the following:

All statistical tests require that the samples should be *random* samples, that is to say, that they should be drawn by means of an operation fundamentally similar to that described in section 1, page 182. **(481)**

While the stipulation **(481)** is probably the most important condition in the whole field of statistics it is a very difficult one to fulfil completely in practice, especially in medical and biological studies. When an investigation has reached the stage of statistical testing, any non-random samples can probably be discarded provided that testing for non-randomness is possible in the case concerned. Although this guards against making an erroneous decision, both time and money will have been wasted. For this reason it is advisable – *before* starting the investigation – to take all possible measures to ensure (maximum) randomness of sampling.
When as in **(479)** there are several permissible tests, no generally valid rules can be laid down as to how the choice should be made. Usually the first tests adopted will be those involving the least amount of calculation. If these do not give the postulated level of significance, they will be followed by more powerful tests from among those permissible. Such a procedure is in order provided that it does not result in the mistake of assuming that a significance is doubly (or more than doubly) guaranteed when two (or more) tests give a significant result. The reason for this is that between many tests there exist correlations not always apparent even to the statistician: to some extent they test in the same manner but with different degrees of sensitivity. An analogy is provided by the viewing of an object under the microscope at three different magnifications: one is unlikely to fall into the error of assuming that its existence is triply confirmed. Similar but less easily recognizable relationships hold for tests between which there are correlations.

Example 19. Given the sample (in chronological order)

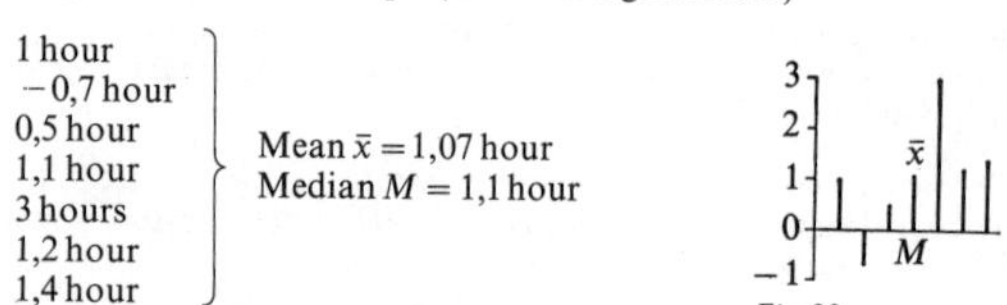

Fig. 23

representing the differences between pairs of observations on the same subject, for example after the administration of two barbiturates. The question is whether these differences differ significantly from zero [$2\alpha=0{,}05$].

In such a case the 6 tests listed in the table on the next page are available (significance limits of these are all given in the statistical tables of this volume).
If it is known that the sample is from a normally distributed population, then *all* of these tests can be tried. In this case the most powerful is the Student test, followed by the Lord and midrange tests, which are only slightly less powerful with samples of this small size. For normally distributed populations the Wilcoxon test is also little inferior to the Student test.

Test	Stipulation regarding form of population	Calculation involved
1 Student (*t*-test). . . .	Normally distributed	The most among these tests
2 Lord.	Normally distributed	About 1/4 of that in 1
3 Midrange (Walsh).	Normally distributed	Less than in 2
4 Walsh	Symmetrical	About the same as in 2
5 Sign	None	None
6 Wilcoxon.	None	About the same as in 2

If nothing is known of the form of the population, then tests 5 and 6 must be used, in accordance with (**479**). In the event of failure of all these only the interpretation given in (**475**) remains.
In example 19 the tests yield the following significances:

Test	Significance
Student	$0{,}025 \leqslant 2\alpha < 0{,}05$
Lord	$0{,}05 < 2\alpha < 0{,}1$
Midrange	$0{,}05 < 2\alpha < 0{,}1$
Walsh	–
Sign	$0{,}05 < 2\alpha$
Wilcoxon.	$2\alpha < 0{,}05$

The Student, Lord, midrange and Wilcoxon tests yield the desired significance while the others more or less fail. This reflects the fact that when two samples are to be tested with respect to a difference in location between their populations, then as a rule for normally distributed populations it is the Student test, for populations of doubtful form the Wilcoxon test that is the more powerful.
As stated in (**481**), all tests are conditional upon the samples being random samples. However, a test of the randomness of this sample made on the basis of runs on the median indicates marked non-randomness with $\alpha \le 0{,}01$. In spite of the obvious significance, the result of the Student and Wilcoxon tests is therefore merely accepted as evidence of a possible difference requiring closer investigation by further experiment.

Common sense in statistical testing

Division of the sample values in example 19 above by 10 leaves the significances resulting from the tests unchanged. This would result in a statistically 'guaranteed' difference in the action of the two barbiturates of 6 minutes on the average – in practice a meaningless difference. This illustrates the importance of looking at the *real* meaning of statistically 'guaranteed' differences before drawing conclusions from them.
It often happens that a significance level is *almost* but not quite reached, 0,054 or 0,06 say, instead of the required 0,05. The line drawn in making decisions must of course be a hard and fast one, but nevertheless in a case such as this the 'common-sense' course is to investigate further. However, if the results again yield not the postulated significance but one only *slightly* in excess of it, then the statement that 'in spite of two series of investigations no significant difference could be shown' is *untrue*. In actual fact both series point clearly in the direction of an existing difference. The only proper course in such circumstances – if changing the experimental conditions does not succeed in reducing the variance – is to carry out a *more extensive* series of investigations with the same significance level [cf. (**463**b) and Fig. 22b, page 193].

10. Parameters

Means, variances and quantiles are dealt with only in a general manner in this section. Special formulae for calculating means and variances of various distributions are given in the sections dealing with these distributions.

10A. Mean and variance of the population

μ_x is the *mean*, σ_x^2 the *variance* of a distribution. In this text the index x will be omitted when there is no danger of confusion arising. The variance is also known as the mean-square deviation. (**482**)

All values conform to the international convention (i.e. 0,1 instead of 0.1).

The square root of the variance is known as the *standard deviation* (σ). (**483**)

The variance and standard deviation *of the mean* are expressed respectively by σ^2/N and $\sigma/\sqrt{N}$ and given the symbols $\sigma_{\bar{x}}^2$ and $\sigma_{\bar{x}}$. (**484**)

The quotient σ/μ is known as the coefficient of variation V. It is therefore the standard deviation in units of the mean. V has meaning only for *positive* values of x. (**485**)

The standard deviation is a measure of the variance. The smaller it is, the steeper the curve of the distribution, the larger it is, the flatter the curve (cf. Fig. 25, page 198). This relationship is the basis of the Chebyshef inequality:

$$\text{Prob}(|x-\mu| \ge k\,\sigma) \le 1/k^2 \quad [k>1]$$

For $1/k^2 = 2\alpha = 0{,}05$ or $0{,}01$, k is respectively $\sim 4{,}5$ or 10. This inequality is valid for *any* population. (**486**)

10B. Transformations

If the variable x is subject to a constant increment a, then

$$X = x \pm a$$

so that

$$\mu_X = \mu_x \pm a, \quad \sigma_X^2 = \sigma_x^2 \qquad \text{(a)}$$

The inverse transformation is

$$\mu_x = \mu_X \mp a, \quad \sigma_x^2 = \sigma_X^2 \qquad \text{(b)}$$

(**487**)

The variance is *unaffected* by a lateral displacement, i.e., it is translation-invariant.
If the variable x is increased or decreased by a constant factor a, then

$$X = a\,x$$

so that

$$\mu_X = a\,\mu_x, \quad \sigma_X^2 = a^2\,\sigma_x^2 \qquad \text{(a)}$$

The inverse transformation is

$$\mu_x = \mu_X/a, \quad \sigma_x^2 = \sigma_X^2/a^2 \qquad \text{(b)}$$

(**488**)

(**487**) and (**488**) are also valid for the estimates $\bar{x}$, $\bar{X}$ and s_x, s_X of μ_x, μ_X and σ_x, σ_X, the calculation of which they often facilitate.

Example 20

(a) Given $x = 145; 145{,}5; 147; 147{,}3$
Then, with $X = x - 145$, $X = 0; 0{,}5; 2; 2{,}3$
from which values $\bar{X}$ and s_X^2 are calculated, when
$\bar{x} = \bar{X} + 145 = 1{,}2 + 145 = 146{,}2$ [$\bar{X}$ from (**491**)]
$s_x^2 = s_X^2 = 1{,}26$ [s_X^2 from (**493**)]

(b) Given $x = 0{,}003\,25; 0{,}001\,60; 0{,}003\,20$
Then, with $X = 10^5\,x$, $X = 325; 160; 320$
from which values $\bar{X}$ and s_X^2 are calculated, when
$\bar{x} = \bar{X}/10^5 = 268{,}\dot{3} \times 10^{-5} = 0{,}002\,68\dot{3}$ [$\bar{X}$ from (**491**)]
$s_x^2 = s_X^2/10^{10} = 8\,808{,}\dot{3} \times 10^{-10} = 8{,}808\,\dot{3} \times 10^{-7}$ [s_X^2 from (**492**)]

A variable x whose distribution has

mean $= 0$
and variance $= 1$

is known as a *standardized* variable, or variable in *standard measure*. (**489**)

If a variable x has the mean $\mu \neq 0$ and the variance $\sigma^2 \neq 1$, then the variable

$$X = \frac{x-\mu}{\sigma} \qquad \text{(a)}$$

is in standard measure. (**490**)

From the standardized variable X the original variable

$$x = \sigma X + \mu \qquad \text{(b)}$$ **(490)**

is obtained.

(489) and **(490)** are in common use in statistics.

10C. Estimates of μ and σ^2 based on ungrouped samples

The *most efficient, unbiased* estimate of the mean μ based on a sample from a normal population with the values $x_1, x_2, ..., x_N$ is

$$\bar{x} = \frac{x_1 + x_2 + \cdots + x_N}{N} = \frac{\Sigma x}{N}$$ **(491)**

[$\bar{x}$ is read as 'x bar']

The *most efficient, unbiased* estimate s^2 of the variance σ^2 is

(a) when μ is known:

$$s^2 = \frac{\Sigma(x-\mu)^2}{N} = \frac{S'_x}{N} \quad \text{[for } S'_x \text{ see (493a) and (493b)]} \qquad \text{(a)}$$

(b) when μ is unknown: **(492)**

$$s^2 = \frac{\Sigma(x-\bar{x})^2}{N-1} = \frac{S_x}{N-1} \quad \text{[for } S_x \text{ see (493)]} \qquad \text{(b)}$$

The calculation of S_x is facilitated by the use of the following sums:

$$S_x = \Sigma(x-\bar{x})^2 \qquad \text{(a)}$$
$$= \Sigma x^2 - N\bar{x}^2 \quad \text{[for } S'_x \text{ write } \mu \text{ instead of } \bar{x}] \qquad \text{(b)}$$
$$= \Sigma x^2 - \bar{x}\,\Sigma x \qquad \text{(c)}$$ **(493)**
$$= \Sigma x^2 - (\Sigma x)^2/N \qquad \text{(d)}$$
$$[= s^2 (N-1)] \qquad \text{(e)}$$

The *most efficient asymptotically unbiased* estimate of σ is s. In practice the bias of s can usually be neglected. Correction factors for eliminating this bias in samples from normally distributed populations are given on page 54, the left-hand table. **(494)**

An upper limit for the standard deviation is[10]

$$s \le \frac{r}{2}\sqrt{\frac{N}{N-1}}$$ **(495)**

where r is the extreme range:

$$r = x_N - x_1 \quad [x_1 \le x_2 \le ... \le x_N]$$

If

$$m = \frac{1}{2}(x_1 + x_N)$$

then

$$\sum_1^N (x_i - \bar{x})^2 \le \sum_1^N (x_i - m)^2 \le \frac{N r^2}{4}$$

This upper limit cannot be improved. It may serve as a check on the calculation of the standard deviation. When only the extreme range and not the form of the distribution is known this upper limit also serves as a conservative limit for the standard deviation.

The most efficient unbiased estimate of $\sigma_{\bar{x}}^2$ is $s_{\bar{x}}^2 = s^2/N$, the most efficient asymptotically unbiased estimate of $\sigma_{\bar{x}}$ is $s_{\bar{x}} = s/\sqrt{N}$. Cf. also **(494)**. **(496)**

Other estimates of σ will be dealt with later.

Example 21 [of **(491)** to **(496)**]. Given the sample of example 19, page 194, then according to formula

(491) $\bar{x} = 7{,}5/7 = 1{,}0714$

(493) $S_x = 15{,}35 - 8{,}0357 = 7{,}3143$

(492) $s^2 = 7{,}3143/6 = 1{,}2190$

(494) $s = \sqrt{1{,}2190} = 1{,}1041$

(496) $s_{\bar{x}} = 1{,}1041/\sqrt{7} = 0{,}4173$

The results should finally be rounded off to an appropriate number of decimal places in order not to imply an accuracy the estimates do not possess.

10D. Estimates of μ and σ^2 based on grouped samples

Given the classes $x_1, x_2, ..., x_n$ with the same class width for all classes $d = x_{i+1} - x_i$ and the frequencies $f_1, f_2, ..., f_n$ ($N = \Sigma f_i$), a provisional mean $\bar{x}'$ is chosen as one of the classes. The classes are now numbered. $\bar{x}'$ receives the number $z = 0$, the classes before receive the numbers $z = -1, -2, ...,$ the classes afterwards the numbers $z = 1, 2, ...$

Classes:	... $(\bar{x}'-2)$	$(\bar{x}'-1)$	$\bar{x}'$	$(\bar{x}'+1)$	$(\bar{x}'+2)$ ...
z:	... -2	-1	0	1	2 ...

Then

$$\bar{x} = \bar{x}' + d\,\frac{\Sigma f z}{N}$$ **(497)**

$$s^2 = \frac{d^2}{N-1}\left(\Sigma f z^2 - \frac{(\Sigma f z)^2}{N}\right)$$ **(498)**

Sheppard's correction

In the grouping of the individual values into classes a small error arises as a result of the random choice of the individual values. This introduces a small error into the estimate of the variance that can be corrected by subtraction of $k = 0{,}08\dot{3}$ (i.e., of 1/12) from the variance estimated in *class units*. This correction (Sheppard's correction) can be dispensed with in the testing of differences for significance but is otherwise to be recommended.

Sheppard's correction: $s^2_{\text{corr.}} = s^2 - \frac{d^2}{12}$ **(499)**

Example 22. Diameter of erythrocytes. Class width $d = 0{,}4$ µm.

Class	Frequency f	Deviation z	Frequency × deviation fz	Frequency × square of deviation fz^2
5,6	5	−4	− 20	80
6,0	78	−3	−234	702
6,4	144	−2	−288	576
6,8	479	−1	−479	479
$7{,}2 = \bar{x}'$	542	0	0	0
7,6	358	+1	+358	358
8,0	279	+2	+558	1116
8,4	99	+3	+297	891
8,8	15	+4	+ 60	240
9,2	1	+5	+ 5	25
	$\Sigma f = N = 2000$		$\Sigma fz = 257$	$\Sigma fz^2 = 4467$

$$\bar{x} = 7{,}2 + 0{,}4 \times \frac{257}{2000} = 7{,}251 \text{ µm}$$

$$s^2 = 0{,}4^2 \times \frac{4467 - 33{,}0}{1999} = 0{,}4^2 \times 2{,}218$$

$s = 0{,}4\sqrt{2{,}218} = 0{,}596$ µm without Sheppard's correction

$s^2 = 0{,}4^2(2{,}218 - 0{,}0833) = 0{,}4^2 \times 2{,}135$

$s = 0{,}4\sqrt{2{,}135} = 0{,}584$ µm with Sheppard's correction

10E. Quantiles of continuous distributions

Definition: In $p = F(x)$, x is known as the *quantile* (p), here given the symbol $Q(p)$ or x_p. Quantiles are thus the *inverse function* of $F(x)$; they are so-called parameters of position. The quantile has also been given the name fractile. On $F(x)$ see also **(401)** and **(402)**.

The quantiles most commonly used are given special names: **(500)**

Quantile	Probability p
Quartile	$0{,}25 \times n$ $[n = 1, 2, 3, 4]$
Median	0,5 [= 2nd quartile]
Decile	$0{,}1 \times n$ $[n = 1, 2, ..., 10]$
Percentile	$0{,}01 \times n$ $[n = 1, 2, ..., 100]$

All values conform to the international convention (i.e. 0,1 instead of 0.1).

Interpretation of a quantile (p) of a continuous population:
$100\,p\%$ of the population lie below the quantile,
$100\,(1-p)\%$ of the population lie above the quantile. **(501)**

Example 23. See Figure 8 (quartiles and median of a normal distribution), page 187.

Estimation

(a) *Ungrouped samples.* The quantile $\mathbf{Q}(p)$ of a population is estimated by calculating the corresponding quantile $Q(p)$ of a sample taken from it. The sample values x are arranged in order of magnitude [cf. (**342**)] and numbered serially, the smallest value receiving the number 1. These *order numbers* are known as the *ranks* of the sample values x, so that

$$x_1 < x_2 < x_3 < \cdots < x_N$$

The quantile $Q(p)$ thus corresponds to the sample value with the rank $R(p)$:

$$R(p) = N\,p + 0{,}5 \quad [\text{for } 1/N \leq p \leq (N-1)/N] \qquad \textbf{(502a)}$$

If $R(p)$ is a whole number, the quantile $Q(p)$ *coincides with* the sample value; if $R(p)$ is a fraction, the quantile $Q(p)$ *lies between* the sample values with ranks adjacent to $R(p)$, i.e., between x_i and x_{i+1}. There would be little point in interpolating between these two values.
If the sequence of ordered sample values contains ties [cf. (**346**)] and $R(p)$ falls on or between the ranks of tied values, then $Q(p)$ is the same as these tied values provided that the number of such ties is small compared with the sample size. In samples with very many ties (few classes and high frequencies) there is no point in determining quantiles in accordance with (**502a**).

Example 24. Given the ranked sample

x:	1,75	1,76	1,76	1,77	1,78	1,79	1,80	1,81	1,82	1,84	1,86
R:	1	2	3	4	5	6	7	8	9	10	11
x:	1,86	1,93	1,95	2,00	2,07	2,18	2,35	2,68	3,56	4,41	
R:	12	13	14	15	16	17	18	19	20	21	

it is required to find the 1st quartile, median and percentile 0,7. In accordance with (**502a**)

$R(0{,}25) = 0{,}25 \times 21 + 0{,}5 = 5{,}75$
[$Q(0{,}25)$ lies between 1,78 and 1,79]

$R(0{,}5) = 0{,}5 \times 21 + 0{,}5 = 11$
[$Q(0{,}5) = 1{,}86$ (note the tie)]

$R(0{,}7) = 0{,}7 \times 21 + 0{,}5 = 15{,}2$
[$Q(0{,}7)$ lies between 2,00 and 2,07]

(b) *Grouped samples.* Given the ranked classes $x_1 \leq x_2 \leq x_3 \leq \cdots \leq x_j \leq \cdots \leq x_n$, with class width $d = x_{i+1} - x_i$, and class frequencies $f_1, f_2, \ldots, f_i, \ldots, f_n$, where $f_1 + f_2 + \cdots + f_n = N$, the sample size.
The cumulative frequencies are written as follows: $f_1 = F(1)$, $f_1 + f_2 = F(2)$, $f_1 + f_2 + f_3 = F(3)$, etc. $f_1 + f_2 + \cdots + f_i = F(i)$. Np is now compared with $F(i)$:
If $Np = F(i)$, then $Q(p) = x_i + \tfrac{1}{2}\,d$.
If Np lies between $F(i)$ and $F(i+1)$, then $Q(p)$ lies between $x_i + \tfrac{1}{2}\,d$ and $x_{i+1} + \tfrac{1}{2}\,d$. **(502b)**

10F. Distribution-free confidence limits for quantiles of continuous distributions (cf. also section 8C, page 192)

Apart from their importance as the inverse function of $F(x)$, quantiles are useful in practice for two reasons: on the one hand their estimates $Q(p)$ can be obtained with a minimum of calculation*; on the other hand, exact confidence limits can be constructed for the parameter $\mathbf{Q}(p)$ with no knowledge at all of the form of the distribution from which the sample is drawn.
The ranks $R(p)$ for distribution-free confidence limits for quantiles with various values of $p \leq 0{,}5$ and samples of size up to $N = 100$ can be read directly from the table on page 103. The ranks $R(p)$ for the median and sample sizes up to $N = 499$ are given in the tables on pages 104–107.

*In the case of large samples the time saved here will be offset by that lost in ranking the sample.

All values conform to the international convention (i.e. 0,1 instead of 0.1).

The procedure is as follows: The limits x_l and x_r corresponding to the sample size N and the probability $p \leq 0{,}5$ are found in the table. If $p > 0{,}5$ it is subtracted from 1, giving $p' = 1 - p < 0{,}5$. For p' the limits x_l and x_r, symbolized by x_l' and x_r', are found in the same way. The ranks $R(p)$ that fix the confidence limits in the sample are then

- for $p \leq 0{,}5$: $R(p)_l = x_l + 1$ and $R(p)_r = x_r$
- for $p > 0{,}5$: $R(p)_l = N - x_r' + 1$ and $R(p)_r = N - x_l'$ **(503)**

Example 25. For the sample in example 24 the 95% confidence limits are as follows:

Quantile	Ranks	95% confidence limits
1st quartile	$1+1=2$ and 10	$1{,}76 < \mathbf{Q}(p) < 1{,}84$
Median	$5+1=6$ and 16	$1{,}79 < \mathbf{Q}(p) < 2{,}07$
Percentile 0,7	$21-12+1=10$ and $21-1=20$	$1{,}84 < \mathbf{Q}(p) < 3{,}56$

10G. Relations between mode, median and mean of continuous distributions

The abscissa x of the maximum value of the density function $f(x)$ is known as the *mode.* **(504)**

In practice the mode is of little importance. On $f(x)$ see (**400**).

In one-peaked *symmetrical* distributions the *mode, median and mean coincide*, but not in non-symmetrical distributions (cf. Fig. 31, page 201). The relationship between the three parameters is expressed by

Median ~ ⅔ mean + ⅓ mode **(505)**

Of main importance in practice is the *identity* of the *median* and the *mean* in *symmetrical* distributions: the distribution-free confidence limits for the median are valid also for the mean. It follows that:

If the mean $\bar{x}$ of a sample coincides with either of the distribution-free confidence limits for the population median or lies outside them, then with a significance probability $\leq 2\alpha$, the sample *does not* originate from a symmetrical distribution. **(506)**

This is the basis of the sign test (cf. section 24D, page 229), which is easily carried out and also independent of the form of the population.

11. The normal distribution

[cf. also section 6, page 187; for the meaning of 'normal' see (**455**)]

11A. Definition and characteristics

The normal distribution is a *continuous* distribution, the probability density function for which is defined by

$$f(x) = \frac{1}{\sigma\sqrt{2\pi}}\,e^{-\frac{1}{2}\left(\frac{x-\mu}{\sigma}\right)^2}$$

[μ: mean; σ: standard deviation; for π and e see pages 9 and 168] **(507)**

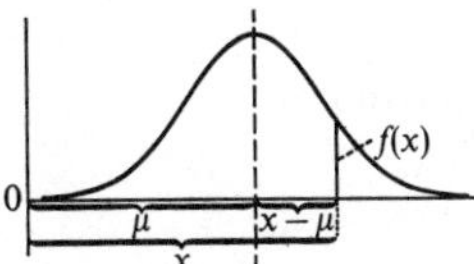

Fig. 24

The curve of the probability density function is *symmetrical* and bell-shaped, that of the cumulative probability distribution $F(x)$ is sigmoid (cf. Figs. 8 and 9, pages 187 and 188). The range of variation of the variable x is from $-\infty$ to ∞. The normal distribution is often criticized on this score since it implies, for example, that the existence of human beings 9 feet tall or more should be 'possible'◊. However,

◊Although they may appear illogical, limits according to probability are more logical than absolute limits. The statement, for instance, that there is an *absolute* limit to the height of the human body at, say, 8′ 3″, would manifestly be untenable.

the word 'possible' is here inappropriate. 'Almost impossible' would be better, since the probability of extreme deviations from the mean decreases rapidly in the normal distribution.

If $\text{Prob}(|x-\mu| \geq k\,\sigma) \leq 2\alpha$, 2α changes with increasing k as follows[11]: **(508)**

k	2α	k	2α
1	$3{,}173\,105 \times 10^{-1}$	6	$1{,}973\,175 \times 10^{-9}$
2	$4{,}550\,026 \times 10^{-2}$	7	$2{,}559\,625 \times 10^{-12}$
3	$2{,}699\,796 \times 10^{-3}$	8	$1{,}244\,192 \times 10^{-15}$
4	$6{,}334\,248 \times 10^{-5}$	9	$2{,}257\,177 \times 10^{-19}$
5	$5{,}733\,031 \times 10^{-7}$	10	$1{,}523\,971 \times 10^{-23}$

Remarks on (**508**): In accordance with the Chebyshef inequality [cf. (**486**)], the probability that in *any* distribution the variable x falls outside the limit $\mu \pm 3\,\sigma$, for example, is less than 1/9; as (**508**) shows, however, in the normal distribution it is only ~3/1000. On the other hand, these much closer limits are valid *only* when the population is *in fact* normal. The inverse deduction should therefore also be noted, namely that should a distribution for which the 3 σ limits are regarded as adequate *not* be normal, then the probability that the variable x falls outside these limits is *not* 3/1000 but may be as large as 1/9. This is an excellent illustration of (**478**).
As with all symmetrical distributions, the mode, median and mean of the normal distribution coincide. Their ordinate is the axis of symmetry of the curve of the probability density function [cf. Fig. 24 and (**505**)]. The most important consequences in practice are the following:

With a significance probability $\leq 2\alpha$, a sample that fails to pass the test for symmetry *does not* originate from a normally distributed population. **(509)**

If a *fairly small* sample passes the symmetry test [cf. also (**474**)], then the population from which it is drawn may still not be normal*. However, in significance tests (cf. page 194, 'Conditions requiring fulfilment') the stipulation of normality may be regarded as *almost* fulfilled. **(510)**

For *small* samples the sign test (cf. page 229) used for testing symmetry is relatively insensitive, that is, it will disclose an actual lack of symmetry in a population much more rarely with small samples than with large ones. For this reason (**510**) is valid only for *fairly small* samples. For small samples therefore, significance tests should be used – provided they are available – in which there are no conditions regarding symmetry or normality.
As (**507**) shows, the normal distribution is *fully* characterized by the two parameters μ and σ. The mean determines the *position* of the distribution with respect to the x axis, the standard deviation the *shape* of the curve: the larger σ is, the flatter the curve (cf. Fig. 25).

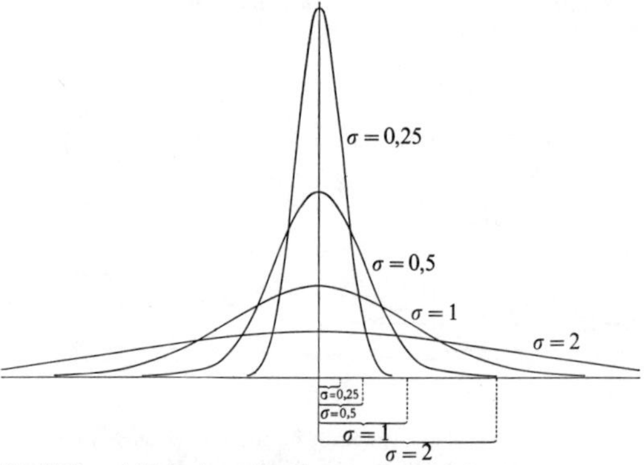

Fig. 25. Normal distributions with various standard deviations.

Since μ and σ can have any values, the number of possible normally distributed populations is infinite. If these are standardized according to (**490**a), they are *all* transformed into a *single* standardized normal distribution.

* Symmetrical distributions that are not normal also exist.

All values conform to the international convention (i.e. 0,1 instead of 0.1).

11B. The standardized normal distribution

If the quotient $(x-\mu)/\sigma$ in (**490**a) is denoted by c, then (**507**) becomes the *standardized normal distribution* (with *mean* 0 and *standard deviation* 1):

$$f(c) = \frac{1}{\sqrt{2\pi}}\, e^{-c^2/2} \qquad \textbf{(511)}$$

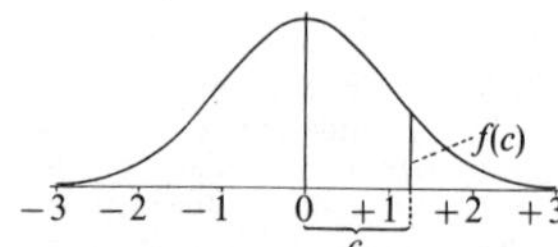

Fig. 26. Standardized normal distribution.

The symmetry of the distribution gives rise to the following relationships:

Probability density function

$f(0) = \max f(c) = 0{,}398\,942$ **(512)**

$f(-c) = f(c)$ **(513)**

Probabilities

$F(0) = \text{Prob}(c<0) = \text{Prob}(c>0) = 0{,}5$ **(514)**

$\text{Prob}(c<-k) = \text{Prob}(c>k)$ (a) **(515)**

$= F(-k) = 1 - F(k)$ (b)

$\text{Prob}(-k \leq c \leq 0) = \text{Prob}(0 \leq c \leq k)$ **(516)**

Quantiles

$Q(0{,}5) = 0$ **(517)**

$Q(p) = -Q(1-p)$ **(518)**

11C. Tables of the standardized normal distribution (pages 26–29)

Page	Table relates to	Left-hand side	Right-hand side
26	$-\infty$ $\quad -c$ $\quad 0$	Inverse function of the integral → $= \text{Quantile } Q(p)$ $= c(p)$ Argument p	$\int_{-\infty}^{c} f(c)\,dc$ $= F(c) = p(c)$ Argument c
27	$-c$ $\quad 0$ $\quad +c$	Inverse function of the integral → $= c(p')$ Argument p'	$\int_{-c}^{c} f(c)\,dc$ $= p'(c)$ Argument c
28	Left-hand side $-c$ $\quad 0$ $\quad +c$	$1 - \int_{-c}^{c} f(c)\,dc$ $= 2P$ Argument c *	
	Right-hand side $0+c$		$\int_{0}^{c} f(c)\,dc$ $= \int_{-c}^{0} f(c)\,dc$ Argument c
29	Upper: ordinate $f(c)$, argument c (cf. Fig. 26) Lower: inverse function of $1 - \int_{-c}^{c} f(c)\,dc$		

* For inverse function see page 29.

11D. Conversion of a normal distribution into the standardized form and vice versa (cf. also section 10B, page 195)

The statement 'normal distribution with mean μ and standard deviation σ' is here abbreviated to 'normal distribution $(\mu;\sigma)$'. **(519)**

The normal distribution $(\mu;\sigma)$ of the variable x is converted into the standardized normal distribution (0; 1) of the variable c (and vice versa) by substituting X of **(490)** by c. **(520)**

In this conversion the probabilities of the converted values remain *unchanged*, so that **(521)**

$$\text{Prob}(x<x_k)=\text{Prob}(c<c_k)$$

Example 26. Given the normal distribution (174; 7), how large are the probabilities of the events $x<160$, $x>181$, $162\le x\le 179$?

From **(521)**

$$\frac{160-174}{7}=-2;\quad \frac{181-174}{7}=1;\quad \frac{162-174}{7}\sim -1{,}71;$$

$$\frac{179-174}{7}\sim 0{,}71$$

whence

$\text{Prob}(c<-2)=F(-2)=0{,}022\,75$ (from the right-hand table on page 26)

$\text{Prob}(c>1)=\text{Prob}(c<-1)$ [cf. **(515a)**] $=0{,}158\,66$ (from the same table)

$\text{Prob}(-1{,}71\le c\le 0{,}71)$: $\text{Prob}(-1{,}71\le c\le 0)$, from **(516)**
$=\text{Prob}(0\le c\le 1{,}71)$, whence the total probability
$\text{Prob}(-1{,}71\le c\le 0{,}71)$
$=\text{Prob}(0\le c\le 1{,}71)+\text{Prob}(0\le c\le 0{,}71)$
$=0{,}456\,37+0{,}261\,15=0{,}717\,52$ (from the right-hand table on page 28).

Example 27. Given the normal distribution of example 26, it is required to find

(a) the one-sided confidence limit x_l for $1-\alpha_l=0{,}95$
(b) the one-sided confidence limit x_r for $1-\alpha_r=0{,}99$
(c) the two-sided confidence limits x_l and x_r for $1-2\alpha=0{,}95$

Solution:

All confidence limits or significance limits are quantiles (α):

(a) c_l is the quantile (α_l), where $\alpha_l=1-0{,}95=0{,}05$. From the left-hand table on page 26, $c_l=-1{,}644\,9$, whence $x_l=-1{,}644\,9\times 7+174=162{,}485\,7$.
(b) c_r is the quantile $(1-\alpha_r)=Q(0{,}99)$. From the left-hand table on page 26, $c_r=2{,}326\,3$, whence $x_r=2{,}326\,3\times 7+174=190{,}284\,1$.
(c) α is here $(1-0{,}95)/2=0{,}025$. Since according to **(518)** the quantile 0,025 is numerically equal to the quantile $1-0{,}025=0{,}975$, only the former need be found in the left-hand table on page 26. This gives $c=-1{,}960$, whence $x_l=-1{,}960\times 7+174=160{,}28$, and $x_r=1{,}960\times 7+174=187{,}72$. Even simpler to obtain are the two-sided limits, namely from the left-hand table on page 27, using the deviation c, which can be read off directly by entering with the probability $1-2\alpha$.

In connection with examples 26 and 27 it should be noted that, in practice, calculations are made with only as many decimal places as are required. However, it is advisable to complete the calculation with the full number of decimal places and then round off the result to the required number.

11E. The probit transformation

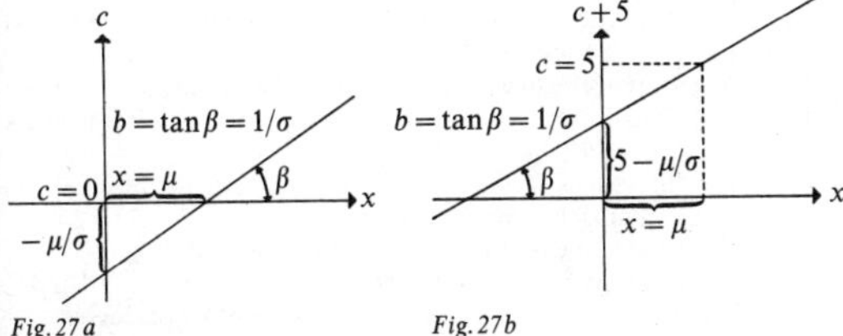

Fig. 27a *Fig. 27b*

The standardized variable $(x-\mu)/\sigma$ can be broken down in accordance with **(34)** into the fractions $-\mu/\sigma$ and x/σ. If $-\mu/\sigma=a$ and $1/\sigma=b$, then

$$c=a+bx\quad [a=-b\mu;\, b=1/\sigma] \qquad \textbf{(522)}$$

In accordance with **(299)**, the curve of **(522)** is a *straight line* (cf. Fig. 27a).

All values conform to the international convention (i.e. 0,1 instead of 0.1).

The straight line of **(522)** passes through the point $(\mu;\,0)$. When μ and σ are known its construction therefore only requires *one* other point to be calculated from **(522)**. **(523)**

If the straight line in Figure 27b is displaced 5 units in the direction of the ordinate axis, then

$$\begin{aligned} c' = \text{probit}^{12} &= c+5=a+bx+5\\ &=-\frac{\mu}{\sigma}+bx+5\\ &=5-b\mu+bx\\ &=a'+b'x\\ \text{where } a' &=5-b\mu \text{ and } b'=b=-\frac{1}{\sigma}\end{aligned} \qquad \textbf{(524)}$$

The straight line of **(524)** passes through the point $(\mu;\,5)$. When μ and σ are known its construction therefore only requires *one* other point to be calculated from **(524)**. **(525)**

Since deviations of more than 5 σ are rare, the displacement of **(522)** to **(524)** means that in practice the majority of probit calculations can be carried out in the upper right quadrant (i.e., $c+5>0$).
If the corresponding $F(c)$ values, which in accordance with **(521)** have the same magnitude as the $F(x)$ values, are now inscribed on the ordinate axis alongside the c or $(c+5)$ scale it will be seen at once that the sigmoid curve can be transformed in this way into a straight line. The following therefore apply to probit calculations on samples:

If the ordinate and abscissa scales are linear scales (cf. the extreme left-hand scale in Fig. 28) and if now in place of $F(x_p)$ the quantiles c_p or probits c_p+5 are plotted in the ordinate direction and x_p in the abscissa direction, then with increasing sample size the points $(x_p;\,c_p)$ or $(x_p;$ probit) will converge stochastically toward the straight line **(522)** or **(524)** provided that the random variable x is normally distributed. **(526)**

If the abscissa axis is divided linearly and the ordinate axis in percentiles $c\times(0{,}01\times n)$ or probits $\times(0{,}01\times n)$, where $n=1,2,\ldots,100$, and if the probabilities $F(c)$ or percentages $100\,F(c)\%$ corresponding to the latter are entered on the ordinate scale (cf. Fig. 28, right-hand vertical scale) and $F(x_p)$ or $100\,F(x_p)\%$ is plotted in the ordinate direction and x_p in the abscissa direction, then with increasing sample size the points $[x_p;\,F(x_p)]$ or $[x_p;\,100\,F(x_p)\%]$ will converge stochastically toward a straight line provided that the random variable x is normally distributed. **(527)**

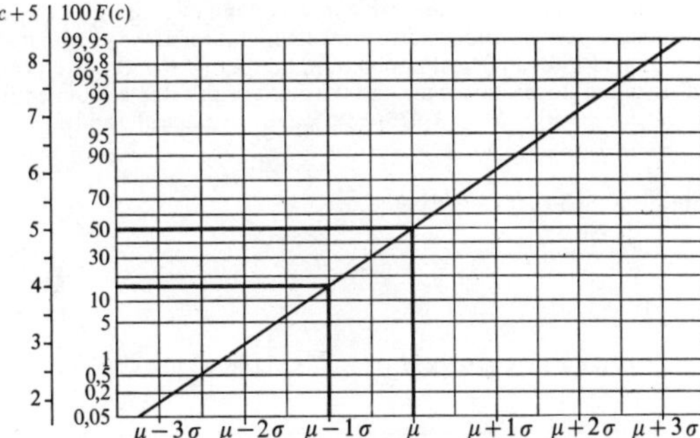

Fig. 28. Probit scale $(=c+5)$ and scale of probability paper.

The operations of **(527)** are carried out on probability paper, those of **(526)** by means of the probit transformation. Here only the latter method, of which further examples are given in later sections, will be used. Tables of probits are given on pages 68 and 69. For descriptions of the *maximum likelihood* method of estimating probit regression lines in those cases where the latter must be used, i.e., when μ and σ cannot be estimated from **(491)** and **(492)**, the reader is referred to the literature[13].

11F. Fitting of normal curves to samples

Normal curves *fitted* to the sample are required when it is desired either to make a test of non-normality (either by eye or formally) or to illustrate this condition. The above-mentioned exact tests for non-normality are more powerful than, for example, the equally exact symmetry test, since the *whole* of the empirical curve of the sample is compared with the normal curve fitted to it, with the result that these tests utilize *all* the information that can be extracted from the sample. For this reason such tests are known as tests of *goodness of fit*. If the test is to be carried out formally, which here amounts to a χ^2-test, two conditions must be met: the sample must be grouped, and the parameters μ and σ must be estimated by means of $\bar{x}$ and s in accordance with (**491**) and (**492**) [cf. the remarks on these equations and also (**430**)]. *In equations used in testing for goodness of fit, μ and σ are replaced by $\bar{x}$ and s.*

(a) *Ungrouped samples.* With ungrouped samples, empirical and fitted probit values can be compared only by eye. From (**500**) and (**502a**) it follows that

$$p_i = F(x_i) = \frac{R_i - 0{,}5}{N} \qquad (528)$$

[R_i: rank of the individual sample value x_i; cf. section 10E, page 196]

The empirical and fitted probits can then be calculated from (**528**) in conjunction with (**524**) to (**526**).

Example 28. Given is the sample of example 24, page 197. The mean $\bar{x}$ is 2,13, and the standard deviation s is 0,671 3. The $F(x_i)$ values are first calculated according to (**528**): $F(x_1) = 0{,}5/21$, $F(x_2) = 1{,}5/21$, etc. [equation (**31**) is used here: $0{,}5/21 + 1/21 + \cdots$]. By multiplying by 100, these values are converted into percentages, which are then used in the table on pages 68 and 69 to obtain the probits. For $x_1, x_2, \ldots$ this gives the empirical probits 3,0, 3,5, 3,8, 4,0, etc. These values are plotted on millimeter paper in accordance with (**526**) to give the result shown in Figure 29.

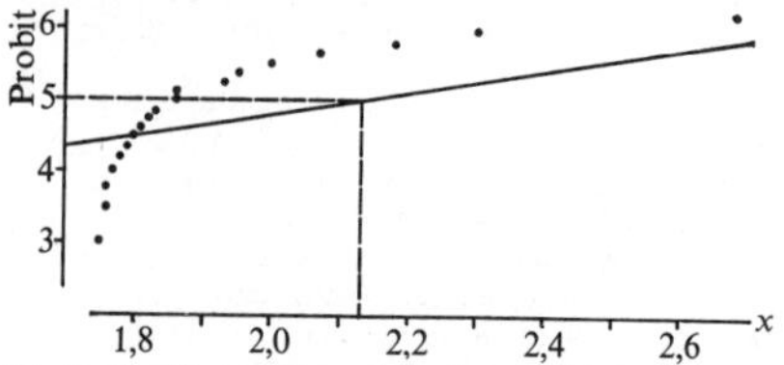

Fig. 29. Empirical probits and fitted probit line for the ungrouped sample of example 24, page 197.

It will at once be seen that the points plotted deviate systematically from a straight line, indicating that it is very unlikely that the sample originates from a normally distributed population. If the sample had originated from a normal population, the points would have been distributed stochastically around the fitted probit line calculated in accordance with (**524**) and (**525**) from $\bar{x}$ and s in place of μ and σ.

(b) *Grouped samples.* In this case

$$f(x_i) = \frac{N\,d}{\sigma} f(c_i) \qquad c_i = \frac{x_i - \mu}{\sigma} \qquad (529)$$

$$F(x_i + \tfrac{1}{2} d) = \Big(\sum_{1}^{i} f_j\Big)/N \qquad (530)$$

[i: ranks of the classes x; $d = x_{i+1} - x_i$: class width; f_i: freqency of the class i]

If both the fitted probability density *and* the cumulative distribution are to be calculated, then $x_i + \tfrac{1}{2} d$ is also used in (**529**) and the calculated ordinates plotted against $x_i + \tfrac{1}{2} d$, that is to say, at the *upper* limit of the class i. (**529**) gives the ordinates for the *middle* of the classes.

Example 29. Given is the sample of example 22, page 196, with $\bar{x} = 7{,}251$, $s = 0{,}584$.

Calculation of the fitted probability density

The calculation is made as follows: The differences $x_i + \tfrac{1}{2} d - \bar{x}$ are multiplied by $1/s$ to obtain the fitted c_i values [this can also be carried out as a simple addition by using equation (**31**)]. For these deviations c, the corresponding ordinates $f(c)$ are obtained from the upper table on page 29 [in this connection see also (**513**)]. Multiplication of these ordinates by $N\,d/s$ gives the required ordinates $f(x_i + \tfrac{1}{2} d)$ (cf. Fig. 30a).

Table 1

$x + \tfrac{1}{2} d$	$x + \tfrac{1}{2} d - \bar{x}$	$(x + \tfrac{1}{2} d - \bar{x})/s = c$	$f(c)$	$f(c) \times N\,d/s = f(x + \tfrac{1}{2} d)$
5,8	−1,451	−2,48	0,018 42	25,2
6,2	−1,051	−1,80	0,078 95	108,2
6,6	−0,651	−1,11	0,215 46	295,2
7,0	−0,251	−0,429	0,363 87	498,5
7,4	0,149	0,255	0,386 18	529,0
7,8	0,549	0,939	0,256 71	351,7
8,2	0,949	1,62	0,107 41	147,1
8,6	1,349	2,31	0,027 68	37,9
9,0	1,749	2,99	0,004 57	6,3
9,4	2,149	3,68	0,000 46	0,6

Calculation of the empirical probits

The values of $F(x_i + \tfrac{1}{2} d)$ are calculated from (**530**), multiplied by 100, and the table on pages 68 and 69 entered to obtain the corresponding probits. The latter are plotted against $x_i + \tfrac{1}{2} d$ as ordinates, giving the points of Figure 30b.

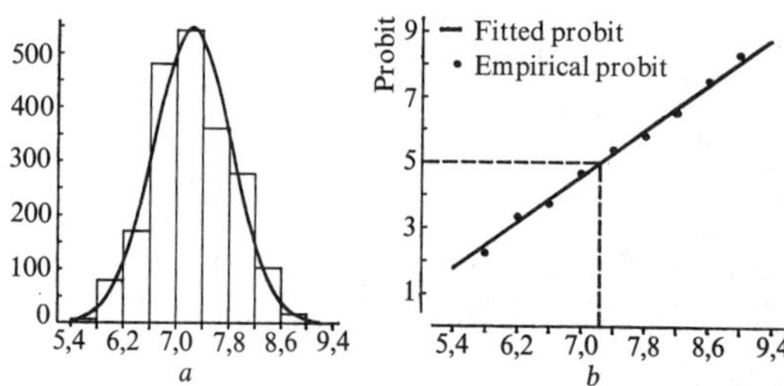

Fig. 30. Fitted probability density (*a*), empirical probits and fitted probit line (*b*) for the sample of example 22, page 196.

Calculation of the fitted probit line

The probit line is constructed according to (**525**). In this example it first passes through the point (7,25; 5). If the value $x = 5{,}4$, say, is taken as the abscissa of the other necessary point, then from (**524**) the corresponding probit is $5 + 1{,}712 \times (5{,}4 - 7{,}25) = 1{,}8$. When a straight line is drawn between these two points it is seen that the empirical probits all lie very close to it. The immediate impression given by Figure 30b is hardly such as to raise doubts that the population from which the sample is taken is other than a normally distributed one. That this impression is misleading, however, is demonstrated below. Note that when the probability density is calculated as shown above, the two points required for the construction of the fitted probit line can be obtained by taking two well separated values from the column headed c of Table 1 and increasing them by 5.

Exact testing for non-normality by the χ^2-test

In this case the test is carried out by means of the c transformation, without probits, as follows:

1. For calculation of the fitted c values for $x_i + \tfrac{1}{2} d$ according to (**522**) see column c of Table 1, which contains these values.
2. The $F(c)$ values corresponding to these fitted c values are obtained from the table on page 26. These are the fitted $F(c)$ values.
3. Multiplication of the fitted $F(c)$ values by the sample size N gives the fitted distribution of the cumulative absolute frequencies $H(x_i + \tfrac{1}{2} d)$.
4. From the differences $H(x_{i+1} + \tfrac{1}{2} d) - H(x_i + \tfrac{1}{2} d)$, the fitted absolute class frequencies f_i' are obtained.
5. From these the values of $(f_i - f_i')^2/f_i = \chi_i^2$ are calculated.
6. The sum of all the χ_i^2 values is the required test statistic χ^2 with degrees of freedom $v = n - 2 - 1$, where n is the number of classes.

The significance probability 2α of the χ^2 value obtained (cf. the table on page 34) is considerably smaller than 0,0005. Hence the population from which the sample originates is definitely not normally distributed, a result completely contrary to the impression gained by eye from the empirical probits (above).

Note that in the above calculation the sequence of the signs of the differences $f_i - f_i'$ should be looked at closely. The occurrence of pluses

All values conform to the international convention (i.e. 0,1 instead of 0.1).

Table 2

$x+\frac{1}{2}d$	$F(c)$	$F(c)\times N = H(x+\frac{1}{2}d)$	$H(x_{i+1}+\frac{1}{2}d) - H(x_i+\frac{1}{2}d) = f_i'$	f_i [cf. (**502b**)]	$(f_i-f_i')^2/f_i' = \chi_i^2$
5,8	0,006 57	13,1	13,1	5	5,01
6,2	0,035 93	71,9	58,8	78	6,27
6,6	0,133 50	267,0	195,1	144	13,38
7,0	0,333 60	667,2	400,2	479	15,52
7,4	0,602 57	1205,1	537,9	542	0,03
7,8	0,826 39	1652,8	447,7	358	17,97
8,2	0,947 38	1894,8	242,0	279	5,66
8,6	0,989 56	1979,1	84,3	99	2,56
9,0	0,998 61	1997,2	18,1	15	0,53
9,4	–*	–*	2,8	1	1,16
			2000,0	2000	$\chi^2 = 68{,}09$
					$\nu = 10-2-1$

*The large deviation 3,68 for the value $x=9{,}4$ is not given in these tables. This is unimportant, however, since as shown by column 4 of this table the differences for the extreme classes are given by H (lowest class) minus 0 and N minus H (highest class).

and minuses should vary randomly. If any systematic trend is detected either Haldane's test (page 229) if there are systematic cycles, or a test of randomness of runs (page 232) provided there are enough classes should be carried out. The reason for this is that if the χ^2-test gives no significant result when the number of classes is large – as in the above example – then it can be assumed with reasonable certainty that the population is normally distributed *provided that there is random variation of the plus and minus runs.* If the latter is not the case then the χ^2-test needs supplementation. The test is also conditional on the classes being *independent* of one another. This is doubtful if the signs follow any systematic cycle.

11G. Standard deviations of the quantiles of samples from normally distributed populations

The formulae given here are only *asymptotically* correct and should therefore only be used for *large* samples (the more extreme the position of the quantile the larger the sample should be), so that in practice they are seldom applicable. When confidence limits for the quantiles of small and medium samples are required it is better to use the procedure given in section 10F, page 197 (distribution-free confidence limits) and *not* calculate them by means of the standard deviations defined in the formulae given here.

(Asymptotic)

$$\text{Standard deviation of } x_p = \sigma_{x_p} = \frac{1}{f(x_p)}\sqrt{\frac{p(1-p)}{N}} \qquad \textbf{(531)}$$

From (**531**) and (**507**) it follows that

$$\left.\begin{matrix}\text{Standard}\\ \text{deviation of}\\ \text{the median}\end{matrix}\right\} x_{0,5} = \sigma_{x_{0,5}} = \sigma\sqrt{\frac{\pi}{2N}} = 1{,}2533\,\sigma\sqrt{\frac{1}{N}} \qquad \textbf{(532)}$$

In a normal distribution the median is identical with the mean μ. The median of a sample is therefore also an estimate of μ. The relative asymptotic efficiency of this estimate according to (**433**), (**484**) and (**532**) is

$$\frac{\sigma/\sqrt{N}}{\sigma\sqrt{\pi/2N}} = \sqrt{\frac{2}{\pi}} \sim 0{,}8$$

that is to say, about 80% of the efficiency of the estimate of μ is made up by $\bar{x}$ according to (**491**).

11H. The logarithmic-normal (lognormal) distribution

The probability density function of this distribution is

$$\left.\begin{aligned} f(x) &= \frac{0{,}4343}{x\times\sigma_{\log x}}\times f(c)\\ c &= \frac{\log x - \mu_{\log x}}{\sigma_{\log x}} \quad [0<x<\infty]\end{aligned}\right\} \textbf{(533)}$$

The estimates of $\mu_{\log x}$ and $\sigma_{\log x}$ are $\bar{x}_{\log x}$ and $s_{\log x}$, calculated according to (**491**) and (**492**) by substituting $\log x$ for x and $(\log x)^2$ for x^2.

The logarithmic-normal distribution is non-symmetrical (cf. Fig. 31a) and has the following characteristics:

$$\text{mode} = \text{antilog}(\mu_{\log x} - 2{,}3026\,\sigma^2_{\log x}) \qquad \textbf{(534)}$$

$$\text{median} = \text{antilog}\,\mu_{\log x} \qquad \textbf{(535)}$$

$$\text{mean} = \text{antilog}(\mu_{\log x} + 1{,}1513\,\sigma^2_{\log x}) \qquad \textbf{(536)}$$

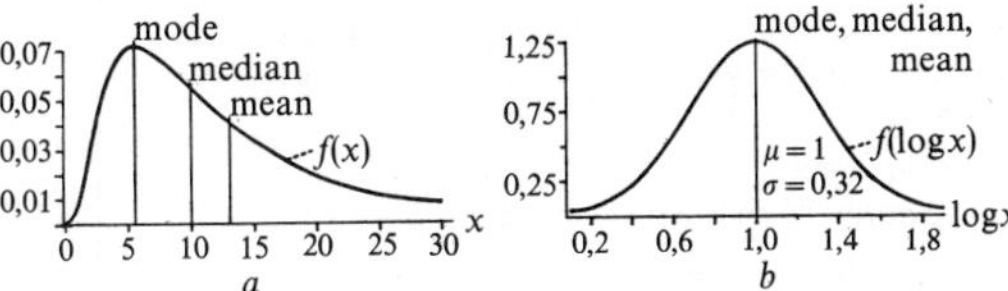

Fig. 31. a Lognormal distribution. *b* Transformation of *a*.

If x is plotted on a logarithmic abscissa scale (or $\log x$ on a linear abscissa scale) the non-symmetrical distribution (**533**) is transformed into the symmetrical normal distribution

$$\left.\begin{aligned} f(\log x) &= \frac{1}{\sigma_{\log x}}\times f(c)\\ c &= \frac{\log x - \mu_{\log x}}{\sigma_{\log x}} \quad [0<x<\infty]\\ &[\text{for } \mu_{\log x} \text{ and } \sigma_{\log x} \text{ see } (\mathbf{533})]\end{aligned}\right\} \textbf{(537)}$$

From (**533**) and (**537**) it follows that

$$f(x) = \frac{0{,}4343}{x}\times f(\log x) \qquad \textbf{(538)}$$

The probability density function of the transformed variable is thus not of the same magnitude as that of the original variable. In Figure 31 note the unequal ordinate scales. The situation is different with the cumulative distribution*, where

$$F(x_p) = F(\log x_p) = p \qquad \textbf{(539)}$$

Similarly for the quantiles

$$x_p = \text{antilog}\,(\log x_p) \qquad \textbf{(540)}$$

and for ungrouped samples

$$\left.\begin{aligned} &R(x_p) = R(\log x_p)\\ &[R\text{: ranks of the individual sample values, cf. section 10E, page 196}]\end{aligned}\right\} \textbf{(541)}$$

From (**537**) and (**539**) to (**541**) it follows that [for (**542**) to (**544**)]:

If a non-symmetrical continuous distribution can be converted into a normal distribution by transformation of the individual values in the manner described in (**537**), then this distribution is a lognormal distribution. } (**542**)

If samples after the transformation in (**537**) can be assumed to come from a normally distributed population [cf. (**509**) and section 11F, page 197], then any *tests* valid for the latter may be applied to these samples. *The results of these tests will also be valid for the untransformed samples.* } (**543**)

For the estimation of the quantiles and their confidence limits in *ungrouped* samples from lognormal populations whose individual values have *not* been transformed, the procedures described in sections 10E and 10F on pages 196 and 197 are applicable *without modification.* } (**544**)

For *grouped* samples the following should be noted: The transformation $x \to \log x$ may be carried out only with the *individual values.* If a sample is grouped into classes it must first be rearranged into an ungrouped sample. The logarithms of the individual values are then obtained, and reformed into a grouped sample, but with *equidistant logarithmic* class limits. If a grouped sample cannot be rearranged because the individual values were not noted, then a logarithmic transformation is *no longer possible.* In taking samples, the individual values should therefore always be noted before they are grouped. } (**545**)

In natural processes many random variables are lognormally distributed. In all cases where the reaction of a body to a given stimulus

*The quantiles of a transformed variable are given by the transformed quantiles of the original variable provided that the transformation was made with an *increasing* function ($\log x$ is an increasing function of x).

is proportional to the intensity of the stimulus and to the size of the body, the form of the distribution is lognormal. In practice, this applies particularly to toxicological and other similar biological studies, where logarithmic transformation of the variable x (dose) is a matter of routine.

11I. The addition theorem for the normal distribution

If $x_1, x_2, \ldots, x_k$ are stochastically independent, normally distributed variables with mean values $\mu_1, \mu_2, \ldots, \mu_k$ and variances $\sigma_1^2, \sigma_2^2, \ldots, \sigma_k^2$, then the variable

$$x = x_1 \pm x_2 \pm \cdots \pm x_k$$

is also normally distributed with mean **(546)**

$$\mu = \mu_1 \pm \mu_2 \pm \cdots \pm \mu_k$$

and variance

$$\sigma^2 = \sigma_1^2 + \sigma_2^2 + \cdots + \sigma_k^2$$

In **(546)** it should be noted that the variances are also *additive* when the mean μ is obtained from *differences*.

11J. The central limit theorem

The importance of the normal distribution lies in the fact that under fairly general conditions, the sum of k stochastically independent variables *of any sort* converges stochastically with increasing k toward a normal distribution with mean **(547)**

$$\mu = \mu_1 + \mu_2 + \cdots + \mu_k$$

and variance

$$\sigma^2 = \sigma_1^2 + \sigma_2^2 + \cdots + \sigma_k^2$$

From **(546)** the sum of independent normally distributed variables is *always* normally distributed, even when k is small. **(547)** is valid for variables distributed in *any* form, however, only when k approaches infinity. In practice, the expression 'infinity' is interpreted liberally. Thus, if for example in **(547)** the distributions all have the *same*, not too non-symmetrical form, then practically speaking their sum is normally distributed even when k is fairly small (50, 100, 200, ...). In other words, there will be a negligible error if the sample distributions are treated as normal.

In this publication, the statistical tables relating to sample distributions are so arranged that samples exceeding the tabulated sizes can for practical purposes be regarded as normally distributed. **(548)**

With *one* exception, *all* the sample distributions dealt with in this volume converge toward the normal distribution in accordance with **(547)**. The exception is the distribution of the extreme range (and of course that of the extreme deviations).

12. Distributions closely allied to the normal distribution

12A. The Student distribution (t-distribution)

If in the standardized *normal* deviation $c = (x-\mu)/\sigma$ the standard deviation σ has to be replaced by its estimate s because σ is unknown and thus has to be estimated from the sample, then the standardized variable

$$t_\nu = \frac{x-\mu}{s_\nu} \quad [s_\nu \text{ independent of } x] \tag{549}$$

has a probability density function **(550)**

$$f(t|\nu) = \frac{\Gamma([\nu+1]/2)}{\Gamma(\nu/2)\sqrt{\nu\pi}}\left(1+\frac{t^2}{\nu}\right)^{-(\nu+1)/2}$$

where

$\Gamma(x/2) = (x/2-1)(x/2-2)\ldots 3\times 2\times 1,$ when x is even

$\Gamma(x/2) = (x/2-1)(x/2-2)\ldots 3/2\times 1/2\times\sqrt{\pi},$ when x is odd

[ν is the number of *degrees of freedom* of t]

The Student distribution is independent of μ and σ; its form is determined only by the number of degrees of freedom ν. The determination of the degrees of freedom will be described later for various individual cases.

All values conform to the international convention (i.e. 0,1 instead of 0.1).

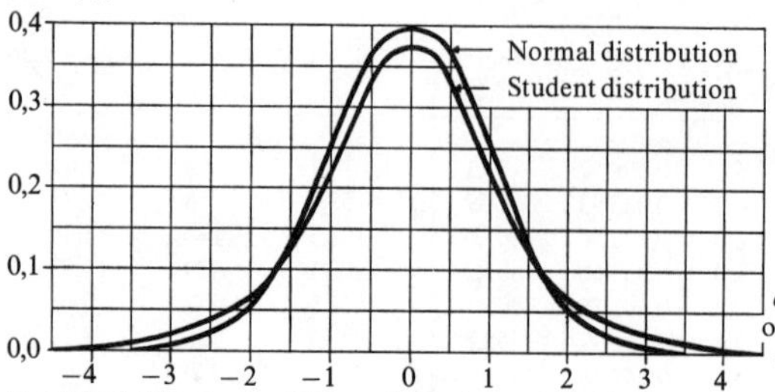

Fig. 32. Probability density of the standardized normal distribution and of the Student distribution with degrees of freedom $\nu = 4$.

The Student distribution (or t-distribution) is very similar to the normal distribution and converges toward it rapidly with increasing degrees of freedom. It is defined for all t from $-\infty$ to ∞. It is continuous, *symmetrical* and bell-shaped, but in contrast to the normal distribution has more probability concentrated in the tails and less in the central part.

Equations **(513)** to **(518)** for the standardized normal distribution derived from the symmetry are also valid for the Student distribution when c is replaced by t. **(551)**

In the tables on pages 30–33 the exact deviations t_0 for degrees of freedom ν between 1 and 200 are given for the following integrals: **(552)**

$$P(\text{of the table}) = \int_{t_0}^{\infty} f(t)\,dt = \text{Prob}(t > t_0) \quad \text{(a)}$$

$$2P(\text{of the table}) = \int_{-\infty}^{-t_0} f(t)\,dt + \int_{t_0}^{\infty} f(t)\,dt = \text{Prob}(t < -t_0) + \text{Prob}(t > t_0) \quad \text{(b)}$$

In *one-tailed* tests (confidence limits) $\alpha = P$, in *two-tailed* tests (confidence limits) $2\alpha = 2P$. (c)

The cumulative distribution $F(t) = \text{Prob}(t \le t_0)$ is [following **(405b)**] (d)

$$F(t_0) = 1 - \text{Prob}(t > t_0) = 1 - P = 1 - \textbf{(552a)}$$

Furthermore

$$\text{Prob}(t^2 > t_0^2|\nu) = 2\,\text{Prob}(t > t_0|\nu) \tag{553}$$

For the relationship between the Student and F-distributions see **(576)**.

12B. The χ^2-distribution

If $x_1, x_2, \ldots$ are stochastically independent observations from the *same normally distributed* population with mean μ and standard deviation σ, then the sum

$$\chi_\nu^2 = c_1^2 + c_2^2 + \cdots + c_i^2 + \cdots + c_\nu^2 = \sum_1^\nu c_i^2 \tag{554}$$

of the squares of the standardized deviations

$$c_i^2 = \left(\frac{x_i-\mu}{\sigma}\right)^2$$

has the probability density function **(555)**

$$f(\chi^2|\nu) = \frac{1}{2^{\nu/2}\,\Gamma(\nu/2)}\,e^{-\chi^2/2}\,(\chi^2)^{(\nu-2)/2} \quad [0 \le \chi^2 < \infty]$$

[ν is the number of degrees of freedom of χ^2; for $\Gamma(\nu/2)$ see **(550)**]

The χ^2-distribution is a continuous, *non-symmetrical* distribution which like the Student distribution – but more slowly – converges toward the normal distribution with increasing degrees of freedom ν (see Fig. 33). It is defined for $\chi^2 \ge 0$, its form dependent only on the degrees of freedom ν. The determination of the latter will be described later for various individual cases [see also **(567)** and **(570)**].

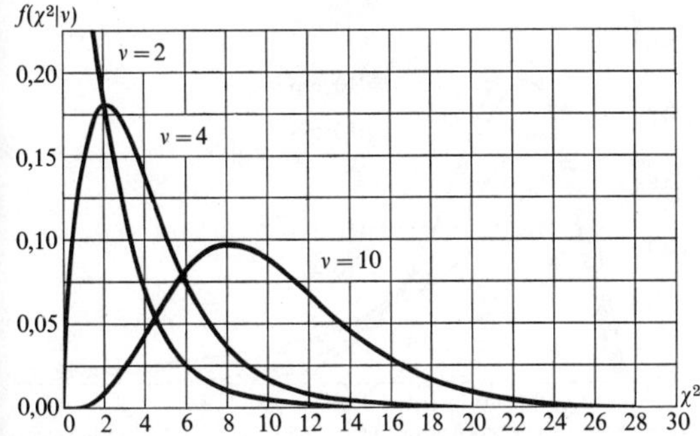

Fig. 33. Probability density functions of the χ^2-distribution with $\nu = 2, 4, 10$.

Parameters

Mode	$= \nu - 2$	(a)	(556)
Mean μ	$= \nu$	(b)	
Variance σ^2	$= 2\nu$	(c)	

Stochastic convergence when $\nu \to \infty$: **(557)**

$\chi^2/\nu \quad \to 1$ (a)

χ^2-distribution $\to$ Normal distribution $(\nu; \sqrt{2\nu})$; fairly slowly (b)

$\sqrt{2\chi^2}$-distribution $\to$ Normal distribution $(\sqrt{2\nu - 1}; 1)$*; faster than (b) (c)

Approximations for quantiles **(558)**

More centrally positioned quantiles [in accordance with (**557**c)]:

$$\chi_p^2 \sim \tfrac{1}{2}\left(c_p + \sqrt{2\nu - 1}\right)^2 \quad [\nu > 30] \qquad \text{(a)}$$

More extreme quantiles[14]:

$$\chi_p^2 \approx \nu\left(1 - \frac{2}{9\nu} + c_p\sqrt{\frac{2}{9\nu}}\right)^3 \quad [\nu > 30] \qquad \text{(b)}$$

For calculation of the quantiles 0,005, 0,025, 0,975 and 0,995 from the confidence limits for λ of the Poisson distribution see (**564**).

Example 30 [of (**558**)]. Comparison between (a) and (b): The quantile $\chi^2_{0,975;\nu=50}$ is required.

(a) $\chi_p^2 \sim \tfrac{1}{2}\left(1{,}96 + \sqrt{100 - 1}\right)^2 = 70{,}922$

(b) $\chi_p^2 \approx 50\left(1 - \frac{2}{450} + 1{,}96\sqrt{\frac{2}{450}}\right)^3 = 71{,}424$. The exact value is 71,420.

In the tables on pages 34–37 the exact deviations χ_0^2 for degrees of freedom ν between 1 and 200 are given for the following integrals: **(559)**

$1\int_r$ (of the table) $= \int_{\chi_0^2}^{\infty} f(\chi^2)\,d\chi^2 = \text{Prob}(\chi^2 > \chi_0^2)$ (a)

$\tfrac{1}{2}\int_r$ (of the table) $= \tfrac{1}{2}$ (**559**a) (b)

$1\int_l$ (of the table) $= \int_0^{\chi_0^2} f(\chi^2)\,d\chi^2 = \text{Prob}(\chi^2 < \chi_0^2) = F(\chi_0^2)$ (c)

$\tfrac{1}{2}\int_l$ (of the table) $= \tfrac{1}{2}$ (**559**c) (d)

(e) For *one-tailed* χ^2-tests $2\alpha = 1\int_r$

Two-tailed χ^2-tests are less common as the distribution is not symmetrical. A variety of two-tailed tests are possible with $2\alpha = \alpha_1 + \alpha_2$, where α_1 is not necessarily equal to $\alpha_2\,(=\alpha)$. For α_1 use $1\int_r$ and for α_2 $1\int_l$.

(f) With *one-sided* confidence limits for σ:

- for *upper* limits $\alpha = 1\int_r$
- for *lower* limits $\alpha = 1\int_l$

A variety of two-sided confidence limits for σ are possible with $2\alpha = \alpha_1 + \alpha_2$, where α_1 is not necessarily equal to $\alpha_2\,(=\alpha)$. For α_1 use $1\int_r$ and for α_2 $1\int_l$.

* According to R.A. Fisher.

All values conform to the international convention (i.e. 0,1 instead of 0.1).

A table of $\sqrt{\nu/\chi_\nu^2}$ for degrees of freedom between 1 and 100 is given on page 54 (*confidence factors for* σ) for the following quantiles: **(560)**

χ_p^2	Column $1-2\alpha$	χ_p^2	Column $1-2\alpha$
0,05 and 0,95	0,90	0,01 and 0,99 ...	0,98
0,025 and 0,975 ..	0,95	0,005 and 0,995 .	0,99

Relationships with other distributions

Normal distribution:

When $\nu = 1$, then $\chi_p^2 = c^2_{(1+p)/2}$, that is $\text{Prob}(\chi^2 < \chi_0^2) = 2\,\text{Prob}(0 < c_0)$ **(561)**

F-Distribution: see (**577**) and (**578**).

Poisson distribution:

$$\text{Prob}(\nu = 2x \mid \chi^2 = \chi_0^2) = \frac{e^{-\chi_0^2/2}(\chi_0^2/2)^x}{x!} \quad [\nu \text{ is even}] \qquad \textbf{(562)}$$
$$= \text{Prob}(x = \nu/2 \mid \lambda = \chi_0^2/2)$$

This distribution is shown in Figure 44 (page 221) with $x = \nu/2$ and $\lambda = \chi_0^2/2$.
If ν is even the following relationship exists between the cumulative distribution functions of the Poisson and the χ^2-distribution:

$$\text{Prob}(\chi^2 > \chi_0^2 \mid \nu = 2k) = \sum_0^{k-1} \frac{e^{-\chi_0^2/2}(\chi_0^2/2)^x}{x!} \quad [\nu \text{ is even}] \qquad \textbf{(563)}$$

For even numbers of degrees of freedom ν the following quantiles can be calculated on the basis of (**563**) from the confidence limits for λ of the Poisson distribution, pages 152 and 154: **(564)**

$\text{Prob}(\chi^2 \le \chi_p^2) = p$	Argument	
0,005	$x = \nu/2$ (page 154)	$\chi_p^2 = 2\lambda_l$
0,025	$x = \nu/2$ (page 152)	$\chi_p^2 = 2\lambda_l$
0,975	$x = (\nu/2) - 1$ (page 152)	$\chi_p^2 = 2\lambda_r$
0,995	$x = (\nu/2) - 1$ (page 154)	$\chi_p^2 = 2\lambda_r$

Example 31 [of (**564**)]

Required:	Solution:
$\chi^2_{0,025;\,\nu=260}$	$x = 130;\ \lambda_l = 108{,}61;\ \chi_p^2 = 217{,}22$
$\chi^2_{0,975;\,\nu=260}$	$x = 129;\ \lambda_r = 153{,}28;\ \chi_p^2 = 306{,}56$

The addition theorem for the χ^2-distribution

In equation (**554**) the sum can be broken up into any number of parts, for example

$$\chi^2 = \underbrace{c_1^2 + c_2^2}_{=\chi_1^2\ [\nu=2]} + \underbrace{c_3^2 + c_4^2 + c_5^2 + c_6^2}_{=\chi_2^2\ [\nu=4]} + \underbrace{c_7^2 + \cdots}_{=\chi_3^2\ [\nu=\ldots]} \text{ etc.}$$

It follows that:

If $\chi_1^2, \chi_2^2, \ldots, \chi_n^2$ are stochastically independent and the χ^2-distributions have the degrees of freedom $\nu_1, \nu_2, \ldots, \nu_n$ respectively, then the sum $\chi^2 = \chi_1^2 + \chi_2^2 + \cdots + \chi_n^2$ likewise has a χ^2-distribution with $\nu = \nu_1 + \nu_2 + \cdots + \nu_n$ degrees of freedom. **(565)**

There is also a division theorem for χ^2 on which the analysis of regression and variance is based.

χ^2 and sample variance

In accordance with (**554**), $\chi^2 = [\Sigma(x-\mu)^2]/\sigma^2$. If μ is replaced by $\bar{x}$, then from (**493**e), $\Sigma(x-\bar{x})^2 = (N-1)s^2$. If now $N-1$ is replaced by ν, then νs^2 is eventually obtained in place of $\Sigma(x-\mu)^2$. Intuitively it is surmised that

$$\chi_\nu^2 = \frac{\nu s_\nu^2}{\sigma^2} \quad [\nu\text{: degrees of freedom of } s^2] \qquad \textbf{(566)}$$

and this is a good guess. It should be noted that (**566**) is a second definition of χ^2 equivalent to (**554**) but valid *only* for *normally* distributed populations.

An important asymptotic property of χ^2

Given is a sample divided into n classes from a population *of any form*. If f_i is the observed frequency of the class i, where $f_1+f_2+\cdots+f_i+\cdots+f_n=N$, then f_i is known as the *empirical* (absolute) *frequency*. If $\boldsymbol{p}_i$ is the *given* or a *hypothetical* probability that the variable x will fall in the class i, where $\boldsymbol{p}_1+\boldsymbol{p}_2+\cdots+\boldsymbol{p}_i+\cdots+\boldsymbol{p}_n=1$, then $N\boldsymbol{p}_i$ is known as the *given* or the *hypothetical* (absolute) *frequency*. The empirical frequencies in the individual classes are random variables. In this case **(567)**

$$\sum_1^n \frac{(f_i-N\boldsymbol{p}_i)^2}{N\boldsymbol{p}_i} \to \chi^2_\nu \quad [\nu\to\infty;\ \nu=n-1]$$

(567) was discovered by K. Pearson. The fact that it is exactly valid only when $\nu\to\infty$ is of little consequence in practice but gives rise to certain restrictions:

In tests for goodness of fit based on **(567)**, the *samples* as a whole should *not* be *too small*, the *hypothetical* (absolute) *frequencies in the individual classes not below* $N\boldsymbol{p}_i=4$. If they are less than this, they should be increased to the required level by combining 2, 3, ... neighboring classes. This is necessary, however, only when the number of classes is small. If ν is greater than (about) 8 and the sample size over 40, then it is permissible for $N\boldsymbol{p}_i$ in isolated classes to be as low as 1. **(568)**

As a rule the hypothetical frequencies are not given:

Theoretical (absolute) frequencies $N\boldsymbol{p}_i$ which have been calculated on the basis of *estimated* parameters are known as *fitted frequencies*; the theoretical distribution corresponding to them is known as the *fitted distribution*. **(569)**

(570)

(a) If k parameters must be estimated in the calculation of fitted frequencies, then the number of degrees of freedom for χ^2 defined by **(567)** is

$$\nu=n-1-k \quad [n\text{: number of classes}]$$

(b) If m samples each grouped into n classes (in an $m\times n$ contingency table) are submitted to a χ^2-test based on **(567)**, then the number of degrees of freedom for χ^2 is

$$\nu=(n-1)(m-1) \quad [n\text{: number of classes}]$$

(c) In the special case, frequently encountered, of the 2×2 table, $\nu=1$.

For an example of a χ^2-test with estimation of parameters see section 11F(b), page 200. Another χ^2-test is described in section 23, page 227, in which further tests for frequency are dealt with.

In conclusion it should be noted that definitions **(554)** and **(566)** differ *fundamentally* from definition **(567)** in spite of the fact that the formulae are very similar: **(554)** and **(566)** are valid only for *normally distributed* populations, **(567)** is valid for populations of *any* form; in **(554)** and **(566)**, $\bar{x}$ and s are *continuous* variables, while in **(567)**, f_i is a *discrete* variable.

When χ^2-tests are carried out with the aid of fitted distributions, care must be taken that the estimates made satisfy condition **(430)** or **(431)**.

12C. The F-distribution (variance-ratio distribution)

In the expression F-distribution, the letter F symbolizes *not* a cumulative distribution but the name of R.A. Fisher, the discoverer of the z-distribution, which is equivalent to the F-distribution[15].

If s_1^2 and s_2^2 are two stochastically independent estimates of the variance σ^2 of the *same normally distributed* population, then in accordance with **(566)**

$$s_1^2=\sigma^2\frac{\chi_1^2}{\nu_1} \text{ and } s_2^2=\sigma^2\frac{\chi_2^2}{\nu_2}$$

It follows that the quotient

$$F=\frac{s_1^2}{s_2^2}=\frac{\chi_1^2/\nu_1}{\chi_2^2/\nu_2} \quad [0\le F<\infty] \qquad \textbf{(571)}$$

(ν_1 and ν_2 are the degrees of freedom of s_1 and s_2 respectively)

has the probability density function

$$f(F)=\frac{\Gamma([\nu_1+\nu_2]/2)}{\Gamma(\nu_1/2)\,\Gamma(\nu_2/2)}\,\nu_1^{\nu_1/2}\,\nu_2^{\nu_2/2}\,\frac{F^{(\nu_1-2)/2}}{(\nu_2+\nu_1F)^{(\nu_1+\nu_2)/2}} \qquad \textbf{(572)}$$

$[0\le F<\infty$; for $\Gamma(\nu/2)$ see **(550)**$]$

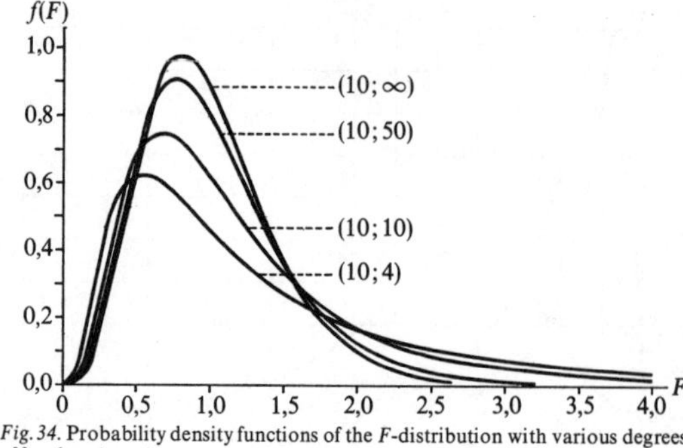

Fig. 34. Probability density functions of the F-distribution with various degrees of freedom $(\nu_1;\nu_2)$.

The F-distribution is a continuous *non-symmetrical* distribution defined for $F\ge 0$.

Parameters

Mean $\mu=\nu_2/(\nu_2-2)$ $[\nu_2>2]$ (a)

Variance $\sigma^2=\left(\frac{\nu_2}{\nu_2-2}\right)^2\times\frac{2(\nu_1+\nu_2-2)}{\nu_1(\nu_2-4)}$ $[\nu_2>4]$ (b) **(573)**

Interchange of ν_1 *and* ν_2

$$F_0(p;\nu_1;\nu_2)=1/[F_0(1-p;\nu_2;\nu_1)] \qquad \textbf{(574)}$$

In **(574)**, p can be $\text{Prob}(F>F_0)$ just as well as $\text{Prob}(F<F_0)$.

The values of F_0 given on pages 38–49 satisfy the following equation:

$$P(\text{of the table})=P_r=\int_{F_0}^{\infty} f(F)\,dF=\text{Prob}(F>F_0) \qquad \textbf{(575)}$$

Relationships to other distributions

Student distribution:

$$\text{Prob}(F>F_0)\,|\,1;\nu_2=\text{Prob}(t^2>t_0^2|\nu_2) = 2\,\text{Prob}(t>t_0|\nu_2) \qquad \textbf{(576)}$$

χ^2-distribution:

When F_p and χ_p^2 denote quantiles

$$F_p(\nu_1;\infty)=\frac{\chi^2_{p;\,\nu_1}}{\nu_1} \quad \text{(a)}$$

$$F_p(\infty;\nu_2)=\frac{\nu_2}{\chi^2_{1-p;\,\nu_2}} \quad \text{(b)} \qquad \textbf{(577)}$$

From **(577)** and **(557a)** it follows that

$F(\nu_1;\infty)\to 1$, when $\nu_1\to\infty$
$F(\infty;\nu_2)\to 1$, when $\nu_2\to\infty$ — that is, $F(\infty;\infty)=1$ **(578)**

Binomial distribution:

$$\text{Prob}\left(F(\nu_1;\nu_2)<\frac{N-x}{x+1}\times\frac{p}{1-p}\right)=\sum_{x+1}^{N}\binom{N}{k}p^k(1-p)^{N-k}$$

where

$$N=\frac{\nu_1+\nu_2}{2}-1 \quad\text{and}\quad x=\frac{\nu_1}{2}-1$$

$[\nu_1$ and ν_2 are even numbers$]$ **(579)**

On the basis of **(579)** the following quantiles F_0 can be calculated from the confidence limits for $\boldsymbol{p}$ of the binomial distribution (pages 89–102):

Prob$(F<F_0)$	Arguments (pages 89–102) Column	N	x	p	Quantile F_0
0,005	99%	$\frac{\nu_1+\nu_2}{2}-1$	$\frac{\nu_1}{2}-1$	p_l	$\frac{\nu_2}{\nu_1}\times\frac{p}{1-p}$
0,025	95%			p_l	
0,975	95%			p_r	
0,995	99%			p_r	

(580)

All values conform to the international convention (i.e. 0,1 instead of 0.1).

Example 32. Find $F_{0,995}(152;36)$.

We have

$N=93 \quad p_r=0{,}8993$ (page 100) $\quad \nu_2/\nu_1=0{,}236842$
$x=75 \quad p/(1-p)=8{,}93049 \quad F_{0,995}(152;36)=2{,}12$

Supplement. Formulae for calculation of F in special cases:

$$F(\nu_1=1;\nu_2=1;\alpha)=\tan^2\frac{(1-\alpha)\pi}{2}\text{ rad} \qquad \textbf{(581)}$$

$$F(\nu_1=2;\nu_2;\alpha)=\frac{\nu_2(1-\alpha^{2/\nu_2})}{2\alpha^{2/\nu_2}} \quad [\nu_2=1,2,3,...] \qquad (a)$$

$$F(\nu_1;\nu_2=2;\alpha)=\frac{2(1-\alpha)^{2/\nu_1}}{\nu_1[1-(1-\alpha)^{2/\nu_1}]} \quad [\nu_1=1,2,3,...] \qquad (b) \qquad \textbf{(582)}$$

Formulae for which $\int_{F_0}^{\infty} f(F)\,dF=\alpha$ can be calculated $\left(F=\frac{s^2_{\nu_1}}{s^2_{\nu_2}}\right)$:

If $\frac{\nu_1 F_0}{\nu_2}<1$,

$$x=\arctan\sqrt{\frac{\nu_1 F_0}{\nu_2}}$$

$$\alpha=1-\frac{\Gamma\left(\frac{\nu_1+\nu_2}{2}\right)}{\Gamma\left(\frac{\nu_1}{2}\right)\Gamma\left(\frac{\nu_2}{2}\right)}\times\frac{\cos^{\nu_2}x\sin^{\nu_1}x}{\frac{\nu_1}{2}}\times\left(1+\frac{\nu_1+\nu_2}{\nu_1+2}\sin^2x+\frac{(\nu_1+\nu_2)(\nu_1+\nu_2+2)}{(\nu_1+2)(\nu_1+4)}\sin^4x+\cdots\right) \qquad (a)$$

If $\frac{\nu_1 F_0}{\nu_2}\geq 1$,

$$x=\arctan\sqrt{\frac{\nu_2}{\nu_1 F_0}}$$

$$\alpha=\frac{\Gamma\left(\frac{\nu_1+\nu_2}{2}\right)}{\Gamma\left(\frac{\nu_1}{2}\right)\Gamma\left(\frac{\nu_2}{2}\right)}\times\frac{\cos^{\nu_1}x\sin^{\nu_2}x}{\frac{\nu_2}{2}}\times\left(1+\frac{\nu_1+\nu_2}{\nu_2+2}\sin^2x+\frac{(\nu_1+\nu_2)(\nu_1+\nu_2+2)}{(\nu_2+2)(\nu_2+4)}\sin^4x+\cdots\right) \qquad (b)$$

(583)

13. The normally distributed population: Confidence and tolerance intervals

(cf. also section 8, page 190)

13A. Confidence intervals for the mean μ

One-sided confidence interval with *single upper* limit

$\text{Prob}(-\infty<\mu<\bar{x}+k\times S\,d)=1-\alpha$ (a)
[cf. also (**584**d)]

One-sided confidence interval with *single lower* limit

$\text{Prob}(\bar{x}-k\times S\,d<\mu<\infty)=1-\alpha$ (b)
[cf. also (**584**d)]

Two-sided confidence interval with *symmetrical* limits

$\text{Prob}(\bar{x}-k\times S\,d<\mu<\bar{x}+k\times S\,d)=1-2\alpha$ (c)
[cf. also (**584**d)]

(584)

Factors $k\times S\,d$ for (**584**a, b, c) (d)

Equations	Degrees of freedom ν of s	k	$S\,d$	Page (c, t or k)
(a), (b)	>200	$\lvert c_\alpha\rvert/\sqrt{N}$	σ or s	26
(a), (b)	≤200	$t_{\nu;\alpha}/\sqrt{N}$	s_ν	30–33
(c)	>200	k_2 or $\lvert c_\alpha\rvert/\sqrt{N}$	σ or s	k_2: 50; c: 26
(c)	≤200	k_2 or $t_{\nu;2\alpha}/\sqrt{N}$	s_ν	k_2: 50; t: 30–33

All values conform to the international convention (i.e. 0,1 instead of 0.1).

In the table on page 50 (for k_2) the number of degrees of freedom $\nu=N-1$ is contained in the argument N. In this table the transition from t to c takes place at $N=201$.

13B. Tolerance intervals

Tolerance intervals without confidence probability

One-sided tolerance interval with *single upper* limit

$\text{Prob}(-\infty<x<m+k\times S\,d)=1-\alpha=\beta_p$ (a)
[cf. also (**585**d)]

One-sided tolerance interval with *single lower* limit

$\text{Prob}(m-k\times S\,d<x<\infty)=1-\alpha=\beta_p$ (b)
[cf. also (**585**d)]

Two-sided tolerance interval with *symmetrical* limits

$\text{Prob}(m-k\times S\,d<x<m+k\times S\,d)=1-2\alpha=\beta_p$ (c)
[cf. also (**585**d)]

(585)

m, k and $S\,d$ for (**585**a, b, c) (d)

Equations	Degrees of freedom ν of s	Known parameters or estimates	m	k	$S\,d$	Page (c, t or k)
(a), (b)	>200	μ,σ or $\bar{x},s$	μ or $\bar{x}$	$\lvert c_\alpha\rvert$	σ or s	26
(a), (b)	≤100	$\bar{x},\sigma$	$\bar{x}$	k_3*	σ	51, col. A
(a), (b)	≤200	μ,s	μ	$t_{\nu;\alpha}$	s	30–33
(a), (b)	≤100	$\bar{x},s$	$\bar{x}$	k_4*	s	51, col. A
(c)	>200	μ,σ or $\bar{x},s$	μ or $\bar{x}$	$\lvert c_\alpha\rvert$	σ or s	26
(c)	≤100	$\bar{x},\sigma$	$\bar{x}$	k_3	σ	51, col. A
(c)	≤200	μ,s	μ	$t_{\nu;2\alpha}$	s	30–33
(c)	≤100	$\bar{x},s$	$\bar{x}$	k_4	s	51, col. A

* β_p in the table is selected as follows: β_p [required] $=1-2\alpha$ [α is given].

Tolerance intervals with confidence probability β_t

Equations (**585**a, b, c) are applicable with the following complementary equation [example of (**585**c)]:

$\text{Prob}[\text{Prob}(m-k\times S\,d<x<m+k\times S\,d)\geq 1-2\alpha]=\beta_t$

(586)

m, k and $S\,d$ for (**585**a, b, c)

Equations	Degrees of freedom ν of s	Known parameters or estimates	m	k	$S\,d$	Page (k)
(a), (b)	≤ 100	$\bar{x},\sigma$	$\bar{x}$	k_5*	σ	51, col. B
(a), (b)	≤ 100	μ,s	μ	k_6*	s	51, col. B
(a), (b)	≤1000	$\bar{x},s$	$\bar{x}$	k_7	s	52, 53
(c)	≤ 100	$\bar{x},\sigma$	$\bar{x}$	k_5	σ	51, col. B
(c)	≤ 100	μ,s	μ	k_6	s	51, col. B
(c)	≤1000	$\bar{x},s$	$\bar{x}$	k_7	s	52, 53

* β_p in the table is selected as follows: $\beta_p=1-2\alpha$ [α is given].

The following equations are valid for the confidence and tolerance factors

(587)

$k_2=t_{2\alpha;\,N-1}\times 1/\sqrt{N}$ for $N\leq 201$ (a)

$\quad=\lvert c_\alpha\rvert\times 1/\sqrt{N}$ for $N>201$ (b)

$k_3=\lvert c_\alpha\rvert\times\sqrt{1+1/N}$ (c)

$k_4=t_{2\alpha;\,N-1}\times\sqrt{1+1/N}$ (d)

k_5: solution of $\int_{c'-k_5}^{c'+k_5} f(c)\,dc=\beta_p \quad [c'=c_{\beta_t}]$ (e)

$k_6=\lvert c_{\alpha_p}\rvert\times\sqrt{(N-1)/\chi^2_{N-1;\,1-\beta_t}}$ (f)

k_7: cf. EISENHART et al.[76]

13C. Confidence intervals for the standard deviation σ

From (**566**) it follows that

$$\left.\begin{array}{l}\text{Prob}(k_l\, s_v < \sigma < k_r\, s_v) = 1 - 2\alpha \\ \left[k_l = \sqrt{v/\chi^2_{v;1-\alpha}};\ k_r = \sqrt{v/\chi^2_{v;\alpha}}\right]\end{array}\right\} \quad (588)$$

Values of k_l and k_r for degrees of freedom between 1 and 100 are given in the left-hand table on page 54.

14. The normally distributed population: Extreme range and extreme deviations

14A. The extreme range

Definition

If x_1 is the lowest and x_n the highest value of a sample of size n, then $x_n - x_1$ is the extreme range w_n of this sample. **(589)**

The standardized extreme range of a sample of size n from a population with standard deviation σ is

$$W_n = \frac{w_n}{\sigma} = \frac{x_n - x_1}{\sigma} \quad (590)$$

The mean extreme range of m samples of size n from one and the same population is

$$\bar{w}_{m,n} = \frac{\sum_1^m w_n}{m} = \frac{\sum_1^m (x_n - x_1)}{m} \quad (591)$$

and the standardized mean extreme range is

$$\bar{W}_{m,n} = \frac{\bar{w}_{m,n}}{\sigma} = \frac{\sum_1^m w_n}{m\sigma} = \frac{\sum_1^m (x_n - x_1)}{m\sigma} \quad (592)$$

Since the extreme range w_n is merely a special case of the mean extreme range $\bar{w}_{m,n}$ with $m = 1$, only the mean extreme range will be referred to in the text that follows.

Mean extreme range as a multiple of σ

The expected value $\mathbf{W}_n$ of the extreme range of random samples of size n from a normally distributed population with unit standard deviation satisfies the relation

$$\bar{W}_{m,n} \underset{(m\to\infty)}{\rightarrow} \mathbf{W}_n \quad (593)$$

The upper right-hand table on page 54 gives values of $\mathbf{W}_n$ for the standardized normal distribution as multiples of σ[17]. (Many authors use the symbol d_n in place of $\mathbf{W}_n$.)

σ as a fraction of the mean extreme range

The quotient

$$\frac{\bar{w}_{m,n}}{\mathbf{W}_n} = \bar{w}_{m,n} \times \mathbf{A}_n \quad (594)$$

gives an unbiased estimate of σ. Values of this quotient are given in the lower right-hand table on page 54.

The relative efficiency of (**594**) compared with that of the estimate s [s^2 from (**492a**)] when $m = 1$ is[18]:

n	2	3	4	5	6	10	15	20	50	100	∞
Efficiency	1,00	0,99	0,98	0,96	0,93	0,85	0,77	0,70	0,49	0,34	0

For n between 2 and 10 there is little difference between the two estimates. Within this range (**594**) is useful as a *rapid method of estimating σ* but *it should not be used in place of s in a standard t-test.* For larger samples the extreme range estimate of σ can likewise be accurately determined by dividing the sample into a number m of *independent* subgroups of the same size between 2 and 10 and determining their extreme ranges. In accordance with (**592**), the mean of these ranges is then the mean extreme range. However, such a subdivision must be effected by a *random selection* among the available sample values. If there is no natural method of doing this (such as using the order in time of obtaining the sample values), random numbers may be used, but the time needed to carry out the subdivision will tend to nullify the advantages of the more rapid calculation.

All values conform to the international convention (i.e. 0,1 instead of 0.1).

Example 33. A sample of size 24, $x_1, x_2, \ldots, x_{24}$, can be subdivided into 12 groups of 2, 8 groups of 3, 6 groups of 4, or 3 groups of 8:

Groups of 2: x_1–x_2, x_3–x_4, ..., x_{23}–x_{24}
Groups of 3: x_1–x_3, x_4–x_6, ..., x_{22}–x_{24}

Overlapping groups must of course be avoided, for example x_1–x_2, x_2–x_3, ..., since these would obviously no longer be independent.

$\sigma_{\bar{x}}$ as a fraction of the mean extreme range

The quotient

$$\frac{\bar{w}_{m,n}}{\mathbf{W}_n\sqrt{m\,n}} = \bar{w}_{m,n} \times \mathbf{A}_{m,n} \quad (595)$$

where $m\,n$ = sample size N, gives an unbiased estimate of the standard deviation $\sigma_{\bar{x}}$ of the estimate $\bar{x}$. Values of the factor $\mathbf{A}_{m,n} = 1/(\mathbf{W}_n \times \sqrt{m\,n})$ are given in the table on page 55.

Example 34. Given a time-ordered sample 3,00, 1,56, 1,34, 2,08, 2,10, 2,67. The estimates of σ and $\sigma_{\bar{x}}$ on the basis of the extreme range or mean extreme range are

(a) 1 extreme range

1,34–3,00: range = 1,66 — $\sigma' = 1{,}66 \times 0{,}39457 = 0{,}655$; $\sigma'_{\bar{x}} = 1{,}66 \times 0{,}16108 = 0{,}267$

(b) 2 extreme ranges

1,34–3,00, 2,08–2,67: mean range = 1,125 — $\sigma' = 1{,}125 \times 0{,}59082 = 0{,}665$; $\sigma'_{\bar{x}} = 1{,}125 \times 0{,}24120 = 0{,}271$

(c) 3 extreme ranges

1,56–3,00, 1,34–2,08, 2,10–2,67: mean range = $0{,}91\dot{6}$ — $\sigma' = 0{,}91\dot{6} \times 0{,}88623 = 0{,}812$; $\sigma'_{\bar{x}} = 0{,}91\dot{6} \times 0{,}36180 = 0{,}332$

For comparison, σ can be estimated using (**492b**) with the result $s = 0{,}63257$. In order to correct the bias of this estimate it must be multiplied by the factor $k_s = 1{,}0509$ (see the left-hand table on page 54, column k_s), giving the result $s = 0{,}665$ and $s_{\bar{x}} = 0{,}271$.
All the above estimates may be regarded as equally valid. Although the agreement between s and the estimates (a) and (b) is striking, this does not mean that estimate (c) is not as good. A further sample from the same population could result in estimates nearer to (c).

14B. Testing extreme ranges and extreme deviations

The studentized extreme range (table on page 58, sample size 2–20)

In the test quotients

$$\frac{x_N - x_1}{s_v} \quad [x_1 < x_2 < \cdots < x_N;\ v\text{: degrees of freedom of } s] \quad (596)$$

s is an estimate calculated from a sample *different* from and *independent* of the sample to be tested but originating from the *same* population.
If the test quotient *attains* or *exceeds* the level in the table corresponding to the degrees of freedom v_s and the sample size N, then the extreme range in question is *too large* (significance probability α).
If σ is known, the levels at $v = \infty$ should be used. If the sample size exceeds the range of the table, testing should be carried out according to (**600d**) for sample sizes between 21 and 25 and according to (**599**) for still larger samples, *if it is desired to test extreme values.*

The studentized extreme deviation (lower table on page 59, sample size 3–9)

In the test quotients

$$\left.\begin{array}{l}\dfrac{x_N - \bar{x}}{s_v} \text{ or } \dfrac{\bar{x} - x_1}{s_v} \\ {[x_1 < x_2 < \cdots < x_N;\ v\text{: degrees of freedom of } s]}\end{array}\right\} \quad (597)$$

s has the same meaning as in (**596**). If σ is known, the levels at $v = \infty$ should be used.
If the test quotient *attains* or *exceeds* the level in the table corresponding to the degrees of freedom v_s and the sample size N, then the extreme deviation in question is *too large* (significance probability α).
If the sample size exceeds the range of the table, testing should be carried out according to (**600c**) and (**600d**) for sample sizes between 10 and 25 and according to (**599**) for still larger samples.

The standardized extreme deviation (upper table on page 59)

We have

$$\text{Prob}(c \leq c_E) = \left(\int_{-\infty}^{c_E} f(c)\,dc\right)^N \quad \text{[for } c_E \text{ see (599)]} \quad \text{(a)}$$

$$\text{Prob}(-c_E \leq c \leq c_E) = \left(\int_{-c_E}^{c_E} f(c)\,dc\right)^N \quad \text{(b)} \qquad \textbf{(598)*}$$

[c_E: standardized extreme deviation; N: sample size]

(**598**a) gives the probability that no deviation from the mean μ is greater than c_E; (**598**b) gives the probability that no deviation from the mean μ is greater than c_E *in absolute value.* In accordance with (**408**b), the corresponding significance probabilities are $1-$(**598**). The table on page 59 gives the probabilities $1-$(**598**a). In the test quotients

$$\frac{x_N-\mu}{\sigma} \text{ or } \frac{\mu-x_1}{\sigma} = c_E \qquad \textbf{(599)}$$

the symbols have the customary meaning. For sample sizes over 25, μ and σ can be replaced by $\bar{x}$ and s. For smaller samples (**597**) should be used.

Testing extreme values of a sample[19] (upper left-hand table on page 60, sample size 3–25)

When *no* independent information on the standard deviation of the population is available, extreme deviations in samples up to a size of 25 can be tested by means of the following quotients:

Sample size N	Quotient	Sample size N	Quotient
3–7....	$\left\lvert\frac{x_N-x_{N-1}}{x_N-x_1}\right\rvert$ (a)	11–13...	$\left\lvert\frac{x_N-x_{N-2}}{x_N-x_2}\right\rvert$ (c)
8–10...	$\left\lvert\frac{x_N-x_{N-1}}{x_N-x_2}\right\rvert$ (b)	14–25...	$\left\lvert\frac{x_N-x_{N-2}}{x_N-x_3}\right\rvert$ (d)

(600)

where $x_1 < x_2 < \dots < x_N$, when a right-hand extreme value is tested,
$x_N < x_{N-1} < \dots < x_1$, when a left-hand extreme value is tested

With samples of over 25, (**599**) should be used with μ and σ replaced by $\bar{x}$ and s.

General considerations in testing extreme values

It is common for extreme values to be ignored, often without comment by the author and without their first being tested statistically. Occasionally they are even eliminated *before* the experimental data are put into the hands of the statistician. This is clearly undesirable, for in some situations extreme values are often the most informative ones in the sample.
If an extreme value is found to be significantly too large after proper statistical testing in accordance with (**597**), (**599**) or (**600**), its rejection is actually justifiable only when a check on the experiment reveals a causal circumstance accounting for its existence. Examples would be an error made in measurements or calculations, the unwitting inclusion of a sick person among healthy persons being investigated, and so on. In such cases the extreme values originate from *other* populations and *ought to be rejected.*
If, however, there is a high degree of probability that the extreme value originates from the same population, the following considerations apply: The smaller the sample the more unlikely it is to contain extreme values of the population. A small sample containing an extreme value can give a completely false picture of the population it represents. In such cases the extreme value *may be ignored.* However, it is advisable to use a small significance probability, at least with larger samples.
A third important consideration to be born in mind in judging extreme values is that the validity of the tests described above is conditional on the population being *normally distributed.* If this is not the case, the tests are practically *worthless* since they are very peculiarly dependent on this condition of normality.

*This formula is derived from (**362**) and (**405**a) or (**407**c).

All values conform to the international convention (i.e. 0,1 instead of 0.1).

Special considerations in testing extreme values

If testing in accordance with (**596**) results in the postulated significance, then at least one of the two extreme values, left or right (*or* possibly the *whole* sample, depending on the situation) must be rejected since they do not originate from that population from which the sample with the calculated s was taken.
It is permissible to test extreme values more than once in the same sample. In this case the sample size must be reduced by 1 after each rejection before a new test is made. The resulting level of significance α_{res} for the total number k of significant tests then has the *very approximate* order of magnitude

$$\alpha_{res} \sim 1-(1-\alpha_1)(1-\alpha_2)\dots(1-\alpha_k)$$

Example 35. The sample of example 24, page 197, is to be tested using (**600**d).

1st test ($N=21$)
Right-hand extreme deviate: $\frac{4{,}41-2{,}68}{4{,}41-1{,}76} = 0{,}653$

Deviate is too large ($\alpha \ll 0{,}005$)

2nd test ($N=20$)
Right-hand extreme deviate: $\frac{3{,}56-2{,}35}{3{,}56-1{,}76} = 0{,}672$

Deviate is too large ($\alpha \ll 0{,}005$)

Only the *5th test* gives no further significant deviation.

After two deletions $\alpha_{res} \sim 1-(\gg 0{,}995)(\gg 0{,}995) < 0{,}01$, if the sample were from a normally distributed population. This is not the case (cf. section 24D, page 229), so that the extreme values may not be rejected.

---

15. The normally distributed population: Comparison of a sample with the hypothetical population

15A. Comparison of the sample and population standard deviations s and σ (or of the variances s^2 and σ^2)

The confidence limits for σ are obtained from (**588**), those for σ^2 analogously by replacing s by s^2 and k by k^2. The hypothetical σ or σ^2 is then compared with these limits and the result interpreted in accordance with (**476**).

15B. Comparison of the sample and population means $\bar{x}$ and μ

Comparison of the estimate $\bar{x}$ with the hypothetical mean is made by means of the test quotients given in (**602**) to (**606**), the numerical value of the quotient being compared with the limit given:

If the test quotient is *smaller* than the limit, then the result is interpreted in accordance with (**474**) or (**475**). If it attains or exceeds the limit, then

	One-tailed test	Two-tailed test
When $\bar{x}-\mu<0$	$\bar{x}<\mu$ [α]	$\bar{x}\neq\mu$ [2α]
When $\bar{x}-\mu>0$	$\bar{x}>\mu$ [α]	
Significance in brackets.		

(601)

The c-test (normal distribution)

Applicability: When σ is known or when the degrees of freedom of s: $N-1>200$

Test quotient	Significance limit	
$\frac{\lvert\bar{x}-\mu\rvert\sqrt{N}}{\sigma}$ or $\frac{\lvert\bar{x}-\mu\rvert\sqrt{N}}{s_{N-1}}$ [$N>201$]	$\lvert c_\alpha\rvert$: page 26	(a)
$\frac{\lvert\bar{x}-\mu\rvert}{s_{N-1}}$ [$N>201$]	$c/\sqrt{N}$ = confidence factor k_2, page 50	(b)

(602)

The t-test (Student distribution)

Applicability: When σ is unknown and the degrees of freedom of s: $N-1 \leq 200$

Test quotient	Significance limit		
$\frac{\lvert\bar{x}-\mu\rvert\sqrt{N}}{s_{N-1}}$ $[N \leq 201]$	t_{N-1}: pages 30–33; $\alpha = P, 2\alpha = 2P$	(a)	(603)
$\frac{\lvert\bar{x}-\mu\rvert}{s_{N-1}}$ $[N \leq 201]$	$t_{N-1}/\sqrt{N}$: confidence factor k_2, page 50	(b)	

Lord's test based on the extreme range[20]

Applicability: Samples of size $N \leq 20$ (a) and $N > 20$ (b)

Test quotient	Significance limit		
$\frac{\lvert\bar{x}-\mu\rvert}{x_N - x_1}$ $[N \leq 20; x_1 < x_2 < \cdots < x_N]$	Page 60, middle left-hand table	(a)	(604)
$\frac{\lvert\bar{x}-\mu\rvert\, m}{[\sum(x_n - x_1)]\,\boldsymbol{A}_{m,n}}$ $[N > 20; mn = N]$	Page 56; $\boldsymbol{A}_{m,n}$: page 55	(b)	
m: number of subgroups of size n (cf. section 14A, page 206) in which $x_1 < x_2 < \cdots < x_n$.			

The midrange test based on the extreme range[21]

Applicability: Samples of size $N \leq 10$

Test quotient	Significance limit	
$\frac{\lvert x_N + x_1 - 2\mu\rvert}{x_N - x_1}$ $[N \leq 10]$	Page 60, upper right-hand table	(605)

Walsh test[21, 22]

Applicability: Samples of size $4 \leq N \leq 15$ from *any symmetrical* population

Test quotient	Significance limit	
Page 60, lower right-hand table	Page 60, lower right-hand table	(606)

The use of **(602b)** and **(603b)** avoids the multiplication by $\sqrt{N}$, with the further advantage that the transition from t to c in using the table on page 50 is quite 'automatic'.

(604) to **(606)** are straightforward *rapid tests* [especially **(605)**]. Within the tabulated range their power is practically the same as that of **(603)**. The Walsh test is suitable not only for normal but also for *any* other symmetrical distribution. In this case, the significance probability for N up to 8 is somewhat higher than that in the table. For $N > 8$ the values in the table are exact.

Example 36. When t is the limit for $\frac{\lvert\bar{x}-\mu\rvert\sqrt{N}}{s}$, then $t\,s$ is the limit for $\lvert\bar{x}-\mu\rvert\sqrt{N}$.

16. The normally distributed population: Comparison of two samples

In comparing two samples, the following hypotheses concerning the parameters of the original populations must be considered:

$$\sigma_1^2 = \sigma_2^2 \begin{cases} \mu_1 = \mu_2 & \text{(a)} \\ \mu_1 \neq \mu_2 & \text{(b)} \end{cases} \quad (607)$$

$$\sigma_1^2 \neq \sigma_2^2 \begin{cases} \mu_1 = \mu_2 & \text{(a)} \\ \mu_1 \neq \mu_2 & \text{(b)} \end{cases} \quad (608)$$

16A. Comparison of variances

The test quotient for the hypothesis $(\sigma_1^2 = \sigma_2^2)$ **(607)** is **(571)**. If $\sigma_1^2 = \sigma_2^2$ where '1' and '2' are randomly assigned it seems reasonable to test the equality by comparing F with the left α and the right α point of the F-distribution $F(\nu_1;\ \nu_2)$. **(609)**

All values conform to the international convention (i.e. 0,1 instead of 0.1).

From **(574)** it follows that the two-tailed test at the 2α level is achieved by using whichever of the two variance estimates is the larger as the numerator and compare the resulting F with the α value. This means that renumbering of the variances with respect to the *indices of the table* is necessary when s_1^2 (from sample 1) is smaller than s_2^2. *The number of degrees of freedom ν_1 in the tables on pages 38–49 is always that of the numerator of* **(571)**. **(609)**

s_1^2 and s_2^2 must be calculated from **(492)**. Their degrees of freedom are $\nu_1 = N_1 - 1$ and $\nu_2 = N_2 - 1$.

If the test quotient is *smaller* than the significance limit F in the table on pages 38–49, then in accordance with **(474)** it can be assumed that $\sigma_1^2 = \sigma_2^2$. In this case the means are tested by the procedure given in section 16B below. If the test quotient *attains* or *exceeds* the significance limit F, then $\sigma_1^2 > \sigma_2^2$ (significance probability $\alpha = P$) or $\sigma_1^2 \neq \sigma_2^2$ (significance probability $2\alpha = P$). The means are tested by the procedure given in section 16C.

16B. Comparison of means when $\sigma_1^2 = \sigma_2^2$

The following symbols are used here:

$$\lvert\bar{x}_1 - \bar{x}_2\rvert = d \text{ and } \lvert\mu_1 - \mu_2\rvert = \boldsymbol{d} \quad (610)$$

The estimate of the common standard deviation $\sigma = \sigma_1 = \sigma_2$ is

$$s = \sqrt{\frac{S_1 + S_2}{N_1 + N_2 - 2}} \quad [\nu_s = \nu_1 + \nu_2 = N_1 + N_2 - 2;\ S_1 \text{ and } S_2 \text{ from } \mathbf{(493)}] \quad (611)$$

The estimate of the standard deviation of the difference $\boldsymbol{d}$ is

$$s_d = s\sqrt{\frac{1}{N_1} + \frac{1}{N_2}} \quad [\nu_{s_d} = N_1 + N_2 - 2;\ s \text{ from } \mathbf{(611)}] \quad (612)$$

If σ is known, s is replaced by σ in **(612)**. If $N_1 = 1$, then $s_d = s\sqrt{1 + 1/N_2}$ [$\nu = N_2 - 1$; cf. also **(452)**, **(587c)** and **(587e)**].

The test quotients for the hypothesis $(\mu_1 = \mu_2 \mid \sigma_1^2 = \sigma_2^2)$ are

- if σ is known or $\nu > 200$: d/σ_d or d/s_d; limit $\lvert c_\alpha\rvert$: page 26 (a)
- when $\nu \leq 200$: d/s_d; limit t_ν, $\alpha = P$, $2\alpha = 2P$: pages 30–33 (b)

(613)

If the test quotient *attains* or *exceeds* the significance limit, then this is considered as evidence that $\mu_1 \neq \mu_2$. In this case it is often desirable to test the hypothesis $(\mu_1 - \mu_2 = \boldsymbol{d} \mid \sigma_1^2 = \sigma_2^2)$:

The test quotients are obtained by replacing d in **(613)** by $\lvert d - \boldsymbol{d}\rvert$. If the quotient exceeds the significance limit, then this is considered as evidence that $\mu_1 - \mu_2 \neq \boldsymbol{d}$. **(614)**

The confidence limits for $\boldsymbol{d}$ are

- two-sided: $\text{Prob}(d - t_{\nu;\alpha} \times s_d \leq \boldsymbol{d} \leq d + t_{\nu;\alpha} \times s_d) = 1 - 2\alpha$ (a)
- one-sided with a single upper limit: $\text{Prob}(\boldsymbol{d} \leq d + t_{\nu;\alpha} \times s_d) = 1 - \alpha$ (b)

(615)

If the test quotient in **(613)** is *smaller* than the significance limit, then it may be assumed in accordance with **(474)** that $\mu_1 = \mu_2$. Since also $\sigma_1^2 = \sigma_2^2$, the conclusion may be drawn that the two samples 1 and 2 originated from the same population with mean μ and variance σ^2. Estimates of these parameters are

$$\bar{x} = \frac{\sum_1^{N_1} x_1 + \sum_1^{N_2} x_2}{N_1 + N_2} = \frac{N_1\bar{x}_1 + N_2\bar{x}_2}{N_1 + N_2} \quad (616)$$

$$s^2 = \frac{S_1 + S_2 + \frac{\left(\sum_1^{N_1} x_1\right)^2}{N_1} + \frac{\left(\sum_1^{N_2} x_2\right)^2}{N_2} - \frac{\left(\sum_1^{N_1} x_1 + \sum_1^{N_2} x_2\right)^2}{N_1 + N_2}}{N_1 + N_2 - 1} = \frac{\nu_1 s_1^2 + \nu_2 s_2^2 + N_1\bar{x}_1^2 + N_2\bar{x}_2^2 - \frac{(N_1\bar{x}_1 + N_2\bar{x}_2)^2}{N_1 + N_2}}{N_1 + N_2 - 1}$$

$[\nu_s = N_1 + N_2 - 1;\ S_1 \text{ and } S_2 \text{ from } \mathbf{(493)}]$ **(617)**

16C. Comparison of means when $\sigma_1^2 \neq \sigma_2^2$

If σ_1 and σ_2 are known, or $N_1+N_2>200$, then

$$\sigma_{\boldsymbol{d}} = \sqrt{\frac{\sigma_1^2}{N_1}+\frac{\sigma_2^2}{N_2}} \text{ and } s_d = \sqrt{\frac{s_1^2}{N_1}+\frac{s_2^2}{N_2}} \qquad \textbf{(618)}$$

and the test quotients

$$\frac{d}{\sigma_{\boldsymbol{d}}} \text{ and } \frac{d}{s_d} \text{ or } \frac{|d-\boldsymbol{d}|}{\sigma_{\boldsymbol{d}}} \text{ and } \frac{|d-\boldsymbol{d}|}{s_d} \qquad \textbf{(619)}$$

have the same limits as (**613**a).

If σ_1 and σ_2 are unknown (the Behrens-Fisher problem), then the test quotients

$$\frac{d}{s_d} \text{ and } \frac{|d-\boldsymbol{d}|}{s_d} \qquad \textbf{(620)}$$

have the same limits as (**613**b)[23], where

$$s_d = \sqrt{\frac{s_1^2}{N_1}+\frac{s_2^2}{N_2}} \qquad \text{(a)}$$

$$\nu = \frac{1}{k^2/\nu_1+(1-k)^2/\nu_2} \qquad \text{(b)}$$

[ν_1 and ν_2: degrees of freedom of s_1 and s_2 respectively]

$$k = \frac{N_2\, s_1^2}{N_2\, s_1^2+N_1\, s_2^2} \qquad \text{(c)} \qquad \textbf{(621)}$$

This is known as Welch's correction.

16D. Testing paired differences

When two analytical methods can be tried out on the same substrate, or two methods of treatment on the same individual, then the *power of a test is considerably greater* if in place of the difference between *two* means, *one* mean calculated from the paired differences is tested.
Let A and B be the methods to be compared, $A_i-B_i=d_i$ the difference between the results given by these methods with the object i, N the total number of objects. A sample of size N of all paired differences d_i is thus obtained and can be tested in accordance with (**602**) to (**606**), usually with a hypothetical mean $\mu=0$. Other even simpler methods of testing paired differences are the sign test (see section 24D, page 229), the Wilcoxon test, and in certain cases appropriate sequential analysis (cf. section 26, page 232).
Methods 16A, B, C, E and 17A, B cannot be used in testing paired differences because of the non-independent nature of the samples.

16E. Tests for two samples using the extreme range[20]

(a) *Two samples of the same size* $N'=N''=N\leq 20$

$x'_N-x'_1$ and $x''_N-x''_1$ are the extreme ranges of these samples; the test quotient is then

$$\frac{|\bar{x}'-\bar{x}''|}{x'_N-x'_1+x''_N-x''_1} \qquad \textbf{(622)}$$

[for limit see page 60, bottom left-hand table]

(b) *Two samples of unequal size*, or of same size but larger than in (a):
The samples are divided respectively into m' and m'' random subgroups of the same size n (cf. section 14A, page 206). The sum of all the extreme ranges of these subgroups from both samples is denoted by S_E. The test quotient is then

$$\frac{|\bar{x}'-\bar{x}''|\sqrt{m'\,m''}}{S_E\times \boldsymbol{A}_{m,n}} \qquad \textbf{(623)}$$

[$m=m'+m''$; for limit see page 56, for $\boldsymbol{A}_{m,n}$ page 55]

17. The normally distributed population: Testing several samples

Given are n samples of sizes

$$N_1, N_2, \ldots, N_i, \ldots, N_n, \text{ where } \sum_1^n N_i = N \qquad \text{(a)}$$

The sums of the individual x values are

$$\sum_1^{N_1} x_1, \sum_1^{N_2} x_2, \ldots, \sum_1^{N_i} x_i, \ldots, \sum_1^{N_n} x_n, \text{ where } \sum_1^n\sum_1^{N_i} x_i = \sum_1^N x \qquad \text{(b)}$$

The sums of the individual squares x^2 are

$$\sum_1^{N_1} x_1^2, \sum_1^{N_2} x_2^2, \ldots, \sum_1^{N_i} x_i^2, \ldots, \sum_1^{N_n} x_n^2, \text{ where } \sum_1^n\sum_1^{N_i} x_i^2 = \sum_1^N x^2 \qquad \text{(c)}$$

The sums of squares calculated in accordance with (**493**) are

$$S_1, S_2, \ldots, S_i, \ldots, S_n, \text{ where } \sum_1^n S_i = S \qquad \text{(d)}$$

The degrees of freedom are

$N_1-1, N_2-1, \ldots, N_i-1, \ldots, N_n-1,$
[symbolized by $\nu_1, \nu_2, \ldots, \nu_i, \ldots, \nu_n$]

$$\text{where } \sum_1^n (N_i-1) = N-n = \nu = \sum_1^n \nu_i \qquad \text{(e)}$$

The means $\bar{x}_1, \bar{x}_2, \ldots, \bar{x}_i, \ldots, \bar{x}_n$ are defined by (**491**) (f)

and the variances $s_1^2, s_2^2, \ldots, s_i^2, \ldots, s_n^2$ by (**492**) (g) **(624)**

17A. Testing variances

The hypothesis $\sigma_1^2=\sigma_2^2=\cdots=\sigma_i^2=\cdots=\sigma_n^2$ is tested by means of Bartlett's test[24].

An estimate of the common variance σ^2 is

$$s^2 = S/\nu \quad [\nu = N-n;\ S, \nu \text{ and } N \text{ from (624d, e and a)}] \qquad \textbf{(625)}$$

The test statistic for s^2 is

$$2{,}3026\left(\nu \log s^2 - \sum_1^n \nu_i \log s_i^2\right)\Big/ k \qquad \text{(a)}$$

[s^2 from (**625**), ν, ν_i and s_i^2 from (**624**e and g)]

where

$$k = 1+\left(\sum_1^n \frac{1}{\nu_i}-\frac{1}{\nu}\right)\Big/ 3(n-1) \quad [\nu \text{ and } \nu_i \text{ from (624e)}] \qquad \text{(b)}$$

When $\nu_1=\nu_2=\cdots=\nu_i=\cdots=\nu_n=\nu_0$, (**626**a and b) become

$$2{,}3026\,\nu\left(\log s^2-(1/n)\sum_1^n \log s_i^2\right)\Big/ k \quad [\text{see (a)}] \qquad \text{(c)}$$

and

$$k = 1+(n+1)/3\nu \quad [\text{see (b)}] \qquad \text{(d)} \qquad \textbf{(626)}$$

The significance limit for the test statistics (**626**a) and (**626**c) is found from the χ^2-distribution with degrees of freedom $\nu=n-1$ (tables on pages 34–37, $2\alpha=1\int_r$). If the test statistic *attains* or *exceeds* the significance limit, then we may suspect that populations with different variances are among those being compared. If the test statistic is *smaller* than the limit, then in accordance with (**474**) it can be assumed that all the populations have the same variance. In this case the means can be further tested as described in section 17B.

17B. Testing means: Simple analysis of variance

In testing the hypothesis $\mu_1=\mu_2=\cdots=\mu_i=\cdots=\mu_n$ the following tabulation is first made [cf. also (**624**)]:

	Sums of squares	Degrees of freedom	Variance
Variance between the samples	S_2	$n-1$	$s_2^2=S_2/(n-1)$
Variance within the samples	S_1	$N-n$	$s_1^2=S_1/(N-n)$
Total	S_T	$N-1$	$s_T^2=S_T/(N-1)$

(627)

where

$$S_2 = \sum_1^n N_i(\bar{x}_i-\bar{x})^2 = \sum_1^n\left(\sum_1^{N_i} x_i\right)^2\Big/ N_i - \left(\sum_1^N x\right)^2\Big/ N \qquad \text{(a)}$$

$$S_1 = S\ [\text{from (624d)}] = S_T - S_2 \qquad \text{(b)}$$

$$S_T = S_1+S_2 = \sum_1^N x^2 - \left(\sum_1^N x\right)^2\Big/ N \qquad \text{(c)}$$

$$\bar{x} = \left(\sum_1^N x\right)\Big/ N \qquad \text{(d)} \qquad \textbf{(628)}$$

In (**628**) a check is made by means of the two identities in (a), (b) and (c).

All values conform to the international convention (i.e. 0,1 instead of 0.1).

In **(627)**, s_2^2 represents the dispersion of the sample means $\bar{x}_i$ around the common mean $\bar{x}$, s_1^2 the dispersion of the individual values around the sample means. If all the samples originate from the same population, so that $\mu_1 = \mu_2 = \cdots = \mu_i = \cdots = \mu_n = \mu$ (the hypothesis in the light of which the variances have been tested), then the variances s_2^2 and s_1^2 should be approximately of the same magnitude. If they are not, then among the samples are some with discrepant means, in which case s_2^2 must be greater than s_1^2. The necessity of carrying out the appropriate F-test is thus avoided when $s_2^2 \le s_1^2$.

The test quotient is

$$s_2^2/s_1^2 \quad [s_2^2 > s_1^2; \text{limit } F, 2\alpha = P\text{: pages 38–49}] \qquad \textbf{(629)}$$

If the test quotient is smaller than the significance limit, then in accordance with **(474)** it can be assumed that all the samples originate from the same population. The estimates of their mean μ and variance σ^2 are

$\bar{x} =$ **(628d)**
$s^2 =$ **(625)** $[\nu_s = N - n]$
with confidence and tolerance intervals constructed as described in **(584)** to **(588)**. **(630)**

If the test quotient *attains* or *exceeds* the significance limit F, then among the means at least two of them are different. Various methods of analysing this situation have been proposed[25]. Here that of Duncan[25] will be used.
The method is dependent on *all samples having the same size* N_0. The standard deviation of a mean $\bar{x}_i$ is first calculated

$$s_{\bar{x}_i} = \sqrt{s^2/N_0} \quad [\nu_{s_{\bar{x}_i}} = N - n; s^2 \text{ from } \textbf{(625)}] \qquad \textbf{(631)}$$

The means $\bar{x}_i$ are now ranked

$$\left.\begin{array}{l}\bar{x}_1 < \bar{x}_2 < \cdots < \bar{x}_i < \cdots < \bar{x}_n \\ {[1, 2, \ldots, i, \ldots, n\text{: ranks } R]}\end{array}\right\} \qquad \textbf{(632)}$$

and the extreme ranges W_i corresponding to the degrees of freedom $\nu_{s_{\bar{x}_i}}$ and the ranks $R = 2, 3, \ldots, n$ are found on page 57. Multiplication of these by the standard deviation of a mean $s_{\bar{x}_i}$ [cf. **(631)**] gives the extreme ranges of the means $W_{\bar{x}_i}$. Subtraction of these from the means $\bar{x}_i$ gives the 'localized extreme ranges' $\bar{x}_i - W_{\bar{x}_i}$. The following conclusions can now be drawn:

The means falling in a 'localized extreme range' $\bar{x}_i - W_{\bar{x}_i}$ cannot be distinguished from each other significantly. **(633)**

The means not distinguishable in **(633)** are underscored (as in example 37) in the order of **(632)**, with the result:

Two means *not* underscored with a common line differ from one another significantly (significance probability α from the table on page 57). **(634)**

....

Example 37. Given 7 samples with the means $\bar{x}_i$ shown below. $N_0 = 5$; $N = 35$; $s_v = 0{,}099$; $\nu_s = 28$. Significance probability $\alpha = 0{,}05$.

From **(631)** the estimated standard deviation of a mean is $s_{\bar{x}_i} = \sqrt{0{,}099/5} \approx 0{,}1407$. The extreme ranges W_i and $W_{\bar{x}_i} = W_i \times s_{\bar{x}_i}$ are given in the table below. The differences $\bar{x}_i - W_{\bar{x}_i}$ are then calculated up to the point where the corresponding underscoring reaches or passes the lowest mean.

R	1	2	3	4	5	6	7
$\bar{x}_i$	1,34	1,36	1,48	1,62	1,74	1,88	2,04
W_i◊		2,90	3,05	3,14	3,21	3,26	3,30
$W_{\bar{x}_i}$		0,408	0,429	0,442	0,451	0,459	0,464
$\bar{x}_i - W_{\bar{x}_i}$					1,289	1,421	1,576
(633)	1,34	1,36	1,48	1,62	1,74	1,88	2,04

The final result is given by **(634)**: 2,04 > 1,34 to 1,48; 1,88 > 1,34 to 1,36.

....

18. The normally distributed population: Regressions of the first kind

Discussion will be limited here to *linear* regression functions.
The functional relationships between two or more variables are often more or less obscured by random influences. Thus the effect of a dose of a drug, for example, will change in a certain way as the dose is increased. The effect will never be an exact function of the dosage, however, and even in the same subject will fluctuate around a curve – the *regression function* – in a random manner. Using statistical methods it is possible to estimate the parameters of the regression function and the required variances.
Although in the above example the dose is *not* a random variable, the effect it brings about is a random variable. In this case the regression is one of the *first kind*. In cases where *both* variables are random variables the regression is one of the *second kind*. A regression of the second kind can be treated as a regression of the first kind when the range of variation of the dependent variable as well as the points at which it is measured are arbitrarily decided beforehand.
In regressions of the first kind there is a *single* regression line, that of y on x, which is used for calculations in both directions – from y to x as well as from x to y. Cf. also section 19, page 215.

18A. Estimation of the parameters of the regression line Y

[cf. also **(298)** to **(311)**]

Ungrouped samples, two variables

Given are n pairs of observations x, y. x is the *independent, non-random* variable, y the *dependent, random* variable.

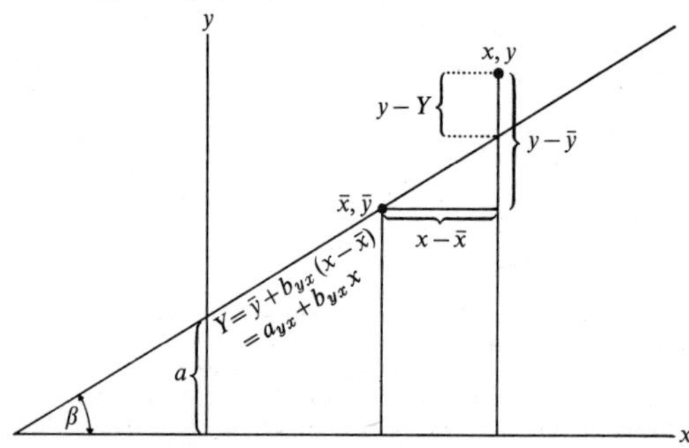

Fig. 35. Linear regression, ungrouped sample.

Estimate Y of the regression line $\mathbf{Y}$:

$$\left.\begin{array}{ll} Y = \bar{y} + b_{yx}(x - \bar{x}) & \text{(a)} \\ = a_{yx} + b_{yx}x & \text{(b)} \end{array}\right\} \qquad \textbf{(635)}$$

[$a_{yx} = \bar{y} - b_{yx}\bar{x}$; $\bar{y}$ and $\bar{x}$ calculated from **(491)**, b_{yx} from **(636)**]

Estimate b_{yx} of the regression coefficient $\boldsymbol{b}_{yx}$:

$$b_{yx} = \frac{s_{xy}}{s_x^2} = \frac{S_{xy}}{S_x} \qquad \textbf{(636)}$$

[s_x^2 and S_x from **(492)** and **(493)**. For s_{xy} see **(637)**. b_{yx} is the tangent of the angle of inclination β_{yx} of the regression line Y. Cf. also **(299)**.]

Estimate s_{xy} of the covariance σ_{xy}:

$$s_{xy} = \frac{\Sigma(x - \bar{x})(y - \bar{y})}{n - 1} = \frac{S_{xy}}{n - 1} \qquad \textbf{(637)}$$

[for S_{xy} see **(638)**]

The calculation of S_{xy} is facilitated by the use of the following sums:

$$\left.\begin{array}{ll} S_{xy} = \Sigma(x - \bar{x})(y - \bar{y}) & \text{(a)} \\ \phantom{S_{xy}} = \Sigma x\,y - \bar{x}\,\Sigma y & \text{(b)} \\ \phantom{S_{xy}} = \Sigma x\,y - \bar{y}\,\Sigma x & \text{(c)} \\ \phantom{S_{xy}} = \Sigma x\,y - \Sigma x\,\Sigma y/n & \text{(d)} \\ {[= s_{xy}(n - 1)]} & \text{(e)} \end{array}\right\} \qquad \textbf{(638)}$$

Estimate $s_{y.x}^2$ of the residual variance $\sigma_{y.x}^2$:

$$\left.\begin{array}{ll} s_{y.x}^2 = \dfrac{\Sigma(Y - y)^2}{n - 2} = \dfrac{S_{y.x}}{n - 2} & \text{(a)} \\ \phantom{s_{y.x}^2} = s_y^2(1 - r^2)\dfrac{n - 1}{n - 2} & \text{(b)} \end{array}\right\} \qquad \textbf{(639)}$$

[for $S_{y.x}$ and r^2 see **(640)** and **(708)**]

$\sigma_{y.x}^2$ is the variance of y when x is fixed. It is *smaller* than the vari-

◊ W_i is obtained by linear interpolation between $\nu = 24$ and $\nu = 30$ in the table on page 57 ($\alpha = 0{,}05$).

All values conform to the international convention (i.e. 0,1 instead of 0.1).

ance $\sigma^2_{y\cdot}$. In very rare cases (with very small correlation or regression coefficients) we can have

$$(1-r^2)\frac{n-1}{n-2}>1 \quad [\text{in which case } s^2_{y.x}>s^2_y]$$

Formula (**639**b) belongs properly in section 19, page 215, but it is more convenient to include it here.
If r is known, values of $1-r^2$ and of its square root can be taken from the table on page 61. Values of $(n-1)/(n-2)$ and of its square root for n between 1 and 250 are given in the table on page 62.

$$\left.\begin{aligned} S_{y.x} &= S_y - b_{yx}\, S_{xy} && \text{(a)}\\ &= S_y - b^2_{yx}\, S_x && \text{(b)}\\ &= S_y\,(1-r^2) && \text{(c)} \end{aligned}\right\} \textbf{(640)}$$

[S_y and S_x from (**493**); S_{xy} from (**638**); b_{yx} from (**636**); r^2 from (**708**)]. The remarks above on (**639**b) apply also to (**640**c).

Estimate $s^2_{b_{yx}}$ of the variance $\sigma^2_{b_{yx}}$:

$$\left.\begin{aligned} s^2_{b_{yx}} &= s^2_{y.x}/S_x && \text{(a)}\\ &= (s^2_y/s^2_x)\times\frac{1-r^2}{n-2} = (S_y/S_x)\times\frac{1-r^2}{n-2} && \text{(b)} \end{aligned}\right\} \textbf{(641)}$$

[s^2_y and s^2_x from (**492**); S_y and S_x from (**493**); $s^2_{y.x}$ from (**639**); r^2 from (**708**)].
The remarks above on (**639**b) apply also to (**641**b).

Estimate $s^2_{\hat{Y}|x}$ of the variance $\sigma^2_{\hat{Y}|x}$ about the regression line $\boldsymbol{Y}$ for a given value of x:

$$\left.\begin{aligned} s^2_{\hat{Y}|x} &= s^2_{y.x}\,(1/n+[x-\bar{x}]^2/S_x) && \text{(a)}\\ &= s^2_{b_{yx}}\,(S_x/n+[x-\bar{x}]^2) && \text{(b)} \end{aligned}\right\} \textbf{(642)}$$

[$\nu=n-2$; S_x from (**493**); $s^2_{y.x}$ from (**639**); $s^2_{b_{yx}}$ from (**641**)]

Special cases of (**642**) are:

Estimate $s^2_{\bar{y}}$ of the variance $\sigma^2_{\bar{y}}$ of the mean $\bar{y}$

$$s^2_{\bar{y}} = s^2_{y.x}/n \quad [\nu=n-2] \qquad \textbf{(643)}$$

Estimate $s^2_{a_{yx}}$ of the variance $\sigma^2_{a_{yx}}$ of the intercept a

$$\left.\begin{aligned} s^2_{a_{yx}} &= s^2_{y.x}(1/n+\bar{x}^2/S_x) && \text{(a)}\\ &= s^2_{b_{yx}}\,(\Sigma x^2)/n && \text{(b)} \end{aligned}\right\} \textbf{(644)}$$

[$\nu=n-2$; $s^2_{b_{yx}}$ from (**641**)]

Example 38. Given the sample:

x	y	x	y	x	y
5,8	2,19	7,0	4,62	8,2	6,58
6,2	3,27	7,4	5,32	8,6	7,41
6,6	3,79	7,8	5,85	9,0	8,29

The y values in this example correspond to the empirical probits of example 29, page 200.

It follows from

(**491**) $\bar{x} = 66{,}6/9 = 7{,}4$
(**493**) $S_x = 502{,}44-492{,}84 = 9{,}6$
(**491**) $\bar{y} = 47{,}32/9 = 5{,}25\dot{7}$
(**493**) $S_y = 280{,}651-248{,}7980\dot{4} = 31{,}8529\dot{5}$
(**492**b) $s^2_y = 31{,}8529\dot{5}/8 = 3{,}981619\dot{4}$
$s_y = 1{,}995399$
(**638**) $S_{xy} = 367{,}62-350{,}168 = 17{,}452$
(**636**) $b_{yx} = 17{,}452/9{,}6 = 1{,}81791\dot{6}$
(**640**) $S_{y.x} = 31{,}8529\dot{5}-31{,}726282 = 0{,}126674$
(**639**) $s^2_{y.x} = 0{,}126674/7 = 0{,}0180963$
$s_{y.x} = 0{,}134522$
(**641**a) $s^2_{b_{yx}} = 0{,}0180963/9{,}6 = 0{,}00188503$
$s_{b_{yx}} = 0{,}0434169$
(**643**) $s^2_{\bar{y}} = 0{,}0180963/9 = 0{,}0020107$
$s_{\bar{y}} = 0{,}0448408$
(**644**a) $s^2_{a_{yx}} = 0{,}0180963\,(1/9+54{,}76/9{,}6) = 0{,}105235$
$s_{a_{yx}} = 0{,}324399$
(**635**a) $Y = 5{,}25\dot{7}+1{,}81791\dot{6}\,(x-7{,}4)$
(**635**b) $= -8{,}194806+1{,}81791\dot{6}\,x$

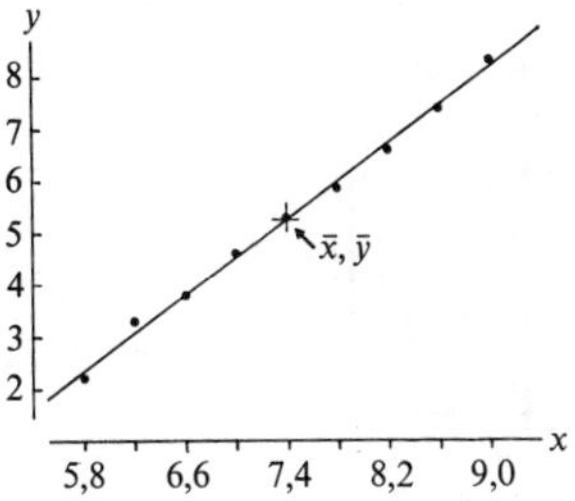

Fig. 36. Probit line of example 38.

A comparison of Figure 36 with Figure 30 (page 200) shows that the two probit lines – obtained by basically different methods – are hardly distinguishable by eye. The slope of the line in Figure 30 is 1/0,584 = 1,7123. As will be shown in example 41, page 213, this differs significantly from the slope 1,8179 in Figure 36.

Grouped samples, two variables

Given are 1, 2, ..., i, ..., k points of measurement (columns) x_i with m_1, m_2, ..., m_i, ..., m_k observations y_{ij}.
x is the *independent, non-random* variable, y the *dependent, random* variable.

(645)

x	1	2	...	i	...	k	
y	11	21	...	i1	...	k1	
	12	22	...	i2	...	k2	
	⋮	⋮		⋮		⋮	
	1j	2j		ij		kj	
	⋮	⋮		⋮		⋮	
	$1m_1$	$2m_2$		im_i		km_k	
	$\sum_{j=1}^{m_1} y_{1j}$	$\sum_{j=1}^{m_2} y_{2j}$	...	$\sum_{j=1}^{m_i} y_{ij}$	...	$\sum_{j=1}^{m_k} y_{kj}$	
	Overall sum $\sum y$; column sum $\sum y_i$						(a; b)
	$\frac{\left(\sum_{j=1}^{m_1} y_{1j}\right)^2}{m_1}$	$\frac{\left(\sum_{j=1}^{m_2} y_{2j}\right)^2}{m_2}$	...	$\frac{\left(\sum_{j=1}^{m_i} y_{ij}\right)^2}{m_i}$	...	$\frac{\left(\sum_{j=1}^{m_k} y_{kj}\right)^2}{m_k}$	
	Overall sum $\sum(\sum y_i)^2/m_i$						(c)
xy	$x_1\sum_{j=1}^{m_1} y_{1j}$	$x_2\sum_{j=1}^{m_2} y_{2j}$	...	$x_i\sum_{j=1}^{m_i} y_{ij}$	...	$x_k\sum_{j=1}^{m_k} y_{kj}$	
	Overall sum $\sum xy$						(d)
y^2	$(11)^2$	$(21)^2$	...	$(i1)^2$	...	$(k1)^2$	
	$(12)^2$	$(22)^2$	...	$(i2)^2$	...	$(k2)^2$	
	⋮	⋮		⋮		⋮	
	$(1j)^2$	$(2j)^2$	...	$(ij)^2$	...	$(kj)^2$	
	⋮	⋮		⋮		⋮	
	$(1m_1)^2$	$(2m_2)^2$	...	$(im_i)^2$	...	$(km_k)^2$	
	$\sum_{j=1}^{m_1} y^2_{1j}$	$\sum_{j=1}^{m_2} y^2_{2j}$	...	$\sum_{j=1}^{m_i} y^2_{ij}$	...	$\sum_{j=1}^{m_k} y^2_{kj}$	
	Overall sum $\sum y^2$; column sum $\sum y_i^2$						(e; f)
x	$m_1 x_1$	$m_2 x_2$	...	$m_i x_i$	...	$m_k x_k$	
	Overall sum $\sum x$						(g)
	$m_1 x_1^2$	$m_2 x_2^2$	...	$m_i x_i^2$	...	$m_k x_k^2$	
	Overall sum $\sum x^2$						(h)
$n=m_1+m_2+\dots+m_i+\dots+m_k$							(i)

All values conform to the international convention (i.e. 0,1 instead of 0.1).

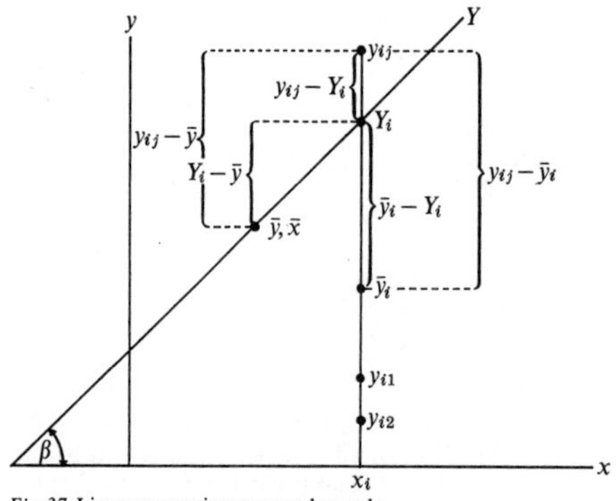

Fig. 37. Linear regression, grouped sample.

(645) allows the following to be calculated:

- column means

$\bar{y}_i = (\sum y_i)/m_i = \mathbf{(645}\text{b}\mathbf{)}/m_i$ **(646)**

- sums of the squares of the deviations of the individual column values from the column means

$S_{y_i} = \sum y_i^2 - (\sum y_i)^2/m_i = \mathbf{(645}\text{f}\mathbf{)} - \mathbf{(645}\text{b}\mathbf{)}^2/m_i$ **(647)**

- overall mean

$\bar{y} = (\sum y)/n = \mathbf{(645}\text{a}\mathbf{)}/\mathbf{(645}\text{i}\mathbf{)}$ **(648)**

- mean of the independent variable

$\bar{x} = (\sum x)/n = \mathbf{(645}\text{g}\mathbf{)}/\mathbf{(645}\text{i}\mathbf{)}$ **(649)**

- sums of the squares of the deviations of x from $\bar{x}$

$S_x = \sum x^2 - (\sum x)^2/n = \mathbf{(645}\text{h}\mathbf{)} - \mathbf{(645}\text{g}\mathbf{)}^2/\mathbf{(645}\text{i}\mathbf{)}$ **(650)**

- sums of products

$S_{xy} = \sum x\,y - \sum x \sum y/n = \mathbf{(645}\text{d}\mathbf{)} - \mathbf{(645}\text{g}\mathbf{)}\,\mathbf{(645}\text{a}\mathbf{)}/\mathbf{(645}\text{i}\mathbf{)}$ **(651)**

- regression coefficient

$b_{yx} = S_{xy}/S_x = \mathbf{(651)}/\mathbf{(650)}$ **(652)**

- sums of the squares for variation within columns

$S_1 = \sum_1^k S_{y_i} = \sum_1^k \mathbf{(647)} \quad [= \sum_{i=1}^{k}\sum_{j=1}^{m_i} (y_{ij}-\bar{y}_i)^2]$ **(653)**

- sums of the squares of the deviations of the column means from the regression line Y

$$S_2 = \sum(\sum y_i)^2/m_i - (\sum y)^2/n - S_3$$
$$= \mathbf{(645}\text{c}\mathbf{)} - \mathbf{(645}\text{a}\mathbf{)}^2/\mathbf{(645}\text{i}\mathbf{)} - \mathbf{(655)}$$
$$[= \sum_{i=1}^{k} m_i\,(\bar{y}_i - Y_i)^2]$$
$[S_3$ from **(655)**$]$ **(654)**

- sums of the squares of the deviations of the regression line from the overall mean

$$S_3 = b_{yx}\,S_{xy} = b_{yx}^2\,S_x = S_{xy}^2/S_x = \mathbf{(652)}\,\mathbf{(651)} = \mathbf{(652)}^2\,\mathbf{(650)}$$
$$[= \sum m_i\,(Y_i - \bar{y})^2]$$ **(655)**

- sums of the squares of the deviations of the individual values from the overall mean

$$S_y = \sum y^2 - (\sum y)^2/n = \mathbf{(645}\text{e}\mathbf{)} - \mathbf{(645}\text{a}\mathbf{)}^2/\mathbf{(645}\text{i}\mathbf{)}$$
$$[= \sum (y_{ij} - \bar{y})^2]$$ **(656)**

Check: $S_1 + S_2 + S_3 = S_y$ **(657)**

- sums of the squares of the residual variations

$S_{y.x} = S_1 + S_2 = S_y - S_3 = \mathbf{(653)} + \mathbf{(654)} = \mathbf{(656)} - \mathbf{(655)}$ **(658)**

- estimated variances

$s_1^2 = S_1/(n-k) = \mathbf{(653)}/(n-k) \quad [v = n-k]$ **(659)**
$s_2^2 = S_2/(k-2) = \mathbf{(654)}/(k-2) \quad [v = k-2]$ **(660)**
$s_3^2 = S_3 = \mathbf{(655)} \quad [v = 1]$ **(661)**
$s_y^2 = S_y/(n-1) = \mathbf{(656)}/(n-1) \quad [v = n-1]$ **(662)**
$s_{y.x}^2 = S_{y.x}/(n-2) = \mathbf{(658)}/(n-2) \quad [v = n-2]$ **(663)**

All values conform to the international convention (i.e. 0,1 instead of 0.1).

The equation of the regression line Y and the estimated variances $s_{b_{yx}}^2, s_{\bar{Y}|x}^2, s_{\bar{y}}^2, s_{a_{yx}}^2$ are obtained from **(635)**, **(641)**, **(642)**, **(643)** and **(644)** by replacing b_{yx} by **(652)**, $s_{y.x}^2$ by **(663)** and S_x by **(650)**.

Example 39. Given the sample:

x	7	8	9
y	1,0 1,4 2,0 2,2	2,0 2,5 2,8 3,1 3,7 4,0	2,9 3,2 3,4 3,9 4,4
$\bar{y}_i$ from **(646)** S_{y_i} from **(647)**	6,6/4 = 1,65 11,8 − 10,89 = 0,91	18,1/6 = 3,01$\dot{6}$ 57,39 − 54,601$\dot{6}$ = 2,788$\dot{3}$	17,8/5 = 3,56 64,78 − 63,368 = 1,412

From formula

(645i) $n = 15$
(648) $\bar{y} = 42{,}5/15 = 2{,}8\dot{3}$
(649) $\bar{x} = (28+48+45)/15 = 8{,}0\dot{6}$
(650) $S_x = (196+384+405) - (28+48+45)^2/15 = 8{,}9\dot{3}$
(651) $S_{xy} = 46{,}2 + 144{,}8 + 160{,}2 - 8{,}0\dot{6} \times 42{,}5 = 8{,}3\dot{6}$
(652) $b_{yx} = 8{,}3\dot{6}/8{,}9\dot{3} = 0{,}936\,567\,164\,1$
(653) $S_1 = 0{,}91 + 2{,}788\dot{3} + 1{,}412 = 5{,}110\dot{3}$
(654) $S_2 = 6{,}6^2/4 + 18{,}1^2/6 + 17{,}8^2/5 - 42{,}5^2/15 - S_3 = 0{,}607\,054\,727\,0$
(655) $S_3 = 0{,}936\,567\,164\,1 \times 8{,}3\dot{6} = 7{,}835\,945\,273$
(656) $S_y = 133{,}97 - 42{,}5^2/15 = 13{,}55\dot{3}$
(657) Check: $5{,}110\dot{3} + 0{,}607\,054\,727 + 7{,}835\,945\,273 = 13{,}55\dot{3}$
(658) $S_{y.x} = 5{,}110\dot{3} + 0{,}607\,055 = 5{,}717\,388$
(663) $s_{y.x}^2 = 5{,}717\,388/13 = 0{,}439\,799$; $s_{y.x} = 0{,}663\,173$
(641a) $s_{b_{yx}}^2 = 0{,}439\,799/8{,}9\dot{3} = 0{,}049\,231\,2$; $s_{b_{yx}} = 0{,}221\,881$
(635) $Y = 2{,}8\dot{3} + 0{,}936\,567\,(x - 8{,}0\dot{6}) = -4{,}721\,64 + 0{,}936\,567\,x$
(659) $s_1^2 = S_1/12 = 0{,}425\,861$
(660) $s_2^2 = S_2/1$
(661) $s_3^2 = S_3$

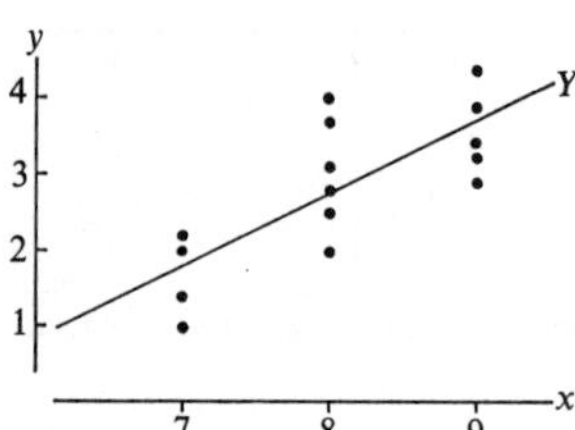

Fig. 38. Regression line of example 39.

18B. Testing the linearity of the regression function

With *ungrouped* samples, general departure from linearity of the regression function can be tested only by eye. The deviations $Y_i - y_i$ should give an impression of randomness and not show any systematic trend (cf. for example Fig. 29 [systematic deviations], on page 200, with Fig. 30b [apparently random deviations], on page 200). With *grouped* samples an exact test is possible, namely by comparing the variance of the column means about the regression line with the variance within the columns.

Test quotient:

$s_2^2/s_1^2 = \mathbf{(660)}/\mathbf{(659)}$
[significance limit F, $P = 2\,\alpha$, $v_2 = k-2$, $v_1 = n-k$: pages 38–49; v_1 of the table $= v_2$ of the test quotient] **(664)**

If the test quotient *attains* or *exceeds* the significance limit, then the regression function is quite possibly non-linear (significance probability $P = 2\,\alpha$).

If the test quotient is *smaller* than the significance limit, then in accordance with **(474)** it can be assumed that the regression is linear. Extrapolation of this interpretation beyond the range of variation of x in the samples should only be done with the greatest caution.

Example 40. In example 39, $s_1^2 = 0{,}425\,861$ and $s_2^2 = 0{,}607\,055$. From **(664)** the value of the test quotient is 1,4255, that of the significance limit $F(1;12)$ for $P = 0{,}05$ is 4,7472. The statistical test therefore does not reject the linearity of the regression function.

18C. Testing the regression coefficient against zero

If the linearity of the regression function is not rejected by the test **(664)**, the next step is to test the regression coefficient against zero, that is, to test the hypothesis $\boldsymbol{b}_{yx} = 0$. In other words, the estimate of the regression coefficient is tested for a significant difference from zero.

Test statistics:

$b_{yx}/s_{b_{yx}}$
[significance limit t, $2P = 2\alpha$, $\nu = n-2$: pages 30–33; b_{yx} from **(636)** or **(652)**; $s_{b_{yx}} = \sqrt{(\mathbf{641a})}$] **(665)**

or

$b_{yx}^2/s_{b_{yx}}^2 = b\,S_{xy}/s_{y.x}^2$
[significance limit $F(1;\nu_2)$, $P = 2\alpha$, $\nu_2 = n-2$: pages 38–49] (a)

or

$b\,S_{xy} - F(1;\nu_2)\,s_{y.x}^2$
[significance limit 0, $F(1;\nu_2)$ as in **(666**a)] (b) **(666)**

With ungrouped samples, $b\,S_{xy}$ is obtained from **(636)** and **(638)**, with grouped samples from **(655)**. $s_{y.x}^2$ is obtained from **(639)** or **(663)**

or

if the correlation coefficient r has been calculated (cf. section 19A, page 215), then when $\boldsymbol{r} = 0$, it follows that
$\boldsymbol{b}_{yx}$ (and $\boldsymbol{b}_{xy}) = 0$ **(667)**

and vice versa. The hypothesis $\boldsymbol{b}_{yx} = 0$ can be tested using r. Significance limit for $|r|$, see page 63 ($\nu = n-2$).

If any of the test statistics in **(665)** to **(667)** *attains* or *exceeds* the corresponding significance limit, then $\boldsymbol{b}_{yx}$ differs significantly from zero. The above tests are special cases of **(668**a) for $b_c = 0$.

18D. Tests on the regression parameters

All the differences specified are approximately *normally distributed.* For degrees of freedom over 200, the deviation $|c_\alpha|$ of the normal distribution (page 26) is therefore adopted as significance limit, for degrees of freedom up to 200 the deviation $t_{P=\alpha}$ or $t_{2P=2\alpha}$ of the Student distribution (pages 30–33).

Test quotients (absolute values should be used):

$(b_{yx} - b_c)/s_{b_{yx}}$ $[\nu = n-2;\ s_{b_{yx}} = \sqrt{(\mathbf{641})}]$ (a)
$(Y|x - Y_c|x)/s_{Y|x}$ $[\nu = n-2;\ s_{Y|x} = \sqrt{(\mathbf{642})}]$ (b)
$(\bar{y} - \mu_c)/s_{\bar{y}}$ $[\nu = n-2;\ s_{\bar{y}} = \sqrt{(\mathbf{643})}]$ (c)
$(a_{yx} - a_c)/s_{a_{yx}}$ $[\nu = n-2;\ s_{a_{yx}} = \sqrt{(\mathbf{644})}]$ (d) **(668)**

Example 41 [of **(668**a)]. Comparison between the regression coefficients of examples 29 (page 200) and 38 (page 211), which have the values 1,7123 and 1,8179 respectively. Since the former was not calculated from **(636)**, it will be considered here as a hypothetical value. The test quotient has the value

$$\frac{1{,}8179 - 1{,}7123}{0{,}043\,42} = 2{,}432 \quad [\nu = 7]$$

The corresponding significance limit $t_{2\alpha=0{,}05}$, page 30, is 2,3646. The two regression coefficients, and therefore the regression lines, thus differ significantly.

18E. Confidence and tolerance limits

Here only the formulae for the two-sided limits will be given, and these in the form of 'estimate $\pm G$' (estimate minus G = lower limit, estimate plus G = upper limit). The corresponding parameters are expected to be included between these two limits.

All values conform to the international convention (i.e. 0,1 instead of 0.1).

Confidence limits

For $\boldsymbol{b}_{yx}$:

$b_{yx} \pm t_{2\alpha}\,s_{b_{yx}}$ $[\nu = n-2 \leq 200;\ s_{b_{yx}} = \sqrt{(\mathbf{641})}]$
$b_{yx} \pm |c_\alpha|\,s_{b_{yx}}$ $[\nu = n-2 > 200;\ s_{b_{yx}} = \sqrt{(\mathbf{641})}]$ **(669)**

For $\boldsymbol{Y}|x$:

$\bar{y} + b_{yx}(x - \bar{x}) \pm t_{2\alpha}\,s_{Y|x}$ $[\nu = n-2 \leq 200;\ s_{Y|x} = \sqrt{(\mathbf{642})}]$
$\bar{y} + b_{yx}(x - \bar{x}) \pm |c_\alpha|\,s_{Y|x}$ $[\nu = n-2 > 200;\ s_{Y|x} = \sqrt{(\mathbf{642})}]$ **(670)**

For μ_y:

$\bar{y} \pm t_{2\alpha}\,s_{\bar{y}}$ $[\nu = n-2 \leq 200;\ s_{\bar{y}} = \sqrt{(\mathbf{643})}]$
$\bar{y} \pm |c_\alpha|\,s_{\bar{y}}$ $[\nu = n-2 > 200;\ s_{\bar{y}} = \sqrt{(\mathbf{643})}]$ **(671)**

For $\boldsymbol{a}_{yx}$:

$a_{yx} \pm t_{2\alpha}\,s_{a_{yx}}$ $[\nu = n-2 \leq 200;\ s_{a_{yx}} = \sqrt{(\mathbf{644})}]$
$a_{yx} \pm |c_\alpha|\,s_{a_{yx}}$ $[\nu = n-2 > 200;\ s_{a_{yx}} = \sqrt{(\mathbf{644})}]$ **(672)**

(670) is a hyperbola (cf. Fig. 39).

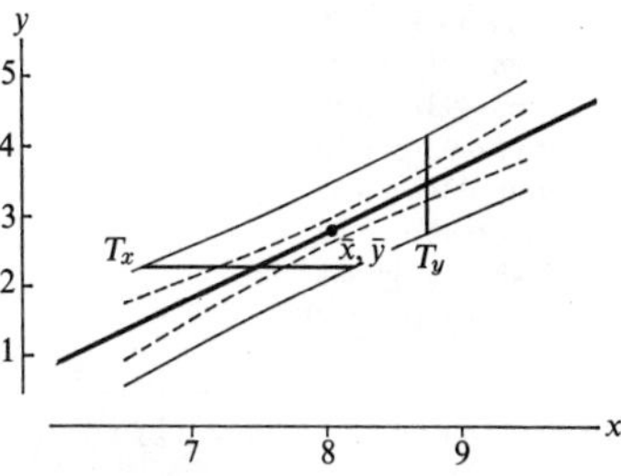

Fig. 39. Confidence and tolerance limits for the regression of Figure 38. - - - Confidence limits for $\boldsymbol{Y}$. —— Tolerance limits for $\boldsymbol{Y}$. T_y: Tolerance interval for $Y|x$. T_x: Tolerance interval for $X|y$.

Tolerance limits for $\boldsymbol{Y}|x$

$= \bar{y} + b_{yx}(x - \bar{x}) \pm t_{2\alpha}\,s_T$
$[\nu = n-2;\ b_{yx}$ from **(636)** or **(652)**] **(673)**

where

$s_T = s_{y.x}\sqrt{1 + 1/n + (x - \bar{x})^2/S_x}$ (a)
$\quad = s_{b_{yx}}\sqrt{(1 + 1/n)\,S_x + (x - \bar{x})^2}$ (b)
$[\nu = n-2;\ S_x$ from **(493)** or **(650)**; $s_{y.x} = \sqrt{(\mathbf{639})}$ or $\sqrt{(\mathbf{663})}$; $s_{b_{yx}} = \sqrt{(\mathbf{641a})}$; $\bar{x} =$ **(491)** or **(649)**] **(674)**

18F. Estimation of x when y is given

$$x|y = \bar{x} + \frac{y - \bar{y}}{b_{yx}} \qquad \mathbf{(675)}$$

Confidence limits for $x|y$ [solution from **(670)** for x]

$$\bar{x} + \frac{y - \bar{y}}{b_{yx}(1-k^2)} \pm \frac{k}{b_{yx}(1-k^2)}\sqrt{(1/n)\,b_{yx}^2(1-k^2)\,S_x + (y - \bar{y})^2} \qquad \mathbf{(676)}$$

where for ungrouped samples b_{yx} and S_x are obtained from **(636)** and **(493)**, for grouped samples from **(652)** and **(650)** and

$$k^2 = \frac{[F(1;\nu_2);\ P = 2\alpha]\,s_{b_{yx}}^2}{b_{yx}^2} \quad [\nu_2 = n-2;\ s_{b_{yx}}^2 \text{ from } \mathbf{(641)}] \qquad \mathbf{(677)}$$

If $k^2 \leq 0{,}05$, then $1 - k^2$ can be taken as 1 in **(676)**.

Tolerance limits for $x|y$ [solution from **(673)** for x]

(676) is used, but with $(1 + 1/n)$ in place of $1/n$ in the term under the root. **(678)**

Example 42. In example 38 (page 211), it is required to calculate x for $y = 5$ and the corresponding confidence and tolerance limits $x|y = 5$.

$$x = 7{,}4 + \frac{5 - 5{,}25\dot{7}}{1{,}81791\dot{6}} = 7{,}2582 \text{ from } \mathbf{(675)}$$

Confidence limits: k^2 is first calculated from **(677)** for $P = 0{,}05$, giving

$$k^2 = \frac{5{,}5914 \times 0{,}001\,885\,42}{1{,}81791\dot{6}^2} = 0{,}003\,190$$

$k = 0{,}05648$

k^2 is less than 0,05, so that $1-k^2$ can be taken as 1 in **(676)**. For purposes of comparison, however, **(676)** is calculated with both values:

	Confidence limits from **(676)**	Tolerance limits from **(678)**
$1-k^2=1$	7,2582 ± 0,0589 = 7,1993 to 7,3171	7,2582 ± 0,5534 = 6,7048 to 7,8116
$1-k^2=0{,}996810$	7,2577 ± 0,0590 = 7,1987 to 7,3167	7,2577 ± 0,5545 = 6,7032 to 7,8122

18G. Comparison of two regression lines of the first kind

Given are the following ungrouped and grouped samples

$(x, y)_1$ and $(x, y)_2$

with the pairs of observations

n_1	and n_2	pairs of observations
$\bar{x}_1$	and $\bar{x}_2$	from **(491)** or **(649)**
$\bar{y}_1$	and $\bar{y}_2$	from **(491)** or **(648)**
S_{x_1}	and S_{x_2}	from **(493)** or **(650)**
S_{y_1}	and S_{y_2}	from **(493)** or **(656)**
$(S_{xy})_1$	and $(S_{xy})_2$	from **(638)** or **(651)**
$(S_{y.x})_1$	and $(S_{y.x})_2$	from **(640)** or **(658)**
$(s^2_{y.x})_1$	and $(s^2_{y.x})_2$	from **(639)** or **(663)**
$(b_{yx})_1=b_1$	and $(b_{yx})_2=b_2$	from **(636)** or **(652)**
Y_1	and Y_2	from **(635)**

In analogy with section 16 (page 208), the following hypotheses must be considered in comparing two linear regressions:

$$(\sigma^2_{y.x})_1=(\sigma^2_{y.x})_2 \begin{cases} \boldsymbol{b}_1=\boldsymbol{b}_2 \begin{cases} \boldsymbol{Y}_1=\boldsymbol{Y}_2 \\ \boldsymbol{Y}_1\neq\boldsymbol{Y}_2 \end{cases} (a) \begin{cases}(a\ c)\\(a\ d)\end{cases} \\ \boldsymbol{b}_1\neq\boldsymbol{b}_2 \quad (b) \end{cases} \qquad (679)$$

$$(\sigma^2_{y.x})_1\neq(\sigma^2_{y.x})_2 \begin{cases} \boldsymbol{b}_1=\boldsymbol{b}_2 \begin{cases} \boldsymbol{Y}_1=\boldsymbol{Y}_2 \\ \boldsymbol{Y}_1\neq\boldsymbol{Y}_2 \end{cases} (a) \begin{cases}(a\ c)\\(a\ d)\end{cases} \\ \boldsymbol{b}_1\neq\boldsymbol{b}_2 \quad (b) \end{cases} \qquad (680)$$

The hypothesis $(\sigma^2_{y.x})_1=(\sigma^2_{y.x})_2$ is tested by means of the quotient

$$(s^2_{y.x})_1/(s^2_{y.x})_2 \qquad (681)$$

[significance limit F, $P=2\alpha$, $\nu_1=n_1-2$, $\nu_2=n_2-2$: pages 38–49]

where the *greater* of the variances is given the index 1.

If the test quotient **(681)** is *smaller* than the significance limit, then **(682)** to **(697)** are valid; if the quotient *attains* or *exceeds* the significance limit, then **(698)** to **(705)** are valid.
If the test quotient **(681)** is *smaller* than the significance limit, then it is reasonable to assume that $(\sigma^2_{y.x})_1=(\sigma^2_{y.x})_2$. The common residual variance $\bar{\sigma}^2_{y.x}$ of the two regression lines can then be estimated under the condition of **(679)** as

$$\bar{s}^2_{y.x}=\frac{(S_{y.x})_1+(S_{y.x})_2}{n_1+n_2-4} \quad [\nu=n_1+n_2-4] \qquad (682)$$

(682) is used to test the hypothesis **(679a)**, i.e., $\boldsymbol{b}_1=\boldsymbol{b}_2$. The test quotient for the difference between the two regression coefficients under the conditions of **(679)** is

$$\frac{b_1-b_2}{s_{D_b}} \quad [\text{significance limit } t;\ 2P=2\alpha;\ \nu=n_1+n_2-4] \qquad (683)$$

$$\text{where } s^2_{D_b}=(682)\times\left(\frac{1}{S_{x_1}}+\frac{1}{S_{x_2}}\right) \qquad (684)$$

If the test quotient **(683)** is *smaller* than the significance limit, then **(685)** to **(697)** are valid. If the quotient *attains* or *exceeds* the significance limit, then the regression lines are not parallel, i.e., $\boldsymbol{b}_1\neq\boldsymbol{b}_2$. In other words:

If the test quotient **(683)** is *smaller* than the significance limit, then the two regression lines may be regarded as *parallel*. **(685)**

The estimate of the common residual variance $\bar{\sigma}^2_{y.x}$ when the conditions of **(679a)** are fulfilled is

$$\bar{s}^2_{y.x}\approx(682) \quad [\nu=n_1+n_2-4]$$
$$=\frac{(S_{y.x})_1+(S_{y.x})_2+\dfrac{(b_1-b_2)^2}{1/S_{x_1}+1/S_{x_2}}}{n_1+n_2-3} \quad [\nu=n_1+n_2-3] \qquad (686)$$

The estimate $\bar{b}_{yx}$ of the common regression coefficient $\boldsymbol{b}_{yx}$ when the conditions of **(679a)** are fulfilled is

$$\bar{b}_{yx}=\frac{(S_{xy})_1+(S_{xy})_2}{S_{x_1}+S_{x_2}} \qquad (687)$$

The estimate $s^2_{\bar{b}_{yx}}$ of the variance $\sigma^2_{\bar{b}_{yx}}$ of the common regression coefficient when the conditions of **(679a)** are fulfilled is

$$s^2_{\bar{b}_{yx}}\approx\frac{(682)}{S_{x_1}+S_{x_2}} \quad [\nu=n_1+n_2-4] \qquad (a)$$
$$=\frac{(686)}{S_{x_1}+S_{x_2}} \quad [\nu=n_1+n_2-3] \qquad (b) \qquad (688)$$

The two lines may be considered as *identical* [hypothesis **(679a c)**] when the test quotient

$$\frac{\hat{b}-\bar{b}}{s_{\hat{b}-\bar{b}}} \qquad (689)$$

[$\nu=n_1+n_2-4$, when $s_{\hat{b}-\bar{b}}=\sqrt{(691a)}$; $\nu=n_1+n_2-3$, when $s_{\hat{b}-\bar{b}}=\sqrt{(691b)}$; $\hat{b}$ from **(690)**; $\bar{b}$ from **(687)**]

is *smaller* than the significance limit t ($2P=2\alpha$, pages 30–33).

$$\hat{b}=\frac{\bar{y}_1-\bar{y}_2}{\bar{x}_1-\bar{x}_2} \qquad (690)$$

$$s^2_{\hat{b}-\bar{b}}\approx(682)\times K \quad [K \text{ from } (692)] \qquad (a)$$
$$=(686)\times K \qquad (b) \qquad (691)$$

$$K=\frac{1}{(\bar{x}_1-\bar{x}_2)^2}\left(\frac{1}{n_1}+\frac{1}{n_2}\right)+\frac{1}{S_{x_1}+S_{x_2}} \qquad (692)$$

The two parallel regression lines do not coincide [hypothesis **(679a d)**] when the test quotient **(689)** *attains* or *exceeds* the significance limit. In this case the vertical and horizontal distances p_y and p_x are often of interest.
The estimate p_y of the *vertical distance* $\boldsymbol{p}_{Y|x}$ and its confidence limits, when the conditions of **(679a d)** are fulfilled, are

$$p_y=|\bar{y}_1-\bar{y}_2-\bar{b}_{yx}(\bar{x}_1-\bar{x}_2)| \quad [\bar{b}_{yx} \text{ from } (687)] \qquad (693)$$

Confidence limits for $\boldsymbol{p}_{Y|x}$

$$\approx(693)\pm t_{2\alpha}\sqrt{(688a)\times[(1/n_1+1/n_2)(S_{x_1}+S_{x_2})+(\bar{x}_1-\bar{x}_2)^2]} \quad [\nu=n_1+n_2-4] \qquad (a)$$
$$=(693)\pm t_{2\alpha}\sqrt{(688b)\times[(1/n_1+1/n_2)(S_{x_1}+S_{x_2})+(\bar{x}_1-\bar{x}_2)^2]} \quad [\nu=n_1+n_2-3] \qquad (b) \qquad (694)$$

The estimate p_x of the *horizontal distance* $\boldsymbol{p}_x$ and its confidence limits, when the conditions of **(679a d)** are fulfilled, are

$$p_x=\left|\bar{x}_1-\bar{x}_2-\frac{\bar{y}_1-\bar{y}_2}{\bar{b}_{yx}}\right| \quad [\bar{b}_{yx} \text{ from } (687)] \qquad (695)$$

Confidence limits for $\boldsymbol{p}_x$

$$\approx \text{or} = \left|\bar{x}_1-\bar{x}_2-\frac{\bar{y}_1-\bar{y}_2}{\bar{b}_{yx}(1-k^2)}\right|\pm\frac{k}{\bar{b}_{yx}(1-k^2)}\times$$
$$\times\sqrt{(1/n_1+1/n_2)(\bar{b}_{yx})^2(1-k^2)(S_{x_1}+S_{x_2})+(\bar{y}_1-\bar{y}_2)^2} \qquad (696)$$

where $\bar{b}_{yx}=(687)$ and either $k=k_1=(697a)$ or $k=k_2=(697b)$. The approximation sign is for $k=k_1$, the equality sign for $k=k_2$.

$$k_1^2=\frac{[F(1;\nu_2);\ P=2\alpha]\ s^2_{\bar{b}_{yx}}}{(\bar{b}_{yx})^2} \quad [\nu_2=n_1+n_2-4;\ s^2_{\bar{b}_{yx}} \text{ from } (688a)] \qquad (a)$$
$$k_2^2=\frac{[F(1;\nu_2);\ P=2\alpha]\ s^2_{\bar{b}_{yx}}}{(\bar{b}_{yx})^2} \quad [\nu_2=n_1+n_2-3;\ s^2_{\bar{b}_{yx}} \text{ from } (688b)] \qquad (b) \qquad (697)$$

When $k\leq 0{,}05$, the term $1-k^2$ in **(696)** can be taken as 1.

If the test quotient **(681)** *attains* or *exceeds* the significance limit, then hypothesis **(680)** is valid, that is to say, $(\sigma^2_{y.x})_1\neq(\sigma^2_{y.x})_2$.

Hypothesis **(680a)**, that $\boldsymbol{b}_1=\boldsymbol{b}_2$, is then tested by means of the quotient **(683)**, where

$$s^2_{D_b}=\frac{(s^2_{y.x})_1}{S_{x_1}}+\frac{(s^2_{y.x})_2}{S_{x_2}} \qquad (a) \qquad (698)$$

All values conform to the international convention (i.e. 0,1 instead of 0.1).

Degrees of freedom $v = $ (**621**b) with

$$k = \frac{(s^2_{y.x})_1 S_{x_2}}{(s^2_{y.x})_1 S_{x_2} + (s^2_{y.x})_2 S_{x_1}} \quad \text{(b)} \quad \textbf{(698)}$$

[significance limit $t_{2\alpha}$, with v from (**621**b) and k from (**698**b)]

If the test quotient (**683**) using (**698**a) is *smaller* than the significance limit, then it can be assumed that $\boldsymbol{b}_1 = \boldsymbol{b}_2$. An estimate of the common regression coefficient is then

$$\bar{b}_{yx} = \frac{(S_{xy})_1/(s^2_{y.x})_1 + (S_{xy})_2/(s^2_{y.x})_2}{S_{x_1}/(s^2_{y.x})_1 + S_{x_2}/(s^2_{y.x})_2} \quad \textbf{(699)}$$

with the estimated variance

$$s^2_{\bar{b}_{yx}} = \frac{1}{S_{x_1}/(s^2_{y.x})_1 + S_{x_2}/(s^2_{y.x})_2} \quad \textbf{(700)}$$

Provided that the sample sizes n_1 and n_2 are *large*, the hypothesis [**680** (a c)] that the two parallel regression lines are *identical* can be tested approximately by means of the quotient (**689**), where

$$\hat{b} = \textbf{(690)}$$

$$s^2_{\hat{b}-\bar{b}} = \frac{1}{(\bar{x}_1 - \bar{x}_2)^2}\left(\frac{(s^2_{y.x})_1}{n_1} + \frac{(s^2_{y.x})_2}{n_2} + \textbf{(700)}\right) \quad \textbf{(701)}$$

[significance limit $|c_\alpha|$: page 26]

If the test quotient (**689**) using (**701**) *attains* or *exceeds* the significance limit, then the two parallel regression lines probably do *not* coincide. In this case, when the conditions of [**680** (a d)] are fulfilled,

- the *vertical* distance is estimated by

$$p_y = \textbf{(693)} \quad [\bar{b}_{yx} \text{ from } \textbf{(699)}] \quad \textbf{(702)}$$

- with confidence limits

$$\approx \textbf{(702)} \pm |c_\alpha| \times \sqrt{\frac{(s^2_{y.x})_1}{n_1} + \frac{(s^2_{y.x})_2}{n_2} + (\bar{x}_1 - \bar{x}_2)^2 \times \textbf{(700)}} \quad \textbf{(703)}$$

- the *horizontal* distance is estimated by

$$p_x = \textbf{(695)} \quad [\bar{b}_{yx} \text{ from } \textbf{(699)}] \quad \textbf{(704)}$$

- with confidence limits

$$\approx \left|\bar{x}_1 - \bar{x}_2 - \frac{\bar{y}_1 - \bar{y}_2}{\bar{b}_{yx}(1-k^2)}\right| \pm \frac{k}{\bar{b}_{yx}(1-k^2)} \times \sqrt{\left(\frac{(s^2_{y.x})_1}{n_1} + \frac{(s^2_{y.x})_2}{n_2}\right)\frac{(\bar{b}_{yx})^2(1-k^2)}{\textbf{(700)}} + (\bar{y}_1 - \bar{y}_2)^2} \quad \textbf{(705)}$$

[$k^2 = c^2_\alpha \times \textbf{(700)}/(\bar{b}_{yx})^2$, c_α: page 26; $c^2_\alpha = \chi^2, v = 1, 1\, \int_r = 2\alpha$: pages 34–37; $\bar{b}_{yx}$ from (**699**)]

When $k \leq 0{,}05$, the term $1 - k^2$ in (**705**) can be taken as 1.

Probit and logit regressions

With appropriate modifications, many of the formulae given in section 18 can be applied to probit and logit regressions. For further details the reader is referred to the literature.

Probit regression[12, 13, 26], tables on pages 68 and 69
Logit regression[27], tables on pages 70 and 71

19. The bivariate normal distribution: Regressions of the second kind

(cf. introduction to section 18, page 210)

Given are n pairs of observations x, y. Both x and y are *random*, normally distributed variables.

Regressions of the second kind are distinguished from those of the first kind by the existence of *two* regression lines

$$Y = \bar{y} + b_{yx}(x - \bar{x}) \quad \text{(a)}$$
$$X = \bar{x} + b_{xy}(y - \bar{y}) \quad \text{(b)} \quad \textbf{(706)}$$

In regressions of the first kind, inferences both from x to y and from y to x are made on the basis of (**706**a) = (**635**), while in regressions of the second kind they are made from x to y on the basis of (**706**a) and from y to x on the basis of (**706**b).

Estimates of the parameters of (**706**) and their variances are made by means of the appropriate formulae in section 18 (page 210). In estimating the parameters of (**706**b), x and y in these formulae must be transposed.

All values conform to the international convention (i.e. 0,1 instead of 0.1).

19A. The correlation coefficient

A further parameter of regressions of the second kind is the correlation coefficient $\boldsymbol{r}$, a measure of the stochastic dependence of the two variables x and y. Its value can lie between -1 and $+1$. If it amounts to either -1 or $+1$, the two variables are totally dependent upon one another, and the two regression lines Y and X coincide. If its value is zero, the variables are independent of one another, and the two regression lines Y and X are at right angles to one another and parallel to the coordinate axes. The remarks in (**361**) apply here too to the expressions 'dependent' and 'independent', so that a realistic interpretation of the correlation coefficient is often difficult or even impossible.

When the correlation coefficient is less than, equal to, or greater than zero, the two regression coefficients b_{yx} and b_{xy} are likewise less than, equal to, or greater than zero. **(707)**

The following relationships are valid for the correlation coefficient

$$\boldsymbol{r} = \frac{\sigma_{xy}}{\sigma_x \sigma_y} \quad \text{(a)}$$

and for its estimate

$$r = \frac{s_{xy}}{s_x s_y} = \frac{S_{xy}}{\sqrt{S_x S_y}} \quad \text{(b)} \quad \textbf{(708)}$$

[S_x and S_y from (**493**), S_{xy} from (**638**)]

The square of the correlation coefficient r^2 is also known as the coefficient (or index) of determination.

From (**708**b) it follows that

$$r = \sqrt{\frac{s_{xy}}{s^2_x} \times \frac{s_{xy}}{s^2_y}} = \sqrt{b_{yx} \times b_{xy}} \quad \textbf{(709)}$$

From (**115**) it therefore follows that the correlation coefficient is also the *geometrical mean* of the two regression coefficients b_{yx} and b_{xy}. Under the hypothesis $\boldsymbol{r} = 0$ when $n \to \infty$, the distribution of the correlation coefficient is asymptotically related to the Student distribution. On the other hand,

$$r\sqrt{\frac{n-2}{1-r^2}}$$

has a distribution of exact Student type with $v = n - 2$ degrees of freedom. The hypothesis can therefore be tested by means of the quotient

$$\frac{|r|}{s_r} \quad [\text{significance limit } t_{2\alpha} \text{ for } n \leq 202] \quad \text{(a)}; \quad [\text{significance limit } |c_\alpha| \text{ for } n > 202] \quad \text{(b)} \quad \textbf{(710)}$$

where

$$s^2_r = \frac{1-r^2}{n-2} \quad [v = n-2; \text{ for } n \leq 202] \quad \text{(a)}$$
$$= \frac{1-r^2}{n-1} \quad [\text{for } n > 202] \quad \text{(b)} \quad \textbf{(711)}$$

(**710**) does not need to be calculated for $v \leq 200$ since the significance limits for r can be taken directly from the table on page 63. They are based on the following formula identical with (**710**a):

$$|r| = \frac{t_{2\alpha}}{\sqrt{v + t^2_{2\alpha}}} \quad [v = n-2] \quad \textbf{(712)}$$

If the test statistics from (**710**) or (**712**) are *smaller* than the corresponding significance limits, then it can be assumed that the correlation coefficient, and in accordance with (**707**) also the two regression coefficients b_{yx} and b_{xy}, do *not* differ from zero.

If the test statistics from (**710**) or (**712**) *attain* or *exceed* the corresponding significance limits, then the correlation coefficient and the two regression coefficients *differ* significantly from zero. If $\boldsymbol{r} \neq 0$, then the distribution of the sample correlation coefficient r is complicated in form. However, its distribution can be approximately normalized by means of R. A. Fisher's z-transformation, as follows:

$$z = \tanh^{-1} r = \tfrac{1}{2} \ln \frac{1+r}{1-r} \quad \text{(a)}$$

and

$$r = \tanh z = \frac{e^{2z} - 1}{e^{2z} + 1} \quad \text{(b)} \quad \textbf{(713)}$$

Cf. also Hyperbolic functions, page 176. Tables for (**713**a) are to be found on page 64 and for (**713**b) on pages 66 and 67.

The variance of z is

$$\sigma_z^2 = \frac{1}{n-3} \quad \text{[cf. also page 64]} \tag{714}$$

The expectation $\boldsymbol{z}$ of z is

$$\boldsymbol{z} \approx \tanh^{-1}\boldsymbol{r} \quad (a)$$
$$= \frac{\boldsymbol{r}}{2(n-1)} + \tanh^{-1}\boldsymbol{r} \quad (b) \tag{715}$$

(**715**b) can as a rule be ignored (see below).
The following is derived from (**713**) to (**715**):

Testing the hypothesis $\boldsymbol{r} = r_0$

Test quotient

$$\frac{|z-z_0|}{\sigma_z} = |z-z_0|\sqrt{n-3} \tag{716}$$

[significance limit $|c_\alpha|$: page 26, or $c_{2\alpha}$: page 29, lower table; z from (**713**a)]

If the test quotient (**716**) is *smaller* than the significance limit, then there is no evidence that the population correlation coefficient differs from r_0.

Confidence limits for $\boldsymbol{r}$

$$\text{Prob}\left[\tanh\left(z - \frac{|c_\alpha|}{\sqrt{n-3}}\right) \le \boldsymbol{r} \le \tanh\left(z + \frac{|c_\alpha|}{\sqrt{n-3}}\right)\right] \approx 1-2\alpha \tag{717}$$

[values for $|c_\alpha|/\sqrt{n-3}$ for $1-2\alpha = 0{,}95$ and $0{,}99$ are given on page 65]

Comparison of two correlation coefficients $\boldsymbol{r}_1$ and $\boldsymbol{r}_2$

Testing the hypothesis $\boldsymbol{r}_1 = \boldsymbol{r}_2$ on the basis of the estimates r_1 and r_2 is effected by means of the following quotient:

$$\frac{|z_1 - z_2|}{\sqrt{\dfrac{1}{n_1-3} + \dfrac{1}{n_2-3}}} \tag{718}$$

[significance limit $|c_\alpha|$, p. 26, or $c_{2\alpha}$, p. 29, lower table]

If the test quotient (**718**) is *smaller* than the significance limit, then it can be assumed that $\boldsymbol{r}_1 = \boldsymbol{r}_2$. The estimate of the common correlation coefficient is then

$$\bar{r} = \tanh\bar{z} = \tanh\frac{(n_1-3)z_1 + (n_2-3)z_2}{n_1+n_2-6} \tag{719}$$

and

$$\sigma_{\bar{z}}^2 = \frac{1}{n_1+n_2-6} \tag{720}$$

The confidence limits for the common correlation coefficient are

$$\text{Prob}[\tanh(\bar{z} - |c_\alpha|\,\sigma_{\bar{z}}) \le \bar{\boldsymbol{r}} \le \tanh(\bar{z} + |c_\alpha|\,\sigma_{\bar{z}})] = 1-2\alpha \tag{721}$$

$[\sigma_{\bar{z}} = \sqrt{(\mathbf{720})}]$

Comparison of several correlation coefficients

Given are k estimates $r_1, r_2, \ldots, r_i, \ldots, r_k$ from k bivariate samples of sizes $n_1, n_2, \ldots, n_i, \ldots, n_k$ respectively.
Testing the hypothesis $\boldsymbol{r}_1 = \boldsymbol{r}_2 = \cdots = \boldsymbol{r}_k = r_0$, where r_0 is a hypothetical known value, is effected by means of the test statistic

$$\sum_1^k (n_i-3)(z_i-z_0)^2 \tag{722}$$

[significance limit χ^2, 1 $\int_r = 2\alpha$, $\nu = k$: pages 34–37; z_i from (**713**a)]

Testing the hypothesis $\boldsymbol{r}_1 = \boldsymbol{r}_2 = \cdots = \boldsymbol{r}_k\ (= \bar{\boldsymbol{r}})$ is effected by means of the test statistic

$$\sum_1^k (n_i-3)(z_i-\bar{z})^2 \tag{723}$$

[significance limit χ^2, 1 $\int_r = 2\alpha$, $\nu = k-1$: pages 34–37]

where

$$\bar{z} = \frac{\sum_1^k (n_i-3)\,z_i}{\sum_1^k (n_i-3)} \tag{724}$$

with variance

$$\sigma_{\bar{z}}^2 = \frac{1}{\sum_1^k (n_i-3)} \tag{725}$$

If the test statistic (**725**) is *smaller* than the significance limit, then it can be assumed that $\boldsymbol{r}_1 = \boldsymbol{r}_2 = \cdots = \boldsymbol{r}_k\ (= \bar{\boldsymbol{r}})$. The estimate $\bar{r}$ of the common correlation coefficient $\bar{\boldsymbol{r}}$ is then approximately

$$\bar{r} \approx \tanh(\bar{z} - a\tanh\bar{z}) \tag{726}$$

where $\bar{z}$ is from (**724**) and

$$a = \frac{\sum_1^k (n_i-3)/(n_i-1)}{2\sum_1^k (n_i-3)} \tag{727}$$

The *confidence limits* for the common correlation coefficient $\bar{\boldsymbol{r}}$ are then approximately

$$\text{Prob}[\tanh(\bar{z} - a\tanh\bar{z} - |c_\alpha|\,\sigma_{\bar{z}}) \le \bar{\boldsymbol{r}} \le \tanh(\bar{z} - a\tanh\bar{z} + |c_\alpha|\,\sigma_{\bar{z}})] \approx 1-2\alpha \tag{728}$$

[$\bar{z}$ from (**724**); a from (**727**); $\sigma_{\bar{z}} = \sqrt{(\mathbf{725})}$; significance limit $|c_\alpha|$: page 26]

Example 43. Given $r = 0{,}3223$, $n = 34$. Does $\boldsymbol{r}$ differ from zero ($2\alpha = 0{,}05$)? Since $\nu = 32$ and the corresponding limit (page 63) is 0,3388, the hypothesis $\boldsymbol{r} = 0$ cannot be rejected.

Example 44. Given $r = 0{,}613$, $n = 42$. Required are the 95% confidence limits for $\boldsymbol{r}$:

$z = 0{,}71371$ (page 64)
$|c_\alpha|\,\sigma_z = 0{,}31385$ (page 65)
$z \pm |c_\alpha|\,\sigma_z = 0{,}400$ to $1{,}027$

whence

$\text{Prob}(\underbrace{0{,}380}_{\text{page 66}} \le \boldsymbol{r} \le \underbrace{0{,}773}_{\text{page 66}}) = 0{,}95$

Example 45

Given are		whence are obtained		
r_i	n_i	z_i	n_i-3	n_i-1
0,555	12	0,62558	9	11
0,590	20	0,67767	17	19
0,670	15	0,81074	12	14
0,621	9	0,72663	6	8
0,733	26	0,93518	23	25
0,800	13	1,09861	10	12
		page 64		

$\bar{z} = 63{,}73451/77 = 0{,}828$ from (**724**); $\tanh\bar{z} = 0{,}6794$ (page 66)
$\chi^2 = 1{,}815$; $\nu = 6-1 = 5$ from (**723**)

The 0,05 significance limit for χ^2, $\nu = 5$, is 11,07 (page 34), whence it follows that the hypothesis $\boldsymbol{r}_1 = \boldsymbol{r}_2 = \cdots = \boldsymbol{r}_k\ (= \bar{\boldsymbol{r}})$ cannot be rejected.

$a = 5{,}073395/154 = 0{,}0329441$ from (**727**)
$\bar{r} = \tanh(0{,}828 - 0{,}0329 \times 0{,}6794) = \tanh 0{,}806 = 0{,}667$ (page 66) from (**726**)
$\sigma_{\bar{z}}^2 = 1/77 = 0{,}012987$; $\sigma_{\bar{z}} = 0{,}11396$ from (**725**)

For $2\alpha = 0{,}05$, $|c_\alpha| = 1{,}96$ (page 26). It follows that $|c_\alpha|\,\sigma_{\bar{z}} = 0{,}223$ and that the 95% confidence limits for $\bar{\boldsymbol{r}}$ from (**728**) are

$\underbrace{\tanh(0{,}806 - 0{,}223)}_{= 0{,}525\ \text{(page 66)}} \le \bar{\boldsymbol{r}} \le \underbrace{\tanh(0{,}806 + 0{,}223)}_{= 0{,}774\ \text{(page 66)}}$

19B. Significance tests (for significance tests with correlation coefficients see section 19A, page 215)

It will be seen that for comparisons of a *single* estimate with a *hypothetical* value the appropriate formulae for a regression of the first kind are valid also for a regression of the second kind. However, when two estimates from two different *samples* [as for example with $(b_{yx})_1-(b_{yx})_2$] are to be compared, then the formulae for a regression of the first kind are no longer valid, although for *high values* of n they are approximately so.

Comparisons between estimates and hypothetical values are made by means of the following test quotients:

Estimate	Hypothetical value	Test quotient
b_{yx}	0	(710) to (712) on the basis of (707)
b_{xy}	0	
b_{yx}	b_c	(668a)
b_{xy}	b_c	(668a)*
$Y\vert x$	$Y_c\vert x$	(668b)
$X\vert y$	$X_c\vert y$	(668b)*
$\bar{y}$	μ_c	(668c)
$\bar{x}$	μ_c	(668c)*
a_{yx}	a_c	(668d)
a_{xy}	a_c	(668d)*

* With x and y transposed.

(729)

Comparison of μ_y with μ_x, that is to say, testing the hypothesis $\mu_y=\mu_x$, is made by means of the test quotient

$$\frac{(\bar{y}-\bar{x})\sqrt{n}}{\sqrt{s_y^2+s_x^2-2s_{xy}}} \qquad (730)$$

[significance limit t, $2P=2\alpha$, $\nu=n-1$: pages 30–33; s_y^2 and s_x^2 from **(492)**, s_{xy} from **(637)**]

Simultaneous comparison of μ_y with μ_{c1} *and* of μ_x with μ_{c2}, that is to say, testing the hypothesis $\mu_y=\mu_{c1}|\mu_x=\mu_{c2}$, is made by means of the test statistic

$$\frac{n(n-2)}{2(1-r^2)}\times\left(\frac{(\bar{x}-\mu_{c2})^2}{S_x}+\frac{(\bar{y}-\mu_{c1})^2}{S_y}-\frac{2S_{xy}(\bar{x}-\mu_{c2})(\bar{y}-\mu_{c1})}{S_xS_y}\right) \qquad (731)$$

[significance limit F, $P=\alpha$, $\nu_1=2$, $\nu_2=n-2$: pages 38–49; S_x and S_y are from **(493)**, S_{xy} from **(638)**, r from **(708)**. Calculation is facilitated by using the relationship $r^2=(S_{xy}/S_xS_y)\times S_{xy}$]

Comparison of a bivariate sample having means $\bar{y}$ and $\bar{x}$ with an *independent* pair of observations x, y, that is to say, testing the hypothesis that (x, y) come from the same (normal) population $(\bar{x}, \bar{y})$, is made by means of the test statistic

$$\frac{n(n-2)}{2(n+1)(1-r^2)}\times\left(\frac{(x-\bar{x})^2}{S_x}+\frac{(y-\bar{y})^2}{S_y}-\frac{2S_{xy}(x-\bar{x})(y-\bar{y})}{S_xS_y}\right) \qquad (732)$$

[significance limits, degrees of freedom, etc. are all as in **(731)**; **(732)** is a special case of **(733)** with $n_1=1$]

Simultaneous comparison of the means of *two* bivariate samples $(x, y)_1$ and $(x, y)_2$, that is to say, testing the hypothesis $(\mu_{y_1}=\mu_{y_2}|\mu_{x_1}=\mu_{x_2})$, is made by means of the following test statistic *when* $\sigma_{y_1}^2=\sigma_{y_2}^2$, $\sigma_{x_1}^2=\sigma_{x_2}^2$, $\boldsymbol{r}_1=\boldsymbol{r}_2$,

$$\frac{n_1n_2(n_1+n_2-3)}{2(n_1+n_2)(1-r^2)}\times\left(\frac{(\bar{x}_1-\bar{x}_2)^2}{S_{x_1}+S_{x_2}}+\frac{(\bar{y}_1-\bar{y}_2)^2}{S_{y_1}+S_{y_2}}-\frac{2[(S_{xy})_1+(S_{xy})_2](\bar{x}_1-\bar{x}_2)(\bar{y}_1-\bar{y}_2)}{(S_{x_1}+S_{x_2})(S_{y_1}+S_{y_2})}\right) \qquad (733)$$

where

$$r^2=\frac{[(S_{xy})_1+(S_{xy})_2]^2}{(S_{x_1}+S_{x_2})(S_{y_1}+S_{y_2})} \qquad (734)$$

[significance limit F, $P=\alpha$, $\nu_1=2$, $\nu_2=n_1+n_2-3$: pages 38–49; otherwise as in **(731)**]

Approximate tests, preliminary to **(733)**, can be made as follows:

Testing the hypothesis $\sigma_{x_1}^2=\sigma_{x_2}^2$ and $\sigma_{y_1}^2=\sigma_{y_2}^2$ from **(609)**

Testing the hypothesis $\boldsymbol{r}_1=\boldsymbol{r}_2$ from **(718)**

For further discussion of tests of the above hypotheses see PEARSON and WILKS[28].

19C. Confidence and tolerance limits

$100(1-\alpha)\%$ confidence and tolerance limits are calculated by means of the formulae below on the basis of the estimates $\bar{x}, \bar{y}, S_x, S_y, S_{xy}$ from a two-dimensional sample. b_{yx} and $s_{b_{yx}}$ are obtained from **(636)** and **(641)**, b_{xy} and $s_{b_{xy}}$ likewise but with x and y transposed. Degrees of freedom of F: $\nu_1=2$, $\nu_2=n-2$; $1-\alpha=1-P$ (pages 38–49).

Confidence limits

$$\mu_y|\mu_x=\bar{y}+b_{yx}(\mu_x-\bar{x})\pm s_{b_{yx}}\sqrt{2FS_x/n-(n-2)(\mu_x-\bar{x})^2} \qquad (735a)$$

$$\mu_x|\mu_y=\bar{x}+b_{xy}(\mu_y-\bar{y})\pm s_{b_{xy}}\sqrt{2FS_y/n-(n-2)(\mu_y-\bar{y})^2} \qquad (735b)$$

(735a) and **(735b)** are identical *confidence ellipses.*

Tolerance limits

$$\boldsymbol{Y}|x=\bar{y}+b_{yx}(x-\bar{x})\pm s_{b_{yx}}\sqrt{2(n+1)FS_x/n-(n-2)(x-\bar{x})^2} \qquad \text{(a)}$$

$$\boldsymbol{X}|y=\bar{x}+b_{xy}(y-\bar{y})\pm s_{b_{xy}}\sqrt{2(n+1)FS_y/n-(n-2)(y-\bar{y})^2} \qquad \text{(b)}$$

(736)

(736a) and **(736b)** are identical *tolerance ellipses* (see below).

The slopes of the main axes X_0, Y_0 of the ellipses defined by **(735)** *and* **(736)** *respectively*, the so-called *orthogonal* regression coefficients, are

$$b_0, -\frac{1}{b_0}=\frac{S_y-S_x}{2S_{xy}}\pm\sqrt{1+\left(\frac{S_y-S_x}{2S_{xy}}\right)^2} \qquad (737)$$

The lengths of the semi-axes of the ellipses of **(735)** *and* **(736)** *are*

$$l_1, l_2=\sqrt{k}\sqrt{S_x+S_y\pm\sqrt{(S_x+S_y)^2-4(S_xS_y-S_{xy}^2)}} \qquad (738)$$

where

$$k=\frac{F}{n(n-2)} \quad \text{for confidence ellipse (735)} \qquad \text{(a)}$$

$$k=\frac{F(n+1)}{n(n-2)} \quad \text{for tolerance ellipse (736)} \qquad \text{(b)}$$

(739)

Construction of ellipses

Rapid method: Calculation from **(737)** and **(738)** and construction from **(315)**.

Exact method: From **(735)** or **(736a)** and/or **(736b)** in conjunction with **(737)** and **(738)**, according to the accuracy required.

The equations of tangents to the confidence or tolerance ellipses parallel to the coordinate axes are:

- horizontal tangents: $y=\bar{y}\pm\sqrt{kS_y}$
- abscissae of the points of contact: $x=\bar{x}\pm b_{xy}\sqrt{kS_y}$ (a)
- vertical tangents: $x=\bar{x}\pm\sqrt{kS_x}$
- ordinates of the points of contact: $y=\bar{y}\pm b_{yx}\sqrt{kS_x}$ (b)

(740)

where

$$k=\frac{2F}{n(n-2)} \quad \text{for confidence ellipse (735)} \qquad \text{(a)}$$

$$k=\frac{2F(n+1)}{n(n-2)} \quad \text{for tolerance ellipse (736)} \qquad \text{(b)}$$

(741)

The lengths of the sides of the rectangle formed by these tangents which circumscribes the ellipse are:

- horizontal sides $\quad l_h=2\sqrt{kS_x}$ (a)
- vertical sides $\quad l_v=2\sqrt{kS_y}$ (b)

[k from **(741)**] (742)

Example 46. Given the bivariate sample:

x	y	x	y	x	y	x	y	x	y
2,6	2,3	3,8	4,5	5,5	4,5	6,5	8,0	8,0	6,5
3,0	3,5	4,2	2,7	5,7	5,7	7,0	6,0	8,0	7,0
3,0	4,0	4,5	5,5	6,0	5,2	7,0	7,0	8,0	8,0
3,5	3,5	4,7	5,7	6,5	6,0	7,5	7,7	10,0	8,0

(a) The parameters are estimated.
(b) Using the formulae for the regression lines Y and X, for the orthogonal regression lines Y_0 and X_0, for the tolerance ellipse for $\boldsymbol{Y}|x$

or $\mathbf{X}|y$, and for the horizontal and vertical tangents to the latter, the lengths of the sides of the rectangle formed by the tangents and the lengths of the semi-axes of the ellipse are calculated.

(c) For purposes of comparison, the tolerance limits for $\mathbf{Y}|x$ and $\mathbf{X}|y$ are calculated using the appropriate formulae for a regression of the first kind.

(d) A comparison is made of the tolerance limits for $\mathbf{Y}|x$ and $\mathbf{X}|y$ of regressions of the second and first kind with $x=\bar{x}$ and $y=\bar{y}$.

(e) $\bar{x}$ and $\bar{y}$ are compared.

(a) Estimates of *parameters*

$\bar{x} = 115{,}0/20 = 5{,}75$ $\quad$ $\bar{y} = 111{,}3/20 = 5{,}565$

$S_x = 740{,}92 - 5{,}75 \times 115 = 79{,}67$ $\quad$ $S_y = 679{,}39 - 5{,}565 \times 111{,}3 = 60{,}005\,5$

$s_x^2 = 79{,}67/19 = 4{,}193\,158$ $\quad$ $s_y^2 = 60{,}005\,5/19 = 3{,}158\,184$

$s_x = 2{,}047\,720$ $\quad$ $s_y = 1{,}777\,128$

$S_{xy} = 700{,}90 - 5{,}75 \times 111{,}3 = 60{,}925$ from (**638**)

$s_{xy} = 60{,}925/19 = 3{,}206\,579$

$r^2 = 60{,}925^2/(79{,}67 \times 60{,}005\,5) = 0{,}776\,435 = (\mathbf{708}\text{b})^2$

$1 - r^2 = 0{,}223\,565$

$r = 0{,}881\,156$

$b_{yx} = 60{,}925/79{,}67 = 0{,}764\,717$ from (**636**)

$b_{xy} = 60{,}925/60{,}005\,5 = 1{,}015\,324$ from (**636**)*

$$b_0, -\frac{1}{b_0} = (60{,}005\,5 - 79{,}67)/(2 \times 60{,}925) \pm$$
$$\pm \sqrt{1 + (60{,}005\,5 - 79{,}67)^2/(2 \times 60{,}925)^2}$$
$$= 0{,}851\,556 \text{ and } -1{,}174\,321 \text{ from } (\mathbf{737})$$

$S_{y.x} = 60{,}005\,5 \times 0{,}223\,565 = 13{,}415\,120$ from (**640**c)

$s_{y.x}^2 = 13{,}415\,120/18 = 0{,}745\,284$ from (**639**a)

$s_{b_{yx}}^2 = 0{,}745\,284/79{,}67 = 0{,}009\,354\,64$ from (**641**a)

$s_{b_{yx}} = 0{,}096\,719\,4$

$S_{x.y} = 79{,}67 \times 0{,}223\,565 = 17{,}811\,410$ from (**640**c)*

$s_{x.y}^2 = 17{,}811\,410/18 = 0{,}989\,523$ from (**639**a)*

$s_{b_{xy}}^2 = 0{,}989\,523/60{,}005\,5 = 0{,}016\,490\,5$ from (**641**a)*

$s_{b_{xy}} = 0{,}128\,415$

(b) *Formulae*

Regression lines

$Y = 5{,}565 + 0{,}764\,717\,(x - 5{,}75) = 1{,}167\,877 + 0{,}764\,717\,x$ from (**706**a)

$X = 5{,}75 + 1{,}015\,324\,(y - 5{,}565) = 0{,}099\,724\,2 + 1{,}015\,324\,y$ from (**706**b)

$X_0;\ y = \bar{y} + b_0\,(x - \bar{x}) = 0{,}668\,555 + 0{,}851\,556\,x$

$Y_0;\ y = \bar{y} - \frac{1}{b_0}(x - \bar{x}) = 12{,}317\,348 - 1{,}174\,321\,x$

Tolerance ellipse (significance limits used):

$F_{P=0,05}(2;18) = 3{,}554\,6$ (from page 40); $t_{P=0,025;\ \nu=18} = 2{,}100\,9$ (from page 30); $t_{P=0,025;\ \nu=19} = 2{,}093\,0$ (from page 30); $F_{P=0,05}(1;18) = 4{,}413\,9$ (from page 40) $= t^2_{P=0,025;\ \nu=18}$.

Tolerance limits for $\mathbf{Y}|x$ (**736**a):

$$1{,}1679 + 0{,}76472\,x \pm 0{,}096\,719\sqrt{594{,}709\,46 - 18\,(x - 5{,}75)^2}$$

Tolerance limits for $\mathbf{X}|y$ (**736**b):

$$0{,}099\,72 + 1{,}015\,3\,y \pm 0{,}128\,42\sqrt{447{,}920\,66 - 18\,(y - 5{,}565)^2}$$

Horizontal tangents (y and x the contact points) [(**740**a) and (**741**b)]:

$y = 0{,}576\,57$ and $10{,}553\,3$

$x = 0{,}685\,12$ and $10{,}814\,9$

Vertical tangents (x and y the contact points) [(**740**b) and (**741**b)]:

$x = 0{,}002\,007\,8$ and $11{,}497\,9$

$y = 1{,}169\,41$ and $9{,}960\,59$

Lengths of the sides of the resulting rectangle [(**742**) and (**741**b)]:

Horizontal sides $l_h = 11{,}496\,0$

Vertical sides $l_v = 9{,}976\,7$

Lengths of the semi-axes of the ellipse [(**738**) and (**739**b)]:

$$\sqrt{\frac{3{,}554\,6 \times 21}{20 \times 18}} \times$$
$$\times \sqrt{79{,}67 + 60{,}005\,5 \pm \sqrt{(139{,}675\,5)^2 - 4\,(4780{,}638\,2 - [60{,}925]^2)}}$$
$$= 7{,}386\,1 \text{ and } 1{,}835\,6$$

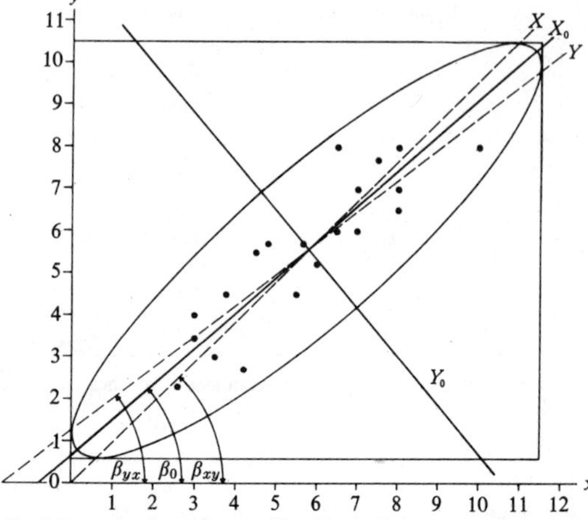

Fig. 40. Regression lines, tolerance ellipse $\mathbf{X}|y$, horizontal and vertical tangents (rectangle).

(c) *Tolerance limits for $\mathbf{Y}|x$ and $\mathbf{X}|y$ calculated from the formulae for a regression of the first kind* ($t_{2P=0,05;\ \nu=18} = 2{,}100\,9$, from page 30)

$\mathbf{Y}|x = 5{,}565 + 0{,}764\,7(x - 5{,}75) \pm 0{,}203\,2 \times \sqrt{83{,}653\,5 + (x - 5{,}75)^2}$ from (**673**)

$\mathbf{X}|y = 5{,}75 + 1{,}407\,0\,(y - 5{,}565) \pm 0{,}373\,9\sqrt{45{,}465\,9 + (y - 5{,}565)^2}$ from (**678**)

(d) *Tolerance limits for $\mathbf{Y}|x$ and $\mathbf{X}|y$, with $x = \bar{x}$ and $y = \bar{y}$, calculated from the formulae for*

	Regression of second kind	*Regression of first kind*
$Y\|\bar{x}$	$5{,}565 \pm 2{,}358\,7$ from (**736**a)	$5{,}565 \pm 1{,}858\,5$ from (**673**)
$X\|\bar{y}$	$5{,}75 \pm 2{,}717\,8$ from (**736**b)	$5{,}75 \pm 2{,}521\,0$ from (**678**)

(e) *Comparison of $\bar{x}$ and $\bar{y}$* ($t_{2P=0,05;\ \nu=19} = 2{,}093\,0$ from page 30)

$$\frac{(5{,}565 - 5{,}75)\sqrt{20}}{\sqrt{4{,}193\,2 + 3{,}158\,2 - 2 \times 3{,}206\,6}} = -0{,}854\,2 \text{ from } (\mathbf{730})$$

The test statistic is smaller than the significance limit, so that the hypothesis $\mu_x = \mu_y$ cannot be rejected.

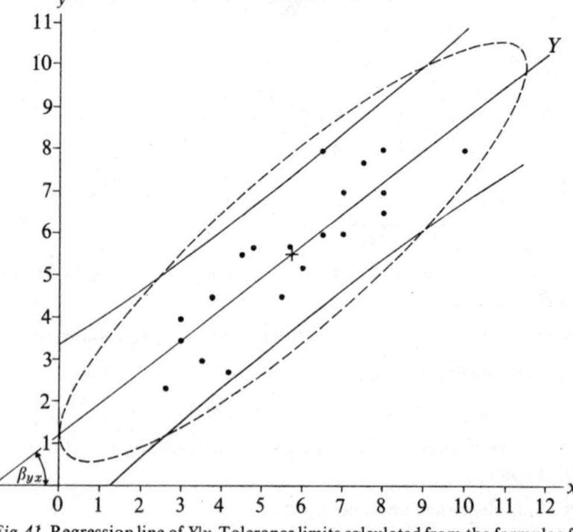

Fig. 41. Regression line of $Y|x$. Tolerance limits calculated from the formulae for a regression of the first kind (hyperbolae) and second kind (ellipse).

* With x and y transposed.

All values conform to the international convention (i.e. 0,1 instead of 0.1).

20. The binomial distribution (cf. also section 5, page 184)

20A. General

E and non-E are two *complementary* events [cf. (**334**) and (**335**)] with the probabilities $\boldsymbol{p}$ and $\boldsymbol{q} = 1 - \boldsymbol{p}$ [cf. (**339**)]. The probability that in N *independent* trials [cf. (**328**), (**357**), and example 10, page 184] the event E will occur exactly $x = 0, 1, 2, ..., N$ times is

$$\left.\begin{array}{l} f(x) = \dot{\boldsymbol{P}}_x = \binom{N}{x} \boldsymbol{p}^x \boldsymbol{q}^{N-x} \\ \dot{\boldsymbol{P}}_0 = \binom{N}{0} \boldsymbol{p}^0 \boldsymbol{q}^N = \boldsymbol{q}^N \\ \dot{\boldsymbol{P}}_1 = \binom{N}{1} \boldsymbol{p}^1 \boldsymbol{q}^{N-1}; ... \\ \dot{\boldsymbol{P}}_N = \binom{N}{N} \boldsymbol{p}^N \boldsymbol{q}^0 = \boldsymbol{p}^N \\ [0 \le \boldsymbol{p} \le 1 \text{ and } \boldsymbol{q} = 1 - \boldsymbol{p}] \end{array}\right\} \quad (743)$$

The individual probabilities $\dot{\boldsymbol{P}}_x$ of (**743**) correspond to the terms of the binomial series developed from $(q+p)^N$ [cf. (**113**)]. For the binomial coefficient $\binom{N}{x}$ cf. (**100**) to (**106**), page 172.

From (**743**) follow the recursion formulae

$$\left.\begin{array}{ll} \dot{\boldsymbol{P}}_{x+1} = \dot{\boldsymbol{P}}_x \times \dfrac{\boldsymbol{p}}{\boldsymbol{q}} \times \dfrac{N-x}{x+1} & \text{(a)} \\ \dot{\boldsymbol{P}}_{x-1} = \dot{\boldsymbol{P}}_x \times \dfrac{\boldsymbol{q}}{\boldsymbol{p}} \times \dfrac{x}{N-x+1} & \text{(b)} \end{array}\right\} \quad (744)$$

Example 47. Calculate all the individual probabilities $\dot{\boldsymbol{P}}_x$ for $\boldsymbol{p} = 0{,}3$ and $N = 7$.
Calculations are made from (**744a**) starting from $x = 0$. $\boldsymbol{p}/\boldsymbol{q} = 3/7$.

$$\dot{\boldsymbol{P}}_0 = \left(\frac{7}{10}\right)^7 = 0{,}0823543$$

$$\dot{\boldsymbol{P}}_1 = \dot{\boldsymbol{P}}_0 \times \frac{3}{7} \times \frac{7}{1} = \dot{\boldsymbol{P}}_0 \times \frac{21}{7} = 0{,}2470629$$

$$\dot{\boldsymbol{P}}_2 = \dot{\boldsymbol{P}}_1 \times \frac{3}{7} \times \frac{6}{2} = \dot{\boldsymbol{P}}_1 \times \frac{18}{14} = 0{,}3176523$$

$$\dot{\boldsymbol{P}}_3 = \dot{\boldsymbol{P}}_2 \times \frac{3}{7} \times \frac{5}{3} = \dot{\boldsymbol{P}}_2 \times \frac{15}{21} = 0{,}2268945$$

A study of the series 21/7, 18/14, 15/21 at once reveals the regular manner in which the numerators and denominators of the recursion factors decrease and increase respectively. The further factors for calculating $\dot{\boldsymbol{P}}_4$, $\dot{\boldsymbol{P}}_5$, ... can therefore be assumed to be 12/28, 9/35, 6/42 and 3/49, giving

$\dot{\boldsymbol{P}}_4 = 0{,}0972405$ $\quad \dot{\boldsymbol{P}}_6 = 0{,}0035721$ $\quad$ Check: $\sum_0^N \dot{\boldsymbol{P}}_x = 1$
$\dot{\boldsymbol{P}}_5 = 0{,}0250047$ $\quad \dot{\boldsymbol{P}}_7 = 0{,}0002187$

The individual probabilities for $N = 1, 2, ..., 99, 100$ and $\boldsymbol{p} = 0{,}01, 0{,}02, ..., 0{,}49, 0{,}50$ can also be obtained using the tables on pages 74–81 (logarithms of binomial coefficients) and 82–88 (logarithms of powers of $\boldsymbol{p}$ and $\boldsymbol{q}$).

Example 48. Calculate $\dot{\boldsymbol{P}}_1$ for $\boldsymbol{p} = 0{,}3$ and $N = 7$.

$\log\binom{7}{1} = 0{,}84510$		(page 74)
$\log \boldsymbol{p}^1 = 0{,}47712 - 1$		(page 86)
$\log \boldsymbol{q}^6 = 0{,}07059 - 1$		(page 86)
$\log \dot{\boldsymbol{P}}_1 = 1{,}39281 - 2 = 0{,}3928 - 1$		
$\dot{\boldsymbol{P}}_1 = 0{,}2471$		(page 11)

For binomial coefficients with $N > 100$ see under 'Binomial Coefficients', page 172. For calculating powers of $\boldsymbol{p}$ and $\boldsymbol{q}$, logarithms with 7 or more places should be used *.
The binomial distribution is a *discrete* distribution. It is *symmetrical* when $\boldsymbol{p} = 0{,}5$, *asymmetrical* when $\boldsymbol{p} \neq 0{,}5$.

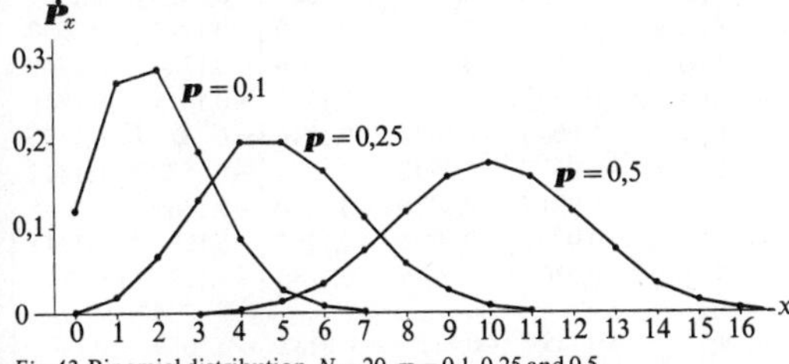

Fig. 42. Binomial distribution, $N = 20$, $\boldsymbol{p} = 0{,}1$, 0,25 and 0,5.

All values conform to the international convention (i.e. 0,1 instead of 0.1).

20B. Parameters of the binomial distribution

As shown by (**743**), the binomial distribution is fully characterized by the probability $\boldsymbol{p}$ and the number of trials N, so that it can be represented by the expression 'binomial distribution ($\boldsymbol{p}$; N)'. Its mean and variance are respectively

$$\mu_x = N\boldsymbol{p} = \text{expectation of } (748) \quad (745)$$

$$\sigma_x^2 = N\boldsymbol{p}\,\boldsymbol{q} = \boldsymbol{q}\,\mu_x = \text{expectation of } (749) \times \frac{N}{N-1} \quad (746)$$

For any given sample size N (N trials) the variance of the binomial distribution is greatest when $\boldsymbol{p} = 0{,}5$, least when $\boldsymbol{p} = 0$ or $\boldsymbol{q} = 0$.
The best estimate of $\boldsymbol{p}$ from a sample of size N in which the event E occurs x times is

$$p = x/N \quad (747)$$

The following are derived from (**745**) to (**747**):

- estimate of μ_x:

$$\bar{x} = N\,p = x \quad (748)$$

- estimate of σ_x^2:

$$s_x^2 = Npq = \frac{x(N-x)}{N} \quad (749)$$

- the mean and variance of the *relative* frequency x/N:

$$\mu_{x/N} = \boldsymbol{p} = \text{expectation of } (747) \quad (750)$$

$$\sigma_{x/N}^2 = \frac{\boldsymbol{p}\,\boldsymbol{q}}{N} = \text{expectation of } (752) \times \frac{N}{N-1} \quad (751)$$

- the corresponding estimate for the mean from (**747**)
- the corresponding estimate for the variance:

$$s_p^2 = \frac{p\,q}{N} = \frac{x(N-x)}{N^3} = \frac{1}{N^2} s_x^2 \quad (752)$$

Example 49. In 64 trials the event x occurs 6 times. Estimate $\boldsymbol{p}$, σ_x^2 and σ_p^2.

$p = 6/64 = 0{,}09375$ from (**747**)
$s_x^2 = 0{,}09375 \times 58 = 5{,}4375$ from (**749**)
$s_p^2 = 5{,}4375/64^2 = 0{,}001327515$ from (**752**)

20C. Cumulative probabilities of the binomial distribution

The calculation of cumulative probabilities in discrete distributions has been dealt with fully in section 5 (page 184). Here some practical applications are indicated.
Let $\boldsymbol{p}$ be the probability of the event E, $\boldsymbol{q}$ that of the event *non-E*. $\dot{\boldsymbol{P}}_x$ is defined in (**743**).

The probability that the event E

- will occur exactly $x = k$ times is given by (**370**) (a)
- will *not* occur exactly $x = k$ times is given by (**371**) (b)
- will occur *at the most* or *less* than $x = k$ times is given by (**372**) (c)
- will occur *at least* or *more* than $x = k$ times is given by (**373**) (d)
- will occur *at least* $x = k$ times *but at the most* $x = s$ times ($k < s$) is given by (**374**) (e)
- will occur *less* than $x = k$ times *or more* than $x = s$ times ($k < s$) is given by (**375**) (f)

(753)

Examples of the calculation of probabilities of this kind are given in section 5, page 184. The following is an additional example.

Example 50. Let $\boldsymbol{p}$ be the probability of the occurrence of an event E in a population. What size N must a sample have if the probability that the event E occurs *at least once* is p^*?
From (**753d**) and (**373**) it follows that

$$\text{Prob}(x \ge 1) = \sum_1^N \dot{\boldsymbol{P}}_x \text{ from } (373b)$$

$$= 1 - \dot{\boldsymbol{P}}_0 \text{ from } (373a)$$

*Tables of $f(x)$ and the cumulative distribution $\sum_x^N f(x)$ for $N = 2, 3, ..., 49$ and $\boldsymbol{p} = 0{,}01, 0{,}02, ..., 0{,}5$ are to be found in the literature[3, 4].

In accordance with (**743**), $\dot{\boldsymbol{P}}_0 = \boldsymbol{q}^N$, whence

$$p^* = 1 - \boldsymbol{q}^N$$

that is

$$N \sim \frac{\log(1-p^*)}{\log \boldsymbol{q}} = \frac{\log(1-p^*)}{\log(1-\boldsymbol{p})} \qquad \textbf{(754)}$$

Application. Let the probability of throwing a six with a die be 1/6. How many throws must be made in order to throw a six at least once with a probability $p^* \geq 0{,}99$?
From (**754**)

$$N \sim \frac{\log(1-0{,}99)}{\log(1-1/6)} = \frac{\log 0{,}01}{\log 5/6} = \frac{-2}{-0{,}079\,181\,25} = 25{,}26$$

It follows that 26 throws must be made in order that, with a probability $p^* \geq 0{,}99$, at least one six will be thrown (with 25 throws p^* would be a little under 0,99).

20D. The binomial and the normal distribution

As shown by Figure 42, with $\boldsymbol{p} = 0{,}5$, the binomial distribution closely resembles the normal distribution even for *fairly small N*. This is not the case with more extreme values of $\boldsymbol{p}$ (cf. $\boldsymbol{p} = 0{,}1$). As shown by Figure 43, however, with increasing N the binomial distribution approximates to the normal distribution even with more extreme values of $\boldsymbol{p}$. In other words:
With increasing N the binomial distribution ($\boldsymbol{p}$; N) tends toward the normal distribution ($N\boldsymbol{p}$, $\sqrt{N\boldsymbol{p}\boldsymbol{q}}$). The closer $\boldsymbol{p}$ lies to 0,5, the greater is this tendency:

$$\binom{N}{x} \boldsymbol{p}^x \boldsymbol{q}^{N-x} \rightarrow \frac{1}{\sqrt{2\pi N \boldsymbol{p}\boldsymbol{q}}}\, e^{-(x-N\boldsymbol{p})^2/2N\boldsymbol{p}\boldsymbol{q}} \qquad \textbf{(755)}$$

[as $N \rightarrow \infty$]

With large N, in accordance with the definitions

$$\text{Prob}(x \leq x_p) = \sum_0^{x_p} \dot{\boldsymbol{P}}_x = p$$

$$\text{Prob}(c \leq c_p) = \int_{-\infty}^{c_p} \text{ of the standardized normal distribution}$$

it follows from (**755**) that

$$\text{Prob}(x \leq x_p) \sim \text{Prob}(c \leq c_p) \qquad \textbf{(756)}$$

where

$$c_p = \frac{x_p - N\boldsymbol{p}}{\sqrt{N\boldsymbol{p}\boldsymbol{q}}} \qquad \textbf{(757)}$$

[for c see page 26, right-hand table]

or

$$x_p = N\boldsymbol{p} + c_p\sqrt{N\boldsymbol{p}\boldsymbol{q}} \qquad \textbf{(758)}$$

[for c see page 26, left-hand table]

With smaller samples, the approximations (**756**) and (**757**) can be improved by using the so-called correction for continuity. In this case, $x + 1/2$ is used in place of x, whence

$$c_p = \frac{x_p + 1/2 - N\boldsymbol{p}}{\sqrt{N\boldsymbol{p}\boldsymbol{q}}} \qquad \textbf{(759)}$$

[for c see page 26, right-hand table]

$$x_p = N\boldsymbol{p} - 1/2 + c_p\sqrt{N\boldsymbol{p}\boldsymbol{q}} \qquad \textbf{(760)}$$

[for c see page 26, left-hand table]

From the definitions

$$\text{Prob}(x \geq x_{p^*}) = 1 - \text{Prob}(x \leq x_{p^*} - 1) = p^*$$

$$\text{Prob}(c \leq c_{1-p^*}) = \int_{-\infty}^{c_{1-p^*}} = 1 - p^*$$

it follows from (**759**) and (**760**) that

$$c_{1-p^*} = \frac{x_{p^*} - 1/2 - N\boldsymbol{p}}{\sqrt{N\boldsymbol{p}\boldsymbol{q}}} \qquad \textbf{(761)}$$

[for c see page 26, right-hand table]

$$x_{p^*} = N\boldsymbol{p} + 1/2 + c_{1-p^*}\sqrt{N\boldsymbol{p}\boldsymbol{q}} \qquad \textbf{(762)}$$

[for c see page 26, left-hand table]

Example 51. Given the binomial distribution ($\boldsymbol{p} = 0{,}1$; $N = 40$), calculate the probabilities $\text{Prob}(x \leq 3) = p$ and $\text{Prob}(x \geq 6) = p^*$.

From (**759**) to (**762**) it follows that

$$c_p = \frac{3{,}5-4}{\sqrt{3{,}6}} = -0{,}264 \text{ from } \textbf{(759)}$$

$p = 0{,}396$ [by linear interpolation in right-hand table, page 26]

$$c_{1-p^*} = \frac{5{,}5-4}{\sqrt{3{,}6}} = 0{,}791 \text{ from } \textbf{(760)}$$

$1 - p^* = 0{,}786$

$p^* = 0{,}214$

The exact values of p and p^*, rounded off to 3 decimal places, are 0,423 and 0,206.

Example 52. For the binomial distribution of example 51, calculate x_p for $p = 0{,}1$ and x_{p^*} for $p^* = 0{,}05$.
From (**759**) to (**762**) it follows that

$c_p = -1{,}2816$, $c_{1-p^*} = 1{,}6449$ } page 26, left-hand table

whence

$$x_p = 3{,}5 - 1{,}2816\sqrt{3{,}6} = 1{,}07 \text{ from } \textbf{(760)}$$

$$x_{p^*} = 4{,}5 + 1{,}6449\sqrt{3{,}6} = 7{,}62 \text{ from } \textbf{(762)}$$

Since x must be a whole number, this gives the results $x_p = 1$ and $x_{p^*} = 8$, which agree with the exact values.

A further very good approximation is[29, 30]

$$\tfrac{1}{2}c \sim \sqrt{(k+1)\boldsymbol{q} + B(\boldsymbol{p},\alpha)} - \sqrt{(N-k)\boldsymbol{p} + B(\boldsymbol{q},\alpha)} \quad \left[\text{when } \sum_{x=0}^{k} \dot{\boldsymbol{P}}_x \sim \alpha \leq 0{,}5\right] \qquad \text{(a)}$$

$$\tfrac{1}{2}c \sim \sqrt{k\boldsymbol{q} + B(\boldsymbol{p},\alpha)} - \sqrt{(N-k+1)\boldsymbol{p} + B(\boldsymbol{q},\alpha)} \quad \left[\text{when } \sum_{x=0}^{k} \dot{\boldsymbol{P}}_x \sim 1-\alpha \geq 0{,}5\right] \qquad \text{(b)}$$

$$B(\boldsymbol{p},\alpha) = \frac{-(7\boldsymbol{q} + \boldsymbol{p}^2)}{18} + \frac{(2\boldsymbol{q} - \boldsymbol{p}^2)c_\alpha^2}{36} \qquad \text{(c)}$$

$$B(\boldsymbol{q},\alpha) = \frac{-(7\boldsymbol{p} + \boldsymbol{q}^2)}{18} + \frac{(2\boldsymbol{p} - \boldsymbol{q}^2)c_\alpha^2}{36} \qquad \text{(d)}$$

The values of $B(\boldsymbol{p},\alpha)$ and $B(\boldsymbol{q},\alpha)$ for certain $\boldsymbol{p}$ and $\boldsymbol{q}$ can be found in the table below. For $\alpha = 0{,}05$ $B(\boldsymbol{p},\alpha)$ and $B(\boldsymbol{q},\alpha)$ may be put equal to zero. Similarly $B(\boldsymbol{p},\alpha)$ and $B(\boldsymbol{q},\alpha)$ may simply be approximated by b_α (see last line in the table below):

$$b_\alpha = \frac{c_\alpha^2 - 4}{12} \qquad \text{(e)}$$

(a)–(e): **(763)**

α		0,005	0,01	0,025	0,05	0,10
$\boldsymbol{p}$						
0,05	$B(\boldsymbol{p},\alpha)$	−0,0199	−0,0843	−0,1671	−0,2270	−0,2830
	$B(\boldsymbol{q},\alpha)$	−0,2175	−0,1902	−0,1552	−0,1299	−0,1062
0,10	$B(\boldsymbol{p},\alpha)$	−0,0207	−0,0815	−0,1595	−0,2160	−0,2689
	$B(\boldsymbol{q},\alpha)$	−0,1963	−0,1756	−0,1490	−0,1297	−0,1117
0,15	$B(\boldsymbol{p},\alpha)$	−0,0226	−0,0796	−0,1528	−0,2057	−0,2553
	$B(\boldsymbol{q},\alpha)$	−0,1763	−0,1620	−0,1436	−0,1302	−0,1177
0,20	$B(\boldsymbol{p},\alpha)$	−0,0258	−0,0788	−0,1469	−0,1961	−0,2422
	$B(\boldsymbol{q},\alpha)$	−0,1576	−0,1494	−0,1389	−0,1314	−0,1243
0,25	$B(\boldsymbol{p},\alpha)$	−0,0302	−0,0790	−0,1417	−0,1871	−0,2296
	$B(\boldsymbol{q},\alpha)$	−0,1400	−0,1379	−0,1351	−0,1332	−0,1313
0,30	$B(\boldsymbol{p},\alpha)$	−0,0358	−0,0803	−0,1374	−0,1788	−0,2175
	$B(\boldsymbol{q},\alpha)$	−0,1236	−0,1274	−0,1322	−0,1356	−0,1389
0,35	$B(\boldsymbol{p},\alpha)$	−0,0426	−0,0826	−0,1339	−0,1711	−0,2059
	$B(\boldsymbol{q},\alpha)$	−0,1084	−0,1179	−0,1300	−0,1387	−0,1469
0,40	$B(\boldsymbol{p},\alpha)$	−0,0505	−0,0859	−0,1312	−0,1641	−0,1948
	$B(\boldsymbol{q},\alpha)$	−0,0945	−0,1094	−0,1286	−0,1425	−0,1555
0,45	$B(\boldsymbol{p},\alpha)$	−0,0597	−0,0902	−0,1294	−0,1577	−0,1842
	$B(\boldsymbol{q},\alpha)$	−0,0817	−0,1020	−0,1280	−0,1469	−0,1645
0,50	$B(\boldsymbol{p},\alpha)$	−0,0701	−0,0956	−0,1283	−0,1520	−0,1741
	$B(\boldsymbol{q},\alpha)$	−0,0701	−0,0956	−0,1283	−0,1520	−0,1741
b_α		+0,2196	+0,1177	−0,0132	−0,1079	−0,1965

All values conform to the international convention (i.e. 0,1 instead of 0.1).

Calculate critical limits k_l and k_r for $x=k$ for given $\boldsymbol{p}$ and N

$$\text{Prob}(k_l \le k \le k_r) \ge 1-2\alpha$$

It follows from (**763**a) to (**763**d) that:

$$k_l, k_r = \text{integer}\Bigg[\overbrace{\boldsymbol{p}(N+1)+(\boldsymbol{q}-\boldsymbol{p})\frac{c_\alpha^2+2}{6}}^{C} \mp \overbrace{\mp\left(1+\frac{|c_\alpha|}{6}\underbrace{\sqrt{2\boldsymbol{p}\boldsymbol{q}(18N+7-c_\alpha^2)-c_\alpha^2-2}}_{A}\right)}^{B}\Bigg] \qquad \textbf{(764)}$$

No limits exist if $A<0$; k_l only exists if $C<B$; k_r only exists if the integer value of $(C+B)>N$.
This is a very good approximation although for $\boldsymbol{p}=\boldsymbol{q}=0{,}5$ (**767**) is even better.

When $\boldsymbol{p}=\boldsymbol{q}$, (**764**) gives

$$\left.\begin{aligned} k_l &= \text{integer}\left[\tfrac{1}{2}\underbrace{\left(N-1-|c_\alpha|\underbrace{\sqrt{N-\frac{c_\alpha^2-1}{6}}}_{A}\right)}_{B}\right] \\ k_r &= N-k_l \end{aligned}\right\} \qquad \textbf{(765)}$$

No limits exist if $A<0$ or $(N-1)<B$.

A further very good approximation for k_l and k_r when $\boldsymbol{p}=\boldsymbol{q}$ can be obtained from the following equation[30]:

$$\left.\begin{aligned} c &= \sqrt{2k+2+\beta}-\sqrt{2N-2k+\beta} \\ \beta &= \frac{(2k+1-N)^2-10N}{12N} \end{aligned}\right\} \qquad \textbf{(766)}$$

Then

$$\left.\begin{aligned} k_l &= \text{integer}\left(A-\sqrt{A^2-B}\right) \\ k_r &= N-k_l \\ A &= \frac{N-1}{2} \\ B &= \frac{(N-1)^2-\frac{c_\alpha^2}{4}\left(4N+\frac{N^2+1}{3N}-c_\alpha^2\right)}{4-\frac{c_\alpha^2}{3N}} \end{aligned}\right\} \qquad \textbf{(767)}$$

20E. The binomial and the Poisson distribution

As shown by Figures 43 and 44, with small values of $\boldsymbol{p}$ the binomial distribution closely resembles the Poisson distribution. The following rule of thumb should be noted:

$$\left.\begin{aligned} &\binom{N}{x}\boldsymbol{p}^x\boldsymbol{q}^{N-x} \approx \frac{e^{-\lambda}\lambda^x}{x!} \quad [\lambda = N\boldsymbol{p}] \\ &\text{if} \\ &\frac{N\boldsymbol{p}\boldsymbol{q}}{N\boldsymbol{p}} \approx 1 \end{aligned}\right\} \qquad \textbf{(768)}$$

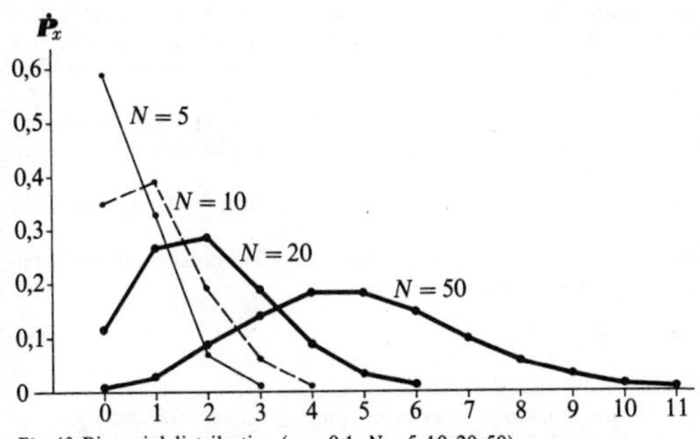

Fig. 43. Binomial distribution ($\boldsymbol{p}=0{,}1$; $N=5, 10, 20, 50$).

All values conform to the international convention (i.e. 0,1 instead of 0.1).

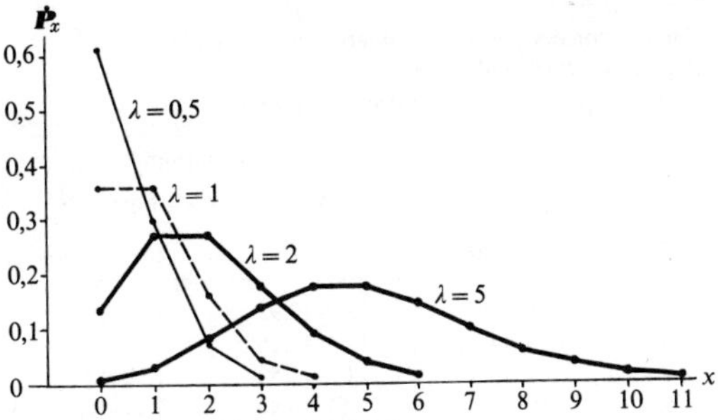

Fig. 44. Poisson distribution ($\lambda = 0{,}5, 1, 2, 5$).

20F. Confidence limits and significance limits

Confidence limits for $\boldsymbol{p}$ (or significance limits for $p=x/N$), pages 89–102

In N trials, the event E occurs $x=k$ times. According to CLOPPER and PEARSON[31], the confidence limits satisfying the equation

$$\text{Prob}(p_l < \boldsymbol{p} < p_r \mid x=k, N) = 1-2\alpha \quad [\alpha < 0{,}25]$$

are the solutions p_l to

$$\sum_{x=k}^{N}\binom{N}{x}p_l^x(1-p_l)^{N-x} = \alpha \qquad \text{(a)}$$

and p_r to

$$\sum_{x=0}^{k}\binom{N}{x}p_r^x(1-p_r)^{N-x} = \alpha \qquad \text{(b)} \qquad \textbf{(769)}$$

For $x=0$ and $x=N$, only *one-sided* $(1-\alpha)$ limits are possible:

– for $x=0$

$$0 \text{ and } p_r = 1-\text{antilog}\left(\frac{\log\alpha}{N}\right) \qquad \text{(a)}$$

– for $x=N$

$$p_l = \text{antilog}\left(\frac{\log\alpha}{N}\right) \text{ and } N \qquad \text{(b)} \qquad \textbf{(770)}$$

For $x=0$ and $x=N$, the confidence limits for $\boldsymbol{p}$ given in the tables on pages 89–102 thus correspond not to $(1-2\alpha)$ but to $(1-\alpha)$ limits.
For $0<x<N$, (**769**) can only be solved iteratively.
Below are given some approximate solutions [derived from (**763**a) to (**763**d)].

Critical limits p_l and p_r for $\boldsymbol{p}$ for given $x=k$ and N

$$\text{Prob}(p_l \le \boldsymbol{p} \le p_r) = 1-2\alpha$$

$$p_{l(k+1)}, p_{r(k)} = \frac{b_r}{2a} \mp \sqrt{\left(\frac{b_r}{2a}\right)^2 - \frac{c_r}{a}} \qquad \text{(a)}$$

or

$$p_{l(k)}, p_{r(k)} = \frac{b_{l,r}}{2a} \mp \sqrt{\left(\frac{b_{l,r}}{2a}\right)^2 - \frac{c_{l,r}}{a}} \qquad \text{(b)}$$

where

$$a = \frac{c_\alpha^4}{18}+\frac{c_\alpha^2}{6}(2N+1)+\left(N+\frac{1}{3}\right)^2 \qquad \text{(c)}$$

$$b_{l,r} = \frac{c_\alpha^4}{18}+\frac{c_\alpha^2}{6}[4(N-A_{l,r})+3] + \frac{2}{3}[A_{l,r}(3N+1)-N]-\frac{2}{9} \qquad \text{(d)} \qquad \textbf{(771)}$$

$$c_{l,r} = \frac{c_\alpha^4}{18}-\frac{c_\alpha^2}{6}(2A_{l,r}-1)+\left(A_{l,r}-\frac{1}{3}\right)^2 \qquad \text{(e)}$$

In (a) to (e)

$$A_{l(k)} = k \qquad \text{(f)}$$

$$A_{r(k)} = k+1 \qquad \text{(g)}$$

For the accuracy of the approximation see the table on next page.

For very small k's (k up to $\sim N/10$) we have, especially for p_l:

$$p_{l,r} = 1-\text{anti-ln}\,\frac{-\lambda_{k(l,r)(1-2\alpha)}}{N-k/2} \quad [\lambda \text{ see } (\textbf{779})] \qquad \textbf{(772)}$$

Comparison between approximations (**771b**) and (**772**) with the exact confidence limits for $\boldsymbol{p}$

$\text{Prob}(p_l \leq \boldsymbol{p} \leq p_r) = 1 - 2\alpha = 0{,}99$; sample size $N = 105$

k	Exact values	Approximations from (**771b**)	Approximations from (**772**)
	$100\,p_l$ $100\,p_r$	$100\,p_l$ $100\,p_r$	$100\,p_l$ $100\,p_r$
5	1,04–12,90	1,09–12,92	1,05–12,89
6	1,49–14,24	1,53–14,26	1,50–14,23
7	1,98–15,54	2,01–15,56	1,99–15,53
8	2,50–16,82	2,53–16,83	2,51–16,80
9	3,05–18,06	3,08–18,08	3,07–18,04
10	3,63–19,29	3,66–19,30	3,65–19,26
11	4,23–20,49	4,25–20,50	4,25–20,46
12	4,85–21,68	4,87–21,69	4,87–21,64
13	5,49–22,85	5,50–22,86	5,51–22,81
14	6,14–24,01	6,15–24,02	6,16–23,95
15	6,80–25,15	6,82–25,16	6,83–25,09
16	7,48–26,29	7,49–26,29	7,51–26,21
17	8,17–27,41	8,18–27,41	8,20–27,32
18	8,87–28,52	8,88–28,52	8,90–28,41
19	9,58–29,62	9,59–29,62	9,61–29,50

Figure 45 shows the confidence intervals for $\boldsymbol{p}$ for all possible values of x for sample sizes $N = 30$ and $N = 10$.

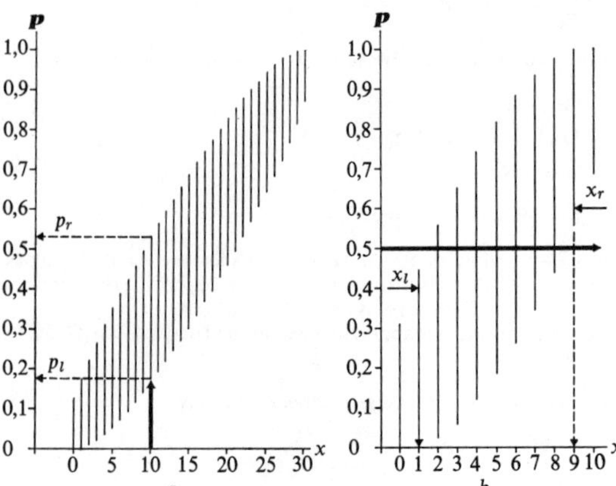

Fig. 45. Binomial distribution. Confidence limits for $\boldsymbol{p}$ ($N = 30$ and $N = 10$).

Significance limits for x (or confidence limits for $N\boldsymbol{p}$*), pages 103–107*

It is assumed that the probability $\boldsymbol{p}$ is known (either on theoretical grounds or from large samples). In a sample *possibly* originating from this population the event E occurs x times. The significance limits for x are in accordance with the conditions (**376**) and (**377**).
The table on page 103 gives such limits for samples of size up to $N = 100$ and for $\boldsymbol{p} = 0{,}05, 0{,}1, \ldots, 0{,}45, 0{,}5$. Further tables on pages 104 and 107 for samples of size up to $N = 499$ and for $\boldsymbol{p} = 0{,}5$.
As shown in Figure 45b, the significance limits for x can be obtained from the confidence limits for $\boldsymbol{p}$ without calculation.

Example 53. Required are the 95% confidence limits for $\boldsymbol{p}$ for a sample of size $N = 10$ and $\boldsymbol{p} = 0{,}5$.

As shown by Figure 45b, the *lower* limit x_l is fixed by that confidence interval for $\boldsymbol{p}$ whose *upper* limit p_r lies *closest* to $\boldsymbol{p}$ *without exceeding it.* (a)

The *upper* limit x_r is fixed by that confidence interval for $\boldsymbol{p}$ whose *lower* limit p_l lies *closest* to $\boldsymbol{p}$ *without falling below it.* (b)

(**773**)

In the table on page 89, $p_r = 44{,}50$ is in accordance with (**773a**) and $p_l = 55{,}50$ in accordance with (**773b**). The required limits for $\boldsymbol{p}$ are therefore $x_l = 1$ and $x_r = 9$.

All values conform to the international convention (i.e. 0,1 instead of 0.1).

According to WILKS[32], the above significance limits correspond to the *distribution-free confidence limits for quantiles* $Q(p)$ (cf. section 10F, page 197) when x_l is replaced by $x_l + 1$ and when p in the table is so chosen that it is of the same magnitude as p in $Q(p)$.

In this connection it should be noted [cf. (**383**)] that the postulated significance probability is reached when x *attains* or *exceeds* in an outward direction from $N\boldsymbol{p}$ the limits x_l or x_r.

Example 54. The hypothetical probability $\boldsymbol{p}$ is 0,05. In 48 trials the event E occurs 7 times. Does this sample originate from the hypothetical population?
For $2\alpha = 0{,}05$, the table on page 103 gives as upper level $x = 7$, so that:

One-tailed test

The sample originates from a population with $\boldsymbol{p} > 0{,}05$ [$\alpha = 0{,}025$]

Two-tailed test

The sample originates from a population with $\boldsymbol{p} \neq 0{,}05$ [$2\alpha = 0{,}05$]

Distribution-free tolerance limits, see section 25, pages 230–232.

20G. Miscellaneous

(a) *Arc-sine transformation,* table on page 73 (cf. also 'Inverse trigonometric functions', page 175)
According to FREEMAN and TUKEY[29], the best transformation $x \to X$ for stabilizing the variance of the binomial distribution when $N\boldsymbol{p} \geq 1$ is in most cases

$$X = \arcsin\sqrt{\frac{x}{N+1}} + \arcsin\sqrt{\frac{x+1}{N+1}}$$

with a variance within $\pm 6\%$ of

$$s_X^2 = \frac{1}{N + \frac{1}{2}} \times \begin{pmatrix}\text{angle in}\\ \text{radians}\end{pmatrix} \text{ or } \frac{821}{N + \frac{1}{2}} \times \begin{pmatrix}\text{angle in}\\ \text{degrees}\end{pmatrix} \qquad (\mathbf{774})$$

The mean $\bar{X}$ of the values thus transformed is approximately $2 \arcsin\sqrt{p}$.
This transformation can be used in analysis of variance and other operations.

(b) With a given p_0, how large must the sample size N be for the event E to occur at least x times with a probability p^*? The solution of this problem for $x = 1$ is given in (**754**).
The simplest approximate solution for $x > 1$ is (when $\boldsymbol{p} < \boldsymbol{q}$)

$$N \sim \frac{1}{p_0}\left(\frac{c^2}{4} + x + c\sqrt{x\,q_0}\right) - 1 \quad [c = c_{p^*} = c_{1-\alpha}] \qquad (\mathbf{775})$$

21. The Poisson distribution

21A. General

E is a random event occurring over a long period of observation◊ an infinite number of times but in a relatively short time◊ (in general the *observation unit* t) only rarely. The probability that in an observation unit t the event will occur $0, 1, 2, \ldots, x$ times is then

$$f(x) = \boldsymbol{P}_x = \frac{e^{-\lambda}\lambda^x}{x!} = \underbrace{\frac{e^{-\lambda}\lambda^0}{0!}}_{=e^{-\lambda}}, \frac{e^{-\lambda}\lambda^1}{1!}, \frac{e^{-\lambda}\lambda^2}{2!} \ldots \qquad (\mathbf{776})$$

[e: base of natural logarithms; for λ see (**779**)]

The Poisson distribution is a discrete non-symmetrical distribution in which, with increasing x, the individual probabilities decrease in a regular manner when $\lambda < 1$, and first increase but then decrease when $\lambda > 1$ (cf. Fig. 44, page 221).
As shown by (**776**), the Poisson distribution is characterized completely by the parameter λ. For this reason it will be written here as Poisson distribution (λ).
Tables of $f(x)$ and the cumulative distribution $\sum_k^{\infty} \boldsymbol{P}_x$ are given by MOLINA[2].
The simplest calculation of several successive individual probabilities is from the recursion formula

$$\boldsymbol{P}_{x+1} = \boldsymbol{P}_x \times \frac{\lambda}{x+1} \qquad (\mathbf{777})$$

◊Time has been chosen as an example. The same argument would apply, for instance, to surfaces and volumes.

Example 55. For the Poisson distribution ($\lambda = 1$) calculate the individual probabilities for x from 0 to 5.

$\dot{P}_0 = 1/e = 0{,}367\,879$ $\quad \dot{P}_3 = \dot{P}_2 \times 1/3 = 0{,}061\,313$

$\dot{P}_1 = \dot{P}_0 \times 1 = 0{,}367\,879$ $\quad \dot{P}_4 = \dot{P}_3 \times 1/4 = 0{,}015\,328$

$\dot{P}_2 = \dot{P}_1 \times 1/2 = 0{,}183\,940$ $\quad \dot{P}_5 = \dot{P}_4 \times 1/5 = 0{,}003\,066$

Calculation of the *cumulative probabilities* is carried out according to the procedure given in section 5, page 184, with N replaced by infinity. It should also be noted that in the Poisson distribution the probability $\text{Prob}(x \geq k)$ should be calculated using the probability $\text{Prob}(x \leq k-1)$, i.e.,

$$\text{Prob}(x \geq k) = 1 - \text{Prob}(x \leq k-1)$$

Example 56. How large must λ be for the event E to occur at least once during the observation unit t with a probability p^*? (This is an unusual problem in the Poisson distribution but sometimes occurs when the latter is used as an approximation to other distributions.) The solution is obtained by using equation (**129**) on page 173. Here the numerical values for various probabilities p^* can also be found. If for example $p^* = 0{,}999$, λ is 6,9.

21B. The addition theorem for the Poisson distribution

If $x_{t_1}, x_{t_2}, \ldots, x_{t_k}$ are stochastically independent random variables◊ with Poisson distributions $(\lambda_{t_1}), (\lambda_{t_2}), \ldots, (\lambda_{t_k})$ respectively, then their sum $x = x_{t_1} + x_{t_2} + \cdots + x_{t_k}$ is likewise a Poisson distribution (λ) with $\lambda = \lambda_{t_1} + \lambda_{t_2} + \cdots + \lambda_{t_k}$. **(778)**

21C. Parameters and their estimates

The mean of the Poisson distribution is

$$\mu_{x_t} = \lambda_t = \text{expectation of } x_t \quad \text{(a)}$$

and the variance

$$\sigma^2_{x_t} = \lambda_t = \text{expectation of } x_t \quad \text{(b)} \qquad \textbf{(779)}$$

[t: observation unit to which x and λ relate]

If a Poisson distribution with observation unit t is used to calculate another Poisson distribution with observation unit $k\,t$, then the mean and variance of the latter are

$$\mu_{x_{kt}}, \sigma^2_{x_{kt}} = k\lambda_t \quad [k>0] \qquad \textbf{(780)}$$

As the mean and variance in the Poisson distribution are the same the following rule of thumb applies:

If the ratio of mean to variance in a *discrete* distribution is approximately 1 (say between 10/9 and 9/10), then a Poisson distribution is likely to approximate to it provided that the variable x can assume high (theoretically, infinitely high) values. **(781)**

Unbiased estimates of λ_t based on n *equal* observation units t are

$$\bar{x}_t = \frac{\sum x_t}{n} = \frac{\sum x_i f_i}{n} \quad \text{(a)}$$

or

$$s_t^2 = \frac{\sum x_t^2 - (\sum x_t)^2/n}{n-1} = \frac{\sum x_i^2 f_i - (\sum x_i f_i)^2/n}{n-1} = \frac{S_t}{n-1} \quad \text{(b)} \qquad \textbf{(782)}$$

$\bar{x}_t$ is the *better* (more efficient) estimate. Since it is also more quickly calculated it is the one usually used. With higher values of n (say $n>5$), however, the additional calculation of $(n-1)\,s_t^2$ [the numerator in (**782**b)] offers the advantage of being able to test whether the ratio $s_t^2/\bar{x}_t$ differs significantly from 1. The test quotient is

$$\frac{(n-1)\,s_t^2}{\bar{x}_t} = \frac{S_t}{\bar{x}_t} \qquad \textbf{(783)}$$

[significance limit χ^2 with $v = n-1$, $2\alpha = 1\int_r$: pages 34–37]

If the test quotient (**783**) *attains* or *exceeds* the significance limit, then the sample probably does not originate from a Poisson distribution. This leads to the following rule of thumb:

When (**783**) is significant, the sample could originate from a binomial distribution when $s_t^2 < \bar{x}_t$, from a binomial distribution with negative index when $s_t^2 > \bar{x}_t$ (cf. also BLISS[33]). **(784)**

Example 57. In 60 minutes 12 events E are observed. $\lambda_{60\,\text{min}} \sim 12/1 = 12$. In accordance with (**780**), the estimate of $\lambda_{1\,\text{min}}$ is then $12/60 = 1/5$.

Example 58. In 60 minutes 12 events E are observed, in 30 minutes (different to the previous 60 minutes) 8. In accordance with (**778**), $\lambda_{90\,\text{min}} \sim 12+8 = 20$, $\lambda_{1\,\text{min}} \sim 20/90$.

Example 59. In 100 independent observation periods of 1 minute each the event E is observed x_i times in f_i observation periods, as follows:

x_i	f_i	$x_i f_i$	$x_i^2 f_i$	
0	5	0	0	$n = 100$
1	30	30	30	$\Sigma x\,[\lambda_{100\,\text{min}}] = 236$
2	24	48	96	$\Sigma x^2 = 778$
3	20	60	180	$\bar{x}_t = 2{,}36$ from (**782**a)
4	12	48	192	$S_t = 778 - 556{,}96 = 221{,}04$ from (**782**b)
5	4	20	100	$\chi^2 = 93{,}661$ and $v = 99$ from (**783**)
6	5	30	180	
7	0			
	100	236	778	

In this case χ^2 lies far inside the significance limit of 0,05 ($0{,}30 < \alpha < 0{,}35$), so that the distribution *could* be a Poisson distribution. A *more efficient* test is provided by calculation of the *fitted* Poisson distribution in accordance with (**776**) with $\lambda = 2{,}36$, multiplication of the value obtained by n and then testing with χ^2 in accordance with (**567**) with degrees of freedom $v = k-2$ from (**570**a), where k = number of classes i.

21D. Transformations

As shown by Figure 44 (page 221), with increasing λ the shape of the Poisson distribution gradually (and fairly rapidly) approaches that of the normal distribution.

$$\frac{e^{-\lambda}\lambda^x}{x!} \to \frac{1}{\sqrt{2\pi\lambda}}\, e^{-(x-\lambda)^2/2\lambda} \quad [\text{as } \lambda \to \infty] \qquad \textbf{(785)}$$

The corresponding approximations are analogous to the approximations of the binomial distribution to the normal distribution using (**759**) to (**762**), with $N\boldsymbol{p}$ replaced by λ.

The following approximations are superior (basic equation by MOLENAAR[30]).

Basic equation:

$$\tfrac{1}{2}c_\alpha = \sqrt{k + \frac{c_\alpha^2 + 11}{18}} - \sqrt{\lambda - \frac{c_\alpha^2+2}{36}} \quad \text{(a)}$$

$$\tfrac{1}{2}c_{1-\alpha} = \sqrt{k - 1 + \frac{c_\alpha^2 + 11}{18}} - \sqrt{\lambda - \frac{c_\alpha^2+2}{36}} \quad \text{(b)} \qquad \textbf{(786)}$$

Critical limits k_l and k_r for k for given λ and α:

$$\text{Prob}(k_l \leq k \leq k_r) \geq 1 - 2\alpha$$

$$k_l, k_r = \text{integer}\left(\lambda + \frac{c_\alpha^2+2}{6} \mp \left[1 + \sqrt{c_\alpha^2\left(\lambda - \frac{c_\alpha^2+2}{36}\right)}\right]\right) \qquad \textbf{(787)}$$

Critical limits λ_l and λ_r for λ for given k and α:

$$\text{Prob}(\lambda_l \leq \lambda \leq \lambda_r) = 1 - 2\alpha$$

$$\lambda_{l(k+1)}, \lambda_{r(k)} = k + \frac{c_\alpha^2+2}{3} \mp \sqrt{c_\alpha^2\left(k + \frac{c_\alpha^2+11}{18}\right)} \quad \text{(a)}$$

$$\lambda_{l(k)}, \lambda_{r(k)} = k + \frac{2c_\alpha^2+1}{6} \mp \left[\frac{1}{2} + \sqrt{c_\alpha^2\left(k + \frac{c_\alpha^2+2}{18} \mp \frac{1}{2}\right)}\right] \quad \text{(b)} \qquad \textbf{(788)}$$

In the equations (**786**) to (**788**) above, k correspond to x.

Example 60. Calculate x_p and x_{1-p^*} (k_l and k_r) for $p = p^* = 0{,}025$ ($\alpha = 0{,}025$) for the Poisson distribution ($\lambda = 99$).

From (**787**)

$$k_l, k_r = 99 + \frac{(1{,}96)^2+2}{6} \mp \left[1 + \sqrt{(1{,}96)^2\left(99 - \frac{(1{,}96)^2+2}{36}\right)}\right]$$

$= 79{,}488$ and $120{,}459$

$=$ (integer) 79 and 120

These correspond to the exact values.

◊ For example, the observation units $t_1, t_2, \ldots, t_k$ must not overlap.

All values conform to the international convention (i.e. 0,1 instead of 0.1).

The following transformation[29] is suitable for stabilizing the variance:

$$\left.\begin{aligned} &X=\sqrt{x}+\sqrt{x+1} \\ &\text{with variance } \sigma_X^2 \sim 1 \\ &\text{and mean } \bar{X} \sim \sqrt{4\lambda+1} \end{aligned}\right\} \quad \textbf{(789)}$$

The relationship between the Poisson and χ^2-distribution is given in **(562)** and **(563)**, whence the following procedure for determining the *exact* values of x_p and x_{p^*} (k_l and k_r):

(a) x_p is required. The value $\chi^2 \leq 2\lambda$ is sought in the column $1\int_l = 1 - p$ of the χ^2-table on pages 34–37. From the degrees of freedom ν of this χ^2 it follows that

$$\left.\begin{aligned} x_p &= \frac{\nu}{2} - 1 \quad [\text{when } \nu \text{ is even}] \\ &= \frac{\nu}{2} - 1{,}5 \quad [\text{when } \nu \text{ is odd}] \end{aligned}\right\} \quad \textbf{(790)}$$

(b) x_{p^*} is required. The value $\chi^2 \geq 2\lambda$ is sought in the column $1\int_l = p^*$ of the χ^2-table on pages 34–37. From the degrees of freedom ν of this χ^2 it follows that

$$\left.\begin{aligned} x_{p^*} &= \frac{\nu}{2} \quad [\text{when } \nu \text{ is even}] \\ &= \frac{\nu}{2} + 0{,}5 \quad [\text{when } \nu \text{ is odd}] \end{aligned}\right\} \quad \textbf{(791)}$$

Example 61. Required are the $(1-2\alpha)$ limits for k when $\lambda = 32$ and $\alpha = 0{,}0005$. The left-hand limit is obtained from **(790)** and is $\chi^2_{0,9995} = 63{,}582 \leq 64$ with $\nu = 31$. $k_l = 31/2 - 1{,}5 = 14$. The right-hand limit is obtained from **(791)** and is $\chi^2_{0,0005} = 64{,}524 \geq 64$ with $\nu = 106$. $k_r = 106/2 = 53$.

21E. Confidence limits and significance limits

Confidence limits for λ (tables on pages 152 and 154)

In analogy with the binomial distribution, confidence limits for λ are solutions to the equations

$$\left.\begin{aligned} &\sum_{k=x}^{k=\infty} \frac{e^{-\lambda_l}\lambda_l^k}{k!} = \alpha \text{ for } \lambda_l \quad [\alpha < 0{,}5] \qquad \text{(a)} \\ &\text{and} \\ &\sum_{k=0}^{k=x} \frac{e^{-\lambda_r}\lambda_r^k}{k!} = \alpha \text{ for } \lambda_r \quad [\alpha < 0{,}5] \qquad \text{(b)} \end{aligned}\right\} \quad \textbf{(792)}$$

For $x = 0$ there is only one $(1-\alpha)$ confidence interval with the solution $\lambda_r = z$ [equation **(129)**, page 173]. The left-hand limit λ_l is zero. For $x > 0$ only iterative solutions are possible.

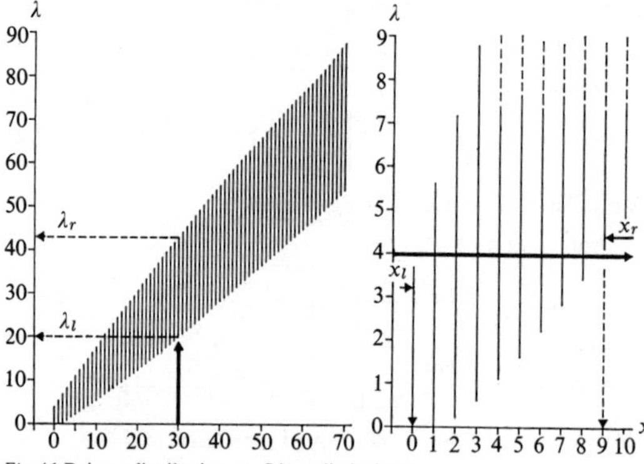

Fig. 46. Poisson distribution, confidence limits for λ.

For confidence intervals other than those in the tables on pages 152 and 154, *exact* limits for λ for given x up to 100 (or 99) can be calculated from the χ^2-table on pages 34–37 as follows:

Given x and α, then

$$\left.\begin{aligned} &\tfrac{1}{2}(\chi^2_{\alpha;\,\nu=2x}) = \lambda_l \qquad \text{(a)} \\ &\tfrac{1}{2}(\chi^2_{1-\alpha;\,\nu=2(x+1)}) = \lambda_r \qquad \text{(b)} \end{aligned}\right\} \quad \textbf{(793)}$$

where χ^2_α and $\chi^2_{1-\alpha}$ denote the α and $(1-\alpha)$ quantiles; α and $1-\alpha$ are to be found under $1\int_l$.

All values conform to the international convention (i.e. 0,1 instead of 0.1).

Example 62. Required are the $(1-2\alpha)$ limits for λ when $x = 98$ and $\alpha = 0{,}05$. For λ_l the table is entered at $\nu = 2 \times 98 = 196$ and $1\int_l = 0{,}05$, giving $\chi_l^2 = 164{,}610$. $\lambda_l = 164{,}610/2 = 82{,}305$. For λ_r the table is entered at $\nu = 2(98+1) = 198$ and $1\int_l = 0{,}95$, giving $\chi_r^2 = 231{,}829$. $\lambda_r = 231{,}829/2 = 115{,}915$.

For higher values of x $(=k)$ a very good approximation is obtained using **(788)**.

Example 63. Required are the $(1-2\alpha)$ confidence limits for λ when $k = 99$ and $\alpha = 0{,}025$.

$$\lambda_l, \lambda_r = 99 + \frac{2(1{,}96)^2+1}{6} \mp \left[\frac{1}{2} + \sqrt{(1{,}96)^2\left(99 + \frac{(1{,}96)^2+2}{18} \mp \frac{1}{2}\right)}\right]$$
$$= 80{,}46 \text{ and } 120{,}53$$

These coincide with the exact values.

Example 64. In 12 minutes 24 events are observed. Calculate the 95% limits for $\lambda_{12\,\text{min}}, \lambda_{1\,\text{min}}, \lambda_{1\,\text{h}}$.
For $x = 24$ in the table on page 152 the limits 15,377 and 35,710 are given.
In accordance with **(780)** these give the following further limits

for $\lambda_{1\,\text{min}}$: 15,377/12 and 35,710/12 = 1,2814 and 2,9758
for $\lambda_{1\,\text{h}}$: 15,377 × 5 and 35,710 × 5 = 76,885 and 178,55

The estimate of the limits for λ_{kt} must always be made on the basis of the number of events x observed during the observation unit t, and *not* on the basis of this number multiplied by k. The following calculation in the case of this example would be wrong:

$x_{1\,\text{min}} = 24/12 = 2$
limits for $x_{1\,\text{min}}$: 0,2422 and 7,2247

or

$x_{1\,\text{h}} = 24 \times 5 = 120$
limits for $x_{1\,\text{h}}$: 99,492 and 143,49

Significance limits for x $(=k)$ when λ is given (tables on pages 153 and 155)

These limits meet the condition **(390)** with N replaced by ∞.
They can be obtained without calculation from the confidence limits for λ, as shown in Figure 46, right. The procedure is exactly analogous to that for determining the corresponding limits for the binomial distribution. For $\alpha \neq 0{,}025$ or $0{,}005$, the left-hand limit is obtained from **(790)**, the right-hand limit from **(791)**. Cf. example 61. For $n > 100$ (or 99), approximations are obtained from **(788)**.

21F. Testing frequencies

(a) *2 samples from two observation units of equal length $t_1 = t_2 = t$*

Given are 2 samples with the *same* length but independent observation unit $t_1 = t_2 = t$, in which the event E occurs x_1 and x_2 times respectively.
The sums $x_1 + x_2 = N$ are calculated. The significance limits for x_1 and x_2 are then x_l and x_r of the table on pages 104–107 for $N = x_1 + x_2$. If x_1 and x_2 *attain* or *exceed* these limits (in an outward direction from ½ N), then the following interpretations may be made:

$$\left.\begin{aligned} &\text{one-tailed test:} \quad \lambda_1 < \lambda_2, \text{ if } x_1 \leq x_l \quad [\text{significance } \alpha] \\ &\phantom{\text{one-tailed test:}} \quad \lambda_1 > \lambda_2, \text{ if } x_1 \geq x_r \quad [\text{significance } \alpha] \\ &\text{two-tailed test:} \quad \lambda_1 \neq \lambda_2, \text{ if } x_1 \text{ and } x_2 \textit{ attain} \text{ or } \textit{exceed} \\ &\phantom{\text{two-tailed test:}} \quad (\text{outwards}) \text{ the levels } x_l \text{ and } x_r \\ &\phantom{\text{two-tailed test:}} \quad [\text{significance } 2\alpha] \end{aligned}\right\} \quad \textbf{(794)}$$

For samples with $x_1 + x_2 > 499$ or $t_1 \neq t_2$ see (b) below.

(b) *Several samples from any number of observation units t_i*

Given are m samples from any number of independent observation units $t_1, t_2, \ldots, t_i, \ldots, t_m$ in which the event E occurs $x_1, x_2, \ldots, x_i, \ldots, x_m$ times. The following are calculated:

$$\lambda_i^* = \frac{x_i}{t_i} \text{ and } \bar{\lambda} = \frac{\Sigma x_i}{\Sigma t_i}$$

and the x_i values transformed into c_i values as follows:

$$\left.\begin{aligned} c_i &= 2\left(\sqrt{x_i+1} - \sqrt{t_i\bar{\lambda}}\right) \quad [\lambda_i^* < \bar{\lambda}] \\ c_i &= 2\left(\sqrt{x_i} - \sqrt{t_i\bar{\lambda}}\right) \quad [\lambda_i^* > \bar{\lambda}] \end{aligned}\right\} \quad \textbf{(795)}$$

1. Compare these transformed data by means of the extreme range test (rapid test).
   The extreme range m is calculated as the difference between the largest c_i and the smallest c_i.
   The significance limits for the extreme range m can be found on page 58 with $N_1 = m$ and $\nu = \infty$. For $m = 2$, i.e. the two-sample problem, these limits are 2,772 ($2\alpha = 0{,}05$) and 3,643 ($2\alpha = 0{,}01$). If the extreme range m *reaches* or *exceeds* the significance limits the interpretation is for $m = 2$:

$$\left.\begin{array}{ll}\text{one-tailed test:} & \lambda_1^* < \lambda_2^*, \text{if } \lambda_1^* - \lambda_2^* < 0 \quad [\text{significance } \alpha] \\ & \lambda_1^* < \lambda_2^*, \text{if } \lambda_1^* - \lambda_2^* > 0 \quad [\text{significance } \alpha] \\ \text{two-tailed test:} & \text{The samples are not all from the same} \\ & \text{population } [\text{significance } 2\alpha]\end{array}\right\} \quad (796)$$

   If $m = 2$ (2 samples) this test is about as good as the χ^2-test.
   If $m > 10$ the extreme range test is not recommended.

2. Comparison by means of the χ^2-test.
   The values of c_i are squared and summed. The test statistic Σc_i^2 is approximately χ^2-distributed with $\nu = m - 1$ degrees of freedom (significance limits pages 34–37).
   The two-sided interpretation when the χ^2-limit is exceeded is: The samples are not all from the same population [significance 2α].

(c) *Confidence limits for the increase in frequency of a rare event*[34]

Given are two samples of sizes N_1 and N_2 in which the fairly *rare* event E occurs with a relative frequency of $p_1 = x_1/N_1$ and $p_2 = x_2/N_2$ respectively. *The samples should be so numbered that* $p_1 < p_2$. The estimate of the proportionate *increase* in relative frequency from sample 1 to sample 2 is then

$$Proc_{1\to 2} = \frac{p_2 - p_1}{p_1} \qquad (797)$$

with the $(1 - 2\alpha)$ confidence limits for $\boldsymbol{Proc}_{1\to 2}$

$$k\left(\frac{1}{p_r} - 1\right) - 1 < \boldsymbol{Proc}_{1\to 2} < k\left(\frac{1}{p_l} - 1\right) - 1 \qquad (798)$$

where $k = N_1/N_2$ and p_r and p_l are obtained from the tables on pages 89–102 for $N = x_1 + x_2$ and $x = x_1$. **(797)** and **(798)** are converted to percentages by multiplying by 100. **(798)** can also be calculated in this way when only the *ratio* N_1/N_2 and the absolute numbers x_1 and x_2 are known. *Interpretation:* When the left-hand limit of **(798)** ≤ 0, then no increase in frequency has occurred.

22. The hypergeometric distribution

22A. General

Given are N balls, of which X are white and $N - X$ red. The probability of drawing exactly x_1 white balls in N_1 draws is then

$$\left.\begin{aligned} f(x_1 \mid X, N, N_1) &= \frac{\binom{X}{x_1}\binom{N-X}{N_1-x_1}}{\binom{N}{N_1}} && \text{(a)} \\ &= \frac{N_1!\,(N-N_1)!\,X!\,(N-X)!}{N!\;x_1!\;(N_1-x_1)!\,(X-x_1)!\,(N-X-N_1+x_1)!} && \text{(b)}\end{aligned}\right\} \quad (799)$$

$f(x_1 \mid X, N, N_1)$ is known as the hypergeometric distribution of x_1 (X, N, N_1 constant).

The corresponding fourfold table is

$$\begin{array}{lll|l} \text{White:} & x_1 & N_1 - x_1 & N_1 \\ \text{Red:} & X - x_1 & N - X - N_1 + x_1 & N - N_1 \\ \hline & X & N - X & N \end{array} \equiv \begin{array}{ll|l} x_1 & N_1 - x_1 & N_1 \\ x_2 & N_2 - x_2 & N_2 \\ \hline X & N - X & N \end{array} \qquad (800)$$

For $N \leq 100$ the calculation of **(799)** is best made from (a) by means of the tables on pages 74–81 (cf. explanation on page 81), for $N > 100$ from (b) by means of the tables on pages 24 and 25. The calculation can also be made with the aid of the recursion formulae:

$$f(x_1 + 1 \mid X) = [f(x_1 \mid X)] \times \frac{(N_1 - x_1)(X - x_1)}{(x_1 + 1)(N - X - N_1 + x_1 + 1)} \qquad (801)$$

and

$$f(x_1 \mid X + 1) = [f(x_1 \mid X)] \times \frac{(N - X - N_1 + x_1)(X + 1)}{(N - X)(X + 1 - x_1)} \qquad (802)$$

All the probabilities $f(x_1 \mid X, N = 20, N_1 = 5)$ and cumulative probabilities $F(x_1 \mid X)$ are given in the tables on the next page, where the same probabilities are shown graphically in Figures 47 and 48.

All values conform to the international convention (i.e. 0,1 instead of 0.1).

A check on calculations of this kind is provided by

$$\left.\begin{aligned} &\sum_{x_1=0}^{x_1=N_1} \text{Prob}(x_1 \mid X = K) = 1 && \text{(a)} \\ &\sum_{X=0}^{X=N-N_1+k_1} \text{Prob}(x_1 = k_1 \mid X) = \frac{N+1}{N_1+1} && \text{(b)}\end{aligned}\right\} \quad (803)$$

Figure 47 clearly demonstrates the symmetry of the relationship

$$\left.\begin{aligned} &\text{Prob}(x_1 = k_1 \mid X = K) = \text{Prob}(x_1 = N_1 - k_1 \mid X = N - K) \\ &\text{whence} \\ &\text{Prob}(x_1 \leq k_1 \mid X = K) = \text{Prob}(x_1 \geq N_1 - k_1 \mid X = N - k)\end{aligned}\right\} \quad (804)$$

22B. Parameters

The mean of x when X, N and N_1 are given is

$$\mu_x = N_1\,\boldsymbol{p} \quad [x \mid N = \boldsymbol{p}] \qquad (805)$$

and the variance is

$$\sigma_x^2 = N_1\,\boldsymbol{p}\,\boldsymbol{q}\left(\frac{N - N_1}{N - 1}\right) \quad [X/N = \boldsymbol{p};\ \boldsymbol{q} = 1 - \boldsymbol{p}] \qquad (806)$$

The variance of the hypergeometric distribution (N, N_1, $\boldsymbol{p}$) is thus *smaller* than that of the binomial distribution ($\boldsymbol{p}$; N_1) by the factor $(N - N_1)/(N - 1)$.

22C. The hypergeometric distribution and other distributions

When $\boldsymbol{p} < 0{,}1$ and N is fairly large (say over 60) the hypergeometric distribution (N, N_1, $\boldsymbol{p}$) approximates to the binomial distribution ($\boldsymbol{p}$; N_1). In this connection it is advisable in significance tests to remain on the safe side. **(807)**

When $N_1/N < 0{,}1$ and N is fairly large the Poisson distribution ($\lambda = N_1\,\boldsymbol{p}$) is a good approximation. **(808)**

When $N_1\,\boldsymbol{p} \geq 4$ (approximately), the normal distribution [**(805)**, $\sqrt{\mathbf{(806)}}$] is a good approximation, whence **(809)**

$$\left.\begin{aligned} c_p &= \frac{x_1 + \tfrac{1}{2} - \mathbf{(805)}}{\sqrt{\mathbf{(806)}}} && \text{(a)} \\ c_{1-p^*} &= \frac{x_1 - \tfrac{1}{2} - \mathbf{(805)}}{\sqrt{\mathbf{(806)}}} && \text{(b)}\end{aligned}\right\} \quad (810)$$

where $+\tfrac{1}{2}$ or $-\tfrac{1}{2}$ can be neglected when N is large.

22D. Significance limits

The significance limits given in the table on pages 137–151 meet the conditions (when N and N_1 are given)

$$\left.\begin{aligned} &\left.\begin{aligned}&\text{Prob}(x_1 \geq k_1 \mid X_l) \leq \alpha \\ &\text{Prob}(x_1 \geq k_1 \mid X_l + 1) > \alpha\end{aligned}\right\} \text{(a)} \\ &\text{and} \\ &\left.\begin{aligned}&\text{Prob}(x_1 \leq k_1 \mid X_r) \leq \alpha \\ &\text{Prob}(x_1 \leq k_1 \mid X_r - 1) > \alpha\end{aligned}\right\} \text{(b)}\end{aligned}\right\} \quad (811)$$

This form of presentation is preferred since it is also convenient in situations in which X is unknown (this does *not* correspond to the situation described at the start of section 22A).
The procedure for finding the upper level (**811**b) for $\alpha = 0{,}05$ is indicated in Figure 48 (horizontal broken line).

With large values of N, **(811)** can be satisfied approximately on the basis of **(810)**, using **(812)**[35] and **(813)**

$$\left.\begin{aligned} X_l, X_r &= \frac{N}{2k}\Bigg(k + 2x_1 - N_1 \mp 1 \mp \\ &\mp \sqrt{k^2 - \frac{2k}{N_1}\left[(x_1 \mp \tfrac{1}{2})^2 + (N_1 - x_1 \pm \tfrac{1}{2})^2\right] + (2x_1 - N_1 \mp 1)^2}\Bigg) \\ &[k = N_1 + (1 - N_1/N)\,c_\alpha^2]\end{aligned}\right\} \quad (812)$$

$$\left.\begin{aligned} X_l, X_r &= \frac{\overbrace{N\,[c_\alpha^2(N - N_1) + (2x_1 \mp 1)(N - 1)]}^{A}}{2\,[c_\alpha^2(N - N_1) + N_1(N - 1)]} \mp \\ &\mp \sqrt{A^2 - \frac{(x_1 \mp \tfrac{1}{2})^2 N^2 (N - 1)}{N_1\,[c_\alpha^2(N - N_1) + N_1(N - 1)]}}\end{aligned}\right\} \quad (813)$$

Hypergeometric distribution: $N = 20$; $N_1 = 5$; individual probabilities $\text{Prob}(x_1 = k_1 \mid X = K)$

x_1	$X = K$																				
	0	1	2	3	4	5	6	7	8	9	10	11	12	13	14	15	16	17	18	19	20
0	1	0,75	0,5526	0,3991	0,2817	0,1937	0,1291	0,0830	0,0511	0,0298	0,0163	0,0081	0,0036	0,0014	0,0004	0,0001					
1		0,25	0,3947	0,4605	0,4696	0,4402	0,3874	0,3228	0,2554	0,1916	0,1354	0,0894	0,0542	0,0293	0,0135	0,0048	0,0010				
2			0,0526	0,1316	0,2167	0,2935	0,3522	0,3874	0,3973	0,3831	0,3483	0,2980	0,2384	0,1761	0,1174	0,0677	0,0310	0,0088			
3				0,0088	0,0310	0,0677	0,1174	0,1761	0,2384	0,2980	0,3483	0,3831	0,3973	0,3874	0,3522	0,2935	0,2167	0,1316	0,0526		
4					0,0010	0,0048	0,0135	0,0293	0,0542	0,0894	0,1354	0,1916	0,2554	0,3228	0,3874	0,4402	0,4696	0,4605	0,3947	0,25	
5						0,0001	0,0004	0,0014	0,0036	0,0081	0,0163	0,0298	0,0511	0,0830	0,1291	0,1937	0,2817	0,3991	0,5526	0,75	1

Hypergeometric distribution: $N = 20$; $N_1 = 5$; cumulative probabilities $\text{Prob}(x_1 \leq k_1 \mid X = K)$

x_1	$X = K$																				
	0	1	2	3	4	5	6	7	8	9	10	11	12	13	14	15	16	17	18	19	20
0	1	0,75	0,5526	0,3991	0,2817	0,1937	0,1291	0,0830	0,0511	0,0298	0,0163	0,0081	0,0036	0,0011	0,0004	0,0001					
1		1	0,9474	0,8596	0,7513	0,6339	0,5165	0,4058	0,3065	0,2214	0,1517	0,0975	0,0578	0,0307	0,0139	0,0049	0,0010				
2			1	0,9912	0,9680	0,9274	0,8687	0,7932	0,7038	0,6045	0,5000	0,3955	0,2962	0,2068	0,1313	0,0726	0,0320	0,0088			
3				1	0,9990	0,9951	0,9861	0,9693	0,9422	0,9025	0,8483	0,7786	0,6935	0,5942	0,4835	0,3661	0,2487	0,1404	0,0526		
4					1	0,9999	0,9996	0,9986	0,9964	0,9919	0,9837	0,9702	0,9489	0,9170	0,8709	0,8063	0,7183	0,6009	0,4474	0,25	
5						1	1	1	1	1	1	1	1	1	1	1	1	1	1	1	1

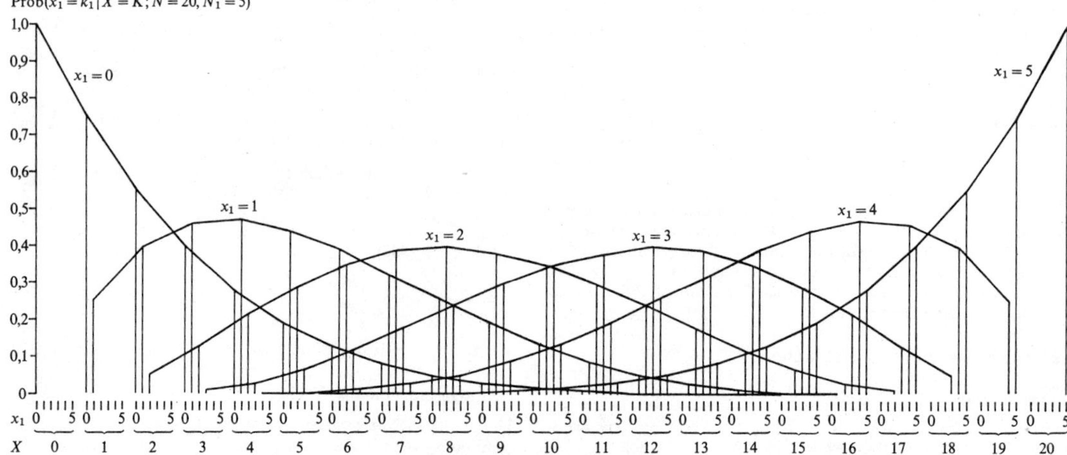

Fig. 47. Hypergeometric distribution. Graphical representation of all possible individual probabilities when N and N_1 are given. The vertical strokes 0–5 represent the probabilities $\text{Prob}(x_1 = 0, 1, \ldots, 5 \mid X = K)$. The curves link the probabilities $\text{Prob}(x_1 = k_1 \mid X = 0, 1, \ldots, 20)$.

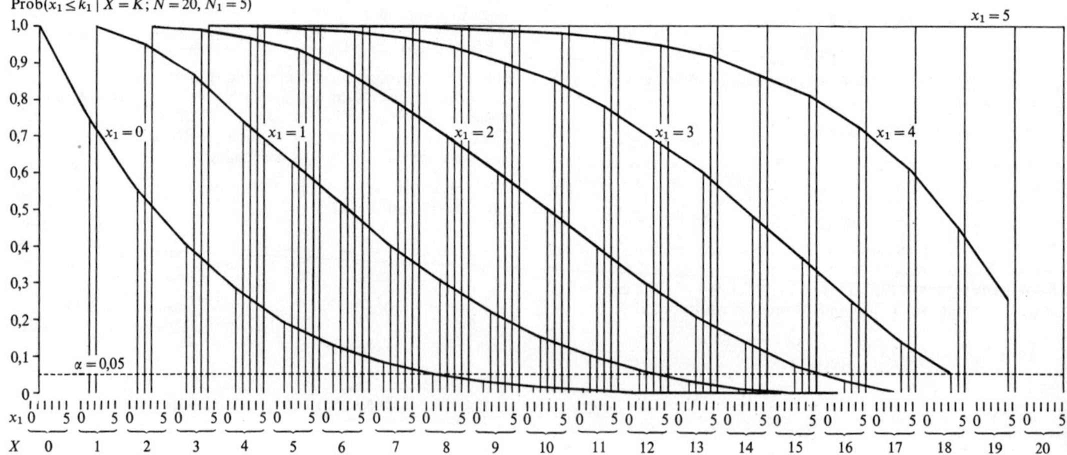

Fig. 48. Hypergeometric distribution. Graphical representation of all possible cumulative probabilities $\text{Prob}(x \leq k_1 \mid X)$ when N and N_1 are given. The vertical strokes 0–5 represent the probabilities $\text{Prob}(x_1 \leq 0, 1, \ldots, 5 \mid X = K)$. The curves link the probabilities $\text{Prob}(x \leq k_1 \mid X - 0, 1, \ldots, 20)$.

All values conform to the international convention (i.e. 0,1 instead of 0.1).

The values obtained from (**812**) and (**813**) are rounded off as follows, e.g.:

result for lower limit = 11,534: $X_l = 11$
result for upper limit = 26,421: $X_r = 27$

When $N > 60$, $N_1 \boldsymbol{p} \geq 4$, $N_2 \boldsymbol{p} \geq 4$ (approximately), the $(1-2\alpha)$ significance limits for x_1 with X given can be obtained approximately as follows:

$$x_l, x_r = N_1 \boldsymbol{p} \mp \left[\tfrac{1}{2} + |c_\alpha| \sqrt{N_1 \boldsymbol{p} \boldsymbol{q} (N-N_1)/(N-1)}\right] \quad \text{[for } \boldsymbol{p} \text{ and } \boldsymbol{q} \text{ see (806)]} \qquad (814)$$

23. Non-parametric tests: nominal data

23A. Introduction

In this section we consider certain non-parametric (or distribution-free) tests applicable to data measured on the simplest of scales: nominal. Nominal data are only classificatory. Examples of nominal data would be sex (females; males), marital status (married, separated, divorced, widowed, single). For further details of these and related tests see the literature, for example SIEGEL[36], HOLLANDER and WOLFE[37] and LEHMANN[38].
We shall distinguish between two situations: one, where the samples drawn are independent and the other where the samples are related or paired. This distinction is also useful in section 24.

23B. Fisher's exact probability test

It is assumed that the data can be classified into two mutually exclusive classes, which we shall call success and failure. Two independent samples have been drawn and the observations classified. The data would typically look like this:

	Sample 1	Sample 2	Total
Success	x_{11}	x_{12}	$x_{11}+x_{12}$
Failure	x_{21}	x_{22}	$x_{21}+x_{22}$
Total	$x_{11}+x_{21}$	$x_{12}+x_{22}$	N

(**815**)

Fisher's exact probability test is particularly useful when the sample sizes are small. It determines whether the proportion of say successes, is the same in the two populations from which the samples were drawn.
It is calculated as follows:

Given that the marginal totals are fixed, the exact probability of observing a particular set of values as in (**815**) is given by the hypergeometric distribution [see (**799**)].

$$p = \frac{\binom{x_{11}+x_{21}}{x_{11}}\binom{x_{12}+x_{22}}{x_{12}}}{\binom{N}{x_{11}+x_{12}}} = \frac{(x_{11}+x_{12})!\,(x_{21}+x_{22})!\,(x_{11}+x_{21})!\,(x_{12}+x_{22})!}{N!\,x_{11}!\,x_{12}!\,x_{21}!\,x_{22}!} \qquad (816)$$

Under the null hypothesis H_0 however, (**816**) only represents a point probability and more extreme combinations of the values of x may be possible given the same marginals. To test the null hypothesis all these probabilities should be summed. If only the probabilities corresponding to one end of the distribution are summed, we get a one-tailed test. As the distribution is not always symmetrical, a two-tailed test is not always obtained by doubling the one-sided probability. The probabilities at the extreme other end may have to be calculated and the probabilities from both ends of the distribution summed.

Example 65.

Suppose the following data have been observed:

	Sample 1	Sample 2	Total
Success	1	5	6
Failure	6	1	7
Total	7	6	13

If we calculate the discrete density function given this particular set of marginals we get:

$p_0 = 0{,}000583$
$p_1 = 0{,}024476$*
$p_2 = 0{,}183566$
$p_3 = 0{,}407925$
$p_4 = 0{,}305944$
$p_5 = 0{,}073427$
$p_6 = 0{,}004079$

$\Sigma p_i = 1{,}000000$

The probability associated with the table is $p_1 = 0{,}024476$ (marked with an asterisk), but both p_0 and p_6 are more extreme. The one-tailed test thus gives $p_0 + p_1 = 0{,}025059$ and the two-tailed test $p_0 + p_1 + p_6 = 0{,}029138$.

23C. χ^2-test

The problem is the same as in section 23B. As N increases the calculation of Fisher's exact probability test becomes more cumbersome, particularly if the smallest x_{ij} is large. An alternative statistic may be [following (**815**)]

$$\chi^2 = \frac{N(x_{11}\ x_{22} - x_{12}\ x_{21})^2}{(x_{11}+x_{12})(x_{21}+x_{22})(x_{11}+x_{21})(x_{12}+x_{22})} \qquad (817)$$

Under H_0 this statistic is approximately χ^2-distributed with degree of freedom $\nu = 1$, i.e. the tables on pages 34–37 may be used to test the null hypothesis. If the test statistic in (**817**) is equal to or greater than the desired significance probability, it is concluded that the probabilities for success (or failure) are not the same for both samples. If the test statistic is smaller than the significance probability, it may be concluded that the probabilities are similar.
Alternatively (**817**) may be sought in the tables on pages 137–151 (for $N \leq 60$) to give the exact significance probability.
To improve the χ^2-approximation, YATES[39] suggested a so-called continuity correction, changing (**817**) to:

$$\chi^2 = \frac{N(|x_{11}\ x_{22} - x_{12}\ x_{21}| - N/2)^2}{(x_{11}+x_{12})(x_{21}+x_{22})(x_{11}+x_{21})(x_{12}+x_{22})} \qquad (818)$$

Formula (**817**) can also be written

$$\chi^2 = \sum_{i=1}^{2}\sum_{j=1}^{2} \frac{(x_{ij}-E_{ij})^2}{E_{ij}} \qquad (819)$$

where $E_{ij} = (x_{1j}+x_{2j})(x_{i1}+x_{i2})/N = N_i M_j / N$, with $N_i = x_{i1} + x_{i2}$ and $M_j = x_{1j} + x_{2j}$. This leads naturally to the extension, where we have m samples rather than 2 and n categories instead of 2. This is often referred to as an $(m \times n)$-contingency table, and (**819**) becomes

$$\chi^2 = \sum_{i=1}^{m}\sum_{j=1}^{n} \frac{(x_{ij}-E_{ij})^2}{E_{ij}} = N\left(\sum_{i=1}^{m}\sum_{j=1}^{n} \frac{x_{ij}^2}{N_i M_j} - 1\right) \qquad (820)$$

This test statistic is approx. χ^2-distributed with $\nu = (m-1)(n-1)$ degrees of freedom under H_0 (tables on pages 34–37). When $\nu = 1$, SIEGEL[36] recommends the use of Fisher's exact probability test if $N < 20$. If $20 \leq N \leq 40$, the χ^2-test (**818**) should be used provided all expected values E_{ij} are 5 or more, otherwise Fisher's test should be used. If $N > 40$, (**818**) should be used. When $\nu > 1$, (**820**) should only be used when no expected values E_{ij} are less than 1 and not less than 20% of the cells have expected values E_{ij} less than 5.

23D. The McNemar test[40]

In sections 23B and 23C we were dealing with independent samples. The McNemar test is useful when we deal with related samples or paired samples or studies in which patients serve as their own control. Assume for example that we have two treatments A and B. All patients are given both treatments. The outcome is recorded as either success or failure. The results could typically be arranged as follows:

		B Success	B Failure
A	Success	x_1	x_2
A	Failure	x_3	x_4

(**821**)

with the sample size $N = x_1 + x_2 + x_3 + x_4$.
It is obvious that x_1 and x_4 offers no inference on the difference between A and B. MCNEMAR showed that under the null hypothesis of no difference between A and B

$$\chi^2_M = \frac{(x_3-x_2)^2}{x_3+x_2} \qquad (822)$$

All values conform to the international convention (i.e. 0,1 instead of 0.1).

(**822**) is approximately χ^2-distributed with degree of freedom $\nu = 1$. Again a continuity correction may be applied to improve the approximation and (**822**) becomes

$$\chi^2_M = \frac{(|x_3 - x_2| - 1)^2}{x_3 + x_2} \qquad \textbf{(823)}$$

Example 66. Suppose we obtained the following result on giving both A and B to the same 10 patients:

		B Success	B Failure
A	Success	1	1
A	Failure	8	0

Using (**822**) we get $\chi^2_M = (8-1)^2/9 = 49/9 = 5{,}444$. If (**823**) is applied we get $\chi^2_M = (|8-1|-1)^2/9 = 36/9 = 4{,}000$; in both cases we may conclude that B is better than A (significance probability $\alpha = 0{,}05$); see table on page 34.

24. Non-parametric tests: ordinal data

24A. Introduction

In this section we shall consider tests which are applicable to data measured on an ordinal scale, i.e. data which have a natural ordering $x_1 \leq x_2 \leq \cdots \leq x_n$ like for example an intelligence quotient. Many psychiatric and psychological measurements result in ordinal type data. For further reading the books by SIEGEL[36], HOLLANDER and WOLFE[37] and LEHMANN[38] are again useful.
These tests depend on a ranking of the data.

(a) *By magnitude (continuous distributions)*
Given are two samples 1 and 2 with the x_1 values 1,06, 1,53, 1,68, 1,68, 1,69, 1,69 and the x_2 values 1,30, 1,55, 1,69, 1.80. These values are ranked as follows:

x_1:	1,06		1,53		1,68	1,68		1,69	1,69	
x_2:		1,30		1,55			1,69			1,80
$R_{1,2}$:	1	2	3	4	5	6	8	8	8	10

$= (7+8+9)/3$ **(824)**

With ties [cf. (**346**)], the procedure is as in (**824**): tied values *within* a sample receive *successive* rank numbers, those *between* the samples the *mean* of the rank numbers at the positions concerned. **(825)**

In the above example, the rank numbers R_1 of the x_1 values are $R_1 = 1, 3, 5, 6, 8$ and 8, and their sum $T_1 = \Sigma R_1 = 31$. **(826)**

With *paired observations*, the n paired differences d_i are calculated as in section 16D, page 209, with all d_i values equal to zero ignored and N reduced accordingly. The *absolute values* of these differences are then ranked and either the rank numbers of all negative differences summed to give T_- or those of all positive differences summed to give T_+. **(827)**

(b) *By order in a series (discrete distributions)*
If in a series of N trials the event E occurs once each in the 2nd, 3rd, 8th and 13th trials, in all N_1 times (for example 4 times), then $R_E = 2, 3, 8$ and 13 respectively and the sum of the R_E numbers $= T_E = 26$. **(828)**

24B. The Wilcoxon two-sample test[41, 42] (or the Mann-Whitney U-test)

Given are two samples from *continuous* distributions of *any* form with means μ_1 and μ_2 respectively. These are so numbered that $N_1 \leq 25$ and $N_2 \leq 50$. The x_1 values are now ranked as in (**824**) and (**825**) to give the sum T_1 of (**826**).

The acceptance regions for T_1 are given in the tables on pages 156–162. If T_1 *attains* the significance levels or *exceeds them in the outward direction* from its expected value, then this may be regarded as evidence that

one-tailed test: $\mu_1 < \mu_2$, if $T_1 \leq T_l$ [significance $\leq \alpha$]
$\mu_1 > \mu_2$, if $T_1 \geq T_r$ [significance $\leq \alpha$]

two-tailed test: $\mu_1 \neq \mu_2$, if $T_1 \leq T_l$ or $T_1 \geq T_r$
[significance $\leq 2\alpha$] **(829)**

Cf. also section 9C, page 193.

Under the null hypothesis, the expectation $\boldsymbol{T}_1$ of the estimate T_1 is

$$\boldsymbol{T}_1 = N_1(N_1 + N_2 + 1)/2 \quad \text{(a)}$$
or
$$6\,\boldsymbol{T}_1 = 3\,N_1(N_1 + N_2 + 1) \quad \text{(b)} \qquad \textbf{(830)}$$

and the variance

$$\sigma^2_{T_1} = N_2\,\boldsymbol{T}_1/6 \quad \text{(a)}$$
or
$$\sigma^2_{6T_1} = 6\,N_2\,\boldsymbol{T}_1 \quad \text{(b)} \qquad \textbf{(831)}$$

For samples outside the scope of the tables the following test quotient can be used

$$(T_1 - \boldsymbol{T}_1)/\sqrt{\sigma^2_{T_1}} \quad \text{(a)}$$
or
$$(6\,T_1 - 6\,\boldsymbol{T}_1)/\sqrt{\sigma^2_{6T_1}} \quad \text{(b)} \qquad \textbf{(832)}$$
[significance limit c_α: page 28]

24C. The Kruskal-Wallis test[43] (H-test)

This test is an extension of the Wilcoxon two-sample test and is useful when we want to test the equality of not two but k population means. Assume we have k independent samples

$$x_{i1}, x_{i2}, ..., x_{in_i} \quad [i = 1, 2, ..., k]$$

from a continuous but otherwise unknown distribution with mean values $\mu_1, \mu_2, ..., \mu_k$. The data are assumed to be ordinal. We want to test the null hypothesis

$$H_0\colon \mu_1 = \mu_2 = ... = \mu_k$$

This is done by calculating the following statistic:

$$H = \frac{12}{N(N+1)} \sum_{i=1}^{k} \frac{R_i^2}{n_i} - 3(N+1) \qquad \textbf{(833)}$$

where $N = \sum_{i=1}^{k} n_i$ and R_i is the sum of the ranks in the i'th sample.
Provided the sample sizes n_i are not too small H is approximately χ^2-distributed with $k-1$ degrees of freedom under H_0. The tables on pages 34–37 can thus be used to test the significance of H. If ties occur the tied observations are given the average rank of the individual ranks. H in (**833**) is then usually corrected to:

$$H_t = H\Bigg/\left(1 - \frac{\Sigma(t^3 - t)}{N^3 - N}\right) \qquad \textbf{(834)}$$

where t is the number of tied observations in a group of identical values.

Example 67. Three groups of patients have been given analgesics A, B and C. Pain relief has been recorded on a scale from 0 to 9. The results are:

A: 2, 4, 3, 7, 0, 6, 3, 5, 3, 6
B: 4, 4, 8, 3, 9, 6, 5, 4
C: 5, 3, 1, 5, 0

Some results are obviously tied and we therefore wish to calculate H_t:

A		B		C	
Score	Rank	Score	Rank	Score	Rank
0	1,5	3	7	0	1,5
2	4	4	11,5	1	3
3	7	4	11,5	3	7
3	7	4	11,5	5	15,5
3	7	5	15,5	5	15,5
4	11,5	6	19		
5	15,5	8	22		
6	19	9	23		
6	19				
7	21				
n_i	10		8		5
R_i	112,5		121		42,5

Ranking all the scores irrespective of A, B and C and summing these for each group gives the R_i's in the table above.

All values conform to the international convention (i.e. 0,1 instead of 0.1).

H can now be calculated from **(833)**

$$H=\frac{12}{23\times 24}\left(\frac{112{,}5^2}{10}+\frac{121^2}{8}+\frac{42{,}5^2}{5}\right)-3\times 24=3{,}152$$

To calculate H_t we need to calculate the correcting factor for ties. There are two scores of 0, three scores of 6, four scores of 4, four scores of 5 and five scores of 3:

$$\begin{aligned}\Sigma(t^3-t) &= (2^3-2)+(3^3-3)+2\times(4^3-4)+(5^3-5)\\ &= 6+24+120+120\\ &= 270\end{aligned}$$

$$\begin{aligned}H_t &= \frac{H}{1-\Sigma(t^3-t)/(N^3-N)}\\ &= 3{,}152/(1-270/121\,44)\\ &= 3{,}224\end{aligned}$$

Using the table on page 34 we find that the probability associated with H_t for $v=k-1=2$ is just under 0,20, i.e., there is no evidence from the existing data that the treatments are different.

24D. The sign test

(a) *Testing a sample for symmetry.* $\tilde{x}$ is calculated, and the sample values, including $\tilde{x}$, are ranked. The number $N(-)$ of samples smaller than $\tilde{x}$ is then counted, and the levels x_l and x_r corresponding to the sample size N and the significance probability 2α sought in the table on pages 104–107. If the number $N(-)$ coincides with either of these levels or lies outside them, then interpretation **(506)** applies.

Example 68. In example 24 on page 197, $\tilde{x}=2{,}130$, $N(-)=16$. For $N=21$ and $2\alpha=0{,}05$, the table on page 105 gives the limits 5–16. With a significance probability of 0,05, the sample *does not* originate from a symmetrical distribution.

(b) *Testing of paired differences (differences between pairs of observations).* In such cases the null hypothesis is that the differences do not on the average differ from zero, or rather that the numbers of differences respectively smaller than and larger than zero are the same. The median is therefore zero. As in (a) above, the number $N(-)$ of differences which are smaller than zero, i.e., negative, is counted; in other words, the number $N(-)$ of *minus signs* is counted. The further procedure is as in (a).

Example 69. Of 400 paired differences, 230 are negative. Do these 400 differences differ on the average from zero ($2\alpha=0{,}05$)? For $2\alpha=0{,}05$ and $N=400$ the table on page 105 gives the limits 179–221, so that the difference from zero is confirmed with the desired significance probability.

Note that if in (a) above $\tilde{x}$ *coincides* with one of the sample values (or in the case of ties, with 2, 3, ... sample values), or if in (b) above 1, 2, ... of the paired differences are equal to zero, then the sample size with which the table is entered must be reduced by 1, 2, ... More powerful, but involving somewhat more calculation, is the Wilcoxon test for paired differences (cf. section 24E). For *small* samples a desired significance can be more easily reached with this test than with the sign test. Cf. also example 19 on page 194. For samples of $N>50$ there is no longer much difference between the two tests (as far as power is concerned; in the Wilcoxon test the amount of calculation involved increases rapidly with increasing sample size). Paired differences can also be examined by sequential analysis (cf. section 26B, page 232).

24E. The Wilcoxon matched-pairs test[42]

The sum T_- is calculated in accordance with **(827)**. The number of ranked paired differences is denoted by n (all zero values are ignored).

Significance limits for the sum T_- are given in the table on page 163. If the differences have been calculated as $d_i=x_{1i}-x_{2i}$ and the sum T_- *attains* the significance limits or *exceeds them in the outward direction* from the expected value of T_-, then it follows that

one-tailed test: $\mu_1>\mu_2$, when $T_-\le T_l$ [significance $\le\alpha$]
$\mu_1<\mu_2$, when $T_-\ge T_r$ [significance $\le\alpha$]
two-tailed test: $\mu_1\ne\mu_2$, when $T_-\le T_l$ or $T_-\ge T_r$ [significance $\le 2\alpha$] **(835)**

All values conform to the international convention (i.e. 0,1 instead of 0.1).

Under the null hypothesis, the expectation $\boldsymbol{T}_-$ of the estimate T_- is

$$\boldsymbol{T}_-=n(n+1)/4 \qquad \textbf{(836)}$$

and the variance is

$$\sigma^2_{T_-}=(2n+1)\boldsymbol{T}_-/6 \qquad \textbf{(837)}$$

For samples outside the scope of the tables the following test quotient can be used:

$$(T_- - \boldsymbol{T}_-)/\sqrt{\sigma^2_{T_-}} \quad \text{[significance limit } c_\alpha\text{: page 26]} \qquad \textbf{(838)}$$

24F. The Friedman test[44]

As the Kruskal-Wallis test is an extension of the Wilcoxon two-sample test in the case of independent samples, so the Friedman test is an extension of the Wilcoxon matched-pairs test in the case of related samples. A typical example is where a group of n patients are each being studied under k different conditions giving data on an ordinal scale.
The results are ranked independently for each patient 1, 2, ..., k and the ranks for each condition then summed to give R_i.
The statistic

$$\chi^2_R=\frac{12}{nk(k+1)}\sum_{i=1}^{k}R_i^2-3n(k+1) \qquad \textbf{(839)}$$

is under the null hypothesis H_0 of no difference between conditions approximately χ^2-distributed with $k-1$ degrees of freedom (when n and/or k is not too small). Thus to test the significance of χ^2_R the tables on pages 34–37 may be used. In the case of ties (within a patient) a correction factor similar to that used in **(834)** may be used and χ^2_R becomes

$$(\chi^2_R)_t=\chi^2_R\bigg/\left(1-\frac{\Sigma(t^3-t)}{n(k^3-k)}\right) \qquad \textbf{(840)}$$

where t is the number of tied observations in a group of identical values [see **(831)**].

Example 70. Assume 10 patients are all given three analgesics A, B and C. Improvements are scored on a scale from 0 to 9:

Patient No.	Scores A	B	C	Rankings A	B	C
1	2	8	8	1	2,5	2,5
2	7	3	4	3	1	2
3	2	2	6	1,5	1,5	3
4	3	1	3	2,5	1	2,5
5	0	9	9	1	2,5	2,5
6	0	1	8	1	2	3
7	6	7	8	1	2	3
8	7	8	5	2	3	1
9	8	9	8	1,5	3	1,5
10	3	5	1	2	3	1
R_i				16,5	21,5	22

$$\chi^2_R=\frac{12\times(16{,}5^2+21{,}5^2+22^2)}{10\times3\times4}-3\times10\times4=1{,}850$$

$$(\chi^2_R)_t=1{,}850\bigg/\left(1-\frac{5(2^3-2)}{10\times24}\right)=2{,}114$$

From page 34 we find that the significance probability associated with $(\chi^2_R)_t$ [as $(\chi^2_R)_t$ is χ^2-distributed with 2 degrees of freedom] is between 0,30 and 0,40, and we conclude that the present data show no evidence of a difference between the three drugs.

24G. Haldane's test for trends in series[45]

The Wilcoxon test can also be used for testing exactly for the possibility that an event E is affected by the order in which it occurs. Examples of this situation are the possibility that the later children of *one* mother may be more liable to a certain disease, the question whether the mortality in, or success of, a particular operation in the *same* hospital is increasing or decreasing, and so on.
The test was developed by HALDANE for such problems independently of WILCOXON.

(a) *Investigation of a series*
T_E is calculated as in (**828**). N_1 is the number of trials (births, operations, etc.) in which the event E has occurred. N_2 is $N-N_1$, where N is the total number of trials in the series being investigated.

The significance limits for T_E are the same as those in section 24B; the interpretation, however, is completely different. *One-tailed test:* If T_E attains or exceeds the *left-hand limit*, then the frequency *decreases* with increasing lateness in the series; if it attains or exceeds the *right-hand limit*, the frequency increases.
Two-tailed test: The order has an influence on the frequency. (**841**)

If all the events in the series cannot be specified, the following sequence, for example, may arise:

Trial	2	3	4	5	6	7	8	9	10	11	12
	+	+	?	–	+	?	+	–	+	?	+
R_E				5				9			
$R_?$			4			7				11	

(**842**)

and the tables on pages 156–162 can no longer be used. In such cases the test criterion (**832**b) is used, with

$$\left.\begin{array}{lll} 6\,T_E = 6\,\Sigma R_E & & (a)\\ 6\,\boldsymbol{T}_E = 6\,N_1\,A/N & & (b)\\ \sigma^2_{6T_E} = 36\,N_1\,N_2\,(NB-A^2)/N^2(N-1) & & (c)\\ A \;= N\,(N+1)/2-\Sigma R_? & & (d)\\ B \;= N\,[1+N\,(2N+3)]/6-\Sigma R^2_? & & (e) \end{array}\right\} \quad (843)$$

If all the events are specified but the sample exceeds the scope of the table, then equations (**830**b) and (**831**b) can be used in conjunction with (**832**b).

(b) *Investigation of several series as samples from the same population*
The successive offspring of 1, 2, 3, ..., *i*, ..., *m* mothers, for example, are to be investigated in respect of a childhood disease that appears to be more common among later births.

The test criterion (**832**b) is used, with

$$\left.\begin{array}{l} 6\,T = \Sigma 6T_i\\ 6\,\boldsymbol{T} = \Sigma 6\boldsymbol{T}_i\\ \sigma^2_{6T} = \Sigma\sigma^2_{6T_i} \end{array}\right\} \quad (844)$$

$6\,\boldsymbol{T}_i$ and $\sigma^2_{6T_i}$ are calculated from (**830**b) and (**831**b) or from (**843**b) and (**843**c) respectively, according to whether all the events in the series i are specified or not.

24H. Spearman's rank correlation coefficient

If the bivariate sample x, y originates from *any continuous* distribution and its values have been not measured but *ranked* [cf. (**342**)], then the interdependence of y and x can be assessed by means of the Spearman coefficient of rank correlation. An alternative correlation coefficient, τ, due to KENDALL[46] has some advantages and some disadvantages (cf. VAN DER WAERDEN[47]).
The Spearman coefficient can be calculated for ranked samples from distributions of any form. When the distribution is a bivariate normal one, the interpretation of this coefficient corresponds to that of the correlation coefficient $\boldsymbol{r}$. How it should be interpreted for other distributions is not clear.
Given are n pairs of observations $(x, y)_i$. The pairs are first separated to form two samples x_i and y_i. The x and y values are then ranked by magnitude, so that for example x_{i5} is the fifth smallest of all x values, y_{i3} the third smallest of all y values. The original pairs of observations are now re-formed, giving for example $(x_5, y_3)_i$. The rank numbers (order numbers), in this case 5 and 3, are given the symbol R as before. The difference between the rank numbers of each pair of observations is now calculated and squared:

$$D_i^2 = (R_{x_i}-R_{y_i})^2 \quad (845)$$

For the pair $(x_5, y_3)_i$ for example, $D_i^2 = (5-3)^2 = 4$.

The estimate of the Spearman coefficient $\boldsymbol{r}_S$ is then

$$r_S = 1-6\sum_1^n D_i^2/(n^3-n) \quad (846)$$

where n is the total number of pairs.

Values of the factor $6/(n^3-n)$ are given in the table on page 164.

All values conform to the international convention (i.e. 0,1 instead of 0.1).

(**846**) is valid only when no ties [cf. (**346**)] occur. However, when the number of ties is small it can still be used. For the procedure when there is a large number of ties see KENDALL[46].

The testing of $\boldsymbol{r}_S$ against zero is made with the significance limits given in the lower table on page 163. It is not necessary to calculate r_S, but only $\Sigma\,D^2$:

If the sum $\Sigma\,D^2$ *attains* or *falls outside* the significance limits, then $\boldsymbol{r}_S$ differs significantly from zero. (a)
If $\Sigma\,D^2$ *falls inside* the significance limits, $\boldsymbol{r}_S$ does not differ from zero. (b) (**847**)

The calculation of r_S is therefore proceeded with only in the case of (**847**a).

KENDALL[46] gives the exact limits for $n = 4$–10. For $n = 11$–30 the approximations given by GLASSER and WINTER[48] may be used. Significance limits in the case of the normal distribution:

$$\pm r_S\sqrt{n-1} = \pm c_\alpha \quad (848)$$

and it follows that

$$\Sigma\,D_i^2 = \frac{n^3-n}{6}\left(1\pm\frac{|c_\alpha|}{\sqrt{n-1}}\right) \quad (849)$$

Significance limits in the case of the Student distribution:

$$\pm r_S\sqrt{\frac{n-2}{1-r_S^2}} = \pm t_\alpha \quad [\nu = n-2] \quad (850)$$

and it follows that

$$\Sigma\,D_i^2 = \frac{n^3-n}{6}\left(1\pm\frac{|t_\alpha|}{\sqrt{n-2+t_\alpha^2}}\right) \quad (851)$$

If the ranked samples originate from *normally distributed* populations, then according to K. PEARSON $\boldsymbol{r}$ and $\boldsymbol{r}_S$ have the following relationship

$$\boldsymbol{r} \simeq 2\sin\frac{\pi}{6}\,\boldsymbol{r}_S \quad (852)$$

For estimates, (**852**) is only approximately valid. A table for calculating r from r_S is given on page 164.

Example 71. Given is the sample of example 46, page 217. This sample has 4 ties with x and 6 with y, an acceptable number with a sample size $n = 20$. The pairs of observations and corresponding ranks R_x and R_y are

x	R_x	y	R_y	D^2	x	R_x	y	R_y	D^2
2,6	1	2,3	1	0	6,0	11	5,2	8	9
3,0	2,5	3,5	3,5	1	6,5	12,5	6,0	12,5	0
3,0	2,5	4,0	5	6,25	6,5	12,5	8,0	19	42,25
3,5	4	3,5	3,5	0,25	7,0	14,5	6,0	12,5	4
3,8	5	4,5	6,5	2,25	7,0	14,5	7,0	15,5	1
4,2	6	2,7	2	16	7,5	16	7,7	17	1
4,5	7	5,5	9	4	8,0	18	6,5	14	16
4,7	8	5,7	10,5	6,25	8,0	18	7,0	15,5	6,25
5,5	9	4,5	6,5	6,25	8,0	18	8,0	19	1
5,7	10	5,7	10,5	0,25	10,0	20	8,0	19	1

$\Sigma\,D^2 = 124$, a sum which lies far outside the 0,002 limit of the lower table on page 163. $\boldsymbol{r}_S$ therefore differs from zero, and calculation is proceeded with in accordance with (**846**). From the upper table on page 164, the factor $6/(20^3-20) = 10^{-4}\times 7{,}51880$, whence it follows that $\boldsymbol{r}_S = 1-(10^{-4}\times 7{,}51880\times 124) = 0{,}906767 \sim 0{,}907$. Assuming that the sample originates from a normally distributed population, $r \sim 0{,}915$ from (**852**) (lower table, page 164). The estimate of $\boldsymbol{r}$ from (**708**) is 0,881.

25. Distribution-free tolerance limits

25A. Distribution-free tolerance limits for samples from continuous distributions

Given is an ordered sample increasing from left (low) to right (high):

Ordered values x:	132	136	143	144	151
Rank:	$x_{(1)}$	$x_{(2)}$	$x_{(3)}$	$x_{(4)}$	$x_{(5)}$
Sample size:	$N = 5$				

Tolerance intervals can now be calculated, e.g. 132–151 or 136–143, etc. Various questions could then be asked, for example: What percentage of the population falls between 132 and 151? In order to answer such questions the rank sums are used, using the ranks of the *left-* (low) and the *right-hand* (high) *limit*. The *left-hand limit* (l) is calculated from the ranks of an increasing ranking and the *right-hand limit* (r) from the ranks of a decreasing ranking. In this way:

The *right-hand limit* of a decreasing ranking is equal to $(N+1)$ minus the *right-hand limit* of an increasing ranking. **(853)**

The rank sum $l+r$ in example 72 for the interval 132–144 is 3 as $l=1$ (in an increasing ranking the intervals is ranked 1 to 4) and $r=2$ (in a decreasing ranking the interval is ranked 2 to 5 or $N+1$ $(=6)$ minus the *right-hand limit* 4 of an increasing ranking).
The same rank sums $l+r$ are normally obtained from different intervals. Conventionally $x_{(0)}=-\infty$ and $x_{(N+1)}=\infty$, so that for a one-sided tolerance interval either the *left-* or the *right-hand limit* is zero.
A sample of size N has N different rank sums formed from

$$\frac{N(N+3)}{2} \tag{854}$$

combinations. As a sample check of the calculations no rank sum is larger than the size of the sample.

Example 72.

Sample size $N=5$.
A Tolerance interval.
B Left-hand and right-hand limits of the tolerance interval by ranks following an increasing ranking.
C Left-hand limit of the tolerance interval by ranks in an increasing ranking and the right-hand limit by ranks in a decreasing ranking.
D The rank sums necessary for the calculations.

Increasing ranking:	1	2	3	4	5
Sample values	132	136	143	144	151
Decreasing ranking:	5	4	3	2	1

A: l – r	B: l r	C: l r	D
$-\infty$–132	$-\infty$–1	0–5	$l+r=5$
132–136	1–2	1–4	
136–143	2–3	2–3	
143–144	3–4	3–2	
144–151	4–5	4–1	
151–$+\infty$	5–$+\infty$	5–0	
$-\infty$–136	$-\infty$–2	0–4	$l+r=4$
132–143	1–3	1–3	
136–144	2–4	2–2	
143–151	3–5	3–1	
144–$+\infty$	4–$+\infty$	4–0	
$-\infty$–143	$-\infty$–3	0–3	$l+r=3$
132–144	1–4	1–2	
136–151	2–5	2–1	
143–$+\infty$	3–$+\infty$	3–0	
$-\infty$–144	$-\infty$–4	0–2	$l+r=2$
132–151	1–5	1–1	
136–$+\infty$	2–$+\infty$	2–0	
$-\infty$–151	$-\infty$–5	0–1	$l+r=1$
132–$+\infty$	1–$+\infty$	1–0	

$(5\times 8/2)=20$ combinations; 5 different rank sums.

It can be seen from this example that one sample can be divided into many tolerance intervals: If for example $N=100$ there are $(100\times 103/2)=5150$ combinations. All the same the tables on pages 108–136 allow us without any calculation at all to obtain the tolerance limits which are independent of the distribution from which we have sampled.

Distribution-free tolerance limits for the one- and two-sample problem

For smaller sizes of the second sample the values in the tables on pages 124–136 are exact as are those on pages 108–123. As the size of the second sample increases the tolerance limits of a sample can be approximated.

All values conform to the international convention (i.e. 0,1 instead of 0.1).

Example 73

(a) Let a sample of size $N=50$ with rank sum $l+r=2$ be given. In the one-sample problem $\beta_p=0{,}9086$ of the population values lie between the tolerance limits with a probability $\beta_t=0{,}95$ (see section 25B below).

Values between the tolerance limits:
$1+1=2$ between the smallest and the largest value
2 above the second smallest value
2 below the second largest value

(b) Let sample one of size $N_1=50$ and rank sum $l+r=2$ and sample two of a different size N_2 be given. N^* is the minimum number of values in sample two which with a probability of at least β_t lie within the $(l+r)$ limits, when both samples are from the same population.

N_2	N^*	$N^*/N_2\sim\beta_p$
10	8	0,8
20	17	0,85
50	44	0,88
100	90	0,90
300	271	0,903

It can be seen that $N^*/N_2\sim\beta_p$ of the two-sample problem, as N_2 increases, tends to β_p of the one-sample problem.

25B. Distribution-free tolerance limits for the one-sample problem
(Tables on pages 108–123)

l: left-hand (lower) tolerance limit
r: right-hand (upper) tolerance limit
N: size of the sample for which tolerance limits are to be determined
β_t, β_p: β_t is the probability that at least 100 β_p% of the population values lie between the tolerance limits l and r (the values in the table are those of β_p)

Exact solution

In each case the most appropriate of the formulae **(855)** to **(858)** is selected and through iteration in β_p the exact value of β_t or $1-\beta_t$ is obtained.

For $l+r=1$ and $l+r=N$ the solutions are **(859)** and **(860)**.

$$1-\beta_t=\sum_{x=N+1-l-r}^{N}\binom{N}{x}\beta_p^x(1-\beta_p)^{N-x} \tag{855}$$

$$1-\beta_t=\sum_{x=0}^{l+r-1}\binom{N}{x}(1-\beta_p)^x\beta_p^{N-x} \tag{856}$$

$$\beta_t=\sum_{x=0}^{N-l-r}\binom{N}{x}\beta_p^x(1-\beta_p)^{N-x} \tag{857}$$

$$\beta_t=\sum_{x=l+r}^{N}\binom{N}{x}(1-\beta_p)^x\beta_p^x \tag{858}$$

If $l+r=1$:

$$\beta_p=e^x;\ x=\frac{\ln(1-\beta_t)}{N} \tag{859}$$

If $l+r=N$:

$$\beta_p=1-e^x;\ x=\frac{\ln\beta_t}{N} \tag{860}$$

Approximation[49]

$$\beta_p\simeq\frac{4[N-½(l+r-1)]-\chi^2}{4[N-½(l+r-1)]+\chi^2}\quad\text{[for }\chi^2\text{ see below]} \tag{861}$$

$$N\simeq ¼\,\chi^2\frac{1+\beta_p}{1-\beta_p}+½(l+r-1)\quad\text{[for }\chi^2\text{ see below]} \tag{862}$$

β_t is then obtained as follows:

$$\chi^2\simeq 4[N-½(l+r-1)]\frac{1-\beta_p}{1+\beta_p}\quad\text{[for }\chi^2\text{ see below]} \tag{863}$$

$[\chi^2=\chi^2_{\beta_t;\,v=2(l+r)};\ \beta_t=1\int_t$: pages 34–37]

25C. Distribution-free tolerance limits for the two-sample problem

(Tables on pages 124–136)

l: left-hand (lower) tolerance limit

r: right-hand (upper) tolerance limit

N_1: size of sample one, which serves as the basis for the determination of the tolerance limits

N_2: size of sample two, which is to be tested as coming from the same population as sample one

β_t, N^*: At least N^* values of sample two lie with a probability of at least β_t between the tolerance limits l and r of sample one when both are samples from the same population.

$$0 \le N^* \le N_2$$
$$1 \le l+r \le N_1$$

$$\dot{P}_{N^*} = \frac{\binom{N^*+N_1-l-r}{N^*}\binom{N_2-N^*+l+r-1}{N_2-N^*}}{\binom{N_1+N_2}{N_2}} \qquad \textbf{(864)}^{50}$$

$$\beta_{t(N^*)} = \sum_{x=N^*}^{N_2} \dot{P}_x \qquad \textbf{(865)}$$

The lower limit of the probability β_t is given in the tables on pages 124–136, i.e.

$$\sum_{x=N^*+1}^{N_2} \dot{P}_x < \beta_{t(N^*)} \le \sum_{x=N^*}^{N_2} \dot{P}_x < \sum_{x=N^*-1}^{N_2} \dot{P}_x \qquad \textbf{(866)}$$

From equation (**864**) it follows:

$$\dot{P}_{N^*=N_2} = \frac{N_1!\,(N_1+N_2-l-r)!}{(N_1+N_2)!\,(N_1-l-r)!} \qquad \text{(a)}^{50}$$

$$\dot{P}_{N^*-1} = \dot{P}_{N^*}\frac{(N_2-N^*+l+r)\,N^*}{(N_1+N^*-l-r)(N_2-N^*+1)} \qquad \text{(b)}^{50}$$

or

$$\dot{P}_{N^*=0} = \frac{N_1!\,(N_2+l+r-1)!}{(N_1+N_2)!\,(l+r-1)!} \qquad \text{(c)}$$

$$\dot{P}_{N^*+1} = \dot{P}_{N^*}\frac{(N_1+N^*-l-r+1)(N_2-N^*)}{(N_2-N^*+l+r-1)(N^*+1)} \qquad \text{(d)}$$

(c) and (d) are used for calculating the smallest N^*

$$\beta_{t(N^*)} = 1 - \sum_{x=0}^{N^*-1} \dot{P}_x \qquad \text{(e)}$$

(a)–(e): **(867)**

Finally further formulae are given for small sample sizes of sample two $N_2 = 1, 2$ and 3:

- to determine the probability β_t for given $N_1, N_2, l+r, N^*$
- to determine the size N_1: How big should N_1 be to obtain a certain β_t-probability even if N_2 is small when both samples are from the same population? (See page 136.)

$N_2 = 1$; $N^* = 1$:

$$\beta_t = 1 - \frac{l+r}{N_1+1} \qquad \textbf{(868)}$$

$$N_1 = \frac{\beta_t + l + r - 1}{1-\beta_t} \quad \text{[integer value !]} \qquad \textbf{(869)}$$

$N_2 = 2$; $N^* = 1$:

$$\beta_t = 1 - \frac{(l+r)(l+r+1)}{(N_1+1)(N_1+2)} \qquad \textbf{(870)}$$

$$N_1 = -\frac{3}{2} + \sqrt{\frac{(l+r)(l+r+1)}{1-\beta_t} + \frac{1}{4}} \quad \text{[integer value !]} \qquad \textbf{(871)}$$

$N_2 = 2$; $N^* = 2$:

$$\beta_t = \left(1-\frac{l+r}{N_1+1}\right)\left(1-\frac{l+r}{N_1+2}\right) \qquad \textbf{(872)}$$

$$N_1 = \frac{l+r}{1-\beta_t} - \frac{3}{2} + \sqrt{\beta_t\left(\frac{l+r}{1-\beta_t}\right)^2 + \frac{1}{4}} \quad \text{[integer value !]} \qquad \textbf{(873)}$$

$N_2 = 3$; $N^* = 1$:

$$\beta_t = 1 - \frac{(l+r)(l+r+1)(l+r+2)}{(N_1+1)(N_1+2)(N_1+3)} \qquad \textbf{(874)}$$

$N_2 = 3$; $N^* = 2$:

$$\beta_t = \left(1-\frac{l+r}{N_1+1}\right)\left(1-\frac{l+r}{N_1+2}\right)\left(1+\frac{2\,(l+r)}{N_1+3}\right) \qquad \textbf{(875)}$$

$N_2 = 3$; $N^* = 3$:

$$\beta_t = \left(1-\frac{l+r}{N_1+1}\right)\left(1-\frac{l+r}{N_1+2}\right)\left(1-\frac{l+r}{N_1+3}\right) \qquad \textbf{(876)}$$

26. Testing for non-randomness

All statistical tests for non-randomness depend on the *chronological* order in which the values $x_1, x_2, \ldots, x_N$ occur in the series of tries $1, 2, \ldots, N$. Here the indices $1, 2, \ldots, i, \ldots, N$ denote *not the rank but the chronological order.*

26A. The mean-square successive difference[51]

The mean-square successive difference δ^2 is defined as

$$\delta^2 = \frac{1}{N-1}\sum_{1}^{N-1}(x_{i+1}-x_i)^2 \quad [N\text{: size of the sample}] \qquad \textbf{(877)}$$

If the sample originates from a normally distributed population, then

$$\text{expectation of } \delta^2 = 2\,\sigma^2 \qquad \textbf{(878)}$$

$\delta^2/2$ is thus an unbiased estimate of σ^2 with

$$\text{efficiency} = \frac{2}{3\,[1+1/(3\,N-4)]} \qquad \textbf{(879)}$$

For $N = 2$, the efficiency is therefore 1; for $N \to \infty$ (asymptotically) it is ⅔.

Since the mean-square successive difference is calculated on the basis of the successive differences $x_{i+1} - x_i$, it is *less sensitive* to *longterm* displacements of the mean and *more sensitive* to rapid *cyclic* influences on the mean than the estimate s^2, which is calculated on the basis of the differences $x_i - \bar{x}$. The ratio

$$\eta = \frac{\delta^2}{s^2} = \frac{\sum_{1}^{N-1}(x_{i+1}-x_i)^2}{\sum_{1}^{N}(x_i-\bar{x})^2} \qquad \textbf{(880)}$$

is therefore an indication of a possible non-random influence on the mean of a *normally distributed* population.

Significance limits for η are given in the left-hand table on page 72. *Interpretation:* If η attains or exceeds the *left-hand limit*, then the mean of the population is affected* by *non-random* long-term factors; if it attains or exceeds the *right-hand limit*, the population mean is affected* by *short-term cyclic* factors (significance α). **(881)**

The approximate limits ($N > 60$) in the table on page 72 have been calculated from

$$\eta_l, \eta_r = 2 \mp 2\,|c_\alpha|\sqrt{\frac{N-2}{(N-1)(N+1)}} \qquad \textbf{(882)}$$

26B. Serial correlation[52]

Given is the sample $x_1, x_2, \ldots, x_N$. Serial correlation is defined as the correlation between the pairs of observations x_i and x_{i+h}. h is known as the lag. For $i+h > N$, $x_{i+h} = x_{i+h-N}$ in the *cyclic* definition. For further details the reader is referred to the literature[52, 53].

With the cyclic definition, serial correlation is a sensitive instrument for revealing periodic influences on a population (or sample when the population is stable).

A measure of the serial correlation with lag h is the serial correlation coefficient $\boldsymbol{r}_h$. Its estimate is

$$r_h = \frac{\Sigma x_i\, x_{i+h} - (\Sigma x_i)^2/n}{\Sigma x_i^2 - (\Sigma x_i)^2/n} \qquad \textbf{(883)}$$

As with other correlation coefficients, its value lies between -1 and $+1$.

The right-hand table on page 72 gives the significance limits for r_h when testing $\boldsymbol{r}_h = 0$ (when $h = 1$) on the assumption that the samples are random samples from a normally distributed population. The approximate limits ($N > 75$) have been calculated from

* The effect can be linear or nonlinear.

All values conform to the international convention (i.e. 0,1 instead of 0.1).

$$r_l, r_r = \frac{-1 \mp |c_\alpha| \sqrt{N-2}}{N-1} \qquad \textbf{(884)}$$

[N: number of values x_i included in the calculation]

For lags other than 1 the same levels can be used, provided that h and N do not possess a common factor. The latter is always the case when N is a prime number. In practice these conditions can be met by deleting one or more individual sample values.

26C. Runs up and down[54, 55]

If $x_1, x_2, ..., x_i, ..., x_N$ are individual sample values from a *continuous* population of *any* form, then a run up of length 1 is defined as the sequence $x_i \to x_{i+1}$ when $x_{i+1} - x_i > 0$. For runs down, $x_{i+1} - x_i < 0$. A sequence of three runs up of length 1 is called a run up of length 3, and so on.
If the sample is a random one not subject to cyclic or constant non-random influences, then the runs up and down should present a random picture, that is to say, there should be no regular runs and not too many long ones or too few short ones.
Runs up and down can be tested by means of the table at the bottom of page 166. Thus a run of length 5 in a sample of size $N=9$, for example, is not likely to be random (significance $\alpha = 0{,}01$). In the same way, a sample of size $N = 12$ is not likely to be a random sample when no run of length 2 is present (significance $1 - \alpha = 0{,}01$).

The number $I\ (l|N)$ of runs up and down of length l and the number $I\ (l+|N)$ of runs of length l and *longer* can be regarded as normally distributed for $N \geq 20$. This can be tested by means of the quotient

$$(I - \boldsymbol{I})/\sqrt{\sigma_I^2} \quad [\text{significance level } |c_\alpha|, \text{page } 26] \qquad \textbf{(885)}$$

The expected value $\boldsymbol{I}$ and the variance σ_I^2 are functions of N; appropriate formulae are to be found in LEVENE and WOLFOWITZ[54]. To some extent the calculations are tedious. The two tables (**886**) and (**887**) give values up to the length usually found in practice; they also show clearly how σ_I^2 for greater lengths converges rapidly toward the expected value $\boldsymbol{I}$. It follows from (**781**) that the distribution of runs up and down very closely approximates, for runs of greater length, to a Poisson distribution (or to approximations to a Poisson distribution) with $\lambda = \boldsymbol{I}$.

26D. Runs above and/or below the median[56]

Runs above and/or below the median can be tested by means of the table on page 166, where a brief explanation of the method will be found.

26E. Runs in samples from binomially distributed populations in which the probabilities p and q are unknown (page 165)

The definition is as follows:

(Time)	1	2	3	4	5	6	7	8	9	10
Series (I)	A	B	A	A	A	B	B	A	B	A
Series (II)	A	B	A	B	A	A	B	A	B	A
Series (III)	A	A	A	A	A	A	B	B	B	B

Each of the series (I), (II), (III) has a size $N = 10$ and contains $N_1 = 4$ B's and $N_2 = 6$ A's (for $N = N_1 + N_2 < 40$, the smaller number is denoted by N_1). In these series the underscored letters in each case form a run. The total number of runs I is 7 in series (I), 9 in series (II), 2 in series (III).

The table on page 165 gives the confidence limits for the estimate I (total$|N_1, N_2$) of the expectation $\boldsymbol{I}$ (total$|N_1, N_2$) of the total number of all runs of both events.

(a) If the left-hand limit is *attained* or *exceeded*, then

$I < \boldsymbol{I}$ [probability α]

or

$I \neq \boldsymbol{I}$ [probability 2α]

Expected value $\boldsymbol{I}\ (l|N)$ and variance of runs up and down of length l **(886)**

Length	Expected value $\boldsymbol{I}\ (l\|N)$ — Exact $\boldsymbol{I}(l\|N) = aN - b$		Asymptotic $\boldsymbol{I}(l\|N) \to \boldsymbol{I}(1+\|N) \times c$ $[N \to \infty]$	Variance $\sigma_I^2 = d \times \boldsymbol{I}(l\|N) + e$		Remarks
l	a	b	c	d	e	
1	$4{,}1\dot{6} \times 10^{-1}$	$-8{,}\dot{3} \times 10^{-2}$	$6{,}25 \times 10^{-1}$	$1{,}01\dot{6}$	$-0{,}397\dot{2}$	Note ‹minus›: – for b and e
2	$1{,}8\dot{3} \times 10^{-1}$	$2{,}\dot{3} \times 10^{-1}$	$2{,}75 \times 10^{-1}$	0,614550	−0,01943342	– for e
3	$5{,}2\dot{7} \times 10^{-2}$	$1{,}30\dot{5} \times 10^{-1}$	$7{,}91\dot{6} \times 10^{-2}$	0,794215	0,00678218	
4	$1{,}15079365 \times 10^{-2}$	$4{,}12698413 \times 10^{-2}$	$1{,}72619048 \times 10^{-2}$	0,935800	0,00083924	
5	$2{,}03373016 \times 10^{-3}$	$9{,}47420634 \times 10^{-3}$	$3{,}05059524 \times 10^{-3}$	0,985361	0,00004629	
6	$3{,}03130511 \times 10^{-4}$	$1{,}73059965 \times 10^{-3}$	$4{,}54695767 \times 10^{-4}$	0,997338	0,00000156	
7	$3{,}91313933 \times 10^{-5}$	$2{,}63999118 \times 10^{-4}$	$5{,}86970899 \times 10^{-5}$	0,999595	0,00000004	
8	$4{,}45927529 \times 10^{-6}$	$3{,}46721180 \times 10^{-5}$	$6{,}68891294 \times 10^{-6}$	0,999947	0,00000000	
9	$4{,}55113302 \times 10^{-7}$	$4{,}00416199 \times 10^{-6}$	$6{,}82669953 \times 10^{-7}$	0,999994	0,00000000	
10	$4{,}20746948 \times 10^{-8}$	$4{,}13038607 \times 10^{-7}$	$6{,}31120422 \times 10^{-8}$	0,999999	0,00000000	

Expected value $\boldsymbol{I}\ (l+|N)$ and variance of runs up and down of length l and longer **(887)**

Length	Expected value $\boldsymbol{I}\ (l+\|N)$ — Exact $\boldsymbol{I}(l+\|N) = aN - b$		Asymptotic $\boldsymbol{I}(l+\|N) \to \boldsymbol{I}(1+\|N) \times c$ $[N \to \infty]$	Variance $\sigma_I^2 = d \times \boldsymbol{I}(l+\|N) + e$		Remarks
$l+$	a	b	c	d	e	
1	$6{,}\dot{6} \times 10^{-1}$	$3{,}\dot{3} \times 10^{-1}$	1	$0{,}2\dot{6}$	$-0{,}2\dot{3}$	Note ‹minus›: – for e
2	$2{,}\dot{5} \times 10^{-1}$	$4{,}1\dot{6} \times 10^{-1}$	$3{,}75 \times 10^{-1}$	$0{,}31\dot{6}$	$0{,}07\dot{2}$	
3	$6{,}\dot{6} \times 10^{-2}$	$1{,}8\dot{3} \times 10^{-1}$	1×10^{-1}	0,710847	0,01729497	
4	$1{,}3\dot{8} \times 10^{-2}$	$5{,}2\dot{7} \times 10^{-2}$	$2{,}08\dot{3} \times 10^{-2}$	0,917857	0,00147817	
5	$\dot{2}{,}3809\dot{5} \times 10^{-3}$	$1{,}15079365 \times 10^{-2}$	$3{,}57142857 \times 10^{-3}$	0,982145	0,00007053	
6	$3{,}47\dot{2} \times 10^{-4}$	$2{,}03373016 \times 10^{-3}$	$5{,}208\dot{3} \times 10^{-4}$	0,996871	0,00000220	
7	$4{,}40917108 \times 10^{-5}$	$3{,}03130511 \times 10^{-4}$	$6{,}61375661 \times 10^{-5}$	0,999535	0,00000005	
8	$4{,}96031746 \times 10^{-6}$	$3{,}91313933 \times 10^{-5}$	$7{,}44047619 \times 10^{-6}$	0,999940	0,00000000	
9	$5{,}01042167 \times 10^{-7}$	$4{,}45927529 \times 10^{-6}$	$7{,}51563251 \times 10^{-7}$	0,999993	0,00000000	
10	$4{,}59288653 \times 10^{-8}$	$4{,}55113302 \times 10^{-7}$	$6{,}88932980 \times 10^{-8}$	0,999999	0,00000000	
11	$3{,}85417052 \times 10^{-9}$	$4{,}20746948 \times 10^{-8}$	$5{,}78125578 \times 10^{-9}$	0,999999	0,00000000	

All values conform to the international convention (i.e. 0,1 instead of 0.1).

(b) If the right-hand limit is *attained* or *exceeded*, then

$I > \boldsymbol{I}$ [probability α]

or

$I \neq \boldsymbol{I}$ [probability 2α]

(c) If I lies between the limits and *attains neither*, then the null hypothesis cannot be rejected.

For N_1 and N_2 values outside the scope of the table, the test quotient **(885)** can be used in conjunction with **(894**a) and **(894**b).

Expected values and variances

– for the number of runs of length l of the event 1 that has occurred a total of N_1 times (N_2 = number of events 2; $N = N_1 + N_2$)

$$\boldsymbol{I}_1(l|N_1, N_2) = N_2(N_2+1)\frac{N_1!(N-l-1)!}{N!(N_1-l)!} \quad \text{(a)}$$

$$\sigma^2 = \boldsymbol{I}\left(1 - \boldsymbol{I} + N_2(N_2-1)\frac{(N-2l-2)!(N_1-l)!}{(N-l-1)!(N_1-2l)!}\right) \quad \text{(b)} \qquad \textbf{(888)}^{57}$$

and asymptotically for higher values of N

$$\boldsymbol{I}_1(l|N_1, N_2) = N p^l q^2 \quad \text{(a)}$$

$$\sigma^2 = \boldsymbol{I}\left(1 - \frac{\boldsymbol{I}}{N}\left[\frac{l^2}{p} + \frac{2}{q} - (l+1)^2\right]\right) \quad \text{(b)} \qquad \textbf{(889)}^{57}$$

$[p = N_1/N; q = 1-p]$

– for the number of runs of length l and *longer* of the event 1

$$\boldsymbol{I}_1(l+|N_1, N_2) = (N_2+1)\frac{N_1!(N-l)!}{N!(N_1-l)!} \quad \text{(a)}$$

$$\sigma^2 = \boldsymbol{I}\left(1 - \boldsymbol{I} + N_2\frac{(N-2l)!(N_1-l)!}{(N-l)!(N_1-2l)!}\right) \quad \text{(b)} \qquad \textbf{(890)}^{57}$$

and asymptotically

$$\boldsymbol{I}_1(l+|N_1, N_2) = N p^l q \quad \text{(a)}$$

$$\sigma^2 = \boldsymbol{I}\left(1 - \frac{\boldsymbol{I}}{N}\left[\frac{l^2 q}{p} + \frac{1}{q}\right]\right) \quad \text{(b)} \qquad \textbf{(891)}^{57}$$

[p and q as in **(889)**]

– for the total number of all runs of the event 1

$$\boldsymbol{I}_1(\text{total}|N_1, N_2) = \boldsymbol{I}_1(1+|N_1, N_2) = \frac{N_1(N_2+1)}{N} \quad \text{(a)}$$

$$\sigma^2 = \frac{\boldsymbol{I}(\boldsymbol{I}-1)}{N-1} \quad \text{(b)} \qquad \textbf{(892)}^{58}$$

and asymptotically

$$\boldsymbol{I}_1(\text{total}|N_1, N_2) = \boldsymbol{I}(1+|N_1, N_2) = Npq \quad \text{(a)}$$

[p and q as in **(889)**]

$$\sigma^2 = \boldsymbol{I}^2/N \quad \text{(b)} \qquad \textbf{(893)}^{57}$$

– for the total number of all runs of events 1 and 2

$$\boldsymbol{I}_{1+2}(\text{total}|N_1, N_2) = \frac{2N_1N_2}{N} + 1 \quad \text{(a)}$$

$$\sigma^2 = \frac{(\boldsymbol{I}-1)(\boldsymbol{I}-2)}{N-1} \quad \text{(b)} \qquad \textbf{(894)}^{59}$$

and asymptotically

$$\boldsymbol{I}_{1+2}(\text{total}|N_1, N_2) = 2Npq \quad [p \text{ and } q \text{ as in } \textbf{(889)}] \quad \text{(a)}$$

$$\sigma^2 = \boldsymbol{I}^2/N \quad \text{(b)} \qquad \textbf{(895)}^{59}$$

The total number of all runs of the event 1 can be tested exactly (within the scope of the tables on pages 137–151) by means of the fourfold table test[58]:

I_1	$N_1 - I_1$	N_1
N_2+1-I_1	$I_1 - 1$	N_2
N_2+1	$N_1 - 1$	N

(896)

26F. The Wald-Wolfowitz test[59]

Given are two samples from *continuous* populations of *any* form. These are ranked as in **(824)** and the total number of all runs (a run being defined as the occurrence of *successive* rank numbers in a sample) counted. Testing of randomness or in this case of the identity of the two populations is carried out by means of the table on page 165 (cf. section 26E) or, for samples outside the scope of this table, by means of the test quotient **(885)** in conjunction with **(894**a) and **(894**b) or **(895**a) and **(895**b).

Example 74. Ranking and determination of runs (1, 2, ... is here a rank order):

Sample 1	1,55	1,58	1,7		1,92			2,2	2,21		
Sample 2				1,91		1,93	2,0			2,3	2,4
$R_{1,2}$	1	2	3	4	5	6	7	8	9	10	11
Run 1 and 2		1		1	1		1		1		1

Total runs: 6, $N = 11$, $N_1 = 6$, $N_2 = 5$

If the total number of runs *attains* or *exceeds* the *left-hand limit* (only this limit can be used in this test), then the samples do not originate from the same population (significance 2α).

26G. Runs in samples from binomially distributed populations in which the probabilities $\boldsymbol{p}$ and $\boldsymbol{q}$ are known

Expected values and variances

– for the number of runs of length l of the event 1 the probability of whose occurrence is $\boldsymbol{p}$ ($\boldsymbol{q} = 1 - \boldsymbol{p}$)

$$\boldsymbol{I}_1(l = N|N, \boldsymbol{p}) = \boldsymbol{p}^N \quad \text{(a)}^{60}$$

$$\sigma^2 = \boldsymbol{I}(1-\boldsymbol{I}) \quad \text{(b)}^{61}$$

$$\boldsymbol{I}_1(l \le N-1|N, \boldsymbol{p}) = \boldsymbol{p}^l\boldsymbol{q}[(N-l-1)\boldsymbol{q}+2] \quad \text{(c)}^{60}$$

$$\sigma^2 = \boldsymbol{I}(1-\boldsymbol{I}) + \varphi(N, l) \quad \text{(d)}^{61}$$

where

$$\varphi(N, l) = 0 \quad [2l \ge N] \quad \text{(e)}^{61}$$

$$\varphi(N, l) = \boldsymbol{p}^{2l}\boldsymbol{q}^2[6 + 6(N-2l-2)\boldsymbol{q} + (N-2l-2)(N-2l-3)\boldsymbol{q}^2] \quad [2 \le 2l \le N-2] \quad \text{(f)}^{61}$$

$$\varphi\left(N, \frac{N-1}{2}\right) = 2\boldsymbol{p}^{N-1}\boldsymbol{q} \quad [N \text{ is odd}] \quad \text{(g)}^{61} \qquad \textbf{(897)}$$

and asymptotically when $N - l \to \infty$

$$\boldsymbol{I}_1(l|N, \boldsymbol{p}) = N\boldsymbol{p}^l\boldsymbol{q}^2 \quad \text{(a)}^{60}$$

$$\sigma^2 = \boldsymbol{I}\left(1 - \boldsymbol{p}^l\boldsymbol{q}^2\left[2\left(l - \frac{\boldsymbol{p}}{\boldsymbol{q}}\right) + 1\right]\right) \quad \text{(b)}^{57} \qquad \textbf{(898)}$$

– for the number of runs of length l and *longer*

$$\boldsymbol{I}_1(l+|N, \boldsymbol{p}) = \boldsymbol{p}^l[(N-l)\boldsymbol{q}+1] \quad \text{(a)}^{60}$$

$$\sigma^2 = \boldsymbol{I}(1-\boldsymbol{I}) + \psi(N, l) \quad \text{(b)}^{61}$$

where

$$\psi(N, l) = 0 \quad [2l \ge N] \quad \text{(c)}^{61}$$

$$\psi(N, l) = \boldsymbol{p}^{2l}\boldsymbol{q}(N-2l)[2 + (N-2l-1)\boldsymbol{q}] \quad [2 \le 2l \le N] \quad \text{(d)}^{61} \qquad \textbf{(899)}$$

and asymptotically when $N - l \to \infty$

$$\boldsymbol{I}_1(l+|N, \boldsymbol{p}) = N\boldsymbol{p}^l\boldsymbol{q} \quad \text{(a)}^{60}$$

$$\sigma^2 = \boldsymbol{I}[1 - \boldsymbol{p}^l\boldsymbol{q}(2l+1)] \quad \text{(b)}^{57} \qquad \textbf{(900)}$$

– for the total number of runs of the event 1

$$\boldsymbol{I}_1(\text{total}|N, \boldsymbol{p}) = \boldsymbol{p}[(N-1)\boldsymbol{q}+1] \quad \text{(a)}^{60}$$

$$\sigma^2 = \boldsymbol{I}(1-\boldsymbol{I}) + (N-2)\boldsymbol{p}^2\boldsymbol{q}[(N-3)\boldsymbol{q}+2] \quad \text{(b)}^{57} \qquad \textbf{(901)}$$

and asymptotically

$$\boldsymbol{I}_1(\text{total}|N, \boldsymbol{p}) = N\boldsymbol{p}\boldsymbol{q} \quad \text{(a)}$$

$$\sigma^2 = \boldsymbol{I}(1 - 3\boldsymbol{p}\boldsymbol{q}) \quad \text{(b)} \qquad \textbf{(902)}^{60}$$

– for the total number of runs of events 1 and 2

$$\boldsymbol{I}_{1+2}(\text{total}|N, \boldsymbol{p}) = 2(N-1)\boldsymbol{p}\boldsymbol{q} + 1 \quad \text{(a)}$$

$$\sigma^2 = 2\boldsymbol{p}\boldsymbol{q}(2[N - (3N-5)\boldsymbol{p}\boldsymbol{q}] - 3) \quad \text{(b)} \qquad \textbf{(903)}^{60}$$

All values conform to the international convention (i.e. 0,1 instead of 0.1).

and asymptotically

$$\mathbf{I}_{1+2}(\text{total}\,|\,N,\mathbf{p}) = 2N\mathbf{p}\,\mathbf{q} \quad \text{(a)}$$
$$\sigma^2 = \mathbf{I}\,(2-3\,\mathbf{p}\,\mathbf{q}) \quad \text{(b)} \qquad \mathbf{(904)}^{60}$$

26H. Runs in samples from multinomially distributed populations

(a) *The probabilities $\mathbf{p}_1, \mathbf{p}_2, ..., \mathbf{p}_i, ..., \mathbf{p}_k$ are unknown*

Expected values and variances

– for the total number of runs of the event i that has occurred a total of N_i times

$$\mathbf{I}_i(\text{total}\,|\,N_i, N) = \frac{N_i(N-N_i+1)}{N} \quad \text{(a)}$$
$$\sigma^2 = \frac{\mathbf{I}(\mathbf{I}-1)}{N-1} \quad \text{(b)} \qquad \mathbf{(905)}^{57}$$

and asymptotically

$$\mathbf{I}_i(\text{total}\,|\,N_i, N) = N\,p_i\,(1-p_i) \quad [p_i = N_i/N] \quad \text{(a)}$$
$$\sigma^2 = \frac{\mathbf{I}^2}{N} \quad \text{(b)} \qquad \mathbf{(906)}^{57}$$

– for the total number of runs of all events

asymptotically

$$\mathbf{I}(\text{total}, N) = N\,(1-\sum_1^k p_i^2) \quad \text{(a)}$$
$$\sigma^2 = N\,[\sum p_i^2 - 2\sum p_i^3 + (\sum p_i^2)^2] \quad \text{(b)} \qquad \mathbf{(907)}^{57}$$

[p_i as in **(906)**]

When $N_1 = N_2 = \cdots = N_k = N_0$, **(907)** becomes

$$\mathbf{I}(\text{total}) = N\,(1-p) \quad \text{(a)}$$
$$\sigma^2 = p\,\mathbf{I} \quad \text{(b)} \qquad \mathbf{(908)}$$

$[p = 1/k;\ N = k\,N_0]$

(b) *The probabilities $\mathbf{p}_i$ are known*

$\mathbf{p}_i$ is the probability that the event i will occur.

Expected values and variances

– for the total number of runs of the event i

$$\mathbf{I}_i(\text{total}\,|\,N, \mathbf{p}_i) = \mathbf{p}_i\,[(N-1)(1-\mathbf{p}_i)+1] \quad \text{(a)}$$
$$\sigma^2 = N\,\mathbf{p}_i\,(1-4\,\mathbf{p}_i+6\,\mathbf{p}_i^2-3\,\mathbf{p}_i^3) + \mathbf{p}_i^2\,(3-8\,\mathbf{p}_i+5\,\mathbf{p}_i^2) \quad \text{(b)} \qquad \mathbf{(909)}^{57}$$

[Formula **(909)** is identical with **(901)** when, in the latter, $\mathbf{p}$ is replaced by $\mathbf{p}_i$]

and asymptotically

$$\mathbf{I}_i(\text{total}\,|\,N, \mathbf{p}_i) = N\mathbf{p}_i\,(1-\mathbf{p}_i) \quad \text{(a)}$$
$$\sigma^2 = \mathbf{I}\,[1-3\,\mathbf{p}_i\,(1-\mathbf{p}_i)] \quad \text{(b)} \qquad \mathbf{(910)}^{57}$$

– for the total number of runs of all events

asymptotically

$$\mathbf{I}(\text{total}) = N\,(1-\sum \mathbf{p}_i^2) \quad \text{(a)}$$
$$\sigma^2 = N\,[\sum \mathbf{p}_i^2 + 2\sum \mathbf{p}_i^3 - 3\,(\sum \mathbf{p}_i^2)^2] \quad \text{(b)} \qquad \mathbf{(911)}^{57}$$

When $\mathbf{p}_1 = \mathbf{p}_2 = \cdots \mathbf{p}_k = \mathbf{p} = 1/k$, **(911)** becomes

$$\mathbf{I}(\text{total}) = N\,(1-\mathbf{p}) \quad \text{(a)}$$
$$\sigma^2 = \mathbf{p}\,\mathbf{I} \quad \text{(b)} \qquad \mathbf{(912)}^{57}$$

27. Sequential analysis

Sequential analysis is one of the more recently developed statistical methods, which is finding a use in the analysis of clinical trials[62]. It is illustrated here by two charts[63] that enable a comparison to be made for example between two drugs, without calculation.

....

Example 75. The effect on patients of drug A is to be compared with that of drug B. Two patients are selected, the toss of a coin deciding which one is to receive drug A and which drug B. They should receive the drugs *simultaneously or in quick succession.* The result is given one of the three ratings

Drug A better
Drug B better
No difference

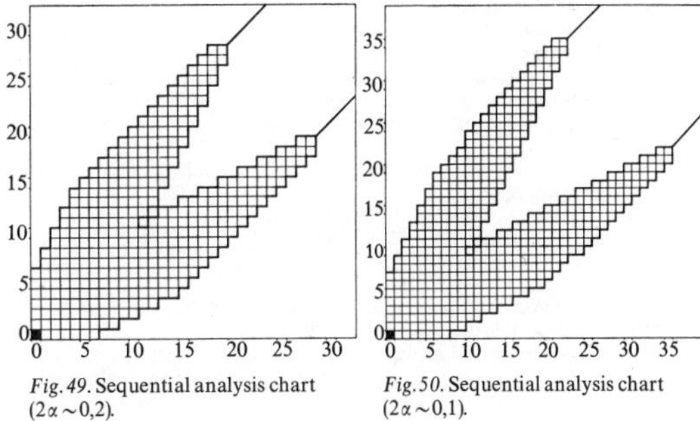

Fig. 49. Sequential analysis chart ($2\alpha \sim 0{,}2$).

Fig. 50. Sequential analysis chart ($2\alpha \sim 0{,}1$).

If drug A is better, a cross is made in the square immediately *above* the black square in the charts (Figs. 49 and 50). If drug B is better, a cross is made in the square immediately *to the right* of the black square. If there is no difference, no entry is made in the charts. A second test is then made in exactly the same way with two different patients and the result entered in the square above or to the right of that marked in the first test, and so on for successive tests. As soon as a barrier is crossed one of the following decisions can be made:

(a) upper barrier crossed: drug A is better
(b) lower barrier crossed: drug B is better
(c) middle barrier crossed: no difference demonstrated

The significance probability for (a) and (b) combined is 2α.

....

All values conform to the international convention (i.e. 0,1 instead of 0.1).

References

1 LAPLACE, P.-S., *Théorie analytique des probabilités*, 3rd ed., Gauthier-Villars, Paris, 1820.
2 MOLINA, E.C., *Poisson's Exponential Binomial Limit*, Van Nostrand, Princeton, 1942.
3 PEARSON, K., *Tables of the Incomplete Beta-Function*, 2nd ed., Cambridge University Press, Cambridge, 1968; *Tables of the Binomial Probability Distribution*, National Bureau of Standards, Applied Mathematics Series 6, Washington, 1949.
4 Harvard University Computation Laboratory, *Tables of the Cumulative Binomial Probability Distribution*, Cambridge, Mass., 1955.
5 LIEBERMAN and OWEN, *Tables of the Hypergeometric Probability Distribution*, Stanford University Press, Stanford, Calif., 1961.
6 RAO, C. R., *Bull. Calcutta math. Soc.*, **37**, 81 (1945).
7 CRAMÉR, H., *Mathematical Methods of Statistics*, Princeton University Press, Princeton, 1968.
8 NEYMAN, J., *Ann. math. Statist.*, **6**, 111 (1935); NEYMAN, J., *Phil. Trans. A*, **236**, 333 (1937); NEYMAN, J., *Biometrika*, **32**, 128 (1941/42).
9 PROSCHAN, F., *J. Amer. statist. Ass.*, **48**, 550 (1953).
10 GUTERMAN, H. E., *Technometrics*, **4**, 134 (1962).
11 *Tables of Normal Probability Functions*, National Bureau of Standards, Applied Mathematics Series 23, Washington, 1953.
12 BLISS, C. I., *Ann. appl. Biol.*, **22**, 134 (1935).
13 FINNEY, D. J., *Probit Analysis*, 3rd ed., Cambridge University Press, Cambridge, 1971; FISHER and YATES, *Statistical Tables for Biological, Agricultural and Medical Research*, 6th ed., Longman, Harlow, 1974; PEARSON and HARTLEY (Eds.), *Biometrika Tables for Statisticians*, 3rd ed., volume 1, Cambridge University Press, Cambridge, 1966.
14 WILSON and HILFERTY, *Proc. nat. Acad. Sci. (Wash.)*, **17**, 684 (1931).
15 FISHER, R. A., On a distribution yielding the error functions of several well-known statistics, *Proceedings of the International Mathematical Congress*, volume 2, Toronto, 1924, page 805.
16 EISENHART et al. (Eds.), *Selected Techniques of Statistical Analysis for Scientific and Industrial Research and Production and Management Engineering*, McGraw-Hill, New York, 1947, page 108.
17 TIPPETT, L. H., *Biometrika*, **17**, 364 (1925).
18 DAVIES and PEARSON, *J. roy. statist. Soc.*, suppl. 1, 76 (1934).
19 DIXON, W. J., *Ann. math. Statist.*, **21**, 488 (1950); DIXON, W. J., *Ann. math. Statist.*, **22**, 68 (1951); DIXON, W. J., *Biometrics*, **9**, 74 (1953).
20 LORD, E., *Biometrika*, **34**, 41 (1947).
21 WALSH, J. E., *Ann. math. Statist.*, **20**, 257 (1949).
22 WALSH, J. E., *J. Amer. statist. Ass.*, **44**, 342 (1949).
23 WELCH, B. L., *Biometrika*, **36**, 293 (1949).
24 BARTLETT, M. S., *Proc. roy. Soc. A*, **160**, 268 (1937).
25 DUNCAN, D. B., *Biometrics*, **11**, 1 (1955).
26 BLISS, C. I., *Biometrics*, **1**, 57 (1945).
27 BERKSON, J., *Biometrics*, **7**, 327 (1951); BERKSON, J., *J. Amer. statist. Ass.*, **48**, 565 (1953).

[28] PEARSON and WILKS, *Biometrika*, **25**, 353 (1933).
[29] FREEMAN and TUKEY, *Ann. math. Statist.*, **21**, 607 (1950).
[30] MOLENAAR, W., *Approximations to the Poisson, Binomial and Hypergeometric Distribution Functions*, Mathematical Centre Tracts 31, Mathematisch Centrum Amsterdam, 1970.
[31] CLOPPER and PEARSON, *Biometrika*, **26**, 404 (1934).
[32] WILKS, S. S., *Bull. Amer. math. Soc.*, **54**, 6 (1948).
[33] BLISS, C. I., *Biometrics*, **9**, 176 (1953).
[34] BROSS, I., *Biometrics*, **10**, 245 (1954).
[35] KATZ, L., *J. Amer. statist. Ass.*, **48**, 256 (1953).
[36] SIEGEL, S., *Nonparametric Statistics for the Behavioral Sciences*, McGraw-Hill, New York, 1958.
[37] HOLLANDER and WOLFE, *Nonparametric Statistical Methods*, Wiley, New York, 1973.
[38] LEHMANN, E. L., *Nonparametrics: Statistical Methods Based on Ranks*, Holden-Day, San Francisco, 1975.
[39] YATES, F., *J. roy. statist. Soc.*, suppl. 1, 217 (1934).
[40] MCNEMAR, Q., *Psychometrika*, **12**, 153 (1947).
[41] WILCOXON, F., *Biometrics*, **1**, 80 (1945).
[42] WILCOXON, F., *Biometrics*, **3**, 119 (1947).
[43] KRUSKAL and WALLIS, *J. Amer. statist. Ass.*, **47**, 583 (1952).
[44] FRIEDMAN, M., *J. Amer. statist. Ass.*, **32**, 675 (1937).
[45] HALDANE and SMITH, *Ann. Eugen. (Lond.)*, **14**, 117 (1947–1949).
[46] KENDALL, M. G., *Rank Correlation Methods*, 4th ed., Griffin, London, 1970.
[47] VAN DER WAERDEN, B. L., *Mathematische Statistik*, 3rd ed., Springer, Berlin, 1971.
[48] GLASSER and WINTER, *Biometrika*, **48**, 444 (1961).
[49] SCHEFFÉ and TUKEY, *Ann. math. Statist.*, **15**, 217 (1944).
[50] DANZIGER and DAVIS, *Ann. math. Statist.*, **35**, 1361 (1964).
[51] VON NEUMANN et al., *Ann. math. Statist.*, **12**, 153 (1941).
[52] ANDERSON, R. L., *Ann. math. Statist.*, **13**, 1 (1942); WALD and WOLFOWITZ, *Ann. math. Statist.*, **14**, 378 (1943).
[53] BENNETT and FRANKLIN, *Statistical Analysis in Chemistry and the Chemical Industry*, Wiley, New York, 1967.
[54] LEVENE and WOLFOWITZ, *Ann. math. Statist.*, **15**, 58 (1944).
[55] WOLFOWITZ, J., *Ann. math. Statist.*, **15**, 163 (1944); OLMSTEAD, P. S., *Ann. math. Statist.*, **17**, 24 (1946).
[56] OLMSTEAD, P. S., *Runs Determined in a Sample by an Arbitrary Cut*, Bell Telephone System, Technical Publications, Monograph 2937, New York, 1958.
[57] MOOD, A. M., *Ann. math. Statist.*, **11**, 367 (1940).
[58] STEVENS, W. L., *Ann. Eugen. (Lond.)*, **9**, 10 (1939).
[59] WALD and WOLFOWITZ, *Ann. math. Statist.*, **11**, 147 (1940).
[60] VON BORTKIEWICZ, L., *Die Iterationen*, Springer, Berlin, 1917.
[61] GEPPERT, M. P., Tübingen, personal communication, 1965.
[62] ARMITAGE, P., *Sequential Medical Trials*, 2nd ed., Blackwell, Oxford, 1975.
[63] BROSS, I., *Biometrics*, **8**, 188 (1952).

All values conform to the international convention (i.e. 0,1 instead of 0.1).

Index

Page numbers are in roman type, proposition numbers in **bold** type

Index

Page numbers are in roman type, proposition numbers in **bold** type

Page numbers are in roman type, proposition numbers in **bold** type

Page numbers are in roman type, proposition numbers in **bold** type

T

U

V

W

Y

Z